Prepare, Apply, Assess and Develop Employability Skills with MyLab Economics

83%

of students said it helped them earn higher grades on homework, exams, or the course

MyLab™ Economics is an online homework, tutorial, and assessment program constructed to work with this text to engage students and improve results. It was designed to help students develop and assess the skills and applicable knowledge that they will need to succeed in their courses and their future careers.

See what students had to say about MyLab Economics:

"Usually when I do homework myself and don't get it I am stuck, but [MyLab Economics] provided the tools necessary to help me learn how to work my way through the trickiest problems."

— Zainul Lughmani,
Binghamton University

Digital Interactives

Economic principles are not static ideas, and learning them shouldn't be either! Digital Interactives are dynamic and engaging assessment activities that promote **critical thinking** and **application** of key economic principles.

Question Help

MyLab Economics homework and practice questions are correlated to the textbook, and many generate algorithmically to give students unlimited opportunity for mastery of concepts. If students get stuck, Learning Aids including Help Me Solve This and eText Pages walk them through the problem and identify helpful information in the text, giving them assistance when they need it most.

"[MyLab Economics] provides ample practice and explanation of the concepts at hand."

— Heather Burkett, University of Nebraska at Omaha

% of students who found learning tool helpful

Dynamic Study Modules help students study chapter topics effectively on their own by continuously assessing their **knowledge application** and performance in real time. These are available as prebuilt Prepare assignments, and are accessible on smartphones, tablets, and computers.

Pearson eText enhances student learning—both in and outside the classroom. Worked examples, videos, and interactive tutorials bring learning to life, while algorithmic practice and self-assessment opportunities test students' understanding of the material. Accessible anytime, anywhere via MyLab or the app.

The **MyLab Gradebook** offers an easy way for students and instructors to view course performance. Item Analysis allows instructors to quickly see trends by analyzing details like the number of students who answered correctly/incorrectly, time on task, and median time spend on a question by question basis. And because it's correlated with the AACSB Standards, instructors can track students' progress toward outcomes that the organization has deemed important in preparing students to be **leaders.**

87% of students would tell their instructor to keep using MyLab Economics

For additional details visit: www.pearson.com/mylab/economics

Microeconomics

Seventh Edition

R. Glenn Hubbard
Columbia University

Anthony Patrick O'Brien
Lehigh University

New York, NY

Vice President, Business, Economics, and UK Courseware: Donna Battista
Director of Portfolio Management: Adrienne D'Ambrosio
Specialist Portfolio Manager: David Alexander
Development Editor: Lena Buonanno
Editorial Assistant: Nicole Nedwidek
Vice President, Product Marketing: Roxanne McCarley
Senior Product Marketer: Tricia Murphy
Product Marketing Assistant: Marianela Silvestri
Manager of Field Marketing, Business Publishing: Adam Goldstein
Senior Field Marketing Manager: Carlie Marvel
Vice President, Production and Digital Studio, Arts and Business: Etain O'Dea
Director of Production, Business: Jeff Holcomb
Managing Producer, Business: Alison Kalil
Content Producer: Christine Donovan
Operations Specialist: Carol Melville
Design Lead: Kathryn Foot

Manager, Learning Tools: Brian Surette
Content Developer, Learning Tools: Sarah Peterson
Managing Producer, Digital Studio and GLP, Media Production and Development: Ashley Santora
Managing Producer, Digital Studio: Diane Lombardo
Digital Studio Producer: Melissa Honig
Digital Studio Producer: Alana Coles
Digital Content Team Lead: Noel Lotz
Digital Content Project Lead: Courtney Kamauf
Project Manager: Heidi Allgair, Cenveo® Publisher Services
Interior Design: Cenveo® Publisher Services
Cover Design: Studio Montage
Cover Photos: Phant/Shutterstock; Mariyana M/Shutterstock
Printer/Binder: LSC Communications, Inc./Kendallville
Cover Printer: Phoenix Color/Hagerstown

Microsoft and/or its respective suppliers make no representations about the suitability of the information contained in the documents and related graphics published as part of the services for any purpose. All such documents and related graphics are provided "as is" without warranty of any kind. Microsoft and/or its respective suppliers hereby disclaim all warranties and conditions with regard to this information, including all warranties and conditions of merchantability, whether express, implied or statutory, fitness for a particular purpose, title and non-infringement. In no event shall Microsoft and/or its respective suppliers be liable for any special, indirect or consequential damages or any damages whatsoever resulting from loss of use, data or profits, whether in an action of contract, negligence or other tortious action, arising out of or in connection with the use or performance of information available from the services.

The documents and related graphics contained herein could include technical inaccuracies or typographical errors. Changes are periodically added to the information herein. Microsoft and/or its respective suppliers may make improvements and/or changes in the product(s) and/or the program(s) described herein at any time. Partial screen shots may be viewed in full within the software version specified.

Microsoft® and Windows® are registered trademarks of the Microsoft Corporation in the U.S.A. and other countries. This book is not sponsored or endorsed by or affiliated with the Microsoft Corporation.

Library of Congress Cataloging-in-Publication Data.

Names: Hubbard, R. Glenn, author. | O'Brien, Anthony Patrick, author.
Title: Microeconomics / R. Glenn Hubbard, Columbia University, Anthony Patrick O'Brien, Lehigh University.
Description: Seventh Edition. | New York : Pearson, [2018] | Revised edition of the authors's Microeconomics, [2017] | Includes index.
Identifiers: LCCN 2017050534| ISBN 9780134737508 | ISBN 0134737504
Subjects: LCSH: Microeconomics.
Classification: LCC HB172 .H83 2018 | DDC 338.5—dc23
LC record available at https://lccn.loc.gov/2017050534

ISBN 10: 0-13-473750-4
ISBN 13: 978-0-13-473750-8

For Constance, Raph, and Will
—*R. Glenn Hubbard*

For Cindy, Matthew, Andrew, and Daniel
—*Anthony Patrick O'Brien*

ABOUT THE **AUTHORS**

Glenn Hubbard, policymaker, professor, and researcher. R. Glenn Hubbard is the dean and Russell L. Carson Professor of Finance and Economics in the Graduate School of Business at Columbia University and professor of economics in Columbia's Faculty of Arts and Sciences. He is also a research associate of the National Bureau of Economic Research and a director of Automatic Data Processing, Black Rock Closed-End Funds, and MetLife. He received a PhD in economics from Harvard University in 1983. From 2001 to 2003, he served as chair of the White House Council of Economic Advisers and chair of the OECD Economic Policy Committee, and from 1991 to 1993, he was deputy assistant secretary of the U.S. Treasury Department. He currently serves as co-chair of the nonpartisan Committee on Capital Markets Regulation. Hubbard's fields of specialization are public economics, financial markets and institutions, corporate finance, macroeconomics, industrial organization, and public policy. He is the author of more than 100 articles in leading journals, including *American Economic Review, Brookings Papers on Economic Activity, Journal of Finance, Journal of Financial Economics, Journal of Money, Credit, and Banking, Journal of Political Economy, Journal of Public Economics, Quarterly Journal of Economics, RAND Journal of Economics,* and *Review of Economics and Statistics.* His research has been supported by grants from the National Science Foundation, the National Bureau of Economic Research, and numerous private foundations.

Tony O'Brien, award-winning professor and researcher. Anthony Patrick O'Brien is a professor of economics at Lehigh University. He received a PhD from the University of California, Berkeley, in 1987. He has taught principles of economics for more than 20 years, in both large sections and small honors classes. He received the Lehigh University Award for Distinguished Teaching. He was formerly the director of the Diamond Center for Economic Education and was named a Dana Foundation Faculty Fellow and Lehigh Class of 1961 Professor of Economics. He has been a visiting professor at the University of California, Santa Barbara, and the Graduate School of Industrial Administration at Carnegie Mellon University. O'Brien's research has dealt with issues such as the evolution of the U.S. automobile industry, the sources of U.S. economic competitiveness, the development of U.S. trade policy, the causes of the Great Depression, and the causes of black–white income differences. His research has been published in leading journals, including *American Economic Review, Quarterly Journal of Economics, Journal of Money, Credit, and Banking, Industrial Relations, Journal of Economic History,* and *Explorations in Economic History.* His research has been supported by grants from government agencies and private foundations.

BRIEF **CONTENTS**

CONTENTS

* These end-of-chapter resource materials repeat in all chapters. Select chapters also include Real-Time Data Exercises.
Students can complete all questions, problems, and exercises in MyLab Economics.

PART 4 Microeconomic Foundations: Consumers and Firms

PART 5 Market Structure and Firm Strategy

PART 6 Labor Markets, Public Choice, and the Distribution of Income

FLEXIBILITY **CHART**

The following chart helps you organize your syllabus based on your teaching preferences and objectives:

Core	Optional	Policy
Chapter 1: Economics: Foundations and Models	**Chapter 1 Appendix:** Using Graphs and Formulas	
Chapter 2: Trade-offs, Comparative Advantage, and the Market System		
Chapter 3: Where Prices Come From: The Interaction of Demand and Supply		
	Chapter 4 Appendix: Quantitative Demand and Supply Analysis	**Chapter 4:** Economic Efficiency, Government Price Setting, and Taxes
		Chapter 5: Externalities, Environmental Policy, and Public Goods
Chapter 6: Elasticity: The Responsiveness of Demand and Supply		
		Chapter 7: The Economics of Health Care
	Chapter 8: Firms, the Stock Market, and Corporate Governance	
	Chapter 8 Appendix: Tools to Analyze Firms' Financial Information	
Chapter 9: Comparative Advantage and the Gains from International Trade		

PREFACE

Our approach in this new edition remains what it was in the first edition, published nearly 15 years ago: to provide students and instructors an economics text that delivers complete economics coverage with many real-world business examples. Our goal has been to teach economics in a "widget-free" way by using real-world business and policy examples. We are gratified by the enthusiastic response from students and instructors who have used the first six editions of this book and who have made it a best-selling economics textbook.

Much has happened in the U.S. and world economies since we prepared the previous edition, including the election of a U.S. president with a distinctive approach to economic policy. We have incorporated many of these developments in the new real-world examples and policy discussions in this edition and also in the digital resources.

New to This Edition

We are grateful to the many instructors and students who made suggestions for improvements in the previous edition. We have done our best to incorporate as many of those suggestions as possible. Here is an overview of the revisions, followed by a more detailed description.

Overview of Changes

- All the chapter openers feature either new companies or have updated information. Students can visit MyLab Economics to watch a brief video that summarizes the key points of each chapter opener.
- Chapters 1–4, include new *An Inside Look* features to help students apply economic thinking to current events and policy debates as they are presented in news articles. Additional news articles and analyses appear weekly on MyLab Economics.
- There are 19 new *Apply the Concept* features (formerly titled *Making the Connection*) to help students tie economic concepts to current events and policy issues. The *Apply the Concept* features that were retained from the previous edition are updated. Students can visit MyLab Economics to watch more than 60 videos in which we summarize the key points in each feature. Related assessment accompanies each video, so students can test their understanding before moving on to a new section of the chapter.
- There are 5 new *Solved Problems* and 8 heavily revised *Solved Problems*. This feature helps students break down and answer economic problems step by step. There are additional Interactive *Solved Problems* on MyLab Economics, where students can receive feedback and tutorial help.
- There is a new category of end-of-chapter material titled *Critical Thinking Exercises*. We were motivated to add this new category of exercises because many instructors have told us that students need help building skills in the following areas: (1) analyzing and interpreting information; (2) applying reasoning and logic to new or unfamiliar ideas and situations; (3) examining ideas and concepts from multiple perspectives; and (4) clearly communicating their findings in a brief paper or class presentation. Students can complete these exercises on MyLab Economics and receive feedback and tutorial help.
- All the figures and tables are updated with the latest data available. Video animations of all the numbered figures and select tables are located on MyLab Economics. Graded practice exercises are included with these animations.

- We have replaced or updated many of the end-of-chapter *Problems and Applications*. In most chapters, one or two problems include graphs or tables for students to analyze. Select chapters have a category titled *Real-Time Data Exercises*, and we updated some of these exercises. Students can complete these exercises on MyLab Economics and receive feedback and tutorial help.

New Content and Features by Chapter

Here is a description of key changes by chapter.

Chapter 1, "Economics: Foundations and Models," opens with a new discussion of why Ford Motor Company manufactures cars in both the United States and Mexico. *An Inside Look* at the end of the chapter presents a news article and analysis of how likely it is that significant numbers of manufacturing jobs will return to the United States from overseas. New *Solved Problem 1.1* analyzes the marginal benefit and marginal cost of speed limits on highways. A new *Apply the Concept* examines why countries trade with each other and how economic concepts can help us evaluate policy debates about tariffs on imports. Taking a principles of economics class requires students to learn different terms, models, and a new way of analyzing real-world events. It can be challenging for students, especially non-majors, to appreciate how this course can help them in a career in business or government or in a nonprofit organization. We therefore decided to add to Chapter 1 a new section that describes economics as a career and highlights the key skills students of any major can gain from studying economics.

Chapter 2, "Trade-offs, Comparative Advantage, and the Market System," opens with an updated discussion of the resource allocation decisions managers at Tesla Motors face. *An Inside Look* at the end of the chapter discusses Tesla's decision to build a factory in Nevada to mass produce lithium-ion batteries for its electric cars. A new *Apply the Concept* illustrates how managers at the nonprofit organization Feeding America use the market mechanism to more efficiently allocate food based on the needs of food programs around the country.

Chapter 3, "Where Prices Come From: The Interaction of Demand and Supply," opens with a new discussion of how Coca-Cola and Pepsi-Cola responded to a fall in demand for sodas by introducing premium bottled water, sometimes called smart water. We use the market for premium bottled water to develop the demand and supply model. *An Inside Look* at the end of the chapter examines how McDonald's responded to shifts in consumer demand by serving breakfast all day and offering online ordering and home delivery. There are three new *Apply the Concepts*: "Virtual Reality Headsets: Will a Substitute Fail for a Lack of Complements?"; "Millennials Shake Up the Markets for Soda, Groceries, Big Macs, and Running Shoes"; and "Forecasting the Demand for Premium Bottled Water."

Chapter 4, "Economic Efficiency, Government Price Setting, and Taxes," opens with a new discussion about the economic link between food riots in Venezuela and the rise in popularity of Uber in the United States. At the end of the chapter, *An Inside Look* examines problems Uber has encountered in attempting to expand its services in the United Kingdom. There are two new *Apply the Concepts*: "The Consumer Surplus from Uber" and "Price Controls Lead to Economic Decline in Venezuela."

Chapter 5, "Externalities, Environmental Policy, and Public Goods," opens with a new discussion of ExxonMobil's support of a carbon tax. Two *Apply the Concepts* in the chapter now incorporate the latest information about government policies toward air pollution and global warming.

Chapter 6, "Elasticity: The Responsiveness of Demand and Supply," opens with a new discussion of how to evaluate the success of the soda tax enacted by several cities, including San Francisco and Philadelphia, in improving people's health and increasing tax revenue.

Chapter 7, "The Economics of Health Care," opens with a new discussion of how insurance companies are dealing with the effects of the Patient Protection and Affordable Care Act of 2010. There is also a discussion of the 2017 debate in Congress over whether that act should be extensively revised.

Chapter 8, "Firms, the Stock Market, and Corporate Governance," opens with a new comparison of the initial public offerings of Snap, Twitter, and Facebook. A new *Apply the Concept* explores why investors are concerned about potential corporate governance issues at Snap and other social media firms.

Chapter 9, "Comparative Advantage and the Gains from International Trade," opens with the decision by Mondelez to move production of Oreo cookies to Mexico to provide context for a new discussion of recent debates about the North American Free Trade Agreement (NAFTA) and the Trans-Pacific Partnership (TPP). A new *Apply the Concept* analyzes who gains and who loses from U.S. trade with China.

Chapter 10, "Consumer Choice and Behavioral Economics," opens with an updated discussion of the problems plaguing the JCPenney department store chain. A new *Apply the Concept* discusses why ticket scalpers have made a larger profit from the hit Broadway musical *Hamilton* than have the show's producers or stars. New *Solved Problem 10.3* analyzes why Tesla doesn't charge workers to park in the lot at its California factory even though the lot has a severe shortage of spaces.

Chapter 11, "Technology, Production, and Costs," opens with an updated discussion of the effects of massive open online courses (MOOCs) on the costs of higher education. A new *Apply the Concept* examines how software company Segment.com rearranged work areas to increase employee output.

Chapter 12, "Firms in Perfectly Competitive Markets," opens with an updated discussion of the difficulty farmers have making an economic profit selling cage-free eggs. A new *Solved Problem* analyzes why a wheat farmer decided to take 170 acres out of production and plant grass, and a new *Apply the Concept* discusses competition in the Asian restaurant market in New York City.

Chapter 13, "Monopolistic Competition: The Competitive Model in a More Realistic Setting," opens with a new discussion of Panera Bread's strategy of differentiating its restaurants by serving only "clean food." A new *Apply the Concept* continues the discussion of that company's strategy. Another new *Apply the Concept* discusses a new phenomenon in the restaurant industry: ghost restaurants that exist only online. New *Solved Problem 13.3* analyzes why Red Robin abandoned its experiment in fast-casual restaurants.

Chapter 14, "Oligopoly: Firms in Less Competitive Markets," opens with an updated discussion of competition in the music streaming business. A new *Apply the Concept* discusses how some bakeries have tried to use government regulations to eliminate competition from home bakers. A new *Solved Problem 14.2* uses game theory to analyze why Spotify and Apple Music offer student discounts.

Chapter 15, "Monopoly and Antitrust Policy," includes a new *Apply the Concept* discussing the reasons for the high prices of some generic drugs.

Chapter 16, "Pricing Strategy," opens with an updated discussion of how Disney uses big data to improve its theme park pricing. A new *Apply the Concept* discusses how firms ranging from airlines to zoos use big data and dynamic pricing to maximize profit.

Chapter 17, "The Markets for Labor and Other Factors of Production," opens with an updated discussion of whether Rio Tinto's extensive use of robots to mine ore in Australia is an indicator of future automation in other industries. Immigration has become a particularly contentious political issue, which led us to add the new section "The Effect of Immigration on the U.S. Labor Market," including new Figure 17.6, which shows annual legal immigration into the United States as a percentage of the U.S. population.

Chapter 18, "Public Choice, Taxes, and the Distribution of Income," opens with a new discussion of proposals to dramatically change how the federal government taxes businesses. We have updated the chapter's discussion to highlight the key points in this debate.

To make room for the new content described earlier, we have cut approximately 17 *Apply the Concepts* and 4 *Solved Problems* from the previous edition and transferred some of them to the book's *Instructor's Manual*, where they are available for instructors who wish to continue using them.

Solving Teaching and Learning Challenges

Many students who take a principles of economics course have difficulty seeing the relevance of the key concepts of opportunity cost, trade-offs, scarcity, and demand and supply to their lives and their careers. This reduces the willingness of some students to prepare for class and to be engaged during class. We address this challenge with contextual learning, a modern organization of content, and an extensive selection of digital assets available on MyLab Economics.

The Foundation:

Contextual Learning and Modern Organization

We believe a course is successful if students can apply what they have learned to both their personal lives and their careers, and if they have developed the analytical skills to understand what they read in the media. That's why we explain economic concepts by using many real-world business examples and applications in the chapter openers, graphs, *Apply the Concept* features, *An Inside Look* features, and end-of-chapter problems. This approach helps majors from all disciplines become educated consumers, voters, and citizens. In addition to our widget-free approach, we have a modern organization and place interesting policy topics early in the book to pique student interest. Here are a few highlights of our approach:

- **A strong set of introductory chapters.** The introductory chapters provide students with a solid foundation in the basics. We emphasize the key ideas of marginal analysis and economic efficiency. In Chapter 4, "Economic Efficiency, Government Price Setting, and Taxes," we use the concepts of consumer and producer surplus to measure the economic effects of price ceilings and price floors as they relate to the familiar examples of rental properties and the minimum wage. (We revisit consumer and producer surplus in Chapter 9, "Comparative Advantage and the Gains from International Trade," where we discuss outsourcing and analyze government policies that affect trade; in Chapter 15, "Monopoly and Antitrust Policy," where we examine the effect of market power on economic efficiency; and in Chapter 16, "Pricing Strategy," where we examine the effect of firm pricing policy on economic efficiency.) In Chapter 8, "Firms, the Stock Market, and Corporate Governance," we provide students with a basic understanding of how firms are organized, raise funds, and provide information to investors. We also illustrate how in a market system entrepreneurs meet consumer wants and efficiently organize production.

- **Early coverage of policy issues.** To expose students to policy issues early in the course, we discuss trade policy in Chapter 1, "Economics: Foundations and Models"; rent control and the minimum wage in Chapter 4, "Economic Efficiency, Government Price Setting, and Taxes"; air pollution, global warming, and public goods in Chapter 5, "Externalities, Environmental Policy, and Public Goods"; government policy toward soda and other sweetened beverages in Chapter 6, "Elasticity: The Responsiveness of Demand and Supply"; and health care policy in Chapter 7, "The Economics of Health Care."

- **Complete coverage of monopolistic competition.** We devote a full chapter, Chapter 13, "Monopolistic Competition: The Competitive Model in a More Realistic Setting," to monopolistic competition prior to covering oligopoly and monopoly in Chapter 14, "Oligopoly: Firms in Less Competitive Markets," and Chapter 15, "Monopoly and Antitrust Policy." Although many instructors cover monopolistic competition very briefly or dispense with it entirely, we think it is an overlooked tool for reinforcing the basic message of how markets work in a context that is much more familiar to students than are the agricultural examples that dominate discussions of perfect competition. We use the monopolistic competition model to introduce the downward-sloping demand curve material usually introduced in a monopoly chapter. This approach helps students grasp the important point that nearly all firms—not just monopolies—face downward-sloping demand curves. Covering monopolistic competition directly after perfect competition also allows for early discussion of topics such as brand management and sources of competitive success. Nevertheless, we wrote the chapter so that instructors who prefer to cover monopoly (Chapter 15, "Monopoly and Antitrust Policy") directly after perfect competition (Chapter 12, "Firms in Perfectly Competitive Markets") can do so without loss of continuity.

- **Extensive, realistic game theory coverage.** In Chapter 14, "Oligopoly: Firms in Less Competitive Markets," we use game theory to analyze competition among oligopolists. Game theory helps students understand how companies with market power make strategic decisions in many competitive situations. We use familiar companies such as Apple, Amazon, Dell, Spotify, and Walmart in our game theory applications.

- **Unique coverage of pricing strategy.** In Chapter 16, "Pricing Strategy," we explore how firms use pricing strategies to increase profits. Students encounter pricing strategies everywhere—when they buy a movie ticket, book a flight for spring break, or research book prices online. We use these relevant, familiar examples to illustrate how companies use strategies such as price discrimination, cost-plus pricing, and two-part tariffs.

MyLab Economics

OVERVIEW

Reach every student by pairing this text with MyLab Economics

MyLab is the teaching and learning platform that empowers you to reach *every* student. By combining trusted author content with digital tools and a flexible platform, MyLab personalizes the learning experience and improves results for each student. Learn more about MyLab Economics at www.pearson.com/mylab/economics.

Deliver trusted content

You deserve teaching materials that meet your own high standards for your course. That's why we partner with highly respected authors to develop interactive content and course-specific resources that you can trust—and that keep your students engaged.

Empower each learner

Each student learns at a different pace. Personalized learning pinpoints the precise areas where each student needs practice, giving all students the support they need—when and where they need it—to be successful.

Teach your course your way

Your course is unique. So whether you'd like to build your own assignments, teach multiple sections, or set prerequisites, MyLab gives you the flexibility to easily create *your* course to fit *your* needs.

Improve student results

When you teach with MyLab, student performance improves. That's why instructors have chosen MyLab for over 15 years, touching the lives of over 50 million students.

FEATURES IN THE BOOK AND SUPPORTING RESOURCES ON MYLAB ECONOMICS

Students and instructors will find the following features in the seventh edition and supporting online resources on MyLab Economics.

Business Cases and An Inside Look *News Articles*

Each chapter-opening case provides a real-world context for learning, sparks students' interest in economics, and helps unify the chapter. The case describes an actual company facing a real situation. The company is integrated in the narrative, graphs, and pedagogical features of the chapter.

Students can visit MyLab Economics to watch a brief video we developed and filmed to summarize the key points of each chapter opener.

An Inside Look is a two-page feature that shows students how to apply the concepts from the chapter to the analysis of a news article. The feature appears at the end of Chapters 1–4. *An Inside Look* presents an excerpt from an article, analysis of the article, a graph(s), and critical thinking questions. Additional articles that are continuously updated are located on MyLab Economics.

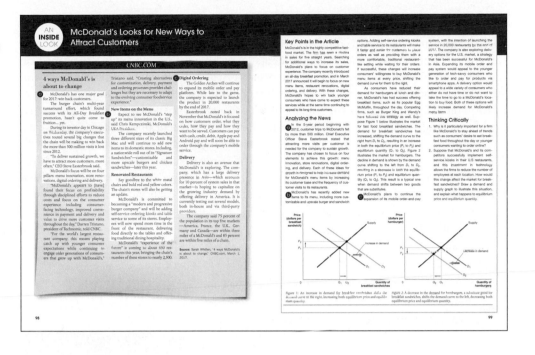

Solved Problems

Many students have great difficulty handling applied economics problems. We help students overcome this hurdle by including in each chapter two or three worked-out problems that analyze real-world economic issues they hear and read about in the news. Our goals are to keep students focused on the main ideas of each chapter and give them a model of how to solve an economic problem by breaking it down step by step. We tie additional exercises in the end-of-chapter *Problems and Applications* section to every *Solved Problem*. Additional *Solved Problems* appear in the *Instructor's Manuals*. In addition, the Test Banks include problems tied to the *Solved Problems* in the main book. Each of the 36 *Solved Problems* in the printed text is accompanied by a similar Interactive *Solved Problem* on MyLab Economics, so students can have more practice and build their problem-solving skills. These interactive tutorials help students learn to think like economists and apply basic problem-solving skills to homework, quizzes, and exams. Each *Solved Problem* on MyLab Economics and in the digital eText also includes at least one additional graded practice exercise for students.

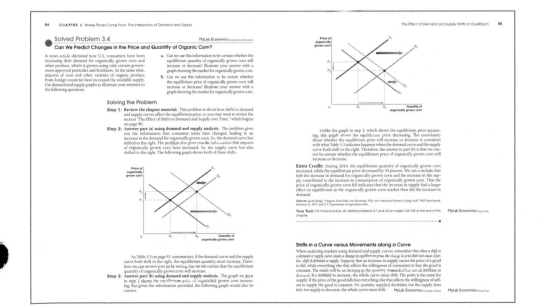

Apply the Concept

Each chapter includes two to four *Apply the Concept* features that provide real-world reinforcement of key concepts and help students learn how to interpret what they read on the Web and in newspapers. Most of the over 60 *Apply the Concept* features use relevant, stimulating, and provocative news stories focused on businesses and policy issues. One-third of them are new to this edition, and most others have been updated. Several discuss health care and trade, which have been at the forefront of recent policy discussions. Each *Apply the Concept* has at least one supporting end-of-chapter problem to allow students to test their understanding of the topic discussed. We prepared and filmed a two- or three-minute video to explain the key point of each *Apply the Concept*. These videos are located on MyLab Economics. We include related assessment with each video, so students can test their understanding. The goal of these videos is to summarize key content and bring the applications to life. In our experience, many students benefit from this type of online learning and assessment.

Apply the Concept   MyLab Economics Video

Forecasting the Demand for Premium Bottled Water

It's important for managers to forecast the demand for their products accurately because doing so helps them determine how much of a good to produce. Firms typically set manufacturing schedules at least a month ahead of time. Premium bottled water is a rapidly growing market, and firms need to carefully plan increases in productive capacity. Firms that fail to produce a large enough quantity to keep pace with increasing demand can lose out to competitors. But will the demand for premium bottled water continue to grow at such a rapid pace?

Sara Stathas/Alamy Stock Photo

How will changes in demographics, income, and tastes shape the market for premium bottled water?

Richard Tedlow of the Harvard Business School has developed a theory of the "three phases of marketing" that can provide some insight into how the markets for many consumer products develop over time. The first phase often has a very large number of firms, each producing a relatively small volume of goods and charging high prices. This phase corresponds to the carbonated soft drink industry in the late nineteenth century, the automobile industry in the early twentieth century, and the personal computer industry in the late 1970s. In the second phase, the market consolidates, with one or a few brands attaining high market shares by selling a large number of units at lower prices. This phase corresponds to the soft drink industry during the middle of the twentieth century, the automobile industry during the 1920s, and the personal computer industry during the 1980s.

Managers at beverage firms will have to take into account a number of factors when estimating the future demand for premium bottled water. Factors that will tend to lead to higher demand for premium bottled water include the popularity of the product with millennials, the trend toward healthier eating habits that has led to declining consumption of carbonated beverages, the taxes on soda that cities have been imposing to both fight obesity and raise tax revenue, and the possibility of attracting consumers who now prefer energy drinks such as Red Bull and sports drinks such as Gatorade. But an obstacle to the rapid growth of demand for premium bottled water comes from doubts raised by some analysts about the benefits from the electrolytes and other ingredients it contains that are not in regular bottled water. If consumers come to believe that these ingredients serve no useful purpose, they may prefer to buy regular bottled water, which typically has a lower price.

As we saw in Chapter 1, economists can use formal models to forecast future values of economic variables. In this case, an economist forecasting the demand for premium bottled water would want to include the factors mentioned in the previous paragraphs as well as other data, including changes over time in demographics and projected income growth.

Sources: Jennifer Maloney, "PepsiCo Gives Its 'Premium' Water a Super Bowl Push," *Wall Street Journal*, January 24, 2017; Quentin Fottrell, "Bottled Water Overtakes Soda as America's No. 1 Drink—Why You Should Avoid Both," marketwatch.com, March 12, 2017; and Richard Tedlow, *New and Improved: The Story of Mass Marketing in America*, Cambridge, MA: Harvard Business School Press, 1996.

Your Turn: Test your understanding by doing related problem 1.17 on page 102 at the end of this chapter.

Don't Let This Happen to You

We know from many years of teaching which concepts students find most difficult. We include in each chapter a box feature called *Don't Let This Happen to You* that alerts students to the most common pitfalls in that chapter's material. We follow up with a related question in the end-of-chapter *Problems and Applications* section. The questions are also available on MyLab Economics, where students can receive instant feedback and tutorial help.

Concept Checks

Each section of each learning objective concludes with a Concept Check on MyLab Economics that contains one or two multiple-choice, true/false, or fill-in questions. These checks act as "speed bumps" that encourage students to stop and check their understanding of fundamental terms and concepts before moving on to the next section. The goal of this digital resource is to help students assess their progress on a section-by-section basis so they can be better prepared for homework, quizzes, and exams.

Don't Let This Happen to You

Remember: A Change in a Good's Price Does *Not* Cause the Demand or Supply Curve to Shift

Suppose a student is asked to draw a demand and supply graph to illustrate how an increase in the price of oranges would affect the market for apples, with other variables being constant. He draws the graph on the left and explains it as follows: "Because apples and oranges are substitutes, an increase in the price of oranges will cause an initial shift to the right in the demand curve for apples, from D_1 to D_2. However, because this initial shift in the demand curve for apples results in a higher price for apples, P_2, consumers will find apples less desirable, and the demand curve will shift to the left, from D_2 to D_3, resulting in a final equilibrium price of P_3." Do you agree or disagree with the student's analysis?

You should disagree. The student has correctly understood that an increase in the price of oranges will cause the demand curve for apples to shift to the right. But, the second demand curve shift the student describes, from D_2 to D_3, will not take place. Changes in the price of a product do not result in shifts in the product's demand curve. Changes in the price of a product result only in movements along a demand curve.

The graph on the right shows the correct analysis. The increase in the price of oranges causes the demand curve for apples to increase from D_1 to D_2. At the original price, P_1, the increase in demand initially results in a shortage of apples equal to $Q_3 - Q_1$. But, as we have seen, a shortage causes the price to increase until the shortage is eliminated. In this case, the price will rise to P_2, where both the quantity demanded and the quantity supplied are equal to Q_2. Notice that the increase in price causes a decrease in the *quantity demanded*, from Q_3 to Q_2, but does *not* cause a decrease in demand.

MyLab Economics Study Plan

Your Turn: Test your understanding by doing related problems 4.13 and 4.14 on page 105 at the end of this chapter.

Graphs and Summary Tables

Graphs are an indispensable part of a principles of economics course but are a major stumbling block for many students. Every chapter except Chapter 1 includes end-of-chapter problems that require students to draw, read, and interpret graphs. Interactive graphing exercises appear on the book's supporting Web site. We use four devices to help students read and interpret graphs:

1. Detailed captions
2. Boxed notes
3. Color-coded curves
4. Summary tables with graphs (see pages 80 and 85 for examples)

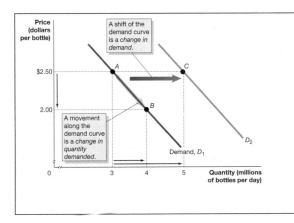

MyLab Economics Animation

Figure 3.3

A Change in Demand versus a Change in Quantity Demanded

If the price of premium bottled water falls from $2.50 to $2.00, the result will be a movement along the demand curve from point A to point B—an increase in quantity demanded from 3 million bottles to 4 million. If consumers' incomes increase, or if another factor changes that makes consumers want more of the product at every price, the demand curve will shift to the right—an increase in demand. In this case, the increase in demand from D_1 to D_2 causes the quantity of premium bottled water demanded at a price of $2.50 to increase from 3 million bottles at point A to 5 million at point C.

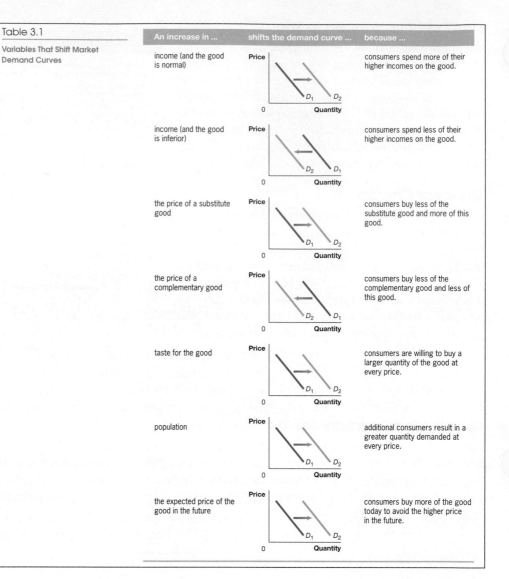

Table 3.1

Variables That Shift Market
Demand Curves

An increase in ...	shifts the demand curve ...	because ...
income (and the good is normal)		consumers spend more of their higher incomes on the good.
income (and the good is inferior)		consumers spend less of their higher incomes on the good.
the price of a substitute good		consumers buy less of the substitute good and more of this good.
the price of a complementary good		consumers buy less of the complementary good and less of this good.
taste for the good		consumers are willing to buy a larger quantity of the good at every price.
population		additional consumers result in a greater quantity demanded at every price.
the expected price of the good in the future		consumers buy more of the good today to avoid the higher price in the future.

Each of the 157 numbered figures in the text has a supporting animated version on MyLab Economics. The goal of this digital resource is to help students understand shifts in curves, movements along curves, and changes in equilibrium values. Having an animated version of a graph helps students who have difficulty interpreting the static version in the printed text. We include graded practice exercises with the animations. In our experience, many students benefit from this type of online learning.

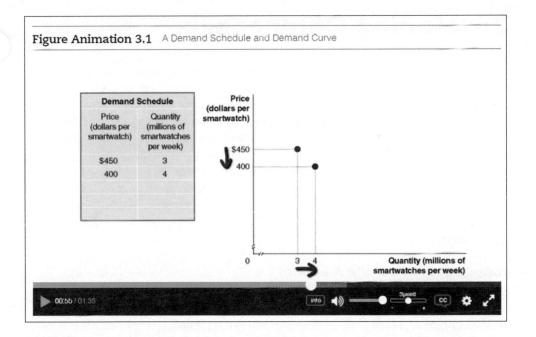

Figure Animation 3.1   A Demand Schedule and Demand Curve

Approximately 35 graphs are continuously updated online with the latest available data from FRED (Federal Reserve Economic Data), which is a comprehensive, up-to-date data set maintained by the Federal Reserve Bank of St. Louis. Students can display a pop-up graph that shows new data. The goal of this digital feature is to help students understand how to work with data and understand how including new data affects graphs.

Review Questions and *Problems and Applications*—Grouped by Learning Objective to Improve Assessment

We group the main end-of-chapter material—*Summary, Review Questions,* and *Problems and Applications*—under learning objectives. The goals of this organization are to make it easier for instructors to assign problems based on learning objectives, both in the book and on MyLab Economics, and to help students efficiently review material that they find difficult. If students have difficulty with a particular learning objective, an instructor can easily identify which end-of-chapter questions and problems support that objective and assign them as homework or discuss them in class. Every exercise in a chapter's *Problems and Applications* section is available on MyLab Economics. Using MyLab Economics, students can complete these and many other exercises online, get tutorial help, and receive instant feedback and assistance on exercises they answer incorrectly. Also, student learning will be enhanced by having the summary material and problems grouped together by learning objective, which allows them to focus on the parts of the chapter they find most challenging. Each major section of the chapter, paired with a learning objective, has at least two review questions and three problems.

As in the previous editions, we include one or more end-of-chapter problems that test students' understanding of the content presented in the *Solved Problem, Apply the Concept,* and *Don't Let This Happen to You* special features in the chapter. Instructors can cover a feature in class and assign the corresponding problem(s) for homework. The Test Bank Files also include test questions that pertain to these special features.

Developing Career Skills

Learning key economic terms, concepts, and models are all important. For a course to be successful, students need to develop the skills and confidence to apply what they've learned outside the classroom. Chapter 1, "Economics: Foundations and Models," now includes a new section that describes economics as a career and the key skills students of any major can gain from studying economics. As described earlier, features such as chapter-opening business cases, *Apply the Concepts*, *Solved Problems*, and end-of-chapter problems provide a real-world context for learning that exposes students to economics as applied in a variety of large and small businesses, government agencies, and nonprofit organizations. *Critical Thinking Exercises*, a new end-of-chapter category in this edition, help build student skills to analyze and interpret information and apply reasoning and logic to new or unfamiliar ideas and situations.

Economics in Your Life & Career

After the chapter-opening real-world business case, we have a feature titled *Economics in Your Life & Career* that adds a personal dimension to the chapter opener by asking students to consider how economics affects their lives and careers. The feature piques the interest of students and emphasizes the connection between the material they are learning and their personal and career decisions

Economics in Your Life & Career

Can You Forecast the Future Demand for Premium Bottled Water?

Firms face many challenges in responding to changes in consumer demand. Firms selling premium bottled water need to forecast future demand in order to determine how much production capacity they will need. If you were a manager for Coca-Cola, PepsiCo, Nestlé, Bai, or another firm selling premium bottled water, what factors would you take into account in forecasting future demand? As you read this chapter, try to answer this question. You can check your answers against those we provide on **page 97** at the end of this chapter.

At the end of the chapter, we use the chapter concepts to answer the questions asked at the beginning of the chapter.

Economics in Your Life & Career

Can You Forecast the Future Demand for Premium Bottled Water?

At the beginning of this chapter, we asked what variables you would take into account in forecasting future demand if you were a manager for a firm selling premium bottled water. In Section 3.1, we discussed the factors that affect the demand for a product and provided a list of the most important variables. In the *Apply the Concept* on page 81, we discussed how economists often use formal models to forecast future demand for a product.

In forecasting demand for premium bottled water, you should take into account factors such as changing demographics, as millennials become a larger fraction of prime-age consumers, and the likelihood that the demand for competing goods, such as carbonated sodas, will decline as consumers turn toward buying healthier products and as more cities impose soda taxes. You may also need to consider whether increased advertising of premium bottled water by large firms such as Coca-Cola and PepsiCo will raise consumer awareness of the product and increase demand for the premium bottled water being sold by other firms as well.

The factors discussed in this chapter provide you with the basic information needed to forecast demand for premium bottled water, although arriving at numerical forecasts requires using statistical analysis that you can learn in more advanced courses.

Instructor Teaching Resources

The authors and Pearson Education have worked together to integrate the text, print, and media resources to make teaching and learning easier.

Supplements Available to Instructors for Download at www.pearsonhighered.com	Features of the Supplement
Instructor's Manual Authored by Edward Scahill of the University of Scranton	• Chapter-by-chapter summaries organized by learning objectives • Extended examples and class exercises • Teaching outlines incorporating key terms and definitions, teaching tips, topics for class discussion • New *Solved Problems* • New *Apply the Concept* features • Solutions to all review questions, problems, and real-time data exercises in the book
Test Bank Authored by Randy Methenitis of Richland College	• 4,000 multiple-choice, true/false, short-answer, and graphing questions. • Test questions are annotated with the following categories: **Difficulty**—1 for straight recall; 2 for some analysis; and 3 for complex analysis **Type**—multiple-choice, true/false, short-answer, essay **Topic**—the term or concept the question supports **Learning outcome** **Page number** in the main book **Special feature** in the main book **The Association to Advance Collegiate Schools of Business** (AACSB) **Guidelines** (see description on the next page)
Computerized TestGen	• Allows instructors to customize, save, and generate classroom tests. • Instructors can edit, add, or delete questions from the Test Banks; analyze test results; and organize a database of tests and student results. • Many options are available for organizing and displaying tests, along with search and sort features. • The software and the Test Banks can be downloaded from www.pearsonhighered.com.
Three Sets of PowerPoint Lecture Presentations Authored by Paul Holmes of Ashland University	• A comprehensive set of PowerPoint slides can be used by instructors for class presentations or by students for lecture preview or review. These slides include all the graphs, tables, and equations in the textbook. Two versions are available—step-by-step mode, in which you can build graphs as you would on a blackboard, and automated mode, in which you use a single click per slide. • A comprehensive set of PowerPoint slides have Classroom Response Systems (CRS) questions built in so that instructors can incorporate CRS "clickers" into their classroom lectures. • Student versions of the PowerPoint slides are available as .pdf files. This version allows students to print the slides and bring them to class for note taking.

What Is the AACSB?

The Association to Advance Collegiate Schools of Business (AACSB) is a not-for-profit corporation of educational institutions, corporations, and other organizations devoted to the promotion and improvement of higher education in business administration and accounting. A collegiate institution offering degrees in business administration or accounting may volunteer for AACSB accreditation review. The AACSB expects a curriculum to include learning experiences in the following categories of Assurance of Learning Standards: Written and Oral Communication; Ethical Understanding and Reasoning; Analytical Thinking; Information Technology; Interpersonal Relations and Teamwork, Diverse and Multicultural Work; Reflective Thinking; and Application of Knowledge. Test Bank questions that test skills relevant to these standards are tagged with the appropriate standard. For example, a question testing the moral questions associated with externalities would receive the Ethical Understanding and Reasoning tag.

Acknowledgements

The guidance and recommendations of the following instructors helped us develop the revision plans for the seventh edition and the supplements package. While we could not incorporate every suggestion from every consultant board member, reviewer, or accuracy checker, we do thank each and every one of you and acknowledge that your feedback was indispensable in developing this text. We greatly appreciate your assistance in making this the best text it could be; you have helped a whole new generation of students learn about the exciting world of economics.

Consultant Board

Shawn Abbott, College of the Siskiyous
Gbenga Ajilore, The University of Toledo
Kalok Chu, Loyola University-Chicago
Eva Dziadula, University of Notre Dame
Robert Gillette, University of Kentucky
William L. Goffe, Pennsylvania State University
Randy Methenitis, Richland College
Christian Raschke, Sam Houston State University
Michael J. Ryan, Western Michigan University
Edward Scahill, University of Scranton

Accuracy Review Board

Our accuracy checkers did a particularly painstaking and thorough job of helping us proof the graphs, equations, and features of the text and supplements. We are grateful for their time and commitment:

Fatma Abdel-Raouf, Goldey-Beacom College
Gbenga Ajilore, The University of Toledo
Harry Ellis, University of North Texas
Robert Gillette, University of Kentucky
Anthony Gyapong, Pennsylvania State University–Abington

Randy Methenitis, Richland College
Brian Rosario, University of California–Davis
Edward Scahill, University of Scranton

Reviewers

The guidance and thoughtful recommendations of many instructors helped us develop and implement a revision plan that improved the book's content, enhanced the figures, and strengthened the assessment features. We extend special thanks to Edward Scahill of the University of Scranton for helping us revise the chapter openers and the solutions to the end-of-chapter questions and problems, to Randy Methenitis of Richland College for helping us revise the *An Inside Look* feature in Chapters 1–4, and to Fernando Quijano for creating all the figures in the book and supplements. We are grateful for the comments and many helpful suggestions received from the following reviewers:

Mark Abajian, University of San Diego
Anna Antus, North Hennepin Community College
Ali Arshad, Central New Mexico Community College
David Barrus, Brigham Young University–Idaho
Leon Battista, Quinnipiac University
Susan Bell, Seminole State College of Florida
Bruce Bellner, The Ohio State University

Jennis Biser, Austin Peay State University

Kelly Blanchard, Purdue University

Michaël Bonnal, University of Tennessee at Chattanooga

Walter Boyle, Fayetteville Technical Community College

Dave Brown, Pennsylvania State University

Regina Cassady, Valencia College

Basanta Chaudhuri, Rutgers University

Mark Cullivan, University of San Diego

Hong Duong, Salisbury University

Edward Durkin, Cuyahoga Community College

Maria Edlin, Middle Tennessee State University

Fatma El-Hamidi, Dietrich School of Arts and Sciences

Irene Foster, The George Washington University

Mark Gius, Quinnipiac University

Brian Goegan, Arizona State University

Timothy Hamilton, Columbia College

Wayne Hickenbottom, University of Texas at Austin

Mike Hilmer, San Diego State University

Mark Isaac, Florida State University

Rus Janis, University of Massachusetts–Amherst

Sarah Jenyk, Youngstown State University

Stephanie Brewer Jozefowicz, Indiana University of Pennsylvania

Shawna Koger, Arlington Public Schools/Metro Community College

Susan Laury, Georgia State University

Jim Lee, Texas A&M University–Corpus Christi

An Li, University of Massachusetts–Amherst

Yan Li, University of Wisconsin–Eau Claire

Svitlana Maksymenko, University of Pittsburgh

David McClough, Ohio Northern University

Scott McGann, Grossmont College

Merve Meral, University of Massachusetts–Dartmouth

Robert Mohr, University of New Hampshire

Mike Munoz, Northwest Vista College

John Nader, Davenport University

John Neri, University of Maryland

Charles Newton, Houston Community College

Eric Nielsen, St. Louis Community College–Meramec

Dan Norgard, Normandale Community College

Nitin Paranjpe, Wayne State University, Oakland University

Azucena Peralta, El Paso Community College

Claudiney Pereira, Arizona State University

Dennis Petruska, Youngstown State University

Ryan Phelps, Stephen F. Austin State University

Cristina Reiser, University of New Mexico

Giacomo Rondina, University of Colorado Boulder

Eric Rothenburg, Kingsborough Community College

Rolando Sanchez, Northwest Vista College

Jonathan Silberman, Oakland University

Richard Slotkin, Pasadena City College

Arjun Sondhi, Wayne State University

Derek Stimel, University of California, Davis

Bedassa Tadesse, University of Minnesota–Duluth

Regina Trevino, University of San Diego

Roger Wehr, University of Texas–Arlington

Elizabeth Wheaton, Southern Methodist University

Daniel Wolman, Nassau Community College

Sourushe Zandvakili, University of Cincinnati

Previous Edition Class Testers, Accuracy Reviewers, and Consultants

The guidance and recommendations of the following instructors helped us shape the previous editions.

Class Testers

We are grateful to both the instructors who class-tested manuscript of the first edition and their students for providing useful recommendations on how to make chapters more interesting, relevant, and accurate:

Charles A. Bennett, Gannon University

Anne E. Bresnock, University of California, Los Angeles, and California State Polytechnic University–Pomona

Linda Childs-Leatherbury, Lincoln University, Pennsylvania

John Eastwood, Northern Arizona University

David Eaton, Murray State University

Paul Elgatian, St. Ambrose University

Patricia A. Freeman, Jackson State University

Robert Godby, University of Wyoming

Frank Gunter, Lehigh University

Ahmed Ispahani, University of La Verne

Brendan Kennelly, Lehigh University and National University of Ireland–Galway

Ernest Massie, Franklin University

Carol McDonough, University of Massachusetts–Lowell

Shah Mehrabi, Montgomery College

Sharon Ryan, University of Missouri–Columbia

Bruce G. Webb, Gordon College

Madelyn Young, Converse College

Susan Zumas, Lehigh University

Accuracy Review Boards

We are grateful to the following accuracy checkers of the previous editions for their hard work on the book and supplements:

Fatma Abdel-Raouf, Goldey-Beacom College

Anne Alexander, University of Wyoming

Clare Battista, California Polytechnic State University

Mohammad Bajwa, Northampton Community College

Cynthia Bansak, St. Lawrence University

Hamid Bastin, Shippensburg University

Doris Bennett, Jacksonville State University

Kelly Hunt Blanchard, Purdue University

Don Bumpass, Sam Houston State University

Charles Callahan III, State University of New York–Brockport

Mark S. Chester, Reading Area Community College
Kenny Christianson, Binghamton University
Ishita Edwards, Oxnard College
Harold Elder, University of Alabama
Harry Ellis, University of North Texas
Can Erbil, Brandeis University
Marc Fusaro, Arkansas Tech University
Sarah Ghosh, University of Scranton
Robert Gillette, University of Kentucky
Maria Giuili, Diablo Valley College
Mark Gius, Quinnipiac University
Robert Godby, University of Wyoming
William L. Goffe, Pennsylvania State University
Edward T. Gullason, formerly, Dowling College
Anthony Gyapong, Pennsylvania State University—
   Abington
Travis Hayes, University of Tennessee–Chattanooga
Carol Hogan, University of Michigan–Dearborn
Anisul M. Islam, University of Houston–Downtown
Aaron Jackson, Bentley College
Nancy Jianakoplos, Colorado State University
Thomas C. Kinnaman, Bucknell University
Mary K. Knudson, University of Iowa
Faik A. Koray, Louisiana State University
Stephan Kroll, California State University–Sacramento
Tony Lima, California State University–East Bay
Randy Methenitis, Richland College
Normal C. Miller, Miami University
David Mitch, University of Maryland–Baltimore County
James A. Moreno, Blinn College
Michael Potepan, San Francisco State University
Mary L. Pranzo, California State University–Fresno
Fernando Quijano, Dickinson State University
Matthew Rafferty, Quinnipiac University
Ratha Ramoo, Diablo Valley College
Jeff Reynolds, Northern Illinois University
Brian Rosario, University of California, Davis
Joseph M. Santos, South Dakota State University
Edward Scahill, University of Scranton
Mark V. Siegler, California State University–Sacramento
Rachel Small, University of Colorado–Boulder
Stephen Smith, Bakersfield College
Rajeev Sooreea, Pennsylvania State University–Altoona
Rebecca Stein, University of Pennsylvania
Ed Steinberg, New York University
Michael Stone, Quinnipiac University
Arlena Sullivan, Jones County Junior College
Wendine Thompson–Dawson, University of Utah
Julianne Treme, University of North Carolina–Wilmington
Robert Whaples, Wake Forest University

Consultant Boards

We received guidance from a dedicated consultant board during the development of the previous editions at several critical junctures. We relied on the board for input on content, figure treatment, and design:

Kate Antonovics, University of California, San Diego
Robert Beekman, University of Tampa
Valerie Bencivenga, University of Texas–Austin
Kelly Blanchard, Purdue University
Susan Dadres, Southern Methodist University
Harry Ellis, Jr., University of North Texas
Sherman T. Folland, Oakland University
Robert Gillette, University of Kentucky
Robert Godby, University of Wyoming
William L. Goffe, Pennsylvania State University
Jane S. Himarios, University of Texas–Arlington
Donn M. Johnson, Quinnipiac University
Mark Karscig, Central Missouri State University
Jenny Minier, University of Kentucky
David Mitch, University of Maryland–Baltimore County
Nicholas Noble, Miami University
Michael Potepan, San Francisco State University
Matthew Rafferty, Quinnipiac University
Helen Roberts, University of Illinois–Chicago
Robert Rosenman, Washington State University
Joseph M. Santos, South Dakota State University
Stephen Snyder, University of Pittsburgh
Martin C. Spechler, Indiana University–Purdue University
   Indianapolis
Robert Whaples, Wake Forest University
Jonathan B. Wight, University of Richmond

Reviewers

ALABAMA
William P. Aldridge, University of Alabama
Doris Bennett, Jacksonville State University
Harold W. Elder, University of Alabama–Tuscaloosa
Wanda Hudson, Alabama Southern Community College
Keith D. Malone, University of North Alabama
Edward Merkel, Troy University
James L. Swofford, University of Southern Alabama
Christopher Westley, Jacksonville State University

ARIZONA
Doug Conway, Mesa Community College
John Eastwood, Northern Arizona University
Price Fishback, University of Arizona
Mehul Rangwala, University of Phoenix
Anne Williams, Gateway Community College

ARKANSAS
Jerry Crawford, Arkansas State University
Marc Fusaro, Arkansas Tech University
Randall Kesselring, Arkansas State University
Dan Marburger, Arkansas State University

CALIFORNIA
Shawn Abbott, College of the Siskiyous
Renatte Adler, San Diego State University

Ercument Aksoy, Los Angeles Valley College
Maneeza Aminy, Golden Gate University
Kate Antonovics, University of California, San Diego
Becca Arnold, Mesa College
Asatar Bair, City College of San Francisco
Diana Bajrami, College of Alameda
Robert Bise, Orange Coast Community College
Victor Brajer, California State University–Fullerton
Anne E. Bresnock, University of California, Los Angeles, and California State Polytechnic University–Pomona
David Brownstone, University of California, Irvine
Maureen Burton, California State Polytechnic University–Pomona
Annette Chamberlin, National College
Anoshua Chaudhuri, San Francisco State University
James G. Devine, Loyola Marymount University
Jose Esteban, Palomar College
Roger Frantz, San Diego State University
Craig Gallet, California State University–Sacramento
Andrew Gill, California State University–Fullerton
Maria Giuili, Diablo Valley College
Julie Gonzalez, University of California–Santa Cruz
Lisa Grobar, California State University–Long Beach
Steve Hamilton, California State University–Fullerton
Dewey Heinsma, Mt. San Jacinto Community College
Jessica Howell, California State University–Sacramento
Greg Hunter, California State University–Pomona
John Ifcher, Santa Clara University
Ahmed Ispahani, University of LaVerne
George A. Jouganatos, California State University–Sacramento
Jonathan Kaplan, California State University–Sacramento
Leland Kempe, California State University–Fresno
Philip King, San Francisco State University
Lori Kletzer, University of California, Santa Cruz
Stephan Kroll, California State University–Sacramento
David Lang, California State University–Sacramento
Carsten Lange, California State Polytechnic University–Pomona
Don Leet, California State University–Fresno
Rose LeMont, Modesto Junior College
Tony Lima, California State University–East Bay
Solina Lindahl, California Polytechnic State University–San Luis Obispo
Roger Mack, DeAnza College
Michael Marlow, California Polytechnic State University
Scott McGann, Grossmont College
Kristen Monaco, California State University–Long Beach
W. Douglas Morgan, University of California, Santa Barbara
Nivedita Mukherji, Oakland University
Solomon Namala, Cerritos College
Andrew Narwold, University of San Diego
Fola Odebunmi, Cypress College

Hanna Paulson, West Los Angeles College
Joseph M. Pogodzinksi, San Jose State University
Michael J. Potepan, San Francisco State University
Mary L. Pranzo, California State University–Fresno
Sasha Radisich, Glendale Community College
Ratha Ramoo, Diablo Valley College
Scott J. Sambucci, California State University–East Bay
Ariane Schauer, Marymount College
Frederica Shockley, California State University–Chico
Mark Siegler, California State University–Sacramento
Jonathan Silberman, Oakland University
Lisa Simon, California Polytechnic State University–San Louis Obispo
Richard Lee Slotkin, Pasadena City College
Stephen Smith, Bakersfield College
Rodney B. Swanson, University of California–Los Angeles
Martha Stuffler, Irvine Valley College
Lea Templer, College of the Canyons
Kristin A. Van Gaasbeck, California State University–Sacramento
Va Nee Van Vleck, California State University–Fresno
Michael Visser, Sonoma State University
Steven Yamarik, California State University–Long Beach
Guy Yamashiro, California State University–Long Beach
Kevin Young, Diablo Valley College
Anthony Zambelli, Cuyamaca College

COLORADO

Mohammed Akacem, Metropolitan State College of Denver
Rhonda Corman, University of Northern Colorado
Dale DeBoer, University of Colorado–Colorado Springs
Debbie Evercloud, University of Colorado–Denver
Karen Gebhardt, Colorado State University
Scott Houser, Colorado School of Mines
Murat Iyigun, University of Colorado at Boulder
Nancy Jianakoplos, Colorado State University
Jay Kaplan, University of Colorado–Boulder
William G. Mertens, University of Colorado–Boulder
Rachael Small, University of Colorado–Boulder
Stephen Weiler, Colorado State University

CONNECTICUT

Christopher P. Ball, Quinnipiac University
Mark Gius, Quinnipiac University
Mark Jablonowski, University of Hartford
Donn M. Johnson, Quinnipiac University
Robert Martel, University of Connecticut
Charles Meyrick, Housatonic Community College
Judith Mills, Southern Connecticut State University
Matthew Rafferty, Quinnipiac University
Christian Zimmermann, University of Connecticut

DELAWARE

Fatma Abdel-Raouf, Goldey-Beacom College
Ali Ataiifar, Delaware County Community College
Andrew T. Hill, University of Delaware

FLORIDA

Frank Albritton, Seminole State College
Herman Baine, Broward Community College
Robert L. Beekman, University of Tampa
William Browning, Florida Gulf Coast University
Eric P. Chiang, Florida Atlantic University
Martine Duchatelet, Barry University
Hadley Hartman, Santa Fe Community College
Richard Hawkins, University of West Florida
Brad Kamp, University of South Florida
Brian Kench, University of Tampa
Carrie B. Kerekes, Florida Gulf Coast University
Thomas McCaleb, Florida State University
Barbara A. Moore, University of Central Florida
Augustine Nelson, University of Miami
Jamie Ortiz, Florida Atlantic University
Deborah Paige, Santa Fe Community College
Robert Pennington, University of Central Florida
Bob Potter, University of Central Florida
Jerry Schwartz, Broward Community College–North
William Stronge, Florida Atlantic University
Nora Underwood, University of Central Florida
Zhiguang Wang, Florida International University
Joan Wiggenhorn, Barry University

GEORGIA

Greg Brock, Georgia Southern University
Donna Fisher, Georgia Southern University
Shelby Frost, Georgia State University
John King, Georgia Southern University
Constantin Ogloblin, Georgia Southern University
Dr. Greg Okoro, Georgia Perimeter College–Clarkston
Michael Reksulak, Georgia Southern University
Bill Yang, Georgia Southern University

IDAHO

Cynthia Hill, Idaho State University
Don Holley, Boise State University
Tesa Stegner, Idaho State University

ILLINOIS

Teshome Abebe, Eastern Illinois University
Ali Akarca, University of Illinois–Chicago
Zsolt Becsi, Southern Illinois University–Carbondale
James Bruehler, Eastern Illinois University
Louis Cain, Loyola University and Northwestern University
Rosa Lea Danielson, College of DuPage
Kevin Dunagan, Oakton Community College
Scott Gilbert, Southern Illinois University
Rajeev K. Goel, Illinois State University
David Gordon, Illinois Valley Community College
Alan Grant, Eastern Illinois University
Rik Hafer, Southern Illinois University–Edwardsville
Alice Melkumian, Western Illinois University
Christopher Mushrush, Illinois State University
Jeff Reynolds, Northern Illinois University
Helen Roberts, University of Illinois–Chicago

Thomas R. Sadler, Western Illinois University
Eric Schulz, Northwestern University
Dennis Shannon, Southwestern Illinois College
Charles Sicotte, Rock Valley Community College
Neil T. Skaggs, Illinois State University
Kevin Sylwester, Southern Illinois University–Carbondale
Wendine Thompson-Dawson, Monmouth College
Tara Westerhold, Western Illinois University
Mark Witte, Northwestern University
Laurie Wolff, Southern Illinois University–Carbondale
Paula Worthington, Northwestern University

INDIANA

Kelly Blanchard, Purdue University
Cecil Bohanon, Ball State University
Kirk Doran, University of Notre Dame
Eva Dziadula, University of Notre Dame
Mary Flannery, University of Notre Dame
Thomas Gresik, University of Notre Dame
Robert B. Harris, Indiana University–Purdue University Indianapolis
Fred Herschede, Indiana University–South Bend
Tom Lehman, Indiana Wesleyan University
Abraham Mathew, Indiana University–Purdue University Indianapolis
John Pomery, Purdue University
Curtis Price, University of Southern Indiana
Rob Rude, Ivy Tech Community College
James K. Self, Indiana University–Bloomington
Esther-Mirjam Sent, University of Notre Dame
Virginia Shingleton, Valparaiso University
Martin C. Spechler, Indiana University–Purdue University Indianapolis
Arun K. Srinivasan, Indiana University–Southeast Campus
Geetha Suresh, Purdue University

IOWA

Terry Alexander, Iowa State University
Paul Elgatian, St. Ambrose University
Jennifer Fuhrman, University of Iowa
Ken McCormick, University of Northern Iowa
Andy Schuchart, Iowa Central Community College
John Solow, University of Iowa
Jonathan Warner, Dordt College

KANSAS

Guatam Bhattacharya, University of Kansas
Amanda Freeman, Kansas State University
Dipak Ghosh, Emporia State University
Alan Grant, Baker University
Wayne Oberle, St. Ambrose University
Jodi Messer Pelkowski, Wichita State University
Martin Perline, Wichita State University
Joel Potter, Kansas State University
Joshua Rosenbloom, University of Kansas

Shane Sanders, Kansas State University
Dosse Toulaboe, Fort Hays State University
Bhavneet Walia, Kansas State University

KENTUCKY

Tom Cate, Northern Kentucky University
Nan-Ting Chou, University of Louisville
David Eaton, Murray State University
Ann Eike, University of Kentucky
Robert Gillette, University of Kentucky
Barry Haworth, University of Louisville
Gail Hoyt, University of Kentucky
Donna Ingram, Eastern Kentucky University
Waithaka Iraki, Kentucky State University
Hak Youn Kim, Western Kentucky University
Martin Milkman, Murray State University
Jenny Minier, University of Kentucky
David Shideler, Murray State University
John Vahaly, University of Louisville

LOUISIANA

Lara Gardner, Southeastern Louisiana University
Jay Johnson, Southeastern Louisiana University
Faik Koray, Louisiana State University
Paul Nelson, University of Louisiana–Monroe
Sung Chul No, Southern University and A&M College
Tammy Parker, University of Louisiana–Monroe
Wesley A. Payne, Delgado Community College
Nancy Rumore, University of Louisiana at Lafayette

MARYLAND

Carey Borkoski, Anne Arundel Community College
Kathleen A. Carroll, University of Maryland–Baltimore
  County
Jill Caviglia Harris, Salisbury University
Dustin Chambers, Salisbury University
Karl Einolf, Mount Saint Mary's University
Marsha Goldfarb, University of Maryland–Baltimore City
Bruce Madariaga, Montgomery College
Shah Mehrabi, Montgomery College
Gretchen Mester, Anne Arundel Community College
David Mitch, University of Maryland–Baltimore County
John Neri, University of Maryland
Henry Terrell, University of Maryland

MASSACHUSETTS

William L. Casey, Jr., Babson College
Arthur Schiller Casimir, Western New England College
Michael Enz, Western New England College
Can Erbil, Brandeis University
Lou Foglia, Suffolk University
Gerald Friedman, University of Massachusetts
Todd Idson, Boston University
Aaron Jackson, Bentley College
Russell A. Janis, University of Massachusetts–Amherst
Anthony Laramie, Merrimack College
Carol McDonough, University of Massachusetts–Lowell
William O'Brien, Worcester State College

Ahmad Saranjam, Bridgewater State College
Howard Shore, Bentley College
Janet Thomas, Bentley College
John Tommasi, University of Massachusetts–Lowell
Gregory H. Wassall, Northeastern University
Bruce G. Webb, Gordon College
Gilbert Wolpe, Newbury College
Jay Zagorsky, Boston University

MICHIGAN

Eric Beckman, Delta College
Jared Boyd, Henry Ford Community College
Victor Claar, Hope College
Dr. Sonia Dalmia, Grand Valley State University
Daniel Giedeman, Grand Valley State University
Allen C. Goodman, Wayne State University
Steven Hayworth, Eastern Michigan University
Gregg Heidebrink, Washtenaw Community College
Carol Hogan, University of Michigan–Dearborn
Marek Kolar, Delta College
Susan J. Linz, Michigan State University
James Luke, Lansing Community College
Ilir Miteza, University of Michigan–Dearborn
John Nader, Grand Valley State University
Norman P. Obst, Michigan State University
Laudo M. Ogura, Grand Valley State University
Robert J. Rossana, Wayne State University
Michael J. Ryan, Western Michigan University
Charles A. Stull, Kalamazoo College
Michael J. Twomey, University of Michigan–Dearborn
Mark Wheeler, Western Michigan University
Wendy Wysocki, Monroe County Community College

MINNESOTA

Mary Edwards, Saint Cloud State University
Phillip J. Grossman, Saint Cloud State University
Monica Hartman, University of St. Thomas
Matthew Hyle, Winona State University
David J. O'Hara, Metropolitan State University–
  Minneapolis
Kwang Woo (Ken) Park, Minnesota State University–
  Mankato
Artatrana Ratha, Saint Cloud State University
Ken Rebeck, Saint Cloud State University
Katherine Schmeiser, University of Minnesota

MISSISSIPPI

Becky Campbell, Mississippi State University
Randall Campbell, Mississippi State University
Patricia A. Freeman, Jackson State University
Arlena Sullivan, Jones County Junior College

MISSOURI

Chris Azevedo, University of Central Missouri
Ariel Belasen, Saint Louis University
Catherine Chambers, University of Central Missouri
Paul Chambers, University of Central Missouri
Kermit Clay, Ozarks Technical Community College

Ben Collier, Northwest Missouri State University
John R. Crooker, University of Central Missouri
Jo Durr, Southwest Missouri State University
Julie H. Gallaway, Southwest Missouri State University
Terrel Gallaway, Southwest Missouri State University
Mark Karscig, Central Missouri State University
Nicholas D. Peppes, Saint Louis Community College–
 Forest Park
Steven T. Petty, College of the Ozarks
Sharon Ryan, University of Missouri–Columbia
Ben Young, University of Missouri–Kansas City

MONTANA
Agnieszka Bielinska-Kwapisz, Montana State University–
 Bozeman
Jeff Bookwalter, University of Montana–Missoula

NEBRASKA
John Dogbey, University of Nebraska–Omaha
Ward Hooker, Central Community College
Allan Jenkins, University of Nebraska–Kearney
James Knudsen, Creighton University
Craig MacPhee, University of Nebraska–Lincoln
Kim Sosin, University of Nebraska–Omaha
Mark E. Wohar, University of Nebraska–Omaha

NEVADA
Michael H. Lampert, Truckee Meadows Community
 College
Bernard Malamud, University of Nevada–Las Vegas
Sheri Perez, College of Southern Nevada
Bill Robinson, University of Nevada–Las Vegas

NEW HAMPSHIRE
Evelyn Gick, Dartmouth College
Neil Niman, University of New Hampshire

NEW JERSEY
Len Anyanwu, Union County College
Maharuk Bhiladwalla, Rutgers University–New
 Brunswick
Giuliana Campanelli-Andreopoulos, William Paterson
 University
Gary Gigliotti, Rutgers University–New Brunswick
John Graham, Rutgers University–Newark
Berch Haroian, William Paterson University
Paul Harris, Camden County College
Jeff Rubin, Rutgers University
Henry Ryder, Gloucester County College
Laura Storino, Rowan University
Donna Thompson, Brookdale Community College

NEW MEXICO
Donald Coes, University of New Mexico
Kate Krause, University of New Mexico
Curt Shepherd, University of New Mexico

NEW YORK
Seemi Ahmad, Dutchess Community College
Chris Annala, State University of New York–Geneseo
Erol Balkan, Hamilton College

John Bockino, Suffolk County Community College–
 Ammerman
Charles Callahan III, State University of New York–
 Brockport
Michael Carew, Baruch College
Sean Corcoran, New York University
Ranjit S. Dighe, City University of New York–Bronx
 Community College
Debra Dwyer, Stony Brook University
Glenn Gerstner, Saint John's University–Queens
Susan Glanz, Saint John's University–Queens
Wayne A. Grove, LeMoyne College
Nancy Howe, Hudson Valley Community College
Christopher Inya, Monroe Community College
Ghassan Karam, Pace University
Clifford Kern, State University of New York–Binghamton
Mary Lesser, Iona College
Anna Musatti, Columbia University
Theodore Muzio, St. John's University, New York
Emre Ozsoz, Fashion Institute of Technology
Howard Ross, Baruch College
Ed Steinberg, New York University
Leonie Stone, State University of New York–Geneseo
Ganti Subrahmanyam, University of Buffalo
Jogindar S. Uppal, State University of New York–Albany
Susan Wolcott, Binghamton University

NORTH CAROLINA
Rita Balaban, University of North Carolina
Otilia Boldea, North Carolina State University
Robert Burrus, University of North Carolina–Wilmington
Lee A. Craig, North Carolina State University
Alexander Deshkovski, North Carolina Central University
Kathleen Dorsainvil, Winston–Salem State University
Lydia Gan, School of Business, University of North
 Carolina–Pembroke
Michael Goode, Central Piedmont Community College
Salih Hakeem, North Carolina Central University
Melissa Hendrickson, North Carolina State University
Haiyong Liu, East Carolina University
Kosmas Marinakis, North Carolina State University
Todd McFall, Wake Forest University
Shahriar Mostashari, Campbell University
Jonathan Phillips, North Carolina State University
Bobby Puryear, North Carolina State University
Jeff Sarbaum, University of North Carolina–Greensboro
Peter Schuhmann, University of North Carolina–
 Wilmington
Robert Shoffner, Central Piedmont Community College
Catherine Skura, Sandhills Community College
Carol Stivender, University of North Carolina–Charlotte
Vera Tabakova, East Carolina University
Eric Taylor, Central Piedmont Community College
Julianne Treme, University of North Carolina–Wilmington
Hui-Kuan Tseng, University of North Carolina at Charlotte

Robert Whaples, Wake Forest University
John Whitehead, Appalachian State University
Gary W. Zinn, East Carolina University
Rick Zuber, University of North Carolina at Charlotte

OHIO

Olugbenga Ajilore, The University of Toledo
Benjamin Blair, Columbus State University
John P. Blair, Wright State University
Bolong Cao, Ohio University–Athens
Kyongwook Choi, Ohio University
James D'Angelo, University of Cincinnati
Darlene DeVera, Miami University
Rudy Fichtenbaum, Wright State University
Tim Fuerst, Bowling Green University
Harley Gill, Ohio State University
Leroy Gill, Ohio State University
Steven Heubeck, Ohio State University
Daniel Horton, Cleveland State University
Michael Jones, University of Cincinnati
Kristen Keith, University of Toledo
Janice Kinghorn, Miami University
Jean Kujawa, Lourdes College
Ernest Massie, Franklin University
Ida A. Mirzaie, Ohio State University
Jay Mutter, University of Akron
Mike Nelson, University of Akron
Nicholas Noble, Miami University
Dennis C. O'Neill, University of Cincinnati
Joseph Palardy, Youngstown State University
Charles Reichheld, Cuyahoga Community College
Teresa Riley, Youngstown State University
Rochelle Ruffer, Youngstown State University
Kate Sheppard, University of Akron
Richard Stratton, University of Akron
Albert Sumell, Youngstown State University
Steve Szheghi, Wilmington College
Melissa Thomasson, Miami University
Yaqin Wang, Youngstown State University
Bert Wheeler, Cedarville University
Kathryn Wilson, Kent State University
Sourushe Zandvakili, University of Cincinnati

OKLAHOMA

David Hudgins, University of Oklahoma
Bill McLean, Oklahoma State University
Denny Myers, Oklahoma City Community College
Ed Price, Oklahoma State University
Abdulhamid Sukar, Cameron University
Zhen Zhu, University of Central Oklahoma

OREGON

Bill Burrows, Lane Community College
Tom Carroll, Central Oregon Community College
Tim Duy, University of Oregon
Alan S. Fudge, Linn-Benton Community College
B. Starr McMullen, Oregon State University

Ted Scheinman, Mount Hood Community College
Larry Singell, University of Oregon
Ayca Tekin-Koru, Oregon State University

PENNSYLVANIA

Bradley Andrew, Juniata College
Mohammad Bajwa, Northampton Community College
Gustavo Barboza, Mercyhurst College
Charles A. Bennett, Gannon University
Cynthia Benzing, West Chester University
Howard Bodenhorn, Lafayette College
Milica Bookman, St. Joseph's University
Robert Brooker, Gannon University
Eric Brucker, Widener University
Shirley Cassing, University of Pittsburgh
Linda Childs-Leatherbury, Lincoln University
Scott J. Dressler, Villanova University
Satyajit Ghosh, University of Scranton
William L. Goffe, Pennsylvania State University
Anthony Gyapong, Pennsylvania State University–
    Abington
Mehdi Haririan, Bloomsburg University
Andrew Hill, Federal Reserve Bank of Philadelphia
Steven Husted, University of Pittsburgh
James Jozefowicz, Indiana University of Pennsylvania
Stephanie Jozefowicz, Indiana University of
    Pennsylvania
Nicholas Karatjas, Indiana University of Pennsylvania
Mary Kelly, Villanova University
Brendan Kennelly, Lehigh University
Thomas C. Kinnaman, Bucknell University
Christopher Magee, Bucknell University
Svitlana Maksymenko, University of Pittsburgh
Katherine McCann, Penn State
Judy McDonald, Lehigh University
Ranganath Murthy, Bucknell University
Hong V. Nguyen, University of Scranton
Cristian Pardo, Saint Joseph's University
Iordanis Petsas, University of Scranton
Denis Raihall, West Chester University
Adam Renhoff, Drexel University
Nicole L. Sadowski, York College of Pennsylvania
Edward Scahill, University of Scranton
Ken Slaysman, York College of Pennsylvania
Rajeev Sooreea, Pennsylvania State University–Altoona
Rebecca Stein, University of Pennsylvania
Sandra Trejos, Clarion University
Peter Zaleski, Villanova University
Ann Zech, Saint Joseph's University
Lei Zhu, West Chester University
Susan Zumas, Lehigh University

RHODE ISLAND

Jongsung Kim, Bryant University
Leonard Lardaro, University of Rhode Island
Nazma Latif-Zaman, Providence College

SOUTH CAROLINA

Calvin Blackwell, College of Charleston
Ward Hooker, Orangeburg–Calhoun Technical College
Woodrow W. Hughes, Jr., Converse College
John McArthur, Wofford College
Victoria Willis-Miller, Piedmont Technical College
Chad Turner, Clemson University
Madelyn Young, Converse College

SOUTH DAKOTA

Joseph M. Santos, South Dakota State University
Jason Zimmerman, South Dakota State University

TENNESSEE

Sindy Abadie, Southwest Tennessee Community College
Charles Baum, Middle Tennessee State University
John Brassel, Southwest Tennessee Community College
Bichaka Fayissa, Middle Tennessee State University
Michael J. Gootzeit, University of Memphis
Travis Hayes, University of Tennessee–Chattanooga
Christopher C. Klein, Middle Tennessee State University
Leila Pratt, University of Tennessee at Chattanooga
Millicent Sites, Carson-Newman College

TEXAS

Carlos Aguilar, El Paso Community College
Rashid Al-Hmoud, Texas Tech University
William Beaty, Tarleton State University
Klaus Becker, Texas Tech University
Alex Brown, Texas A&M University
Jack A. Bucco, Austin Community College–Northridge and Saint Edward's University
Don Bumpass, Sam Houston State University
Marilyn M. Butler, Sam Houston State University
Mike Cohick, Collin County Community College
Cesar Corredor, Texas A&M University
Steven Craig, University of Houston
Patrick Crowley, Texas A&M University–Corpus Christi
Richard Croxdale, Austin Community College
Susan Dadres, Southern Methodist University
David Davenport, McLennan Community College
Harry Ellis, Jr., University of North Texas
Paul Emberton, Texas State University
Diego Escobari, Texas A&M University
Christi Esquivel, Navarro College
Nicholas Feltovich, University of Houston–Main
Charles Harold Fifield, Baylor University
Jamal G. Husein, Angelo State University
Mark Frank, Sam Houston State University
Alejandro Gelves, Midwestern State University
Edgar Ghossoub, University of Texas–San Antonio
Richard Gosselin, Houston Community College–Central
Sheila Amin Gutierrez de Pineres, University of Texas–Dallas
Tina J. Harvell, Blinn College–Bryan Campus
James W. Henderson, Baylor University

Jane S. Himarios, University of Texas–Arlington
James Holcomb, University of Texas–El Paso
Jamal Husein, Angelo State University
Ansul Islam, University of Houston–Downtown
Karen Johnson, Baylor University
Kathy Kelly, University of Texas–Arlington
Thomas Kemp, Tarrant County College–Northwest
Jim Lee, Texas A&M University–Corpus Christi
Ronnie W. Liggett, University of Texas–Arlington
Akbar Marvasti, University of Houston–Downtown
James Mbata, Houston Community College
Kimberly Mencken, Baylor University
Randy Methenitis, Richland College
Carl Montano, Lamar University
James Moreno, Blinn College
Camille Nelson, Texas A&M University
Michael Nelson, Texas A&M University
Charles Newton, Houston Community College–Southwest College
John Pisciotta, Baylor University
Shofiqur Rahman, University of Texas–El Paso
Sara Saderion, Houston Community College–Southwest College
George E. Samuels, Sam Houston State University
David Schutte, Mountain View College
Ivan Tasic, Texas A&M University
David Torres, University of Texas–El Paso
Ross vanWassenhove, University of Houston
Roger Wehr, University of Texas–Arlington
Jim Wollscheid, Texas A&M University–Kingsville
J. Christopher Wreh, North Central Texas College
David W. Yoskowitz, Texas A&M University–Corpus Christi
Inske Zandvliet, Brookhaven College

UTAH

Chris Fawson, Utah State University
Lowell Glenn, Utah Valley State College
Aric Krause, Westminster College
Arden Pope, Brigham Young University

VERMONT

Nancy Brooks, University of Vermont

VIRGINIA

Lee Badgett, Virginia Military Institute
Lee A. Coppock, University of Virginia
Erik Craft, University of Richmond
Janelle Davenport, Hampton University
Philip Heap, James Madison University
George E. Hoffer, Virginia Commonwealth University
Oleg Korenok, Virginia Commonwealth University
Larry Landrum, Virginia Western Community College
Frances Lea, Germanna Community College
Carrie Meyer, George Mason University
John Min, Northern Virginia Community College
Eugene Bempong Nyantakyi, West Virginia University

James Roberts, Tidewater Community College–Virginia Beach
Robert Rycroft, University of Mary Washington
Araine A. Schauer, Mary Mount College
Sarah Stafford, The College of William & Mary
Bob Subrick, James Madison University
Susanne Toney, Hampton University
Michelle Vachris, Christopher Newport University
James Wetzel, Virginia Commonwealth University
George Zestos, Christopher Newport University

WASHINGTON

Genevieve Briand, Washington State University
Lisa Citron, Cascadia College
Andrew Ewing, University of Washington
Stacey Jones, Seattle University
Dean Peterson, Seattle University
Robert Rosenman, Washington State University

WEST VIRGINIA

Jacqueline Agesa, Marshall University
Richard Agesa, Marshall University
Robin S. McCutcheon, Marshall University College of Business

WISCONSIN

Peng Huang, Ripon College
Marina Karabelas, Milwaukee Area Technical College
Elizabeth Sawyer Kelly, University of Wisconsin–Madison
Pascal Ngoboka, University of Wisconsin–River Falls
Kevin Quinn, St. Norbert College
John R. Stoll, University of Wisconsin–Green Bay

WYOMING

Robert Godby, University of Wyoming

DISTRICT OF COLUMBIA

Leon Battista, American Enterprise Institute
Robert Berman, American University
Michael Bradley, George Washington University
Colleen M. Callahan, American University
Eliane P. Catilina, Graduate School USA
Robert Feinberg, American University
Walter Park, American University
Ralph Sonenshine, American University

INTERNATIONAL

Minh Quang Dao, Carleton University–Ottawa, Canada

A Word of Thanks

Once again, we benefited greatly from the dedication and professionalism of the Pearson Economics team. Portfolio Manager David Alexander's energy and support were indispensable. David helped mold the presentation and provided words of encouragement whenever our energy flagged. Content Editor Lena Buonanno worked tirelessly to ensure that this text was as good as it could be and to coordinate the many moving parts involved in a project of this magnitude. This new edition posed particular challenges, and we remain astonished at the amount of time, energy, and unfailing good humor she brings to this project. As we worked on the first edition, former Director of Key Markets David Theisen provided invaluable insight into how best to structure a principles text. His advice helped shape nearly every chapter. We extend our thanks to Tricia Murphy, our Product Marketing Manager, and Carlie Marvel, our Field Marketer, for their energy and creativity in presenting our book and digital products to both professors and students.

Christine Donovan managed the entire production process and the extensive supplement package that accompanies the book. Editorial Assistant Nicole Nedwidek assisted the team in completing several tasks, including review surveys and summaries, to help produce both the book and media resources.

We received excellent research assistance on previous editions from Dante DeAntonio, Ed Timmons, Matthew Saboe, David Van Der Goes, and Jason Hockenberry. We thank Elena Zeller, Jennifer Brailsford, Ellen Vandevort Wolf, Emily Webster, Mollie Sweet, Jayme Wagner, and Rebecca Barney for their careful proofreading of first- and second-round page proofs. Over all editions of our books, we received helpful feedback and recommendations from Lehigh University faculty colleagues Frank R. Gunter, Thomas J. Hyclak, and Robert J. Thornton.

As instructors, we recognize how important it is for students to view graphs that are clear and accessible. We are fortunate to have Fernando Quijano render all the figures in our books and also our supplements. Market feedback on the figures continues to be positive. We extend our thanks to Fernando not only for collaborating with us and creating the best figures possible but also for his patience with our demanding schedule.

This seventh edition has several media components, which required skilled and patient creators and developers. We extend special thanks to Andy Taylor of Hodja Media for preparing the video clips and to Paul Graf of the University of Indiana–Bloomington for preparing the graph animations. These videos and animations are an important part of our revision.

A good part of the burden of an undertaking on this scale is borne by our families. We appreciate the patience, support, and encouragement of our wives and children.

Why Does Ford Assemble Cars in Both the United States and Mexico?

Until recently, did most U.S. firms operate only within the United States? Although some people believe so, in fact, many U.S. firms have been producing goods abroad for decades. For example, Henry Ford founded the Ford Motor Company in Dearborn, Michigan, in 1903. By the next year, Ford was assembling cars in Ontario, Canada. Ford began assembling cars in Manchester, England, in 1911, and in Mexico in 1925. Clearly, for many decades, Ford has been a multinational corporation, manufacturing and selling its cars around the world. In 2017, though, Ford's non-U.S. operations, particularly those in Mexico, were the subject of political controversy.

Some of the cars Ford assembles in Mexico are sold there, but Ford also exports cars from Mexico to the United States and other countries. In 2017, in an attempt to increase manufacturing employment in the United States, President Donald Trump considered imposing a 35 percent tariff—in effect, a tax—on cars that Ford and other U.S. companies assembled in Mexico for sale in the United States. If the tariff were enacted, U.S. car companies would have to pay the U.S. government an amount equal to 35 percent of the price of these cars at the border. The tariff would increase the prices consumers would pay for these cars and, therefore, reduce their sales. President Trump argued that the tariffs would give U.S. car companies an *economic incentive* to assemble more cars in the United States, which would increase employment in U.S. manufacturing.

U.S. car companies were assembling some cars in Mexico because in a *market system*, firms respond to economic incentives. In this case, the lower wages the companies can pay Mexican workers and the lower prices for auto parts in Mexico reduced Ford's costs by more than $1,000 per car. Typically, technological progress creates economic incentives for firms to change how they produce goods and services. For example, robotics can lead automobile manufacturers to automate some jobs, reducing

Jonathan Ernst/Reuters/Alamy Stock Photo

employment in the industry. Firms also respond to changes in consumer tastes, as when more people become interested in buying electric cars. But sometimes firms respond to incentives from changes in government policy. For instance, in 1994, the governments of Canada, Mexico, and the United States agreed to the North American Free Trade Agreement (NAFTA), which made it easier for U.S. firms like Ford to ship products from Mexico to the United States. In 2017, some policymakers in Washington believed that a tariff on imports to the United States from Mexico was needed to reverse the economic incentives in NAFTA.

In this chapter and the remainder of this book, we will see how economics provides us with the tools to analyze how firms, consumers, and workers respond to economic incentives and how government policymakers can attempt to reach their objectives by changing those incentives.

AN INSIDE LOOK on **page 20** discusses how likely it is that significant numbers of manufacturing jobs will return to the United States from overseas.

Sources: Dee-Ann Durbin, "Made in Mexico, Popular on U.S. Highways," Associated Press, February 8, 2017; David Welch and David Merrill, "Why Trump Tariffs on Mexican Cars Probably Won't Stop Job Flight," bloomberg. com, January 4, 2017; and Allan Nevins and Frank Ernest Hill, *Ford: Expansion and Challenge, 1915–1933*, New York: Charles Scribner's Sons, 1957, Ch. 14.

Chapter Outline & Learning Objectives

Economics in Your Life & Career

Should You Consider a Career in Manufacturing?

In the late 1940s and early 1950s, a third of workers in the United States were employed in manufacturing. Traditionally, many high school graduates viewed working on a manufacturing assembly line as a way to earn a middle-class income. Many college graduates in engineering, accounting, management, and other fields have also found employment in manufacturing. But will manufacturing be a good source of careers in the future? In December 2016, total employment in U.S. manufacturing was 12.3 million. But the U.S. Bureau of Labor Statistics forecasts that by 2024, this number will decline to 11.4 million. What is the basis for this forecast, and how reliable is it? As you read this chapter, try to answer this question. You can check your answer against the one we provide on **page 19** at the end of this chapter.

In this book, we use economics to answer questions such as the following:

- What determines the prices of goods and services from bottled water to smartphones to automobiles?
- Why have health care costs risen so rapidly?
- Why do firms engage in international trade, and how do government policies, such as tariffs, affect international trade?
- Why does the government control the prices of some goods and services, and what are the effects of those controls?

Economists do not always agree on the answer to every question, and there are lively debates on some issues. Because new economic questions are constantly arising, economists are always developing new methods to analyze them.

All the topics we discuss in this book illustrate a basic fact of life: To attain our goals, we must make choices. We must make choices because we live in a world of **scarcity**, which means that although our wants are *unlimited*, the resources available to fulfill those wants are *limited*. You might want to own a BMW and spend each summer vacationing at five-star European hotels, but unless Bill Gates is a close and generous relative, you probably lack the funds to fulfill these wants. Every day, you make choices as you spend your limited income on the many goods and services available. The finite amount of time you have also limits your ability to attain your goals. If you spend an hour studying for your economics midterm, you have one hour less to study for your history midterm. Firms and the government are in the same situation as you: They must also attain their goals with limited resources. **Economics** is the study of the choices consumers, business managers, and government officials make to attain their goals, given their scarce resources.

We begin this chapter by discussing three important economic ideas that we will return to many times in the following chapters: *People are rational, people respond to economic incentives,* and *optimal decisions are made at the margin.* Then, we consider the three fundamental questions that any economy must answer: *What* goods and services will be produced? *How* will the goods and services be produced? and *Who* will receive the goods and services produced? Next, we consider the role of *economic models* in analyzing economic issues. **Economic models** are simplified versions of reality used to analyze real-world economic situations. We will explore why economists use models and how they construct them. Finally, we will discuss the difference between microeconomics and macroeconomics, and we will preview some important economic terms.

Scarcity A situation in which unlimited wants exceed the limited resources available to fulfill those wants.

Economics The study of the choices people make to attain their goals, given their scarce resources.

Economic model A simplified version of reality used to analyze real-world economic situations.

Market A group of buyers and sellers of a good or service and the institution or arrangement by which they come together to trade.

1.1 Three Key Economic Ideas

LEARNING OBJECTIVE: Explain these three key economic ideas: People are rational, people respond to economic incentives, and optimal decisions are made at the margin.

Whether your goal is to buy a smartphone or find a part-time job, you will interact with other people in *markets.* A **market** is a group of buyers and sellers of a good or service and the institution or arrangement by which they come together to trade. Examples of markets are the markets for smartphones, houses, haircuts, stocks and bonds, and labor. Most of economics involves analyzing how people make choices and interact in markets. Here are the three important ideas about markets that we'll return to frequently:

1. People are rational.
2. People respond to economic incentives.
3. Optimal decisions are made at the margin.

People Are Rational

Economists generally assume that people are rational. This assumption does *not* mean that economists believe everyone knows everything or always makes the "best" decision. It means that economists assume that consumers and firms use all available information as they act to achieve their goals. Rational individuals weigh the benefits and costs of each action, and they choose an action only if the benefits outweigh the costs. For example, if Apple charges a price of $649 for its new iPhone, economists assume that the managers at Apple have estimated that this price will earn the company the most profit. Even though the managers may be wrong—maybe a price of $625 or $675 would be more profitable—economists assume that the managers at Apple have acted rationally, on the basis of the information available to them, in choosing the price of $649. Although not everyone behaves rationally all the time, the assumption of rational behavior is very useful in explaining most of the choices that people make.   **MyLab Economics** Concept Check

People Respond to Economic Incentives

People act from a variety of motives, including envy, compassion, and religious belief. While not ignoring other motives, economists emphasize that consumers and firms consistently respond to *economic incentives*. This point may seem obvious, but it is often overlooked. For example, according to an article in the *Wall Street Journal*, the FBI couldn't understand why banks were not taking steps to improve security in the face of an increase in robberies: "FBI officials suggest that banks place uniformed, armed guards outside their doors and install bullet-resistant plastic, known as a 'bandit barrier,' in front of teller windows." FBI officials were surprised that few banks took their advice. But the article also reported that installing bullet-resistant plastic costs $10,000 to $20,000, and a well-trained security guard receives $50,000 per year in salary and benefits. The average loss in a bank robbery is only about $1,200. The economic incentive to banks is clear: It is less costly to put up with bank robberies than to take additional security measures. FBI agents may be surprised by how banks respond to the threat of robberies—but economists are not.

In each chapter, the *Apply the Concept* feature discusses a news story or another application related to the chapter material. Read this *Apply the Concept* for a discussion of whether people respond to economic incentives even when deciding how much to eat and how much to exercise.   **MyLab Economics** Concept Check

Apply the Concept   MyLab Economics Video

Does Health Insurance Give People an Incentive to Become Obese?

Obesity is a factor in a variety of diseases, including heart disease, stroke, diabetes, and hypertension, making it a significant health problem in the United States. Body mass index (BMI) is a measurement of a person's weight relative to the person's height. According to the U.S. Centers for Disease Control and Prevention (CDC), an adult with a body mass index (BMI) of 30 or greater is considered *obese*. For example, a 5'6" adult with a BMI of 30 is 40 pounds overweight.

The following two maps show the dramatic increase in obesity between 1994 and 2015. In 1994, in a majority of states, only between 10 percent and 14 percent of the adult population was obese, and in no state was more than 20 percent of the adult population obese. By 2015, in every state, at least 20 percent of the adult population was obese, and in 44 states, at least 25 percent of the adult population was obese.

Many people who suffer from obesity have underlying medical conditions. For these people, obesity is a medical problem that they cannot control. The fact that obesity has increased, though, indicates that for some people, obesity is the result of diet and lifestyle choices. Potential explanations for the increase in obesity include greater intake of high-calorie fast foods, insufficient exercise, and a decline in the physical

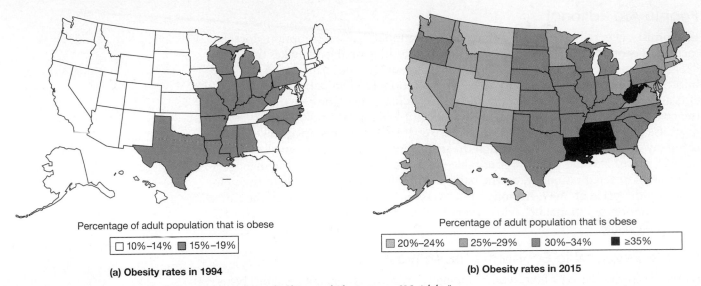

Percentage of adult population that is obese

| ☐ 10%–14% | ■ 15%–19% |

(a) Obesity rates in 1994

Percentage of adult population that is obese

| ☐ 20%–24% | ■ 25%–29% | ■ 30%–34% | ■ ≥35% |

(b) Obesity rates in 2015

Source: Centers for Disease Control and Prevention, "Prevalence of Self-Reported Obesity among U.S. Adults."

activity associated with many jobs. The CDC recommends that teenagers get a minimum of 60 minutes of aerobic exercise per day, a standard that only 15 percent of high school students meet. In 1960, 50 percent of jobs in the United States required at least moderate physical activity. Today, only 20 percent of jobs do. As a result, a typical worker today who may work at a computer is burning off about 130 *fewer* calories per workday than a worker in the 1960s who was more likely to have worked in a manufacturing plant.

In addition to eating too much and not exercising enough, could having health insurance be a cause of obesity? Obese people tend to suffer more medical problems and so incur higher medical costs. Obese people with health insurance that will reimburse them for only part of their medical bills, or who have no health insurance, must pay some or all of these higher medical bills themselves. People with health insurance that covers most of their medical bills will not suffer as large a monetary cost from being obese. In other words, by reducing some of the costs of obesity, health insurance may give people an economic incentive to gain weight.

At first glance, this argument may seem implausible. Some people suffer from medical conditions that can make physical activity difficult or that can cause weight gain even with moderate eating, so they may become obese, regardless of which type of health insurance they have. The people who are obese because of poor eating habits or lack of exercise probably don't consider health insurance when deciding whether to have a slice of chocolate cake or to watch Netflix instead of going to the gym. But if economists are correct about the importance of economic incentives, then we would expect that if we hold all other personal characteristics—such as age, gender, and income—constant, people with health insurance will be more likely to be overweight than people without health insurance.

Jay Bhattacharya and Kate Bundorf of Stanford University, Noemi Pace of the University of Venice, and Neeraj Sood of the University of Southern California, have analyzed the effects of health insurance on weight. Using a sample that followed nearly 80,000 people from 1989 to 2004, they found that after controlling for factors including age, gender, income, education, and race, people with health insurance were significantly more likely to be overweight than people without health insurance. Having private health insurance increased BMI by 1.3 points. Having public health insurance, such as Medicaid, which is a program under which the government provides health care to low-income people, increased BMI by 2.3 points. These findings do not mean that health insurance is the sole cause, or even the most important cause, of obesity. The findings do suggest that people respond to economic incentives even when making decisions about what they eat and how much they exercise. In Section 1.3, we will see that economists modify conclusions as they collect additional data.

Note: The exact formula for the body mass index is BMI = (Weight in pounds/Height in inches^2) × 703.

Sources: Centers for Disease Control and Prevention, "Prevalence of Self-Reported Obesity among U.S. Adults," www.cdc. gov; Katherine M. Flegal, Margaret D. Carroll, Cynthia L. Ogden, and Lester R. Curtin, "Prevalence and Trends in Obesity among U.S. Adults, 1999–2008," *Journal of the American Medical Association*, Vol. 303, No. 3, January 20, 2010, pp. 235–241; Jay Bhattacharya, Kate Bundorf, Noemi Pace, and Neeraj Sood, "Does Health Insurance Make You Fat?" in Michael Grossman and Naci H. Mocan, eds., *Economic Aspects of Obesity*, Chicago: University of Chicago Press, 2011; and Tara Parker-Pope, "Less Active at Work, Americans Have Packed on Pounds," *New York Times*, May 25, 2011.

Your Turn: Test your understanding by doing related problems 1.7 and 1.8 on page 23 at the end of this chapter.

MyLab Economics Study Plan

Optimal Decisions Are Made at the Margin

Some decisions are "all or nothing." For instance, when an entrepreneur decides whether to open a new restaurant, she starts the new restaurant or she doesn't. When you decide whether to attend graduate school, you either enroll in graduate school or you don't. But rather than being all or nothing, most decisions in life involve doing a little more or a little less. If you are trying to decrease your spending and increase your saving, the decision is not really between saving all the money you earn or spending it all. Rather, many small choices are involved, such as whether to buy a caffè mocha at Starbucks every day or just once a week.

Economists use the word *marginal* to mean "extra" or "additional." Should you watch another hour of television or spend that hour studying? The *marginal benefit* (MB) of watching more television is the additional enjoyment you receive. The *marginal cost* (MC) is the reduction in your test score from having studied a little less. Should Apple produce an additional 300,000 iPhones? Firms receive *revenue* from selling goods. Apple's marginal benefit is the additional revenue it receives from selling 300,000 more iPhones. Apple's marginal cost is the additional cost—for wages, parts, and so forth—of producing 300,000 more iPhones. *Economists reason that the optimal decision is to continue any activity up to the point where the marginal benefit equals the marginal cost—that is, to the point where* MB = MC. Often we apply this rule without consciously thinking about it. Usually you will know whether the additional enjoyment from watching a television program is worth the additional cost you pay by not spending that hour studying without giving the decision a lot of thought. In business situations, however, firms often have to make careful calculations to determine, for example, whether the additional revenue received from increasing production is greater or less than the additional cost of the production. Economists refer to analysis that involves comparing marginal benefits and marginal costs as **marginal analysis**.

In each chapter, you will see the feature *Solved Problem*. This feature will increase your understanding of the material by leading you through the steps of solving an applied economic problem. After reading the problem, test your understanding by doing the related problems that appear at the end of the chapter. You can also complete Solved Problems on www.pearson.com/mylab/economics and receive tutorial help.

MyLab Economics Concept Check

Marginal analysis Analysis that involves comparing marginal benefits and marginal costs.

Solved Problem 1.1

MyLab Economics Interactive Animation

The Marginal Benefit and Marginal Cost of Speed Limits

In an opinion column in the *New York Times*, economists Sendhil Mullainathan of Harvard University and Richard Thaler of the University of Chicago noted, "We do not post 10-mile-per-hour speed limits on all highways, even though that would be safer." Why is a 10-mile-per-hour speed limit unlikely to be optimal? How could a state highway department use marginal analysis to decide whether to increase the speed limit on a highway from 55 to 65 miles per hour?

Solving the Problem

Step 1: **Review the chapter material.** This problem is about making decisions, so you may want to review the section "Optimal Decisions Are Made at the Margin," which appears on this page.

Step 2: **Discuss how we can decide what the optimal speed limit is and why it is unlikely to be 10 miles per hour.** The faster people drive, the more likely they are to have accidents because the less time they have to react to problems on the highway. In addition, the faster a car or truck is traveling, the more likely it is that an accident will cause damage to the vehicles involved and injuries to the vehicles' occupants. These are the main costs of increasing the speed limit. These costs will increase with each additional mile per hour the speed limit is increased. In other words, the marginal cost from increasing the speed limit is positive.

Increasing the speed limit has benefits as well. The higher the speed limit, the faster people and freight will reach their destinations. These benefits will increase with each additional mile per hour the speed limit is increased, so the marginal benefit from increasing the speed limit is positive. The optimal speed limit will be the one where the marginal cost of decreased safety equals the marginal benefit of faster travel. We know that we have reached the optimal speed limit when increasing the limit further would result in marginal cost being greater than marginal benefit.

A 10-mile-per-hour speed limit would result in very long travel times. So, we can reasonably conclude that a 10-mile-per-hour speed limit isn't optimal because the marginal benefit from increasing it is likely to be much greater than the marginal cost.

Step 3: **Explain how a state highway department could use marginal analysis to decide whether to increase the speed limit on a highway from 55 to 65 miles per hour.** Increasing the speed limit by 10 miles per hour will reduce travel times for people and freight—so there will be a marginal benefit—but will likely also increase the number of accidents and the damage from those accidents. The state highway department should try to estimate the dollar values of the marginal cost and marginal benefit of making the change. If the marginal benefit is greater than the marginal cost, the speed limit should be increased. Although it can be difficult to assign dollar values to the marginal benefit and marginal cost of an action, marginal analysis captures the steps you can follow to make optimal decisions in many situations.

Extra Credit: Suppose that the highway department calculates that increasing the speed limit will result in reduced travel time valued at $100 million. This information would not be enough to decide that the speed limit should be raised because it represents only the marginal benefit from the higher speed limit. If the dollar value of more severe accidents from greater speed turns out to be $125 million, then the marginal cost of increasing the speed limit would be greater than the marginal benefit, and the speed limit should not be raised. Marginal benefit and marginal cost both have to be considered in arriving at an optimal decision.

Source: Sendhil Mullainathan and Richard Thaler, "Waiting in Line for the Illusion of Security," *New York Times*, May 27, 2016.

MyLab Economics Study Plan   **Your Turn:** For more practice, do related problems 1.9 and 1.10 on page 23 at the end of this chapter.

1.2 The Economic Problem That Every Society Must Solve

LEARNING OBJECTIVE: Discuss how an economy answers these questions: What goods and services will be produced? How will the goods and services be produced? Who will receive the goods and services produced?

Because we live in a world of scarcity, any society faces the *economic problem* that it has only a limited amount of economic resources—such as workers, machines, and raw materials—and so can produce only a limited amount of goods and services. Therefore, every society faces **trade-offs**: Producing more of one good or service means producing less of another good or service. The best measure of the cost of producing a good or service is the value of what has to be given up to produce it. The **opportunity cost** of any activity—such as producing a good or service—is the highest-valued alternative that must be given up to engage in that activity. The concept of opportunity cost is very important in economics and applies to individuals, firms, and society as a whole. For instance, suppose that you earn a salary of $100,000 per year working as a manager for Ford. You decide to leave your job and open your own management consulting firm. In this case, the opportunity cost of the labor you supply to your own firm is the $100,000 you give up by not working for Ford, *even if you do not explicitly pay yourself a salary*. As in this example, opportunity costs often do not involve actual payments of money.

Trade-offs force society to make choices when answering three fundamental questions:

1. *What* goods and services will be produced?
2. *How* will the goods and services be produced?
3. *Who* will receive the goods and services produced?

Throughout this book, we will return to these questions many times. For now, we briefly introduce each question.

What Goods and Services Will Be Produced?

How will society decide whether to produce more economics textbooks or more smartphones? More daycare facilities or more football stadiums? Of course, "society" doesn't make decisions; only individuals make decisions. The answer to the question of what will be produced is determined by the choices that consumers and people working for firms or the government make. Every day, you help decide which goods and services firms will produce when you choose to buy an iPhone instead of a Samsung Galaxy or a caffè mocha rather than a chai tea. Similarly, managers at Apple must choose whether to devote the company's scarce resources to making more iPhones or more smartwatches. Members of Congress and the president must choose whether to spend more of the federal government's limited budget on breast cancer research or on repairing highways. In each case, consumers, managers of firms, and government policymakers face the problem of scarcity by trading off one good or service for another. And each choice made comes with an opportunity cost, measured by the value of the best alternative given up. **MyLab Economics** Concept Check

How Will the Goods and Services Be Produced?

Firms choose how to produce the goods and services they sell. In many cases, firms face a trade-off between using more workers and using more machines. For example, a local service station has to choose whether to provide car repair services using more diagnostic computers and fewer auto mechanics or fewer diagnostic computers and more auto mechanics. Similarly, movie studios have to choose whether to produce animated films using highly skilled animators to draw them by hand or fewer animators and more computers. In deciding whether to move production offshore to China, firms may need to choose between a production method in the United States that uses fewer workers and more machines and a production method in China that uses more workers and fewer machines. **MyLab Economics** Concept Check

Who Will Receive the Goods and Services Produced?

In the United States, who receives the goods and services produced depends largely on how income is distributed. The higher a person's income, the more goods and services he or she can buy. Often, people are willing to give up some of their income—and, therefore, some of their ability to purchase goods and services—by donating to charities to increase the incomes of poorer people. Americans donate more than $370 billion per year to charity, or an average donation of about $2,900 for each household in the country. An important policy question, however, is whether the

Trade-off The idea that, because of scarcity, producing more of one good or service means producing less of another good or service.

Opportunity cost The highest-valued alternative that must be given up to engage in an activity.

government should intervene to make the distribution of income more equal. Such intervention already occurs in the United States because people with higher incomes pay a larger fraction of their incomes in taxes and because the government makes payments to people with low incomes. There is disagreement over whether the current attempts to redistribute income are sufficient or whether there should be more or less redistribution. **MyLab Economics** Concept Check

Centrally Planned Economies versus Market Economies

Centrally planned economy An economy in which the government decides how economic resources will be allocated.

Market economy An economy in which the decisions of households and firms interacting in markets allocate economic resources.

To answer the three questions—what, how, and who—societies organize their economies in two main ways. A society can have a **centrally planned economy** in which the government decides how economic resources will be allocated. Or a society can have a **market economy** in which the decisions of households and firms interacting in markets allocate economic resources.

From 1917 to 1991, the most important centrally planned economy in the world was that of the Soviet Union, which was established when Vladimir Lenin and the Communist Party staged a revolution and took control of the Russian Empire. In the Soviet Union, the government decided what goods to produce, how the goods would be produced, and who would receive the goods. Government employees managed factories and stores. The objective of these managers was to follow the government's orders rather than to satisfy the wants of consumers. Centrally planned economies like that of the Soviet Union have not been successful in producing low-cost, high-quality goods and services. As a result, the standard of living of the average person in a centrally planned economy tends to be low. All centrally planned economies have also been political dictatorships. Dissatisfaction with low living standards and political repression finally led to the collapse of the Soviet Union in 1991. Today, only North Korea still has a completely centrally planned economy.

All high-income democracies, including the United States, Canada, Japan, and the countries of Western Europe, have market economies. Market economies rely primarily on privately owned firms to produce goods and services and to decide how to produce them. Markets, rather than the government, determine who receives the goods and services produced. In a market economy, firms must produce goods and services that meet the wants of consumers, or the firms will go out of business. In that sense, it is ultimately consumers who decide what goods and services will be produced. Because firms in a market economy compete to offer the highest-quality products at the lowest price, they are under pressure to use the lowest-cost methods of production. For example, as we saw in the chapter opener, Ford moved some production to Mexico to lower its production costs in the face of competition from both foreign and domestic car firms.

In a market economy, the income of an individual is determined by the payments he receives for what he or she has to sell. If you become a civil engineer, and firms are willing to pay a salary of $85,000 per year for someone with your training and skills, you will have this amount of income to purchase goods and services. If you also buy a house that you rent out, your income will be even higher. One of the attractive features of markets is that they reward hard work. Generally, the more extensive the training you have received and the longer the hours you work, the higher your income will be. Of course, luck—both good and bad—also plays a role here. Someone might have a high income because she won the state lottery, while someone else might have a low income because he has severe medical problems. We can conclude that market economies respond to the question "Who receives the goods and services produced?" with the answer "Those who are most willing and able to buy them." **MyLab Economics** Concept Check

The Modern "Mixed" Economy

In the 1800s and early 1900s, the U.S. government engaged in relatively little regulation of markets for goods and services. Beginning in the mid-1900s, government intervention in the economy dramatically increased in the United States and other market economies. This increase was primarily caused by the high rates of unemployment and business bankruptcies during the Great Depression of the 1930s. Some government intervention was also intended to raise the incomes of the elderly, the sick, and people with limited skills. For example, in the 1930s, Congress established the *Social Security system*, which provides government payments to retired and disabled workers, and enacted *minimum wage* legislation, which sets a floor on the wages employers can pay workers in many occupations. In more recent years, government intervention in the economy has also expanded to meet goals such as protecting the environment, promoting civil rights, and providing medical care to low-income and elderly people.

Some economists argue that the extent of government intervention makes it no longer accurate to refer to the economies of the United States, Canada, Japan, and Western Europe as pure market economies. Instead, they should be called *mixed economies*. A **mixed economy** is still primarily a market economy because most economic decisions result from the interaction of buyers and sellers in markets. However, the government plays a significant role in the allocation of resources. As we will see in later chapters, economists continue to debate the role government should play in a market economy.

Mixed economy An economy in which most economic decisions result from the interaction of buyers and sellers in markets but in which the government plays a significant role in the allocation of resources.

One of the most important developments in the international economy in recent years has been the movement of China from being a centrally planned economy to being a mixed economy. The Chinese economy suffered decades of economic stagnation following the takeover of the government in 1949 by Mao Zedong and the Communist Party. Although China remains a political dictatorship, the production of most goods and services is now determined in the market rather than by the government. The result has been rapid economic growth that has lifted more than a billion people in China out of poverty. **MyLab Economics** Concept Check

Efficiency and Equity

Market economies tend to be more efficient than centrally planned economies. There are two types of efficiency. **Productive efficiency** occurs when a good or service is produced at the lowest possible cost. **Allocative efficiency** occurs when production is in accordance with consumer preferences. Markets tend to be efficient because they promote competition and facilitate voluntary exchange. With **voluntary exchange**, both the buyer and the seller of a product are made better off by the transaction. We know that they are both made better off because, otherwise, the buyer would not have agreed to buy the product or the seller would not have agreed to sell it. Productive efficiency is achieved when competition among firms forces them to produce goods and services at the lowest cost. Allocative efficiency is achieved when the combination of competition among firms and voluntary exchange between firms and consumers results in firms producing the mix of goods and services that consumers prefer the most. Competition will result in firms continuing to produce and sell goods and services as long as the additional benefit to consumers is greater than the additional cost of production. In this way, the mix of goods and services produced will match consumer preferences.

Productive efficiency A situation in which a good or service is produced at the lowest possible cost.

Allocative efficiency A state of the economy in which production is in accordance with consumer preferences; in particular, every good or service is produced up to the point where the last unit provides a marginal benefit to society equal to the marginal cost of producing it.

Voluntary exchange A situation that occurs in markets when both the buyer and the seller of a product are made better off by the transaction.

Although markets promote efficiency, they don't guarantee it. Inefficiency can arise from various sources. For instance, it may take some time for firms to learn how to efficiently produce a good or service. When smartphones were introduced, firms did not instantly achieve productive efficiency because it took time to discover the lowest-cost method of producing this good. As we will discuss in later chapters, inefficiency can also arise if governments interfere with voluntary exchange in markets. For example, many governments limit the imports of some goods from foreign countries. This limitation reduces efficiency by keeping goods from being produced at the lowest cost, a point we discuss further in the *Apply the Concept* on page 15. The production of some goods damages the environment. In this case, government intervention can increase efficiency because without such intervention, firms may ignore the costs of environmental damage and thereby fail to produce the goods at the lowest possible cost.

Equity The fair distribution of economic benefits.

Not everyone will consider a particular outcome to be desirable, even if the outcome is economically efficient. Many people prefer economic outcomes that they consider fair or equitable, even if those outcomes are less efficient. **Equity** is harder to define than efficiency because there isn't an agreed-upon definition of fairness. For some people, equity means a more equal distribution of economic benefits than would result from an emphasis on efficiency alone. For example, some people support raising taxes on people with higher incomes to provide the funds for programs that aid the poor. Although governments may increase equity by reducing the incomes of high-income people and increasing the incomes of the poor, these policies may reduce efficiency. People have less incentive to open new businesses, work hard, and save if the government takes a significant amount of the income they earn from working or saving. The result is that fewer goods and services are produced, and less saving takes place. As this example illustrates, *there is often a trade-off between efficiency and equity.* Government policymakers frequently confront this trade-off.

MyLab Economics Study Plan

MyLab Economics Concept Check

Economic Models

LEARNING OBJECTIVE: Explain how economists use models to analyze economic events and government policies.

As mentioned at the start of the chapter, economic models are simplified versions of reality. Many professions rely on models: An engineer may use a computer model of a bridge to help test whether it will withstand high winds, or a biologist may make a physical model of a nucleic acid to better understand its properties. Economists rely on economic models, or theories, to analyze real-world issues ranging from the effects of tariffs on the prices of imported goods to the most efficient policies for reducing pollution. (This book uses the words *model* and *theory* interchangeably.) One purpose of economic models is to make economic ideas sufficiently explicit and concrete so that individuals, firms, or the government can use them to make decisions. For example, we will see in Chapter 3 that the model of demand and supply is a simplified version of how the prices of products are determined by the interactions among buyers and sellers in markets.

Economists use economic models to answer questions such as "How many people will be employed in manufacturing in 2024?" Economists at the U.S. Bureau of Labor Statistics (BLS) build models that allow them to forecast future employment in different occupations. The BLS models provide estimates of future demand for U.S. manufacturing production and estimates of how many employees manufacturing firms will require to produce that level of output. As mentioned at the beginning of the chapter, the BLS forecasts that employment in manufacturing will decline significantly by 2024.

Sometimes economists use an existing model to analyze a real-world problem or issue, but in other cases, they have to develop a new model. To develop a model, economists generally follow these steps:

1. Decide on the assumptions to use.
2. Formulate a testable hypothesis.
3. Use economic data to test the hypothesis.
4. Revise the model if it fails to explain the economic data well.
5. Retain the revised model to help answer similar economic questions in the future.

The Role of Assumptions in Economic Models

Any model is based on assumptions because models have to be simplified to be useful. Economic models make *behavioral assumptions* about the motives of consumers and firms. Economists assume that consumers will buy the goods and services that will maximize their well-being or their satisfaction. Similarly, economists assume that firms act to maximize their profits. These assumptions are simplifications because they do not describe the motives of every consumer and every firm. How can we know whether the assumptions in a model are too simplified or too limiting? We can determine the usefulness of assumptions by forming hypotheses based on the assumptions and then testing the hypotheses using real-world information.

MyLab Economics Concept Check

Forming and Testing Hypotheses in Economic Models

An **economic variable** is something measurable that can have different values, such as the number of people employed in manufacturing. In an economic model, a hypothesis is a statement about an economic variable that may be either correct or incorrect. An example of a hypothesis in an economic model is the statement that increased use of industrial robots and information technology in U.S. factories has resulted in a decline in manufacturing employment. The hypothesis may be correct if the main effect of industrial robots has been to replace assembly line workers, thereby reducing employment. Or the hypothesis may be incorrect if the use of robots and other information technology has increased firms' demand for software programmers and other technology workers, thereby increasing employment. An economic hypothesis is usually about a *causal relationship*; in this case, the hypothesis states that increased use of robots and information technology causes, or leads to, lower employment in manufacturing.

Before we can accept a hypothesis, we have to test it by analyzing statistics on the relevant economic variables. In our example, we would gather statistics on how the use of industrial robots and information technology in manufacturing has changed over time, on employment in manufacturing, and perhaps on other variables. Testing a hypothesis can be tricky. For example, showing that employment in manufacturing declined at the same time that use of robots increased would not be enough to demonstrate that the increased use of robots *caused* the decline in employment. Just because two things are correlated—that is, they happen at the same time—does not mean that one caused the other. For example, suppose that at the same time that use of robots in U.S. manufacturing was increasing, U.S. manufacturing firms faced declining sales due to increased competition from foreign firms. In that case, the declining sales, rather than the increased use of robots, may explain the decrease in U.S. manufacturing employment. Over a period of time, many economic variables change, which complicates the testing of hypotheses. In fact, when economists disagree about a hypothesis, it is often because of disagreements over interpreting the statistical analysis used to test the hypothesis.

Note that hypotheses must be statements that could, in principle, turn out to be incorrect. Statements such as "Increasing employment in manufacturing is good" or "Increasing employment in manufacturing is bad" are value judgments rather than hypotheses because it is not possible to disprove them.

Economists accept and use an economic model if it leads to hypotheses that are confirmed by statistical analysis. In many cases, the acceptance is tentative, however, pending the gathering of new data or further statistical analysis. In fact, economists often refer to a hypothesis having been "not rejected" rather than having been "accepted" by statistical analysis. But what if statistical analysis clearly rejects a hypothesis? For example, what if a model leads to a hypothesis that increased use of industrial robots will cause a decline in manufacturing employment, but the data reject this hypothesis? In this case, the model should be reconsidered. It may be that an assumption used in the model was too simplified or too limiting. For example, perhaps the model ignored the fact that the mix of products being manufactured in the United States was changing. For example, perhaps the assembly of electric cars requires more workers than does the assembly of gasoline-powered cars. Or perhaps the model did not include the effect of tariffs on the demand for U.S. manufactured goods because such tariffs had typically been low. If tariffs sharply increase, the model may not be able to accurately estimate the relationship between changes in the use of industrial robots and changes in employment.

As we saw at the beginning of the chapter, the U.S. Bureau of Labor Statistics (BLS) has forecast that total employment in U.S. manufacturing will decline from 12.3 million in December 2016 to 11.4 million in 2024. The BLS periodically analyzes the accuracy of its projections. It has had difficulty accurately projecting manufacturing employment. For example, in 2000, the BLS projected that in 2010, 19,047,000 people would be employed in manufacturing. In fact, in 2010, only 11,529,000 people were employed in manufacturing. The BLS concluded that this large error was the result of its model

Economic variable Something measurable that can have different values, such as the number of people employed in manufacturing.

failing to account for the extent to which U.S. firms would move manufacturing operations overseas, how quickly firms would improve their ability to produce the same output with fewer works, and the lasting effects of the severe 2007–2009 recession. Analyzing its errors helps the BLS to improve its models and employment projections.

The process of developing models, testing hypotheses, and revising models occurs not just in economics but also in disciplines such as physics, chemistry, and biology. This process is often called the *scientific method*. Economics is a *social science* because it applies the scientific method to the study of the interactions among individuals. **MyLab Economics** Concept Check

Positive and Normative Analysis

Positive analysis Analysis concerned with what is.

Normative analysis Analysis concerned with what ought to be.

Throughout this book, as we build economic models and use them to answer questions, bear in mind the following important distinction: **Positive analysis** is concerned with *what is*, and **normative analysis** is concerned with *what ought to be*. Economics is about positive analysis, which measures the costs and benefits of different courses of action.

We can use the federal government's minimum wage law to compare positive and normative analysis. In 2017, under this law, it was illegal for an employer to hire a worker at a wage less than $7.25 per hour. (Some states and cities had enacted higher minimum wages.) Without the minimum wage law, some firms and workers would voluntarily agree to a lower wage. Because of the minimum wage law, some workers have difficulty finding jobs, and some firms end up paying more for labor than they otherwise would have. A positive analysis of the federal minimum wage law uses an economic model to estimate how many workers have lost their jobs because of the law, its effect on the costs and profits of businesses, and the gains to workers receiving the minimum wage. After economists complete this positive analysis, the decision as to whether the minimum wage law is a good or a bad idea is a normative one and depends on how people evaluate the trade-off involved. Supporters of the law believe that the losses to employers and workers who are unemployed as a result of the law are more than offset by the gains to workers who receive higher wages than they would without the law. Opponents of the law believe the losses are greater than the gains. The assessment by any individual depends, in part, on that person's values and political views. The positive analysis an economist provides would play a role in the decision but can't by itself decide the issue one way or the other.

In each chapter, you will see a *Don't Let This Happen to You* box like the one below. These boxes alert you to common pitfalls in thinking about economic ideas. After reading this box, test your understanding by working the related problem or problems at the end of the chapter. **MyLab Economics** Concept Check

Don't Let This Happen to You

Don't Confuse Positive Analysis with Normative Analysis

"Economic analysis has shown that the minimum wage law is a bad idea because it causes unemployment." Is this statement accurate? As of 2017, the federal minimum wage law prevents employers from hiring workers at a wage of less than $7.25 per hour. This wage is higher than some employers are willing to pay some workers. If there were no minimum wage law, some workers who currently cannot find any firm willing to hire them at $7.25 per hour would be able to find employment at a lower wage. Therefore, positive economic analysis indicates that the minimum wage law causes unemployment. (In Chapter 4, we'll explore why economists disagree about *how much* unemployment the minimum wage law causes.) But some workers who

have jobs benefit from the minimum wage law because they are paid a higher wage than they otherwise would be. In other words, the minimum wage law creates both losers—the workers who become unemployed and the firms that have to pay higher wages—and winners—the workers who receive higher wages.

Should we value the gains to the winners more than we value the losses to the losers? The answer involves normative analysis. Positive economic analysis can show the consequences of a particular policy, but it cannot tell us whether the policy is "good" or "bad." So, the statement at the beginning of this box is inaccurate.

MyLab Economics Study Plan

Your Turn: Test your understanding by doing related problems 3.6 and 3.7 on page 25 at the end of this chapter.

Economics as a Social Science

Because economics studies the actions of individuals, it is a social science. Economics is therefore similar to other social science disciplines, such as psychology, political science, and sociology. Economics differs from other social sciences because it puts more emphasis on how the decisions of individuals explain outcomes such as the prices firms charge or the policies governments enact. Economics considers individual decision making in every context, not just in the context of business. Economists have studied issues such as why people have difficulty losing weight or attaining other goals, why people sometimes ignore relevant information when making decisions, and how couples decide to divide up household chores. Government policymakers have also increasingly relied on economic analysis when evaluating laws or regulations. As we will see throughout this book, economists have played an important role in influencing government policies in areas such as the environment, health care, and efforts to reduce poverty.　　　　　　　　　　　　　　　**MyLab Economics** Concept Check

Apply the Concept　　　　　　　　　　**MyLab Economics** Video

What Can Economics Contribute to the Debate over Tariffs?

What effect would proposed tariffs on imports of goods from Mexico and other countries have on the U.S. economy? Governments typically impose tariffs to raise revenue or to discourage imports by raising the selling prices of imported goods. If imports of goods decline, production and employment at domestic firms that compete with imports may increase. For example, a tariff on imports of cars assembled in Mexico would raise their prices and lead U.S. consumers to buy more cars assembled in the United States. We can create a preliminary list of potential winners and losers in a country that imposes a tariff: The government gains from collecting the tariff revenue, and domestic firms and their workers gain from the higher prices of competing imported goods. Consumers lose because they pay higher prices for goods on which the tariff has been enacted. If some of the imported goods are used as inputs or are sold by domestic firms—for example, Walmart may sell imported tires on which Congress has enacted a tariff—those firms will also lose from the tariff.

Erika Skogg/National Geographic/Getty images

Because of its fertile soil and warm climate, Colombia has a comparative advantage in coffee bean production relative to the United States.

Economics can provide valuable information to policymakers and the general public as they consider actions such as implementing tariffs. As we will discuss further in Chapters 2 and 9, economic analysis shows that trade between countries occurs primarily on the basis of comparative advantage. A country has a comparative advantage if it can produce a good at a lower opportunity cost than competitors. For example, due to the climate and soil in Colombia, coffee can be grown there without requiring the transfer of significant resources from producing other goods and services—so the opportunity cost of producing coffee in Colombia is low. The United States is not well suited for producing coffee, so the opportunity cost of producing coffee in the United States is very high. We can conclude that Colombia has a comparative advantage relative to the United States in producing coffee. Imposing a tariff on imports to the United States of Colombian coffee would reduce economic efficiency by shifting production of coffee from Colombia, where it can be grown at a low cost, to the United States, where it can only be grown at a high cost.

Economists can use models to estimate the dollar amounts gained by the winners from the imposition of a tariff, the amount lost by the losers, and the size of the loss of economic efficiency. Economic analysis of tariffs typically shows that the dollar losses from the government imposing a tariff are larger than the dollar gains, so the tariff causes a net loss for the country as a whole.

Although economic analysis can contribute to the debate over policy proposals by measuring their likely effects, it cannot by itself decide whether a proposal should be enacted. Policymakers and a majority of the general public may decide to enact a tariff because they place a higher value on the gains to some groups—workers and firms struggling to compete against imported goods—than on the losses to other groups—consumers as a whole. In other words, policymakers and the general public would be making a normative judgment in favor of tariffs. Ultimately policymakers and the general public are responsible for weighing trade-offs and deciding whether a proposal should be enacted.

Sources: John D. Stoll, "Donald Trump, GM, Ford and the Made-in-Mexico Car," *Wall Street Journal*, January 3, 2017; Mary Anastasia O'Grady, "Texas and the Real Forgotten Man," *Wall Street Journal*, February 12, 2017; and David Welch and David Merrill, "Why Trump Tariffs on Mexican Cars Probably Won't Stop Job Flight," bloomberg.com, January 4, 2017.

MyLab Economics Study Plan

Your Turn: Test your understanding by doing related problem 3.8 on page 25 at the end of this chapter.

1.4 Microeconomics and Macroeconomics

LEARNING OBJECTIVE: Distinguish between microeconomics and macroeconomics.

Microeconomics The study of how households and firms make choices, how they interact in markets, and how the government attempts to influence their choices.

Macroeconomics The study of the economy as a whole, including topics such as inflation, unemployment, and economic growth.

Economic models can be used to analyze decision making in many areas. We group some of these areas together as *microeconomics* and others as *macroeconomics*. **Microeconomics** is the study of how households and firms make choices, how they interact in markets, and how the government attempts to influence their choices. **Macroeconomics** is the study of the economy as a whole, including topics such as inflation, unemployment, and economic growth. Table 1.1 gives examples of microeconomic and macroeconomic issues.

The division between microeconomics and macroeconomics is not a bright line. Many economic situations have *both* a microeconomic aspect and a macroeconomic aspect. For example, the level of total investment by firms in new machinery and equipment helps to determine how rapidly the economy grows—which is a macroeconomic issue. But to understand how much new machinery and equipment firms decide to purchase, we have to analyze the incentives individual firms face—which is a microeconomic issue.

MyLab Economics Study Plan

MyLab Economics Concept Check

Table 1.1

Issues in Microeconomics and Macroeconomics

Examples of Microeconomic Issues	Examples of Macroeconomic Issues
• How consumers react to changes in product prices	• Why economies experience periods of recession and increasing unemployment
• How firms decide what prices to charge for the products they sell	• Why, over the long run, some economies have grown much faster than others
• Which government policy would most efficiently reduce obesity	• What determines the inflation rate
• The costs and benefits of approving the sale of a new prescription drug	• What determines the value of the U.S. dollar in exchange for other currencies
• The most efficient way to reduce air pollution	• Whether government intervention can reduce the severity of recessions

1.5 Economic Skills and Economics as a Career

LEARNING OBJECTIVE: Describe economics as a career and the key skills you can gain from studying economics.

How do economists do what they do? The following analogy may be helpful: When people are thinking of buying a house, they may hire a structural engineer as a consultant to examine the house and prepare a report. The engineer's report is likely to both *describe* any problems with the house—like cracks in the foundation—and *advise* the potential buyer how to fix the problems and the likely cost.

You have seen that economics is about making choices. Economists spend much of their time describing how individuals, businesses, and governments make choices and analyzing the results of the choices. Then, like a structural engineer advising a homeowner how to fix a leaky basement, economists advise on how better decisions can be made.

In this book, we will explore economic principles that you will find very useful in understanding what is happening in the world of economics and business and in your everyday life. Individuals can use economic principles to improve how they make important decisions, such as what career to pursue, what financial investment to make, or whether to lease or buy a car. Managers in businesses can also use economic principles to improve how they make important decisions, such as what prices to charge for their products, whether to begin selling their products in a foreign market, or whether to invest in new software. Government policymakers use economic principles to make decisions, such as whether to raise taxes on cigarettes to discourage teenage smoking, whether to raise interest rates to reduce the threat of inflation, or whether to allocate additional funds to research on cancer or to research on heart disease.

Many businesses, government agencies, and nonprofit organizations—including hospitals, museums, and charities—hire economists. Colleges and universities also hire economists to teach and to carry out academic research on business, the economy, and economic policy.

The Bureau of Labor Statistics (www.bls.gov/ooh/Life-Physical-and-Social-Science/Economists.htm#tab-2) lists activities economists often perform while pursuing careers in these organizations:

- An economist working for Ford Motor Company may forecast the demand for electric cars over the next 10 years.
- An economist working for Goldman Sachs, a Wall Street investment firm, may use economic models to forecast future values of interest rates.
- An economist working for McDonald's may assess whether the firm should open additional restaurants in China.
- An economist working for the U.S. Federal Trade Commission may gather and analyze data relevant to deciding whether two firms should be allowed to reduce competition in a market by merging to form a combined firm, as when chemical companies Dow Chemical and DuPont proposed merging in 2017.
- An economist working for one of the regional Federal Reserve Banks may forecast trends in employment and production in that region.
- A journalist who majored in economics and is working for the *Wall Street Journal* may report on the Federal Reserve, interpreting monetary policy for the paper's readers.
- An economist working for the World Bank, an international economic organization with the mission of reducing poverty and increasing economic growth, might write a report analyzing the effectiveness of a development program in a low-income country.

A first step for many students in deciding whether to pursue a career in economics is to seek a summer internship with a firm or an agency that employs economists.

Many of the choices we discuss in this book will be those that business firms make. Economics has developed a set of tools designed specifically to help business firms make better decisions. It is not too surprising that more chief executive officers of Fortune 500 firms majored in economics than in any other subject. But many students who do not pursue a career in economics can still benefit from the skills they learn by taking economics classes.   **MyLab Economics** Concept Check   **MyLab Economics** Study Plan

1.6 # A Preview of Important Economic Terms

LEARNING OBJECTIVE: Define important economic terms.

In the following chapters, you will encounter certain important terms again and again. Becoming familiar with these terms is a necessary step in learning economics. Here we provide a brief introduction to some of these terms. We will discuss them all in greater depth in later chapters:

- ***Firm, company, or business.*** A *firm* is an organization that produces a good or service. Most firms produce goods or services to earn a profit, but there are also nonprofit firms, such as universities and some hospitals. Economists use the terms *firm, company*, and *business* interchangeably.

- **Entrepreneur.** An *entrepreneur* is someone who operates a business. In a market system, entrepreneurs decide what goods and services to produce and how to produce them. An entrepreneur starting a new business puts his or her own funds at risk. If an entrepreneur is wrong about what consumers want or about the best way to produce goods and services, his or her funds can be lost. Losing money in a failed business is not unusual: In the United States, about half of new businesses fail within four years. Without entrepreneurs willing to assume the risk of starting and operating businesses, economic progress would be impossible in a market system.

- **Innovation.** There is a distinction between an *invention* and an *innovation*. An *invention* is a new good or a new process for making a good. An *innovation* is the practical application of an invention. (*Innovation* may also be used more broadly to refer to any significant improvement in a good or in the means of producing a good.) Much time often passes between the appearance of a new idea and its development for widespread use. For example, the Wright brothers first achieved self-propelled flight at Kitty Hawk, North Carolina, in 1903, but the Wright brothers' plane was very crude, and it wasn't until the introduction of the DC-3 by Douglas Aircraft in 1936 that regularly scheduled intercity airline flights became common in the United States. Similarly, the first digital electronic computer—the ENIAC—was developed in 1945, but the first IBM personal computer was not introduced until 1981, and widespread use of computers did not have a significant effect on the productivity of U.S. businesses until the 1990s.

- **Technology.** A firm's *technology* is the processes it uses to produce goods and services. In the economic sense, a firm's technology depends on many factors, such as the skill of its managers, the training of its workers, and the speed and efficiency of its machinery and equipment.

- **Goods.** *Goods* are tangible merchandise, such as books, computers, or Blu-ray players.

- **Services.** *Services* are activities performed for others, such as providing haircuts or investment advice.

- **Revenue.** A firm's *revenue* is the total amount received for selling a good or service. We calculate it by multiplying the price per unit by the number of units sold.

- **Profit.** A firm's *profit* is the difference between its revenue and its costs. Economists distinguish between *accounting profit* and *economic profit*. In calculating accounting profit, we exclude the costs of some economic resources that the firm does not pay for explicitly. In calculating economic profit, we include the opportunity costs of all resources used by the firm. When we refer to *profit* in this book, we mean economic profit. It is important not to confuse *profit* with *revenue*.

- **Household.** A *household* consists of all persons occupying a home. Households are suppliers of factors of production—particularly labor—used by firms to make goods and services. Households also demand goods and services produced by firms and governments.

- **Factors of production, economic resources, or inputs.** Firms use *factors of production* to produce goods and services. The main factors of production are labor, capital, natural resources—including land—and entrepreneurial ability. Households earn income by supplying the factors of production to firms. Economists use the terms *factors of production, economic resources*, and *inputs* interchangeably.

- **Capital.** In everyday speech, the word *capital* can refer to *financial capital* or to *physical capital*. Financial capital includes stocks and bonds issued by firms, bank accounts, and holdings of money. In economics, though, *capital* refers to physical capital, which includes manufactured goods that are used to produce other goods and services. Examples of physical capital are computers, factory buildings, machine tools, warehouses, and trucks. The total amount of physical capital available in a country is called its *capital stock*.

- *Human capital.* *Human capital* refers to the accumulated training and skills that workers possess. For example, college-educated workers generally have more skills and are more productive than workers who have only high school degrees; therefore, college-educated workers have more human capital.   **MyLab Economics** Concept Check   **MyLab Economics** Study Plan

Continued from page 3

Economics in Your Life & Career

Should You Consider a Career in Manufacturing?

At the beginning of this chapter, we posed the question "What is the basis for the BLS's forecast that manufacturing employment will decline by 2024, and how reliable is this forecast?" As we saw in this chapter, the BLS uses economic models to forecast future employment in U.S. manufacturing. In recent years, the BLS has had difficulty accurately forecasting manufacturing employment. For example, in 2000, the BLS forecast that manufacturing employment would increase over the following 10 years, when in fact it declined substantially. The BLS analyzes errors like these in attempting to improve its forecasts. So, it is likely that the BLS's forecasts will become more accurate over time, but it would be a mistake to expect the forecasts to be exact.

Conclusion

Economics is a group of useful ideas about how individuals make choices given their scarce resources. Economists have put these ideas into practice by developing economic models. Consumers, business managers, and government policymakers use these models every day to help make choices. In this book, we explore many key economic models and give examples of how to apply them in the real world.

Reading the news is an important part of understanding the current business climate and learning how to apply economic concepts to a variety of real-world events. At the end of each of the first four chapters, you will see a two-page feature titled *An Inside Look*. This feature consists of an excerpt from an article that relates to the company or economic issue introduced at the start of the chapter and also to the concepts discussed in the chapter. A summary and an analysis with a supporting table or graph highlight the key economic points of the article. Read the following *An Inside Look* for a discussion of how likely it is that significant numbers of manufacturing jobs will return to the United States from overseas. Test your understanding by answering the *Thinking Critically* questions.

Is Manufacturing Returning to the United States?

24/7 WALL ST.

Manufacturers Bringing the Most Jobs Back to America

The loss of American manufacturing jobs to foreign labor has been a central theme of several presidential candidates' campaigns. However, the trend of offshoring may be slowing, according to one organization.

According to non-profit advocacy group the Reshoring Initiative, offshoring resulted in a net loss of approximately 220,000 manufacturing jobs from 2000 to 2003. However, according to the group, the country added roughly as many jobs due to foreign investment and reshoring as it lost to offshoring last year. Some of the largest U.S.-based companies, likely for both public relations and practical reasons, have begun building factories domestically for operations that would likely have gone overseas a few years ago.

Offshoring, or shifting production from U.S. plants to foreign facilities, is a relatively recent phenomenon that has taken a considerable toll on the U.S. economy. In an interview with 24/7 Wall St., Harry Moser, founder and president of the Reshoring Initiative, explained that recent developments have made the prospect of manufacturing domestically much more feasible. Moser cited economic troubles and rising wages in China as one of the primary drivers of this recent trend.

Indeed, lower labor costs and fewer regulations in countries such as China have created an incentive for U.S. companies to relocate production there. Consequently, U.S. manufacturing has taken a major hit.

A study by the Economic Policy Institute found that the U.S. lost roughly 2.4 million manufacturing jobs to China alone from 2001 to 2013.

However, the same market forces that have pushed American jobs overseas are now bringing some of those jobs back. Recently, labor costs in places such as China have been rising, and when paired with high international shipping costs, offshore production presents less of a discount than it once did. Recently, General Electric shifted production of a water heater from China to a plant in Louisville, Kentucky. The move brought hundreds of manufacturing and engineering jobs back to the U.S.

While the reshoring phenomenon is primarily a byproduct of expensive labor abroad and high shipping costs, bringing manufacturing jobs back to the United States is often beneficial to a company's image. For example, Walmart contracted General Electric to manufacture high efficiency light bulbs in its plants in Ohio and Illinois as a part of Walmart's brand-boosting Made in USA initiative. Similarly, Farouk Systems, Inc. cites image as a primary reason for reshoring jobs. Along with Walmart and General Electric, Farouk Systems ranks among the companies bringing the most jobs back from overseas.

A variety of other logistical factors are also making reshoring more practical for businesses. In the era of Amazon, in which consumers expect quick turnaround on products, it can be more practical for companies to manufacture products in-country to have the product ready for customers faster and avoid shipping expenses. Moser further explained that reshoring can often improve the quality of the manufacturing product. "Many have done it because of the consumer preference for made in America products," Moser added.

The extent to which these factory openings are truly a sign of an American manufacturing renaissance or merely a pause from the ongoing departure of the industry from U.S. shores is still unclear. One certainty is that it will take more than a few thousand jobs to reverse the trend of decades of offshoring and heavy reliance on foreign imports. . . . It is perhaps much easier to make the argument that the service sector is experiencing a true revival. While several years ago it was common practice for American companies to offshore customer support call center jobs, many American companies and customer service contractors are adding or plan to add jobs in the U.S. As of last year, there were roughly five million Americans employed in some 66,000 call centers across the country. . . .

Source: Manufacturers Bringing The Most Jobs Back to America by Michael B. Sauter and Samuel Stebbins. Copyright © April 19, 2016. Used with permission from 24/7 Wall St.

Key Points in the Article

Over the past few decades, many U.S. manufacturing companies relocated production overseas, a practice known as offshoring. The firms were responding to economic incentives such as lower labor costs and limited government regulations. Recently, however, some of these manufacturing jobs have been returning to the United States, a practice known as reshoring. Again, firms have been responding to economic incentives, including rising foreign wages, high international shipping costs, improved product quality in U.S. plants, and faster delivery times. According to the advocacy group the Reshoring Initiative, the United States added about as many jobs due to reshoring and foreign investment as it lost to offshoring in 2015, and some of the largest U.S.-based companies are now building domestic manufacturing facilities that would have likely been built in foreign countries only a few years ago.

Analyzing the News

a The table below lists the eight U.S. companies that returned the most manufacturing jobs to the United States through reshoring from 2011 to 2016. These companies have shifted production from foreign factories to new or expanded factories in the United States for a variety of reasons, including rising foreign labor costs. One key economic idea is that people are rational, and economists assume that consumers and firms use all available information as they act to achieve their goals. Economists would therefore conclude that managers at these reshoring companies are acting rationally in using all available information in making the decision to move manufacturing back to the United States.

b Another key economic idea is that people respond to economic incentives. The Economic Policy Institute conducted a study that showed that approximately 2.4 million U.S. manufacturing jobs were offshored to China from 2001 to 2013, primarily due to lower wages and fewer regulations in that country. These factors created economic incentives for managers at U.S. manufacturing companies to move production to China in order to produce goods at a lower cost than would be possible in the United States. Recently, however, labor costs in China and some other countries have been rising, as has the cost to ship internationally. These cost increases have reduced the economic incentive to produce goods overseas and resulted in some manufacturing jobs returning to the United States.

c Other reasons some manufacturing jobs are returning to the United States include a growing expectation by consumers that their orders will be delivered quickly and an increasing preference by U.S. consumers for products made in the United States. These reasons also reflect the key economic ideas that people are rational and that they respond to economic incentives. When interacting in markets, sellers want to supply the goods that buyers desire. If buyers have increased their preference for domestically produced goods and want their orders to be delivered quickly, firms are acting rationally when they reshore manufacturing jobs to the United States.

Thinking Critically

1. During the 2016 presidential campaign, President Trump proposed enacting a 45 percent tariff on imports from China. How might a tariff of this magnitude provide an economic incentive for companies like General Electric to return additional manufacturing jobs from China to the United States through reshoring?

2. Evaluate the following statement in terms of positive analysis and normative analysis: "The table shows that General Motors brought back more than 2,300 manufacturing jobs to the United States through reshoring from Canada and Mexico from 2011 to 2016. Reshoring is a good idea because it increases employment in the United States."

Manufacturers Bringing the Most Jobs Back to the United States, 2011–2016

Company	Total Jobs Reshored (estimate)	Countries from Which Jobs Were Reshored	Industry
Ford	3,200	Mexico, Spain	Transportation equipment
Boeing	2,700	Not available	Transportation equipment
General Electric	2,656	China, Mexico	Electrical equipment and appliances
General Motors	2,345	Mexico, Canada	Transportation equipment
Caterpillar	2,100	Japan, Mexico	Machinery
Flextronics (Apple)	1,700	Not available	Computers
Farouk Systems	1,200	China	Electronic appliances
Mars	1,000	Not available	Food

Source: The Reshoring Initiative

CHAPTER SUMMARY AND PROBLEMS

Key Terms

Allocative efficiency, p. 11

Centrally planned economy, p. 10

Economic model, p. 4

Economic variable, p. 13

Economics, p. 4

Equity, p. 12

Macroeconomics, p. 16

Marginal analysis, p. 7

Market, p. 4

Market economy, p. 10

Microeconomics, p. 16

Mixed economy, p. 11

Normative analysis, p. 14

Opportunity cost, p. 9

Positive analysis, p. 14

Productive efficiency, p. 11

Scarcity, p. 4

Trade-off, p. 9

Voluntary exchange, p. 11

1.1 Three Key Economic Ideas, pages 4–8

LEARNING OBJECTIVE: Explain these three key economic ideas: People are rational, people respond to economic incentives, and optimal decisions are made at the margin.

MyLab Economics Visit www.pearson.com/mylab/economics to complete these exercises online and get instant feedback.

Summary

Economics is the study of the choices consumers, business managers, and government officials make to attain their goals, given their scarce resources. We must make choices because of **scarcity**, which means that although our wants are unlimited, the resources available to fulfill those wants are limited. A **market** is a group of buyers and sellers who trade a good or service. Economists assume that people are rational in the sense that consumers and firms use all available information as they take actions intended to achieve their goals. Rational individuals weigh the benefits and costs of each action and choose an action only if the benefits outweigh the costs. Although people act from a variety of motives, ample evidence indicates that they respond to economic incentives. Economists use the word **marginal** to mean extra or additional. The optimal decision is to continue any activity up to the point where the marginal benefit equals the marginal cost.

Review Questions

1.1 Briefly discuss the meaning of each of the following economic ideas: People are rational, people respond to economic incentives, and optimal decisions are made at the margin.

1.2 What is scarcity? Why is scarcity central to the study of economics?

Problems and Applications

1.3 Discuss whether you agree with the following statement: "The problem with economics is that it assumes that consumers and firms always make the correct decisions. But we know that everyone makes mistakes."

1.4 According to the FBI Bank Crime Statistics, there were more than 4,000 bank robberies in the United States in

2015, an increase of 3.9 percent over 2014. The FBI claims that banks have made themselves easy targets by refusing to install clear acrylic partitions, called *bandit barriers,* that separate bank tellers from the public. According to a special agent with the FBI, "Bandit barriers are a great deterrent. We've talked to guys who rob banks, and as soon as they see a bandit barrier, they go find another bank." Despite this finding, many banks have been reluctant to install these barriers. Wouldn't banks have a strong incentive to install bandit barriers to deter robberies? Why, then, do so many banks not install them?

Sources: U.S. Department of Justice, Federal Bureau of Investigation, "Bank Crime Statistics 2015," and "Bank Crime Statistics 2014"; and Richard Cowen, "FBI Says Banks Are to Blame for Rise in Robberies," NorthJersey.com, March 10, 2009.

1.5 The grading system plays an important role in student learning. In their book *Effective Grading: A Tool for Learning and Assessment in College,* Barbara Walvoord and Virginia Anderson stated that "grading infuses everything that happens in the classroom." They also argued that grading "needs to be acknowledged and managed from the first moment that an instructor begins planning a class."

a. How could the grading system a teacher uses affect the incentives of students to learn the course material?

b. If teachers put too little weight in the grading scale on a certain part of the course, such as readings outside the textbook, how might students respond?

c. Teachers often wish that students came to class prepared, having read the upcoming material. How could a teacher design the grading system to motivate students to come to class prepared?

Source: Barbara E. Walvoord and Virginia Johnson Anderson, *Effective Grading: A Tool for Learning and Assessment in College,* 2nd ed., San Francisco: Jossey-Bass, 2010, p. 1.

1.6 The federal government subsidizes some loans to college students. Typically, the more students who participate in these programs and the more they borrow, the higher the cost to the federal government. In 2011, President Barack Obama convinced Congress to pass these changes to the federal student loan programs: (1) Payments were capped at 10 percent of a borrower's discretionary income; (2) any unpaid balances for people working for government or in the nonprofit sector were forgiven after making 120 monthly payments (10 years' worth of payments); and (3) people working in the private sector had their loans forgiven after making 240 monthly payments (20 years of payments).

a. As a result of these changes in the federal student loan program, would you predict that the total amount that students borrowed under these programs increased or decreased? Briefly explain.

b. As part of his 2016 federal budget proposal, President Obama recommended significant changes to the federal student loan programs. Given your answer to part (a), do you think President Obama was likely to have recommended changes that would increase or changes that would decrease the payments that borrowers would have to make? Briefly explain.

c. How might President Obama and his advisers have failed to correctly forecast the effects of the 2011 changes to the loan programs?

Sources: Allesandra Lanza, "What Obama's 2016 Budget Proposal Means for Student Borrowers," usnews.com, February 11, 2015; and Josh Mitchell, "Student-Debt Forgiveness Plans Skyrocket, Raising Fears over Costs, Higher Tuition," *Wall Street Journal*, April 22, 2014.

1.7 **(Related to the Apply the Concept on page 5)** Many universities and corporations offer a health and wellness program that helps their employees improve or maintain their health and get paid (a relatively small amount) for doing so. The programs vary but typically consist of employees completing a health assessment, receiving a program for healthy living, and monitoring their monthly health activities.

a. Why would universities and corporations pay employees to improve or maintain their health?

b. How does health insurance affect the incentive of employees to improve or maintain their health?

c. Would a wellness program increase or decrease the health insurance premiums that an insurance company would charge the university or corporation to provide insurance coverage? Briefly explain.

1.8 **(Related to the Apply the Concept on page 5)** Jay Bhattacharya and Kate Bundorf of Stanford University have found evidence that people who are obese and who work for firms that provide health insurance receive lower wages than workers at those firms who are not obese. At firms that do not provide health insurance, obese workers do not receive lower wages than workers who are not obese.

a. Why might firms that provide workers with health insurance pay a lower wage to obese workers than to workers who are not obese?

b. Is Bhattacharya and Bundorf's finding relevant to the question of whether health insurance provides people with an incentive to become obese? Briefly explain.

Source: Jay Bhattacharya and M. Kate Bundorf, "The Incidence of the Health Care Costs of Obesity," *Journal of Health Economics*, Vol. 28, No. 3, May 2009, pp. 649–658.

1.9 **(Related to Solved Problem 1.1 on page 7)** For many years, McDonald's used frozen beef patties to make its hamburgers. It recently began market testing how consumers in the United States would respond to hamburgers made of fresh beef that had never been frozen. In early 2017, McDonald's expanded the market test from only 55 restaurants to more than 300. The switch to fresh, never-frozen beef patties would be a huge undertaking involving "how [the beef] is transported to the restaurants, how it is stored when it arrives and how much it affects employees' process of making burgers." If you were a manager at McDonald's, how would you go about analyzing whether to switch to fresh, never-frozen beef patties? In your answer, consider whether your decision would have to be all or nothing—all fresh, never-frozen beef patties in all McDonald's hamburgers—and whether you would have to switch in all McDonald's locations around the world (in 119 countries) or just in certain countries.

Sources: Samantha Bomkamp, "McDonald's Expands Fresh Beef Test Again," chicago.tribune.com, March 17, 2017.

1.10 **(Related to Solved Problem 1.1 on page 7)** Late in the semester, a friend tells you, "I was going to drop my psychology course so I could concentrate on my other courses, but I had already put so much time into the course that I decided not to drop it." What do you think of your friend's reasoning? Would it make a difference to your answer if your friend has to pass the psychology course at some point to graduate? Briefly explain.

1.11 In a paper written by Bentley College economists Patricia M. Flynn and Michael A. Quinn, the authors state:

> We find evidence that Economics is a good choice of major for those aspiring to become a CEO [chief executive officer]. When adjusting for the size of the pool of graduates, those with undergraduate degrees in Economics are shown to have had a greater likelihood of becoming an S&P 500 CEO than any other major.

A list of famous economics majors published by Marietta College includes business leaders Elon Musk, Warren Buffett, Steve Ballmer, David Rockefeller, Arnold Schwarzenegger, Bill Belichick, Diane von Furstenberg, and Sam Walton, as well as Presidents George H.W. Bush, Gerald Ford, Ronald Reagan, and Donald Trump, and Supreme Court Justice Sandra Day O'Connor. Why might studying economics be particularly good preparation for being the top manager of a corporation or a leader in government?

Sources: Patricia M. Flynn and Michael A. Quinn, "Economics: A Good Choice of Major for Future CEOs," *Social Science Research Network*, November 28, 2006; and *Famous Economics Majors*, Marietta College, Marietta, Ohio, November 21, 2014.

1.2 The Economic Problem That Every Society Must Solve, pages 8–12

LEARNING OBJECTIVE: Discuss how an economy answers these questions: What goods and services will be produced? How will the goods and services be produced? Who will receive the goods and services produced?

MyLab Economics Visit www.pearson.com/mylab/economics to complete these exercises online and get instant feedback.

Summary

Society faces **trade-offs**: Producing more of one good or service means producing less of another good or service. The **opportunity cost** of any activity—such as producing a good or service—is the highest-valued alternative that must be given up to engage in that activity. The choices of consumers, firms, and governments determine what goods and services will be produced. Firms choose how to produce the goods and services they sell. In the United States, who receives the goods and services produced depends largely on how income is distributed in the marketplace. In a **centrally planned economy**, most economic decisions are made by the government. In a **market economy**, most economic decisions are made by consumers and firms. Most economies, including that of the United States, are **mixed economies** in which most economic decisions are made by consumers and firms but in which the government also plays a significant role. There are two types of efficiency: (1) **Productive efficiency**, which occurs when a good or service is produced at the lowest possible cost, and (2) **allocative efficiency**, which occurs when production corresponds with consumer preferences. **Voluntary exchange** is a situation that occurs in markets when both the buyer and the seller of a product are made better off by the transaction. **Equity** usually involves a fair distribution of economic benefits. Government policymakers often face a trade-off between equity and efficiency.

Review Questions

2.1 Why does scarcity imply that every society and every individual face trade-offs?

2.2 What are the three economic questions that every society must answer? Briefly discuss the differences in the way centrally planned, market, and mixed economies answer these questions.

2.3 What is the difference between productive efficiency and allocative efficiency?

2.4 What is the difference between efficiency and equity? Why do government policymakers often face a trade-off between efficiency and equity?

Problems and Applications

2.5 According to *Forbes* magazine, in 2017, Bill Gates was the world's richest person, with wealth of $86 billion. Does Bill Gates face scarcity? Does everyone? Are there any exceptions?

Source: "The World's Billionaires," forbes.com, March 20, 2017.

2.6 Consider an organization that exists to help the poor. The members of the organization are discussing alternative methods of aiding the poor, when a proponent of one particular method asserts, "If even one poor person is helped with this method, then all our time and money would have been worth it." If you were a member of the organization, how would you reply to this assertion?

2.7 College football attendance, especially student attendance, has been on the decline. In 2016, home attendance at major college football games declined for the sixth consecutive year and was the lowest since 2000. The opportunity cost of engaging in an activity is the value of the best alternative that must be given up to engage in that activity. How does your opportunity cost of attending a game compare with the opportunity cost facing a college student 15 years ago? Can this change account for the decline in college football attendance? Briefly explain.

Source: Jon Solomon, "College Football Attendance in 2016: Crowds Decline for Sixth Straight Year," cbssports.com, December 16, 2016.

2.8 In a market economy, why does a firm have a strong incentive to be productively efficient and allocatively efficient? What does the firm earn if it is productively and allocatively efficient, and what happens if it is not?

2.9 Alberto Chong of Georgia State University and several colleagues conducted an experiment to test the efficiency of government postal services around the world. They mailed letters to nonexistent businesses in 159 countries and kept track of how many of the letters were returned. Was this test most relevant to evaluating the productive efficiency or the allocative efficiency of these postal services? Briefly explain.

Source: Alberto Chong, Rafael La Porta, Florencio Lopez-de-Silanes, and Andrei Shleifer, "Letter Grading Government Efficiency," *Journal of the European Economic Association*, Vol. 12, No. 2, April 2014, pp. 277–299.

2.10 The Food and Drug Administration (FDA) is part of the federal government's Department of Health and Human Services. Among its other functions, the FDA evaluates the safety and effectiveness of drugs and medical devices. FDA approval had to be granted before OraSure was allowed to market its home HIV test. In a centrally planned economy, the government decides how resources will be allocated. In a market economy, the decisions of households and firms interacting in markets allocate resources. Briefly explain which statement is more accurate: (a) The regulation of the production and sale of drugs and medical devices in the United States is an example of how resources are allocated in a centrally planned economy, or (b) the regulation of the production and sale of drugs and medical devices in the United States is an example of how resources are allocated in a market economy.

2.11 Would you expect a centrally planned economy to be better at productive efficiency or allocative efficiency? Be sure to define *productive efficiency* and *allocative efficiency* in your answer.

2.12 Leonard Fleck, a philosophy professor at Michigan State University, has written:

When it comes to health care in America, we have limited resources for unlimited health care needs. We want everything contemporary medical technology can offer that will improve the length or quality of our lives as we age. But as presently healthy taxpayers, we want costs controlled.

Why is it necessary for all economic systems to limit services such as health care? How does a market system prevent people from getting as many goods and services as they want?

Source: Leonard Fleck, *Just Caring: Health Care Rationing and Democratic Deliberation*, New York: Oxford University Press, 2009.

2.13 Suppose that your college decides to give away 1,000 tickets to the football game against your school's biggest rival. The athletic department elects to distribute the tickets by giving them away to the first 1,000 students who show up at the department's office at 10 A.M. the following Monday.

    a. Which groups of students will be most likely to try to get the tickets? Think of specific examples and then generalize.

    b. What is the opportunity cost to students of distributing the tickets this way?

    c. Productive efficiency occurs when a good or service (such as the distribution of tickets) is produced at the lowest possible cost. Is this an efficient way to distribute the tickets? If possible, think of a more efficient method of distributing the tickets.

    d. Is this an equitable way to distribute the tickets? Briefly explain.

1.3   Economic Models, pages 12–16

LEARNING OBJECTIVE: Explain how economists use models to analyze economic events and government policies.

MyLab Economics   Visit www.pearson.com/mylab/economics to complete these exercises online and get instant feedback.

Summary

An **economic variable** is something measurable that can have different values, such as the number of people employed in manufacturing. Economists rely on economic models when they apply economic ideas to real-world problems. **Economic models** are simplified versions of reality used to analyze real-world economic situations. Economists accept and use an economic model if it leads to hypotheses that are confirmed by statistical analysis. In many cases, the acceptance is tentative, however, pending the gathering of new data or further statistical analysis. Economics is a *social science* because it applies the scientific method to the study of the interactions among individuals. Economics is concerned with positive analysis rather than normative analysis. **Positive analysis** is concerned with what is. **Normative analysis** is concerned with what ought to be. As a social science, economics considers human behavior in every context of decision making, not just in business.

Review Questions

3.1 Why do economists use models? How are economic data used to test models?

3.2 Describe the five steps economists follow to arrive at a useful economic model.

3.3 What is the difference between normative analysis and positive analysis? Is economics concerned mainly with normative analysis or positive analysis? Briefly explain.

Problems and Applications

3.4 Suppose an economist develops an economic model and finds that it works great in theory but fails in practice. What should the economist do next?

3.5 Dr. Strangelove's theory is that the price of mushrooms is determined by the activity of subatomic particles that exist in another universe parallel to ours. When the subatomic particles are emitted in profusion, the price of mushrooms is high. When subatomic particle emissions are low, the price of mushrooms is also low. How would you go about testing Dr. Strangelove's theory? Discuss whether this theory is useful.

3.6 **(Related to the Don't Let This Happen to You on page 14)** Briefly explain which of the following statements represent positive analysis and which represent normative analysis.

    a. A 50-cent-per-pack tax on cigarettes will lead to a 12 percent reduction in smoking by teenagers.

    b. The federal government should spend more on AIDS research.

    c. Rising wheat prices will increase bread prices.

    d. The price of coffee at Starbucks is too high.

3.7 **(Related to the Don't Let This Happen to You on page 14)** Warren Buffett is the chief executive officer of the investment firm Berkshire Hathaway and one of the wealthiest people in the world. In an editorial in the *Wall Street Journal*, Buffett argued that economic policies in the United States should be designed so that people who are willing to work receive enough income to live a "decent lifestyle." He argued that an expansion of the Earned Income Tax Credit (EITC) would be superior to an increase in the minimum wage as a means to reach this goal. The EITC is a program under which the federal government makes payments to low-income workers. Is Buffett correct that it is the role of the federal government to make sure people who work will have enough income to live a "decent lifestyle"?

Source: Warren Buffett, "Better Than Raising the Minimum Wage," *Wall Street Journal*, May 21, 2015.

3.8 **(Related to the Apply the Concept on page 15)** The *Apply the Concept* feature explains that there are both positive and normative aspects to the debate over whether the federal government should enact tariffs on imports of cars from Mexico. What economic statistics would be most useful in evaluating the positive elements in this debate? Assuming that these statistics are available or could be gathered, are they likely to resolve the normative issues in this debate?

3.9 **(Related to the Chapter Opener on page 2)** According to an article on reuters.com, Fiat Chrysler Automobiles, the firm that sells Dodge and Chrysler cars and trucks in the

United States, decided to invest $1 billion to modernize two of its U.S. production plants. The article described the possible effect of President Trump's trade policies on Fiat Chrysler's decision.

   a. What trade policies was the article referring to? How would those policies affect Fiat Chrysler's decision about whether to expand production in the United States?

   b. The article also implied that Fiat Chrysler's decision might have been affected by the possibility that the Trump administration will relax environmental regulations, such as a rule requiring companies to increase their cars' miles per gallon, and attempt to reduce the taxes corporations pay on their profits. Why would these two factors affect Fiat Chrysler's decision?

   c. Which groups are likely to gain, and which groups are likely to lose as a result of Fiat Chrysler's decision to produce more cars in U.S. plants rather than in overseas plants?

Source: Bernie Woodall and David Sheparhson, "Fiat Chrysler to Add U.S. Jobs as Trump Puts Spotlight on Industry," reuters.com, January 9, 2017.

3.10 Suppose you are building an economic model to forecast the number of people employed in U.S. manufacturing in 2024. Should your model take into account possible changes in economic policy enacted by the president and Congress? Briefly explain.

3.11 To receive a medical license in the United States, a doctor must complete a residency program at a hospital. Hospitals are not free to expand their residency programs in a particular medical specialty without approval from a residency review committee (RRC), which is made up of physicians in that specialty. A hospital that does not abide by the rulings of the RRC runs the risk of losing its accreditation from the Accreditation Council for Graduate Medical Education (ACGME). The RRCs and ACGME argue that this system ensures that residency programs do not expand to the point where they are not providing residents with high-quality training.

   a. How does this system help protect consumers?

   b. Is it possible that this system protects the financial interests of doctors more than the well-being of consumers? Briefly explain.

   c. Discuss whether you consider this system to be good or bad. Is your conclusion an example of normative economics or of positive economics? Briefly explain.

Sources: Brian Palmer, "We Need More Doctors, Stat!" *Slate*, June 27, 2011; and Sean Nicholson, "Barriers to Entering Medical Specialties," Wharton School, September 2003.

1.4 Microeconomics and Macroeconomics, page 16

LEARNING OBJECTIVE: Distinguish between microeconomics and macroeconomics.

MyLab Economics   Visit **www.pearson.com/mylab/economics** to complete these exercises online and get instant feedback.

Summary

Microeconomics is the study of how households and firms make choices, how they interact in markets, and how the government attempts to influence their choices. **Macroeconomics** is the study of the economy as a whole, including topics such as inflation, unemployment, and economic growth.

Review Question

4.1 Briefly discuss the difference between microeconomics and macroeconomics.

4.2 Is every economic issue either strictly microeconomic or strictly macroeconomic? Briefly explain.

Problems and Applications

4.3 Briefly explain whether each of the following is primarily a microeconomic issue or a macroeconomic issue.

   a. The effect of higher cigarette taxes on the quantity of cigarettes sold

   b. The effect of higher income taxes on the total amount of consumer spending

   c. The reasons the economies of East Asian countries grow faster than the economies of sub-Saharan African countries

   d. The reasons for low rates of profit in the airline industry

4.4 Briefly explain whether you agree with the following assertion:

   Microeconomics is concerned with things that happen in one particular place, such as the unemployment rate in one city. In contrast, macroeconomics is concerned with things that affect the country as a whole, such as how the rate of teenage smoking in the United States would be affected by an increase in the tax on cigarettes.

Critical Thinking Exercises

CT1.1 For this exercise, your instructor may assign you to a group. As you saw in this chapter, an economy must answer three key questions: what to produce, how to produce it, and who receives the goods and services produced. High-income countries like the United States, have capitalist economic systems, which economists call *market economies*. This exercise focuses on the ideas about capitalism that you and other students bring to this class so we can connect what you already know with how economists think about the economic system (and they think a lot about it!). Using the concepts in this chapter, explain common complaints you have about capitalism or that you have heard from others. Be sure to use the following terms or concepts in your analysis: *market, market economy, equity, allocative efficiency, centrally planned economy, normative analysis,* and *positive analysis.* Each member of the group should describe at least one complaint about capitalism and use at least one of the terms or concepts listed above. Each group should then produce a one-page paper for this analysis to either turn in or to discuss in class.

CT1.2 Suppose that you're very athletic. For example, you may like to run, swim, play volleyball, or bike. You would like to perform better at your next competition. Perhaps you want to run a 5-kilometer race 1 minute faster or perhaps you want your team to advance further in a team sports competition, like volleyball. What concept can you use from this chapter to design your training program? *Hint:* This question is not about using concepts like markets, positive or normative analysis, or assuming that people act rationally, but there is one concept introduced in this chapter that is applicable to improving your athletic performance.

Appendix

LEARNING OBJECTIVE: Use graphs and formulas to analyze economic situations.

Using Graphs and Formulas

Graphs are used to illustrate key economic ideas. Graphs appear not just in economics textbooks but also on Web sites and in newspaper and magazine articles that discuss events in business and economics. Graphs serve two useful purposes: (1) They simplify economic ideas, and (2) they make the ideas more concrete so they can be applied to real-world problems. Economic, business, and policy issues can be complicated, but a graph can help cut through complications and highlight the key relationships needed to understand the issue. In that sense, a graph can be like a street map.

Suppose you take a bus to New York City to see the Empire State Building. After arriving at the Port Authority Bus Terminal, you will probably use Google Maps or a similar app to find your way to the Empire State Building.

Maps are simplified versions of reality. The following map shows the streets in this part of New York City and some of the most important buildings. The map does not show most stores, most buildings, or the names, addresses, and telephone numbers of the people who live and work in the area. In fact, the map shows almost nothing about the messy reality of life in this section of New York City, except how the streets are laid out, which is the essential information you need to get from the Port Authority Bus Terminal to the Empire State Building.

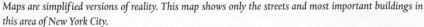

Maps are simplified versions of reality. This map shows only the streets and most important buildings in this area of New York City.

Think about someone who says, "I know how to get around in the city, but I just can't figure out how to read a map." It certainly is possible to find your destination in a city without a map, but it's a lot easier with one. The same is true of using graphs in economics. It is possible to arrive at a solution to a real-world problem in economics and business without using graphs, but it is usually a lot easier if you use them.

With practice, you will become familiar with the graphs and formulas in this text, and you will know how to use them to analyze problems that would otherwise seem very difficult. What follows is a brief review of how graphs and formulas are used.

Graphs of One Variable

Figure 1A.1 displays values for *market shares* in the U.S. automobile market, using two common types of graphs. Market shares show the percentage of industry sales accounted for by different firms. In this case, the information is for firms grouped by where the firm is headquartered: U.S.-based firms,[1] Japanese-based firms, European-based firms, and Korean-based firms. Panel (a) displays the information about market shares as a *bar graph*, with the market share of each group of firms represented by the height of its bar. Panel (b) displays the same information as a *pie chart*, with the market share of each group of firms represented by the size of its slice of the pie.

Information about an economic variable is also often displayed in a *time-series graph*, like Figure 1A.2, which shows on a coordinate grid how the values of a variable change over time. In a coordinate grid, we can measure the value of one variable along the vertical axis (or *y*-axis) and the value of another variable along the horizontal axis (or *x*-axis). The point where the vertical axis intersects the horizontal axis is called the *origin*. At the origin, the value of both variables is zero. The points on a coordinate grid represent values of the two variables.

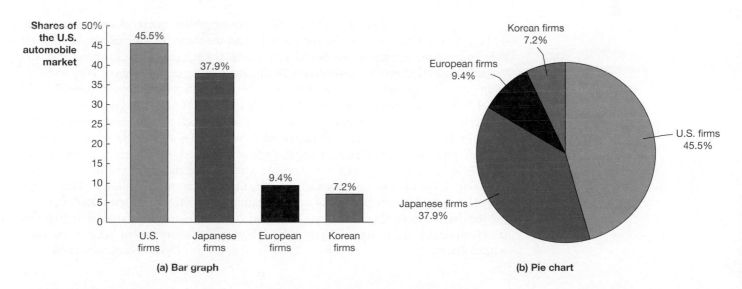

(a) Bar graph   (b) Pie chart

MyLab Economics Animation

Figure 1A.1   **Bar Graph and Pie Chart**

Values for an economic variable are often displayed as a bar graph or a pie chart. In this case, panel (a) shows market share data for the U.S. automobile industry as a bar graph, with the market share of each group of firms represented by the height of its bar. Panel (b) displays the same information as a pie chart, with the market share of each group of firms represented by the size of its slice of the pie.

Source: "Auto Sales," *Wall Street Journal*, February 1, 2017.

---

[1] In this case, the category "U.S.-based firms" includes Chrysler, which while a member of the traditional U.S. "Big Three" automobile firms and producing most of its vehicles in North America, has been owned by the Italian-based Fiat Chrysler Automobiles NV since 2009.

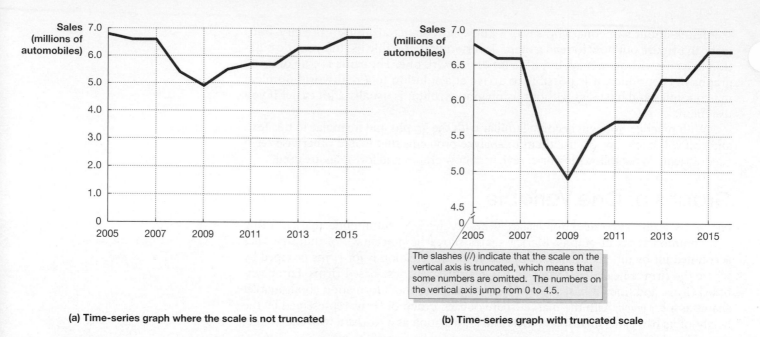

(a) Time-series graph where the scale is not truncated

(b) Time-series graph with truncated scale

The slashes (//) indicate that the scale on the vertical axis is truncated, which means that some numbers are omitted. The numbers on the vertical axis jump from 0 to 4.5.

MyLab Economics Animation

Figure 1A.2 Time-Series Graphs

Both panels present time-series graphs of Ford Motor Company's worldwide sales during each year from 2005 to 2016. In panel (a), the vertical axis starts at 0, and the distance between each pair of values shown is the same. In panel (b), the scale on the vertical axis is truncated, so although it starts at 0, it then jumps to 4.5 million. As a result, the fluctuations in Ford's sales appear smaller in panel (a) than in panel (b).

Source: Ford Motor Company, *Annual Report*, various years.

In Figure 1A.2, we measure the number of automobiles and trucks sold worldwide by Ford Motor Company on the vertical axis, and we measure time on the horizontal axis. In time-series graphs, the height of the line at each date shows the value of the variable measured on the vertical axis. Both panels of Figure 1A.2 show Ford's worldwide sales during each year from 2005 to 2016. The difference between panel (a) and panel (b) illustrates the importance of the scale used in a time-series graph. In panel (a), the vertical axis starts at 0, and the distance between each pair of values shown is the same. In this panel, the decline in Ford's sales during 2008 and 2009 appears relatively small. In panel (b), the scale on the vertical axis is truncated, which means that although it starts at zero, it jumps to 4.5 million. As a result, the distance on the vertical axis from 0 to 4.5 million is much smaller than the distance from 4.5 million to 5.0 million. The slashes (//) near the bottom of the axis indicate that the scale is truncated. In panel (b), the decline in Ford's sales during 2008 and 2009 appears much larger than in panel (a). (Technically, the horizontal axis in both panels is also truncated because we start with 2005, not 0.)

MyLab Economics Concept Check

Graphs of Two Variables

We often use graphs to show the relationship between two variables. Suppose you are interested in the relationship between the price of a cheese pizza and the quantity of pizzas sold per week in the town of Statesboro, Georgia. A graph showing the relationship between the price of a good and the quantity of the good demanded at each price is called a *demand curve*. (As we will discuss later, in drawing a demand curve for a good, we have to hold constant any variables other than price that might affect the willingness of consumers to buy the good.) Figure 1A.3 shows the data collected on price and quantity. The figure shows a two-dimensional grid on which we measure the price of

Price (dollars per pizza)	Quantity (pizzas per week)	Point
$15	50	A
14	55	B
13	60	C
12	65	D
11	70	E

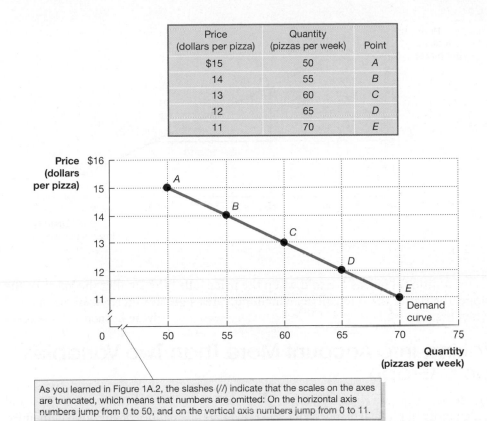

As you learned in Figure 1A.2, the slashes (//) indicate that the scales on the axes are truncated, which means that numbers are omitted: On the horizontal axis numbers jump from 0 to 50, and on the vertical axis numbers jump from 0 to 11.

MyLab Economics Animation

Figure 1A.3

Plotting Price and Quantity Points in a Graph

The figure shows a two-dimensional grid on which we measure the price of pizza along the vertical axis (or y-axis) and the quantity of pizza sold per week along the horizontal axis (or x-axis). Each point on the grid represents one of the price and quantity combinations listed in the table. By connecting the points with a line, we can better illustrate the relationship between the two variables.

pizza along the y-axis and the quantity of pizza sold per week along the x-axis. Each point on the grid represents one of the price and quantity combinations listed in the table. We can connect the points to form the demand curve for pizza in Statesboro, Georgia. Notice that the scales on both axes in the graph are truncated. In this case, truncating the axes allows the graph to illustrate more clearly the relationship between price and quantity by excluding low prices and quantities.

Slopes of Lines

Once you have plotted the data in Figure 1A.3, you may be interested in how much the quantity of pizza sold increases as the price decreases. The *slope* of a line tells us how much the variable we are measuring on the y-axis changes as the variable we are measuring on the x-axis changes. We can use the Greek letter delta (Δ) to stand for the change in a variable. The slope is sometimes called the rise over the run. So, we have several ways of expressing slope:

$$\text{Slope} = \frac{\text{Change in value on the vertical axis}}{\text{Change in value on the horizontal axis}} = \frac{\Delta y}{\Delta x} = \frac{\text{Rise}}{\text{Run}}.$$

Figure 1A.4 reproduces the graph from Figure 1A.3. Because the slope of a straight line is the same at any point, we can use any two points in the figure to calculate the slope of the line. For example, when the price of pizza decreases from $14 to $12, the quantity of pizza sold increases from 55 per week to 65 per week. Therefore, the slope is:

$$\text{Slope} = \frac{\Delta \text{Price of pizza}}{\Delta \text{Quantity of pizza}} = \frac{(\$12 - \$14)}{(65 - 55)} = \frac{-2}{10} = -0.2.$$

The slope of this line shows us how responsive consumers in Statesboro, Georgia, are to changes in the price of pizza. The larger the value of the slope (ignoring the negative sign), the steeper the line will be, which indicates that not

MyLab Economics Animation

Figure 1A.4

Calculating the Slope of a Line

We can calculate the slope of a line as the change in the value of the variable on the *y*-axis divided by the change in the value of the variable on the *x*-axis. Because the slope of a straight line is constant, we can use any two points in the figure to calculate the slope of the line. For example, when the price of pizza decreases from $14 to $12, the quantity of pizza demanded increases from 55 per week to 65 per week. So, the slope of this line equals −2 divided by 10, or −0.2.

many additional pizzas are sold when the price falls. The smaller the value of the slope, the flatter the line will be, which indicates a greater increase in pizzas sold when the price falls. **MyLab Economics** Concept Check

Taking into Account More Than Two Variables on a Graph

The demand curve in Figure 1A.4 shows the relationship between the price of pizza and the quantity of pizza demanded, but we know that the quantity of any good demanded depends on more than just the price of the good. For example, the quantity of pizza demanded in a given week in Statesboro, Georgia, can be affected by other variables—the price of hamburgers, whether an advertising campaign by local pizza parlors has begun that week, and so on. Allowing the values of any other variables to change will cause the position of the demand curve in the graph to change.

Suppose that the demand curve in Figure 1A.4 was drawn holding the price of hamburgers constant, at $1.50. If the price of hamburgers rises to $2.00, some consumers will switch from buying hamburgers to buying pizza, and more pizzas will be demanded at every price. The result on the graph will be to shift the line representing the demand curve to the right. Similarly, if the price of hamburgers falls from $1.50 to $1.00, some consumers will switch from buying pizza to buying hamburgers, and fewer pizzas will be demanded at every price. The result on the graph will be to shift the line representing the demand curve to the left.

The table in Figure 1A.5 shows the effect of a change in the price of hamburgers on the quantity of pizza demanded. On the graph, suppose that at first we are on the line labeled Demand curve$_1$. If the price of pizza is $14 (point A), an increase in the price of hamburgers from $1.50 to $2.00 increases the quantity of pizzas demanded from 55 to 60 per week (point B) and shifting the demand curve to the right to Demand curve$_2$. Or, if we start on Demand curve$_1$ and the price of pizza is $12 (point C), a decrease in the price of hamburgers from $1.50 to $1.00 decreases the quantity of pizzas demanded from 65 to 60 per week (point D) and shifts the demand curve to the left to Demand curve$_3$. By shifting the demand curve, we have taken into account the effect of changes in the value of a third variable—the price of hamburgers. We will use this technique of shifting curves to allow for the effects of additional variables many times in this book. **MyLab Economics** Concept Check

Positive and Negative Relationships

We can use graphs to show the relationships between any two variables. Sometimes the relationship between the variables is *negative*, meaning that as one variable increases in value, the other variable decreases in value. This was the case with the price of pizza and the quantity of pizzas demanded. The relationship between two variables can also be *positive*, meaning that the values of both variables increase or

| Quantity (pizzas per week) | | | |
Price (dollars per pizza)	When the Price of Hamburgers = $1.00	When the Price of Hamburgers = $1.50	When the Price of Hamburgers = $2.00
$15	45	50	55
14	50	55	60
13	55	60	65
12	60	65	70
11	65	70	75

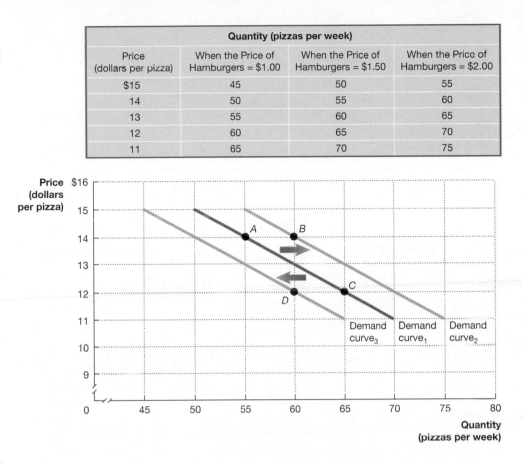

MyLab Economics Animation

Figure 1A.5

Showing Three Variables on a Graph

The demand curve for pizza shows the relationship between the price of pizzas and the quantity of pizzas demanded, *holding constant other factors that might affect the willingness of consumers to buy pizza.* If the price of pizza is $14 (point A), an increase in the price of hamburgers from $1.50 to $2.00 increases the quantity of pizzas demanded from 55 to 60 per week (point B) and shifts the demand curve to Demand curve$_2$. Or, if we start on Demand curve$_1$ and the price of pizza is $12 (point C), a decrease in the price of hamburgers from $1.50 to $1.00 decreases the quantity of pizza demanded from 65 to 60 per week (point D) and shifts the demand curve to Demand curve$_3$.

decrease together. For example, when the level of total income—or *disposable personal income*—received by households in the United States increases, the level of total *consumption spending*, which is spending by households on goods and services, also increases. The table in Figure 1A.6 shows the values (in billions of dollars) for income and consumption spending for 2013–2016. The graph plots the data from the table,

Year	Disposable Personal Income (billions of dollars)	Consumption Spending (billions of dollars)
2013	$12,396	$11,361
2014	13,023	11,863
2015	13,520	12,284
2016	14,046	12,753

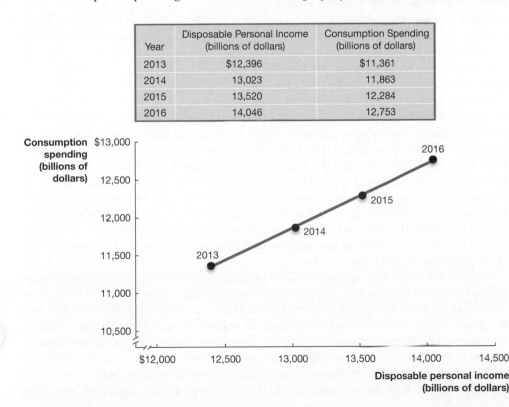

MyLab Economics Animation

Figure 1A.6

Graphing the Positive Relationship between Income and Consumption

In a positive relationship between two economic variables, as one variable increases, the other variable also increases. This figure shows the positive relationship between disposable personal income and consumption spending. As disposable personal income in the United States has increased, so has consumption spending.

Source: U.S. Department of Commerce, Bureau of Economic Analysis.

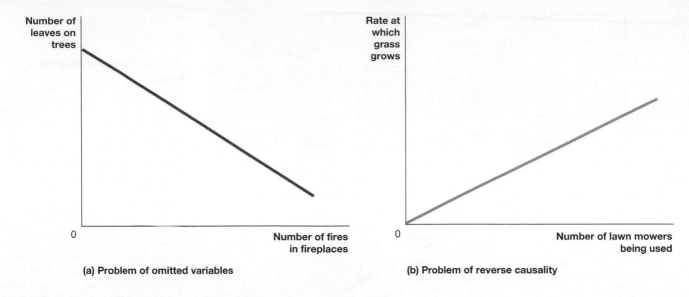

(a) Problem of omitted variables   (b) Problem of reverse causality

MyLab Economics Animation

Figure 1A.7   **Determining Cause and Effect**

Using graphs to draw conclusions about cause and effect can be hazardous. In panel (a), we see that there are fewer leaves on the trees in a neighborhood when many homes have fires burning in their fireplaces. We cannot draw the conclusion that using fireplaces causes the leaves to fall because we have an *omitted variable*—the season of the year.

In panel (b), we see that more lawn mowers are used in a neighborhood during times when the grass grows rapidly and fewer lawn mowers are used when the grass grows slowly. Concluding that using lawn mowers *causes* the grass to grow faster would be making the error of *reverse causality*.

with disposable personal income measured along the horizontal axis and consumption spending measured along the vertical axis.   **MyLab Economics** Concept Check

Determining Cause and Effect

When we graph the relationship between two variables, we usually want to draw conclusions about whether changes in one variable are causing changes in the other variable. Doing so can, however, lead to mistakes. Suppose that over the course of a year, you graph the number of homes in a neighborhood that have a fire burning in the fireplace and the number of leaves on trees in the neighborhood and you get a relationship like that shown in panel (a) of Figure 1A.7: The more fireplaces in use in the neighborhood, the fewer leaves the trees have. Can we draw the conclusion from this graph that using a fireplace causes trees to lose their leaves? We know, of course, that such a conclusion is incorrect. In spring and summer, there are relatively few fireplaces being used, and the trees are full of leaves. In the fall, as trees begin to lose their leaves, fireplaces are used more frequently. And in winter, many fireplaces are being used and many trees have lost all their leaves. The reason that the graph in Figure 1A.7 is misleading in terms of cause and effect is that there is obviously an *omitted variable* in the analysis—the season of the year. An omitted variable is one that affects the other variables in the analysis, and its omission can lead to false conclusions about cause and effect.

Although in our example the omitted variable is obvious, there are many debates about cause and effect where the existence of an omitted variable has not been clear. For instance, it has been known for many years that people who smoke cigarettes suffer from higher rates of lung cancer than do nonsmokers. For some time, tobacco companies and some scientists argued that there was an omitted variable—perhaps failure to exercise or poor diet—that made some people both more likely to smoke and more likely to develop lung cancer. If this omitted variable existed, then the finding that smokers were more likely to develop lung cancer would not have been evidence that smoking *caused* lung cancer. In this case, however, nearly all scientists eventually concluded that the omitted variable did not exist and that, in fact, smoking does cause lung cancer.

A related problem in determining cause and effect is known as *reverse causality*. The error of reverse causality occurs when we conclude that changes in variable X cause changes in variable Y when, in fact, it is actually changes in variable Y that cause changes in variable X. For example, panel (b) of Figure 1A.7 plots the number of lawn mowers being used in a neighborhood against the rate at which grass on lawns in the neighborhood is growing. We could conclude from this graph that using lawn mowers *causes* the grass to grow faster. We know, however, that in reality, the causality is in the other direction: Rapidly growing grass during the spring and summer causes the increased use of lawn mowers, and slowly growing grass in the fall or winter or during periods of low rainfall causes the decreased use of lawn mowers.

Once again, in our example, the potential error of reverse causality is obvious. In many economic debates, however, cause and effect can be more difficult to determine. For example, changes in the money supply, or the total amount of money in the economy, tend to occur at the same time as changes in the total amount of income people in the economy earn. A famous debate in economics was about whether the changes in the money supply caused the changes in total income or whether the changes in total income caused the changes in the money supply. Each side in the debate accused the other side of committing the error of reverse causality.   **MyLab Economics** Concept Check

Are Graphs of Economic Relationships Always Straight Lines?

The graphs of relationships between two economic variables that we have drawn so far have been straight lines. The relationship between two variables is *linear* when it can be represented by a straight line. Few economic relationships are actually linear. For example, if we carefully plot data on the price of a product and the quantity demanded at each price, holding constant other variables that affect the quantity demanded, we will usually find a curved—or *nonlinear*—relationship rather than a linear relationship. In practice, however, it is often useful to approximate a nonlinear relationship with a linear relationship. If the relationship is reasonably close to being linear, the analysis is not significantly affected. In addition, it is easier to calculate the slope of a straight line, and it is also easier to calculate the area under a straight line. So, in this textbook, we often assume that the relationship between two economic variables is linear, even when we know that this assumption is not precisely correct.   **MyLab Economics** Concept Check

Slopes of Nonlinear Curves

In some situations, we need to take into account the nonlinear nature of an economic relationship. For example, panel (a) of Figure 1A.8 shows the hypothetical relationship between Apple's total cost of producing iPhones and the quantity of iPhones produced. The relationship is curved rather than linear. In this case, the cost of production is increasing at an increasing rate, which often happens in manufacturing. In other words, as we move up the curve, its slope becomes larger. (Remember that with a straight line, the slope is always constant.) To see why, first remember that we calculate the slope of a curve by dividing the change in the variable on the y-axis by the change in the variable on the x-axis. As we move from point A to point B, the quantity produced increases by 1 million iPhones, while the total cost of production increases by $50 million. Farther up the curve, as we move from point C to point D, the change in quantity is the same—1 million iPhones—but the change in the total cost of production is now much larger—$250 million. Because the change in the y variable has increased, while the change in the x variable has remained the same, we know that the slope has increased.

To measure the slope of a nonlinear curve at a particular point, we measure the slope of the line that is tangent to that curve at that point. This tangent line will touch the curve only at that point. We can measure the slope of the tangent line just as we

(a) The slope of a nonlinear curve is not constant

(b) The slope of a nonlinear curve is measured by the slope of the tangent line

MyLab Economics Animation

Figure 1A.8 **The Slope of a Nonlinear Curve**

The relationship between the quantity of Apple iPhones produced and the total cost of production is curved rather than linear. In panel (a), when we move from point A to point B, the quantity produced increases by 1 million iPhones, while the total cost of production increases by $50 million. Farther up the curve, as we move from point C to point D, the change in quantity is the same—1 million iPhones—but the change in the total cost of production is now much larger—$250 million.

Because the change in the y variable has increased, while the change in the x variable has remained the same, we know that the slope has increased. In panel (b), we measure the slope of the curve at a particular point by calculating the slope of the tangent line at that point. The slope of the tangent line at point B is 75, and the slope of the tangent line at point C is 150.

would measure the slope of any other straight line. In panel (b), the tangent line at point B has a slope equal to:

$$\frac{\Delta \text{Cost}}{\Delta \text{Quantity}} = \frac{75}{1} = 75.$$

The tangent line at point C has a slope equal to:

$$\frac{\Delta \text{Cost}}{\Delta \text{Quantity}} = \frac{150}{1} = 150.$$

Once again, we see that the slope of the curve is larger at point C than at point B.

MyLab Economics Concept Check

Formulas

We have just seen that graphs are an important economic tool. In this section, we will review several useful formulas and show how to use them to summarize data and calculate important relationships.

Formula for a Percentage Change

The *percentage change* is the change in some economic variable, usually from one period to the next, expressed as a percentage. A key macroeconomic measure is the real gross domestic product (GDP). GDP is the value of all the final goods and services produced in a country during a year. "Real" GDP is corrected for the effects of inflation. When economists say that the U.S. economy grew 1.6 percent during 2016, they mean that real GDP was 1.6 percent higher in 2016 than it was in 2015. The formula for making this calculation is:

$$\left(\frac{GDP_{2016} - GDP_{2015}}{GDP_{2015}}\right) \times 100$$

or, more generally, for any two periods:

$$\text{Percentage change} = \left(\frac{\text{Value in the second period} - \text{Value in the first period}}{\text{Value in the first period}}\right) \times 100.$$

In this case, real GDP was $16,397 billion in 2015 and $16,660 billion in 2016. So, the growth rate of the U.S. economy during 2016 was:

$$\left(\frac{\$16,660 - \$16,397}{\$16,397}\right) \times 100 = 1.6\%.$$

Notice that it doesn't matter that in using the formula, we ignored the fact that GDP is measured in billions of dollars. In fact, when calculating percentage changes, *the units don't matter*. The percentage increase from $16,397 billion to $16,660 billion is exactly the same as the percentage increase from $16,397 to $16,660.   **MyLab Economics** Concept Check

Formulas for the Areas of a Rectangle and a Triangle

Areas that form rectangles and triangles on graphs can have important economic meaning. For example, Figure 1A.9 shows the demand curve for Pepsi. Suppose that the price is currently $2.00 and that 125,000 bottles of Pepsi are sold at that price. A firm's *total revenue* is equal to the amount it receives from selling its product, or the quantity sold multiplied by the price. In this case, total revenue will equal 125,000 bottles times $2.00 per bottle, or $250,000.

The formula for the area of a rectangle is:

$$\text{Area of a rectangle} = \text{Base} \times \text{Height}.$$

In Figure 1A.9, the shaded rectangle also represents the firm's total revenue because its area is given by the base of 125,000 bottles multiplied by the price of $2.00 per bottle.

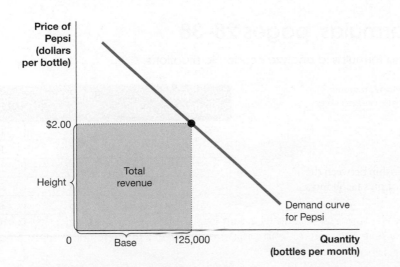

MyLab Economics Animation

Figure 1A.9

Showing a Firm's Total Revenue on a Graph

The area of a rectangle is equal to its base multiplied by its height. Total revenue is equal to quantity multiplied by price. Here, total revenue is equal to the quantity of 125,000 bottles times the price of $2.00 per bottle, or $250,000. The area of the shaded rectangle shows the firm's total revenue.

MyLab Economics Animation

Figure 1A.10

The Area of a Triangle

The area of a triangle is equal to 1/2 multiplied by its base multiplied by its height. The area of the shaded triangle has a base equal to 150,000 − 125,000, or 25,000, and a height equal to $2.00 − $1.50, or $0.50. Therefore, its area is equal to 1/2 × 25,000 × $0.50, or $6,250.

We will see in later chapters that areas that are triangles can also have economic significance. The formula for the area of a triangle is:

$$\text{Area of a triangle} = \frac{1}{2} \times \text{Base} \times \text{Height}.$$

The shaded area in Figure 1A.10 is a triangle. The base equals 150,000 − 125,000, or 25,000. Its height equals $2.00 − $1.50, or $0.50. Therefore, its area equals 1/2 × 25,000 × $0.50, or $6,250. Notice that the shaded area is a triangle only if the demand curve is a straight line, or linear. Not all demand curves are linear. However, the formula for the area of a triangle will usually still give a good approximation, even if the demand curve is not linear.

MyLab Economics Study Plan   MyLab Economics Concept Check

Summary of Using Formulas

You will encounter several other formulas in this book. Whenever you use a formula, you should follow these steps:

1. Make sure you understand the economic concept the formula represents.
2. Make sure you are using the correct formula for the problem you are solving.
3. Make sure the number you calculate using the formula is economically reasonable. For example, if you are using a formula to calculate a firm's revenue and your answer is a negative number, you know you made a mistake somewhere.   MyLab Economics Concept Check

MyLab Economics Study Plan

Using Graphs and Formulas, pages 28–38

LEARNING OBJECTIVE: Use graphs and formulas to analyze economic situations.

MyLab Economics   Visit **www.pearson.com/mylab/economics** to complete these exercises online and get instant feedback.

Problems and Applications

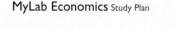

1A.1 The table on the right shows the relationship between the price of custard pies and the number of pies Jacob buys per week:

Price (dollars per pie)	Quantity of Pies	Week
$3.00	6	July 2
2.00	7	July 9
5.00	4	July 16
6.00	3	July 23
1.00	8	July 30
4.00	5	August 6

a. Is the relationship between the price of pies and the number of pies Jacob buys a positive relationship or a negative relationship?

b. Plot the data from the table on a graph similar to Figure 1A.3 on page 31. Draw a straight line that best fits the points.

c. Calculate the slope of the line.

1A.2 The following table gives information about the quantity of glasses of lemonade demanded on sunny and overcast days:

Price (dollars per glass)	Quantity (glasses of lemonade per day)	Weather
$0.80	30	Sunny
0.80	10	Overcast
0.70	40	Sunny
0.70	20	Overcast
0.60	50	Sunny
0.60	30	Overcast
0.50	60	Sunny
0.50	40	Overcast

Plot the data from the table on a graph similar to Figure 1A.5 on page 33. Draw two straight lines representing the two demand curves—one for sunny days and one for overcast days.

1A.3 Using the information in Figure 1A.2 on page 30, calculate the percentage change in Ford's auto sales from one year to the next. During which year did sales fall at the highest rate?

1A.4 Real GDP in 2014 was $15,982 billion. Real GDP in 2015 was $16,397 billion. What was the percentage change in real GDP from 2014 to 2015? What do economists call the percentage change in real GDP from one year to the next?

1A.5 Assume that the demand curve for Pepsi passes through the following two points:

Price per bottle of Pepsi (in dollars)	Quantity (bottles)
$2.50	100,000
1.25	200,000

a. Draw a graph with a linear demand curve that passes through these two points.

b. Show on the graph the areas representing total revenue at each price. Give the value for total revenue at each price.

1A.6 What is the area of the triangle shown in the following figure?

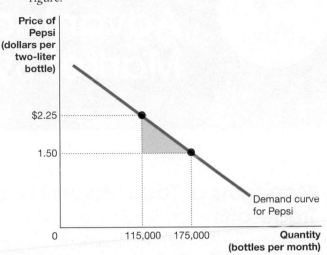

1A.7 Calculate the slope of the total cost curve at point A and at point B in the following figure.

2

Trade-offs, Comparative Advantage, and the Market System

Managers at Tesla Motors Face Trade-offs

Are electric cars the wave of the future? If you're like most drivers, you probably like the idea of skipping the gas station in favor of powering up your car by plugging it into an electric outlet. Electric cars, though, have struggled to succeed in the marketplace for two key reasons: (1) The lithium batteries that power electric cars are costly, forcing up the prices of the cars, and (2) the batteries available today need to be recharged every 100 to 300 miles, making the cars impractical for long trips.

Tesla Motors is an American-based automobile manufacturer founded in 2003 by billionaire Elon Musk, who also started the online payment system PayPal and the private space firm SpaceX. Although in 2017, the firm held only a tiny 0.3 percent share of the U.S. car market, its goal is to become the first firm to sell large numbers of electric cars. Tesla is building a nationwide network of fast-charging stations to make it easier for drivers to make longer trips. Tesla's early models were priced at over $60,000. In 2017, the company introduced its new Model 3, with a lower price of $35,000, aimed at luring customers away from gasoline-powered cars such as the Toyota Camry and Honda Accord.

Tesla manufactures its cars in a single factory in Fremont, California. To compete in the automobile market, Tesla's managers must make many strategic decisions. For example, during the first half of 2017, Tesla sold a total of about 50,000 Model S sedans, with a base price of $68,000, and Model Xs, a sport utility vehicle (SUV), with a base price of $85,500. With a limited capacity to manufacture cars in its Fremont plant, Tesla had to decide whether it would be more profitable to produce more units of its Model S and Model X or to use that capacity to produce the Model 3. Ultimately, Tesla's plan to gain a significant share of the automobile market led its managers to decide to allocate resources to producing the Model 3, even though doing so meant it would be able to produce fewer units of its other models.

Tesla's managers must also decide how to sell and service its cars. Tesla has had difficulty opening company-owned

Joe White/Retuers

dealerships to sell its cars because some states have laws that require car manufacturers to sell through independent dealerships, which Tesla is unwilling to do. In those states, Tesla sells its cars only online and relies on company-owned service centers to provide maintenance and repair services. Some economists have questioned whether Tesla will be able to meet its future sales goals without selling cars through independent dealerships as most other car companies do.

Tesla's managers also face other key decisions. For instance, they intend to eventually manufacture 1 million vehicles annually. Doing so will likely require building at least one additional factory in which to assemble the cars, as well as additional factories to manufacture the battery cells that power the cars. Like other decisions managers make, this one involves a trade-off: Devoting more resources to building additional factories would leave fewer resources available for expanding production in its two existing car and battery factories.

AN INSIDE LOOK on **page 64** discusses the reasons Tesla decided to build a large battery plant in Nevada.

Sources: Dana Hull, "Tesla Keeping Model 3 Steady as Musk to Lose CFO, Seek Cash," bloomberg.com, February 22, 2017; and Tim Higgins, "Tesla Narrowly Misses 80,000-Vehicle Sales Goal in 2016," *Wall Street Journal*, January 3, 2017.

Chapter Outline & Learning Objectives

2.1 **Production Possibilities Frontiers and Opportunity Costs,** page 42
Use a production possibilities frontier to analyze opportunity costs and trade-offs.

2.2 **Comparative Advantage and Trade,** page 48
Describe comparative advantage and explain how it serves as the basis for trade.

2.3 **The Market System,** page 54
Explain the basics of how a market system works.

Economics in Your Life & Career

The Trade-offs When You Buy a Car

Although electric cars are much in the news and are increasing in popularity, most people still buy conventional gasoline-powered cars. When you buy a gasoline-powered car, you probably consider factors such as safety and fuel efficiency. To increase fuel efficiency, automobile manufacturers make some cars that are small and light. Large cars absorb more of the impact of an accident than do small cars, so people are usually safer driving large cars. What do these facts tell us about the relationship between safety and fuel efficiency? If you were a manager at an automobile company, how might you evaluate the relationship between safety and fuel efficiency when designing cars? As you read the chapter, try to answer these questions. You can check your answers against those provided on **page 63** at the end of this chapter.

Scarcity A situation in which unlimited wants exceed the limited resources available to fulfill those wants.

In a market system, managers are continually making decisions like those made by Tesla's managers. These decisions reflect a key fact of economic life: *Scarcity requires trade-offs.* **Scarcity** exists because we have unlimited wants but only limited resources available to fulfill those wants. Goods and services are scarce. So, too, are the economic resources, or *factors of production*—workers, capital, natural resources, and entrepreneurial ability—used to make goods and services. Your time is scarce, which means you face trade-offs: If you spend an hour studying for an economics exam, you have one less hour to spend studying for a psychology exam or going to the movies. If your university decides to use some of its scarce budget to buy new computers for the computer labs, those funds will not be available to buy new books for the library or to resurface the student parking lots. If Tesla decides to devote some of the scarce workers and machinery in its Fremont assembly plant to producing more Model 3s, those resources will not be available to produce more Model Ss.

Households and firms make many of their decisions in markets. Trade is a key activity that takes place in markets. Trade results from the decisions of millions of households and firms around the world. By engaging in trade, people can raise their incomes. In this chapter, we provide an overview of how the market system coordinates the independent decisions of these millions of households and firms. We begin our analysis of the economic consequences of scarcity and how a market system works by introducing an important economic model: the *production possibilities frontier.*

2.1 Production Possibilities Frontiers and Opportunity Costs

LEARNING OBJECTIVE: Use a production possibilities frontier to analyze opportunity costs and trade-offs.

As we saw in the chapter opener, Tesla operates an automobile factory in Fremont, California, where it assembles three vehicle models: Model S and Model 3 sedans, and Model X SUVs. Because the firm's resources—workers, machinery, materials, and entrepreneurial ability—are limited, Tesla faces a trade-off: Resources devoted to producing one model are not available for producing the other models. Chapter 1 explained that economic models can be useful in analyzing many questions. We can use a simple model called the *production possibilities frontier* to analyze the trade-offs Tesla faces in its Fremont plant. A **production possibilities frontier (PPF)** is a curve showing the maximum attainable combinations of two goods that can be produced with available resources and current technology. In Tesla's case, the company produces three vehicle models at its Fremont plant, using workers, materials, robots, and other machinery.

Production possibilities frontier (PPF) A curve showing the maximum attainable combinations of two goods that can be produced with available resources and current technology.

Graphing the Production Possibilities Frontier

Figure 2.1 uses a production possibilities frontier to illustrate that the key trade-off Tesla faced in 2017 was allocating resources between its two original models (Model S and Model X) and its new Model 3. The numbers from the table are plotted in the graph. The line in the graph represents Tesla's production possibilities frontier. If Tesla uses all its resources to produce its original models, it can produce 80 per day—point A at one end of the production possibilities frontier. If Tesla uses all its resources to produce its new Model 3, it can produce 80 per day—point E at the other end of the production possibilities frontier. If Tesla devotes resources to producing both its orginal models and the Model 3, it could be at a point like B, where it produces 60 of its original models and 20 Model 3s.

All the combinations either on the frontier—like points A, B, C, D, and E—or inside the frontier—like point F—are *attainable* with the resources available. Combinations on the frontier are *efficient* because all available resources are being fully utilized, and the

Tesla's Production Choices at Its Fremont Plant		
Choice	Quantity of Original Models Produced per Day	Quantity of Model 3s Produced per Day
A	80	0
B	60	20
C	40	40
D	20	60
E	0	80

MyLab Economics Animation

Figure 2.1

Tesla's Production Possibilities Frontier

Tesla faces a trade-off: To build one more of its original Model S and Model X cars, it must build one fewer of its new Model 3. The production possibilities frontier illustrates the trade-off Tesla faces. Combinations on the production possibilities frontier—like points A, B, C, D, and E—are *efficient* because the maximum output is being obtained from the available resources. Combinations inside the frontier—like point F—are *inefficient* because some resources are not being used. Combinations outside the frontier—like point G—are *unattainable* with current resources.

fewest possible resources are being used to produce a given amount of output. Combinations inside the frontier—like point F—are *inefficient* because maximum output is not being obtained from the available resources—perhaps because the assembly line is not operating at its capacity. Tesla might like to be beyond the frontier—at a point like G, where it would be producing 60 of its original models and 50 of its Model 3s per day—but points beyond the production possibilities frontier are *unattainable*, given the firm's current resources. To produce the combination at G, Tesla would need more machines and more workers.

Notice that if Tesla is producing efficiently and is on the production possibilities frontier, the only way to produce one more Model 3 is to produce one less of its original models. Recall from Chapter 1 that the **opportunity cost** of any activity is the highest-valued alternative that must be given up to engage in that activity. For Tesla, the opportunity cost of producing one more Model 3 is the number of original models the company will not be able to produce because it has shifted those resources to producing the additional Model 3. For example, if Tesla moves from point B to point C, the opportunity cost of producing 20 more Model 3s per day is the 20 fewer original models that it can produce.

What point on the production possibilities frontier is best? We can't tell without further information. If consumer demand for Model 3s is greater than the demand for the original models (as Tesla expected), the company is likely to choose a point closer to E. If demand for the original models is greater than the demand for Model 3s, the company is likely to choose a point closer to A.   **MyLab Economics** Concept Check

Opportunity cost The highest-valued alternative that must be given up to engage in an activity.

Solved Problem 2.1

MyLab Economics Interactive Animation

Drawing a Production Possibilities Frontier for Tesla Motors

Suppose, for simplicity, that during any given week, the machinery and number of workers at Tesla Motors's Fremont plant cannot be increased. So the number of original models or Model 3s the company can produce during the week depends on how many hours are devoted to assembling each of the different models. Assume that Model 3s are more difficult to assemble, so if Tesla devotes an hour to assembling its original Model S or Model X, it will produce 15 vehicles, but if Tesla devotes an hour to producing Model 3s, it will produce only 10 vehicles. Assume that the plant can run for 8 hours per day.

a. Use the information given to fill in the missing cells in the following table:

Choice	Hours Spent Making Original Models	Hours Spent Making Model 3s	Quantity Produced per Day Original Models	Quantity Produced per Day Model 3s
A	8	0		
B	7	1		
C	6	2		
D	5	3		
E	4	4		
F	3	5		
G	2	6		
H	1	7		
I	0	8		

b. Use the data in the table to draw a production possibilities frontier graph illustrating Tesla's trade-off between assembling original models and assembling Model 3s. Label the vertical axis "Quantity of original models produced per day." Label the horizontal axis "Quantity of Model 3s produced per day." Make sure to label the values where Tesla's production possibilities frontier intersects the vertical and horizontal axes.

c. Label the points representing choice D and choice E. If Tesla is at choice D, what is its opportunity cost of making 10 more Model 3s?

Solving the Problem

Step 1: **Review the chapter material.** This problem is about using production possibilities frontiers to analyze trade-offs, so you may want to review the section "Graphing the Production Possibilities Frontier," which begins on page 42.

Step 2: **Answer part (a) by filling in the table.** If Tesla can assemble 15 original models in 1 hour, then with choice A, it can assemble 120 original models and 0 Model 3s. Because Tesla can assemble 10 Model 3s in 1 hour, with choice B, it will produce 105 original models and 10 Model 3s. Using similar reasoning, you can fill in the remaining cells in the table as follows:

Choice	Hours Spent Making Original Models	Hours Spent Making Model 3s	Quantity Produced per Day Original Models	Quantity Produced per Day Model 3s
A	8	0	120	0
B	7	1	105	10
C	6	2	90	20
D	5	3	75	30
E	4	4	60	40
F	3	5	45	50
G	2	6	30	60
H	1	7	15	70
I	0	8	0	80

Step 3: **Answer part (b) by drawing the production possibilities frontier graph.** Using the data from the table in step 2, you should draw a graph that looks like this:

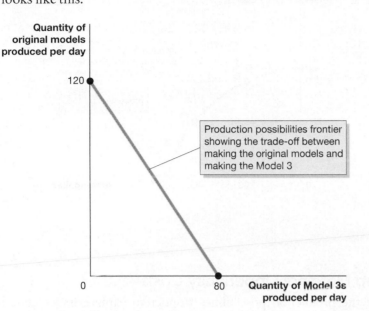

If Tesla devotes all 8 hours to assembling original models, it will produce 120 of them. Therefore, Tesla's production possibilities frontier will intersect the vertical axis at 120 original models produced. If Tesla devotes all 8 hours to assembling Model 3s, it will produce 80 of them. Therefore, Tesla's production possibilities frontier will intersect the horizontal axis at 80 Model 3s produced.

Step 4: **Answer part (c) by labeling choices D and E on your graph.** The points for choices *D* and *E* can be plotted using the information from the table:

Moving from choice *D* to choice *E* increases Tesla's production of Model 3s by 10 but lowers its production of original models by 15. Therefore, Tesla's opportunity cost of producing 10 more Model 3s is producing 15 fewer original models.

Your Turn: For more practice, do related problem 1.10 on page 67 at the end of this chapter.   MyLab Economics Study Plan

Figure 2.2

Increasing Marginal Opportunity Costs

As the economy moves down the production possibilities frontier, it experiences *increasing marginal opportunity costs* because increasing automobile production by a given quantity requires larger and larger decreases in tank production. For example, to increase automobile production from 0 to 200—moving from point *A* to point *B*—the economy has to give up only 50 tanks. But to increase automobile production by another 200 vehicles—moving from point *B* to point *C*—the economy has to give up 150 tanks.

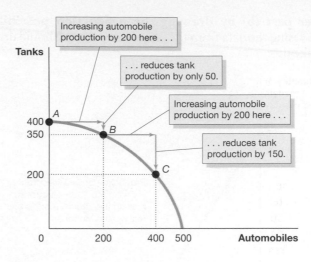

Increasing Marginal Opportunity Costs

We can use the production possibilities frontier to explore issues concerning the economy as a whole. Suppose we divide all the goods and services produced in the economy into just two types: military goods and civilian goods. In Figure 2.2, tanks represent military goods and automobiles represent civilian goods. If all the country's resources are devoted to producing military goods, 400 tanks can be produced in one year. If all resources are devoted to producing civilian goods, 500 automobiles can be produced in one year. Devoting resources to producing both goods results in the economy being at other points along the production possibilities frontier.

Notice that this production possibilities frontier is bowed outward rather than being a straight line. Because the curve is bowed out, the opportunity cost of automobiles in terms of tanks depends on where the economy currently is on the production possibilities frontier. For example, to increase automobile production from 0 to 200—moving from point *A* to point *B*—the economy has to give up only 50 tanks. But to increase automobile production by another 200 vehicles—moving from point *B* to point *C*—the economy has to give up 150 tanks.

As the economy moves down the production possibilities frontier, it experiences *increasing marginal opportunity costs* because increasing automobile production by a given quantity requires larger and larger decreases in tank production. Increasing marginal opportunity costs occur because some workers, machines, and other resources are better suited to one use than to another. At point *A*, some resources that are well suited to producing automobiles—such as workers who have years of experience on automobile assembly lines—are now producing tanks. Shifting these resources into producing automobiles by moving from point *A* to point *B* allows a substantial increase in automobile production without much loss of tank production. But as the economy moves down the production possibilities frontier, more and more resources that are better suited to tank production are switched to automobile production. As a result, the increases in automobile production become increasingly smaller, while the decreases in tank production become increasingly larger. We would expect in most situations that production possibilities frontiers will be bowed outward rather than linear, as we assumed in the Tesla example discussed earlier.

The idea of increasing marginal opportunity costs illustrates an important economic concept: *The more resources already devoted to an activity, the smaller the payoff to devoting additional resources to that activity.* For example:

- The more hours you have already spent studying economics, the smaller the increase in your test grade from each additional hour you spend—and the greater the opportunity cost of using the hour in that way.

- The more funds a firm has devoted to research and development during a given year, the smaller the amount of useful knowledge it receives from each additional dollar spent—and the greater the opportunity cost of using the funds in that way.
- The more funds the federal government spends cleaning up toxic waste dumps during a given year, the smaller the reduction in pollution from each additional dollar spent—and, once again, the greater the opportunity cost of using the funds in that way. MyLab Economics Concept Check

Economic Growth

At any given time, the total resources available to any economy are fixed. For example, if the United States produces more automobiles, it must produce less of something else—tanks in our example. The capital stock is the amount of machinery and other physical capital available in an economy. Over time, the resources available to an economy may increase because both the labor force and the capital stock increase. When the amount of resources increases, the economy's production possibilities frontier shifts outward, making it possible to produce both more automobiles and more tanks. Panel (a) of Figure 2.3 shows that over time, the economy can move from point A to point B, producing more tanks and more automobiles.

Similarly, technological change makes it possible to produce more goods with the same number of workers and the same amount of machinery, which also shifts the production possibilities frontier outward. Technological change need not affect all sectors equally. Panel (b) of Figure 2.3 shows the results of technological change in the automobile industry that increases the quantity of automobiles workers can produce per year while leaving unchanged the quantity of tanks they can produce.

Outward shifts in the production possibilities frontier represent **economic growth** because they allow the economy to increase the production of goods and services, which ultimately raises the standard of living. In the United States and other high-income countries, the market system has aided the process of economic growth, which over the past 200 years has greatly increased the well-being of the average person. MyLab Economics Concept Check

Economic growth The ability of the economy to increase the production of goods and services.

MyLab Economics Study Plan

(a) Shifting out the production possibilities frontier

(b) Technological change in the automobile industry

MyLab Economics Animation

Figure 2.3 **Economic Growth**

Panel (a) shows that as more economic resources become available and technological change occurs, the economy can move from point A to point B, producing more tanks and more automobiles. Panel (b) shows the results of technological change in the automobile industry that increases the quantity of vehicles workers can produce per year while leaving unchanged the maximum quantity of tanks they can produce. Outward shifts in the production possibilities frontier represent *economic growth*.

Comparative Advantage and Trade

2.2

LEARNING OBJECTIVE: Describe comparative advantage and explain how it serves as the basis for trade.

Trade The act of buying and selling.

We can use the concepts of the production possibilities frontier and opportunity cost to understand the basic economic activity of *trade*. Markets are fundamentally about **trade**, which is the act of buying and selling. Sometimes we trade directly, as when children trade one baseball card for another baseball card. But often we trade indirectly: We sell our labor services as, say, an accountant, a salesperson, or a nurse for money, and then we use the money earned to buy goods and services. Although in these cases trade takes place indirectly, ultimately the accountant, salesperson, or nurse is trading his or her services for food, clothing, and other goods and services. One of the great benefits of trade is that it makes it possible for people to become better off by increasing both their production and their consumption.

Specialization and Gains from Trade

Consider the following situation: You and your neighbor both have fruit trees on your properties. Initially, suppose you have only apple trees and your neighbor has only cherry trees. In this situation, if you both like apples and cherries, there is an obvious opportunity for both of you to gain from trade: You trade some of your apples for some of your neighbor's cherries, making you both better off. But what if there are apple and cherry trees growing on both of your properties? In that case, there can still be gains from trade. For example, your neighbor might be very good at picking apples, and you might be very good at picking cherries. It would make sense for your neighbor to concentrate on picking apples and for you to concentrate on picking cherries. You can then trade some of the cherries you pick for some of the apples your neighbor picks. But what if your neighbor is actually better at picking both apples and cherries than you are?

We can use production possibilities frontiers (*PPFs*) to show how your neighbor can benefit from trading with you *even though she is better than you are at picking both apples and cherries*. (For simplicity, and because it will not have any effect on the conclusions we draw, we will assume that the *PPFs* in this example are straight lines.) The table in Figure 2.4 shows how many apples and how many cherries you and your neighbor can pick in one week. We can use the data in the table to construct *PPFs* for you and your neighbor. Panel (a) shows your *PPF*. If you devote all your time to picking apples, you can pick 20 pounds of apples per week. If you devote all your time to picking cherries, you can pick 20 pounds per week. Panel (b) shows that if your neighbor devotes all her time to picking apples, she can pick 30 pounds. If she devotes all her time to picking cherries, she can pick 60 pounds.

The *PPFs* in Figure 2.4 show how many apples and cherries you and your neighbor can consume *without trade*. Suppose that when you don't trade with your neighbor, you pick and consume 8 pounds of apples and 12 pounds of cherries per week. This combination of apples and cherries is represented by point *A* in panel (a) of Figure 2.5. When your neighbor doesn't trade with you, she picks and consumes 9 pounds of apples and 42 pounds of cherries per week. This combination of apples and cherries is represented by point *C* in panel (b).

After years in which you each pick and consume your own apples and cherries, suppose your neighbor makes the following proposal: Next week she will trade you 15 pounds of her cherries for 10 pounds of your apples. Should you accept this proposal? As we can see in Figure 2.5, you should accept because you will end up with more apples and more cherries to consume. To take advantage of her proposal, you should specialize in picking only apples rather than splitting your time between picking apples and picking cherries. We know specializing will allow you to pick 20 pounds of apples. You can trade 10 pounds of apples to your neighbor for 15 pounds of her cherries. The result is that you will be able to consume 10 pounds of apples and 15 pounds of cherries (point *B* in panel (a) of Figure 2.5). You are clearly

	You		**Your Neighbor**	
	Apples	Cherries	Apples	Cherries
Devote all time to picking apples	20 pounds	0 pounds	30 pounds	0 pounds
Devote all time to picking cherries	0 pounds	20 pounds	0 pounds	60 pounds

MyLab Economics Animation

Figure 2.4   **Production Possibilities for You and Your Neighbor, without Trade**

The table shows how many pounds of apples and how many pounds of cherries you and your neighbor can each pick in one week. We can use the data from the table to construct *PPF*s for you and your neighbor. Panel (a) shows your *PPF*. If you devote all your time to picking apples and none

to picking cherries, you can pick 20 pounds. If you devote all your time to picking cherries, you can pick 20 pounds. Panel (b) shows that if your neighbor devotes all her time to picking apples, she can pick 30 pounds. If she devotes all her time to picking cherries, she can pick 60 pounds.

(a) Your production and consumption with trade

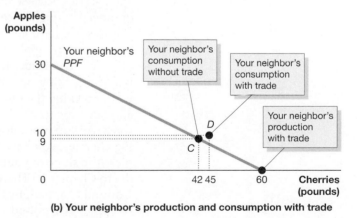

(b) Your neighbor's production and consumption with trade

MyLab Economics Animation

Figure 2.5   **Gains from Trade**

When you don't trade with your neighbor, you pick and consume 8 pounds of apples and 12 pounds of cherries per week—point *A* in panel (a). When your neighbor doesn't trade with you, she picks and consumes 9 pounds of apples and 42 pounds of cherries per week—point *C* in panel (b). If you specialize in picking apples, you can pick 20 pounds. If your neighbor specializes in picking cherries, she can pick

60 pounds. If you trade 10 pounds of your apples for 15 pounds of your neighbor's cherries, you will be able to consume 10 pounds of apples and 15 pounds of cherries—point *B* in panel (a). Your neighbor can now consume 10 pounds of apples and 45 pounds of cherries—point *D* in panel (b). You and your neighbor are both better off as a result of the trade.

Table 2.1

A Summary of the Gains
from Trade

	You		Your Neighbor	
	Apples (in pounds)	Cherries (in pounds)	Apples (in pounds)	Cherries (in pounds)
Production and consumption *without* trade	8	12	9	42
Production *with* trade	20	0	0	60
Consumption *with* trade	10	15	10	45
Gains from trade (increased consumption)	2	3	1	3

better off as a result of trading with your neighbor: You can now consume 2 more pounds of apples and 3 more pounds of cherries than you were consuming without trading. You have moved beyond your *PPF*!

Your neighbor has also benefited from the trade. By specializing in picking only cherries, she can pick 60 pounds. She trades 15 pounds of cherries to you for 10 pounds of apples. She can then consume 10 pounds of apples and 45 pounds of cherries (point D in panel (b) of Figure 2.5). This combination is 1 more pound of apples and 3 more pounds of cherries than she was consuming before trading with you. She also has moved beyond her *PPF*. Table 2.1 summarizes the changes in production and consumption that result from your trade with your neighbor. (In this example, we chose one specific rate of trading cherries for apples—15 pounds of cherries for 10 pounds of apples. There are, however, many other rates of trading cherries for apples that would also make you and your neighbor better off.)   **MyLab Economics** Concept Check

Absolute Advantage versus Comparative Advantage

Perhaps the most remarkable aspect of the preceding example is that your neighbor benefits from trading with you even though she is better than you at picking both apples and cherries. **Absolute advantage** is the ability of an individual, a firm, or a country to produce more of a good or service than competitors, using the same amount of resources. Your neighbor has an absolute advantage over you in picking both apples and cherries because she can pick more of each fruit than you can in the same amount of time. Although it seems that your neighbor should pick her own apples *and* her own cherries, we have just seen that she is better off specializing in picking cherries and leaving picking apples to you.

We can consider further why both you and your neighbor benefit from specializing in picking only one fruit. First, think about the opportunity cost to each of you of picking the two fruits. We saw from the *PPF* in Figure 2.4 that if you devoted all your time to picking apples, you would be able to pick 20 pounds of apples per week. As you move down your *PPF* and shift time away from picking apples to picking cherries, you have to give up 1 pound of apples for each pound of cherries you pick (the slope of your *PPF* is −1). (For a review of calculating slopes, see the appendix to Chapter 1.) Therefore, your opportunity cost of picking 1 pound of cherries is 1 pound of apples. By the same reasoning, your opportunity cost of picking 1 pound of apples is 1 pound of cherries. Your neighbor's *PPF* has a different slope, so she faces a different trade-off: As she shifts time from picking apples to picking cherries, she has to give up 0.5 pound of apples for every 1 pound of cherries she picks (the slope of your neighbor's *PPF* is −0.5). As she shifts time from picking cherries to picking apples, she gives up 2 pounds of cherries for every 1 pound of apples she picks. Therefore, her opportunity cost of picking 1 pound of apples is 2 pounds of cherries, and her opportunity cost of picking 1 pound of cherries is 0.5 pound of apples.

Absolute advantage The ability of an individual, a firm, or a country to produce more of a good or service than competitors, using the same amount of resources.

	Opportunity Cost of Picking 1 Pound of Apples	Opportunity Cost of Picking 1 Pound of Cherries
You	1 pound of cherries	1 pound of apples
Your neighbor	2 pounds of cherries	0.5 pound of apples

Table 2.2

Opportunity Costs of Picking Apples and Cherries

Table 2.2 summarizes the opportunity costs for you and your neighbor of picking apples and cherries. Note that even though your neighbor can pick more apples in a week than you can, the *opportunity cost* of picking apples is higher for her than for you because when she picks apples, she gives up more cherries than you do. So, even though she has an absolute advantage over you in picking apples, it is more costly for her to pick apples than it is for you. The table also shows that her opportunity cost of picking cherries is lower than yours. **Comparative advantage** is the ability of an individual, a firm, or a country to produce a good or service at a lower opportunity cost than competitors. In picking apples, your neighbor has an *absolute advantage* over you, while you have a *comparative advantage* over her. Your neighbor has both an absolute advantage and a comparative advantage over you in picking cherries. As we have seen, you are better off specializing in picking apples, and your neighbor is better off specializing in picking cherries.   **MyLab Economics** Concept Check

Comparative advantage The ability of an individual, a firm, or a country to produce a good or service at a lower opportunity cost than competitors.

Comparative Advantage and the Gains from Trade

We have just arrived at an important economic principle: *The basis for trade is comparative advantage, not absolute advantage.* The fastest apple pickers do not necessarily do much apple picking. If the fastest apple pickers have a comparative advantage in some other activity—picking cherries, playing Major League Baseball, or being industrial engineers—they are better off specializing in that activity. Individuals, firms, and countries are better off if they specialize in producing goods and services for which they have a comparative advantage and obtain the other goods and services they need by trading. We will return to the important concept of comparative advantage in Chapter 9, which is devoted to the subject of international trade.   **MyLab Economics** Concept Check

MyLab Economics Study Plan

Don't Let This Happen to You

Don't Confuse Absolute Advantage and Comparative Advantage

First, make sure you know the definitions:

- **Absolute advantage.** The ability of an individual, a firm, or a country to produce more of a good or service than competitors, using the same amount of resources. In our example, your neighbor has an absolute advantage over you in both picking apples and picking cherries.
- **Comparative advantage.** The ability of an individual, a firm, or a country to produce a good or service at a lower opportunity cost than competitors. In our example, your neighbor has a comparative advantage in picking cherries, but you have a comparative advantage in picking apples.

Keep these two key points in mind:

1. It is possible to have an absolute advantage in producing a good or service without having a comparative advantage. This is the case with your neighbor picking apples.
2. It is possible to have a comparative advantage in producing a good or service without having an absolute advantage. This is the case with your picking apples.

MyLab Economics Study Plan

Your Turn: Test your understanding by doing related problem 2.5 on page 69 at the end of this chapter.

Solved Problem 2.2

Comparative Advantage and the Gains from Trade

Suppose that Canada and the United States both produce maple syrup and honey, which are sold for the same price in both countries. These are the combinations of the two goods that each country can produce in one day, using the same amounts of capital and labor:

Canada		United States	
Honey (in tons)	Maple Syrup (in tons)	Honey (in tons)	Maple Syrup (in tons)
0	60	0	50
10	45	10	40
20	30	20	30
30	15	30	20
40	0	40	10
		50	0

a. Which country has a comparative advantage in producing maple syrup? Which country has a comparative advantage in producing honey?

b. Suppose that Canada is currently producing 30 tons of honey and 15 tons of maple syrup, and the United States is currently producing 10 tons of honey and 40 tons of maple syrup. Demonstrate that Canada and the United States can both be better off if they specialize in producing only one good and trade for the other.

c. Illustrate your answer to part (b) by drawing a *PPF* for Canada and a *PPF* for the United States. Show on your *PPFs* the combinations of honey and maple syrup produced and consumed in each country before and after trade.

Solving the Problem

Step 1:   Review the chapter material. This problem is about comparative advantage, so you may want to review the section "Absolute Advantage versus Comparative Advantage," which begins on page 50.

Step 2:   Answer part (a) by calculating which country has a comparative advantage in each activity. Remember that a country has a comparative advantage in producing a good if it can produce the good at the lowest opportunity cost. When Canada produces 1 more ton of honey, it produces 1.5 tons less of maple syrup. When the United States produces 1 more ton of honey, it produces 1 ton less of maple syrup. Therefore, for the United States, the opportunity cost of producing honey—1 ton of maple syrup—is lower than for Canada—1.5 tons of maple syrup. When Canada produces 1 more ton of maple syrup, it produces 0.67 ton less of honey. When the United States produces 1 more ton of maple syrup, it produces 1 ton less of honey. Therefore, Canada's opportunity cost of producing maple syrup—0.67 ton of honey—is lower than that of the United States—1 ton of honey. We can conclude that the United States has a comparative advantage in the production of honey and Canada has a comparative advantage in the production of maple syrup.

Step 3:   Answer part (b) by showing that specialization makes Canada and the United States better off. We know that Canada and the United States should each specialize where it has a comparative advantage. If both countries specialize, Canada will produce 60 tons of maple syrup and 0 tons of honey, and the United States will produce 0 tons of maple syrup and 50 tons of honey. After both countries specialize, the United States could then trade 30 tons of honey to Canada for 40 tons of maple syrup. (Other mutually beneficial trades are possible as well.) We can summarize the results in a table:

	Before Trade		After Trade	
	Honey (in tons)	Maple Syrup (in tons)	Honey (in tons)	Maple Syrup (in tons)
Canada	30	15	30	20
United States	10	40	20	40

The United States is better off after trade because it can consume the same amount of maple syrup and 10 more tons of honey. Canada is better off after trade because it can consume the same amount of honey and 5 more tons of maple syrup.

Step 4: **Answer part (c) by drawing the *PPFs*.**

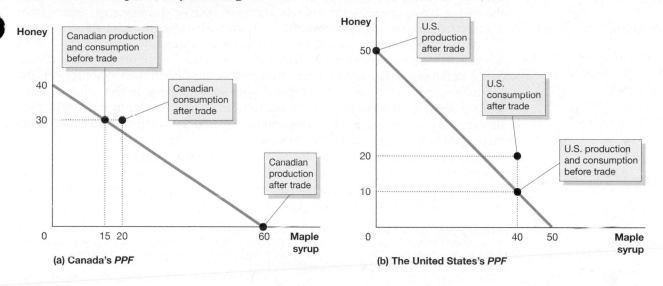

(a) Canada's *PPF*

(b) The United States's *PPF*

Your Turn: For more practice, do related problems 2.6 and 2.7 on page 69 at the end of this chapter.

MyLab Economics Study Plan

Apply the Concept

MyLab Economics Video

Comparative Advantage, Opportunity Cost, and Housework

Among roommates, married couples, and other people living together, dividing up the household chores can be a source of stress. Traditionally with married couples, women did most of the housework, such as preparing meals, cleaning, and doing laundry. In 1965, married women with children averaged about 32 hours of housework per week, while married men averaged only 4 hours. Today, women average about 15.5 hours of housework, while men average about 10 hours.

Housework doesn't seem to be part of buying, selling, and the usual topics of business and economics. In fact, we can use basic economic concepts to analyze housework. Consider first the most efficient way to divide up household chores. Suppose Jack and Jill need to decide how they will get the cooking and laundry done. Assume that Jack has an absolute advantage over Jill in both chores, but he has a big advantage over Jill in cooking—he takes much less time to prepare very tasty meals—but is only a little faster than Jill in doing laundry. In other words, assuming that they have the same amount of time available to do housework, Jack has a comparative advantage in cooking, while Jill has a comparative advantage in doing laundry. So rather than Jack and Jill both doing some of the cooking and some of the laundry, they would be better off if Jack follows his comparative advantage and does all the cooking, while Jill follows her comparative advantage and does all the laundry.

Economics can also provide some insight into the decline in the number of hours spent on housework since the 1960s. Combined, men and women now spend more than 30 percent fewer hours on housework. This decline has been partly driven by technology, particularly improvements in household appliances, such as dishwashers and microwave ovens. The decline in the number of hours women devote to housework also reflects the greater job opportunities available to women today than in the 1960s. The opportunity cost to a woman of spending time on housework and childcare is the wage she gives up by not spending that time in paid work. If a woman could work for an hour at a wage of $20 but spends that hour doing household chores, the opportunity cost of the time spent on chores is $20. As job opportunities for women and the wages those jobs pay have increased, so has the opportunity cost of doing housework. So in

What's the most efficient way to divide up household chores?

Rolf Bruderer/Flirt/Glow Images

addition to taking advantage of improved appliances, many families have found that the cost of hiring specialists in household chores, such as cleaning services and lawn care services, is lower than the cost of the wife (or husband) performing those chores.

As women's wages have risen relative to men's wages, the opportunity cost to women of doing housework has increased more than has the opportunity cost to men. So we would expect that in addition to women devoting fewer hours to housework, the gap between the hours women and men devote would narrow. In fact, while in 1965, women devoted 28 more hours per week to housework than did men, in 2016, they devoted only 6 more hours. The average number of hours women devoted to paid work increased from 8 hours per week to 20 hours.

Of course, changes in social attitudes also help explain changes in how men and women allocate their time. But we have seen that the basic economic concepts of comparative advantage and opportunity cost provide important insights into the not-so-wonderful world of household chores.

Sources: U.S. Bureau of Labor Statistics, "American Time Use Survey—2016," June 27, 2017; Kim Parker and Wendy Wang, "Modern Parenthood: Roles of Moms and Dads Converge as They Balance Work and Family," pewsocialtrends.org, March 14, 2013; Emily Oster, "You're Dividing the Chores Wrong," *Slate*, November 21, 2012; and Ellen Byron, "A Truce in the Chore Wars," *New York Times*, December 4, 2012.

MyLab Economics Study Plan

Your Turn: Test your understanding by doing related problems 2.14 and 2.15 on pages 69–70 at the end of this chapter.

The Market System

2.3

LEARNING OBJECTIVE: Explain the basics of how a market system works.

We have seen that households, firms, and the government face trade-offs and incur opportunity costs because resources are scarce. We have also seen that trade allows people to specialize according to their comparative advantage. By engaging in trade, people can raise their incomes and their standard of living. Of course, trade in the modern world is much more complex than the examples we have considered so far. Trade today involves the decisions of millions of people around the world. How are all of these decisions coordinated? In the United States and most other countries, trade is carried out in markets. Markets also determine the answers to the three fundamental questions discussed in Chapter 1:

1. What goods and services will be produced?
2. How will the goods and services be produced?
3. Who will receive the goods and services produced?

Market A group of buyers and sellers of a good or service and the institution or arrangement by which they come together to trade.

Recall that a **market** is a group of buyers and sellers of a good or service and the institution or arrangement by which they come together to trade. Markets take many forms: They can be physical places, such as the pizza parlors in your city or the New York Stock Exchange, or virtual places, such as eBay. In a market, the buyers are demanders of goods or services, and the sellers are suppliers of goods or services. Households and firms interact in two types of markets: product markets and factor markets. **Product markets** are markets for goods—such as smartphones—and services—such as medical treatment. In product markets, households are demanders and firms are suppliers. **Factor markets** are markets for the *factors of production*. **Factors of production** are the inputs used to make goods and services. Factors of production are divided into four broad categories:

Product market A market for goods—such as computers—or services—such as medical treatment.

Factor market A market for the factors of production, such as labor, capital, natural resources, and entrepreneurial ability.

Factors of production Labor, capital, natural resources, and other inputs used to make goods and services.

1. *Labor* includes all types of work, from the part-time labor of teenagers working at McDonald's to the work of senior managers in large corporations.
2. *Capital* refers to physical capital, such as computers, office buildings, and machine tools, used to produce other goods.
3. *Natural resources* include land, water, oil, iron ore, and other raw materials (or "gifts of nature") that are used in producing goods.

4. An *entrepreneur* is someone who operates a business. *Entrepreneurial ability* is the ability to bring together the other factors of production to successfully produce and sell goods and services.

The Circular Flow of Income

Two key groups participate in markets:

1. *Households* are all the individuals in a home. A household may consist of one person or several persons. Households are suppliers of factors of production—particularly labor—employed by firms to make goods and services. Households use the income they receive from selling the factors of production to purchase the goods and services supplied by firms. We are familiar with households as suppliers of labor because most people earn most of their income by going to work, meaning they are selling their labor services to firms in the labor market. But households own the other factors of production as well, either directly or indirectly, by owning the firms that own these resources. All firms are owned by households. Small firms, like a neighborhood restaurant, might be owned by one person. Large firms, like Apple, are owned by millions of households that buy shares of stock in them. When firms pay profits to the people who own them, the firms are paying for using the capital and natural resources that are supplied to them by those owners. So, we can generalize by saying that in factor markets, households are suppliers and firms are demanders.

2. *Firms* are suppliers of goods and services. Firms use the funds they receive from selling goods and services to buy or hire the factors of production needed to make the goods and services.

We can use a simple economic model called the **circular-flow diagram** to see how participants in markets are linked. Figure 2.6 shows that in factor markets, households supply labor and other factors of production in exchange for wages and other

Circular-flow diagram A model that illustrates how participants in markets are linked.

MyLab Economics Animation

Figure 2.6

The Circular-Flow Diagram

Households and firms are linked together in a circular flow of production, income, and spending. The blue arrows show the flow of the factors of production. In factor markets, households supply labor, entrepreneurial ability, and other factors of production to firms. Firms use these factors of production to make goods and services that they supply to households in product markets. The red arrows show the flow of goods and services from firms to households. The green arrows show the flow of funds. In factor markets, households receive wages and other payments from firms in exchange for supplying the factors of production. Households use these wages and other payments to purchase goods and services from firms in product markets. Firms sell goods and services to households in product markets, and they use the funds to purchase the factors of production from households in factor markets.

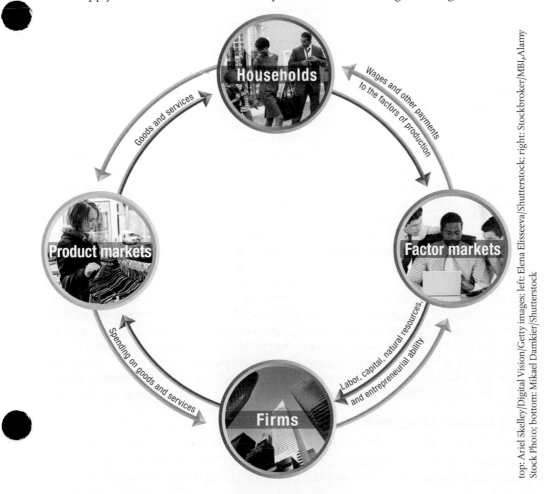

top: Ariel Skelley/Digital Vision/Getty images; left: Elena Elisseeva/Shutterstock; right: Stockbroker/MBI/Alamy Stock Photo; bottom: Mikael Damkier/Shutterstock payments from firms. In product markets, households use the payments they earn in factor markets to purchase the goods and services supplied by firms. Firms produce these goods and services using the factors of production supplied by households. In the figure, the blue arrows show the flow of factors of production from households through factor markets to firms. The red arrows show the flow of goods and services from firms through product markets to households. The green arrows show the flow of funds from firms through factor markets to households and the flow of spending from households through product markets to firms.

Like all economic models, the circular-flow diagram is a simplified version of reality. Figure 2.6 leaves out (1) the important role of government in buying goods from firms and in making payments, such as Social Security or unemployment insurance payments, to households; (2) the roles played by banks, the stock and bond markets, and other parts of the *financial system* in aiding the flow of funds from lenders to borrowers; and (3) the fact that some goods and services purchased by domestic households are produced in foreign countries and some goods and services produced by domestic firms are sold to foreign households. (We explore the government, the financial system, and the international sector in later chapters.) Despite these simplifications, the circular-flow diagram in Figure 2.6 helps us see how product markets, factor markets, and their participants are linked together. One of the great wonders of the market system is that it manages to successfully coordinate the independent activities of so many households and firms. **MyLab Economics** Concept Check

The Gains from Free Markets

Free market A market with few government restrictions on how a good or service can be produced or sold or on how a factor of production can be employed.

A **free market** exists when the government places few restrictions on how goods and services can be produced or sold or on how factors of production can be employed. Governments in all modern economies intervene more than is consistent with a fully free market. In that sense, we can think of the free market as being a benchmark against which we can judge actual economies. There are relatively few government restrictions on economic activities in the United States, Canada, Western Europe, Hong Kong, Singapore, and Estonia. So these countries come close to the free market benchmark. In countries such as Cuba and North Korea, the free market system has been rejected in favor of centrally planned economies with extensive government control over product and factor markets. Countries that come closest to the free market benchmark have been more successful than countries with centrally planned economies in providing their people with rising living standards.

The Scottish philosopher Adam Smith is considered the father of modern economics because his book, *An Inquiry into the Nature and Causes of the Wealth of Nations*, published in 1776, was an early and very influential argument for the free market system. Smith was writing at a time when extensive government restrictions on markets were common. In many parts of Europe, the *guild system* prevailed. Under this system, governments would give guilds, or organizations of producers, the authority to control the production of a good. For example, the shoemakers' guild controlled who was allowed to produce shoes, how many shoes they could produce, and what price they could charge. In France, the cloth makers' guild even dictated the number of threads in the weave of the cloth.

Smith argued that such restrictions reduced the income and wealth of a country and its people by restricting the quantity of goods produced. Some people at the time supported the restrictions of the guild system because it was in their financial interest to do so. If you were a member of a guild, the restrictions served to reduce the competition you faced. But other people believed that the alternative to the guild system was economic disorder. Smith argued that these people were wrong and that a country could enjoy a smoothly functioning economic system if firms were freed from restrictions placed on their operations either by guilds or directly by governments. **MyLab Economics** Concept Check

The Market Mechanism

In Smith's day, defenders of restrictions on how firms operate argued that if, for example, the shoemakers' guild did not control shoe production, either too many or too few shoes would be produced. In contrast, Smith maintained that prices would do a better job of coordinating the activities of buyers and sellers than the guilds could. A key to understanding Smith's argument is the assumption that *individuals usually act in a rational, self-interested way.* In particular, individuals take the actions that are most likely to make themselves better off financially. This assumption of rational, self-interested behavior underlies nearly all economic analysis. In fact, economics can be distinguished from other disciplines that study human behavior—such as sociology and psychology—by its emphasis on the assumption of self-interested behavior. Adam Smith understood— as economists today understand—that people's motives can be complex. But when we analyze people in the act of buying and selling, the motivation of financial reward usually provides the best explanation for the actions people take.

For example, suppose that a significant number of consumers switch from buying conventional gasoline-powered cars to buying either gasoline/electric-powered hybrid cars, such as the Toyota Prius, or all-electric cars, such as the Tesla Model 3. Firms will find that they can charge relatively higher prices for hybrid cars and electric cars than they can for gasoline-powered cars. The self-interest of these firms will lead them to respond to consumers' wishes by producing more hybrid and electric cars and fewer gasoline-powered cars. Or suppose that consumers decide that they want to eat less bread, pasta, and other foods that contain gluten. Then the prices firms can charge for gluten-free bread and pasta will increase. The self-interest of firms will lead them to produce more gluten-free bread and pasta and less regular bread and pasta, which, in fact, is what has happened over the past 10 years.

Note that for the market mechanism to work in response to changes in consumers' wants, *prices must be flexible.* The *relative price* is the price of one good or service relative to the prices of other goods or services. Changes in relative prices provide information, or a signal, to both consumers and firms. For example, consumers worldwide have increased their demand for cattle and poultry. Because corn is fed to cattle and poultry, prices for corn have increased relative to prices for other crops. Many farmers in the United States received this price signal and responded by increasing the amount of corn they planted and decreasing the amount of soybeans and wheat. One Kansas farmer was quoted as saying, "It seemed to me there was $100 to $150 per acre more money in the corn than there was in the beans. That's the kind of math that a lot of guys were using." In recent years, the United States has experienced record corn crops. Similarly, falling prices for DVDs and music CDs were a signal to movie studios and record companies to devote fewer resources to these products and more resources to making movies and music available to stream online.

In the United States today, governments at the federal, state, and local levels set or regulate the prices of only about 10 to 20 percent of goods and services. The prices of other goods and services are free to change as consumer preferences change and as costs of production change.

In the case where consumers want more of a product, and in the case where they want less of a product, the market system responds without a guild or the government giving orders about how much to produce or what price to charge. Economists have used Adam Smith's metaphor of the *invisible hand* to describe how the market leads firms to provide consumers with the goods they want. Firms respond *individually* to changes in prices by making decisions that *collectively* end up satisfying the preferences of consumers. **MyLab Economics** Concept Check

Apply the Concept   MyLab Economics Video

A Story of the Market System in Action: How Do You Make an iPad?

Apple produces the iPad. Because Apple's headquarters is in Cupertino, California, it seems reasonable to assume that iPads are also manufactured in that state. A poll by the *New York Times* showed that, in fact, a majority of people interviewed believed that iPads are manufactured in the United States, if not specifically in California. Although engineers at Apple designed the iPad, the company produces none of the components

Qilai Shen/Bloomberg/Getty Images

The market coordinates the activities of many people spread around the world who contribute to making an iPad.

of the iPad, and it doesn't assemble the components into finished products. Far from being produced entirely by one company in one country, the iPad requires the coordinated activities of thousands of workers and dozens of firms spread around the world.

Foxconn, which is based in Taiwan, assembles most iPads in factories in China and Brazil and ships them to Apple for sale in the United States. Pegatron, another Taiwanese firm with factories in China, also assembles some iPads. Although Foxconn and Pegatron do final assembly, they don't make any of the components and, in fact, charge Apple only about $6 for assembling each iPad.

Multiple firms can supply a particular component for an iPad model. The following table lists just some of the firms that have supplied Apple with iPad components.

Firm	Location of the Firm	iPad Component Supplied
AKM	Japan	Motion sensor
AU Optronics	Taiwan	Display
Avago Technologies	United States (Pennsylvania)	Wireless technology
Bosch Sensortec	Germany	Accelerometer
Broadcom	United States (California)	Touchscreen controller and wireless chip
Cirrus Logic	United States (Texas)	Audio chip
Corning	United States (New York)	Glass screen cover
Dialog Semiconductor	Germany	Power management chip
Elpida	United States (Idaho)	System memory
Infineon Technologies	Germany	Semiconductors
LG Electronics	South Korea	Display
Quicomm	United Kingdom	Wireless section
Samsung	South Korea	Display, flash memory, and applications processor
Sharp	Japan	Display
SK Hynix	South Korea	Flash memory
Skyworks Solutions	United States (Massachusetts)	Wireless technology
STMicroelectronics	France/Italy	Motion sensors
Texas Instruments	United States (Texas)	Touchscreen controller
Toshiba	Japan	Flash memory
TriQuint Semiconductor	United States (Oregon)	Wireless technology

Each of these suppliers in turn relies on its own suppliers. For example, Broadcom designs the touchscreen controller for the iPad and supplies it to Apple, but it does not manufacture the components of the controller or assemble them. To manufacture the components, Broadcom relies on SilTerra, based in Malaysia; SMIC, based in mainland China; and Taiwan Semiconductor Manufacturing Corporation (TSMC) and UMC, based in Taiwan. TSMC's factories are for the most part not in Taiwan but in mainland China and Eastern Europe. To assemble the components, Broadcom uses several companies, including Amkor Technology, based in Chandler, Arizona, and STATS ChipPAC, based in Singapore.

All told, an iPad contains hundreds of parts that are designed, manufactured, and assembled by firms around the world. Many of these firms are not even aware of which other firms are also producing components for the iPad. Few of the managers of these firms have met managers of the other firms or shared knowledge of how their particular components are produced. In fact, no one person—from Tim Cook, the chief executive officer of Apple, on down—possesses the knowledge of how to produce all the components that are assembled into an iPad. Instead, the invisible hand of the market has led these firms to contribute their knowledge and resources to the process that ultimately results in an iPad available for sale in a store in the United States. Apple has so efficiently organized the process of producing the iPad that you can order a custom iPad with a personal engraving and have it delivered from an assembly plant in China or Brazil to your doorstep in the United States in as little as three days.

Sources: Don Reisinger, "iPad Air 2 Models Cost Apple $275 to $358, Teardowns Reveal," cnet.com, October 29, 2014; Marjorie Connelly, "Poll Finds Consumer Confusion on Where Apple Devices Are Made," *New York Times*, January 25, 2012; Andrew Rassweiler, "Still Air: Apple iPad Air 2 Largely Holds the Line on Features and Costs, IHS Teardown Reveals," technology.ihs.com, October 28, 2014; and Eva Dou and Tripp Mickle, "Apple Supplier Foxconn Plans Expansion in U.S.," *Wall Street Journal*, December 7, 2016.

Your Turn: Test your understanding by doing related problems 3.8 and 3.9 on page 70 at the end of this chapter.

MyLab Economics Study Plan

The Role of the Entrepreneur in the Market System

Entrepreneurs are central to a market system. An **entrepreneur** is someone who operates a business. Entrepreneurs first determine what goods and services they believe consumers want and then decide how to produce those goods and services most profitably, using the available factors of production—labor, capital, and natural resources. Successful entrepreneurs are able to search out opportunities to provide new goods and services. Frequently these opportunities are created by new technology. Consumers and existing businesses often do not at first realize that the new technology makes new products feasible. For example, even after the development of the internal combustion engine had made automobiles practicable, Henry Ford remarked: "If I had asked my customers what they wanted, they would have said a faster horse." Because consumers often cannot evaluate a new product before it exists, some of the most successful entrepreneurs, such as the late Steve Jobs of Apple, rarely use *focus groups*, or meetings with consumers in which the consumers are asked what new products they would like to see. Instead, entrepreneurs think of products that consumers may not even realize they need, such as, in Jobs's case, an MP3 player—the iPod—or a tablet computer—the iPad. Entrepreneurs are important to the economy because they are often responsible for making new products widely available to consumers, as Henry Ford did with the automobile and Steve Jobs did with the iPod.

The firms that entrepreneurs found are typically small at first, as Apple and Ford were. Table 2.3 on the next page lists some of the important products entrepreneurs at small firms introduced during the twentieth century.

Entrepreneurs put their own funds at risk when they start businesses. If they are wrong about what consumers want or about the best way to produce goods and services, they can lose those funds. In fact, it is not unusual for entrepreneurs who eventually achieve great success to fail at first. For instance, early in their careers, both Henry Ford and Sakichi Toyoda, who eventually founded the Toyota Motor Corporation, started companies that quickly failed. Research by Richard Freeman of Harvard University has shown that a typical entrepreneur earns less than an employee at a large firm who has the same education and other characteristics. Few entrepreneurs make the fortunes earned by Mark Zuckerberg (Facebook), Steve Jobs (Apple), or Bill Gates (Microsoft).

Entrepreneurs make vital contributions to economic growth through their roles in responding to consumer wants and introducing new products. Government policies that encourage entrepreneurship are also likely to increase economic growth and raise the standard of living. In the next section, we consider the legal framework required for a successful market in which entrepreneurs can succeed.   MyLab Economics Concept Check

Entrepreneur Someone who operates a business, bringing together the factors of production—labor, capital, and natural resources—to produce goods and services.

The Legal Basis of a Successful Market System

In a free market, government does not restrict how firms produce and sell goods and services or how they employ factors of production. But the absence of such government restrictions is not enough for the market system to succeed in providing people

Table 2.3

Important Products Introduced
by Entrepreneurs at Small Firms

Biotechnology	Inventor
Biomagnetic imaging	Raymond Damadian
Biosynthetic insulin	Herbert Boyer
DNA fingerprinting	Alec Jeffries
High-resolution CAT scanner	Robert Ledley
Communication	**Inventor**
FM radio	Edwin Howard Armstrong
Consumer Goods	**Inventor**
Air conditioning	William Haviland Carrier
Disposable diaper	Marion Donovan
Oral contraceptives	Carl Djerassi
Quick-frozen foods	Clarence Birdseye
Safety razor	King Gillette
Soft contact lens	Kevin Tuohy
Zipper	Gideon Sundback
Information Technology	**Inventor**
Integrated circuit	Jack Kilby
Microprocessor	Ted Hoff
Optical scanner	Everett Franklin Lindquist
Personal computer	Steve Jobs and Steve Wozniak
Supercomputer	Seymour Cray
Vacuum tube (television)	Philo Farnsworth
Transportation	**Inventor**
Airplane	Orville and Wilbur Wright
Automobile, mass produced	Henry Ford
Automobile windshield wiper	Mary Anderson
Helicopter	Igor Sikorsky
Hydraulic brake	Malcolm Lockheed
Overnight delivery service	Fred Smith

Sources: William J. Baumol, *The Microtheory of Innovative Entrepreneurship*, Princeton, NJ: Princeton University Press, 2010; Lemelson-MIT Program; and various other sources. Note that historians sometimes dispute the identity of the person who first commercially developed a particular product.

with a high standard of living. Government has to take active steps to provide a *legal environment* that will allow markets to operate efficiently.

Protection of Private Property For the market system to work well, individuals must be willing to take risks. Someone with $250,000 can be cautious and keep it safely in a bank—or even in cash, if the person doesn't trust banks. But the market system won't work unless a significant number of people are willing to risk their funds by investing them in businesses. Investing in businesses is risky in any country. Many businesses fail every year in the United States and other high-income countries. But in high-income countries, someone who starts a new business or invests in an existing business doesn't have to worry that the government, the military, or criminal gangs might decide to seize the business or demand payments for not destroying it. Unfortunately, in many low-income countries, business owners are not well protected from having their businesses seized by the government or from having their profits taken by criminals. Where these problems exist, opening a business can be extremely risky. Cash can be concealed easily, but a business is difficult to conceal or move.

Property rights are the rights individuals or firms have to the exclusive use of their property, including the right to buy or sell it. Property can be physical property, such as a store or factory. Property can also be intangible, such as the right to an idea. Two amendments to the U.S. Constitution guarantee property rights: The Fifth Amendment states that the federal government shall not deprive any person "of life, liberty, or property, without due process of law." The Fourteenth Amendment extends this guarantee to the actions of state governments: "No state . . . shall deprive any person of life, liberty, or property, without due process of law." Similar guarantees exist in every high-income country. Unfortunately, in many developing countries, such guarantees do not exist or are poorly enforced.

In any modern economy, *intellectual property rights* are very important. Intellectual property includes books, films, software, and ideas for new products or new ways of producing products. To protect intellectual property, the federal government grants a *patent* that gives an inventor—often a firm—the exclusive right to produce and sell a new product for a period of 20 years from the date the patent was filed. For instance, because Apple has a patent on its Siri voice-recognition software for smartphones and other devices, other firms cannot sell their own versions of Siri. The government grants patents to encourage firms to spend money on the research and development necessary to create new products. If other companies could freely copy Siri, Apple would not have spent the funds necessary to develop it. Just as a new product or a new method of making a product receives patent protection, new books, films, and software receive *copyright* protection. Under U.S. law, the creator of a book, film, or piece of music has the exclusive right to use the creation during the creator's lifetime. The creator's heirs retain this exclusive right for 70 years after the death of the creator.

In providing copyright protection for only a limited time, Congress provides economic incentives to creators while eventually—after the period of copyright has ended—allowing the creators' works to be freely available to others. The longer the period of copyright, the longer the creator (or the creators' family) can restrict others from using the work.

Enforcement of Contracts and Property Rights Business activity often involves someone agreeing to carry out some action in the future. For example, you may borrow $20,000 to buy a car and promise the bank—by signing a loan contract—that you will pay back the money over the next five years. Or Facebook may sign a licensing agreement with a small technology company, agreeing to use that company's technology for a period of several years in return for a fee. Usually these agreements take the form of legal contracts. For the market system to work, businesses and individuals have to rely on these contracts being carried out. If one party to a legal contract does not fulfill its obligations—perhaps the small company had promised Facebook exclusive use of its technology but then begins licensing it to other companies—the other party can go to court to have the agreement enforced. Similarly, if you believe that the federal or state government has violated your property rights under the Fifth or Fourteenth Amendments, you can go to court to have your rights enforced.

But going to court to enforce a contract or property rights will be successful only if the court system is independent and judges are able to make impartial decisions on the basis of the law. In the United States and other high-income countries, the court systems have enough independence from other parts of the government and enough protection from intimidation by outside forces—such as criminal gangs—that they are able to make their decisions based on the law. In many developing countries, the court systems lack this independence and will not provide a remedy if the government violates property rights, or if a person with powerful political connections decides to violate a business contract.

If property rights are not well enforced, fewer goods and services will be produced. This reduces economic efficiency, leaving the economy inside its production possibilities frontier.   **MyLab Economics** Concept Check

Property rights The rights individuals or firms have to the exclusive use of their property, including the right to buy or sell it.

Jim West/Alamy Stock Photo

Feeding America uses the market mechanism to improve its allocation of food donations.

Apply the Concept

Managers at Feeding America Use the Market Mechanism to Reduce Hunger

Charitable giving doesn't seem to have much to do with markets. When donors give money, clothing, or food to a charity, they typically don't expect anything in exchange—beyond a possible tax deduction. In 1979, retired businessman John van Hengel started Feeding America. This charity collects donations of food from farmers, supermarkets, food processing plants, and governments and distributes the food to thousands of food pantries and food programs operated by churches, schools, and community centers around the country. These programs give the donated food away free or at a very low price to low-income families.

By 2004, Feeding America was providing 1.8 billion pounds of food per year to millions of low-income people, but the organization's managers realized that they could serve even more people if they could operate more efficiently. In particular, the managers were concerned that food was sometimes not allocated in ways that were consistent with the needs of local food programs. For example, potatoes might be shipped to food programs in Idaho—the country's leading potato growing state—or milk might be shipped to food programs that lacked the refrigeration capacity to keep it fresh long enough to distribute. In 2005, Feeding America asked Canice Prendergast, Don Eisenstein, and Harry Davis, professors at the University of Chicago's Booth School of Business, to design a more efficient way of allocating food to local food programs.

Feeding America had been allocating food by calculating how many low-income people lived in an area and then shipping a target number of pounds of food to food programs in the area. All food, whether fruit, bread, milk, or pasta, that weighed the same was treated the same in making allocations to local food programs. The food programs were not allowed to choose which foods they wanted to receive. Because Feeding America provided on average only about 20 percent of the total food donations local food programs received, it might ship food—for example, bread and breakfast cereal—the local program already had, while failing to ship food, such as fruits and vegetables, that the program needed.

The business professors advising Feeding American proposed changing the food allocation system to one that resembled a market. Each food program was given a number of "shares" that they could use in bidding against other food programs for the types of food that best met the needs of the low-income people using their program. In addition, any local program that had surplus food was allowed to sell it to other local programs in exchange for shares. Although this new system does not involve money, it operates like a market—in which consumers determine prices by competing against each other in buying goods. Goods for which consumers have a greater preference tend to have higher prices than goods for which consumers have a lesser preference; for instance, in supermarkets, organic produce often sells for a higher price than nonorganic produce. Similarly, food programs turned out to have a stronger preference for fresh fruits and vegetables than for pasta. Under the previous system, a pound of fresh fruit would have been treated the same as a pound of pasta in calculating how much food Feeding America would allocate to a local program. But when under the new system local food banks were allowed to bid for food with shares, the price of a pound of fruit or vegetables was 116 times higher than the price of a pound of pasta.

Because under the new system food is allocated in a way that more closely fits the needs of local food programs, Feeding America is able to provide food to thousands more low-income people than was possible under the old system. In addition, because less food is wasted, people and organizations have been willing to donate more food to the program. Finally, Feeding America's managers have used the knowledge of which types of foods local food programs prefer to guide the types of food they ask companies to donate. For instance, in addition to fruits and vegetables, programs are willing to pay more shares for peanut butter and frozen chicken because these foods are easy to store. Even many critics of using a market mechanism to allocate food donations eventually embraced the system, including the director of one Michigan food program whose initial reaction was: "I am a socialist. That's why I run a food bank. I don't believe in markets."

The success of Feeding America's revised procedures for allocating food donations shows how powerfully market mechanisms can increase efficiency and raise living standards.

Sources: Sendhil Mullainathan, "Sending Potatoes to Idaho? How the Free Market Can Fight Poverty," *New York Times*, October 7, 2016; Canice Prendergast, "The Allocation of Food to Food Banks," Working Paper, University of Chicago, Booth School of Business, October 11, 2016; Ray Fisman and Tim Sullivan, "The Invisible Helping Hand," slate.com, June 7, 2016; and feedingamerica.org.

Your Turn: Test your understanding by doing related problem 3.16 on page 71 at the end of this chapter.

MyLab Economics Study Plan

Continued from page 41

Economics in Your Life & Career

The Trade-offs When You Buy a Car

At the beginning of the chapter, we asked you to think about two questions: What is the relationship between safety and fuel efficiency for gasoline-powered cars? and If you were a manager at an automobile company, how might you evaluate the relationship between safety and fuel efficiency when designing cars?

To answer the first question, you have to recognize that there is a trade-off between safety and fuel efficiency. With the technology available at any particular time, an automobile manufacturer can increase fuel efficiency by making a car smaller and lighter. But driving a lighter car increases your chances of being injured if you have an accident. The trade-off between safety and fuel efficiency would look much like the relationship in Figure 2.1 on page 43. To answer the second question, to increase both safety and fuel efficiency, automobile makers would have to discover new technologies that allow them to make cars lighter and safer at the same time. Such new technologies would make points like *G* in Figure 2.1 attainable. As a manager at an automobile company, you would need to take into account federal regulations that require certain levels of safety and fuel efficiency. Assuming that you had met those regulatory requirements, consumer preferences would determine how you would trade off safety versus fuel efficiency in designing cars.

Conclusion

We have seen that by trading in markets, people are able to specialize and pursue their comparative advantage. Trading on the basis of comparative advantage makes the participants better off. The key role of markets is to facilitate trade. In fact, the market system is a very effective means of coordinating the decisions of millions of consumers, workers, and firms. At the center of the market system is the consumer. To be successful, firms must respond to the preferences of consumers. These preferences are communicated to firms through prices. We continue to explore how markets work in Chapter 3, when we develop the model of demand and supply.

Before moving on to Chapter 3, read *An Inside Look* on the next page for a discussion of Tesla's Gigafactory in Nevada.

Tesla Bets Big on Nevada Battery Plant

ZACKS.COM

So, What Actually Is Tesla's Gigafactory?

Since 2014, electric car maker **Tesla Inc.** has been constructing what they call a Gigafactory. But what, exactly, does that mean? What makes it different from a regular manufacturing plant?

According to Tesla, one of its goals as a company is to expedite the process of transitioning to global sustainable transportation. In order to do this, enough vehicles must be produced to sway change in the automobile industry as a whole. Tesla plans to have a production rate of 500,000 electric cars every year by the second half of this decade, which will require a huge supply of lithium-ion batteries, a type of rechargeable battery.

Thus, the Gigafactory was born.

The name "Gigafactory" is a term that comes from Tesla's planned battery production amount per year of 35 gigawatt-hours (GWh). In quantifiable terms, "giga" is a measurement unit that stands for "billions"; one GWh is the same as generating one billion watts for one hour, or one million times more than that one kilowatt-hour (kWh).

The Tax Deal

Tesla's Gigafactory is located outside the city of Sparks, Nevada, but the state had to go through a somewhat arduous process to win the factory deal. Three additional states were in the running: Arizona, Texas, and New Mexico.

According to The Verge, Nevada won the deal after the state controversially "offered an incentives package that was the largest in Nevada history, and became one of the 15 largest nationally. Over the next 20 years, Tesla could take in nearly $1.3 billion in tax benefits for building its Gigafactory in Nevada … [a]ssuming Tesla meets its obligations under the deal, it will spend 20 years free from sales tax, and 10 years free from property tax, while it receives millions of dollars more in tax credits…."

Production Plan

Since the idea of the Gigafactory was conceived out of the necessity to increase the supply of lithium-ion batteries, it makes sense that the factory would utilize renewable production methods. The entire plant will be powered by renewable energy sources in order to achieve net zero energy. Most notably, the majority of the manufacturing processes will be under one roof, a choice that could potentially reduce cost, waste, and enhance innovation.

Tesla began lithium-ion battery cell production this past January, and the cells will be used in the company's Powerwall energy storage products. By 2018, Tesla expects the cost of its batteries to decline by over one-third thanks to large-scale production at the Gigafactory. Tesla also anticipates annual lithium-ion battery production of the factory to reach near its original goal of 35 gigawatt-hours by

the same year, which equals the total global production from 2014. Tesla hopes to reach full capacity by 2020.

The company also announced plans to invest $350 million in the Gigafactory for the production of electric motors and gearbox components for its Model 3 sedan, its highly-anticipated mass-market vehicle. The investment will create about 500 jobs.

Future of the Gigafactory

Last January, electronics company Panasonic agreed to invest up to $1.6 billion in Tesla's Gigafactory. Kazuhiro Tsuga, President of Panasonic, said that "We are sort of waiting on the demand from Tesla. If Tesla succeeds and the electric vehicle becomes mainstream, the world will be changed and we will have lots of opportunity to grow."

Tesla is even considering building more Gigafactories. CEO Elon Musk has referred to the Nevada plant as "Gigafactory 1" in the past, and during the company's fiscal 2016 earnings release back in February, the electric car maker informed its shareholders [about] plans of two or three more potential Gigafactory plants.

"Later this year, we expect to finalize locations for Gigafactories 3, 4, and 5 (Gigafactory 2 is the Tesla solar plant in New York)," said the company in its earnings report….

Source: Madeleine Johnson, "So, What Actually Is Tesla's Gigafactory?" zacks.com, June 6, 2017.

Key Points in the Article

Tesla opened a large factory near Sparks, Nevada, to mass produce lithium-ion batteries. Tesla will use the batteries in its electric cars and in energy storage products the firm will sell to consumers and to other firms. Known as the Gigafactory, the multi-billion-dollar manufacturing facility will greatly increase the world's productive capacity for lithium-ion batteries. These batteries are a critical component of Tesla's cars, and the company hopes that by building such a large facility, it will be able to produce batteries at a lower cost per unit. Tesla will also be manufacturing batteries for its Powerwall energy storage products at its new facility as the company expands beyond the production of electric automobiles.

Analyzing the News

a Increasing battery production is vital to Tesla's success, so the strategic decisions of where, when, and how large to build a battery factory were important. When ultimately deciding to build the Gigafactory near Sparks, Nevada, managers at Tesla were choosing how to allocate resources. The investment in the factory represents a trade-off because it took resources away from other potential projects. Managers believed the best use of

Tesla's scarce resources was to build the battery plant because doing so allowed them to produce enough batteries to meet their production goals for cars and energy storage products.

b At its Nevada plant, Tesla is producing batteries for its automobiles as well as for home and commercial use, so it must choose how many of each product to produce. Like all other companies, Tesla faces trade-offs in choosing which goods to produce. Suppose Tesla must choose between producing batteries for its Model 3 sedan and batteries for its Powerwall energy storage product, and it has the capacity to produce 600,000 batteries in 2018. This capacity is represented by PPF_{2018} in the figure below. This curve shows that Tesla would have to sacrifice production (and therefore sales) of one type of battery to produce more of the other. If the market grows for both its Model 3 sedan and its Powerwall home batteries, Tesla will need to produce a larger number of total batteries, which is represented by PPF_{2022} in the figure.

c Future production was also a consideration for Tesla managers as they decided how to allocate resources. The company needed to look at the longer term when considering the trade-offs in allocating resources to the construction of the Nevada plant and also possible addi-

tional Gigafactories. Tesla partnered with Panasonic, the world's leading battery cell manufacturer, which agreed to invest up to $1.6 billion in the Nevada factory. These longer-term considerations play an integral part in Tesla's goal of gaining a comparative advantage in battery manufacturing and in successfully expanding its clean-energy business.

Thinking Critically

1. Suppose that from 2018 to 2022, the resources Tesla uses to produce its batteries remain constant, while improvements in technology allow Tesla to produce a larger quantity of Powerwall batteries but no additional batteries for the Model 3 sedan. Draw a graph that illustrates this technology change. Be sure to show both the 2018 PPF and the new 2022 PPF. What is the opportunity cost to Tesla of producing one Model 3 sedan battery in 2018? Is the opportunity cost higher or lower in 2022?

2. Assume that the figure below accurately represents Tesla's PPFs for 2018 and 2022. Now suppose that in 2022, Tesla receives orders for 750,000 Model 3 sedan batteries and 350,000 Powerwall batteries. Explain whether Tesla can fill all these orders.

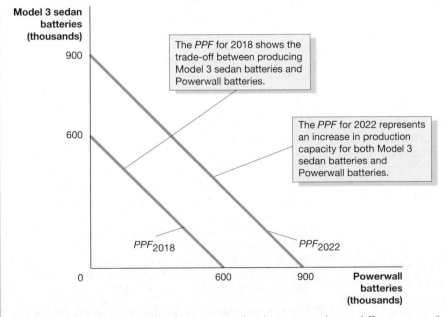

The PPF for 2018 shows the trade-off between producing Model 3 sedan batteries and Powerwall batteries.

The PPF for 2022 represents an increase in production capacity for both Model 3 sedan batteries and Powerwall batteries.

These *PPFs* show the trade-off Tesla's managers face between producing different types of batteries and how that trade-off may change over time.

Key Terms

2.1 Production Possibilities Frontiers and Opportunity Costs, pages 42–47

LEARNING OBJECTIVE: Use a production possibilities frontier to analyze opportunity costs and trade-offs.

MyLab Economics Visit **www.pearson.com/mylab/economics** to complete these exercises online and get instant feedback.

Summary

The **production possibilities frontier (PPF)** is a curve that shows the maximum attainable combinations of two goods that can be produced with available resources. The *PPF* is used to illustrate the trade-offs that arise from **scarcity**. Points on the *PPF* are technically efficient. Points inside the *PPF* are inefficient, and points outside the *PPF* are unattainable. The **opportunity cost** of any activity is the highest-valued alternative that must be given up to engage in that activity. Because of increasing marginal opportunity costs, *PPFs* are usually bowed out rather than straight lines. This illustrates the important economic concept that the more resources that are already devoted to any activity, the smaller the payoff from devoting additional resources to that activity is likely to be. **Economic growth** is illustrated by an outward shift in the *PPF*.

Review Questions

1.1 What do economists mean by *scarcity*? Can you think of anything that is not scarce according to the economic definition?

1.2 What is a production possibilities frontier? How can we show efficiency on a production possibilities frontier? How can we show inefficiency? What causes a production possibilities frontier to shift outward?

1.3 What does increasing marginal opportunity costs mean? What are the implications of this idea for the shape of the production possibilities frontier?

Problems and Applications

1.4 Draw a production possibilities frontier that shows the trade-off between the production of cotton and the production of soybeans.

  a. Show the effect that a prolonged drought would have on the initial production possibilities frontier.

  b. Suppose that genetic modification makes soybeans resistant to insects, allowing yields to double. Show the effect of this technological change on the initial production possibilities frontier.

1.5 **(Related to the Chapter Opener on page 40)** One of the trade-offs Tesla faces is between safety and the maximum range someone can drive an electric car before having to recharge it. For example, adding steel to a car makes it safer but also heavier, which results in fewer miles between recharges. Draw a hypothetical production possibilities frontier that Tesla engineers face that shows this trade-off.

1.6 According to an article in the *Wall Street Journal*, Staples Inc., an office supply store, "has found a new use for some of its roomy office-supply stores: make parts of them into offices." Because many businesses now store their records digitally and many consumers shop online rather than in stores, Staples no longer needs as much floor space for filing cabinets and some other products. To use the surplus space, Staples has undertaken a partnership with Workbar, an office-sharing firm, to offer small business owners and professionals shared workspaces inside select Staples retail stores. In these circumstances, does Staples incur a cost from using some of the space in its retail stores for office workspaces? If Staples does incur a cost, briefly explain what the cost would be.

Source: Drew FitzGerald and Suzanne Kapner, "Staples Finds New Use for Its Stores: Office Space," *Wall Street Journal*, April 4, 2016.

1.7 An economist remarked that "the cost of consuming a book is the combination of the retail price and the opportunity cost of the time spent reading." Isn't the cost of consuming a book just the price you pay to buy the book? Why include the cost of the time spent reading the book in the cost of consuming the book?

Source: Craig L. Garthwaite, "Demand Spillovers, Combative Advertising, and Celebrity Endorsements," *American Economic Journal: Applied Economics*, Vol. 6, No. 2, April 2014, p. 78.

1.8 Suppose we can divide all the goods produced by an economy into two types: consumption goods and capital goods. Capital goods, such as machinery, equipment, and computers, are goods used to produce other goods.

a. Use a production possibilities frontier graph to illustrate the trade-off to an economy between producing consumption goods and producing capital goods. Is it likely that the production possibilities frontier in this situation will be a straight line (as in Figure 2.1 on page 43) or bowed out (as in Figure 2.2 on page 46)? Briefly explain.

b. Suppose a technological change occurs and has a favorable effect on the production of capital goods but not consumption goods. Show the effect on the production possibilities frontier.

c. Suppose that Lichtenstein and Luxembourg currently have identical production possibilities frontiers but that Lichtenstein devotes only 5 percent of its resources to producing capital goods over each of the next 10 years, while Luxembourg devotes 30 percent. Which country is likely to experience more rapid economic growth in the future? Illustrate using a production possibilities frontier graph. Your graph should include production possibilities frontiers for Lichtenstein and Luxembourg today and in 10 years.

1.9 Use the following production possibilities frontier for a country to answer the questions.

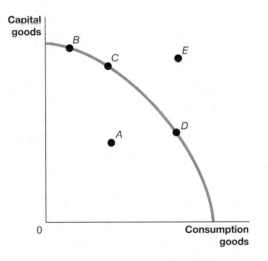

a. Which point or points are unattainable? Briefly explain why.

b. Which point or points are efficient? Briefly explain why.

c. Which point or points are inefficient? Briefly explain why.

d. At which point is the country's future growth rate likely to be the highest? Briefly explain why.

1.10 **(Related to Solved Problem 2.1 on page 44)** You have exams in economics and chemistry coming up, and you have 5 hours available for studying. The following table shows the trade-offs you face in allocating the time you will spend studying each subject:

	Hours Spent Studying		Midterm Score	
Choice	Economics	Chemistry	Economics	Chemistry
A	5	0	95	70
B	4	1	93	78
C	3	2	90	84
D	2	3	86	88
E	1	4	81	90
F	0	5	75	91

a. Use the data in the table to draw a production possibilities frontier graph. Label the vertical axis "Score on economics exam" and label the horizontal axis "Score on chemistry exam." Make sure to label the values where your production possibilities frontier intersects the vertical and horizontal axes. (Note that the origin in your graph will not occur at the values 0,0.)

b. Label the points representing choice C and choice D. If you are at choice C, what is your opportunity cost of increasing your chemistry score by 4 points?

c. Under what circumstances would choice A be sensible?

1.11 Suppose the U.S. president is attempting to decide whether the federal government should spend more on research to find a cure for heart disease. Imagine that you are the president's economic advisor and need to prepare a report discussing the relevant factors the president should consider. Use the concepts of opportunity cost and trade-offs to discuss some of the main issues you would deal with in your report.

1.12 State government Medicaid programs provide medical insurance to poor and disabled people. A news article described a new prescription drug that costs as much as "$94,000 for one 12-week treatment regimen" to treat hepatitis C, a liver disease. Several states restricted access to the new drug under their Medicaid programs to patients who are most acutely ill (stage 3 or stage 4) with hepatitis C. State Medicaid programs are paid for, in part, out of state budgets. What trade-offs do state governments face when new prescription drugs are introduced with much higher prices than existing drugs? Do you agree with states providing expensive new drugs only to the patients who are most ill from a disease? Briefly explain.

Sources: Lisa Schencker, "State Switches Stance on Hepatitis C Drugs, Expands Access, but Not All Medicaid Patients Qualify," chicagotribune.com, September 12, 2016.

1.13 Lawrence Summers served as secretary of the Treasury in the Clinton administration and as director of the National Economic Council in the Obama administration. He has been quoted as giving the following defense of the economic approach to policy issues:

There is nothing morally unattractive about saying: We need to analyze which way of spending money on health care will produce more benefit and which less, and using our money as efficiently as we can. I don't think there is anything immoral about seeking to achieve environmental benefits at the lowest possible costs.

Would it be more ethical to reduce pollution without worrying about the cost or by taking the cost into account? Briefly explain.

Source: David Wessel, "Precepts from Professor Summers," *Wall Street Journal*, October 17, 2002.

1.14 In *The Wonderful Wizard of Oz* and his other books about the Land of Oz, L. Frank Baum observed that if people's wants were limited enough, most goods would not be scarce. According to Baum, this was the case in Oz:

> There were no poor people in the Land of Oz, because there was no such thing as money.... Each person was given freely by his neighbors whatever he required for his use, which is as much as anyone may reasonably desire. Some tilled the lands and raised great crops of grain, which was divided equally among the whole population, so that all had enough. There were many tailors and dressmakers and shoemakers and the like, who made things that any who desired them might

wear. Likewise there were jewelers who made ornaments for the person, which pleased and beautified the people, and these ornaments also were free to those who asked for them. Each man and woman, no matter what he or she produced for the good of the community, was supplied by the neighbors with food and clothing and a house and furniture and ornaments and games. If by chance the supply ever ran short, more was taken from the great storehouses of the Ruler, which were afterward filled up again when there was more of any article than people needed....

> You will know, by what I have told you here, that the Land of Oz was a remarkable country. I do not suppose such an arrangement would be practical with us.

Briefly explain whether you agree with Baum that the economic system in Oz wouldn't work in the contemporary United States.

Source: L. Frank Baum, *The Emerald City of Oz*, 1910, pp. 30–31.

2.2 Comparative Advantage and Trade, pages 48–54

LEARNING OBJECTIVE: Describe comparative advantage and explain how it serves as the basis for trade.

 MyLab Economics Visit **www.pearson.com/mylab/economics** to complete these exercises online and get instant feedback.

Summary

Fundamentally, markets are about **trade**, which is the act of buying and selling. People trade on the basis of comparative advantage. An individual, a firm, or a country has a **comparative advantage** in producing a good or service if it can produce the good or service at the lowest opportunity cost. People are usually better off specializing in the activity for which they have a comparative advantage and trading for the other goods and services they need. It is important not to confuse comparative advantage with absolute advantage. An individual, a firm, or a country has an **absolute advantage** in producing a good or service if it can produce more of that good or service using the same amount of resources. It is possible to have an absolute advantage in producing a good or service without having a comparative advantage.

Review Questions

2.1 What is absolute advantage? What is comparative advantage? Is it possible for a country to have a comparative advantage in producing a good without also having an absolute advantage? Briefly explain.

2.2 What is the basis for trade: absolute advantage or comparative advantage? How can an individual or a country gain from specialization and trade?

Problems and Applications

2.3 Look again at the information in Figure 2.4 on page 49. Choose a rate of trading cherries for apples different from the rate used in the text (15 pounds of cherries for 10

pounds of apples) that will allow you and your neighbor to benefit from trading. Prepare a table like Table 2.1 on page 50 to illustrate your answer.

2.4 Using the same amount of resources, the United States and Canada can both produce lumberjack shirts and lumberjack boots, as shown in the following production possibilities frontiers:

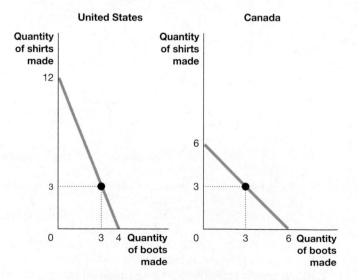

a. Which country has a comparative advantage in producing lumberjack boots? Which country has a comparative advantage in producing lumberjack shirts? Briefly explain.

b. Does either country have an absolute advantage in producing both goods? Briefly explain.

c. Suppose that both countries are currently producing three pairs of boots and three shirts. Show that both can be better off if they each specialize in producing one good and then trade for the other.

2.5 **(Related to the Don't Let This Happen to You on page 51)** A columnist for *Forbes* argues, "Even if China is always better than Spain at producing textiles, if the best thing that Spain could be doing is textiles, then that's what Spain should be doing."

   a. What does the columnist mean by "China is always better than Spain" in producing textiles (which include clothing, sheets, and similar products)? Was the columnist arguing that China has an absolute advantage over Spain in producing textiles, a comparative advantage, or both? Briefly explain.

   b. The columnist noted that, in fact, Spain exports significant quantities of textiles. If his description of the situation in China and Spain is accurate, briefly explain how Spanish firms are able to export textiles in competition with Chinese firms.

   Source: Tim Worstall, "Inditex's Zara and the Power of Comparative Advantage," forbes.com, July 7, 2015.

2.6 **(Related to Solved Problem 2.2 on page 52)** Suppose the United Kingdom and Norway both produce oil and fish oil, which are sold for the same prices in both countries. The following table shows the combinations of both goods that each country can produce in a day, measured in thousands of barrels, using the same amounts of capital and labor:

United Kingdom		Norway	
Oil	Fish oil	Oil	Fish Oil
0	8	0	4
2	6	1	3
4	4	2	2
6	2	3	1
8	0	4	0

   a. Which country has a comparative advantage in producing oil? Briefly explian.

   b. Can these two countries gain from trading oil and fish oil with each other? Briefly explain.

2.7 **(Related to Solved Problem 2.2 on page 52)** Suppose that France and Germany both produce schnitzel and wine. The following table shows combinations of the goods that each country can produce in a day:

France		Germany	
Wine (bottles)	Schnitzel (pounds)	Wine (bottles)	Schnitzel (pounds)
0	8	0	15
1	6	1	12
2	4	2	9
3	2	3	6
4	0	4	3
		5	0

   a. Which country has a comparative advantage in producing wine? Which country has a comparative advantage in producing schnitzel?

   b. Suppose that France is currently producing 1 bottle of wine and 6 pounds of schnitzel, and Germany is currently producing 3 bottles of wine and 6 pounds of schnitzel. Demonstrate that France and Germany can both be better off if they specialize in producing only one good and then trade for the other.

2.8 Can an individual or a country produce beyond its production possibilities frontier? Can an individual or a country consume beyond its production possibilities frontier? Briefly explain.

2.9 If Nicaragua can produce with the same amount of resources twice as much coffee as Colombia, explain how Colombia could have a comparative advantage in producing coffee.

2.10 Imagine that the next time the New England Patriots play the Miami Dolphins at Gillette Stadium in Foxborough, Massachusetts, Patriots star quarterback Tom Brady has a temporary lack of judgment and plans to sell Patriots memorabilia during the game because he realizes that he can sell five times more Patriots products than anyone in the stadium sports gear store. Likewise, imagine that you are a creative and effective manager at work and that you tell your employees that during the next six months, you plan to clean the offices because you can clean five times better than the cleaning staff. What error in judgment are both you and Tom making? Why shouldn't you and Tom do what you are better than anyone else at doing?

2.11 After Russia seized what had formerly been the Ukrainian territory of Crimea in February 2014, the United States and many other countries imposed economic sanctions that reduced the ability of Russia to engage in international trade. A columnist writing in the *New York Times* noted, "If sanctions push Russia onto a path of greater self-reliance, its manufacturing and service industries will surely grow faster." If the columnist is correct about the effect of the sanctions, are the sanctions likely to improve the economic well-being of the average Russian in the long run? Briefly explain.

   Source: Anatole Kaletsky, "Reasons to Welcome a Ukraine Deal," *New York Times*, September 18, 2014.

2.12 In colonial America, the population was spread thinly over a large area, and transportation costs were very high because it was difficult to ship products by road for more than short distances. As a result, most of the free population lived on small farms, where people not only grew their own food but also usually made their own clothes and very rarely bought or sold anything for money. Explain why the incomes of these farmers were likely to rise as transportation costs fell. Use the concept of comparative advantage in your answer.

2.13 During the 1928 U.S. presidential election campaign, Herbert Hoover, the Republican candidate, argued that the United States should import only products that could not be produced here. Briefly explain whether this policy would be likely to raise average income in the United States.

2.14 **(Related to the Apply the Concept on page 53)** In discussing dividing up household chores, Emily Oster, an economist at the University of Chicago, advised, "No, you shouldn't always unload the dishwasher because you're better at it." If you are better at unloading the dishwasher, why shouldn't you be the one to unload it?

Source: Emily Oster, "You're Dividing the Chores Wrong," *Slate*, November 21, 2012.

2.15 **(Related to the Apply the Concept on page 53)** The chapter mentions that in 1965, married women with children did an average of 32 hours of housework per week, while men did an average of only 4 hours of housework—a total

of 36 hours of housework. In 2016, the estimated average weekly hours of housework for women declined to 15.7, while the hours worked by men increased to about 9.7—a total of 25.4 hours of housework. Does the decrease in the total number of hours of housework—from 36 to 25.4— mean that families are willing to live in messier homes? Briefly explain.

Source: U.S. Bureau of Labor Statistics, "American Time Use—2016," June 27, 2017.

2.3 The Market System, pages 54–63

LEARNING OBJECTIVE: Explain the basics of how a market system works.

Summary

A **market** is a group of buyers and sellers of a good or service and the institution or arrangement by which they come together to trade. **Product markets** are markets for goods and services, such as computers and medical treatment. **Factor markets** are markets for the **factors of production**, such as labor, capital, natural resources, and entrepreneurial ability. A **circular-flow diagram** shows how participants in product markets and factor markets are linked. Adam Smith argued in his 1776 book *The Wealth of Nations* that in a **free market**, in which the government does not control the production of goods and services, changes in prices lead firms to produce the goods and services most desired by consumers. If consumers demand more of a good, its price will rise. Firms respond to rising prices by increasing production. If consumers demand less of a good, its price will fall. Firms respond to falling prices by producing less of a good. An **entrepreneur** is someone who operates a business. In the market system, entrepreneurs are responsible for organizing the production of goods and services. The market system will work well only if there is protection for **property rights**, which are the rights of individuals and firms to use their property.

Review Questions

3.1 What is a circular-flow diagram, and what does it demonstrate?

3.2 What are the two main categories of participants in markets? Which participants are of greatest importance in determining what goods and services are produced?

3.3 What is a free market? In what ways does a free market economy differ from a centrally planned economy?

3.4 What is an entrepreneur? Why do entrepreneurs play a key role in a market system?

3.5 Under what circumstances are firms likely to produce more of a good or service? Under what circumstances are firms likely to produce less of a good or service?

3.6 What are property rights? What role do they play in the working of a market system? Why are independent courts important for a well-functioning economy?

Problems and Applications

3.7 Identify whether each of the following transactions will take place in the factor market or in the product market

and whether households or firms are supplying the good or service or demanding the good or service.
   a. Tariq buys a Tesla Model 3.
   b. Tesla increases employment at its Fremont plant.
   c. Tariq works 20 hours per week at McDonald's.
   d. Tariq sells the land he owns to McDonald's so that it can build a new restaurant.

3.8 **(Related to the Apply the Concept on page 57)** The late Nobel Prize–winning economist Kenneth Arrow of Stanford University once wrote that the argument that the outcomes in a market system "may be very different from, and even opposed to, intentions is surely the most important intellectual contribution that economic thought has made." Briefly explain how it is possible for the outcomes in a market system to be different from what firms and consumers intended them to be. Why is this idea such an important intellectual contribution?

Sources: Kenneth J. Arrow, "Economic Equilibrium," *Encyclopedia of the Social Sciences*, 1968; and Encyclopedia.com.

3.9 **(Related to the Apply the Concept on page 57)** In a famous essay on the market system, the economist Leonard Read discussed how a pencil sold by the U.S. firm Eberhard Faber Pencil Company (now owned by Paper Mate) was made. He noted that logging companies in California and Oregon grew the cedar wood used in the pencil. The wood was milled into pencil-width slats at a factory in San Leandro, California. The graphite for the pencil was mined in Sri Lanka and mixed with clay purchased from a firm in Mississippi and wax from a firm in Mexico. The rubber was purchased from a firm in Indonesia. Was it necessary for the managers of all these firms to know how the components they produced were assembled into a pencil? Was it necessary for the chief executive officer of the Eberhard Faber Company to know this information? Briefly explain.

Source: Leonard E. Read, *I, Pencil: My Family Tree as Told to Leonard E. Read*, Irvington-on-Hudson, NY: The Foundation for Economic Education, Inc., December 1958.

3.10 Evaluate the following argument: "Adam Smith's analysis of the market system is based on a fundamental flaw: He assumes that people are motivated by self-interest. But this isn't true. I'm not selfish, and most people I know aren't selfish."

3.11 Writing in the *New York Times*, Michael Lewis argued that "a market economy is premised on a system of incentives designed to encourage an ignoble human trait: self-interest." Do you agree that self-interest is an "ignoble human trait"? What incentives does a market system provide to encourage self-interest?

Source: Michael Lewis, "In Defense of the Boom," *New York Times,* October 27, 2002.

3.12 Some economists have been puzzled that although entrepreneurs take on the risk of losing money by starting new businesses, on average their incomes are lower than those of people with similar characteristics who go to work at large firms. The late William Baumol believed part of the explanation for this puzzle may be that entrepreneurs are like people who buy lottery tickets. On average, people who don't buy lottery tickets are left with more money than people who buy tickets because lotteries take in more money than they give out. Baumol argued that "the masses of purchasers who grab up the [lottery] tickets are not irrational if they receive an adequate payment in another currency: psychic rewards."

    a. What are "psychic rewards"?

    b. What psychic rewards might an entrepreneur receive?

    c. Do you agree with Baumol that an entrepreneur is like someone buying a lottery ticket? Briefly explain.

Source: William J. Baumol, *The Microtheory of Innovative Entrepreneurship,* Princeton, NJ: Princeton University Press, 2010.

3.13 In the foreword to a report on property rights around the world, Peruvian economist Hernando De Soto noted, "Countries that have weak property rights also struggle to develop strong, innovative economic markets."

    a. What did De Soto mean by "strong, innovative economic markets"?

    b. Why would such markets be important for a country that is hoping to raise the standard of living of its residents? What do property rights have to do with developing such markets?

Source: Hernando De Soto, "Foreword," *International Property Rights Index, 2016,* internationalpropertyrightsindex.org.

3.14 According to an article on Phillyburbs.com, some farmers in rural Pennsylvania caused a "stink" by using pig manure for fertilizer. The farmers purchased the pig manure, which is an organic fertilizer, from a nearby pork processing plant and spread it across the fields where they grow corn and soybeans. The article asserted that the farmers switched to pig manure because of the skyrocketing price of chemical fertilizers. Some of the residents of the town of Milford complained about the smell, but the article said that the farmers were "likely protected under Pennsylvania's Right to Farm Act, which allows farmers to engage in practices that are common to agriculture."

    a. What price signal did the farmers respond to in their switch to the organic pig manure fertilizer?

    b. According to the Pennsylvania Right to Farm Act, do the farmers or the townspeople have the property right to the smell of the air around the farms? (Some of the residents did ask the township to urge the farmers to plow under the manure to reduce its stench.)

Source: Amanda Cregan, "Milford Farmers Switch to Pig Manure Causing a Stink for Neighbors," Phillyburbs.com, March 6, 2013.

3.15 The British historian Thomas Macaulay once remarked that copyrights are "a tax on readers." In what sense are copyrights a tax on readers? If copyrights are a tax on readers, why do governments enact them?

3.16 **(Related to the Apply the Concept on page 62)** The *Apply the Concept* feature explains that the Feeding American charity asked three professors at the University of Chicago's Booth School of Business to design a more efficient way of allocating food to local food programs and that the professors proposed changing the food allocation system to one that resembled a market.

    a. Under the new system, the "shares" each food program receives would be the equivalent to what economic variable that consumers use in the marketplace to bid for goods and services?

    b. The number of shares a food program needs to receive certain types of food would be equivalent to what economic variable in the marketplace for goods and services?

    c. One of the University of Chicago professors advising Feeding America noted, "Much of the food that is distributed through food banks often originates with donors—large manufacturers or distributors—far from [local food bank's] needy clients." Why might this fact make it more likely that a market mechanism would improve the well-being of people receiving food from local food banks?

Source: Canice Prendergast, "The Allocation of Food to Food Banks," Working Paper, University of Chicago, Booth School of Business, October 11, 2016.

Critical Thinking Exercises

CT2.1 For this exercise, your instructor may assign you to a group. Can you think of a good or service that is produced entirely by one company without the purchase of *any* raw materials or other goods or services from another company? First, each member of the group should propose at least one company that might meet this criterion by writing it down on a piece of paper and not showing it to other group members. Second, after each group member has written down a response, the members should then reveal their responses, and the group should discuss whether each company does indeed produce a good or service without any raw materials or goods and services from another company. If you cannot think of many such companies, which concepts from this chapter do you think this conclusion might illustrate?

CT2.2 On YouTube, watch one or two of the short videos on the "Primitive Technology" channel, www.youtube.com/channel/UCAL3JXZSzSm8AlZyD3nQdBA. You'll likely find it quite impressive how this single man can make so many different products, such as a hammer, a sling, and a hut, using only raw materials found in a forest and his Internet research. But how might an economist evaluate the efficiency of one person alone producing so many different products with no help from anyone else?

Note: See https://primitivetechnology.wordpress.com/about/ for more information on these videos.

3

Where Prices Come From:
The Interaction of Demand and Supply

How Smart Is Your Water?

What does a firm do when its primary product starts to fall out of fashion? The Coca-Cola Company and PepsiCo, Inc., have faced that question in recent years. Between 2004 and 2016, measured by volume, sales in the United States of carbonated beverages like Coke and Pepsi declined by more than 25 percent, while sales of bottled water increased by more than 50 percent. In 2016, sales of bottled water were greater than sales of carbonated beverages for the first time. This change resulted from a shift in consumer tastes as many people, particularly millennials, increased their demand for healthier beverages that don't contain sugar or artificial sweeteners.

In 1994, Pepsi responded to increased consumer demand for bottled water by introducing Aquafina water, and in 1999, Coke responded by introducing Dasani water. Neither company, though, had found selling bottled water to be as profitable as selling soda. As a result of decades of advertising, Coke and Pepsi are two of the most recognizable brand names in the world. The companies also have networks of bottling plants and commitments from supermarkets to provide them with extensive shelf space. Other companies have had trouble competing with Coke and Pepsi, which together account for nearly 75 percent of the market for carbonated beverages. The Aquafina and Dasani brands are not nearly as well known, however, so other companies have been better able to compete in the bottled water market, limiting Coke and Pepsi to less than 20 percent of that market.

By 2017, Coke and Pepsi were attempting to increase their profits in the bottled water market by introducing premium water or smart water brands. With regular bottled water, firms filter tap water or spring water to remove impurities. With premium water, like Pepsi's LIFEWTR and Coke's smartwater, firms also add ingredients, typically electrolytes. Although many nutritionists are skeptical that premium water is any better for you than regular bottled water, demand for premium bottled water has been increasing rapidly. Both Coke and Pepsi have been able to

Andrew Toth/ Stringer/Getty Images

charge higher prices for their premium water brands than they do for their carbonated beverages. But the firms were facing determined competition from Nestlé's Perrier brand and Danone's Evian brand, among many others.

Although premium water was a hot product in 2017, there are no guarantees in a market system. Will Coke and Pepsi and their competitors be able to continue charging higher prices for premium water than for regular bottled water, or will competition force down prices and make selling premium bottled water no more profitable than selling regular bottled water? Although competition is not always good news for firms trying to sell products, it is great news for consumers because it increases the choice of available products and lowers the prices consumers pay for those products.

AN INSIDE LOOK on **page 98** discusses how McDonald's has responded to shifts in consumer demand by serving breakfast all day, allowing customers to order food online, and offering home delivery.

Sources: Jennifer Maloney, "Coca-Cola Needs to Be More Than Just Coke, Its Next Chief Says," *Wall Street Journal*, February 23, 2017; Jennifer Maloney, "PepsiCo Gives Its 'Premium' Water a Super Bowl Push," *Wall Street Journal*, January 24, 2017; and Feliz Solomon, "Coca-Cola and Pepsi Now Have Something Else in Common," fortune.com, December 7, 2016.

Chapter Outline & Learning Objectives

Economics in Your Life & Career

Can You Forecast the Future Demand for Premium Bottled Water?

Firms face many challenges in responding to changes in consumer demand. Firms selling premium bottled water need to forecast future demand in order to determine how much production capacity they will need. If you were a manager for Coca-Cola, PepsiCo, Nestlé, Bai, or another firm selling premium bottled water, what factors would you take into account in forecasting future demand? As you read this chapter, try to answer this question. You can check your answers against those we provide on **page 97** at the end of this chapter.

Perfectly competitive market A market that meets the conditions of having (1) many buyers and sellers, (2) all firms selling identical products, and (3) no barriers to new firms entering the market.

I n Chapter 1, we explored how economists use models to predict human behavior. In Chapter 2, we used the production possibilities frontiers (*PPF*) model to analyze scarcity and trade-offs. In this chapter and the next, we explore the model of demand and supply, which is the most powerful tool in economics, and use the model to explain how prices are determined.

Economic models are simplified versions of reality that are based on assumptions. In some cases, the assumptions of a model may not describe exactly the economic situation we are analyzing. For example, the model of demand and supply assumes that we are analyzing a **perfectly competitive market**, which is a market where there are many buyers and sellers, all the products sold are identical, and there are no barriers to new firms entering the market. These assumptions are very restrictive and apply exactly to only a few markets, such as the markets for wheat and other agricultural products. However, the model of demand and supply has proven to be very useful in analyzing markets where competition among sellers is intense, even if there are relatively few sellers and the products being sold are not identical. In recent studies, the model of demand and supply has been successful in analyzing markets with as few as four buyers and four sellers. As we will see in this chapter, this model is often successful in predicting changes in quantities and prices in many markets.

We begin studying the model of demand and supply by discussing consumers and the demand side of the market, and then we turn to firms and the supply side. Throughout this text, we will apply this model to understand business, the economy, and economic policy.

3.1 The Demand Side of the Market
LEARNING OBJECTIVE: List and describe the variables that influence demand.

We saw in Chapter 2 that in a market system, consumers ultimately determine which goods and services will be produced. The most successful businesses are the ones that respond best to consumer demand. But what determines consumer demand for a product? Certainly, many factors influence the willingness of consumers to buy a particular product. For example, consumers who are considering buying premium bottled water, such as Bai's Antiwater or Coca-Cola's smartwater, will make their decisions based on, among other factors, the income they have available to spend and the effectiveness of the advertising campaigns of the companies that sell premium bottled water. For most consumers, the primary factor in their buying decision is the price of the product. So, we focus on this factor first. As we discuss demand, keep in mind that we are considering not what a consumer *wants* to buy but what the consumer is both *willing* and *able* to buy.

Demand Schedules and Demand Curves

Demand schedule A table that shows the relationship between the price of a product and the quantity of the product demanded.

Quantity demanded The amount of a good or service that a consumer is willing and able to purchase at a given price.

Demand curve A curve that shows the relationship between the price of a product and the quantity of the product demanded.

Market demand The demand by all the consumers of a given good or service.

Tables that show the relationship between the price of a product and the quantity of the product demanded are called **demand schedules**. The table in Figure 3.1 shows the quantity of premium bottled water consumers would be willing and able to buy per day at five different prices. The amount of a good or service that a consumer is willing and able to purchase at a given price is called the **quantity demanded**. The graph in Figure 3.1 plots the numbers from the table as a **demand curve**, which shows the relationship between the price of a product and the quantity of the product demanded. (Note that, for convenience, we made the demand curve in Figure 3.1 a straight line, or linear. There is no reason that all demand curves need to be straight lines.) The demand curve in Figure 3.1 shows the **market demand**, which is the demand by all the consumers of a given good or service. The market for a product, such as restaurant meals, that is sold locally would include all the consumers in a city or a relatively small area. The market for a product, such as premium bottled water, that is sold internationally would include all the consumers in the world.

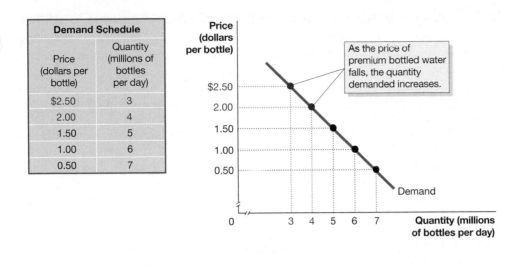

Demand Schedule	
Price (dollars per bottle)	Quantity (millions of bottles per day)
$2.50	3
2.00	4
1.50	5
1.00	6
0.50	7

As the price of premium bottled water falls, the quantity demanded increases.

MyLab Economics Animation

Figure 3.1

A Demand Schedule and Demand Curve

As the price of premium bottled water changes, consumers change the quantity they are willing and able to buy. We can show this as a *demand schedule* in a table or as a *demand curve* on a graph. The table and graph both show that as the price of premium bottled water falls, the quantity demanded increases. When the price of water is $2.50 per bottle, consumers buy 3 million bottles per day. When the price falls to $2.00, consumers buy 4 million bottles. Therefore, the demand curve for premium bottled water is downward sloping.

The demand curve in Figure 3.1 slopes downward because consumers will buy more premium bottled water as the price falls. When the price of a bottle of water is $2.50, consumers buy 3 million bottles per day. When the price falls to $2.00, consumers buy 4 million. Buyers demand a larger quantity of a product as the price falls because the product becomes less expensive relative to other products and because they can afford to buy more at a lower price. **MyLab Economics** Concept Check

The Law of Demand

The inverse relationship between the price of a product and the quantity of the product demanded is called the **law of demand**: Holding everything else constant, when the price of a product falls, the quantity demanded of the product will increase, and when the price of a product rises, the quantity demanded of the product will decrease. The law of demand holds for any market demand curve. Economists have found only a very few exceptions to this law. **MyLab Economics** Concept Check

Law of demand A rule that states that, holding everything else constant, when the price of a product falls, the quantity demanded of the product will increase, and when the price of a product rises, the quantity demanded of the product will decrease.

What Explains the Law of Demand?

It makes sense that consumers will buy more of a good when its price falls and less of a good when its price rises, but let's look more closely at why this result holds. When the price of a product falls, consumers buy a larger quantity because of two effects:

1. The **substitution effect** refers to the change in the quantity demanded of a good that results because a change in price makes the good more or less expensive *relative* to other goods that are *substitutes*. When the price of premium bottled water falls, people will substitute buying premium bottled water for other goods, such as regular bottled water or carbonated soft drinks, like Coke and Pepsi.

2. The **income effect** of a price change refers to the change in the quantity demanded of a good that results because a change in the good's price increases or decreases consumers' purchasing power. *Purchasing power* is the quantity of goods a consumer can buy with a fixed amount of income. When the price of a good falls, the increased purchasing power of consumers' incomes will usually lead them to purchase a larger quantity of the good. When the price of a good rises, the decreased purchasing power of consumers' incomes will usually lead them to purchase a smaller quantity of the good.

Substitution effect The change in the quantity demanded of a good that results from a change in price, making the good more or less expensive relative to other goods that are substitutes.

Income effect The change in the quantity demanded of a good that results from the effect of a change in the good's price on consumers' purchasing power.

Although we can analyze them separately, the substitution effect and the income effect occur simultaneously whenever a price changes. So, a fall in the price of premium bottled water leads consumers to buy more bottles both because the bottles are now less expensive relative to substitute products and because the purchasing power of consumers' incomes has increased. **MyLab Economics** Concept Check

Holding Everything Else Constant: The *Ceteris Paribus* Condition

Ceteris paribus ("all else equal") condition The requirement that when analyzing the relationship between two variables—such as price and quantity demanded—other variables must be held constant.

Notice that the definition of the law of demand contains the phrase *holding everything else constant*. In constructing the market demand curve for premium bottled water, we focused only on the effect that changes in the price of premium bottled water would have on the quantity consumers would be willing and able to buy. We were holding constant other variables that might affect the willingness of consumers to buy premium bottled water. Economists refer to the necessity of holding all variables other than price constant in constructing a demand curve as the **ceteris paribus condition**. *Ceteris paribus* means "all else equal" in Latin.

What would happen if we allowed a change in a variable—other than price—that might affect the willingness of consumers to buy premium bottled water? Consumers would then change the quantity they demanded at each price. We can illustrate this effect by shifting the market demand curve. A shift of a demand curve is *an increase or a decrease in demand*. A movement along a demand curve is *an increase or a decrease in the quantity demanded*. As Figure 3.2 shows, the demand curve shifts to the right if consumers decide to buy more premium bottled water at each price, and the demand curve shifts to the left if consumers decide to buy less at each price. **MyLab Economics** Concept Check

Variables That Shift Market Demand

Many variables other than price can influence market demand. These five are the most important:

- Income
- Prices of related goods
- Tastes
- Population and demographics
- Expected future prices

We next discuss how changes in each of these variables affect the market demand curve.

Income The income that consumers have available to spend affects their willingness and ability to buy a good. Suppose that the market demand curve in Figure 3.1 on page 75 represents the willingness of consumers to buy premium bottled water when average household income is $56,000. If average household income rises to $58,000, the demand for premium bottled water will increase, shifting the demand curve to the right. A good is a **normal good** when the demand for the good increases following a rise in income and decreases following a fall in income. Most goods are

Normal good A good for which the demand increases as income rises and decreases as income falls.

MyLab Economics Animation

Figure 3.2

Shifting the Demand Curve

When consumers increase the quantity of a product they want to buy at a given price, the demand curve shifts to the right, from D_1 to D_2. When consumers decrease the quantity of a product they want to buy at a given price, the demand curve shifts to the left, from D_1 to D_3.

normal goods, but some goods are *inferior goods*. A good is an **inferior good** when the demand for it decreases following a rise in income and increases following a fall in income. For instance, as your income rises, you might buy fewer cans of tuna or packages of instant noodles and buy more salmon or whole grain pasta. So, for you, canned tuna and instant noodles would be examples of inferior goods—not because they are of low quality but because you buy less of them as your income increases.

Inferior good A good for which the demand increases as income falls and decreases as income rises.

Prices of Related Goods The prices of other goods can also affect consumers' demand for a product. Consumers who buy premium bottled water could buy regular bottled water instead. Goods and services that can be used for the same purpose are called **substitutes**. When two goods are substitutes, the more you buy of one, the less you will buy of the other. A decrease in the price of a substitute causes the demand curve for a good to shift to the left. An increase in the price of a substitute causes the demand curve for a good to shift to the right.

Substitutes Goods and services that can be used for the same purpose.

Suppose that the market demand curve in Figure 3.1 on page 75 represents the willingness and ability of consumers to buy premium bottled water during a day when the average price of regular bottled water is $0.75. If the average price of regular bottled water falls to $0.65, consumers will demand fewer bottles of premium water at every price, which shifts the demand curve for premium bottled water to the left.

Apply the Concept

MyLab Economics Video

Virtual Reality Headsets: Will a Substitute Fail for a Lack of Complements?

Firms can increase their profits if they successfully introduce a product that better serves a known consumer need than do existing products. Coke and Pepsi have used this strategy in trying to convince consumers that premium bottled water is superior to regular bottled water. Similarly, when firms such as Sony, Facebook, and HTC began selling virtual reality headsets, they hoped that consumers would consider them a superior alternative to existing game consoles, such as the Sony PlayStation and the Microsoft Xbox.

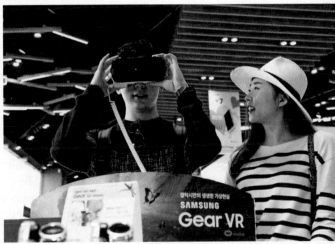

Bloomberg/Getty images

Is the success of virtual reality headsets being held back by a lack of complements?

But to be an effective substitute for game consoles, virtual reality headsets were dependent on important complementary products—games that could be played using the headsets. Existing games that are playable on game consoles can't be played on virtual reality headsets. So, makers of these headsets were dependent on firms that develop and sell games and other software to release titles that could be used with the headsets. In early 2017, not many game developers were doing so. Although Sony had heavily advertised its PlayStation VR goggles during the 2016 holiday season, it had sold fewer than 1 million units. Some game developers considered those sales to be too low to take the risk of spending the funds needed to develop virtual reality games.

Sony and the other firms selling virtual reality headsets had difficulty selling enough headsets to convince game developers they would be able to make a profit selling games for the headsets. But a key reason that sales of headsets lagged was that many consumers didn't believe there were enough games and other software available to justify buying headsets rather than game consoles. The firms making headsets hoped the problem could gradually be overcome as the number of games increased and as consumers became more familiar with the product. As one industry analyst put it, "This is going to be a long slog, as the technology continues to improve, more content becomes available and awareness increases."

Until then, the success of virtual reality headsets as a substitute for game consoles was being held back by the limited availability of a complementary good: games and other software that could be used with the headsets.

Sources: Takashi Mochizuki, "Sony's Virtual-Reality Headset Confronts Actual Reality of Modest Sales," *Wall Street Journal*, February 27, 2017; Joshua Brustein, "Will VR Ever Matter?" bloomberg.com, October 20, 2016; and Nick Wingfield, "Sticker Shock, and Maybe Nausea, Hamper Sales of Virtual Reality Gear," *New York Times*, January 8, 2017.

MyLab Economics Study Plan

Your Turn: Test your understanding by doing related problem 1.12 on page 101 at the end of this chapter.

Complements Goods and services that are used together.

Goods and services that are used together—such as hot dogs and hot dog buns—are called **complements**. When two goods are complements, the more consumers buy of one, the more they will buy of the other. A decrease in the price of a complement causes the demand curve for a good to shift to the right. An increase in the price of a complement causes the demand curve for a good to shift to the left.

When working out at the gym, many people drink a premium water such as Water Joe, Pepsi's LIFEWTR, or Fiji Water. So, for many people, premium bottled water and a gym membership are complements. Suppose that the market demand curve in Figure 3.1 on page 75 represents the willingness of consumers to buy premium bottled water at a time when the average price of a gym membership is $40 per month. If the price of gym memberships drops to $30 per month, consumers will buy more gym memberships *and* more premium bottled water, so the demand curve for premium bottled water will shift to the right.

Tastes An advertising campaign for a product can influence consumer demand. For example, PepsiCo paid millions of dollars to advertise LIFEWTR during the 2017 Super Bowl. If other firms making premium bottled water begin to advertise heavily, consumers are likely to buy more of it at every price, and the demand curve will shift to the right. An economist would say that the advertising campaign has affected consumers' *taste* for premium bottled water. Taste is a catchall category that refers to the many subjective elements that can enter into a consumer's decision to buy a product. Sometimes trends play a substantial role. For example, the popularity of low-carbohydrate diets caused a decline in demand for some goods, such as bread and donuts, and an increase in demand for fish. In general, when consumers' taste for a product increases, the demand curve will shift to the right, and when consumers' taste decreases, the demand curve will shift to the left.

Population and Demographics As the population of a country increases, the number of consumers will increase, as will the demand for most products. The **demographics** of a population refers to its characteristics, with respect to age, race, and gender. As the demographics of a country or region change, the demand for particular goods will increase or decrease because different categories of people tend to have different preferences for those goods. For instance, the U.S. Census Bureau forecasts that Hispanics will increase from 18 percent of the U.S. population in 2016 to 29 percent in 2060. This increase will expand demand for Spanish-language books, Web sites, and cable television channels, among other goods and services.

Demographics The characteristics of a population with respect to age, race, and gender.

NC1 Wenn Photos/Newscom

Millennials have a greater demand for bottled water and smaller demand for soda than do older generations.

Apply the Concept

MyLab Economics Video

Millennials Shake Up the Markets for Soda, Groceries, Big Macs, and Running Shoes

Changing demographics can affect the demand for products. The usefulness of some products varies with age. For example, when birth rates are high, the demand for baby products such as formula and diapers increases. Similarly, when there are more older people, the demand for nursing homes increases. Many retail analysts believe that *tastes* for products may also differ across generations, so that some products that are popular with older generations may be much less popular with younger generations. There are no exact definitions of generations, but the following chart shows common labels.

Years Born	Generation Label	Age Range in 2017	Number of People in the Generation in 2017
1946–1964	Baby boom generation	53–71	79 million
1965–1984	Generation X	33–52	83 million
1985–2004	Millennials, or generation Y	13–32	87 million

The millennials outnumber the two generations that preceded them, but the size of each generation doesn't tell the whole story for retailers. Market research indicates that consumers between the ages of 18 and 49 account for a large fraction of all retail sales. This fact helps explain why firms are willing to pay high prices to run commercials on television programs, such as AMC's *The Walking Dead*, that this "prime demographic" watches. Note that the whole of the baby boom generation is now older than this demographic. Members of generation X are also beginning to age out of this group, and over time millennials will begin to make up the bulk of this demographic.

Because of their importance as consumers, firms become concerned if millennials don't have a strong demand for their products. For instance, according to the *Wall Street Journal*, only 20 percent of millennials have ever eaten a Big Mac, McDonald's most important menu item. Millennials are more likely to visit "fast-casual" restaurants, such as Panera Bread, than they are fast-food restaurants, such as McDonald's or Burger King. Millennials are also less likely to play golf or to enter marathons or other races or even to run noncompetitively. Many millennials prefer to attend fitness classes or to work out on their own. As fewer young people play golf, sales of golf equipment, rounds of golf at golf courses, and ratings of golf tournaments on television have all declined. Sales of running shoes and other running gear have also declined. The reduced demand for these products from millennials helped push retail chains Sports Authority, Bob's Stores, and Eastern Mountain Sports into bankruptcy and forced Dick's Sporting Goods to close some of its stores.

Millennials are also less likely to shop at grocery stores, preferring online retailers like Amazon Fresh or using smartphone apps like Seamless and Grubhub to order from restaurants. Spending at grocery stores by people aged 25 to 34 dropped by more than 25 percent between 1990 and 2016, after adjusting for inflation. As we saw in the chapter opener, in 2016, for the first time U.S. consumers purchased more bottled water than carbonated beverages. As a result, many traditional beverage companies like Coca-Cola and PepsiCo have begun to increase their production of bottled water. In particular, by 2017, these companies were heavily promoting premium bottled water brands, such as smartwater and LIFEWTR. As one of PepsiCo's top managers put it, "What we see developing is a premium water segment of the water category, driven heavily by millennials." But these companies faced the challenge of convincing millennials and other consumers that the electrolytes and other ingredients added to premium bottled water were enough to justify paying a significantly higher price than for regular bottled water. As one skeptical appraisal said, "To put it simply, in most situations plain old water will suffice. Unless you're running a marathon or partaking in an intense hike."

Regardless of whether the demand for premium water continues to expand rapidly, as firms make plans for the long run, they have to take into account how changing demographics may affect demand for their products.

Sources: Julie Jargon, "McDonald's Knows It's Losing the Burger Battle—Can It Come Back?" *Wall Street Journal*, October 6, 2016; Sara Germano, "Dick's Drops Brands as It Expands In-house Labels," *Wall Street Journal*, March 7, 2017; Heather Haddon, "Grocers Feel Chill from Millennials," *Wall Street Journal*, October 27, 2016; John Kell, "PepsiCo to Launch Premium Water Brand LIFEWTR," fortune.com, December 9, 2016; and Hayley Sugg, "Pepsi's New Enhanced Water Brand Follows Trend," cookinglight.com, February 8, 2017.

Your Turn: Test your understanding by doing related problems 1.13 and 1.14 on page 101 at the end of this chapter.

MyLab Economics Study Plan

Expected Future Prices Consumers choose not only which products to buy but also when to buy them. For instance, if enough consumers become convinced that houses will be selling for lower prices in three months, the demand for houses will decrease now, as some consumers postpone their purchases to wait for the expected price decrease. Alternatively, if enough consumers become convinced that the price of houses will be higher in three months, the demand for houses will increase now, as some consumers try to beat the expected price increase.

Table 3.1 summarizes the most important variables that cause market demand curves to shift. Note that the table shows the shift in the demand curve that results from an *increase* in each of the variables. A *decrease* in these variables would cause the demand curve to shift in the opposite direction. **MyLab Economics** Concept Check

Table 3.1

Variables That Shift Market Demand Curves

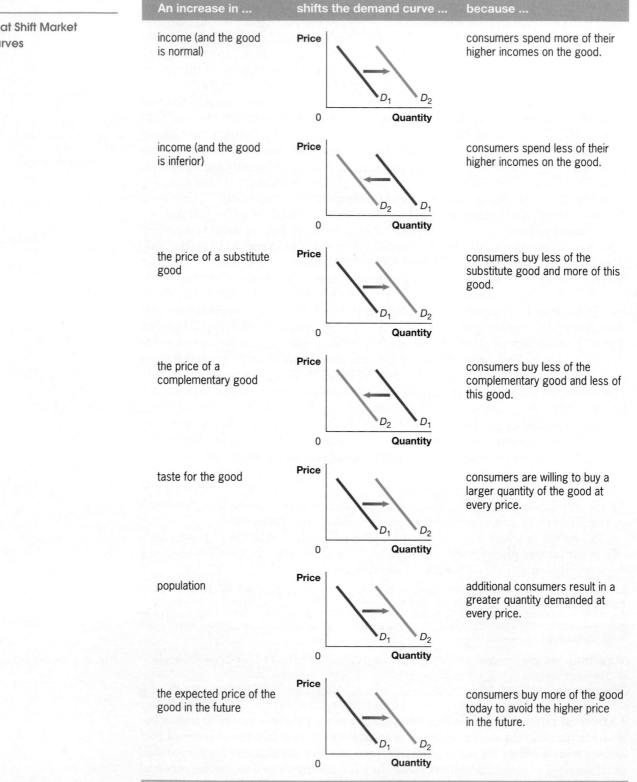

An increase in ...	shifts the demand curve ...	because ...
income (and the good is normal)		consumers spend more of their higher incomes on the good.
income (and the good is inferior)		consumers spend less of their higher incomes on the good.
the price of a substitute good		consumers buy less of the substitute good and more of this good.
the price of a complementary good		consumers buy less of the complementary good and less of this good.
taste for the good		consumers are willing to buy a larger quantity of the good at every price.
population		additional consumers result in a greater quantity demanded at every price.
the expected price of the good in the future		consumers buy more of the good today to avoid the higher price in the future.

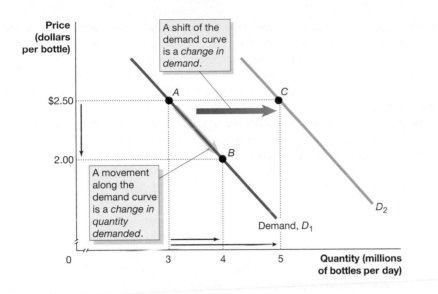

Figure 3.3

A Change in Demand versus a Change in Quantity Demanded

If the price of premium bottled water falls from $2.50 to $2.00, the result will be a movement along the demand curve from point A to point B—an increase in quantity demanded from 3 million bottles to 4 million. If consumers' incomes increase, or if another factor changes that makes consumers want more of the product at every price, the demand curve will shift to the right—an increase in demand. In this case, the increase in demand from D_1 to D_2 causes the quantity of premium bottled water demanded at a price of $2.50 to increase from 3 million bottles at point A to 5 million at point C.

A Change in Demand versus a Change in Quantity Demanded

It is important to understand the difference between a *change in demand* and a *change in quantity demanded*. A change in demand refers to a shift of the demand curve. A shift occurs if there is a change in one of the variables—*other than the price of the product*—that affects the willingness of consumers to buy the product. A change in quantity demanded refers to a movement along the demand curve as a result of a change in the product's price. Figure 3.3 illustrates this important distinction. If the price of premium bottled water falls from $2.50 to $2.00, the result will be a movement along the demand curve from point A to point B—an increase in quantity demanded from 3 million bottles to 4 million. If consumers' incomes increase, or if another factor changes that makes consumers want more of the product at every price, the demand curve will shift to the right—an increase in demand. In this case, the increase in demand from D_1 to D_2 causes the quantity of premium bottled water demanded at a price of $2.50 to increase from 3 million bottles at point A to 5 million at point C.   **MyLab Economics** Concept Check

Apply the Concept   MyLab Economics Video

Forecasting the Demand for Premium Bottled Water

It's important for managers to forecast the demand for their products accurately because doing so helps them determine how much of a good to produce. Firms typically set manufacturing schedules at least a month ahead of time. Premium bottled water is a rapidly growing market, and firms need to carefully plan increases in productive capacity. Firms that fail to produce a large enough quantity to keep pace with increasing demand can lose out to competitors. But will the demand for premium bottled water continue to grow at such a rapid pace?

Richard Tedlow of the Harvard Business School has developed a theory of the "three phases of marketing" that can provide some insight into how the markets for many consumer products develop over time. The first phase often has a very large number of firms, each producing a relatively small volume of goods and charging high prices. This phase corresponds to the carbonated soft drink industry in the late nineteenth century, the automobile industry in the early twentieth century, and the personal computer industry in the late 1970s. In the second phase, the market consolidates, with one or a few brands attaining high market shares by selling a large number of units at lower prices. This phase corresponds to the soft drink industry during the middle of the twentieth century, the automobile industry during the 1920s, and the personal computer industry during the 1980s.

Sara Stathas/Alamy Stock Photo

How will changes in demographics, income, and tastes shape the market for premium bottled water?

The third phase of marketing involves a rapid multiplication of products introduced by the dominant firms. Carbonated soft drinks, automobiles, and personal computers are all currently in this phase. For instance, Coca-Cola and Pepsi are the dominant firms in the carbonated soft drink industry, but they offer an incredible variety of products, from basic Coke and Pepsi to caffeine-free, Diet Cherry Coke, and Black Cherry French Vanilla Diet Pepsi Jazz.

The premium bottled water industry is probably in the second phase of marketing, with Coca-Cola, PepsiCo, Danone, and Nestlé each having market shares of at least 10 percent, and dozens of smaller firms making up the remainder of the market. Whether these smaller firms will be able to thrive or whether the industry will face rapid consolidation and move quickly into the third phase of marketing is crucial to managers planning the future at these firms.

Managers at beverage firms will have to take into account a number of factors when estimating the future demand for premium bottled water. Factors that will tend to lead to higher demand for premium bottled water include the popularity of the product with millennials, the trend toward healthier eating habits that has led to declining consumption of carbonated beverages, the taxes on soda that cities have been imposing to both fight obesity and raise tax revenue, and the possibility of attracting consumers who now prefer energy drinks such as Red Bull and sports drinks such as Gatorade. But an obstacle to the rapid growth of demand for premium bottled water comes from doubts raised by some analysts about the benefits from the electrolytes and other ingredients it contains that are not in regular bottled water. If consumers come to believe that these ingredients serve no useful purpose, they may prefer to buy regular bottled water, which typically has a lower price.

As we saw in Chapter 1, economists can use formal models to forecast future values of economic variables. In this case, an economist forecasting the demand for premium bottled water would want to include the factors mentioned in the previous paragraphs as well as other data, including changes over time in demographics and projected income growth.

Sources: Jennifer Maloney, "PepsiCo Gives Its 'Premium' Water a Super Bowl Push," *Wall Street Journal*, January 24, 2017; Quentin Fottrell, "Bottled Water Overtakes Soda as America's No. 1 Drink—Why You Should Avoid Both," marketwatch. com, March 12, 2017; and Richard Tedlow, *New and Improved: The Story of Mass Marketing in America*, Cambridge, MA: Harvard Business School Press, 1996.

MyLab Economics Study Plan

Your Turn: Test your understanding by doing related problem 1.17 on page 102 at the end of this chapter.

The Supply Side of the Market
LEARNING OBJECTIVE: List and describe the variables that influence supply.

Quantity supplied The amount of a good or service that a firm is willing and able to supply at a given price.

Just as many variables influence the willingness and ability of consumers to buy a particular good or service, many variables influence the willingness and ability of firms to supply a good or service. The most important of these variables is price. The amount of a good or service that a firm is willing and able to supply at a given price is the **quantity supplied**. Holding other variables constant, when the price of a good rises, producing the good is more profitable, and the quantity supplied will increase. When the price of a good falls, selling the good is less profitable, and the quantity supplied will decrease. In addition, as we saw in Chapter 2, devoting more and more resources to the production of a good results in increasing marginal costs. For example, if Coca-Cola, PepsiCo, Fiji, Bai, and other firms increase production of premium bottled water during a given time period, they are likely to find that the cost of producing additional bottles increases as they run existing factories for longer hours and pay higher prices for electrolytes and other ingredients and higher wages for workers. With higher marginal costs, firms will supply a larger quantity only if the price is higher.

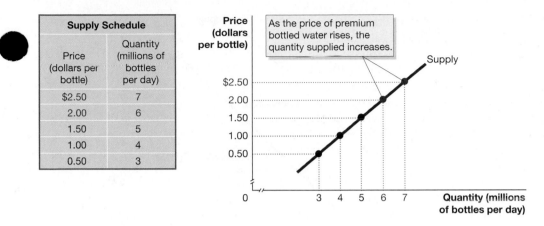

Supply Schedule	
Price (dollars per bottle)	Quantity (millions of bottles per day)
$2.50	7
2.00	6
1.50	5
1.00	4
0.50	3

As the price of premium bottled water rises, the quantity supplied increases.

MyLab Economics Animation

Figure 3.4

A Supply Schedule and Supply Curve

As the price of producing premium bottled water changes, Coca-Cola, PepsiCo, Fiji, Bai, and other firms change the quantity they are willing to supply. We can show this as a *supply schedule* in a table or as a *supply curve* on a graph. The supply schedule and supply curve both show that as the price of premium bottled water rises, firms will increase the quantity they supply. At a price of $2.00 per bottle, firms will supply 6 million bottles per day. At a price of $2.50, firms will supply 7 million.

Supply Schedules and Supply Curves

A **supply schedule** is a table that shows the relationship between the price of a product and the quantity of the product supplied. The table in Figure 3.4 is a supply schedule showing the quantity of premium bottled water that firms would be willing to supply per month at different prices. The graph in Figure 3.4 plots the numbers from the table as a **supply curve**, which shows the relationship between the price of a product and the quantity of the product supplied. The supply schedule and supply curve both show that as the price of premium bottled water rises, firms will increase the quantity they supply. At a price of $2.00 per bottle, firms will supply 6 million bottles per day. At a higher price of $2.50, firms will supply 7 million. (Once again, we are assuming for convenience that the supply curve is a straight line, even though not all supply curves are actually straight lines.)   MyLab Economics Concept Check

Supply schedule A table that shows the relationship between the price of a product and the quantity of the product supplied.

Supply curve A curve that shows the relationship between the price of a product and the quantity of the product supplied.

The Law of Supply

The *market supply curve* in Figure 3.4 is upward sloping. We expect most supply curves to be upward sloping, according to the **law of supply**, which states that, holding everything else constant, increases in price cause increases in the quantity supplied, and decreases in price cause decreases in the quantity supplied. Notice that the definition of the law of supply—like the definition of the law of demand—contains the phrase *holding everything else constant*. If only the price of the product changes, there is a movement along the supply curve, which is *an increase or a decrease in the quantity supplied*. As Figure 3.5 shows, if any other variable that affects the willingness of firms to supply a good changes, the supply curve will shift, which is *an increase or a decrease in supply*. When firms increase the quantity of a product they want to sell at a given price, the supply curve shifts to the right. The shift from S_1 to S_3 represents *an increase in supply*. When firms decrease the quantity of a product they want to sell at a given price, the supply curve shifts to the left. The shift from S_1 to S_2 represents *a decrease in supply*.   MyLab Economics Concept Check

Law of supply A rule that states that, holding everything else constant, increases in price cause increases in the quantity supplied, and decreases in price cause decreases in the quantity supplied.

Variables That Shift Market Supply

Many variables other than price can affect market supply. These five are the most important:

- Prices of inputs
- Technological change
- Prices of related goods in production
- Number of firms in the market
- Expected future prices

We next discuss how changes in each of these variables affect the market supply curve.

Prices of Inputs The factor most likely to cause the supply curve for a product to shift is a change in the price of an input. An *input* is anything used in the production of a good or service. For instance, if the price of electrolytes used in many premium

MyLab Economics Animation

Figure 3.5

Shifting the Supply Curve

When firms increase the quantity of a product they want to sell at a given price, the supply curve shifts to the right. The shift from S_1 to S_3 represents an *increase in supply*. When firms decrease the quantity of a product they want to sell at a given price, the supply curve shifts to the left. The shift from S_1 to S_2 represents a *decrease in supply*.

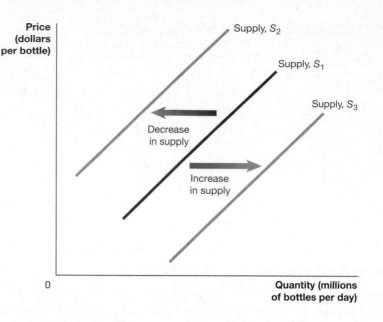

Technological change A positive or negative change in the ability of a firm to produce a given level of output with a given quantity of inputs.

bottled waters or the price of plastic bottles rises, the cost of producing premium bottled water will increase, making it less profitable at every price. The supply of premium bottled water will decline, and the market supply curve will shift to the left. Similarly, if the price of an input falls, the supply of premium bottled water will increase, and the market supply curve will shift to the right.

Technological Change A second factor that causes a change in supply is **technological change**, which is a positive or negative change in the ability of a firm to produce a given level of output with a given quantity of inputs. Positive technological change occurs whenever a firm is able to produce more output using the same amount of inputs. In other words, the *productivity* of the firm's workers or machines has increased. For example, suppose that PepsiCo develops a better way to lay out the plants where LIFEWTR is bottled so that it can produce more bottles per day, using the same number of workers and amount of machinery. If a firm can produce more output with the same amount of inputs, its costs will be lower, and the good will be more profitable to produce at any given price. As a result, when positive technological change occurs, the firm will increase the quantity supplied at every price, and its supply curve will shift to the right.

Negative technological change is relatively rare, although it could result from an earthquake or another natural disaster or from a war that reduces the ability of firms to supply as much output with a given amount of inputs. Negative technological change will raise firms' costs, and firms will earn lower profits from producing the good. Therefore, negative technological change will cause the market supply curve to shift to the left.

Prices of Related Goods in Production Firms often choose which good or service they will produce. Alternative goods that a firm could produce are called *substitutes in production*. Many of the firms that produce premium bottled water also produce other beverages, such as regular bottled water, juices, or carbonated soft drinks. For example, PepsiCo produces Aquafina bottled water, Tropicana orange juice, and Pepsi-Cola, among other beverages. If the price of carbonated soft drinks decreases relative to the price of premium bottled water, soft drinks will become less profitable, and Coca-Cola, PepsiCo, and other firms will shift some of their productive capacity away from soft drinks and toward premium bottled water. The firms will offer more bottles of premium water for sale at every price, so the supply curve for premium bottled water will shift to the right.

Goods that are produced together are called *complements in production*. For example, the same geological formations that contain oil usually also contain natural gas. If the price of oil rises, oil companies that begin pumping more oil from these formations will also produce more natural gas. As a result, an increase in the price of oil will cause the supply curve for natural gas—a complement in production—to shift to the right.

Number of Firms in the Market A change in the number of firms in the market will change supply. When new firms *enter* a market, the supply curve shifts to the right, and when existing firms leave, or *exit*, a market, the supply curve shifts to the left. In early 2017, for instance, PepsiCo entered the market for premium bottled water when it introduced LIFEWTR, which shifted the market supply curve to the right.

Expected Future Prices If a firm expects that the price of its product will be higher in the future, it has an incentive to decrease supply now and increase it in the future. For instance, if Coca-Cola believes that prices for premium bottled water are temporarily low—perhaps because of a recession—it may store some of its production of smartwater today to sell later on, when it expects prices to be higher.

Table 3.2 summarizes the most important variables that cause market supply curves to shift. Note that the table shows the shift in the supply curve that results from an *increase* in each of the variables. A *decrease* in these variables would cause the supply curve to shift in the opposite direction. MyLab Economics Concept Check

Table 3.2

Variables That Shift Market Supply Curves

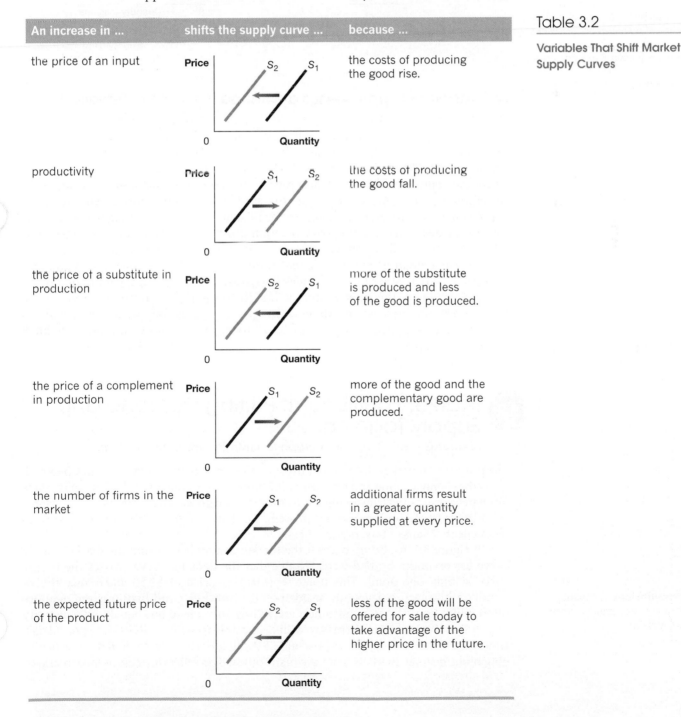

An increase in ...	shifts the supply curve ...	because ...
the price of an input		the costs of producing the good rise.
productivity		the costs of producing the good fall.
the price of a substitute in production		more of the substitute is produced and less of the good is produced.
the price of a complement in production		more of the good and the complementary good are produced.
the number of firms in the market		additional firms result in a greater quantity supplied at every price.
the expected future price of the product		less of the good will be offered for sale today to take advantage of the higher price in the future.

MyLab Economics Animation

Figure 3.6

A Change in Supply versus a Change in Quantity Supplied

If the price of premium bottled water rises from \$2.00 to \$2.50, the result will be a movement up the supply curve from point *A* to point *B*—an increase in the quantity supplied by Coca-Cola, PepsiCo, Bai, and other firms from 6 million bottles to 7 million. If the price of an input decreases, or if another factor changes that causes sellers to supply more of the product at every price, the supply curve will shift to the right—an increase in supply. In this case, the increase in supply from S_1 to S_2 causes the quantity of premium bottled water supplied at a price of \$2.50 to increase from 7 million at point *B* to 9 million at point *C*.

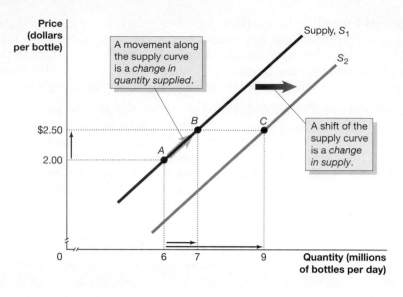

MyLab Economics Study Plan

A Change in Supply versus a Change in Quantity Supplied

We noted in Section 3.1 the important difference between a change in demand and a change in quantity demanded. There is a similar difference between a *change in supply* and a *change in quantity supplied*. A change in supply refers to a shift of the supply curve. The supply curve will shift when there is a change in one of the variables—*other than the price of the product*—that affects the willingness of suppliers to sell the product. A change in quantity supplied refers to a movement along the supply curve as a result of a change in the product's price. Figure 3.6 illustrates this important distinction. If the price of premium bottled water rises from \$2.00 to \$2.50, the result will be a movement up the supply curve from point *A* to point *B*—an increase in quantity supplied from 6 million to 7 million. If the price of an input decreases, or if another factor changes that causes sellers to supply more of a product at every price, the supply curve will shift to the right—an increase in supply. In this case, the increase in supply from S_1 to S_2 causes the quantity of premium bottled water supplied at a price of \$2.50 to increase from 7 million at point *B* to 9 million at point *C*.   MyLab Economics Concept Check

---

3.3 # Market Equilibrium: Putting Demand and Supply Together

LEARNING OBJECTIVE: Use a graph to illustrate market equilibrium.

The purpose of markets is to bring buyers and sellers together. As we saw in Chapter 2, instead of being chaotic and disorderly, the interaction of buyers and sellers in markets ultimately results in firms being led to produce the goods and services that consumers want most. To understand this process, we first need to see how markets work to reconcile the plans of buyers and sellers.

In Figure 3.7, we bring together the market demand curve and the market supply curve for premium bottled water. Notice that the demand curve crosses the supply curve at only one point. This point represents a price of \$1.50 and a quantity of 5 million bottles per day. Only at this point of **market equilibrium** is the quantity of premium bottled water consumers are willing and able to buy equal to the quantity of premium bottled water firms are willing and able to sell. In this case, the *equilibrium price* is \$1.50, and the *equilibrium quantity* is 5 million bottles. As we noted at the beginning of the chapter, markets that have many buyers and sellers are competitive markets,

Market equilibrium A situation in which quantity demanded equals quantity supplied.

MyLab Economics Animation

Figure 3.7

Market Equilibrium

Where the demand curve crosses the supply curve determines market equilibrium. In this case, the demand curve for premium bottled water crosses the supply curve at a price of $1.50 and a quantity of 5 million bottles. Only at this point is the quantity of premium bottled water consumers are willing to buy equal to the quantity that Coca-Cola, PepsiCo, Bai, and other firms are willing to sell: The quantity demanded is equal to the quantity supplied.

and equilibrium in these markets is a **competitive market equilibrium**. In the market for premium bottled water, there are many buyers but only about 45 firms. Whether 45 firms are enough for our model of demand and supply to apply to this market is a matter of judgment. In this chapter, we are assuming that the market for premium bottled water has enough sellers to be competitive.

Competitive market equilibrium A market equilibrium with many buyers and sellers.

How Markets Eliminate Surpluses and Shortages

A market that is not in equilibrium moves toward equilibrium. Once a market is in equilibrium, it remains in equilibrium. To see why, consider what happens if a market is not in equilibrium. Suppose that the price in the market for premium bottled water was $2.00 rather than the equilibrium price of $1.50. As Figure 3.8 shows, at a price of $2.00, the quantity of bottles supplied would be 6 million, and the quantity of bottles demanded would be 4 million. When the quantity supplied is greater than

MyLab Economics Animation

Figure 3.8

The Effect of Surpluses and Shortages on the Market Price

When the market price is above equilibrium, there will be a *surplus*. A price of $2.00 for premium bottled water results in 6 million bottles being supplied but only 4 million being demanded, or a surplus of 2 million. As Coca-Cola, PepsiCo, Bai, and other firms cut the price to dispose of the surplus, the price will fall to the equilibrium price of $1.50. When the market price is below equilibrium, there will be a *shortage*. A price of $0.50 results in 7 million bottles being demanded but only 3 million being supplied, or a shortage of 4 million. As firms find that consumers who are unable to find premium bottled water available for sale are willing to pay higher prices to get it, the price will rise to the equilibrium price of $1.50.

Surplus A situation in which the quantity supplied is greater than the quantity demanded.

Shortage A situation in which the quantity demanded is greater than the quantity supplied.

the quantity demanded, there is a **surplus** in the market. In this case, the surplus is equal to 2 million bottles (6 million − 4 million = 2 million). When there is a surplus, firms will have unsold goods piling up, which gives them an incentive to increase their sales by cutting the price. Cutting the price will simultaneously increase the quantity demanded and decrease the quantity supplied. This adjustment will reduce the surplus, but as long as the price is above $1.50, there will be a surplus, and downward pressure on the price will continue. Only when the price falls to $1.50 will the market be in equilibrium.

If, however, the price were $0.50, the quantity demanded would be 7 million bottles, and the quantity supplied would be 3 million, as shown in Figure 3.8. When the quantity demanded is greater than the quantity supplied, there is a **shortage** in the market. In this case, the shortage is equal to 4 million bottles (7 million − 3 million = 4 million). When a shortage occurs, some consumers will be unable to buy premium bottled water at the current price. In this situation, firms will realize that they can raise the price without losing sales. A higher price will simultaneously increase the quantity supplied and decrease the quantity demanded. This adjustment will reduce the shortage, but as long as the price is below $1.50, there will be a shortage, and upward pressure on the price will continue. Only when the price rises to $1.50 will the market be in equilibrium.

At a competitive market equilibrium, all consumers willing to pay the market price will be able to buy as much of the product as they want, and all firms willing to accept the market price will be able to sell as much of the product as they want. As a result, there will be no reason for the price to change unless either the demand curve or the supply curve shifts. **MyLab Economics** Concept Check

Demand and Supply Both Count

Keep in mind that the interaction of demand and supply determines the equilibrium price. Neither consumers nor firms can dictate what the equilibrium price will be. No firm can sell anything at any price unless it can find a willing buyer, and no consumer can buy anything at any price without finding a willing seller. **MyLab Economics** Concept Check

Solved Problem 3.3

MyLab Economics Interactive Animation

Demand and Supply Both Count: A Tale of Two Letters

Which letter is likely to be worth more: one written by Abraham Lincoln or one written by his assassin, John Wilkes Booth? Lincoln is one of the greatest presidents, and many people collect anything he wrote. The demand for letters written by Lincoln surely would seem to be much greater than the demand for letters written by Booth. Yet, when R.M. Smythe and Co. auctioned off on the same day a letter written by Lincoln and a letter written by Booth, the Booth letter sold for $31,050, and the Lincoln letter sold for only $21,850. Use a demand and supply graph to explain how the Booth letter has a higher market price than the Lincoln letter, even though the demand for letters written by Lincoln is greater than the demand for letters written by Booth.

Solving the Problem

Step 1: **Review the chapter material.** This problem is about prices being determined at market equilibrium, so you may want to review the section "Market Equilibrium: Putting Demand and Supply Together," which begins on page 86.

Step 2: **Draw demand curves that illustrate the greater demand for Lincoln's letters.** Begin by drawing two demand curves. Label one "Demand for Lincoln's letters" and the other "Demand for Booth's letters." Make sure that the Lincoln demand curve is much farther to the right than the Booth demand curve.

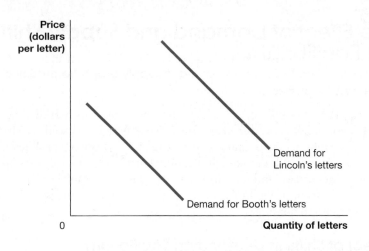

Step 3: **Draw supply curves that illustrate the equilibrium price of Booth's letters being higher than the equilibrium price of Lincoln's letters.** Based on the demand curves you have just drawn, think about how it might be possible for the market price of Lincoln's letters to be lower than the market price of Booth's letters. This outcome can occur only if the supply of Lincoln's letters is much greater than the supply of Booth's letters. Draw on your graph a supply curve for Lincoln's letters and a supply curve for Booth's letters that will result in an equilibrium price of Booth's letters of $31,050 and an equilibrium price of Lincoln's letters of $21,850. You have now solved the problem.

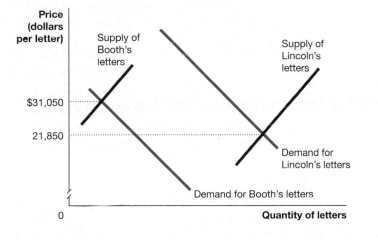

Extra Credit: The explanation for this puzzle is that both demand and supply count when determining market price. The demand for Lincoln's letters is much greater than the demand for Booth's letters, but the supply of Booth's letters is very small. Historians believe that only eight letters written by Booth exist today. (Note that the supply curves for letters written by Booth and by Lincoln are upward sloping, even though only a fixed number of each of these letters is available and, obviously, no more can be produced. The upward slope of the supply curves occurs because the higher the price, the larger the quantity of letters that will be offered for sale by people who currently own them.)

Your Turn: For more practice, do related problems 3.5, 3.6, and 3.7 on pages 103–104 at the end of this chapter.

MyLab Economics Study Plan

The Effect of Demand and Supply Shifts on Equilibrium

LEARNING OBJECTIVE: Use demand and supply graphs to predict changes in prices and quantities.

We have seen that the interaction of demand and supply in markets determines the quantity of a good that is produced and the price at which it is sold. We have also seen that several variables cause demand curves to shift and other variables cause supply curves to shift. As a result, demand and supply curves in most markets are constantly shifting, and the prices and quantities that represent equilibrium are constantly changing. In this section, we look at how shifts in demand and supply curves affect equilibrium price and quantity.

The Effect of Shifts in Demand on Equilibrium

Because premium bottled water is a normal good, when incomes increase, the market demand curve shifts to the right. Figure 3.9 shows the effect of a demand curve shifting to the right, from D_1 to D_2. This shift causes a shortage at the original equilibrium price, P_1. To eliminate the shortage, the equilibrium price rises to P_2, and the equilibrium quantity rises from Q_1 to Q_2. In contrast, if the price of a substitute good, such as regular bottled water, were to fall, the demand for premium bottled water would decrease, shifting the demand curve to the left. When the demand curve shifts to the left, both the equilibrium price and quantity will decrease. **MyLab Economics** Concept Check

The Effect of Shifts in Supply on Equilibrium

When PepsiCo entered the market by selling LIFEWTR, the market supply curve for premium bottled water shifted to the right. Figure 3.10 shows the supply curve shifting from S_1 to S_2. When the supply curve shifts to the right, there will be a surplus at the original equilibrium price, P_1. The surplus is eliminated as the equilibrium price falls to P_2 and the equilibrium quantity rises from Q_1 to Q_2. If an existing firm exits the market, the supply curve will shift to the left, causing the equilibrium price to rise and the equilibrium quantity to fall. **MyLab Economics** Concept Check

The Effect of Shifts in Demand and Supply over Time

Whenever only demand or only supply shifts, we can easily predict the effect on equilibrium price and quantity. But, what happens if *both* curves shift? For

MyLab Economics Animation

Figure 3.9

The Effect of an Increase in Demand on Equilibrium

Increases in income will cause the equilibrium price and quantity to rise:
1. Because premium bottled water is a normal good, as income increases, the quantity demanded increases at every price, and the market demand curve shifts to the right, from D_1 to D_2, which causes a shortage at the original price, P_1.
2. The equilibrium price rises from P_1 to P_2.
3. The equilibrium quantity rises from Q_1 to Q_2.

MyLab Economics Animation

Figure 3.10

The Effect of an Increase in Supply on Equilibrium

If a firm enters a market, as PepsiCo entered the market for premium bottled water, the equilibrium price will fall, and the equilibrium quantity will rise:

1. As PepsiCo enters the market, a larger quantity of premium bottled water will be supplied at every price, so the market supply curve shifts to the right, from S_1 to S_2, which causes a surplus at the original price, P_1.
2. The equilibrium price falls from P_1 to P_2.
3. The equilibrium quantity rises from Q_1 to Q_2.

instance, in many markets, the demand curve shifts to the right over time as population and income increase. The supply curve also often shifts to the right as new firms enter the market and positive technological change occurs. Whether the equilibrium price in a market rises or falls over time depends on whether demand shifts to the right more than does supply. Panel (a) of Figure 3.11 shows that when demand shifts to the right more than supply, the equilibrium price rises, while panel (b) shows that when supply shifts to the right more than demand, the equilibrium price falls.

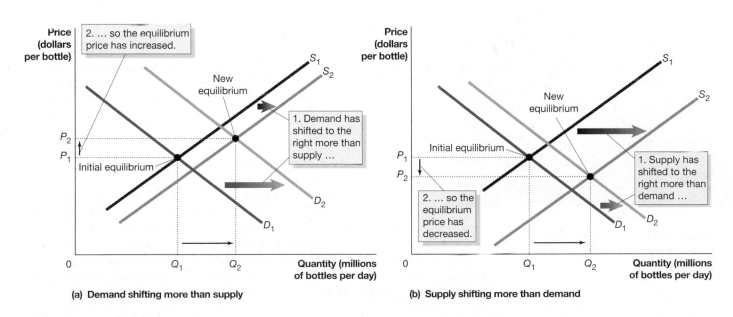

(a) Demand shifting more than supply

(b) Supply shifting more than demand

MyLab Economics Animation

Figure 3.11   Shifts in Demand and Supply over Time

Whether the price of a product rises or falls over time depends on whether demand shifts to the right more than supply.

In panel (a):
1. Demand shifts to the right more than supply.
2. The equilibrium price rises from P_1 to P_2.

In panel (b):
1. Supply shifts to the right more than demand.
2. The equilibrium price falls from P_1 to P_2.

Table 3.3

How Shifts in Demand and
Supply Affect Equilibrium Price
(*P*) and Quantity (*Q*)

The entry in red shows that if the demand
curve shifts to the right and the supply
curve also shifts to the right, the equilibrium quantity will increase, while the
equilibrium price may increase, decrease,
or remain unchanged.

	Supply Curve Unchanged	Supply Curve Shifts to the Right	Supply Curve Shifts to the Left
Demand curve unchanged	*Q* unchanged *P* unchanged	*Q* increases *P* decreases	*Q* decreases *P* increases
Demand curve shifts to the right	*Q* increases *P* increases	*Q* increases *P* increases, decreases, or is unchanged	*Q* increases, decreases, or is unchanged *P* increases
Demand curve shifts to the left	*Q* decreases *P* decreases	*Q* increases, decreases, or is unchanged *P* decreases	*Q* decreases *P* increases, decreases, or is unchanged

Table 3.3 summarizes all possible combinations of shifts in demand and supply over time and the effects of the shifts on equilibrium price (*P*) and quantity (*Q*). For example, the entry in red in the table shows that if the demand curve shifts to the right and the supply curve also shifts to the right, the equilibrium quantity will increase, while the equilibrium price may increase, decrease, or remain unchanged. To make sure you understand each entry in the table, draw demand and supply graphs to check whether you can reproduce the predicted changes in equilibrium price and quantity. If the entry in Table 3.3 indicates that the equilibrium price or quantity can increase, decrease, or remain unchanged, draw three graphs similar to panels (a) or (b) of Figure 3.11—one showing the equilibrium price or quantity increasing, one showing it decreasing, and one showing it unchanged. **MyLab Economics** Concept Check

Apply the Concept

MyLab Economics Video

Lower Demand for Orange Juice—But Higher Prices?

Joe Raedle/Getty Images News/ Getty Images

*Citrus greening disease in Brazil and
the United States decreased the supply
of oranges.*

For many years, Florida orange growers used the advertising slogan "A morning without orange juice is like a day without sunshine." And many Americans agreed, regularly drinking a glass of orange juice with their breakfast. In recent years, though, many consumers have replaced orange juice in their diets with bottled water, tea, coffee, smoothies, or energy drinks. Although assessments of the nutritional value of orange juice vary, some consumers have decided to switch to beverages with fewer calories and less sugar. Between 2011 and 2016, sales of orange juice in the United States declined by more than 15 percent. A 2017 *Wall Street Journal* article quoted an analyst at Deutsche Bank as saying, "People are shifting to low-calorie, natural products."

Ordinarily, when demand for a product is falling, consumers who continue to buy it will pay a lower price. This outcome results from the demand curve shifting to the left, which causes a lower equilibrium price—provided that the supply curve doesn't shift. In fact, though, in recent years the supply curve for orange juice has shifted to the left, largely because of problems in growing oranges in Brazil and the United States, the two leading orange growing countries. Orange groves in both Brazil and Florida had been suffering from an incurable disease called citrus greening, which causes oranges to shrivel and to produce bitter fruit. During the 2016–2017 growing season, Florida produced fewer oranges than in any year since the 1960s.

The following figure shows the market for orange juice. Because of a change in consumer tastes, the demand curve has shifted to the left. Because of citrus greening reducing the orange crops in Brazil and Florida, the supply curve has also shifted to the left. In early 2017, a 64-ounce bottle of orange juice was selling for about $4.00, up from about $3.25 two years earlier. At the same time, total U.S. consumption of orange juice had fallen from the equivalent of 371 million bottles in 2015 to 338 million bottles in 2017.

In recent years, the orange juice market has experienced decreases in both demand and supply. If the decrease in demand had been larger than the decrease in supply, we would have seen the price of orange juice decline. Because the price of orange juice has actually increased, we know the decrease in supply must have been larger than the decrease in demand. (To convince yourself of this last point, try drawing another version of the figure in which the demand and supply curves both shift to the left, but the equilibrium price decreases.)

Sources: Ellen Byron, "Last on the Shelf: How Products Dwindle Out of Favor," *Wall Street Journal*, January 10, 2017; Hayley Peterson, "Orange Juice Is Being Called a Massive Scam—And Now It's Disappearing from Breakfast in America," businessinsider.com, October 13, 2016; Fabiana Batista, "Too Much Water Is Diluting Juice from World's No. 1 Orange Crop," bloomberg.com, February 13, 2017; Arian Campo-Flores, "Florida Orange Production Forecast Lowered to 70 Million Boxes," *Wall Street Journal*, February 10, 2017; and data from the U.S. Department of Agriculture.

Your Turn: Test your understanding by doing related problem 4.6 on page 104 at the end of this chapter.

MyLab Economics Study Plan

Solved Problem 3.4

Can We Predict Changes in the Price and Quantity of Organic Corn?

A news article discussed how U.S. consumers have been increasing their demand for organically grown corn and other produce, which is grown using only certain government-approved pesticides and fertilizers. At the same time, imports of corn and other varieties of organic produce from foreign countries have increased the available supply. Use demand and supply graphs to illustrate your answers to the following questions.

a. Can we use this information to be certain whether the equilibrium quantity of organically grown corn will increase or decrease? Illustrate your answer with a graph showing the market for organically grown corn.

b. Can we use this information to be certain whether the equilibrium price of organically grown corn will increase or decrease? Illustrate your answer with a graph showing the market for organically grown corn.

Solving the Problem

Step 1: **Review the chapter material.** This problem is about how shifts in demand and supply curves affect the equilibrium price, so you may want to review the section "The Effect of Shifts in Demand and Supply over Time," which begins on page 90.

Step 2: **Answer part (a) using demand and supply analysis.** The problem gives you the information that consumer tastes have changed, leading to an increase in the demand for organically grown corn. So, the demand curve has shifted to the right. The problem also gives you the information that imports of organically grown corn have increased. So, the supply curve has also shifted to the right. The following graph shows both of these shifts.

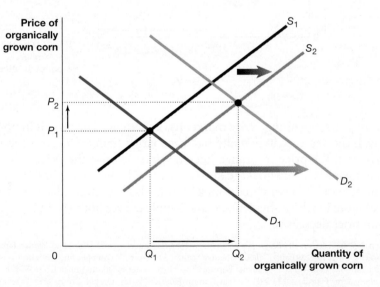

As Table 3.3 on page 92 summarizes, if the demand curve and the supply curve both shift to the right, the equilibrium quantity must increase. Therefore, we can answer part (a) by stating that we are certain that the equilibrium quantity of organically grown corn will increase.

Step 3: **Answer part (b) using demand and supply analysis.** The graph we drew in step 2 shows the equilibrium price of organically grown corn increasing. But given the information provided, the following graph would also be correct.

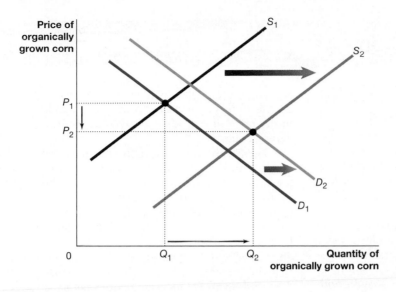

Unlike the graph in step 2, which shows the equilibrium price increasing, this graph shows the equilibrium price decreasing. The uncertainty about whether the equilibrium price will increase or decrease is consistent with what Table 3.3 indicates happens when the demand curve and the supply curve both shift to the right. Therefore, the answer to part (b) is that we cannot be certain whether the equilibrium price of organically grown corn will increase or decrease.

Extra Credit: During 2016, the equilibrium quantity of organically grown corn increased, while the equilibrium price decreased by 30 percent. We can conclude that *both* the increase in demand for organically grown corn and the increase in the supply contributed to the increase in consumption of organically grown corn. That the price of organically grown corn fell indicates that the increase in supply had a larger effect on equilibrium in the organically grown corn market than did the increase in demand.

Sources: Jacob Bunge, "Organic Food Sales Are Booming; Why Are American Farmers Crying Foul?" *Wall Street Journal*, February 21, 2017; and U.S. Department of Agriculture data.

Your Turn: For more practice, do related problems 4.7 and 4.8 on pages 104–105 at the end of this chapter.   MyLab Economics Study Plan

Shifts in a Curve versus Movements along a Curve

When analyzing markets using demand and supply curves, remember that *when a shift in a demand or supply curve causes a change in equilibrium price, the change in price does not cause a further shift in demand or supply.* Suppose that an increase in supply causes the price of a good to fall, while everything else that affects the willingness of consumers to buy the good is constant. The result will be an increase in the quantity demanded but not an increase in demand. For demand to increase, the whole curve must shift. The point is the same for supply: If the price of the good falls but everything else that affects the willingness of sellers to supply the good is constant, the quantity supplied decreases, but the supply does not. For supply to decrease, the whole curve must shift.   MyLab Economics Concept Check   MyLab Economics Study Plan

Don't Let This Happen to You

Remember: A Change in a Good's Price Does *Not* Cause the Demand or Supply Curve to Shift

Suppose a student is asked to draw a demand and supply graph to illustrate how an increase in the price of oranges would affect the market for apples, with other variables being constant. He draws the graph on the left and explains it as follows: "Because apples and oranges are substitutes, an increase in the price of oranges will cause an initial shift to the right in the demand curve for apples, from D_1 to D_2. However, because this initial shift in the demand curve for apples results in a higher price for apples, P_2, consumers will find apples less desirable, and the demand curve will shift to the left, from D_2 to D_3, resulting in a final equilibrium price of P_3." Do you agree or disagree with the student's analysis?

You should disagree. The student has correctly understood that an increase in the price of oranges will cause the demand curve for apples to shift to the right. But, the second demand curve shift the student describes, from D_2 to D_3, will not take place. Changes in the price of a product do not result in shifts in the product's demand curve. Changes in the price of a product result only in movements along a demand curve.

The graph on the right shows the correct analysis. The increase in the price of oranges causes the demand curve for apples to increase from D_1 to D_2. At the original price, P_1, the increase in demand initially results in a shortage of apples equal to $Q_3 - Q_1$. But, as we have seen, a shortage causes the price to increase until the shortage is eliminated. In this case, the price will rise to P_2, where both the quantity demanded and the quantity supplied are equal to Q_2. Notice that the increase in price causes a decrease in the *quantity demanded*, from Q_3 to Q_2, but does *not* cause a decrease in demand.

MyLab Economics Study Plan

Your Turn: Test your understanding by doing related problems 4.13 and 4.14 on page 105 at the end of this chapter.

Continued from page 73

Economics in Your Life & Career

Can You Forecast the Future Demand for Premium Bottled Water?

At the beginning of this chapter, we asked what variables you would take into account in forecasting future demand if you were a manager for a firm selling premium bottled water. In Section 3.1, we discussed the factors that affect the demand for a product and provided a list of the most important variables. In the *Apply the Concept* on page 81, we discussed how economists often use formal models to forecast future demand for a product.

In forecasting demand for premium bottled water, you should take into account factors such as changing demographics, as millennials become a larger fraction of prime-age consumers, and the likelihood that the demand for competing goods, such as carbonated sodas, will decline as consumers turn toward buying healthier products and as more cities impose soda taxes. You may also need to consider whether increased advertising of premium bottled water by large firms such as Coca-Cola and PepsiCo will raise consumer awareness of the product and increase demand for the premium bottled water being sold by other firms as well.

The factors discussed in this chapter provide you with the basic information needed to forecast demand for premium bottled water, although arriving at numerical forecasts requires using statistical analysis that you can learn in more advanced courses.

Conclusion

The interaction of demand and supply determines market equilibrium. The model of demand and supply is a powerful tool for predicting how changes in the actions of consumers and firms will cause changes in equilibrium prices and quantities. As we have seen in this chapter, we can use the model to analyze markets that do not meet all the requirements for being perfectly competitive. As long as there is intense competition among sellers, the model of demand and supply can often successfully predict changes in prices and quantities. We will use this model in the next chapter to analyze economic efficiency and the results of government-imposed price floors and price ceilings.

Before moving on to Chapter 4, read *An Inside Look* on the next page for a discussion of strategies McDonald's is using to reverse a trend of declining sales.

McDonald's Looks for New Ways to Attract Customers

CNBC.COM

4 ways McDonald's is about to change

(a) McDonald's has one major goal for 2017: win back customers.

The burger chain's multi-year turnaround effort, which found success with its All-Day Breakfast promotion, hasn't quite come to fruition...yet.

During its investor day in Chicago on Wednesday, the company's executives touted several big changes that the chain will be making to win back the more than 500 million visits it lost since 2012.

"To deliver sustained growth, we have to attract more customers, more often," CEO Steve Easterbrook said.

McDonald's focus will be on four pillars: menu innovation, store renovations, digital ordering and delivery.

"McDonald's appears to [have] found their focus on profitability through disciplined efforts to reduce costs and focus on the consumer experience including consumer-facing technology, improved convenience in payment and delivery and value to drive more customer visits throughout the day," Darren Tristano, president of Technomic, told CNBC.

"For the world's largest restaurant company, this means playing catch up with younger consumer expectations while continuing to engage older generations of consumers that grew up with McDonald's,"

Tristano said. "Creating alternatives for customization, delivery, payment and ordering processes provides challenges but they are necessary to adapt to the evolving consumer foodservice experience."

New Items on the Menu

(b) Expect to see McDonald's "step up" its menu innovation in the U.S., said Chris Kempczinski, McDonald's USA President.

The company recently launched three different sizes of its classic Big Mac and will continue to add new items to its domestic stores. Including, a nationwide roll out of its "Signature Sandwiches"—customizable and more upscale burgers and chicken sandwiches—later this year.

Renovated Restaurants

Say goodbye to the white metal chairs and bold red and yellow colors. The chain's stores will also be getting an update.

McDonald's is committed to becoming a "modern and progressive burger company" and will be adding self-service ordering kiosks and table service to some of its stores. Employees will now spend more time in the front of the restaurant, delivering food directly to the tables and offering traditional dining hospitality.

McDonald's "experience of the future" is coming to about 650 restaurants this year, bringing the chain's number of these stores to nearly 2,500.

(c) Digital Ordering

The Golden Arches will continue to expand its mobile order and pay platform. While late to the game, the company is expected to launch the product in 20,000 restaurants by the end of 2017.

Easterbrook noted back in November that McDonald's is focused on how customers order, what they order, how they pay and how they want to be served. Customers can pay with cash, credit, debit, Apple pay and Android pay and will soon be able to order through the company's mobile service.

Delivery

Delivery is also an avenue that McDonald's is exploring. The company, which has a large delivery presence in Asia—which accounts for 10 percent of system sales in that market—is hoping to capitalize on the growing industry demand by offering delivery in America. It is currently testing out several models, both in-house and via third-party providers.

The company said 75 percent of the population in its top five markets —America, France, the U.K., Germany and Canada—are within three miles of a McDonald's and 85 percent are within five miles of a chain.

Source: Sarah Whitten, "4 ways McDonald's is about to change," CNBC.com, March 1, 2017.

Key Points in the Article

McDonald's is in the highly competitive fast-food market. The firm has seen a decline in sales for five straight years. Searching for additional ways to increase its sales, McDonald's plans to focus on customer experience. The company recently introduced an all-day breakfast promotion, and in March 2017 announced it will begin to focus on new menu items, restaurant renovations, digital ordering, and delivery. With these changes, McDonald's hopes to win back younger consumers who have come to expect these services while at the same time continuing to appeal to its long-time customers.

Analyzing the News

(a) In the 5-year period beginning with 2012, customer trips to McDonald's fell by more than 500 million. Chief Executive Officer Steve Easterbrook stated that attracting more visits per customer is needed for the company to sustain growth. The company has chosen to focus on four elements to achieve this growth: menu innovation, store renovations, digital ordering, and delivery. Each of these ideas for growth is designed to help increase demand for McDonald's menu items by increasing its customer base and the frequency of customer visits to its restaurants.

(b) McDonald's has recently added new items to its menu, including more customizable and upscale burger and sandwich options. Adding self-service ordering kiosks and table service to its restaurants will make it faster and easier for customers to place orders as well as providing them with a more comfortable, traditional restaurant-like setting while waiting for their orders. If successful, these changes will increase consumers' willingness to buy McDonald's menu items at every price, shifting the demand curve for them to the right.

As consumers have reduced their demand for hamburgers at lunch and dinner, McDonald's has had success offering breakfast items, such as its popular Egg McMuffin, throughout the day. Competing firms, such as Burger King and Wendy's have followed this strategy as well. Suppose Figure 1 below illustrates the market for fast food breakfast sandwiches. The demand for breakfast sandwiches has increased, shifting the demand curve to the right from D_1 to D_2, resulting in an increase in both the equilibrium price (P_1 to P_2) and equilibrium quantity (Q_1 to Q_2). Figure 2 illustrates the market for hamburgers. The decline in demand is shown by the demand curve shifting to the left from D_1 to D_2, resulting in a decrease in both the equilibrium price (P_1 to P_2) and equilibrium quantity (Q_1 to Q_2). This result is a typical one when demand shifts between two goods that are substitutes.

(c) McDonald's plans to continue the expansion of its mobile order-and-pay system, with the intention of launching the service in 20,000 restaurants by the end of 2017. The company is also exploring delivery options for the U.S. market, a strategy that has been successful for McDonald's in Asia. Expanding its mobile order and pay system would appeal to the younger generation of tech-savvy consumers who like to order and pay for products via smartphone apps. A delivery option would appeal to a wide variety of consumers who either do not have time or do not want to take the time to go to a McDonald's location to buy food. Both of these options will likely increase demand for McDonald's menu items.

Thinking Critically

1. Why is it particularly important for a firm like McDonald's to stay ahead of trends such as consumers' desire to eat breakfast food throughout the day or younger consumers wanting to order online?

2. Suppose that McDonald's and its competitors successfully implement self-service kiosks in their U.S restaurants, and this investment in technology allows the firms to reduce the number of employees at each location. How would this change affect the market for breakfast sandwiches? Draw a demand and supply graph to illustrate this situation, and explain what happens to equilibrium price and equilibrium quantity.

Figure 1: An increase in demand for breakfast sandwiches shifts the demand curve to the right, increasing both equilibrium price and equilibrium quantity.

Figure 2: A decrease in the demand for hamburgers, a substitute good for breakfast sandwiches, shifts the demand curve to the left, decreasing both equilibrium price and equilibrium quantity.

CHAPTER SUMMARY AND PROBLEMS

Key Terms

Ceteris paribus ("all else equal") condition, p. 76

Competitive market equilibrium, p. 87

Complements, p. 78

Demand curve, p. 74

Demand schedule, p. 74

Demographics, p. 78

Income effect, p. 75

Inferior good, p. 77

Law of demand, p. 75

Law of supply, p. 83

Market demand, p. 74

Market equilibrium, p. 86

Normal good, p. 76

Perfectly competitive market, p. 74

Quantity demanded, p. 74

Quantity supplied, p. 82

Shortage, p. 88

Substitutes, p. 77

Substitution effect, p. 75

Supply curve, p. 83

Supply schedule, p. 83

Surplus, p. 88

Technological change, p. 84

3.1 The Demand Side of the Market, pages 74–82

LEARNING OBJECTIVE: List and describe the variables that influence demand.

MyLab Economics   Visit **www.pearson.com/mylab/economics** to complete these exercises online and get instant feedback.

Summary

The model of demand and supply is the most powerful tool in economics. The model applies exactly only to **perfectly competitive markets**, where there are many buyers and sellers, all the products sold are identical, and there are no barriers to new sellers entering the market. But the model can also be useful in analyzing markets that don't meet all these requirements.

The **quantity demanded** is the amount of a good or service that a consumer is willing and able to purchase at a given price. A **demand schedule** is a table that shows the relationship between the price of a product and the quantity of the product demanded. A **demand curve** is a graph that shows the relationship between the price of a product and the quantity of the product demanded. **Market demand** is the demand by all consumers of a given good or service. The **law of demand** states that *ceteris paribus*—holding everything else constant—the quantity of a product demanded increases when the price falls and decreases when the price rises. Demand curves slope downward because of the **substitution effect**, which is the change in quantity demanded that results from a price change making one good more or less expensive relative to another good, and the **income effect**, which is the change in quantity demanded of a good that results from the effect of a change in the good's price on consumer purchasing power. Changes in income, the prices of related goods, tastes, population and demographics, and expected future prices all cause the demand curve to shift. **Substitutes** are goods that can be used for the same purpose. **Complements** are goods that are used together. A **normal good** is a good for which demand increases as income increases. An **inferior good** is a good for which demand decreases as income increases. **Demographics** refers to the characteristics of a population with respect to age, race, and gender. A change in demand refers to a shift of the demand curve. A change in quantity demanded refers to a movement along the demand curve as a result of a change in the product's price.

Review Questions

1.1 What is a demand schedule? What is a demand curve?

1.2 What do economists mean when they use the Latin expression *ceteris paribus*?

1.3 What is the difference between a change in demand and a change in quantity demanded?

1.4 What is the law of demand? Use the substitution effect and the income effect to explain why an increase in the price of a product causes a decrease in the quantity demanded.

1.5 What are the main variables that will cause the demand curve to shift? Give an example of each.

Problems and Applications

1.6 For each of the following pairs of products, briefly explain which are complements, which are substitutes, and which are unrelated.
   a. New cars and used cars
   b. Houses and washing machines
   c. UGG boots and Pepsi's LIFEWTR
   d. Pepsi's LIFEWTR and Diet Coke

1.7 The Toyota Prius is a gasoline/electric hybrid car that gets 54 miles to the gallon. An article in the *Wall Street Journal* noted that sales of the Prius had been hurt by low gasoline prices and that "Americans are now more likely to trade in a hybrid or an electric vehicle for an SUV." Does the article indicate that gasoline-powered cars and gasoline are substitutes or complements? Does it indicate that gasoline-powered cars and hybrids are substitutes or complements? Briefly explain.
   Source: Sean McClain, "Toyota's Prius Pays Price for Cheap Gasoline," *Wall Street Journal*, September 6, 2016.

1.8 **[Related to the Chapter Opener on page 72]** In recent years, a number of cities have passed taxes on carbonated sodas to help reduce obesity and raise tax revenues. An article in the *New York Times* observed, "With that public momentum, a soda tax may be coming to a city near you." If this forecast is correct, what will be the effect on the demand for premium bottled water? Briefly explain.
   Source: Anahad O'Connor and Margot Sanger-Katz, "As Soda Taxes Gain Wider Acceptance, Your Bottle May Be Next," *New York Times*, November 26, 2016.

1.9 State whether each of the following events will result in a movement along the demand curve for McDonald's Quarter Pounder hamburgers or whether it will cause the curve to shift. If the demand curve shifts, indicate whether it will shift to the left or to the right and draw a graph to illustrate the shift.

   a. The price of Burger King's Whopper hamburger declines.

   b. McDonald's distributes coupons for $1.00 off the purchase of a Quarter Pounder.

   c. Because of a shortage of potatoes, the price of French fries increases.

   d. McDonald's switches to using fresh, never-frozen beef patties in its Quarter Pounders.

   e. The U.S. economy enters a period of rapid growth in incomes.

1.10 Suppose that the following table shows the quantity demanded of UGG boots at five different prices in 2018 and 2019.

	Quantity Demanded (thousands of pairs of boots)	
Price	2018	2019
$160	5,000	4,000
170	4,500	3,500
180	4,000	3,000
190	3,500	2,500
200	3,000	2,000

Name two different variables that, if their values were to change, would cause the quantity demanded of UGG boots to change from 2018 to 2019, as indicated in the table.

1.11 Suppose that the curves in the following graph represent two demand curves for traditional chicken wings (basket of six) at Buffalo Wild Wings. What would cause a movement from point A to point B on D_1? Name two variables that, if their values were to change, would cause a movement from point A to point C.

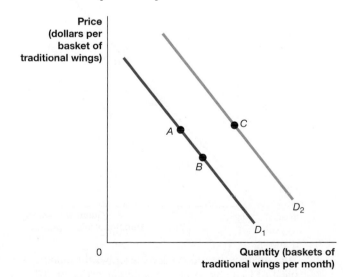

1.12 **[Related to the Apply the Concept on page 77]** A news article about virtual reality headsets observed, "For any hardware platform, it is critical to attract outside developers and build a virtuous cycle in which popular software titles drive hardware sales, which in turn brings in more software developers." The article referred to two types of software: games, such as *Final Fantasy*, that were already available for video game consoles, and software intended only for use with virtual reality headsets. As both these types of software become available, are they likely to make virtual reality headsets closer or less close substitutes for video game consoles? Briefly explain.

Source: Takashi Mochizuki, "Sony's Virtual-Reality Headset Confronts Actual Reality of Modest Sales," *Wall Street Journal*, February 27, 2017.

1.13 **[Related to the Apply the Concept on page 78]** From 1979 to 2015, China had a policy that allowed couples to have only one child. (Since 2016, couples have been allowed to have two children.) The one-child policy caused a change in the demographics of China. Between 1980 and 2015, the share of the population aged 14 and under decreased from 36 percent to 17 percent. And, as parents attempted to ensure that the lone child was a son, the number of male children relative to female children increased. Choose three goods and explain how the demand for them has been affected by China's one-child policy.

Sources: World Bank, *World Development Indicators*, April 2016; and "China New 'Two Child' Policy Increases Births by 7.9 Percent, Government Says," cbsnews.com, January 23, 2017.

1.14 **[Related to the Apply the Concept on page 78]** Would you pay $12 for a cup of coffee? Starbucks is betting enough people will say "yes," as it launches a chain of luxury coffee shops called Starbucks Reserve. Which generation(s) do you expect Starbucks Reserve to attract: baby boomers (ages 53 and over), generation X (ages 33 to 52), or millennials (ages 13 to 32)? Briefly explain. To be successful as a luxury coffee bar, how does Starbucks need to distinguish Starbucks Reserve coffee shops from its standard Starbucks coffee shops?

Source: Julie Jargon, "Middle-Market Woes Inspire Starbucks's Bet on Luxury Coffee," *Wall Street Journal*, December 5, 2016.

1.15 Suppose the following table shows the price of a base model Toyota Prius hybrid and the quantity of Priuses sold for three years. Do these data indicate that the demand curve for Priuses is upward sloping? Briefly explain.

Year	Price	Quantity
2016	$31,880	35,265
2017	30,550	33,250
2018	33,250	36,466

1.16 Consider the following two uses of the word *demand* in news articles:

   a. An article in the *Wall Street Journal* noted that an "increase in the price of oil quickly reduces demand for oil."

   b. A different article in the *Wall Street Journal* noted, "Electric cars are poised to reduce U.S. gasoline demand by 5% over the next two decades."

Do you agree with how these two articles use the word *demand*? Briefly explain.

Sources: Josh Zumbrun, "Oil's Plunge Could Help Send Its Price Back Up," *Wall Street Journal*, February 22, 2015; and Lynn Cook and Alison Sider, "U.S. Gasoline Demand Is Likely to Slide," *Wall Street Journal*, June 20, 2016.

1.17 **Related to the Apply the Concept on page 81]** An article on marketwatch.com stated, "While the fizzy soda drinks companies have experienced an annual volume sales decline since 2003, bottled water grew every year over the last two decades, except 2009 during the depths of the Great Recession."

a. What factors have caused a decline in sales of carbonated ("fizzy") beverages? Is it likely that those factors will lead to further declines in demand in the future? Briefly explain.

b. Why might sales of bottled water be likely to decline during a recession, when employment and household incomes fall? Would sales of premium bottled water be likely to decline by more or by less during a recession than sales of regular bottled water? Briefly explain.

Source: Quentin Fottrell, "Bottled Water Overtakes Soda as America's No. 1 Drink—Why You Should Avoid Both," marketwatch.com, March 12, 2017.

3.2 The Supply Side of the Market, pages 82–86

LEARNING OBJECTIVE: List and describe the variables that influence supply.

MyLab Economics Visit **www.pearson.com/mylab/economics** to complete these exercises online and get instant feedback.

Summary

The **quantity supplied** is the amount of a good that a firm is willing and able to supply at a given price. A **supply schedule** is a table that shows the relationship between the price of a product and the quantity of the product supplied. A **supply curve** is a curve that shows the relationship between the price of a product and the quantity of the product supplied. When the price of a product rises, producing the product is more profitable, and a greater amount will be supplied. The **law of supply** states that, holding everything else constant, the quantity of a product supplied increases when the price rises and decreases when the price falls. Changes in the prices of inputs, technology, the prices of related goods in production, the number of firms in a market, and expected future prices all cause the supply curve to shift. **Technological change** is a positive or negative change in the ability of a firm to produce a given level of output with a given quantity of inputs. A change in supply refers to a shift of the supply curve. A change in quantity supplied refers to a movement along the supply curve as a result of a change in the product's price.

Review Questions

2.1 What is a supply schedule? What is a supply curve?

2.2 What is the difference between a change in supply and a change in quantity supplied?

2.3 What is the law of supply? What are the main variables that cause a supply curve to shift? Give an example of each.

Problems and Applications

2.4 Briefly explain whether each of the following statements describes a change in supply or a change in quantity supplied.

    a. To take advantage of high prices for snow shovels during a snowy winter, Alexander Shovels, Inc., decides to increase output.

    b. The success of Pepsi's LIFEWTR and Coke's smartwater leads more firms to begin producing premium bottled water.

    c. In the six months following the Japanese earthquake and tsunami in 2011, production of automobiles in Japan declined by 20 percent.

2.5 According to a news story about the International Energy Agency, the agency forecast that "the current slide in [oil] prices won't [reduce] global supply." Would a decline in oil prices ever cause a reduction in the supply of oil? Briefly explain.

Source: Sarah Kent, "Plunging Oil Prices Won't Dent Supply in Short Term," *Wall Street Journal*, December 12, 2014.

2.6 Suppose that the curves in the following graph represent two supply curves for traditional chicken wings (basket of six) at Buffalo Wild Wings. What would cause a movement from point A to point B on S_1? Name two variables that, if their values were to change, would cause a movement from point A to point C.

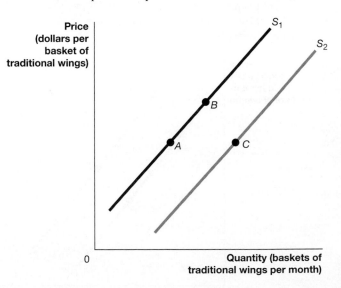

2.7 Suppose that the following table shows the quantity supplied of UGG boots at five different prices in 2018 and 2019.

	Quantity Supplied (thousands of pairs of boots)	
Price	2018	2019
$160	3,000	2,000
170	3,500	2,500
180	4,000	3,000
190	4,500	3,500
200	5,000	4,500

Name two different variables that, if their values were to change, would cause the quantity supplied of UGG boots to change from 2018 to 2019, as indicated in the table.

2.8 In most cities, firms that own office buildings can renovate them for use as residential apartments. According to a news story, in many cities "residential rents are surpassing office rents." Predict the effect of this trend on the supply of office space in these cities. Use a graph to illustrate your answer.

Source: Eliot Brown, "Developers Turn Former Office Buildings into High-End Apartments," *Wall Street Journal*, May 7, 2014.

2.9 Oil prices plummeted from over $100 per barrel in mid-2014 to under $30 in early 2016. According to a Reuters article, oil traders in 2015 and 2016 put massive amounts of oil in storage (even on tankers at sea), anticipating higher prices in the future. The article noted that in early 2017, "traders are turning the spigots to drain the priciest storage tanks holding U.S. crude stockpiles as strengthening markets make it unprofitable to store for future sale." What effect would the strategy of stockpiling crude oil have had for the supply of oil in 2015 and 2016? Use a graph to illustrate your answer.

Source: Catherine Ngai and Liz Hampton, "Traders Drain Pricey U.S. Oil Storage as OPEC Deal Bites," reuters.com, February 24, 2017.

3.3 Market Equilibrium: Putting Demand and Supply Together, pages 86–89

LEARNING OBJECTIVE: Use a graph to illustrate market equilibrium.

MyLab Economics Visit **www.pearson.com/mylab/economics** to complete these exercises online and get instant feedback.

Summary

Market equilibrium occurs where the demand curve intersects the supply curve. A **competitive market equilibrium** has a market equilibrium with many buyers and sellers. Only at this point is the quantity demanded equal to the quantity supplied. Prices above equilibrium result in **surpluses**, with the quantity supplied being greater than the quantity demanded. Surpluses cause the market price to fall. Prices below equilibrium result in **shortages**, with the quantity demanded being greater than the quantity supplied. Shortages cause the market price to rise.

Review Questions

3.1 What do economists mean by *market equilibrium*?

3.2 What do economists mean by *shortage*? By *surplus*?

3.3 What happens in a market if the current price is above the equilibrium price? What happens if the current price is below the equilibrium price?

Problems and Applications

3.4 Briefly explain whether you agree with the following statement: "When there is a shortage of a good, consumers eventually give up trying to buy it, so the demand for the good declines, and the price falls until the market is finally in equilibrium."

3.5 [Related to Solved Problem 3.3 on page 88] In *The Wealth of Nations*, Adam Smith discussed what has come to be known as the "diamond and water paradox":

> Nothing is more useful than water: but it will purchase scarce anything; scarce anything can be had in exchange for it. A diamond, on the contrary, has scarce any value in use; but

a very great quantity of other goods may frequently be had in exchange for it.

Graph the market for diamonds and the market for water. Show how it is possible for the price of water to be much lower than the price of diamonds, even though the demand for water is much greater than the demand for diamonds.

Source: Adam Smith, *An Inquiry into the Nature and Causes of the Wealth of Nations*, Vol. I, Oxford, UK: Oxford University Press, 1976; original edition, 1776.

3.6 [Related to Solved Problem 3.3 on page 88] An article discusses the market for autographs by Mickey Mantle, the superstar center fielder for the New York Yankees during the 1950s and 1960s, "At card shows, golf outings, charity dinners, Mr. Mantle signed his name over and over." One expert on sports autographs was quoted as saying, "He was a real good signer…. He is not rare." Yet the article quoted another expert as saying, "Mr. Mantle's autograph ranks No. 3 of most-popular autographs, behind Babe Ruth and Muhammad Ali." A baseball signed by Mantle is likely to sell for the relatively high price of $250 to $400. By contrast, baseballs signed by Whitey Ford, a teammate of Mantle's on the Yankees, typically sell for less than $150. Use one graph to show both the demand and supply for autographs by Whitey Ford and the demand and supply for autographs by Mickey Mantle. Show how it is possible for the price of Mantle's autographs to be higher than the price of Ford's autographs, even though the supply of Mantle autographs is larger than the supply of Ford autographs.

Source: Beth DeCarbo, "Mantle Autographs Not Rare, but Collectors Don't Care," *Wall Street Journal*, August 4, 2008.

3.7 [Related to Solved Problem 3.3 on page 88] Comic book fans eagerly compete to buy copies of *Amazing Fantasy* No. 15, which contains the first appearance of the superhero Spider-Man. At the same time the publisher printed copies of the comic for the U.S. market, with the price printed on the cover in cents, it printed copies for the U.K. market, with the price printed on the cover in British pence. About 10 times as many U.S. copies of *Amazing Fantasy* No. 15 have survived as U.K. copies. Yet in auctions that occurred at about the same time, a U.S. copy sold for $29,000, while a U.K. copy in the same condition sold for only $10,755. Use a demand and supply graph to explain how the U.S. version of the comic has a higher price than the U.K. version, even though the supply of the U.S. version is so much greater than the supply of the U.K. version.

Source: Auction price data from *GPA Analysis for CGC Comics*, www.comics.gpanalysis.com.

3.8 If a market is in equilibrium, is it necessarily true that all buyers and sellers are satisfied with the market price? Briefly explain.

3.9 A news story from 2017 about the oil market stated, "crude oil prices fell … in part [due to] renewed concerns about the global supply glut."
  a. What does the article mean by a "glut"? What does a glut imply about the quantity demanded of oil relative to the quantity supplied?
  b. What would be the effect of the glut on oil prices?
  c. Briefly explain what would make the glut start to shrink.

Source: Paul Ebeling, "Crude Oil Prices Falling, Traders Worry About Global Supply Glut," livetradingnews.com, March 27, 2017.

3.4 The Effect of Demand and Supply Shifts on Equilibrium, pages 90–97

LEARNING OBJECTIVE: Use demand and supply graphs to predict changes in prices and quantities.

MyLab Economics Visit **www.pearson.com/mylab/economics** to complete these exercises online and get instant feedback.

Summary

In most markets, demand and supply curves shift frequently, causing changes in equilibrium prices and quantities. Over time, if demand increases more than supply, equilibrium price will rise. If supply increases more than demand, equilibrium price will fall.

Review Questions

4.1 Draw a demand and supply graph to show the effect on the equilibrium price in a market in the following situations.
  a. The demand curve shifts to the right.
  b. The supply curve shifts to the left.

4.2 If, over time, the demand curve for a product shifts to the right more than the supply curve does, what will happen to the equilibrium price? What will happen to the equilibrium price if the supply curve shifts to the right more than the demand curve? For each case, draw a demand and supply graph to illustrate your answer.

Problems and Applications

4.3 [Related to the Chapter Opener on page 72] Suppose the demand for premium bottled water increases rapidly during 2018. At the same time, six more firms begin producing premium bottled water. A student remarks that, because of these events, we can't know for certain whether the price of premium bottled water will rise or fall. Briefly explain whether you agree. Be sure to include a demand and supply graph of the market for premium bottled water to illustrate your answer.

4.4 According to an article in the *Wall Street Journal*, in early 2017, President Donald Trump was considering whether to reverse a requirement by the Environmental Protection Agency that oil refiners increase the amount of ethanol they blend with gasoline. If the requirement were to remain, the result would be an increase in demand for ethanol, which is made from corn. Many U.S. farmers can use the same acreage to grow either corn or soybeans. Use a demand and supply graph to analyze the effect on the equilibrium price of soybeans resulting from an increase in the demand for corn.

Source: Siobhan Hughes, Natalie Andrews, and Kristina Peterson, "Senate Looks to Move Fast on Trump Administration Hearings, Health Law," *Wall Street Journal*, January 8, 2017.

4.5 According to a news article on bloomberg.com, the demand for coffee is increasing as "millennials' seemingly unquenchable thirst for coffee is helping to push global demand to a record." At the same time, coffee crops in Brazil and Asia have been hampered by dry weather and droughts. The article noted that "consumption is rising as supplies are getting tighter."
  a. Use a demand and supply graph of the coffee market to illustrate how the equilibrium quantity of coffee can increase as a result of these events. Be sure that all curves on your graphs are properly labeled, that you show any shifts in those curves, and that you indicate the initial and final equilibrium points.
  b. The article contains a chart showing changes in worldwide sales of coffee from 2006 through 2016. The chart is labeled "World demand has expanded in the past decade." Are data on the quantity of coffee sold and data on the demand for coffee the same thing? Can the quantity of coffee sold increase if the demand for coffee hasn't increased? Briefly explain.

Source: Marvin G. Perez, "Coffee-Loving Millennials Push Demand to a Record," bloomberg.com, October 30, 2016.

4.6 [Related to the Apply the Concept on page 92] Suppose that many cities begin to pass taxes on carbonated sodas, while at the same time scientists discover a cure for citrus greening, which is reducing orange crops in Florida and Brazil. Use a demand and supply graph to illustrate your answers to the following questions.
  a. Can we use this information to be certain whether the equilibrium price of orange juice will increase or decrease?
  b. Can we use this information to be certain whether the equilibrium quantity of orange juice will increase or decrease?

4.7 [Related to Solved Problem 3.4 on page 94] The demand for watermelons is highest during summer and lowest during winter. Yet watermelon prices are normally lower in summer than in winter. Use a demand and supply graph to demonstrate how this is possible. Be sure to carefully label the curves in your graph and to clearly indicate the equilibrium summer price and the equilibrium winter price.

4.8 [Related to Solved Problem 3.4 on page 94] According to one observer of the lobster market: "After Labor Day, when the vacationers have gone home, the lobstermen usually have a month or more of good fishing conditions, except for the occasional hurricane." Use a demand and supply graph to explain whether lobster prices are likely to be higher or lower during the fall than during the summer.

Source: Jay Harlow, "Lobster: An Affordable Luxury," www.Sallyhernstein.com.

4.9 Years ago, an apple producer argued that the United States should enact a tariff, or a tax, on imports of bananas. His reasoning was that "the enormous imports of cheap bananas into the United States tend to curtail the domestic consumption of fresh fruits produced in the United States."

    a. Was the apple producer assuming that apples and bananas are substitutes or complements? Briefly explain.

    b. If a tariff on bananas acts as an increase in the cost of supplying bananas in the United States, use two demand and supply graphs to show the effects of the apple producer's proposal. One graph should show the effect on the banana market in the United States, and the other graph should show the effect on the apple market in the United States. Be sure to label the change in equilibrium price and quantity in each market and any shifts in the demand and supply curves.

Source: Douglas A. Irwin, *Peddling Protectionism: Smoot-Hawley and the Great Depression*, Princeton, NJ: Princeton University Press, 2011, p. 22.

4.10 In early 2017, an article in the *Financial Times* about the oil market quoted the chief economist of oil company BP as saying, "Pricing pressure is likely to come from the supply side, because of strong growth in US shale oil (crude oil found within shale formations), and the demand side as the rise of renewable energy, including electric vehicles, gradually slows growth in oil consumption." After reading this article, a student argues: "From this information, we would expect that the price of oil will fall, but we don't know whether the equilibrium quantity of oil will increase or decrease." Is the student's analysis correct? Illustrate your answer with a demand and supply graph.

Source: Andrew Ward, "BP Warns of Price Pressures from Long-Term Oil Glut," *Financial Times*, January 25, 2017.

4.11 Historically, the production of many perishable foods, such as dairy products, was highly seasonal. As the supply of those products fluctuated, prices tended to fluctuate tremendously—typically by 25 to 50 percent or more—over the course of the year. One effect of mechanical refrigeration, which was commercialized on a large scale in the last decade of the nineteenth century, was that suppliers could store perishable foods from one season to the next. Economists have estimated that as a result of refrigerated storage, wholesale prices rose by roughly

10 percent during peak supply periods, while they fell by almost the same amount during the off season. Use a demand and supply graph for each season to illustrate how refrigeration affected the market for perishable food.

Source: Lee A. Craig, Barry Goodwin, and Thomas Grennes, "The Effect of Mechanical Refrigeration on Nutrition in the U.S.," *Social Science History*, Vol. 28, No. 2, Summer 2004, pp. 327–328.

4.12 If the equilibrium price and quantity of a product were $100 and 1,000 units per month in 2017 and $150 and 800 units per month in 2018, did this product experience a larger shift in its demand curve or in its supply curve from 2017 to 2018? Briefly explain.

4.13 [Related to the Don't Let This Happen to You on page 96] A student writes the following: "Increased production leads to a lower price, which in turn increases demand." Do you agree with his reasoning? Briefly explain.

4.14 [Related to the Don't Let This Happen to You on page 96] A student was asked to draw a demand and supply graph to illustrate the effect on the market for premium bottled water of a fall in the price of electrolytes used in some brands of premium bottled water, holding everything else constant. She drew the following graph and explained it as follows:

> Electrolytes are an input to some brands of premium bottled water, so a fall in the price of electrolytes will cause the supply curve for premium bottled water to shift to the right (from S_1 to S_2). Because this shift in the supply curve results in a lower price (P_2), consumers will want to buy more premium bottled water, and the demand curve will shift to the right (from D_1 to D_2). We know that more premium bottled water will be sold, but we can't be sure whether the price of premium bottled water will rise or fall. That depends on whether the supply curve or the demand curve has shifted farther to the right. I assume that the effect on supply is greater than the effect on demand, so I show the final equilibrium price (P_3) as being lower than the initial equilibrium price (P_1).

Explain whether you agree with the student's analysis. Be careful to explain exactly what—if anything—you find wrong with her analysis.

4.15 The following four graphs represent four market scenarios, each of which would cause either a movement along the supply curve for premium bottled water or a shift of the supply curve. Match each scenario with the appropriate graph.

a. A decrease in the supply of sports drinks
b. A drop in the average household income in the United States from $56,000 to $52,000
c. An improvement in the bottling technology for premium bottled water
d. An increase in the prices of electrolytes used in premium bottled water

4.16 Proposals have been made to increase government regulation of firms providing childcare services by, for instance, setting education requirements for childcare workers. Suppose that these regulations increase the quality of childcare and cause the demand for childcare services to increase. At the same time, assume that complying with the new government regulations increases the costs of firms providing childcare services. Draw a demand and supply graph to illustrate the effects of these changes in the market for childcare services. Briefly explain whether the total quantity of childcare services purchased will increase or decrease as a result of the regulations.

4.17 Which of the following graphs best represents what happens in the market for hotel rooms at a ski resort during the winter? Briefly explain. From the graph you picked, what would be the result during the winter if hotel rates stayed at their summer level?

4.18 The following graphs show the supply and demand curves for two markets. One of the markets is for electric automobiles, and the other is for a cancer-fighting drug, without which lung cancer patients will die. Briefly explain which graph most likely represents each market.

Critical Thinking Exercises

CT3.1 For this exercise, your instructor may assign you to a group. Which curve did you find more difficult to understand: the demand curve or the supply curve? What specific difficulties did you have in understanding that curve? Working together, explain your thinking in a one-paragraph report you will either submit to your instructor or discuss with the rest of the class.

CT3.2 Graphs simplify economic ideas and make them more concrete. Consider the data available on these two Web sites:

- www.eia.gov/dnav/pet/pet_pri_gnd_a_epmr_pte_dpgal_w.htm provides data on the retail price of gasoline (what we pay at the pump) for both the United States overall and for different regions and states.
- www.eia.gov/dnav/pet/PET_CONS_REFMG_D_NUS_VTR_MGALPD_M.htm provides data on gasoline sales for the United States.

If you were to use a graph to explain changes in these data over time, would you use a graph of the demand curve, a graph of the supply curve, or a graph of a market? Write a paragraph to explain your thinking.

CT3.3 Review Figure 3.9 on page 90 and its analysis of the market for premium bottled water. The figure shows several different changes occurring: (a) a shift in a curve, (b) some event external to the market that affects the market, (c) and a new equilibrium. What is the order in which these three different changes occur? In the analysis of other markets that you will carry out later in the course, must the order of these three changes stay the same as in this example, or can the order be different?

4

Economic Efficiency, Government Price Setting, and Taxes

What Do Food Riots in Venezuela and the Rise of Uber in the United States Have in Common?

In 2016 and 2017, news stories described riots in Venezuela as crowds stormed supermarkets and street gangs fought over food. Food deliveries to stores were made under armed guard, and in some cities the government had to send in troops to protect stores from looting. As one news story put it: "Venezuela is convulsing from hunger."

In many cities in the United States, you can't legally operate a taxi unless you have a permit from the city government. For example, New York City requires taxi drivers to purchase a medallion. The number of medallions issued is limited, and until recently, the price of a medallion could exceed $1 *million*. By 2017, though, people could hail a ride using a mobile app from firms such as Uber or Lyft. Drivers who want to work for these firms sign up, agree to meet certain requirements, and use their own vehicles to pick up riders. Hundreds of thousands of riders in New York City began using these services, which drove the price of a taxi medallion to as little as $250,000.

What's the connection between food riots in Venezuela and the rise of Uber in the United States? Both cases were ultimately the result of governments intervening to change equilibrium prices determined by the market. As we saw in Chapter 3, in a competitive market equilibrium, all consumers willing to pay the market price will be able to buy as much of the product as they want, and all firms willing to accept the market price will be able to sell as much of the product as they want. But this observation doesn't mean that all consumers and firms will be *happy* with the market price. Consumers would typically prefer to pay a lower price, and firms would prefer to receive a higher price. In some cases, either buyers or sellers can convince the government to enact *price controls*, which are legally binding maximum or minimum prices. In Venezuela, the government's attempts to expand control over private businesses led to disruptions in the supply of many

Bloomberg/Getty images

goods, including food. As market prices rose as a result of the reductions in supply, the government imposed rules that kept prices from rising to their new equilibrium levels. The result was food shortages that led to riots.

In New York and other cities, government limits on the supply of taxis pushed the price of a ride well above the competitive market level. High prices provided Travis Kalanick, the founder of Uber, and other entrepreneurs the opportunity to earn a profit using mobile technology to offer ride-hailing services at a lower price than taxis were charging.

As we'll see in this chapter, when governments interfere with the prices determined by markets, they create both winners and losers, and they typically reduce economic efficiency.

AN INSIDE LOOK on **page 132** explores problems Uber has encountered in attempting to expand its services in the United Kingdom.

Sources: Nicholas Casey, "Venezuelans Ransack Stores as Hunger Grips the Nation," *New York Times*, June 19, 2016; Maria Ramirez and Kejal Vyas, "Venezuela Deploys Troops after Weekend Riots," *Wall Street Journal*, December 19, 2016; Elena Holodny, "Uber and Lyft Are Demolishing New York City Taxi Drivers," businnessinsider.com, October 12, 2016; and Emma G. Fitzsimmons and Winnie Hu, "The Downside of Ride-Hailing: More New York City Gridlock," *New York Times*, March 6, 2017.

Chapter Outline & Learning Objectives

Economics in Your Life & Career

As a Member of the City Council, Should You Support Rent Control?

Suppose you have been elected to your city council. A group of renters have become concerned that rising rents are making it difficult for them to find affordable apartments. They propose that the city council enact a rent control law that will keep rents in the future from rising above their current levels. If you and the other city council members vote to enact this law, is it likely that in the future it will be easier for renters to find an affordable apartment in your city? Who in your city would benefit, and who would lose from this law? As you read the chapter, try to answer these questions. You can check your answers against the ones we provide on **page 131** at the end of this chapter.

In a competitive market, the price adjusts to ensure that the quantity demanded equals the quantity supplied. As a result, in equilibrium, every consumer willing to pay the market price is able to buy as much of the product as the consumer wants, and every firm willing to accept the market price can sell as much as it wants. Consumers would naturally prefer to pay a lower price, and sellers would prefer to receive a higher price. Normally, consumers and firms have no choice but to accept the equilibrium price if they wish to participate in the market.

Occasionally, however, consumers or firms persuade the government to intervene to try to lower or raise the market price of a good or service:

- Consumers sometimes succeed in having the government impose a **price ceiling**, which is a legally determined maximum price that sellers may charge. Rent control, which puts a legal limit on the rent that landlords can charge for an apartment, is an example of a price ceiling.

- Firms sometimes succeed in having the government impose a **price floor**, which is a legally determined minimum price that sellers may receive. In markets for farm products such as milk, the federal government has been setting price floors above the equilibrium market price since the 1930s.

Another way the government intervenes in markets is by imposing taxes. The government relies on the revenue raised from taxes to finance its operations. But taxes also affect the decisions that consumers and firms make.

Each of these government interventions has predictable negative consequences for economic efficiency. Economists have developed the concepts of *consumer surplus*, *producer surplus*, and *deadweight loss* to help policymakers and voters analyze the economic effects of price ceilings, price floors, and taxes.

Price ceiling A legally determined maximum price that sellers may charge.

Price floor A legally determined minimum price that sellers may receive.

 4.1 **Consumer Surplus and Producer Surplus**

LEARNING OBJECTIVE: Distinguish between the concepts of consumer surplus and producer surplus.

Consumer surplus measures the dollar benefit consumers receive from buying goods or services in a particular market. Producer surplus measures the dollar benefit firms receive from selling goods or services in a particular market. Economic surplus in a market is the sum of consumer surplus and producer surplus. As we will see, *when the government imposes a price ceiling or a price floor, the amount of economic surplus in a market is reduced*. In other words, price ceilings and price floors reduce the total benefit to consumers and firms from buying and selling in a market. To understand why this is true, we need to understand how consumer surplus and producer surplus are determined.

Consumer Surplus

Consumer surplus is the difference between the highest price a consumer is willing to pay for a good or service and the actual price the consumer pays. Suppose you want to stream the movie *Wonder Woman*. Before you check the price to rent it on iTunes or Amazon, you decide that $5.99 is the highest price you would be willing to pay. On iTunes, you find that the rental price is actually $3.99, so you rent the movie. Your consumer surplus in this example is $2: the difference between the $5.99 you were willing to pay and the $3.99 you actually paid.

We can use the demand curve to measure the total consumer surplus in a market. Demand curves show the willingness of consumers to purchase a product at different prices. Consumers are willing to purchase a product up to the point where the marginal benefit of consuming a product is equal to its price. The **marginal benefit** is the additional benefit to a consumer from consuming one more unit of a good or service. As a simple example, suppose there are only four consumers in the market for chai tea: Theresa, Tom, Terri, and Tim. Because these four consumers have different tastes for tea and different incomes, the marginal benefit each of them receives from consuming

Consumer surplus The difference between the highest price a consumer is willing to pay for a good or service and the actual price the consumer pays.

Marginal benefit The additional benefit to a consumer from consuming one more unit of a good or service.

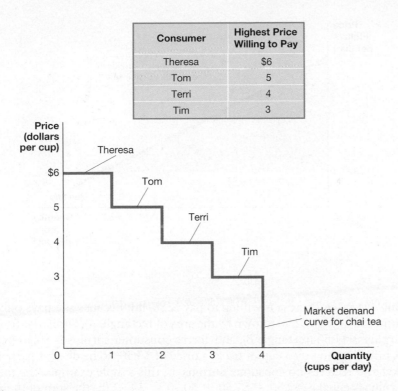

Consumer	Highest Price Willing to Pay
Theresa	$6
Tom	5
Terri	4
Tim	3

MyLab Economics Animation

Figure 4.1

Deriving the Demand Curve for Chai Tea

With four consumers in the market for chai tea, the demand curve is determined by the highest price each consumer is willing to pay. At prices above $6, no tea is sold because $6 is the highest price any consumer is willing to pay. At prices of $3 and below, each of the four consumers is willing to buy one cup of tea.

a cup of tea will be different. Therefore, the highest price each is willing to pay for a cup of tea is also different. In Figure 4.1, the information from the table is used to construct a demand curve for chai tea. At prices above $6 per cup, no tea is sold because $6 is the highest price any of the consumers is willing to pay. At a price of $5, both Theresa and Tom are willing to buy tea, so two cups are sold. At prices of $3 and below, all four consumers are willing to buy tea, and four cups are sold.

Suppose the market price of tea is $3.50 per cup. As Figure 4.2 shows, the demand curve allows us to calculate the total consumer surplus in this market. Panel (a) shows

(a) Consumer surplus with a market price of $3.50

(b) Consumer surplus with a market price of $3.00

MyLab Economics Animation

Figure 4.2   Measuring Consumer Surplus

Panel (a) shows the consumer surplus for Theresa, Tom, and Terri when the price of tea is $3.50 per cup. Theresa's consumer surplus is equal to the area of rectangle A and is the difference between the highest price she would pay—which is $6—and the market price of $3.50. Tom's consumer surplus is equal to the area of rectangle B, and Terri's consumer surplus

is equal to the area of rectangle C. Total consumer surplus in this market is equal to the sum of the areas of rectangles A, B, and C, or the total area below the demand curve and above the market price. In panel (b), consumer surplus increases by the dark blue area as the market price declines from $3.50 to $3.00.

MyLab Economics Animation

Figure 4.3

Total Consumer Surplus in the Market for Chai Tea

The demand curve shows that most buyers of chai tea would have been willing to pay more than the market price of $2.00. For each buyer, consumer surplus is equal to the difference between the highest price he or she is willing to pay and the market price actually paid. Therefore, the total amount of consumer surplus in the market for chai tea is equal to the area below the demand curve and above the market price. Consumer surplus represents the benefit to consumers in excess of the price they paid to purchase a product.

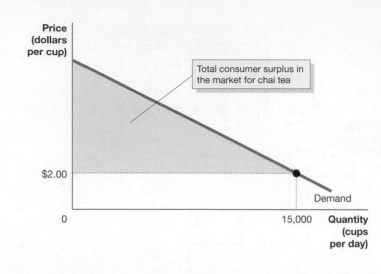

that the highest price Theresa is willing to pay is $6, but because she pays only $3.50, her consumer surplus is $2.50 (shown by the area of rectangle A). Similarly, Tom's consumer surplus is $1.50 (rectangle B), and Terri's consumer surplus is $0.50 (rectangle C). Tim is unwilling to buy a cup of tea at a price of $3.50, so he doesn't participate in this market and receives no consumer surplus. In this simple example, the total consumer surplus is equal to $2.50 + $1.50 + $0.50 = $4.50 (or the sum of the areas of rectangles A, B, and C). Panel (b) shows that a lower price will increase consumer surplus. If the price of tea falls from $3.50 per cup to $3.00, Theresa, Tom, and Terri each receive $0.50 more in consumer surplus (shown by the dark blue areas), so the total consumer surplus in the market rises to $6.00. Tim now buys a cup of tea but doesn't receive any consumer surplus because the price is equal to the highest price he is willing to pay. In fact, Tim is indifferent between buying the cup or not; his well-being is the same either way.

The market demand curves shown in Figures 4.1 and 4.2 do not look like the typical smooth demand curve because in this case we have only a small number of consumers, each consuming a single cup of tea. With many consumers, the market demand curve for chai tea will have the normal smooth shape shown in Figure 4.3. In this figure, the quantity demanded at a price of $2.00 is 15,000 cups per day. We can calculate total consumer surplus in Figure 4.3 the same way we did in Figures 4.1 and 4.2—by adding up the consumer surplus received on each unit purchased. Once again, we can draw an important conclusion: *The total amount of consumer surplus in a market is equal to the area below the demand curve and above the market price.* Consumer surplus is shown as the shaded area in Figure 4.3 and represents the benefit to consumers in excess of the price they paid to purchase a product—in this case, chai tea. **MyLab Economics** Concept Check

Apply the Concept

MyLab Economics Video

The Consumer Surplus from Uber

Consumer surplus allows us to measure the benefit consumers receive in excess of the price they pay to purchase a product. As we noted in the chapter opener, in many cities, local governments have artificially reduced the quantity of taxi services supplied by legally restricting the number of taxis allowed to operate. The government restrictions on taxis generally do not apply to Uber, Lyft, and other ride-hailing services that use mobile apps. As a result, the services have become very popular among both drivers and riders. In 2017, in New York City alone, more than 50,000 people had signed up as drivers with the services, and hundreds of thousands of consumers were using the services each day.

The enthusiastic response by consumers to the ride-hailing services indicates that they have resulted in a substantial increase in consumer surplus. Peter Cohen and Jonathan Hall, economists who work for Uber, along with Robert Hahn of the University of Oxford and Steven Levitt and Robert Metcalfe of the University of Chicago, have estimated the consumer surplus attributed to Uber. Uber practices "surge pricing," which means that the firm varies the prices its drivers charge depending on the weather, the time of day, the availability of drivers in the area, and whether an event such as a football game or a New Year's Eve celebration is occurring. The firm has particularly good data available for economists to use in estimating its demand curve because it has so many riders and because it has information both on the quantity of rides accepted at a particular price and the quantity of rides not accepted because a potential rider decides that a surge price is higher than he or she wishes to pay.

The economists analyzed data on millions of instances of riders using the app to get pricing information for a potential trip—including both sessions where the rider went ahead, summoned a driver, and paid for a trip and sessions where the rider decided against making the trip. The data were for Uber's basic UberX service in its four largest markets: New York, San Francisco, Chicago, and Los Angeles. To carry out the analysis, the economists estimated the demand curve for Uber's service and then computed the shaded area shown in the following graph.

The economists analyzed a six-month period in 2015, during which consumers took about 111 million trips using Uber in these four cities. The demand curve shows the marginal benefit consumers receive from using Uber rather than making the trip some other way or not making the trip at all. The shaded area below the demand curve and above the $13.30 base price that Uber charges represents the difference between the price consumers would have paid rather than do without Uber's service and the $13.30 they did pay. The shaded area in the graph represents the total consumer surplus in the market for Uber's service. Cohen and his colleagues estimate that the value of this area is $2.88 billion per year. Extrapolating this result to the country as a whole, they estimate that the total consumer surplus from Uber during 2015 was $6.76 billion. This value is one year's benefit to the consumers who used Uber's ride-hailing service.

Note: This figure illustrates the approach of Cohen and his colleagues but doesn't reproduce it exactly. Among other simplifications, the figure assumes that the demand curve for Uber's service is linear.

Sources: Peter Cohen et al., "Using Big Data to Estimate Consumer Surplus: The Case of Uber," National Bureau of Economic Research, Working Paper No. 22627, September 2016; Adam Creighton, "Uber's Pricing Formula Has Allowed Economists to Map Out a Real Demand Curve," *Wall Street Journal*, September 19, 2016; and Jayson Derrick, "What Would Be the Social Cost if Uber Vanishes?" finance.yahoo.com, September 8, 2016.

Your Turn: For more practice do related problem 1.13 on page 135 at the end of this chapter.

Producer Surplus

Just as demand curves show the willingness of consumers to buy a product at different prices, supply curves show the willingness of firms to supply a product at different prices. The willingness to supply a product depends on the cost of producing it. Firms will supply an additional unit of a product only if they receive a price equal to the additional cost of producing that unit. **Marginal cost** is the additional cost to a firm of producing one more unit of a good or service. Consider the marginal cost to the firm Heavenly Tea of producing one more cup of tea: In this case, the marginal cost includes the ingredients to make the tea and the wages paid to the worker preparing the tea. Often, the marginal cost of producing a good increases as more of the good is produced during a given period of time. Increasing marginal cost is the key reason that supply curves are upward sloping.

Marginal cost The additional cost to a firm of producing one more unit of a good or service.

Panel (a) of Figure 4.4 shows Heavenly Tea's producer surplus. For simplicity, we show Heavenly producing only a small quantity of tea. The figure shows that Heavenly's marginal cost of producing the first cup of tea is $1.25, its marginal cost of producing the second cup is $1.50, and so on. The marginal cost of each cup of tea is the lowest price Heavenly is willing to accept to supply that cup. The supply is therefore also a marginal cost curve. Suppose the market price of tea is $2.00 per cup. On the first cup of tea, the price is $0.75 higher than the lowest price that Heavenly is willing to accept. **Producer surplus** is the difference between the lowest price a firm would be willing to accept for a good or service and the price it actually receives. Therefore, Heavenly's producer surplus on the first cup is $0.75 (shown by the area of rectangle A), its producer surplus on the second cup is $0.50 (rectangle B), and its producer surplus on the third cup is $0.25 (rectangle C). Heavenly will not be willing to supply the fourth cup because the marginal cost of producing it is greater than the market price. Heavenly's total producer surplus is equal to $0.75 + $0.50 + $0.25 = $1.50 (or the sum of the areas of rectangles A, B, and C). A higher price will increase producer surplus. For example, if the market price of chai tea rises from $2.00 to $2.25, Heavenly's producer surplus will increase from $1.50 to $2.25. (Make sure you understand how the new level of producer surplus was calculated.)

Producer surplus The difference between the lowest price a firm would be willing to accept for a good or service and the price it actually receives.

(a) Producer surplus for Heavenly Tea

(b) Total producer surplus in the market for chai tea

MyLab Economics Animation

Figure 4.4 **Measuring Producer Surplus**

Panel (a) shows Heavenly Tea's producer surplus. The lowest price Heavenly Tea is willing to accept to supply a cup of tea is equal to its marginal cost of producing that cup. When the market price of tea is $2.00, Heavenly receives producer surplus of $0.75 on the first cup (the area of rectangle A), $0.50 on the second cup (rectangle B), and $0.25 on the third cup (rectangle C). In panel (b), the total amount of producer surplus tea sellers receive from selling chai tea can be calculated by adding up for the entire market the producer surplus received on each cup sold. In the figure, total producer surplus is equal to the shaded area above the supply curve and below the market price.

The supply curve shown in panel (a) of Figure 4.4 does not look like the typical smooth supply curve because we are looking at a single firm producing only a small quantity of tea. With many firms, the market supply curve for chai tea will have the normal smooth shape shown in panel (b) of Figure 4.4. In panel (b), the quantity supplied at a price of $2.00 is 15,000 cups per day. We can calculate total producer surplus in panel (b) the same way we did in panel (a): by adding up the producer surplus received on each cup sold. Therefore, *the total amount of producer surplus in a market is equal to the area above the market supply curve and below the market price*. The total producer surplus tea sellers receive from selling chai tea is shown as the shaded area in panel (b) of Figure 4.4.   MyLab Economics Concept Check

What Consumer Surplus and Producer Surplus Measure

We have seen that consumer surplus measures the benefit to consumers from participating in a market, and producer surplus measures the benefit to producers from participating in a market. It is important to be clear about what these concepts are measuring:

- Consumer surplus measures the *net* benefit to consumers from participating in a market rather than the *total* benefit. That is, if the price of a product were zero, the consumer surplus in a market would be all of the area under the demand curve. When the price is not zero, consumer surplus is the area below the demand curve and above the market price. So, consumer surplus in a market is equal to the total benefit consumers receive minus the total amount they must pay to buy the good or service.

- Producer surplus measures the *net* benefit received by producers from participating in a market. If producers could supply a good or service at zero cost, the producer surplus in a market would be all of the area below the market price. When cost is not zero, producer surplus is the area below the market price and above the supply curve. So, producer surplus in a market is equal to the total dollar amount firms receive from consumers minus the cost of producing the good or service.   MyLab Economics Concept Check   MyLab Economics Study Plan

4.2 The Efficiency of Competitive Markets

LEARNING OBJECTIVE: Explain the concept of economic efficiency.

Recall that a *competitive market* is a market with many buyers and many sellers. An important advantage of the market system is that it results in efficient economic outcomes. But what does *economic efficiency* mean? The concepts we have developed so far in this chapter give us two ways to think about the economic efficiency of competitive markets. We can think in terms of marginal benefit and marginal cost. We can also think in terms of consumer surplus and producer surplus. As we will see, these two approaches lead to the same outcome, but using both can increase our understanding of economic efficiency.

Marginal Benefit Equals Marginal Cost in Competitive Equilibrium

Figure 4.5 again shows the market for chai tea. Recall that the demand curve shows the marginal benefit received by consumers, and the supply curve shows the marginal cost of production. For this market to achieve economic efficiency, the marginal benefit from the last unit sold should equal the marginal cost of production. In the figure, this equality occurs at competitive equilibrium where 15,000 cups per day are produced and marginal benefit and marginal cost are both equal to $2.00. This outcome is economically efficient because every cup of chai tea has been produced where the marginal benefit to buyers is greater than or equal to the marginal cost to producers.

To further understand why the level of output at competitive equilibrium is efficient, consider what the situation would be if output were at a different level. Suppose that output of chai tea is 14,000 cups per day. Figure 4.5 shows that at this level

MyLab Economics Animation

Figure 4.5

Marginal Benefit Equals Marginal Cost Only at Competitive Equilibrium

In a competitive market, equilibrium occurs at a quantity of 15,000 cups and a price of $2.00 per cup, where marginal benefit equals marginal cost. This level of output is economically efficient because every cup has been produced for which the marginal benefit to buyers is greater than or equal to the marginal cost to producers.

of output, the marginal benefit from the last cup sold is $2.20, while the marginal cost is only $1.80. This level of output is not efficient because 1,000 more cups could be produced for which the additional benefit to consumers would be greater than the additional cost of production. Consumers would willingly purchase those cups, and tea sellers would willingly supply them, making both consumers and sellers better off. Similarly, if the output of chai tea is 16,000 cups per day, the marginal cost of the 16,000th cup is $2.20, while the marginal benefit is only $1.80. Tea sellers would only be willing to supply this cup at a price of $2.20, which is $0.40 higher than consumers would be willing to pay. In fact, consumers would not be willing to pay the price tea sellers would need to receive for any cup beyond the 15,000th.

To summarize: *Equilibrium in a competitive market results in the economically efficient level of output, at which marginal benefit equals marginal cost.* **MyLab Economics** Concept Check

Economic Surplus

Economic surplus The sum of consumer surplus and producer surplus.

Economic surplus in a market is the sum of consumer surplus and producer surplus. In a competitive market, with many buyers and sellers and no government restrictions, economic surplus is at a maximum when the market is in equilibrium. To see this point, let's look at the market for chai tea shown again in Figure 4.6. The consumer surplus in this market is the blue area below the demand curve and above the line indicating the equilibrium price of $2.00. The producer surplus is the red area above the supply curve and below the price line. **MyLab Economics** Concept Check

MyLab Economics Animation

Figure 4.6

Economic Surplus Equals the Sum of Consumer Surplus and Producer Surplus

The economic surplus in a market is the sum of the blue area, representing consumer surplus, and the red area, representing producer surplus.

MyLab Economics Animation

Figure 4.7

When a Market Is Not in Equilibrium, There Is a Deadweight Loss

Economic surplus is maximized when a market is in competitive equilibrium. When a market is not in equilibrium, there is a deadweight loss. For example, when the price of chai tea is $2.20 instead of $2.00, consumer surplus declines from an amount equal to the sum of areas A, B, and C to just area A. Producer surplus increases from the sum of areas D and E to the sum of areas B and D. At competitive equilibrium, there is no deadweight loss. At a price of $2.20, there is a deadweight loss equal to the sum of triangles C and E.

	At Competitive Equilibrium	At a Price of $2.20
Consumer surplus	A + B + C	A
Producer surplus	D + E	B + D
Deadweight loss	None	C + E

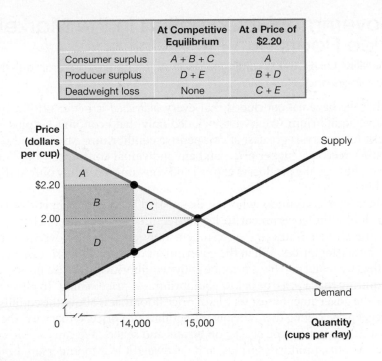

Deadweight Loss

To show that economic surplus is maximized at equilibrium, consider a situation in which the price of chai tea is *above* the equilibrium price, as shown in Figure 4.7. At a price of $2.20 per cup, the number of cups consumers are willing to buy per day falls from 15,000 to 14,000. At competitive equilibrium, consumer surplus is equal to the sum of areas A, B, and C. At a price of $2.20, fewer cups are sold at a higher price, so consumer surplus declines to just the area of A. At competitive equilibrium, producer surplus is equal to the sum of areas D and E. At the higher price of $2.20, producer surplus changes to be equal to the sum of areas B and D. The sum of consumer and producer surplus—economic surplus—has been reduced to the sum of areas A, B, and D. Notice that this sum is less than the original economic surplus by an amount equal to the sum of triangles C and E. Economic surplus has declined because at a price of $2.20, all the cups between the 14,000th and the 15,000th, which would have been produced in competitive equilibrium, are not being produced. These "missing" cups are not providing any consumer or producer surplus, so economic surplus has declined. The reduction in economic surplus resulting from a market not being in competitive equilibrium is called the **deadweight loss**. In the figure, deadweight loss is equal to the sum of the triangles C and E.   MyLab Economics Concept Check

Deadweight loss The reduction in economic surplus resulting from a market not being in competitive equilibrium.

Economic Surplus and Economic Efficiency

Consumer surplus measures the benefit to consumers from buying a particular product, such as chai tea. Producer surplus measures the benefit to firms from selling a particular product. Therefore, economic surplus—which is the sum of the benefit to firms plus the benefit to consumers—is the best measure we have of the benefit to society from the production of a particular good or service. Economic surplus gives us a second way of characterizing the economic efficiency of a competitive market: *Equilibrium in a competitive market results in the greatest amount of economic surplus, or total net benefit to society, from the production of a good or service.* Anything that causes the market for a good or service not to be in competitive equilibrium reduces the total benefit to society from the production of that good or service.

Now we can give a more general definition of *economic efficiency* in terms of our two approaches: **Economic efficiency** is a market outcome in which the marginal benefit to consumers of the last unit produced is equal to its marginal cost of production and in which the sum of consumer surplus and producer surplus is at a maximum.   MyLab Economics Concept Check

Economic efficiency A market outcome in which the marginal benefit to consumers of the last unit produced is equal to its marginal cost of production and in which the sum of consumer surplus and producer surplus is at a maximum.

MyLab Economics Study Plan

4.3 Government Intervention in the Market: Price Floors and Price Ceilings

LEARNING OBJECTIVE: Explain the economic effect of government-imposed price floors and price ceilings.

Notice that we have *not* concluded that every *individual* is better off if a market is at competitive equilibrium. We have concluded only that economic surplus, or the *total* net benefit to society, is greatest at competitive equilibrium. Any individual producer would rather receive a higher price, and any individual consumer would rather pay a lower price, but usually producers can sell and consumers can buy only at the competitive equilibrium price.

Producers or consumers who are dissatisfied with the competitive equilibrium price can lobby the government to legally require that producers charge a different price. In the United States, the government only occasionally overrides the market outcome by setting prices. When the government does intervene, it can attempt to aid either sellers by requiring that a price be above equilibrium—a price floor—or aid buyers by requiring that a price be below equilibrium—a price ceiling. To affect the market outcome, the government must set a legal price floor that is above the equilibrium price or set a legal price ceiling that is below the equilibrium price. Otherwise, the price ceiling or price floor will not be *binding* on buyers and sellers. We can use the concepts of consumer surplus, producer surplus, and deadweight loss to understand more clearly why price floors and price ceilings reduce economic efficiency.

Price Floors: Government Policy in Agricultural Markets

The Great Depression of the 1930s was the worst economic disaster in U.S. history, affecting every sector of the economy. Many farmers could sell their products only at very low prices, so they convinced the federal government to set price floors for many agricultural products, such as wheat and corn. Government intervention in agriculture—often called the *farm program*—has continued ever since. To understand how a price floor in an agricultural market works, suppose that the equilibrium price in the wheat market is $6.50 per bushel, but the government decides to set a price floor of $8.00 per bushel. As Figure 4.8 shows, the price of wheat rises from $6.50 to $8.00, and the quantity of wheat sold falls from 2.0 billion bushels per year to 1.8 billion. Initially, suppose that production of wheat also falls to 1.8 billion bushels.

MyLab Economics Animation

Figure 4.8

The Economic Effect of a Price Floor in the Wheat Market

If wheat farmers convince the government to impose a price floor of $8.00 per bushel, the amount of wheat sold will fall from 2.0 billion bushels per year to 1.8 billion. If we assume that farmers produce 1.8 billion bushels, producer surplus then increases by rectangle *A*—which is transferred from consumer surplus—and falls by triangle *C*. Consumer surplus declines by rectangle *A* plus triangle *B*. There is a deadweight loss equal to triangles *B* and *C*, representing the decline in economic efficiency due to the price floor. In reality, a price floor of $8.00 per bushel will cause farmers to expand their production from 2.0 billion to 2.2 billion bushels, resulting in a surplus of wheat.

The producer surplus received by wheat farmers increases by an amount equal to the area of rectangle A and decreases by an amount equal to the area of triangle C. (This is the same result we saw in the market for chai tea in Figure 4.7.) The area of rectangle A represents a transfer from consumer surplus to producer surplus. The total fall in consumer surplus is equal to the sum of the areas of rectangle A and triangle B. Wheat farmers benefit from this program, but consumers lose. There is also a deadweight loss equal to the areas of triangles B and C because economic efficiency declines as the price floor reduces the amount of economic surplus in the market for wheat. In other words, the price floor has caused the marginal benefit of the last bushel of wheat to be greater than the marginal cost of producing it. We can conclude that a price floor reduces economic efficiency.

We assumed initially that farmers reduce their production of wheat to the amount consumers are willing to buy. In fact, as Figure 4.8 shows, a price floor will cause the quantity of wheat that farmers want to supply to increase from 2.0 billion to 2.2 billion bushels. Because the higher price also reduces the amount of wheat consumers want to buy, the result is a surplus of 0.4 billion bushels of wheat (the 2.2 billion bushels supplied minus the 1.8 billion demanded).

The federal government's farm programs have often resulted in large surpluses of wheat and other agricultural products. In response, the government has usually either bought the surplus food or paid farmers to restrict supply by taking some land out of cultivation. Because both of these options are expensive, Congress passed the Freedom to Farm Act of 1996. The intent of the act was to phase out price floors and government purchases of surpluses and return to a free market in agriculture. To allow farmers time to adjust, the federal government began paying farmers *subsidies*, or cash payments based on the number of acres planted. Although the subsidies were originally scheduled to be phased out, Congress has passed additional farm bills that have resulted in the continuation of subsidies requiring substantial federal government spending. In 2017, the Congressional Budget Office estimated that the farm program would result in federal spending of more than $66.5 billion over the following 10 years.   **MyLab Economics** Concept Check

Apply the Concept   MyLab Economics Video

Price Floors in Labor Markets: The Debate over Minimum Wage Policy

The minimum wage may be the most controversial "price floor." Supporters see the minimum wage as a way of raising the incomes of low-skilled workers. Opponents argue that it results in fewer jobs and imposes large costs on small businesses.

Since 2009, the national minimum wage as set by Congress has been $7.25 per hour for most occupations. It is illegal for an employer to pay less than this wage in these occupations. Although only about 4 percent of workers in the United States earn the minimum wage or less, many people are concerned that workers who receive the minimum wage or a wage a little above the minimum are not earning a "living wage" that would allow them to escape from poverty. Some members of Congress have introduced legislation to raise the minimum wage in several steps to $12 per hour. In recent years, protests in a number of cities brought pressure on fast-food restaurants and other employers to voluntarily raise the minimum wage they paid to $15 per hour. Several cities and states are increasing their minimum wage, typically in a series of steps phased in over several years. Currently, only a few cities and states plan to eventually raise their minimum wage as high as $15 per hour. In 2017, President Donald Trump and a majority of Congress seemed unlikely to support raising the federal minimum wage.

For many workers, the legal minimum wage is irrelevant because it is well below the wage employers are voluntarily willing to pay them. But for some low-skilled workers—such as restaurant workers—the minimum wage is above the wage they would otherwise receive. The following figure shows the effect of the minimum wage on employment in the market for low-skilled labor.

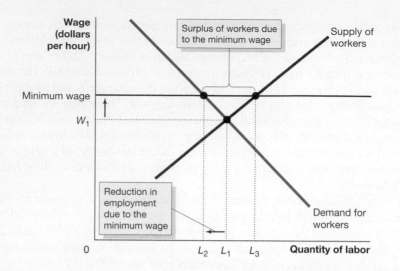

Without a minimum wage, the equilibrium wage would be W_1 and the number of workers hired would be L_1. With a minimum wage set above the equilibrium wage, the number of workers employers demand declines from L_1 to L_2, and the quantity of labor supplied increases to L_3, leading to a surplus of workers unable to find jobs equal to $L_3 - L_2$. The quantity of labor supplied increases because the higher wage attracts more people to work. For instance, some teenagers may decide that working after school is worthwhile at the minimum wage of $7.25 per hour but would not be worthwhile at a lower wage.

This analysis is very similar to our analysis of the wheat market in Figure 4.8. Just as a price floor in the wheat market leads to less wheat being consumed, a price floor in the labor market should lead to fewer workers being hired. Views differ sharply among economists, however, concerning how large a reduction in employment the minimum wage causes. The U.S. Congressional Budget Office (CBO) estimates that raising the minimum wage to $10.10 per hour, as President Barack Obama had proposed in 2015, would result in a decline in employment of 500,000 workers. Some economists believe that the effects of the minimum wage on employment are far smaller, however. For instance, David Card of the University of California, Berkeley, and Alan Krueger of Princeton University conducted a study of fast-food restaurants in New Jersey and Pennsylvania. Their study indicated that the effect of past minimum wage increases on employment has been very small. This study has been controversial, and other economists have examined similar data and come to the different conclusion that the minimum wage leads to a significant decrease in employment.

Whatever the extent of employment losses from the minimum wage, because it is a price floor, it will cause a deadweight loss, just as a price floor in the wheat market does. Therefore, many economists favor alternative policies for attaining the goal of raising the incomes of low-skilled workers. One policy many economists support is the *earned income tax credit*, which reduces the amount of tax that low-income wage earners pay to the federal government. Workers with very low incomes who do not owe any tax receive a payment from the government. Unlike with the minimum wage, the earned income tax credit can increase the incomes of low-skilled workers without reducing employment. The earned income tax credit also places a lesser burden on the small businesses that employ many low-skilled workers and may cause a smaller loss of economic efficiency.

Sources: Steven Greenhouse, "How the $15 Minimum Wage Went from Laughable to Viable," *New York Times*, April 1, 2016; U.S. Bureau of Labor Statistics, "Characteristics of Minimum Wage Workers, 2015," BLS Reports 1061, April 2016; U.S. Congressional Budget Office, "The Effects of a Minimum-Wage Increase on Employment and Family Income," February 2014; David Card and Alan B. Krueger, *Myth and Measurement: The New Economics of the Minimum Wage*, Princeton, NJ: Princeton University Press, 1995; and David Neumark and William Wascher, "Minimum Wages and Employment: A Case Study of the Fast-Food Industry in New Jersey and Pennsylvania: Comment," *American Economic Review*, Vol. 90, No. 5, December 2000, pp. 1362–1396.

MyLab Economics Study Plan   **Your Turn:** Test your understanding by doing related problem 3.9 on page 137 at the end of this chapter.

Price Ceilings: Government Rent Control Policy in Housing Markets

Support for governments setting price floors typically comes from sellers, and support for governments setting price ceilings typically comes from consumers. For example, when there is a sharp increase in gasoline prices, some policymakers and consumer groups will propose that the government impose a price ceiling on the market for gasoline. A number of cities impose rent control, which puts a ceiling on the maximum rent that landlords can charge for an apartment.

Figure 4.9 shows the market for apartments in a city that has rent control. Without rent control, the equilibrium rent would be $2,500 per month, and 2,000,000 apartments would be rented. With a maximum legal rent of $1,500 per month, landlords reduce the quantity of apartments supplied to 1,900,000. The fall in the quantity of apartments supplied can be the result of landlords converting some apartment buildings into offices, selling apartments off as condominiums, or converting multi-unit buildings into single-family homes. During World War II, governments imposing rent controls resulted in the largest increase in home ownership in U.S. history because many landlords sold off rental housing that was no longer profitable to rent to tenants. Over time, landlords may even abandon some rental housing. At one time in New York City, rent control resulted in landlords abandoning whole city blocks of apartment houses because they were unable to cover their costs with the rents the government allowed them to charge. In London, when rent controls were applied to rooms and apartments located in a landlord's own home, the quantity of these apartments supplied decreased by 75 percent.

In Figure 4.9, with the rent ceiling of $1,500 per month, the quantity of apartments demanded rises to 2,100,000, resulting in a shortage of 200,000 apartments. Consumer surplus increases by rectangle A and falls by triangle B. Rectangle A would have been part of producer surplus if rent control were not in place. With rent control, it is part of consumer surplus. Rent control causes the producer surplus that landlords receive to fall by rectangle A plus triangle C. Triangles B and C represent the deadweight loss, which results from rent control reducing the amount of economic surplus in the market for apartments. Rent control has caused the marginal benefit of the last apartment rented to be greater than the marginal cost of supplying it. We can conclude that a price ceiling, such as rent control, reduces economic efficiency. The appendix to this chapter shows how we can make quantitative estimates of the deadweight loss and provides an example of the changes in consumer surplus and producer surplus that can result from rent control.

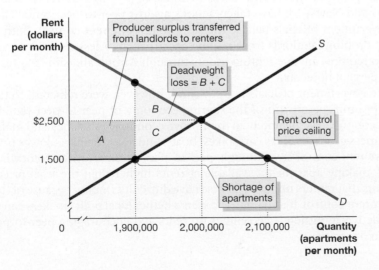

MyLab Economics Animation

Figure 4.9

The Economic Effect of a Rent Ceiling

Without rent control, the equilibrium rent is $2,500 per month. At that price, 2,000,000 apartments would be rented. If the government imposes a rent ceiling of $1,500 per month, the quantity of apartments supplied decreases to 1,900,000, and the quantity of apartments demanded increases to 2,100,000, resulting in a shortage of 200,000 apartments. Producer surplus equal to the area of rectangle A is transferred from landlords to renters, and there is a deadweight loss equal to the areas of triangles B and C.

Don't Let This Happen to You

Don't Confuse "Scarcity" with "Shortage"

At first glance, the following statement seems correct: "There is a shortage of every good that is scarce." In everyday conversation, we describe a good as "scarce" if we have trouble finding it. For instance, if you are looking for a gift for a child, you might call the latest hot toy "scarce" if you are willing to buy it at its listed price but can't find it online or in any store. But recall that economists have a broader definition of *scarce*. In the economic sense, almost everything—except undesirable

things like garbage—is scarce. A shortage of a good occurs only if the quantity demanded is greater than the quantity supplied at the current price. Therefore, the preceding statement— "There is a shortage of every good that is scarce"—is incorrect. In fact, there is no shortage of most scarce goods.

MyLab Economics Study Plan

Your Turn: Test your understanding by doing related problem 3.12 on page 138 at the end of this chapter.

Renters as a group benefit from rent controls—total consumer surplus is larger— but landlords lose. Because of the deadweight loss, the total loss to landlords is greater than the gain to renters. Notice also that although renters as a group benefit, the number of renters is reduced, so some renters are made worse off by rent controls because they are unable to find an apartment at the legal rent. **MyLab Economics** Concept Check

Black Markets and Peer-to-Peer Sites

When governments regulate prices by enacting price ceilings or price floors, buyers and sellers often find a way around the regulations. As a result, renters may be worse off and landlords may be better off than Figure 4.9 makes it seem. We have assumed that renters and landlords actually abide by the price ceiling, but sometimes they don't. Because rent control leads to a shortage of apartments, renters who would otherwise not be able to find apartments have an incentive to offer landlords rents *above* the legal maximum. The result is a **black market** in which buying and selling take place at prices that violate government price regulations.

Black market A market in which buying and selling take place at prices that violate government price regulations.

Online peer-to-peer rental sites like Airbnb have provided landlords and tenants another way to avoid rent controls. Landlords can use these sites to convert a regular yearly rental into a series of short-term rentals for which they can charge above the legal maximum rent. Tenants can also use the sites to make a profit from rent controls. In San Francisco in recent years, some tenants have moved out of the city but kept their rent-controlled apartments and rented them using peer-to-peer rental sites. Both San Francisco and New York have taken actions against peer-to-peer rental sites because some government officials believe the sites undermine rent control. Both cities have laws that prohibit landlords from renting apartments for less than 30 days. San Francisco also requires anyone renting rooms through Airbnb and similar sites to pay the city's 14 percent hotel tax.

Some government officials in both cities, however, were reluctant to take actions that might limit the growth of the sharing economy of peer-to-peer rental sites. The sharing economy has the potential to improve economic efficiency and make available to consumers goods, such as cars, bikes, boats, and apartments, at lower prices. When cities have rent control laws, though, peer-to-peer sites perform a somewhat different function, making apartments available at rents higher than the legal price ceiling— apartments that renters might otherwise have difficulty finding because of the shortage caused by rent control. It remains to be seen whether local policymakers can resolve the conflict between putting legal ceilings on rents and encouraging peer-to-peer sites to operate in their cities.

Solved Problem 4.3

What's the Economic Effect of a Black Market in Renting Apartments?

In many cities that have rent controls, such as New York and San Francisco, the actual rents paid can be much higher than the legal maximum. Because rent controls cause a shortage of apartments, desperate tenants are often willing to pay landlords rents that are higher than the law allows, perhaps by writing a check for the legally allowed rent and paying an additional amount in cash. Look again at

Figure 4.9 on page 121. Suppose that competition among tenants results in the black market rent rising to $3,500 per month. At this rent, tenants demand 1,900,000 apartments. Draw a graph showing the market for apartments and compare this situation with the one shown in Figure 4.9. Be sure to note any differences in consumer surplus, producer surplus, and deadweight loss.

Solving the Problem

Step 1: Review the chapter material. This problem is about price controls in the market for apartments, so you may want to review the section "Price Ceilings: Government Rent Control Policy in Housing Markets," which begins on page 121.

Step 2: Draw a graph similar to Figure 4.9, with the addition of the black market price.

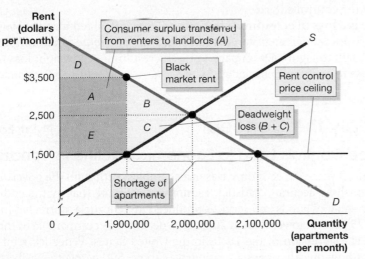

Step 3: Analyze the changes from Figure 4.9. The black market rent is now $3,500 per month—even higher than the original competitive equilibrium rent shown in Figure 4.9. So, consumer surplus declines by an amount equal to the sum of the areas of rectangle A and rectangle E. The remaining consumer surplus is triangle D. Note that rectangle A, which would have been part of consumer surplus without rent control, represents a transfer from renters to landlords. Compared with the situation shown in Figure 4.9, producer surplus has increased by an amount equal to the sum of the areas of rectangles A and E, and consumer surplus has declined by the same amount. Deadweight loss is equal to the sum of the areas of triangles B and C, the same as in Figure 4.9.

Extra Credit: This analysis leads to a surprising result: With an active black market in apartments, rent control may leave renters as a group worse off—with less consumer surplus—than if there were no rent control. There is one more possibility to consider, however. If enough landlords become convinced that they can get away with charging rents above the legal ceiling, the quantity of apartments supplied will increase. Eventually, the market could even end up at the competitive equilibrium, with an equilibrium rent of $2,500 and equilibrium quantity of 2,000,000 apartments. In that case, the rent control price ceiling becomes nonbinding—not because it was set below the equilibrium price but because the government didn't effectively enforce it.

Your Turn: For more practice, do related problem 3.13 on page 138 at the end of this chapter.   MyLab Economics Study Plan

Rent controls can also lead to an increase in racial and other types of illegal discrimination. With rent controls, more renters are looking for apartments than there are apartments to rent. Landlords are more likely to indulge their prejudices by refusing to rent to people from groups they don't like, even if doing so is illegal. In cities without rent controls, landlords face more competition, which makes it more difficult to reject tenants on the basis of irrelevant characteristics, such as race. **MyLab Economics** Concept Check

The Results of Government Price Controls: Winners, Losers, and Inefficiency

When the government imposes price floors or price ceilings, three important results occur:

1. **Some people win.** The winners from rent control are the people who are paying less for rent because they live in rent-controlled apartments. Landlords may also gain if they break the law by charging rents above the legal maximum for their rent-controlled apartments, provided that those illegal rents are higher than the competitive equilibrium rents would be.
2. **Some people lose.** The losers from rent control are the landlords of rent-controlled apartments who abide by the law and renters who are unable to find apartments to rent at the controlled price.
3. **There is a loss of economic efficiency.** Rent control reduces economic efficiency because fewer apartments are rented than would be rented in a competitive market (refer again to Figure 4.9 on page 121). The resulting deadweight loss measures the decrease in economic efficiency. **MyLab Economics** Concept Check

Apply the Concept   MyLab Economics Video

Price Controls Lead to Economic Decline in Venezuela

In 2017, the Venezuelan economy was in a shambles. Although the government was no longer publishing accurate statistics, economists estimate that by the end of 2017 real GDP—the value of goods and services produced in Venezuela, corrected for inflation—would be 25 percent lower than in 2015. That decline was comparable to the worst years of the Great Depression of the 1930s in the United States. Venezuela's inflation rate, a measure of how quickly prices are rising, was above 500 percent—easily the highest in the world. The unemployment rate was above 10 percent, and Caracas, the country's capital, had the highest murder rate of any capital city in the world. As we saw in the chapter opener, some desperate people in Venezuela engaged in food riots at supermarkets.

Many economists believe the problems with the Venezuelan economy are due to the policies of Hugo Chavez, who was elected president in 1999, and Nicolas Maduro, who became president following Chavez's death in 2013. Under Chavez, the government seized control of thousands of private firms, including firms in the oil industry—the source of most of Venezuela's exports. The government seized large farms and redistributed the land to low-income Venezuelans, many of whom had no experience in farming, lacked access to loans needed to finance purchases of seeds, fertilizers, and pesticides, and were not connected to distribution networks to sell their crops. One farmer was quoted as saying, "They encouraged me to seize this land from its previous owner, but now I can't get loans, and the state agricultural store doesn't have seeds, fertilizers or insecticides. How can I plant crops with nothing?"

Disruptions to Venezuela's agricultural sector led to a sharp reduction in food production. For several years, the Venezuelan government was able to ensure that sufficient food would be available in supermarkets by using its oil revenues to buy imported food. But a large decline in oil prices beginning in 2014 meant the government could no longer pay for food imports. The falling supply of food would ordinarily have resulted in price increases that would have increased the quantity of food grown domestically. But the Venezuelan government imposed price controls that kept prices well below their new equilibrium levels. In an interview, Nicholas Casey, a reporter for the *New York Times*, described the resulting shortages:

> [You] go outside as early as 5 a.m, sometimes 4:30, you see people lining up in front of stores to try to see what's going to be there when they open their doors. And sometimes even these stores—after you're waiting through a line that might be 500, 1,000 people sometimes … you get to the front of the line, and you find that they've only got cooking oil. They don't have flour. They don't have any of the basic things that you need there.

The price controls resulted in a thriving black market in many goods run by what Venezuelans call *bachaqueros*. These small-scale entrepreneurs buy up food and other groceries at the below-market controlled prices and resell them to consumers who would otherwise be unable to buy these goods. Consider the case of cornmeal, which is used to make arepa, a corn pancake that is an important part of most Venezuelans' diet. In late 2016, the government price ceiling for a 2-pound bag of cornmeal was 190 bolivars, the Venezuelan currency (its symbol is Bs). The equilibrium market price of cornmeal was about 975 bolivars, but few supermarkets had any for sale. Many Venezuelans had to buy cornmeal on the black market at a price of 3,500 bolivars. The figure below, which is similar to Figure 4.9, illustrates the situation.

The figure shows that most consumers are worse off because of the price controls. Less cornmeal is available for sale (Q_1 rather than the market equilibrium quantity Q_2), and at the price ceiling, there is a shortage of cornmeal equal to $Q_3 - Q_1$. Although a few consumers may be able to buy cornmeal at the low price ceiling price of 190 bolivars, most supermarkets have no cornmeal available on their shelves, forcing many consumers to pay the black market price of 3,500 bolivars. Note that the situation for Venezuelan consumers may be worse than the figure indicates. Although the high black market price might provide an incentive for some farmers to expand their production of cornmeal, news reports indicate that domestic production has increased very little. Instead, some black market sellers, particularly those living along the border with Colombia, are buying cornmeal at controlled prices and smuggling it out of Venezuela, were it can be sold in Colombia at the market equilibrium price. Although this price is below the black market price, people selling on the black market in Venezuela risk being arrested by the government. So, the actual amount of cornmeal available to Venezuelan consumers might be less than Q_1 shown in the figure.

Tragically, news reports indicate that hunger is widespread in Venezuela, and economists estimate that more than 80 percent of the population is living in poverty.

Sources: Nicholas Casey, "No Food, No Medicine, No Respite: A Starving Boy's Death in Venezuela, *New York Times*, December 25, 2016; Patrick Gillespie and Osmary Hernandez, "Venezuela's Food Prices Skyrocket as People Go Hungry," cnn.com, October 21, 2016; "Venezuela's Leaders Ignore Reality," *Economist*, January 26, 2017; Terry Gross, "Bust Times in Oil-Rich Venezuela: 'The Banks Don't Have Money to Give Out,'" Fresh Air interview with Nicholas Casey, npr.org, June 8, 2016; Peter Wilson, "Venezuelan Food Shortages Bode Ill for Chavez's Re-election," usatoday.com,

August 13, 2012; and Mery Mogollon, "Packs of Black-Market Foot Soldiers Raid Venezuela Markets," latimes.com, April 1, 2015.

MyLab Economics Study Plan   **Your Turn:** Test your understanding by doing related problems 3.14 and 3.15 on page 138 at the end of this chapter.

Positive and Normative Analysis of Price Ceilings and Price Floors

Are rent controls, government farm programs, and other price ceilings and price floors bad? As we saw in Chapter 1, questions of this type do not have right or wrong answers. Economists are generally skeptical of government attempts to interfere with competitive market equilibrium. Economists know the role competitive markets have played in raising the average person's standard of living. They also know that too much government intervention has the potential to reduce the ability of the market system to produce similar increases in living standards in the future. The situation in Venezuela today appears to fit this description.

But recall the difference between positive and normative analysis. Positive analysis is concerned with *what is*, and normative analysis is concerned with *what should be*. Our analysis in this chapter of rent control and the U.S. farm program is positive analysis. We discussed the economic results of these programs. Whether these programs are desirable or undesirable is a normative question. Whether the gains to the winners more than make up for the losses to the losers and for the decline in economic efficiency is a matter of judgment and not strictly an economic question. Price ceilings and price floors continue to exist partly because people who understand their downside still believe they are good policies and therefore support them. The policies also persist because many people who support them do not understand the economic analysis in this chapter and

MyLab Economics Study Plan   so do not understand the drawbacks to these policies.   **MyLab Economics** Concept Check

The Economic Effect of Taxes

LEARNING OBJECTIVE: Analyze the economic effect of taxes.

Supreme Court Justice Oliver Wendell Holmes once remarked, "Taxes are what we pay for a civilized society." When the government taxes a good or service, however, it affects the market equilibrium for that good or service. Just as with a price ceiling or price floor, one result of a tax is a decline in economic efficiency. Analyzing taxes is an important part of the field of economics known as *public finance*. In this section, we will use the model of demand and supply and the concepts of consumer surplus, producer surplus, and deadweight loss to analyze the economic effect of taxes.

The Effect of Taxes on Economic Efficiency

Whenever a government taxes a good or service, less of that good or service will be produced and consumed. For example, a tax on cigarettes will raise the cost of smoking and reduce the amount of smoking that takes place. We can use a demand and supply graph to illustrate this point. Figure 4.10 shows the market for cigarettes.

Without the tax, the equilibrium price of cigarettes would be $5.00 per pack, and 4 billion packs of cigarettes would be sold per year (point A). If the federal government requires sellers of cigarettes to pay a $1.00-per-pack tax, then their cost of selling cigarettes will increase by $1.00 per pack. This increase in cost causes the supply curve for cigarettes to shift up by $1.00 because sellers will now require a price that is $1.00 greater to supply the same quantity of cigarettes. In Figure 4.10, the supply curve shifts up by $1.00 to show the effect of the tax, and there is a new equilibrium price of $5.90 and a new equilibrium quantity of 3.7 billion packs (point B).

The federal government will collect tax revenue equal to the tax per pack multiplied by the number of packs sold, or $3.7 billion. The area shaded in green in Figure 4.10 represents the government's tax revenue. Consumers will pay a higher price

Price the consumer pays after the $1.00-per-pack tax is imposed

Tax revenue

Price received by producers after paying the tax

$1.00-per-pack federal tax on cigarettes shifts the supply curve up by $1.00

Deadweight loss or excess burden from tax

MyLab Economics Animation

Figure 4.10

The Effect of a Tax on the Market for Cigarettes

Without the tax, market equilibrium occurs at point A. The equilibrium price of cigarettes is $5.00 per pack, and 4 billion packs of cigarettes are sold per year. A $1.00-per-pack tax on cigarettes will cause the supply curve for cigarettes to shift up by $1.00, from S_1 to S_2. The new equilibrium occurs at point B. The price of cigarettes will increase by $0.90, to $5.90 per pack, and the quantity sold will fall to 3.7 billion packs. The tax on cigarettes will increase the price paid by consumers from $5.00 to $5.90 per pack. Producers will receive a price of $5.90 per pack (point B), but after paying the $1.00 tax, they will be left with $4.90 (point C). The government will receive tax revenue equal to the green-shaded box. Some consumer surplus and some producer surplus will become tax revenue for the government, and some will become deadweight loss, shown by the yellow-shaded area.

of $5.90 per pack. Although sellers appear to be receiving a higher price per pack, once they have paid the tax, the price they receive falls from $5.00 per pack to $4.90 per pack. There is a loss of consumer surplus because consumers are paying a higher price. The price producers receive falls, so there is also a loss of producer surplus. Therefore, the tax on cigarettes has reduced *both* consumer surplus and producer surplus. Some of the reduction in consumer and producer surplus becomes tax revenue for the government. The rest of the reduction in consumer and producer surplus is equal to the deadweight loss from the tax, shown by the yellow-shaded triangle in the figure.

We can conclude that the true burden of a tax is not just the amount consumers and producers pay the government but also includes the deadweight loss. The deadweight loss from a tax is called the *excess burden* of the tax. *A tax is efficient if it imposes a small excess burden relative to the tax revenue it raises.* One contribution economists make to government tax policy is to advise policymakers on which taxes are most efficient.   **MyLab Economics** Concept Check

Tax Incidence: Who Actually Pays a Tax?

The answer to the question "Who pays a tax?" seems obvious: Whoever is legally required to send a tax payment to the government pays the tax. But there can be an important difference between who is legally required to pay the tax and who actually *bears the burden* of the tax. Economists call the actual division of the burden of a tax between buyers and sellers **tax incidence**. For example, as of April 2017, the federal government levied an excise tax of 18.4 cents per gallon of gasoline sold. Gas station owners collect this tax and forward it to the federal government, but who actually bears the burden of the tax?

Tax incidence The actual division of the burden of a tax between buyers and sellers in a market.

Determining Tax Incidence on a Demand and Supply Graph Suppose that currently the federal government does not impose a tax on gasoline. In Figure 4.11, equilibrium in the retail market for gasoline occurs at the intersection of the demand curve and supply curve, S_1. The equilibrium price is $2.50 per gallon, and the equilibrium quantity is 144 billion gallons per year. Now suppose that the federal government imposes a 10-cents-per-gallon tax. As a result of the tax, the supply curve for gasoline will shift up by 10 cents per gallon. At the new equilibrium, where the demand curve intersects the supply curve, S_2, the price has risen by 8 cents per gallon, from $2.50 to $2.58. Notice that only in the extremely unlikely case that demand is a vertical line will the market price rise by the full amount of the tax. Consumers are paying 8 cents more per gallon. Sellers of gasoline receive a new higher price of $2.58 per gallon, but after paying the 10-cents-per-gallon tax, they are left with $2.48 per gallon, or 2 cents less than they were receiving in the old equilibrium.

Although the sellers of gasoline are responsible for collecting the tax and sending the tax receipts to the government, they do not bear most of the burden of the tax.

Figure 4.11

The Incidence of a Tax on Gasoline

With no tax on gasoline, the price would be $2.50 per gallon, and 144 billion gallons of gasoline would be sold each year. A 10-cents-per-gallon excise tax shifts the supply curve up, from S_1 to S_2, raises the price consumers pay from $2.50 to $2.58, and lowers the price sellers receive from $2.50 to $2.48. Therefore, consumers pay 8 cents of the 10-cents-per-gallon tax on gasoline, and sellers pay 2 cents.

In this case, consumers pay 8 cents of the tax because the market price has risen by 8 cents, and sellers pay 2 cents of the tax because after sending the tax to the government, they are receiving 2 cents less per gallon of gasoline sold. Expressed in percentage terms, consumers pay 80 percent of the tax, and sellers pay 20 percent of the tax.

Solved Problem 4.4

When Do Consumers Pay All of a Sales Tax Increase?

A student makes the following statement: "If the federal government raises the sales tax on gasoline by $0.25, then the price of gasoline will rise by $0.25. Consumers can't get by without gasoline, so they have to pay the whole amount of any increase in the sales tax." Under what circumstances will the student's statement be true? Use a graph of the market for gasoline to illustrate your answer.

Solving the Problem

Step 1: **Review the chapter material.** This problem is about tax incidence, so you may want to review the section "Tax Incidence: Who Actually Pays a Tax?" which begins on page 127.

Step 2: **Draw a graph like Figure 4.11 to illustrate the circumstances when consumers will pay all of an increase in a sales tax.**

Step 3: **Use the graph to evaluate the statement.** The graph shows that consumers will pay all of an increase in a sales tax only if the demand curve is a vertical line. It is very unlikely that the demand for gasoline would look like this because we expect that for every good, an increase in price will cause a decrease in the quantity demanded. Because the demand curve for gasoline is not a vertical line, the statement is incorrect.

Your Turn: For more practice, do related problem 4.8 on page 140 at the end of the chapter.

MyLab Economics Study Plan

Does It Make a Difference Whether the Government Collects a Tax from Buyers or Sellers? We have already seen the important distinction between who is legally required to pay a tax and who actually bears the burden of a tax. We can reinforce this point by noting explicitly that the incidence of a tax does *not* depend on whether the government collects a tax from the buyers of a good or from the sellers. Figure 4.12 illustrates this point by showing the effect on equilibrium in the market for gasoline if a 10-cents-per-gallon tax is imposed on buyers rather than on sellers. That is, we are now assuming that instead of sellers having to collect the 10-cents-per-gallon tax at the pump, buyers are responsible for keeping track of how many gallons of gasoline they purchase and sending the tax to the government. (Of course, it would be very difficult for buyers to keep track of their purchases or for the government to check whether they were paying all of the taxes they owe. That is why the government collects the tax on gasoline from sellers.)

Figure 4.12 is similar to Figure 4.11 except that it shows the gasoline tax being imposed on buyers rather than on sellers. In Figure 4.12, the supply curve does not shift because nothing has happened to change the quantity of gasoline sellers are willing to supply at any given price. The demand curve has shifted, however, because consumers now have to pay a 10-cent tax on every gallon of gasoline they buy. Therefore, at every quantity, they are willing to pay a price 10 cents lower than they would have paid without the tax. In the figure, we indicate the effect of the tax by shifting the demand curve down by 10 cents, from D_1 to D_2. Once the tax has been imposed and the demand curve has shifted down, the new equilibrium quantity of gasoline is 140 billion gallons, which is exactly the same as in Figure 4.11.

The new equilibrium price after the tax is imposed appears to be different in Figure 4.12 than in Figure 4.11, but if we include the tax, buyers will pay the same price, and sellers will receive the same price in both figures. To see this point, notice that in Figure 4.11, buyers pay sellers a price of $2.58 per gallon. In Figure 4.12, they pay sellers only $2.48, but they must also pay the government a tax of 10 cents per gallon. So, the total price buyers pay remains $2.58 per gallon. In Figure 4.11, sellers receive $2.58 per gallon from buyers, but after they pay the tax of 10 cents per gallon, they are left with $2.48, which is the same amount they receive in Figure 4.12.   **MyLab Economics** Concept Check

MyLab Economics Animation

Figure 4.12

The Incidence of a Tax on Gasoline Paid by Buyers

With no tax on gasoline, the demand curve is D_1. If a 10-cents-per-gallon tax is imposed that consumers are responsible for paying, the demand curve shifts down by the amount of the tax, from D_1 to D_2. In the new equilibrium, consumers pay a price of $2.58 per gallon, including the tax. Producers receive $2.48 per gallon. The result is the same as when producers were responsible for paying the tax.

Apply the Concept

MyLab Economics Video

Is the Burden of the Social Security Tax Really Shared Equally between Workers and Firms?

Most people who receive paychecks have several different taxes withheld by their employers, who forward the taxes directly to the government. In fact, after getting their first job, many people are shocked when they discover the gap between their gross pay and their net pay after taxes have been deducted. The largest tax many people of low or moderate income pay is FICA, which stands for the Federal Insurance Contributions Act. FICA funds the Social Security and Medicare programs, which provide income and health care to elderly and disabled people. FICA is sometimes called the *payroll tax*. When Congress passed the act, it wanted employers and workers to equally share the burden of the tax. In 2017, FICA was 15.3 percent of wages, with workers paying 7.65 percent, which is withheld from their paychecks, and employers paying the other 7.65 percent.

But does requiring workers and employers to each pay half the tax mean that the burden of the tax is also shared equally? Our discussion in this chapter shows that the answer is "no." In the labor market, employers are buyers, and workers are sellers. As we saw in the example of the federal tax on gasoline, whether the tax is collected from buyers or from sellers does not affect the incidence of the tax. Most economists believe, in fact, that the burden of FICA falls almost entirely on workers. The following figure, which shows the market for labor, illustrates why.

In the market for labor, the demand curve represents the quantity of labor demanded by employers at various wages, and the supply curve represents the quantity of labor supplied by workers at various wages. The intersection of the demand curve and the supply curve determines the equilibrium wage. In both panels, the equilibrium wage without a Social Security payroll tax is $10 per hour. For simplicity, let's assume that the payroll tax equals $1 per hour of work. In panel (a), we assume that employers must pay the tax. The tax causes the demand for labor curve to shift down by $1 at every quantity of labor because firms must now pay a $1 tax for every hour of labor they hire. We have drawn the supply curve for labor as being very steep because most economists believe the quantity of labor supplied by workers does not change much as the wage rate changes. In panel (a), after the tax is imposed, the equilibrium wage declines from $10 per hour to $9.05 per hour. Firms are now paying a total of $10.05 for every hour of work they hire: $9.05 in wages to workers and $1 in tax to the government. In other words, workers have paid $0.95 of the $1 tax, and firms have paid only $0.05.

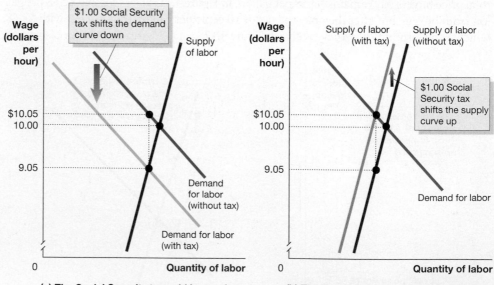

(a) The Social Security tax paid by employers

(b) The Social Security tax paid by workers

Panel (b) shows that this result is exactly the same when the tax is imposed on workers rather than on firms. In this case, the tax causes the supply curve for labor to shift up by $1 at every quantity of labor because workers must now pay a tax of $1 for every hour they work. After the tax is imposed, the equilibrium wage increases to $10.05 per hour. But workers receive only $9.05 after they have paid the $1.00 tax. Once again, workers have paid $0.95 of the $1 tax, and firms have paid only $0.05.

Although the figure presents a simplified analysis, it reflects the conclusion of most economists who have studied the incidence of FICA: Even though Congress requires employers to pay half the tax and workers to pay the other half, in fact, the burden of the tax falls almost entirely on workers. This conclusion would not be changed even if Congress revised the law to require either employers or workers to pay all of the tax. The forces of demand and supply working in the labor market, and not Congress, determine the incidence of the tax.

Your Turn: Test your understanding by doing related problems 4.9 and 4.10 on page 140 at the end of this chapter.

MyLab Economics Study Plan

Continued from page 109

Economics in Your Life & Career

As a Member of the City Council, Should You Support Rent Control?

At the beginning of the chapter, we posed the following questions: If you and the other city council members vote to enact a rent control law, is it likely that in the future it will be easier for renters to find an affordable apartment in your city? Who in your city would benefit, and who would lose from the law?

This chapter has shown that although rent control can keep rents lower than they might otherwise be, it can also lead to a permanent shortage of apartments. Renters may have to search for a long time to find a suitable apartment, and landlords may even ask renters to make additional payments, in violation of the rent control law, which would make the actual rent paid higher than the controlled rent. Finding an apartment in a city after enactment of rent control will typically be more difficult. People who are able to find an apartment at the controlled rent will benefit if the city council enacts the law, while landlords and renters who are unable to find an apartment at the controlled rent will lose. As the chapter also notes, whether rent control should be enacted is a normative question—one that you and the rest of the city council will have to answer.

Conclusion

Our discussion of the model of demand and supply shows that markets free from government intervention eliminate surpluses and shortages and do a good job of responding to the wants of consumers. We have seen that both consumers and firms sometimes try to use the government to change market outcomes in their favor. The concepts of consumer surplus, producer surplus, and deadweight loss allow us to measure the benefits consumers and producers receive from competitive market equilibrium. These concepts also allow us to measure the effects of government price floors and price ceilings and the economic effect of taxes.

Read *An Inside Look* on the next page for a discussion of problems Uber has encountered in attempting to expand its services in the United Kingdom.

CNBC.COM

Meet the Lawyer Trying to Make US Tech Giants Pay More Taxes. His First Target: Uber

Lawyer Jolyon Maugham took an Uber on Monday in London, but it was no normal ride. He was on his way to deliver a letter to the ride-hailing service's headquarters that could kick off legal proceedings potentially costing the U.S. start-up millions of dollars.

Maugham's case revolves around how much tax Uber pays in the U.K. and, if successful, could have wide-reaching implications across Europe. Britain has something called value-added tax (VAT), which is paid when you buy goods or services. The current rate is 20 percent.

Uber pays no VAT in the U.K. because the ride-hailing app does not class its drivers as employees. Instead it says it is connecting riders to drivers.

"Uber says that it is a business-to-business service. It says that it is supplying the taxi drivers with an introduction service but that proposition suffers from two deficiencies. The first is that it doesn't really accord with what you and I would think of as reality because we think that Uber is a consumer facing brand, it's not a business facing brand. So it doesn't look like reality looks like," Maugham told CNBC by phone on Friday.

"In an employment tribunal case last year, they found that Uber was engaging its drivers as workers and it also went on to say, and this is the necessary logical consequence of the first proposition, that Uber is supplying transportation services and it is making a VAT-able supply."

The lawyer is referring to a landmark U.K. case last year in which judges ruled that Uber drivers are not self-employed and should get all the benefits of full workers' rights such as holiday pay and pensions. Uber has appealed the decision and it is still ongoing. The company also said that its drivers, not the company, pay VAT. If you are self-employed, you can be liable to pay VAT if your turnover for a 12-month period is over £83,000 ($103,552). But it is unlikely an Uber driver would make this in a year.

"Drivers who use the Uber app are subject to the same VAT laws as any other transportation provider in the U.K.," an Uber spokesperson told CNBC by email.

Maugham said that he hopes this will go to the High Court in London to be heard next month. What's at stake here for Uber is large sums of money as well as implications that could span across other jurisdictions. If Uber loses, it will have to increase fares by 20 percent to accommodate for VAT, and could be liable to pay tax on previous revenues it earned. The company has not released its financials in the U.K. for 2016, but Maugham believes it could be liable to pay £200 million ($249 million) in VAT for last year. If Uber loses any potential case, its VAT payments could be assessed across the entire European Union (EU).

A rise in fares is not something that will please most Uber users given they use the service for the cheaper prices and convenience. The lawyer said he was not worried about any backlash from the public.

"I think there will be a much larger constituency that believes that nobody is above the law, and everybody has to pay taxes that parliament demand. Unless these big powerful corporations pay their taxes, society cannot operate. There will be people who will be irritated they have to pay more for their Uber taxi, but [I] think they will be in the minority," Maugham told CNBC.

The affairs of U.S. technology firms in Europe have been in focus over the past few years. Last year, the European Commission, the European Union's executive arm, said Ireland must recover 13 billion euros ($14 billion) in "illegal tax benefits" it granted to Apple. The iPhone maker has appealed the decision. And Google agreed to pay the U.K. £130 million in back taxes last year, in a move that was criticized at the time as a "sweetheart deal." Google at the time said it was going to be paying more tax in the U.K. moving forward.

Maugham said he is going after Uber because the public sees such stories which leads to distrust in the government. He wants to put pressure on the government "to take this behavior more seriously." …

Source: Arjun Kharpal, "Meet the Lawyer Trying to Make US Tech Giants Pay More Taxes. His First Target: Uber," cnbc.com, March 24, 2017.

Key Points in the Article

British lawyer Joylon Maugham has brought a lawsuit against Uber to require the ride-hailing company to pay the United Kingdom's value-added tax (VAT), which is similar to the U.S. sales tax. Uber argues that its drivers are already subject to the same VAT laws that apply to other transportation providers. Uber classifies its drivers as self-employed, and requires the self-employed to pay VAT only if yearly earnings are over £83,000 (approximately $103,000), which is more than most Uber drivers earn. In a 2016 case, however, judges in the United Kingdom ruled that Uber drivers are not self-employed, which would mean that the company, and not its drivers, is subject to the VAT. Uber has appealed this decision, but if unsuccessful, Uber will have to raise fares to cover the 20 percent VAT and could be ordered to pay the tax on past earnings as well.

Uber is not the only U.S. company operating in Europe to be confronted about taxes in recent years. In 2016, the European Union told Ireland that it must recover €13 billion in tax benefits granted to Apple, and Google agreed to pay back taxes to the United Kingdom and also to pay more taxes in the future.

Analyzing the News

(a) Like many other European countries, the United Kingdom charges a value-added tax (VAT) on the purchase of goods and services. The current VAT is 20 percent. Uber has not been paying the VAT, arguing that the company doesn't employ its drivers but instead acts only as an intermediary that connects drivers and passengers. A lawyer has challenged Uber's claim that the company is not required to pay the tax, and, if successful, the result could cost Uber millions of dollars as well as set a precedent for other European countries in which Uber operates.

(b) A court ruled in 2016 that Uber drivers are not self-employed, a decision that Uber has appealed. If Uber loses the appeal, it will have to increase fares as its costs rise because of the VAT. The figure below shows a hypothetical example of the effect of this tax on the market for ride-hailing services like those offered by Uber and Lyft. Without the tax, the equilibrium price is £30 per ride, with a quantity of 12,000 rides being provided each day. With a 20 percent tax (£6), the supply curve shifts up by £6, increasing the price the consumer pays to £33, decreasing the price ride-hailing firms receive to £27, and decreasing the quantity of rides being provided to 8,500. The tax revenue is equal to £51,000 per day (£6 per ride × 8,500 rides). The imposition of the 20 percent tax on Uber rides will generate revenue for the government, but it will also reduce economic efficiency by reducing consumer and producer surplus. Consumers will pay a higher price for rides, which reduces consumer surplus, and firms will receive a lower price per ride, which reduces producer surplus. Some of the reduction in consumer and producer surplus will become tax revenue, but the rest is deadweight loss from the tax, a result of the decrease in the number of rides due to the imposition of the tax. Economic efficiency could also be reduced across Europe if Uber and other ride-hailing services are required to pay a VAT in additional countries.

(c) Uber is just one of several U.S. companies facing increased taxes in Europe. In 2016, the European Commission cited both Apple and Google as companies not paying their fair share of taxes. As with Uber, tax increases for these companies will result in higher prices as less of their goods and services will be produced and consumed; the tax increases will also reduce economic efficiency.

Thinking Critically

1. The figure shows the market for rides before and after the imposition of a 20 percent tax. How can we use the figure to measure the effect the tax has on economic efficiency? Redraw the graph and show the area representing the excess burden created by the implementation of the tax.

2. Uber and other ride-hailing firms may be required to start paying the U.K.'s VAT. The figure shows a hypothetical example of the effects of this tax on the market for rides in the United Kingdom. Redraw the graph to show what would happen if riders, instead of ride-hailing firms, were responsible for directly paying the tax to the government. Explain any differences in price, quantity, and tax incidence.

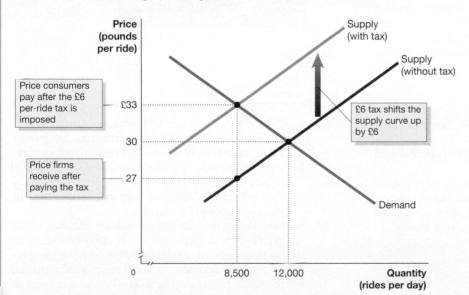

The British government's imposing a 20 percent VAT shifts the supply curve up by £6 in the market for rides arranged using ride-hailing apps, increasing the price paid by the consumer from £30 to £33 and decreasing the price received by ride-hailing firms from £30 to £27.

CHAPTER SUMMARY
AND PROBLEMS

Key Terms

Black market, p. 122

Consumer surplus, p. 110

Deadweight loss, p. 117

Economic efficiency, p. 117

Economic surplus, p. 116

Marginal benefit, p. 110

Marginal cost, p. 114

Price ceiling, p. 110

Price floor, p. 110

Producer surplus, p. 114

Tax incidence, p. 127

 4.1 Consumer Surplus and Producer Surplus, pages 110–115

LEARNING OBJECTIVE: Distinguish between the concepts of consumer surplus and producer surplus.

MyLab Economics Visit www.pearson.com/mylab/economics to complete these exercises online and get instant feedback.

Summary

Although most prices are determined by demand and supply in markets, the government sometimes imposes *price ceilings* and *price floors*. A **price ceiling** is a legally determined maximum price that sellers may charge. A **price floor** is a legally determined minimum price that sellers may receive. Economists analyze the effects of price ceilings and price floors by using the concepts of *consumer surplus, producer surplus,* and *deadweight loss*. **Marginal benefit** is the additional benefit to a consumer from consuming one more unit of a good or service. The demand curve is also a marginal benefit curve. **Consumer surplus** is the difference between the highest price a consumer is willing to pay for a good or service and the actual price the consumer pays. The total amount of consumer surplus in a market is equal to the area below the demand curve and above the market price. **Marginal cost** is the additional cost to a firm of producing one more unit of a good or service. The supply curve is also a marginal cost curve. **Producer surplus** is the difference between the lowest price a firm is willing to accept for a good or service and the price it actually receives. The total amount of producer surplus in a market is equal to the area above the supply curve and below the market price.

Review Questions

1.1 What is marginal benefit? Why is the demand curve referred to as a marginal benefit curve?

1.2 What is marginal cost? Why is the supply curve referred to as a marginal cost curve?

1.3 What is consumer surplus? How does consumer surplus change as the equilibrium price of a good rises or falls?

1.4 What is producer surplus? How does producer surplus change as the equilibrium price of a good rises or falls?

Problems and Applications

1.5 On a shopping trip, Melanie decided to buy a light blue coat that had a price tag of $79.95. When she brought the coat to the store's sales clerk, Melanie was told that the coat was on sale, and she would pay 20 percent less than the price on the tag. After the discount was applied, Melanie paid $63.96, $15.99 less than the original price.

Was the value of Melanie's consumer surplus from this purchase $79.95? $63.96? $15.99? Or some other amount? Briefly explain.

1.6 (Related to the Chapter Opener on page 108) Uber is an app people use to arrange transportation with drivers who use their own cars for this purpose. Customers pay for their rides with the Uber smartphone app. Uber's prices fluctuate with the demand for the service. This "surge pricing" can result in different prices for the same distance traveled at different times of day or days of the week. Annie Lowrey, a writer for the *New York Times*, explained that she paid $13 for a 10 P.M. 2-mile trip in downtown Washington, DC, on New Year's Eve. Three hours later she paid $47 for the return trip to her home. Did she receive negative consumer surplus on her return trip? Briefly explain.

Source: Annie Lowrey, "Is Uber's Surge-Pricing an Example of High Tech Gouging?" *New York Times*, January 10, 2014.

1.7 Consider the information given in the following table on four consumers in the market for premium bottled water.

Consumer	Highest Price Willing to Pay
Jill	$4
Jose	3
Josh	2
Jordan	1

a. If the price of a bottle of premium bottled water is $1.50, what is the total consumer surplus received by these consumers? Illustrate your answer with a graph.

b. Suppose the price of premium bottled water rises to $2.50. Now what is the consumer surplus received by these consumers? Illustrate your answer by using the graph you prepared in part (a).

1.8 Suppose that a frost in Florida reduces the size of the orange crop, which causes the supply curve for oranges to shift to the left. Briefly explain whether consumer surplus will increase or decrease and whether producer surplus will increase or decrease. Use a demand and supply graph to illustrate your answers.

1.9 An article in the *Wall Street Journal* discussed research at Ohio State University that may lead to producing carbon black—an important input in automobile tire making—out of eggshells, tomato skins, and other food waste. According to the article, this research could lead to a reduction in the cost of producing tires.

a. Assuming that the research is successful, use a demand and supply graph to show the effect of these falling costs on consumer surplus in the market for tires.

b. Can we be certain whether these falling costs will increase producer surplus? Briefly explain.

Source: Daniel Akst, "Making Tire Filler from Eggshells" *Wall Street Journal*, March 9, 2017.

1.10 A student makes the following argument: "When a market is in equilibrium, there is no consumer surplus. We know this because in equilibrium, the market price is equal to the price consumers are willing to pay for the good." Briefly explain whether you agree with the student's argument.

1.11 In the following graph, is the consumer surplus larger with demand curve D_1 or demand curve D_2? Briefly explain. Compare the producer surplus with demand curve D_1 and with demand curve D_2.

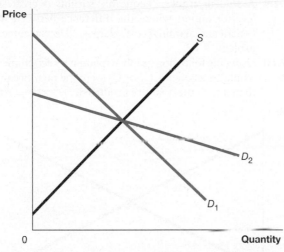

1.12 Assume that the following graph illustrates the market for a breast cancer–fighting drug, without which breast cancer patients cannot survive. What is the consumer surplus in this market? How does it differ from the consumer surplus in the markets you have studied up to this point?

1.13 (Related to the Apply the Concept on page 112) The *Apply the Concept* states that the value of the area representing consumer surplus from Uber's service was $2.88 billion per year for the four cities involved in the study. Use the information from the graph in the *Apply the Concept* to show how this value was calculated. (For a review of how to calculate the area of a triangle, see the appendix to Chapter 1.)

1.14 The following graph shows the market for tickets to a concert that will be held in a local arena that seats 15,000 people. What is the producer surplus in this market? How does it differ from the producer surplus in the markets you have studied up to this point?

4.2 **The Efficiency of Competitive Markets, pages 115–117**

LEARNING OBJECTIVE: Explain the concept of economic efficiency.

MyLab Economics Visit **www.pearson.com/mylab/economics** to complete these exercises online and get instant feedback.

Summary

Equilibrium in a competitive market is economically efficient. **Economic surplus** is the sum of consumer surplus and producer surplus. **Economic efficiency** is a market outcome in which the marginal benefit to consumers from the last unit produced is equal to the marginal cost of production and in which the sum of consumer surplus and producer surplus is at a maximum. When the market price is above or below the equilibrium price, there is a reduction in economic surplus. The reduction in economic surplus resulting from a market not being in competitive equilibrium is called the **deadweight loss**.

Review Questions

2.1 Define *economic surplus* and *deadweight loss*.

2.2 What is economic efficiency? Why do economists define efficiency in this way?

Problems and Applications

2.3 An article about record high avocado prices discussed how avocado crops had suffered from hot weather, droughts, and an invasive beetle that kills avocado trees. Use a demand and supply graph of the avocado market to illustrate the effect of the hot weather, droughts, and invasive beetle. How are producer surplus and consumer surplus affected? Briefly explain.

Source: Rafi Letzter, "Avocado Prices Just Hit a Record High, and Show No Signs of Coming Down. Here's Why," businessinsider.com, November 3, 2016.

2.4 Briefly explain whether you agree with the following statement: "A lower price in a market always increases economic efficiency in that market."

2.5 Briefly explain whether you agree with the following statement: "If at the current quantity, marginal benefit is greater than marginal cost, there will be a deadweight loss in the market. However, there is no deadweight loss when marginal cost is greater than marginal benefit."

2.6 According to an article in the *Wall Street Journal*, restaurant chains, including Subway, McDonald's, and Chick-fil-A, have begun serving only chickens that were raised without being fed antibiotics. Using this method of raising chickens increases their cost. Suppose that consumers react to the news of restaurants selling antibiotic-free chicken sandwiches by increasing their demand for the sandwiches. Can you tell whether economic surplus will increase in the market for chicken sandwiches? Use a graph of the market for chicken sandwiches to illustrate your answer.

Source: Jacob Bunge, "Perdue Farms Eliminated Antibiotics from Chicken Supply," *Wall Street Journal*, October 6, 2016.

2.7 Briefly explain whether you agree with the following statement: "If consumer surplus in a market increases, producer surplus must decrease."

2.8 Using the following graph, show the effects on consumer surplus and producer surplus of an increase in supply from S_1 to S_2. By how much does economic surplus increase?

2.9 A student argues: "Economic surplus is greatest at the level of output where the difference between marginal benefit and marginal cost is largest." Do you agree? Briefly explain.

2.10 Using the following graph, explain why economic surplus would be smaller if Q_1 or Q_3 were the quantity produced than if Q_2 is the quantity produced.

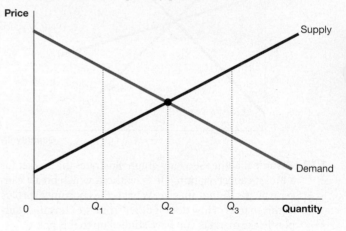

4.3 **Government Intervention in the Market: Price Floors and Price Ceilings, pages 118–126**

LEARNING OBJECTIVE: Explain the economic effect of government-imposed price floors and price ceilings.

MyLab Economics   Visit **www.pearson.com/mylab/economics** to complete these exercises online and get instant feedback.

Summary

Producers or consumers who are dissatisfied with the equilibrium in a market can attempt to convince the government to impose a price floor or a price ceiling. Price floors usually increase producer surplus, decrease consumer surplus, and cause a deadweight loss. Price ceilings usually increase consumer surplus, reduce producer surplus, and cause a deadweight loss. The results of the government imposing price ceilings and price floors are that some people win, some people lose, and a loss of economic efficiency occurs. Price ceilings and price floors can lead to a **black market**, in which buying and selling take place at prices that violate government price regulations. Positive analysis is concerned with *what is*, and normative analysis is concerned with *what should be*. Positive analysis shows that price ceilings and price floors cause deadweight losses. Whether these policies are desirable or undesirable, though, is a normative question.

Review Questions

3.1 Why do some consumers tend to favor price controls while others tend to oppose them?

3.2 Do producers tend to favor price floors or price ceilings? Briefly explain.

3.3 What is a black market? Under what circumstances do black markets arise?

3.4 Can economic analysis provide a final answer to the question of whether the government should intervene in markets by imposing price ceilings and price floors? Briefly explain.

Problems and Applications

3.5 The following graph shows the market for apples. Assume that the government has imposed a price floor of $10 per crate.

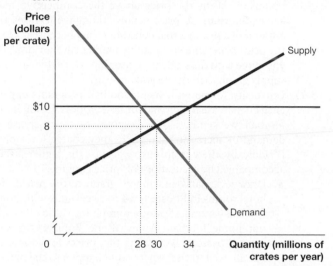

a. How many crates of apples will be sold to consumers after the price floor has been imposed?

b. Will there be a shortage or a surplus of apples? If there is a shortage or a surplus, how large will it be?

c. Will apple producers benefit from the price floor? If so, explain how they will benefit.

3.6 Use the information on the kumquat market in the table to answer the following questions.

Price (per crate)	Quantity Demanded (millions of crates per year)	Quantity Supplied (millions of crates per year)
$10	120	20
15	110	60
20	100	100
25	90	140
30	80	180
35	70	220

a. What are the equilibrium price and quantity? How much revenue do kumquat producers receive when the market is in equilibrium? Draw a graph showing the market equilibrium and the area representing the revenue kumquat producers receive.

b. Suppose the federal government decides to impose a price floor of $30 per crate. Now how many crates of kumquats will consumers purchase? How much revenue will kumquat producers receive? Assume that the government does not purchase any surplus kumquats. On your graph from part (a), show the price floor, the change in the quantity of kumquats purchased, and the revenue kumquat producers receive after the price floor is imposed.

c. Suppose the government imposes a price floor of $30 per crate and purchases any surplus kumquats from producers. Now how much revenue will kumquat producers receive? How much will the government spend on purchasing surplus kumquats? On your graph from part (a), show the area representing the amount the government spends to purchase the surplus kumquats.

3.7 Suppose that the government sets a price floor for milk that is above the competitive equilibrium price and that the government does not purchase any surplus milk.

a. Draw a graph showing this situation. Be sure your graph shows the competitive equilibrium price, the price floor, the quantity that would be sold in competitive equilibrium, and the quantity that would be sold with the price floor.

b. Compare the economic surplus in this market when there is a price floor and when there is not.

3.8 In Allentown, Pennsylvania, in the summer of 2014, the average price of a gallon of gasoline was $3.68—a 22-cent increase from the year before. Many consumers were upset by the increase. One consumer was quoted in a local newspaper as saying, "It's crazy. The government should step in." Suppose the government had stepped in and imposed a price ceiling equal to the old price of $3.46 per gallon.

a. Draw a graph showing the effect of the price ceiling on the market for gasoline. Be sure that your graph shows:
  i. The price and quantity of gasoline before and after the price ceiling is imposed
  ii. The areas representing consumer surplus and producer surplus before and after the price ceiling is imposed
  iii. The area of deadweight loss

b. Will the consumer who was complaining about the increase in the price of gasoline definitely be made better off by the price ceiling? Briefly explain.

Source: Sam Kennedy, "Valley Feeling Pain at the Pump," (Allentown, PA) *Morning Call*, June 21, 2014.

3.9 (Related to the Apply the Concept on page 119) An article in the *Wall Street Journal* noted that a study by the U.S. Congressional Budget Office "estimated raising the minimum wage to $10.10 an hour would reduce U.S. employment by 500,000 but lift 900,000 Americans out of poverty." Why might raising the minimum wage reduce employment? How would it raise some people out of poverty? What effect might these estimates have on a *normative* analysis of the minimum wage?

Source: Julie Jargon and Eric Morath, "As Wage Debate Rages, Some Have Made the Shift," *Wall Street Journal*, April 8, 2014.

3.10 If San Francisco were to repeal its rent control law, would the prices for short-term rentals in the city listed on Airbnb and other peer-to-peer sites be likely to rise or fall? Briefly explain.

3.11 The competitive equilibrium rent in the city of Lowell is currently $1,000 per month. The government decides to enact rent control and establish a price ceiling of $750 per month for apartments. Briefly explain whether rent control is likely to make each of the following people better or worse off.

a. Someone currently renting an apartment in Lowell

b. Someone who will be moving to Lowell next year and who intends to rent an apartment

c. A landlord who intends to abide by the rent control law

d. A landlord who intends to ignore the law and illegally charge the highest rent possible for his apartments

3.12 **(Related to the Don't Let This Happen to You on page 122)** Briefly explain whether you agree with the following statement: "If there is a shortage of a good, it must be scarce, but there is not a shortage of every scarce good."

3.13 **(Related to Solved Problem 4.3 on page 123)** Use the information on the market for apartments in Bay City in the table to answer the following questions.

Rent	Quantity Demanded	Quantity Supplied
$500	375,000	225,000
600	350,000	250,000
700	325,000	275,000
800	300,000	300,000
900	275,000	325,000
1,000	250,000	350,000

a. In the absence of rent control, what is the equilibrium rent, and what is the equilibrium quantity of apartments rented? Draw a demand and supply graph of the market for apartments to illustrate your answer. In equilibrium, will there be any renters who are unable to find an apartment to rent or any landlords who are unable to find a renter for an apartment?

b. Suppose the government sets a ceiling of $600 per month on rents. What is the quantity of apartments demanded, and what is the quantity of apartments supplied?

c. Assume that all landlords abide by the law in part (b). Use a demand and supply graph to illustrate the effect of this price ceiling on the market for apartments. Be sure to indicate on your graph each of the following: (i) the area representing consumer surplus after the price ceiling has been imposed, (ii) the area representing producer surplus after the price ceiling has been imposed, and (iii) the area representing the deadweight loss after the price ceiling has been imposed.

d. Assume that the quantity of apartments supplied is the same as you determined in (b), but now assume that landlords ignore the law and rent this quantity of apartments for the highest rent they can get. Briefly explain what this rent will be.

3.14 **(Related to the Apply the Concept on page 124)** According to an article in the *New York Times*, the Venezuelan government "imposes strict price controls that are intended to make a range of foods and other goods more affordable for the poor. They are often the very products that are the hardest to find."

a. Why would imposing price controls on goods make the goods hard to find?

b. One of the goods subject to price controls was toothpaste. Draw a graph to illustrate this situation. On your graph, be sure to indicate the areas representing consumer surplus, producer surplus, and deadweight loss.

Source: William Neuman, "With Venezuelan Cupboards Bare, Some Blame Price Controls," *New York Times*, April 20, 2012.

3.15 **(Related to the Apply the Concept on page 124)** According to a news story, in late 2016, a recent college graduate

in Caracas, Venezuela, hadn't eaten meat in a month. He was quoted as saying it was "not because we can't find meat, but because it's very expensive." Meat, like other food in Venezuela, was subject to a price ceiling. Why then was it very expensive? Illustrate your answer with a graph.

Source: Patrick Gillespie and Osmary Hernandez, "Venezuela's Food Prices Skyrocket as People Go Hungry," cnn.com, October 21, 2016.

3.16 A student makes the following argument: "A price floor reduces the amount of a product that consumers buy because it keeps the price above the competitive market equilibrium. A price ceiling, though, increases the amount of a product that consumers buy because it keeps the price below the competitive market equilibrium." Do you agree with the student's reasoning? Use a demand and supply graph to illustrate your answer.

3.17 University towns with major football programs experience an increase in demand for hotel rooms during home football weekends. Hotels respond to the increase in demand by increasing the prices they charge for rooms. Periodically, there is an outcry against the higher prices, accompanied by accusations of "price gouging."

a. Draw a demand and supply graph of the market for hotel rooms in Boostertown for weekends with home football games and another graph for weekends without home football games. If the Boostertown city council passes a law stating that prices for rooms are not allowed to rise, what would happen to the market for hotel rooms during home football game weekends? Show your answer on your graph.

b. If the prices of hotel rooms are not allowed to increase, what will be the effect on out-of-town football fans?

c. How might the city council's law affect the supply of hotel rooms over time? Briefly explain.

d. University towns are not the only places that face peak and nonpeak "seasons." Can you think of other locations that face a large increase in demand for hotel rooms during particular times of the year? Why do we typically not see laws limiting the prices hotels can charge during peak seasons?

3.18 Suppose that initially the gasoline market is in equilibrium, at a price of $2.50 per gallon and a quantity of 45 million gallons per month. Then a war in the Middle East disrupts imports of oil into the United States, shifting the supply curve for gasoline from S_1 to S_2. The price of gasoline begins to rise, and consumers protest. The federal government responds by setting a price ceiling of $2.50 per gallon. Use the graph to answer the following questions.

a. If there were no price ceiling, what would be the equilibrium price of gasoline, the quantity of gasoline demanded, and the quantity of gasoline supplied? Now assume that the price ceiling is imposed and that there is no black market in gasoline. What are the price of gasoline, the quantity of gasoline demanded, and the quantity of gasoline supplied? How large is the shortage of gasoline?

b. Assume that the price ceiling is imposed, and there is no black market in gasoline. Show on the graph the areas representing consumer surplus, producer surplus, and deadweight loss.

c. Now assume that there is a black market, and the price of gasoline rises to the maximum that consumers are willing to pay for the amount supplied by producers, at $2.50 per gallon. Show on the graph the areas representing producer surplus, consumer surplus, and deadweight loss.

d. Are consumers made better off with the price ceiling than without it? Briefly explain.

3.19 An editorial in the *Economist* magazine discusses the fact that in most countries—including the United States—it is illegal for individuals to buy or sell body parts, such as kidneys.

a. Draw a demand and supply graph for the market for kidneys. Show on your graph the legal maximum price of zero and indicate the quantity of kidneys supplied at this price. (*Hint:* Because we know that some kidneys are donated, the quantity supplied will not be zero.)

b. The editorial argues that buying and selling kidneys should be legalized:

> With proper regulation, a kidney market would be a big improvement over the current sorry state of affairs. Sellers could be checked for disease and drug use, and cared for after operations. ... Buyers would get better kidneys, faster. Both sellers and buyers would do better than in the illegal market, where much of the money goes to middlemen.

Do you agree with this argument? Should the government treat kidneys like other goods and allow the market to determine the price?

Source: "Psst, Wanna Buy a Kidney?" *Economist,* November 18, 2006.

4.4 The Economic Effect of Taxes, pages 126–131

LEARNING OBJECTIVE: Analyze the economic effect of taxes.

MyLab Economics Visit **www.pearson.com/mylab/economics** to complete these exercises online and get instant feedback.

Summary

Most taxes result in a loss of consumer surplus, a loss of producer surplus, and a deadweight loss. The true burden of a tax is not just the amount consumers and producers pay to the government but also includes the deadweight loss. The deadweight loss from a tax is called the excess burden of the tax. **Tax incidence** is the actual division of the burden of a tax. In most cases, consumers and firms share the burden of a tax levied on a good or service.

Review Questions

4.1 What is meant by *tax incidence?*

4.2 What do economists mean by an *efficient tax?*

4.3 Does who is legally responsible for paying a tax—buyers or sellers—make a difference in the amount of tax each pays? Briefly explain.

4.4 As explained in the chapter, economic efficiency is a market outcome in which the marginal benefit to consumers of the last unit produced is equal to its marginal cost of production. Using this explanation of economic efficiency, explain why a tax creates a deadweight loss.

Problems and Applications

4.5 Suppose that the current equilibrium price of a quarter-pound hamburger is $5, and 10 million quarter-pound hamburgers are sold per month. After the federal government imposes a tax of $0.50 per hamburger, the equilibrium price of hamburgers rises to $5.20, and the equilibrium quantity falls to 9 million. Illustrate this situation with a demand and supply graph. Be sure your graph shows the equilibrium price before and after the tax; the equilibrium quantity before and after the tax; and the areas representing consumer surplus after the tax, producer surplus after the tax, tax revenue collected by the government, and deadweight loss.

4.6 The following graph shows the effect of a tax imposed on soft drinks. Use this graph to answer the questions.

a. Which areas in the graph represent the excess burden (deadweight loss) of the tax?

b. Which areas represent the revenues collected by the government from the tax?

c. Would economists consider this tax to be efficient? Briefly explain.

4.7 Use the following graph of the market for cigarettes to answer the questions.

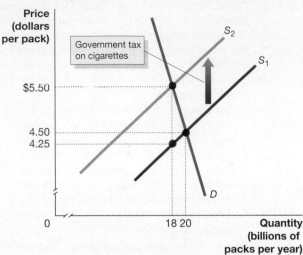

a. According to the graph, how much is the government tax on cigarettes?

b. What price do producers receive after paying the tax?

c. How much tax revenue does the government collect?

d. How would the graph be different if the tax were collected from the buyers of cigarettes?

e. If the tax were collected from buyers, what would be the new equilibrium price that buyers pay producers of cigarettes?

f. Including the tax, what would be the total amount that cigarette buyers pay per pack?

4.8 (Related to Solved Problem 4.4 on page 128) Suppose the federal government decides to impose a sales tax of $1.00 per pizza. Briefly explain whether you agree with the following statement, made by a representative of the pizza industry:

> The pizza industry is very competitive. As a result, pizza sellers will have to pay the whole tax because they are unable to pass any of it on to consumers in the form of higher prices. Therefore, a sales tax of $1.00 per pizza will result in pizza sellers receiving $1.00 less on each pizza sold, after paying the tax.

Illustrate your answer with a graph.

4.9 (Related to the Apply the Concept on page 130) According to a news story, Pennsylvania's liquor tax is "paid by the seller—the restaurant or bar owner—when the seller buys liquor from state-run wine and spirit stores." Briefly explain the effect of how liquor taxes in Pennsylvania are collected has on the price of a glass of wine a consumer purchases in a restaurant in the state.

Source: Matt Assad, "How Booze Brings Heady Development," (Allentown, PA) *Morning Call*, February 22, 2015.

4.10 (Related to the Apply the Concept on page 130) Suppose the government imposes a payroll tax of $1 per hour of work and collects the tax from employers. Use a graph for the market for labor to show the effect of the payroll tax, assuming the special case of a vertical supply curve of labor. By how much does the new equilibrium wage that employers pay workers fall?

Critical Thinking Exercises

CT4.1 For this exercise, your instructor may assign you to a group. The chapter describes how a market can be economically efficient. Before you took this class, you might have heard someone say that "markets are efficient." Compare the description of efficiency in this chapter with what you thought about efficiency prior to taking this class. Write up your thoughts in a paragraph (that you may be asked to turn in or to discuss in class). In your group, each member should make the comparison. Then, as a group, prepare a one-paragraph summary of what you discussed and be prepared to turn in the summary or discuss it with the class.

CT4.2 Suppose that the mayor of New York abolishes rent control. A friend of yours who lives in New York complains about the higher apartment rents that result. This friend has never taken an economics class. Explain to your friend why the apartment market is now more efficient because rent control has been abolished. Your explanation should be two paragraphs long and contain a visual, such as a graph or table, that illustrates your argument. Include in your answer whether you think it's likely that your friend will change her opinion of rent control on the basis of your analysis.

CT4.3 In 1948, the United States experienced a potato surplus. Watch the video clip "Farm Journalist Potato Surplus" located in the MyLab course available for this text. For there to be a surplus, what must be happening in this market? Explain your reasoning in a paragraph and be sure to use an appropriate graph.

Appendix

Quantitative Demand and Supply Analysis

LEARNING OBJECTIVE: Use quantitative demand and supply analysis.

Graphs help us understand economic change *qualitatively*. For instance, a demand and supply graph can tell us that if household incomes rise, the demand curve for a normal good will shift to the right, and the price of the good will rise. Often, though, economists, business managers, and policymakers want to know more than the qualitative direction of change; they want a *quantitative estimate* of the size of the change.

In this chapter, we carried out a qualitative analysis of rent controls. We saw that imposing rent controls involves a trade-off: Renters as a group gain, but landlords lose, and the market for apartments becomes less efficient, as shown by the deadweight loss. To better evaluate rent controls, we need to know more than just that these gains and losses exist; we need to know how large they are. A quantitative analysis of rent controls will tell us how large the gains and losses are.

Demand and Supply Equations

The first step in a quantitative analysis is to supplement our use of demand and supply curves with demand and supply *equations*. Economists use data on prices, quantities, and other economic variables to statistically estimate equations for demand and supply curves. For example, suppose that economists have estimated that the demand for apartments in New York City is:

$$Q^D = 4,750,000 - 1,000P,$$

and the supply of apartments is:

$$Q^S = -1,000,000 + 1,300P.$$

We have used Q^D for the quantity of apartments demanded per month, Q^S for the quantity of apartments supplied per month, and P for the apartment rent, in dollars per month. In reality, both the quantity of apartments demanded and the quantity of apartments supplied will depend on more than just the rental price of apartments in New York City. The demand for apartments in New York City will also depend, for instance, on the average incomes of families in the New York area and on the rents of apartments in the surrounding cities. For simplicity, we will ignore these other factors.

With no government intervention, we know that at competitive market equilibrium, the quantity demanded must equal the quantity supplied, or:

$$Q^D = Q^S.$$

We can use this equation, which is called an *equilibrium condition*, to solve for the equilibrium monthly apartment rent by setting the quantity demanded from the demand equation equal to the quantity supplied from the supply equation:

$$4,750,000 - 1,000P = -1,000,000 + 1,300P$$

$$5,750,000 = 2,300P$$

$$P = \frac{5,750,000}{2,300} = \$2,500.$$

We can then substitute this price back into either the supply equation or the demand equation to find the equilibrium quantity of apartments rented:

Figure 4A.1

Graphing Demand and Supply Equations

After statistically estimating demand and supply equations, we can use the equations to draw demand and supply curves. In this case, the equilibrium rent for apartments is $2,500 per month, and the equilibrium quantity of apartments rented is 2,250,000. The demand equation tells us that at a rent of $4,750, the quantity of apartments demanded will be zero. The supply equation tells us that at a rent of $769, the quantity of apartments supplied will be zero. The areas representing consumer surplus and producer surplus are also indicated on the graph.

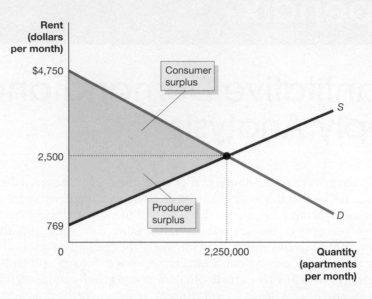

$$Q^D = 4,750,000 - 1,000P = 4,750,000 - 1,000(2,500) = 2,250,000,$$

or:

$$Q^S = -1,000,000 + 1,300P = -1,000,000 + 1,300(2,500) = 2,250,000.$$

Figure 4A.1 illustrates the information from these equations in a graph. The figure shows the values for rent when both the quantity supplied and the quantity demanded are zero. These values can be calculated from the demand and supply equations by setting Q^D and Q^S equal to zero and solving for price:

$$Q^D = 0 = 4,750,000 - 1,000P$$

$$P = \frac{4,750,000}{1,000} = \$4,750$$

and:

$$Q^S = 0 = -1,000,000 + 1,300P$$

$$P = \frac{-1,000,000}{-1,300} = \$769.23.$$

MyLab Economics Concept Check

Calculating Consumer Surplus and Producer Surplus

Figure 4A.1 shows consumer surplus and producer surplus in this market.

Recall that the sum of consumer surplus and producer surplus equals the net benefit that renters and landlords receive from participating in the market for apartments. We can use the values from the demand and supply equations to calculate the value of consumer surplus and producer surplus. Remember that consumer surplus is the area below the demand curve and above the line representing market price. Notice that this area forms a right triangle because the demand curve is a straight line—it is *linear*. As we noted in the appendix to Chapter 1, the area of a triangle is equal to ½ × Base × Height. In this case, the area is:

$$\frac{1}{2} \times (2,250,000) \times (4,750 - 2,500) = \$2,531,250,000.$$

So, this calculation tells us that the consumer surplus in the market for rental apartments in New York City is about $2.5 billion per month.

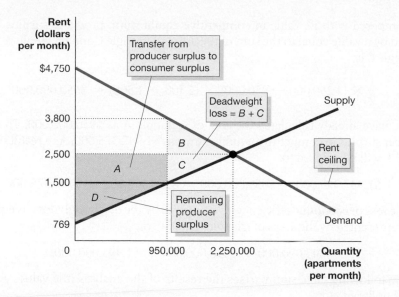

MyLab Economics Animation

Figure 4A.2

Calculating the Economic Effect of Rent Controls

Once we have estimated equations for the demand and supply of rental housing, a graph can guide our numerical estimates of the economic effects of rent control. Consumer surplus falls by an amount equal to the area of triangle B and increases by an amount equal to the area of rectangle A. Producer surplus falls by an amount equal to the sum of the areas of rectangle A and triangle C. The remaining producer surplus is equal to the area of triangle D. Deadweight loss is equal to the sum of the areas of triangles B and C.

We can calculate producer surplus in a similar way. Remember that producer surplus is the area above the supply curve and below the line representing market price. Because the supply curve is also a straight line, producer surplus in the figure is equal to the area of the triangle:

$$\frac{1}{2} \times 2,250,000 \times (2,500 - 769) = \$1,947,375,000.$$

This calculation tells us that the producer surplus in the market for rental apartments in New York City is about \$1.9 billion per month.

We can use the same type of analysis to measure the effect of rent control on consumer surplus, producer surplus, and economic efficiency. For instance, suppose the city imposes a rent ceiling of \$1,500 per month. Figure 4A.2 can help guide us as we measure the effect.

First, we can calculate the quantity of apartments that will actually be rented by substituting the rent ceiling of \$1,500 into the supply equation:

$$Q^S = -1,000,000 + (1,300 \times 1,500) = 950,000.$$

We also need to know the price on the demand curve when the quantity of apartments is 950,000. We can do this by substituting 950,000 for quantity in the demand equation and solving for price:

$$950,000 = 4,750,000 - 1,000P$$

$$P = \frac{-3,8000,000}{-1,000} = \$3,800.$$

Compared with its value in competitive equilibrium, consumer surplus has been reduced by a value equal to the area of triangle B but increased by a value equal to the area of rectangle A. The area of triangle B is:

$$\frac{1}{2} \times (2,250,000 - 950,000) \times (3,800 - 2,500) = \$845,000,000,$$

and the area of rectangle A is Base × Height, or:

$$(\$2,500 - \$1,500) \times (950,000) = \$950,000,000.$$

The value of consumer surplus in competitive equilibrium was \$2,531,250,000. As a result of the rent ceiling, it will be increased to:

$$(\$2,531,250,000 + 950,000,000) - \$845,000,000 = \$2,636,250,000.$$

Compared with its value in competitive equilibrium, producer surplus has been reduced by a value equal to the sum of the areas of triangle C and rectangle A. The area of triangle C is:

$$\frac{1}{2} \times (2,250,000 - 950,000) \times (2,500 - 1,500) = \$650,000,000.$$

We have already calculated the area of rectangle A as \$950,000,000. The value of producer surplus in competitive equilibrium was \$1,947,375,000. As a result of the rent ceiling, it will be reduced to:

$$\$1,947,375,000 - \$650,000,000 - \$950,000,000 = \$347,375,000.$$

The loss of economic efficiency, as measured by the deadweight loss, is equal to the value represented by the areas of triangles B and C, or:

$$\$845,000,000 + \$650,000,000 = \$1,495,000,000.$$

The following table summarizes the results of the analysis (the values are in millions of dollars):

Consumer Surplus		Producer Surplus		Deadweight Loss	
Competitive Equilibrium	Rent Control	Competitive Equilibrium	Rent Control	Competitive Equilibrium	Rent Control
\$2,531	\$2,636	\$1,947	\$347	\$0	\$1,495

Qualitatively, we know that imposing rent control will make consumers better off, make landlords worse off, and decrease economic efficiency. The advantage of the analysis we have just gone through is that it puts dollar values on the qualitative results. We can now see how much consumers have gained, how much landlords have lost, and how great the decline in economic efficiency has been. Sometimes the quantitative results can be surprising. Notice, for instance, that after the imposition of rent control, the deadweight loss is actually much greater than the remaining producer surplus. Of course, these results are dependent on the numbers we chose for the demand and supply curve equations. Choosing different numbers would have changed the results.

Economists often study issues where the qualitative results of actions are apparent, even to non-economists. You don't have to be an economist to understand who wins and who loses from rent control or that if a company cuts the price of its product, its sales will increase. Business managers, policymakers, and the general public do, however, need economists to measure quantitatively the effects of different actions—including policies such as rent control—so that they can better assess the results of these actions.

MyLab Economics Study Plan

MyLab Economics Concept Check

 4A

Quantitative Demand and Supply Analysis, pages 141–144

LEARNING OBJECTIVE: Use quantitative demand and supply analysis.

MyLab Economics Visit **www.pearson.com/mylab/economics** to complete these exercises online and get instant feedback.

Review Questions

4A.1 In a linear demand equation, what economic information is conveyed by the intercept on the price axis? Similarly, what economic information is conveyed by the intercept on the price axis in a linear supply equation?

4A.2 Suppose you were assigned the task of choosing a price that maximizes economic surplus in a market. What price would you choose? Why?

4A.3 Consumer surplus is used as a measure of a consumer's net benefit from purchasing a good or service. Explain why consumer surplus is a measure of net benefit.

4A.4 Why would economists use the term *deadweight loss* to describe the effect on consumer surplus and producer surplus from a price control?

Problems and Applications

4A.5 Suppose that you have been hired to analyze the effect on employment from the imposition of a minimum wage in the labor market. Further suppose that you estimate the demand and supply functions for labor, where L stands for the quantity of labor (measured in thousands of workers) and W stands for the wage rate (measured in dollars per hour):

$$\text{Demand: } L^D = 100 - 4W$$

$$\text{Supply: } L^S = 6W$$

First, calculate the free market equilibrium wage and quantity of labor. Now suppose the proposed minimum wage is $12. How large will the surplus of labor in this market be?

4A.6 The following graphs illustrate the markets for two different types of labor. Suppose that an identical minimum wage is imposed in both markets. In which market will the minimum wage have the largest impact on employment? Why?

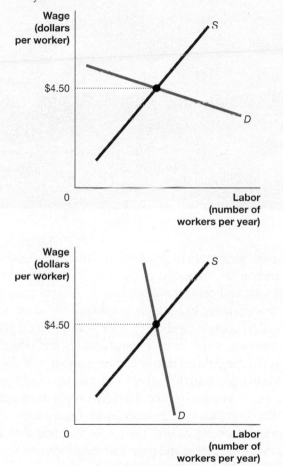

4A.7 Suppose that you are the vice president of operations of a manufacturing firm that sells an industrial lubricant in a competitive market. Further suppose that your economist gives you the following demand and supply functions:

$$\text{Demand: } Q^D = 45 - 2P$$

$$\text{Supply: } Q^S = -15 + P$$

What is the consumer surplus in this market? What is the producer surplus?

4A.8 The following graph shows a market in which a price floor of $3.00 per unit has been imposed. Calculate the values of each of the following.

a. The deadweight loss
b. The transfer of producer surplus to consumers or the transfer of consumer surplus to producers
c. Producer surplus after the price floor is imposed
d. Consumer surplus after the price floor is imposed

4A.9 Construct a table like the one in this appendix on page 144 but assume that the rent ceiling is $2,000 rather than $1,500.

Externalities, Environmental Policy, and Public Goods

Why Does ExxonMobil Want to Pay a Carbon Tax?

Why would the head of an oil company advocate taxing the company's own product? In 2017, ExxonMobil's chief executive officer (CEO), Darren Woods, did just that. He confirmed the company's support for a carbon tax, under which the federal government would tax energy consumption on the basis of the carbon content of the energy. For example, oil refiners like ExxonMobil would pay a tax on the carbon content of the oil they were refining into products such as gasoline and home heating oil, and electric utilities like Pacific, Gas, & Electric (PG&E) would pay a tax on the carbon content of the coal and natural gas they burn to generate electricity. The burning of fossil fuels like oil and coal generates carbon dioxide, CO_2, a "greenhouse gas" that most scientists believe contributes to global warming.

Public opinion polls show that a majority of people believe that the government should regulate greenhouse gases. Most economists agree that government policy should attempt to reduce these gases, but they disagree with the public about which government policies would be best. The public tends to support government rules that require firms to use particular methods to reduce pollution—for example, by requiring that automobile companies produce cars with better fuel efficiency. Many economists believe that using these *command-and-control policies* is a less economically efficient way to reduce pollution than is using *market-based policies* that rely on economic incentives rather than on administrative rules.

A carbon tax is an example of a market-based policy that provides households and firms with an economic incentive to reduce their use of those fuels by raising their price. Government policies to reduce pollution, including the carbon tax, have been controversial, however. Some businesses oppose the carbon tax because they believe it

KingWu/iStock/Getty Images

will raise their costs of production. Other businesses view the carbon tax favorably, particularly in comparison with command-and-control policies that they see as more costly and less effective. In addition, command-and-control policies can be complex and difficult for government regulators to administer, so oil firms, electric utilities, and other firms subject to the policies face uncertainty about how they will be able to operate in the future. A carbon tax would provide these firms with greater certainty. According to an article in the *Wall Street Journal*, a spokesman for ExxonMobil argued, "A straightforward carbon tax . . . is far preferable to the patchwork of current and potential regulations on the state, federal and international levels."

As we will see in this chapter, economic analysis plays an important role in the debate over environmental policies.

Sources: Amy Harder and Bradley Olsen, "Exxon Touts Carbon Tax to Oil Industry," *Wall Street Journal*, June 30, 2016; Suzanne McCarron, "Letter: Exxon Favors a Carbon Tax," *New York Times*, December 30, 2016; and Paola Sapienza and Luigi Zingales, "Economic Experts vs. Average Americans," *American Economic Review, Papers and Proceedings*, Vol. 103, No. 3, May 2013, pp. 636–642.

Chapter Outline & Learning Objectives

Economics in Your Life & Career

Giving Advice on the "Best" Level of Pollution

Policymakers debate alternative approaches for achieving the goal of reducing carbon dioxide emissions. Suppose you have taken a job in Washington, DC, as a policy aide to a U.S. senator. The senator asks you, "If carbon dioxide emissions hurt the environment, shouldn't the federal government take action to eliminate them completely?" How do you respond? As you read this chapter, try to answer this question. You can check your answer against the one we provide on **page 173** at the end of this chapter.

Externality A benefit or cost that affects someone who is not directly involved in the production or consumption of a good or service.

Pollution is a part of economic life. Consumers create air pollution by burning gasoline to power their cars and natural gas to heat their homes. Firms create air pollution when they produce electricity, pesticides, or plastics, among other products. Utilities such as electric power plants produce sulfur dioxide when they burn coal to generate electricity. Sulfur dioxide contributes to acid rain, which can damage trees, crops, and buildings. The burning of fossil fuels generates carbon dioxide and other greenhouse gases that can increase global warming.

Pollution is just one example of an **externality**, which is a benefit or cost that affects someone who is not directly involved in the production or consumption of a good or service. In the case of air pollution, there is a *negative externality* because, for example, people with asthma may bear a cost even though they were not involved in the buying or selling of the electricity that caused the pollution. In the case of medical research, there is a *positive externality* because people who are not directly involved in producing it or paying for it can benefit.

A competitive market usually does a good job of producing the economically efficient quantity of a good or service, but not when there is an externality in the market. When there is a negative externality, the market may produce a quantity of the good that is greater than the efficient amount. When there is a positive externality, the market may produce a quantity that is less than the efficient amount. Government interventions in the economy—such as the price floors on agricultural products or price ceilings on rents we discussed in Chapter 4, Section 4.3—can reduce economic efficiency. But, when there are externalities, government intervention may actually *increase* economic efficiency and enhance the well-being of society. The way in which government intervenes is important, however. Economists can help policymakers ensure that government programs are as efficient as possible.

In this chapter, we explore how best to deal with the problems resulting from pollution and other externalities. We also look at *public goods*, such as national defense, which may not be produced at all unless the government produces them.

5.1　Externalities and Economic Efficiency

LEARNING OBJECTIVE: Identify examples of positive and negative externalities and use graphs to show how externalities affect economic efficiency.

When you consume a Big Mac, only you benefit, but when you consume a college education, other people also benefit. College-educated people are less likely to commit crimes, and by being better-informed voters, they are more likely to contribute to better government policies. So, although you capture most of the benefits of your college education, you do not capture all of them.

When you buy a Big Mac, the price you pay covers all of the cost McDonald's incurs in producing the Big Mac. When you buy electricity from a utility that burns coal and generates carbon dioxide, though, the price you pay covers some of the costs the utility incurs but does not cover the cost of the damage carbon dioxide does to the environment.

So, there is a *positive externality* in the production of college educations because people who do not pay for them will nonetheless benefit from them. There is a *negative externality* in the generation of electricity. For example, if fish and wildlife have disappeared from a lake because of acid rain generated by a utility, people who live near the lake incur a cost—even though they may not purchase electricity from that utility.

The Effect of Externalities

Externalities interfere with the *economic efficiency* of a market equilibrium. A competitive market achieves economic efficiency by maximizing the sum of consumer surplus and producer surplus (see Chapter 4, Section 4.2). *But that result holds only if there are no externalities in production or consumption.* An externality can cause a difference between the *private cost* of production and the *social cost*:

- The **private cost** is the cost borne by the producer of a good or service.
- The **social cost** is the total cost of producing a good or service, and it is equal to the private cost plus any external cost, such as the cost of pollution.

Unless there is an externality, the private cost and the social cost are equal.

An externality can also cause a difference between the *private benefit* from consumption and the *social benefit*:

- The **private benefit** is the benefit received by the consumer of a good or service.
- The **social benefit** is the total benefit from consuming a good or service, and it is equal to the private benefit plus any external benefit, such as the benefit to others resulting from your college education.

Unless there is an externality, the private benefit and the social benefit are equal.

Private cost The cost borne by the producer of a good or service.

Social cost The total cost of producing a good or service, including both the private cost and any external cost.

Private benefit The benefit received by the consumer of a good or service.

Social benefit The total benefit from consuming a good or service, including both the private benefit and any external benefit.

How a Negative Externality in Production Reduces Economic Efficiency

Typically, economists assume that the producer of a good or service must bear all the costs of production. But we now know that this assumption is not always true. In the production of electricity, private costs are borne by the utility, but some external costs of pollution are borne by people who are not customers of the utility. The social cost of producing electricity is the sum of the private cost plus the external cost. Figure 5.1 shows the effect on the market for electricity of a negative externality in production.

S_1 is the market supply curve and represents only the private costs that utilities have to bear in generating electricity. Firms will supply an additional unit of a good or service only if they receive a price equal to the additional cost of producing that unit, so a supply curve represents the *marginal cost* of producing a good or service (see Chapter 4, Section 4.1). If utilities also had to bear the cost of pollution, the supply curve would be S_2, which represents the true marginal social cost of generating electricity. The equilibrium with price $P_{Efficient}$ and quantity $Q_{Efficient}$ is efficient. The equilibrium with price P_{Market} and quantity Q_{Market} is not efficient.

To see why, remember that an equilibrium is economically efficient if economic surplus—which is the sum of consumer surplus plus producer surplus—is at a maximum (see Chapter 4, Section 4.2). When economic surplus is at a maximum, the net benefit to society from the production of the good or service is at a maximum.

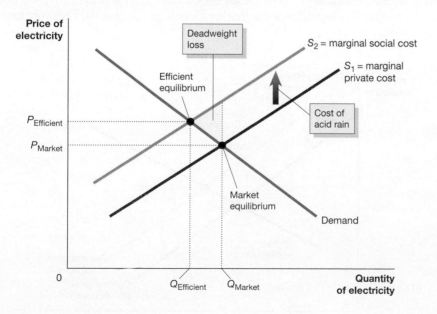

MyLab Economics Animation

Figure 5.1

The Effect of Pollution on Economic Efficiency

Because utilities do not bear the cost of acid rain, they produce electricity beyond the economically efficient level. Supply curve S_1 represents only the marginal private cost that the utility has to pay. Supply curve S_2 represents the marginal social cost, which includes the costs to those affected by acid rain. If the supply curve were S_2 rather than S_1, market equilibrium would occur at price $P_{Efficient}$ and quantity $Q_{Efficient}$, the economically efficient level of output. But, when the supply curve is S_1, the market equilibrium occurs at price P_{Market} and quantity Q_{Market} where there is a deadweight loss equal to the area of the yellow triangle. Because of the deadweight loss, this equilibrium is not efficient.

With an equilibrium quantity of $Q_{Efficient}$, economic surplus is at a maximum, and the equilibrium is efficient. But, with an equilibrium quantity of Q_{Market}, economic surplus is reduced by the deadweight loss—equal to the yellow triangle in Figure 5.1—and the equilibrium is not efficient. The deadweight loss occurs because the supply curve is above the demand curve for the production of the units of electricity between $Q_{Efficient}$ and Q_{Market}. That is, the additional cost—including the external cost—of producing these units is greater than the marginal benefit to consumers, as represented by the demand curve. In other words, because of the cost of the pollution, economic efficiency would be improved if less electricity were produced.

We can conclude the following: *When there is a negative externality in producing a good or service, too much of the good or service will be produced at market equilibrium.*

How a Positive Externality in Consumption Reduces Economic Efficiency
We have seen that a negative externality interferes with achieving economic efficiency. The same holds true for a positive externality. In earlier chapters, we assumed that the demand curve represents all the benefits that come from consuming a good. But a college education generates benefits that are not captured by the student receiving the education and so are not included in the market demand curve for college educations. Figure 5.2 shows the effect of a positive externality in consumption on the market for college educations.

If students receiving a college education could capture all its benefits, the demand curve would be D_2, which represents the marginal social benefits. The actual demand curve is D_1, however, which includes only the marginal private benefits received by students. The efficient equilibrium would occur at price $P_{Efficient}$ and quantity $Q_{Efficient}$. At this equilibrium, economic surplus is maximized. The market equilibrium, at price P_{Market} and quantity Q_{Market}, will not be efficient because the demand curve is above the supply curve for production of the units between Q_{Market} and $Q_{Efficient}$. That is, the marginal benefit—including the external benefit—of producing these units is greater than the marginal cost. As a result, there is a deadweight loss equal to the area of the yellow triangle. Because of the positive externality, economic efficiency would be improved if more college educations were produced.

We can conclude the following: *When there is a positive externality in consuming a good or service, too little of the good or service will be produced at market equilibrium.*

MyLab Economics Concept Check

Externalities and Market Failure

We have seen that because of externalities, the efficient level of output may not occur in either the market for electricity or the market for college educations. These are examples

MyLab Economics Animation

Figure 5.2

The Effect of a Positive Externality on Economic Efficiency

People who do not consume college educations can still benefit from them. As a result, the marginal social benefit from a college education is greater than the marginal private benefit to college students. Because the market demand curve D_1 includes only the marginal private benefit, the quantity of college educations produced, Q_{Market}, is too low. If the market demand curve were D_2 instead of D_1, the level of college educations produced would be $Q_{Efficient}$, which is the efficient level. At the market equilibrium of Q_{Market}, there is a deadweight loss equal to the area of the yellow triangle.

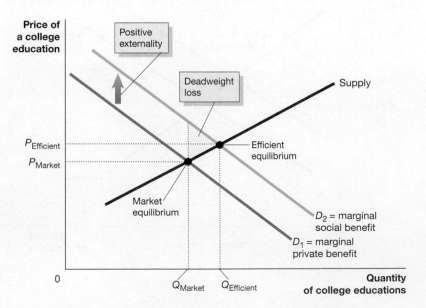

of **market failure**—situations in which the market fails to produce the efficient level of output. In Section 5.3, we will discuss possible solutions to problems of externalities. But, first, we need to consider why externalities occur.   MyLab Economics Concept Check

What Causes Externalities?

Governments need to guarantee *property rights* in order for a market system to function well (see Chapter 2, Section 2.3). **Property rights** refer to the rights individuals or businesses have to the exclusive use of their property, including the right to buy or sell it. Property can be tangible or physical, such as a store or factory. Property can also be intangible, such as the right to an idea. Most of the time, the governments of the United States and other high-income countries do a good job of enforcing property rights, but in certain situations, property rights do not exist or cannot be legally enforced.

Consider the following situation: Lee owns land that includes a lake. A paper company wants to lease some of Lee's land to build a paper mill that will discharge pollutants into his lake. Because Lee owns the lake, he can charge the paper company the cost of cleaning up the pollutants. The result is that the cost of the pollution is a private cost to the paper company and is included in the price of the paper it sells. There is no externality, the efficient level of paper is produced, and there is no market failure.

Now suppose that the paper company again builds its paper mill on privately owned land but discharges its pollutants into a lake that is owned by the state government rather than by an individual. In the absence of any government regulations, the company can discharge pollutants into the lake without having to pay a fee. The cost of the pollution will be external to the company because it doesn't have to pay the cost of cleaning it up. The paper mill will produce a quantity of paper that is greater than the economically efficient level, and a market failure will occur. Or, suppose that Lee owns the lake, but the pollution is caused by acid rain generated by an electric utility hundreds of miles away. The law does not allow Lee to charge the electric utility for the damage caused by the acid rain. Even though someone is damaging Lee's property, he cannot enforce his property rights in this situation. Once again, there is an externality, and the market failure will result in too much electricity being produced.

If you buy a house, the government will protect your right to exclusive use of that house. No one else can use the house without your permission. Because of your property rights in the house, your private benefit from the house and the social benefit are the same. When you buy a college education, however, other people are able to benefit from it. You have no property right that will enable you to prevent them from benefiting or to charge them for the benefits they receive. As a result, there is a positive externality, and the market failure will result in too few college educations being supplied.

We can conclude the following: *Externalities and market failures result from incomplete property rights or from the difficulty of enforcing property rights in certain situations.*

MyLab Economics Concept Check
MyLab Economics Study Plan

Market failure A situation in which the market fails to produce the efficient level of output.

Property rights The rights individuals or businesses have to the exclusive use of their property, including the right to buy or sell it.

5.2 Private Solutions to Externalities: The Coase Theorem

LEARNING OBJECTIVE: Discuss the Coase theorem and explain how private bargaining can lead to economic efficiency in a market with an externality.

As noted at the beginning of this chapter, government intervention may increase economic efficiency and enhance the well-being of society when externalities are present. It is also possible, however, for people to find private solutions to the problem of externalities.

Can the market cure market failure? In an influential article written in 1960, Ronald Coase, formerly of the University of Chicago, winner of the 1991 Nobel Prize in Economics, argued that under some circumstances, private solutions to the problem of externalities will occur. To understand Coase's argument, we need to recognize that completely eliminating an externality usually is not economically efficient. Consider pollution, for example. There is, in fact, an *economically efficient level of pollution reduction.*

At first, this seems paradoxical. Pollution is bad, and you might think the efficient amount of a bad thing is zero. But it isn't zero.

The Economically Efficient Level of Pollution Reduction

Chapter 1, Section 1.1, introduced the important idea that the optimal decision is to continue any activity up to the point where the marginal benefit equals the marginal cost. This result applies to reducing pollution just as much as it does to other activities. Sulfur dioxide emissions contribute to smog and acid rain. As sulfur dioxide emissions—or any other type of pollution—decline, society benefits: Fewer trees die, fewer buildings are damaged, and fewer people suffer breathing problems. But, a key point is that the additional benefit—that is, the *marginal benefit*—received from eliminating another ton of sulfur dioxide *declines* as sulfur dioxide emissions are reduced. To see why, consider what happens if utilities generate electricity without attempting to reduce sulfur dioxide emissions. In this situation, many smoggy days will occur in the cities of the Midwest and Northeast. Even healthy people may experience breathing problems. As sulfur dioxide emissions are reduced, the number of smoggy days will fall, and healthy people will no longer experience breathing problems. Eventually, if sulfur dioxide emissions fall to low levels, people with asthma will no longer be affected. Further reductions in sulfur dioxide emissions will have little additional benefit. The same will be true of the other benefits from reducing sulfur dioxide emissions: As the reductions increase, the additional benefits from fewer buildings and trees being damaged and lakes polluted will decline.

Apply the Concept

MyLab Economics Video

The Clean Air Act: How a Government Policy Reduced Infant Mortality

Red_pepper82/iStock/Getty Images

Some studies link passage of the Clean Air Act of 1970 to a decline in infant mortality.

The United States has made tremendous progress in reducing air pollution since Congress passed and President Richard Nixon signed into law the Clean Air Act in 1970. By 2017, total emissions of the six main air pollutants had fallen by at least 50 percent, with carbon monoxide emissions having fallen more than 70 percent and lead emissions having fallen more than 99 percent. Over the same period, real U.S. gross domestic product (GDP)—which measures the value, corrected for inflation, of all the final goods and services produced in the country—more than tripled, energy consumption increased by half, and the number of miles traveled by all vehicles doubled.

As we have seen, when levels of pollution are high, the marginal benefit of reducing pollution is also high. We would expect, then, that the benefit of reducing air pollution in 1970 was much higher than the benefit from a proportional reduction in air pollution would be today, when the level of pollution is much lower. Several studies have shown that the benefits from the reductions in air pollution that occurred in the period immediately after passage of the Clean Air Act were indeed large. We can briefly discuss three of those studies.

Kenneth Y. Chay of Brown University and Michael Greenstone of the University of Chicago noted that the exposure of pregnant women to high levels of air pollution can be damaging to their unborn children, possibly by reducing lung functioning. This damage would increase the chance that the infant would die in the first weeks after being born. In the two years following passage of the Clean Air Act, there was a sharp reduction in air pollution and also in infant mortality. The decline was mainly due to a reduction in deaths within one month of birth. Of course, other factors may also have contributed to the decline in infant mortality, but Chay and Greenstone used statistical analysis to isolate the effect of the decline in air pollution. They concluded that "1,300 fewer infants died in 1972 than would have in the absence of the Clean Air Act."

Nicholas J. Sanders of Cornell University and Charles Stoecker of Tulane University analyzed the effect of the Clean Air Act on reducing the stress fetuses in the womb suffer as a result of pollution. They concluded that in 1972, the reduction in pollution due to the Clean Air Act prevented 9,900 fetal deaths.

Further research by economists Adam Isen, of the U.S. Department of the Treasury, Maya Rossin-Slater, of the University of California, Santa Barbara, and W. Reed Walker, of the University of California, Berkeley, indicates that a reduction in exposure to pollution had a lasting effect on people who were small children at the time the act was passed. They estimate that as a result of improved health, the 1.5 million children born each year into the counties that had been the most polluted earn about $4,300 more as adults than they would have if pollution had not been reduced.

Sources: Kenneth Y. Chay and Michael Greenstone, "Air Quality, Infant Mortality, and the Clean Air Act of 1970," National Bureau of Economic Research, Working Paper No. 10053, October 2003; Nicholas J. Sanders and Charles Stoecker, "Where Have All the Young Men Gone? Using Sex Ratios to Measure Fetal Death Rates," *Journal of Health Economics*, Vol. 41, May 2015, pp. 30–45; and Adam Isen, Maya Rossin-Slater, and W. Reed Walker, "Every Breath You Take—Every Dollar You'll Make: The Long-Term Consequences of the Clean Air Act of 1970," *Journal of Political Economy*, forthcoming.

Your Turn: Test your understanding by doing related problem 2.8 on page 176 at the end of this chapter.

MyLab Economics Study Plan

What about the marginal cost to electric utilities of reducing pollution? To reduce sulfur dioxide emissions, utilities have to switch from burning high-sulfur coal to burning more costly fuel, or they have to install pollution control devices, such as scrubbers. As the level of pollution falls, further reductions become increasingly costly. Reducing emissions or other types of pollution to very low levels can require complex and expensive new technologies. For example, Arthur Fraas, formerly of the federal Office of Management and Budget, and Vincent Munley, of Lehigh University, have shown that the marginal cost of removing 97 percent of pollutants from municipal wastewater is more than twice as high as the marginal cost of removing 95 percent.

The *net benefit* to society from reducing pollution is equal to the difference between the benefit of reducing pollution and the cost. For us to maximize the net benefit to society, sulfur dioxide emissions—or any other type of pollution—should be reduced up to the point where the marginal benefit from another ton of reduction is equal to the marginal cost. Figure 5.3 illustrates this conclusion.

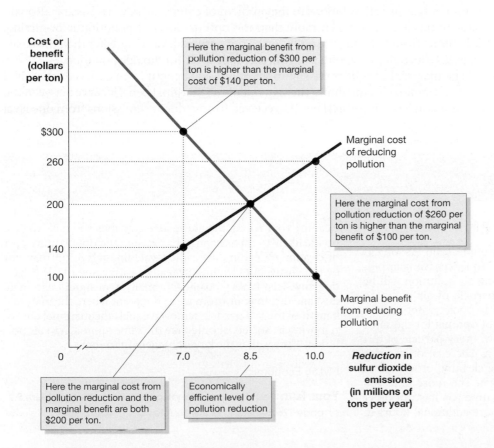

MyLab Economics Animation

Figure 5.3

The Marginal Benefit from Pollution Reduction Should Equal the Marginal Cost

If the reduction of sulfur dioxide emissions is 7.0 million tons per year, the marginal benefit of $300 per ton is greater than the marginal cost of $140 per ton. Further reductions in emissions will increase the net benefit to society. If the reduction of sulfur dioxide emissions is 10.0 million tons, the marginal cost of $260 per ton is greater than the marginal benefit of $100 per ton. An increase in sulfur dioxide emissions will increase the net benefit to society. Only when the reduction is 8.5 million tons is the marginal benefit equal to the marginal cost. This level is the economically efficient level of pollution reduction.

In Figure 5.3, we measure *reductions* in sulfur dioxide emissions on the horizontal axis. We measure the marginal benefit and marginal cost in dollars from eliminating another ton of sulfur dioxide emissions on the vertical axis. As reductions in pollution increase, the marginal benefit declines and the marginal cost increases. The economically efficient amount of pollution reduction occurs where the marginal benefit equals the marginal cost. The figure shows that, in this case, the economically efficient reduction of sulfur dioxide emissions is 8.5 million tons per year. In a program begun in 1990, this is the reduction Congress decided should occur by 2010. At that level of emission reduction, the marginal benefit and the marginal cost of the last ton of sulfur dioxide emissions eliminated are both $200 per ton. Suppose instead that the emissions target is only 7.0 million tons per year. The figure shows that, at that level of reduction, the last ton of reduction adds $300 to the benefits received by society, but it adds only $140 to the costs of utilities. There is a net benefit to society of $160 from this ton of pollution reduction. In fact, the figure shows a net benefit to society from pollution reduction for every ton from 7.0 million to 8.5 million. Only when sulfur dioxide emissions are reduced by 8.5 million tons per year will marginal benefit fall enough and marginal cost rise enough that the two are equal.

Now suppose Congress had set the target for sulfur dioxide emissions reduction at 10.0 million tons per year. Figure 5.3 shows that the marginal benefit at that level of reduction falls to only $100 per ton and the marginal cost rises to $260 per ton. The last ton of reduction actually *reduces* the net benefit to society by $160 per ton. In fact, every ton of reduction beyond 8.5 million reduces the net benefit to society.

To summarize:

- If the marginal benefit of reducing pollution is greater than the marginal cost, further reductions will make society better off.
- If the marginal cost of reducing pollution is greater than the marginal benefit, further reductions will actually make society worse off. **MyLab Economics** Concept Check

The Basis for Private Solutions to Externalities

In arguing that private solutions to the problem of externalities were possible, Ronald Coase emphasized that when more than the optimal level of pollution is occurring, the benefits from reducing the pollution to the optimal level are greater than the costs. Figure 5.4 illustrates this point using the example of sulfur dioxide pollution.

The marginal benefit curve shows the additional benefit from each reduction in a ton of sulfur dioxide emissions. The area under the marginal benefit curve between the two emission levels is the *total* benefit received from reducing emissions from one level

Don't Let This Happen to You

Remember That It's the *Net* Benefit That Counts

Why not *completely* eliminate anything unpleasant? As long as any person suffers any unpleasant consequences from air pollution, the marginal benefit of reducing air pollution will be positive. Therefore, removing every particle of air pollution will result in the largest *total* benefit to society. But removing every particle of air pollution is not optimal for the same reason that it is not optimal to remove every particle of dirt or dust from a room when cleaning it. The cost of cleaning your room is not just the price of the cleaning products but also the opportunity cost of your time. The more time you devote to cleaning your room, the less time you have for other activities. As you devote more and more additional hours to cleaning your room, the alternative activities you have to give up are likely to increase in value, raising the opportunity cost of cleaning: Cleaning instead of watching television may not be too costly, but cleaning instead of eating any meals or getting any sleep is very costly. Optimally, you should eliminate dust and dirt in your room up to the point where the marginal benefit of the last particle removed equals the marginal cost of removing it. Society should take the same approach to air pollution. The result is the largest *net* benefit to society.

MyLab Economics Study Plan

Your Turn: Test your understanding by doing related problem 2.9 on page 176 at the end of this chapter.

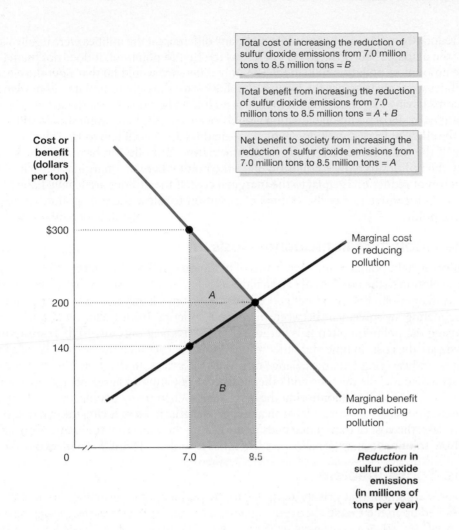

Total cost of increasing the reduction of sulfur dioxide emissions from 7.0 million tons to 8.5 million tons = B

Total benefit from increasing the reduction of sulfur dioxide emissions from 7.0 million tons to 8.5 million tons = A + B

Net benefit to society from increasing the reduction of sulfur dioxide emissions from 7.0 million tons to 8.5 million tons = A

MyLab Economics Animation

Figure 5.4

The Benefits of Reducing Pollution to the Optimal Level Are Greater Than the Costs

Increasing the reduction in sulfur dioxide emissions from 7.0 million tons to 8.5 million tons results in total benefits equal to the sum of the areas of A and B under the marginal benefit curve. The total cost of this decrease in pollution is equal to the area of B under the marginal cost curve. The total benefits are greater than the total costs by an amount equal to the area of A. Because the total benefits from reducing pollution are greater than the total costs, it is possible for those receiving the benefits to arrive at a private agreement with polluters to pay them to reduce pollution.

to another. For instance, in Figure 5.4, the total benefit from increasing the reduction in sulfur dioxide emissions from 7.0 million tons to 8.5 million tons is the sum of the areas of A and B. The marginal cost curve shows the additional cost from each reduction in a ton of emissions. The *total* cost of reducing emissions from one level to another is the area under the marginal cost curve between the two emission levels. The total cost from increasing the reduction in emissions from 7.0 million tons to 8.5 million tons is the area of B. The net benefit from reducing emissions is the difference between the total cost and the total benefit, which is equal to the area of A.

In Figure 5.4, the benefits from further reductions in sulfur dioxide emissions are much greater than the costs. In the appendix to Chapter 1, we reviewed the formula for calculating the area of a triangle, which is ½ × base × height, and the formula for the area of a rectangle, which is base × height. Using these formulas, we can calculate the value of the total benefits from the reduction in emissions and the value of the total costs. The value of the benefits (A + B) is $375 million. The value of the costs (B) is $255 million. If the people who would benefit from a reduction in pollution could get together, they could offer to pay the electric utilities $255 million to reduce the pollution to the optimal level. After making the payment, they would still be left with a net benefit of $120 million. In other words, a private agreement to reduce pollution to the optimal level is possible, without any government intervention.   **MyLab Economics** Concept Check

Do Property Rights Matter?

In discussing the bargaining between the electric utilities and the people suffering the effects of the utilities' pollution, we assumed that the electric utilities were not legally liable for the damage they were causing. In other words, the property of the victims of pollution was not legally protected from damage, so the victims would have to pay the utilities to reduce the pollution. But would it make any difference if the utilities were legally liable for the damages? Surprisingly, as Coase was the first to point out, it does not matter for the amount of pollution reduction. The only difference would be that now the electric utilities would have to pay the victims of pollution for the right to pollute rather than the victims having to pay the utilities to reduce pollution. Because the marginal benefits and marginal costs of pollution reduction would not change, the bargaining should still result in the efficient level of pollution reduction—in this case, 8.5 million tons.

If the utilities are not legally liable, the victims of pollution have an incentive to pay the utilities to reduce pollution up to the point where the marginal benefit of the last ton of reduction is equal to the marginal cost. If the utilities are legally liable, they have an incentive to pay the victims of pollution to allow them to pollute up to the same point. **MyLab Economics** Concept Check

The Problem of Transactions Costs

Transactions costs The costs in time and other resources that parties incur in the process of agreeing to and carrying out an exchange of goods or services.

Unfortunately, polluters and the victims of pollution can have difficulty arriving at a private solution to the problem of externalities. One important reason is that there are often both many polluters and many people suffering from the negative effects of pollution. Negotiating an agreement between the people suffering from pollution and the firms causing the pollution often fails because of the *transactions costs* involved. **Transactions costs** are the costs in time and other resources that parties incur in the process of agreeing to and carrying out an exchange of goods or services. In this case, the transactions costs would include the time and other costs of negotiating an agreement, drawing up a binding contract, and monitoring the agreement. When many people are involved, the transactions costs are often higher than the net benefits from reducing the externality. In that case, the cost of transacting ends up exceeding the gain from the transaction, and a private solution to an externality problem is not feasible. **MyLab Economics** Concept Check

The Coase Theorem

Coase theorem The argument of economist Ronald Coase that if transactions costs are low, private bargaining will result in an efficient solution to the problem of externalities.

Coase's argument that private solutions to the problem of externalities are possible is summed up in the **Coase theorem**: *If transactions costs are low, private bargaining will result in an efficient solution to the problem of externalities.* We have seen the basis for the Coase theorem in the preceding example of pollution by electric utilities: Because the benefits from reducing an externality are often greater than the costs, private bargaining can lead to an efficient outcome. But we have also seen that this outcome will occur only if transactions costs are low, and in the case of pollution, they usually are not. In general, private bargaining is most likely to reach an efficient outcome if the number of parties bargaining is small.

In practice, we must add a couple of other qualifications to the Coase theorem. In addition to low transactions costs, private solutions to the problem of externalities will occur only if all parties to the agreement have full information about the costs and benefits associated with the externality, and all parties must be willing to accept a reasonable agreement. For example, if those suffering from the effects of pollution do not have information on the costs of reducing pollution, it is unlikely that the parties can reach an agreement. Unreasonable demands can also hinder an agreement. For instance, in the example of pollution by electric utilities, we saw that the total benefit of reducing sulfur dioxide emissions was $375 million. Even if transactions costs are very low, if the utilities insist on being paid more than $375 million to reduce emissions, no agreement will be reached because the amount paid exceeds the value of the reduction to those suffering from the emissions. **MyLab Economics** Concept Check

MyLab Economics Study Plan

 Apply the Concept **MyLab Economics** Video

How Can You Defend Your Knees on a Plane Flight?

Imagine that you are on a plane, peacefully using your laptop on the tray table. Then, with no warning, the person in front of you forcefully reclines her seat, banging your knees and—much worse!—cracking the screen of your laptop. Unfortunately, this problem has become common. Until a few years ago, most seats in the coach section of airplanes had 32 inches of space from the front of one seat to the back of the seat in the next row. But airlines have been reconfiguring their planes to fit more seats. Today, many coach seats have only 29 inches of space, and those missing 3 inches can make a big difference, particularly if you have long legs!

Clearly, there is an externality involved when someone reclines a seat. The person reclining gets the benefit of a more comfortable position, but as the person in the seat behind, you have to bear the cost of a seat reclining into your space. But is it your space? If you had a property right to the space, you could choose to make the person in front of you pay a fee to recline her chair. But the airlines own the space, and their policy is to allow people to recline their seats. The airlines' views became clear following incidents involving the Knee Defender, a device invented by Ira Goldman. When you slip Goldman's gadget over the bars on your tray table, it prevents the seat in front of you from being reclined. Fights broke out over the use of the gadget, so most major U.S. airlines banned its use.

Because the airlines give passengers the right to recline their seats, what can you do if the person in front of you is squeezing your knees or making it impossible for you to use your laptop on your tray table? If the cost to you from these problems is greater than the benefit to the person in front of you from reclining, there should be a payment that you can make to that person in exchange for not reclining. That's the solution that Josh Barro, a frequent flier and *New York Times* columnist, suggested: "If my reclining bothers you, you can pay me to stop." He was skeptical that many people really are bothered by having the seat in front of them reclined: "If they really cared that much, someone would have opened his wallet and paid me by now."

Applying Coase's theorem, Barro's analysis seems to be correct: If the cost to you from having the seat in front of yours reclined is greater than the benefit to the recliner, you should make a payment to the recliner. Because this outcome rarely occurs, people reclining must get a larger benefit than the cost imposed on people behind them. But economist Donald Marron of the Urban Institute argues that this analysis holds only if we assume that the transactions costs of negotiating an agreement are low. If many people don't like the idea of negotiating with a stranger about a payment for not reclining a seat, then the transactions costs might be too high for the efficient outcome to occur.

Ronald Coase passed away in 2013, so we may never know how he dealt with the issue of someone in front of him reclining his or her seat.

Sources: Scott McCartney, "Airline Seat Battles: Be Kind, Don't Recline?" *Wall Street Journal*, September 3, 2014; Josh Barro, "Don't Want Me to Recline My Airline Seat? You Can Pay Me," *New York Times*, August 27, 2014; Donald Marron, "Who Owns the Right to Recline? Property Rights in the Sky," dmarron.com, August 26, 2014; and Adam Levine-Weinberg, "It's No Surprise Airlines Have Banned the 'Knee Defender,'" fool.com, September 7, 2014.

Your Turn: Test your understanding by doing related problems 2.10 and 2.11 on page 176 at the end of this chapter.

MyLab Economics Study Plan

Jason Hetherington/The Image Bank/ Getty Images

If you were on a plane, would you be willing to pay the passenger in front of you to not recline her seat?

5.3 Government Policies to Deal with Externalities

LEARNING OBJECTIVE: Analyze government policies to achieve economic efficiency in a market with an externality.

When private solutions to externalities are not feasible, how should the government intervene? British economist A. C. Pigou of Cambridge University was the first to analyze market failure systematically and to suggest an answer to that question.

Imposing a Tax When There Is a Negative Externality

Pigou argued that to deal with a negative externality in production, the government should impose a tax equal to the cost of the externality. The effect of such a tax is shown in Figure 5.5, which reproduces the negative externality from acid rain shown in Figure 5.1 on page 149.

MyLab Economics Animation

Figure 5.5

When There Is a Negative Externality, a Tax Can Lead to the Efficient Level of Output

Because utilities do not bear the cost of acid rain, they produce electricity beyond the economically efficient level. If the government imposes a tax equal to the cost of acid rain, the utilities will internalize the externality. As a consequence, the supply curve will shift up, from S_1 to S_2. The market equilibrium quantity changes from Q_{Market}, where an inefficiently high level of electricity is produced, to $Q_{Efficient}$, the economically efficient equilibrium quantity. The price of electricity will rise from P_{Market}—which does not include the cost of acid rain—to $P_{Efficient}$—which does include the cost. Consumers pay the price $P_{Efficient}$, while producers receive the price P, which is equal to $P_{Efficient}$ minus the amount of the tax.

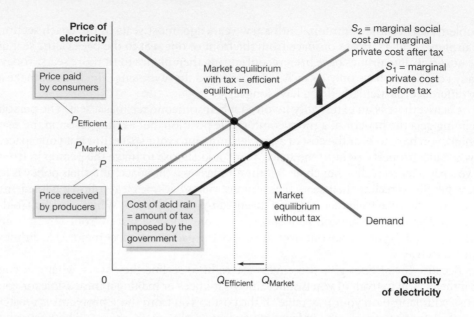

By imposing a tax on the production of electricity equal to the cost of acid rain, the government will cause electric utilities to *internalize* the externality. As a consequence, the cost of the acid rain will become a private cost borne by the utilities, and the supply curve for electricity will shift from S_1 to S_2. The result will be a decrease in the equilibrium output of electricity from Q_{Market} to the efficient level, $Q_{Efficient}$. The price consumers pay for electricity will rise from P_{Market} (which does not include the cost of acid rain) to $P_{Efficient}$ (which does include the cost). Producers will receive a price P, which is equal to $P_{Efficient}$ minus the amount of the tax. **MyLab Economics** Concept Check

Providing a Subsidy When There Is a Positive Externality

Pigou reasoned that the government can deal with a positive externality in consumption by giving consumers a subsidy, or payment, equal to the value of the externality. The effect of such a subsidy is shown in Figure 5.6, which reproduces the positive externality from college education shown in Figure 5.2 on page 150.

MyLab Economics Animation

Figure 5.6

When There Is a Positive Externality, a Subsidy Can Bring about the Efficient Level of Output

People who do not consume college educations can benefit from them. As a result, the social benefit from a college education is greater than the private benefit to college students. If the government pays a subsidy equal to the external benefit, students will internalize the externality. The subsidy will cause the demand curve to shift up, from D_1 to D_2. As a result, the market equilibrium quantity will shift from Q_{Market}, where an inefficiently low level of college educations is supplied, to $Q_{Efficient}$, the economically efficient equilibrium quantity. Producers receive the price $P_{Efficient}$, while consumers pay the price P, which is equal to $P_{Efficient}$ minus the amount of the subsidy.

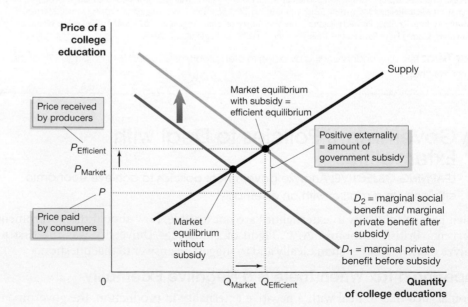

By paying college students a subsidy equal to the external benefit from a college education, the government will cause students to *internalize* the externality. That is, the external benefit from a college education will become a private benefit received by college students, and the demand curve for college educations will shift from D_1 to D_2. The equilibrium quantity of college educations supplied will increase from Q_{Market} to the efficient level, $Q_{Efficient}$. Producers receive the price $P_{Efficient}$, while consumers pay the price P, which is equal to $P_{Efficient}$ minus the amount of the subsidy. In fact, the government does heavily subsidize college educations. All states have government-operated universities that charge tuitions well below the cost of providing the education. The state and federal governments also provide students with grants and low-interest loans that subsidize college educations. The economic justification for these programs is that college educations provide an external benefit to society.

Apply the Concept   MyLab Economics Video

Should the Government Tax Cigarettes and Soda?

Generally, governments use Pigovian taxes to deal with negative externalities in *production*. Governments also impose taxes—sometimes called *sin taxes*—on products such as cigarettes and alcohol. Some policymakers have argued that these products generate negative externalities in *consumption*, so a tax on them can increase economic efficiency. Recently, several cities have begun taxing sweetened sodas, on the grounds that they cause a negative externality by raising medical costs. For example, in 2017, the city of Philadelphia began collecting a 1.5-cent per ounce tax on sweetened beverages. Just as governments can deal with a positive externality in consumption by giving consumers a subsidy, they can deal with a negative externality by imposing a tax.

As the following figure shows, by imposing a tax on soda, the government will cause consumers to internalize the externality. That is, the external cost to drinking soda will become a private cost paid by consumers. Because consumers now have to pay a tax on soda, at every quantity, they are willing to pay less than they would have without the tax, so the demand curve for soda will shift down by the amount of the tax, from D_1 to D_2. The equilibrium quantity of sodas consumed will decrease from Q_{Market} to the efficient level, $Q_{Efficient}$. (Note that as we saw in Chapter 4, pages 129–131, we get the same result whether the government imposes a tax on the buyers of a good or on the sellers.)

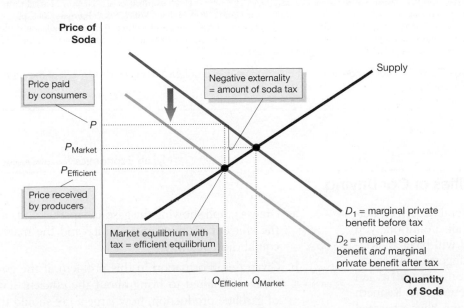

But do people actually cause a negative externality by smoking and drinking sweetened sodas? It might seem that they don't because consumers of cigarettes and sodas bear the costs of any health problems they experience. In fact, though, the higher medical expenses from treating the complications of cigarette smoking or obesity are not paid entirely by the smokers or soda drinkers. A smoker who receives health insurance through his employer may increase the costs of that insurance, which all the workers at the firm will pay. Similarly, taxpayers partly pay for the health care of someone who is over age 65 and is enrolled in the federal government's Medicare program. The costs of medical care that smokers or soda drinkers do not pay themselves represent a negative externality.

There is a complication to this conclusion, however: Smokers and people who are obese tend to die early. This tragic outcome means that people in both groups may have been paying taxes to help pay for Social Security and Medicare benefits that they will never receive. They may also have made payments into company and public employee pension plans and purchased long-term care insurance, but they may not have lived long enough to receive many pension payments or to have spent time in a nursing home. So, there are offsetting effects: While alive, smokers and obese people may impose costs on others who bear the expense of their higher medical costs, but because they are likely to die early, they provide a financial gain to recipients of Social Security, Medicare, company and public employee pension plans, and purchasers of long-term care insurance.

W. Kip Viscusi of Vanderbilt University has studied the case of tobacco smoking and concluded that the external costs and benefits roughly offset each other, meaning that there doesn't appear to be a significant negative externality from smoking. Studies of obesity have arrived at somewhat conflicting results: A study of obesity in the Netherlands found that the cost savings from premature death offset the additional lifetime medical costs of obese people. But another study using U.S. data found that obesity did lead to a net increase in lifetime medical costs, even taking into account the shorter average life spans of obese people.

There may also be costs to smoking and obesity beyond additional medical costs. Smokers may inflict costs on others because of secondhand smoke or because smoking during pregnancy can lead to low birth weights and other health problems for babies. Airlines have noted that they spend more on fuel costs because of the increasing weight of passengers.

Economists and policymakers continue to debate whether the government should use taxes to deal with negative externalities in consumption.

Sources: Jennifer Kaplan, "Philadelphia's Soda Sellers Say Tax Has Reduced Sales by as Much as 50%," bloomberg.com, February 17, 2017; W. Kip Viscusi, "Cigarette Taxation and the Social Consequences of Smoking," in James Poterba, ed., *Tax Policy and the Economy*, Vol. 9, Cambridge: MIT Press, 1995; Pieter H. M. van Baal, et al., "Lifetime Medical Costs of Obesity: Prevention No Cure for Increasing Health Expenditure," *PLoS Medicine*, Vol. 5, No. 2, February 2008, pp. 242–249; Pierre-Carl Michaud, et al., "Understanding the Economic Consequences of Shifting Trends in Population Health," National Bureau of Economic Research, Working Paper No. 15231, August 2009; and "Feds Say Obesity Epidemic Hurts Airlines by Increasing Fuel Costs," Associated Press, November 5, 2004.

MyLab Economics Study Plan

Your Turn: Test your understanding by doing related problem 3.9 on pages 177–178 at the end of this chapter.

Solved Problem 5.3

MyLab Economics Interactive Animation

Dealing with the Externalities of Car Driving

When you drive a car, you generate several negative externalities: You cause some additional air pollution, you increase the chances that other drivers will have an accident, and you cause some additional congestion on roads, causing other drivers to spend more time in traffic. Ian Parry of the International Monetary Fund and Kenneth Small of the University of California, Irvine, have estimated that these external costs amount to about $1.00 per gallon of gasoline. Taxes on gasoline vary by state and currently average about $0.50 per gallon.

a. Draw a graph showing the gasoline market. Indicate the efficient equilibrium quantity and the market equilibrium quantity.

b. Given the information in this problem, if the government wanted to bring about the efficient level of gasoline production, how large a tax should the government impose on gasoline? Will the price consumers pay for gasoline rise by the full amount of the tax? Briefly explain using your graph from part (a).

Solving the Problem

Step 1: **Review the chapter material.** This problem is about the government using a tax to deal with a negative externality, so you may want to review the section "Government Policies to Deal with Externalities," which begins on page 157.

Step 2: **Answer part (a) by drawing a graph of the gasoline market.** In this case, the tax is levied on the consumption of gasoline rather than on its production, so your graph should show the demand curve representing marginal social benefit being below the demand curve showing marginal private benefit. (Of course, the government actually collects the tax from sellers rather than from consumers, but we get the same result whether the government imposes a tax on the buyers of a good or on the sellers.) Your graph should also show the market equilibrium quantity of gasoline, Q_{Market}, being greater than the efficient equilibrium quantity, $Q_{Efficient}$.

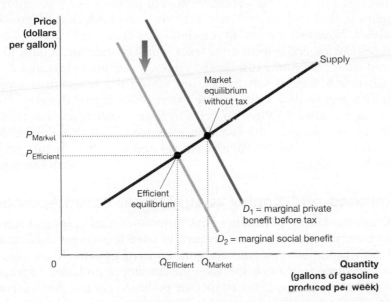

Step 3: **Answer part (b) by explaining the size of the necessary tax, indicating the tax on your graph from part (a), and explaining the effect of the tax on the equilibrium price.** If Parry and Small are correct that the external cost from consuming gasoline is $1.00 per gallon, then the tax per gallon should be raised from $0.50 to $1.00 per gallon. You should show the effect of the increase in the tax on your graph.

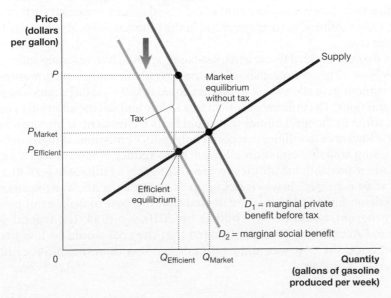

The graph shows that although the tax shifts down the demand curve for gasoline, the price consumers pay increases by less than the amount of the tax. To see this, note that the price consumers pay rises from P_{Market} to P, which is smaller than the per gallon tax, which equals the vertical distance between $P_{\text{Efficient}}$ and P.

Source: Ian W. H. Parry and Kenneth A. Small, "Does Britain or the United States Have the Right Gasoline Tax?" *American Economic Review*, Vol. 95, No. 4, September 2005, pp. 1276–1289.

MyLab Economics Study Plan

Your Turn: For more practice, do related problems 3.10, 3.11, and 3.12 on page 178 at the end of this chapter.

Pigovian taxes and subsidies
Government taxes and subsidies intended to bring about an efficient level of output in the presence of externalities.

Because Pigou was the first economist to propose using government taxes and subsidies to deal with externalities, they are sometimes called **Pigovian taxes and subsidies**. Note that a Pigovian tax eliminates deadweight loss and improves economic efficiency, unlike most other taxes, which are intended simply to raise revenue and can reduce consumer surplus and producer surplus and create a deadweight loss (see Chapter 4, Section 4.4). In fact, one reason that economists support Pigovian taxes as a way to deal with negative externalities is that the government can use the revenues raised by Pigovian taxes to lower other taxes that reduce economic efficiency. For instance, the Canadian province of British Columbia has enacted a Pigovian tax on carbon dioxide emissions and uses the revenue raised to reduce personal income taxes.   MyLab Economics Concept Check

Command-and-Control versus Market-Based Approaches

Command-and-control approach
A policy that involves the government imposing quantitative limits on the amount of pollution firms are allowed to emit or requiring firms to install specific pollution control devices.

Although the federal government has sometimes used taxes and subsidies to deal with externalities, it has more frequently used a *command-and-control approach* to deal with pollution. A **command-and-control approach** involves the government imposing quantitative limits on the amount of pollution firms are allowed to emit or requiring firms to install specific pollution control devices. For example, in the 1980s, the federal government required auto manufacturers such as Ford and General Motors to install catalytic converters to reduce auto emissions on all new automobiles.

Congress could have used a command-and-control approach to achieve its goal of reducing sulfur dioxide emissions by 8.5 million tons per year by 2010. However, this approach would not have been an economically efficient solution to the problem because utilities can have very different costs of reducing sulfur dioxide emissions. Some utilities that already used low-sulfur coal could reduce emissions further only at a high cost. Other utilities, particularly those in the Midwest, were able to reduce emissions at a lower cost.

Congress decided to use a market-based approach to reducing sulfur dioxide emissions by setting up a *cap-and-trade system* of tradable emission allowances. The federal government gave allowances to utilities equal to the total target amount of sulfur dioxide emissions. The utilities were then free to buy and sell the allowances on the Chicago Mercantile Exchange. Utilities that could reduce emissions at low cost did so and sold their allowances to utilities that could only reduce emissions at high cost.

Using tradable emission allowances to reduce acid rain was a success in that it made it possible for utilities to meet Congress's emissions goal at a much lower cost than expected. Just before Congress enacted the allowances program in 1990, the Edison Electric Institute estimated that the cost to utilities of complying with the program would be $7.4 billion by 2010. By 1994, the federal government's General Accounting Office estimated that the cost would be less than $2 billion. In practice, the cost was almost 90 percent less than the initial estimate, or only about $870 *million*.   MyLab Economics Concept Check

The End of the Sulfur Dioxide Cap-and-Trade System

The dollar value of the total benefits of reducing sulfur dioxide emissions turned out to be at least 25 times as large as the costs. Despite its successes, however, the sulfur dioxide cap-and-trade system had effectively ended by 2013. Over the years, research showed that sulfur dioxide emissions had caused more illnesses than had been initially thought. In response to these findings, President George W. Bush proposed legislation lowering the cap on sulfur dioxide emissions, but Congress did not pass the legislation. Court rulings kept the Environmental Protection Agency (EPA) from using regulations to set up a new trading system for sulfur dioxide allowances with a lower cap. As a result, the EPA reverted to the previous system of setting limits on sulfur dioxide emissions at the state or individual power plant level.

Because nationwide trading of emission allowances was no longer possible, the allowances lost their value. Many economists continue to believe that using market-based policies, such as the sulfur dioxide cap-and-trade system, is an efficient way to deal with the externalities of pollution. But in the end, any policy requires substantial political support to be enacted and maintained.   **MyLab Economics** Concept Check

Are Tradable Emission Allowances Licenses to Pollute?

Tradable emission allowances face a political problem. While many environmentalists support these allowances, other environmentalists have criticized the allowances for being "licenses to pollute." These environmentalists argue that just as the government does not issue licenses to rob banks or drive drunk, it should not issue licenses to pollute. But, this criticism ignores one of the central lessons of economics: Because resources are scarce, trade-offs exist. Resources that are spent on reducing one type of pollution are not available to reduce other types of pollution or for any other use. Because reducing acid rain using tradable emission allowances cost utilities $870 million per year, rather than $7.4 billion, as originally estimated, society saved more than $6.5 billion per year.   **MyLab Economics** Concept Check

Apply the Concept   MyLab Economics Video

Should the United States Enact a Carbon Tax to Fight Global Warming?

In the past 35 years, the global temperature has increased about 0.75 degree Fahrenheit (or 0.40 degree Celsius) compared with the average for the period between 1951 and 1980. The following graph shows changes in temperature in the years since 1880.

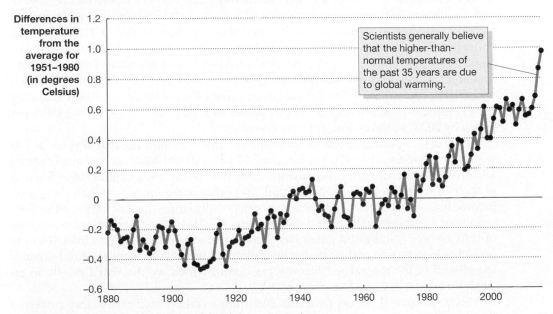

Source: NASA, Goddard Institute for Space Studies, data.giss.nasa.gov/gistemp.

Over the centuries, global temperatures have gone through many long periods of warming and cooling. Nevertheless, most scientists are convinced that the recent warming trend is not part of the natural fluctuations in temperature but is primarily a result of the burning of fossil fuels, such as coal, natural gas, and petroleum. Burning these fuels releases carbon dioxide, which accumulates in the atmosphere as a "greenhouse gas." Greenhouse gases cause some of the heat released from the earth to be reflected back, increasing temperatures. Worldwide annual carbon dioxide emissions increased from about 198 million metric tons of carbon in 1850 to 3,855 million metric tons in 1930 and to 35,700 million metric tons in 2015.

If greenhouse gases continue to accumulate in the atmosphere, according to some estimates, global temperatures could increase by 3 degrees Fahrenheit or more during the next 100 years. Such an increase in temperature could lead to significant changes in climate, which might result in more hurricanes and other violent weather conditions, disrupt farming in many parts of the world, and lead to increases in sea levels, which could result in flooding in coastal areas.

Although most economists and policymakers agree that emitting carbon dioxide results in a significant negative externality, there is extensive debate over which policies should be adopted for three key reasons. First, there are disagreements about how rapidly global warming is likely to occur and what the economic cost will be. Second, carbon dioxide emissions are a worldwide problem; sharp reductions in carbon dioxide emissions only in the United States and Europe, for instance, would not be enough to stop global warming. But coordinating policy across countries has proven difficult. Third, policymakers and economists debate the relative effectiveness of different policies.

In 2015, representatives from 195 nations meeting in Paris agreed to voluntary efforts to restrict emissions of greenhouse gases. The same year, the Obama administration introduced the Clean Power Plan, which would have required states to reduce power plant emissions to 32 percent below 2005 levels by 2030. In 2017, though, the Trump administration decided to withdraw from the Paris agreement and cancel the Clean Power Plan regulations. Some members of the Trump administration argued that the Clean Power Plan's goals would be difficult to meet without disrupting the country's power supply.

Many economists favor a carbon tax as a market-based policy to reduce carbon dioxide emissions. In 2017, economists working at the U.S. Department of the Treasury's Office of Tax Analysis estimated that the marginal social cost of carbon dioxide emissions was about $49 per metric ton. A carbon tax would be intended to replace other regulations on the emissions of carbon dioxide, relying instead on market forces responding to an increase in the price of products that result in carbon dioxide emissions. For example, a $49 per ton carbon tax would raise the price of gasoline by about $0.44 per gallon. This price increase would lead some consumers to switch from cars and trucks with poor fuel mileage to vehicles, including electric cars and trucks, with higher fuel mileage. The federal government's Corporate Average Fuel Economy (CAFE) standards, which require car companies to achieve an average of 54.5 miles per gallon by 2025, would no longer be necessary.

Treasury Department economists estimate that a carbon tax that was set at $49 per ton and increased to $70 per ton over 10 years would raise tax revenue of about $2.2 trillion over that period. Because lower-income households spend a larger fraction of their incomes on gasoline, heating oil, and other energy products than do higher-income households, they would bear a proportionally larger share of the tax. Most proposals for a carbon tax, including one made in 2017 by former Republican secretaries of state George Schultz and James Baker, include a way of refunding to lower-income households some part of their higher tax payments, possibly by increasing and expanding eligibility for the earned income tax credit, which we discussed briefly in an *Apply the Concept* in Chapter 4, pages 119–120.

Some policymakers opposed implementing a carbon tax because they preferred the command-and-control approach of directly regulating emissions. Other opponents worried that a tax generating trillions of dollars of revenue might disrupt the economy in unanticipated ways, even if most of the revenue was refunded back to households. As of late 2017, it seemed doubtful that Congress would pass a carbon tax. The debate over policies to deal with global warming is likely to continue for many years.

Sources: Coral Davenport, "Trump Lays Plans to Reverse Obama's Climate Change Legacy," *New York Times*, March 21, 2017; Coral Davenport, "Nations Approve Landmark Climate Accord in Paris," *New York Time*, December 12, 2015; Jessica Shankleman and Joe Ryan, "Trump Likely to Withdraw from Paris Climate Pact, Ebell Says," bloomberg.com, January 17, 2017; John Horowitz, Julie-Anne Cronin, Hannah Hawkins, Laura Konda, and Alex Yuskavage, "Methodology for Analyzing a Carbon Tax," Office of Tax Analysis, Working Paper No. 115, January 2017; and George P. Shultz and James A. Baker III, "A Conservative Answer to Climate Change," *Wall Street Journal*, February 7, 2017.

Your Turn: Test your understanding by doing related problems 3.15 and 3.16 on page 179 at the end of this chapter.

MyLab Economics Study Plan

5.4 Four Categories of Goods

LEARNING OBJECTIVE: Categorize goods on the basis of whether they are rival or excludable and use graphs to illustrate the efficient quantities of public goods and common resources.

We can explore further the question of when the market is likely to succeed in supplying the efficient quantity of a good by understanding that goods differ on the basis of whether their consumption is *rival* and *excludable*:

- **Rivalry** occurs when one person's consumption of a unit of a good means no one else can consume it. If you consume a Big Mac, for example, no one else can consume it.
- **Excludability** means that anyone who does not pay for a good cannot consume it. If you don't pay for a Big Mac, McDonald's can exclude you from consuming it. The consumption of a Big Mac is therefore rival and excludable.

The consumption of some goods, however, can be either *nonrival* or *nonexcludable*:

- *Nonrival* means that one person's consumption does not interfere with another person's consumption.
- *Nonexcludable* means that it is impossible to exclude others from consuming the good, whether they have paid for it or not.

Figure 5.7 shows four possible categories into which goods can fall:

1. A **private good** is both rival and excludable. Food, clothing, haircuts, and many other goods and services fall into this category. One person's consuming a unit of these goods keeps other people from consuming that unit, and no one can consume these goods without buying them. Although we didn't state it explicitly, when we analyzed the demand and supply for goods and services in earlier chapters, we assumed that the goods and services were all private goods.

2. A **public good** is both nonrival and nonexcludable. Public goods are often, although not always, supplied by a government rather than by private firms. The

Rivalry The situation that occurs when one person's consumption of a unit of a good means no one else can consume it.

Excludability The situation in which anyone who does not pay for a good cannot consume it.

Private good A good that is both rival and excludable.

Public good A good that is both nonrival and nonexcludable.

MyLab Economics Animation
Figure 5.7

Four Categories of Goods

Goods and services can be divided into four categories on the basis of whether people can be excluded from consuming them and whether they are rival in consumption. A good or service is rival in consumption if one person consuming a unit of the good means that another person cannot consume that unit.

	Excludable	Nonexcludable
Rival	**Private Goods** *Examples:* Big Macs Running shoes	**Common Resources** *Examples:* Tuna in the ocean Public pasture land
Nonrival	**Quasi-Public Goods** *Examples:* Cable TV Toll road	**Public Goods** *Examples:* National defense Court system

classic example of a public good is national defense. Your consuming national defense does not interfere with your neighbor consuming it, so consumption is nonrival. You also cannot be excluded from consuming it, whether you pay for it or not. No private firm would be willing to supply national defense because everyone can consume national defense whether they pay for it or not. The behavior of consumers in this situation is called **free riding** because individuals benefit from a good—in this case, national defense—without paying for it.

Free riding Benefiting from a good without paying for it.

3. A *quasi-public good* is excludable but not rival. An example is cable television. People who do not pay for cable television do not receive it, but one person watching it doesn't prevent other people from watching it. Another example is a toll road. Anyone who doesn't pay the toll doesn't get on the highway, but one person using the highway doesn't interfere with someone else using the highway (unless so many people are using the highway that it becomes congested). Goods that fall into this category are called *quasi-public goods*.

Common resource A good that is rival but not excludable.

4. A **common resource** is rival but not excludable. Forest land in many poor countries is a common resource. If one person cuts down a tree, no one else can use that tree. But if no one has a property right to the forest, no one can be excluded from using it. As we will discuss in more detail later in this section, people often overuse common resources.

We analyzed the demand and supply for private goods in earlier chapters. For the remainder of this chapter, we focus on the categories of public goods and common resources. To determine the optimal quantity of a public good, we have to modify our usual demand and supply analysis to take into account that a public good is both nonrival and nonexcludable.

The Demand for a Public Good

We can determine the market demand curve for a good or service by adding up the quantity of the good demanded by each consumer at each price. To keep things simple, let's consider the case of a market with only two consumers. Figure 5.8 shows that the market demand curve for hamburgers depends on the individual demand curves of Jill and Joe.

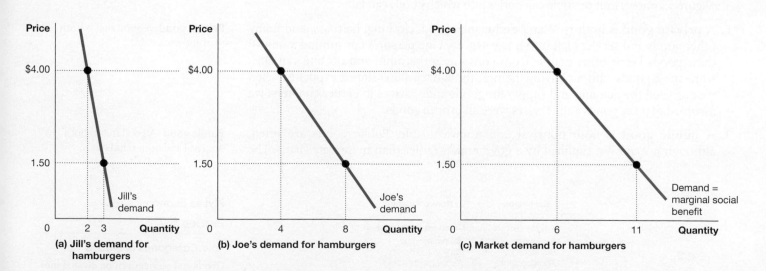

Figure 5.8   **Constructing the Market Demand Curve for a Private Good**

The market demand curve for private goods is determined by adding horizontally the quantity of the good demanded at each price by each consumer. For instance, in panel (a), Jill demands 2 hamburgers when the price is $4.00, and in panel (b), Joe demands 4 hamburgers when the price is $4.00. So, a quantity of 6 hamburgers and a price of $4.00 is a point on the market demand curve in panel (c).

At a price of $4.00, Jill demands 2 hamburgers per week and Joe demands 4. Adding horizontally, the combination of a price of $4.00 per hamburger and a quantity demanded of 6 hamburgers will be a point on the market demand curve for hamburgers. At a price of $1.50, Jill demands 3 hamburgers per week and Joe demands 8. Adding horizontally, the combination of a price of $1.50 per hamburger and a quantity demanded of 11 hamburgers will be another point on the market demand curve. A consumer's demand curve for a good represents the marginal benefit the consumer receives from the good, so when we add together the consumers' demand curves, we have not only the market demand curve but also the marginal social benefit curve for this good, assuming that there is no externality in consumption.

How can we find the demand curve or marginal social benefit curve for a public good? Once again, for simplicity, assume that Jill and Joe are the only consumers. Unlike with a private good, where Jill and Joe can end up consuming different quantities, with a public good, they will consume *the same quantity*. Suppose that Jill owns a service station on an isolated rural road, and Joe owns a car dealership next door. These are the only two businesses around for miles. Both Jill and Joe are afraid that unless they hire a security guard at night, their businesses may be burgled. Like national defense, the services of a security guard are in this case a public good: Once hired, the guard will be able to protect both businesses, so the good is nonrival. It also will not be possible to exclude either business from being protected, so the good is nonexcludable.

To arrive at a demand curve for a public good, we don't add quantities at each price, as with a private good. Instead, we add the price each consumer is willing to pay for each quantity of the public good. This value represents the total dollar amount consumers as a group would be willing to pay for that quantity of the public good. In other words, to find the demand curve, or marginal social benefit curve, for a private good, we add the demand curves of individual consumers horizontally; for public goods, we add individual demand curves vertically. Figure 5.9 shows how the marginal social benefit curve for security guard services depends on the individual demand curves of Jill and Joe.

The figure shows that Jill is willing to pay $8 per hour for the guard to provide 10 hours of protection per night. Joe would suffer a greater loss from a burglary, so he is willing to pay $10 per hour for the same amount of protection. Adding the dollar amount that each is willing to pay gives us a price of $18 per hour and a quantity of 10 hours as a point on the marginal social benefit curve for security guard services. The figure also shows that because Jill is willing to spend $4 per hour for 15 hours of guard services and Joe is willing to pay $5, a price of $9 per hour and a quantity of 15 hours is another point on the marginal social benefit curve for security guard services.   **MyLab Economics** Concept Check

The Optimal Quantity of a Public Good

We know that to achieve economic efficiency, a good or service should be produced up to the point where the sum of consumer surplus and producer surplus is maximized, or, alternatively, where the marginal social cost equals the marginal social benefit. Therefore, the optimal quantity of security guard services—or any other public good—will occur where the marginal social benefit curve intersects the supply curve. As with private goods, in the absence of an externality in production, the supply curve represents the marginal social cost of supplying the good. Figure 5.10 shows that the optimal quantity of security guard services supplied is 15 hours, at a price of $9 per hour.

Will the market provide the economically efficient quantity of security guard services? One difficulty is that the individual preferences of consumers, as shown by their demand curves, are not revealed in this market. This difficulty does not arise with private goods because consumers must reveal their preferences in order to purchase private goods. If the market price of Big Macs is $4.00, Joe either reveals that he is willing to pay that much by buying it or he does without it. In our example, neither

MyLab Economics Animation

Figure 5.9

Constructing the Demand Curve for a Public Good

To find the demand curve for a public good, we add up the price at which each consumer is willing to purchase each quantity of the good. In panel (a), Jill is willing to pay $8 per hour for a security guard to provide 10 hours of protection. In panel (b), Joe is willing to pay $10 for that level of protection. Therefore, in panel (c), the price of $18 per hour and the quantity of 10 hours will be a point on the demand curve for security guard services.

(a) Jill's demand for security guard services

(b) Joe's demand for security guard services

(c) Total demand for security guard services

MyLab Economics Animation

Figure 5.10

The Optimal Quantity of a Public Good

The optimal quantity of a public good is produced where the sum of consumer surplus and producer surplus is maximized, which occurs where the demand curve intersects the supply curve. In this case, the optimal quantity of security guard services is 15 hours, at a price of $9 per hour.

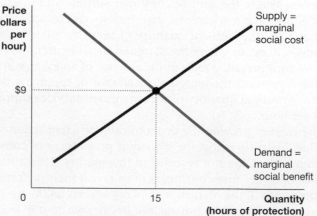

Jill nor Joe can be excluded from consuming the services provided by a security guard once either hires one, and, therefore, neither has an incentive to reveal her or his preferences. In this case, though, with only two consumers, it is likely that private bargaining will result in an efficient quantity of the public good. This outcome is not likely for a public good—such as national defense—that is supplied by the government to millions of consumers.

Governments sometimes use *cost–benefit analysis* to determine what quantity of a public good should be supplied. For example, before building a dam on a river, the federal government will attempt to weigh the costs against the benefits. The costs include the opportunity cost of other projects the government cannot carry out if it builds the dam. The benefits include improved flood control or new recreational opportunities on the lake formed by the dam. However, for many public goods, including national defense, the government does not use a formal cost–benefit analysis. Instead, the quantity of national defense supplied is determined by a political process involving Congress and the president. Even here, of course, Congress and the president realize that trade-offs are involved: The more resources used for national defense, the fewer resources are available for other public or private goods.   MyLab Economics Concept Check

Solved Problem 5.4   MyLab Economics Interactive Animation

Determining the Optimal Level of Public Goods

Suppose, once again, that Jill and Joe run businesses that are next door to each other on an isolated road, and both need a security guard. Their demand schedules for security guard services are as follows:

Joe		Jill	
Price (dollars per hour)	Quantity (hours of protection)	Price (dollars per hour)	Quantity (hours of protection)
$20	0	$20	1
18	1	18	2
16	2	16	3
14	3	14	4
12	4	12	5
10	5	10	6
8	6	8	7
6	7	6	8
4	8	4	9
2	9	2	10

The supply schedule for security guard services is as follows:

Price (dollars per hour)	Quantity (hours of protection)
$8	1
10	2
12	3
14	4
16	5
18	6
20	7
22	8
24	9

a. Draw a graph that shows the optimal level of security guard services. Be sure to label the curves on the graph.

b. Briefly explain why 8 hours of security guard protection is not an optimal quantity.

Solving the Problem

Step 1: **Review the chapter material.** This problem is about determining the optimal level of public goods, so you may want to review the section "The Optimal Quantity of a Public Good," which begins on page 167.

Step 2: **Begin by deriving the demand curve or marginal social benefit curve for security guard services.** To calculate the marginal social benefit of guard services, we need to add the prices that Jill and Joe are willing to pay at each quantity:

Demand, or Marginal Social Benefit	
Price (dollars per hour)	Quantity (hours of protection)
$38	1
34	2
30	3
26	4
22	5
18	6
14	7
10	8
6	9

Step 3: **Answer part (a) by plotting the demand (marginal social benefit) and supply (marginal social cost) curves.** The graph shows that the optimal level of security guard services is 6 hours.

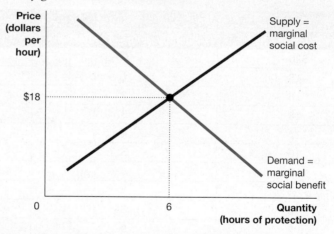

Step 4: **Answer part (b) by explaining why 8 hours of security guard protection is not an optimal quantity.** For each hour beyond 6, the supply curve is above the demand curve. Therefore, the marginal social benefit received will be less than the marginal social cost of supplying these hours. This results in a deadweight loss and a reduction in economic surplus.

MyLab Economics Study Plan   **Your Turn:** For more practice, do related problem 4.6 on page 180 at the end of this chapter.

Common Resources

In England during the Middle Ages, each village had an area of pasture, known as a *commons*, on which any family in the village was allowed to graze its cows or sheep without charge. Of course, the grass one family's cow ate was not available for another family's cow, so consumption was rival. But every family in the village had the right to use the commons, so it was nonexcludable. Without some type of limit on usage, the commons would be overgrazed. To see why, consider the economic incentives facing

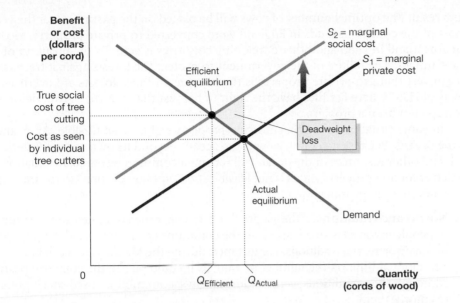

MyLab Economics Animation

Figure 5.11

Overuse of a Common Resource

For a common resource such as wood from a forest, the efficient level of use, $Q_{Efficient}$, is determined by the intersection of the demand curve, which represents the marginal social benefit received by consumers, and S_2, which represents the marginal social cost of cutting the wood. Because each individual tree cutter ignores the external cost, the equilibrium quantity of wood cut is Q_{Actual}, which is greater than the efficient quantity. At the actual equilibrium level of output, there is a deadweight loss, equal to the area of the yellow triangle.

a family that was thinking of buying another cow and grazing it on the commons. The family would gain the benefits from increased milk production, but adding another cow to the commons would create a negative externality by reducing the amount of grass available for the cows of other families. Because this family—and the other families in the village—did not take this negative externality into account when deciding whether to add another cow to the commons, too many cows would be added. The grass on the commons would eventually be depleted, and no family's cow would get enough to eat.

The Tragedy of the Commons The tendency for a common resource to be overused is called the **tragedy of the commons**. The forests in many poor countries are a modern example. When a family chops down a tree in a public forest, it takes into account the benefits of gaining firewood or wood for building, but it does not take into account the costs of deforestation. Haiti, for example, was once heavily forested. Today, perhaps half of the country's original forests have been cut down, primarily to be burned to create charcoal for heating and cooking. Because the mountains no longer have tree roots to hold the soil, heavy rains now often lead to devastating floods.

Figure 5.11 shows that with a common resource such as wood from a forest, the efficient level of use, $Q_{Efficient}$, is determined by the intersection of the demand curve, which represents the marginal social benefit received by consumers, and S_2, which represents the marginal social cost of cutting the wood. As in our discussion of negative externalities, the social cost is equal to the private cost of cutting the wood plus the external cost. In this case, the external cost represents the fact that the more wood each person cuts, the less wood there is available for others and the greater the deforestation, which increases the chances of floods. Because each individual tree cutter ignores the external cost, the equilibrium quantity of wood cut is Q_{Actual}, which is greater than the efficient quantity. At the actual equilibrium level of output, there is a deadweight loss, equal to the area of the yellow triangle in Figure 5.11.

Is There a Way out of the Tragedy of the Commons? Notice that our discussion of the tragedy of the commons is very similar to our earlier discussion of negative externalities. The source of the tragedy of the commons is the same as the source of negative externalities: lack of clearly defined and enforced property rights. For instance, suppose that instead of being held as a collective resource, a piece of pastureland is owned by one person. That person will take into account the effect of adding another cow on the grass available to cows already using the pasture.

Tragedy of the commons The tendency for a common resource to be overused.

As a result, the optimal number of cows will be placed on the pasture. Over the years, most of the commons lands in England were converted to private property. Most of the forestland in Haiti and other developing countries is actually the property of the government. The failure of the government to protect the forests against trespassers or convert them to private property is the key reason those forests are overused. In areas of Haiti where families have the right to harvest the trees they grow, deforestation has not been a problem.

In some situations, though, enforcing property rights is *not* feasible. An example is the oceans. Because no country owns the oceans beyond its own coastal waters, the fish and other resources of the ocean will remain a common resource. In situations in which enforcing property rights is not feasible, two types of solutions to the tragedy of the commons are possible:

1. **Norms and traditions.** If the geographic area concerned is limited and the number of people involved is small, access to the commons can be restricted through community norms and traditions. For instance, during the Middle Ages each family had a traditional limit on the number of animals it could put on the common pasture. Although these traditions were not formal laws, communities used social pressure to enforce them.

2. **Laws.** If the geographic area or the number of people involved is large, legal restrictions on access to the commons are required. These restrictions can take several different forms, including taxes, quotas, and tradable permits. By setting a tax equal to the external cost, governments can ensure that the efficient quantity of a resource is used. In the United States, the government has used quotas to limit access to pools of oil that are beneath property owned by many different persons. The quotas specify the quantity of oil that can be pumped during a given period of time.

MyLab Economics Study Plan

MyLab Economics Concept Check

Continued from page 147

Economics in Your Life & Career

Giving Advice on the "Best" Level of Pollution

At the beginning of this chapter, we asked you to think about what advice you would give as a policy aide to a U.S. senator on the "best" level of carbon emissions. Conceptually, this is a straightforward question to answer: The efficient level of carbon emissions is the level for which the marginal benefit of reducing carbon emissions exactly equals the marginal cost of reducing carbon emissions. In practice, however, this question is very difficult to answer. For example, scientists disagree about how much carbon emissions are contributing to climate change and what the damage from climate change will be. In addition, the cost of reducing carbon emissions depends on the method of reduction used. As a result, neither the marginal benefit curve nor the marginal cost curve for reducing carbon emissions is known with certainty. This uncertainty makes it difficult for policymakers to determine the economically efficient level of carbon emissions and is the source of much of the current debate. In any case, economists agree that the total cost of *completely* eliminating carbon emissions is much greater than the total benefit. So, at least you can provide the senator you work for with that conclusion!

Conclusion

We saw in Chapter 4 that government interventions in the economy, such as imposing price ceilings and price floors, can reduce economic efficiency. But in this chapter, we have seen that the government plays an important role in the economy when the absence of well-defined and enforceable property rights keeps the market from operating efficiently. For instance, because no one has a property right to clean air, in the absence of government intervention, firms will produce too great a quantity of products that generate air pollution. We have also seen that public goods are nonrival and nonexcludable, so the government often supplies them.

Visit **MyLab Economics** for a news article and analysis related to the concepts in this chapter.

CHAPTER SUMMARY
AND PROBLEMS

Key Terms

Coase theorem, p. 156

Command-and-control approach, p. 162

Common resource, p. 166

Excludability, p. 165

Externality, p. 148

Free riding, p. 166

Market failure, p. 151

Pigovian taxes and subsidies, p. 162

Private benefit, p. 149

Private cost, p. 149

Private good, p. 165

Property rights, p. 151

Public good, p. 165

Rivalry, p. 165

Social benefit, p. 149

Social cost, p. 149

Tragedy of the commons, p. 171

Transactions costs, p. 156

 5.1 Externalities and Economic Efficiency, pages 148–151

LEARNING OBJECTIVE: Identify examples of positive and negative externalities and use graphs to show how externalities affect economic efficiency.

MyLab Economics Visit www.pearson.com/mylab/economics to complete these exercises online and get instant feedback.

Summary

An **externality** is a benefit or cost to parties who are not involved in a transaction. Pollution and other externalities in production cause a difference between the **private cost** borne by the producer of a good or service and the **social cost**, which includes any external cost, such as the cost of pollution. An externality in consumption causes a difference between the **private benefit** received by the consumer and the **social benefit**, which includes any external benefit. If externalities exist in production or consumption, the market will not produce the optimal level of a good or service. This outcome is referred to as **market failure**. Externalities arise when property rights do not exist or cannot be legally enforced. **Property rights** are the rights individuals or businesses have to the exclusive use of their property, including the right to buy or sell it.

Review Questions

1.1 What is an externality? Give an example of a positive externality, and give an example of a negative externality.

1.2 When does the private cost of producing a good differ from the social cost? Give an example. When does the private benefit from consuming a good differ from the social benefit? Give an example.

1.3 What is economic efficiency? How do externalities affect the economic efficiency of a market equilibrium?

1.4 What is market failure? When is market failure likely to arise?

1.5 Briefly explain the relationship between property rights and the existence of externalities.

Problems and Applications

1.6 A neighbor's barking dog can be both a positive externality and a negative externality. Under what circumstances would a dog's bark be a positive externality? Under what circumstances would a dog's bark be a negative externality?

1.7 Yellowstone National Park is in bear country. The National Park Service, at its Yellowstone Web site, states the following about camping and hiking in bear country:

> Do not leave packs containing food unattended, even for a few minutes. Allowing a bear to obtain human food even once often results in the bear becoming aggressive about obtaining such food in the future. Aggressive bears present a threat to human safety and eventually must be destroyed or removed from the park. Please obey the law and do not allow bears or other wildlife to obtain human food.

What negative externality does obtaining human food pose for bears? What negative externality do bears obtaining human food pose for future campers and hikers?

Source: National Park Service, Yellowstone National Park, "Backcountry Camping and Hiking," www.nps.gov/yell/planyourvisit/backcountryhiking.htm.

1.8 Every year at the beginning of flu season, many people, including the elderly, get a flu shot to reduce their chances of contracting the flu. One result is that people who do *not* get a flu shot are less likely to contract the flu.

a. What type of externality (negative or positive) arises from getting a flu shot?

b. On the graph that follows, show the effects of this externality by drawing in and labeling any additional curves that are needed and by labeling the efficient quantity and the efficient price of flu shots. Label the area representing deadweight loss in this market.

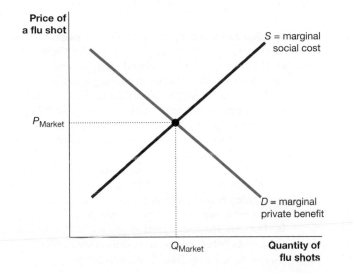

1.9 John Cassidy, a writer for the *New Yorker*, wrote a blog post arguing against New York City's having installed bike lanes. Cassidy complained that the bike lanes had eliminated traffic lanes on some streets as well as some on-street parking. A writer for the *Economist* disputed Cassidy's argument with the following comment: "I hate to belabour the point, but driving, as it turns out, is associated with a number of negative externalities." What externalities are associated with driving? How do these externalities affect the debate over whether big cities should install more bike lanes?

Sources: John Cassidy, "Battle of the Bike Lanes," *New Yorker*, March 8, 2011; and "The World Is His Parking Spot," *Economist*, March 9, 2011.

1.10 In a study at a large state university, students were randomly assigned roommates. Researchers found that, on average, males assigned to roommates who reported drinking alcohol in the year before entering college earned GPAs one-quarter point lower than those assigned to nondrinking roommates. For males who drank frequently before college, being assigned to a roommate who also drank frequently before college reduced their GPAs by two-thirds of a point. Draw a graph showing the price of alcohol and the quantity of alcohol consumption on college campuses. Include in the graph the demand for drinking and the private and social costs of drinking. Label any deadweight loss that arises in this market.

Source: Michael Kremer and Dan M. Levy, "Peer Effects and Alcohol Use among College Students," *Journal of Economic Perspectives*, Vol. 22, No. 3, Summer 2008, pp. 189–206.

1.11 Tom and Jacob are college students. Each of them will probably get married later and have two or three children. Each knows that if he studies more in college, he'll get a better job and earn more money. Earning more will enable them to spend more on their future families for things such as orthodontia, nice clothes, admission to expensive colleges, and travel. Tom thinks about the benefits to his potential children when he decides how much studying to do. Jacob doesn't.

a. What type of externality arises from studying?
b. Draw a graph showing this externality, contrasting the responses of Tom and Jacob. Who studies more? Who acts more efficiently? Briefly explain.

1.12 In recent years, companies have used fracking, or hydraulic fracturing, in drilling for oil and natural gas that previously could not be profitably recovered. According to an article in the *New York Times*, "horizontal drilling has enabled engineers to inject millions of gallons of high-pressure water directly into layers of shale to create the fractures that release the gas. Chemicals added to the water dissolve minerals, kill bacteria that might plug up the well, and insert sand to prop open the fractures." Experts are divided about whether fracking results in significant pollution, but some people worry that chemicals used in fracking might lead to pollution of underground supplies of water used by households and farms.

a. First, assume that fracking causes no significant pollution. Use a demand and supply graph to show the effect of fracking on the market for natural gas.
b. Now assume that fracking does result in pollution. On your graph from part (a), show the effect of fracking. Be sure to carefully label all curves and all equilibrium points.
c. In your graph in part (b), what has happened to the efficient level of output and the efficient price in the market for natural gas compared with the situation before fracking? Can you be certain that the efficient level of output and the efficient price have risen or fallen as a result of fracking? Briefly explain.

Source: Susan L. Brantley and Anna Meyendorff, "The Facts on Fracking," *New York Times*, March 13, 2013.

1.13 In an article in the agriculture magazine *Choices*, Oregon State University economist JunJie Wu made the following observation about the conversion of farmland to urban development:

> Land use provides many economic and social benefits, but often comes at a substantial cost to the environment. Although most economic costs are figured into land use decisions, most environmental externalities are not. These environmental "externalities" cause a divergence between private and social costs for some land uses, leading to an inefficient land allocation. For example, developers may not bear all the environmental and infrastructural costs generated by their projects. Such "market failures" provide a justification for private conservation efforts and public land use planning and regulation.

What does the author mean by *market failures* and *inefficient land allocation*? Explain why the author describes inefficient land allocation as a market failure. Illustrate your argument with a graph showing the market for land to be used for urban development.

Source: JunJie Wu, "Land Use Changes: Economic, Social, and Environmental Impacts," *Choices*, Vol. 23, No. 4, Fourth Quarter 2008, pp. 6–10.

5.2 Private Solutions to Externalities: The Coase Theorem, pages 151–157

LEARNING OBJECTIVE: Discuss the Coase theorem and explain how private bargaining can lead to economic efficiency in a market with an externality.

MyLab Economics Visit www.pearson.com/mylab/economics to complete these exercises online and get instant feedback.

Summary

Externalities and market failures result from incomplete property rights or from the difficulty of enforcing property rights in certain situations. When an externality exists and the efficient quantity of a good is not being produced, the total cost of reducing the externality is usually less than the total benefit. **Transactions costs** are the costs in time and other resources that parties incur in the process of agreeing to and carrying out an exchange of goods or services. According to the **Coase theorem**, if these costs are low, private bargaining will result in an efficient solution to the problem of externalities.

Review Questions

2.1 What do economists mean by "an economically efficient level of pollution"?

2.2 What is the Coase theorem? Why do the parties involved in an externality have an incentive to reach an efficient solution?

2.3 What are transactions costs? When are we likely to see private solutions to the problem of externalities?

Problems and Applications

2.4 Is it ever possible for an *increase* in pollution to make society better off? Briefly explain, using a graph like Figure 5.3 on page 153.

2.5 If the marginal cost of reducing a certain type of pollution is zero, should all of that type of pollution be eliminated? Briefly explain.

2.6 Discuss the factors that determine the marginal cost of reducing crime. Discuss the factors that determine the marginal benefit of reducing crime. Would it be economically efficient to reduce the amount of crime to zero? Briefly explain.

2.7 In discussing the reduction of air pollution in the developing world, Richard Fuller of the Blacksmith Institute, an environmental organization, observed, "It's the 90/10 rule. To do 90 percent of the work only costs 10 percent of the money. It's the last 10 percent of the cleanup that costs 90 percent of the money." Why should it be any more costly to clean up the last 10 percent of polluted air than to clean up the first 90 percent? What trade-offs would be involved in cleaning up the final 10 percent?

Source: Tiffany M. Luck, "The World's Dirtiest Cities," *Forbes*, February 26, 2008.

2.8 (Related to the Apply the Concept on page 152) In the first years following the passage of the Clean Air Act in 1970, air pollution declined sharply, and there were important health benefits, including a decline in infant mortality. According to an article in the *Economist*, however, recently some policymakers "worry that the EPA is constantly tightening restrictions on pollution, at ever higher cost to business but with diminishing returns in terms of public health."

  a. Why might additional reductions in air pollution come at "ever higher cost"? What does the article mean by arguing that these reductions will result in "diminishing returns in terms of public health"?

  b. How should the federal government decide whether further reductions in air pollution are needed?

Source: "Soaring Emissions," *Economist*, June 2, 2011.

2.9 (Related to the Don't Let This Happen to You on page 154) Mabel is an advocate for a "zero tolerance" policy regarding all illegal street drugs, including cocaine, marijuana, and heroin. Mabel has witnessed high crime and violence in her neighborhood and believes that only if police arrest and prosecute anyone who sells or uses illegal drugs will she and her neighbors and their children live without fear. Is the policy that Mabel endorses economically efficient? Briefly explain.

2.10 (Related to the Apply the Concept on page 156) Ira Goldman invented the Knee Defender, which keeps the airline seat in front of a passenger from reclining. He argues that airlines have sold the space between two seats to the person occupying the seat but also to the person in the seat in front of that seat by allowing the occupant of that seat to recline it. Assume that Goldman is correct. According to the Coase theorem, does this airline policy make it impossible for passengers to achieve an economically efficient outcome with respect to the issue of reclining seats? Briefly explain.

Source: Damon Darlin, "In Defense of the Knee Defender," *New York Times*, August 28, 2014.

2.11 (Related to the Apply the Concept on page 156) An article in the *Economist* about the struggle among airline passengers over reclining seats offered the following observation: "Given that airlines are unlikely to increase the [distance between] their seats any time soon, better that all planes come with fixed, non-reclining chairs in the first place." Would the change proposed result in an economically efficient outcome? Briefly explain.

Source: "Upright and Uptight," *Economist*, June 7, 2014.

5.3 Government Policies to Deal with Externalities, pages 157–165

LEARNING OBJECTIVE: Analyze government policies to achieve economic efficiency in a market with an externality.

MyLab Economics Visit www.pearson.com/mylab/economics to complete these exercises online and get instant feedback.

Summary

When private solutions to externalities are unworkable, the government sometimes intervenes. One way to deal with a negative externality in production is to impose a tax equal to the cost of the externality. The tax causes the producer of the good to internalize the externality. The government can deal with a positive externality in consumption by giving consumers a subsidy, or payment, equal to the value of the externality. Government taxes and subsidies intended to bring about an efficient level of output in the presence of externalities are called **Pigovian taxes and subsidies**. Although the federal government has sometimes used subsidies and taxes to deal with externalities, in dealing with pollution it has more often used a command-and-control approach. A **command-and-control approach** involves the government imposing quantitative limits on the amount of pollution allowed or requiring firms to install specific pollution control devices. Direct pollution controls of this type are not economically efficient, however. As a result, economists generally prefer reducing pollution by using market-based policies.

Review Questions

3.1 What is a Pigovian tax? How large should a Pigovian tax be to achieve efficiency?

3.2 What does it mean for a producer or consumer to internalize an externality? What would cause a producer or consumer to internalize an externality?

3.3 Why do most economists prefer tradable emission allowances to the command-and-control approach to pollution?

Problems and Applications

3.4 A column in the *New York Times* notes that many economists "support Pigovian taxes because, in some sense, we are already paying them." In what sense might consumers in a market be "paying" a Pigovian tax even if the government hasn't imposed an explicit tax?

Source: Adam Davidson, "Should We Tax People for Being Annoying?" *New York Times*, January 8, 2013.

3.5 Many antibiotics are no longer effective in eliminating infections because bacteria have evolved to become resistant to them. Some bacteria are now resistant to all but one or two existing antibiotics. In 2015, the Obama administration proposed subsidizing research aimed at developing new antibiotics.

a. Are there externalities involved in the market for antibiotics that would require a government subsidy to achieve an economically efficient outcome? Briefly explain.

b. Many people have health insurance that covers the majority of the cost of their prescription drugs, including antibiotics. Does that fact make the case for a government subsidy of the production of antibiotics stronger or weaker? Briefly explain.

Source: Sabrina Tavernise and Michael D. Shear, "Obama Seeks to Double Funding to Fight Antibiotic Resistance," *New York Times*, March 27, 2015.

3.6 A column in the *New York Times* has the headline "Should We Tax People for Being Annoying?"

a. Do annoying people cause a negative externality? Should they be taxed? Do crying babies on a bus or plane cause a negative externality? Should the babies (or their parents) be taxed?

b. Do people who plant flowers and otherwise have beautiful gardens visible from the street cause a positive externality? Should these people receive a government subsidy?

c. Should every negative externality be taxed? Should every positive externality be subsidized? How might the government decide whether using Pigovian taxes and subsidies is appropriate?

Source: Adam Davidson, "Should We Tax People for Being Annoying?" *New York Times*, January 8, 2013.

3.7 An article in the *Economist* noted that Uber, the ride-hailing app, "is said to worsen traffic problems" and observed that the result is a negative externality.

a. Explain the reasoning behind the argument that using Uber might generate a negative externality.

b. If Uber generates a negative externality, should the government impose a tax on each ride? Should the government also tax rides in taxis? Should it tax rides in private cars? Briefly explain.

Source: "Internet Firms' Legal Immunity Is under Threat," *Economist*, February 11, 2017.

3.8 In 2017, President Donald Trump was considering a major increase on federal government spending on infrastructure, including building and repairing bridges, highways, rail lines, and subways. An article in the *Economist* argued, "Just as economists talk of 'negative externalities' (from, say, pollution), infrastructure can have positive externalities that are not captured by investors but will benefit society."

a. Explain what positive externalities infrastructure spending might generate.

b. If infrastructure spending generates a positive externality, what effect should this have on government policy?

Source: "Are Big Infrastructure Projects Castles in the Air or Bridges to Nowhere?" *Economist*, January 16, 2017.

3.9 **(Related to the Apply the Concept on page 159)** Eric Finkelstein, an economist at Duke University, argued that the external costs from being obese are larger than the external costs from smoking because "the mortality effect for obesity is much smaller than it is for smoking and the costs start much earlier in life."

a. What does Finkelstein mean by the "mortality effect"? Why would the mortality effect of obesity being smaller than the mortality effect of smoking result in obesity having a larger external cost?

b. Tobacco taxes have been more politically popular than taxes on soda. Why might the general public be more willing to support cigarette taxes than soda taxes?

Source: David Leonhardt, "Obama Likes Some Sin Taxes More Than Others," *New York Times*, April 10, 2013.

3.10 **(Related to Solved Problem 5.3 on page 160)** Solved Problem 5.3 contains the statement "Of course, the government actually collects the tax from sellers rather than from consumers, but we get the same result whether the government imposes a tax on the buyers of a good or on the sellers." Demonstrate that this statement is correct by solving the problem, assuming that the increase in the tax on gasoline shifts the supply curve rather than the demand curve.

3.11 **(Related to Solved Problem 5.3 on page 160)** The fumes from dry cleaners can contribute to air pollution. Suppose the following graph illustrates the situation in the dry cleaning market.

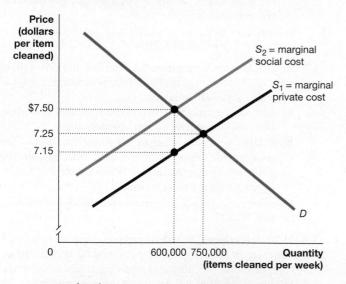

a. Explain how a government can use a tax on dry cleaning to bring about the efficient level of production. What should the value of the tax be?

b. How large is the deadweight loss (in dollars) from excessive dry cleaning, according to the graph?

3.12 **(Related to Solved Problem 5.3 on page 160)** Companies that produce toilet paper bleach the paper to make it white. Some paper plants discharge the bleach into rivers and lakes, causing substantial environmental damage. Suppose the following graph illustrates the situation in the toilet paper market.

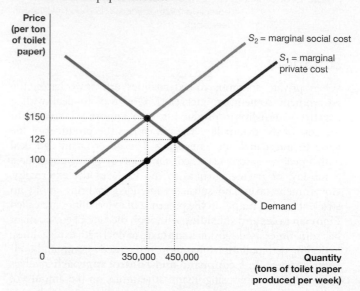

Explain how the federal government can use a tax on toilet paper to bring about the efficient level of production. What should the value of the tax be?

3.13 The following graph illustrates the situation in the dry cleaning market, assuming that the marginal social cost of the pollution *increases* as the quantity of items cleaned per week increases. The graph includes two demand curves: one for a smaller city, D_S, and the other for a larger city, D_L.

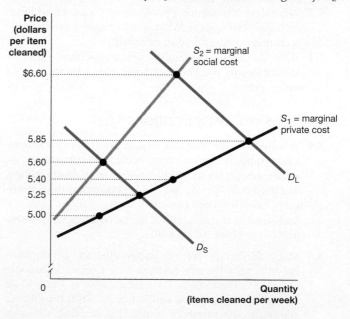

a. Explain why the marginal social cost curve has a different slope than the marginal private cost curve.

b. What tax per item cleaned will achieve economic efficiency in the smaller city? In the larger city? Explain why the efficient tax is different in the two cities.

3.14 **(Related to the Chapter Opener on page 146)** In a letter to the *New York Times*, Suzanne McCarron, an executive at ExxonMobil, argued that a carbon tax would "allow market forces to drive solutions."

a. According to McCarron, what problem would a carbon tax solve?

b. How would a carbon tax allow market forces to "drive solutions"?

Source: Suzanne McCarron, "Letter: Exxon Favors a Carbon Tax," *New York Times*, December 30, 2016.

3.15 **(Related to the Apply the Concept on page 163)** An economist for the Brookings Institution argued that "a price on carbon would minimize the cost of steering economic activity away from the greenhouse gas emissions that threaten the climate."

a. In what sense does a carbon tax put a price on carbon?

b. How would a carbon tax steer economic activity away from greenhouse gas emissions?

c. Why might a carbon tax be less costly to the economy than a command-and-control approach to reducing greenhouse gases? Why might a command-and-control approach to pollution control still be more politically popular than a carbon tax? Include in your answer a brief discussion of the difference between the normative analysis and positive analysis of this policy issue.

Source: Fred Dews, "10 Things You Should Know about the Carbon Tax," brookings.edu, May 4, 2016.

3.16 **(Related to the Apply the Concept on page 163)** An economics student made the following comment about a proposed carbon tax:

I read that a tax on carbon would have a greater negative effect on low-income consumers than high-income consumers, but I disagree. Business executives spend a lot of money and time traveling—both by car and plane. Many rich people have homes that are considerably larger than the average family's home. Heating and air conditioning bills are certainly greater for larger homes than smaller homes. The cost of a carbon tax would surely be greater for those with the highest incomes.

Explain whether you agree that a carbon tax would impose a greater burden on high-income consumers than low-income consumers.

5.4 Four Categories of Goods, pages 165–172

LEARNING OBJECTIVE: Categorize goods on the basis of whether they are rival or excludable and use graphs to illustrate the efficient quantities of public goods and common resources.

MyLab Economics Visit **www.pearson.com/mylab/economics** to complete these exercises online and get instant feedback.

Summary

There are four categories of goods: private goods, public goods, quasi-public goods, and common resources. **Private goods** are both rival and excludable. **Rivalry** means that when one person consumes a unit of a good, no one else can consume that unit. **Excludability** means that anyone who does not pay for a good cannot consume it. **Public goods** are both nonrival and nonexcludable. Private firms are usually not willing to supply public goods because of free riding. **Free riding** involves benefiting from a good without paying for it. *Quasi-public goods* are excludable but not rival. **Common resources** are rival but not excludable. The **tragedy of the commons** refers to the tendency for a common resource to be overused. The tragedy of the commons results from a lack of clearly defined and enforced property rights. We find the market demand curve for a private good by adding the quantity of the good demanded by each consumer at each price. We find the demand curve for a public good by adding vertically the price each consumer would be willing to pay for each quantity of the good. The optimal quantity of a public good occurs where the demand curve intersects the curve representing the marginal cost of supplying the good.

Review Questions

4.1 Define *rivalry* and *excludability* and use these terms to discuss the four categories of goods.

4.2 What is free riding? How is free riding related to the need for public goods?

4.3 What is the tragedy of the commons? How can it be avoided?

Problems and Applications

4.4 The merry-go-round in Ross Park, a public park in Binghamton, New York, was first installed in 1920 and has been periodically refurbished by the city in the years since. There is no entry fee to visit the park or to ride the merry-go-round. Is the merry-go-round a public good? Briefly explain.

Source: Greater Binghamton, "Carousels," www.visitbinghamton.org/ebrochures/carousels.pdf.

4.5 In writing about the increased popularity of national parks in the United States, such as Yosemite, Yellowstone, and the Grand Canyon, environmental economist Margaret Walls wrote:

When one person's visit to a park doesn't appreciably diminish the experience for others, the fee to use the park should be zero. That doesn't apply when the public good starts to experience congestion problems . . . the Park Service should . . . [charge] a significantly higher fee at the most popular parks during the summer months.

Are Yosemite and other national parks public goods? Briefly explain.

Source: Margaret A. Walls, "Protecting Our National Parks: Entrance Fees Can Help," *Resources*, No. 193, Fall 2016.

4.6 **(Related to Solved Problem 5.4 on page 169)** Suppose that Joe and Jill are the only two people in the small town of Andover. Andover has land available to build a park of no more than 9 acres. Joe and Jill's demand schedules for the park are as follows:

Joe	
Price per Acre	Number of Acres
$10	0
9	1
8	2
7	3
6	4
5	5
4	6
3	7
2	8
1	9

Jill	
Price per Acre	Number of Acres
$15	0
14	1
13	2
12	3
11	4
10	5
9	6
8	7
7	8
6	9

The supply schedule is as follows:

Price per Acre	Number of Acres
$11	1
13	2
15	3
17	4
19	5
21	6
23	7
25	8
27	9

   a. Draw a graph showing the optimal size of the park. Be sure to label the curves on the graph.
   b. Briefly explain why a park of 2 acres is not optimal.
4.7 As readers of Herman Melville's 1851 novel *Moby Dick* know, at one time oil made from whale blubber was an important source of energy that was widely used by households and firms in oil lamps. Other sources of energy replaced whale oil in the second half of the nineteenth century, and today many Americans consider whales only as a source of entertainment on visits to aquariums and whale watching excursions. But some species of whales—including baleen and gray whales—are in danger of extinction. The U.S. Department of Agriculture estimates that more than 9 billion chickens are raised for food annually. Chickens, unlike whales, are not threatened with extinction. Briefly explain why.
4.8 Nancy Folbre, an economist at the University of Massachusetts, Amherst, argued, "We must take responsibility for governing the commons—not just the quaint oldfashioned village green, but things that cannot easily be privatized—[such as] clean air." Do you agree that clean air is like a common pasture in England in the Middle Ages? Briefly explain.

Source: Nancy Folbre, "Taking Responsibility for the Commons," *New York Times*, February 26, 2009.

4.9 Vaccines don't provide immunity from disease for some people. But if most people get vaccinated against a disease, such as measles, then the population achieves "herd immunity," which means that there are so few cases of the disease that even people for whom vaccinations are ineffective are unlikely to contract the disease. An article in the *Economist* argued that "herd immunity is a classic public good."

a. Do you agree with this statement?

b. The same article argued that there is an incentive to "'free ride' off the contributions of others" by not getting vaccinated. What does the author mean by "free ride"? If the author is correct, what will be the effect of this free riding?

c. Given your answer to part (b), why do most people vaccinate their children against childhood diseases, and why do many adults get vaccinated against influenza?

Source: "Resorting to Freedom," *Economist*, February 4, 2015.

4.10 Put each of the following goods or services into one of the categories shown in Figure 5.7 on page 165. That is, categorize them as private goods, public goods, quasi-public goods, or common resources.

a. A television broadcast of baseball's World Series

b. Home mail delivery

c. Education in a public school

d. Education in a private school

e. Hiking in a park surrounded by a fence

f. Hiking in a park not surrounded by a fence

g. An apple

4.11 A columnist for the *Wall Street Journal* argued that high-speed Internet connections are now a public good: "We're going to have to transition to the building of public infrastructure and away from the revolution being the domain of private enterprise. It's not enough for Google to roll out high speed fiber to a handful of cities."

a. In what ways is the infrastructure for high-speed Internet connections like automobile highways? In what ways is it different from highways?

b. As of 2017, private firms have constructed most of the infrastructure for high-speed Internet connections, while governments have constructed most highways. Is it still possible that the infrastructure for high-speed Internet connections is a public good despite this fact? Briefly explain.

c. Do you agree with the columnist that we should think of the infrastructure for high-speed Internet connections as being like a public good? Is there any information you would need to know before deciding?

Source: Christopher Mims, "The Future Is Here. It Just Needs a Big Push," *Wall Street Journal*, January 19, 2016.

4.12 William Easterly in *The White Man's Burden* shared the following account by New York University Professor Leonard Wantchekon of how Professor Wantchekon's village in Benin, Africa, managed the local fishing pond when he was growing up:

> To open the fishing season, elders performed ritual tests at Amlé, a lake fifteen kilometers from the village. If the fish were large enough, fishing was allowed for two or three days. If they were too small, all fishing was forbidden, and anyone who secretly fished the lake at this time was outcast, excluded from the formal and informal groups that formed the village's social structure. Those who committed this breach of trust were often shunned by the whole community; no one would speak to the offender, or even acknowledge his existence for a year or more.

What economic problem were the village elders trying to prevent? Do you think their solution was effective?

Source: William Easterly, *The White Man's Burden: Why the West's Efforts to Aid the Rest Have Done So Much Ill and So Little Good*, New York: Penguin Books, 2006, p. 94.

Critical Thinking Exercises

CT5.1 You and a friend are discussing the role of government in the economy. Her viewpoint is that governments should not interfere with the operation of markets. After reading this chapter and Chapter 4, could you convince her to change her viewpoint? Write a paragraph in your own words giving the argument you would make to your friend. Be sure to include a graph to illustrate your argument.

CT5.2 The chapter describes an "efficient level of pollution." Going beyond being able to answer a test question on this topic, did the concepts in this chapter convince you there is an efficient level of pollution? Briefly explain in your own words.

Elasticity: The Responsiveness of Demand and Supply

Do Soda Taxes Work?

In recent years, a number of cities, including San Francisco, Chicago, and Philadelphia, have enacted taxes on soda, energy drinks, iced tea, and other sweetened beverages. Do such taxes work? The answer depends on what policy goals city governments are trying to achieve. A tax on soda can have positive effects on health because drinking sweetened beverages has been linked to obesity, diabetes, and other health problems. In 2016, when San Francisco enacted a 2-cents-per-ounce tax on sweetened beverages, a member of the California state senate argued, "These drinks are undermining public health and helping explode health care costs and insurance rates for the taxpayer." A tax on soda also raises revenue for the city enacting it. For example, when Philadelphia imposed a tax of 1.5 cents per ounce on sweetened beverages in 2016, Mayor Jim Kenney stated, "The purpose of the tax was to raise money for important needs."

Notice that these two purposes for enacting a soda tax can be at odds with each other. The tax revenue a city raises equals the tax per ounce of soda multiplied by the number of ounces of soda sold. For example, if the tax is 1.5 cent per ounce and 6 billion ounces of soda are sold in the city that year, the tax will raise $90 million. Philadelphia hoped to raise $400 million from its soda tax over a five-year period. But as the tax raises the prices consumers pay for sweetened beverages, grocery stores and supermarkets will sell a smaller quantity of these beverages. The greater the decline in the quantity of soda demanded, the greater the health effect of the tax . . . but the less revenue the city will raise from the tax.

Firms selling soda are also concerned with how much the quantity of soda demanded falls following a tax increase.

Matt Rourke/AP Images

In Philadelphia, PepsiCo indicated that its sales fell by 40 percent after the tax took effect. An owner of a supermarket chain in Chicago was quoted as saying that following passage of a soda tax in that city, many of his customers began buying their soda in nearby Indiana, where there was no soda tax.

All businesses have a financial incentive to determine how much their sales will fall as prices increase. Governments also have an incentive to determine how consumers will react if the price of a product such as soda rises following a tax increase. In this chapter, we will explore how economists measure the responsiveness of the quantity demanded and the quantity supplied to changes in the market price.

Sources: Jennifer Kaplan, "Philadelphia's Soda Sellers Say Tax Has Reduced Sales by as Much as 50%," bloomberg.com, February 17, 2017; "Soda Taxes a Healthy Trend," sfchronicle.com, January 27, 2017; Candice Choi and Kristen de Groot, "'Soda Tax' Stakes Escalate in Pivotal Philadelphia Fight," *New York Times*, March 17, 2017; and Charles Thomas, "Hundreds Protest Tax on Sugary Drinks in Cook County," abc7chicago.com, October 31, 2016.

Chapter Outline & Learning Objectives

Economics in Your Life & Career

Would PepsiCo and One of Its Bottlers Prefer a National or Local Soda Tax?

In 2017, several city governments had taxes on soda, but there was no national soda tax. Suppose that Congress and the president are considering enacting such a tax. You are an economist working for PepsiCo, and the firm's managers ask you to evaluate the effect of the tax on the firm's sales of its sodas and sweetened energy drinks. In particular, you are asked to consider whether a national soda tax might be better than widespread local soda taxes (assuming that the national tax would replace the local taxes). Would your evaluation change if you were employed by a local Pepsi bottler rather than by PepsiCo? As you read this chapter, try to answer these questions. You can check your answers against those we provide on **page 207** at the end of this chapter.

Elasticity A measure of how much one economic variable responds to changes in another economic variable.

Whether you manage a beverage distributor, a clothing store, or a service station, you need to know how an increase or a decrease in the price of your products will affect the quantity consumers are willing to buy. We know that cutting the price of a good increases the quantity demanded and that raising the price reduces the quantity demanded. But the critical question is: *How much* will the quantity demanded change as a result of a price increase or decrease? Economists use the concept of **elasticity** to measure how one economic variable—such as the quantity demanded—responds to changes in another economic variable—such as the price. For example, the responsiveness of the quantity demanded of a good to changes in its price is called the *price elasticity of demand*. Knowing the price elasticity of demand allows you to compute the effect of a price change on the quantity demanded. This knowledge is important to a business in determining the price that will maximize profit.

In addition to a good's price, consumer income and the prices of related goods also affect the quantity of the good that consumers demand. As a manager, you can apply the concept of elasticity to measure the responsiveness of demand to these other variables. With many economic issues, we are also interested in the responsiveness of the quantity supplied of a good to changes in its price, which is called the *price elasticity of supply*.

In this chapter, we will see that elasticity is an important concept not just for business managers but for policymakers as well. For example, if the government wants to discourage smoking, it can raise the price of cigarettes by increasing the tax on them. If policymakers know the price elasticity of demand for cigarettes, they can calculate how many fewer packs of cigarettes smokers will demand at a higher price.

6.1 The Price Elasticity of Demand and Its Measurement

LEARNING OBJECTIVE: Define and calculate the price elasticity of demand.

We know from the law of demand that when the price of a product falls, the quantity demanded of the product increases. But the law of demand tells firms only that the demand curves for their products slope downward. It is more useful to have a measure of the responsiveness of the quantity demanded to a change in price. This measure is called the **price elasticity of demand**.

Measuring the Price Elasticity of Demand

Price elasticity of demand The responsiveness of the quantity demanded to a change in price, measured by dividing the percentage change in the quantity demanded of a product by the percentage change in the product's price.

We might measure the price elasticity of demand by using the slope of the demand curve because the slope tells us how much quantity changes as price changes, but this approach has a drawback: The measurement of slope is sensitive to the units chosen for quantity and price. For example, suppose a soda tax causes an increase in the price of soda of $1 per 2-liter bottle, which decreases the quantity demanded from 10.2 million bottles to 10.1 million bottles per day. The change in quantity is −0.1 million gallons, and the change in price is $1, so the slope is −0.1/1 = −0.1. But:

- If we measure price in cents, rather than in dollars, the slope is −0.1/100 = −0.001.
- If we measure price in dollars and bottles in thousands, instead of millions, the slope is −100/1 = −100.
- If we measure price in cents and bottles in thousands, the slope is −100/100 = −1.

Clearly, the value we compute for the slope can change dramatically, depending on the units we use for quantity and price.

To avoid this confusion over units, economists use *percentage changes* when measuring the price elasticity of demand. Percentage changes are not dependent on units of measurement. (For a review of calculating percentage changes, see the appendix to Chapter 1.) No matter what units we use to measure the quantity of soda, 10 percent more soda is 10 percent more soda. Therefore, the price elasticity of demand is measured by dividing the percentage change in the quantity demanded by the percentage change in the product's price. Or:

$$\text{Price elasticity of demand} = \frac{\text{Percentage change in quantity demanded}}{\text{Percentage change in price}}.$$

It's important to remember that *the price elasticity of demand is not the same as the slope of the demand curve.*

If we calculate the price elasticity of demand for a price cut, the percentage change in price will be negative, and the percentage change in quantity demanded will be positive. Similarly, if we calculate the price elasticity of demand for a price increase, the percentage change in price will be positive, and the percentage change in quantity demanded will be negative. Therefore, the price elasticity of demand is always negative. In comparing elasticities, though, we are usually interested in their relative size. So, we often drop the minus sign and compare their *absolute values*. For example, although -3 is actually a smaller number than -2, we say that a price elasticity of -3 is larger than a price elasticity of -2.   **MyLab Economics** Concept Check

Elastic Demand and Inelastic Demand

If the quantity demanded is very responsive to changes in price, the percentage change in quantity demanded will be *greater* than the percentage change in price, and the price elasticity of demand will be greater than 1 in absolute value. In this case, demand is **elastic**. For example, if a 10 percent decrease in the price of bagels results in a 20 percent increase in the quantity of bagels demanded, then:

$$\text{Price elasticity of demand} = \frac{20\%}{-10\%} = -2,$$

and we can conclude that the demand for bagels is elastic.

When the quantity demanded is not very responsive to price, however, the percentage change in quantity demanded will be *less* than the percentage change in price, and the price elasticity of demand will be less than 1 in absolute value. In this case, demand is **inelastic**. For example, if a 10 percent decrease in the price of wheat results in a 5 percent increase in the quantity of wheat demanded, then:

$$\text{Price elasticity of demand} = \frac{5\%}{-10\%} = -0.5,$$

and we can conclude that the demand for wheat is inelastic.

In the special case where the percentage change in quantity demanded is equal to the percentage change in price, the price elasticity of demand equals -1 (or 1 in absolute value). In this case, demand is **unit elastic**.   **MyLab Economics** Concept Check

An Example of Calculating Price Elasticities

Suppose you own a grocery, and you are trying to decide whether to cut the price of a 2-liter bottle of Coca-Cola. You are currently at point A in Figure 6.1, selling 1,000 bottles per day at a price of $1.50 per bottle. How many more bottles you will sell by cutting the price to $1.35 depends on the price elasticity of demand for Coca-Cola at your grocery store. Let's consider two possibilities: If D_1 is the demand curve for Coca-Cola at your grocery, your sales will increase to 1,200 bottles per day, point B. But if D_2 is your demand curve, your sales will increase only to 1,050 bottles per day, point C. We might expect—correctly, as we will see—that between these points, demand curve D_1 is *elastic* and demand curve D_2 is *inelastic*.

To confirm that D_1 is elastic between these points and that D_2 is inelastic, we need to calculate the price elasticity of demand for each curve. In calculating price elasticity between two points on a demand curve, though, we face a problem because we get a different value for price increases than for price decreases. Suppose we calculate the

Elastic demand The case where the percentage change in quantity demanded is *greater* than the percentage change in price, so the price elasticity is *greater* than 1 in absolute value.

Inelastic demand The case where the percentage change in quantity demanded is *less* than the percentage change in price, so the price elasticity is *less* than 1 in absolute value.

Unit-elastic demand The case where the percentage change in quantity demanded is *equal to* the percentage change in price, so the price elasticity is equal to 1 in absolute value.

MyLab Economics Animation

Figure 6.1

Elastic and Inelastic Demand

Along D_1, cutting the price from $1.50 to $1.35 increases the number of bottles demanded from 1,000 to 1,200 per day. Because the percentage change in quantity demanded is greater than the percentage change in price (in absolute value), demand is elastic between point A and point B. Along D_2, cutting the price from $1.50 to $1.35 increases the number of bottles demanded only from 1,000 to 1,050 per day. Because the percentage change in quantity demanded is smaller than the percentage change in price (in absolute value), demand is inelastic between point A and point C.

MyLab Economics Concept Check

price elasticity for D_1 as the price is cut from $1.50 to $1.35. This 10 percent price cut increases the quantity demanded from 1,000 bottles to 1,200 bottles, or by 20 percent. Therefore, the price elasticity of demand between points A and B is $20\%/-10\% = -2.0$.

Now let's calculate the price elasticity for D_1 as the price is *increased* from $1.35 to $1.50. This 11.1 percent price increase causes a decrease in the quantity demanded from 1,200 bottles to 1,000 bottles, or by 16.7 percent. So, now our measure of the price elasticity of demand between points A and B is $-16.7\%/11.1\% = -1.5$. It can be confusing to have different values for the price elasticity of demand between the same two points on the same demand curve. As we will see in the next section, economists use a formula that allows them to avoid this confusion when calculating elasticities.

The Midpoint Formula

We can use the *midpoint formula* to ensure that we have only one value of the price elasticity of demand between the same two points on a demand curve. The midpoint formula uses the *average* of the initial and final quantities and the initial and final prices. If Q_1 and P_1 are the initial quantity and price, and Q_2 and P_2 are the final quantity and price, the midpoint formula is:

$$\text{Price elasticity of demand} = \frac{(Q_2-Q_1)}{\left(\dfrac{Q_1+Q_2}{2}\right)} \div \frac{(P_2-P_1)}{\left(\dfrac{P_1+P_2}{2}\right)}.$$

The midpoint formula may seem challenging at first, but the numerator is just the change in quantity divided by the average of the initial and final quantities, and the denominator is just the change in price divided by the average of the initial and final prices.

Let's apply the formula to calculating the price elasticity of D_1 in Figure 6.1. Between point A and point B on D_1, the change in quantity is 200, and the average of the two quantities is 1,100. Therefore, there is an 18.2 percent change in quantity demanded. The change in price is $-$0.15, and the average of the two prices is $1.425. Therefore, there is a -10.5 percent change in price. So, the price elasticity of demand is $18.2\%/-10.5\% = -1.7$. Notice these three results from calculating the price elasticity of demand using the midpoint formula:

1. As we suspected from examining Figure 6.1, demand curve D_1 is elastic between points A and B.
2. The value for the price elasticity calculated using the midpoint formula is between the two values we calculated above.

3. The midpoint formula will give us the same value whether we are moving from the higher price to the lower price or from the lower price to the higher price.

We can also use the midpoint formula to calculate the elasticity of demand between point A and point C on D_2. In this case, there is a 4.9 percent change in quantity and a -10.5 percent change in price. So, the elasticity of demand is $4.9\%/-10.5\% = -0.5$. Once again, as we suspected, demand curve D_2 is price inelastic between points A and C.   MyLab Economics Concept Check

Solved Problem 6.1   MyLab Economics Interactive Animation

Calculating the Price Elasticity of Demand

Suppose you own a grocery, and you are currently selling Coca-Cola for $1.50 per 2-liter bottle. At this price, you can sell 2,000 bottles per day. You are considering cutting the price to $1.30 to attract consumers who have been buying their Coca-Cola at competing grocery stores. The following graph shows two possible increases in the quantity of Coca-Cola sold as a result of your price cut. Use the information in the following graph to calculate the price elasticity between these two prices on each of the demand curves. Use the midpoint formula in your calculations. State whether each demand curve is elastic or inelastic between these two prices.

Solving the Problem

Step 1: **Review the chapter material.** This problem requires calculating the price elasticity of demand, so you may want to review the material in the section "The Midpoint Formula," which begins on page 186.

Step 2: **To begin using the midpoint formula, calculate the average quantity and the average price for demand curve D_1.**

$$\text{Average quantity} = \frac{2,000 + 2,500}{2} = 2,250$$

$$\text{Average price} = \frac{\$1.50 + \$1.30}{2} = \$1.40$$

Step 3: **Now calculate the percentage change in the quantity demanded and the percentage change in price for demand curve D_1.**

$$\text{Percentage change in quantity demanded} = \frac{2,500 - 2,000}{2,250} \times 100 = 22.2\%$$

$$\text{Percentage change in price} = \frac{\$1.30 - \$1.50}{\$1.40} \times 100 = -14.3\%$$

Step 4: **Divide the percentage change in the quantity demanded by the percentage change in price to arrive at the price elasticity for demand curve D_1.**

$$\text{Price elasticity of demand} = \frac{22.2\%}{-14.3\%} = -1.6$$

Because the elasticity is greater than 1 in absolute value, D_1 is price *elastic* between these two prices.

Step 5: **Calculate the price elasticity of demand curve D_2 between these two prices.**

$$\text{Percentage change in quantity demanded} = \frac{2,100 - 2,000}{2,050} \times 100 = 4.9\%$$

$$\text{Percentage change in price} = \frac{\$1.30 - \$1.50}{\$1.40} \times 100 = -14.3\%$$

$$\text{Price elasticity of demand} = \frac{4.9\%}{-14.3\%} = -0.3$$

Because the elasticity is less than 1 in absolute value, D_2 is price *inelastic* between these two prices.

MyLab Economics Study Plan   **Your Turn:** For more practice, do related problem 1.8 on page 210 at the end of this chapter.

When Demand Curves Intersect, the Flatter Curve Is More Elastic

Remember that *elasticity* is not the same thing as *slope*. While slope is calculated using changes in quantity and price, elasticity is calculated using percentage changes. But it *is* true that if two demand curves intersect:

- The demand curve with the smaller slope (in absolute value)—the flatter demand curve—is more elastic.
- The demand curve with the larger slope (in absolute value)—the steeper demand curve—is less elastic.

In Figure 6.1 on page 186, for a given change in price, demand curve D_1 is more elastic than demand curve D_2.   MyLab Economics Concept Check

Polar Cases of Perfectly Elastic and Perfectly Inelastic Demand

Perfectly inelastic demand The case where the quantity demanded is completely unresponsive to price and the price elasticity of demand equals zero.

Although they do not occur frequently, you should be aware of the extreme, or *polar*, cases of price elasticity. If a demand curve is a vertical line, it is **perfectly inelastic**. In this case, the quantity demanded is completely unresponsive to price, and the price elasticity of demand equals zero. No matter how much price may increase or decrease, the quantity remains the same. For only a very few products will the quantity demanded be completely unresponsive to the price, making the demand curve a vertical line. The drug insulin is an example. Some diabetics must take a certain amount of insulin each day. If the price of insulin declines, it will not affect the required dose and therefore will not increase the quantity demanded. Similarly, a price increase will not affect the required dose or decrease the quantity demanded. (Of course, some diabetics may not be able to afford insulin at a higher price. If so, even for this good the demand curve may not be completely vertical and, therefore, not perfectly inelastic.)

Perfectly elastic demand The case where the quantity demanded is infinitely responsive to price and the price elasticity of demand equals infinity.

If a demand curve is a horizontal line, it is **perfectly elastic**. In this case, the quantity demanded is infinitely responsive to price, and the price elasticity of demand equals infinity. If a demand curve is perfectly elastic, an increase in price causes the quantity demanded to fall to zero. Once again, perfectly elastic demand curves are rare, and it is important not to confuse *elastic* with *perfectly elastic*. Table 6.1 on the next page summarizes the different price elasticities of demand.   MyLab Economics Concept Check

MyLab Economics Study Plan

Table 6.1

Summary of the Price Elasticity of Demand

If demand is . . .	then the absolute value of price elasticity is . . .	
elastic	greater than 1	**Price** 1. An 11 percent cut in price ... $1.50 1.35 Demand 0 1,000 1,200 **Quantity** 2. ... causes an 18 percent increase in quantity demanded.
inelastic	less than 1	**Price** 1. An 11 percent cut in price ... $1.50 1.35 Demand 0 1,000 1,050 **Quantity** 2. ... causes a 5 percent increase in quantity demanded.
unit elastic	equal to 1	**Price** 1. An 11 percent cut in price... $1.50 1.35 Demand 0 1,000 1,116 **Quantity** 2. ... causes an 11 percent increase in quantity demanded.
perfectly elastic	equal to infinity	**Price** Demand Any increase in price causes quantity demanded to fall to 0. $1.50 0 **Quantity**
perfectly inelastic	equal to 0	**Price** Demand $1.65 1. An increase or a decrease in price ... 1.50 1.35 0 1,000 **Quantity** 2. ... causes no change in quantity demanded.

Don't Let This Happen to You

Don't Confuse Inelastic with Perfectly Inelastic

You may be tempted to simplify the concept of elasticity by assuming that any demand curve described as being inelastic is *perfectly* inelastic. You should never make this assumption because perfectly inelastic demand curves are rare. For example, consider the following problem: "Use a demand and supply graph to show how a decrease in supply affects the equilibrium quantity of gasoline. Assume that the demand for gasoline is inelastic." The following graph would be an *incorrect* answer to this problem:

Most economists believe that the demand for gasoline is inelastic, but it is not *perfectly* inelastic. When the price of gasoline rises, the quantity demanded falls. So, the correct answer to this problem would use a graph showing a typical downward-sloping demand curve rather than a vertical demand curve:

MyLab Economics Study Plan

Your Turn: Test your understanding by doing related problem 1.10 on page 210 at the end of this chapter.

6.2 The Determinants of the Price Elasticity of Demand

LEARNING OBJECTIVE: List and explain the determinants of the price elasticity of demand.

We have seen that the demand for some products may be elastic, while the demand for other products may be inelastic. In this section, we examine why price elasticities differ among products. The key determinants of the price elasticity of demand are:

- The availability of close substitutes for the good
- The passage of time
- Whether the good is a luxury or a necessity
- The definition of the market
- The share of the good in the consumer's budget

Availability of Close Substitutes

How consumers react to a change in the price of a product depends on whether there are alternative products. So the availability of substitutes is the most important determinant of the price elasticity of demand. For example, when the price of gasoline rises, consumers have few alternatives, so the quantity demanded falls only a little. But if the price of pizza rises, consumers have many alternative foods they can eat, so the quantity demanded is likely to fall substantially. In fact, a key constraint on a firm's pricing policies is how many close substitutes exist for its product. In general, *if a product has more substitutes available, it will have a more elastic demand. If a product has fewer substitutes available, it will have a less elastic demand.*   MyLab Economics Concept Check

Passage of Time

It usually takes consumers some time to adjust their buying habits when prices change. If the price of chicken falls, for example, it takes a while before consumers decide to change from eating chicken for dinner once a week to eating it twice a week. If the price of gasoline increases, it also takes a while for consumers to decide to begin taking public transportation, to buy more fuel-efficient cars, or to find new jobs closer to where they live. *The more time that passes, the more elastic the demand for a product becomes.*   MyLab Economics Concept Check

Luxuries versus Necessities

Goods that are luxuries usually have more elastic demand curves than goods that are necessities. For example, the demand for milk is inelastic because milk is a necessity, and the quantity that people buy is not very dependent on its price. Tickets to a concert are a luxury, so the demand for concert tickets is much more elastic than the demand for bread. *The demand curve for a luxury is more elastic than the demand curve for a necessity.*   MyLab Economics Concept Check

Definition of the Market

In a narrowly defined market, consumers have more substitutes available. For example, if you own a service station and raise the price you charge for gasoline, many of your customers will switch to buying from a competitor. So, the demand for gasoline at one particular station is likely to be elastic. The demand for gasoline as a product, in contrast, is inelastic because consumers have few alternatives (in the short run) to buying it. *The more narrowly we define a market, the more elastic demand will be.*   MyLab Economics Concept Check

Share of a Good in a Consumer's Budget

Goods that take only a small fraction of a consumer's budget tend to have less elastic demand than goods that take a large fraction. For example, most people buy table salt infrequently and in relatively small quantities. The share of an average consumer's budget that is spent on salt is very low. So, even a doubling of the price of salt is likely to result in only a small decline in the quantity of salt demanded. "Big-ticket items," such as houses, cars, and furniture, take up a larger share in the average consumer's budget. Increases in the prices of these goods are likely to result in significant declines in the quantity demanded. In general, *the demand for a good will be more elastic the larger the share of the good in the average consumer's budget.*   MyLab Economics Concept Check

Some Estimated Price Elasticities of Demand

Table 6.2 shows some estimated short-run price elasticities of demand. It's important to remember that estimates of the price elasticities of different goods can vary, depending on the data used and the time period over which the estimates were made. The results given in the table are consistent with our discussion of the determinants of price elasticity. Goods for which there are few substitutes, such as cigarettes, gasoline, and health insurance, are price inelastic, as are broadly defined goods, such as bread and soda. Particular brands of products such as Coca-Cola, Tide, and Post Raisin Bran are price elastic.

Table 6.2 also shows that:

- The demand for books or DVDs bought from a particular retailer is typically price elastic. Note, though, that the demand for books from Amazon is inelastic, which indicates that consumers do not consider ordering from other online sites to be good substitutes for ordering from Amazon.

Table 6.2

Estimated Real-World Price
Elasticities of Demand

Product	Estimated Elasticity	Product	Estimated Elasticity
Books (Barnes & Noble)	−4.00	Water (residential use)	−0.38
Books (Amazon)	−0.60	Chicken	−0.37
DVDs (Amazon)	−3.10	Cocaine	−0.28
Post Raisin Bran	−2.50	Cigarettes	−0.25
New automobiles	−1.95	Beer	−0.29
Tide (liquid detergent)	−3.92	Catholic school attendance	−0.19
Coca-Cola	−1.22	Residential natural gas	−0.09
Grapes	−1.18	Gasoline	−0.06
Soda	−0.70	Milk	−0.04
Restaurant meals	−0.67	Sugar	−0.04
Health insurance (low-income households)	−0.65	Uber ride-hailing service (four large cities)	−0.50
Bread	−0.40		

Source: See Text Credits at the back of the book for complete source list.

- An increase in the price of grapes will lead some consumers to substitute other fruits, so demand for grapes is price elastic.
- Similarly, an increase in the price of new automobiles will lead some consumers to buy used automobiles or to continue driving their current cars, so demand for automobiles is also price elastic.
- The demand for necessities, such as natural gas and water, is price inelastic. In the four large cities from which the Uber data were collected, judging from the estimated price elasticity, consumers consider the ride-hailing service to be a necessity.

MyLab Economics Study Plan

MyLab Economics Concept Check

6.3 The Relationship between Price Elasticity of Demand and Total Revenue

LEARNING OBJECTIVE: Explain the relationship between the price elasticity of demand and total revenue.

Total revenue The total amount of funds a seller receives from selling a good or service, calculated by multiplying price per unit by the number of units sold.

Knowing the price elasticity of demand allows a firm to calculate how changes in price will affect its **total revenue**, which is the total amount of funds it receives from selling a good or service. Total revenue is calculated by multiplying price per unit by the number of units sold.

- When demand is inelastic, price and total revenue move in the same direction: An increase in price raises total revenue, and a decrease in price reduces total revenue.
- When demand is elastic, price and total revenue move inversely: An increase in price reduces total revenue, and a decrease in price raises total revenue.

To understand the relationship between price elasticity and total revenue, consider Figure 6.2. Panel (a) shows a demand curve for soda that is inelastic between point A and point B. (It was demand curve D_2 in Figure 6.1 on page 186.) The total revenue you receive from selling soda in your grocery store at point A equals the price, $1.50, multiplied by the 1,000 bottles sold, or $1,500. This amount equals the areas of rectangles C and D in the figure because together the rectangles have a height of $1.50 and a base of 1,000 bottles. Because this demand curve is inelastic between point A and point B, cutting the price to $1.35 (point B) reduces total revenue. The new total revenue is shown by the areas of rectangles D and E and is equal to $1.35 multiplied by 1,050 bottles, or $1,417.50. Total revenue falls because the increase in the quantity demanded is not

(a) Cutting price when demand is inelastic reduces total revenue.

(b) Cutting price when demand is elastic increases total revenue.

MyLab Economics Animation

Figure 6.2 **The Relationship between Price Elasticity and Total Revenue**

When demand is inelastic, a cut in price will decrease total revenue. In panel (a), at point A, the price is $1.50, 1,000 bottles are sold, and the total revenue you receive equals $1.50 × 1,000 bottles, or $1,500. At point B, cutting the price to $1.35 increases the quantity demanded to 1,050 bottles, but the fall in price more than offsets the increase in quantity. As a result, revenue falls to $1.35 × 1,050 gallons, or $1,417.50.

When demand is elastic, a cut in the price will increase total revenue. In panel (b), at point A, the areas of rectangles C and D are still equal to $1,500. But at point B, the areas of rectangles D and E are equal to $1.35 × 1,200 bottles, or $1,620. In this case, the increase in the quantity demanded is large enough to offset the fall in price, so total revenue increases.

large enough to make up for the decrease in price. As a result, the $67.50 increase in revenue gained as a result of the price cut—rectangle E—is less than the $150 in revenue lost—rectangle C.

Panel (b) of Figure 6.2 shows a demand curve that is elastic between point A and point B. (It was demand curve D_1 in Figure 6.1.) With this demand curve, cutting the price increases total revenue. At point A, the areas of rectangles C and D are still equal to $1,500, but at point B, the areas of rectangles D and E are equal to $1.35 multiplied by 1,200 bottles, or $1,620. Here, total revenue rises because the increase in the quantity demanded is large enough to offset the lower price. As a result, the $270 increase in revenue gained as a result of the price cut—rectangle E—is greater than the $150 in revenue lost—rectangle C.

A less common possibility than those shown in Figure 6.2 is that demand is unit elastic. In that case, a small change in price is exactly offset by a proportional change in the quantity demanded, leaving revenue unaffected. Therefore, when demand is unit elastic, neither a decrease nor an increase in price affects revenue. Table 6.3 summarizes the relationship between price elasticity and revenue.

Elasticity and Revenue with a Linear Demand Curve

Along most demand curves, elasticity is not constant at every point. For example, a straight-line, or linear, demand curve for renting movies on iTunes or another site is shown in panel (a) of Figure 6.3. (For simplicity, small quantities are used.) The numbers from the table are plotted in the graphs. The demand curve shows that when the price drops by $1 per movie, consumers always respond by renting 2 more movies per month. When the price is high and the quantity demanded is low, demand is elastic.

Table 6.3

The Relationship between Price Elasticity and Revenue

If demand is . . .	then . . .	because . . .
elastic	an increase in price reduces revenue	the decrease in quantity demanded is proportionally *greater* than the increase in price.
elastic	a decrease in price increases revenue	the increase in quantity demanded is proportionally *greater* than the decrease in price.
inelastic	an increase in price increases revenue	the decrease in quantity demanded is proportionally *smaller* than the increase in price.
inelastic	a decrease in price reduces revenue	the increase in quantity demanded is proportionally *smaller* than the decrease in price.
unit elastic	an increase in price does not affect revenue	the decrease in quantity demanded is proportionally *the same as* the increase in price.
unit elastic	a decrease in price does not affect revenue	the increase in quantity demanded is proportionally *the same as* the decrease in price.

(a) Demand curve for movies

(b) Total revenue curve

Price	Quantity Demanded	Total Revenue
$8	0	$0
7	2	14
6	4	24
5	6	30
4	8	32
3	10	30
2	12	24
1	14	14
0	16	0

MyLab Economics Animation

Figure 6.3   Elasticity Is Not Constant along a Linear Demand Curve

The data from the table are plotted in the graphs. Panel (a) shows that as we move down the demand curve for renting movies, the price elasticity of demand declines. In other words, at higher prices, demand is elastic, and at lower prices, demand is inelastic.

Panel (b) shows that as the quantity of movies rented increases from 0, revenue will increase until it reaches a maximum of $32 when 8 movies are rented. As purchases increase beyond 8 movies, revenue falls because demand is inelastic on this portion of the demand curve.

Demand is elastic because a $1 drop in price is a smaller percentage change when the price is high, and an increase of 2 movies is a larger percentage change when the quantity of movies rented is low. By similar reasoning, we can see why demand is inelastic when the price is low and the quantity demanded is high.

Panel (a) in Figure 6.3 shows that when price is between $8 and $4 and quantity demanded is between 0 movies and 8 movies, demand is elastic. Panel (b) shows that over this same range, total revenue will increase as price falls. For example, in panel (a), as price falls from $7 to $6, the quantity demanded increases from 2 to 4, and in panel (b), total revenue increases from $14 to $24. Similarly, when price is between $4 and $0 and the quantity demanded is between 8 and 16, demand is inelastic. Over this same range, total revenue will decrease as price falls. For example, as price falls from $3 to $2 and the quantity demanded increases from 10 to 12, total revenue decreases from $30 to $24.

MyLab Economics Concept Check   MyLab Economics Study Plan

Solved Problem 6.3

MyLab Economics Interactive Animation

Price and Revenue Don't Always Move in the Same Direction

New York City officials believed they needed more revenue to maintain 35 city-owned recreation centers. To raise the additional revenue, the city's parks department increased the annual membership fee to use the centers from $75 to $150. According to an article in the *New York Times*, "the department had hoped to realize $4 million in new revenue, but in fact, it lost about $200,000." The article also explains that the parks department had expected a 5 percent decline in memberships due to the price increase.

a. What did the parks department believe about the price elasticity of demand for memberships in its recreation centers?

b. Is demand for memberships actually elastic or inelastic? Briefly explain. Illustrate your answer with a graph showing the demand curve for memberships as the parks department believed it to be and as it actually is.

Solving the Problem

Step 1: **Review the chapter material.** This problem deals with the effect of a price change on a firm's revenue, so you may want to review the section "The Relationship between Price Elasticity of Demand and Total Revenue," which begins on page 192.

Step 2: **Answer part (a) by explaining how the parks department viewed the demand for memberships.** Looking at Table 6.3, we can conclude that managers at the parks department must have thought the demand for memberships was inelastic because they believed that revenue would increase if they raised the price. The managers estimated that the quantity of memberships demanded would fall by 5 percent following the 100 percent price increase. Therefore, they must have believed that the price elasticity of demand for memberships was $-5\%/100\% = -0.05$.

Step 3: **Answer part (b) by explaining whether the demand for memberships is actually elastic or inelastic and by drawing a graph to illustrate your answer.** Because revenue fell when the parks department raised the price, we know that demand for memberships must be elastic. In the following graph, D_1 shows the demand for memberships as the parks department believed it to be. Moving along this demand curve from point A to point B, an increase in the price from $75 to $150 causes a decline of only Q_1 to Q_2 in the quantity of memberships demanded. D_2 shows the demand curve as it actually is. Moving along this demand curve from point A to point C, the increase in price causes a much larger decline of Q_1 to Q_3 in memberships demanded.

Source: Lisa W. Foderaro, "Public Recreation Centers Looking to Stem Exodus," *New York Times*, February 15, 2013.

MyLab Economics Study Plan

Your Turn: For more practice, do related problems 3.8 and 3.9 on page 212 at the end of this chapter.

Apply the Concept

MyLab Economics Video

Why Does Amazon Care about Price Elasticity?

Hachette is a large book publisher whose authors include James Patterson, J. K. Rowling, and J. D. Salinger. In 2014, Hachette and Amazon disagreed on pricing of e-books. Hachette was charging between $14.99 and $19.99 for its e-books, but Amazon wanted the publisher to lower the price to only $9.99. Amazon pressured Hachette by reducing discounts on the publisher's hardcover books, not allowing Amazon customers to preorder the publisher's books, and delaying shipping some of its books by two to three weeks.

But why did Amazon want Hachette to lower the price of e-books? In a posting on its Web site, Amazon asserted, "We've quantified the price elasticity of e-books from repeated measurements across many titles." Amazon estimated that the price elasticity of demand for e-books is −1.35. The following table uses Amazon's estimate to show how sales revenue would change in response to a decrease in the price of e-books.

Price of Book	Copies Sold at That Price	Total Revenue at That Price
$14.99	100,000	$1,499,000
$9.99	174,000	$1,738,260

Amazon concluded, "At $9.99, even though the customer is paying less, the total pie is bigger and there is more to share amongst [Amazon, Hachette, and the author of the book]."

If Amazon's analysis is correct, why would Hachette resist cutting the prices of e-books? Hachette believed that while the demand for bestsellers by authors such as James Patterson and J. K. Rowling might be price elastic, the demand for other e-books it published by less-well-known authors or on obscure subjects was price inelastic. For those books, cutting the price would reduce Hachette's revenue. In addition, Hachette believed that lower prices on e-books might come at the expense of sales of hardcover copies of those books, on which the publisher made higher profits. Eventually, Amazon and Hachette reached an agreement that allowed Hachette

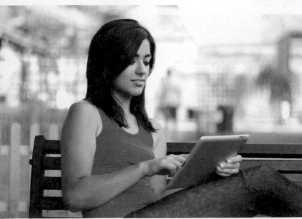

Kacso Sandor/123RF

Amazon and book publishers have debated the benefit of lowering e-book prices.

to determine the prices its e-books would sell for on Amazon's site. Amazon signed similar agreements with other publishers. In the following years, prices of e-books have risen on Amazon.

The results of the higher prices, though, weren't what the publishers had hoped for, as they were accompanied by falling revenue. The *Wall Street Journal* quoted an executive at a publishing company as observing, "The new business model for e-books is having a significant impact. . . . There's no question that publishers' net receipts have gone down." Amazon appeared to be correct about the demand for e-books being price elastic. The publishers, though, believed they would still gain from higher e-book prices pushing more consumers toward buying hardcover editions of those books.

Sources: Jeffrey A. Trachtenberg, "E-Book Sales Fall after New Amazon Contracts," *Wall Street Journal*, September 3, 2015; The Amazon Books Team, "Announcement Update re: Amazon/Hachette Business Interruption," Amazon.com, July 29, 2014; Farhad Manjoo, "Amazon Wants Cheaper E-books. But Should It Get to Enforce Prices?" *New York Times*, August 1, 2014; Tom Ryan, "Amazon Explains Digital Pricing Elasticity," retailwire.com, August 4, 2014; David Streitfeld, "Amazon and Hachette Resolve Dispute," *New York Times*, November 13, 2014; and Brent Kendall, "Supreme Court Turns Away Apple Appeal in E-books Antitrust Case," *Wall Street Journal*, March 7, 2016.

Your Turn: Test your understanding by doing related problems 3.10 and 3.11 on page 212 at the end of this chapter.

MyLab Economics Study Plan

6.4 Other Demand Elasticities

LEARNING OBJECTIVE: Define and calculate the cross-price elasticity of demand and the income elasticity of demand and explain their determinants.

Elasticity is an important concept in economics because it allows us to quantify the responsiveness of one economic variable to changes in another economic variable. In addition to price elasticity, two other demand elasticities are important:

1. Cross-price elasticity of demand
2. Income elasticity of demand

Cross-Price Elasticity of Demand

Suppose you work at Apple, and you need to predict the effect of an increase in the price of Samsung's Galaxy smartphone on the quantity of Apple iPhones demanded, holding other factors constant. You can do this by calculating the **cross-price elasticity of demand**, which is the percentage change in the quantity of Apple iPhones demanded divided by the percentage change in the price of Galaxy smartphones—or, in general:

$$\text{Cross-price elasticity of demand} = \frac{\text{Percentage change in quantity demanded of one good}}{\text{Percentage change in price of another good}}.$$

The cross-price elasticity of demand is positive or negative, depending on whether the two products are substitutes or complements. Recall that substitutes are products that can be used for the same purpose, such as two brands of smartphones. Complements are products that are used together, such as iPhones and applications that can be downloaded from online stores. An increase in the price of a substitute will lead to an increase in the quantity demanded, so the cross-price elasticity of demand will be positive. An increase in the price of a complement will lead to a decrease in the quantity demanded, so the cross-price elasticity of demand will be negative. Of course, if the two products are unrelated—such as iPhones and peanut butter—the cross-price elasticity of demand will be zero. Table 6.4 summarizes the key points about the cross-price elasticity of demand.

Cross-price elasticity of demand is important to firm managers because it allows them to measure whether products sold by other firms are close substitutes for their products. For example, PepsiCo and Coca-Cola both spend heavily on advertising, each hoping to convince consumers that its cola tastes better than its rival's. How can these

Cross-price elasticity of demand
The percentage change in the quantity demanded of one good divided by the percentage change in the price of another good.

Table 6.4

Summary of Cross-Price Elasticity of Demand

If the products are . . .	then the cross-price elasticity of demand will be . . .	Example
substitutes	positive.	Two brands of smartphones
complements	negative.	iPhones and applications downloaded from online stores
unrelated	zero.	iPhones and peanut butter

firms tell whether their advertising campaigns have been effective? One way is by seeing whether the cross-price elasticity of demand has changed. If, for instance, Coca-Cola has a successful advertising campaign, when it increases the price of Coke, the percentage increase in sales of Pepsi should be smaller. In other words, the value of the cross-price elasticity of demand should have declined.   **MyLab Economics** Concept Check

Income Elasticity of Demand

Income elasticity of demand A measure of the responsiveness of the quantity demanded to changes in income, measured by the percentage change in the quantity demanded divided by the percentage change in income.

The **income elasticity of demand** measures the responsiveness of the quantity demanded to changes in income. It is calculated as follows:

$$\text{Income elasticity of demand} = \frac{\text{Percentage change in quantity demanded}}{\text{Percentage change in income}}.$$

We know that if the quantity demanded of a good increases as income increases, the good is a *normal good* (see Chapter 3, Section 3.1). Normal goods are often further subdivided into *luxuries* and *necessities*. A good is a luxury if the quantity demanded is very responsive to changes in income so that a 10 percent increase in income results in more than a 10 percent increase in the quantity demanded. Expensive jewelry and vacation homes are examples of luxuries. A good is a necessity if the quantity demanded is not very responsive to changes in income so that a 10 percent increase in income results in less than a 10 percent increase in the quantity demanded. Food and clothing are examples of necessities. A good is *inferior* if the quantity demanded falls when income increases. Ground beef with a high fat content is an example of an inferior good. We should note that *normal good*, *inferior good*, *necessity*, and *luxury* are labels economists use for goods with different income elasticities; the labels are not intended to be value judgments about the worth of these goods.

Because most goods are normal goods, during periods of economic expansion when consumer income is rising, most firms can expect—holding other factors constant—that the quantity demanded of their products will increase. Sellers of luxuries can expect particularly large increases. During recessions, falling consumer income can cause firms to experience increases in demand for inferior goods. For example, the demand for bus trips increases as consumers cut back on air travel, and supermarkets find that the demand for canned tuna increases relative to the demand for fresh salmon. Table 6.5 summarizes the key points about the income elasticity of demand.   **MyLab Economics** Concept Check

MyLab Economics Study Plan

Table 6.5

Summary of Income Elasticity of Demand

If the income elasticity of demand is . . .	then the good is . . .	Example
positive but less than 1	normal and a necessity.	Bread
positive and greater than 1	normal and a luxury.	Caviar
negative	inferior.	High-fat meat

Apply the Concept

MyLab Economics Video

Price Elasticity, Cross-Price Elasticity, and Income Elasticity in the Market for Alcoholic Beverages

Many public policy issues are related to the consumption of alcoholic beverages. These issues include underage drinking, drunk driving, and the possible beneficial effects of red wine in lowering the risk of heart disease. Knowing how responsive the demand for alcohol is to changes in price provides insight into these policy issues. Christopher Ruhm of the University of Virginia and colleagues estimated statistically the following elasticities. (*Spirits* refers to all beverages, other than beer and wine, that contain alcohol.)

Price elasticity of demand for beer	−0.30
Cross-price elasticity of demand between beer and wine	−0.83
Cross-price elasticity of demand between beer and spirits	−0.50
Income elasticity of demand for beer	0.09

These results indicate that the demand for beer is inelastic. A 10 percent increase in the price of beer will result in a 3 percent decline in the quantity of beer demanded. Somewhat surprisingly, both wine and spirits are complements for beer rather than substitutes. A 10 percent increase in the price of wine will result in an 8.3 percent *decrease* in the quantity of beer demanded. Previous studies of the price elasticity of beer found that beer was a substitute for other alcoholic drinks. Ruhm and his colleagues argued that their results are more reliable because they use Uniform Product Code (UPC) scanner data on prices and quantities sold in grocery stores. They noted that these price data are more accurate than the data used in many previous studies that included the prices of only one brand each of beer, wine, and whiskey.

The results in the table also show that a 10 percent increase in income will result in a 0.9 percent *increase* in the quantity of beer demanded. So, beer is a normal good. According to the definitions given earlier, beer would be classified as a necessity because it has an income elasticity that is positive but less than 1.

Source: Christopher J. Ruhm, et al., "What U.S. Data Should Be Used to Measure the Price Elasticity of Demand for Alcohol?" *Journal of Health Economics*, Vol. 31, No. 6, December 2012.

Your Turn: Test your understanding by doing related problem 4.8 on page 213 at the end of this chapter.

MyLab Economics Study Plan

6.5 Using Elasticity to Analyze the Disappearing Family Farm

LEARNING OBJECTIVE: Use price elasticity and income elasticity to analyze economic issues.

The concepts of price elasticity and income elasticity can help us understand many economic issues. For example, some people are concerned that the family farm is becoming an endangered species in the United States. Although food production has been growing steadily, the number of farms and farmers continue to dwindle. In 1950, the United States had more than 5 million farms, and more than 23 million people lived on farms. By 2017, only about 2 million farms remained, and fewer than 3 million people lived on them. The federal government has several programs that are intended to aid farmers (see Chapter 4, Section 4.3). Many of these programs have been aimed at helping small, family-operated farms, but growth in farm production, combined with low price and income elasticities for most food products, have made it difficult for owners of family farms to earn a profit.

MyLab Economics Animation

Figure 6.4

Elasticity and the Disappearing Family Farm

In 1950, U.S. farmers produced 1.0 billion bushels of wheat at a price of $19.23 per bushel. Over the next 67 years, rapid increases in farm productivity caused a large shift to the right in the supply curve for wheat. The income elasticity of demand for wheat is low, so the demand for wheat increased relatively little over this period. Because the demand for wheat is also inelastic, the large shift in the supply curve and the small shift in the demand curve resulted in a sharp decline in the price of wheat, from $19.23 per bushel in 1950 to $3.85 in 2017.

Source: U.S. Department of Agriculture, *Wheat Yearbook Tables*, March 10, 2017.

Productivity measures the ability of firms to produce goods and services with a given amount of economic inputs, such as workers, machines, and land. Productivity has grown very rapidly in U.S. agriculture. In 1950, the average U.S. wheat farmer harvested about 17 bushels from each acre of wheat planted. By 2017, because of the development of superior strains of wheat and improvements in farming techniques, the average American wheat farmer harvested 53 bushels per acre. So, even though the total number of acres devoted to growing wheat declined from about 62 million to about 44 million, total wheat production rose from about 1.0 billion bushels to about 2.3 billion.

Unfortunately for U.S. farmers, this increase in wheat production resulted in a substantial decline in wheat prices. Two key factors explain this decline: (1) The demand for wheat is inelastic, and (2) the income elasticity of demand for wheat is low. Even though the U.S. population has increased greatly since 1950 and the income of the average American is much higher than it was in 1950, the demand for wheat has increased only moderately. For all of the additional wheat to be sold, the price has had to decline. Because the demand for wheat is inelastic, the price decline has been substantial. Figure 6.4 illustrates these points.

A large shift in supply, a small shift in demand, and an inelastic demand curve combined to drive down the price of wheat from $19.23 per bushel in 1950 to $3.85 in 2017. (We measure the price in 1950 in terms of prices in 2017 to adjust for the general increase in prices since 1950.) With low prices, only the most efficiently run farms have been able to remain profitable. Small family-run farms have found it difficult to survive, and many of these farms have disappeared. The markets for most other food products are similar to the market for wheat. They are characterized by output growth and low income and price elasticities. The result is the paradox of U.S. farming: ever more abundant and cheaper food, supplied by fewer and fewer farms. U.S. consumers have benefited, but most family farmers have not. **MyLab Economics** Concept Check

MyLab Economics Study Plan

Solved Problem 6.5

MyLab Economics Interactive Animation

Using Price Elasticity to Analyze the Effects of a Soda Tax

Some economists, health professionals, and policymakers argue in favor of a soda tax because they believe that people who drink sweetened beverages can experience health problems. Some city governments also believe that a soda tax is a good way to raise tax revenues. If the main goal of a soda tax is to reduce consumption of sweetened beverages, will the tax be more effective if the demand for sweetened beverages is elastic or if it is inelastic? What about if the main goal is to raise tax revenue for a city government? Assume that the tax is $0.75 per bottle of soda and that prior to the tax being imposed, the equilibrium quantity of soda sold in the city was 90,000 bottles per day and the equilibrium price was $1.75 per bottle. Illustrate your answer with a graph of the market for soda in the city and summarize the key results in a table.

Solving the Problem

Step 1: **Review the chapter material.** This problem deals with the effect of a price change on quantity demanded and revenue, so you may want to review the section "The Relationship between Price Elasticity of Demand and Total Revenue," which begins on page 192. (Note: To review the effects on a market of a government imposing a tax, see Chapter 4, Section 4.4.)

Step 2: **Answer the question by explaining the effect of the price elasticity of demand for soda on the effectiveness of a soda tax in attaining policymakers' goals and by drawing a graph to illustrate your answer.** We know from Chapter 4, Section 4.4 that the effect of the soda tax will be to shift up the supply curve for soda by the amount of the tax from Supply (without tax) to Supply (with tax). Your graph should show that the tax causes the equilibrium quantity of bottles sold per day to fall by less when the demand is price inelastic than when demand is price elastic and for the equilibrium price to rise by more. As drawn, using hypothetical values, the equilibrium quantity demanded falls from 90,000 to 80,000 when demand is price inelastic, and from 90,000 to 70,000 when demand is price elastic. The equilibrium price rises from $1.75 per bottle to $2.25 when demand is price inelastic, and from $1.75 to $2.00 when demand is elastic. Given these values, when the demand for soda is price inelastic, the city government collects tax revenue of $0.75 per bottle multiplied by 80,000 bottles, or $60,000 per day. When the demand for soda is price elastic, the city government collects only $52,500 per day.

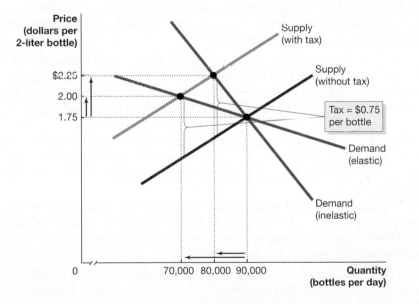

We can summarize the information from the graph in the following table:

	When Demand for Soda Is Price Inelastic	When Demand for Soda Is Price Elastic
Decline in equilibrium quantity	Smaller	Larger
Increase in equilibrium price	Larger	Smaller
Effect on discouraging soda consumption	Smaller effect	Larger effect
Effect on city tax revenue	More tax revenue collected	Less tax revenue collected

We can conclude that the tax is more effective at reducing consumption of soda when demand is price elastic but more effective at raising tax revenue for the city when demand is price inelastic.

MyLab Economics Study Plan

Your Turn: For more practice, do related problems 5.2 and 5.3 on page 214 at the end of this chapter.

6.6 The Price Elasticity of Supply and Its Measurement

LEARNING OBJECTIVE: Define price elasticity of supply and explain its determinants and how it is measured.

We can use the concept of elasticity to measure the responsiveness of firms to a change in price, just as we used it to measure the responsiveness of consumers. We know from the law of supply that when the price of a product increases, the quantity supplied increases. To measure how much the quantity supplied increases when price increases, we use the *price elasticity of supply*.

Measuring the Price Elasticity of Supply

Price elasticity of supply The responsiveness of the quantity supplied to a change in price, measured by dividing the percentage change in the quantity supplied of a product by the percentage change in the product's price.

As we did with the price elasticity of demand, we calculate the **price elasticity of supply** by using percentage changes:

$$\text{Price elasticity of supply} = \frac{\text{Percentage change in quantity supplied}}{\text{Percentage change in price}}.$$

Notice that because supply curves are upward sloping, the price elasticity of supply will be a positive number. We categorize the price elasticity of supply the same way we categorize the price elasticity of demand:

- If the price elasticity of supply is less than 1, then supply is *inelastic*. For example, economists have estimated that over a period of a year, the price elasticity of supply of gasoline from U.S. oil refineries is about 0.20. So, gasoline supply is inelastic: A 10 percent increase in the price of gasoline will result in only a 2 percent increase in the quantity supplied.
- If the price elasticity of supply is greater than 1, then supply is *elastic*. For example, if the price of wheat increases by 10 percent and the quantity of wheat that farmers supply increases by 15 percent, the price elasticity of supply is 1.5. So wheat supply is elastic.
- If the price elasticity of supply is equal to 1, the supply is *unit elastic*. For example, if the price of bottled water increases by 10 percent and the quantity of bottled water that firms supply increases by 10 percent, the price elasticity of supply equals 1. So bottled water supply is unit elastic.

As with other elasticity calculations, when we calculate the price elasticity of supply, we hold constant the values of other variables. MyLab Economics Concept Check

Determinants of the Price Elasticity of Supply

Whether supply is elastic or inelastic depends on the ability and willingness of firms to alter the quantity they produce as price increases. Often, firms have difficulty increasing the quantity of the product they supply during any short period of time. For example, a pizza parlor cannot produce more pizzas on any one night than is possible using the ingredients in the kitchen. Within a day or two, the business can buy more ingredients, and within a few months, it can hire more cooks and install additional ovens. As a result, the supply curve for pizza and most other products will be inelastic if we measure it over a short period of time, but the supply curve will be increasingly elastic the longer the period of time over which we measure it. Products that require resources that are themselves in fixed supply are an exception to this rule. For example, a French winery may rely on a particular variety of grape. If all the land on which that grape can be grown is already planted in vineyards, then the supply of that wine will be inelastic even over a long period.   **MyLab Economics** Concept Check

Apply the Concept   **MyLab Economics** Video

Why Are Oil Prices So Unstable?

Bringing oil to market is a long process. Oil companies hire geologists to locate fields for exploratory oil well drilling. If substantial amounts of oil are present, the company begins full-scale development of the field. From exploration to pumping significant amounts of oil can take years. This long process is the reason for the low short-run price elasticity of supply for oil. Because there are no close substitutes for oil, the short-run price elasticity of demand for oil is also low.

As the world economy recovered from the deep recession of 2007–2009, the demand for oil increased rapidly in a number of countries, particularly China, India, Russia, and Brazil. As the following graph shows, when supply is inelastic, an increase in demand can cause a large increase in price. The shift in the demand curve from D_1 to D_2 causes the equilibrium quantity of oil to increase by less than 5 percent, from 85 million barrels per day in 2009 to 89 million in 2011, but the equilibrium price to increase 175 percent, from $40 to $110 per barrel.

Since the 1970s, the world oil market has been heavily influenced by the Organization of the Petroleum Exporting Countries (OPEC). OPEC has 11 members, including Saudi Arabia, Kuwait, Iran, Venezuela, and Nigeria. Together, OPEC members own 75 percent of the world's proven oil reserves. In recent years, though, production of oil in the United States has increased rapidly as a result of widespread adoption of a new technology called hydraulic fracturing, or *fracking*. Fracking involves injecting a mixture of water, sand, and chemicals into a rock formation at high pressure to release oil and natural gas that could not have been recovered using traditional methods. Largely due to fracking, oil production in the United States rose from 5.6 million barrels per day in 2011 to 9.2 million in 2017.

As the following graph shows, this expansion in U.S. production combined with greater production from some OPEC member countries caused a significant increase in the world supply of oil. (Production in some other regions, such as the North

Sea, has been declining.) The price of oil declined from $110 in 2011 to $47 in 2017. The extent of the price change reflected not only the size of the increase in supply but also the low short-run price elasticity of demand for oil.

The combination of a low price elasticity of demand and a low price elasticity of supply means that even relatively small increases or decreases in the demand or supply of oil can result in large swings in its equilibrium price. Over the past 40 years, the price has been as low as $10 per barrel and as high as $140. These price swings are likely to continue in the future.

Sources: Data are from the U.S. Energy Administration's website: https://www.eia.gov/petroleum/data.php

MyLab Economics Study Plan

Your Turn: Test your understanding by doing related problems 6.4 and 6.5 on page 215 at the end of this chapter.

Polar Cases of Perfectly Elastic and Perfectly Inelastic Supply

Although it occurs infrequently, supply can fall into one of the polar cases of price elasticity. If a supply curve is a vertical line, it is *perfectly inelastic*. In this case, the quantity supplied is completely unresponsive to price, and the price elasticity of supply equals zero. Regardless of how much price may increase or decrease, the quantity remains the same. Over a brief period of time, the supply of some goods and services may be perfectly inelastic. For example, a parking lot may have only a fixed number of parking spaces. If demand increases, the price to park in the lot may rise, but no more spaces will become available. Of course, if demand increases permanently, over a longer period of time, the owner of the lot may buy more land and add additional spaces.

If a supply curve is a horizontal line, it is *perfectly elastic*. In this case, the quantity supplied is infinitely responsive to price, and the price elasticity of supply equals infinity. If a supply curve is perfectly elastic, a very small increase in price causes a very large increase in the quantity supplied. Just as with demand curves, it is important not to confuse a supply curve being elastic with its being perfectly elastic and not to confuse a supply curve being inelastic with its being perfectly inelastic. Table 6.6 summarizes the different price elasticities of supply. **MyLab Economics** Concept Check

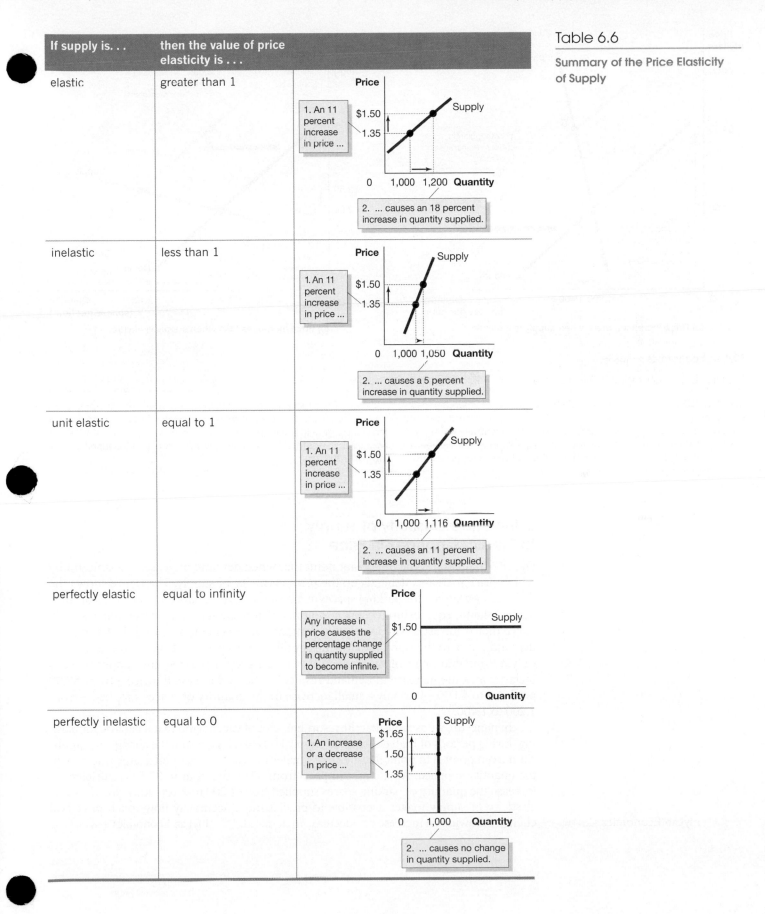

Table 6.6

Summary of the Price Elasticity of Supply

If supply is...	then the value of price elasticity is ...	
elastic	greater than 1	Price. 1. An 11 percent increase in price ... $1.50, 1.35. Supply. 0, 1,000, 1,200 Quantity. 2. ... causes an 18 percent increase in quantity supplied.
inelastic	less than 1	Price. 1. An 11 percent increase in price ... $1.50, 1.35. Supply. 0, 1,000, 1,050 Quantity. 2. ... causes a 5 percent increase in quantity supplied.
unit elastic	equal to 1	Price. 1. An 11 percent increase in price ... $1.50, 1.35. Supply. 0, 1,000, 1,116 Quantity. 2. ... causes an 11 percent increase in quantity supplied.
perfectly elastic	equal to infinity	Price. Any increase in price causes the percentage change in quantity supplied to become infinite. $1.50. Supply. 0 Quantity.
perfectly inelastic	equal to 0	Price. Supply. $1.65, 1.50, 1.35. 1. An increase or a decrease in price ... 0, 1,000 Quantity. 2. ... causes no change in quantity supplied.

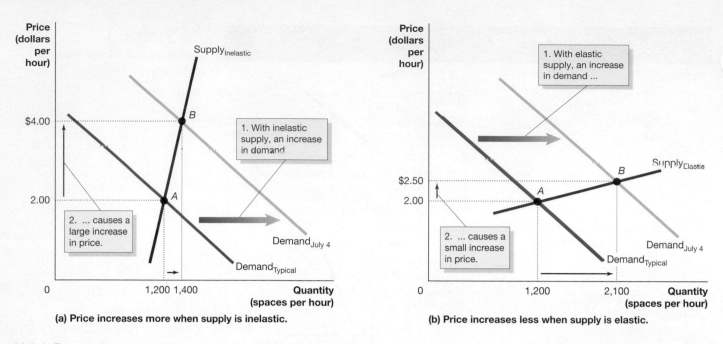

MyLab Economics Animation

Figure 6.5   **Changes in Price Depend on the Price Elasticity of Supply**

In panel (a), Demand_Typical represents the typical demand for parking spaces on a summer weekend at a beach resort. Demand_July4 represents demand on July 4. Because supply is inelastic, the shift in equilibrium from point A to point B results in a large increase in price—from $2.00 per hour to $4.00—but only a small increase in the quantity of spaces supplied—from 1,200 to 1,400. In panel (b), supply is elastic. As a result, the change in equilibrium from point A to point B results in a smaller increase in price and a larger increase in the quantity supplied. An increase in price from $2.00 per hour to $2.50 is sufficient to increase the quantity of parking supplied from 1,200 to 2,100.

Using Price Elasticity of Supply to Predict Changes in Price

Figure 6.5 illustrates the important point that when demand increases, the amount by which price increases depends on the price elasticity of supply. The figure shows the demand and supply for parking spaces at a beach resort. In panel (a), on a typical summer weekend, equilibrium occurs at point A, where Demand_Typical intersects a supply curve that is inelastic. The increase in demand for parking spaces on July 4 shifts the demand curve to the right, moving the equilibrium to point B. Because the resort has only a limited amount of vacant land that it can use for parking, the supply curve is inelastic and the increase in demand results in a large increase in price—from $2.00 per hour to $4.00—but only a small increase in the quantity of spaces supplied—from 1,200 to 1,400.

In panel (b), we assume that the resort has a lot of vacant land that it can use for parking during periods of high demand, so supply is elastic. As a result, the change in equilibrium from point A to point B results in a smaller increase in price and a larger increase in the quantity supplied. An increase in price from $2.00 per hour to $2.50 is sufficient to increase the quantity of parking spaces supplied from 1,200 to 2,100. Knowing the price elasticity of supply makes it possible to predict more accurately how much price will change following an increase or a decrease in demand.   MyLab Economics Concept Check

MyLab Economics Study Plan

Continued from page 183

Economics in Your Life & Career

Would PepsiCo and One of Its Bottlers Prefer a National or Local Soda Tax?

At the beginning of the chapter, we asked you to consider two scenarios: First, if you worked as an economist for PepsiCo, how would you evaluate the effect of a national soda tax? Second, we asked how your answer might change if you were employed by a local Pepsi bottler.

As we saw in Table 6.2 on page 192, the demand for soda is price inelastic, so although a soda tax will reduce sales of Pepsi's sweetened beverages, the effect will be smaller than it would be if the demand were price elastic. Although Pepsi's sales would decline less if soda taxes were limited to a few cities, the firm might prefer a uniform national tax rather than face widespread local taxes because a national tax would make planning easier and reduce uncertainty. A high tax in one city and a low tax in another city might end up shifting sales from one city to the other in a way that would have a negative effect on local Pepsi bottlers.

A local Pepsi bottler will have a strong preference for a uniform national tax over a local tax. As we saw in the chapter opener, the Pepsi bottler in Philadelphia experienced a sharp 40 percent decrease in sales after the city enacted a soda tax. Because the tax did not apply to the city's suburbs or to other neighboring towns, some consumers in Philadelphia switched to buying their soda outside the city limits. Because Pepsi for sale outside of Philadelphia is a close substitute for Pepsi sold in the city, the demand for Pepsi in Philadelphia turned out to be price elastic.

Conclusion

Computing elasticities is important in economics because it allows us to measure how one variable changes in response to changes in another variable. For example, by calculating the price elasticity of demand for its product, a firm can make a quantitative estimate of the effect of a price change on the revenue it receives. Similarly, by calculating the price elasticity of demand for cigarettes, the government can better estimate the effect of an increase in cigarette taxes on smoking. Table 6.7 on the next page summarizes the different elasticities we discussed in this chapter.

Table 6.7

Summary of Elasticities

PRICE ELASTICITY OF DEMAND

Formula: $\dfrac{\text{Percentage change in quantity demanded}}{\text{Percentage change in price}}$

Midpoint formula: $\dfrac{(Q_2 - Q_1)}{\left(\dfrac{Q_1 + Q_2}{2}\right)} \div \dfrac{(P_2 - P_1)}{\left(\dfrac{P_1 + P_2}{2}\right)}$

	Absolute Value of Price Elasticity	Effect on Total Revenue of an Increase in Price
Elastic	Greater than 1	Total revenue falls
Inelastic	Less than 1	Total revenue rises
Unit elastic	Equal to 1	Total revenue unchanged

CROSS-PRICE ELASTICITY OF DEMAND

Formula: $\dfrac{\text{Percentage change in quantity demanded of one good}}{\text{Percentage change in price of another good}}$

Types of Products	Value of Cross-Price Elasticity
Substitutes	Positive
Complements	Negative
Unrelated	Zero

INCOME ELASTICITY OF DEMAND

Formula: $\dfrac{\text{Percentage change in quantity demanded}}{\text{Percentage change in income}}$

Types of Products	Value of Income Elasticity
Normal and a necessity	Positive but less than 1
Normal and a luxury	Positive and greater than 1
Inferior	Negative

PRICE ELASTICITY OF SUPPLY

Formula: $\dfrac{\text{Percentage change in quantity supplied}}{\text{Percentage change in price}}$

	Value of Price Elasticity
Elastic	Greater than 1
Inelastic	Less than 1
Unit elastic	Equal to 1

Visit **MyLab Economics** for a news article and analysis related to the concepts in this chapter.

CHAPTER SUMMARY
AND PROBLEMS

Key Terms

Cross-price elasticity of demand, p. 197

Elastic demand, p. 185

Elasticity, p. 184

Income elasticity of demand, p. 198

Inelastic demand, p. 185

Perfectly elastic demand, p. 188

Perfectly inelastic demand, p. 188

Price elasticity of demand, p. 184

Price elasticity of supply, p. 202

Total revenue, p. 192

Unit-elastic demand, p. 185

6.1 The Price Elasticity of Demand and Its Measurement, pages 184–190

LEARNING OBJECTIVE: Define and calculate the price elasticity of demand.

MyLab Economics Visit www.pearson.com/mylab/economics to complete these exercises online and get instant feedback.

Summary

Elasticity measures how much one economic variable responds to changes in another economic variable. The **price elasticity of demand** measures how responsive the quantity demanded is to changes in price. The price elasticity of demand is equal to the percentage change in the quantity demanded divided by the percentage change in price. If the quantity demanded changes more than proportionally when price changes, the price elasticity of demand is greater than 1 in absolute value, and demand is **elastic**. If the quantity demanded changes less than proportionally when price changes, the price elasticity of demand is less than 1 in absolute value, and demand is **inelastic**. If the quantity demanded changes proportionally when price changes, the price elasticity of demand is equal to 1 in absolute value, and demand is **unit elastic**. **Perfectly inelastic demand** curves are vertical lines, and **perfectly elastic demand** curves are horizontal lines. Relatively few products have perfectly elastic or perfectly inelastic demand curves.

Review Questions

1.1 Write the formula for the price elasticity of demand. Why isn't elasticity just measured by the slope of the demand curve?

1.2 If a 10 percent increase in the price of Cheerios causes a 25 percent reduction in the number of boxes of Cheerios demanded, what is the price elasticity of demand for Cheerios? Is the demand for Cheerios elastic or inelastic?

1.3 What is the midpoint formula for calculating price elasticity of demand? How else can you calculate the price elasticity of demand? What is the advantage of using the midpoint formula?

1.4 Draw a graph of a perfectly inelastic demand curve. Think of a product that would have a perfectly inelastic demand curve. Explain why demand for this product would be perfectly inelastic.

Problems and Applications

1.5 **(Related to the Chapter Opener on page 182)** A study of the consumption of beverages in Mexico found that "overall, for soft drinks a 10% price increase decreases the quantity consumed by 10.6%." Given this information, calculate the price elasticity of demand for soda in Mexico. Is demand price elastic or price inelastic? Briefly explain.

Source: M. A. Colchero, et al., "Price Elasticity of the Demand for Sugar Sweetened Beverages and Soft Drinks in Mexico," *Economics and Human Biology*," Vol. 19, December 2015, pp. 129–137.

1.6 Suppose that the following table gives data on the price of rye and the number of bushels of rye sold in 2017 and 2018:

Year	Price (dollars per bushel)	Quantity (bushels)
2017	$3	8 million
2018	2	12 million

a. Calculate the change in the quantity of rye demanded divided by the change in the price of rye. Measure the quantity of rye in bushels.

b. Calculate the change in the quantity of rye demanded divided by the change in the price of rye, but this time measure the quantity of rye in millions of bushels. Compare your answer to the one you computed in (a).

c. Assuming that the demand curve for rye did not shift between 2017 and 2018, use the information in the table to calculate the price elasticity of demand for rye. Use the midpoint formula in your calculation. Compare the value for the price elasticity of demand to the values you calculated in (a) and (b).

1.7 Jacob Goldstein, a correspondent for National Public Radio, discussed the effect that a tax on sugared soft drinks would have on consumers: "How much would a tax drive down consumption? Economists call this issue 'price elasticity of demand'—how much demand goes down as price increases." Briefly explain whether you agree with Goldstein's definition of price elasticity of demand.

Source: Jacob Goldstein, "Would a Soda Tax Be a Big Deal?" *Planet Money*, March 10, 2010.

1.8 **(Related to Solved Problem 6.1 on page 187)** You own a hot dog stand that you set up outside the student union every day at lunchtime. Currently, you are selling hot dogs for a price of $3 each, and you sell 30 hot dogs a day. You are considering cutting the price to $2. The following graph shows two possible increases in the quantity sold as a result of your price cut. Use the information in the graph to calculate the price elasticity of demand between these two prices on each of the demand curves. Use the mid-point formula to calculate the price elasticities.

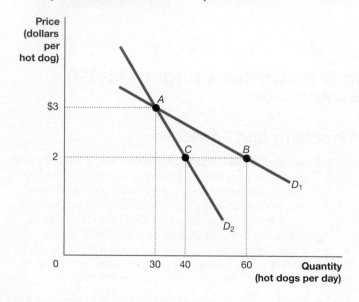

1.9 In 1916, Ford Motor Company sold 500,000 Model T Fords at a price of $440 each. Henry Ford believed that he could increase sales of the Model T by 1,000 cars for every dollar he cut the price. Use this information to calculate the price elasticity of demand for Model T Fords. Use the midpoint formula in your calculation.

1.10 **(Related to the Don't Let This Happen to You on page 190)** The publisher of a magazine gives her staff the following information:

Current price	$2 per issue
Current sales	150,000 copies per month
Current total costs	$450,000 per month

The publisher tells the staff, "Our costs are currently $150,000 more than our revenues each month. I propose to eliminate this problem by raising the price of the magazine to $3 per issue. This will result in our revenue being exactly equal to our cost." Do you agree with the publisher's analysis? Explain. (*Hint:* Remember that a firm's revenue is calculated by multiplying the price of the product by the quantity sold.)

 6.2 **The Determinants of the Price Elasticity of Demand, pages 190–192**

LEARNING OBJECTIVE: List and explain the determinants of the price elasticity of demand.

MyLab Economics Visit www.pearson.com/mylab/economics to complete these exercises online and get instant feedback.

Summary

The main determinants of the price elasticity of demand for a good are the availability of close substitutes, the passage of time, whether the good is a necessity or a luxury, how narrowly the market for the good is defined, and the share of the good in the consumer's budget.

Review Questions

2.1 What are the key determinants of the price elasticity of demand for a product? Which determinant is the most important?

2.2 Is the demand for most agricultural products elastic or inelastic? Briefly explain.

Problems and Applications

2.3 Briefly explain whether the demand for each of the following products is likely to be elastic or inelastic:
   a. Milk
   b. Frozen cheese pizza
   c. Gasoline
   d. Prescription medicine

2.4 According to a news story about the bus system in the Lehigh Valley in Pennsylvania, "Ridership fell 14 percent … after a 33 percent increase" in bus fares. Based on this information, is the demand for bus trips price elastic or price inelastic? Explain your answer in terms of the five determinants of price elasticity.
Source: Dan Hartzell, "U.S. Transit Use Highest Since 1956," (Allentown, PA) *Morning Call*, March 13, 2014.

2.5 One study found that the price elasticity of demand for soda is −0.78, while the price elasticity of demand for Coca-Cola is −1.22. Coca-Cola is a type of soda, so why isn't its price elasticity the same as the price elasticity for soda as a product?
Source: Kelly D. Brownell and Thomas R. Frieden, "Ounces of Prevention—The Public Policy Case for Taxes on Sugared Beverages," *New England Journal of Medicine*, April 30, 2009, pp. 1805–1808.

2.6 The price elasticity of demand for crude oil in the United States has been estimated to be −0.06 in the short run and −0.45 in the long run. Why would the demand for crude oil be more price elastic in the long run than in the short run?
Source: John C. B. Cooper, "Price Elasticity of Demand for Crude Oil: Estimate for 23 Countries," *OPEC Review*, Vol. 27, March 2003, pp. 1–8.

2.7 The entrance fee into Yellowstone National Park in northwestern Wyoming is "$30 for a private, noncommercial vehicle; $25 for a motorcycle or a snowmobile; or $15 for each visitor 16 and older entering by foot, bike, ski, etc." The fee provides the visitor with a seven-day entrance permit into Yellowstone and nearby Grand Teton National Park.

a. Would you expect the demand for entry into Yellowstone National Park for visitors in private, noncommercial vehicles to be elastic or inelastic? Briefly explain.

b. There are three general ways to enter the park: in a private, noncommercial vehicle; on a motorcycle; and by foot, bike, or ski. Which way would you expect to have the largest price elasticity of demand, and which would you expect to have the smallest price elasticity of demand? Briefly explain.

Source: National Park Service, "Yellowstone National Park: Basic Information," www.nps.gov/yell/planyourvisit/basicinfo.htm.

6.3 The Relationship between Price Elasticity of Demand and Total Revenue, pages 192–197

LEARNING OBJECTIVE: Explain the relationship between the price elasticity of demand and total revenue.

MyLab Economics Visit www.pearson.com/mylab/economics to complete these exercises online and get instant feedback.

Summary

Total revenue is the total amount of funds received by a seller of a good or service. When demand is inelastic, a decrease in price reduces total revenue, and an increase in price raises total revenue. When demand is elastic, a decrease in price increases total revenue, and an increase in price decreases total revenue. When demand is unit elastic, an increase or a decrease in price leaves total revenue unchanged.

Review Questions

3.1 If the demand for orange juice is inelastic, will an increase in the price of orange juice increase or decrease the revenue that orange juice sellers receive?

3.2 The price of organic apples falls, and apple growers find that their revenue increases. Is the demand for organic apples elastic or inelastic?

Problems and Applications

3.3 In recent years, increases in the number of visitors to national parks such as Yellowstone and Grand Canyon have resulted in over $12 billion in deferred maintenance costs. In response to the overcrowding that has contributed to the cost overruns, the Park Service has considered limiting the number of daily visits to the parks and soliciting corporate sponsorships. Margaret Walls, a research director and senior fellow at Resources for the Future, has offered another suggestion: Increase entrance fees. But she warned: "Figuring out an efficient and fair fee structure will not be easy. It requires detailed data on visitation, for starters, as well as analysis to shed light on price elasticities of demand for different groups of visitors at different locations." Why is it important for the Park Service to have estimates of price elasticities of demand before raising entrance fees to the national parks?

Source: Margaret A. Walls, "Protecting Our National Parks: New Entrance Fees Can Help," *Resources*, No. 193, Fall 2016.

3.4 An article in the *New York Times* about the New York Metropolitan Opera (the Met) suggested that the popularity of opera might be increased if the Met reduced its ticket prices. But the article observed that such ticket price cuts would be possible only if the Met received a gift from "a very deep-pocketed donor." What were the authors of the article assuming would happen to the Met's revenue following the cut in ticket prices? What were they assuming about the price elasticity of demand for tickets to the Met? Briefly explain.

Source: Zachary Woolfe et al., "The Met Opera Is Struggling. How Can It Fill Those Empty Seats?" *New York Times*, May 4, 2016.

3.5 Economists' estimates of price elasticities can differ somewhat, depending on the time period and on the markets in which the price and quantity data used in the estimates were gathered. An article in the *New York Times* contained the following statement from the Centers for Disease Control and Prevention: "A 10 percent increase in the price of cigarettes reduces consumption by 3 percent to 5 percent." Given this information, compute the range of the price elasticity of demand for cigarettes. Explain whether the demand for cigarettes is elastic, inelastic, or unit elastic. If cigarette manufacturers raise prices, will their revenue increase or decrease? Briefly explain.

Source: Shaila Dewan, "States Look at Tobacco to Balance the Budget," *New York Times*, March 20, 2009.

3.6 When San Francisco and other cities in California adopted soda taxes, an opinion column in the *New York Times* observed, "Often, the taxes don't even pinch the budgets of low-income families, because they respond by drinking less soda." What does the columnist mean when he writes that soda taxes don't "pinch the budgets" of low-income families? Shouldn't an increase in the price of soda resulting from a tax always increase the amount that families have to spend to buy soda? Briefly explain.

Source: David Leonhardt, "Fight Big Soda," *New York Times*, October 6, 2016.

3.7 Use the following graph for Yolanda's Frozen Yogurt Stand to answer the questions.

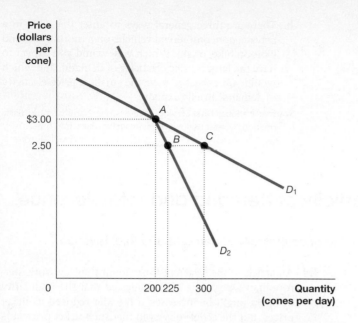

a. Use the midpoint formula to calculate the price elasticity of demand for D_1 between point A and point C and the price elasticity of demand for D_2 between point A and point B. Which demand curve is more elastic, D_1 or D_2? Briefly explain.

b. Suppose Yolanda is initially selling 200 cones per day at a price of $3.00 per cone. If she cuts her price to $2.50 per cone and her demand curve is D_1, what will be the change in her revenue? What will be the change in her revenue if her demand curve is D_2?

3.8 **(Related to Solved Problem 6.3 on page 195)** In 2017, the Metropolitan Transportation Authority (MTA) in New York City raised the price of a monthly subway pass from $116.50 to $121.00. According to an article in the *New York Times*, "Officials at the authority have said they must raise fares every two years to pay for the rising costs of providing service."

a. In order for the MTA's strategy for covering its rising costs to be successful, what must be true about the price elasticity of demand for subway passes?

b. Suppose that the MTA's strategy in (a) doesn't succeed. What then must be true about the price elasticity of demand for subway passes? On the same graph, draw a demand curve for subway passes assuming that the MTA's strategy succeeds and a second demand curve assuming that the strategy fails. For each demand curve, your graph should indicate the areas representing the revenue the MTA receives following the price increase.

Source: Emma G. Fitzsimmons, "M.T.A. Votes to Raise Fares and Tolls: What You Need to Know," *New York Times*, January 25, 2017.

3.9 **(Related to Solved Problem 6.3 on page 195)** According to an article in the *Wall Street Journal*, reporting on Coca-Cola's results for the fourth quarter of 2016: "Higher pricing . . . drove revenue growth of 8%." Based on this

information, is the demand for the beverages Coke sells price elastic or price inelastic? Briefly explain.

Source: Jennifer Maloney and Anne Steele, "Coke's Profit Falls as Restructuring Continues," *Wall Street Journal*, February 9, 2017.

3.10 **(Related to the Apply the Concept on page 196)** According to an article in the *New York Times*, some small publishers have argued that Amazon has been increasing the prices it charges for their books on its Web site. Amazon was increasing the prices by reducing the discount it offered consumers on the retail prices of the books. One small nonfiction publisher said that Amazon had reduced the discount on its books from about 30 percent to about 16 percent. According to the author of the article: "For this publisher, that means less revenue and less profit as some buyers reject the more expensive books."

a. Does the fact that some buyers will no longer buy the publisher's books at a higher price necessarily mean the publisher will earn less revenue? Briefly explain.

b. What must be true about the price elasticity of demand for the publisher's books for the author's statement to be correct?

Source: David Streitfeld, "As Competition Wanes, Amazon Cuts Back Discounts," *New York Times*, July 4, 2013.

3.11 **(Related to the Apply the Concept on page 196)** Amazon allows authors who self-publish their e-books to set the prices they charge. One author was quoted as saying, "I am able to drop prices and, by sheer volume of sales, increase my income." Was the demand for her books price elastic or price inelastic? Briefly explain.

Source: David Streitfeld, "For the Indie Writers of Amazon, It's Publish or Perish," *New York Times*, January 4, 2015.

3.12 The Delaware River Joint Toll Bridge Commission increased the toll from $0.50 to $1.00 on the bridges on Route 22 and Interstate 78 from New Jersey to Pennsylvania. Use the information in the following table to answer the questions. (Assume that besides the toll change, nothing occurred during these months that would affect consumer demand.)

Number of Vehicles Crossing the Bridge			
Month	Toll	Route 22 Bridge	Interstate 78 Bridge
November	$0.50	519,337	728,022
December	$1.00	433,691	656,257

a. Calculate the price elasticity of demand for each bridge, using the midpoint formula.

b. How much total revenue did the commission collect from these bridges in November? How much did it collect in December? Relate your answer to your answer in (a).

Source: Garrett Therolf, "Frugal Drivers Flood Free Bridge," (Allentown, PA) *Morning Call*, January 20, 2003.

6.4 Other Demand Elasticities, pages 197–199

LEARNING OBJECTIVE: Define and calculate the cross-price elasticity of demand and the income elasticity of demand and explain their determinants.

Summary

In addition to the price elasticity of demand, other important demand elasticities are the **cross-price elasticity of demand**, which is equal to the percentage change in the quantity demanded of one good divided by the percentage change in the price of another good, and the **income elasticity of demand**, which is equal to the percentage change in the quantity demanded by the percentage change in income.

Review Questions

4.1 Define the *cross-price elasticity of demand*. What does it mean if the cross-price elasticity of demand is negative? What does it mean if the cross-price elasticity of demand is positive?

4.2 Define the *income elasticity of demand*. How does the income elasticity of a normal good differ from the income elasticity of an inferior good? Is it possible to tell from the income elasticity of demand whether a product is a luxury good or a necessity good?

Problems and Applications

4.3 When lettuce prices doubled, from about $1.50 per head to about $3.00, the reaction of one consumer was quoted in a newspaper article: "I will not buy [lettuce] when it's $3 a head," she said, adding that other green vegetables can fill in for lettuce. "If bread were $5 a loaf we'd still have to buy it. But lettuce is not that important in our family."
  a. For this consumer's household, which product has the higher price elasticity of demand: bread or lettuce? Briefly explain.
  b. Is the cross-price elasticity of demand between lettuce and other green vegetables positive or negative for this consumer? Briefly explain.
  Source: Justin Bachman, "Sorry, Romaine Only," Associated Press, March 29, 2002.

4.4 (**Related to the Chapter Opener on page 182**) A study of consumers in Mexico found that the cross-price elasticity of demand between soda and milk was 0.11, while the cross-price elasticity of demand between soda and candy was −0.32. Is soda a substitute or a complement for milk? Is soda a substitute or a complement for candy? Briefly explain.
  Source: M. A. Colchero et al., "Price Elasticity of the Demand for Sugar Sweetened Beverages and Soft Drinks in Mexico," *Economics and Human Biology*," Vol. 19, December 2015, pp. 129–137.

4.5 In the following graph, the demand for hot dog buns has shifted to the right because the price of hot dogs has fallen from $2.20 to $1.80 per package. Use the midpoint formula to calculate the cross-price elasticity of demand between hot dogs and hot dog buns.

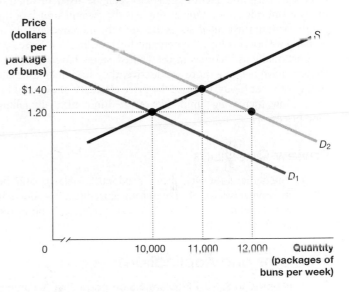

4.6 Are the cross-price elasticities of demand between the following pairs of products likely to be positive or negative? Briefly explain.
  a. Iced coffee and iced tea
  b. French fries and ketchup
  c. Steak and chicken
  d. Blu-ray players and Blu-ray discs

4.7 Rank the following four goods from lowest income elasticity of demand to highest income elasticity of demand. Briefly explain your ranking.
  a. Bread
  b. Pepsi
  c. Mercedes-Benz automobiles
  d. Laptop computers

4.8 (**Related to the Apply the Concept on page 199**) The elasticities reported in this *Apply the Concept* were calculated using price data for many brands of beer. Why might price elasticity estimates be less reliable if they use data for only one brand of beer?

4.9 Consider firms selling three goods: Firm A sells a good with an income elasticity of demand less than zero; Firm B sells a good with an income elasticity of demand greater than zero but less than one; and Firm C sells a good with an income elasticity of demand greater than one. In a recession when incomes fall, which firm is likely to see its sales decline the most? Which firm is likely to see its sales increase the most? Briefly explain.

6.5 Using Elasticity to Analyze the Disappearing Family Farm, pages 199–202

LEARNING OBJECTIVE: Use price elasticity and income elasticity to analyze economic issues.

MyLab Economics Visit **www.pearson.com/mylab/economics** to complete these exercises online and get instant feedback.

Summary

Price elasticity and income elasticity can be used to analyze many economic issues. One example is the disappearance of the family farm in the United States. Because the income elasticity of demand for food is low, the demand for food has not increased proportionally as incomes in the United States have grown. As farmers have become more productive, they have increased the supply of most foods. Because the price elasticity of demand for food is low, increasing supply has resulted in continually falling food prices.

Review Questions

5.1 The demand for agricultural products is inelastic, and the income elasticity of demand for agricultural products is low. How do these facts help explain the decline of the family farm in the United States?

Problems and Applications

5.2 (Related to Solved Problem 6.5 on page 200) According to a study by the U.S. Centers for Disease Control and Prevention, the price elasticity of demand for cigarettes is −0.25. Americans purchase about 360 billion cigarettes each year.
  a. If the federal tax on cigarettes were increased enough to cause a 50 percent increase in the price of cigarettes, what would be the effect on the quantity of cigarettes demanded?
  b. Is raising the tax on cigarettes a more effective way to reduce smoking if the demand for cigarettes is elastic or if it is inelastic? Briefly explain.
Source: "Response to Increases in Cigarette Prices by Race/Ethnicity, Income, and Age Groups—United States, 1976–1993," *Morbidity and Mortality Weekly Report,* July 31, 1998.

5.3 (Related to Solved Problem 6.5 on page 200) Suppose that the long-run price elasticity of demand for gasoline is −0.55. Assume that the price of gasoline is currently $3.00 per gallon, the equilibrium quantity of gasoline is 140 billion gallons per year, and the federal government decides to increase the excise tax on gasoline by $1.00 per gallon. Suppose that in the long run, the price of gasoline increases by $0.70 per gallon after the $1.00 excise tax is imposed.
  a. What is the new quantity of gasoline demanded after the tax is imposed? How effective would a gas tax be in reducing consumption of gasoline in the long run?
  b. How much does the federal government receive from the tax?

5.4 According to an article in the *Wall Street Journal,* in 2017, farmers in the United States were facing a fourth consecutive year of falling farm incomes. The article states that a "deepening downturn in the U.S. agricultural economy" was the result of years of bumper harvests. Shouldn't increases in the amount of agricultural products farmers sell be good news for them and raise their incomes? Briefly explain.
Source: Jesse Newman, "U.S. Farm Income Seen Falling for Fourth Straight Year," *Wall Street Journal,* February 7, 2017.

5.5 Corruption has been a significant problem in Iraq. Opening and running a business there usually requires paying multiple bribes to government officials. We can think of there being a demand and supply for bribes, with the curves having the usual shapes: The demand for bribes will be downward sloping because the smaller the bribe, the more business owners will be willing to pay it. The supply of bribes will be upward sloping because the larger the bribe, the more government officials will be willing to run the risk of breaking the law by accepting the bribe. Suppose that the Iraqi government introduces a new policy to reduce corruption that raises the cost to officials of accepting bribes—perhaps by increasing the jail term for accepting a bribe. As a result, the supply curve for bribes will shift to the left. If we measure the burden on the economy from corruption by the total value of the bribes paid, what must be true of the demand for bribes if the government policy is to be effective? Illustrate your answer with a demand and supply graph. Be sure to show on your graph the areas representing the burden of corruption before and after the government policy is enacted.
Source: Frank R. Gunter, *The Political Economy of Iraq: Restoring Balance in a Post-Conflict Society,* Cheltenham, UK: Edward Elgar, 2013, Chapter 4.

5.6 The head of the United Kumquat Growers Association makes the following statement:

> The federal government is considering implementing a price floor in the market for kumquats. The government will not be able to buy any surplus kumquats produced at the price floor or to pay us any other subsidy. Because the demand for kumquats is elastic, I believe this program will make us worse off, and I say we should oppose it.

Explain whether you agree with this reasoning.

5.7 Review the concept of economic efficiency from Chapter 4, pages 115–117, before answering the following question: Will there be a greater loss of economic efficiency from a price ceiling when demand is elastic or inelastic? Illustrate your answer with a demand and supply graph.

The Price Elasticity of Supply and Its Measurement, pages 202–208

6.6

LEARNING OBJECTIVE: Define price elasticity of supply and explain its determinants and how it is measured.

MyLab Economics Visit **www.pearson.com/mylab/economics** to complete these exercises online and get instant feedback.

Summary

The **price elasticity of supply** is equal to the percentage change in quantity supplied divided by the percentage change in price. The supply curves for most goods are inelastic over a short period of time, but they become increasingly elastic over longer periods of time. Perfectly inelastic supply curves are vertical lines, and perfectly elastic supply curves are horizontal lines. Relatively few products have perfectly elastic or perfectly inelastic supply curves.

Review Questions

6.1 Write the formula for the price elasticity of supply. If an increase of 10 percent in the price of frozen pizzas results in a 9 percent increase in the quantity of frozen pizzas supplied, what is the price elasticity of supply for frozen pizzas? Is the supply of pizzas elastic or inelastic?

6.2 What is the main determinant of the price elasticity of supply?

Problems and Applications

6.3 To legally operate a taxi in New York City, a driver must have a medallion issued by the New York City Taxi and Limousine Commission, an agency of the city's government. In 2017 the number of medallions was 13,587. In recent years the taxi industry in New York and other large cities has encountered competition from companies such as Uber, an app-based service that offers rides from drivers who own their own cars. Uber varies the prices it charges based on the demand for rides, with rides during busier periods, such as Saturday nights, having higher prices.
   a. What does the limitation on their number imply about the price elasticity of supply of taxi medallions?
   b. Is the supply of Uber rides more or less elastic than the supply of taxi rides in New York City? Briefly explain.
   Source: Matthew Flamm, "Have Taxis Finally Hit Rock Bottom?" crainsnewyork.com, April 11, 2017.

6.4 **(Related to the Apply the Concept on page 203)** An article in the *Wall Street Journal* notes that although U.S. oil production has increased rapidly in recent years, the increase has still amounted to only 5 percent of world production.

Still, that increase has been "enough to help trigger a price collapse." Briefly explain under what circumstances a small increase in supply can lead to a large decline in equilibrium price.
   Source: Georgi Kantchev and Bill Spindle, "Shale-Oil Producers Ready to Raise Output," *Wall Street Journal*, May 13, 2015.

6.5 **(Related to the Apply the Concept on page 203)** Suppose that instead of being highly inelastic, the demand for oil is highly elastic.
   a. Given the situation illustrated by the first graph in the *Apply the Concept* on page 203, would the resulting price change be larger, smaller, or the same as the actual price change shown in the graph? Briefly explain.
   b. Given the situation illustrated by the second graph in the *Apply the Concept* on page 203, would the resulting price change be larger, smaller, or the same as the actual price change shown in the graph? Briefly explain.

6.6 Use the midpoint formula for calculating elasticity to calculate the price elasticity of supply between point *A* and point *B* for each panel of Figure 6.5 on page 206.

6.7 An article in the *Wall Street Journal* described the production of cocoa beans used to make chocolate in African countries such as Ghana and Ivory Coast. The article explained that when prices of cocoa beans rise, it can take two to four years for new trees to produce the pods in which the beans are grown. If the demand for chocolate were to increase, all else equal, would you expect the price of chocolate to be greater after one year or after four years? Use a graph to illustrate your answer.
   Source: Alexandra Wexler, "Chocolate Makers Fight a Melting Supply of Cocoa," *Wall Street Journal*, January 13, 2016.

6.8 Suppose that on most days, the price of a rose is $1, and 8,000 roses are purchased. On Valentine's Day, the price of a rose jumps to $2, and 30,000 roses are purchased.
   a. Draw a demand and supply graph that shows why the price jumps.
   b. Based on this information, what do we know about the price elasticity of demand for roses? What do we know about the price elasticity of supply for roses? Calculate values for the price elasticity of demand and the price elasticity of supply or explain why you can't calculate these values.

6.9 Use the graph of the market for basketball tickets at State University on the next page to answer the questions.

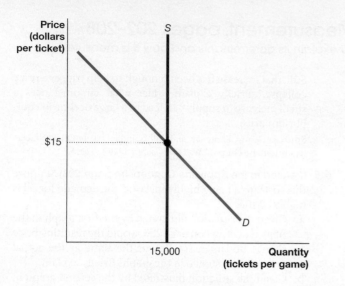

a. What is the price elasticity of supply in this case?

b. Suppose the basketball team at State University goes undefeated in the first half of the season, and the demand for basketball tickets increases. Show the effects of this increase in demand on the graph. What happens to the equilibrium price and quantity of tickets? Briefly explain.

c. If the State University basketball team continues to do very well in future years, what is likely to happen to the price elasticity of supply of tickets to its games? Briefly explain.

Critical Thinking Exercises

CT6.1 Survey a group of 10 people and find *one* good that all of them purchase each month. That common good might be pizza, Starbucks coffee, bottled water, gigabytes of data on their phone plan, or gasoline. Ask each person three questions about that good: (1) Roughly what is the current price you pay for the good? (2) How much of the good do you consume each month? and (3) How much of the good would you consume if the price of the good doubled? Enter the data you gather in a spreadsheet and estimate this group's elasticity of demand for the good, using the midpoint formula. Does your result make sense to you? Briefly explain.

CT6.2 From the following tables, what types of elasticity can you calculate? Briefly explain.

Quantity of Gasoline an Average Consumer Purchases per Month	Price of Gasoline	Income per Month of the Average Consumer
100 gallons	$2.50	$4,000
120 gallons	2.60	4,500

Quantity of Gasoline an Average Consumer Purchases per Month	Price of Gasoline	Income per Month of the Average Consumer
100 gallons	$2.60	$4,000
120 gallons	$2.60	$4,500

The Economics of Health Care

Where Will You Find Health Insurance?

When Donald Trump took office as president in January 2017, he pledged to "repeal and replace" the Patient Protection and Affordable Care Act (ACA). The ACA was enacted by President Barack Obama and Congress in 2010 and is often referred to as "Obamacare." During 2017, two bills to revise the ACA failed in Congress, reflecting the lack of political consensus about the role of the federal government in the health care system. One controversial feature of the ACA was the fine imposed on individuals who do not have health insurance. In 2017, if you did not have health insurance, you were fined $695 or 2.5 percent of your income, whichever amount was higher. Many young, healthy individuals chose to pay the fine, which was typically lower than the premiums they would have to pay to buy health insurance.

This outcome was bad news for companies like Humana that sell insurance policies on the health insurance marketplaces established by the ACA. Under the ACA, insurance companies were not allowed to charge higher premiums for older people or people with chronic medical problems ("preexisting conditions"). Insurance companies were also required to include in every policy coverage for contraceptives, physical examinations, tests to screen for diseases, and certain other services without any additional charge to the policyholder. If you did not expect to use those services, you might prefer to buy a policy with more limited coverage. Insurance companies would be able to charge lower premiums for such policies, but weren't allowed to offer them under the ACA.

As more younger and healthier people did not buy individual health insurance policies, the remaining consumers on the health insurance marketplaces became, on average, older and less healthy—and more likely to file claims with the insurance companies. If Humana and other insurance companies responded by raising their premiums, they ran the risk of even fewer young and healthy people buying policies, which would require further premium increases, and so on. Humana and some other companies responded by leaving the insurance marketplaces. In 2016, 85 percent of people enrolled in the health insurance marketplaces had

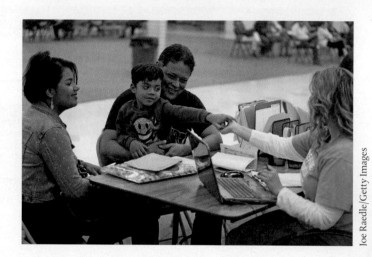

Joe Raedle/Getty Images

a choice of at least three insurance companies from which to buy a policy; in 2017, only 57 percent had that choice. In more than 1,000 counties nationwide, only one insurance company was left offering policies on the marketplaces.

Some people participate in their employers' health insurance plan rather than buy an individual policy on the health insurance marketplaces. But as the costs of medical services continue to rise, employers are increasing the amounts they deduct from worker paychecks to pay for the insurance, and they are offering plans with higher deductibles, which means workers are paying more before insurance begins covering their medical expenses.

The increasing health care costs individuals and businesses face are reflected in trends in health care spending in the overall economy, which increased from about 5 percent of gross domestic product (GDP) in 1960 to more than 18 percent in 2017. In this chapter, we will discuss the role economic analysis can play in the debate over health care policy in the United States.

Sources: Anna Wilde Mathews and Stephanie Armour, "Humana's Decision to Pull Out of Health Exchanges Pressures Republicans," *Wall Street Journal*, February 15, 2017; Zachary Tracer, "Trump Points to Humana Exit from Obamacare as Sign of Failure," bloomberg.com, February 14, 2017; Cynthia Cox et al., "2017 Premium Changes and Insurer Participation in the Affordable Care Act's Health Insurance Marketplaces," kff.org, November 1, 2016; and U.S. Centers for Medicare & Medicaid Studies, "National Health Expenditure Data," www.cms.gov.

Chapter Outline & Learning Objectives

Economics in Your Life & Career

Is Your Take-Home Pay Affected by What Your Employer Spends on Your Health Insurance?

If you work for a firm that offers health insurance, the firm will withhold some amount from each of your paychecks to pay for the insurance. Typically, firms pay the majority of the cost of health insurance for their employees. In 2016, on average, employees paid only 18 percent of the cost of coverage for themselves or 29 percent of the cost of coverage for their family. Your paycheck probably doesn't show the amount your employer pays on your behalf for health insurance, but does that amount affect your take-home pay? As you read this chapter, try to answer this question. You can check your answer against the one we provide on **page 245** at the end of this chapter.

Source: The Kaiser Family Foundation and Health Research and Educational Trust, *Employer Health Benefits, 2016 Annual Survey*, September 14, 2016.

Health care Goods and services, such as prescription drugs, consultations with a doctor, and surgeries, that are intended to maintain or improve a person's health.

Health care refers to goods and services, such as prescription drugs, consultations with a doctor, and surgeries, that are intended to maintain or improve a person's health. Health care makes up more than one-sixth of the U.S. economy—about the size of the entire economy of France. Improvements in health care are an important part of the tremendous increase in living standards people in the United States and other high-income countries have experienced over the past 100 years. Health care has seen rapid technological change, with new products, such as MRI units and other diagnostic equipment; prescription drugs to treat cancer, high blood pressure, diabetes, and AIDS; vaccinations for meningitis and other illnesses; and new surgical techniques, such as cardiac catheterizations for treatment of heart disease.

Health care is provided through markets, just as are most other goods and services, such as smartphones and haircuts. So, we can apply to health care the tools of economic analysis we used in previous chapters. But the government plays a larger role in the market for health care than it does in other markets. In the United States, doctors and hospitals that supply most health care are primarily private firms, but the government provides some health care services directly through the Veterans Health Administration, which is part of the U.S. Department of Veterans Affairs, and indirectly through the Medicare and Medicaid programs. In addition, under the Affordable Care Act (ACA), the government regulates the health insurance policies that insurance companies offer.

In addition to having a large role for government, the market for health care differs from most markets in other ways. Most importantly, a typical consumer of health care doesn't pay the full price for that care. Most people have private health insurance, either provided through their employers or purchased on the government-run health insurance marketplaces, or they are enrolled in the Medicare or Medicaid programs. Consumers who have insurance make different decisions about the quantity of health care they wish to consume than they would if they were paying the full cost of the services. So, to analyze the market for health care, we need to use economic tools beyond those introduced in previous chapters. We begin our analysis of health care with an overview of health care around the world.

7.1 The Improving Health of People in the United States

LEARNING OBJECTIVE: Use data to discuss trends in U.S. health over time.

Two hundred years ago, the whole world was very poor by modern standards. Today, an average person in a high-income country has a standard of living well beyond what even the richest people in the past could have imagined. One aspect of this higher standard of living is the improved health the average person enjoys. For example, in the late 1700s, England had the highest level of income per person of any large country. But the average person in England had a short life span, and many people suffered from diseases—such as cholera, yellow fever, dysentery, and smallpox—that have disappeared from high-income countries today. The average life expectancy at birth was only 38 years, and 30 percent of the population died before reaching age 30. Even people who survived to age 20 could expect to live only an average of 34 more years. Today, the average life expectancy at birth in the United Kingdom and other high-income countries is around 80 years. People in eighteenth-century England were also short by modern standards. The average height of an adult male was 5 feet, 5 inches compared with 5 feet, 9 inches today.

In this section, we discuss the health of people in the United States. In Section 7.2, we compare the health care systems in the United States and other countries.

Variable	1850	2016
Life expectancy at birth	38.3 years	78.8 years
Average height (adult males)	5'7"	5'9.3"
Infant mortality (death of a child under 1 year of age)	228.9 per 1,000 live births	5.8 per 1,000 live births

Table 7.1

Health in the United States, 1850 and 2016

Note: The data on height for 1850 include only native-born white and black male citizens. The data on height for 2016 were gathered in 2007–2010 and represent the median height of adult males 20 years and older.

Sources: Susan B. Carter et al., eds., *Historical Statistics of the United States: Millennium Edition*; U.S. National Center for Health Statistics, *Anthropometric Reference Data for Children and Adults: United States, 2007–2010*, October 2012; and Centers for Disease Control and Prevention, *National Vital Statistics Reports*, various issues.

Changes over Time in U.S. Health

When economists measure changes over time in the standard of living in a country, they usually look first at increases in income per person. However, changes in health are also important because health is an essential part of a person's well-being and, therefore, of his or her standard of living. The health of the average person in the United States improved significantly during the 1800s and 1900s, and by and large, it continues to improve today.

Table 7.1 compares three indicators of health in the United States in 1850 and 2016. Individuals in the United States today are taller, live much longer, and are much less likely to die in the first months of life than was true 165 years ago. Economists often use height as a measure of long-run changes in the average well-being of a population. A person's height depends partly on genetics—that is, tall parents tend to have tall children—but also on a person's *net nutritional status*. Net nutritional status depends on a person's food intake relative to the work the person has to perform, whether the person is able to remain warm in cold weather, and the diseases to which the person is exposed. Over time, people in the United States and other high-income countries have, on average, become taller, which is an indication that their nutritional status has improved.   **MyLab Economics** Concept Check

Reasons for Long-Run Improvements in U.S. Health

For most of the country's history, the health of people in the United States has steadily improved, with life expectancies increasing and death rates decreasing. Panel (a) of Figure 7.1 shows for the years 1900–2016 the increase in life expectancy and the decline in the mortality rate, or death rate, measured as deaths per 100,000 people. Note that the mortality rate is "age adjusted," which means that it is not affected by changes in the number of people in each age group. Life expectancy at birth in the United States increased from 47.3 years in 1900 to 78.8 years in 2016. Panel (b) shows for recent years the change in the overall mortality rate of the U.S. population, measured as deaths per 100,000 people, and the age-adjusted mortality rates for several diseases. In the panel, the mortality rates in 1981 are set equal to 100, and the rates for 2015 are measured relative to their 1981 levels. The overall mortality rate decreased by more than 25 percent between 1981 and 2015. Over this same period, deaths from cancer and from cardiovascular disease, such as heart attacks and strokes, declined significantly. Cancer deaths were 23 percent lower in 2015 than they were in 1981, while deaths from cardiovascular disease declined by 60 percent. Deaths from diabetes and kidney disease both increased during this period, largely due to the effects of increasing obesity. The overall decline in death rates in the United States since 1981 has been due to changes in lifestyle, particularly a decline in smoking, and advances in new diagnostic equipment, prescription drugs, and surgical techniques.

What explains increases in life expectancy and declines in death rates over the longer time span since 1850? Improvements in sanitation and in the distribution of food during the late 1800s and early 1900s led to better health during that period. More generally, the late Nobel Laureate Robert Fogel of the University of Chicago and Roderick Floud of Gresham College, along with coauthors, described a process by which better health makes it possible for people to work harder as they become taller, stronger, and

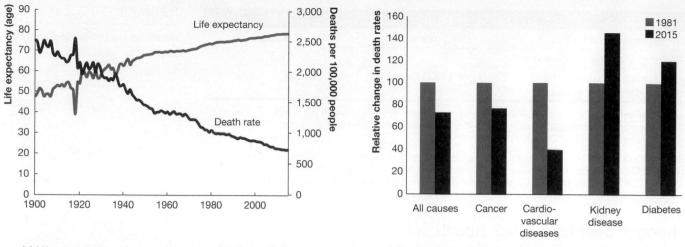

(a) Life expectancy at birth and the death rate per 100,000 people in the United States

(b) Changes in mortality rates

MyLab Economics Animation

Figure 7.1   **The Improving Health of the U.S. Population**

Panel (a) shows that since 1900, life expectancy has increased and mortality rates have decreased in the United States. Panel (b) shows that since 1981, there have been significant decreases in rates of death due to cardiovascular diseases and cancer. Rates of death due to kidney disease and diabetes have increased, primarily because of an increase in obesity. Note that in panel (a), the increase in mortality and decrease in life expectancy in 1918 are due to the severe influenza epidemic of that year.

Sources: For panel (a): Susan B. Carter et al., eds., *Historical Statistics of the United States: Millennium Edition*, Series Ab644; and Centers for Disease Control and Prevention, *National Vital Statistics Reports*, various issues; for panel (b): Centers for Disease Control and Prevention, *National Vital Statistics Reports*, various issues; and Jiaquan Xu, et al., "National Center for Health Statistics, Data Brief 267: Mortality in the United States, 2015," December 2016.

MyLab Economics Study Plan

more resistant to disease. Working harder raises a country's total income, making it possible for the country to afford better sanitation, more food, and a better system for distributing the food. In effect, improving health shifts out a country's production possibilities frontier. Higher incomes also allow the country to devote more resources to research and development, including medical research. The United States has been a pioneer in the development of medical technology, new surgical techniques, and new pharmaceuticals, which have played important roles in lengthening life spans and reducing the death toll from diseases.

MyLab Economics Concept Check

 7.2   Health Care around the World

LEARNING OBJECTIVE: Compare the health care systems and health care outcomes in the United States and other countries.

In the United States, private firms provide most health care, through either doctors' practices or hospitals. The main exception is the care the government provides through the network of hospitals operated by the federal government's Veterans Health Administration, although some cities also own and operate hospitals. Governments in most countries outside the United States have a more substantial direct role in paying for or providing health care. Policymakers and economists debate the effects of greater government involvement in the health care system on health outcomes such as life expectancy, infant mortality, and successful treatment of diseases.

The U.S. Health Care System

Health insurance A contract under which a buyer agrees to make payments, or *premiums*, in exchange for the provider's agreeing to pay some or all of the buyer's medical bills.

One important difference among health care systems in different countries is the way people pay for their health care. Most people in the United States have *health insurance* that helps them pay their medical bills. **Health insurance** is a contract under which a buyer agrees to make payments, or *premiums*, in exchange for the provider's agreeing to pay some or all of the buyer's medical bills. Figure 7.2 shows the sources of health insurance in the United States in 2016. About 49 percent of people received health insurance through their employer, and about 7 percent directly purchased an individual or

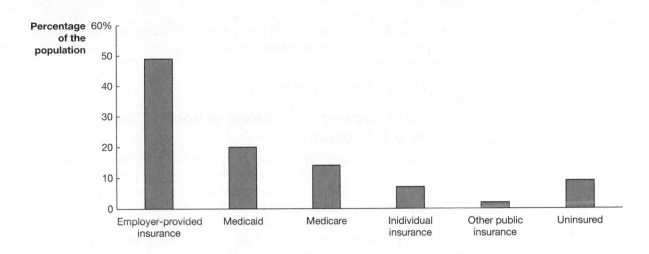

MyLab Economics Animation

Figure 7.2   **Sources of Health Insurance in the United States, 2016**

In 2016, about 49 percent of people received health insurance through their employer and about 7 percent directly purchased an individual or family health insurance policy from an insurance company. About 35 percent of people received health insurance through a government program, including Medicaid, Medicare, and other public insurance (including the program run by the Department of Veterans Affairs). About 9 percent of people were uninsured.

Note: Because some people have more than one type of health insurance, the sum of the values for each category shown is greater than 100 percent.

Source: Kaiser Family Foundation estimates based on data in U.S. Census Bureau, *Current Population Survey*, March 2017.

family health insurance policy from an insurance company, often using the state health insurance marketplaces Congress established under the Affordable Care Act. About 35 percent of people received health insurance through a government program including Medicaid, Medicare, and the program run by the Department of Veterans Affairs.

Most people who have private health insurance receive it through their employer. According to a survey of employers by the Kaiser Family Foundation, in 2016, 98 percent of firms employing more than 200 workers and 55 percent of firms employing between 3 and 199 workers offered health insurance as a fringe benefit (that is, a type of non-wage compensation) to their employees. Private health insurance companies can be either not-for-profit firms, such as some of the Blue Cross and Blue Shield organizations, or for-profit firms, such as Humana, Aetna, and John Hancock, which typically also sell other types of insurance. Private health insurance companies sell *group plans* to employers to cover all of their employees and individual plans directly to the public. Some health insurance plans reimburse doctors and hospitals on a **fee-for-service** basis, which means that doctors and hospitals receive a payment for each service they provide. Other health insurance plans are organized as *health maintenance organizations* (HMOs), which typically reimburse doctors mainly by paying a flat fee per patient rather than paying a fee for each individual office visit or other service provided.

Fee-for-service A system under which doctors and hospitals receive a payment for each service they provide.

About 9 percent of people were not covered by health insurance in 2016. This percentage was lower than in previous years, partly as a result of Congress passing the Affordable Care Act, but still represented more than 28 million uninsured people. Many people lack health insurance because their incomes are low, and they believe they cannot afford to buy private health insurance, even with government subsidies. Some low-income people either do not qualify for Medicaid or choose not to participate in that program. More than 70 percent of uninsured people live in families in which at least one member has a job. These individuals either were not offered health insurance through their employers or chose not to purchase it. Some young people opt out of employer-provided health insurance because they are healthy and do not believe that the cost of the premium their employer charges for the insurance is worth the benefit of having the insurance. More than half the uninsured were younger than age 35. Although most large firms offer their employees health insurance, fewer than two-thirds accept it. The remaining employees are covered by a spouse's policy, are not eligible for coverage, or have decided to go uninsured because they do not want to pay the premium for the insurance. The uninsured must pay for their own medical bills *out of pocket*, with money from their own income, just as they pay their other bills, or receive care from doctors or hospitals either free or below the normal price. **MyLab Economics** Concept Check

Apply the Concept

MyLab Economics Video

The Increasing Importance of Health Care in the U.S. Economy

When you graduate from college, you are much more likely than your parents or grandparents were to get a job in health care. There are many types of jobs in health care, from doctors and nurses to managers at hospitals and nursing homes to researchers and salespeople at pharmaceutical firms. As the following maps show, in 1990, manufacturing was the largest source of employment in most states, and in no state was health care the largest employer. By 2000, manufacturing was still the largest employer in 27 states, but health care had become the largest employer in two states. The results for 2016 are strikingly different, with manufacturing the largest employer in only 7 states and health care the largest employer in 35 states.

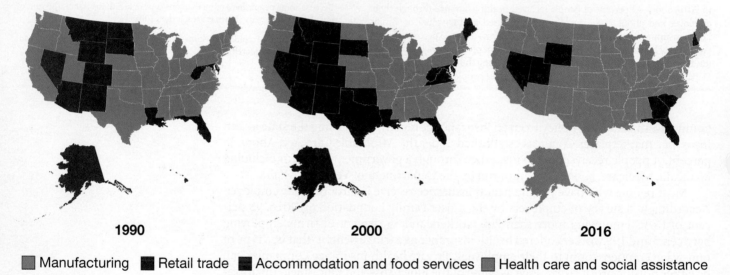

1990   2000   2016

■ Manufacturing ■ Retail trade ■ Accommodation and food services ■ Health care and social assistance

In 1990, almost twice as many people in the United States worked in manufacturing as worked in health care. Today, employment in health care has doubled, while employment in manufacturing has declined by more than 30 percent. And these trends are likely to continue. The U.S. Bureau of Labor Statistics forecasts that 13 of the 20 fastest-growing occupations over the next 10 years will be in health care.

What explains these trends? We discuss explanations for rising health care spending in the United States in Section 7.4. For now, note that the growth of employment in health care is similar to that in other service industries, such as retail stores and restaurants, and that the growth of employment in the health care and service industries is much faster than that in goods-producing industries, such as manufacturing. In addition, there is evidence that as people's incomes grow, their demand for health care grows faster than their demand for most other goods and services. The average age of the U.S. population is also increasing, and older people have a greater demand for health care. Finally, the Affordable Care Act has increased the demand for health care among low-income people in two ways: by providing subsidies to buy health insurance for people whose incomes fall below a certain level and by expanding the Medicaid system.

Whatever changes Congress may make to the Affordable Care Act, it seems likely that health care will continue to be a booming sector of the economy and an important source of new jobs in the coming decades.

Sources: U.S. Bureau of Labor Statistics; U.S. Census Bureau; Rani Molla, "How America's Top Industries Have Changed," *Wall Street Journal*, July 28, 2014; and "Why Nurses Are the New Auto Workers," *Economist*, July 25, 2014.

MyLab Economics Study Plan   **Your Turn:** Test your understanding by doing related problem 2.9 on page 247 at the end of this chapter.

The Health Care Systems of Canada, Japan, and the United Kingdom

In many countries, such as Canada, Japan, and the United Kingdom, the government either supplies health care directly by operating hospitals and employing doctors and nurses or pays for most health care expenses, even if hospitals are not government owned and doctors are not government employees. In this section, we look briefly at the health care systems in these three countries.

Canada Canada has a **single-payer health care system**, in which the government provides *national health insurance* to all Canadian residents. Each of the 10 Canadian provinces has its own system, although each system must meet the federal government's requirement of covering 100 percent of the cost of all medically necessary procedures. Individuals pay nothing for doctor's visits or hospital stays; instead, they pay for medical care indirectly through the taxes they pay to the provincial and federal governments. As in the United States, most doctors and hospitals are private businesses, but unlike in the United States, doctors and hospitals are required to accept the fees that are set by the government. Also as in the United States, doctors and hospitals are typically reimbursed on a fee-for-service basis.

Single-payer health care system A system, such as the one in Canada, in which the government provides health insurance to all of the country's residents.

Japan Japan has a system of *universal health insurance* under which every resident of the country is required to enroll either in one of the many nonprofit health insurance societies that are organized by industries or professions or in the health insurance program provided by the national government. The system is funded by a combination of premiums paid by employees and firms and a payroll tax similar to the tax that funds the Medicare program in the United States. Unlike the Canadian system, the Japanese system requires substantial *copayments*, under which patients pay as much as 30 percent of their medical bills, while health insurance pays for the rest. Japanese health insurance does not pay for most preventive care, such as annual physical exams, or for medical expenses connected with pregnancies, unless complications result. Health insurance in the United States and Canada typically does cover these expenses. As in the United States, most doctors in Japan do not work for the government, and there are many privately owned hospitals. The number of government-run hospitals, though, is greater than in the United States.

The United Kingdom In the United Kingdom, the government, through the National Health Service (NHS), owns nearly all hospitals and directly employs nearly all doctors. (Note that England, Scotland, Wales, and Northern Ireland run their health care systems independently, although their main features are the same.) This system contrasts with those in the United States, Canada, and Japan, where the government employs relatively few doctors and owns relatively few hospitals. Because there are few private insurance plans and private hospitals in the United Kingdom, its health care system is often called **socialized medicine**. With 1.4 million employees, the NHS is the largest government-run health care system in the world. Apart from a small copayment for prescriptions, the NHS supplies health care services without charge to patients and receives its funding from income taxes. The NHS concentrates on preventive care and care for acute conditions. Nonemergency care, also called *elective care*—such as hip replacements, knee surgery following a sports injury, or reconstructive surgery following a mastectomy—is a low priority. The NHS's goals result in waiting lists for elective care that can be very long, with patients sometimes waiting a year or more for a procedure that would be available in a few weeks or less in the United States. To avoid the waiting lists, more than 10 percent of the population also has private health insurance, frequently provided by employers, which the insured use to pay for elective care. The NHS essentially trades off broader coverage for longer waiting times and performing fewer procedures, particularly nonemergency surgeries. **MyLab Economics** Concept Check

Socialized medicine A health care system under which the government owns most of the hospitals and employs most of the doctors.

MyLab Economics Animation

Figure 7.3

Levels of Income per Person and Spending per Person on Health Care

The United States is well above the line showing the average relationship between income per person and health care spending per person, which indicates that the United States spends more on health care per person than do other countries, even taking into account the relatively high levels of income in the United States.

Note: Income per person is measured as real GDP per person.

Source: Organization for Economic Co-operation and Development, *OECD Health Data 2016*, November 2016.

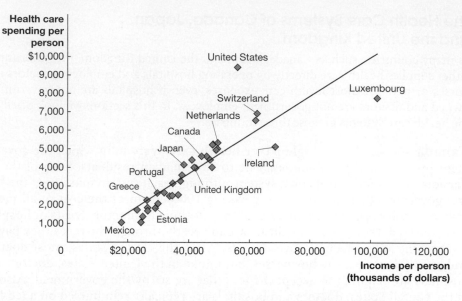

Comparing Health Care Outcomes around the World

We have seen that the way health care systems are organized varies significantly across countries. Health care outcomes and the amounts countries spend on health care are also quite different. In Figure 7.3, each green diamond represents a combination of health care spending per person and income per person for 35 high-income countries. The figure shows that, typically, the higher the level of income per person in a country, the higher the level of spending per person on health care. This result is not surprising because health care is a *normal good*. We know that as income increases, so does spending on normal goods (see Chapter 3, Section 3.1). The line in the figure shows the average relationship between income per person and health care spending per person. The diamonds for most countries are fairly close to the line, but note that the diamond representing the United States is significantly above the line. Being well above the line indicates that health care spending per person in the United States is higher than in other countries, even taking into account the relatively high income levels in the United States. In Section 7.4, we will discuss explanations for the high level of health care spending in the United States.

Has the high level of health care spending in the United States resulted in better health outcomes? Are people in the United States healthier, and do they have their medical problems addressed more rapidly than do people in other countries? Table 7.2 compares several health outcomes for the countries that are members of the Organization for Economic Co-operation and Development (OECD), a group of 35 high-income countries. The table shows that the United States does relatively poorly with respect to infant mortality, while it does somewhat below average with respect to life expectancy at birth but about average with respect to life expectancy at age 65. People in the United States are significantly more likely to be obese than are people in other high-income countries, which can lead to developing diabetes and other health problems.

The United States rates well in the availability of medical equipment that can be used in diagnosing and treating illness. Table 7.2 shows that the United States has more than twice as many MRI units per person and over 50 percent more CT scanners per person than the average of high-income countries, although the United States has relatively fewer of these machines than does Japan. The United States also appears to do well in cancer treatment, with a lower rate of cancer deaths, particularly given that people in the United States are more likely to develop cancer, and a relatively low mortality ratio from cancer. The mortality ratio measures the rate at which people die from cancer relative to the rate at which they are diagnosed with cancer. A low cancer mortality ratio indicates that the U.S. health care system does a relatively good job of reducing the death rate among people diagnosed with cancer. **MyLab Economics** Concept Check

Table 7.2

Health Outcomes in High-Income Countries

Health Care Outcome	United States	Canada	Japan	United Kingdom	OECD Average
Life Expectancy					
Life expectancy at birth	78.8 years	81.0 years	83.7 years	81.4 years	80.6 years
Male life expectancy at age 65	18.0 years	18.8 years	19.3 years	18.8 years	17.9 years
Female life expectancy at age 65	20.5 years	21.7 years	24.2 years	21.3 years	21.3 years
Infant mortality (deaths per 1,000 live births)	6.0	4.9	2.1	3.9	4.0
Health Problems					
Obesity (percentage of the population with BMI > 30)	38.2%	28.0%	3.9%	25.6%	22.3%
Diagnostic Equipment					
MRI units per 1,000,000 population	38.1	8.9	51.7	6.1	15.7
CT scanners per 1,000,000 population	41.0	14.7	107.1	8.0	26.4
Cancer					
Cancer per 100,000 population	318.0	295.7	217.1	272.9	269.8
Deaths from cancer per 100,000 population	189.5	207.5	179.0	221.9	202.1
Risk of dying of cancer before age 75	11.2%	10.8%	9.3%	11.3%	11.5%
Mortality ratio for cancer	33.3%	34.9%	43.2%	40.3%	40.4%

Sources: Organization for Economic Co-operation and Development, *OECD Health Statistics, 2016*, most recent data available, typically 2014, but 2012 for the data in the last two rows on cancer; and World Health Organization, Agency for Research on Cancer, "Globocan 2012: Estimated Cancer Incidence, Mortality, and Prevalence Worldwide in 2012." For cancer data, the final column uses the average for European Union countries rather than for OECD countries. Data on death from cancers are standardized for age differences across countries.

How Useful Are Cross-Country Comparisons of Health Outcomes?

Health economists and other researchers disagree strongly about the usefulness of cross-country comparisons of health outcomes in measuring the effectiveness of different health care systems. Here are some factors that make cross-country comparisons in health outcomes difficult:

- **Data problems.** Countries do not always collect data on diseases and other health problems in the same way. So, there are not enough consistent data available to compare health outcomes for more than a few diseases.
- **Problems with measuring health care delivery.** The easiest outcomes to measure are deaths because a specific event has occurred. So, measures of life expectancy, infant mortality, and mortality rates from some diseases, such as cancer, are available across countries. But much of health care involves treatment for injuries, simple surgeries, writing of pharmaceutical prescriptions, and other activities for which outcomes are difficult to measure. For example, although the United Kingdom does well in many of the measures shown in Table 7.2, patients often have long waiting times for elective surgeries, such as joint replacements, that can be arranged much more quickly in some other countries, including the United States. Economists have difficulty measuring the cost to patients of these waiting times.
- **Problems with distinguishing health care effectiveness from lifestyle choices.** Health outcomes depend partly on the effectiveness of doctors and hospitals in delivering medical services. But they also depend on the choices of individuals. For example, in the United States, the high rates of obesity and hospitalizations for

diabetes—which can be a complication of obesity—may be caused more by the decisions individuals make about diet and exercise than by the effectiveness of the U.S. health care system.

* **Problems with determining consumer preferences.** In most markets, we can assume that the quantities and prices we observe reflect the interactions of the preferences of consumers (demand) with the costs to firms of producing goods and services (supply). Given their incomes and preferences, consumers compare the prices of different goods and services when making their buying decisions. The prices firms charge represent the costs of providing the good or service. In the market for health care, however, the government plays the dominant role in supplying the service in most countries other than the United States, so the cost of the service is not fully represented in its price, which in some countries is zero. Even in countries where consumers must pay for medical services, the prices they pay usually do not represent the cost of providing the service. In the United States, for instance, consumers with private health insurance typically pay only 10 to 20 percent of the price as a copayment. For these reasons, it is difficult to determine whether some countries do a better job than others in providing health care services whose cost and effectiveness are consistent with consumer preferences.

MyLab Economics Study Plan

MyLab Economics Concept Check

7.3 Information Problems and Externalities in the Market for Health Care

LEARNING OBJECTIVE: Define information problems and externalities and explain how they affect the market for health care.

Asymmetric information A situation in which one party to an economic transaction has less information than the other party.

The market for health care is significantly affected by the problem of **asymmetric information**, which occurs when one party to an economic transaction has less information than the other party. Understanding the concept of asymmetric information can help us analyze the actions of buyers and sellers of health care and health insurance and the actions of the government in the health care market. The consequences of asymmetric information may be easier to understand if we first consider its effect on the market for used automobiles, which is the market in which economists first began to carefully study this problem.

Adverse Selection and the Market for "Lemons"

Nobel Laureate George Akerlof of Georgetown University pointed out that the seller of a used car will always have more information on the true condition of the car than will potential buyers. For example, a car that has not had its oil changed regularly can have damage that even a trained mechanic may have difficulty detecting.

If potential buyers of used cars know that they will have difficulty distinguishing good used cars from bad used cars, or "lemons," they will take this fact into account in the prices they are willing to pay. Consider the following simple example: Suppose that half of the 2015 Honda Civics offered for sale have been well maintained and are good, reliable used cars. The other half have been poorly maintained and are lemons that will be unreliable. Suppose that potential buyers of 2015 Civics would be willing to pay $10,000 for a reliable one but only $5,000 for an unreliable one. The sellers know how well they have maintained their cars and whether they are reliable, but the buyers do not have this information and so have no way of distinguishing the reliable used cars from the unreliable ones.

In this situation, buyers will generally offer a price somewhere between the price they would be willing to pay for a good car and the price they would be willing to pay for a lemon. With a 50–50 chance of buying a good car or a lemon, buyers might offer $7,500, which is halfway between the price they would pay if they knew for certain the car was a good one and the price they would pay if they knew it was a lemon.

Unfortunately for used car buyers, a major glitch arises at this point. From the buyers' perspective, given that they don't know whether any particular car offered for sale is a good car or a lemon, an offer of $7,500 seems reasonable. But the sellers do know whether the cars they are offering are good cars or lemons. To a seller of a good car, an offer of $7,500 is $2,500 below the true value of the car, and the seller will be reluctant to sell. But to a seller of a lemon, an offer of $7,500 is $2,500 above the true value of the car, and the seller will be quite happy to sell. As sellers of lemons take advantage of knowing more about the cars they are selling than buyers do, buyers in the used car market will fall victim to **adverse selection**: Most used cars offered for sale will be lemons. In other words, because of asymmetric information, the market has selected adversely the cars that will be offered for sale. Notice as well that the problem of adverse selection reduces the total quantity of used cars bought and sold in the market because few good cars are offered for sale. **MyLab Economics** Concept Check

Adverse selection The situation in which one party to a transaction takes advantage of knowing more than the other party to the transaction.

Asymmetric Information in the Market for Health Insurance

Asymmetric information problems are particularly severe in the markets for all types of insurance, including health insurance. To understand this point, first consider how insurance works. Insurance companies provide the service of *risk pooling* when they sell policies to households. For example, if you own a $150,000 house but do not have a fire insurance policy, a fire that destroys your house can be a financial catastrophe. But an insurance company can pool the financial risk of your house burning down by selling fire insurance policies to you and thousands of other homeowners. Homeowners are willing to accept the certain cost represented by the premium they pay for insurance in return for eliminating the uncertain—but potentially very large —cost should their house burn down.

Notice that for the insurance company to cover all of its costs, the total amount it receives in premiums must be greater than the amount it pays out in claims to policyholders. To survive, insurance companies have to predict accurately the amount they are likely to pay out to policyholders. For instance, if an insurance company predicts that the houses of only 2 percent of policyholders will burn down during a year when 5 percent of houses actually burn down, the company will suffer losses. However, if the company predicts that 8 percent of houses will burn down when only 5 percent actually do, the company will have charged premiums that are too high. A company that charges premiums that are too high will lose customers to other companies and may eventually be driven out of business.

Adverse Selection in the Market for Health Insurance Health insurance companies face a key obstacle to accurately predicting the number of claims policyholders will make: Buyers of health insurance policies always know more about the state of their health—and, therefore, how likely they are to submit medical bills for payment—than do the insurance companies. In other words, insurance companies face an adverse selection problem because sick people are more likely to want health insurance than are healthy people. If insurance companies have trouble determining who is healthy and who is sick, they are likely to sell policies to more sick people than they had expected, with the result that the premiums they charge will be too low to cover their costs.

An insurance company faces a financial problem if the premiums it is charging are too low to cover the costs of the claims being submitted. The company might try to increase the premiums it charges, but this may make the adverse selection problem worse. If premiums rise, then younger, healthier people who rarely visit the doctor may respond to the increase in premiums by dropping their insurance. The higher premiums make the adverse selection problem worse for the insurance company because it will have fewer healthy policyholders than it had before the premium increase. The situation is similar to that facing a used car buyer who knows that adverse selection is a problem in the used car market and decides to compensate for it by lowering the price he is willing to pay for a car. The lower price will reduce the number of sellers of good cars willing to sell to him, making his adverse selection problem worse.

One way to deal with the problem of adverse selection is for the government to require every person to buy insurance. Doing so would increase the ability of insurance companies to engage in risk pooling. Most states require all drivers to buy automobile

Moral hazard Actions people take after they have entered into a transaction that make the other party to the transaction worse off.

insurance so that both high-risk and low-risk drivers will carry insurance. The Patient Protection and Affordable Care Act (ACA), passed in 2010, requires residents of the United States to buy health insurance or pay a fine. This provision of the law is known as the *individual mandate* and has been controversial. We discuss it further in Section 7.4.

Moral Hazard in the Market for Health Insurance The insurance market is subject to a second consequence of asymmetric information. **Moral hazard** refers to actions people take after they have entered into a transaction that make the other party to the transaction worse off. Moral hazard in the insurance market occurs when people change their behavior after becoming insured. For example, once a firm has taken out a fire insurance policy on a warehouse, its managers might be reluctant to install an expensive sprinkler system. Similarly, someone with health insurance may visit the doctor for treatment of a cold or other minor illness, which he would not do if he lacked insurance. Or someone with health insurance might engage in risky activities, such as riding a motorcycle, which she would not do if she lacked insurance.

One way to think about the basic moral hazard problem with insurance is to note that normally there are two parties to an economic transaction: the buyer and the seller. The insurance company becomes a third party to the purchase of medical services because the insurance company, rather than the patient, pays for some or all of the service. For this reason, economists refer to traditional health insurance as a *third-party payer* system. Because of this system, consumers of health care do not pay a price that reflects the full cost of providing the service. This lower price leads consumers to use more health care than they otherwise would.

Don't Let This Happen to You

Don't Confuse Adverse Selection with Moral Hazard

The two key consequences of asymmetric information are adverse selection and moral hazard. It is easy to mix up these concepts. One way to keep the concepts straight is to remember that:

- Adverse selection refers to what happens at the time of entering into a transaction. An example would be an insurance company selling a life insurance policy to a terminally ill person because the company lacks full information on the person's health.

- Moral hazard refers to what happens after entering into a transaction, such as a nonsmoker buying a life insurance policy and then starting to smoke four packs of cigarettes a day.

It may help to remember that *a* comes before *m* alphabetically, just as *a*dverse selection comes before *m*oral hazard.

MyLab Economics Study Plan

Your Turn: Test your understanding by doing related problems 3.9 and 3.10 on page 248 at the end of this chapter.

Principal–agent problem A problem caused by agents pursuing their own interests rather than the interests of the principals who hired them.

Third-party payer health insurance can also lead to another consequence of moral hazard, known as the *principal–agent problem*, because some doctors may be led to take actions that are not necessarily in the best interests of their patients, such as increasing their incomes by prescribing unnecessary tests or other treatments for which the doctors receive payment. The **principal–agent problem** results from agents—in this case, doctors—pursuing their own interests rather than the interests of the principals—in this case, patients—who hired them. If patients had to pay the full price of lab tests, MRI scans, and other procedures, they would be more likely to question whether the procedures were really necessary. Because health insurance pays most of the bill for these procedures, patients are more likely to accept them. Note that the fee-for-service aspect of most health insurance in the United States can make the principal–agent problem worse because doctors and hospitals are paid for each service performed, whether or not the service was necessary or effective.

The number of medical procedures performed in the United States has been continually increasing. Many doctors argue that the increasing number of medical procedures is not the result of third-party payer health insurance. Instead, the increase is due to the improved effectiveness of the procedures in diagnosing illness and the tendency of some doctors to practice "defensive medicine" because they fear that if they fail to correctly diagnose an illness, a patient may file a *malpractice lawsuit* against them.

How Insurance Companies Deal with Adverse Selection and Moral Hazard Insurance companies can take steps to reduce adverse selection and moral hazard problems. For example, insurance companies can use deductibles and coinsurance (or copayments) to reduce moral hazard. A deductible requires the policyholder to pay a certain dollar amount before the insurance begins paying claims. With coinsurance, the insurance company pays only a percentage of any claim. Suppose you have a health insurance policy with a $200 deductible and 20 percent coinsurance, and you receive a medical bill for $1,000. You must pay the first $200 of the bill and 20 percent of the remaining $800. Deductibles and coinsurance make the policies less attractive to people who intend to file many claims, thereby reducing the adverse selection problem. Deductibles and coinsurance also provide policyholders with an incentive to avoid filing claims, thereby reducing the moral hazard problem. Deductibles have been increasing in many employer-provided health insurance plans. According to a survey by the Kaiser Family Foundation, in 2006 only 10 percent of workers were enrolled in plans with deductibles of $1,000 per year or more, but by 2016, 51 percent of workers were enrolled in such plans. Notice, though, that deductibles and coinsurance reduce, but do not eliminate, adverse selection and moral hazard. People who anticipate having large medical bills will still have a greater incentive than healthy people to buy insurance, and people with health insurance are still more likely to visit the doctor even for a minor illness than are people without health insurance.

Prior to the passage of the ACA in 2010, to reduce the problem of adverse selection, insurance companies typically limited coverage of *preexisting conditions*, which are medical problems, such as heart disease or cancer, that the buyer already has before purchasing insurance. Critics argue that by excluding coverage of preexisting conditions, insurance companies were forcing people with serious illnesses to pay the entire amount of what might be very large medical bills or to go without medical care. Some people with chronic or terminal illnesses found it impossible to buy an individual health insurance policy. The insurance companies argued that if they did not exclude coverage of preexisting conditions, they might have been unable to offer any health insurance policies or might have been forced to charge premiums that were so high as to cause relatively healthy people to not renew their policies, which would have made adverse selection problems worse. To some extent, the debate over coverage of preexisting conditions is a normative one. Ordinarily, in a market system, people who cannot afford a good or service must do without it. However, many people do not want others to be without health insurance because they cannot afford it. As we will discuss in the next section, Congress included significant restrictions on the ability of insurance companies to limit coverage of preexisting conditions when it passed the ACA.   **MyLab Economics** Concept Check

Externalities in the Market for Health Care

For most goods and services, we assume that the consumer receives all the benefits from consuming the good and that the firm producing the good bears all of the costs of production. Some goods or services, though, involve an *externality*, which is a benefit or cost that affects someone who is not directly involved in the production or consumption of a good or service. For example, if a utility burns coal to produce electricity, the result will be air pollution, which causes a *negative externality* because people with asthma or other breathing problems may bear a cost even though they were not involved in buying or selling the electricity that caused the pollution. College education may result in a *positive externality* because college-educated people are less likely to commit crimes and, by being better-informed voters, are more likely to contribute to better government policies. So, although you receive most of the benefits of your college education, other people also receive some of the benefits.

Externalities interfere with the economic efficiency of a market equilibrium. A competitive market achieves economic efficiency by maximizing the sum of consumer surplus and producer surplus (see Chapter 4, Section 4.1). But when there is a negative externality in production, as with air pollution, the market will produce more than the efficient quantity. When there is a positive externality in consumption, as with college educations, the market will produce less than the efficient quantity. (A more complete discussion of externalities appears in Chapter 5, "Externalities, Environmental Policy, and Public Goods.")

Many economists believe that several aspects of health care involve externalities. For example, anyone vaccinated against a communicable disease not only protects herself or himself but also reduces the chances that people who have not been vaccinated will contract the disease. The positive externality from vaccinations causes a difference between the *private benefit* from being vaccinated and the *social benefit*. The *private benefit* is the benefit you receive as a consumer of a good or service. The *social benefit* is the total benefit from consuming a good or service, and it is equal to the private benefit plus any external benefit, such as the benefit to others from a reduced chance of getting a disease for which you have been vaccinated. Because of the positive externality, the social benefit of vaccinations is greater than the private benefit.

Figure 7.4 shows the market for vaccinations. If people receiving vaccinations could capture all the benefits, the demand curve would be D_2, which represents the marginal social benefit. The actual demand curve is D_1, however, which represents only the marginal private benefit received by people getting vaccinations. The efficient equilibrium would occur at price $P_{Efficient}$ and quantity $Q_{Efficient}$. At this equilibrium, economic surplus is maximized. The market equilibrium, at price P_{Market} and quantity Q_{Market}, will not be efficient because the demand curve is above the supply curve for production of the vaccinations between Q_{Market} and $Q_{Efficient}$. That is, the marginal benefit—including the external benefit—for producing these vaccinations is greater than the marginal cost. As a result, there is a deadweight loss equal to the area of the yellow triangle. Because of the positive externality, economic efficiency would be improved if more people were vaccinated.

Figure 7.4 assumes that the market for vaccinations is like the market for goods such as hamburgers, with consumers paying the full price of the vaccinations. In practice, people with health insurance pay a reduced price for vaccinations, and the government often provides further subsidies to the firms that produce vaccines. One reason for the government subsidies is to overcome the effects of the positive externality.

Externalities are important in health care markets, though economists and policymakers continue to debate the extent to which they require significant government involvement in health care.   **MyLab Economics** Concept Check

MyLab Economics Animation

Figure 7.4

The Effect of a Positive Externality on the Market for Vaccinations

People who do not get vaccinated still benefit from other people being vaccinated. As a result, the marginal social benefit from vaccinations is greater than the marginal private benefit to people being vaccinated. Because only the marginal private benefit is represented in the market demand curve D_1, the quantity of vaccinations produced, Q_{Market}, is too low. If the market demand curve were D_2 instead of D_1, the level of vaccinations would be $Q_{Efficient}$, which is the efficient level. At the market equilibrium of Q_{Market}, there is a deadweight loss equal to the area of the yellow triangle.

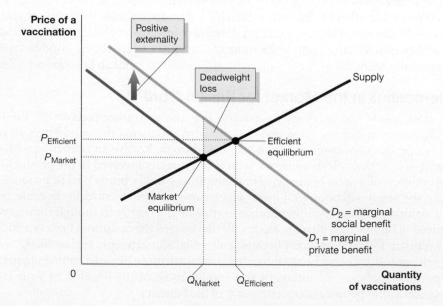

Should the Government Run the Health Care System?

Some members of Congress have proposed expanding the federal government's role in health care by adopting a system similar to the single-payer system used in Canada, under which the government would provide health care to all residents of the United States. What role the federal government should play in health care is a controversial public policy issue.

Is Health Care a Public Good? Economists categorize goods on the basis of whether they are *rival* and *excludable*. Rivalry occurs when one person consuming a unit of a good means no one else can consume it. If you consume a salad from Panera Bread, for example, no one else can consume it. Excludability means that anyone who does not pay for a good cannot consume it. If you don't pay for a salad, for example, Panera can exclude you from consuming it. A *public good* is both nonrival and nonexcludable. Public goods are often, although not always, supplied by a government rather than by private firms. The classic example of a public good is national defense. Your consuming national defense does not interfere with your neighbor consuming it, so consumption is nonrival. You also cannot be excluded from consuming it, whether you pay for it or not. No private firm would be willing to supply national defense because everyone can consume national defense without paying for it.

Is health care a public good that government should supply—or, at least, pay for? Is it a private good, like furniture, clothing, or computers, that private firms should supply and consumers should pay for without government aid? Should private firms supply most health care, subject to some government regulation? Economists differ in their answers to these questions because the delivery of health care involves a number of complex issues, but we can consider briefly some of the most important points. Because public goods must be both nonrival and nonexcludable, health care does not qualify as a public good under the usual definition. More than one person cannot simultaneously "consume" the same surgical operation performed by a particular doctor in a particular hospital. And someone who will not pay for an operation can be excluded from consuming it. (Most states require hospitals to treat patients who are too poor to pay for treatment, and many doctors will treat poor people at a reduced price. But health care does not fit the definition of a public good because there is nothing about health care that keeps people who do not pay for it from being excluded from consuming it.)

Do Externalities in Health Care Justify More Government Intervention? Aspects of the delivery of health care have convinced some economists that government intervention is justified. For example, consuming certain types of health care generates positive externalities. Being vaccinated against a communicable disease, such as influenza or meningitis, reduces not only the chance that the person vaccinated will catch the disease but also the probability that an epidemic of the disease will occur. Therefore, the market may supply an inefficiently small quantity of vaccinations unless vaccinations receive a government subsidy.

Do Information Problems with Health Care Justify More Government Intervention? Information problems are also important in the market for private health insurance. Consumers who buy health insurance often know much more about the state of their health than do the companies selling health insurance. This information problem may raise costs to insurance companies when the pool of people being insured is small, making insurance companies less willing to offer health insurance to consumers the companies suspect may file too many claims. Economists debate how important information problems are in health care markets and whether government intervention is required to reduce them.

Or Should There Be Greater Reliance on Market-Based Policies? Many economists believe that market-based policies are the best approach to improving the health care system. As we saw in Table 7.2 on page 227, the United States has a mixed record on health outcomes. The United States is, however, a world leader in innovation in medical technology and prescription drugs. The market-oriented approach to reforming health care starts with the goal of improving health care outcomes while preserving incentives for U.S. firms to continue with innovations in medical screening equipment, surgical procedures, and prescription drugs. Presently, markets are delivering inaccurate signals to consumers because when buying health care, unlike when buying most other goods and services, consumers pay a price well below the true cost of providing the service. Under current tax laws, people do not pay taxes on health insurance benefits they receive from their employers, and this benefit encourages them to want generous coverage that reduces incentives to control costs. As we will discuss in Section 7.4, market-based approaches to health care reform attempt to address these issues.

It remains an open question whether the U.S. health care system will continue to move toward greater government intervention, which is the approach adopted in most other countries, or whether market-based reforms will be implemented. Because health care is so important to consumers and because health care is an increasingly large part of the U.S. economy, the role of the government in the health care system is likely to be the subject of intense debate for some time to come.

MyLab Economics Study Plan   **MyLab Economics** Concept Check

7.4 The Debate over Health Care Policy in the United States

LEARNING OBJECTIVE: Explain the major issues involved in the debate over health care policy in the United States.

Shortly after taking office in January 2009, President Barack Obama proposed far-reaching changes in the U.S. health care system. The result was the Patient Protection and Affordable Care Act (ACA), which Congress passed in March 2010. The act was controversial, with every Republican member of Congress and 34 Democratic members voting against it. Since passage of the ACA, economists have vigorously debated its effects on health care and the economy. During 2017, bills to significantly amend the ACA failed in Congress, although other proposals to amend the ACA appeared likely to follow.

Before discussing the details of the ACA and the debate over the legislation's effect, we explore the issue of rising health care costs, which played an important role in the health care debate.

The Rising Cost of Health Care

Figure 7.5 illustrates a key fact underlying the debate over health care policy in the United States: Health care's share of gross domestic product (GDP), which is the total value of output in the economy, is increasing. Panel (a) shows that spending on health care was less than 6 percent of GDP in 1965 but had risen to nearly 18 percent in 2017 and is projected to continue rising in future years. In other words, an increasing percentage of total production in the United States is being devoted to health care. Panel (b) shows increases in health care spending per person in the United States and 10 other high-income countries. Spending on health care has grown faster in the United States than in other countries.

Does it matter that spending on health care is an increasing share of total spending and output in the U.S. economy? The shares of different products in total spending change frequently. For instance, in the United States, the shares of spending on smartphones or streaming movies were much greater in 2017 than in 2010. Spending on food as a share of total spending has been declining for decades. Economists interpret these changes as reflecting in part consumers' preferences: Consumers choose to spend relatively more of their incomes on smartphones and relatively less on food. As we have seen, though, most people pay for health care by relying on third-party payers, such as employer-provided health insurance or government-provided Medicare or Medicaid. Out-of-pocket spending, spending on health care that consumers pay out of their own incomes rather than through health insurance, has been declining.

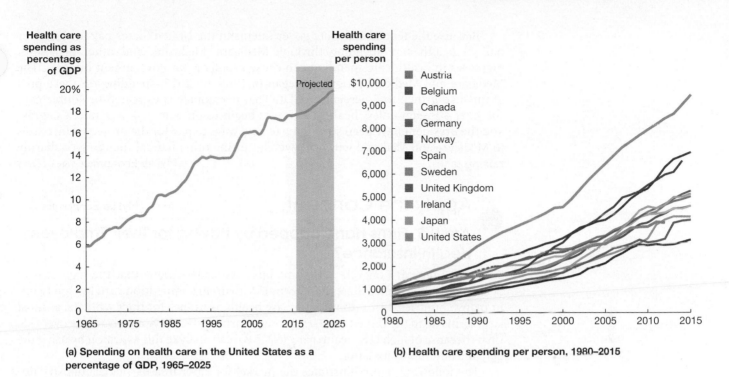

(a) Spending on health care in the United States as a percentage of GDP, 1965–2025

(b) Health care spending per person, 1980–2015

MyLab Economics Real-time Data

Figure 7.5 **Spending on Health Care around the World**

Panel (a) shows that health care spending has been a rising percentage of GDP in the United States. Health care spending rose from less than 6 percent of GDP in 1965 to nearly 18 percent in 2017 and it is projected to rise further in future years. (The projected increases are shown by the line in the shaded area.)

Panel (b) shows that health care spending per person has been growing faster in the United States than in other high-income countries.

Sources: For panel (a): U.S. Department of Health and Human Services, Centers for Medicare & Medicaid Services; for panel (b): Organization for Economic Co-operation and Development, *OECD Health Data 2016*, November 2016.

Figure 7.6 shows that out-of-pocket spending on health care as a percentage of all spending on health care has fallen steadily since 1960. In 1960, 48 percent of all health care spending was out of pocket, while today only about 10 percent is. As a result, in recent years, consumers of health care have been directly paying for only a small fraction of the true cost of providing health care, with third-party payers picking up the remainder. As average incomes rise, consumers might be expected to spend a rising share of the increase on health care. But because consumers do not pay the full cost of increases in health care spending, they may not be willing to buy as much health care as they currently receive if they had to pay the full price.

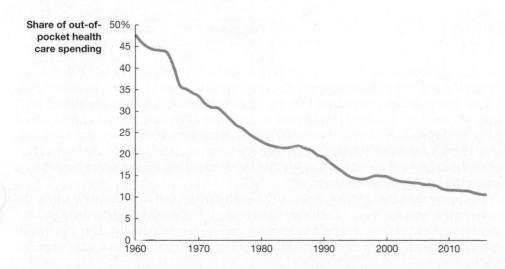

MyLab Economics Animation

Figure 7.6

The Declining Share of U.S. Out-of-Pocket Health Care Spending

Out-of-pocket spending on health care has declined sharply as a fraction of all health care spending, while the fraction of spending accounted for by third-party payers, such as firms or the government, has increased.

Source: U.S. Department of Health and Human Services, Centers for Medicare & Medicaid Services.

Because the federal and state governments in the United States pay for just over half of health care spending through Medicare, Medicaid, and other programs, increases in health care spending can cause problems for government budgets. The Medicare and Medicaid programs began in 1965. By 2017, spending on these programs had grown to 7 percent of GDP. That percentage is expected to double over the next 40 years unless health care costs begin to grow at a slower rate. Congress and the president have been struggling to find ways to pay for the projected increases in Medicare and Medicaid without severely cutting other federal spending or sharply raising taxes. **MyLab Economics** Concept Check

Apply the Concept
MyLab Economics Video

Are U.S. Firms Handicapped by Paying for Their Employees' Health Insurance?

Some members of Congress and some business leaders argue that the high cost of health care in the United States handicaps U.S. firms in competition with foreign firms. In many countries, firms do not purchase health insurance for their workers, as most large firms do in the United States. Do foreign firms in fact have an advantage over U.S. firms because of high U.S. health care costs? We can analyze this assertion by using the demand and supply for labor.

The following figure illustrates the market for labor in a particular industry (for example, automobiles). The demand curve is downward sloping because the lower the wage, the larger the quantity of workers firms will demand. The supply curve is upward sloping because as the wage rises, more workers will want to work in this industry. (A more complete discussion of the labor market appears in Chapter 17, "The Markets for Labor and Other Factors of Production.")

Equilibrium in this labor market occurs where the quantity of labor demanded equals the quantity of labor supplied. On the vertical axis, we measure the wage, so the graph shows the determination of the equilibrium wage. When choosing among jobs, however, workers don't just consider the wages firms offer; they also take into account *fringe benefits*, such as employer contributions to retirement accounts or employer-provided health insurance. It would therefore be more accurate to describe the intersection of the labor demand and labor supply curves as determining *the equilibrium compensation* rather than the equilibrium wage.

Suppose the United States moved to a health care system like Canada's, where the government pays for most health care from taxes. If labor markets determine equilibrium compensation, what would happen if firms no longer paid for their employees' health insurance? The Congressional Budget Office (CBO) undertakes studies of policy issues for Congress. In an overview of proposals for reforming health insurance in the United States, the CBO addressed this question:

> Some observers have asserted that domestic producers that provide health insurance to their workers face higher costs for compensation than competitors based in countries where insurance is not employment based and that fundamental changes to the health insurance system could reduce or eliminate that disadvantage. However, such a cost reduction is unlikely to occur.... The equilibrium level of overall compensation in the economy is determined by the supply of and the demand for labor. Fringe benefits (such as health insurance) are just part of that compensation. Consequently, the costs of fringe benefits are borne by workers largely in the form of lower cash wages than they would receive if no such benefits were provided by their employer. Replacing employment-based health care with a government-run system could reduce employers' payments for their workers' insurance, but the amount that they would have to pay in overall compensation would remain essentially unchanged.

To give an example, suppose a firm was paying its workers $50,000 in wages and paying $10,000 per worker for health insurance, thereby providing total compensation of $60,000. If the government began paying all health care expenses, it might appear that the firm's labor costs would drop by $10,000 per worker. But if the firm offered its employees only $50,000 in wages as their total compensation, many would leave to work for other firms. The firm would have to pay its employees an additional $10,000 in wages so that the total compensation it offered would be at the equilibrium level of $60,000 for the industry. In other words, basic demand and supply analysis indicates that having firms rather than the government provide health insurance to workers changes the *composition* of the compensation that firms pay workers but does not change the *amount* of compensation that firms pay.

Source: Congressional Budget Office, "Key Issues in Analyzing Major Health Insurance Proposals," December 2008, p. 167.

Your Turn: Test your understanding by doing related problem 4.10 on page 250 at the end of this chapter.

MyLab Economics Study Plan

Explaining Increases in Health Care Spending

In this section, we briefly discuss some explanations for why health care's share of the U.S. economy has been continually increasing. We start by reviewing explanations that policymakers and journalists sometimes offer but that are unlikely to account for most of the increases in health care costs.

Factors That Do *Not* Explain Sustained Increases in Health Care Spending The two panels of Figure 7.5 on page 235 show that spending on health care has been growing faster than the economy as a whole for at least the past several decades. Explaining the rapid growth of health care spending requires identifying factors that have more than a one-time effect. For example, because the U.S. health care system relies on many independent hospitals, medical practices, and insurance companies, some observers argue that it generates more paperwork, duplication, and waste than systems in other countries. Even if this observation is correct, it cannot account for health care's rising share of GDP unless paperwork and waste are *increasing* year after year, which seems unlikely.

Unlike in most other countries, it is relatively easy in the United States for patients who have been injured by medical errors to sue doctors and hospitals for damages. The Congressional Budget Office (CBO) estimates, though, that the payments to settle malpractice lawsuits plus the premiums doctors pay for malpractice insurance amount to less than 1 percent of health care costs. Other economists believe that the CBO estimate is too low and that the costs of malpractice lawsuits, including the costs of unnecessary tests and procedures doctors order to avoid being sued, are as much as 7 percent of total health care costs. Still, these costs have not been significantly increasing over time.

Somewhere between 1 and 4 percent of health care costs are due to uninsured patients receiving treatments at hospital emergency rooms that could have been provided less expensively in doctors' offices. But once again, prior to the implementation of the ACA, this cost was not increasing rapidly enough to account for much of the increase in health care costs as a percentage of GDP, and as the implementation of the ACA has led to a decrease in the number of uninsured people, this cost has declined.

In the next sections, we discuss three factors that many economists believe help explain the sustained increases in health care spending.

"Cost Disease" in the Health Care Sector Some economists argue that health care suffers from a problem often encountered in service industries. In the sectors of the economy that produce goods, such as the manufacturing sector, *productivity*, or the amount of output each worker can produce in a given period, increases steadily. These increases in productivity occur because over time firms provide workers with more machinery and equipment, including computers and software, with which to work, and because technological progress results in improvements in machinery and equipment and in other parts of the production process. As workers produce more goods, firms are able to pay them higher wages. By contrast, in service-producing industries, increasing output per worker is more difficult. In medicine, MRI units, CT scanners, and other medical technology have improved diagnosis and treatment, but most medicine still requires a face-to-face meeting between a doctor or medical technologist and a patient. As wages rise in industries in which productivity is increasing rapidly, service industries in which productivity is increasing less rapidly must match these wage increases or lose workers. Because increases in wages are not offset by increases in productivity in service industries, the cost to firms of supplying services increases.

William Baumol of New York University has labeled the tendency for low productivity in service industries to lead to higher costs in those industries as "the cost disease of the service sector." Health care probably suffers from this cost disease because growth in labor productivity in the health care sector has been less than half as fast as labor productivity growth in the economy as a whole. This slow growth in productivity can help explain why the cost of health care has been rising rapidly, thereby increasing health care's share of total spending and output.

The Aging of the Population and Advances in Medical Technology As people age, they increase their spending on health care. Firms continue to develop new prescription drugs and medical equipment that typically have higher costs than the drugs and equipment they replace. The aging of the U.S. population and the introduction of higher-cost drugs and medical equipment interact to drive up spending on the federal government's Medicare program and on health care generally. People over age 65 disproportionately use many newly introduced drugs and diagnostic tools. Partly as a result, health care spending on people over age 65 is six times greater than spending on people aged 18 to 24 and four times greater than on people aged 25 to 44. In 2017, about 58 million people were enrolled in Medicare, and that number is expected to grow to 74 million by 2025. As we have seen, even in the absence of the development of new drugs and other medical technology, low rates of productivity in the health care sector could be expected to drive up costs. In fact, as Figure 7.7 illustrates, the CBO estimates that more of the increase in federal spending on Medicare and Medicaid benefits will be due to increases in the cost of providing health care rather than to the aging of the population. In the figure, "effect of excess cost growth" refers to the extent to which health care costs per person grow faster than GDP per person. An aging population and increases in the cost of providing health care are key reasons health care spending is an increasing percentage of GDP.

Distorted Economic Incentives As we noted earlier, some part of the increase in health care spending over the years results from consumers' choosing to allocate more of their incomes to health care as their incomes rise. But as we have also seen,

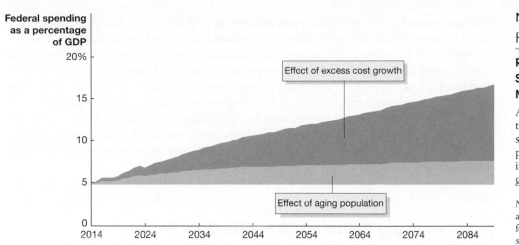

MyLab Economics Animation

Figure 7.7

Reasons for Rising Federal Spending on Medicare and Medicaid

Although the aging of the U.S. population will increase federal government spending on the Medicare and Medicaid programs, increases in the cost of providing health care will have a larger effect on government spending on these programs.

Note: In addition to spending on the Medicare and Medicaid programs, the figure includes federal spending on the Children's Health Insurance Program (CHIP) and federal spending on subsidies to the health insurance marketplaces established under the ACA.

Source: U.S. Congressional Budget Office.

consumers usually pay less than the true cost of medical treatment because a third party—typically an insurance company or the government—often pays most of the bill. For example, once they have satisfied their insurance plan's deductible, consumers who have health insurance provided by their employers usually pay only a small amount—perhaps $20— for a visit to a doctor's office, when the true cost of the visit might be $80 or $90. The result is that consumers demand a larger quantity of health care services than they would if they paid a price that better represented the cost of providing the services.

Figure 7.8 illustrates this situation. If consumers paid the full price of medical services, their demand would be D_1. The marginal benefit to consumers from medical services would equal the marginal cost of producing the services, and the equilibrium quantity would be at the efficient level $Q_{\text{Efficient}}$. However, because consumers pay only a fraction of the true cost of medical services, their demand increases to D_2. In this equilibrium, the quantity of medical services produced increases to Q_{Market}, which is beyond the efficient level. The marginal cost of producing these additional units is greater than the marginal benefit consumers receive from them. As a result, there is a deadweight loss equal to the area of the yellow triangle. Doctors and other suppliers of medical services receive a price, P_{Market}, that is well above the price, P, paid by consumers. Note that the effect of a third-party payer is common to nearly all health care systems, whether

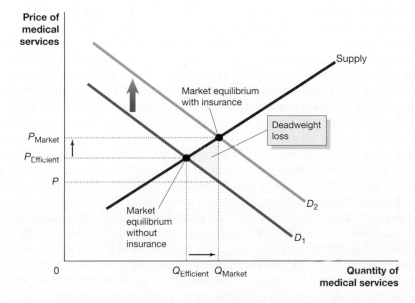

MyLab Economics Animation

Figure 7.8

The Effect of the Third-Party Payer System on the Demand for Medical Services

If consumers paid the full price of medical services, their demand would be D_1, and the equilibrium quantity would be at the efficient level $Q_{\text{Efficient}}$. Because consumers pay only a fraction of the true cost of medical services, their demand is D_2, and the equilibrium quantity of medical services produced increases to Q_{Market}, which is beyond the efficient level. There is a deadweight loss equal to the yellow triangle. Doctors and other suppliers of medical services receive a price, P_{Market}, that is well above the price, P, paid by consumers.

the government provides health care directly, as is done in the United Kingdom, or whether many people have private health insurance, as in the United States.

In important ways, health insurance is different from other types of insurance. As we discussed earlier, the basic idea of insurance is that the financial risk of an unpredictable, high-cost event—a house fire or a serious car accident—is pooled among the many consumers who buy insurance. Health insurance, though, also typically covers many planned expenses, such as routine health checkups, annual physicals, and contraceptives, and other low-cost events, such as treatment for minor illnesses. By disguising the true cost of these routine expenses, health insurance encourages overuse of health care services.

We discuss the role of economic incentives in health care further in the next section.   MyLab Economics Concept Check

The Continuing Debate over Health Care Policy

As we have seen, the United States has been unusual among high-income countries in relying on private health insurance, usually purchased through employers or the health insurance marketplaces, to provide health care coverage to the majority of the population. Most other high-income countries either provide health care directly, as the United Kingdom does, through government-owned hospitals and government-employed doctors, or provide health insurance to all residents, as Canada does, without directly employing doctors or owning hospitals. There have been several attempts to reorganize the U.S. health care system to make it more like the systems in other countries. In 1945, President Harry Truman proposed a plan for *national health insurance*, under which anyone could purchase health insurance from the federal government. The health insurance would have covered treatment received from doctors and hospitals that agreed to enroll in the system. Congress declined to enact the plan. In 1993, President Bill Clinton proposed a health care plan intended to provide universal insurance coverage. While somewhat complex, the plan was based on requiring most businesses to provide health insurance to their employees and new government-sponsored health alliances that would ensure coverage for anyone who otherwise would not have health insurance. After a prolonged political debate, Congress chose not to enact President Clinton's plan.

Patient Protection and Affordable Care Act (ACA) Health care reform legislation passed by Congress and signed by President Barack Obama in 2010.

The Patient Protection and Affordable Care Act In 2009, President Barack Obama proposed health care legislation that after much debate and significant changes was signed into law as the **Patient Protection and Affordable Care Act (ACA)** in March 2010. The act was long and complex at more than 20,000 pages and touched nearly every aspect of health care in the United States. Here is a summary of only the main provisions of the act:

- **Individual mandate.** The act requires that, with limited exceptions, every resident of the United States have health insurance that meets certain basic requirements. Individuals who do not acquire health insurance are subject to a fine. In 2017 the fine was $695 or 2.5 percent of income, whichever was greater. (The fine will rise with inflation in future years.) For example, in 2017 an adult with an income of $40,000 per year paid a fine of $1,000 if he or she did not have health insurance.
- **State health insurance marketplaces.** Each state must establish a marketplace called an Affordable Insurance Exchange. Separate marketplaces were established for individuals and small businesses with fewer than 50 employees. The marketplaces offer health insurance policies that meet certain specified requirements. Although the marketplaces were intended to be run by a state government agency or a nonprofit firm, a majority of states decided to allow the federal government to run their marketplaces. Private insurance companies compete by offering policies on the marketplaces to individuals and small businesses. Low-income individuals and small businesses with 25 or fewer employees are eligible for tax credits to offset the costs of buying health insurance. The purpose of the marketplaces is to allow greater risk pooling and lower administrative costs than existed in the market for health insurance policies sold to individuals or small businesses. If successful, greater risk pooling and lower administrative costs make it possible for individuals

and small businesses to buy polices with lower premiums than were formerly available. In 2017, about 11 million people purchased health insurance policies through the marketplace. As we saw in the chapter opener, though, some insurance firms, including Humana, Aetna, and UnitedHealth, had pulled out of the marketplaces in at least some states. These firms found that adverse selection problems—with the proportion of older, sicker patients turning out to be higher than expected—and higher administrative costs resulted in their suffering losses on the policies they offered in the marketplaces.

- **Employer mandate.** Every firm with more than 200 full-time employees must offer health insurance to its employees and must automatically enroll them in the plan. In 2017, firms with 50 or more full-time employees must offer health insurance that meets certain requirements or pay a fee of up to $3,390 to the federal government for every employee who receives a tax credit from the federal government for obtaining health insurance through a health insurance marketplace. A worker is a full-time employee if he or she works at least 30 hours per week.

- **Regulation of health insurance.** Insurance companies are required to participate in a high-risk pool that will insure individuals with preexisting medical conditions who have been unable to buy health insurance for at least six months. All individual and group policies must provide coverage for dependent children up to age 26. Lifetime dollar maximums on coverage are prohibited. Limits are also placed on the size of deductibles and on the waiting period before coverage becomes effective.

- **Changes to Medicare and Medicaid.** Eligibility for Medicaid was originally expanded to persons with incomes up to 138 percent of the federal poverty line, although a 2012 Supreme Court decision resulted in the states being allowed to opt out of this requirement. In an attempt to control increases in health care costs, the Independent Payment Advisory Board (IPAB) was established and given the power to reduce Medicare payments for prescription drugs and the use of diagnostic equipment and other technology if Medicare spending exceeds certain levels. Some Medicare reimbursements to hospitals and doctors were reduced.

- **Taxes.** Several new taxes help fund the program. Workers earning more than $200,000 pay higher Medicare payroll taxes, and people who earn more than $200,000 pay a new 3.8 percent tax on their investment income. Beginning in 2018, a tax is scheduled to be imposed on employer-provided health insurance plans that have a value above $10,200 for an individual or $27,500 for a family—so-called *Cadillac plans*. In 2017, Congress was considering proposals to repeal this tax. Pharmaceutical firms, health insurance firms, and firms producing medical devices also pay new taxes.

Solved Problem 7.4

MyLab Economics Interactive Animation

Recent Trends in U.S. Health Care

An article in the *New York Times* on the effects of the Patient Protection and Affordable Care Act (ACA) and other developments in the U.S. health care system through the end of 2016 mentioned these three trends:

1. Deductibles increased in many employer-provided health care plans, as well as in the policies offered on the ACA health insurance marketplaces.
2. There was an increase in the number of surgeries and other medical procedures performed in doctor's offices or clinics rather than in higher-cost hospital settings.

3. There was a decline in patients being readmitted to hospitals after the ACA imposed penalties on hospitals that readmit too many patients.

   a. Use a graph of the market for medical services to show the effect of these trends, holding constant other factors affecting the market for medical services. Be sure to explain any shifts in the demand curve or supply curve.
   b. Assuming that these are the only changes happening in the market for medical services, can we be certain whether they will result in an increase or decrease in the equilibrium price of medical services? In the equilibrium quantity of medical services? Briefly explain.

Solving the Problem

Step 1: **Review the chapter material.** This problem is about explaining changes in health care spending, so you may want to review the section "Explaining Increases in Health Care Spending," which begins on page 237.

Step 2: **Answer part (a) by drawing a graph of the market for medical services that shows the effect of the three trends and by explaining shifts in the curves.** The first trend—higher deductibles—reduces moral hazard and adverse selection problems by increasing the quantity of medical services that employees and people who receive insurance on the ACA health insurance exchanges purchase out-of-pocket. Employees are likely to visit doctors less frequently for minor illnesses such as colds. So, the demand curve for medical services will shift to the left. The second trend—the increase in the number of surgeries and other medical procedures performed outside hospitals—reduces the cost of providing these types of medical services, which will shift the supply curve for medical services to the right. The third trend—a decline in the number of patients being readmitted to hospitals—should reduce the cost of hospitalizations because more patients are being successfully treated in a single stay. This trend will also cause the supply curve for medical services to shift to the right.

Your graph should look like the one below.

Step 3: **Answer part (b) by explaining whether these trends will increase or decrease the equilibrium price and quantity of medical services.** The graph in part (a) shows both the equilibrium price and the equilibrium quantity declining. We can be certain that the equilibrium price will decline because the shift of the demand curve to the left and the shift of the supply curve to the right both cause the equilibrium price to decline. However, we can't be certain that the equilibrium quantity will decline because the effect of the supply curve shifting to the right is to make the equilibrium quantity *increase*. Whether the equilibrium quantity declines depends on whether the demand curve shifts more or less than the supply curve shifts. Although two of the trends listed affect supply and only one affects demand, we do not know the size of the shift that results from any of the trends, so we can't tell with certainty what the effect will be on the equilibrium quantity.

Extra Credit: The cost of medical care has continued to increase. In 2017, however, economists were analyzing the reasons for a slowdown in the *rate* of that increase. The trends mentioned in this problem were among the likely factors. The quantity of medical services continued to increase, at least partly as a result of the effects of the Affordable Care Act. The act provides subsidies to buy health insurance for people whose incomes fall below a certain level and has expanded the Medicaid system, thereby increasing the demand for health care among low-income people.

Source: Margot Sanger-Katz, "Grading Obamacare: Successes, Failures and 'Incompletes,'" *New York Times*, February 5, 2017.

Your Turn: For more practice, do related problem 4.12 on page 250 at the end of this chapter.

MyLab Economics Study Plan

The Debate over the ACA Since its passage, the ACA has remained the source of considerable debate among policymakers and economists. As mentioned in the chapter opener, President Trump took office in January 2017, vowing to "repeal and replace" the act. Changes to the act proposed by the Trump administration focused on incorporating market-based incentives intended to reduce the costs of providing health care and to improve economic incentives. Other critics of the act, including Vermont senator and 2016 Democratic presidential candidate Bernie Sanders, argued that the act should be amended (or replaced) to allow for an expanded role for the government in health care similar to the role played by governments in other high-income countries.

As we discussed in the previous section, some economists and policymakers believe that information problems and externalities in the market for health care are sufficiently large that the government should either provide health care directly through government-owned hospitals and government-employed doctors or pay for health care through national health insurance (that is, a single-payer system). Those in favor of moving toward greater government involvement in health care often raise three arguments:

1. A single-payer system would reduce the paperwork and waste caused by the current system.
2. The current Medicare system—which is essentially a single-payer system for people over age 65—has had lower administrative costs than have private health insurance companies.
3. The systems in most other high-income countries have lower levels of health care spending per person and lower rates of increase in total health care spending, while providing good health outcomes.

Some economists and policymakers support **market-based reforms**, which involve changing the market for health care so that it becomes more like the markets for other goods and services. With such reforms, the prices consumers pay and suppliers receive would do a better job of conveying information on consumer demand and supplier costs. The expectation is that increased competition among doctors, hospitals, pharmaceutical companies, and other providers of health care would reduce costs and increase economic efficiency. Economists who support market-based reforms as the best way to improve the health care system were disappointed that the ACA did not adopt this approach. Currently, markets are delivering inaccurate signals to consumers because when buying health care, unlike when buying most other goods and services, consumers pay a price well below the true cost of providing the service.   **MyLab Economics** Concept Check

Market-based reforms Changes in the market for health care that would make it more like the markets for other goods and services.

Apply the Concept   MyLab Economics Video

How Much Is That MRI Scan?

Magnetic resonance imaging (MRI) units play an important role in modern medicine. First introduced in the early 1980s, they allow doctors to see inside the body's soft tissues to identify medical problems such as tumors and torn muscles. As we noted in Section 7.2, MRI units are more widely available in the United States than in most other countries. We would normally expect that when a product is widely available, competition among firms will result in the price of the product being about the same everywhere. Customers would not buy a best-selling book from Amazon.com if the price were 50 percent higher than on BarnesandNoble.com.

Does competition equalize the prices of medical services? The evidence indicates that it doesn't. The data in the following table demonstrate that the prices of abdominal MRI scans vary widely. In most cities in the United States, the most expensive MRI scan has a price that is more than double the least expensive scan. And prices for MRI scans also vary widely across cities.

City	Highest Price	Lowest Price	Difference
San Francisco, California	$5,500	$725	$4,775
Chicago, Illinois	4,700	330	4,370
New York, New York	4,900	550	4,350
Houston, Texas	4,600	575	4,025
Atlanta, Georgia	4,400	825	3,575
Baton Rouge, Louisiana	4,200	700	3,500
Omaha, Nebraska	4,100	650	3,450
Lexington, Kentucky	4,000	675	3,325
Orlando, Florida	3,300	750	2,550
Charlotte, North Carolina	2,250	650	1,600

Two reporters looking at prices for shoulder MRI scans in Pensacola, Florida, found that Sacred Heart Hospital was charging $800 for a shoulder MRI scan, while Pensacola Open MRI & Imaging, a private firm located less than a mile away, was charging only $450 for the same scan. Pensacola Open MRI & Imaging was actually using newer MRI units that give higher-resolution images, so it was charging less for a better service. How can some providers of medical services charge hundreds or thousands of dollars more than competitors and remain in business? The answer is that most patients are not concerned about prices because they either do not pay them or they pay only a small fraction of them. Patients typically rely on doctors to refer them to a facility for an MRI scan or other procedure and make little or no effort to determine the price the facility charges. A goal of market-based reforms of the health care system is to give patients an incentive to pay more attention to the prices of medical services.

Sources: Caitlin Kenney, "Shopping for an MRI," www.npr.org, November 6, 2009; MRI prices from newchoicehealth. com, March 30, 2017.

MyLab Economics Study Plan **Your Turn:** Test your understanding by doing related problem 4.13 on page 250 at the end of this chapter.

Supporters of market-based reforms note that employees have to pay federal income and payroll taxes on the wages their employers pay them, but in most circumstances they do not pay taxes on the value of the health insurance their employers provide them. This feature of the tax laws encourages employees to want generous health care coverage; in fact, if offered the choice between a $1,000 salary increase or increased health care coverage worth $1,000, many people would choose the increased health care coverage because it would be tax free (although someone who was young and healthy and did not expect to have medical bills would probably choose the increase in salary). The size of this tax break is quite substantial—more than $250 billion in 2015. But individuals typically get no tax break when buying an individual health insurance policy or when they spend money on health care out of pocket.[1]

Some economists have proposed making the tax treatment of employer-provided health insurance the same as the tax treatment of individually purchased health insurance and out-of-pocket health care spending. They argue that this change could, potentially, significantly reduce spending on health care without reducing the effectiveness of the health care received. Such tax law changes would make it more likely that employer-provided health insurance would focus on large medical bills—such as those resulting from hospitalizations—while consumers would pay prices closer to the

---

[1] Individuals receive a deduction on their federal income tax only if their medical expenses are greater than 10 percent of their income. Only a relatively small number of individuals have expenses high enough to use that deduction. Self-employed individuals can typically deduct the cost of health insurance from their income when paying their federal income tax.

costs of providing routine medical care. John Cogan of the Hoover Institution, Glenn Hubbard of Columbia University, and Daniel Kessler of Stanford University estimated that repealing the tax preference for employer-provided health insurance would reduce spending by people enrolled in these programs by 33 percent.

Currently, the U.S. health care system is a world leader in innovation in medical technology and prescription drugs. About two-thirds of pharmaceutical patents are issued to U.S. firms and about two-thirds of research on new medicines is carried out in the United States. One goal of market-based reforms would be to ensure that U.S. firms continue with innovations in medical screening equipment, surgical procedures, and prescription drugs. Executives of U.S. pharmaceutical firms have voiced concern over whether aspects of the ACA will affect their ability to profitably bring new prescription drugs to market. In particular, managers at these firms worry that the new Independent Payment Advisory Board (IPAB) might reduce the payments Medicare would make for new prescription drugs.

Both critics of the ACA who favor greater government involvement in health care and those who favor market reforms raise questions about the act's individual mandate, which requires every U.S. resident to have health insurance. The mandate was considered necessary because otherwise healthy people might avoid buying insurance until they become ill. Because insurance companies would not be allowed to deny coverage for preexisting conditions, they would end up paying large medical bills for people who had not been paying premiums to support the system while they were healthy. People who do not buy insurance are subject to fines under the act, but there were questions about how effective the fines would be in pushing people to buy insurance. In 2016, several million people paid the fine rather than buy insurance.   **MyLab Economics** Study Plan

Continued from page 219

Economics in Your Life & Career

Is Your Take-Home Pay Affected by What Your Employer Spends on Your Health Insurance?

At the beginning of this chapter, we asked you to think about this question: Your paycheck doesn't show the amount your employer pays on your behalf for health insurance, but does that amount affect your take-home pay? The *Apply the Concept* on page 236 shows that the equilibrium compensation that workers receive in labor markets is made up partly of wages and partly of fringe benefits such as health insurance. So, while the amount that a firm pays on your behalf for health insurance may not affect your total compensation, it will affect the amount of your take-home pay. For a given level of compensation, the more a firm pays for your health insurance, the less it will pay you in wages.

A related question is why a firm would buy health insurance for you rather than increase your wages by the same amount and let you buy your own insurance. We have seen that there are two important reasons so many people receive health insurance from their employers: (1) The wage an employer pays you is taxable income to you, but the money an employer spends to buy health insurance for you is not taxable; and (2) insurance companies are typically willing to charge lower premiums for group insurance, particularly to large employers, because risk pooling is improved and adverse selection and moral hazard problems are lower than with individual policies.

Conclusion

In this chapter, we have seen that economic analysis can provide important insights into the market for health care. As with many other policy issues, though, economic analysis can help inform the debate but cannot resolve it. Because health care is so important to consumers and health care services are such a large part of the U.S. economy, the role of the government in the health care system is likely to be the subject of intense debate for years to come.

Visit **MyLab Economics** for a news article and analysis related to the concepts in this chapter.

Key Terms

Adverse selection, p. 229

Asymmetric information, p. 228

Fee-for-service, p. 223

Health care, p. 220

Health insurance, p. 222

Market-based reforms, p. 243

Moral hazard, p. 230

Patient Protection and Affordable Care Act (ACA), p. 240

Principal–agent problem, p. 230

Single-payer health care system, p. 225

Socialized medicine, p. 225

7.1 The Improving Health of People in the United States, pages 220–222

LEARNING OBJECTIVE: Use data to discuss trends in U.S. health over time.

MyLab Economics Visit www.pearson.com/mylab/economics to complete these exercises online and get instant feedback.

Summary

Health care refers to goods and services, such as prescription drugs and consultations with a doctor, that are intended to maintain or improve health. Over time, the health of people in most countries has improved. In the United States, as a result of improving health, life expectancy has increased, death rates have decreased, infant mortality has decreased, and the average person has become taller.

Review Questions

1.1 Briefly discuss the most important differences between the market for health care and the markets for other goods and services.

1.2 Briefly describe changes over time in the health of the average person in the United States.

1.3 How can improvements in health increase a country's total income? How can increases in a country's total income improve health?

Problems and Applications

1.4 In what sense have improvements in the health of the average American caused the U.S. production possibilities frontier to shift out? Panel (a) in Figure 7.1 on page 222 indicates that life expectancy in the United States declined in 1918. What effect did this decline in life expectancy likely have on the U.S. production possibilities frontier? Briefly explain.

1.5 The widespread acceptance in the late 1800s of the idea that bacteria causes diseases helped lead to a public health movement. This movement eventually brought sewers, clean drinking water, and garbage removal to all U.S. cities. What effect did the public health movement in the United States in the late 1800s and early 1900s have on the country's production possibilities frontier?

1.6 Between 1830 and 1890, the height of the average adult male in the United States declined by about 2 inches at the same time that average incomes more than tripled. Did the standard of living in the United States increase during this period? What insight into the health and well-being of the U.S. population might the decline in height provide? Briefly explain.

7.2 Health Care around the World, pages 222–228

LEARNING OBJECTIVE: Compare the health care systems and health care outcomes in the United States and other countries.

MyLab Economics Visit www.pearson.com/mylab/economics to complete these exercises online and get instant feedback.

Summary

Health insurance is a contract under which a buyer agrees to make payments, or premiums, in exchange for the provider agreeing to pay some or all of the buyer's medical bills. A majority of people in the United States live in households that have private health insurance, which they typically obtain through an employer. Other people have health insurance through the Veteran's Administration or the Medicare and Medicaid programs. In 2016, about 9 percent of people in the United States lacked health insurance. Many health insurance plans operate on a **fee-for-service** basis, under which doctors and hospitals receive a payment for each service they provide. Most countries outside the United States have greater government involvement in their health care systems. Canada has a **single-payer health care system**, in which the government provides national health insurance to all Canadian residents. In the United Kingdom, the government owns most hospitals and employs most doctors, so the health care system is referred to as **socialized medicine**. The United States spends more per person on health care than do other high-income countries; has lower life expectancy, higher infant mortality, and a greater incidence of obesity than do other high-income countries; and has more medical technology per person and has lower mortality rates for people diagnosed with cancer than do other high-income countries. Data and other problems make it difficult to compare health care outcomes across countries.

Review Questions

2.1 Define the following terms:
   a. Health insurance
   b. Fee-for-service
   c. Single-payer health care system
   d. Socialized medicine

2.2 What are the main sources of health insurance in the United States?

2.3 Briefly compare the health care systems in Canada, Japan, and the United Kingdom with the health care system in the United States.

2.4 What is meant by the phrase "health outcome"? How do health outcomes in the United States compare with those of other high-income countries? What problems arise in attempting to compare health outcomes across countries?

Problems and Applications

2.5 An article in the *Economist* noted that the National Health Service (NHS) in the United Kingdom "provides health care free at the point of use."
   a. What does "free at the point of use" mean? Is health care actually free to residents of the United Kingdom? Briefly explain.
   b. The same article suggested that funding problems at the NHS could be alleviated by "reducing demand for unnecessary treatments" and noted that while two-thirds of the 35 countries in the Organization for Economic Co-operation and Development (OECD) charge patients for an appointment with a general practitioner, the NHS does not. Is there a possible connection between the NHS's funding problem and its failure to charge patients for doctor appointments? Briefly explain.

   Source: "Accident and Emergency," *Economist*, September 10, 2016.

2.6 In an opinion column about improving the performance of doctors in the United States, a health economist observed that "it's very hard to measure the things we really care about, like quality of life and improvements in functioning." Why is it difficult to measure outcomes like these? Does the economist's observation have relevance to comparisons in health outcomes across countries? Briefly explain.

   Source: Aaron E. Carroll, "The Problem with 'Pay for Performance' in Medicine," *New York Times*, July 28, 2014.

2.7 An article in the *Economist* on evaluating health outcomes is subtitled "To Improve Health Care, Governments Need to Use the Right Data." Among the data not currently being collected in most countries, the article mentioned "how soon after surgery patients get back to work." Why don't governments currently collect such data? Why might such data be important in evaluating the effectiveness of a country's health care system?

   Source: "Measuring Health Care," *Economist*, February 1, 2014.

2.8 An article in the *Wall Street Journal* discussed Aspire Health, a startup firm that believes that it can use software to "predict which patients are likely to die in the next year and reduce their medical bills substantially by offering them palliative care at home.... Palliative care focuses on easing symptoms such as pain and shortness of breath that are often overlooked amid aggressive efforts to save seriously ill patients."
   a. Should providing palliative care to very ill patients, who are typically elderly, be an important goal of a health care system? Are there other goals that should have a higher priority? (*Note:* This question is basically a normative one without a definitive correct or incorrect answer. You are being asked to consider what the goals of a health care system *should be*.)
   b. Would it be possible to measure how successful the health care systems of different countries are in providing palliative care? If so, how might it be done?

   Source: Melinda Beck, "Can a Death-Predicting Algorithm Improve Care?" *Wall Street Journal*, December 2, 2016.

2.9 **(Related to the Apply the Concept on page 224)** A report from the American Council on Competitiveness noted that "there has been some recent progress in the digital health sector, which aims to better integrate information and software technologies into all aspects of healthcare." The report also concluded that "the U.S. has rather poor health outcomes relative to other developed countries and stands out as having exceptionally low healthcare productivity when measuring outcomes against spending."
   a. Briefly discuss the evidence for and against U.S. health care performing poorly relative to other countries when comparing outcomes to spending.
   b. If the U.S. health care sector makes increasing use of information technology, will it be likely to employ more workers or fewer workers than if it fails to widely adopt this technology? Briefly explain.

   Source: Jonathan Rothwell, "No Recovery: An Analysis of Long-Term U.S. Productivity Decline," U.S. Council on Competitiveness, 2016, pp. 54 and 76.

7.3 Information Problems and Externalities in the Market for Health Care, pages 228–234

LEARNING OBJECTIVE: Define information problems and externalities and explain how they affect the market for health care.

MyLab Economics   Visit **www.pearson.com/mylab/economics** to complete these exercises online and get instant feedback.

Summary

The market for health care is affected by the problem of **asymmetric information**, which occurs when one party to an economic transaction has less information than the other party. **Adverse selection**, the situation in which one party to a transaction takes advantage of knowing more than the other party to the transaction, is a problem for firms selling health insurance policies because it results in people who are less healthy being more likely to buy insurance than people who are healthier. **Moral hazard**, actions people take after they have entered into a transaction that make the other party to the transaction worse off, is also a problem for insurance companies because once people have health insurance, they are likely to make more visits to their doctors and in other ways increase their use of medical services. Moral hazard can also involve a **principal–agent problem**, in which doctors may order more lab tests, MRI scans, and other procedures than they would if their patients lacked health insurance. Insurance companies use deductibles and copayments to reduce the problems of adverse selection and moral hazard. There may be externalities involved with medicine and health care because, for example, people who are vaccinated against influenza or other diseases may not receive all of the benefits from having been vaccinated, and people who become obese may not bear all of the costs from their obesity.

Review Questions

3.1 Define the following terms:
   a. Asymmetric information
   b. Adverse selection
   c. Moral hazard
   d. Principal–agent problem

3.2 What are the asymmetric information problems in the market for health insurance?

3.3 How do health insurance companies deal with asymmetric information problems?

3.4 What is an externality? Are there externalities in the market for health care? Briefly explain.

Problems and Applications

3.5 Suppose you see a 2015 Honda Civic hatchback advertised in the campus newspaper for $9,000. If you could be sure that the car is reliable, you would be willing to pay $10,000 for it. If you could be sure that the car is unreliable, you would be willing to pay $5,000 for it. Under what circumstances should you buy the car?

3.6 What is the *lemons problem*? Is there a lemons problem in the market for health insurance? Briefly explain.

3.7 An article in the *Economist* referred to "the basic logic of the insurance industry—that it is impossible to predict who will be hit by what misfortune when, and that people should therefore pool their risks." In what sense does insurance involve pooling risks? How does the problem of adverse selection affect the ability of insurance to provide the benefit of pooling risk?
   Source: "Risk and Reward," *Economist*, May 12, 2015.

3.8 Under the Social Security retirement system, the federal government collects a tax on most people's wage income and makes payments to retired workers above a certain age who are covered by the system. (The age to receive full Social Security retirement benefits varies based on the year the worker was born.) The Social Security retirement system is sometimes called a program of social insurance. Is Social Security an insurance program in the same sense as a health insurance policy that a company provides to its workers? Briefly explain.

3.9 **(Related to the Don't Let This Happen to You on page 230)** Briefly explain whether you agree with the following statement: "The reluctance of healthy young adults to buy health insurance creates a moral hazard problem for insurance companies."

3.10 **(Related to the Don't Let This Happen to You on page 230)** While teaching the concepts of asymmetric information, a professor asked his students for examples of adverse selection or moral hazard in marriage. One of the students, who happened to be married, replied: "Your spouse doesn't bring you flowers anymore!" Would the student's reply be an example of adverse selection or moral hazard? Briefly explain.

3.11 A news article noted that some features of the U.S. health care system contribute "to the high cost of medical care by encouraging hospitals and doctors to perform tests and procedures regardless of the value to a patient." What features is the article referring to? Why would hospitals and doctors perform tests that may not be of any value to patients?
   Source: Reed Abelson, "Industry Group to Back Results-Focused Care," *New York Times*, January 28, 2015.

3.12 An opinion column in the *Wall Street Journal* observed about "defensive medicine" that "many physicians maintain that fear of lawsuits significantly affects the practice of medicine, and that reform of the malpractice system is crucial for containing costs." Is there another economic explanation—apart from fear of lawsuits—for why doctors may end up ordering unnecessary tests and other medical procedures? Briefly explain.
   Source: Amitabh Chandra, Anupam B. Jena, and Seth A. Seabury, "Defensive Medicine May Be Costlier Than It Seems," *Wall Street Journal*, February 7, 2013.

3.13 An article in the *Economist* argued that the real problem with health insurance is:

   The healthy people who decide not to buy insurance out of rational self-interest, and who turn out to be right. By not buying insurance, those (largely young) healthy people will be failing to subsidize the people insurance is meant for: the ones who end up getting sick.

   a. Why is it rational for healthy people not to buy health insurance?
   b. Do you agree that health insurance is meant for people who end up getting sick?
   c. Why is the situation described here a problem for a system of health insurance? If it is a problem, suggest possible solutions.

   Source: "Romney on Health Care: To Boldly Go Where He Had Already Been Before," *Economist*, May 13, 2011.

3.14 **(Related to the Chapter Opener on page 218)** An article on the usnews.com site about the Patient Protection and Afford Care Act (ACA) reported that "the participation (enrollment) of the prized 'young invincibles' . . . has been elusive." ("Young invincibles" refers to 18- to 34-year-olds who don't buy health insurance because they expect to remain healthy.) The article noted that the number of people with preexisting conditions enrolled in the health insurance marketplaces has risen relative to the number of young invincibles and asserted that this "imbalance has caused premiums to rise, which can also cause some healthier beneficiaries to avoid plans."
   a. Why is the participation of young invincibles important to the success of the ACA health insurance marketplaces?
   b. Why would an increase in the ratio of people with preexisting conditions to young invincibles result in

increases in premiums? What economic problem that occurs in the market for health care does this increase illustrate?

c. If the ratio of people with preexisting conditions to young invincibles continues to rise, what will be the consequences for the health insurance marketplaces?

Source: Kimberly Leonard, "'Young Invincibles' Remain Elusive for Obamacare," usnews.com, September 7, 2016.

3.15 Explain whether you agree with the following statement:

> Providing health care is obviously a public good. If one person becomes ill and doesn't receive treatment, that person may infect many other people. If many people become ill, then the output of the economy will be negatively affected. Therefore, providing health care is a public good that should be supplied by the government.

7.4 The Debate over Health Care Policy in the United States, pages 234–245

LEARNING OBJECTIVE: Explain the major issues involved in the debate over health care policy in the United States.

MyLab Economics Visit www.pearson.com/mylab/economics to complete these exercises online and get instant feedback.

Summary

In 2010, Congress passed the **Patient Protection and Affordable Care Act (ACA)**, which significantly reorganized the U.S. health care system. Spending on health care in the United States has been growing rapidly as a percentage of GDP, and spending per person on health care has been growing more rapidly than in other high-income countries. Third-party payers, such as employer-provided health insurance and the Medicare and Medicaid programs, have financed an increasing fraction of health care spending, while out-of-pocket payments have sharply declined as a fraction of total health care spending. Several explanations have been offered for the rapid increase in health care spending in the United States: Slow rates of growth of labor productivity in health care may be driving up costs, the U.S. population is becoming older, medical technology and new prescription drugs have higher costs, and the tax system and the reliance on third-party payers have distorted the economic incentives of consumers and suppliers of health care. The ACA has several important provisions: (1) an individual mandate that requires every resident of the United States to obtain health insurance or be fined; (2) the establishment of health exchanges that will be run by the state or federal governments and provide a means for individuals and small businesses to purchase health insurance; (3) an employer mandate that requires every firm with more than 200 employees to offer health insurance to them; (4) increased regulation of health insurance companies; (5) expansion of eligibility for Medicaid and the establishment of the Independent Payment Advisory Board (IPAB), which has the power to reduce Medicare payments for prescription drugs and for the use of diagnostic equipment and other technology if Medicare spending exceeds certain levels; and (6) increased taxes on people with incomes above $200,000. Some critics of the ACA argue that it does not go far enough in increasing government involvement in the health care system, while other critics argue that health care reform should rely more heavily on **market-based reforms**, which involve changing the market for health care so that it becomes more like the markets for other goods and services.

Review Questions

4.1 What is the Patient Protection and Affordable Care Act (ACA)? Briefly list its major provisions.

4.2 In the United States, what has been the trend in health care spending as a percentage of GDP? Compare the increases in health care spending per person in the United States with the increases in health care spending per person in other high-income countries. What implications do current trends in health care spending have for the growth of federal government spending in the United States?

4.3 Briefly discuss how economists explain the rapid increases in health care spending.

4.4 What arguments do economists and policymakers who believe that the federal government should have a larger role in the health care system make in criticizing the ACA?

4.5 What arguments do economists and policymakers who believe that market-based reforms are the key to improving the health care system make in criticizing the ACA?

Problems and Applications

4.6 Figure 7.7 on page 239 shows that the Congressional Budget Office forecasts that less than half of future increases in spending on Medicare and Medicaid as a percentage of GDP will be due to the aging of the population. What factors explain most of the increase?

4.7 Improvements in technology usually result in lower costs of production or new and improved consumer goods and services. Assume that an improvement in medical technology results in an increase in life expectancy for people 65 years of age and older. How would this technological advance be likely to affect expenditures on health care?

4.8 Some economists and policymakers have argued that one way to control federal government spending on Medicare is to have a board of experts decide whether new medical technologies are worth their higher costs. If the board decided that they are *not* worth the costs, Medicare would not pay for them. Other economists and policymakers argue that the costs to beneficiaries should more closely represent the costs of providing medical services. This result might be attained by raising premiums, deductibles, and copayments or by "means testing," which would limit the Medicare benefits that high-income individuals receive. Political columnist David Brooks summarized these two ways to restrain the growth of spending on Medicare: "From the top, a body of experts can be empowered to make rationing decisions. . . . Alternatively, at the bottom, costs can be shifted to beneficiaries with premium supports to help them handle the burden."

a. What are "rationing decisions"? How would these decisions restrain the growth of Medicare spending?

b. How would shifting the costs of Medicare to beneficiaries restrain the growth of Medicare spending? What does Brooks mean by "premium supports"?

c. Should Congress and the president be concerned about the growth of Medicare spending? If so, which of these approaches should they adopt, or is there a third approach that might be better? (*Note:* This question is normative and has no definitive answer. It is intended to lead you to consider possible approaches to the Medicare program.)

Source: David Brooks, "The Missing Fifth," *New York Times,* May 9, 2011.

4.9 The late Nobel Laureate Robert Fogel of the University of Chicago argued, "Expenditures on health care are driven by demand, which is spurred by income and by advances in biotechnology that make health interventions increasingly effective."

a. If Fogel was correct, should policymakers be concerned by projected increases in health care spending as a percentage of GDP?

b. What objections do some economists raise to Fogel's analysis of what is driving increases in spending on health care?

Source: Robert Fogel, "Forecasting the Cost of U.S. Healthcare," *The American,* September 3, 2009.

4.10 **(Related to the Apply the Concept on page 236)** Employees in most circumstances do not pay taxes on the value of the health insurance provided by their employers. If employees were taxed on the value of the employer-provided health insurance, what would you expect to happen to the overall compensation employers pay employees? To the value of health insurance provided by employers? To the wages paid to employees? Briefly explain.

4.11 Suppose consumers pay less than the true cost of medical services because a third party, such as an insurance company or the government, pays most of the bill. In the following graph, D_1 represents the demand for medical services if consumers paid the full price of medical services; D_2 represents the demand for medical services when consumers pay only a fraction of the true cost of medical services; and S represents the supply of medical services. Use the graph to answer the following questions. Briefly explain your answers.

a. What is the equilibrium market price received by doctors and other suppliers of medical services?

b. What is the efficient quantity of medical services?

c. What is the price paid by consumers of medical services?

d. Which area represents the deadweight loss resulting from consumers not paying the full price of medical services?

4.12 **(Related to Solved Problem 7.4 on page 241)** In 2017, an article in the *Wall Street Journal* discussed trends in the health care sector. The article noted the "adoption of new health information technology," using "advanced algorithms and natural-language processing technologies to read and reformat" data on patients. Assuming that health information technology continues to advance, use a graph of the market for medical services to show the effect. Explain any shifts in the demand curve or supply curve and the effect on the equilibrium price and quantity of medical services.

Sources: Jonathan D. Rockoff and Peter Loftus, "Facing Criticism, Drug Makers Keep Lid on Price Increases," *Wall Street Journal,* February 26, 2017; and Sara Castellanos, "A New Tool to Analyze Medical Records," *Wall Street Journal,* January 25, 2017.

4.13 **(Related to the Apply the Concept on page 243)** A column in the *Wall Street Journal* observed, "Independent websites like Edmunds.com, AutoTrader.com and Kelley Blue Book publish detailed pricing information [on automobiles] for consumers and do so for free. Consumers want such information and businesses see opportunity in providing it, even for free, in order to attract eyeballs for advertising. . . . Such information doesn't exist in health care." Why aren't there Web sites that offer pricing data on health care and make a profit from selling advertisements?

Source: Holman W. Jenkins, Jr., "The Young Won't Buy ObamaCare," *Wall Street Journal,* June 18, 2013.

4.14 Some firms offer their employees a health care plan with high deductibles, sometimes as much as $4,500 per year. What effect do high-deductible plans have on how often employees visit doctors or otherwise use health care services? If the federal government were to require that employer health care plans have deductibles that were no greater than $200 per year, would the employees in these plans be better off? Would the employers offering these plans be worse off? Briefly explain.

Critical Thinking Exercises

CT7.1 After graduation, you accept a job with a new small startup. Your manager asks you to evaluate health insurance plans and identify which plan is most likely to help attract good employees. One idea she proposes is to offer health insurance to employees with no deductibles and no copays. What advice might you give your manager? After hearing your advice, she asks if offering more generous health insurance will increase the total employee compensation she will need to offer employees over the next 10 years. How would you answer her, using concepts from the chapter?

CT7.2 From your local paper, bloomberg.com, cnn.com, or another site, locate two articles that advocate specific changes in the U.S. health care system. Avoid news articles that only describe the debate over health care. Instead, try to locate articles that present arguments in favor of *specific changes*. How would you describe the differences between the proposals presented in the two articles? Would it be possible for Congress and the president to enact both proposals? Briefly explain.

Firms, the Stock Market, and Corporate Governance

Is Snapchat the Next Facebook . . . or the Next Twitter?

You probably can't imagine a world without Facebook, Twitter, and Snapchat. These social media applications ("apps") are all businesses that started small but grew rapidly. To finance that growth, they needed to raise funds. Some businesses raise funds by borrowing from banks. Once firms grow large enough, they can become *public firms* and sell stocks and bonds to investors in financial markets, such as the New York Stock Exchange. Firms that do not sell stock are called *private firms*. Facebook, Twitter, and Snapchat have all made the transition to being public firms.

Once a firm goes public, it has access to greater financing but also faces pressure from investors to earn a profit. During its first year as a public company, Facebook struggled to meet the expectations of its investors. From the time Mark Zuckerberg started Facebook in 2004 as a sophomore in college until the company went public with an *initial public offering (IPO)* of stock in 2012, he was the unquestioned leader of the company. But when the firm was losing money, investors questioned Zuckerberg's leadership. Advertising is the main source of revenue for social media apps. Eventually, Zuckerberg found a better way to target advertising on the Facebook app. By late 2017, the firm's stock price had increased from its initial price of $38 a share to over $170 a share.

But the situations at Twitter and Snapchat seemed less promising. When Twitter became a public company with an IPO in 2013, its stock sold for $45 per share. In early 2017, Twitter announced that its losses at the end of 2016 had doubled to $167 million as it struggled to increase its revenue from selling advertising. During that same period, Facebook had earned a profit of $3.57 *billion*. The price of Twitter's stock fell to less than $17 per share in late 2017.

As Stanford University undergraduates, Evan Spiegel and Bobby Murphy developed the Snapchat app, which allows photographs to automatically disappear shortly

Stillbeyou/Alamy Stock Photo

after being sent. Snapchat's parent firm, Snap, became a public company with an IPO in March 2017. Investors wondered whether the company would become as successful as Facebook or struggle as Twitter has. Although Snapchat is especially popular among teenagers, popularity can be difficult to turn into revenue. Twitter and Snap both struggled to convince firms to advertise on their apps. Both companies tried to increase their appeal to advertisers by getting users to spend more time on their app: Twitter live streamed some NFL games, and Snap allowed users to search its popular Stories feature.

As we will see in this chapter, the ability of firms such as Facebook, Twitter, and Snap to raise funds in financial markets is crucial to the health of the economy. Financial markets are also an important source of investment opportunities to households as they accumulate savings to buy houses, pay for college, and prepare for retirement.

Sources: Deepa Seetharaman and Ezequiel Minaya, "Twitter Rethinks Ad Strategy in Effort to Translate User Growth into Additional Revenue," *Wall Street Journal*, February 9, 2017; Georgia Wells, "Snapchat Launches New Search Tool in Quest for More Engagement," *Wall Street Journal*, March 31, 2017; and Mike Shields, "Neither Trump Nor the NFL Delivered Big Rewards for Twitter," *Wall Street Journal*, February 9, 2017.

Chapter Outline & Learning Objectives

Economics in Your Life & Career

Would You Recommend That Snapchat or Twitter Start Charging Users?

You can use Facebook or Twitter for free—or can you? Social media apps don't charge you directly; instead, they earn their revenue primarily by displaying ads as you use the app. Most sites collect data about your Web searches and browsing habits and then display ads for products they think you might buy. But many people see these targeted ads as an invasion of their privacy.

Suppose you work as an economist for a social media company and you are asked to consider a proposal to begin charging app users in exchange for their not having to see advertisements. What factors would you need to take into account in evaluating this proposal? As you read this chapter, try to answer this question. You can check your answer against the one we provide on **page 271** at the end of this chapter.

I n this chapter, we look at firms: how they are organized, how they raise funds, and the information they provide to investors. As we have discussed in earlier chapters, firms in a market system are responsible for organizing the factors of production to produce goods and services. Entrepreneurs start firms to earn a profit by offering a good or service. To succeed, entrepreneurs must meet consumers' wants by producing new or better goods and services or by finding ways to produce existing goods and services at a lower cost so that they can be sold at a lower price than by competing firms. Entrepreneurs also need access to sufficient funds, and they must be able to efficiently organize production. As the typical firm in many industries has become larger over the past 100 years, the task of efficiently organizing production has become more difficult. In the final section of this chapter, we look at problems of *corporate governance* that are particularly likely to occur in large firms. We also look at the steps firms and the government have taken to overcome these problems.

8.1 Types of Firms

LEARNING OBJECTIVE: Categorize the major types of firms in the United States.

In studying a market economy, it is important to understand the basics of how firms operate. In the United States, there are three main categories of firms:

1. A **sole proprietorship** is a firm owned by a single individual. Although most sole proprietorships are small, some employ many workers and earn large profits.
2. A **partnership** is a firm owned jointly by two or more—sometimes many—persons. Most law and accounting firms are partnerships. Some of them can be quite large. For instance, in 2017, the Baker McKenzie law firm based in Chicago had more than 1,500 partners.
3. A **corporation** is a legal form of business that provides owners with protection from losing more than their investment in the firm should the business fail. Most large firms are organized as corporations.

Who Is Liable? Limited and Unlimited Liability

A key distinction among the three types of firms is that the owners of sole proprietorships and partnerships have unlimited liability, which means there is no legal distinction between the personal assets of the owners of the firm and the assets of the firm. An **asset** is anything of value owned by a person or a firm. If a sole proprietorship or a partnership owes a lot of money to the firm's suppliers or employees, the suppliers and employees have a legal right to sue the firm for payment, even if it means the firm's owners have to sell some of their personal assets, such as stocks or bonds, to pay their debts. In other words, with sole proprietorships and partnerships, the owners are not legally distinct from the firms they own.

It may seem fair that the owners of a firm should be responsible for the firm's debts. But in the early 1800s, many state legislatures in the United States realized that unlimited liability was a significant problem for any firm that was attempting to raise funds from large numbers of investors. An investor might be interested in making a relatively small investment in a firm but might be unwilling to become a partner in the firm for fear of placing at risk all of his or her personal assets if the firm were to fail. To get around this problem, state legislatures began to pass *general incorporation laws*, which allowed firms to more easily be organized as corporations. Under the corporate form of business, the owners of a firm have **limited liability**, which means that if the firm fails, the owners can never lose more than the amount they have invested in the firm. In other words, the owners of the firm do not risk losing their personal assets. In fact, in the eyes of the law, a corporation is a legal "person," separate from its owners. Limited liability has made it possible for corporations to raise funds by issuing shares of stock to large numbers of investors. For example, if you buy a share of Twitter stock, you

---

Sole proprietorship A firm owned by a single individual and not organized as a corporation.

Partnership A firm owned jointly by two or more persons and not organized as a corporation.

Corporation A legal form of business that provides owners with protection from losing more than their investment should the business fail.

Asset Anything of value owned by a person or a firm.

Limited liability A legal provision that shields owners of a corporation from losing more than they have invested in the firm.

Table 8.1

Differences among Business Organizations

	Sole Proprietorship	**Partnership**	**Corporation**
Advantages	• Control by owner • No layers of management	• Ability to share work • Ability to share risks	• Limited personal liability • Greater ability to raise funds
Disadvantages	• Unlimited personal liability • Limited ability to raise funds	• Unlimited personal liability • Limited ability to raise funds	• Costly to organize • Possible double taxation of income

are a part owner of the firm, but if Twitter were to go bankrupt, you would not be personally responsible for any of Twitter's debts. Therefore, you could not lose more than the amount you paid for the stock.

Organizing a firm as a corporation also has some disadvantages. In the United States, corporate profits are taxed twice—once at the corporate level and again when investors in the firm receive a share of the firm's profits. Corporations generally are larger than sole proprietorships and partnerships and are therefore more difficult to organize and run. Table 8.1 reviews the advantages and disadvantages of the three types of business organizations.   MyLab Economics Concept Check

Corporations Earn the Majority of Revenue and Profits

Figure 8.1 gives basic statistics on the three types of business organizations. Panel (a) shows that almost three-quarters of all firms are sole proprietorships. Panels (b) and (c) show that although only 18 percent of all firms are corporations, they account for a majority of the revenue and profit earned by all firms. *Profit* is the difference between revenue and the total cost to a firm of producing the goods and services it offers for sale.

There are nearly 5.9 million corporations in the United States, but only 37,000 have annual revenues of more than $50 million. We can think of these 37,000 firms—including Apple, McDonald's, and Snap—as representing "big business." These large firms earn more than 80 percent of the total profits of all corporations in the United States.   MyLab Economics Concept Check

| (a) Number of firms | (b) Revenue | (c) Profit |

MyLab Economics Animation

Figure 8.1   **Business Organizations: Sole Proprietorships, Partnerships, and Corporations**

The three types of firms in the United States are sole proprietorships, partnerships, and corporations. Panel (a) shows that only 18 percent of all firms are corporations. Yet, as panels (b) and (c) show, corporations account for a majority of the revenue and profit earned by all firms.

Source: Internal Revenue Service, *Statistics of Income*, Fall 2016.

Apply the Concept

MyLab Economics Video

Why Are Fewer Young People Starting Businesses?

We have seen that although a large majority of all firms are sole proprietorships, they account for only a small fraction of the total revenue and profit earned by all firms. In fact, more than 70 percent of people work at firms that have 50 or more employees. Does this mean that small businesses are not important to the U.S. economy?

On the contrary, most economists would argue that small businesses are vital to the health of the economy. Starting a small firm provides an entrepreneur with a vehicle for bringing a new product or process to market. During the late nineteenth and early twentieth centuries, Thomas Edison, Henry Ford, and the Wright brothers introduced important products shortly after starting what were initially very small firms. In more recent years, Bill Gates, Steve Jobs, Michael Dell, and Mark Zuckerberg decided that the best way to develop their ideas was by founding Microsoft, Apple, Dell Computer, and Facebook rather than by working for large corporations.

In most years, more than 400,000 new firms open in the United States, and, of these, more than 95 percent employ fewer than 20 workers. In a typical year, new small firms create 3.3 million jobs, which is more than 40 percent of all new jobs. Looking only at newly started firms, more than 85 percent of jobs created are created by small firms.

Because of the importance of small firms, some economists and policymakers have been concerned by a slowdown in recent years in the number of firms started. As the following graph shows, in the late 1970s, about 16 percent of all firms were less than a year old. In recent years, only about 8 percent of firms were less than a year old. In absolute numbers, in recent years business startups have been running about 25 percent below the levels of just 10 years ago. The decline in starting new businesses is not concentrated in one industry or geographic area but has occurred across industries, including the information and high-tech sectors, and in most states and cities. In fact, one study of census data indicates that during the 2010–2014 period, more than half of new businesses were started in just five cities: New York, Miami, Los Angeles, Houston, and Dallas.

The decline in starting new firms has been particularly large among people under the age of 35. At first, this trend may seem surprising because of the publicity received by high-tech startups such as Twitter, Facebook, Snap, Uber, and Airbnb, all of which were started by young entrepreneurs. But while in the 1990s about one-third of all new firms were started by people younger than 35, today fewer than one-quarter are.

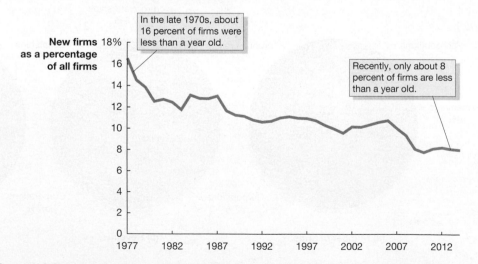

Source: U.S. Census Bureau, "Business Dynamics Statistics, Firm Characteristics Data Tables," September 2016.

Economists have not reached a consensus on the reasons for the decline in business startups. Some economists believe that despite the publicity received by innovative high-tech firms, the overall U.S. economy is experiencing a slowdown in technological progress. With fewer new technologies being introduced, there are fewer opportunities to start firms selling new goods and services. Some economists believe that an increase in government regulations has raised the costs of starting and running a small business. In particular, state and local governments have imposed licensing requirements on many occupations. According to a study by the Bureau of Labor Statistics, while in the 1950s only 5 percent of workers were in an occupation that required a license, today nearly 25 percent are. More than 1,100 occupations require a license in at least one state. In 2016, a study of New York City businesses by the city comptroller found that "nearly one third of . . . business owners report waiting six months or longer to complete the necessary approvals to open their business, and 13% take more than a year." In a rare example of agreement over policy, during the 2016 presidential campaign, Hillary Clinton and Donald Trump agreed that the federal government should reduce barriers to people wanting to open new businesses.

Many economists and policymakers worry that without an increase in young entrepreneurs starting new firms, the U.S. economy will become less dynamic and less able to sustain high rates of economic growth.

Sources: Janet Adamy, "The Five Megacities Where Business Startups Have Boomed," *Wall Street Journal*, February 1, 2017; Nicole Schubert and Jennifer Fermino, "Controller Scott Stringer Plans to Cut Red Tape Strangling Approvals for NYC Small Businesses," *New York Daily News*, March 28, 2016; Ian Hathaway and Robert E. Litan, "What's Driving the Decline in the Firm Formation Rate? A Partial Explanation," *Brookings Economic Studies*, November 20, 2014; Morris M. Kleiner and Alan B. Krueger, "Analyzing the Extent and Influence of Occupational Licensing on the Labor Market," *Journal of Labor Economics*, Vol. 31, No. S1 (Part 2), April 2013, pp. S173–S202; David Neumark, Brandon Wall, and Junfu Zhang, "Do Small Businesses Create More Jobs? New Evidence for the United States from the National Establishment Time Series," *Review of Economics and Statistics*, Vol. 93, No. 1, February 2011, pp. 16–29.

Your Turn: Test your understanding by doing related problems 1.8 and 1.9 on page 274 at the end of this chapter.

MyLab Economics Study Plan

The Structure of Corporations and the Principal–Agent Problem

Large corporations account for a majority of revenue and profit in the economy, so it is important to know how they are managed. Most large corporations have a similar management structure. The way in which a corporation is structured and the effect that structure has on the corporation's behavior is referred to as **corporate governance**. Figure 8.2 shows the structure of the typical corporation.

Unlike the owners of family businesses, the top management of a large corporation does not generally own a large share of the firm's stock, so large corporations have a **separation of ownership from control**. Although the shareholders actually own the firm, the top management controls the firm's day-to-day operations. Because top managers own only a small percentage of the firm's stock, they may decrease the firm's profit by spending money to purchase private jets or schedule management

Corporate governance The way in which a corporation is structured and the effect that structure has on the corporation's behavior.

Separation of ownership from control A situation in a corporation in which the top management, rather than the shareholders, controls day-to-day operations.

MyLab Economics Animation

Figure 8.2   **The Structure of the Typical Corporation**

A corporation's shareholders elect a board of directors to represent their interests. The board of directors appoints a chief executive officer (CEO) to run the day-to-day operations of the corporation. Sometimes the board of directors also appoints other members of top management, such as the chief financial officer (CFO). At other times, the CEO appoints other members of top management.

Members of top management—sometimes called C-suite executives—including the CEO and CFO, often serve on the board of directors. They are called inside directors. Members of the board of directors who do not have a direct management role in the firm are called outside directors. The outside directors are intended to act as a check on the decisions of top managers.

Principal–agent problem A problem caused by an agent pursuing the agent's own interests rather than the interests of the principal who hired the agent.

meetings at luxurious resorts. The conflict between the interests of shareholders and the interests of the top management is called the **principal–agent problem**.[1] This problem occurs when agents—in this case, a firm's top management—pursue their own interests rather than the interests of the principal who hired them—in this case, the shareholders of the corporation. Because the outside directors are not involved with the daily operations of the firm, they may have difficulty deciding whether the actions top managers take really are in the best interests of shareholders. To reduce the effects of the principal–agent problem, many boards of directors in the 1990s began to tie the salaries of top managers to the firm's profit or to the price of the firm's stock. They hoped this step would give top managers an incentive to make the firm as profitable as possible, thereby benefiting its shareholders. Sometimes, though, top managers act in ways that increase the profit of the firm in the short run—and the salaries and bonuses of the top managers—but actually reduce the profit of the firm in the long run.

MyLab Economics Study Plan

MyLab Economics Concept Check

 ## 8.2 How Firms Raise Funds

LEARNING OBJECTIVE: Explain how firms raise the funds they need to operate and expand.

Owners and managers of firms operate them to earn a profit. To succeed, a firm must raise funds to pay for its operations, including paying its employees and buying or renting computers and other machinery and equipment. In fact, a central challenge for anyone running a firm, whether that person is a sole proprietor or a top manager of a large corporation, is raising the funds needed to operate and expand the business. Suppose you develop a new social media app, and you decide to start a business using $100,000 you have saved in a bank. You use the $100,000 to rent an office, buy computers and other information technology, and pay other startup expenses. Your firm is a great success, and you decide to expand it by moving to a larger office and buying more information technology. As the owner of a small business, you can raise the funds for this expansion in three ways:

1. If you are making a profit, you could reinvest the profit back into your firm. Profits that are reinvested in a firm rather than taken out of the firm and paid to the firm's owners are called *retained earnings*.
2. You could raise funds by recruiting additional owners to invest in the firm. This arrangement would increase the firm's *financial capital*.
3. You could borrow the funds from relatives, friends, or a bank.

The managers of a large public firm have some additional ways to raise funds, as we will see in the next section.

Sources of External Funds

Unless firms rely on retained earnings, they have to raise the *external funds* they need from those who have funds available to invest. It is the role of an economy's *financial system* to transfer funds from savers to firms and other borrowers.

Indirect finance A flow of funds from savers to borrowers through financial intermediaries such as banks. Intermediaries raise funds from savers to lend to firms (and other borrowers).

Most firms raise external funds in two ways. The first way, called **indirect finance**, relies on financial intermediaries such as banks. If you put $1,000 in a checking account or in a certificate of deposit (CD), the bank will loan most of those funds to borrowers. The bank will combine your funds with those of other depositors and, for example, make a $100,000 loan to a local business. Small businesses rely heavily on bank loans as their primary source of external funds.

A second way for firms to acquire external funds is through *financial markets*. Raising funds in these markets, such as the New York Stock Exchange on Wall Street in

---

[1] In Chapter 7, we saw that the principal–agent problem arises from moral hazard that can occur because of asymmetric information. In this case, the asymmetric information involves top managers knowing more about how the firm is actually run than do the firm's shareholders.

New York City, is called **direct finance**. Direct finance usually takes the form of the borrower selling a *financial security* to the lender. A financial security is a document—often in electronic form—that states the terms under which the funds pass from the buyer of the security (who is lending funds) to the borrower. *Bonds* and *stocks* are the two main types of financial securities. Typically, only large corporations are able to sell bonds and stocks on financial markets. Investors are generally unwilling to buy securities issued by small and medium-sized firms because the investors lack sufficient information on the financial health of smaller firms.

Bonds **Bonds** are financial securities that represent promises to repay a fixed amount of funds. When Apple sells a bond to raise funds, it promises to pay the purchaser of the bond an interest payment each year for the term of the bond, as well as a payment of the loan amount, or the *principal*, at the end of the term. Apple may need to raise many millions of dollars to build new offices, but each individual bond has a principal, or *face value*, of $1,000, which is the amount each bond purchaser is lending Apple. So, Apple must sell many bonds to raise all the funds it needs. Suppose Apple promises it will pay interest of $40 per year to anyone who buys one of its bonds. The interest payments on a bond are called **coupon payments**. The **interest rate** is the cost of borrowing funds, usually expressed as a percentage of the amount borrowed. We can calculate the interest rate on the bond, called the *coupon rate*, by dividing the coupon by the face value of the bond. In this case, the coupon rate is:

$$\frac{\$40}{\$1,000} = 0.04, \text{ or } 4\%.$$

Many bonds that corporations issue have terms, or *maturities*, of 30 years. In this example, if you bought a bond from Apple, Apple would pay you $40 per year for 30 years, and at the end of the thirtieth year, Apple would repay the $1,000 principal to you.

The interest rate that a corporation selling a bond has to pay depends in part on how likely bond buyers— investors— think that the corporation is to default, or not make the promised coupon or principal payments. The higher the *default risk* on a bond, the higher the interest rate will be. For example, investors see the federal government as being very unlikely to default on its bonds, so federal government bonds pay a lower interest rate than do bonds of a firm such as Apple. In turn, Apple pays a lower interest rate on its bonds than does a corporation that investors believe is not as likely to make its bond payments. The interest rate on bonds also depends on how high investors expect the inflation rate to be. The higher the inflation rate, the fewer goods and services investors can buy with any given coupon payment, and the higher coupon payment investors will require before being willing to buy a bond. For example, suppose that Apple is able to sell bonds with a coupon of $40 when investors expect the inflation rate in future years will be 2 percent. If investors come to expect that the inflation rate will rise to 4 percent, they may be unwilling to buy Apple's bonds unless the firm raises the coupon rate to $60.

Apply the Concept

MyLab Economics Video

The Rating Game: Are the Federal Government or State Governments Likely to Default on Their Bonds?

Federal regulations require that before they can sell bonds to investors, firms and governments must first have bonds rated by one of the credit-rating agencies. The three largest rating agencies are Moody's Investors Service, Standard & Poor's Corporation, and Fitch Ratings. These private firms rate bonds by giving them letter grades—AAA or Aaa being the highest—that reflect the likelihood that the firm or government will be able to make the payments on the bond. The following table shows the ratings:

Direct finance A flow of funds from savers to firms through financial markets, such as the New York Stock Exchange.

Bond A financial security that represents a promise to repay a fixed amount of funds.

Coupon payment An interest payment on a bond.

Interest rate The cost of borrowing funds, usually expressed as a percentage of the amount borrowed.

	Moody's Investors Service	Standard & Poor's (S&P)	Fitch Ratings	Meaning of the Ratings
Investment-grade bonds	Aaa	AAA	AAA	Highest credit quality
	Aa	AA	AA	Very high credit quality
	A	A	A	High credit quality
	Baa	BBB	BBB	Good credit quality
Non-investment-grade bonds	Ba	BB	BB	Speculative
	B	B	B	Highly speculative
	Caa	CCC	CCC	Substantial default risk
	Ca	CC	CC	Very high levels of default risk
	C	C	C	Exceptionally high levels of default risk (for Moody's: "typically in default")
	—	D	D	Default

Note: The entries in the "Meaning of the Ratings" column are slightly modified from those that Fitch uses. The other two rating agencies have similar descriptions. For each rating from Aa to Caa, Moody's adds a numerical modifier of 1, 2, or 3. The rating Aa1 is higher than the rating Aa2, and the rating Aa2 is higher than the rating Aa3. Similarly, Standard & Poor's and Fitch Ratings add a plus (+) or minus (−) sign. The rating AA+ is higher than the rating AA, and the rating AA is higher than the rating AA−.

Source: *Money, Banking, and the Financial System*, 3rd ed., by R. Glenn Hubbard and Anthony Patrick O'Brien. Copyright © 2018 by Pearson Education, Inc. Reprinted and electronically reproduced by permission of Pearson Education, Inc., New York.

Investors can use the ratings in deciding how much risk they are willing to accept when buying a bond. Generally, the lower the rating, the higher the interest rate an investor will receive but also the higher the risk that the issuer of the bond will default.

The rating agencies charge firms and governments—rather than investors—for their services. This arrangement raises the question of whether rating agencies face a conflict of interest. Some economists and policymakers are concerned that because firms issuing bonds can choose which of the agencies to hire to rate their bonds, the agencies may have an incentive to give higher ratings than might be justified in order to keep the firms' business.

Some investors worry that the U.S. government might someday default on the bonds that it has sold. Over the past 15 years, the federal government has been spending more than it has been collecting in taxes. The result is a federal budget deficit, which forces the Treasury to sell bonds equal to the amount of the deficit. The budget deficit was particularly large during and immediately after the 2007–2009 recession, which resulted in sharp declines in tax receipts and increases in government spending. Forecasts from the U.S. Congressional Budget Office indicate that large budget deficits will continue indefinitely because spending on Social Security, Medicare, Medicaid, and other government programs is expected to increase faster than tax revenues.

In 2011, Standard & Poor's (S&P) decided that because of these continuing deficits, it would downgrade U.S. Treasury bonds from AAA to AA+. Never before had a rating agency given Treasury bonds less than an AAA rating. Is it likely that the U.S. Treasury will default on its bonds? S&P argued that while a default is still unlikely, the continuing large deficits increased the chance that someday the Treasury might not make the interest payments on its bonds. Most investors, though, appear confident that the Treasury will not default and are willing to buy Treasury bonds despite the historically low interest rates on the bonds.

Some investors worry that some U.S. state governments might default on their bonds. Many states have substantial obligations to make pension payments to retired teachers and other public employees. Making these payments may be difficult without large increases in taxes or cuts in other state spending. During 2016, S&P reduced the ratings on bonds issued by four states. As a result, interest rates on the bonds issued by these states rose. But even the state of Illinois, with a bond rating of just BBB, had the interest rate on its bonds rise only to 4 percent. Although this rate was about 1.5 percentage points higher than the rates on bonds issued by states with better credit ratings, it was still low enough to indicate that investors did not believe there was substantial risk that Illinois would fail to make the payments on its bonds.

Sources: Greg Ip, "Sovereign Default: It's Not Personal, Just Business," *Wall Street Journal*, May 25, 2016; Reuters, "S&P Cuts Illinois' Credit Rating on State's 'Weak' Management," cnbc.com, October 1, 2016; and Cyrus Sanati, "S.E.C. Urges Changes to Ratings-Agency Rules," *New York Times*, August 28, 2009.

Your Turn: Test your understanding by doing related problems 2.8 and 2.9 on page 275 at the end of this chapter.

MyLab Economics Study Plan

Stocks When you buy a newly issued bond from a firm, you are lending funds to that firm. When you buy **stock** issued by a firm, you are actually buying part ownership of that firm. A corporation selling stock is doing the same thing the owner of a small business does when he or she takes on a partner: The firm is increasing its financial capital by bringing additional owners into the firm. Any one shareholder usually owns only a small fraction of the total shares of stock issued by a corporation.

Many small investors buy shares of *mutual funds* rather than directly buying stocks issued by individual companies. Mutual funds, such as Fidelity Investment's Magellan Fund, sell shares to investors and use the funds to invest in a portfolio of financial assets, such as stocks and bonds. By buying shares in a mutual fund, small investors reduce the costs they would pay to buy many individual stocks and bonds. Small savers who have only enough money to buy a few individual stocks and bonds can use mutual funds to *diversify*, which lowers their investment risk because most mutual funds hold a large number of stocks and bonds. If a firm issuing a stock or bond declares bankruptcy, causing the stock or bond to lose all of its value, the effect on a mutual fund's portfolio is likely to be small. The effect might be devastating, though, to a small investor who invested most of his or her savings in the stock or bond. Because mutual funds are willing to buy back their shares at any time, they also provide savers with easy access to their money.

Exchange-traded funds (ETFs) are similar to mutual funds in that when you buy shares in an ETF, you are buying a claim to a portfolio of stocks or bonds. But mutual funds can only be bought from or sold back to the firm that issues them. ETFs can be bought and sold to other investors in financial markets, just like individual stocks or bonds. And while mutual funds can only be sold at the end of the trading day (4:30 P.M. on the New Stock Exchange), ETFs can be bought and sold throughout the day.

A shareholder is entitled to a portion of the corporation's profits, if there are any. Corporations generally keep some of their profits as retained earnings to finance future expansion. The remaining profits are paid to shareholders as **dividends**. If a firm uses its retained earnings to grow and earn an economic profit, its share price rises, which provides a *capital gain* for investors. If a corporation is unable to make a profit, it usually does not pay a dividend. Under the law, corporations must make payments on any debt they have before making payments to their owners. That is, a corporation must make promised payments to bondholders before it can make any dividend payments to shareholders. Unlike bonds, stocks do not have a maturity date, so the firm is not obliged to return the investor's funds at any particular date.   MyLab Economics Concept Check

Stock A financial security that represents partial ownership of a firm.

Dividends Payments by a corporation to its shareholders.

Stock and Bond Markets Provide Capital—and Information

The original purchasers of stocks and bonds may resell them to other investors. In fact, most of the buying and selling of stocks and bonds that takes place each day involves investors reselling existing stocks and bonds to each other rather than corporations selling new stocks and bonds to investors. The buyers and sellers of stocks and bonds together make up the *stock and bond markets*. There is no single place where stocks and bonds are bought and sold. Some trading of stocks and bonds takes place in buildings known as *exchanges*, such as the New York Stock Exchange or the Tokyo Stock Exchange. In the United States, the stocks and bonds of the largest corporations are traded on the New York Stock Exchange. The development of computer technology has spread the trading of stocks and bonds outside exchanges to *securities dealers* linked by computers. These dealers comprise the *over-the-counter market*. The stocks of many high-technology firms—including Apple, Snap, Twitter, and Facebook—are traded in the most important of the over-the-counter markets, the *National Association of Securities Dealers Automated Quotations* system, which is referred to by its acronym, NASDAQ. Today, even stocks and bonds that are traded on exchanges like the New York Stock Exchange are typically traded electronically rather than face-to-face by dealers on the floor of the exchange.

Shares of stock represent claims on the profits of the firms that issue them. Therefore, as the fortunes of the firms change and they earn more or less profit, the prices of the stock the firms have issued should also change. Similarly, bonds represent claims to receive coupon payments and one final payment of the principal. Therefore, a particular bond that was issued in the past may have its price go up or down, depending on whether the coupon payments being offered on newly issued bonds are higher or lower than those on existing bonds. If you hold a bond with a coupon of $30 per year, and similar newly issued bonds have coupons of $40 per year, the price of your bond will fall because it is less attractive to investors. The price of a bond will also be affected by changes in *default risk*, which reflects investors' expectations of the issuing firm's ability to make the coupon payments. For example, if investors begin to believe that a firm may soon go out of business and stop making coupon payments to its bondholders, the price of the firm's bonds will fall to very low levels.

Changes in the value of a firm's stocks and bonds provide important information for a firm's managers, as well as for investors. An increase in the stock price means that investors are more optimistic about the firm's profit prospects, and the firm's managers might want to expand the firm's operations as a result. By contrast, a decrease in the firm's stock price indicates that investors are less optimistic about the firm's profit prospects, so management may want to shrink the firm's operations. Similarly, changes in the value of the firm's bonds imply changes in the cost of external funds to finance the firm's investment in research and development or in new factories. A higher bond price indicates a lower cost of new external funds, while a lower bond price indicates a higher cost of new external funds. **MyLab Economics** Concept Check

The Fluctuating Stock Market

When economists, investors, and policymakers are interested in measuring the performance of the stock market, they don't do so by following the price of any one company—even a company as large and important as Apple, Walmart, or General Motors. Instead,

Don't Let This Happen to You

When Snap Shares Are Sold, Snap Doesn't Get the Money

Shares of Snap, the parent company of the social media app Snapchat, are a popular investment, with investors buying and selling shares often as their views about the value of the firm shift. That's great for Snap, right? Think of Snap collecting all that money as shares change hands and the stock price goes up. *Wrong*. Snap raises funds in a primary market, but its shares trade in a secondary market. Those trades don't put money into Snap's hands, but they do give important information to the firm's managers. Let's see why.

Primary markets are markets in which firms sell newly issued stocks and bonds to initial buyers. Businesses can raise funds in a primary financial market in two ways—by borrowing (selling bonds) or selling shares of stock—which result in different types of claims on the borrowing firm's future income. Although you may hear about stock market fluctuations every day in news updates, bonds actually account for more of the funds raised by borrowers. The total value of bonds in the United States is typically about twice the value of stocks.

In *secondary markets*, stocks and bonds that have already been issued are sold by one investor to another. When Snap sells shares to the public, it is turning to a primary market for new funds. (When a private company goes public by selling stock for the first time, the stock sale is called an *initial public offering* [IPO].) Once Snap's shares are issued, investors trade the shares in the secondary market. Snap does not receive any new funds when its shares are traded. The initial seller of a stock or bond raises funds from an investor only in the primary market. Secondary markets convey information to firms' managers and investors by determining the prices of stocks and bonds. For example, a major increase in Snap's stock price conveys the market's optimism about the firm, and Snap may decide to raise funds to expand. So, secondary markets are valuable sources of information for corporations that are considering raising funds.

Primary and secondary markets are both important, but they play different roles. As an investor, you principally trade stocks and bonds in a secondary market. If you become a corporate manager, you may help decide how to raise new funds to expand the firm where you work.

MyLab Economics Study Plan

Your Turn: Test your understanding by doing related problem 2.11 on page 275 at the end of this chapter.

they measure the overall performance of the stock market by using *stock market indexes*, which are averages of stock prices.

The most widely followed stock market indexes are the three that appear on the first page of the *Wall Street Journal*'s Web site: the Dow Jones Industrial Average, the S&P 500, and the NASDAQ Composite Index. Although the Dow is an average of the prices of the stocks of just 30 large firms, including Coca-Cola, Microsoft, and Walt Disney, it is the most familiar index to many individual investors. The S&P 500 index includes the 30 stocks that are in the Dow as well as stocks issued by 470 other large companies, each of which has a market capitalization of at least $5 billion. Because these firms are so large, the total value of their stocks represents about 80% of the value of all publicly traded U.S. firms. The NASDAQ Composite Index includes the more than 3,000 stocks that are traded in the NASDAQ over-the-counter market. Some firms in the NASDAQ Composite Index, such as Microsoft and Intel, are also included in the Dow and in the S&P 500, but the NASDAQ includes stocks issued by many smaller technology firms that are not included in the other indexes.

There are two key points about index numbers, like the stock market indexes, to keep in mind:

1. The numbers are not measured in dollars or any other units. Indexes are set equal to 100 in a particular year, called the *base year*. Because indexes are designed to show movements in a variable over time, the year chosen as the base year is not important.
2. The values of index numbers aren't meaningful by themselves; changes in their values are important. For instance, the value of the S&P 500 was 2095 in 2016. No one is particularly interested in that value by itself, but the fact that the S&P 500 increased from 2061 in 2015 to 2095 in 2016 is interesting because it tells us that this measure of stock prices increased by:

$$\left(\frac{2095 - 2061}{2061}\right) \times 100 = 1.6 \text{ percent.}$$

(For a review of how to calculate percentage increases, see the appendix to Chapter 1.) This increase is relatively small when compared to the long-run increase in stock prices, which has averaged about 10 percent per year.

Figure 8.3 shows movements from 1999 to 2017 in the three most widely followed stock indexes. (The shaded areas represent months in which the U.S. economy

(a) Dow Jones Industrial Average   (b) S&P 500   (c) NASDAQ Composite Index

MyLab Economics Real-time Data

Figure 8.3   **Movements in Stock Market Indexes, 1999 to 2017**

The performance of the U.S. stock market is often measured by market indexes, which are averages of stock prices. The three most important indexes are the Dow Jones Industrial Average, the S&P 500, and the NASDAQ Composite Index. During the period from 1999 to 2017, the three indexes followed similar patterns, rising when the U.S. economy was expanding and falling when the economy was in recession. Note that in all three panels, the vertical axis does not start at zero.

was in a business cycle recession, when the production and profits of many firms were falling.)

As we have seen, ownership of a firm's stock represents a claim on the firm's profits. So, the larger the firm's profits are, the higher its stock price will be. When the overall economy is expanding, incomes, employment, and spending will all increase, as will corporate profits. When the economy is in a recession, incomes, employment, and spending will fall, as will corporate profits. Therefore, we would expect that stock prices will rise when the economy is expanding and fall when the economy is in recession. We see this pattern reflected in the three stock market indexes shown in Figure 8.3. All three indexes follow a roughly similar pattern: increases in stock prices during the economic expansion of the late 1990s; declines after the "dot-com crash" of 2000 and the recession of 2001; increases from late 2001 to late 2007; declines as the U.S. economy entered a recession at the end of 2007; and then increases beginning in early 2009. In 2017, as recovery from the recession continued, all three indexes had reached their highest values ever.   **MyLab Economics** Concept Check

Apply the Concept   MyLab Economics Video

Why Are Many People Poor Stock Market Investors?

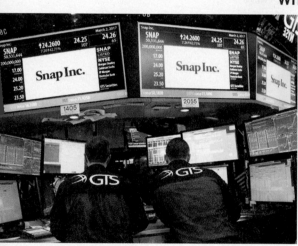

Monika Graff/UPI/Newscom

New information about Snap's future profitability would cause the price of its stock to change.

You've probably heard this standard advice about investing: "Buy low and sell high." That is, you should buy shares of stocks and other financial assets when their prices are low and sell them when their prices are high. Unfortunately, many people do the opposite. For instance, many people bought shares of Apple stock when it was selling for more than $130 per share in May 2015 and sold when it was below $94 per share in April 2016 . . . only to regret the sale when the price bounced back to $143 per share in April 2017.

Stock prices are difficult to predict, but many people convince themselves that a stock whose price has been rising will continue to rise and that a stock whose price has been falling will continue to fall. As a result, people end up buying high and selling low rather than the reverse. Studies have shown that individual investors consistently earn lower returns on their investments when they frequently buy and sell stock hoping to predict changes in stock prices.

But why are stock prices so difficult to predict? The key reason is that stock prices are based less on the *current* profitability of firms than on their *expected* future profitability. After all, few investors would be willing to pay a high price for a stock that was profitable today but was expected to suffer large losses tomorrow. Similarly, investors in the fall of 2017 were willing to pay $14 per share for Snap even though the firm was suffering losses because they expected it would earn profits in the future. If you look carefully at Figure 8.3, you can see that stock prices start to rise when investors begin to expect that an economic recovery will soon begin rather than after the recovery has already begun.

Many Wall Street investment professionals spend a lot of time and money gathering all possible information about the future profitability of firms, hoping to buy stock in the most profitable firms. As a result, all of the information about a firm that is available in newspapers, financial magazines, cable business shows, and online is reflected in the firm's stock price. For example, if at the end of a particular day, Snap is selling for $15 per share, that price reflects all the information available about Snap's future profitability. What might cause Snap's stock price to change? *Only new information about its future profitability.* For example, if Snap releases new data showing that its advertising sales on Snapchat have been lower than investors had expected, its stock price will fall.

Even highly paid professional investors cannot consistently predict stock prices. The managers of mutual funds and ETFs who try to earn high returns by frequently buying and selling stocks are rarely able to beat the stock market averages, such as the S&P 500. One study found that, in a typical year, only one-third of mutual fund managers were able to earn their investors a higher return than a small investor could earn by investing in an index mutual fund that buys only the stocks in the S&P 500. Only 10 percent of mutual fund managers earned a higher return than an index fund for two consecutive years.

Whichever way you—or Wall Street professionals—predict stock prices will move in the future, you are as likely to be wrong as you are to be right.

Sources: Morgan Housel, "Three Mistakes Investors Keep Making Again and Again," *Wall Street Journal*, September 12, 2014; Chris Dieterich, "Hedge Fund Short Bets Are Going the Wrong Way . . . Again," *Wall Street Journal*, February 7, 2017; Deepa Seetharaman, "A Rival's Shadow Looms Over Snapchat IPO," *Wall Street Journal*, February 5, 2017; and Howard Gold, "Almost No One Can Beat the Market," marketwatch.com, October 25, 2013.

Your Turn: Test your understanding by doing related problem 2.12 on page 275 at the end of this chapter.

MyLab Economics Study Plan

Solved Problem 8.2

MyLab Economics Interactive Animation

Why Does Warren Buffett Like Mutual Funds?

Warren Buffett is considered one of the greatest investors who has ever lived. His ability to predict which firms' stocks are likely to rise in price helped make him one of the richest people in the world. Yet Buffett advises that individual investors not try to pick individual stocks but instead use 90 percent of their savings to buy shares in mutual funds that charge low fees, such as those offered by the Vanguard Group. Is it likely that anyone investing mostly in mutual funds will become as wealthy as Buffett? Why would Buffett give this advice?

Solving the Problem

Step 1: **Review the chapter material.** This problem is about investing in the stock market, so you may want to review the section "The Fluctuating Stock Market," which begins on page 262, and the *Apply the Concept* "Why Are Many People Poor Stock Market Investors?" which begins on page 264.

Step 2: **Answer the first question by explaining whether investing in low-cost mutual funds is a way to become as wealthy as Warren Buffett.** Most investors who have become wealthy have done so by making large investments in just a few firms. Mutual funds typically hold large numbers of stocks and bonds, so even if one or two of the stocks do extremely well, the total investment return from the fund will be held back by the smaller increases (or losses) in the other stocks in the fund. By investing in mutual funds, you can accumulate significant amounts to pay for a house, a college education, or retirement. Many people who have earned only middle-class incomes have accumulated a million dollars or more by retirement age by investing in low-cost mutual funds. But no one is known to have become fabulously wealthy with this approach to saving.

Step 3: **Answer the second question by explaining why Warren Buffett would advise most people to put their savings in mutual funds, even though they are unlikely to become wealthy by doing so.** Mutual funds give individual investors a low-cost way to diversify. Although it's possible to earn a high return investing in the stocks of individual firms, it's also easy for a small investor to lose all of his or her money if those firms run into financial problems. As Buffett put it in one of his annual letters to investors in his company, Berkshire Hathaway: "Active investment management by professionals—in aggregate—[will] over a period of years underperform the returns achieved by rank amateurs who simply [sit] still . . . [by investing] in an unmanaged low-cost index fund."

Extra Credit: Warren Buffett may have become a billionaire by being better than other investors at predicting the future profits of the firms he invests in. Or he may have become a billionaire because he was lucky that the firms he invested in did particularly well—in which case he may not be better at forecasting the future profitability of firms than are other investors. Given that nearly all other equally intelligent and hard-working professional investors have been unable to consistently "beat the market" by earning higher returns than those earned by the typical low-cost, well-diversified mutual fund, it is impossible to know with certainty the true reasons for Buffett's success.

Source: Warren Buffett, *Letter to Berkshire Shareholders*, February 25, 2017, p. 21.

MyLab Economics Study Plan   **Your Turn:** For more practice, do related problem 2.13 on page 275 at the end of this chapter.

8.3 Using Financial Statements to Evaluate a Corporation

LEARNING OBJECTIVE: Describe the information corporations include in their financial statements.

To raise funds, a firm's managers must persuade potential lenders or investors that the firm will be profitable. Before a firm can sell new issues of stocks or bonds, it must first provide investors and financial regulators with information about its finances. To borrow from a bank, a firm must also provide the bank with financial information.

The Securities and Exchange Commission (SEC) requires publicly owned firms to report their performance in financial statements prepared using standard accounting methods, often referred to as *generally accepted accounting principles*. Such disclosure reduces the cost to investors of gathering information about firms, but it doesn't eliminate these costs—for two reasons. First, some firms may be too young to have much information for potential investors to evaluate. Second, managers may try to present the required information in the most favorable way so that investors will overvalue their securities.

Private firms also collect information on business borrowers and sell the information to lenders and investors. If the information-gathering firms do a good job, lenders and investors purchasing the information will be better able to judge the quality of borrowing firms. Some firms—including Moody's Investors Service, Standard & Poor's Corporation, Value Line, and Dun & Bradstreet—collect information from businesses and sell it to subscribers. Buyers include individual investors, libraries, and financial intermediaries. You can find some of these publications in your college library or through online information services.

What kind of information do investors and firm managers need? A firm must answer three basic questions: What to produce? How to produce it? What price to charge? To answer these questions, a firm's managers need two pieces of information: The first is the firm's revenues and costs, and the second is the value of the property and other assets the firm owns and the firm's debts, or other **liabilities**, that it owes to households and other firms. Potential investors in the firm also need this information to decide whether to buy the firm's stocks or bonds. The information can be found in the firm's *financial statements*, principally its income statement and balance sheet, which we discuss next.

> **Liability** Anything owed by a person or a firm.

The Income Statement

> **Income statement** A financial statement that shows a firm's revenues, costs, and profit over a period of time.

A firm's **income statement** shows its revenues, costs, and profit over a period of time. Corporations issue annual income statements, although the 12-month *fiscal year* covered may be different from the calendar year to better represent the seasonal pattern of the business. We explore income statements in greater detail in the appendix to this chapter.

Accounting Profit An income statement shows a firm's revenue, costs, and profit for the firm's fiscal year. To determine profitability, the income statement starts with the firm's revenue and subtracts its operating expenses and taxes paid. The remainder, *net income*, is the **accounting profit** of the firm.

Economic Profit Accounting profit provides information on a firm's current net income, measured according to accepted accounting standards. Accounting profit is not, however, the ideal measure of a firm's profit because it doesn't include some of the firm's costs. *Economic profit* provides a better indication than accounting profit of how successful a firm is because economic profit is calculated using all of a firm's costs. Firms making an economic profit will remain in business and may even expand. Firms making an *economic loss* are unlikely to remain in business in the long run. To understand how economic profit is calculated, remember that economists always measure cost as *opportunity cost*. The **opportunity cost** of any activity is the highest-valued alternative that must be given up to engage in that activity. Costs are either *explicit* or *implicit*. When a firm spends money, an **explicit cost** results. If a firm incurs an opportunity cost but does not spend money, an **implicit cost** results. For example, firms incur an explicit labor cost when they pay wages to employees. Firms have many other explicit costs as well, such as the cost of the electricity used to light their buildings or the costs of advertising or insurance.

Some costs are implicit, however. The most important of these is the opportunity cost to investors of the funds they have invested in the firm. Economists use the term *normal rate of return* to refer to the minimum amount that investors must earn on the funds they invest in a firm, expressed as a percentage of the amount invested. If a firm fails to provide investors with at least a normal rate of return, it will not be able to remain in business over the long run because investors will not continue to invest their funds in the firm. For example, by 2013, once-popular teen clothing retailer Wet Seal was suffering from falling sales due to declining customer traffic in malls and competition from online sellers. Many investors expected the firm to eventually declare bankruptcy, and as a result, the price of its stock dropped from $5 per share to less than $1 per share. In 2017, the firm closed all its stores, and its remaining assets were sold off. The return (in dollars) that investors require to continue investing in a firm is a true cost to the firm and should be subtracted from the firm's revenues to calculate its profit.

The rate of return that investors require to continue investing in a firm varies from firm to firm. If the investment is risky—as would be the case with a biotechnology startup—investors may require a high rate of return to compensate them for the risk. Investors in firms in more established industries, such as electric utilities, may require lower rates of return. The exact rate of return investors require to invest in any particular firm is difficult to calculate, which also makes it difficult for an accountant to include the return as a cost on an income statement. Firms have other implicit costs, besides the return investors require, that can also be difficult to calculate. As a result, the rules of accounting generally require that only explicit costs be included in the firm's financial records. *Economic costs* include both explicit costs *and* implicit costs. **Economic profit** is equal to a firm's revenues minus its economic costs. Because accounting profit excludes some implicit costs, it is larger than economic profit.

MyLab Economics Concept Check

The Balance Sheet

A firm's **balance sheet** shows its financial position on a particular day, usually the end of a quarter or year. Recall that an asset is anything of value that a firm owns, and a liability is a debt or an obligation owed by a firm. Subtracting the value of a firm's liabilities from the value of its assets leaves its *net worth*. We can think of the net worth as what the firm's owners would be left with if the firm were closed, its assets were sold, and its liabilities were paid off. Investors can determine a firm's net worth by inspecting its balance sheet. We analyze balance sheets in more detail in the appendix to this chapter.

MyLab Economics Concept Check

Accounting profit A firm's net income, measured as revenue minus operating expenses and taxes paid.

Opportunity cost The highest-valued alternative that must be given up to engage in an activity.

Explicit cost A cost that involves spending money.

Implicit cost A nonmonetary opportunity cost.

Economic profit A firm's revenues minus all of its implicit and explicit costs.

Balance sheet A financial statement that sums up a firm's financial position on a particular day, usually the end of a quarter or year.

MyLab Economics Study Plan

8.4 Recent Issues in Corporate Governance Policy

LEARNING OBJECTIVE: Discuss the debate over corporate governance policy.

Accurate and easy-to-understand financial statements help a firm's managers make decisions and provide information to investors who are considering buying the firm's stock or bonds. In fact, the information in financial statements helps guide resource allocation in the economy.

Firms disclose financial statements in periodic filings to the federal government and in *annual reports* to shareholders. An investor is more likely to buy a firm's stock if the firm's income statement shows a large after-tax profit and if its balance sheet shows a large net worth. The top management of a firm has at least two reasons to attract investors and keep the firm's stock price high. First, a higher stock price increases the funds the firm can raise when it sells a given amount of stock. Second, to reduce the principal–agent problem, boards of directors often tie the salaries of top managers to the firm's stock price or to the profitability of the firm.

Top managers clearly have an incentive to maximize the profit reported on the income statement and the net worth reported on the balance sheet. If top managers make good decisions, the firm's profit will be high, and the firm's assets will be large relative to its liabilities. Problems that surfaced during the early 2000s, however, revealed that at some firms, top managers inflated profits and concealed liabilities that should have been listed on their balance sheets. At other firms, managers took on more risk than they disclosed to investors. We will explore problems with corporate governance and the government's reaction to these problems by discussing the accounting scandals of the early 2000s and problems that many financial firms encountered during the recession of 2007–2009.

The Accounting Scandals of the Early 2000s

In the early 2000s, the top managers of several well-known firms, including Enron, an energy trading firm, and WorldCom, a telecommunications firm, falsified their firms' financial statements in order to mislead investors about how profitable the firms actually were. Several top managers were sentenced to long prison terms, and some of the firms, including Enron, went out of business.

How was it possible for corporations such as Enron and WorldCom to falsify their financial statements? The federal government regulates how financial statements are prepared, but this regulation cannot by itself guarantee the accuracy of the statements. All firms that issue stock to the public have certified public accountants who work for outside firms *audit* their financial statements. Unfortunately, as the Enron and World-Com scandals revealed, top managers who are determined to deceive investors about the true financial condition of their firms can also deceive outside auditors.

To guard against future scandals, new federal legislation was enacted in 2002. The landmark *Sarbanes-Oxley Act* of 2002 requires that CEOs personally certify the accuracy of financial statements. The Sarbanes-Oxley Act also requires that financial analysts and auditors disclose whether any conflicts of interest might exist that would limit their independence in evaluating a firm's financial condition. On balance, most observers acknowledge that the Sarbanes-Oxley Act increased confidence in the U.S. corporate governance system. However, as we will discuss in the next section, problems during 2007–2009 at financial firms again raised questions about whether corporations were adequately disclosing information to investors. **MyLab Economics** Concept Check

Corporate Governance and the Financial Crisis of 2007–2009

Beginning in 2007 and lasting into 2009, the U.S. economy suffered its worst financial crisis since the Great Depression of the 1930s. At the heart of the crisis was a problem in the market for home mortgages. When people buy houses, they typically borrow the money by taking out a mortgage loan from a bank or another financial institution. The house they are buying is pledged as collateral for the loan, meaning that the bank can take possession of the house and sell it if the borrower defaults by failing to make the payments on the loan. In a process called *securitization*, banks and other financial firms bundled many mortgages together into *mortgage-backed securities*, which are very similar to bonds in that the investor who buys one receives regular interest payments. In this case, owners of the securities would receive payments that came from the payments being made on the original mortgage loans.

By the early 2000s, banks and other financial institutions were loosening the standards for granting mortgages. Lenders began granting mortgages to *subprime borrowers*, whose credit histories included failing to pay all their bills on time, and *Alt-A borrowers*, who failed to document that their incomes were high enough to afford their mortgage payments. The ease of obtaining a mortgage increased demand for housing and caused prices to soar.

This *housing bubble* began to deflate in mid-2006, with prices in many cities beginning a sharp downturn. By 2007, many borrowers—particularly subprime and Alt-A borrowers—began to default on their mortgages. These defaults were bad news for anyone owning mortgage-backed securities because the value of these securities depended on steady payments being made on the underlying mortgages. As prices of these securities plunged, the result was a financial crisis as many financial institutions suffered heavy losses, and some of the largest of them remained in business only because they received aid from the federal government. Some economists argue that the firms did a poor job of correctly assessing the risk of the investments they made in these securities. This failure may be an indication of poor corporate governance if top managers were unable to effectively monitor the employees who were deciding to invest in risky securities.   MyLab Economics Concept Check

Government Regulation in Response to the Financial Crisis

During the financial crisis, many investors complained that they weren't aware of the riskiness of some of the assets—particularly mortgage-backed securities—on the balance sheets of financial firms. Some observers believed that the managers of many financial firms had intentionally misled investors about the riskiness of these assets. Others argued that the managers themselves had not understood how risky the assets were. As the crisis passed, in July 2010, Congress overhauled the regulation of the financial system with the passage of the **Wall Street Reform and Consumer Protection Act**, referred to as the **Dodd-Frank Act**. Among its provisions, the act created the Consumer Financial Protection Bureau, housed in the Federal Reserve—the central bank of the United States—to write rules intended to protect consumers in their borrowing and investing activities. The act also established the Financial Stability Oversight Council, which includes representatives from all the major federal financial regulatory bodies, including the SEC and the Federal Reserve. The council is intended to identify and act on risks to the financial system. Economists are divided in their opinions about whether the Dodd-Frank Act will significantly reduce the risk of future financial crises. In 2017, President Donald Trump argued that Dodd-Frank was doing more harm than good to the financial system and that its provisions should be modified.   MyLab Economics Concept Check

Wall Street Reform and Consumer Protection Act (Dodd-Frank Act) Legislation passed during 2010 that was intended to reform regulation of the financial system.

Did Principal–Agent Problems Help Cause the 2007–2009 Financial Crisis?

As we have seen, the process of securitizing mortgages played an important role in the financial crisis of 2007–2009. Beginning in the 1990s, private investment banks began to securitize mortgages. Unlike commercial banks, whose main activities are accepting deposits and making loans, investment banks had traditionally concentrated on providing advice to corporations on selling new stocks and bonds and on *underwriting* the issuance of stocks and bonds by guaranteeing a price to the firm selling them.

Why did investment banks take on so much risk by originating securities backed by mortgages granted to borrowers who had a significant likelihood of defaulting on the loans? Michael Lewis, a financial journalist and former Wall Street bond salesman, argued that a key reason was a change in how the investment banks were organized.

Traditionally, large Wall Street investment banks had been organized as partnerships, but by 2000, they had all converted to being publicly traded corporations. As we have seen, in a partnership, the funds of the relatively small group of owners are put directly at risk, and the principal–agent problem is reduced because there is little separation of ownership from control. With a publicly traded corporation, on the other hand, the principal–agent problem can be severe. Lewis argued:

> No investment bank owned by its employees would have . . . bought and held $50 billion in [exotic mortgage-backed securities] . . . or even allow [these securities] to be sold to its customers. The hoped-for short-term gain would not have justified the long-term hit.

Issues of corporate governance will clearly continue to be a concern for economists, policymakers, and investors. **MyLab Economics** Concept Check

Apply the Concept

MyLab Economics Video

Should Investors Worry about Corporate Governance at Snapchat?

We saw in the chapter opener that advertising is the main factor determining whether a social media app will be profitable. In 2017, Facebook had succeeded in attracting substantial advertising and was very profitable. Twitter, in contrast, struggled to attract advertising and was suffering losses. In March 2017, as Snap began selling stock in an *initial public offering* (IPO), many investors were uncertain whether the Snapchat app would earn enough advertising revenue to become profitable.

But some investors were concerned as well about potential corporate governance issues at Snap. Snap's IPO was unusual in that investors buying newly issued shares would not have the voting rights that shareholders typically have. Snap has three classes of stock:

Lucas Jackson/REUTERS/Alamy Stock Photo

Snap's co-founders, Evan Spiegel and Bobby Murphy, own 90 percent of the voting shares in the company, which worries some investors.

Class of Stock	Voting Rights	Relevance to Snap's IPO
Class A	No voting rights	The IPO consisted only of Class A shares, meaning that investors who bought them would have no votes in electing members of Snap's board of directors.
Class B	1 vote per share	Class B shares were sold to early investors who had provided funds to the firm prior to the IPO.
Class C	10 votes per share	Evan Spiegel and Bobby Murphy, Snap's cofounders, retained all of the Class C shares.

The result of this structure is that Spiegel and Murphy own 90 percent of the voting shares in the company, giving them much more control than top managers typically have at a public company. As a financial columnist for the *New York Times* put it, "The only way the two founders are ever really going to lose control of Snap is if both die."

Google and Facebook also have issued non-voting shares, but Snap became the first firm in the history of U.S. financial markets to have an IPO that consisted entirely of non-voting shares. Does Snap's governance structure matter? Many investors apparently don't think so because on the day of its IPO, March 2, 2017, Snap had no trouble selling 200 million Class A shares, which raised $3.4 billion for the firm. Other investors, though, particularly some pension funds and other institutional investors, were unwilling to invest in Snap because of the firm's governance structure. They worried that without the ability to elect outside directors, there would be no chance to bring in new top managers if Spiegel and Murphy failed to make the Snapchat app profitable.

Similarly, it wouldn't be possible for the directors to sell the firm to outside investors even if doing so would likely increase the value of the Class A shares. As one investor put it, Snap's governance structure "reduces the role of a board [of directors] member to that of an adviser who works at the behest or pleasure of the founder."

Spiegel and Murphy, and the founders of other technology firms, argue, though, that they have good reason to limit the voting rights of shareholders. They believe that shareholders with voting rights can push top management into making decisions that might help boost profit in the short run but that will be bad for the firm—and its shareholders—in the long term. As an article in the *Wall Street Journal* put it, "They wanted to decide what Snap should do and which products to create whether or not anyone else agreed." Academic studies have shown that the stock prices of companies that issue non-voting shares perform about as well as the stock prices of companies that do not issue non-voting shares.

In the end, many investors seemed to believe that Snap's future success would depend more on its ability to expand its advertising revenue by attracting users beyond its core audience of teenagers and young adults than on its corporate governance structure.

Sources: Maureen Farrell, "Tech Founders Want IPO Riches without Those Pesky Shareholders," *Wall Street Journal*, April 3, 2017; Steven Davidoff Solomon, "Snap's Plan Is Most Unfriendly to Outsiders," *New York Times*, February 3, 2017; Maureen Farrell, "In Snap IPO, New Investors to Get Zero Votes, while Founders Keep Control," *Wall Street Journal*, January 16, 2017; and Justin Fox, "Snap's Experiment in Totalitarian Capitalism," bloomberg.com, March 6, 2017.

Your Turn: Test your understanding by doing related problems 4.5 and 4.6 on page 276 at the end of this chapter.

MyLab Economics Study Plan

Continued from page 253

Economics in Your Life & Career

Would You Recommend That Snapchat or Twitter Start Charging Users?

At the beginning of the chapter, we asked what factors you, as an economist for a social media company, would consider in evaluating a proposal for the app to start charging users in exchange for their not having to view advertisements. One factor to consider is how much the app should charge users. A business columnist suggested that after five free tweets, Twitter should charge users 2 cents per tweet. To evaluate this strategy, you would need to gather information on how responsive users of the app would be to being charged for the service. In part, this responsiveness would depend on how annoyed the typical app user is by targeted ads. Some people actually find the information in targeted ads useful and would prefer to see the ads rather than pay any fee.

In practice, people have become increasingly reluctant to pay anything to download and use an app. Some free apps are downloaded millions of times, while very similar apps that charge a small fee have significantly fewer downloads. In a given year, only about one-third of smartphone or tablet owners will pay for any apps. App developers have mostly adopted the business model of allowing their apps to be downloaded and used for free while trying to still earn money from users. For instance, the popular games *Clash of Clans* and *Candy Crush Saga* can be downloaded and played for free. The developers earn a profit from people who pay to play the game faster, get extra turns, or otherwise receive benefits not available to those who play for free. The usefulness of social media apps increases as more people use them. If only a few people were on Facebook, Twitter, or Snapchat, these apps wouldn't be much fun. So, these apps can't afford the significant decline in users that would likely occur if they began to charge a fee. The remaining users who were paying would likely find the apps less fun because fewer people would be on them, and they might gradually stop using them.

So, as an economist working for one of these social media companies, you might advise them that charging app users is probably not a good way to increase revenue.

Conclusion

In a market system, firms make independent decisions about which goods and services to produce, how to produce them, and what prices to charge. In modern high-income countries, such as the United States, large corporations account for a majority of the sales and profits earned by firms. Generally, the managers of these corporations do a good job of representing the interests of stockholders while providing the goods and services demanded by consumers. As the business scandals of the early 2000s and the problems with financial firms in 2007–2009 showed, however, the principal–agent problem can sometimes become severe. Economists debate the costs and benefits of regulations proposed to address these problems.

Visit **MyLab Economics** for a news article and analysis related to the concepts in this chapter.

CHAPTER SUMMARY
AND PROBLEMS

Key Terms

Accounting profit, p. 267

Asset, p. 254

Balance sheet, p. 267

Bond, p. 259

Corporate governance, p. 257

Corporation, p. 254

Coupon payment, p. 259

Direct finance, p. 259

Dividends, p. 261

Economic profit, p. 267

Explicit cost, p. 267

Implicit cost, p. 267

Income statement, p. 266

Indirect finance, p. 258

Interest rate, p. 259

Liability, p. 266

Limited liability, p. 254

Opportunity cost, p. 267

Partnership, p. 254

Principal–agent problem, p. 258

Separation of ownership from control, p. 257

Sole proprietorship, p. 254

Stock, p. 261

Wall Street Reform and Consumer Protection Act (Dodd-Frank Act), p. 269

8.1 ## Types of Firms, pages 254–258
LEARNING OBJECTIVE: Categorize the major types of firms in the United States.

MyLab Economics Visit www.pearson.com/mylab/economics to complete those exercises online and get instant feedback.

Summary

There are three types of firms: A **sole proprietorship** is a firm owned by a single individual and not organized as a corporation; a **partnership** is a firm owned jointly by two or more persons and not organized as a corporation; and a **corporation** is a legal form of business that provides its owners with limited liability. An **asset** is anything of value owned by a person or a firm. The owners of sole proprietorships and partnerships have unlimited liability, which means there is no legal distinction between the personal assets of the owners of the business and the assets of the business. The owners of corporations have **limited liability**, which means they can never lose more than their investment in the firm. Although only 18 percent of firms are corporations, they account for the majority of revenue and profits earned by all firms. **Corporate governance** refers to the way in which a corporation is structured and the effect the structure has on the firm's behavior. Most corporations have a similar management structure: The shareholders elect a board of directors that appoints the corporation's top managers, such as the chief executive officer (CEO). Because top managers often do not own a large fraction of the stock in the corporation, large corporations have a **separation of ownership from control**. When top managers have less incentive to increase the corporation's profits than to increase their own salaries and their own enjoyment, corporations can suffer from the **principal–agent problem**. The principal-agent problem exists when the principals—in this case, the shareholders of the corporation—have difficulty getting the agent—the corporation's top management—to carry out their wishes.

Review Questions

1.1 What are the three major types of firms in the United States? Briefly discuss the most important characteristics of each type.

1.2 What is limited liability? Why does the government grant limited liability to the owners of corporations? Why is limited liability more important for firms trying to raise funds from a large number of investors than for firms trying to raise funds from a small number of investors?

1.3 What does it mean to describe large corporations as having a separation of ownership from control? How is the separation of ownership from control related to the principal–agent problem?

Problems and Applications

1.4 Suppose that shortly after graduating from college, you decide to start your own business. Will you be likely to organize the business as a sole proprietorship, a partnership, or a corporation? Explain your reasoning.

1.5 An article discussing the reasons that the Connecticut state legislature passed a general incorporation law in 1837 observed that prior to the passage of the law, investors were afraid that large businesses "were not a safe bet for their money." Briefly explain the author's reasoning.

Source: Anne Rajotte, "Connecticut's General Incorporation Law Was the First of Its Kind," ctstatelibrary.org, June 10, 2014.

1.6 Evaluate the following argument:

I would like to invest in the stock market, but I think that buying shares of stock in a corporation is too risky. Suppose I buy $10,000 of Twitter stock, and the company ends up going bankrupt. Because as a stockholder I'm part owner of the company, I might be responsible for paying hundreds of thousands of dollars of the company's debts.

1.7 According to an article in the *Economist*, historian David Faure argued that the Chinese economy failed to grow rapidly during the nineteenth century because "family-run companies . . . could not raise sufficient capital to exploit the large-scale opportunities tied to the rise of the steam engine, notably railways and (with limited exceptions) global shipping and automated manufacturing."

How did the United States solve the problem of firms raising enough funds to operate railroads and other large-scale businesses?

Source: "The PCCW Buy-out in Court," *Economist*, April 21, 2009.

1.8 **(Related to the Apply the Concept on page 256)** Two economists at the Brookings Institution argued that "new firms rather than existing ones have accounted for a disproportionate share of disruptive and thus highly productivity enhancing innovations in the past—the automobile, the airplane, the computer and personal computer, air conditioning, and Internet search, to name just a few."

   a. Why might new firms be more likely than older firms to introduce "disruptive" innovations?

   b. Assuming that these economists are correct about the most important source of productivity enhancing innovations, what are the implications for the future of the U.S. economy of recent trends in the formation of new businesses?

Source: Ian Hathaway and Robert E. Litan, "What's Driving the Decline in the Firm Formation Rate? A Partial Explanation," *Brookings Economic Studies*, November 20, 2014.

1.9 **(Related to the Apply the Concept on page 256)** While running for president, former Secretary of State Hillary Clinton published a position paper outlining how, if elected, she would make it easier to start a small business. One of her proposals was:

> Any state and locality willing to make starting a business cheaper and easier and meaningfully streamline unnecessary licensing

programs will receive federal funding to support innovative programs and offset forgone licensing revenue.

   a. Why might this proposal be expected to increase the rate at which small businesses are formed?

   b. Given your answer to part (a), why did state and local governments pass such licensing requirements in the first place?

Source: "Hillary Clinton Will Make Life Easier for Small Business at Every Step of the Way," hillaryclinton.com, August 23, 2016.

1.10 The principal–agent problem arises almost everywhere in the business world, and it also crops up even closer to home. Discuss the principal–agent problem that exists in the college classroom. Who is the principal? Who is the agent? What potential conflicts in objectives exist between this principal and this agent?

1.11 Salespeople, whether selling life insurance, automobiles, or pharmaceuticals, typically get paid on commission instead of a straight hourly wage. How does paying a commission help solve the principal–agent problem between the owners of a business and their salespeople?

1.12 Private equity firms, such as Blackstone and Kohlberg Kravis Roberts & Co., search for firms where the managers appear not to be maximizing profits. A private equity firm can buy stock in these firms and have its employees elected to the firms' boards of directors and may even acquire control of the targeted firm and replace the top management. Does the existence of private equity firms reduce any problems in corporate governance? Briefly explain.

8.2   How Firms Raise Funds, pages 258–266

LEARNING OBJECTIVE: Explain how firms raise the funds they need to operate and expand.

MyLab Economics   Visit **www.pearson.com/mylab/economics** to complete these exercises online and get instant feedback.

Summary

Firms rely on retained earnings—which are profits kept by the firm and not paid out to the firm's owners—or on using the savings of households for the funds they need to operate and expand. With **direct finance**, the savings of households flow directly to businesses when investors buy **stocks** and **bonds** in financial markets. With **indirect finance**, savings flow indirectly to businesses when households deposit money in savings and checking accounts in banks and the banks lend these funds to businesses. Federal, state, and local governments also sell bonds in financial markets, and households also borrow funds from banks. When a firm sells a bond, it is borrowing money from the buyer of the bond. Firms make **coupon payments** to buyers of bonds. The **interest rate** is the cost of borrowing funds, usually expressed as a percentage of the amount borrowed. When a firm sells stock, it is selling part ownership of the firm to the buyer of the stock. **Dividends** are payments by a corporation to its shareholders. The original purchasers of stocks and bonds may resell them in stock and bond markets, such as the New York Stock Exchange. The performance of the U.S. stock market is often measured using stock market indexes. The three most widely followed stock indexes are the Dow Jones Industrial Average, the S&P 500, and the NASDAQ Composite Index.

Review Questions

2.1 What is the difference between direct finance and indirect finance? If you borrow money from a bank to buy a new car, are you using direct finance or indirect finance?

2.2 Why is a bond considered to be a loan but a share of stock is not? Why do corporations issue both bonds and shares of stock?

2.3 How do the stock and bond markets provide information to businesses? Why do stock and bond prices change over time?

Problems and Applications

2.4 Suppose that a firm in which you have invested is losing money. Would you rather own the firm's stock or the firm's bonds? Briefly explain.

2.5 Suppose you originally invested in a firm when it was small and unprofitable. Now the firm has grown to be large and profitable. Would you be better off if you had bought the firm's stock or the firm's bonds? Briefly explain.

2.6 If you deposit $20,000 in a savings account at a bank, you might earn 1 percent interest per year. Someone who borrows $20,000 from a bank to buy a new car might have to pay an interest rate of 6 percent per year on the loan. Knowing this, why don't you just lend your money directly to the car buyer and cut out the bank?

2.7 **(Related to the Chapter Opener on page 252)** Were the shares of stock issued as a result of Snap's initial public offering (IPO) sold in a primary market or a secondary market? Was the IPO an example of direct finance or indirect finance?

2.8 **(Related to the Apply the Concept on page 259)** According to an article by Reuters News Agency, in November 2016, Fitch Ratings cut its rating on McDonald's bonds from BBB+ to BBB.
   a. What is Fitch's top bond rating? Under what circumstances would Fitch, or the other bond rating agencies, be likely to cut the rating on a firm's bonds?
   b. What will be the likely result of this rating's cut for the interest rate McDonald's will have to pay when it sells new bonds? Briefly explain.
   Source: "Fitch Downgrades McDonald's IDR to 'BBB'; Outlook Stable," reuters.com, November 7, 2016.

2.9 **(Related to the Apply the Concept on page 259)** Investors use the bond ratings from Moody's, S&P, and Fitch to determine which bonds they will buy and the prices they are willing to pay for them. The rating services charge the firms and governments that issue bonds, rather than investors, for their services. Critics argue that the rating agencies may give higher ratings than are justified in order to continue to sell their services to bond issuing firms. To avoid this impression, why don't Moody's, S&P, and Fitch sell their services directly to investors?

2.10 What effect would the following events be likely to have on the price of Google's stock?
   a. A competitor launches a search engine that is better than Google's.

   b. The corporate income tax is abolished.
   c. Google's board of directors becomes dominated by close friends and relatives of its top management.
   d. The price of wireless Internet connections in developing countries unexpectedly drops, so more and more people worldwide use the Internet.
   e. Google announces a profit of $10 billion, but investors anticipated that Google would earn a profit of $11 billion.

2.11 **(Related to the Don't Let This Happen to You on page 262)** Briefly explain whether you agree with the following statement: "The total value of the shares of Microsoft stock traded on the NASDAQ last week was $500 million, so the firm actually received more revenue from stock sales than from selling software."

2.12 **(Related to the Apply the Concept on page 264)** A column in the *Wall Street Journal* listed "trying to forecast what stocks will do next" as one of the three mistakes investors make repeatedly. Briefly explain why trying to forecast stock prices would be a mistake for the average investor.
   Source: Morgan Housel, "Three Mistakes Investors Keep Making Again and Again," *Wall Street Journal*, September 12, 2014.

2.13 **(Related to Solved Problem 8.2 on page 265)** In a letter to his company's stockholders, Warren Buffett offered the following opinion: "Most investors, of course, have not made the study of business prospects a priority in their lives. . . . I have good news for these non-professionals: The typical investor doesn't need this skill." Briefly explain Buffett's reasoning.
   Source: Warren Buffett, *Letter to Berkshire Shareholders*, March 1, 2014, p. 20.

8.3 **Using Financial Statements to Evaluate a Corporation, pages 266–267**
LEARNING OBJECTIVE: Describe the information corporations include in their financial statements.

MyLab Economics Visit **www.pearson.com/mylab/economics** to complete these exercises online and get instant feedback.

Summary

A firm's **income statement** shows its revenues, costs, and profit over a period of time. A firm's **balance sheet** shows its financial position on a particular day, usually the end of a quarter or year. A balance sheet records a firm's assets and liabilities. A **liability** is anything owed by a person or a firm. Firms report their **accounting profit** on their income statements. Accounting profit does not always include all of a firm's **opportunity cost**. **Explicit cost** is a cost that involves spending money. **Implicit cost** is a nonmonetary opportunity cost. Because accounting profit excludes some implicit costs, it is larger than **economic profit**.

Review Questions

3.1 What is the difference between a firm's assets and its liabilities? Give an example of an asset and an example of a liability.

3.2 What is the difference between a firm's balance sheet and its income statement?

3.3 Distinguish between a firm's explicit costs and its implicit costs and between a firm's accounting profit and its economic profit.

3.4 Would a business be expected to survive in the long run if it earned a positive accounting profit but a negative economic profit? Briefly explain.

Problems and Applications

3.5 Paolo currently has $100,000 invested in bonds that earn him 4 percent interest per year. He wants to open a pizza restaurant and is considering either selling the bonds and using the $100,000 to start his restaurant or borrowing $100,000 from a bank, which would charge him an annual interest rate of 6 percent. He finally decides to sell the bonds and not take out the bank loan. He reasons: "Because I already have the $100,000 invested in the bonds, I don't have to pay anything to use the money. If I take out the bank loan, I have to pay interest, so my costs of producing pizza will be higher if I take out the loan than if I sell the bonds." Evaluate Paolo's reasoning.

3.6 Paolo and Alfredo are twins who both want to open pizza restaurants. Their parents have always liked Alfredo best, and they buy two pizza ovens and give both to him. Unfortunately, Paolo must buy his own pizza ovens.

Does Alfredo have a lower cost of producing pizza than Paolo does because Alfredo received his pizza ovens as a gift, while Paolo had to pay for his? Briefly explain.

3.7 Dane decides to give up a job earning $200,000 per year as a corporate lawyer and converts the duplex that he owns into a UFO museum. (He had been renting out the duplex for $20,000 a year.) His explicit costs are $75,000 per year paid to his assistants and $10,000 per year for utilities. Fans flock to the museum to see his collection of extraterrestrial paraphernalia, which he could easily sell on eBay for $1,000,000. Over the course of the year, the museum brings in revenues of $200,000.

    a. How much is Dane's accounting profit for the year?

    b. Is Dane earning an economic profit? Explain.

3.8 Snap was founded in 2011, but it wasn't until 2017 that it filed its first annual report with the Securities and Exchange Commission (SEC). Briefly explain why.

3.9 Jay Ritter, a professor at the University of Florida, was quoted in the *Wall Street Journal* as saying about Facebook: "It's entirely possible for a company to have solid growth prospects while its stock is overvalued."

    a. What does it mean to describe a stock as "overvalued"?

    b. Why might a firm's stock be overvalued despite the firm having "solid growth prospects"?

    Source: Mark Hulbert, "A Year after Its Debut, Facebook Still Looks Overpriced," *Wall Street Journal*, May 17, 2013.

8.4   ## Recent Issues in Corporate Governance Policy, pages 268–271

LEARNING OBJECTIVE: Discuss the debate over corporate governance policy.

Summary

Because their compensation often rises with the profitability of the corporation that employs them, top managers have an incentive to overstate the profits reported on their firm's income statements. During the early 2000s, it became clear that the top managers of several large corporations had done this, even though intentionally falsifying financial statements is illegal. The *Sarbanes-Oxley Act* of 2002 took several steps intended to increase the accuracy of financial statements and increase the penalties for falsifying them. The financial crisis of 2007–2009 revealed that many financial firms held assets that were far riskier than investors had realized. Congress passed the **Wall Street Reform and Consumer Protection Act (Dodd-Frank Act)** in July 2010 to address some of the issues raised by the financial crisis of 2007–2009.

Review Questions

4.1 What is the Sarbanes-Oxley Act? Why did Congress pass it?

4.2 What was the source of the problems encountered by many financial firms during the crisis of 2007–2009?

Problems and Applications

4.3 Tronc is a publishing firm that owns several newspapers, including the *Los Angeles Times* and the *Chicago Tribune*. In early 2017, one of Tronc's largest investors sent the corporation a letter stating that he was "troubled by the company's corporate governance, or lack thereof." In particular, he was unhappy with a limit of 25 percent on how many of the corporation's shares he could own and with an attempt to remove him from the board of directors.

    a. What is corporate governance? In whose interest should corporations be governed? Briefly explain.

    b. Is limiting the percentage of a firm's stock that one person can hold an example of good corporate governance or bad corporate governance? Briefly explain.

    Sources: Lukas I. Alpert, "Tronc's Second-Largest Shareholder Raises Corporate Governance Questions," *Wall Street Journal*, March 27, 2017.

4.4 According to an article in the *Wall Street Journal*: "There is infrequent turnover among directors at S&P 500 corporations, where the median director was 63 years old. . . . The research found that at 24% of the companies, a majority of the board had been in place for at least 10 years." Is having members of boards of directors serve for longer periods likely to be good news or bad news for corporate governance? Briefly explain.

    Source: Joann S. Lublin, "Corporate Heavyweights Back Governance Practices," *Wall Street Journal*, July 21, 2016.

4.5 **(Related to the Apply the Concept on page 270)** An opinion columnist in the *New York Times* asserted that "Snap Inc. is aiming to adopt the most shareholder-unfriendly governance in an initial public offering, ever."

    a. What did the columnist mean by "governance"?

    b. Why would he consider Snap's governance to be "shareholder-unfriendly"? If Snap's governance is shareholder unfriendly, why would investors have bought Snap's stock when the company engaged in an IPO in March 2017?

    Source: Steven Davidoff Solomon, "Snap's Plan Is Most Unfriendly to Outsiders," *New York Times*, February 3, 2017.

4.6 **(Related to the Apply the Concept on page 270)** An opinion columnist for bloomberg.com observed, "A lot of people seem to think that committed, long-term shareholders should get more say than those who can bail out at any moment."

    a. What does the columnist mean by a shareholder who can bail out at any moment?

    b. What is the argument in favor of long-term shareholders having more say in running a corporation than shareholders who can bail out at any moment? How did Snap attempt to achieve this goal?

    c. Is there a good argument against giving long-term shareholders more say in running a corporation? Briefly explain.

    Source: Justin Fox, "Snap's Experiment in Totalitarian Capitalism," bloomberg.com, March 6, 2017.

Critical Thinking Exercises

CT8.1 For this exercise, your instructor may assign you to a group. What did you find surprising in this chapter, based on what you knew before you read it? Compare your answers with those of others in your group. Write a paragraph on each topic that at least two students in the group found surprising and explain why the members of the group were surprised.

CT8.2 This chapter described the concept of a firm's balance sheet. Individuals and households have balance sheets as well, and the broad categories in them are the same as those on a firm's balance sheet. That is, an asset is something that an individual owns, a liability is something that an individual owes, and net worth is the difference between the value of assets and the value of liabilities. Construct a balance sheet for yourself. You can make estimates about the type and value of assets, liabilities, and net worth. The focus of this exercise is on what counts as assets and liabilities for an individual.

CT8.3 Many news articles on firms describe recent changes in their finances. Locate and read one recent article on a firm's balance sheet or income statement from sources such as a local newspaper, cnn.com, or bloomberg.com. What significant changes does the article report about the firm's balance sheet or income statement?

Appendix

Tools to Analyze Firms' Financial Information

As we saw in the chapter, firms are not just "black boxes" transforming inputs into output. The majority of business revenue and profit are earned by large corporations. Unlike founder-dominated firms, the typical large corporation is run by managers who generally do not own a controlling interest in the firm. Large firms raise funds from outside investors, and outside investors seek information on firms and the assurance that the managers of firms will act in the interests of the investors.

This chapter shows how corporations raise funds by issuing stocks and bonds. This appendix provides more detail to support that discussion. We begin by analyzing *present value* as a key concept in determining the prices of financial securities. We then provide greater information on *financial statements* issued by corporations, using Twitter as an example.

Using Present Value to Make Investment Decisions

Firms raise funds by selling equity (stock) and debt (bonds and loans) to investors and lenders. If you own a share of stock or a bond, you will receive payments in the form of dividends or coupons over a number of years. Most people value funds they already have more highly than funds they will receive some time in the future. For example, you would probably not trade $1,000 you already have for $1,000 you will not receive for one year. The longer you have to wait to receive a payment, the less value it will have for you. One thousand dollars you will not receive for two years is worth less to you than $1,000 you will receive after one year. The value you give today to money you will receive in the future is called the future payment's **present value**. The present value of $1,000 you will receive in one year will be less than $1,000.

Present value The value in today's dollars of funds to be paid or received in the future.

Why is the $1,000 you will not receive for one year less valuable to you than the $1,000 you already have? The most important reason is that if you have $1,000 today, you can use that $1,000 today. You can buy goods and services with the money and receive enjoyment from them. The $1,000 you receive in one year does not have direct use to you now.

Also, prices will likely rise during the year you are waiting to receive your $1,000. So, when you finally do receive the $1,000 in one year, you will not be able to buy as much with it as you could with $1,000 today. Finally, there is some risk that you will not receive the $1,000 in one year. The risk may be very great if an unreliable friend borrows $1,000 from you and vaguely promises to pay you back in one year. The risk may be very small if you lend money to the federal government by buying a U.S. Treasury bond. In either case, though, there is at least some risk that you will not receive the funds promised.

When someone lends money, the lender expects to be paid back both the amount of the loan and some additional interest. Say you are willing to lend $1,000 today if you are paid back $1,100 one year from now. In this case, you are charging $100/$1,000 = 0.10, or 10 percent interest on the funds you have loaned. Economists would say that you value $1,000 today as equivalent to the $1,100 to be received one year in the future.

Notice that $1,100 can be written as $1,000 $\times$ (1 + 0.10). That is, the value of money received in the future is equal to the value of money in the present multiplied by 1 plus the interest rate, with the interest rate expressed as a decimal. Or:

$$\$1,100 = \$1,000 \times (1 + 0.10).$$

Notice, also, that if we divide both sides by (1 + 0.10), we can rewrite this formula as:

$$\$1,000 = \frac{\$1,100}{(1 + 0.10)}.$$

The rewritten formula states that the present value is equal to the future value to be received in one year divided by 1 plus the interest rate. This formula is important because you can use it to convert any amount to be received in one year into its present value. Writing the formula generally, we have:

$$\text{Present value} = \frac{\text{Future value}_1}{(1 + i)}.$$

The present value of funds to be received in one year—Future value$_1$—can be calculated by dividing the amount of those funds to be received by 1 plus the interest rate. With an interest rate of 10 percent, the present value of $1,000,000 to be received one year from now is:

$$\frac{\$1,000,000}{(1 + 0.10)} = \$909,090.91.$$

This formula allows us to calculate the value today of funds that will be received in one year. But financial securities such as stocks and bonds involve promises to pay funds over many years. Therefore, it would be useful if we could expand this formula to calculate the present value of funds to be received more than one year in the future.

Go back to the original example, where we assumed you were willing to loan out your $1,000 for one year, provided that you received 10 percent interest. Suppose you are asked to lend the funds for two years and that you are promised 10 percent interest per year for each year of the loan. That is, you are lending $1,000, which at 10 percent interest will grow to $1,100 after one year, and you are agreeing to loan that $1,100 for a second year at 10 percent interest. So, after two years, you will be paid back $1,100 $\times$ (1 + 0.10), or $1,210. Or:

$$\$1,210 = \$1,000 \times (1 + 0.10) \times (1 + 0.10),$$

or:

$$\$1,210 = \$1,000 \times (1 + 0.10)^2.$$

This equation can also be rewritten as:

$$\$1,000 = \frac{\$1.210}{(1 + 0.10)^2}.$$

To put this equation in words, the $1,210 you receive two years from now has a present value equal to $1,210 divided by the quantity 1 plus the interest rate squared. If you agree to lend out your $1,000 for three years at 10 percent interest, you will receive:

$$\$1,331 = \$1,000 \times (1 + 0.10)^3.$$

Notice, again, that:

$$\$1,000 = \frac{\$1,331}{(1 + 0.10)^3}.$$

You can probably see a pattern here. We can generalize the concept to say that the present value of funds to be received n years in the future—whether n is 1, 20, or 85 does not matter—equals the amount of the funds to be received divided by the quantity 1 plus the interest rate raised to the nth power. For instance, with an interest rate of 10 percent, the value of $1,000,000 to be received 25 years in the future is:

$$\text{Present value} = \frac{\$1,000,000}{(1 + 0.10)^{25}} = \$92,296.$$

Or, more generally:

$$\text{Present value} = \frac{\text{Future value}_n}{(1 + i)^n},$$

where Future value$_n$ represents funds that will be received in n years.

Solved Problem 8A.1

MyLab Economics Interactive Animation

How to Receive Your Contest Winnings

Suppose you win a contest and are given the choice of the following prizes:

Prize 1: $50,000 to be received right away, with four additional payments of $50,000 to be received each year for the next 4 years

Prize 2: $175,000 to be received right away

Explain which prize you would choose and the basis for your decision.

Solving the Problem

Step 1: **Review the material.** This problem involves applying the concept of present value, so you may want to review the section "Using Present Value to Make Investment Decisions," which begins on page 278.

Step 2: **Explain the basis for choosing the prize.** Unless you need cash immediately, you should choose the prize with the highest present value.

Step 3: **Calculate the present value of each prize.** Prize 2 consists of one payment of $175,000 received right away, so its present value is $175,000. Prize 1 consists of five payments spread out over time. To find the present value of the prize, we must find the present value of each of these payments and add them together. To calculate present value, we must use an interest rate.

Let's assume an interest rate of 10 percent. In that case, the present value of Prize 1 is:

$$\$50,000 + \frac{\$50,000}{(1 + 0.10)} + \frac{\$50,000}{(1 + 0.10)^2} + \frac{\$50,000}{(1 + 0.10)^3} + \frac{\$50,000}{(1 + 0.10)^4}$$

$$= \$50,000 + \$45,454.55 + \$41,322.31 + \$37,565.74 + \$34,150.67$$

$$= \$208,493.27$$

Step 4: **State your conclusion.** Prize 1 has the greater present value, so you should choose it rather than Prize 2.

Your Turn: For more practice, do related problems 8A.6, 8A.7, 8A.8, and 8A.9 on page 286 at the end of this appendix.

MyLab Economics Study Plan

Using Present Value to Calculate Bond Prices

Anyone who buys stocks or bonds is really buying a promise to receive certain payments—dividends in the case of stocks or coupons in the case of bonds. The price investors are willing to pay for a financial asset should be equal to the value of the payments they will receive as a result of owning the asset. Because most of the coupon or dividend payments will be received in the future, it is their present value that matters. We therefore have the following important idea: *The price of a financial asset should be equal to the present value of the payments to be received from owning that asset.*

Let's look at an example. Suppose that in 1990, General Electric issued a bond with an $80 coupon that will mature in 2020. It is now 2018, and that bond has been bought and sold by investors many times. You are considering buying it. If you buy the bond, you will receive two years of coupon payments plus a final payment of the bond's principal, or face value, of $1,000. Suppose, once again, that you need an interest rate of 10 percent to invest your funds. If the bond has a coupon of $80, the present value of the payments you receive from owning the bond—and, therefore, the present value of the bond—will be:

$$\text{Present value} = \frac{\$80}{(1 + 0.10)} + \frac{\$80}{(1 + 0.10)^2} + \frac{\$1,000}{(1 + 0.10)^2} = \$965.29.$$

That is, the present value of the bond will equal the present value of the three payments you will receive during the two years you own the bond. You should, therefore, be willing to pay $965.29 to own this bond and have the right to receive these payments from GE. This process of calculating present values of future payments is used to determine bond prices, with one qualification: The relevant interest rate used by investors in the bond market to calculate the present value and, therefore, the price of an existing bond is usually the coupon rate on comparable newly issued bonds. Therefore, the general formula for the price of a bond is:

$$\text{Bond price} = \frac{\text{Coupon}_1}{(1 + i)} + \frac{\text{Coupon}_2}{(1 + i)^2} + \cdots + \frac{\text{Coupon}_n}{(1 + i)^n} + \frac{\text{Face value}}{(1 + i)^n}.$$

where:

- $Coupon_1$ is the coupon payment to be received after one year.

- $Coupon_2$ is the coupon payment to be received after two years.

- $Coupon_n$ is the coupon payment received in the year the bond matures.

- The ellipsis takes the place of the coupon payments—if any—received between the second year and the year when the bond matures.

- Face value is the amount that will be received when the bond matures.

- i is the interest rate on comparable newly issued bonds.   **MyLab Economics** Concept Check

Using Present Value to Calculate Stock Prices

When you own a firm's stock, you are legally entitled to your share of the firm's profit. Remember that the payments a firms makes to its shareholders are called *dividends*. The price of a share of stock should equal the present value of the dividends investors expect to receive as a result of owning that stock. Therefore, the general formula for the price of a stock is:

$$\text{Stock price} = \frac{\text{Dividend}_1}{(1 + i)} + \frac{\text{Dividend}_2}{(1 + i)^2} + \ldots$$

Notice that this formula looks very similar to the one we used to calculate the price of a bond, with two important differences:

1. Unlike a bond, a share of stock has no maturity date, so we have to calculate the present value of an infinite number of dividend payments. It may seem that the stock's price must be infinite as well, but remember that dollars you don't receive for many years are worth very little today. For instance, a dividend payment of $10 that will be received 40 years in the future is worth only a little more than $0.20 today at a 10 percent interest rate.
2. You know with certainty the coupon payments you will receive from owning the bond because they are set when the bond is issued and cannot be changed (unless the firm that issued the bond declares bankruptcy). However, you don't know for sure what the dividend payments from owning a stock will be. How large a dividend payment you will receive depends on how profitable the company will be in the future.

Although it is possible to forecast the future profitability of a company, this cannot be done with perfect accuracy. To emphasize this point, some economists rewrite the basic stock price formula by adding a superscript e to each dividend term to emphasize that these are *expected* dividend payments. Because the future profitability of companies is often very difficult to forecast, it is not surprising that differences of opinion exist over what the price of a particular stock should be. Some investors will be optimistic about the future profitability of a company and will, therefore, believe that the company's stock should have a high price. Other investors might be pessimistic and believe that the company's stock should have a low price.   **MyLab Economics** Concept Check

A Simple Formula for Calculating Stock Prices

It is possible to simplify the formula for determining the price of a stock. If we assume that dividends will grow at a constant rate, we get the following equation:

$$\text{Stock price} = \frac{\text{Dividend}}{(i - \text{Growth rate})}.$$

In this equation, Dividend is the dividend expected to be received one year from now, and Growth rate is the rate at which those dividends are expected to grow. If a company pays a dividend of $1 per share to be received one year from now and Growth rate is 10 percent, the company is expected to pay a dividend of $1.10 the following year, $1.21 the year after that, and so on.

Now suppose that IBM will pay a dividend of $5 per share at the end of the year, the consensus of investors is that these dividends will increase at a rate of 5 percent per year for the indefinite future, and the interest rate is 10 percent. Then the price of IBM's stock should be:

$$\text{Stock price} = \frac{\$5.00}{(0.10 - 0.05)} = \$100.00.$$

In recent years, investors have debated whether the high prices of the stocks of many high-tech firms, including Twitter and Snap, were justified, given that many of these companies had not made any profit yet and so had not paid any dividends. Is there any way that a rational investor would pay a high price for the stock of a company that is currently not earning profits? The formula for determining stock prices shows that it is possible, provided that the investor's assumptions are optimistic enough! For example, suppose that a stock analyst predicts that Snap will soon be earning $1 per share of stock. That is, Snap's total earnings divided by the number of shares of its stock outstanding would be $1. Suppose Snap pays out that $1 in dividends and that the $1 will grow rapidly over the years, by, say, 7 percent per year. Then the formula indicates that the price of Snap's stock should be:

$$\text{Stock price} = \frac{\$1.00}{(0.10 - 0.07)} = \$33.33.$$

If you are sufficiently optimistic about the future prospects of a company, a high stock price can be justified even if the company is not currently earning a profit. But investors in stocks must be careful. Suppose investors decide that the growth rate of Snap's dividend is likely to be only 4 percent per year instead of 7 percent because they expect the firm to have trouble attracting older consumers to its Snapchat app, which would reduce the firm's profitability. Then our formula indicates that the price of Snap's stock should be:

$$\text{Stock price} = \frac{\$1.00}{(0.10 - 0.04)} = \$16.67.$$

This price is only half the price determined assuming a more optimistic growth rate. We can conclude that investors use information about a firm's profitability and growth prospects to determine what the firm is worth. **MyLab Economics** Concept Check

Going Deeper into Financial Statements

Corporations disclose substantial information about their business operations and financial position to actual and potential investors. Some of this information meets the demands of participants in financial markets and of information-collection agencies, such as Moody's Investors Service, which develops credit ratings that help investors judge how risky corporate bonds are. Other information meets the legal reporting requirements of the U.S. Securities and Exchange Commission.

Key sources of information about a corporation's profitability and financial position are its principal financial statements—the *income statement* and the *balance sheet*. These important information sources were first introduced in the chapter. In the following section we go into more detail, using recent data for Twitter as an example.

Revenue		$2,530	Revenue from sales
Operating expenses			
	Cost of revenue	932	
	Research and development	714	Categories of costs
	Sales and marketing	958	
	General and administrative	293	
Total operating expenses		2,897	Total cost
Loss from operations		(367)	
Other income		(74)	Operating income = Revenue − Operating expenses
Income before income taxes		(441)	
Income taxes		(16)	Before-tax accounting profit
Net income (accounting loss)		(457)	After-tax accounting loss

Note: All numbers are in millions of dollars.

MyLab Economics Animation

Figure 8A.1 Twitter's Income Statement for 2016

Twitter's income statement shows the company's revenue, costs, and profit for 2016. The difference between its revenue ($2,530 million) and its operating expenses ($2,897 million) is its operating income (a loss of $367 million). Most corporations also have interest expenses and income from investments, such as government and corporate bonds. In this case, Twitter paid more in interest than it earned on its investments, so its *income before*

income taxes was a loss of $441 million. After paying taxes, Twitter had a net loss, or accounting loss, of $457 million for the year.

Note: Negative values in the figure are shown in parentheses.

Source: Twitter, *Annual Report, 2016.*

Analyzing Income Statements

As discussed in the chapter, a firm's income statement summarizes its revenues, costs, and profit over a period of time. Figure 8A.1 shows Twitter's income statement for 2016.

Twitter's income statement presents the results of the company's operations during the year. Listed first are the revenues it earned, largely from selling advertising on its app, from January 1, 2016, to December 31, 2016: $2,530 million. Listed next are Twitter's operating expenses, the most important of which is its *cost of revenue*—which is commonly known as *cost of sales* or *cost of goods sold*: $932 million. Cost of revenue is the direct cost of producing the products sold, including in this case the salaries of the computer programmers Twitter hires to write the software for its app. Twitter also has substantial costs for researching and developing its products ($714 million) and for sales and marketing them ($958 million). General and administrative expenses ($293 million) include costs such as the salaries of top managers.

The difference between a firm's revenue and its costs is its *profit*. Profit shows up in several forms on an income statement. A firm's *operating income* is the difference between its revenue and its operating expenses. Most corporations, including Twitter, also have interest expenses and income from investments, such as government and corporate bonds. In this case, Twitter paid more in interest than it earned on its investments. Because its costs were greater than its revenue, Twitter's *income before income taxes* was a loss of $441 million. (A loss in financial statements is indicated by the use of parentheses.) Twitter paid $16 million in taxes, so its *net income* after taxes was a loss of $457 million. The fact that Twitter could experience a loss while still having a high stock price is an indication that investors were expecting Twitter to earn significant profits in the future. The net income that firms report on their income statements is referred to as their after-tax *accounting profit*.   MyLab Economics Concept Check

Analyzing Balance Sheets

As discussed in the chapter, while a firm's income statement reports the firm's activities for a period of time, a firm's balance sheet summarizes its financial position on a particular day, usually the end of a quarter or year. To understand how a balance sheet

Assets		Liabilities and Stockholders' Equity	
Current assets	$4,747	Current liabilities	$ 584
Property and equipment	784	Long-term liabilities	1,681
Goodwill	1,185	Total liabilities	2,265
Other assets	154	Stockholders' equity	4,605
Total assets	$6,870	Total liabilities and stockholders' equity	$6,870

Note: All values are in millions of dollars.

MyLab Economics Animation

Figure 8A.2

Twitter's Balance Sheet as of December 31, 2016

Corporations list their assets on the left of their balance sheets and their liabilities on the right. The difference between the value of a firm's assets and the value of its liabilities equals the net worth of the firm, or stockholders' equity. Stockholders' equity is listed on the right side of the balance sheet. Therefore, the value of the left side of the balance sheet must always equal the value of the right side.

Source: Twitter, *Annual Report, 2016.*

is organized, first recall that an asset is anything of value that the firm owns, and a liability is a debt or an obligation that the firm owes. Subtracting the value of a firm's liabilities from the value of its assets leaves its *net worth*. Because a corporation's stockholders are its owners, net worth is often listed as **stockholders' equity** on a balance sheet. Using these definitions, we can state the balance sheet equation (also called the basic accounting equation) as follows:

$$\text{Assets} - \text{Liabilities} = \text{Stockholders Equity},$$

or:

$$\text{Assets} = \text{Liabilities} + \text{Stockholders Equity}.$$

This equation tells us that the value of a firm's assets must equal the value of its liabilities plus the value of stockholders' equity. An important accounting convention dating back to the beginning of modern bookkeeping in fifteenth-century Italy holds that balance sheets should list assets on the left side and liabilities and net worth, or stockholders' equity, on the right side. Notice that this means that *the value of the left side of the balance sheet must always equal the value of the right side.* Figure 8A.2 shows Twitter's balance sheet as of December 31, 2016.

Two of the entries on the asset side of the balance sheet may be unfamiliar:

1. *Current assets* are assets that the firm could convert into cash quickly, such as the balance in its checking account or its accounts receivable, which is money currently owed to the firm for products that have been delivered but not yet paid for.
2. *Goodwill* represents the difference between the purchase price of a company and the market value of its assets. It represents the ability of a business to earn an economic profit from its assets. For example, if you buy a restaurant that is located on a busy intersection and you employ a chef with a reputation for preparing delicious food, you may pay more than the market value of the tables, chairs, ovens, and other assets. This additional amount you pay will be entered on the asset side of your balance sheet as goodwill.

We can note two entries on the liabilities side of the balance sheet:

1. *Current liabilities* are short-term debts such as accounts payable, which is money owed to suppliers for goods received but not yet paid for, or bank loans that will be paid back in less than one year.
2. *Long-term liabilities* are long-term bank loans, the value of outstanding corporate bonds, and other long-term debts.   **MyLab Economics** Concept Check

Stockholders' equity The difference between the value of a corporation's assets and the value of its liabilities; also known as *net worth.*

MyLab Economics Study Plan

Key Terms

8A **Tools to Analyze Firms' Financial Information, pages 278–285**

LEARNING OBJECTIVE: Explain the concept of present value and describe the information contained on a firm's income statement and balance sheet.

MyLab Economics   Visit www.pearson.com/mylab/economics to complete these exercises online and get instant feedback.

Review Questions

8A.1 Why is money you receive at some future date worth less to you than money you receive today? If the interest rate rises, what effect does this have on the present value of payments you receive in the future?

8A.2 Give the formula for calculating the present value of a bond that will pay a coupon of $100 per year for 10 years and that has a face value of $1,000.

8A.3 Compare the formula for calculating the present value of the payments you will receive from owning a bond to the formula for calculating the present value of the payments you will receive from owning a stock. What are the key similarities? What are the key differences?

8A.4 How is operating income calculated? How does operating income differ from net income? How does net income differ from accounting profit?

8A.5 What is the key difference between a firm's income statement and its balance sheet? What is listed on the left side of a balance sheet? What is listed on the right side?

Problems and Applications

8A.6 **(Related to Solved Problem 8A.1 on page 280)** If the interest rate is 10 percent, what is the present value of a bond that matures in 2 years, pays $85 1 year from now, and pays $1,085 2 years from now?

8A.7 **(Related to Solved Problem 8A.1 on page 280)** Before the 2017 National Football League season, the New York Giants signed defensive lineman Jason Pierre-Paul to a contract that would pay him an immediate $5 million signing bonus and the following amounts: $2.5 million for the 2017 season, $17.5 million for the 2018 season, $19.5 million for the 2019 season, and $17.5 million for the 2020 season. Assume that Pierre-Paul receives each of his four seasonal salaries as a lump-sum payment at the end of the year.
   a. One newspaper article said that "Pierre-Paul's deal is worth $62 million." Do you agree that $62 million was the value of this contract? Briefly explain.
   b. What was the present value of Pierre-Paul's contract at the time he signed it, assuming an interest rate of 10 percent?
   c. If you use an interest rate of 5 percent, what was the present value of Pierre-Paul's contract?

Sources: Bill Pennington, "Jason Pierre-Paul Agrees to Four-Year Contract with Giants," *New York Times*, March 17, 2017; the terms of the contract are from sportrac.com.

8A.8 **(Related to Solved Problem 8A.1 on page 280)** A winner of the Pennsylvania Lottery was given the choice of receiving $18 million at once or $1,440,000 per year for 25 years.
   a. If the winner had opted for the 25 annual payments, how much in total would she have received?

b. At an interest rate of 10 percent, what would be the present value of the 25 payments?

c. At an interest rate of 5 percent, what would be the present value of the 25 payments?

d. What interest rate would make the present value of the 25 payments equal to the one payment of $18 million? (This question is difficult and requires the use of a financial calculator or a spreadsheet. *Hint:* If you are familiar with the Excel spreadsheet program, use the RATE function. You can answer parts (b) and (c) by using the Excel PV [Present Value] function.)

8A.9 **(Related to Solved Problem 8A.1 on page 280)** Before the start of the 2000 baseball season, the New York Mets decided that they didn't want Bobby Bonilla playing for them any longer. But Bonilla had a contract with the Mets for the 2000 season that would have obliged the Mets to pay him $5.9 million. When the Mets released Bonilla, he agreed to take the following payments in lieu of the $5.9 million the Mets would have paid him in the year 2000: He would receive 25 equal payments of $1,193,248.20 each July 1 from 2011 to 2035. If you were Bobby Bonilla, which would you rather have had, the lump-sum $5.9 million in 2000 or the 25 payments beginning in 2011? Explain the basis for your decision.

Source: Mike Sielski, "There's No Accounting for This," *Wall Street Journal*, July 1, 2010.

8A.10 Suppose that eLake, an online auction site, is paying a dividend of $2 per share. You expect this dividend to grow 2 percent per year, and the interest rate is 10 percent. What is the most you would be willing to pay for a share of stock in eLake? If the interest rate is 5 percent, what is the most you would be willing to pay? When interest rates in the economy decline, would you expect stock prices in general to rise or fall? Briefly explain.

8A.11 Suppose you buy the bond of a large corporation at a time when the inflation rate is very low. If the inflation rate increases during the time you hold the bond, what is likely to happen to the price of the bond?

8A.12 Use the information in the following table for calendar year 2016 to prepare an income statement for McDonald's Corporation. Be sure to include entries for operating income and net income.

Revenue from company restaurants	$15,295 million
Revenue from franchised restaurants	9,327 million
Cost of operating company-owned restaurants	12,699 million
Income taxes	2,180 million
Interest expense	885 million
General and administrative cost	2,460 million
Cost of restaurant leases	1,718 million

Source: McDonalds Corp., *Annual Report*, 2016.

8A.13 Use the information in the following table on the financial situation of Starbucks Corporation as of October 2, 2016 (the end of the firm's financial year), to prepare a balance sheet for the firm. Be sure to include an entry for stockholders' equity.

Current assets	$4,761 million
Current liabilities	4,547 million
Property and equipment	4,534 million
Long-term liabilities	3,892 million
Goodwill	1,720 million
Other assets	3,316 million

Source: Starbucks Corp., *Annual Report, 2016.*

8A.14 The *current ratio* is equal to a firm's current assets divided by its current liabilities. Use the information in Figure 8A.2 on page 285 to calculate Twitter's current ratio on December 31, 2016. Investors generally prefer that a firm's current ratio be greater than 1.5. What problems might a firm encounter if the value of its current assets is low relative to the value of its current liabilities?

Comparative Advantage and the Gains from International Trade

9

President Trump, Oreo Cookies, and Free Trade

Does it matter if the cookies you buy are made in the United States or in Mexico? In 2016, Mondelez International, Inc., a U.S. food company that makes Oreo cookies, announced that it would eliminate 600 jobs at its Chicago factory and begin producing Oreos in a plant in Mexico. Decisions like these played a major role in the 2016 presidential election. As a candidate, Donald Trump promised to renegotiate the North American Free Trade Agreement (NAFTA), a 1994 treaty that removed restrictions on trade and investment among the United States, Canada, and Mexico. Trump blamed NAFTA, which he called "the single worst trade deal ever approved in this country" for causing a loss of jobs in the United States as U.S. firms moved some of their operations to other countries.

President Trump pulled the United States out of negotiations on the Trans-Pacific Partnership (TPP), an agreement that had been intended to reduce trade barriers between the United States and 11 other countries, including Canada, Japan, Mexico, and Vietnam. Many economists, however, support trade agreements like NAFTA and the TPP, arguing that they benefit U.S. consumers by reducing the prices they pay for food, clothing, and many other goods. These economists maintain that the agreements improve economic efficiency because they result in goods being produced at the lowest opportunity cost. Some U.S. firms also support these trade agreements. In 2016, the value of the industrial equipment that U.S.-based Caterpillar Inc. exported to Mexico was worth $33 million more than the parts Caterpillar imported from Mexico. Trade analyst Chris Rogers noted the advantages to the company from having a "flexible, cross-border supply chain . . . to move parts and completed vehicles to where the optimal labor cost and skill sets are, without . . . tariff hurdles."

Kristoffer Tripplaar/Alamy Stock Photo

But those arguments in favor of free trade are unconvincing to workers who have lost their jobs. More than 2 million U.S. manufacturing jobs may have been lost to Chinese imports since 1999. Although trade with China has created other jobs throughout the United States, President Trump carried several Midwestern states during the 2016 election in part because of discontent over the loss of manufacturing jobs there.

Does eliminating government restrictions on international trade help or hurt workers and consumers in the United States? Few government policies are as hotly debated as those involving international trade. In this chapter, we will explore the economics of trade and the debate over trade policies.

Sources: Azam Ahmed and Elizabeth Malkin, "For Commerce Pick Wilbur Ross, 'Inherently Bad' Deals Paid Off," *New York Times*, February 25, 2017; Jacob M. Schlesinger, Andrew Tangel, and Valerie Bauerlein, "NAFTA's Net U.S. Impact Is Modest," *Wall Street Journal*, January 27, 2017; and "Trade, at What Price?" *Economist*, April 2, 2016.

Chapter Outline & Learning Objectives

Economics in Your Life & Career

Should a Member of Congress Support a Tariff on Running Shoes?

Suppose that you are an aide to a member of Congress who is considering whether to vote for a bill that would eliminate the U.S. tariff on running shoes. She asks you to prepare a memorandum recommending how she should vote, taking into account both the economic interests of the firms and workers in her district and the broader interests of the U.S. economy as a whole. What facts and conclusions from the economic analysis of international trade should you include in your memorandum? As you read this chapter, try to answer this question. You can check your answer against the one we provide on **page 314** at the end of this chapter.

T*rade* is simply the act of buying or selling. Is there a difference between trade that takes place within a country and international trade? Within the United States, domestic trade makes it possible for consumers in Ohio to eat salmon caught in Alaska and for consumers in Montana to drive cars built in Michigan or Kentucky. Similarly, international trade makes it possible for consumers in the United States to drink wine from France and use smartphones assembled in China. One significant difference between domestic trade and international trade is that international trade is more controversial. At one time, nearly all the televisions, shoes, clothing, and toys bought in the United States were also produced here. Today, firms in other countries produce most of these goods. This shift has benefited U.S. consumers because foreign-made goods have lower prices or higher quality than the U.S.-made goods they have replaced. At the same time, though, many U.S. firms that produced these goods have gone out of business, and their workers have had to find other jobs. Some cities in the industrial Midwest have been devastated as factories have closed down and few new firms have replaced them. Some families who had worked for several generations in the same factory have been faced with accepting major income declines or moving elsewhere to find jobs. Cities and towns in New England and in the Carolinas and Georgia have faced similar difficulties as shoe, clothing, textile, and furniture factories have closed in the face of foreign competition. Not surprisingly, opinion polls show that many Americans favor reducing international trade because they believe doing so will preserve jobs in the United States. But is this belief accurate?

We can use the tools of demand and supply to analyze markets for internationally traded goods and services. We have seen that trade in general—whether within a country or between countries—is based on the principle of comparative advantage (see Chapter 2, Section 2.2). In this chapter, we look more closely at the role of comparative advantage in international trade. We also use the concepts of consumer surplus, producer surplus, and deadweight loss (see Chapter 4, Section 4.2) to analyze government policies that interfere with trade. With this background, we can return to the political debate over whether the United States benefits from international trade. We begin by looking at the role international trade plays in the U.S. economy.

9.1 The United States in the International Economy

LEARNING OBJECTIVE: Discuss the role of international trade in the U.S. economy.

International trade has grown tremendously over the past 50 years, due primarily to three factors: the decreasing costs of shipping products around the world, the spread of inexpensive and reliable communications, and changes in government policies. Firms can use large container ships to send their products across oceans at low cost. Businesspeople today can travel to Europe or Asia, using fast, inexpensive, and reliable air transportation. The Internet, cellphones, and text messaging allow managers to communicate instantaneously and at a very low cost with customers and suppliers around the world. These and other improvements in transportation and communication have created an integrated global marketplace that earlier generations of businesspeople could only dream of.

Over the past 50 years, many governments have changed policies to facilitate international trade. For example, tariff rates have fallen. A **tariff** is a tax imposed by a government on *imports* into a country. **Imports** are goods and services purchased domestically that have been produced in other countries. In the 1930s, the United States charged an average tariff rate above 50 percent. Today, the rate is less than 1.5 percent. In North America, most tariffs between Canada, Mexico, and the United States were eliminated following the passage of the North American Free Trade Agreement (NAFTA) in 1994.

Tariff A tax imposed by a government on imports.

Imports Goods and services purchased domestically that are produced in other countries.

In Europe, 28 countries have formed the European Union, which has eliminated all tariffs among member countries, greatly increasing both imports and **exports**, which are goods and services produced domestically and sold in other countries. In 2017, though, the policy of reducing government restrictions on trade seemed newly in doubt. In Europe, the United Kingdom was withdrawing from the European Union and possibly facing new barriers to trading with the remaining members. And, as we saw in the chapter opener, the Trump administration had withdrawn from negotiations aimed at concluding the Trans-Pacific Partnership (TPP), which was to have been an agreement to increase trade between the United States and 11 other countries around the Pacific Ocean, including Canada, Japan, Mexico, and Vietnam. The Trump administration wished to renegotiate NAFTA, and doing so could result in greater barriers to trade among the United States, Mexico, and Canada.

Exports Goods and services produced domestically and sold in other countries.

The Importance of Trade to the U.S. Economy

U.S. consumers are buying increasing quantities of goods and services produced in other countries. At the same time, U.S. businesses are selling increasing quantities of goods and services to consumers in other countries. Figure 9.1 shows that since 1970, both exports and imports have tended to increase as a fraction of U.S. gross domestic product (GDP). GDP is the value of all the final goods and services produced in a country during a year. World trade declined sharply during the severe worldwide recession of 2007–2009 and has grown relatively slowly since that time. The slowdown in trade seems to have been caused by slower income growth in some countries, including China, Brazil, and many countries in Europe, combined with some firms deciding to produce fewer of their products in foreign countries. In the United States, imports and exports have been growing more slowly than GDP in the past few years. Despite this slowdown, exports and imports increased from being less than 6 percent of U.S. GDP in 1970 to being more than 12 percent in 2016.

Not all sectors of the U.S. economy are affected equally by international trade. For example, although it's difficult to import or export some services, such as haircuts and appendectomies, a large percentage of U.S. agricultural production is exported. Each year, the United States exports about 50 percent of its wheat and rice crops and 20 percent of its corn crop.

Many U.S. manufacturing industries also depend on trade. About 20 percent of U.S. manufacturing jobs depend directly or indirectly on exports. In some industries, such as pharmaceutical drugs, output is directly exported. In other industries, such as steel, output is used to make other products, such as bulldozers or machine tools, that are then exported. In all, about two-thirds of U.S. manufacturing industries depend on exports for at least 10 percent of jobs.   **MyLab Economics** Concept Check

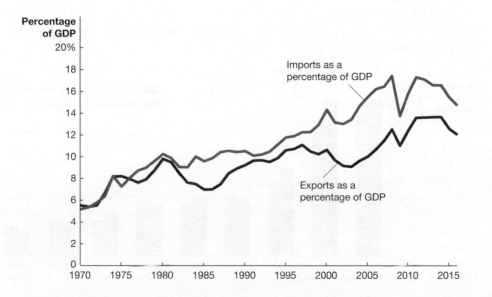

MyLab Economics Real-time data

Figure 9.1

The Increasing Importance of International Trade to the United States

Exports and imports of goods and services as a percentage of total production—measured by GDP—show the importance of international trade to an economy. In 2016, both imports and exports were much larger fractions of U.S. GDP than they were in 1970.

Source: U.S. Department of Commerce, Bureau of Economic Analysis.

Figure 9.2

The Eight Leading Exporting Countries

China is the leading exporting country, accounting for 12.1 percent of total world exports. The United States is second, with a 10.3 percent share. The values are the shares of total world exports of merchandise and commercial services.

Source: World Trade Organization, *International Trade Statistics*, 2016.

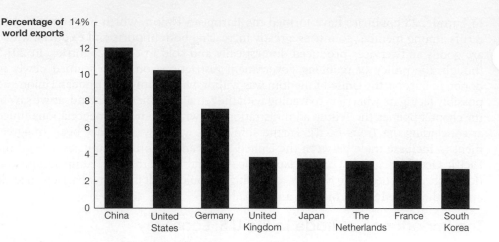

U.S. International Trade in a World Context

The United States is the second-largest exporter in the world, just behind China, as Figure 9.2 illustrates. Six of the other seven leading exporting countries are also high-income countries. Although China is still a relatively low-income country, the rapid growth of the Chinese economy over the past 35 years has resulted in its becoming the largest exporter. Three of the top exporting countries are in East Asia, four are in Western Europe, and one is in North America.

Figure 9.3 shows that international trade is less important to the United States than it is to many other countries, with imports and exports being lower percentages of GDP. In some smaller countries, such as Belgium and the Netherlands, imports and exports make up more than half of GDP. In the larger European economies, imports and exports make up one-quarter to one-half of GDP.

9.2 Comparative Advantage in International Trade

LEARNING OBJECTIVE: Explain the difference between comparative advantage and absolute advantage in international trade.

Why have businesses around the world increasingly looked for markets in other countries? Why have consumers increasingly purchased goods and services made in other countries? People trade for one reason: Trade makes them better off. Whenever a buyer and seller agree to a sale, they must both believe they are better off; otherwise, there would be no sale. This outcome must hold whether the buyer and seller live in the same city or in different countries. As we will see, governments are more likely to interfere with international trade than they are with domestic trade, but the reasons for the interference are more political than economic.

Figure 9.3

International Trade as a Percentage of GDP

International trade is still less important to the United States than it is to most other countries.

Source: Organization for Economic Co-operation and Development, *Country Statistical Profiles*, April 2017.

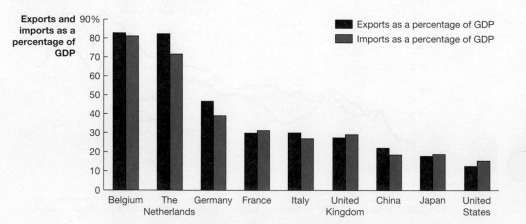

A Brief Review of Comparative Advantage

Recall that **comparative advantage** is the ability of an individual, a firm, or a country to produce a good or service at a lower opportunity cost than competitors. **Opportunity cost** is the highest-valued alternative that must be given up to engage in an activity. People, firms, and countries specialize in economic activities in which they have a comparative advantage. In trading, we benefit from the comparative advantage of other people (or firms or countries), and they benefit from our comparative advantage.

A good way to think of comparative advantage is to recall the example of you and your neighbor picking fruit (see Chapter 2, Section 2.2). Your neighbor is better at picking both apples and cherries than you are. Why, then, doesn't your neighbor pick both types of fruit? Because the opportunity cost to your neighbor of picking her own apples is very high: She is a particularly skilled cherry picker, and every hour spent picking apples is an hour taken away from picking cherries. You can pick apples at a much lower opportunity cost than your neighbor, so you have a comparative advantage in picking apples. Your neighbor can pick cherries at a much lower opportunity cost than you can, so she has a comparative advantage in picking cherries. Your neighbor is better off specializing in picking cherries, and you are better off specializing in picking apples. You can then trade some of your apples for some of your neighbor's cherries, and both of you will end up with more of each fruit. (If you have trouble following the point here, refer to Chapter 2, Tables 2.1 and 2.2.)   MyLab Economics Concept Check

> **Comparative advantage** The ability of an individual, a firm, or a country to produce a good or service at a lower opportunity cost than competitors.
>
> **Opportunity cost** The highest-valued alternative that must be given up to engage in an activity.

Comparative Advantage and Absolute Advantage

The principle of comparative advantage can explain why people pursue different occupations. It can also explain why countries produce different goods and services. International trade involves many countries importing and exporting many different goods and services. Countries are better off if they specialize in producing the goods for which they have a comparative advantage. They can then trade for the goods for which other countries have a comparative advantage.

We can illustrate why specializing on the basis of comparative advantage makes countries better off with a simple example involving just two countries and two products. Suppose the United States and China produce only smartphones and wheat. Assume that each country uses only labor to produce each good and that there are no differences between Chinese and U.S. smartphones or between Chinese and U.S. wheat. Table 9.1 shows how much each country can produce of each good with one hour of labor.

Notice that Chinese workers are more productive than U.S. workers in making both goods. In one hour, Chinese workers can produce six times as many smartphones and one and one-half times as many bushels of wheat as U.S. workers. China has an *absolute advantage* over the United States in producing both goods. **Absolute advantage** is the ability to produce more of a good or service than competitors when using the same amount of resources. In this case, China can produce more of both goods using the same amount of labor as the United States.

It might seem at first that China has nothing to gain from trading with the United States because it has an absolute advantage in producing both goods. However, China is better off specializing in producing only smartphones and obtaining the wheat it needs by exporting smartphones to the United States in exchange for wheat. The reason China benefits from trade is that although it has an *absolute advantage* in the production of both goods, it has a *comparative advantage* only in the production of smartphones. The United States has a comparative advantage in the production of wheat.

> **Absolute advantage** The ability to produce more of a good or service than competitors when using the same amount of resources.

	Output per Hour of Work	
	Smartphones	Wheat (bushels)
China	12	6
United States	2	4

Table 9.1

An Example of Chinese Workers Being More Productive Than U.S. Workers

Table 9.2

The Opportunity Costs of Producing Smartphones and Wheat

The table shows the opportunity cost each country faces in producing smartphones and wheat. For example, the first entry in the "Wheat" column shows that China must give up 2 smartphones for every bushel of wheat it produces.

	Opportunity Costs	
	Smartphones	**Wheat (bushels)**
China	0.5 bushel of wheat	2 smartphones
United States	2 bushels of wheat	0.5 smartphone

If it seems contrary to common sense that China should import wheat from the United States even though China can produce more wheat per hour of labor, think about the opportunity cost to each country of producing each good. If China wants to produce more wheat, it has to switch labor away from smartphone production. Every hour of labor switched from producing smartphones to producing wheat reduces smartphone production by 12 and increases wheat production by 6 bushels. China has to give up 12 smartphones for every 6 bushels of wheat it produces. Therefore, the opportunity cost to China of producing 1 more bushel of wheat is 12/6, or 2 smartphones.

If the United States switches one hour of labor from smartphones to wheat, production of smartphones falls by 2, and production of wheat rises by 4 bushels. Therefore, the opportunity cost to the United States of producing 1 more bushel of wheat is 2/4, or 0.5 smartphone. The United States has a lower opportunity cost of producing wheat and, therefore, has a comparative advantage in making this product. By similar reasoning, we can see that China has a comparative advantage in producing smartphones. Table 9.2 summarizes the opportunity cost each country faces in producing these goods.

MyLab Economics Study Plan

MyLab Economics Concept Check

 9.3 ## How Countries Gain from International Trade

LEARNING OBJECTIVE: Explain how countries gain from international trade.

Can China really gain from producing only smartphones and trading with the United States for wheat? To see that it can, assume at first that China and the United States do not trade with each other. A situation in which a country does not trade with other countries is called **autarky**. Assume that in autarky, each country has 1,000 hours of labor available to produce the two goods, and each country produces the quantities of the two goods shown in Table 9.3. Because there is no trade, these quantities also represent consumption of the two goods in each country.

Autarky A situation in which a country does not trade with other countries.

Increasing Consumption through Trade

Suppose now that China and the United States begin to trade with each other. The **terms of trade** is the ratio at which a country can trade its exports for imports from other countries. For simplicity, let's assume that the terms of trade end up with China and the United States being willing to trade one smartphone for one bushel of wheat, even though we know that in reality the price of a smartphone is much higher than the price of a bushel of wheat.

Terms of trade The ratio at which a country can trade its exports for imports from other countries.

Once trade has begun, the United States and China can exchange wheat for smartphones or smartphones for wheat. For example, if China specializes by using all 1,000 available hours of labor to produce smartphones, it will be able to produce 12,000

Table 9.3

Production without Trade

	Production and Consumption	
	Smartphones	**Wheat (bushels)**
China	9,000	1,500
United States	1,500	1,000

Without Trade

Production and Consumption

	Smartphones	Wheat
China	9,000	1,500
United States	1,500	1,000

MyLab Economics Animation

Table 9.4

Gains from Trade for China and the United States

With Trade

	Production with Trade		Trade		Consumption with Trade	
	Smartphones	Wheat	Smartphones	Wheat	Smartphones	Wheat
China	12,000	0	Export 1,500	Import 1,500	10,500	1,500
United States	0	4,000	Import 1,500	Export 1,500	1,500	2,500

With trade, the United States and China specialize in the good they have a comparative advantage in producing . . .

. . . and export some of that good in exchange for the good the other country has a comparative advantage in producing.

Gains from Trade

Increased Consumption

China	1,500 Smartphones
United States	1,500 Bushels of wheat

The increased consumption made possible by trade represents the gains from trade.

smartphones. It could then export 1,500 smartphones to the United States in exchange for 1,500 bushels of wheat. (Remember that we are assuming the terms of trade are 1 smartphone for 1 bushel of wheat.) China ends up with 10,500 smartphones and 1,500 bushels of wheat. Compared with the situation before trade, China has the same number of bushels of wheat but 1,500 more smartphones. If the United States specializes in producing wheat, it will be able to produce 4,000 bushels of wheat. It could then export 1,500 bushels of wheat to China in exchange for 1,500 smartphones. The United States ends up with 2,500 bushels of wheat and 1,500 smartphones. Compared with the situation before trade, the United States has the same number of smartphones but 1,500 more bushels of wheat. Trade has allowed both countries to increase the quantities of goods consumed. Table 9.4 summarizes the gains from trade for the United States and China.

By trading, China and the United States are able to consume more than they could without trade. This outcome is possible because world production of both goods increases after trade. (In this example, our "world" consists of just the United States and China.)

Why does total production of smartphones and wheat increase when China specializes in producing smartphones and the United States specializes in producing wheat? A domestic analogy helps answer this question: If a company shifts production from an old factory to a more efficient modern factory, its output will increase. Similarly, if a farmer shifts from growing wheat on land that is suffering from soil exhaustion to land that is fertile, the farmer's wheat output will increase. The same thing happens in our example. Producing wheat in China and smartphones in the United States is inefficient. Shifting production to the more efficient country—the one with the comparative advantage—increases total production. The key point is: *Countries gain from specializing in producing goods in which they have a comparative advantage and trading for goods in which other countries have a comparative advantage.*

MyLab Economics Concept Check

Solved Problem 9.3

The Gains from Trade

The first discussion of comparative advantage appears in *On the Principles of Political Economy and Taxation*, a book written by the British economist David Ricardo in 1817. Ricardo provided a famous example of the gains from trade, using wine and cloth production in Portugal and England. The following table is adapted from Ricardo's example, with cloth measured in sheets and wine measured in kegs:

	Output per Year of Labor	
	Cloth	Wine
Portugal	100	150
England	90	60

a. Explain which country has an absolute advantage in the production of each good.

b. Explain which country has a comparative advantage in the production of each good.

c. Suppose that Portugal and England currently do not trade with each other. Each country has 1,000 workers, so each has 1,000 years of labor time to use in producing cloth and wine, and the countries are currently producing the amounts of each good shown in the following table:

	Cloth	Wine
Portugal	18,000	123,000
England	63,000	18,000

Show that Portugal and England can both gain from trade. Assume that the terms of trade are that one sheet of cloth can be traded for one keg of wine.

Solving the Problem

Step 1: Review the chapter material. This problem is about absolute and comparative advantage and the gains from trade, so you may want to review the sections "Comparative Advantage in International Trade," which begins on page 292, and "How Countries Gain from International Trade," which begins on page 294.

Step 2: Answer part (a) by determining which country has an absolute advantage. Remember that a country has an absolute advantage over another country when it can produce more of a good using the same resources. The first table in the problem shows that Portugal can produce more cloth *and* more wine with 1 year's worth of labor than can England. Therefore, Portugal has an absolute advantage in the production of both goods, and England does not have an absolute advantage in the production of either good.

Step 3: Answer part (b) by determining which country has a comparative advantage. A country has a comparative advantage when it can produce a good at a lower opportunity cost. To produce 100 sheets of cloth, Portugal must give up producing 150 kegs of wine. Therefore, Portugal's opportunity cost of producing 1 sheet of cloth is 150/100, or 1.5 kegs of wine. England has to give up producing 60 kegs of wine to produce 90 sheets of cloth, so its opportunity cost of producing 1 sheet of cloth is 60/90, or 0.67 keg of wine. The opportunity costs of producing wine can be calculated in the same way. The following table shows the opportunity cost to Portugal and England of producing each good.

	Opportunity Costs	
	Cloth	Wine
Portugal	1.5 kegs of wine	0.67 sheet of cloth
England	0.67 keg of wine	1.5 sheets of cloth

Portugal has a comparative advantage in wine because its opportunity cost is lower. England has a comparative advantage in cloth because its opportunity cost is lower.

Step 4: Answer part (c) by showing that both countries can benefit from trade. By now it should be clear that both countries will be better off if they specialize in producing the good for which they have a comparative advantage and trade for the other good. The following table is very similar to Table 9.4 and shows one example of trade making both countries better off. (To test your understanding, construct another example.)

Without Trade	Production and Consumption	
	Cloth	Wine
Portugal	18,000	123,000
England	63,000	18,000

With Trade	Production with Trade		Trade		Consumption with Trade	
	Cloth	Wine	Cloth	Wine	Cloth	Wine
Portugal	0	150,000	Import 18,000	Export 18,000	18,000	132,000
England	90,000	0	Export 18,000	Import 18,000	72,000	18,000

Gains from Trade	Increased Consumption
Portugal	9,000 wine
England	9,000 cloth

Your Turn: For more practice, do related problems 3.5 and 3.6 on page 317 at the end of this chapter.

MyI ab Economics Study Plan

Why Don't We See Complete Specialization?

In our example of two countries producing only two products, each country specializes in producing one of the goods. In the real world, many goods and services are produced in more than one country. For example, the United States, Japan, Germany, China, Canada, Mexico, India, and other countries produce automobiles. We do not see complete specialization in the real world for three main reasons:

1. **Not all goods and services are traded internationally.** For example, even if Japan had a comparative advantage in the production of medical services, it would be difficult for it to specialize in producing medical services and then export them. There is no easy way for U.S. patients who need appendectomies to receive them from surgeons in Japan.

2. **Production of most goods involves increasing opportunity costs.** Recall that production of most goods involves increasing opportunity costs (see Chapter 2, Section 2.1). Although we didn't include this fact in our example, if the United States devotes more workers to producing wheat, the opportunity cost of producing more wheat will increase. At some point, the opportunity cost of producing wheat in the United States may rise to the level of the opportunity cost of producing wheat in China. When that happens, international trade will no longer push the United States further toward specialization. The same will be true of China: The increasing opportunity cost of producing smartphones will cause China to stop short of complete specialization.

3. **Tastes for products differ.** Most products are *differentiated*. Smartphones, laptops, cars, and televisions—to name just a few products—have a variety of features. When buying automobiles, some people look for reliability and fuel efficiency, others look for room to carry seven passengers, and still others want styling and high performance. So, some car buyers prefer Toyota Prius hybrids, and some prefer Chevy Suburbans, and others prefer BMWs. As a result, Japan, the United States, and Germany may each have a comparative advantage in producing different types of automobiles.   MyLab Economics Concept Check

Does Anyone Lose as a Result of International Trade?

In our smartphone and wheat example, consumption increases in both the United States and China as a result of trade. Everyone gains, and no one loses. Or do they? In our example, we referred repeatedly to "China" or the "United States" producing smartphones or wheat. But countries do not produce goods—firms do. In a world without trade, there would be smartphone firms and wheat farms in both China and the United States. In a world with trade, there would be only Chinese smartphone firms and U.S. wheat farms. Chinese wheat farms and U.S. smartphone firms would be competed out of business. Overall, total employment would not change, and production would increase as a result of trade. Nevertheless, the owners of Chinese wheat farms, the owners of U.S. smartphone firms, and the people who work for them are worse off as a result of trade. The losers from trade are likely to try to persuade the Chinese and U.S. governments to interfere with trade by barring imports of the competing products from the other country or by imposing high tariffs on them.   MyLab Economics Concept Check

Don't Let This Happen to You

Remember That Trade Creates Both Winners and Losers

The following statement is from a Federal Reserve publication: "Trade is a win–win situation for all countries that participate." People sometimes interpret statements like this to mean that there are no losers from international trade. But notice that the statement refers to *countries*, not individuals. When countries participate in trade, they make their consumers better off by increasing the quantity of goods and services available to them.

As we have seen, however, expanding trade eliminates the jobs of workers employed at companies that are less efficient than foreign companies. Trade also creates new jobs at companies that export products to foreign markets. But it may be difficult for workers who lose their jobs because of trade to easily

find others. That is why in the United States the federal government uses the *Trade Adjustment Assistance (TAA)* program to provide funds for workers who have lost their jobs due to international trade. Qualified unemployed workers can use these funds to pay for retraining, searching for new jobs, or relocating to areas where new jobs are available. This program—and similar programs in other countries—recognizes that there are losers from international trade as well as winners.

Source: Federal Reserve Bank of Dallas, "International Trade and the Economy," www.dallasfed.org/educate/everyday/ev7.html.

MyLab Economics Study Plan

Your Turn: Test your understanding by doing related problem 3.11 on page 318 at the end of this chapter.

Apply the Concept   MyLab Economics Video

Who Gains and Who Loses from U.S. Trade with China?

Early in his administration, President Donald Trump criticized what he saw as unbalanced trade between the United States and China and warned, "We can no longer have massive trade deficits . . . and job losses." From Mao Zedong's founding of the People's Republic of China in 1949 until the mid-1970s, China was a centrally planned economy that rejected free markets and had very little trade with the United States. Beginning in the 1970s, when Deng Xiaoping succeeded Mao as leader of China, the government adopted market-based reforms of the economy and began exporting significant quantities of goods to the United States and other countries. This process accelerated after China became a member of the World Trade Organization (WTO) in 2001, which gave it greater access to world markets.

The following figure shows the growth since 2000 in U.S. imports from China and U.S. exports to China. While U.S. exports of goods to China were more than four times higher in 2016 than in 2000, the dollar increase in U.S. imports of goods from China was much larger. As a result, the gap between U.S. imports of goods from China and exports to China (the U.S. trade deficit with China) had swelled to nearly $300 billion. Some economists and policymakers have labeled the surge in Chinese imports beginning in 2001 the *China shock*.

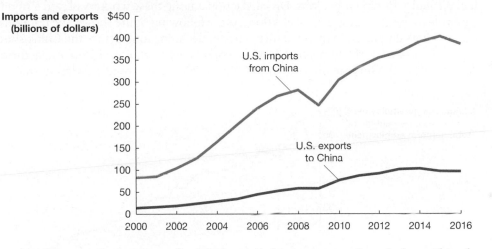

The following figure shows the distribution of U.S. imports of goods from China by broad product categories. Many of the products the United States currently imports from China were at one time manufactured in the United States. Chinese firms were able to win a large share of these markets typically by offering goods at lower prices than U.S. firms (or firms in other foreign countries that were also competing in the U.S. market). These lower prices have benefited U.S. consumers. Lower-income consumers in particular have benefitted from the low prices of textile products, such as clothing, sheets, and towels. Smartphones and other consumer electronics products would have much higher prices if they were assembled in the United States rather than in China and other foreign countries. (However, as we saw in the *Apply the Concept* in Chapter 2, page 57, U.S. firms have been able to produce some components of iPads and other consumer electronics.)

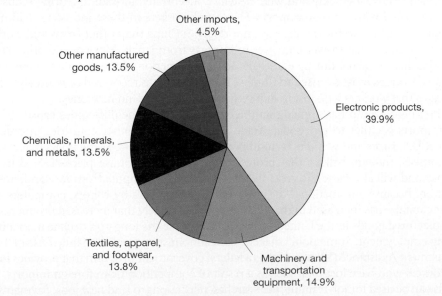

Because consumers pay lower prices for goods imported from China, they have more of their income available to spend on other goods and services produced in the United States. A family that buys low-price Chinese-made clothes at Walmart can more easily afford to dine out at the local Red Lobster restaurant or to buy fresh fruits and vegetables grown at local farms. In this sense, the losses suffered by U.S. firms (and their workers) that have been forced out of business by Chinese competitors have resulted in gains to other U.S. firms (and their workers).

But David Autor of the Massachusetts Institute of Technology and other economists studying the effects of the China shock on the U.S. economy point out that the firms most hurt by Chinese imports have been concentrated in certain states, particularly in the Midwest and Southeast. As noted in the chapter opener, some cities in these areas have been devastated as local manufacturing plants have closed and workers have had difficulty finding other jobs. Dissatisfaction among these workers played a significant role in the 2016 presidential election. As the following figure shows, the fraction of U.S. workers employed in manufacturing began declining long before the China shock began. In 1944, nearly 38 percent of U.S. workers were employed in manufacturing. At the start of the surge in imports from China in 2001, only about 12 percent were.

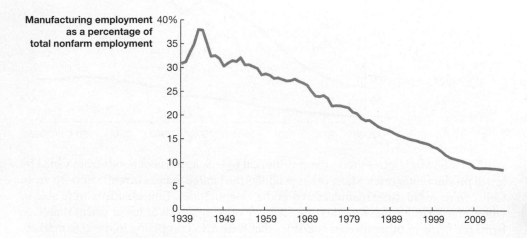

Autor, David Dorn of the University of Zurich, and Gordon Hanson of the University of California, San Diego estimate that between 1999 and 2011, the China shock resulted in the loss of 2.4 million jobs and may have accounted for 25 percent of the decline in manufacturing jobs during those years. Although total employment in the United States increased by substantially more than this amount over the same period, the job losses happened relatively quickly and were heavily concentrated in manufacturing industries that competed with Chinese imports. Firms and workers in these industries had more difficulty adjusting to the increase in imports from China than other firms and workers had to the somewhat slower increases in imports from Japan, Mexico, and other countries that had occurred during earlier decades. The fraction of the population employed declined in areas most exposed to Chinese imports and has recovered only slowly, which indicates that workers who lost their jobs have struggled to find new ones.

President Trump has argued that the best response to the difficulties caused by rising imports is either to renegotiate trade agreements with other countries in order to protect U.S. firms and workers or to impose tariffs on imports. Some policymakers and economists, though, believe that protecting U.S. firms will raise prices U.S. consumers pay and will also raise the costs to U.S. firms that buy inputs from foreign firms. In addition, because automation—the replacement of workers by robots, computers, and other capital—has increased in manufacturing, it is unlikely that increased production of manufactured goods in the United States would reverse the long-run decline in manufacturing employment. Some policymakers and economists support expanded use of Trade Adjustment Assistance (TAA), which is a federal government program that provides funds to workers who have lost their jobs as a result of competition from foreign imports. The funds can be used for job training, job searches, relocations to find new jobs, payments for health insurance, and replacement of lost wages. But studies by the Department of Labor, which administers the program, indicate that significant numbers of workers who lost their jobs as a result of the China shock had not found new jobs paying comparable wages by the time their TAA benefits had run out, which is typically two years.

The effects of the China surge have led policymakers and economists to reassess the balance between winners and losers from international trade and to consider whether current policies to help the losers are adequate.

Sources: Chun Han Wong, "China Digs in on Trade as Trump Warns of 'Very Difficult' Summit," *Wall Street Journal*, March 31, 2017; Bob Davis and Jon Hilsenrath, "How the China Shock, Deep and Swift, Fueled the Rise of Trump," *Wall Street Journal*, August 11, 2016; David H. Autor, David Dorn, and Gordon H. Hanson, "The China Shock: Learning from Labor-Market Adjustment to Large Changes in Trade," *Annual Review of Economics*, Vol. 8, 2016, pp. 205–240; David H. Autor, David Dorn, and Gordon H. Hanson, "The China Syndrome: Local Labor Market Effects of Import Competition in the United States," *American Economic Review*, Vol. 103, No. 6, October 2013, pp. 2121–2168; and data from the U.S. International Trade Commission and from the Federal Reserve Bank of St. Louis.

Your Turn: Test your understanding by doing related problems 3.12 and 3.13 on page 318 at the end of this chapter.

MyLab Economics Study Plan

Where Does Comparative Advantage Come From?

Among the main sources of comparative advantage are the following:

- **Climate and natural resources.** This source of comparative advantage is the most obvious. Because of geology, Saudi Arabia has a comparative advantage in the production of oil. Because of climate and soil conditions, Costa Rica has a comparative advantage in the production of bananas, and the United States has a comparative advantage in the production of wheat.

- **Relative abundance of labor and capital.** Some countries, such as the United States, have many highly skilled workers and a great deal of machinery. Other countries, such as China, have many unskilled workers and relatively little machinery. As a result, the United States has a comparative advantage in the production of goods that require highly skilled workers or sophisticated machinery, such as aircraft and computer software. China has a comparative advantage in the production of goods, such as furniture, clothing, and children's toys, that require unskilled workers and small amounts of simple machinery. In fact, many economists believe that the surge in Chinese imports to the United States and other countries following China's admittance to the World Trade Organization (WTO) was fueled by the low cost of producing manufactured goods using low-wage, unskilled workers. These workers had become available to manufacturing firms after economic reforms allowed large numbers of workers to leave unproductive collective farms and state-owned companies for higher-paid factory work.

- **Technology.** Broadly defined, *technology* is the processes firms use to turn inputs into goods and services. At any given time, firms in different countries do not all have access to the same technologies. In part, this difference is a result of past investments countries have made in higher education or in supporting research and development. Some countries are strong in *product technologies*, which involve the ability to develop new products. For example, firms in the United States have pioneered the development of such products as radios, televisions, digital computers, airliners, medical equipment, and many prescription drugs. Other countries are strong in *process technologies*, which involve the ability to improve the processes used to make existing products. For example, Japanese-based firms, such as Toyota and Honda, have succeeded by greatly improving the processes for designing and manufacturing automobiles.

- **External economies.** It is difficult to explain the location of some industries on the basis of climate, natural resources, the relative abundance of labor and capital, or technology. For example, why does southern California have a comparative advantage in making movies or Switzerland in making watches or New York in providing financial services? The answer is that once an industry becomes established in an area, firms located in that area gain advantages over firms located elsewhere. The advantages include the availability of skilled workers, the opportunity to interact with other firms in the same industry, and proximity to suppliers. These advantages result in lower costs to firms located in the area. Because these lower costs result from increases in the size of the industry in an area, economists refer to them as **external economies**.

External economies Reductions in a firm's costs that result from an increase in the size of an industry.

MyLab Economics Concept Check   MyLab Economics Study Plan

Government Policies That Restrict International Trade

9.4

LEARNING OBJECTIVE: Analyze the economic effects of government policies that restrict international trade.

Free trade Trade between countries that is without government restrictions.

Free trade, or trade between countries without government restrictions, makes consumers better off. We can expand on this idea by using the concepts of consumer surplus and producer surplus (see Chapter 4, Section 4.1). Figure 9.4 shows the market in the United States for the biofuel ethanol, which can be used as a substitute for gasoline. The figure shows the situation of autarky, where the United States does not trade with other countries. The equilibrium price of ethanol is $2.00 per gallon, and the equilibrium quantity is 6.0 billion gallons per year. The blue area represents consumer surplus, and the red area represents producer surplus.

Now suppose that the United States begins importing ethanol from Brazil and other countries that produce ethanol for $1.00 per gallon. Because the world market for ethanol is large, we will assume that the United States can buy as much ethanol as it wants without causing the *world price* of $1.00 per gallon to rise. Therefore, once imports of ethanol are allowed into the United States, U.S. firms will not be able to sell ethanol at prices higher than the world price of $1.00, and the U.S. price will become equal to the world price.

Figure 9.5 shows the result of allowing imports of ethanol into the United States. With the price lowered from $2.00 to $1.00, U.S. consumers increase their purchases from 6.0 billion gallons to 9.0 billion gallons. Equilibrium moves from point *F* to point *G*. In the new equilibrium, U.S. producers have reduced the quantity of ethanol they supply from 6.0 billion gallons to 3.0 billion gallons. Imports will equal 6.0 billion gallons, which is the difference between U.S. consumption and U.S. production.

Under autarky, consumer surplus would be area *A* in Figure 9.5. With imports, the reduction in price increases consumer surplus, so it is now equal to the sum of areas *A*, *B*, *C*, and *D*. Although the lower price increases consumer surplus, it reduces producer surplus. Under autarky, producer surplus was equal to the sum of areas *B* and *E*. With imports, it is equal to only area *E*. Recall that economic surplus equals the sum of consumer surplus and producer surplus. Moving from autarky to allowing imports increases economic surplus in the United States by an amount equal to the sum of areas *C* and *D*.

MyLab Economics Animation

Figure 9.4

The U.S. Market for Ethanol under Autarky

This figure shows the market for ethanol in the United States, assuming autarky, where the United States does not trade with other countries. The equilibrium price of ethanol is $2.00 per gallon, and the equilibrium quantity is 6.0 billion gallons per year. The blue area represents consumer surplus, and the red area represents producer surplus.

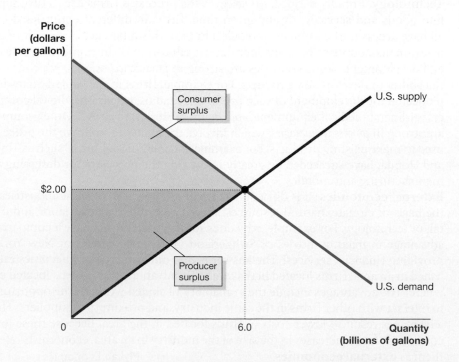

	Under Autarky	With Imports
Consumer Surplus	A	A + B + C + D
Producer Surplus	B + E	E
Economic Surplus	A + B + E	A + B + C + D + E

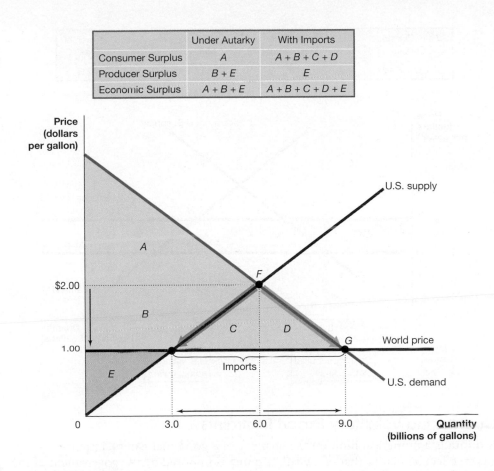

MyLab Economics Animation

Figure 9.5

The Effect of Imports on the U.S. Ethanol Market

When imports are allowed into the United States, the price of ethanol falls from $2.00 to $1.00. U.S. consumers increase their purchases from 6.0 billion gallons to 9.0 billion gallons. Equilibrium moves from point F to point G. U.S. producers reduce the quantity of ethanol they supply from 6.0 billion gallons to 3.0 billion gallons. Imports equal 6.0 billion gallons, which is the difference between U.S. consumption and U.S. production. Consumer surplus equals the sum of areas A, B, C, and D. Producer surplus equals the area E.

We can conclude that international trade helps consumers but hurts firms that are less efficient than foreign competitors. As a result, these firms and their workers are often strong supporters of government policies that restrict trade. These policies usually take one of two forms: (1) *tariffs* or (2) *quotas* and *voluntary export restraints*.

Tariffs

The most common interferences with trade are *tariffs*, which are taxes imposed by a government on goods imported into the country. Like any other tax, a tariff increases the cost of selling a good. Figure 9.6 shows the effect of a tariff of $0.50 per gallon on ethanol imports into the United States. The $0.50 tariff raises the price of ethanol in the United States from the world price of $1.00 per gallon to $1.50 per gallon. At this higher price, U.S. ethanol producers increase the quantity they supply from 3.0 billion gallons to 4.5 billion gallons. U.S. consumers, though, cut back their purchases of ethanol from 9.0 billion gallons to 7.5 billion gallons. Imports decline from 6.0 billion gallons (9.0 billion − 3.0 billion) to 3.0 billion gallons (7.5 billion − 4.5 billion). Equilibrium moves from point G to point H.

By raising the price of ethanol from $1.00 to $1.50, the tariff reduces consumer surplus by the sum of areas A, T, C, and D. Area A is the increase in producer surplus from the higher price. The government collects tariff revenue equal to the tariff of $0.50 per gallon multiplied by the 3.0 billion gallons imported. Area T represents the government's tariff revenue. Areas C and D represent losses to U.S. consumers that are not captured by anyone. These areas are deadweight loss and represent the decline in economic efficiency resulting from the ethanol tariff. Area C shows the effect of U.S. consumers being forced to buy from U.S. producers that are less efficient than foreign producers, and area D shows the effect of U.S. consumers buying less ethanol than they would have at the world price. As a result of the tariff, economic surplus has been reduced by the sum of areas C and D.

We can conclude that the tariff succeeds in helping U.S. ethanol producers but hurts U.S. consumers and the efficiency of the U.S. economy.   **MyLab Economics** Concept Check

Figure 9.6

The Effects of a Tariff on Ethanol

Without a tariff on ethanol, U.S. producers will sell 3.0 billion gallons of ethanol, U.S. consumers will purchase 9.0 billion gallons, and imports will be 6.0 billion gallons. The U.S. price will equal the world price of $1.00 per gallon. The $0.50-per-gallon tariff raises the price of ethanol in the United States to $1.50 per gallon, and U.S. producers increase the quantity they supply to 4.5 billion gallons. U.S. consumers reduce their purchases to 7.5 billion gallons. Equilibrium moves from point G to point H. The ethanol tariff causes a loss of consumer surplus equal to the area $A + C + T + D$. The area A is the increase in producer surplus due to the higher price. The area T is the government's tariff revenue. The areas C and D represent deadweight loss.

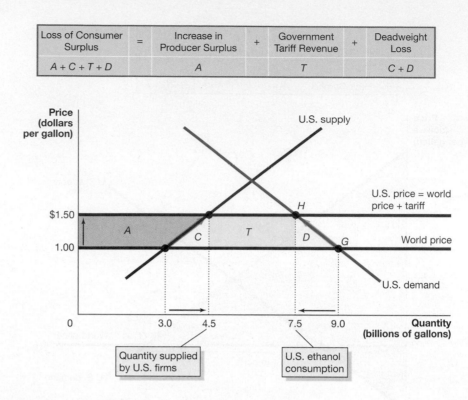

Loss of Consumer Surplus	=	Increase in Producer Surplus	+	Government Tariff Revenue	+	Deadweight Loss
$A + C + T + D$		A		T		$C + D$

Quota A numerical limit a government imposes on the quantity of a good that can be imported into the country.

Voluntary export restraint (VER) An agreement negotiated between two countries that places a numerical limit on the quantity of a good that can be imported by one country from the other country.

Quotas and Voluntary Export Restraints

A **quota** is a numerical limit on the quantity of a good that can be imported, and it has an effect similar to that of a tariff. A quota is imposed by the government of the importing country. A **voluntary export restraint (VER)** is an agreement negotiated between two countries that places a numerical limit on the quantity of a good that can be imported by one country from the other country. In the 1980s, the United States and Japan negotiated a VER that limited the quantity of automobiles the United States would import from Japan. The Japanese government agreed to the VER primarily because it was afraid that if it did not, the United States would impose a tariff or quota on imports of Japanese automobiles. Quotas and VERs have similar economic effects.

The main purpose of most tariffs and quotas is to reduce the foreign competition that domestic firms face. For many years, Congress has imposed a quota on sugar imports to protect U.S. sugar producers. Figure 9.7 shows the actual statistics for the U.S. sugar market in 2016. The effect of a quota is very similar to the effect of a tariff. By limiting imports, a quota forces the domestic price of a good above the world price. In this case, the sugar quota limits sugar imports to 6.7 billion pounds per year (shown by the bracket in Figure 9.7), forcing the U.S. price of sugar up to $0.28 per pound, or $0.10 higher than the world price of $0.18 per pound. The U.S. price is above the world price because the quota keeps foreign sugar producers from selling the additional sugar in the United States that would drive the U.S. price down to the world price. At a price of $0.28 per pound, U.S. producers increase the quantity of sugar they supply from the 9.6 billion pounds they would supply at the world price to 18.0 billion pounds, and U.S. consumers cut back their purchases of sugar from the 27.0 billion pounds they would purchase at the world price to the 24.7 billion pounds they are willing to purchase at the higher U.S. price. If there were no import quota, equilibrium would be at the world price (point E), but with the quota, equilibrium is at the U.S. price (point F). **MyLab Economics** Concept Check

Measuring the Economic Effect of the Sugar Quota

We can use the concepts of consumer surplus, producer surplus, and deadweight loss to measure the economic impact of the sugar quota. Without a sugar quota, the world price of $0.18 per pound would also be the U.S. price. In Figure 9.7, without a sugar quota, consumer surplus would equal the area above the $0.18 price line and below

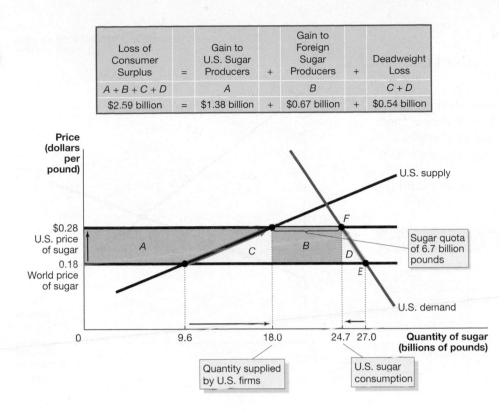

Loss of Consumer Surplus	=	Gain to U.S. Sugar Producers	+	Gain to Foreign Sugar Producers	+	Deadweight Loss
$A + B + C + D$	=	A	+	B	+	$C + D$
$2.59 billion	=	$1.38 billion	+	$0.67 billion	+	$0.54 billion

Price (dollars per pound)

$0.28 U.S. price of sugar

0.18 World price of sugar

U.S. supply

F

Sugar quota of 6.7 billion pounds

A C B D

E

U.S. demand

9.6   18.0   24.7 27.0   **Quantity of sugar (billions of pounds)**

Quantity supplied by U.S. firms

U.S. sugar consumption

MyLab Economics Animation

Figure 9.7

The Economic Effect of the U.S. Sugar Quota

Without a sugar quota, U.S. sugar producers would have sold 9.6 billion pounds of sugar, U.S. consumers would have purchased 27.0 billion pounds of sugar, and imports would have been 17.4 billion pounds. The U.S. price would have equaled the world price of $0.18 per pound. Because the sugar quota limits imports to 6.7 billion pounds (the bracket in the graph), the price of sugar in the United States rises to $0.28 per pound, and U.S. producers supply 18.0 billion pounds. U.S. consumers purchase 24.7 billion pounds rather than the 27.0 billion pounds they would purchase at the world price. Without the import quota, equilibrium would be at point E; with the quota, equilibrium is at point F. The sugar quota causes a loss of consumer surplus equal to the area $A + B + C + D$. The area A is the gain to U.S. sugar producers. The area B is the gain to foreign sugar producers. The areas C and D represent deadweight loss. The total loss to U.S. consumers in 2016 was $2.59 billion.

Note: The quota amount shown in the figure includes some imports outside the quota, including imports from Mexico.

the demand curve. The sugar quota causes the U.S. price to rise to $0.28 and reduces consumer surplus by the area $A + B + C + D$. Without a sugar quota, producer surplus received by U.S. sugar producers would be equal to the area below the $0.18 price line and above the supply curve. The higher U.S. price resulting from the sugar quota increases the producer surplus of U.S. sugar producers by an amount equal to area A.

A foreign producer must have a license from the U.S. government to import sugar under the quota system. Therefore, a foreign sugar producer that is lucky enough to have an import license also benefits from the quota because it is able to sell sugar in the U.S. market at $0.28 per pound instead of $0.18 per pound. Area B is the gain to foreign sugar producers. Areas A and B represent transfers from U.S. consumers of sugar to U.S. and foreign producers of sugar. Areas C and D represent losses to U.S. consumers that are not captured by anyone. These areas are deadweight loss and represent the decline in economic efficiency resulting from the sugar quota. Area C shows the effect of U.S. consumers being forced to buy from U.S. producers that are less efficient than foreign producers, and area D shows the effect of U.S. consumers buying less sugar than they would have at the world price.

Figure 9.7 provides enough information to calculate the dollar value of each of the four areas. The table in the figure shows the results of these calculations. The total loss to consumers from the sugar quota was $2.59 billion in 2016. About 53 percent of the loss to consumers, or $1.38 billion, was gained by U.S. sugar producers as increased producer surplus. About 26 percent, or $0.67 billion, was gained by foreign sugar producers as increased producer surplus, and about 21 percent, or $0.54 billion, was a deadweight loss to the U.S. economy. The U.S. International Trade Commission estimates that eliminating the sugar quota would result in the loss of about 3,000 jobs in the U.S. sugar industry. The cost to U.S. consumers of saving these jobs is equal to $2.59 billion/3,000, or about $860,000 per job each year. In fact, this cost is an underestimate because eliminating the sugar quota would result in new jobs being created, particularly in the candy industry. Over the years, several U.S. candy companies—including the makers of Life Savers and Star Brite mints—have moved factories to other countries to escape the effects of the sugar quota. Partly as a result of the sugar quota, total employment in U.S. chocolate and candy firms that use sugar as an input declined by one-third between 1996 and 2016.   **MyLab Economics** Concept Check

Solved Problem 9.4

Measuring the Economic Effect of a Quota

Suppose that the United States currently both produces and imports apples. The U.S. government then decides to restrict international trade in apples by imposing a quota that allows imports of only 4 million boxes of apples into the United States each year. The figure shows the results of imposing the quota.

Fill in the following table, using the prices, quantities, and letters in the figure:

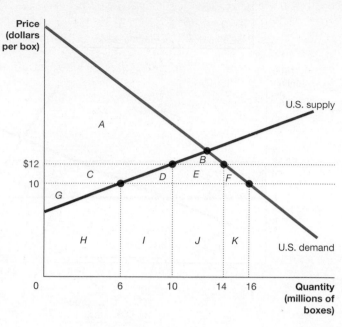

	Without Quota	With Quota
World price of apples		
U.S. price of apples		
Quantity supplied by U.S. firms		
Quantity demanded by U.S. consumers		
Quantity imported		
Area of consumer surplus		
Area of domestic producer surplus		
Area of deadweight loss		

Solving the Problem

Step 1: Review the chapter material. This problem is about measuring the economic effects of a quota, so you may want to review the sections "Quotas and Voluntary Export Restraints," and "Measuring the Economic Effect of the Sugar Quota," which both begin on page 304.

Step 2: Fill in the table. After studying Figure 9.7, you should be able to fill in the table. Remember that consumer surplus is the area below the demand curve and above the market price.

	Without Quota	With Quota
World price of apples	$10	$10
U.S. price of apples	$10	$12
Quantity supplied by U.S. firms	6 million boxes	10 million boxes
Quantity demanded by U.S. consumers	16 million boxes	14 million boxes
Quantity imported	10 million boxes	4 million boxes
Area of consumer surplus	$A + B + C + D + E + F$	$A + B$
Area of domestic producer surplus	G	$G + C$
Area of deadweight loss	No deadweight loss	$D + F$

Your Turn: For more practice, do related problem 4.11 on page 320 at the end of this chapter.

The High Cost of Preserving Jobs with Tariffs and Quotas

The sugar quota is not the only government policy that imposes a high cost on U.S. consumers to save jobs at U.S. firms. The tariff on shoe imports has been estimated to cost U.S. consumers $300,000 per year for each job saved just for women's shoes and rubber shoes. In 2009, the United States imposed a tariff on imports of Chinese tires. As a result, U.S. consumers spent about $1.1 billion more per year on tires. The tariff saved an estimated 1,200 jobs in the U.S. tire industry, at a cost of $900,000 per year per job saved.

Just as the sugar quota costs jobs in the candy industry, other tariffs and quotas cost jobs outside the industries immediately affected. For example, in 1991, the United States imposed tariffs on flat-panel displays used in laptop computers. The tariff was good news for U.S. producers of these displays but bad news for companies producing laptop computers. Toshiba, Sharp, and Apple all closed their U.S. laptop production facilities and moved production overseas. In fact, whenever one industry receives tariff or quota protection, other domestic industries lose jobs. The 2009 tariff on imports of Chinese tires may have cost more than 3,000 jobs in retail stores because the higher price of tires left consumers with less to spend on other goods and services.   **MyLab Economics** Concept Check

Apply the Concept   **MyLab Economics** Video

Smoot-Hawley, the Politics of Tariffs, and the Cost of Protecting a Vanishing Industry

In the 1920s, Congress and the president responded to the financial hardship U.S. farmers faced. As a result of that response, in 2017 many U.S. businesses that import foreign-made shoes into the United States paid tariffs of 35 percent or more on the value of the shoes. Sound illogical? The politics of tariffs can certainly seem to be.

Here is the connection between farmers in the 1920s and shoes today: The 1920s were a period of rapid economic progress in the United States, with the mass production of automobiles, the expansion of electricity use in homes and businesses, improvements in public health, a boom in housing construction, and the development of network radio and talking films. But the incomes of many farmers declined, partly because of increasing agricultural production from foreign competitors. During the 1928 presidential election, Herbert Hoover, the Republican Party candidate, promised that if elected, he would aid farmers by raising tariffs on agricultural goods imported into the United States.

After Hoover won the election, Congress in 1929 considered a new tariff bill. During congressional negotiations, the number of products on which tariffs would be raised quickly expanded beyond agricultural products, in a process known as *logrolling*. Logrolling refers to members of Congress promising to support each other's legislation. In this case, a member of Congress from a district with many dairy farms who wanted the tariff on milk increased would seek out a member of Congress from a district with shoe factories and negotiate along these lines: "If you vote to increase tariffs on milk, I'll vote to increase tariffs on shoes." The law Congress finally passed in 1930, the *Smoot-Hawley Tariff Act*, raised tariffs to the highest level in U.S. history. As a percentage of the value of imports covered by the law, tariffs reached nearly 60 percent.

The process of logrolling can lead to very detailed and complex tariffs as members of Congress attempt to protect specific firms in their districts from competition from foreign producers. For example, the 2017 tariff on shoes contains

i4images/Alamy Stock Photo

How does the Smoot-Hawley Tariff Act of 1930 affect what you pay for your shoes today?

hundreds of entries, many aimed at very specific types of shoes. Here are *just a few* of those entries:

Type of Shoe	Tariff
Footwear designed to be worn over, or in lieu of, other footwear as a protection against water, oil, grease, or chemicals or cold or inclement weather	37.5%
Parts of footwear (including uppers whether or not attached to soles other than outer soles); removable insoles, heel cushions and similar articles; gaiters, leggings and similar articles, and parts thereof: Valued over $3/pair but not over $6.50	63 cents per pair plus 26.2%
Tennis shoes, basketball shoes, gym shoes, training shoes and the like, costing more than $12 per pair	20.0%
Footwear with open toes or open heels; footwear of the slip-on type, that is held to the foot without the use of laces or buckles or other fasteners, the foregoing except footwear of subheading 6402.99.20 and except footwear having a foxing or a foxing-like band wholly or almost wholly of rubber or plastics applied or molded at the sole and overlapping the upper: Having outer soles with textile materials having the greatest surface area in contact with the ground, but not taken into account under the terms of additional U.S. note 5 to this chapter	12.5%
House slippers valued not over $3 per pair having outer soles with textile materials having the greatest surface area in contact with the ground, but not taken into account under the terms of additional U.S. note 5 to this chapter	12.5%
Footwear with outer soles of rubber, plastics, leather or composition leather and uppers of textile materials: Having soles (or mid-soles, if any) of rubber or plastics which are affixed to the upper exclusively with an adhesive (any mid-soles also being affixed exclusively to one another and to the sole with an adhesive); the foregoing except footwear having uppers of vegetable fibers and having outer soles with textile materials having the greatest surface area in contact with the ground, but not taken into account under the terms of additional U.S. note 5 to this chapter	7.5%
Sandals and similar footwear of plastics, produced in one piece by molding	3.0%

Are you having trouble understanding the entries in the table? Imagine being the owner of a small business in 2017 who wants to import shoes. You will have a lot of difficulty determining what tariff to pay, given the complexity of the law.

Canada, the largest trading partner of the United States, reacted to passage of the Smoot-Hawley Tariff Act by enacting large increases in tariffs on U.S. imports. Other countries raised tariffs as well, resulting in a *trade war* that led to a sharp decrease in global trade and helped increase the severity of the Great Depression of the 1930s.

Since the end of World War II in 1945, the United States and most other countries have greatly reduced tariffs on most goods. But the United States continues to impose high tariffs on shoes 85 years after the passage of Smoot-Hawley. During that time, employment in the U.S. shoe industry has fallen from 275,000 workers to fewer than 15,000, as more than 98 percent of the shoes sold in the United States are imported. The total cost to U.S. consumers from higher shoe prices due to the tariff is more than $2 billion per year. The fact that high tariffs on shoes have survived despite few shoes being manufactured in the United States anymore demonstrates how difficult it can sometimes be to remove government protection for an industry once the protection has been enacted.

One way to avoid logrolling when passing tariff laws is for Congress to give the president *fast-track authority* when negotiating trade agreements with other countries. Under fast-track authority, once the president has finished negotiating an agreement with other countries, Congress can either pass or reject the agreement but cannot change any of its provisions. Fast-track authority would have prevented the vote trading that occurred during the Congressional deliberations over Smoot-Hawley. Some members of Congress have recently become skeptical about the merits of free trade, so it seems less likely that Congress will grant presidents fast-track authority in the future.

Sources: U.S. International Trade Commission, *Official Harmonized Tariff Schedule of the United States (2017)*, http://hts.usitc.gov; Carl Hulse and Gardiner Harris, "House Republicans and White House Try to Revive Trade Bill Stalled by Democrats," *New York Times*, June 15, 2015; and Blake W. Krueger, "A Shoe Tariff with a Big Footprint," *Wall Street Journal*, November 22, 2012.

MyLab Economics Study Plan   **Your Turn:** Test your understanding by doing related problems 4.13 and 4.14 on page 320 at the end of this chapter.

Gains from Unilateral Elimination of Tariffs and Quotas

It is easier for policymakers to gain political support for reducing or eliminating tariffs or quotas if it is done as part of an agreement with other countries that requires those countries to eliminate some of their tariffs or quotas. But as the example of the sugar quota shows, *the U.S. economy would experience a gain in economic surplus from the elimination of tariffs and quotas even if other countries did not reduce their tariffs and quotas.*   **MyLab Economics** Concept Check

Other Barriers to Trade

In addition to tariffs and quotas, governments sometimes erect other barriers to trade. For example, all governments require that imports meet certain health and safety requirements. Sometimes, however, governments use these requirements to shield domestic firms from foreign competition. For example, a government may impose stricter health and safety requirements on imported goods than on goods produced by domestic firms.

Many governments also restrict imports of certain products on national security grounds. The argument is that in time of war, a country should not be dependent on imports of critical war materials. Once again, these restrictions are sometimes used more to protect domestic companies from competition than to protect national security. For years, the U.S. government would buy military uniforms only from U.S. manufacturers, even though uniforms are not a critical war material. The Defense Department gives each army recruit a voucher to purchase a pair of athletic shoes for training. New Balance has attempted to force the Defense Department to require the vouchers be used only to purchase U.S.-made shoes. Many officials in the Defense Department didn't see soldiers training in foreign-made running shoes as a threat to national security.   **MyLab Economics** Concept Check

MyLab Economics Study Plan

9.5 | The Debate over Trade Policies and Globalization

LEARNING OBJECTIVE: Evaluate the debate over trade policies and globalization.

The debate over whether the U.S. government should regulate international trade has continued since the founding of the country. One particularly controversial attempt to restrict trade took place during the Great Depression of the 1930s. At that time, the United States and other countries attempted to help domestic firms by raising tariffs on imports. The United States started the process by passing the Smoot-Hawley Tariff Act in 1930, which raised average tariff rates to nearly 60 percent. As other countries retaliated by raising their tariffs, international trade collapsed.

By the end of World War II in 1945, government officials in the United States and Europe were looking for a way to reduce tariffs and revive international trade. To help achieve this goal, they set up the General Agreement on Tariffs and Trade (GATT) in 1948. Countries that joined the GATT agreed not to impose new tariffs or import quotas. In addition, a series of *multilateral negotiations*, called *trade rounds*, took place, in which countries agreed to reduce tariffs from the very high levels of the 1930s.

In the 1940s, most international trade was in goods, and the GATT agreement covered only goods. In the following decades, trade in services and products incorporating *intellectual property*, such as software programs and movies, grew in importance. Many GATT members pressed for a new agreement that would cover services and intellectual property, as well as goods. A new agreement was negotiated, and in January 1995, the GATT was replaced by the **World Trade Organization (WTO)**, headquartered in Geneva, Switzerland. More than 150 countries are currently members of the WTO.

World Trade Organization (WTO) An international organization that oversees international trade agreements.

Why Do Some People Oppose the World Trade Organization?

During the years immediately after World War II, many low-income, or developing, countries enacted high tariffs and restricted investment by foreign companies. When these policies failed to produce much economic growth, many of these countries

Globalization The process of countries becoming more open to foreign trade and investment.

decided during the 1980s to become more open to foreign trade and investment. This process became known as **globalization**. Most developing countries joined the WTO and began to follow its policies.

During the 1990s, opposition to globalization began to increase. Over the years, protests, which have sometimes turned violent, have occurred in cities hosting WTO meetings. Why would attempts to reduce trade barriers with the objective of increasing income around the world cause such a furious reaction? The opposition to the WTO comes from three sources. First, some opponents are specifically against the globalization process that began in the 1980s and became widespread in the 1990s. Second, other opponents have the same motivation as the supporters of tariffs in the 1930s—to erect trade barriers to protect domestic firms from foreign competition. Third, some critics of the WTO support globalization in principle but believe that the WTO favors the interests of the high-income countries at the expense of the low-income countries. Let's look more closely at the sources of opposition to the WTO.

Anti-globalization Many of those who protest at WTO meetings distrust globalization. Some believe that free trade and foreign investment destroy the distinctive cultures of many countries. As developing countries began to open their economies to imports from the United States and other high-income countries, the imports of food, clothing, movies, and other goods began to replace the equivalent local products. So, a teenager in Thailand might be eating in a McDonald's restaurant, wearing Levi's jeans and a Ralph Lauren shirt, listening to a song by Lady Gaga on his iPhone, before downloading *Wonder Woman* to his iPad. Globalization has increased the variety of products available to consumers in developing countries, but some people argue that this is too high a price to pay for what they see as damage to local cultures.

Globalization has also allowed multinational corporations to relocate factories from high-income countries to low-income countries. These new factories in Indonesia, Malaysia, Pakistan, and other countries pay much lower wages than are paid in the United States, Europe, and Japan and often do not meet the environmental or safety regulations that are imposed in high-income countries. Some factories use child labor, which is illegal in high-income countries. Some people have argued that firms with factories in developing countries should pay workers wages as high as those paid in high-income countries. They also believe these firms should abide by the health, safety, and environmental regulations that exist in the high-income countries.

The governments of most developing countries have resisted these proposals. They argue that when the currently rich countries were poor, they also lacked environmental or safety standards, and their workers were paid low wages. They argue that it is easier for rich countries to afford high wages and environmental and safety regulations than it is for poor countries. They also point out that many jobs that seem to have very low wages based on the standards of high-income countries are often better than the alternatives available to workers in low-income countries.

Protectionism The use of trade barriers to shield domestic firms from foreign competition.

"Old-Fashioned" Protectionism The anti-globalization argument against free trade and the WTO is relatively new. Another argument against free trade, called *protectionism*, has been around for centuries. **Protectionism** is the use of trade barriers to shield domestic firms from foreign competition. Some of the recent opposition to free trade in the United States appears to be protectionist. For as long as international trade has existed, governments have attempted to restrict it to protect domestic firms. As we saw with the analysis of the sugar quota, protectionism causes losses to consumers and eliminates jobs in the domestic industries that buy the protected product. In addition, by reducing the ability of countries to produce according to comparative advantage, protectionism reduces incomes.

Why, then, does protectionism attract support, and why has support for protectionist policies increased recently among some policymakers in the United States? Protectionism is usually justified on the basis of one of the following arguments:

- **Saving jobs.** President Trump and other supporters of protectionist policies argue that free trade reduces employment by driving domestic firms out of business. It is true that when more-efficient foreign firms drive less-efficient domestic firms out of business, jobs are lost, but jobs are also lost when more-efficient domestic firms drive less-efficient domestic firms out of business. Economists have traditionally argued that these job losses are rarely permanent. In the U.S. economy, jobs are lost and new jobs are created continually. No economic study has ever found a long-term connection between the total number of jobs available in the United States as a whole and the level of tariff protection for domestic industries. But, as we discussed in the *Apply the Concept* on page 298, recent studies of the effects of the surge of imports from China that began in 2001 have shown that employment losses in areas most affected by imports have proven to be long-lasting. People living in some cities and towns that were home to firms that have closed because of competition from foreign imports have experienced significant hardships. Some of these areas have suffered from declining populations as workers have left to find jobs elsewhere, and the lower incomes of many people who remain have resulted in reduced sales by local businesses. The main streets in some of these towns have many boarded-up storefronts, and local governments have struggled to maintain services in the face of declining tax revenue. But, as we have also seen, trade restrictions destroy jobs in some industries at the same time that they preserve jobs in others. The U.S. sugar quota may have saved jobs in the U.S. sugar industry, but it has also destroyed jobs in the U.S. candy industry.

- **Protecting high wages.** Some people worry that firms in high-income countries will have to start paying much lower wages to compete with firms in developing countries. For the country as a whole, this fear is misplaced, however, because free trade actually raises living standards by increasing economic efficiency. When a country practices protectionism and produces goods and services it could obtain more inexpensively from other countries, it reduces its standard of living. The United States could ban imports of coffee and begin growing it domestically. But doing so would entail a very high opportunity cost because coffee could only be grown in the continental United States in greenhouses and would require large amounts of labor and equipment. The coffee would have to sell for a very high price to cover these costs. Suppose the United States did ban coffee imports. Eliminating the ban at some future time would cause U.S. coffee workers to lose their jobs, but the standard of living in the United States would rise as coffee prices declined and labor, machinery, and other resources were moved out of coffee production and into production of goods and services for which the United States has a comparative advantage. But again, recent experience indicates that while trade contributes to raising the standard of living of the country as a whole, it can lead to long-lived declines in income in areas that are most exposed to competition from imports. Such a decline appears to have taken place in areas of the Midwest and Southeast where firms were most exposed to competition from Chinese imports.

- **Protecting infant industries.** It is possible that firms in a country may have a comparative advantage in producing a good, but because the country begins production of the good later than other countries, its firms initially have higher costs. Producing some goods and services involves substantial "learning by doing." As workers and firms produce more of the good or service, they gain experience and become more productive. Over time, these firms will have lower costs and can charge lower prices. As the firms in the "infant industry" gain experience, they will be able to compete successfully with foreign producers. Under free trade, however, they may not get a chance. The established foreign producers can sell the product at a lower price and drive domestic producers out of business before they gain enough experience to compete. To economists, the infant industry argument is the most persuasive of the protectionist arguments. It has a significant drawback, however. Tariffs eliminate the need for firms in an infant industry to become productive enough to compete with foreign firms. After World War II, the governments of many developing countries used the infant industry argument to justify high tariff rates. Unfortunately, most of their infant industries never grew up, and they continued for years as inefficient drains on their economies.

- **Protecting national security.** A country will typically not want to rely on other countries for goods that are critical to its military defense. For example, the United States would probably not want to import all its jet fighter engines from China. The definition of which goods are critical to military defense is a slippery one, however. In fact, it is rare for an industry to ask for protection without raising the issue of national security, even if its products have mainly nonmilitary uses. **MyLab Economics** Concept Check

Apply the Concept

MyLab Economics Video

Protecting Consumer Health or Protecting U.S. Firms from Competition?

Lucenet Patrice/Oredia/Alamy Stock Photo

Are restrictions on catfish imports protecting the health of U.S. consumers or the interests of U.S. producers?

The World Trade Organization and other international agreements limit the use of tariffs and quotas. So to protect firms from foreign competition, governments sometimes regulate imports by claiming that they pose a threat to consumer health or safety.

Is imported catfish safe for U.S. consumers to eat, or does it contain bacteria and dangerous chemicals? The U.S. states that produce the most catfish are Alabama, Arkansas, Mississippi, and Texas. In 2008, members of Congress from those states pushed through legislation setting up a catfish inspection office in the U.S. Department of Agriculture (USDA). By 2014, the office had spent $20 million but had not actually inspected any imported catfish. The money had been spent on just setting up offices and paying administrators' salaries. That year, Congress set a deadline for the inspection program to begin. In the following years, the office has spent $14 million annually inspecting catfish.

Vietnam and other countries that export catfish to the United States have objected that the real purpose of the inspections is to erect a barrier to trade. Those governments argue that the inspections violate the commitments of the United States under the World Trade Organization not to erect barriers to trade. A study by the U.S. Government Accountability Office indicated that the health risk to U.S. consumers from imported catfish was very low, even without the proposed inspections. Some members of Congress from states that do not produce catfish also argue that new inspections of imported catfish were unnecessary and result in U.S. consumers paying higher prices. Despite these arguments, an attempt in Congress to eliminate the USDA's catfish inspection office failed in 2016.

Policymakers are often caught in a dilemma over imports. Firms want to reduce or eliminate sales lost to imports, but imposing trade barriers reduces economic efficiency, lowers incomes, and invites retaliation from foreign governments. Although some imported goods can, in fact, pose threats to the health and safety of U.S. consumers, some health and safety regulations are intended to protect the U.S. firms involved rather than U.S. consumers.

Sources: William R. Jones, "Waste and Duplication in the USDA Catfish Inspection Program," statement before the Subcommittee on Health, Committee on Energy and Commerce, U.S. House of Representatives, December 7, 2016; David Williams, "The Catfish (Inspection Program) that Survived Commonsense," thehill.com, December 7, 2016; Bruce Einhorn and Chau Mai, "The Catfish Wars Could Derail U.S.–Asia Trade," businessweek.com, June 30, 2014; and U.S. Government Accountability Office, *Seafood Safety: Responsibility for Inspecting Catfish Should Not Be Assigned to USDA*, GAO 12-411, May 2012.

MyLab Economics Study Plan   **Your Turn:** Test your understanding by doing related problems 5.9 and 5.10 on page 322 at the end of this chapter.

Dumping

In recent years, the United States has extended protection to some domestic industries by using a provision in the WTO agreement that allows governments to impose tariffs in the case of *dumping*. **Dumping** is selling a product for a price below its cost of production. Using tariffs to offset the effects of dumping is controversial, despite being allowed under the WTO agreement.

Dumping Selling a product for a price below its cost of production.

In practice, it is difficult to determine whether foreign companies are dumping goods because the true production costs of a good are not easy for governments to calculate. As a result, the WTO allows countries to determine that dumping has occurred if a product is exported for a lower price than it sells for on the home market. There is a problem with this approach, however. Often there are good business reasons for a firm to sell a product for different prices to different consumers. For example, the airlines charge business travelers higher ticket prices than leisure travelers. Firms also use "loss leaders"—products that are sold below cost, or even given away free—when introducing a new product or, in the case of retailing, to attract customers who will also buy full-price products. For example, during the holiday season, Walmart sometimes offers toys at prices below what it pays to buy them from manufacturers. It's unclear why these normal business practices should be unacceptable when used in international trade.   MyLab Economics Concept Check

Positive versus Normative Analysis (Once Again)

Economists emphasize the burden on the economy imposed by tariffs, quotas, and other government restrictions on free trade. Does it follow that these interferences are bad? Remember that positive analysis concerns what *is*, while normative analysis concerns what *ought to be*. Measuring the effect of the sugar quota on the U.S. economy is an example of positive analysis. Asserting that the sugar quota is bad public policy and should be eliminated is normative analysis. The sugar quota—like all other interferences with trade—makes some people better off and some people worse off, and it reduces total income and consumption. Whether increasing the profits of U.S. sugar companies and the number of workers they employ justifies the costs imposed on consumers and the reduction in economic efficiency is a normative question.

Most economists do not support interferences with trade, such as the sugar quota, because they believe that markets should be as free as possible. But the opposite view is certainly intellectually respectable. It is possible for someone to understand the costs of tariffs and quotas but still believe that they are a good idea, perhaps because he or she believes unrestricted free trade would cause too much disruption to the economy.

The success of industries in getting the government to erect barriers to foreign competition depends partly on some members of the public knowing the costs of trade barriers but supporting them anyway. However, two other factors are also at work:

1. The costs that tariffs and quotas impose on consumers are large in total but relatively small per person. For example, the sugar quota imposes a total burden of $2.59 billion per year on consumers. Spread across 325 million Americans, the burden is only about $8 per person—too little for most people to worry about, even if they know the burden exists.
2. The jobs lost to foreign competition are easy to identify, but the jobs created by foreign trade are less easy to identify.

In other words, the industries that benefit from tariffs and quotas benefit a lot—for example, the sugar quota increases the profits of U.S. sugar producers by $1.38 billion per year—while each consumer loses relatively little. This concentration of benefits and widely spread burdens makes it easy to understand why members of Congress receive strong pressure from some industries to enact tariffs and quotas and relatively little pressure from the general public to reduce them.   MyLab Economics Concept Check

MyLab Economics Study Plan

Continued from page 289

Economics in Your Life & Career

Should a Member of Congress Support a Tariff on Running Shoes?

At the beginning of the chapter, we asked you to suppose you are an aide to a member of Congress who is considering whether to vote for a bill that would eliminate the U.S. tariff on running shoes. We asked what facts and conclusions from the economic analysis of international trade you should include in your memorandum advising the member on her vote.

The *Apply the Concept* "Smoot-Hawley, the Politics of Tariffs, and the Cost of Protecting a Vanishing Industry" on page 307 notes that currently the federal government imposes a tariff of 35 percent on most imported running shoes. The cost to consumers from this tariff is estimated to be about $2 billion per year. So, one factor to include in your memo is that local businesses in the member's district that sell running shoes and local consumers who buy them would both benefit from removing the tariff. A possibly more important factor, though, influencing the member's vote will be whether there are any shoe factories in her district. If so, it may be difficult politically to vote to eliminate the tariff on running shoes, even though the gain to other local businesses and to local consumers is likely to be greater in dollar terms than the losses to the owners of the shoe factory and its workers. As the *Apply the Concept* also noted, logrolling during the writing of the 1930 Smoot-Hawley Tariff Act is a reason the shoe tariff was enacted and a key reason it survives to the present. Even if there is no shoe factory in the member's district, other members of Congress who do have shoe factories in their districts may offer to trade their votes on issues that concern your member in exchange for her vote to uphold the shoe tariff. Such is the mixture of positive and normative considerations that result in tariffs and other laws!

Conclusion

There are few issues economists agree upon more than the economic benefits of free trade. However, there are few political issues as controversial as government policy toward trade. Some people who would be reluctant to see the government interfere with domestic trade support interference with international trade. The damage high tariffs inflicted on the world economy during the 1930s shows what can happen when governments around the world abandon free trade. Whether future episodes of that type can be avoided is by no means certain.

Visit **MyLab Economics** for a news article and analysis related to the concepts in this chapter.

Key Terms

Absolute advantage, p. 293	External economies, p. 301	Protectionism, p. 310	Voluntary export restraint (VER), p. 304
Autarky, p. 294	Free trade, p. 302	Quota, p. 304	
Comparative advantage, p. 293	Globalization, p. 310	Tariff, p. 290	World Trade Organization (WTO), p. 309
Dumping, p. 313	Imports, p. 290	Terms of trade, p. 294	
Exports, p. 291	Opportunity cost, p. 293		

9.1 The United States in the International Economy, pages 290–292

LEARNING OBJECTIVE: Discuss the role of international trade in the U.S. economy.

MyLab Economics Visit www.pearson.com/mylab/economics to complete these exercises online and get instant feedback.

Summary

International trade has been increasing in recent decades, in part because of reductions in *tariffs* and other barriers to trade. A **tariff** is a tax imposed by a government on imports. The quantity of goods and services the United States imports and exports has been continually increasing. **Imports** are goods and services bought domestically but produced in other countries. **Exports** are goods and services produced domestically and sold to other countries. Today, the United States is the second-leading exporting country in the world behind China, and about 20 percent of U.S. manufacturing jobs depend on exports.

Review Questions

1.1 Briefly explain whether the value of U.S. exports is typically larger or smaller than the value of U.S. imports. Are imports and exports now a smaller or larger fraction of GDP than they were 40 years ago?

1.2 Briefly explain whether you agree with the following statement: "International trade is more important to the U.S. economy than it is to most other economies."

Problems and Applications

1.3 If the United States were to stop trading goods and services with other countries, which U.S. industries would be likely to see their sales decline the most? Briefly explain.

1.4 Briefly explain whether you agree with the following statement: "Japan has always been much more heavily involved in international trade than are most other nations. In fact, today Japan exports a larger fraction of its GDP than Germany, the United Kingdom, or the United States."

1.5 Why might a smaller country, such as the Netherlands, be more likely to import and export larger fractions of its GDP than would a larger country, such as China or the United States?

9.2 Comparative Advantage in International Trade, pages 292–294

LEARNING OBJECTIVE: Explain the difference between comparative advantage and absolute advantage in international trade.

MyLab Economics Visit www.pearson.com/mylab/economics to complete these exercises online and get instant feedback.

Summary

Comparative advantage is the ability of an individual, a firm, or a country to produce a good or service at the lowest **opportunity cost**. **Absolute advantage** is the ability to produce more of a good or service than competitors when using the same amount of resources. Countries trade on the basis of comparative advantage, not on the basis of absolute advantage.

Review Questions

2.1 What is the difference between absolute advantage and comparative advantage? If a country has an absolute advantage in producing a good, will it always be an exporter of that good? Briefly explain.

2.2 A World Trade Organization (WTO) publication called comparative advantage "arguably the single most powerful insight in economics." What is comparative advantage? What makes it such a powerful insight?

Source: World Trade Organization, "Understanding the WTO," www.wto.org/english/thewto_e/whatis_e/tif_e/fact3_e.htm.

Problems and Applications

2.3 A book on the Roman Empire made the following observation: "Romans bought their pots from professional potters, and bought their defence from professional soldiers. From both they got a quality product—much better than if they had had to do their soldiering and potting themselves." Briefly explain what economic concept the author is illustrating in this passage. How does he know that Romans got better pots and better defense by relying on this economic concept?

Source: Bryan Ward-Perkins, *The Fall of Rome and the End of Civilization*, Oxford: Oxford University Press, 2005, p. 49.

2.4 In the 2016 Summer Olympic Games, Ashton Eaton (from the United States) won a gold medal in the decathlon, which requires athletes to compete in 10 different track and field events. In one of these events Eaton ran a 100-meter race in 10.46 seconds. In a separate event, Usain Bolt (from Jamaica) won a gold medal by running 100 meters in 9.81 seconds.
  a. Which performance—Eaton's or Bolt's—is better explained by the concept of comparative advantage? Briefly explain.
  b. Based on their performance at the 2016 Olympic Games, can we say whether Eaton or Bolt was the better athlete? Briefly explain.

2.5 An article in the *New York Times* quoted an economist as arguing that "global free trade and the European single market . . . encourage countries to specialize in sectors where they enjoy comparative advantage. Germany's [comparative advantage] is in cars and machine tools." For the author's observation to be correct, must Germany be able to produce more cars and machine tools per hour worked than do France, Italy, Spain, and Germany's other trading partners? Briefly explain.

Source: Anatole Kaletsky, "In Disguise, a Budget That Britain Needs," *New York Times*, March 24, 2014.

2.6 Briefly explain whether you agree with the following argument: "Unfortunately, Bolivia does not have a comparative advantage with respect to the United States in the production of any good or service." (*Hint:* You do not need any specific information about the economies of Bolivia or the United States to be able to answer this question.)

2.7 The following table shows the hourly output per worker for Greece and Italy measured as quarts of olive oil and pounds of pasta.

	Output per Hour of Work	
	Olive Oil	Pasta
Greece	4	2
Italy	4	8

Calculate the opportunity cost of producing olive oil and pasta in both Greece and Italy.

2.8 Using the numbers in the following table, explain which country has a comparative advantage in producing smartphones.

	Output per Hour of Work	
	Smartphones	Fitness Bracelets
Switzerland	8	10
Canada	5	3

2.9 Patrick J. Buchanan, a political commentator and former presidential candidate, argued in his book on the global economy that there is a flaw in David Ricardo's theory of comparative advantage:

> Classical free trade theory fails the test of common sense. According to Ricardo's law of comparative advantage . . . if America makes better computers and textiles than China does, but our advantage in computers is greater than our advantage in textiles, we should (1) focus on computers, (2) let China make textiles, and (3) trade U.S. computers for Chinese textiles.... The doctrine begs a question. If Americans are more efficient than Chinese in making clothes … why surrender the more efficient American industry? Why shift to a reliance on a Chinese textile industry that will take years to catch up to where American factories are today?

Do you agree with Buchanan's argument? Briefly explain.

Source: Patrick J. Buchanan, *The Great Betrayal: How American Sovereignty and Social Justice Are Being Sacrificed to the Gods of the Global Economy*, Boston: Little, Brown & Company, 1998, p. 66.

9.3 How Countries Gain from International Trade, pages 294–301

LEARNING OBJECTIVE: Explain how countries gain from international trade.

MyLab Economics   Visit **www.pearson.com/mylab/economics** to complete these exercises online and get instant feedback.

Summary

Autarky is a situation in which a country does not trade with other countries. The **terms of trade** is the ratio at which a country can trade its exports for imports from other countries. When a country specializes in producing goods for which it has a comparative advantage and trades for the other goods it needs, the country will have a higher level of income and consumption. We do not see complete specialization in production for three reasons: (1) Not all goods and services are traded internationally, (2) production of most goods involves increasing opportunity costs, and (3) tastes for products differ across countries. Although the population of a country as a whole benefits from trade, firms—and their workers—that are unable to compete with lower-cost foreign producers lose. Among the main sources of comparative advantage are climate and natural resources, relative abundance of labor and capital, technology, and external economies. **External economies**

are reductions in a firm's costs that result from an increase in the size of an industry.

Review Questions

3.1 Briefly explain how international trade increases a country's consumption.

3.2 What is meant by a country specializing in the production of a good? Is it typical for countries to be completely specialized? Briefly explain.

3.3 What are the main sources of comparative advantage?

3.4 Does everyone gain from international trade? If not, explain which groups lose.

Problems and Applications

3.5 (Related to Solved Problem 9.3 on page 296) The following table shows the hourly output per worker in two industries in Chile and Argentina.

	Output per Hour of Work	
	Hats	Beer (barrels)
Chile	8	6
Argentina	1	2

a. Explain which country has an absolute advantage in the production of hats and which country has an absolute advantage in the production of beer.

b. Explain which country has a comparative advantage in the production of hats and which country has a comparative advantage in the production of beer.

c. Suppose that Chile and Argentina currently do not trade with each other. Each has 1,000 hours of labor to use producing hats and beer, and the countries are currently producing the amounts of each good shown in the following table.

	Hats	Beer (barrels)
Chile	7,200	600
Argentina	600	800

Using this information, give a numerical example of how Chile and Argentina can both gain from trade. Assume that after trading begins, one hat can be exchanged for one barrel of beer.

3.6 (Related to Solved Problem 9.3 on page 296) A political commentator makes the following statement:

> The idea that international trade should be based on the comparative advantage of each country is fine for rich countries like the United States and Japan. Rich countries have educated workers and large quantities of machinery and equipment. These advantages allow them to produce every product more efficiently than poor countries can. Poor countries like Kenya and Uruguay have nothing to gain from international trade based on comparative advantage.

Do you agree with this argument? Briefly explain.

3.7 The following data summarize the trade between Canada and the United States in 2015 and 2016.

	Exports from the United States to Canada (billions of U.S. dollars)	Exports from Canada to the United States (billions of U.S. dollars)
2015	$ 280.6	$ 296.2
2016	266.8	278.1

In both years, the value of Canada's exports to the United States exceeded the value of U.S. exports to Canada. Can we conclude that foreign trade between the two countries benefited Canada more than it benefited the United States? Briefly explain.

Source: U.S. Department of Commerce, Census Bureau, Economic Indicators Division.

3.8 An article in the *New Yorker* stated, "The main burden of trade-related job losses and wage declines has fallen on middle- and lower-income Americans. But . . . the very people who suffer most from free trade are often, paradoxically, among its biggest beneficiaries." Explain how it is possible that middle- and lower-income Americans are both the biggest losers and at the same time the biggest winners from free trade.

Source: James Surowiecki, "The Free-Trade Paradox," *New Yorker,* May 26, 2008.

3.9 Hal Varian, chief economist at Google, made the following two observations about international trade:

1. Trade allows a country "to produce more with less."

2. "There is little doubt who wins [from trade] in the long run: consumers."

Briefly explain whether you agree with either or both of these observations.

Source: Hal R. Varian, "The Mixed Bag of Productivity," *New York Times,* October 23, 2003.

3.10 Suppose the following graph shows Tanzania's production possibilities frontier (PPF) for cashew nuts and mangoes. Assume that the output per hour of work is 8 bushels of cashew nuts or 2 bushels of mangoes and that Tanzania has 1,000 hours of labor. Without trade, Tanzania evenly splits its labor hours between cashews and mangoes and produces and consumes at point A.

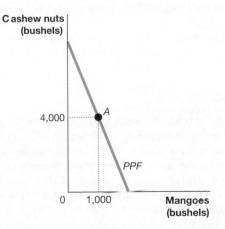

a. Suppose Tanzania opens trade with Kenya, and Kenya's output per hour of work is 1 bushel of cashew nuts or 1 bushel of mangoes. Having the comparative advantage, Tanzania completely specializes in cashew nuts. How many bushels of cashew nuts can Tanzania produce? Denote this point on the graph as point *B*.

b. Suppose Tanzania keeps 5,000 bushels of cashew nuts and exports the remaining 3,000 bushels. If the terms of trade are 1 bushel of mangoes for 2 bushels of cashew nuts, how many bushels of mangoes will Tanzania get in exchange? Denote on the graph the quantity of cashew nuts and mangoes that Tanzania consumes with trade and label this point as point *C*. How does point *C* with trade compare to point *A* without trade?

c. With trade, is Tanzania producing on its *PPF*? With trade, is Tanzania consuming on its *PPF*?

3.11 (Related to the Don't Let This Happen to You on page 298) Former President Barack Obama once described a trade agreement reached with the government of Colombia as a "'win–win' for both our countries." Is everyone in both countries likely to win from the agreement? Briefly explain.

Source: Kent Klein, "Obama: Free Trade Agreement a 'Win–Win' for US, Colombia," voanews.com.

3.12 (Related to the Apply the Concept on page 298) An article in the *Wall Street Journal* discussing the effect of Chinese imports on the U.S. economy made the following observation: "[China's] emergence as a trade powerhouse rattled the American economy more violently than economists and policy makers anticipated at the time. . . . The U.S. workforce adapted more slowly than expected."

a. What does the article mean that China's emergence as a trade powerhouse rattled the U.S. economy?

b. Why didn't economists and policymakers expect the economic effect of imports from China to be as great as it turned out to be?

c. In what sense has the U.S. workforce adapted more slowly than expected?

Source: Bob Davis and Jon Hilsenrath, "How the China Shock, Deep and Swift, Fueled the Rise of Trump," *Wall Street Journal*, August 11, 2016.

3.13 (Related to the Apply the Concept on page 298) An article in the *Economist* discussing the effects of Chinese imports on U.S. jobs referred to the "China-shock literature" and included a graph showing for the period from 1990 to 2016 the decrease in U.S. manufacturing employment as a percentage of the working-age population along with the increase in imports of goods from China as a percentage of GDP.

a. What does the article mean by the "China-shock literature?"

b. What has caused most of the decline in U.S. manufacturing employment since the 1940s?

c. The article noted that "places in America more exposed to these Chinese imports [were] typically those with lots of labor-intensive manufacturing." Why would places with lots of labor-intensive manufacturing be more exposed to Chinese imports?

Source: "Trade with China: Shock Horror," *Economist*, March 11, 2017

3.14 An article in the *New York Times* discussed the number of innovative food companies, particularly those selling natural foods, that have become established in Boulder, Colorado, in recent years. According to the article, Boulder has a large number of people with experience in managing food companies, lenders who know the industry, food distributors, and food processing plants. The article quoted one entrepreneur as asserting: "There's an ecosystem here that supports food entrepreneurs that you just don't find in other places. Everything you need, including a lot of experience and expertise, is right here." What advantages does being located in Boulder give to startup natural food firms? In what circumstances can natural food firms located elsewhere overcome these advantages? Are Boulder's advantages likely to persist over time?

Source: Stephanie Strom, "Foodies Know: Boulder Has Become a Hub for New Producers," *New York Times*, February 4, 2017.

9.4 Government Policies That Restrict International Trade, pages 302–309

LEARNING OBJECTIVE: Analyze the economic effects of government policies that restrict international trade.

MyLab Economics Visit **www.pearson.com/mylab/economics** to complete these exercises online and get instant feedback.

Summary

Free trade is trade between countries without government restrictions. Government policies that interfere with trade usually take the form of *tariffs, quotas,* or *voluntary export restraints*. A **quota** is a numerical limit imposed by a government on the quantity of a good that can be imported into the country. A **voluntary export restraint (VER)** is an agreement negotiated between two countries that places

a numerical limit on the quantity of a good that can be imported by one country from the other country. The federal government's sugar quota costs U.S. consumers $2.59 billion per year, or about $860,000 per year for each job saved in the sugar industry. Saving jobs by using tariffs and quotas is often very expensive.

Review Questions

4.1 What is a tariff? What is a quota? Give an example, other than a quota, of a nontariff barrier to trade.

4.2 Who gains and who loses when a country imposes a tariff or a quota on imports of a good?

Problems and Applications

4.3 Political commentator B. Bruce-Briggs once wrote the following in the *Wall Street Journal*: "This is not to say that the case for international free trade is invalid; it is just irrelevant. It is an 'if only everybody' . . . argument . . . . In the real world almost everybody sees benefits in economic nationalism." What do you think he means by "economic nationalism"? Do you agree that a country benefits from free trade only if every other country also practices free trade? Briefly explain.

Source: B. Bruce-Biggs, "The Coming Overthrow of Free Trade," *Wall Street Journal*, February 24, 1983.

4.4 **(Related to the Chapter Opener on page 288)** While running for the 2016 Democratic nomination for president, Vermont Senator Bernie Sanders opposed the Trans-Pacific Partnership in part because he believed that as a result of the agreement, "the U.S. will lose more than 130,000 jobs to Vietnam and Japan alone." Do you agree that reducing barriers to trade reduces the number of jobs available to workers in the United States? Briefly explain.

Source: Bernie Sanders, "Senator Bernie Sanders: The Trans-Pacific Trade (TPP) Agreement Must Be Defeated," www.sanders.senate.gov/download/the-trans-pacific-trade-tpp-agreement-must-be-defeated?inline=file.

4.5 The United States produces beef and also imports beef from other countries.
   a. Draw a graph showing the demand and supply of beef in the United States. Assume that the United States can import as much as it wants at the world price of beef without causing the world price of beef to increase. Be sure to indicate on your graph the quantity of beef imported. Assume that the world price of beef is lower than the U.S. price.
   b. Now show on your graph the effect of the United States imposing a tariff on beef. Be sure to indicate on your graph the quantity of beef sold by U.S. producers before and after the tariff is imposed, the quantity of beef imported before and after the tariff, and the price of beef in the United States before and after the tariff.
   c. Discuss who benefits and who loses when the United States imposes a tariff on beef.

4.6 A student makes the following argument:

> Tariffs on imports of foreign goods into the United States will cause the foreign companies to add the amount of the tariff to the prices they charge in the United States for those goods. Instead of putting a tariff on imported goods, we should ban importing them. Banning imported goods is better than putting tariffs on them because U.S. producers benefit from the reduced competition, and U.S. consumers don't have to pay the higher prices caused by tariffs.

Briefly explain whether you agree with the student's reasoning.

4.7 A columnist for bloomberg.com offered the following observation about economic legislation: "History shows that concentrated opposition beats diffuse support every time."

   a. Briefly explain what this columnist means.
   b. Does his observation apply to tariffs? Briefly explain.

Source: Peter Coy, "Show Us Your Tax Reforms," bloomberg.com, March 30, 2017.

4.8 The following graph shows the effect on consumer surplus, producer surplus, government tariff revenue, and economic surplus of a tariff of $1 per unit on imports of plastic combs into the United States. Use the areas denoted by letters in the graph to answer the following questions.

   a. Which area shows the losses to U.S. consumers of buying a smaller quantity of combs than they would have if they could have purchased them at the world price?
   b. Which area shows the losses to U.S. consumers of having to buy combs from U.S. producers who are less efficient than foreign producers?
   c. Which areas show the deadweight loss to the U.S. economy as a result of the tariff on combs?

4.9 The following graph shows the situation after the U.S. government removes a tariff on imports of canned tuna.

   a. Which areas show the gain in consumer surplus?
   b. Which area shows the loss in producer surplus?
   c. Which area shows the loss in government tariff revenue?
   d. Which areas show the gain in economic surplus?

4.10 According to an editorial in the *Washington Post*, "Sugar protectionism is a burden on consumers and a job-killer."
   a. In what sense does the United States practice "sugar protectionism"?
   b. In what way is sugar protectionism a burden on consumers? In what way is it a job-killer?
   c. If sugar protectionism has the bad effects stated in the editorial, why don't Congress and the president eliminate it?

   Source: "Sourball," *Washington Post*, March 22, 2010.

4.11 **(Related to Solved Problem 9.4 on page 306)** Suppose that the United States currently both produces kumquats and imports them. The U.S. government then decides to restrict international trade in kumquats by imposing a quota that allows imports of only 6 million pounds of kumquats into the United States each year. The following figure shows the results of imposing the quota.

Fill in the table below using the letters in the figure.

	Without Quota	With Quota
World price of kumquats		
U.S. price of kumquats		
Quantity supplied by U.S. firms		
Quantity demanded		
Quantity imported		
Area of consumer surplus		
Area of domestic producer surplus		
Area of deadweight loss		

4.12 Suppose the government is considering imposing either a tariff or a quota on canned peaches. Assume that the proposed quota has the same effect on the U.S. price of canned peaches as the proposed tariff. Use the graph to answer the following questions.

   a. If the government imposes a tariff, which area shows the government tariff revenue?
   b. If the government imposes a quota, which area shows the gain to foreign producers of canned peaches?
   c. As a consumer of peaches, would you prefer that the government impose the tariff or the quota? Briefly explain.

4.13 **(Related to the Apply the Concept on page 307)** An economic analysis of a proposal to impose a quota on steel imports into the United States indicated that the quota would save 3,700 jobs in the steel industry but cost about 35,000 jobs in other U.S. industries. Why would a quota on steel imports cause employment to decline in other industries? Which other industries is a steel quota likely to affect?

   Source: Douglas A. Irwin, *Free Trade under Fire*, Princeton, NJ: Princeton University Press, 2002, p. 82.

4.14 **(Related to the Apply the Concept on page 307)** For several years, the United States imposed a tariff on tire imports. According to an analysis by economists Gary Clyde Hufbauer and Sean Lowry of the Peterson Institute, of the additional $1.1 billion consumers spent on tires as a result of the tariff on Chinese tires, the workers whose jobs were saved in the U.S. tire industry received only about $48 million in wages. Wouldn't it have been cheaper for the federal government to have raised taxes on U.S. consumers and given the money to tire workers rather than to have imposed a tariff? If so, why didn't the federal government adopt this alternative policy?

   Source: Gary Clyde Hufbauer and Sean Lowry, "US Tire Tariffs: Saving Few Jobs at High Cost," Peterson Institute for International Economics, Policy Brief Number PB12-9, April 2012.

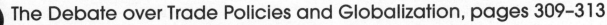

9.5 The Debate over Trade Policies and Globalization, pages 309–313

LEARNING OBJECTIVE: Evaluate the debate over trade policies and globalization.

Summary

The **World Trade Organization (WTO)** is an international organization that enforces trade agreements among members. The WTO has promoted **globalization**, the process of countries becoming more open to foreign trade and investment. Some critics of the WTO argue that globalization has damaged local cultures around the world. Other critics oppose the WTO because they believe in **protectionism**, which is the use of trade barriers to shield domestic firms from foreign competition. The WTO allows countries to use tariffs in cases of **dumping**, when an imported product is sold for a price below its cost of production.

Review Questions

5.1 What events led to the General Agreement on Tariffs and Trade (GATT)? Why did the WTO eventually replace the GATT?

5.2 What is globalization? Why are some people opposed to globalization? What is protectionism? Who benefits and who loses from protectionist policies? What are the main arguments people use to justify protectionism?

5.3 What is dumping? Who benefits and who loses from dumping? What problems arise when anti-dumping laws are implemented?

Problems and Applications

5.4 In 2017, shortly after President Trump took office, the U.S. Department of Commerce considered imposing tariffs on European steel companies it accused of dumping steel on the U.S. market. An article in the *Wall Street Journal* quoted Secretary of Commerce Wilbur Ross as asserting, "A healthy steel industry is critical to our economy and manufacturing base, yet our steel industry today is under assault from foreign producers that dump and subsidize their exports." What is dumping? If the United States imposes tariffs on imports of steel from Europe, briefly explain who is likely to gain and who is likely to lose.

Source: Andrea Thomas and Ulrike Dauer, "Germany Hits Back at U.S. Proposals of Anti-dumping Tariffs on Steel Imports," *Wall Street Journal*, March 31, 2017.

5.5 Steven Landsburg, an economist at the University of Rochester, wrote the following in an article in the *Wall Street Journal*:

> Free trade is not only about the right of American consumers to buy at the cheapest possible price; it's also about the right of foreign producers to earn a living. Steelworkers in West Virginia struggle hard to make ends meet. So do steelworkers in South Korea. To

protect one at the expense of the other, solely because of where they happened to be born, is a moral outrage.

How does the U.S. government protect steelworkers in West Virginia at the expense of steelworkers in South Korea? Is Landsburg making a positive statement or a normative statement? A few days later, Tom Redburn published an article disagreeing with Landsburg. Redburn argued that caring about the welfare of people in the United States more than about the welfare of people in other countries isn't "some evil character flaw." According to Redburn, "A society that ignores the consequences of economic disruption on those among its citizens who come out at the short end of the stick is not only heartless, it also undermines its own cohesion and adaptability."

Which of the two arguments do you find most convincing?

Sources: Steven E. Landsburg, "Who Cares if the Playing Field Is Level?" *Wall Street Journal*, June 13, 2001; and Tom Redburn, "Economic View: Of Politics, Free Markets, and Tending to Society," *New York Times*, June 17, 2001.

5.6 Suppose you are explaining the benefits of free trade and someone states, "I don't understand all the principles of comparative advantage and gains from trade. I just know that if I buy something produced in America, I create a job for an American, and if I buy something produced in Brazil, I create a job for a Brazilian." Do you agree with this statement? When the United States imports products for which it does not have a comparative advantage, does this mean there are fewer jobs in the United States? In the example in Section 9.3 with China and the United States producing and trading smartphones and wheat, when the United States imports smartphones from China, does the number of jobs in the United States decline? Briefly explain.

5.7 Every year, the Gallup Poll asks a sample of people in the United States whether they believe foreign trade provides "an opportunity for economic growth through increased U.S. exports" or whether they believe foreign trade represents "a threat to the economy from foreign imports." The following table shows the responses for 2 years.

	View of Foreign Trade		
Year	Favorable to Foreign Trade	Unfavorable	State of the U.S. Economy
2008	41%	52%	Deep economic recession
2017	72%	23%	Economic expansion

a. Do you believe that foreign trade helps or hurts the economy? (Be sure to define what you mean by "helps" or "hurts.")

b. Why might the general public's opinion of foreign trade be substantially different during an economic recession, when production and employment are falling, than during an economic expansion, when production and employment are increasing?

c. Typically polls show that people in the United States under 30 years of age have a more favorable opinion of foreign trade than do people age 65 and over. Why might younger people have a more favorable view of foreign trade than older people?

Source: Art Swift, "In US, Record-High 72% See Foreign Trade as Opportunity," gallup.com, February 16, 2017.

5.8 At one time, Eastman Kodak was the world's largest producer of photographic film, employing nearly 145,000 workers worldwide, including thousands at its headquarters in Rochester, New York. The firm eventually laid off most of those workers because its sales declined as it failed to adjust to digital photography as quickly as many of its foreign competitors. A member of Congress from Rochester described the many new firms that were now located in buildings that were formerly owned by Kodak. A *New York Times* columnist concluded, "which, of course, is precisely the way globalization is supposed to work." Briefly explain what the columnist meant. Do you agree with his conclusion?

Does the outcome in Rochester show that globalization is good? Briefly explain.

Source: Joe Nocera, "Don't Blame NAFTA," *New York Times*, January 23, 2015.

5.9 **(Related to the Apply the Concept on page 312)** According to an opinion column in the *New York Times*, because of attempts to make it more difficult to import catfish into the United States, many Vietnamese businesses that export catfish shifted from exporting to the United States to exporting to China. Briefly explain who gained and who lost as a result of this adjustment by Vietnamese businesses resulting from U.S. trade restrictions.

Source: Roger Cohen, "Of Catfish Wars and Shooting Wars," *New York Times*, March 26, 2015.

5.10 **(Related to the Apply the Concept on page 312)** In 2016, an editorial in the *Wall Street Journal* was in favor of, "repealing the notorious catfish program that has become a byword for Washington waste and protectionism? This should be an easy call." Why would a federal government program to inspect catfish be considered an example of protectionism? If repealing the program is "an easy call," as the editorial asserts, why was the program still in place in 2017, more than a year after the editorial was published?

Source: "A Chance of a Catfish Vote," *Wall Street Journal*, July 6, 2016.

Critical Thinking Exercises

CT9.1 As we saw in this chapter, comparative advantage is an important economic concept. We often use a table and some arithmetic to explain it, but how might you use words to explain comparative advantage to someone not taking this course, such as a roommate, a family member, or a friend? *Hint:* You might want to explain the concept using just two people or perhaps two businesses that trade goods and services with each other, where one is more efficient in the production of all goods and services and yet both benefit from trading with each other.

CT9.2 A key part of this chapter is the section "Where Does Comparative Advantage Come From?" starting on page 301. The section explains the main sources of comparative advantage among countries. Comparative advantage also applies to people. Describe some sources of comparative advantage between people; that is, why might one person have a comparative advantage in the production of a good or service relative to another person?

CT9.3 In Chapter 3, we used the demand and supply model to understand markets. Can we also use this model to understand comparative advantage?

Consumer Choice and Behavioral Economics

J.C. Penney Customers Didn't Buy into "Everyday Low Prices"

In 2010, the J.C. Penney department store chain had nearly 600 "sales," and it sold almost three-quarters of its products at prices marked down by at least 50 percent. However, these sales were illusions because Penney had raised prices before discounting them. The company also often required customers to clip coupons to get the sale price. Soon after being named chief executive officer (CEO) of J.C. Penney in 2011, Ron Johnson, who had had a successful career as head of Apple's retail stores, decided to try a new pricing strategy of "everyday low prices" that eliminated most sales and coupons. But the new pricing policy backfired. Penney's sales plunged 25 percent in 2012, and the company fired Johnson after only 17 months. In 2017, Penney was still struggling. With its revenue and profits remaining well below 2010 levels, the company announced that it was closing 140 of its 1,000 stores and would reduce employment by 6,000 workers.

What was wrong with Johnson's pricing policy? First, the everyday low prices ended up being higher than the sale prices under the previous pricing policy. Some customers noticed and switched to shopping at Walmart and other department stores. Some economists, though, believe that Johnson ran into an even bigger problem: Although economists generally assume that people have enough information to make optimal buying decisions, this assumption may not always be accurate. For example, many consumers have only a rough idea of the typical price of a pair of jeans or a shirt. These consumers have difficulty knowing whether everyday low prices really are low. Instead, they wait for sales and use coupons because they believe doing so allows them to buy at lower-than-normal prices.

Mark Lennihan/AP Images

As Alexander Chernev of Northwestern University put it, "J.C. Penney might say it's a fair price, but why should consumers trust J.C. Penney?" He argued that consumers "want a great deal," which they believe they get only if a store is having a sale or if they use coupons.

We can better understand the failure of Penney's pricing strategy by using insights from *behavioral economics*, which is the study of situations in which people make choices that do not appear to be economically rational. Firms must understand consumer behavior to determine what strategies are likely to be most effective in selling their products. In this chapter, we will examine how consumers make decisions about which products to buy.

Sources: Ed Lin, "J.C. Penney Stock Could Be in a Beauty of a Mess," barrons.com, March 29, 2017; Stephanie Clifford and Catherine Rampell, "Sometimes, We Want Prices to Fool Us," *New York Times*, April 13, 2013; Wendy Liebmann, "What Will We Learn from Ron Johnson's Mistake?" *Forbes*, May 8, 2013; and Brad Tuttle, "The 5 Big Mistakes That Led to Ron Johnson's Ouster at JC Penney," *Time*, April 9, 2013.

Chapter Outline & Learning Objectives

Economics in Your Life & Career

How Should You Price Tickets to a Hit Broadway Show?

Suppose you work for a producer of a show running at the Richard Rodgers Theatre on Broadway in New York City, or suppose you work for a concert promoter who books bands to play at the 40 Watt Club in Athens, Georgia. The producer asks you for advice on what to charge for tickets. The answer seems easy: Charge the highest price that will sell all the available tickets.

Charging a lower price would seem to reduce the profit that could be earned from the show. In fact, though, charging the highest price is *not* the strategy most Broadway producers or concert promoters use. Why not? As you read this chapter, try to answer this question. You can check your answer against the one we provide on **page 351** at the end of this chapter.

We begin this chapter by exploring how consumers make decisions. We have seen that economists usually assume that people act in a rational, self-interested way. In explaining consumer behavior, economists believe people make choices that will leave them as satisfied as possible, given their *tastes*, their *incomes*, and the *prices* of the goods and services available to them. We will see how downward-sloping demand curves result from the economic model of consumer behavior. We will also explore how in certain situations, knowing which decision is the best one can be difficult. In these cases, economic reasoning provides a tool for consumers to improve their decision making. Finally, we will see that *experimental economics* has shown that factors such as social pressure and notions of fairness can affect consumer behavior. We will look at how businesses take these factors into account when setting prices. In the appendix to this chapter, we extend the analysis by using indifference curves and budget lines to understand consumer behavior.

10.1 Utility and Consumer Decision Making

LEARNING OBJECTIVE: Define utility and explain how consumers choose goods and services to maximize their utility.

We have seen that the model of demand and supply is a powerful tool for analyzing how prices and quantities are determined. We have also seen that, according to the *law of demand*, whenever the price of a good falls, the quantity demanded increases. In this section, we will show how the economic model of consumer behavior leads to the law of demand.

An Overview of the Economic Model of Consumer Behavior

Imagine browsing the Web sites of your favorite stores, trying to decide how to spend your clothing budget. If you had an unlimited budget, your decision would be easy: Just buy as much of everything as you want. Given that you have a limited budget, what do you do? Economists assume that consumers act so as to make themselves as well off as possible. Therefore, you should choose the one combination of clothes that makes you as well off as possible from among the combinations that you can afford. Stated more generally, the economic model of consumer behavior predicts that consumers will choose to buy the combination of goods and services that makes them as well off as possible from among all the combinations that their budgets allow them to buy.

    Although this prediction may seem obvious and not particularly useful, we will see that it leads to conclusions that are useful—but not obvious.   **MyLab Economics** Concept Check

Utility

The amount of satisfaction you receive from consuming a particular combination of goods and services depends on your tastes or preferences. There is an old saying that "there's no accounting for taste," and economists don't try to. If you buy a bottle of Coca-Cola's smartwater instead of a bottle of PepsiCo's LIFEWTR for the same price, you must receive more enjoyment or satisfaction from drinking smartwater. Economists refer to the enjoyment or satisfaction people receive from consuming goods and services as **utility**. So we can say that the goal of a consumer is to spend available income so as to maximize utility. But utility is a difficult concept to measure because there is no way of knowing exactly how much enjoyment or satisfaction someone receives from consuming a product. Similarly, it is not possible to compare utility across consumers. There is no way of knowing for sure whether Jill receives more or less satisfaction than Jack from drinking a bottle of smartwater.

    Two hundred years ago, economists hoped to measure utility in units called *utils*. The util would be an objective measure in the same way that temperature is: If it is 75 degrees in New York and 75 degrees in Los Angeles, it is just as warm in both cities. These economists wanted to say that if Jack's utility from drinking a bottle of

Utility The enjoyment or satisfaction people receive from consuming goods and services.

smartwater is 10 utils and Jill's utility is 5 utils, then Jack receives exactly twice the satisfaction from drinking a bottle of smartwater as Jill does. In fact, it is *not* possible to measure utility across people. It turns out that none of the important conclusions of the economic model of consumer behavior depend on utility being directly measurable (a point we demonstrate in the appendix to this chapter). Nevertheless, the economic model of consumer behavior is easier to understand if we assume that utility is something directly measurable, like temperature. **MyLab Economics** Concept Check

The Principle of Diminishing Marginal Utility

To make the model of consumer behavior more concrete, let's see how a consumer makes decisions in a case involving just two products: pizza and Coke. To begin, consider how the utility you receive from consuming a good changes with the quantity of the good you consume. Suppose that you arrive at a Super Bowl party where the hosts are serving pizza and you are very hungry. In this situation, you are likely to receive quite a lot of enjoyment, or utility, from consuming the first slice of pizza. Suppose this satisfaction is measurable and is equal to 20 units of utility, or utils. After eating the first slice, you decide to have a second slice. Because you are no longer as hungry, the satisfaction you receive from eating the second slice of pizza is less than the satisfaction you received from eating the first slice. Consuming the second slice increases your utility by only an *additional* 16 utils, which raises your *total* utility from eating the 2 slices to 36 utils. If you continue eating slices, each additional slice gives you less and less additional satisfaction.

The table in Figure 10.1 shows the relationship between the number of slices of pizza you consume while watching the Super Bowl and the amount of utility you receive. The second column in the table shows the total utility you receive from eating a particular number of slices. The third column shows the additional utility, or **marginal utility (MU)**, you receive from consuming 1 additional slice. (Remember that in economics, *marginal* means *additional*.) For example, as you increase your consumption from 2 slices to 3 slices, your total utility increases from 36 to 46, so your marginal utility from consuming the third slice is 10 utils. As the table shows, by the time you eat the fifth slice of pizza that evening, your marginal utility is very low: only 2 utils. If you were to eat a sixth slice, you would feel slightly ill, and your marginal utility would actually be a *negative* 3 utils.

> **Marginal utility (MU)** The change in total utility a person receives from consuming one additional unit of a good or service.

Figure 10.1 also plots the numbers from the table as graphs. Panel (a) shows how your total utility rises as you eat the first 5 slices of pizza and then falls as you eat the sixth slice. Panel (b) shows how your marginal utility declines with each additional slice you eat and finally becomes negative when you eat the sixth slice. The height of the marginal utility line at any quantity of pizza in panel (b) represents the change in utility as a result of consuming that additional slice. For example, the change in utility as a result of consuming 4 slices instead of 3 is 6 utils, so the height of the marginal utility line in panel (b) for the fourth slice is 6 utils.

The relationship illustrated in Figure 10.1 between consuming additional units of a product during a period of time and the marginal utility received from consuming each additional unit is called the **law of diminishing marginal utility**. For nearly every good or service, the more you consume during a period of time, the less you increase your total satisfaction from each additional unit you consume. **MyLab Economics** Concept Check

> **Law of diminishing marginal utility** The principle that consumers experience diminishing additional satisfaction as they consume more of a good or service during a given period of time.

The Rule of Equal Marginal Utility per Dollar Spent

The key challenge for consumers is to decide how to allocate their limited incomes among all the products they want to buy. Every consumer has to make trade-offs: If you have $100 to spend on entertainment for the month, then the more movies you rent or buy online, the fewer movies you can see in the theater. Economists refer to the limited amount of income you have available to spend on goods and services as your **budget constraint**. The principle of diminishing marginal utility helps us understand how consumers can best spend their limited incomes on the products available to them.

> **Budget constraint** The limited amount of income available to consumers to spend on goods and services.

MyLab Economics Animation

Figure 10.1

Total and Marginal Utility from Eating Pizza on Super Bowl Sunday

The table shows that for the first 5 slices of pizza, the more you eat, the more your total satisfaction, or utility, increases. If you eat a sixth slice, you start to feel ill from eating too much pizza, and your total utility falls. Each additional slice increases your utility by less than the previous slice, so your marginal utility from each slice is less than your marginal utility from the one before. Panel (a) shows your total utility rising as you eat the first 5 slices and falling with the sixth slice. Panel (b) shows your marginal utility falling with each additional slice you eat and becoming negative with the sixth slice. The height of the marginal utility line at any quantity of pizza in panel (b) represents the change in utility as a result of consuming that additional slice. For example, the change in utility as a result of consuming 4 slices instead of 3 is 6 utils, so the height of the marginal utility line in panel (b) for the fourth slice is 6 utils.

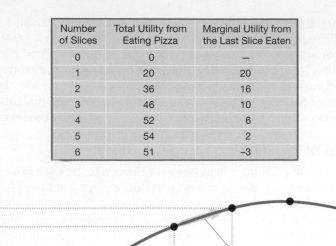

Number of Slices	Total Utility from Eating Pizza	Marginal Utility from the Last Slice Eaten
0	0	—
1	20	20
2	36	16
3	46	10
4	52	6
5	54	2
6	51	−3

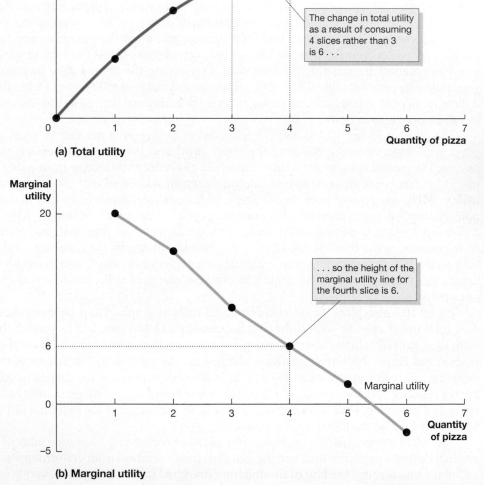

(a) Total utility

The change in total utility as a result of consuming 4 slices rather than 3 is 6 . . .

. . . so the height of the marginal utility line for the fourth slice is 6.

(b) Marginal utility

Suppose you attend a Super Bowl party at a restaurant, and you have $10 to spend on refreshments. Pizza is selling for $2 per slice, and Coke is selling for $1 per cup. Table 10.1 shows the relationship between the amount of pizza you eat, the amount of Coke you drink, and the amount of satisfaction, or utility, you receive. The values for pizza are repeated from the table in Figure 10.1. The values for Coke also follow the principle of diminishing marginal utility.

How many slices of pizza and how many cups of Coke should you buy if you want to maximize your utility? If you did not have a budget constraint, you would buy 5 slices of pizza and 5 cups of Coke because that would give you total utility of 107 (= 54 + 53) which is the maximum utility you can achieve. Eating another slice of pizza or drinking another cup of Coke during the evening would lower your utility.

Number of Slices of Pizza	Total Utility from Eating Pizza	Marginal Utility from the Last Slice	Number of Cups of Coke	Total Utility from Drinking Coke	Marginal Utility from the Last Cup
0	0	—	0	0	—
1	20	20	1	20	20
2	36	16	2	35	15
3	46	10	3	45	10
4	52	6	4	50	5
5	54	2	5	53	3
6	51	−3	6	52	−1

MyLab Economics Animation

Table 10.1

Total Utility and Marginal Utility from Eating Pizza and Drinking Coke

Unfortunately, you do have a budget constraint: You have only $10 to spend. To buy 5 slices of pizza (at $2 per slice) and 5 cups of Coke (at $1 per cup), you would need $15.

To select the best way to spend your $10, remember this key economic principle: *Optimal decisions are made at the margin.* That is, most of the time economic decision makers—consumers, firms, and the government—are faced with decisions about whether to do a little more of one thing or a little more of an alternative. In this case, you are choosing to consume a little more pizza or a little more Coke. Tesla chooses whether to manufacture more high-price Models S cars or more lower-price Model 3 cars in its California factory. Congress and the president choose whether to spend more for research on heart disease or more to repair highways. Everyone faces a budget constraint, and everyone faces trade-offs.

The key to making the best consumption decision is to maximize utility by following *the rule of equal marginal utility per dollar spent.* As you decide how to spend your income, you should buy pizza and Coke up to the point where the last slice of pizza and the last cup of Coke purchased give you equal increases in utility *per dollar.* By using this approach, you will maximize your total utility, given your budget constraint.

It is important to remember that to follow this rule, you must equalize your marginal utility per dollar spent, *not* your marginal utility from each good. (Or, to use a familiar phrase, you want to get "the most bang for your buck.") Buying season tickets for your favorite National Football League (NFL) team or for the symphony or buying a BMW may give you a lot more satisfaction than drinking a cup of Coke, but the NFL tickets may well give you less satisfaction *per dollar spent.* To decide how many slices of pizza and cups of Coke to buy, you must convert the values for marginal utility in Table 10.1 into marginal utility per dollar. You can do this by dividing marginal utility by the price of each good, as shown in Table 10.2.

In column (3), we calculate marginal utility per dollar spent on pizza. Because the price of pizza is $2 per slice, the marginal utility per dollar from eating 1 slice

(1) Number of Slices of Pizza	(2) Marginal Utility (MU_{Pizza})	(3) Marginal Utility per Dollar $\left(\dfrac{MU_{Pizza}}{P_{Pizza}}\right)$	(4) Cups of Coke	(5) Marginal Utility (MU_{Coke})	(6) Marginal Utility per Dollar $\left(\dfrac{MU_{Coke}}{P_{Coke}}\right)$
1	20	10	1	20	20
2	16	8	2	15	15
3	10	5	3	10	10
4	6	3	4	5	5
5	2	1	5	3	3
6	−3	−1.5	6	−1	−1

MyLab Economics Animation

Table 10.2

Converting Marginal Utility to Marginal Utility per Dollar

Table 10.3

Equalizing Marginal Utility per Dollar Spent

Combinations of Pizza and Coke with Equal Marginal Utilities per Dollar	Marginal Utility per Dollar (MU/P)	Total Spending	Total Utility
1 slice of pizza and 3 cups of Coke	10	$2 = $3 = $5	20 + 45 = 65
3 slices of pizza and 4 cups of Coke	5	$6 + $4 = $10	46 + 50 = 96
4 slices of pizza and 5 cups of Coke	3	$8 + $5 = $13	52 + 53 = 105

equals 20 divided by $2, or 10 utils per dollar. Similarly, we show in column (6) that because the price of Coke is $1 per cup, the marginal utility per dollar from drinking 1 cup of Coke equals 20 divided by $1, or 20 utils per dollar. To maximize the total utility you receive, you must make sure that the utility per dollar of pizza for the last slice of pizza is equal to the utility per dollar of Coke for the last cup. Table 10.2 shows that there are three combinations of slices of pizza and cups of Coke where marginal utility per dollar is equalized. Table 10.3 lists the combinations, the total amount of money needed to buy each combination, and the total utility received from consuming each combination.

As shown in the bottom row of the table, if you buy 4 slices of pizza, the last slice gives you 3 utils per dollar. If you buy 5 cups of Coke, the last cup also gives you 3 utils per dollar, so you have equalized your marginal utility per dollar. Unfortunately, as the third column in the table shows, to buy 4 slices and 5 cups, you would need $13, and you have only $10. The top row of the table shows that you could also equalize your marginal utility per dollar by buying 1 slice and 3 cups, but that would cost just $5, leaving you with $5 not spent. As the middle row shows, only when you buy 3 slices and 4 cups have you equalized your marginal utility per dollar and spent neither more nor less than the $10 available.

We can summarize the two conditions for maximizing utility as follows:

1. $\dfrac{MU_{Pizza}}{P_{Pizza}} = \dfrac{MU_{Coke}}{P_{Coke}}$

This condition states that the marginal utility per dollar spent must be the same for both goods.

2. Spending on pizza + Spending on Coke = Amount available to be spent

This condition is the budget constraint, which states that total spending on both goods must equal the amount available to be spent.

Of course, these conditions for maximizing utility apply not just to pizza and Coke but to any pairs of goods.   **MyLab Economics** Concept Check

Solved Problem 10.1

MyLab Economics Interactive Animation

Finding the Optimal Level of Consumption

The following table shows Lee's utility from consuming ice cream cones and bottles of smartwater:

Number of Ice Cream Cones	Total Utility from Ice Cream Cones	Marginal Utility from Last Cone	Number of Bottles of Smartwater	Total Utility from Bottles of Smartwater	Marginal Utility from Last Bottle
0	0	—	0	0	—
1	30	30	1	40	40
2	55	25	2	75	35
3	75	20	3	101	26
4	90	15	4	119	18
5	100	10	5	134	15
6	105	5	6	141	7

a. Ed inspects this table and concludes, "Lee's optimal choice would be to consume 4 ice cream cones and 5 bottles of smartwater because with that combination, his marginal utility from ice cream cones is equal to his marginal utility from smartwater." Do you agree with Ed's reasoning? Briefly explain.

b. Suppose that Lee has an unlimited budget to spend on ice cream cones and bottles of smartwater. Under these circumstances, how many ice cream cones and how many bottles of smartwater will he consume? (Assume that Lee cannot consume more than 6 ice cream cones or 6 cans of smartwater.)

c. Suppose that Lee has $7 per week to spend on ice cream cones and bottles of smartwater. The price of an ice cream cone is $2, and the price of a bottle of smartwater is $1. If Lee wants to maximize his utility, how many ice cream cones and how many bottles of smartwater should he buy?

Solving the Problem

Step 1: Review the chapter material. This problem involves finding the optimal consumption of two goods, so you may want to review the section "The Rule of Equal Marginal Utility per Dollar Spent," which begins on page 327.

Step 2: Answer part (a) by analyzing Ed's reasoning. Ed's reasoning is incorrect. To maximize utility, Lee needs to equalize marginal utility *per dollar* for the two goods.

Step 3: Answer part (b) by determining how Lee would maximize utility with an unlimited budget. With an unlimited budget, consumers maximize utility by continuing to buy each good as long as their utility is increasing. In this case, Lee will maximize utility by buying 6 ice cream cones and 6 bottles of smartwater, given that we are assuming he cannot buy more than 6 units of either good.

Step 4: Answer part (c) by determining Lee's optimal combination of ice cream cones and bottles of smartwater. Lee will maximize his utility if he spends his $7 per week so that the marginal utility of ice cream cones divided by their price is equal to the marginal utility of smartwater divided by its price. We can use the following table to solve this part of the problem:

| | Ice Cream Cones | | Bottles of Smartwater | |
Quantity	MU	$\dfrac{MU}{P}$	MU	$\dfrac{MU}{P}$
1	30	15	40	40
2	25	12.5	35	35
3	20	10	26	26
4	15	7.5	18	18
5	10	5	15	15
6	5	2.5	7	7

Lee will maximize his utility by buying 1 ice cream cone and 5 bottles of smartwater. At this combination, the marginal utility of each good divided by its price equals 15. He has also spent all of his $7.

Your Turn: For more practice, do related problems 1.9 and 1.10 on pages 352–353 at the end of this chapter.

MyLab Economics Study Plan

What if the Rule of Equal Marginal Utility per Dollar Does Not Hold?

The idea of getting the maximum utility by equalizing the ratio of marginal utility to price for the goods you are buying can be difficult to grasp, so it is worth thinking about it in another way. Suppose that instead of buying 3 slices of pizza and 4 cups of Coke, you buy 4 slices and 2 cups. This combination costs $10, so you would meet your

Don't Let This Happen to You

Equalize Marginal Utilities *per Dollar*

Harry likes to read e-books and watch movies on his tablet. The following table gives Harry's utility from buying books and movies.

	Harry's Utility from Buying Books and Movies				
Quantity of Books	Total Utility from Books	Marginal Utility from Last Book	Quantity of Movies	Total Utility from Movies	Marginal Utility from Last Movie
0	0	—	0	0	—
1	50	50	1	60	60
2	85	35	2	105	45
3	110	25	3	145	40
4	130	20	4	175	30
5	140	10	5	195	20
6	145	5	6	210	15

Can you determine from this table the optimal combination of books and movies for Harry? It is very tempting to say that Harry should buy 4 books and 5 movies because his marginal utility from books is equal to his marginal utility from movies with that combination. In fact, we can't be sure this is the best combination because we are lacking some critical information: Harry's budget constraint—how much he has available to spend on books and movies—and the prices of books and movies.

Let's say that Harry has $100 to spend this month, the price of an e-book is $10, and the price of an online movie is $20. (Harry insists on buying his movies instead of renting them!) Using the information from the first table, we can now calculate Harry's marginal utility per dollar for both goods, as shown in the following table.

	Harry's Marginal Utility and Marginal Utility per Dollar from Buying Books and Movies				
Quantity of Books	Marginal Utility from Last Book (MU_{Books})	Marginal Utility per Dollar $\left(\dfrac{MU_{Books}}{P_{Books}}\right)$	Quantity of Movies	Marginal Utility from Last Movie (MU_{Movies})	Marginal Utility per Dollar $\left(\dfrac{MU_{Movies}}{P_{Movies}}\right)$
1	50	5	1	60	3
2	35	3.5	2	45	2.25
3	25	2.5	3	40	2
4	20	2	4	30	1.5
5	10	1	5	20	1
6	5	0.5	6	15	0.75

Harry's marginal utility per dollar is the same for two combinations of books and movies, as shown in the following table:

Combinations of Books and Movies with Equal Marginal Utilities per Dollar	Marginal Utility per Dollar (MU/P)	Total Spending	Total Utility
5 books and 5 movies	1	$50 + $100 = $150	140 + 195 = 335
4 books and 3 movies	2	$40 + $60 = $100	130 + 145 = 275

Unfortunately, 5 books and 5 movies would cost Harry $150, and he has only $100. The best Harry can do is to buy 4 books and 3 movies. This combination provides him with the maximum amount of utility attainable, given his budget constraint.

The key point is the same as in Solved Problem 10.1 on page 330: Consumers maximize their utility when they equalize marginal utility *per dollar* for every good they buy, *not* when they equalize marginal utility.

MyLab Economics Study Plan

Your Turn: Test your understanding by doing related problem 1.12 on page 353 at the end of this chapter.

budget constraint by spending all the money available to you, but would you have gotten the maximum amount of utility? No, you wouldn't have. From the information in Table 10.2 on page 329, we can list the additional utility per dollar you are getting from the last slice and the last cup and the total utility from consuming 4 slices and 2 cups:

Marginal utility per dollar for the fourth slice of pizza = 3 utils per dollar

Marginal utility per dollar for the second cup of Coke = 15 utils per dollar

Total utility from 4 slices of pizza and 2 cups of Coke = 87 utils

Obviously, the marginal utilities per dollar are not equal. The last cup of Coke gave you considerably more satisfaction per dollar than did the last slice of pizza. Therefore, you can raise your total utility by buying less pizza and more Coke. Buying 1 less slice of pizza frees up $2 that will allow you to buy 2 more cups of Coke. Eating 1 less slice of pizza reduces your utility by 6 utils, but drinking 2 additional cups of Coke raises your utility by 15 utils (make sure you see this), for a net increase of 9. You end up equalizing your marginal utility per dollar (5 utils per dollar for both the last slice and the last cup) and raising your total utility from 87 to 96 utils.   **MyLab Economics** Concept Check

The Income Effect and Substitution Effect of a Price Change

We can use the rule of equal marginal utility per dollar to analyze how consumers adjust their buying decisions when a price changes. Suppose you are back at the restaurant for the Super Bowl party, but this time the price of pizza is $1.50 per slice, rather than $2. You still have $10 to spend on pizza and Coke.

When the price of pizza was $2 per slice and the price of Coke was $1 per cup, your optimal choice was to consume 3 slices of pizza and 4 cups of Coke. The fall in the price of pizza to $1.50 per slice has two effects on the quantity of pizza you consume.

The Income Effect When the price of a good falls, you have more purchasing power. In our example, 3 slices of pizza and 4 cups of Coke now cost a total of only $8.50 instead of $10.00. An increase in purchasing power is essentially the same thing as an increase in income. The change in the quantity of pizza you will demand because of this increase in purchasing power—holding all other factors constant— is the **income effect** of the price change. Recall that if a product is a *normal good*, a consumer increases the quantity demanded as the consumer's income rises, but if a product is an *inferior good*, a consumer decreases the quantity demanded as the consumer's income rises (see Chapter 3, Section 3.1). So, if we assume that pizza is a normal good for you, the income effect of a fall in price causes you to consume more pizza. If pizza were an inferior good for you, the income effect of a fall in the price would have caused you to consume less pizza.

Income effect The change in the quantity demanded of a good that results from the effect of a change in price on consumer purchasing power, holding all other factors constant.

The Substitution Effect When the price of pizza falls, pizza becomes cheaper *relative* to Coke, and the marginal utility per dollar for each slice of pizza you consume increases. If we hold constant the effect of the price change on your purchasing power and just focus on the effect of the price being lower relative to the price of the other good, we have isolated the **substitution effect** of the price change. The lower price of pizza relative to the price of Coke has reduced the *opportunity cost* to you of consuming pizza because now you have to give up less Coke to consume the same quantity of pizza. Therefore, the substitution effect from the fall in the price of pizza relative to the price of Coke causes you to eat more pizza and drink less Coke. In this case, both the income effect and the substitution effect of the fall in price cause you to eat more pizza. If the price of pizza had risen, both the income effect and the substitution effect would have caused you to eat less pizza. Table 10.4 summarizes the effect of a price change on the quantity demanded.

Substitution effect The change in the quantity demanded of a good that results from a change in price making the good more or less expensive relative to other goods, holding constant the effect of the price change on consumer purchasing power.

We can use Table 10.5 to determine the effect of the fall in the price of pizza on your optimal consumption. Table 10.5 has the same information as Table 10.2, with one change: The marginal utility per dollar from eating pizza has been changed to reflect the new lower price of $1.50 per slice. Examining the table, we can see that the

Table 10.4

Income Effect and Substitution
Effect of a Price Change

When price ...	consumer purchasing power ...	The income effect causes quantity demanded to ...	The substitution effect causes the opportunity cost of consuming a good to ...
decreases,	increases.	increase for a normal good and decrease for an inferior good.	decrease when the price decreases, which causes the quantity of the good demanded to increase.
increases,	decreases.	decrease for a normal good and increase for an inferior good.	increase when the price increases, which causes the quantity of the good demanded to decrease.

fall in the price of pizza will result in you eating 1 more slice of pizza, so your optimal consumption now becomes 4 slices of pizza and 4 cups of Coke. You will be spending all of your $10, and the last dollar you spend on pizza will provide you with about the same marginal utility per dollar as the last dollar you spend on Coke. You will not be receiving exactly the same marginal utility per dollar spent on the two products. As Table 10.5 shows, the last slice of pizza gives you 4 utils per dollar, and the last cup of Coke gives you 5 utils per dollar. But this is as close as you can come to equalizing marginal utility per dollar for the two products, unless you can buy a fraction of a slice of pizza or a fraction of a cup of Coke.

MyLab Economics Study Plan

MyLab Economics Concept Check

 10.2 # Where Demand Curves Come From

LEARNING OBJECTIVE: Use the concept of utility to explain the law of demand.

According to the *law of demand*, whenever the price of a product falls, the quantity demanded increases (see Chapter 3, Section 3.1). Now that we have covered the concepts of total utility, marginal utility, and the budget constraint, we can look more closely at why the law of demand holds.

In our example of optimal consumption of pizza and Coke at the Super Bowl party, we found the following:

$$\text{Price of pizza} = \$2 \text{ per slices} \rightarrow \text{Quantity of pizza demanded} = 3 \text{ slices}$$

$$\text{Price of pizza} = \$1.50 \text{ per slice} \rightarrow \text{Quantity of pizza demanded} = 4 \text{ slices}$$

In panel (a) of Figure 10.2, we plot the two points showing the optimal number of slices of pizza you choose to consume at each price. In panel (b), we draw a line connecting the two points. This downward-sloping line represents your demand curve for pizza. We could find more points on the line by changing the price of pizza and using

MyLab Economics Animation

Table 10.5

Adjusting Optimal Consumption
to a Lower Price of Pizza

Number of Slices of Pizza	Marginal Utility from Last Slice (MU_{Pizza})	Marginal Utility per Dollar ($\dfrac{MU_{Pizza}}{P_{Pizza}}$)	Number of Cups of Coke	Marginal Utility from Last Cup (MU_{Coke})	Marginal Utility per Dollar ($\dfrac{MU_{Coke}}{P_{Coke}}$)
1	20	13.33	1	20	20
2	16	10.67	2	15	15
3	10	6.67	3	10	10
4	6	4	4	5	5
5	2	1.33	5	3	3
6	−3	−2	6	−1	−1

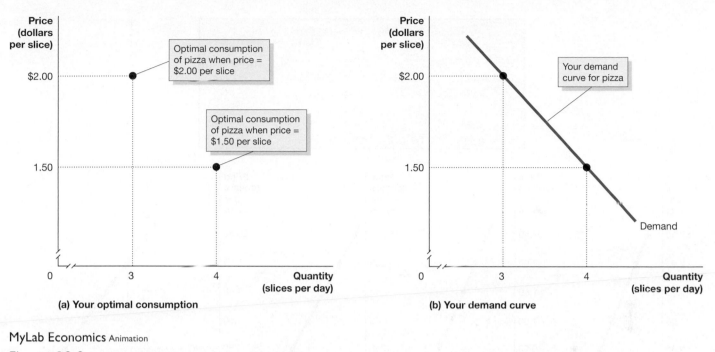

Figure 10.2 **Deriving the Demand Curve for Pizza**

A consumer responds optimally to a fall in the price of a product by consuming more of that product. In panel (a), the price of pizza falls from $2 per slice to $1.50, and the optimal quantity of slices you consume rises from 3 to 4. When we graph this result in panel (b), we have your demand curve.

the information in Table 10.2 to find the new optimal number of slices of pizza you would demand at each price.

To this point in the chapter, we have been looking at an individual demand curve. Economists, though, are typically interested in market demand curves. We can construct the market demand curve from the individual demand curves for all the consumers in the market. To keep things simple, let's assume that there are only three consumers in the market for pizza: you, David, and Lori. The table in Figure 10.3 shows the individual demand schedules for the three consumers. Because consumers differ in their incomes and their preferences for products, we would not expect every consumer to demand the same quantity of a given product at each price. The final column gives the market demand, which is simply the sum of the quantities demanded by each of the three consumers at each price. For example, at a price of $1.50 per slice, your quantity demanded is 4 slices, David's is 6 slices, and Lori's is 5 slices. So, at a price of $1.50, a quantity of 15 slices is demanded in the market. The graphs in the figure show that we can obtain the market demand curve by adding horizontally the individual demand curves.

Remember that according to the law of demand, market demand curves always slope downward. We now know that this result holds because the income and substitution effects of a decrease in price cause consumers to increase the quantity of the good they demand. There is a complicating factor, however. As we discussed earlier, only for a normal good will the income effect lead consumers to increase the quantity of the good they demand when the price falls. For an inferior good, the income effect leads consumers to *decrease* the quantity of the good they demand. The substitution effect, in contrast, results in consumers increasing the quantity they demand of both normal and inferior goods when the price falls. So, when the price of an inferior good falls, the income effect and substitution effect work in opposite directions: The income effect causes consumers to decrease the quantity of the good they demand, while the substitution effect causes consumers to increase the quantity of the good they demand. Is it possible, then, that consumers might actually buy less of a good when the price falls? If they did, the demand curve would be upward sloping. **MyLab Economics** Concept Check

MyLab Economics Study Plan

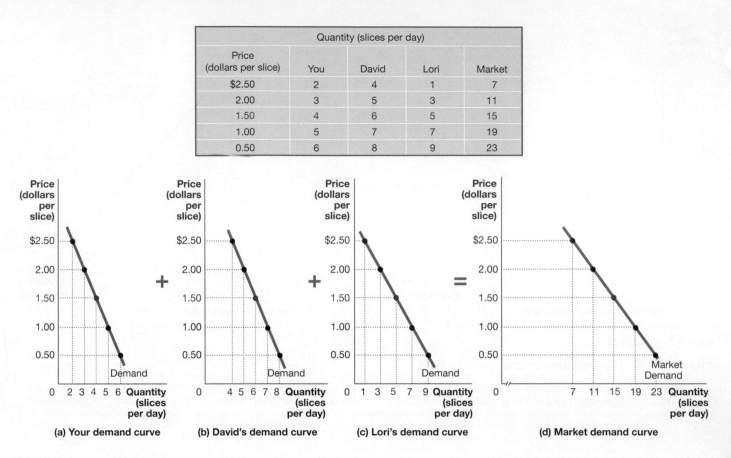

Quantity (slices per day)				
Price (dollars per slice)	You	David	Lori	Market
$2.50	2	4	1	7
2.00	3	5	3	11
1.50	4	6	5	15
1.00	5	7	7	19
0.50	6	8	9	23

(a) Your demand curve

(b) David's demand curve

(c) Lori's demand curve

(d) Market demand curve

MyLab Economics Animation

Figure 10.3   **Deriving the Market Demand Curve from Individual Demand Curves**

The table shows that the total quantity demanded in a market is the sum of the quantities demanded by each buyer. We can find the market demand curve by adding horizontally the individual demand curves in panels (a), (b), and (c).

For instance, at a price of $1.50, your quantity demanded is 4 slices, David's is 6 slices, and Lori's is 5 slices. Therefore, panel (d) shows that a price of $1.50 and a quantity demanded of 15 is a point on the market demand curve.

Apply the Concept

MyLab Economics Video

Are There Any Upward-Sloping Demand Curves in the Real World?

Giles Angel/Alamy Stock Photo

Rice is a Giffen good in poor parts of China.

For a demand curve to be upward sloping, the good would have to be an inferior good, and the income effect would have to be larger than the substitution effect. Economists have understood the conditions for an upward-sloping demand curve since the possibility was first discussed by the British economist Alfred Marshall in the 1890s. Marshall wrote that his friend, Sir Robert Giffen, had told him that when the price of bread rose, very poor people in British cities would actually buy more bread rather than less. Since that time, goods with upward-sloping demand curves have been called *Giffen goods*.

For more than a century, finding an actual Giffen good proved impossible. A close examination of the data showed that Giffen had been mistaken and that poor people in British cities bought less bread when prices rose, so their demand curves were downward sloping. Other possible candidates for being Giffen goods were also found to actually have downward-sloping demand curves. Finally, in 2006, Robert Jensen of Brown University and Nolan Miller of Harvard discovered two Giffen goods. They reasoned that to be a Giffen good, with an income effect larger than its substitution effect, a good must be inferior and make up a very large portion of consumers' budgets. Jensen and Miller knew that very poor people in the Hunan region of China spent most of their incomes on rice, while in the Gansu province, very poor people spent most of their income on wheat-based foods, such as buns and noodles. In both places, poor people ate meat when their incomes made it possible because they preferred the taste of meat, even though it did not supply as many calories as the rice or wheat they could purchase for the same price.

Jensen and Miller carried out the following experiment: In Hunan, for a five-month period, they gave a selected number of poor families coupons that would allow them to buy rice at a lower price. Families could not use the coupons for any other purpose. In Gansu, they gave a selected number of poor families coupons to buy wheat at a lower price. Jensen and Miller then observed the purchases of the families during the time they received the coupons and during the period immediately thereafter. In Hunan, during the months they received the coupons, the families bought less rice and more meat, and in Gansu, they bought less wheat and more meat. Because in Hunan, families bought less rice when the price was lower, their demand curves for rice were upward sloping. Similarly, in Gansu, families bought less wheat when the price was lower, so their demand curves for wheat were upward sloping. After more than a century of searching, economists had finally discovered examples of a Giffen good.

Source: Robert T. Jensen and Nolan H. Miller, "Giffen Behavior and Subsistence Consumption," *American Economic Review*, Vol. 98, No. 4, September 2008, pp. 1553–1577.

Your Turn: Test your understanding by doing related problems 2.9 and 2.10 on page 354 at the end of this chapter.

MyLab Economics Study Plan

10.3 Social Influences on Decision Making

LEARNING OBJECTIVE: Explain how social influences can affect consumption choices.

Sociologists and anthropologists have argued that social factors such as culture, customs, and religion are very important in explaining the choices people make. Economists have traditionally seen such factors as being relatively unimportant, if they take them into consideration at all. Recently, however, some economists have begun to study how social factors influence consumer choice.

For example, people seem to receive more utility from consuming goods they believe are popular. As the late Gary Becker, a Nobel Prize winner in economics, and Kevin Murphy put it:

> The utility from drugs, crime, going bowling, owning a Rolex watch, voting Democratic, dressing informally at work, or keeping a neat lawn depends on whether friends and neighbors take drugs, commit crimes, go bowling, own Rolex watches, vote Democratic, dress informally, or keep their lawns neat.

This reasoning can help explain why one restaurant is packed, while another restaurant that serves essentially the same food and has similar decor has many fewer customers. Consumers decide which restaurant to go to not only on the basis of food and decor but also on the basis of the restaurant's popularity. People receive utility from being seen eating at a popular restaurant because they believe it makes them appear knowledgeable and fashionable. Whenever consumption takes place publicly, some consumers base their purchasing decisions on what other consumers are buying. Examples of public consumption include eating in restaurants, attending sporting events or the theater, wearing clothes or jewelry, and driving cars. In all these cases, the decision to buy a product depends partly on the characteristics of the product and partly on how many other people are buying the product.

The Effects of Celebrity Endorsements

In some cases, it is not just the number of people who use a product that makes it desirable but which other people use it. If consumers believe that media stars or professional athletes use a product, demand for the product will often increase. For example, New

England Patriots quarterback Tom Brady is one of the biggest stars in the National Football League, so it may not be surprising that companies including Under Armour sportswear, UGG footwear, and Beautyrest mattresses have lined up to have him endorse their products. Brady makes around $7 million per year from his endorsements.

Tom Brady is a great football player, but why do consumers care what products he uses? They may believe Brady has better information than they do about the products he endorses. The average football fan might believe that if Brady endorses Under Armour sportswear, maybe Under Armour makes better sportswear. It seems more likely, however, that people buy products associated with Tom Brady or other celebrities because using these products makes them feel closer to the celebrity endorser or because it makes them appear to be fashionable. **MyLab Economics** Concept Check

Network Externalities

Network externality A situation in which the usefulness of a product increases with the number of consumers who use it.

Technology can play a role in explaining why consumers buy products that many other consumers are already buying. There is a **network externality** in the consumption of a product if the usefulness of the product increases with the number of consumers who use it.

There's Strength in Numbers If you owned the only phone in the world, it would not be very useful. The usefulness of phones increases as the number of people who own them increases. Similarly, your willingness to buy an Apple iPad depends in part on the number of other people who own iPads. The more people who own iPads, the more applications, or "apps," other firms will produce for the iPad, and the more novels, textbooks, newspapers, and magazines publishers will make available for downloading to the iPad, and, therefore, the more useful an iPad is to you.

Do Switching Costs Cause Inferior Technologies to Survive? Some economists have suggested the possibility that network externalities may have a significant downside because they might result in consumers buying products that contain inferior technologies. This outcome could occur because network externalities can create significant *switching costs* related to changing products: When a product becomes established, consumers may find switching to a new product that contains a better technology too costly. The selection of products may be *path dependent*: Because of switching costs, the technology that was first available may have advantages over better technologies that were developed later. In other words, the path along which the economy has developed in the past is important.

One possible example of path dependence and the use of an inferior technology is the QWERTY order of the letters along the top row of most computer keyboards. This order became widely used when manual typewriters were developed in the late nineteenth century. The metal keys on manual typewriters would stick together if a user typed too quickly, so the QWERTY keyboard was designed to slow down typists and minimize the problem of the keys sticking together. With computers, the problem that QWERTY was developed to solve no longer exists, so keyboards could be changed to have letters in a more efficient layout. But because the overwhelming majority of people have learned to use keyboards with the QWERTY layout, there might be significant costs to them if they had to switch, even if a new layout ultimately made them faster typists.

Other products that have supposedly embodied inferior technologies are VHS video recorders—supposedly inferior to Sony Betamax recorders—and the Windows computer operating system—supposedly inferior to the Macintosh operating system.

Do Network Externalities Result in Market Failure? Some economists have argued that because of path dependence and switching costs, network externalities can result in *market failure*, which is the situation in which the market fails to produce the efficient level of output (see Chapter 5, Section 5.1). If network externalities result in market failure, government intervention in these markets might improve economic efficiency. Many economists are skeptical, however, that network externalities really do lead to consumers being locked into products with inferior technologies.

In particular, economists Stan Leibowitz of the University of Texas, Dallas, and Stephen Margolis of North Carolina State University have argued that, in practice, the gains from using a superior technology are larger than the losses due to switching costs. After carefully studying the cases of the QWERTY keyboard, VHS video recorders, and the Windows computer operating system, they have concluded that there is no good evidence that the alternative technologies were actually superior. The implications of network externalities for economic efficiency remain controversial among economists.   **MyLab Economics** Concept Check

Does Fairness Matter?

If people were only interested in making themselves as well off as possible in a material sense, they would not be concerned with fairness. There is a great deal of evidence, however, that people like to be treated fairly and that they usually attempt to treat others fairly, even if doing so makes them worse off financially. Tipping servers in restaurants is an example. In the United States, diners in restaurants typically add 15 to 20 percent to their food bills as tips to their servers. Tips are not *required*, but most people consider not tipping to be very unfair, unless the service has been exceptionally bad. You could argue that people leave tips not to be fair but because they are afraid that if they don't leave a tip, the next time they visit the restaurant, they will receive poor service. Studies have shown, however, that most people leave tips at restaurants even while on vacation or in other circumstances where they are unlikely to visit the restaurant again.

There are many other examples of people parting with money when they are not required to do so and when they receive nothing material in return. The most obvious example is making donations to charity. Apparently, donating money to charity or leaving tips in restaurants that they will never visit again gives people more utility than they would receive from keeping the money and spending it on themselves.

A Test of Fairness in the Economic Laboratory: The Ultimatum Game

Experiment Economists have used experiments to understand the role that fairness plays in consumer decision making. *Experimental economics* has been widely used during the past two decades, and a number of experimental economics laboratories exist in the United States and Europe. Economists Maurice Allais, Reinhard Selten, and Vernon Smith were awarded the Nobel Prize in Economics in part because of their contributions to experimental economics. Experiments make it possible to focus on a single aspect of consumer behavior. The *ultimatum game*, first popularized by Werner Güth of the Max Planck Institute of Economics in Germany, is an experiment that tests whether fairness is important in consumer decision making. Various economists have conducted the ultimatum game experiment under slightly different conditions but with generally the same result.

Figure 10.4 illustrates the ultimatum game. A group of volunteers—often college students—are divided into pairs. One member of each pair is the "allocator," and the other member of the pair is the "recipient." The allocator is given an amount of money, say $20, and decides how much each member of the pair will get. There are no restrictions on how the allocator divides up the money. The allocator could keep it all, give it

Allocator offers division of $20.00

Recipient accepts offer   Recipient rejects offer

Allocator and recipient receive money.   Allocator and recipient receive nothing.

MyLab Economics Animation

Figure 10.4

The Ultimatum Game

In the ultimatum game, an allocator divides an amount of money between himself or herself and the recipient. If the recipient rejects the division of money, neither player receives anything. In experiments, most recipients would rather receive nothing than receive what they believe to be an unfair division of the money.

all to the recipient, or anything in between. The recipient must then decide whether to accept the allocation or reject it. If the recipient decides to accept the allocation, each member of the pair gets to keep his or her share. If the recipient decides to reject the allocation, both members of the pair receive nothing.

If neither the allocator nor the recipient cares about fairness, optimal play in the ultimatum game is straightforward: The allocator should propose a division of the money in which the allocator receives $19.99 and the recipient receives $0.01. The allocator has maximized his or her gain. The recipient should accept the division because the alternative is to reject it and receive nothing at all: Even a penny is better than nothing. In fact, when the ultimatum game experiment is carried out, both allocators and recipients act as if fairness is important. Allocators usually offer recipients at least a 40 percent share of the money, and recipients almost always reject offers of less than a 10 percent share.

Why do allocators offer recipients more than a negligible amount? It might be that allocators do not care about fairness but fear that recipients do care and will reject offers they consider unfair. This possibility was tested in an experiment known as the *dictator game* carried out by Daniel Kahneman (a psychologist who shared the 2002 Nobel Prize in Economics), Jack Knetsch, and 2017 Economics Nobel Laureate Richard Thaler, using students at Cornell University. In this experiment, the allocators were given only two possible divisions of $20: either $18 for themselves and $2 for the recipient or an even division of $10 for themselves and $10 for the recipient. One important difference from the ultimatum game was that *the recipient was not allowed to reject the division*. Of the 161 allocators, 122 chose the even division of the $20. Because there was no possibility of the $18/$2 split being rejected, the allocators must have chosen the even split because they valued acting fairly.

Why would recipients in the ultimatum game ever reject any division of the money in which they receive even a very small amount, given that even a small amount of money is better than nothing? Apparently, most people value fairness enough that they will refuse to participate in transactions they consider unfair, even if they are worse off financially as a result.

Are the Results of Economic Experiments Reliable?
Economists have conducted the ultimatum game and the dictator game many times in different countries, using different groups of people. Therefore, most economists believe that the results of the game provide strong evidence that people value fairness. Some economists question this conclusion, though. They argue that the experimental situation is artificial, so results may not hold up in the real world. Although allocators in the dictatorship game give money to the other player, whose identity is not known to the allocator, in the real world, people rarely just hand money to strangers. So, it is possible that the fairness observed in the experiments may be the result of people wanting to avoid appearing selfish rather than people valuing fairness. For instance, in the ultimatum game, anyone who kept $19.99 and gave the other person only $0.01 might be afraid of appearing selfish in the eyes of the economist conducting the experiment. Particularly because the dollar amounts in the experiment are small, wanting to please the person conducting the experiment may be the main motive behind the choices made.

There is some experimental evidence that when the amount being divided is large, recipients in ultimatum games will accept even very uneven divisions. Steffen Andersen of the Copenhagen Business School and colleagues conducted the dictator game with poor villagers in India, whose average daily wage was about 100 rupees. In their experiments, the amounts to be divided varied from 20 rupees to 20,000 rupees. They found that the larger the amount at stake, the smaller the share the allocator offered the recipient. When the amount was 20,000 rupees—or the equivalent of about 200 days' pay—allocators offered recipients, on average, a share of about 12 percent. Despite being offered this low share, only 4 percent of recipients rejected the offer. The results indicate that, as economists might expect, the more costly it is to a recipient to reject an unfair offer, the less likely the recipient is to do so.

This recent research does not completely reverse the usual interpretation of the results of the ultimatum and dictator games. However, the research does show that the results of the games are not as clear-cut as many economists had thought.

Business Implications of Fairness If consumers value fairness, how does this affect firms? One consequence is that firms will sometimes not raise prices of goods and services, even when there is a large increase in demand, because they are afraid their customers will consider the price increases unfair and may buy elsewhere.

Consider three examples where it seems that businesses could increase their profits by raising prices:

- When the dance rock band LCD Soundsystem played a concert at New York's Madison Square Garden, the tickets were priced at $50 each. But, demand for the tickets was so high that tickets sold online for as much as $2,500 each. Why didn't the band or the concert promoter charge more than $50 for the tickets?

- Each year, many more people would like to buy tickets to see the Super Bowl than there are tickets for them to buy at the price the National Football League (NFL) charges. Why doesn't the NFL raise prices?

- When the restaurant Next opened in Chicago, it used a unique approach to pricing. The restaurant sold tickets that entitled the buyer to a dinner, including drinks and tip. The restaurant sold the tickets for $45 to $75, depending on the dinner chosen. The tickets were resold online for prices from $500 to $3,000. Why didn't Next increase its ticket prices?

In each of these cases, it appears that a firm could increase its profit by raising prices. The seller would be selling the same quantity—of seats at a concert or in a football stadium, or meals in a restaurant—at a higher price, so profit should increase. Economists have provided two explanations for why firms sometimes do not raise prices in these situations. Gary Becker has suggested that the products involved—concerts, football games, or restaurant meals—are all products that buyers consume together with other buyers. In those situations, the amount consumers wish to buy may be related to how much of the product other people are consuming. People like to consume, and be seen consuming, a popular product—ones where the quantity demanded appears to be much greater than the quantity supplied. If rock bands, the NFL, and popular restaurants increased their prices enough to equate the quantity of tickets demanded with the quantity supplied, they might find that they had also eliminated their popularity.

Daniel Kahneman, Jack Knetsch, and Richard Thaler have offered another explanation for why firms don't always raise prices when doing so would seem to increase their profit. In surveys of consumers, these researchers found that most people considered it fair for firms to raise their prices following an increase in costs but unfair to raise prices following an increase in demand. For example, Kahneman, Knetsch, and Thaler conducted a survey in which people were asked their opinion of the following situation: "A hardware store has been selling snow shovels for $15. The morning after a large snowstorm, the store raises the price to $20." Eighty-two percent of respondents said that they considered the hardware store's actions to be unfair. Kahneman, Knetsch, and Thaler have concluded that firms may sometimes not raise their prices even when the quantity demanded of their product is greater than the quantity supplied out of fear that, in the long run, they will lose customers who believe the price increases were unfair.

These explanations for why firms don't always raise prices to a level that would equate the quantity demanded with the quantity supplied share the same basic idea: Sometimes firms will give up some profit in the short run to keep their customers happy and increase their profit in the long run.   **MyLab Economics** Concept Check   **MyLab Economics** Study Plan

Apply the Concept   **MyLab Economics** Video

Who Made the Most Profit from the Broadway Musical *Hamilton*?

For the year 2016, the answer to the question is not Lin-Manuel Miranda, the star and creator of the musical on the life of Alexander Hamilton, nor the rest of the cast. Nor is it the show's producers, nor the people who provided the financing for the show,

Giles Angel/Alamy Stock Photo

How much would you pay for a ticket to the musical Hamilton?

nor the owners of the Richard Rodgers Theatre where the Broadway show is performed. The people who made the most profit from *Hamilton* were scalpers—people who buy tickets at their original price and then resell them at a higher price.

For as long as there have been ticketed sporting events, concerts, and plays, there have been ticket scalpers. In ancient Rome, the Roman Colosseum seated 50,000 spectators for gladiatorial contests and other events. Although the Roman government distributed tickets for free, enterprising people would accumulate as many as they could and resell them for cash or goods. Before the Internet, scalpers typically waited outside a sports arena, concert hall, or theater, eyeing the crowd for people who seemed as if they needed tickets, hoping to make a deal for cash on the spot. At one time, scalping tickets was illegal in many cities and states, so scalpers needed to avoid police officers stationed outside events.

Today, most ticket reselling has moved online, to popular sites such as StubHub and SeatGeek, and most local governments have repealed their bans on scalping. These sites have provided an easy way for people who find they can no longer attend an event to resell their tickets. But professional ticket resellers have also used the sites to boost their profits. Using sophisticated software programs called "ticket bots," professional resellers buy large blocks of tickets the moment they are available for sale. The professional resellers then list the tickets on StubHub or other sites at several times their face value. Although use of ticket bots is illegal in most states, theaters and other venues can have difficulty identifying whether a particular purchase has been made by a human or a bot.

A column in the *New York Times* gathered data on the last 100 performances before Lin-Manuel Miranda left the cast of *Hamilton* on July 9, 2016. The average face value of tickets was $189, while the average resale ticket sold for $1,120—or nearly six times as much. The average resale price for a ticket to Miranda's last performance on July 9 was $10,900. For the last 32 performances before July 9, ticket resellers made a profit of $10.5 million—or nearly four times the $2.7 million profit the show's producers earned. Why didn't the producers just raise ticket prices so that the quantity demanded equaled the 1,321 tickets (which is the number of seats in the Richard Rodgers Theatre) available for each performance? The producers did raise ticket prices beginning in January 2017. The price for a ticket to the best seats increased from $475 to $849, and prices for most other seats increased from a range of $139 to $177 to a range of $179 to $199.

But these increases still left prices far below what tickets were selling for on the resale market. The producers were reluctant to raise ticket prices any higher because they were afraid of a negative reaction among theater fans. As the research of Kahneman, Knetsch, and Thaler has shown, consumers see it as more fair for firms to raise prices after an increase in costs than as a result of an increase in demand. The costs for staging *Hamilton* were no higher than for other musicals, so increasing ticket prices would have been based only on the high demand for the show. The owners of the theater, the show's producers, and the show's cast all intend to be involved with shows in the future and were reluctant to raise prices to the levels necessary to equate the quantity of tickets demanded to the supply for fear of damaging their reputations.

To make sure they could earn profits from future shows, the producers of *Hamilton* had no good alternative but to let scalpers earn a sizable profit off their show.

Sources: Tiff Fehr, "How Scalpers Make Their Millions with 'Hamilton,'" *New York Times*, July 29, 2016; "The War on Ticket Bots Is Unlikely to Be Won," *Economist*, January 5, 2017; Michael Paulson, "'Hamilton' Raises Ticket Prices: The Best Seats Will Now Cost $849," *New York Times*, June 8, 2016; Keith Veronese, "Pottery Shards Were the First Ever Ticket Stubs," io9.gizmodo.com, April 27, 2012; and Daniel Kahneman, Jack Knetsch, and Richard Thaler, "Fairness as a Constraint on Profit Seeking: Entitlements in the Market," *American Economic Review*, Vol. 76, No. 4, September 1986, pp. 728–741.

MyLab Economics Study Plan   **Your Turn:** Test your understanding by doing related problems 3.7 and 3.8 on page 355 at the end of this chapter.

Solved Problem 10.3

Why Doesn't Tesla Charge Its Employees to Park Their Cars?

Tesla manufactures electric cars in a factory in California. There are a total of 4,500 parking spaces at the factory, while Tesla has about 16,000 employees working there (although some work on different shifts). According to an article in the *Wall Street Journal*, the shortage of parking spaces is prompting many employees to park in unauthorized places, including up on grass medians. Some employees arrive hours before their shifts begin to secure spaces. Some employees pay other employees for spaces.

a. Use a graph to illustrate the demand and supply for parking spaces as it is now at Tesla's factory. Indicate on your graph the market price, the quantity of park-

ing spaces supplied, the quantity of parking spaces demanded, and any shortage or surplus of spaces.

b. Now suppose that Tesla decides to auction off the right to park in the lot. On your graph from part (a) show what the equilibrium price and equilibrium quantity will now be.

c. Would the auction approach to allocating parking spaces in part (b) be more economically efficient than the approach that Tesla actually uses? Briefly explain.

d. Is Tesla likely to adopt the auction approach to solving its parking problems given in part (b)? Briefly explain.

Source: Tim Higgins, "Elon Musk Has an Awkward Problem at Tesla: Employee Parking," *Wall Street Journal*, April 11, 2017.

Solving the Problem

Step 1: **Review the chapter material.** This problem involves the reasons firms don't always raise prices, so you may want to review the section "Business Implications of Fairness," on page 341. (To answer part (c), it would be helpful to review the discussion of economic efficiency in Chapter 4, Section 4.2.)

Step 2: **Answer part (a) by drawing a graph of the demand and supply for parking spaces, indicating the requested information.** Note that because the quantity of parking spaces is fixed at 4,500, the supply curve is a vertical line. Because Tesla doesn't charge its employees to park in the lot, the market price is 0. We don't know the actual quantity of parking spaces demanded at a price of 0, so let's label it Q_1. At a price of 0, there is a shortage of parking spaces equal to $Q_1 - 4,500$.

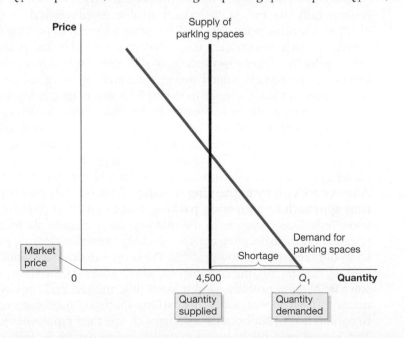

Step 3: **Answer part (b) by showing on your graph the effect of Tesla's auctioning off the right to park in the lot.** If Tesla auctions off the right to park in the lot, bidding among employees should cause the price to rise so that the quantity demanded falls to match the fixed quantity supplied of 4,500 spaces. We don't know exactly what this price will be, so just label it P_1 in your graph. The price has risen from 0 to P_1, the equilibrium quantity is 4,500, and the shortage has been eliminated.

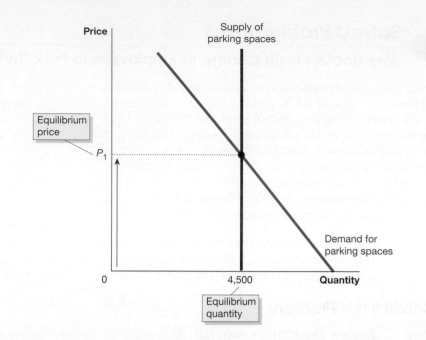

Step 4: **Answer part (c) by explaining that the auction approach to allocating parking spaces in part (b) is economically efficient.** We saw in Chapter 4 that the demand curve measures the marginal benefit consumers receive from consuming a product. At equilibrium in a market, we expect to see the efficient outcome where the price equals the marginal benefit consumers receive from consuming the last unit of the good or service. As the figure in Step 2 shows, with a price of zero, the marginal benefit from the 4,500th parking space is far above the price, so the outcome in not efficient. When Tesla auctions off the right to park in the lot, the price will rise to P_1 and the outcome is economically efficient. At P_1, the quantity demanded equals the quantity supplied. At any other price, there will be either a surplus of parking spaces or a shortage, which was the case when the price was 0. Looked at another way, for the price to perform the function of allocating a scarce resource—parking spaces—to its highest valued use as measured by marginal benefit, Tesla would need to allow the price to rise to P_1. Some of its employees will value a parking space at the factory more highly than others for various reasons, including whether they have access to public transportation and whether they have other commitments that make it impossible to arrive at the lot early enough to be sure of finding a space. Unless the price is allowed to adjust, people who place a lower value on the spaces may still end up parking in them.

Step 5: **Answer part (d) by explaining whether Tesla is likely to adopt the auction approach to allocating parking spaces given in part (b).** The situation Tesla faces is similar to the one popular Broadway shows or popular restaurants face in deciding whether to charge a market-clearing price. Doing so would seem to increase profit in the short run but may reduce profit in the long run by irritating customers who value fairness. Similarly, Tesla could solve its parking problem (and make a little money) and improve the economic efficiency of allocating its parking spaces by auctioning off the right to park in its lot. But because few firms charge their employees for parking, Tesla's employees might be upset if they had to pay for it. Tesla's managers might worry that employees who are upset may not work as hard or may even quit. It's worth noting that the article in the *Wall Street Journal* discussing Tesla's parking problems doesn't indicate that the firm is even considering charging its employees to use its parking lot.

MyLab Economics Study Plan   **Your Turn:** For more practice, do related problem 3.9 on page 355 at the end of this chapter.

10.4 Behavioral Economics: Do People Make Rational Choices?

LEARNING OBJECTIVE: Describe the behavioral economics approach to understanding decision making.

When economists say that consumers and firms are behaving "rationally," they mean that consumers and firms are taking actions that are appropriate to reach their goals, given the information available to them. Some economists study situations in which people do not appear to be making choices that are economically rational. This area of economics is called **behavioral economics**. Why might consumers or businesses not act rationally? The most obvious reason is that they do not realize that their actions are inconsistent with their goals. One of the objectives of economics is to suggest ways to make better decisions. In this section, we discuss ways in which people can improve their decisions by avoiding some common pitfalls. We also use ideas from behavioral economics to analyze how consumers make decisions when shopping.

Behavioral economics The study of situations in which people make choices that do not appear to be economically rational.

Pitfalls In Decision Making

People commonly commit the following three mistakes when making decisions:

1. They take into account monetary costs but ignore nonmonetary opportunity costs that don't involve explicitly spending money.
2. They fail to ignore sunk costs.
3. They are unrealistic about their future behavior.

Ignoring Nonmonetary Opportunity Costs Remember that the **opportunity cost** of any activity is the highest-valued alternative that must be given up to engage in that activity. For example, if you own something you could sell, you incur an opportunity cost if you use it yourself. It is often difficult for people to think of opportunity costs in these terms.

Opportunity cost The highest-valued alternative that must be given up to engage in an activity.

Consider the following example: The NFL ran a lottery that allowed the winners to purchase Super Bowl tickets at their face value, which was either $325 or $400, depending on where in the stadium the seats were located. Economist Alan Krueger of Princeton surveyed the lottery winners, asking them two questions:

Question 1: If you had not won the lottery, would you have been willing to pay $3,000 for your ticket?
Answer 1: Ninety-four percent answered that they would not have paid $3,000 for a ticket.
Question 2: If after winning your ticket (and before arriving in Florida for the Super Bowl) someone had offered you $3,000 for your ticket, would you have sold it?
Answer 2: Ninety-two percent answered that they would not have sold their ticket for $3,000.

But these answers are contradictory! If someone offers you $3,000 for your ticket, then by using the ticket rather than selling it, you incur an opportunity cost of $3,000. There really is a $3,000 cost involved in using that ticket, even though you do not pay $3,000 in cash. The two alternatives—either paying $3,000 or not receiving $3,000—amount to exactly the same thing.

If the ticket is really *not* worth $3,000 to you, you should sell it. If it is worth $3,000 to you, you should be willing to pay $3,000 in cash to buy it. Not being willing to sell a ticket you already own for $3,000 while at the same time not being willing to buy a ticket for $3,000 if you didn't already own one is inconsistent behavior. The inconsistency comes from a failure to take into account nonmonetary opportunity costs. Behavioral economists believe this inconsistency is caused by the **endowment effect**, which is the tendency of people to be unwilling to sell a good they already own even if they are offered a price that is greater than the price they would be willing to pay to buy the good if they didn't already own it.

Endowment effect The tendency of people to be unwilling to sell a good they already own even if they are offered a price that is greater than the price they would be willing to pay to buy the good if they didn't already own it.

The failure to take into account opportunity costs is a very common error in decision making. Suppose, for example, that a friend is in a hurry to have his room cleaned—it's the Friday before parents' weekend—and he offers you $50 to do it for him. You turn him down and spend the time cleaning your own room, even though you know somebody down the hall who would be willing to clean your room for $20. Leave aside complicating details—the guy who asked you to clean his room is a real slob, or you don't want the person who offered to clean your room for $20 to go through your stuff—and you should see the point we are making. The opportunity cost of cleaning your own room is $50—the amount your friend offered to pay you to clean his room. It is inconsistent to turn down an offer from someone else to clean your room for $20 when you are doing it for yourself at a cost of $50. The key point here is this: *Nonmonetary opportunity costs are just as real as monetary costs, and people should take them into account when making decisions.*

There are many examples of businesses taking advantage of the tendency of consumers to ignore nonmonetary costs. For example, some firms sell products with mail-in rebates. Rather than have a mail-in rebate of $10, why not just cut the price by $10? Companies are relying on the fact that failing to mail in a rebate form once you have already paid for a product is a nonmonetary opportunity cost rather than a direct monetary cost. In fact, only a small percentage of customers actually mail in rebates.

Failing to Ignore Sunk Costs

Sunk cost A cost that has already been paid and cannot be recovered.

A **sunk cost** is a cost that has already been paid and cannot be recovered. Once you have paid money and can't get it back, you should ignore that money in any later decisions you make. Consider the following two situations:

Situation 1: You bought a ticket to a play for $75. The ticket is nonrefundable and must be used on Tuesday night. An hour before the play will begin (too late to successfully resell your ticket on StubHub or another site), a friend calls and invites you to a local comedy club to see a comedian you both like who is appearing only on Tuesday night. Your friend offers to pay the cost of going to the club.

Situation 2: It's Tuesday afternoon, and you are about to buy a ticket for that night's performance of the same play as in situation 1. As you are logging on to the theater's site to buy the ticket, your friend calls and invites you to the comedy club.

Would your decision to go to the play or the comedy club be different in situation 1 than in situation 2? Most people would say that in situation 1, they would go to the play because otherwise they would lose the $75 they had paid for the ticket. In fact, the $75 is "lost" no matter what you do because the ticket is nonrefundable, and you don't have time to resell it. The only real issue for you to decide is whether you would prefer to see the play or prefer to go with your friend to the comedy club. If you would prefer to go to the club, the fact that you have already paid $75 for the ticket to the play is irrelevant. Your decision should be the same in situation 1 as in situation 2.

Apply the Concept

MyLab Economics Video

A Blogger Who Understands the Importance of Ignoring Sunk Costs

These days, there are thousands, if not millions, of blogs (or "Web logs") on which people post their thoughts on topics ranging from politics and sports to their favorite hobbies. For most bloggers who spend hours a day writing up their latest ideas and providing links to relevant material on the Web, the only compensation is interacting with other people who share their interests. Very few blogs become so successful that they attract paid advertising and earn their owners a good income. One example of a successful blogger is Arnold Kim, who began one of the earliest blogs about Apple products in 2000, during his fourth year of medical school. He continued blogging on his site, MacRumors.com, over the next eight years, while pursuing a medical career as a nephrologist (a doctor who treats kidney problems).

Jay Paul/The New York Times/Redux Pictures

Arnold Kim, founder of MacRumors.com, gave up a medical career to blog full time.

By 2008, Kim's site had become very successful, attracting 4.4 million people and more than 40 million page views each month. He was earning more than $100,000 per year from paid advertising by companies such as Verizon, Audible.com, and CDW. But the tasks of compiling rumors about new Apple products, keeping an Apple buying guide up to date, and monitoring multiple discussion boards on the site became more than he could handle as a part-time job. Kim enjoyed working on the Web site and believed that ultimately it could earn him more than he was earning as a doctor. Still, he hesitated to abandon his medical career because he had invested nearly $200,000 in his education.

But the $200,000, as well as the years he had spent in medical school, completing a residency in internal medicine, and completing a fellowship in nephrology, were sunk costs. Kim realized that he needed to ignore these sunk costs in order to make a rational decision about whether to continue in medicine or to become a full-time blogger. After calculating that he would make more from his Web site than from his medical career—and taking into account that by working from home he could spend more time with his young daughter—he decided to blog full time. He was quoted as saying that, "on paper it was an easy decision." Despite competition from many new blogs, MacRumors continued to do well, being viewed by 12.5 million people per month in mid-2017, and Kim's income had risen above what he would have made as a doctor.

Knowing that it is rational to ignore sunk costs can be important in making key decisions in life.

Sources: Brian X. Chen, "Arnold Kim Celebrates 10 Years as Apple Rumor King," www.wired.com, February 23, 2010; Brian Stelter, "My Son, the Blogger: An M.D. Trades Medicine for Apple Rumors," *New York Times*, July 21, 2008; Dan Frommer, "Nephrologist to Mac Blogger: The Unlikely Career Path of MacRumors' Arnold Kim," www.businessinsider.com, July 13, 2008; and "Macrumors Traffic," www.quantcast.com, April 12, 2017.

Your Turn: Test your understanding by doing related problems 4.9, 4.10, and 4.11 on page 356 at the end of this chapter.   MyLab Economics Study Plan

---

Being Unrealistic about Future Behavior As we saw in Chapter 1, obesity is an increasing problem in the United States. Why do some people end up eating too much? One possibility is that they receive more utility from eating high-calorie foods than they would from being thin. A more likely explanation, however, is that many people eat a lot today because they expect to eat less tomorrow. But they never do eat less, and so they end up overweight. (Of course, some people also suffer from medical problems that lead to weight gain.) Similarly, some people continue smoking today because they expect to be able to give it up sometime in the future. Unfortunately, for many people that time never comes, and they suffer the health consequences of years of smoking. In both these cases, people are overvaluing the utility from current choices—eating chocolate cake or smoking—and undervaluing the utility to be received in the future from being thin or not getting lung cancer.

Economists who have studied this question argue that many people have preferences that are not consistent over time. In the long run, you would like to be thin or give up smoking or achieve some other goal, but each day, you make decisions (such as to eat too much or smoke) that are not consistent with this long-run goal. If you are unrealistic about your future behavior, you underestimate the costs of choices—such as overeating or smoking—that you make today. A key way of avoiding this problem is to be realistic about your future behavior, although that can be difficult to do!

Taking into account nonmonetary opportunity costs, ignoring sunk costs, and being more realistic about future behavior are three ways in which consumers are able to improve the decisions they make.   MyLab Economics Concept Check

"Nudges": Using Behavioral Economics to Guide Behavior

Richard Thaler, winner of the 2017 Nobel Prize in economics, has popularized the idea of devising *nudges* to lead people to making better decisions. For example, because many people are unrealistic about their future behavior, they save too little for retirement.

As a result, some firms find that fewer than the expected number of employees enroll in voluntary retirement savings plans known as 401(k) plans. Although these employees have a long-run goal of saving enough to enjoy a comfortable retirement, in the short run, they spend more than is consistent with attaining their goal. At the suggestion of behavioral economists, many firms now automatically enroll employees in these retirement plans, giving them the option to leave the plan if they choose to. To a fully rational employee, the decision about whether to save through a 401(k) plan should be independent of the minor amount of paperwork involved in either enrolling in a plan or leaving a plan in which the employer has enrolled the employee. In practice, though, automatically enrolling employees in a plan means that to leave the plan, the employees must confront the inconsistency between their short-run actions of spending too much and their long-run goal of a comfortable retirement. Rather than confront their inconsistency, most employees choose to remain in the plan.

Behavioral economics has also been used to improve health care. Many people with serious illnesses fail to regularly take their prescription medication. Even though they have the long-run goal of becoming well, the short-run inconvenience of taking the medication causes them to skip some doses. Using insights from behavioral economics, the designers of the Wellth app deposit $150 into a patient's account. Each morning the app sends the patient a reminder to take his medicine. If he snaps a selfie of himself taking the medicine each day for 90 days, he gets to keep the $150. He has money subtracted for each day he fails to take his medicine. The app designers claim that the app can reduce by more than 40 percent hospital readmissions due to patients failing to take their prescriptions.

Doctors who prescribe antibiotics for medical problems, such as a cold or the flu, for which antibiotics are ineffective, contribute to the spread of antibiotic-resistant bacteria. Some doctors are overconfident about knowing when it is appropriate to prescribe antibiotics. Accordingly, studies show that providing doctors with information on nonantibiotic treatments is not an effective way of reducing overuse of antibiotics. It is much more effective to send doctors e-mails showing how their rates of prescribing antibiotics compare with the rates of "top performing" doctors. Similarly, many doctors are overconfident in their ability to avoid illnesses they may contract as a result of failing to wash their hands while seeing patients. Signs posted in hospitals reminding doctors that they are risking their own health by not washing their hands have been less effective in increasing hand washing than have signs reminding doctors that they are risking their patients' health by not washing their hands.   **MyLab Economics** Concept Check

The Behavioral Economics of Shopping

In Section 10.1, we analyzed how consumers can choose the products they buy in order to maximize utility. In this section, we briefly consider problems consumers may encounter that keep them from making optimal consumption choices when shopping.

In discussing how consumers maximize utility, we used simple examples in which people were choosing the optimal quantity of two goods, subject to a budget constraint. Consider, though, a typical trip to the supermarket. Someone shopping for a family of four might end up buying 25 or more products. A consumer in that situation is unlikely to equate the ratios of the marginal utilities to the prices for all these products when deciding the quantities to buy. Does it matter that consumers often make consumption choices that are not optimal in this sense? Economists are divided in their answers to this question. Many economists make these two points in arguing that it doesn't matter:

1. The assumptions in most scientific models, including economic models, are not literally correct. In the model of consumer choice, for example, unrealistic assumptions are necessary to simplify a complex reality by focusing on the most important factors involved in decision making.
2. Models are best judged by the success of their predictions rather than by the realism of their assumptions. Predictions based on the model of consumer choice have been successful in predicting many types of consumer behavior.

Rules of Thumb Behavioral economists argue that it *does* matter that consumers usually do not make optimal consumption choices. These economists believe that there are benefits to analyzing *how* consumers actually make decisions. The model we have used in this chapter assumes that:

- When people shop, they have full information on the prices of products, including information on differences in prices across stores.
- People can make complicated calculations such as computing the ratios of marginal utilities to prices across many products.

In fact, people often make choices on the basis of only limited information and without the time or capacity to calculate their optimal choices. As a result, rather than make optimal choices, people often use *rules of thumb*, which are guides to decision making that may not produce optimal choices. For example, you may decide that a particular supermarket has the lowest prices for the products you buy, without continually checking whether this assumption is correct. If a new supermarket with lower prices opens, at least for a period, you may continue shopping at the old supermarket, even though doing so is no longer optimal.

Anchoring How do shoppers decide whether the price of a product is high or low? Behavioral economists use the word *anchoring* to describe one aspect of how consumers evaluate prices. If people are uncertain about a value, such as a price, they often relate—or anchor—that value to some other known value, even if the second value is irrelevant. Psychologists Amos Tversky and Daniel Kahneman carried out an experiment to illustrate the effects of anchoring. They constructed a wheel that when spun always stopped on a value of either 10 or 65. For each group of participants in the experiment, they spun the wheel and then asked that group: "What is your best guess of the percentage of African nations in the United Nations?" When the wheel stopped on a value of 10 when spun for that group, the average answer was 25 percent. When the wheel stopped on 65, the average answer was 45 percent. Even though the value from the spin of the wheel had no relevance to the question being asked, the value anchored the participants' responses. In another experiment, conducted by Brian Wansink of Cornell University, Robert Kent of the University of Delaware, and Stephen Hoch of the University of Pennsylvania, three supermarkets offered cans of Campbell's soup for sale at a 12-percent reduction in price. On one day during the sale, a display sign stated "Limit of 12 per person"; on another day, a display sign said "No limit per person." On the day when the sign limited sales, the supermarkets sold an average of 7 cans per person. On the day when the sign stated there was no limit on sales, the supermarkets sold 3.3 cans per person. The number 12 on the sign had anchored the shoppers' decisions on how many cans to buy.

Consumers often lack the information to evaluate whether the price of a good is "high" or "low." Stores can take advantage of this lack of information to anchor consumers' estimates by marking a high "regular price" on a product, which makes the discounted "sale price" appear to be a bargain even if the product is very rarely offered for sale at the regular price.

MyLab Economics Study Plan   **MyLab Economics** Concept Check

Apply the Concept

MyLab Economics Video

J.C. Penney Meets Behavioral Economics

We saw at the beginning of this chapter that after a very successful career as the head of Apple's retail stores, Ron Johnson was recruited to become the CEO of the J.C. Penney department store chain. Johnson instituted a new pricing strategy of offering goods at "everyday low prices" and rarely discounting prices below those levels. The new strategy failed, as Penney's revenue declined. Johnson was fired as CEO after only 17 months.

Ideas from behavioral economics can help explain what went wrong. First, Johnson assumed that consumers would understand that the everyday low prices really were low, at least compared with the very high regular prices that Penney had

Bebeto Matthews/AP Images

Consumers generally respond strongly to sales that offer discounted prices, so a strategy that replaces sales with low fixed prices is not likely to be effective.

previously used when calculating the discounts it advertised during a sale. However, there is substantial evidence that some consumers are not well aware of prices even for goods they buy regularly. One study of supermarket shoppers asked people the prices of goods they had just placed in their shopping carts. Fewer than half the shoppers could accurately recall the prices, and one-quarter couldn't even offer a guess, even though they had placed the goods in their carts less than a minute earlier. Another study asked people who were about to enter a department store questions about the prices of goods they frequently purchased. Only about one-third could give accurate answers. When asked to evaluate whether a specific price of a good they frequently purchased was high or low, about 15 percent of people identified prices that were actually high as being good deals and prices that were actually low as being bad deals.

Studies of retail sales show that consumers purchase a significant fraction of goods at discount prices. For example, a study of checkout scanner data from nine supermarkets showed that while liquid laundry detergent was offered at discount prices only about one-quarter of the time, nearly half of detergent was purchased at the sale prices. Because consumers respond so strongly to sales that offer discounted prices, a strategy that replaces sales with low fixed prices is not likely to be effective.

Why do consumers respond to sales? Why wasn't J.C. Penney able to convince consumers that everyday low prices really were low? One possibility is that by displaying both a high "regular price" and a low "sale price," sales provide consumers with an "anchor," or reference point, to interpret the prices being offered. A sale price seems low if offered as a markdown from a higher regular price even if—because of sales and the use of coupons—few people ever buy the good at the regular price. Without the anchor of the regular price, consumers can have difficulty deciding whether an everyday low price is actually low, particularly because some consumers enter a store with little idea of what typical prices are. As the Northwestern professor quoted in the chapter opener put it: "J.C. Penney might say it's a fair price, but why should consumers trust J.C. Penney?"

By largely eliminating sales, Johnson disregarded some of the insights of behavioral economics. As a result, J.C. Penney suffered losses, and Johnson lost his job.

Sources: Stephanie Clifford and Catherine Rampell, "Sometimes, We Want Prices to Fool Us," *New York Times*, April 13, 2013; Daniel Kahneman, *Thinking, Fast and Slow*, New York: Farrar, Strauss and Giroux, 2011; Julio Rotemberg, "Behavioral Aspects of Price Setting, and Their Policy Implications," National Bureau of Economic Research, Working Paper 13754, January 2008; Marc Vanhuele and Xavier Drèze, "Measuring the Price Knowledge Shoppers Bring to the Store," *Journal of Marketing*, Vol. 66, No. 4, October 2002, pp. 72–85; Peter R. Dickson and Alan G. Sawyer, "The Price Knowledge and Search of Supermarket Shoppers," *Journal of Marketing*, Vol. 54, No. 3, July 1990, pp. 42–53; and Igal Hendel and Aviv Nevo, "Measuring the Implications of Sales and Consumer Inventory Behavior," *Econometrica*, Vol. 74, No. 6, November 2006, pp. 1637–1673.

MyLab Economics Study Plan   **Your Turn:** Test your understanding by doing related problem 4.15 on page 357 at the end of this chapter.

Continued from page 325

Economics in Your Life & Career

How Should You Price Tickets to a Hit Broadway Show?

At the beginning of this chapter, we asked you to give advice on ticket pricing for a theater or concert venue and to explain why most theater producers and concert promoters do not charge the highest price that will allow them to sell all the available tickets.

We have seen in the chapter that many consumers act as if they believe fairness is important. In particular, consumers often object to price increases they believe result from a firm experiencing an increase in demand rather than an increase in cost. As a result, many theater producers or concert promoters are reluctant to charge very high prices to performances of a hot show or band because they believe that doing so will alienate their customers and make it harder to sell tickets to future shows. These producers and promoters believe that allowing ticket scalpers to take some of their profit in the short run is acceptable because charging lower prices helps increase their profit in the long run.

Conclusion

In a market system, consumers are in the driver's seat. Goods are produced only if consumers want them to be. Therefore, how consumers make their decisions is an important area for economists to study. Economists expect that consumers will spend their incomes so that the last dollar spent on each good provides them with equal additional amounts of satisfaction, or utility. In practice, there are significant social influences on consumer decision making, particularly when a good or service is consumed in public. Fairness also seems to be an important consideration for most consumers. Finally, many consumers could improve the decisions they make if they would take into account nonmonetary opportunity costs, ignore sunk costs, and be more realistic about their future behavior.

In this chapter, we studied consumers' choices. In the next several chapters, we will study firms' choices.

Visit **MyEconLab** for a news article and analysis related to the concepts in this chapter.

Key Terms

Behavioral economics, p. 345

Budget constraint, p. 327

Endowment effect, p. 345

Income effect, p. 333

Law of diminishing marginal utility, p. 327

Marginal utility (MU), p. 327

Network externality, p. 338

Opportunity cost, p. 345

Substitution effect, p. 333

Sunk cost, p. 346

Utility, p. 326

 10.1 Utility and Consumer Decision Making, pages 326–334

LEARNING OBJECTIVE: Define utility and explain how consumers choose goods and services to maximize their utility.

MyLab Economics Visit **www.pearson.com/mylab/economics** to complete these exercises online and get instant feedback.

Summary

Utility is the enjoyment or satisfaction that people receive from consuming goods and services. The goal of a consumer is to spend available income so as to maximize utility. **Marginal utility** is the change in total utility a person receives from consuming one additional unit of a good or service. The **law of diminishing marginal utility** states that consumers receive diminishing additional satisfaction as they consume more of a good or service during a given period of time. The **budget constraint** is the amount of income consumers have available to spend on goods and services. To maximize utility, consumers should make sure they spend their income so that the last dollar spent on each product gives them the same marginal utility. The **income effect** is the change in the quantity demanded of a good that results from the effect of a change in the price on consumer purchasing power. The **substitution effect** is the change in the quantity demanded of a good that results from a change in price making the good more or less expensive relative to other goods, holding constant the effect of the price change on consumer purchasing power.

Review Questions

1.1 What is the economic definition of *utility*? Is it possible to measure utility?

1.2 What is the definition of *marginal utility*? What is the law of diminishing marginal utility? Why is marginal utility more useful than total utility in consumer decision making?

1.3 What is meant by a consumer's *budget constraint*? What is the rule of equal marginal utility per dollar spent?

1.4 How does a change in the price of a product cause both a substitution effect and an income effect?

Problems and Applications

1.5 Does the law of diminishing marginal utility hold true in every situation? Is it possible to think of goods for which consuming additional units, at least initially, will result in increasing marginal utility?

1.6 In a forbes.com column, Patrick Rishe, an economist at Washington University, noted that in recent years, the National Football League has significantly expanded the number of games it broadcasts. As a result, he argued: "The NFL has oversaturated the market with its product.... TV ratings, consequently, have fallen. At least in part, diminishing marginal utility is a likely explanation as to why." Briefly explain his reasoning.

Source: Patrick Rishe, "2016 NFL TV Ratings Decline: Has Diminishing Marginal Utility Set In?" forbes.com, December 6, 2016.

1.7 If consumers should allocate their income so that the last dollar spent on every product gives them the same amount of additional utility, how should they decide the amount of their income to save?

1.8 You have six hours to study for two exams tomorrow. The following table shows the relationship between hours of study and test scores.

Economics		Psychology	
Hours	Score	Hours	Score
0	54	0	54
1	62	1	60
2	69	2	65
3	75	3	69
4	80	4	72
5	84	5	74
6	87	6	75

a. Use the rule for determining optimal purchases to decide how many hours you should study each subject. Treat each point on an exam as 1 unit of utility and assume that you consider an extra point on an economics exam to have the same value as an extra point on a psychology exam.

b. Now suppose that you are a psychology major and that you value each point you earn on a psychology exam as being worth three times as much as each point you earn on an economics exam. Now how many hours should you study each subject?

1.9 (Related to **Solved Problem 10.1** on page 330) Joe has $16 to spend on Twinkies and Ho-Hos. Twinkies have a price of $1 per pack, and Ho-Hos have a price of $2 per pack. Use the information in these graphs to determine the number of Twinkies and Ho-Hos packs Joe should buy to maximize his utility. Briefly explain your reasoning.

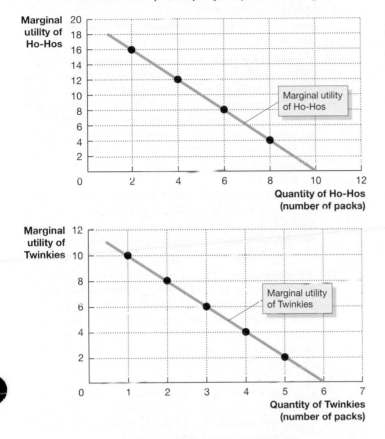

Marginal utility of Ho-Hos

Marginal utility of Twinkies

1.10 (Related to Solved Problem 10.1 on page 330) José has $55 to spend on apples and oranges. Given the information

in the following table, is José maximizing utility? Briefly explain.

	Price	Quantity	Total Utility	Marginal Utility of Last Unit
Apples	$0.50	50	1,000	20
Oranges	$0.75	40	500	30

1.11 Maya spends her $50 budget on two goods, cans of tuna and bottles of ginger ale. Initially, the marginal utility per dollar she spends on tuna is equal to the marginal utility per dollar she spends on ginger ale. Then the price of ginger ale decreases, while her income and the price of tuna do not change. Determine whether each of the following statements about what happens as a result of the decrease in the price of ginger ale is true or false and briefly explain why.

   a. Her marginal utility from consuming ginger ale increases.

   b. The marginal utility per dollar she spends on ginger ale increases.

   c. Because of the substitution effect, Maya will buy more ginger ale. Therefore, we can conclude that ginger ale is a normal good.

   d. As Maya adjusts to the change in the price of ginger ale, her marginal utility per dollar spent on tuna will increase.

1.12 (Related to the Don't Let This Happen to You on page 332) LaToya is buying corn chips and soda. She has 4 bags of corn chips and 5 bottles of soda in her shopping cart. The marginal utility of the fourth bag of corn chips is 10, and the marginal utility of the fifth bottle of soda is also 10. Is LaToya maximizing utility? Briefly explain.

10.2 Where Demand Curves Come From, pages 334–337

LEARNING OBJECTIVE: Use the concept of utility to explain the law of demand.

MyLab Economics   Visit www.pearson.com/mylab/economics to complete these exercises online and get instant feedback.

Summary

When the price of a good falls, the ratio of the marginal utility to price rises. This change leads consumers to buy more of that good. As a result, whenever the price of a product falls, the quantity demanded increases. We saw in Chapter 3, Section 3.1 that this relationship is known as the *law of demand*. The market demand curve can be constructed from the individual demand curves for all the consumers in the market.

Review Questions

2.1 Explain how a downward-sloping demand curve results from consumers adjusting their consumption choices to changes in price.

2.2 How is the market demand curve derived from consumers' individual demand curves?

2.3 What would need to be true for a demand curve to be upward sloping?

Problems and Applications

2.4 Considering only the income effect, if the price of an inferior good declines, would a consumer want to buy a larger quantity or a smaller quantity of the good? Does your answer mean that the demand curves for inferior goods should slope upward? Briefly explain.

2.5 The chapter states that "when the price of an inferior good falls, the income effect and substitution effect work in opposite directions." Explain what this statement means.

2.6 Suppose the market for ice cream cones is made up of three consumers: Tiago, Terrell, and Tim. Use the information in the following table to construct the market demand curve for ice cream cones. Show the information in a table and in a graph.

Price	Tiago Quantity Demanded (cones per week)	Terrell Quantity Demanded (cones per week)	Tim Quantity Demanded (cones per week)
$1.75	2	1	0
1.50	4	3	2
1.25	6	4	3
1.00	7	6	4
0.75	9	7	5

2.7 Marty and Ann discussed the rule of equal marginal utility per dollar spent, a topic that was recently covered in the economics course they were both taking:

Marty: "When I use my calculator to divide the marginal utility of pizza by a price of zero, I don't get an answer. This result must mean that if pizza were being sold for a price of zero, the quantity demanded would be infinite."
Ann: "Marty, that can't be true. No producer would be willing to 'sell' pizza, or any other product, for a zero price. Quantity demanded cannot be infinite, so zero prices cannot appear on demand curves and demand schedules."

Suppose that Marty and Ann ask you for advice in resolving their disagreement. What would you tell them?

2.8 Consider two goods: pizza and Coke. Along an individual's demand curve for pizza, as the price of pizza falls, does the marginal utility per dollar spent on pizza always equal the marginal utility per dollar spent on Coke? In other words, does the rule of equal marginal utility per dollar spent hold as the price changes and you move up or down the demand curve? How can the rule hold, given that the price of pizza changes along the demand curve? If you need help to answer this problem, look back at the discussion of Figure 10.2 on page 335.

2.9 (Related to the Apply the Concept on page 336) A columnist on forbes.com noted that many poor people have diets that are high in carbohydrates, such as potatoes, rice, or bread, with relatively little protein from meat or fish. He said that as a consumer in this situation, if the price

of the carbohydrates in your diet rises, "you'll cut out the more expensive fish, bacon or pork in order to buy more of that basic carbohydrate. And that's what a Giffen Good is." Explain his reasoning that in this situation the carbohydrate is a Giffen good.

Source: Tim Worstall, "Being Quoted in the New York Times Is Great, But . . . ," forbes.com, November 23, 2014.

2.10 (Related to the Apply the Concept on page 336) In studying the consumption of very poor families in China, Robert Jensen and Nolan Miller found that in both Hunan and Gansu, "Giffen behavior is most likely to be found among a range of households that are poor (but not too poor or too rich)."
  a. What do Jensen and Miller mean by "Giffen behavior"?
  b. Why would the poorest of the poor be less likely than people with slightly higher incomes to exhibit this behavior?
  c. Why must a good make up a very large portion of consumers' budgets to be a Giffen good?

Source: Robert T. Jensen and Nolan H. Miller, "Giffen Behavior and Subsistence Consumption," *American Economic Review*, Vol. 98, No. 4, September 2008, p. 1569.

2.11 According to the U.S. Energy Information Administration, the average price of heating oil fell to under $3.00 a gallon during the winter of 2014–2015, the lowest price in more than four years. About 6.2 million U.S. households in the Northeast rely on the fuel to heat their homes. For the following questions, assume that no factor that affects the demand for heating oil, other than its price, changed during the winter of 2014–2015.
  a. If households in the Northeast increased their consumption of heating oil in the winter of 2014–2015, can we conclude that for these households, heating oil was a normal good? Briefly explain.
  b. If households in the Northeast decreased their consumption of heating oil in the winter of 2014–2015, can we conclude that for these households heating oil is an inferior good? Briefly explain.
  c. If households in the Northeast decreased their consumption of heating oil in the winter of 2014–2015, can we conclude that for these households heating oil is a Giffen good? Briefly explain.

Source: Jon Kamp, "Cheaper Hearing Oil Fuels Billions in Savings in Northeast," *Wall Street Journal*, January 16, 2015.

(10.3) Social Influences on Decision Making, pages 337–344

LEARNING OBJECTIVE: Explain how social influences can affect consumption choices.

MyLab Economics Visit www.pearson.com/mylab/economics to complete these exercises online and get instant feedback.

Summary

Social factors can have an effect on consumption. For example, the amount of utility people receive from consuming a good often depends on how many other people they know who also consume the good. There is a **network externality** in the consumption of a product if the usefulness of the product increases with the number of consumers who use it. There is evidence that people like to be treated fairly and that they usually attempt to treat others fairly, even if doing so makes them worse off financially. This result has been demonstrated in laboratory experiments such as the ultimatum game. When firms set prices, they take into account consumers' preference for fairness. For example, hardware stores often do not increase the price of snow shovels to take advantage of a temporary increase in demand following a snowstorm.

Review Questions

3.1 In which of the following situations are social influences on consumer decision making likely to be greater: choosing a restaurant for dinner or choosing which brand of toothpaste to buy? Briefly explain.

3.2 What are network externalities? For what types of products are network externalities likely to be important? What is path dependence?

3.3 How does the fact that consumers apparently value fairness affect the pricing decisions that businesses make?

Problems and Applications

3.4 Which of the following products are most likely to have significant network externalities? Briefly explain.
   a. Smartphones
   b. Dog food
   c. Board games
   d. LCD televisions
   e. 3D televisions

3.5 Writing about a trip to Switzerland in an article in the *New York Times*, economist Daniel Hamermesh noted that electrical outlets in Switzerland use an unusual three-prong plug. Adapters for that type of plug are not typically included in adapter sets, so he and his wife weren't able to plug their computers into their hotel's outlets. Hamermesh wondered: "Why does Switzerland renounce the network externalities that would come with using standard European plugs with their standard 220-volt electricity?" How is Switzerland "renouncing network externalities" by not using standard European plugs?
   Source: Daniel Hamermesh, "If Switzerland Would Only Change Its Plugs," *New York Times*, September 23, 2008.

3.6 An article in the *Wall Street Journal* reported that customers who shopped at Neiman Marcus and other high-end retailers were becoming more resistant to paying high prices for clothing and accessories:

> High-end [retailers] which raised prices incessantly over the past decade, are learning the hard way that even wealthy customers are hunting for better deals and selection, whether online or at shops run by individual brands. . . . Neiman's Chief Executive Karen Katz . . . reduced snob appeal by allowing Neiman shoppers to use Visa and MasterCard. Previously, the stores only accepted American Express or Neiman credit cards.

   a. What does the article mean by "snob appeal"? Is there an economic explanation for it? Briefly explain.
   b. Why might losing snob appeal be a problem for high-end retailers like Neiman Marcus?
   Source: Suzanne Kapner and Ryan Dezember, "Neiman Marcus Finds Even Wealthy Shoppers Want Better Deals," *Wall Street Journal*, April 16, 2017.

3.7 **(Related to the Apply the Concept on page 341)** An article in the *Economist* noted that for the Broadway musical *Hamilton*, "Every time the show's producers release a new block [of tickets] to sell, they immediately get snapped up by 'ticket bots,' high-speed ticket-buying software." The musical's producer called the ticket bots "computerized cheaters."
   a. How do people earn a profit from using the bots to buy tickets?
   b. Is there a strategy the musical's producer could use to eliminate the profit earned by the ticket bots? If so, why doesn't he use it?
   Source: "The War on Ticket Bots Is Unlikely to Be Won," *Economist*, January 5, 2017.

3.8 **(Related to the Apply the Concept on page 341)** In an opinion column in the *New York Times*, advocating increased legal penalties for people who use ticket bots, Lin-Manuel Miranda, the star and creator of the musical *Hamilton*, wrote, "I want the thousands of tickets for shows, concerts and sporting events that are now purchased by bots and resold at higher prices to go into the general market so that you have a chance to get them."
   a. What does he mean by the "general market"?
   b. Suppose that ticket bots were eliminated, and theaters were able to enforce a limit of each person being allowed to buy only four tickets. Is it likely that most of the people attending a hit Broadway musical like *Hamilton* would pay face value for their tickets? Briefly explain.
   Source: Lin-Manuel Miranda, "Stop the Bots from Killing Broadway," *New York Times*, June 7, 2016.

3.9 **(Related to Solved Problem 10.3 on page 343)** An article in the *Wall Street Journal* on the parking problems at Tesla's Fremont, California, factory noted that "Tesla has tried to encourage alternatives to driving, such as biking, public transportation and the shuttle buses provided from around the Bay Area."
   a. If Tesla auctioned off the right to park in its lot, would the firm need to provide other encouragement for employees to use alternative means of transportation? Briefly explain.
   b. Is the most economically efficient allocation of parking spaces in Tesla's lot likely to result from auctioning off the right to park or from keeping parking free while encouraging employees to use alternative means of getting to work? Briefly explain.
   c. Given your answer to part (b), why hasn't Tesla considered charging employees for parking in its lot?
   Source: Tim Higgins, "Elon Musk Has an Awkward Problem at Tesla: Employee Parking," *Wall Street Journal*, April 11, 2017.

10.4 Behavioral Economics: Do People Make Rational Choices?
pages 345–350

LEARNING OBJECTIVE: Describe the behavioral economics approach to understanding decision making.

MyLab Economics Visit **www.pearson.com/mylab/economics** to complete these exercises online and get instant feedback.

Summary

Behavioral economics is the study of situations in which people act in ways that are not economically rational. **Opportunity cost** is the highest-valued alternative that must be given up to engage in an activity. People would improve their decision making if they took into account nonmonetary opportunity costs. People sometimes ignore nonmonetary opportunity costs because of the **endowment effect**—the tendency of people to be unwilling to sell something they already own even if they are offered a price that is greater than the price they would be willing to pay to buy the good if they didn't already own it. People would also improve their decision making if they ignored *sunk costs*. A **sunk cost** is a cost that has already been paid and cannot be recovered. Finally, people would improve their decision making if they were more realistic about their future behavior. Behavioral economics gives insights into consumer behavior that can guide business strategies.

Review Questions

4.1 What does it mean to be economically rational?

4.2 Define *behavioral economics*. What are the three common mistakes that consumers often make? Give an example of each mistake.

4.3 Does using rules of thumb increase or decrease the likelihood of a consumer making an optimal choice? Briefly explain.

4.4 What is anchoring? How might a firm use anchoring to influence consumer choices in order to increase sales?

Problems and Applications

4.5 Marvin visits his aunt and uncle, who live in Milwaukee. The Milwaukee Bucks basketball team is scheduled to play a home game against the Golden State Warriors during Marvin's visit. An online broker has a ticket for sale in Section 212 of the arena where the game will be played, but the price, $75, is more than Marvin is willing to pay. From another online ticket broker he buys a ticket for $50 for a seat in Section 212 of the arena. On the day of the game, a friend of Marvin's uncle offers to pay Marvin $75 for his ticket. He declines the offer. How can Marvin's refusal to sell his ticket be explained?

4.6 Richard Thaler, winner of the 2017 Nobel Prize in Economics, was first to use the term *endowment effect* to describe placing a higher value on something already owned than would be placed on the object if not currently owned. According to an article in the *Economist*:

> Dr. Thaler, who recently had some expensive bottles of wine stolen, observes that he is "now confronted with precisely one of my own experiments: these are bottles I wasn't planning to sell and now I'm going to get a cheque from an insurance company and most of these bottles I will not buy. I'm a good enough economist to know there's a bit of an inconsistency there."

Based on Thaler's statement, how do his stolen bottles of wine illustrate the endowment effect? Why did he make the statement: "I'm a good enough economist to know there's a bit of an inconsistency there"?

Source: "It's Mine, I Tell You," *Economist*, June 19, 2008.

4.7 Suppose that you are a big fan of the Harry Potter books. You would love to own a copy of the very first printing of the first book, but unfortunately you can't find it for sale for less than $5,000. You are willing to pay at most $200 for a copy but can't find one at that price until one day, in a used bookstore, you see a copy selling for $10, which you immediately buy. Are you being irrational if you keep the copy rather than sell it?

4.8 Someone who owns a townhouse wrote to a real estate advice columnist to ask whether he should sell his townhouse or wait and sell it in the future, when he hoped that prices would be higher. The columnist replied: "Ask yourself: Would you buy this townhouse today as an investment? Because every day you don't sell it, you're buying it." Do you agree with the columnist? In what sense are you buying something if you don't sell it? Should the owner's decision about whether to sell depend on what price he originally paid for the townhouse?

Source: Edith Lane, "Contract Exclusion OK?" (Allentown, PA) *Morning Call*, May 22, 2011.

4.9 (Related to the Apply the Concept on page 346) Baseball writer Rob Neyer described attending a Red Sox game at Fenway Park in Boston and having a seat in the sun on a hot, humid day: "Granted, I could have moved under the overhang and enjoyed today's contest from a nice, cool, shady seat. But when you paid forty-five dollars for a ticket in the fourth row, it's tough to move back to the twenty-fourth [row]." Briefly evaluate Neyer's reasoning.

Source: Rob Neyer, *Feeding the Green Monster*, New York: iPublish. com, 2001, p. 50.

4.10 (Related to the Apply the Concept on page 346) In 2012, the San Francisco Giants Major League Baseball team signed pitcher Matt Cain to a contract that paid him a salary of $20 million per year from 2013 through 2017. The annual salaries were all guaranteed, and the Giants had to pay Cain whether he performed well or not—and they had to pay him even if the team released him and he no longer played for the Giants. During 2016, Cain pitched ineffectively, and at the beginning of the 2017 season, it was uncertain whether the Giants would keep him as a regular player. Giants General Manager Bobby Evans was quoted as saying that in the decision on Cain, his salary wasn't a factor: "It's really not about the money at this point." Is Evans's analysis correct? Should the salary the Giants are paying Cain matter in deciding whether to keep him on the team? Would the team's decision be affected if Cain were receiving the Major League Baseball minimum salary of $535,000? Briefly explain.

Source: Daniel Mano, "Bobby Evans Explains Matt Cain's Uncertain Status with Giants," mercurynews.com, March 14, 2017.

4.11 (Related to the Apply the Concept on page 346) The following excerpt is from a letter sent to a financial advice columnist: "My wife and I are trying to decide how to invest a $250,000 windfall. She wants to pay off our $114,000 mortgage, but I'm not eager to do that because we refinanced only nine months ago, paying $3,000 in fees and costs." Briefly discuss what effect the $3,000 refinancing cost should have on this couple's investment decision.

Source: Liz Pulliam, *Los Angeles Times* advice column, March 24, 2004.

4.12 Andrea grew up enjoying her Italian grandmother's home-cooked meals. Chicken and pasta with meatballs were her favorite foods. But after Andrea graduated from college, found a job, and got married, she became a vegetarian and no longer ate chicken or meatballs. Briefly explain which of the following statements provides the most likely explanation of Andrea's decision to become a vegetarian:

• When Andrea was young, she was unrealistic about her future behavior. Therefore, she did not act rationally.

- Andrea was not working when she was young. After she graduated from college and became employed, her income rose. We can conclude that for Andrea, chicken, meatballs, and other meat products are inferior goods.
- Social influences explain Andrea's decision to become a vegetarian. More people, including celebrities from the entertainment field, have become vegetarians. Andrea became a vegetarian because she now feels a kinship with these celebrities, and being a vegetarian makes her appear to be fashionable.

4.13 In an article in the *Quarterly Journal of Economics*, Ted O'Donoghue and Matthew Rabin made the following observation: "People have self-control problems caused by a tendency to pursue immediate gratification in a way that their 'long-run selves' do not appreciate." What do they mean by people's "long-run selves"? Give two examples of people pursuing immediate gratification that their long-run selves would not appreciate.

Source: Ted O'Donoghue and Matthew Rabin, "Choice and Procrastination," *Quarterly Journal of Economics*, Vol. 116, No. 1, February 2001, pp. 125–126.

4.14 Shawn Van Dyke, a construction industry consultant, wrote on a home building site:

> Brains do some pretty funny things when making a buying decision. If you understand your customers' brain activities, then you can use this knowledge to help increase your sales and deliver on value. . . . There's an old question in advertising. "How do you sell a $2,000 watch? Put it next to a $10,000 watch." This is an example of price anchoring.

a. What is price anchoring?
b. Explain why Van Dyke cited the "old advertising question" as an example of price anchoring.

Source: Shawn Van Dyke, "The Psychology of Price Anchoring," finchomebuilding.com, December 26, 2016.

4.15 (Related to the Apply the Concept on page 349) The *Economist* offered the following two options for subscribing:

1. $56 per year for an online-only subscription
2. $125 per year for a print plus online access subscription

A large majority of subscribers chose option 1. But the magazine would have preferred to sell more $125 subscriptions because it can charge higher rates to advertisers in the print magazine than it can online. The magazine decided to rely on insights from behavioral economics to try to increase the number of people choosing the $125 subscriptions. It began offering the following three options:

1. $56 per year for an online-only subscription
2. $125 per year for a print plus online access subscription
3. $125 per year for a print-only subscription

A large majority of subscribers now chose option 2 rather than option 1. What insights from behavioral economics that were discussed in this chapter can help explain this result?

Source: Mukul Patki, "5 Behavioral Economics Principles Marketers Can't Afford to Ignore," *Forbes*, March 1, 2013.

4.16 (Related to the Chapter Opener on page 324) An article in the *New York Times* about J.C. Penney's pricing strategy under former CEO Ron Johnson observed, "Penney had pulled up the anchor, only to see many of its customers sail away."
a. In behavioral economics, what is an "anchor"?
b. In what sense did Penney "pull up the anchor"?
c. Why did Penney follow this strategy, and what was the result?

Source: Stephanie Clifford and Catherine Rampell, "Sometimes We Want Prices to Fool Us," *New York Times*, April 13, 2013.

Critical Thinking Exercises

CT10.1 You're in a store like REI, Cabela's, or Bass Pro Shops that specializes in selling outdoor clothing and accessories. On the front of a rack of rain jackets, you see one with a price tag of $400 and think, "Why does the store even put this jacket on the rack? Hardly anyone would pay that much for just a rain jacket. Doesn't the store understand opportunity cost? By putting that jacket on the rack, it doesn't have room for an affordable jacket that more customers are likely to buy." Identify the concept from this chapter that can explain why the store puts such an expensive jacket on a rack.

CT10.2 You are talking to a recently retired person who saved for years in order to travel and see the world. The more this person travels, the happier he is. Does this observation mean that the *law of diminishing marginal utility* is wrong? Briefly explain.

CT10.3 For this exercise, your instructor may assign you to a group. Each member of each group should think of an example of when he or she has experienced one of the "pitfalls in decision making" described in Section 10.4 and write down the example. Next, the group members should share their examples with each other. Finally, someone in the group should write a brief report of about a page that summarizes the pitfalls that members of the group have experienced and explains how avoiding these pitfalls would improve decision making.

Appendix

LEARNING OBJECTIVE:
Use indifference curves and
budget lines to understand
consumer behavior.

Using Indifference Curves and Budget Lines to Understand Consumer Behavior

Consumer Preferences

In this chapter, we analyzed consumer behavior using the assumption that satisfaction, or *utility*, is measurable in utils. Although this assumption made our analysis easier to understand, it is unrealistic. In this appendix, we use the more realistic assumption that consumers are able to *rank* different combinations of goods and services in terms of how much utility they provide. For example, a consumer is able to determine whether he or she prefers 2 slices of pizza and 1 can of Coke or 1 slice of pizza and 2 cans of Coke, even if the consumer is unsure exactly how much utility he or she would receive from consuming these goods. This approach has the advantage of allowing us to actually draw a map of a consumer's preferences.

To begin with, suppose that a consumer is presented with the following alternatives, or *consumption bundles*:

Consumption Bundle *A*	Consumption Bundle *B*
2 slices of pizza and 1 can of Coke	1 slice of pizza and 2 cans of Coke

We assume that the consumer will always be able to decide which of the following is true:

* The consumer prefers bundle *A* to bundle *B*.
* The consumer prefers bundle *B* to bundle *A*.
* The consumer is indifferent between bundle *A* and bundle *B*. That is, the consumer would be equally happy to receive either bundle, so we can say that the consumer receives equal utility from the two bundles.

For consistency, we also assume that the consumer's preferences are *transitive*. For example, if a consumer prefers pepperoni pizza to mushroom pizza and prefers mushroom pizza to anchovy pizza, the consumer must prefer pepperoni pizza to anchovy pizza.

Indifference Curves

Indifference curve A curve that shows the combinations of consumption bundles that give the consumer the same utility.

Given the assumptions in the preceding section, we can draw a map of a consumer's preferences by using indifference curves. An **indifference curve** shows combinations of consumption bundles that give the consumer the same utility. In reality, consumers choose among consumption bundles containing many goods and services, but to make the discussion easier to follow, we will assume that only two goods are involved. Nothing important would change if we expanded the discussion to include many goods instead of just two.

The table in Figure 10A.1 gives Dave's preferences for pizza and Coke. The graph plots the information from the table. Every possible combination of pizza and Coke will have an indifference curve passing through it, although in the figure we have shown only four of Dave's indifference curves. Dave is indifferent among all the consumption bundles that are on the same indifference curve. So, he is indifferent among bundles *E*, *B*, and *F* because they all lie on indifference curve I_3. Even though Dave has 4 fewer cans of Coke with bundle *B* than with bundle *E*, the additional slice of pizza he has in bundle *B* results in his having the same amount of utility at both points.

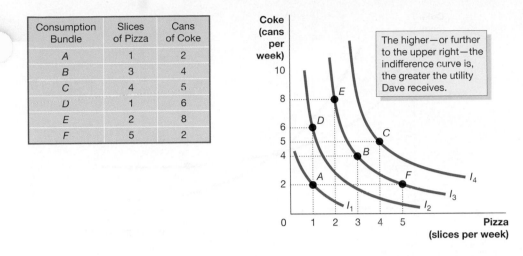

Consumption Bundle	Slices of Pizza	Cans of Coke
A	1	2
B	3	4
C	4	5
D	1	6
E	2	8
F	5	2

The higher—or further to the upper right—the indifference curve is, the greater the utility Dave receives.

MyLab Economics Animation

Figure 10A.1

Plotting Dave's Preferences for Pizza and Coke

Every possible combination of pizza and Coke will have an indifference curve passing through it, although in the graph we show just four of Dave's indifference curves. Dave is indifferent among all the consumption bundles that are on the same indifference curve. So, he is indifferent among bundles E, B, and F because they all lie on indifference curve I_3. Moving to the upper right in the graph increases the quantities of both goods available for Dave to consume. Therefore, the further to the upper right the indifference curve is, the greater the utility Dave receives.

Even without looking at Dave's indifference curves, we know he will prefer consumption bundle D to consumption bundle A because in D he receives the same quantity of pizza as in A but 4 additional cans of Coke. But we need to know Dave's preferences, as shown by his indifference curves, to know how he will rank bundle B and bundle D. Bundle D contains more Coke but less pizza than bundle B, so Dave's ranking will depend on how much pizza he would be willing to give up to receive more Coke. The higher the indifference curve—that is, the further to the upper right on the graph—the greater the amounts of both goods that are available for Dave to consume and the greater his utility. In other words, Dave receives more utility from the consumption bundles on indifference curve I_2 than from the consumption bundles on indifference curve I_1, more utility from the bundles on I_3 than from the bundles on I_2, and so on.   MyLab Economics Concept Check

The Slope of an Indifference Curve

Remember that the slope of a curve is the ratio of the change in the variable on the vertical axis to the change in the variable on the horizontal axis. Along an indifference curve, the slope tells us the rate at which the consumer is willing to trade off one product for another while keeping the consumer's utility constant. Economists call this rate the **marginal rate of substitution (MRS)**.

We expect that the MRS will change as we move down an indifference curve. In Figure 10A.1, at a point like E on indifference curve I_3, Dave's indifference curve is relatively steep. As we move down the curve, it becomes less steep, until it becomes relatively flat at a point like F. This is the usual shape of indifference curves: They are bowed in, or convex. A consumption bundle like E contains a lot of Coke and not much pizza. We would expect that Dave could give up a significant quantity of Coke for a smaller quantity of additional pizza and still have the same level of utility. Therefore, the MRS will be high. As we move down the indifference curve, Dave moves to bundles, like B and F, that have more pizza and less Coke. At those points, Dave is willing to trade less Coke for pizza, and the MRS declines.   MyLab Economics Concept Check

Marginal rate of substitution (MRS) The rate at which a consumer would be willing to trade off one good for another.

Can Indifference Curves Ever Cross?

Remember that we assume that consumers have transitive preferences. That is, if Dave prefers consumption bundle X to consumption bundle Y and prefers consumption bundle Y to consumption bundle Z, he must prefer bundle X to bundle Z. If indifference curves cross, this assumption is violated. To understand why, look at Figure 10A.2, which shows two of Dave's indifference curves crossing.

Because bundle X and bundle Z are both on indifference curve I_1, Dave must be indifferent between them. Similarly, because bundle X and bundle Y are on indifference curve I_2, Dave must be indifferent between them. The assumption of transitivity means that Dave should also be indifferent between bundle Z and bundle Y. We know he won't be,

MyLab Economics Animation

Figure 10A.2

Indifference Curves Cannot Cross

Because bundle X and bundle Z are both on indifference curve I_1, Dave must be indifferent between them. Similarly, because bundle X and bundle Y are on indifference curve I_2, Dave must be indifferent between them. The assumption of transitivity means that Dave should also be indifferent between bundle Z and bundle Y. We know he won't be, however, because bundle Y contains more pizza and more Coke than bundle Z. So, Dave will definitely prefer bundle Y to bundle Z, which violates the assumption of transitivity. Therefore, none of Dave's indifference curves can cross.

however, because bundle Y contains more pizza and more Coke than bundle Z. So, Dave will definitely prefer bundle Y to bundle Z, which violates the assumption of transitivity. Therefore, none of Dave's indifference curves can cross.   MyLab Economics Concept Check

The Budget Constraint

Remember that a consumer's *budget constraint* is the amount of income he or she has available to spend on goods and services. Suppose that Dave has $10 per week to spend on pizza and Coke. The table in Figure 10A.3 shows the combinations that he

MyLab Economics Animation

Figure 10A.3

Dave's Budget Constraint

Dave's budget constraint shows the combinations of slices of pizza and cans of Coke he can buy with $10. The price of Coke is $1 per can, so if he spends all of his $10 on Coke, he can buy 10 cans (bundle G). The price of pizza is $2 per slice, so if he spends all of his $10 on pizza, he can buy 5 slices (bundle L). As he moves down his budget constraint from bundle G, he gives up 2 cans of Coke for every slice of pizza he buys. Any consumption bundles along the line or inside the line are affordable. Any bundles that lie outside the line are unaffordable.

Combinations of Pizza and Coke Dave Can Buy with $10			
Consumption Bundle	Slices of Pizza	Cans of Coke	Total Spending
G	0	10	$10.00
H	1	8	10.00
I	2	6	10.00
J	3	4	10.00
K	4	2	10.00
L	5	0	10.00

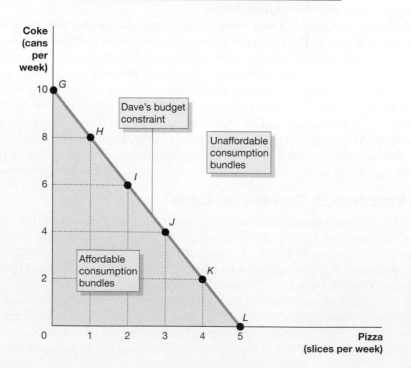

can afford to buy if the price of pizza is $2 per slice and the price of Coke is $1 per can. As you can see, all the points lie on a straight line. This line represents Dave's budget constraint. The line intersects the vertical axis at the maximum number of cans of Coke Dave can afford to buy with $10, which is consumption bundle *G*. The line intersects the horizontal axis at the maximum number of slices of pizza Dave can afford to buy with $10, which is consumption bundle *L*. As he moves down his budget constraint from bundle *G*, he gives up 2 cans of Coke for every slice of pizza he buys.

Any consumption bundle along the line or inside the line is *affordable* for Dave because he has the income to buy those combinations of pizza and Coke. Any bundle that lies outside the line is *unaffordable* because those bundles cost more than the income Dave has available to spend.

The slope of the budget constraint is constant because the budget constraint is a straight line. The slope of the line equals the change in the number of cans of Coke divided by the change in the number of slices of pizza. In this case, moving down the budget constraint from one point to another point, the change in the number of cans of Coke equals −2, and the change in the number of slices of pizza equals 1, so the slope equals −2/1, or −2. Notice that with the price of pizza equal to $2 per slice and the price of Coke equal to $1 per can, the slope of the budget constraint is equal to the ratio of the price of pizza to the price of Coke (multiplied by −1). In fact, this result will always hold: *The slope of the budget constraint is equal to the ratio of the price of the good on the horizontal axis divided by the price of the good on the vertical axis multiplied by −1.*

MyLab Economics Concept Check

Choosing the Optimal Consumption of Pizza and Coke

Dave would like to be on the highest possible indifference curve because higher indifference curves represent more pizza and more Coke. But Dave can only buy the bundles that lie on or inside his budget constraint. In other words, *to maximize utility, a consumer needs to be on the highest indifference curve, given his budget constraint.*

Figure 10A.4 plots the consumption bundles from Figure 10A.1 on page 359 along with the budget constraint from Figure 10A.3. The figure also shows the indifference

MyLab Economics Animation

Figure 10A.4

Finding Optimal Consumption

Dave would like to be on the highest possible indifference curve, but he cannot reach indifference curves such as I_4 that are outside his budget constraint. Dave's optimal combination of slices of pizza and cans of Coke is at point *B*, where his budget constraint just touches—or is *tangent* to—the highest indifference curve he can reach. At point *B*, he buys 3 slices of pizza and 4 cans of Coke.

curves that pass through each consumption bundle. In Figure 10A.4, the highest indifference curve shown is I_4. Unfortunately, Dave lacks the income to purchase consumption bundles—such as C—that lie on I_4. He has the income to purchase bundles such as A and D, but he can do better. If he consumes bundle B, he will be on the highest indifference curve he can reach, given his budget constraint of $10. The resulting combination of 3 slices of pizza and 4 cans of Coke represents Dave's optimal consumption of pizza and Coke, given his preferences and his budget constraint. Notice that at point B, Dave's budget constraint just touches—or is *tangent* to—I_3. In fact, bundle B is the only bundle on I_3 that Dave is able to purchase for $10.

Apply the Concept

MyLab Economics Video

Apple Determines the Optimal Mix of iPhone Features

Consumers have different preferences, which helps explain why many firms offer products with a variety of features. For example, Apple sells its iPhones with different screen sizes, processors, displays, cameras, battery lives, and amounts of memory. We can use the model of consumer choice to analyze a simplified version of the situation managers at Apple face in deciding which features to offer consumers.

Assume that consumers have $500 each to spend on an iPhone and that they are concerned with only two smartphone features: screen size and memory. Because larger screens and larger memories increase Apple's cost of producing smartphones, consumers face a trade-off: The larger the screen, the smaller the amount of memory. Consumers in panel (a) of the following figure prefer screen size to memory. For this group, the point of tangency between a typical consumer's indifference curve and the budget constraint shows an optimal choice of a 5.5-inch screen and 128 gigabytes (GB) of memory. Consumers in panel (b) prefer memory to screen size. For this group, the point of tangency between a typical consumer's indifference curve and the budget constraint shows an optimal choice of a 4.7-inch screen and 256 GB of memory.

(a) Consumers who prefer screen size to memory capacity

(b) Consumers who prefer memory capacity to screen size

Apple and other companies use market research methods such as surveys and focus groups to gather information about consumer preferences. With knowledge of consumers' preferences and data on the costs of producing different smartphone components, Apple can determine the mix of features to offer consumers.

MyLab Economics Study Plan   **Your Turn:** Test your understanding by doing related problem 10A.8 on page 370 at the end of this appendix.

Deriving the Demand Curve

Suppose the price of pizza falls from $2 per slice to $1 per slice. How will this change affect Dave's decision about which combination of pizza and Coke is optimal? First, notice what happens to Dave's budget constraint when the price of pizza falls. As Figure 10A.5 shows, when the price of pizza is $2 per slice, the maximum number of slices Dave can buy is 5. After the price of pizza falls to $1 per slice, Dave can buy a maximum of 10 slices. His budget constraint rotates outward from point A to point B to represent this. (Notice that the fall in the price of pizza does not affect the maximum number of cans of Coke Dave can buy with his $10.)

When his budget constraint rotates outward, Dave is able to purchase consumption bundles that were previously unaffordable. Panel (a) of Figure 10A.6 shows that the combination of 3 slices of pizza and 4 cans of Coke was optimal when the price of pizza was $2 per slice, but the combination of 7 slices of pizza and 3 cans of Coke is optimal when the price of pizza falls to $1. The lower price of pizza causes Dave to consume more pizza and less Coke and to end up on a higher indifference curve.

The change in Dave's optimal consumption of pizza as the price changes explains why demand curves slope downward. Dave adjusted his consumption of pizza as follows:

Price of pizza = $2 per slice → Quantity of pizza demanded = 3 slices

Price of pizza = $1 per slice → Quantity of pizza demanded = 7 slices

In panel (b) of Figure 10A.6, we plot the two points of optimal consumption and draw a line to connect the points. This downward-sloping line is Dave's demand curve for pizza. We could find more points on the demand curve by changing the price of pizza and finding the new optimal number of slices of pizza Dave would demand.

Remember that according to the law of demand, demand curves always slope downward. We have just shown that the law of demand results from the optimal adjustment by consumers to changes in prices. A fall in the price of a good will rotate *outward* the budget constraint and make it possible for a consumer to reach higher indifference curves. As a result, the consumer will increase the quantity of the good demanded. An increase in price will rotate *inward* the budget constraint and force the consumer to a lower indifference curve. As a result, the consumer will decrease the quantity of the good demanded.   **MyLab Economics** Concept Check

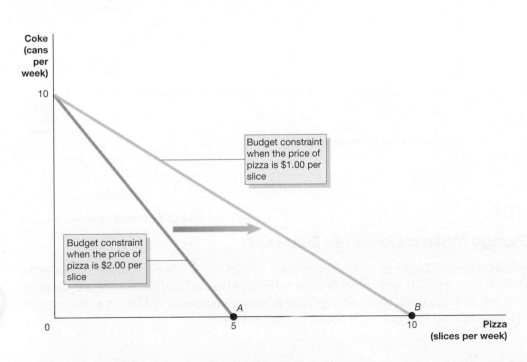

Coke (cans per week)

Budget constraint when the price of pizza is $1.00 per slice

Budget constraint when the price of pizza is $2.00 per slice

A

B

0   5   10   Pizza (slices per week)

MyLab Economics Animation

Figure 10A.5

How a Price Decrease Affects the Budget Constraint

A fall in the price of pizza from $2 per slice to $1 per slice increases the maximum number of slices Dave can buy with $10 from 5 to 10. The budget constraint rotates outward from point A to point B to show the effect of the price decrease.

MyLab Economics Animation

Figure 10A.6

How a Price Change Affects Optimal Consumption

In panel (a), a fall in the price of pizza results in Dave's consuming less Coke and more pizza:

1. A fall in the price of pizza rotates the budget constraint outward because Dave can now buy more pizza with his $10.
2. In the new optimum on indifference curve I_2, Dave changes the quantities he consumes of both goods. His consumption of Coke falls from 4 cans to 3 cans.
3. In the new optimum, Dave's consumption of pizza increases from 3 slices to 7 slices.

In panel (b), Dave responds optimally to the fall in the price of pizza from $2 per slice to $1 per slice by increasing the quantity of slices he consumes from 3 slices to 7 slices. When we graph this result, we have Dave's demand curve for pizza.

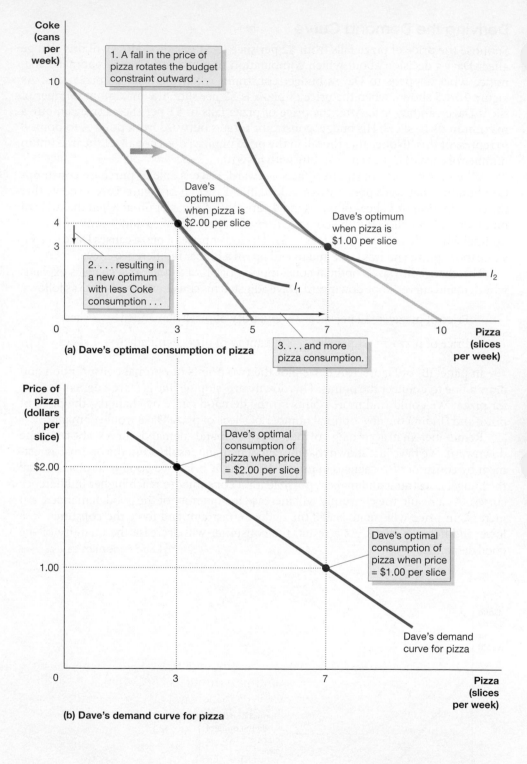

(a) Dave's optimal consumption of pizza

(b) Dave's demand curve for pizza

Solved Problem 10A.1

MyLab Economics Interactive Animation

When Does a Price Change Make a Consumer Better Off?

Dave has $300 to spend each month on pizzas and streaming movies. Pizzas and movies both have a price of $10, and Dave is maximizing his utility by buying 20 pizzas and 10 movies. Suppose Dave still has $300 to spend, but the price of movies rises to $20, while the price of pizzas drops to $5. Is Dave better or worse off than he was before the price change? Use a budget constraint–indifference curve graph to illustrate your answer.

Solving the Problem

Step 1: **Review the chapter material.** This problem concerns the effect of price changes on optimal consumption, so you may want to review the section "Deriving the Demand Curve," which begins on page 363.

Step 2: **Solve the problem by drawing the appropriate graph.** We begin by drawing the budget constraint, indifference curve, and point of optimal consumption for the original prices:

Now draw a graph that shows the results of the price changes. Notice that in this problem, the prices of *both* goods change. You can determine the position of the new budget constraint by calculating the maximum quantity of pizzas and movies Dave can buy after the price changes. You should also note that after the price changes, Dave can still buy his original optimal consumption bundle—20 pizzas and 10 movies—by spending all his $300, so his new budget constraint must pass through this point.

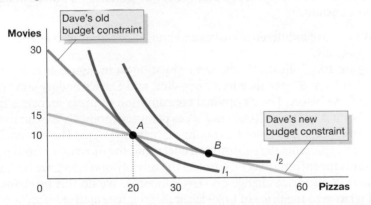

At the new prices, Dave can buy a maximum of 60 pizzas or 15 movies. Both his old and new budget constraints pass through the consumption bundle at point A. This consumption bundle is no longer optimal, however, because with the new prices, it is possible for him to reach an indifference curve that is higher than I_1. We can draw in the new highest indifference curve he can reach—I_2—and show the new optimal consumption bundle—point B.

Because Dave can now reach a higher indifference curve, we can conclude that he is better off as a result of the price change.

Your Turn: For more practice, do related problem 10A.10 on page 370 at the end of this appendix.

MyLab Economics Study Plan

The Income Effect and the Substitution Effect of a Price Change

We saw in this chapter that a price change has these two effects on the quantity of a good consumed:

1. The *substitution effect* is the change in the quantity demanded of a good that results from a change in price making the good more or less expensive relative to other

MyLab Economics Animation

Figure 10A.7

Income and Substitution Effects of a Price Change

Following a decline in the price of pizza, Dave's optimal consumption of pizza increases from 3 slices per week (point A) to 7 slices per week (point C). We can think of this movement from point A to point C as taking place in two steps: The movement from point A to point B along indifference curve I_1 represents the substitution effect, and the movement from point B to point C represents the income effect. Dave increases his consumption of pizza from 3 slices per week to 5 slices per week because of the substitution effect of a fall in the price of pizza and from 5 slices per week to 7 slices per week because of the income effect.

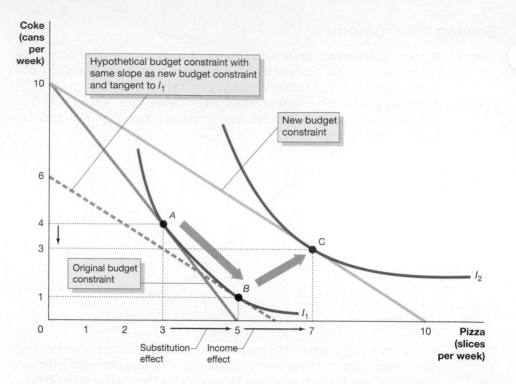

goods, holding constant the effect of the price change on consumer purchasing power.

2. The *income effect* is the change in the quantity demanded of a good that results from the effect of a change in price on consumer purchasing power, holding all other factors constant.

We can use indifference curves and budget constraints to analyze these two effects more precisely.

Figure 10A.7 illustrates the same situation as in Figure 10A.6: The price of pizza has fallen from $2 per slice to $1 per slice, and Dave's budget constraint has rotated outward. As before, Dave's optimal consumption of pizza increases from 3 slices per week (point A in Figure 10A.7) to 7 slices per week (point C). We can think of this movement from point A to point C as taking place in two steps: The movement from point A to point B represents the substitution effect, and the movement from point B to point C represents the income effect. To isolate the substitution effect, we have to hold constant the effect of the price change on Dave's income. We do this by changing the price of pizza relative to the price of Coke *but at the same time holding his utility constant by keeping Dave on the same indifference curve*. In Figure 10A.7, in moving from point A to point B, Dave remains on indifference curve I_1. Point A is a point of tangency between I_1 and Dave's original budget constraint. Point B is a point of tangency between I_1 and a new, *hypothetical* budget constraint that has a slope equal to the new ratio of the price of pizza to the price of Coke. At point B, Dave has increased his consumption of pizza from 3 slices to 5 slices. Because we are still on indifference curve I_1, we know that this increase is Dave's response only to the change in the relative price of pizza and, therefore, that the increase represents the substitution effect of the fall in the price of pizza.

At point B, Dave has not spent all his income. Remember that the fall in the price of pizza has increased Dave's purchasing power. In Figure 10A.7, we illustrate the additional pizza Dave consumes because of the income effect of increased purchasing power by the movement from point B to point C. Notice that in moving from point B to point C, the price of pizza relative to the price of Coke is constant because the slope of the new budget constraint is the same as the slope of the hypothetical budget constraint that is tangent to I_1 at point B.

We can conclude that Dave increases his consumption of pizza from 3 slices per week to 5 slices per week because of the substitution effect of a fall in the price of pizza

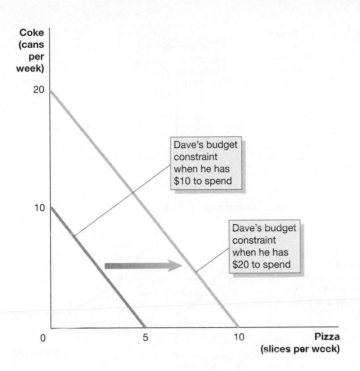

MyLab Economics Animation
Figure 10A.8

How a Change in Income Affects the Budget Constraint

When the income Dave has to spend on pizza and Coke increases from $10 to $20, his budget constraint shifts outward. With $10, Dave could buy a maximum of 5 slices of pizza or 10 cans of Coke. With $20, he can buy a maximum of 10 slices of pizza or 20 cans of Coke.

and from 5 slices per week to 7 slices per week because of the income effect. Recall from our discussion of income and substitution effects in this chapter that the income effect of a price decline causes consumers to buy more of a normal good and less of an inferior good. Because the income effect causes Dave to increase his consumption of pizza, pizza must be a normal good for him. MyLab Economics Concept Check

How a Change in Income Affects Optimal Consumption

Suppose that the price of pizza remains at $2 per slice, but the income Dave has to spend on pizza and Coke increases from $10 to $20. Figure 10A.8 shows how this change affects his budget constraint. With an income of $10, Dave could buy a maximum of 5 slices of pizza or 10 cans of Coke. With an income of $20, he can buy 10 slices of pizza or 20 cans of Coke. The additional income allows Dave to increase his consumption of both pizza and Coke and to move to a higher indifference curve.

Figure 10A.9 shows Dave's new optimum. Dave is able to increase his consumption of pizza from 3 to 7 slices per week and his consumption of Coke from 4 to 6 cans per week. MyLab Economics Concept Check

The Slope of the Indifference Curve, the Slope of the Budget Line, and the Rule of Equal Marginal Utility per Dollar Spent

In this chapter, we saw that consumers maximize utility when they consume each good up to the point where the marginal utility per dollar spent is the same for every good. This condition seems different from the one we stated earlier in this appendix that to maximize utility, a consumer needs to be on the highest indifference curve, given his budget constraint. In fact, the two conditions are equivalent. To see this, begin by looking at Figure 10A.10, which again combines Dave's indifference curve and budget constraint. Remember that at the point of optimal consumption, the indifference curve and the budget constraint are tangent, so they have the same slope. Therefore, *at the point of optimal consumption, the marginal rate of substitution (MRS) is equal to the ratio of the price of the product on the horizontal axis to the price of the product on the vertical axis.*

The slope of the indifference curve tells us the rate at which a consumer is *willing* to trade off one good for the other. The slope of the budget constraint tells us the

MyLab Economics Animation

Figure 10A.9

How a Change in Income Affects Optimal Consumption

An increase in income leads Dave to consume more Coke and more pizza:

1. An increase in income shifts Dave's budget constraint outward because he can now buy more of both goods.
2. In the new optimum on indifference curve I_2, Dave changes the quantities he consumes of both goods. His consumption of Coke increases from 4 to 6 cans.
3. In the new optimum, Dave's consumption of pizza increases from 3 to 7 slices.

rate at which a consumer is *able* to trade off one good for the other. Only at the point of optimal consumption is the rate at which a consumer is willing to trade off one good for the other equal to the rate at which the consumer can trade off one good for the other.

The Rule of Equal Marginal Utility per Dollar Spent Revisited

Recall from this chapter the *rule of equal marginal utility per dollar*, which states that to maximize utility, consumers should spend their income so that the last dollar spent on each product gives them the same marginal utility. We can use our indifference curve and budget constraint analysis to see why this rule holds. When we move from one

MyLab Economics Animation

Figure 10A.10

At the Optimum Point, the Slopes of the Indifference Curve and Budget Constraint Are the Same

At the point of optimal consumption, the marginal rate of substitution is equal to the ratio of the price of the product on the horizontal axis to the price of the product on the vertical axis.

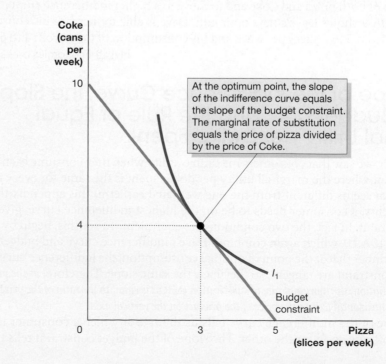

point on an indifference curve to another, we end up with more of one product and less of the other product but the same amount of utility. For example, as Dave moves down an indifference curve, he consumes less Coke and more pizza, but he has the same amount of utility.

Remember that marginal utility (MU) tells us how much additional utility a consumer gains (or loses) from consuming more (or less) of a good. So when Dave consumes less Coke by moving down an indifference curve, he loses utility equal to:

$$-\text{Change in the quantity of Coke} \times MU_{Coke},$$

but he consumes more pizza, so he gains utility equal to:

$$\text{Change in the quantity of Pizza} \times MU_{Pizza}.$$

We know that the gain in utility from the additional pizza is equal to the loss from the smaller quantity of Coke because Dave's total utility remains the same along an indifference curve. Therefore, we can write:

$$-(\text{Change in the quantity of Coke} \times MU_{Coke}) = (\text{Change in the quantity of pizza} \times MU_{Pizza}).$$

Loss in utility from consuming less Coke

Gain in utility from consuming more pizza

If we rearrange terms, we have:

$$\frac{-\text{Change in the quantity of Coke}}{\text{Change in the quantity of Pizza}} = \frac{MU_{Pizza}}{MU_{Coke}}.$$

Because the expression:

$$\frac{-\text{Change in the quantity of Coke}}{\text{Change in the quantity of Pizza}}$$

is the slope of the indifference curve, it is equal to the MRS (multiplied by -1). So, we can write:

$$\frac{-\text{Change in the quantity of Coke}}{\text{Change in the quantity of Pizza}} = MRS = \frac{MU_{Pizza}}{MU_{Coke}}.$$

The slope of Dave's budget constraint equals the price of pizza divided by the price of Coke (multiplied by -1). We saw earlier in this appendix that at the point of optimal consumption, the MRS equals the ratio of the prices of the two goods. Therefore:

$$\frac{MU_{Pizza}}{MU_{Coke}} = \frac{P_{Pizza}}{P_{Coke}}.$$

We can rewrite this to show that at the point of optimal consumption:

$$\frac{MU_{Pizza}}{P_{Pizza}} = \frac{MU_{Coke}}{P_{Coke}}.$$

This last expression is the rule of equal marginal utility per dollar that we first developed in this chapter. So we have shown how this rule follows from the indifference curve and budget constraint approach to analyzing consumer choice.   MyLab Economics Concept Check   MyLab Economics Study Plan

Key Terms

Indifference curve, p. 358

Marginal rate of substitution (MRS), p. 359

10.A Using Indifference Curves and Budget Lines to Understand Consumer Behavior, pages 358–369

LEARNING OBJECTIVE: Use indifference curves and budget lines to understand consumer behavior.

MyLab Economics   Visit **www.pearson.com/mylab/economics** to complete these exercises online and get instant feedback.

Review Questions

10A.1 What are the two assumptions economists make about consumer preferences?

10A.2 What is an indifference curve? What is a budget constraint?

10A.3 How do consumers choose the optimal consumption bundle?

Problems and Applications

10A.4 Jacob receives an allowance of $5 per week. He spends all his allowance on ice cream cones and bottles of smartwater soda.

  a. If the price of ice cream cones is $0.50 per cone and the price of bottles of smartwater is $1 per bottle, draw a graph showing Jacob's budget constraint. Be sure to indicate on the graph the maximum number of ice cream cones and the maximum number of bottles of smartwater that Jacob can buy.

  b. Jacob buys 8 ice cream cones and 1 bottle of smartwater. Draw an indifference curve representing Jacob's choice, assuming that he has chosen the optimal combination.

  c. Suppose that the price of ice cream cones rises to $1 per cone. Draw Jacob's new budget constraint and his new optimal consumption of ice cream cones and bottles of smartwater.

10A.5 Suppose that Jacob's allowance in problem 10A.4 climbs from $5 to $10 per week.

  a. Show how the increased allowance alters Jacob's budget constraint.

  b. Draw a set of indifference curves showing how Jacob's choice of ice cream cones and bottles of smartwater changes when his allowance increases. Assume that both goods are normal.

  c. Draw a set of indifference curves showing how Jacob's choice of ice cream cones and bottles of smartwater changes when his allowance increases. Assume that smartwater is a normal good but ice cream is an inferior good.

10A.6 Suppose that Calvin considers Pepsi and Coke to be perfect substitutes. They taste the same to him, and he gets exactly the same amount of enjoyment from drinking a can of Pepsi or a can of Coke.

  a. Will Calvin's indifference curves showing his trade-off between Pepsi and Coke have the same curvature as the indifference curves drawn in the figures in this appendix? Briefly explain.

  b. How will Calvin decide whether to buy Pepsi or Coke?

10A.7 In the following budget constraint–indifference curve graph, Nikki has $200 to spend on tops and pants.

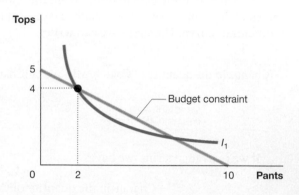

  a. What is the price of tops? What is the price of pants?

  b. Is Nikki making the optimum choice if she buys 4 tops and 2 pants? Explain how you know this.

10A.8 (Related to the Apply the Concept on page 362) Marilou and Hunter both purchase milk and doughnuts at the same Quik Mart. They have different tastes for milk and doughnuts and different incomes. They both buy some milk and some doughnuts, but they buy considerably different quantities of the two goods. Can we conclude that their marginal rate of substitution between milk and doughnuts is the same? Draw a graph showing their budget constraints and indifference curves and explain.

10A.9 Sunsweet decides that prune juice has a bad image, so it launches a slick advertising campaign to convince young people that prune juice is very hip. The company hires Taylor Swift, Beyoncé, and Bruno Mars to endorse its product. The campaign works! Prune juice sales soar, even though Sunsweet hasn't cut the price. Draw a budget constraint and indifference curve diagram with Sunsweet prune juice on one axis and other drinks on the other axis and show how the celebrity endorsements have changed things.

10A.10 (Related to Solved Problem 10A.1 on page 364) Dave has $300 to spend each month on pizzas and online movies. Pizzas and movies both currently have a price of $10, and Dave is maximizing his utility by buying 20 pizzas and 10 movies. Suppose Dave still has $300 to spend, but the price of a pizza rises to $12, while the price of a movie drops to $6. Is Dave better or worse off than he was before the price change? Use a budget constraint–indifference curve graph to illustrate your answer.

10A.11 The following graph illustrates the combination of apples and oranges (point *A*) that maximizes Yolanda's total utility, given her budget. Suppose the price of oranges doubles, while the price of apples and Yolanda's income both stay the same.

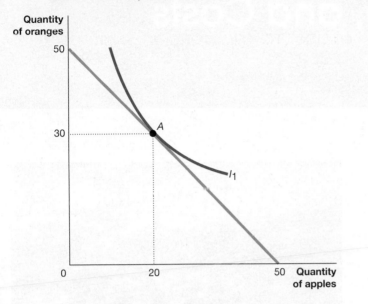

a. Draw a new budget constraint to reflect the increase in the price of oranges.
b. Based on the assumptions regarding consumer preferences listed at the beginning of this appendix, sketch in a new indifference curve to reflect the new optimal combination of apples and oranges now that the price of oranges has doubled.
c. Are there any circumstances in which the new optimal combination of apples and oranges will include a larger quantity of oranges (compared to the original combination)? Briefly explain.

10A.12 An article in the *Wall Street Journal* noted that as a result of lower gasoline prices, sales "improved notably over the last two months at Back Yard Burgers, a dining chain based in Nashville, Tenn." A student is asked to use an indifference curve and budget constraint graph to show the effect on a consumer of lower gasoline prices, making the following assumptions:

1. The consumer has $120 per month to spend on gasoline and burgers.
2. The price of gasoline falls from $3.00 per gallon to $2.00 per gallon.
3. The price of burgers is unchanged at $6.

The student draws the following graph.

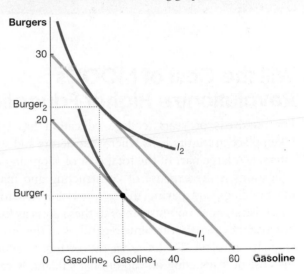

Comment on whether the student has correctly drawn each of the following.
a. The consumer's original budget constraint before the decline in the price of gasoline
b. The consumer's budget constraint after the decline in the price of gasoline
c. The change in the quantity of gasoline the consumer buys after the decline in the price of gasoline

Source: Nick Timiraos, "Pump Prices Prime Economy for Growth," *Wall Street Journal*, December 11, 2014.

Will the Cost of MOOCs Revolutionize Higher Education?

For hundreds of years, college education has typically taken place in lecture halls where instructors and students interact. A large part of the total cost of supplying college educations is the expense of constructing and maintaining buildings and paying the salaries of instructors and administrators. Economists refer to these costs as *fixed costs* because they remain the same regardless of the number of students enrolled. The *marginal cost* of higher education, the cost of instructing one additional student, is very low as long as there are empty seats in classrooms. But once classrooms are full, the marginal cost rises significantly because a school would need to build more classrooms and hire more instructors. For instance, the Georgia Institute of Technology (Georgia Tech) has to cap enrollment in its on-campus master's degree in computer science at 300 students because that is the capacity of the available facilities.

Technology has started changing colleges' costs. Some colleges now offer massive open online courses (MOOCs). The fixed cost of an online course is relatively high because instructors must develop new syllabi, exams, and teaching notes, as well as determine when and how to interact with their students. But after the courses are placed online, the cost of providing instruction to an additional student is close to zero because instruction is not limited by the size of a classroom. Because the marginal cost is low, after the fixed costs are covered, colleges can earn substantial revenues from MOOCs, even if they charge students low prices for these courses. In 2017, Georgia Tech's online master's degree in computer science enrolled more than 4,500 students at a price of $510 for a three-credit course—only about one-tenth the price of taking the course as a regular student on Georgia Tech's campus.

Early results for MOOCs have been mixed. Although some students do well in online courses, dropout rates tend

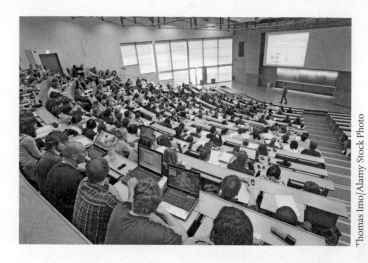

Thomas Imo/Alamy Stock Photo

to be higher than for traditional courses. In MOOCs with large enrollments, instructors cannot interact with individual students. But the results for Georgia Tech's online master's degree in computer science look promising. A study by Joshua Goodman and colleagues at the Harvard Kennedy School found that graduation rates were high, and the quality of students enrolled online was comparable to the quality of students enrolled in the traditional on-campus program. The cost advantages of online instruction and the potential to expand undergraduate and postgraduate education to students who would not otherwise receive it suggest that MOOCs will not be a passing fad.

In this chapter, we will analyze the types of costs involved in the production of a good or service and see how those costs affect how firms operate.

Sources: Kevin Carey, "An Online Education Breakthrough? A Master's Degree for a Mere $7,000," *New York Times*, September 28, 2016; Joshua Goodman, Julia Melkers, and Amanda Pallais, "Can Online Delivery Increase Access to Education?" Harvard Kennedy School Faculty Research, Working Paper Series RWP16-035, September 2016; Steve Maas, "Do Online Courses Increase Access to Education?" pbs.org, January 24, 2017; and "The Digital Degree," *Economist*, June 28, 2014.

Chapter Outline & Learning Objectives

Economics in Your Life & Career

Using Cost Concepts in Your Online Business

Suppose you are considering starting a Web site to sell iPhone cases. You locate a Taiwanese manufacturer who will sell you the cases for $10 each. Your friend José already is running such a site, and you plan to buy the same computers and software that he uses. Like José, you intend to rent a small building in an industrial park where you can have an office and storage space for your inventory. You plan to sell the cases for $15 each.

You find out that José is selling more cases per month than you expect to sell and that he is selling them for only $13. You wonder how José makes a profit at the lower price. As José sells more cases per month, will his firm's costs be lower than your firm's costs? As you read the chapter, see if you can answer this question. You can check your answer against the one we provide on **page 392** at the end of this chapter.

In Chapter 10, we looked behind the demand curve to better understand consumer decision making. In this chapter, we look behind the supply curve to better understand firm decision making. Earlier chapters showed that supply curves are upward sloping because marginal cost increases as firms increase the quantity of a good that they supply. In this chapter, we look more closely at why this relationship between production and cost holds. In the appendix to this chapter, we extend the analysis by using isoquants and isocost lines to better understand how firms choose inputs to produce goods. Once we have an understanding of production and cost, we can proceed in the following chapters to understand how firms decide what level of output to produce and what price to charge.

11.1 Technology: An Economic Definition
LEARNING OBJECTIVE: Define technology and give examples of technological change.

Technology The processes a firm uses to turn inputs into outputs of goods and services.

Technological change A change in the ability of a firm to produce a given level of output with a given quantity of inputs.

The basic activity of a firm is to use *inputs*, such as workers, machines, and natural resources, to produce *outputs* of goods and services. A pizza parlor, for example, uses inputs such as pizza dough, pizza sauce, cooks, and ovens to produce pizza. A firm's **technology** is the processes it uses to turn inputs into outputs of goods and services. Notice that this economic definition of technology is broader than the everyday definition. In everyday language, *technology* usually refers only to the development of new products. In the economic sense, a firm's technology depends on many factors, such as the skills of its managers, the training of its workers, and the speed and efficiency of its machinery and equipment. A pizza parlor's technology of pizza production, for example, includes not only the capacity of its pizza ovens and how quickly they bake the pizza but also how quickly the cooks can prepare the pizza for baking and how well the firm's manager motivates the workers and arranges the facilities to allow the cooks to quickly prepare the pizzas and get them in the ovens.

Whenever a firm experiences positive **technological change**, it is able to produce more output using the same inputs or the same output using fewer inputs. Positive technological change can come from many sources. For example, a firm's managers may increase production or sales by rearranging the layout of a retail store or the floor of a factory, by creating a training program for workers, or by installing faster or more reliable machinery or equipment. It is also possible for a firm to experience negative technological change. If a firm, for example, hires less-skilled workers or if a hurricane damages its facilities, the quantity of output it can produce from a given quantity of inputs may decline.

MyLab Economics Study Plan

MyLab Economics Concept Check

Apply the Concept

MyLab Economics Video

Would You Please Be Quiet? Technological Change at Segment.com

Segment.com is a firm located in San Francisco that develops and sells enterprise software. This software allows companies to gather data on customers; track the data across computers, smartphones, and other devices; and manage the companies' social media presence. Segment's office is located in what was once a warehouse. With 20,000 square feet of space, 30-foot ceilings, and an industrial appearance, the space has a very cool look that has helped the firm attract millennial software engineers. And like many tech firms that occupy similar facilities, Segment uses an open-office approach, in which, rather than having individual offices, most of its roughly 100 employees work from desks that are not divided by walls from the other desks in the workspace.

But CEO Peter Reinhardt found that the office layout was causing a problem. "Focus" is one of Segment's four core values—naturally enough for a firm that needs its software engineers to devote concentrated attention to often difficult programming issues. But many engineers complained that they had trouble focusing because they were distracted by noise. Reinhardt considered asking employees to talk less:

"But demanding 'be quiet!' is horrible in a collaborative work environment." He was also puzzled by the fact that clients visiting the office sometimes remarked on how quiet it was—the opposite of what his engineers were telling him.

Reinhardt asked the engineers to design an app to record decibel levels and install the app on iPads around the office. Data from the app showed that because of the acoustics of the building, the level of noise differed significantly in different areas. Where the engineers were working turned out to be the loudest area, while the entrance area where clients were greeted was the quietest. Reinhardt decided to rearrange where his employees worked: The engineers and product development people were moved to the quietest area, while people in sales and marketing, who often talked on the phone, were moved to the loudest area.

According to Reinhardt, the result of the rearranged work areas was an increase in output equivalent to hiring 10 to 15 additional workers. Put another way, Segment.com was able to produce more output with the same number of workers. The firm had experienced positive technological change, not by installing faster computers or other hardware but by reorganizing its workplace.

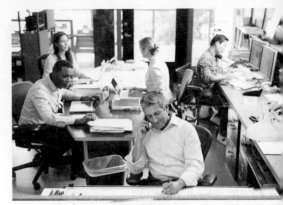

Monkey Business Images/Shutterstock

Reorganizing a workspace to improve efficiency is one example of a positive technological change.

Sources: Peter Reinhardt, "Improving Our Focus by Measuring Sound Levels," segment.com, October 19, 2016; and Rachel Feintzeig, "How One Firm Lowered Its Open-Office Noise," *Wall Street Journal*, November 15, 2016.

Your Turn: Test your understanding by doing related problem 1.5 on page 394 at the end of this chapter.

MyLab Economics Study Plan

11.2 The Short Run and the Long Run in Economics

LEARNING OBJECTIVE: Distinguish between the economic short run and the economic long run.

When firms analyze the relationship between their level of production and their costs, they separate the time period involved into the short run and the long run. In the **short run**, at least one of the firm's inputs is fixed. In particular, in the short run, the firm's technology and the size of its physical plant—its factory, store, or office—are both fixed, while some other inputs, including the number of workers the firm hires, are variable. In the **long run**, the firm is able to vary all its inputs and can adopt new technology and increase or decrease the size of its physical plant.

The actual length of calendar time before the short run becomes the long run differs from firm to firm. A pizza parlor may have a short run of just a few weeks before it is able to increase its physical plant by adding another pizza oven and some tables and chairs. General Motors, in contrast, may have a short run of a year or more before it can increase the capacity of one of its automobile assembly plants by installing new equipment.

Short run The period of time during which at least one of a firm's inputs is fixed.

Long run The period of time in which a firm can vary all its inputs, adopt new technology, and increase or decrease the size of its physical plant.

The Difference between Fixed Costs and Variable Costs

Total cost is the cost of all the inputs a firm uses in production. We have just seen that in the short run, some inputs are fixed and others are variable. The costs of the fixed inputs are called *fixed costs*, and the costs of the variable inputs are called *variable costs*. We can also think of **variable costs** as the costs that change as output changes. Similarly, **fixed costs** are costs that remain constant as output changes. A typical firm's variable costs include its labor costs, raw material costs, and costs of electricity and other utilities. Typical fixed costs include lease payments for factory or retail space, payments for fire insurance, and payments for online and television advertising. All of a firm's costs are either fixed or variable, so we can state the following:

Total cost The cost of all the inputs a firm uses in production.

Variable costs Costs that change as output changes.

Fixed costs Costs that remain constant as output changes.

$$Total\ cost = Fixed\ cost + Variable\ cost$$

or, using symbols:

$$TC = FC + VC.$$ **MyLab Economics** Concept Check

Apply the Concept

MyLab Economics Video

Fixed Costs in the Publishing Industry

An editor at Cambridge University Press gives the following estimates of the annual fixed cost for a medium-size academic book publisher:

Cost	Amount
Salaries and benefits	$625,000
Rent	75,000
Utilities	20,000
Supplies	6,000
Postage	5,000
Travel	9,000
Subscriptions, etc.	5,000
Miscellaneous	5,000
Total	$750,000

The wages of this editor are a fixed cost to the publisher.

Elena Elisseeva/Shutterstock

Academic book publishers hire editors, designers, and production and marketing managers who help prepare books for publication. Because these employees work on several books simultaneously, the number of people the company hires does not go up and down with the quantity of books the company publishes during any particular year. Publishing companies therefore consider the salaries and benefits of people in these job categories to be fixed costs.

In contrast, for a company that *prints* books, the quantity of workers varies with the quantity of books printed. The wages and benefits of the workers operating the printing presses, for example, would be a variable cost.

The other costs listed in the table are typical of fixed costs at many firms.

Source: *Handbook for Academic Authors*, 5th edition, by Beth Luey. Copyright © 2010 by Cambridge University Press. Reprinted by permission.

Your Turn: Test your understanding by doing related problems 2.7, 2.8, and 2.9 on page 395 at the end of this chapter.

MyLab Economics Study Plan

Implicit Costs versus Explicit Costs

Opportunity cost The highest-valued alternative that must be given up to engage in an activity.

Explicit cost A cost that involves spending money.

Implicit cost A nonmonetary opportunity cost.

Remember that economists always measure cost as **opportunity cost**, which is the highest-valued alternative that must be given up to engage in an activity. As we saw in Chapter 8, Section 8.3, costs are either *explicit* or *implicit*. When a firm spends money, it incurs an **explicit cost**. When a firm experiences a nonmonetary opportunity cost, it incurs an **implicit cost**.

For example, suppose that Jill Johnson owns a pizza restaurant. Her explicit costs include the wages she pays her workers and the payments she makes for rent and electricity. But some of Jill's most important costs are implicit. Before opening her own restaurant, Jill earned a salary of $30,000 per year managing a restaurant for someone else. To start her restaurant, Jill quit her job, withdrew $50,000 from her bank account—where she was earning interest of $3,000 per year—and used the funds to equip her restaurant with tables, chairs, a cash register, and other equipment. To open her own business, Jill had to give up the $30,000 salary and the $3,000 in interest. This $33,000 is an implicit cost because it does not represent payments that Jill has to make. Nevertheless, giving up this $33,000 per year is a real cost to Jill.

In addition, during the course of the year, the $50,000 worth of tables, chairs, and other physical capital in Jill's store will lose some of its value partly due to wear and tear and partly due to better furniture, cash registers, and so forth becoming available. *Economic depreciation* is the difference between what Jill paid for her capital at the beginning of the year and what she would receive if she sold the capital at the end of the year.

Jill's Explicit Costs	Amount
Pizza dough, tomato sauce, and other ingredients	$20,000
Wages	48,000
Interest payments on her loan to buy pizza ovens	10,000
Electricity	6,000
Lease payment for her restaurant	24,000
Jill's Implicit Costs	
Forgone salary	30,000
Forgone interest	3,000
Economic depreciation	10,000
Total	**$151,000**

Table 11.1

Jill Johnson's Costs per Year

If Jill could sell the capital for $40,000 at the end of the year, the $10,000 in economic depreciation represents another implicit cost. (Note that the whole $50,000 she spent on the capital is not a cost because she still has the equipment at the end of the year, although it is now worth only $40,000.)

Table 11.1 lists Jill's costs. The rules of accounting generally require that only explicit costs be used for purposes of keeping the company's financial records and for paying taxes (see Chapter 8, Section 8.3). Therefore, explicit costs are sometimes called *accounting costs. Economic costs* include both accounting costs and implicit costs.   **MyLab Economics** Concept Check

The Production Function

Let's look at the relationship in the short run between Jill Johnson's level of production and her costs. We can use a simpler example than the one in Table 11.1 by assuming that Jill employs only labor—workers—and one type of capital—pizza ovens—to produce a single good: pizzas. Many firms use more than two inputs and produce more than one good, but it is easier to understand the relationship between output and cost by focusing on the case of a firm using only two inputs and producing only one good. In the short run, Jill doesn't have time to build a larger restaurant, install additional pizza ovens, or redesign the layout of her restaurant. So, in the short run, she can increase or decrease the quantity of pizzas she produces only by increasing or decreasing the number of workers she employs.

The first three columns of Table 11.2 show the relationship between the quantity of workers and ovens Jill uses per week and the quantity of pizzas she can produce. The relationship between the inputs employed by a firm and the maximum output it can produce with those inputs is called the firm's **production function**. Because a firm's technology is the processes it uses to turn inputs into output, the production function represents the firm's technology. The first three columns of Table 11.2 show Jill's *short-run* production function because we are assuming that the time period is too short for Jill to increase or decrease the quantity of ovens she is using.   **MyLab Economics** Concept Check

Production function The relationship between the inputs employed by a firm and the maximum output it can produce with those inputs.

MyLab Economics Animation

Table 11.2

Short-Run Production and Cost at Jill Johnson's Restaurant

Quantity of Workers	Quantity of Pizza Ovens	Quantity of Pizzas per Week	Cost of Pizza Ovens (fixed cost)	Cost of Workers (variable cost)	Total Cost of Pizzas per Week	Cost per Pizza (average total cost)
0	2	0	$800	$0	$800	—
1	2	200	800	650	1,450	$7.25
2	2	450	800	1,300	2,100	4.67
3	2	550	800	1,950	2,750	5.00
4	2	600	800	2,600	3,400	5.67
5	2	625	800	3,250	4,050	6.48
6	2	640	800	3,900	4,700	7.34

A First Look at the Relationship between Production and Cost

Table 11.2 shows Jill Johnson's costs. We can determine the total cost of producing a given quantity of pizzas if we know how many workers and ovens are required to produce that quantity and how much Jill has to pay for those workers and ovens. Suppose Jill has taken out a bank loan to buy two pizza ovens. The cost of the loan is $800 per week. Therefore, her fixed costs are $800 per week. If Jill pays $650 per week to each worker, her variable costs depend on how many workers she hires. In the short run, Jill can increase the quantity of pizzas she produces only by hiring more workers. Table 11.2 shows that if she hires 1 worker, she produces 200 pizzas during the week; if she hires 2 workers, she produces 450 pizzas; and so on. For a particular week, Jill's total cost of producing pizzas is equal to the $800 she pays on the loan for the ovens plus the amount she pays to hire workers. If Jill decides to hire 4 workers and produce 600 pizzas, her total cost is $3,400: $800 to lease the ovens and $2,600 to hire the workers. Her cost per pizza is equal to her total cost of producing pizzas divided by the quantity of pizzas produced. If she produces 600 pizzas at a total cost of $3,400, her cost per pizza, or *average total cost*, is $3,400/600 = $5.67. A firm's **average total cost** is always equal to its total cost divided by the quantity of output produced.

Average total cost Total cost divided by the quantity of output produced.

Panel (a) of Figure 11.1 uses the numbers in the next-to-last column of Table 11.2 to graph Jill's total cost. Panel (b) uses the numbers in the last column to graph her average total cost. Notice in panel (b) that Jill's average cost curve has a roughly U shape. As production increases from low levels, average total cost falls. Average total cost then rises at higher levels of production. To understand why the average total cost curve has this U shape, we first need to look more closely at the technology of producing pizzas, as shown by the production function for Jill's restaurant. Then we need to look at how this technology determines the relationship between production and cost.

MyLab Economics Study Plan | MyLab Economics Concept Check

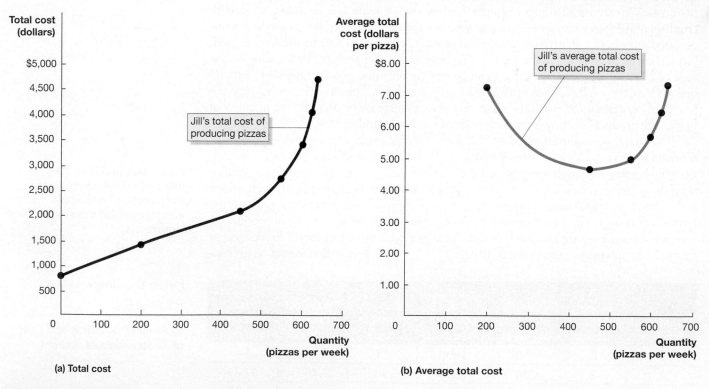

(a) Total cost

(b) Average total cost

MyLab Economics Animation

Figure 11.1 **Graphing Total Cost and Average Total Cost at Jill Johnson's Restaurant**

We can use the information from Table 11.2 to graph the relationship between the quantity of pizzas Jill produces and her total cost and average total cost. Panel (a) shows that total cost increases as the level of production increases. Panel (b) shows that her average total cost is roughly U shaped: As production increases from low levels, average total cost falls before rising at higher levels of production.

The Marginal Product of Labor and the Average Product of Labor

LEARNING OBJECTIVE: Explain and illustrate the relationship between the marginal product of labor and the average product of labor.

To better understand the choices Jill faces, given the technology available to her, think first about what happens if she hires only one worker. That one worker will have to perform several different activities, including taking orders from customers, baking the pizzas, bringing the pizzas to the customers' tables, and ringing up sales on the cash register. If Jill hires two workers, some of these activities can be divided up: One worker could take the orders, ring up the sales, and bring the pizzas to the customers' tables, and the other worker could prepare and bake the pizzas. With such a division of tasks, Jill will find that hiring two workers actually allows her to produce more than twice as many pizzas as she could produce with just one worker.

The additional output a firm produces as a result of hiring one more worker is called the **marginal product of labor**. We can calculate the marginal product of labor by determining how much total output increases as each additional worker is hired, which we do for Jill's restaurant in Table 11.3.

When Jill hires only one worker, she increases output from 0 pizzas to 200 pizzas per week. So, the marginal product of labor for the first worker is 200 pizzas. When she hires two workers, she produces 450 pizzas per week. Hiring the second worker increases her output by 250 pizzas per week. For the second worker, the marginal product of labor rises to 250 pizzas. This increase in marginal product results from the *division of labor* and from *specialization*. By dividing the tasks to be performed—the division of labor—Jill reduces the time workers lose moving from one activity to the next. She also allows them to become more specialized at their tasks. For example, a worker who concentrates on preparing and baking pizzas will become skilled at doing so quickly.

> **Marginal product of labor** The additional output a firm produces as a result of hiring one more worker.

The Law of Diminishing Returns

In the short run, the quantity of pizza ovens Jill leases is fixed, so as she hires more workers, the marginal product of labor eventually begins to decline. At some point, Jill uses up the gains from the division of labor and from specialization and starts to experience the effects of the **law of diminishing returns**. This law states that adding more of a variable input, such as labor, to the same amount of a fixed input, such as capital, will eventually cause the marginal product of the variable input to decline. For Jill, the marginal product of labor begins to decline when she hires the third worker. Hiring three workers raises the quantity of pizzas she produces from 450 per week to 550. But the increase in the quantity of pizzas—100—is less than the increase when she hired the second worker—250—so the marginal product of labor has declined.

If Jill kept adding more and more workers to the same quantity of pizza ovens, workers would eventually begin to get in each other's way, and the marginal product of labor would actually become negative. When the marginal product is negative, the level of total output declines. No firm would in reality hire so many workers as to experience a negative marginal product of labor and falling total output. **MyLab Economics** Concept Check

> **Law of diminishing returns** The principle that, at some point, adding more of a variable input, such as labor, to the same amount of a fixed input, such as capital, will cause the marginal product of the variable input to decline.

Quantity of Workers	Quantity of Pizza Ovens	Quantity of Pizzas	Marginal Product of Labor
0	2	0	—
1	2	200	200
2	2	450	250
3	2	550	100
4	2	600	50
5	2	625	25
6	2	640	15

MyLab Economics Animation

Table 11.3

The Marginal Product of Labor at Jill Johnson's Restaurant

Graphing Production

Panel (a) in Figure 11.2 graphs the relationship between the quantity of workers Jill hires and her total output of pizzas, using the numbers from Table 11.3. Panel (b) graphs the marginal product of labor. In panel (a), output increases as more workers are hired, but the increase in output does not occur at a constant rate. Because of specialization and the division of labor, output at first increases at an increasing rate, with each additional worker hired causing production to increase by a *larger* amount than did the hiring of the previous worker. But after the second worker has been hired, hiring more workers while keeping the quantity of ovens constant results in diminishing returns. When the point of diminishing returns is reached, production increases at a decreasing rate. Each additional worker Jill hires after the second worker causes production to increase by a *smaller* amount than did the hiring of the previous worker.

(a) Total output

(b) Marginal product of labor

When the marginal product of labor is increasing, total output increases at an increasing rate.

When the marginal product of labor is decreasing, but still positive, total output increases, but at a decreasing rate.

MyLab Economics Animation

Figure 11.2 **Total Output and the Marginal Product of Labor**

In panel (a), output increases as more workers are hired, but the increase in output does not occur at a constant rate. Because of specialization and the division of labor, output at first increases at an increasing rate, with each additional worker hired causing production to increase by a *greater* amount than did the hiring of the previous worker. When the point of diminishing returns is reached, production increases at a decreasing rate. Each

additional worker Jill hires after the second worker causes production to increase by a *smaller* amount than did the hiring of the previous worker. In panel (b), the *marginal product of labor* is the additional output produced as a result of hiring one more worker. The marginal product of labor rises initially because of the effects of specialization and division of labor, and then it falls because of the effects of diminishing returns.

In panel (b), the marginal product of labor curve rises initially because of the effects of specialization and the division of labor, and then it falls because of the effects of diminishing returns.

MyLab Economics Concept Check

Apply the Concept

MyLab Economics Video

Adam Smith's Famous Account of the Division of Labor in a Pin Factory

The Wealth of Nations, written in Scotland by Adam Smith in 1776, is the first book to have discussed some of the key ideas of economics. Smith considered the concept of the division of labor important enough to discuss in the first chapter of the book. He illustrated the concept by using an example of a pin factory. The following is an excerpt from his account of how pin making was divided into a series of tasks:

> One man draws out the wire, another straightens it, a third cuts it, a fourth points it, a fifth grinds it at the top for receiving the head; to make the head requires two or three distinct operations; to put it on is a ... [distinct operation], to whiten the pins is another; it is even a trade by itself to put them into the paper; and the important business of making a pin is, in this manner, divided into eighteen distinct operations.

Because the labor of pin making was divided up in this way, an average worker was able to produce about 4,800 pins per day. Smith estimated that a single worker operating by himself each of the machines used in pin making would make only about 20 pins per day. Smith concluded, "The greatest improvement in the productive powers of labor ... [has] been the effects of the division of labor." More than 240 years later, economists agree with Smith's conclusion, and understanding the gains from the division of labor and specialization remains relevant to most business situations today.

Source: Adam Smith, *An Inquiry into the Nature and Causes of the Wealth of Nations*, Vol. I, Oxford, UK: Oxford University Press, 1976 (originally published 1776), pp. 14–15.

Your Turn: Test your understanding by doing related problem 3.7 on page 396 at the end of this chapter.

The gains from division of labor and specialization are as important to firms today as they were in the eighteenth century, when Adam Smith first discussed them.

MyLab Economics Study Plan

The Relationship between Marginal Product and Average Product

The marginal product of labor tells us how much total output changes as the quantity of workers hired changes. We can also calculate the **average product of labor**, which is the total output produced by a firm divided by the quantity of workers. For example, using the numbers in Table 11.3, if Jill hires 4 workers to produce 600 pizzas, the average product of labor is 600/4 = 150.

We can state the relationship between the marginal and average products of labor this way: *The average product of labor is the average of the marginal products of labor.* For example, the numbers from Table 11.3 on page 379 show that the marginal product of the first worker Jill hires is 200, the marginal product of the second worker is 250, and the marginal product of the third worker is 100. Therefore, the average product of labor for three workers is 183.3:

Average product of labor The total output produced by a firm divided by the quantity of workers.

$$183.3 = (200 + 250 + 100)/3$$

| Average product of labor for three workers | Marginal product of labor of first worker | Marginal product of labor of second worker | Marginal product of labor of third worker |

By taking the average of the marginal products of the first three workers, we have the average product of the three workers.

Whenever the marginal product of labor is greater than the average product of labor, the average product of labor must be increasing. This statement is true for the same reason that a person 6 feet, 2 inches tall entering a room where the average height is 5 feet, 9 inches raises the average height of people in the room. Whenever the marginal product of labor is less than the average product of labor, the average product of labor must be decreasing. The marginal product of labor equals the average product of labor at the quantity of workers for which the average product of labor is at its maximum.

MyLab Economics Concept Check

An Example of Marginal and Average Values: College Grades

The relationship between the marginal product of labor and the average product of labor is the same as the relationship between the marginal and average values of any variable. To see this point more clearly, think about the familiar relationship between a student's grade point average (GPA) in one semester and his overall, or cumulative, GPA. The table in Figure 11.3 shows Paul's college grades for each semester, beginning with fall of his first year. The graph in Figure 11.3 plots the grades from the table. Just as each additional worker hired adds to a firm's total production, each additional semester

MyLab Economics Animation

Figure 11.3

Marginal and Average GPAs

The relationship between marginal and average values for a variable can be illustrated using GPAs. We can calculate the GPA Paul earns in a particular semester (his "marginal GPA"), and we can calculate his cumulative GPA for all the semesters he has completed so far (his "average GPA"). Paul's GPA is only 1.50 in the fall semester of his first year. In each following semester through the fall of his junior year, his GPA for the semester increases—raising his cumulative GPA. In Paul's junior year, even though his semester GPA declines from fall to spring, his cumulative GPA rises. Only in the fall of his senior year, when his semester GPA drops below his cumulative GPA, does his cumulative GPA decline.

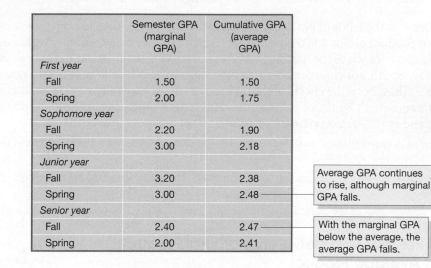

	Semester GPA (marginal GPA)	Cumulative GPA (average GPA)
First year		
Fall	1.50	1.50
Spring	2.00	1.75
Sophomore year		
Fall	2.20	1.90
Spring	3.00	2.18
Junior year		
Fall	3.20	2.38
Spring	3.00	2.48
Senior year		
Fall	2.40	2.47
Spring	2.00	2.41

Average GPA continues to rise, although marginal GPA falls.

With the marginal GPA below the average, the average GPA falls.

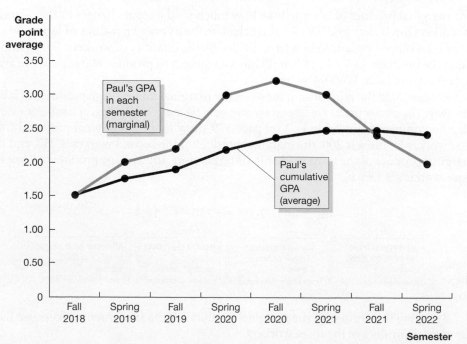

adds to Paul's total grade points. We can calculate what hiring each individual worker adds to total production (marginal product), and we can calculate the average production of the workers hired so far (average product).

Similarly, we can calculate the GPA Paul earns in a particular semester (his "marginal GPA"), and we can calculate his cumulative GPA for all the semesters he has completed so far (his "average GPA"). As the table shows, Paul gets off to a weak start in the fall semester of his first year, earning only a 1.50 GPA. In each subsequent semester through the fall of his junior year, his GPA for the semester increases from the previous semester—raising his cumulative GPA. As the graph shows, however, his cumulative GPA does not increase as rapidly as his semester-by-semester GPA because his cumulative GPA is held back by the low GPAs of his first few semesters. Notice that in Paul's junior year, even though his semester GPA declines from fall to spring, his cumulative GPA rises. Only in the fall of his senior year, when his semester GPA drops below his cumulative GPA, does his cumulative GPA decline.   **MyLab Economics** Concept Check

MyLab Economics Study Plan

11.4 The Relationship between Short-Run Production and Short-Run Cost

LEARNING OBJECTIVE: Explain and illustrate the relationship between marginal cost and average total cost.

We have seen that technology determines the values of the marginal product of labor and the average product of labor. In turn, the marginal and average products of labor affect the firm's costs. Keep in mind that the relationships we are discussing are *short-run* relationships: We are assuming that the time period is too short for the firm to change its technology or the size of its physical plant.

The average total cost curve in panel (b) of Figure 11.1 on page 378 for Jill Johnson's restaurant has a U shape. As we will soon see, the U shape of the average total cost curve is determined by the shape of the curve that shows the relationship between *marginal cost* and the level of production.

Marginal Cost

One of the key ideas in economics is that optimal decisions are made at the margin (see Chapter 1, Section 1.1). Consumers, firms, and government officials usually make decisions about doing a little more or a little less. As Jill Johnson considers whether to hire additional workers to produce additional pizzas, she needs to consider how much she will add to her total cost by producing the additional pizzas. **Marginal cost** is the change in a firm's total cost from producing one more unit of a good or service. We can calculate marginal cost for a particular increase in output by dividing the change in total cost by the change in output. We can express this idea mathematically (remember that the Greek letter delta, Δ, means, "change in"):

Marginal cost The change in a firm's total cost from producing one more unit of a good or service.

$$MC = \frac{\Delta TC}{\Delta Q}.$$

In the table in Figure 11.4, we use this equation to calculate Jill's marginal cost of producing pizzas. The values for the other columns in the table are from Table 11.2 and Table 11.3.   **MyLab Economics** Concept Check

Why Are the Marginal and Average Cost Curves U Shaped?

Notice in the graph in Figure 11.4 that Jill's marginal cost of producing pizzas declines at first and then increases, giving the marginal cost curve a U shape. The table in Figure 11.4 also shows the marginal product of labor. This table helps us understand the important relationship between the marginal product of labor and the marginal cost of production:

- The marginal product of labor is *rising* for the first two workers, but the marginal cost of the pizzas produced by these workers is *falling*.

Figure 11.4

Jill Johnson's Marginal Cost and Average Total Cost of Producing Pizzas

We can use the information in the table to calculate Jill's marginal cost and average total cost of producing pizzas. For the first two workers hired, the marginal product of labor is increasing, which causes the marginal cost of production to fall. For the last four workers hired, the marginal product of labor is falling, which causes the marginal cost of production to increase. Therefore, the marginal cost curve falls and then rises—that is, it has a U shape—because the marginal product of labor rises and then falls. As long as marginal cost is below average total cost, average total cost will be falling. When marginal cost is above average total cost, average total cost will be rising. The relationship between marginal cost and average total cost explains why the average total cost curve also has a U shape.

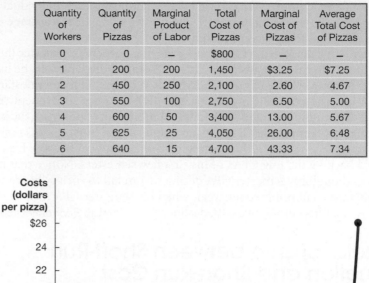

Quantity of Workers	Quantity of Pizzas	Marginal Product of Labor	Total Cost of Pizzas	Marginal Cost of Pizzas	Average Total Cost of Pizzas
0	0	—	$800	—	—
1	200	200	1,450	$3.25	$7.25
2	450	250	2,100	2.60	4.67
3	550	100	2,750	6.50	5.00
4	600	50	3,400	13.00	5.67
5	625	25	4,050	26.00	6.48
6	640	15	4,700	43.33	7.34

- The marginal product of labor is *falling* for the last four workers, but the marginal cost of pizzas produced by these workers is *rising*.

We can generalize what the table shows us: *When the marginal product of labor is rising, the marginal cost of output is falling. When the marginal product of labor is falling, the marginal cost of output is rising.*

One way to understand the relationship between the marginal product of labor and the marginal cost of output is to notice that the only additional cost to Jill from producing more pizzas is the additional wages she pays to hire more workers. She pays each new worker the same $650 per week. So the marginal cost of the additional pizzas each worker makes depends on that worker's additional output, or marginal product. As long as the additional output from each new worker is rising, the marginal cost of that output is falling. When the additional output from each new worker is falling, the marginal cost of that output is rising. *We can conclude that the marginal cost of output falls and then rises—forming a U shape—because the marginal product of labor rises and then falls.*

The relationship between marginal cost and average total cost follows the usual relationship between marginal and average values. As long as marginal cost is below average total cost, average total cost falls. When marginal cost is above average total cost, average total cost rises. Marginal cost equals average total cost when average total cost is at its lowest point. Therefore, the average total cost curve has a U shape because the marginal cost curve has a U shape.

Solved Problem 11.4

Calculating Marginal Cost and Average Cost

Santiago Delgado owns a copier store. He leases two copy machines for which he pays $12.50 each per day. He cannot increase the number of machines he leases without giving the office machine company six weeks' notice. He can hire as many workers as he wants, at a cost of $50 per day per worker. These are the only two inputs he uses to produce copies.

a. Fill in the remaining columns in the table by using the definitions of costs.

b. Draw the average total cost curve and marginal cost curve for Santiago's store. Do these curves have the expected shape? Briefly explain.

Quantity of Workers	Quantity of Copies per Day	Fixed Cost	Variable Cost	Total Cost	Average Total Cost	Marginal Cost
0	0					
1	625					
2	1,325					
3	2,200					
4	2,600					
5	2,900					
6	3,100					

Solving the Problem

Step 1: **Review the chapter material.** This problem requires you to understand definitions of costs, so you may want to review the section "The Difference between Fixed Costs and Variable Costs," which begins on page 375, and the section "Why Are the Marginal and Average Cost Curves U Shaped?" which begins on page 383.

Step 2: **Answer part (a) by using the definitions of costs to fill in the table.** Santiago's fixed cost is the amount he pays to lease the copy machines. He uses two copy machines and pays $12.50 each to lease them, so his fixed cost is $25. Santiago's variable cost is the amount he pays to hire workers. He pays $50 per worker per day. His total cost is the sum of his fixed cost and his variable cost. His average total cost is his total cost divided by the quantity of copies he produces that day. His marginal cost is the change in total cost divided by the change in output. For example, his marginal cost of producing 1,325 copies per day, rather than 625 copies, is:

$$MC = (\$125 - \$75)/(1{,}325 - 625) = \$0.07.$$

Quantity of Workers	Quantity of Copies per Day	Fixed Cost	Variable Cost	Total Cost	Average Total Cost	Marginal Cost
0	0	$25	$0	$25	—	—
1	625	25	50	75	$0.12	$0.08
2	1,325	25	100	125	0.09	0.07
3	2,200	25	150	175	0.08	0.06
4	2,600	25	200	225	0.09	0.13
5	2,900	25	250	275	0.09	0.17
6	3,100	25	300	325	0.10	0.25

Step 3: **Answer part (b) by drawing the average total cost and marginal cost curves for Santiago's store and by explaining whether they have the usual shape.** Use the numbers from the table to draw your graph:

We expect average total cost and marginal cost curves to have a U shape, which Santiago's cost curves do. Both cost curves fall and then rise in the same way as the cost curves in Figure 11.4 on page 384.

MyLab Economics Study Plan   **Your Turn:** For more practice, do related problem 4.7 on page 397 at the end of this chapter.

11.5 Graphing Cost Curves

LEARNING OBJECTIVE: Graph average total cost, average variable cost, average fixed cost, and marginal cost.

Average fixed cost Fixed cost divided by the quantity of output produced.

Average variable cost Variable cost divided by the quantity of output produced.

We have seen that we calculate average total cost by dividing total cost by the quantity of output produced. Similarly, we can calculate **average fixed cost** by dividing fixed cost by the quantity of output produced. And we can calculate **average variable cost** by dividing variable cost by the quantity of output produced. We can present these three measures of cost mathematically (with Q representing the level of output) as:

$$\text{Average total cost} = ATC = \frac{TC}{Q}$$

$$\text{Average fixed cost} = AFC = \frac{FC}{Q}$$

$$\text{Average variable cost} = AVC = \frac{VC}{Q}$$

Finally, notice that average total cost is the sum of average fixed cost plus average variable cost:

$$ATC = AFC + AVC.$$

The only fixed cost Jill incurs in operating her restaurant is the $800 per week she pays on the bank loan for her pizza ovens. Her variable costs are the wages she pays her workers. The table and graph in Figure 11.5 show Jill's costs.

We will use graphs like the one in Figure 11.5 in the next several chapters to analyze how firms decide the level of output to produce and the price to charge. Before going further, be sure you understand the following three key facts about Figure 11.5:

1. The marginal cost (*MC*), average total cost (*ATC*), and average variable cost (*AVC*) curves are all U shaped, and the marginal cost curve intersects both the average

Quantity of Workers	Quantity of Ovens	Quantity of Pizzas	Cost of Ovens (fixed cost)	Cost of Workers (variable cost)	Total Cost of Pizzas	ATC	AFC	AVC	MC
0	2	0	$800	$0	$800	–	–	–	–
1	2	200	800	650	1,450	$7.25	$4.00	$3.25	$3.25
2	2	450	800	1,300	2,100	4.67	1.78	2.89	2.60
3	2	550	800	1,950	2,750	5.00	1.45	3.54	6.50
4	2	600	800	2,600	3,400	5.67	1.33	4.33	13.00
5	2	625	800	3,250	4,050	6.48	1.28	5.20	26.00
6	2	640	800	3,900	4,700	7.34	1.25	6.09	43.33

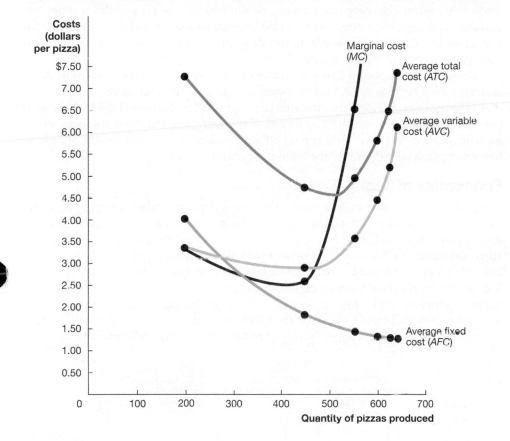

MyLab Economics Animation

Figure 11.5

Costs at Jill Johnson's Restaurant

Jill's costs of making pizzas are shown in the table and plotted in the graph. Notice three important facts about the graph:

1. The marginal cost (MC), average total cost (ATC), and average variable cost (AVC) curves are all U shaped, and the marginal cost curve intersects both the average variable cost curve and the average total cost curve at their minimum points.
2. As output increases, average fixed cost (AFC) gets smaller and smaller.
3. As output increases, the difference between average total cost and average variable cost decreases. Make sure you can explain why each of these three facts is true.

You should spend time becoming familiar with this graph because it is one of the most important graphs in microeconomics.

variable cost curve and the average total cost curve at their minimum points. When marginal cost is below either average variable cost or average total cost, it causes them to decrease. When marginal cost is above average variable cost or average total cost, it causes them to increase. Therefore, when marginal cost equals average variable cost or average total cost, they must be at their minimum points.

2. As output increases, average fixed cost gets smaller and smaller. In calculating average fixed cost, we are dividing something that gets larger and larger—output—into something that remains constant—fixed cost. Firms often refer to this process of lowering average fixed cost by selling more output as "spreading the overhead" (where "overhead" refers to fixed cost).

3. As output increases, the difference between average total cost and average variable cost decreases. The difference between average total cost and average variable cost is average fixed cost, which gets smaller as output increases. **MyLab Economics** Concept Check

MyLab Economics Study Plan

11.6 Costs in the Long Run

LEARNING OBJECTIVE: Explain how firms use the long-run average cost curve in their planning.

The distinction between fixed cost and variable cost applies to the short run but *not* to the long run. For example, in the short run, Jill Johnson has a fixed cost of $800 per week because she signed a loan agreement with a bank when she bought her pizza ovens. But in the long run, the cost of buying more pizza ovens becomes variable because Jill can choose whether to expand her business by buying more of them. The same would be true of any other fixed cost a company like Jill's might have. Once a company has purchased a fire insurance policy, the cost of the policy is fixed. But when the policy expires, the company must decide whether to renew it, and the cost becomes variable. The important point is that *in the long run, all costs are variable; there are no fixed costs in the long run.* In other words, in the long run, total cost equals variable cost, and average total cost equals average variable cost.

Managers of successful firms simultaneously consider how they can most profitably run their current store, factory, or office and also whether in the long run they would be more profitable if they became larger or smaller. Jill must consider how to run her current restaurant, which has only two pizza ovens, and she must also plan what to do when her current bank loan is paid off and the lease on her store ends. Should she buy more pizza ovens? Should she lease a larger restaurant?

Economies of Scale

Short-run average cost curves represent the costs a firm faces when some input, such as the quantity of machines it uses, is fixed. The **long-run average cost curve** shows the lowest cost at which a firm is able to produce a given quantity of output in the long run, when no inputs are fixed. A firm may experience **economies of scale**, which means the firm's long-run average cost falls as it increases the quantity of output it produces. We can see the effects of economies of scale in Figure 11.6, which shows the relationship between short-run and long-run average cost curves. Managers can use long-run average cost curves for planning because they show the effect on cost of expanding output by, for example, building a larger factory or restaurant. **MyLab Economics** Concept Check

---

Long-run average cost curve A curve that shows the lowest cost at which a firm is able to produce a given quantity of output in the long run, when no inputs are fixed.

Economies of scale The situation in which a firm's long-run average cost falls as it increases the quantity of output it produces.

MyLab Economics Animation

Figure 11.6

The Relationship between Short-Run Average Cost and Long-Run Average Cost

If a small car company expects to sell only 20,000 cars per year, it will be able to produce cars at the lowest average cost of $52,000 per car if it builds the small factory represented by the *ATC* curve on the left of the figure. A larger factory will be able to produce 200,000 cars per year at a lower cost of $27,000 per car. An automobile factory producing 200,000 cars per year and a factory producing 400,000 cars per year will experience constant returns to scale and will have the same average cost. An automobile factory assembling 200,000 cars per year will have reached minimum efficient scale. Very large automobile factories will experience diseconomies of scale, and their average costs will rise as production increases beyond 400,000 cars per year.

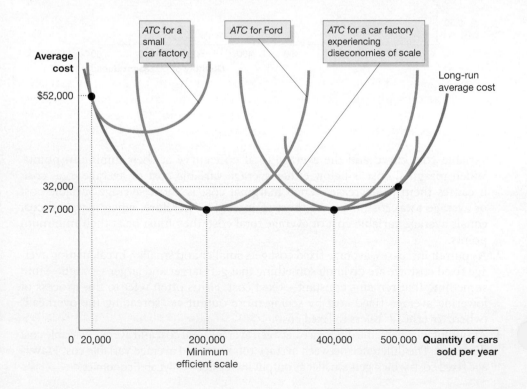

Long-Run Average Cost Curves for Automobile Factories

Figure 11.6 shows long-run average cost in the automobile industry. If a small company expects to sell only 20,000 cars per year (as Tesla Motors did in 2016), then it will be able to assemble cars at the lowest average cost of $52,000 per car if it builds a small factory, as represented by the *ATC* curve on the left of the figure. A much larger factory, such as those operated by Ford, General Motors, and Toyota, will be able to produce 200,000 cars per year at a lower average cost of $27,000 per car. This decline in average cost from $52,000 to $27,000 represents the economies of scale that exist in manufacturing automobiles. Why would the larger automobile factory have lower average costs? One important reason is that a company like Ford produces 10 times as many cars per year in one of its factories as Tesla produces in its factory, but it might need only 6 times as many workers. This saving in labor cost would reduce Ford's average cost of selling cars.

In general, firms may experience economies of scale for a number of reasons, with these being the most important:

1. As in the case of automobile production, the firm's technology may make it possible to increase production with a smaller proportional increase in at least one input.
2. Both workers and managers can become more specialized, enabling them to become more productive, as output expands.
3. Large firms, like Ford, Walmart, or Apple, may be able to purchase inputs at lower costs than smaller competitors. In fact, as Apple and Walmart expanded, their bargaining power with their suppliers increased, and their average costs fell.
4. As a firm expands, it may be able to borrow money at a lower interest rate, thereby lowering its costs.

Economies of scale do not continue indefinitely as the firm increases its output. The long-run average cost curve in most industries has a flat segment that often stretches over a substantial range of output. As Figure 11.6 shows, an automobile factory producing 200,000 cars per year and a factory producing 400,000 cars per year have the same average cost. Over this range of output, firms in the industry experience **constant returns to scale**. As these firms increase their output, they increase their inputs, such as the size of the factory and the quantity of workers, proportionally. The level of output at which all economies of scale are exhausted is known as **minimum efficient scale**. An automobile factory producing 200,000 cars per year has reached minimum efficient scale. Firms that produce at less than minimum efficient scale may have difficulty surviving because they will be producing output at higher cost than competitors.

Very large automobile factories experience increasing average costs as managers begin to have difficulty coordinating the operation of the factory. Figure 11.6 shows that for production above 400,000 cars per year, firms in the industry experience **diseconomies of scale**. For instance, Toyota found that as it expanded production at its Georgetown, Kentucky, plant and its plants in China, its managers had difficulty keeping average cost from rising. According to the president of Toyota's Georgetown plant, "Demand for … high volumes saps your energy. Over a period of time, it eroded our focus … [and] thinned out the expertise and knowledge we painstakingly built up over the years." One analysis of the problems Toyota faced in expanding production concluded, "It is the kind of paradox many highly successful companies face: Getting bigger doesn't always mean getting better."

Constant returns to scale The situation in which a firm's long-run average costs remain unchanged as it increases output.

Minimum efficient scale The level of output at which all economies of scale are exhausted.

Diseconomies of scale The situation in which a firm's long-run average cost rises as the firm increases output.

Solved Problem 11.6

MyLab Economics Interactive Animation

Using Long-Run Average Cost Curves to Understand Business Strategy

In 2017, Pon Holdings, maker of Santa Cruz bicycles, proposed buying Accell Group, maker of Raleigh bicycles. According to an article in the *Wall Street Journal*: "Their combined scale could help the companies eliminate duplicate operating costs, broaden their portfolio of bikes to appeal to a larger customer base and help secure better pricing from suppliers." At the time of the proposed deal, Pon was selling about 800,000 bicycles per year, and Accell was selling about 1.5 million. (In the end, the deal did not take place.)

a. What must have been true of Pon Holdings's position on its long-run average cost curve for it to have expected to benefit from this deal?

b. Use a long-run average cost curve for Pon to illustrate the effect Pon expected from purchasing Accell. Can we determine whether Pon would have reached minimum efficient scale as a result of this deal? Briefly explain.

Solving the Problem

Step 1: **Review the chapter material.** This problem is about the long-run average cost curve, so you may want to review the material in the section "Costs in the Long Run," which begins on page 388.

Step 2: **Answer part (a) by explaining where Pon must have been on its long-run average cost curve at the time it proposed purchasing Accell Group.** Pon expected that its increase in scale from purchasing Accell would have reduced its average cost. Therefore, Pon must have been producing a quantity that is below minimum efficient scale.

Step 3: **Answer part (b) by drawing a long-run average cost graph for Pon and by explaining whether it is possible to determine if the firm would have reached minimum efficient scale as a result of the deal.** For Pon's strategy to be successful, it must have been below minimum efficient scale. In the following graph, we assume that Pon was currently producing at point A on its long-average cost curve, where its bicycle output equals 800,000 and average cost equals Average $cost_1$. By purchasing Accell, Pon would have expanded production to point B, where it would be producing 2,300,000. Pons's average total cost would have been reduced to Average $cost_2$.

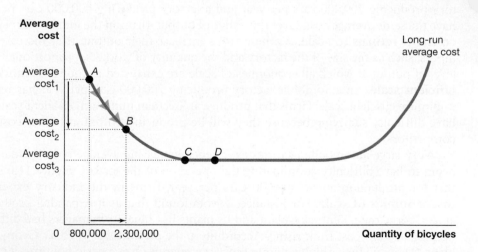

As drawn, the graph shows that Pon is still below minimum efficient scale at point B. It is possible that the purchase of Accell would have pushed Pon to minimum efficient scale at point C or beyond minimum efficient scale at point D. In both cases, Pon would have reduced its average cost to Average $cost_3$. We don't have enough information to know with certainty whether Pon expected the deal to result in its being at point B, point C, or point D. All we can say is that Pon expected its average cost to fall, and it expected to move down its long-run average cost curve, but it did not expect to become so large that it would have experienced diseconomies of scale.

Source: Ben Dummett, "Dutch Deal Would Unite Biking Brands," *Wall Street Journal*, April 11, 2017.

MyLab Economics Study Plan · **Your Turn:** For more practice, do related problems 6.7, 6.8, and 6.9 on page 400 at the end of this chapter.

Over time, most firms in an industry will build factories or stores that are at least as large as the minimum efficient scale but not so large that diseconomies of scale occur. For example, in the automobile industry, most factories produce between 200,000 and 400,000 cars per year. However, firms often do not know the exact shape of their long-run average cost curves. As a result, they may mistakenly build factories or stores that are either too large or too small.   **MyLab Economics** Concept Check

MyLab Economics Study Plan

Apply the Concept

MyLab Economics Video

The Colossal River Rouge: Diseconomies of Scale at Ford Motor Company

When Henry Ford started the Ford Motor Company in 1903, automobile companies produced cars in small workshops, using highly skilled workers. Ford introduced two new ideas to the automobile industry that allowed him to take advantage of economies of scale. First, Ford used identical—or, interchangeable—parts so that unskilled workers could assemble the cars. Second, instead of having groups of workers moving from one stationary automobile to the next, he had the workers remain stationary, while the automobiles moved along an assembly line. Ford built a large factory at Highland Park, outside Detroit, where he used these ideas to produce the famous Model T at an average cost well below what his competitors could match using older production methods in smaller factories.

Ford believed that he could produce automobiles at an even lower average cost by building a still larger plant along the River Rouge in Dearborn, Michigan. Unfortunately, Ford's River Rouge plant was too large and suffered from diseconomies of scale. Ford's managers had great difficulty coordinating the production of automobiles in such a large plant. The following description of the River Rouge plant comes from a biography of Ford by Allan Nevins and Frank Ernest Hill:

CSU Archives/Everett Collection Inc/Alamy Stock Photo

Was Ford's River Rouge plant in Dearborn, Michigan too big?

> A total of 93 separate structures stood on the [River Rouge] site…. Railroad trackage covered 93 miles, conveyors 27 [miles]. About 75,000 men worked in the great plant. A force of 5000 did nothing but keep it clean, wearing out 5000 mops and 3000 brooms a month, and using 86 tons of soap on the floors, walls, and 330 acres of windows. The Rouge was an industrial city, immense, concentrated, packed with power…. By its very massiveness and complexity, it denied men at the top contact with and understanding of those beneath, and gave those beneath a sense of being lost in inexorable immensity and power.

Beginning in 1927, Ford produced the Model A—its only car model at that time—at the River Rouge plant. Ford failed to achieve economies of scale and actually *lost money* on each of the four Model A body styles.

Ford could not raise the price of the Model A to make it profitable because at a higher price, the car could not compete with similar models produced by competitors such as General Motors and Chrysler. Ford eventually reduced the cost of making the Model A by constructing smaller factories spread out across the country. These smaller factories assembled the Model A at a lower average cost than was possible at the River Rouge plant.

Source: Allan Nevins and Frank Ernest Hill, *Ford: Expansion and Challenge, 1915–1933*, New York: Scribner, 1957, pp. 293, 295.

Your Turn: Test your understanding by doing related problem 6.10 on page 400 at the end of this chapter.

MyLab Economics Study Plan

Don't Let This Happen to You

Don't Confuse Diminishing Returns with Diseconomies of Scale

The concepts of diminishing returns and diseconomies of scale may seem similar, but they are actually unrelated. Diminishing returns applies only to the short run, when at least one of the firm's inputs, such as the quantity of machinery it uses, is fixed. The law of diminishing returns tells us that in the short run, hiring more workers will, at some point, result in less additional output. Diminishing returns explains why marginal cost curves eventually slope upward.

Diseconomies of scale apply only in the long run, when the firm is free to vary all its inputs, can adopt new technology, and can vary the amount of machinery it uses and the size of its facility. Diseconomies of scale explain why long-run average cost curves eventually slope upward.

MyLab Economics Study Plan

Your Turn: Test your understanding by doing related problems 6.12 and 6.13 on page 400 at the end of this chapter.

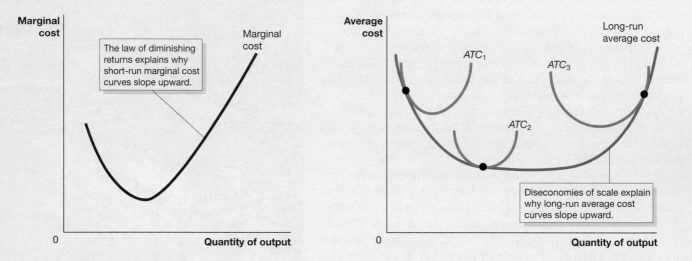

Continued from page 373

Economics in Your Life & Career

Using Cost Concepts in Your Online Business

At the beginning of the chapter, we asked you to suppose that you are about to start a Web site to sell iPhone cases. Both you and your friend José can buy cases from the manufacturer for $10 each. But because José sells more cases per month than you expect to be able to sell, his costs per case are lower than yours. We asked you to think about why this might be true.

In this chapter, we have seen that firms often experience declining average costs as the quantity they sell increases. A key reason José's average costs might be lower than yours has to do with fixed costs. Because you will have the same computers and software and rent an office similar to José's, you may be paying about the same amount for equipment and an office lease. You may also be paying about the same amounts for utilities, insurance, and advertising. All these are fixed costs because they do not change as the quantity of cases you sell changes. Because José's fixed costs are the same as yours but he is selling more cases, his average fixed costs are lower than yours, and, therefore, so are his average total costs. With lower average total costs, he can sell his cases for a lower price than you do and still make a profit.

Conclusion

In this chapter, we discussed the relationship between a firm's technology, production, and costs. We encountered a number of definitions of costs. Because we will use these definitions in later chapters, it is useful to bring them together in Table 11.4 for you to review.

We have seen the important relationship between a firm's level of production and its costs. This information is vital to all firms as they attempt to decide the optimal level of production and the optimal prices to charge for their products. We will explore this point further in the next chapter.

Visit **MyLab Economics** for a news article and analysis related to the concepts in this chapter.

Term	Definition	Symbols and Equations
Total cost	The cost of all the inputs used by a firm, or fixed cost plus variable cost	TC
Fixed costs	Costs that remain constant as a firm's level of output changes	FC
Variable costs	Costs that change as a firm's level of output changes	VC
Marginal cost	An increase in total cost resulting from producing another unit of output	$MC = \dfrac{\Delta TC}{\Delta Q}$
Average total cost	Total cost divided by the quantity of output produced	$ATC = \dfrac{TC}{Q}$
Average fixed cost	Fixed cost divided by the quantity of output produced	$AFC = \dfrac{FC}{Q}$
Average variable cost	Variable cost divided by the quantity of output produced	$AVC = \dfrac{VC}{Q}$
Implicit cost	A nonmonetary opportunity cost	—
Explicit cost	A cost that involves spending money	—

Table 11.4

A Summary of Definitions of Cost

Key Terms

Average fixed cost, p. 386	Economies of scale, p. 388	Long-run average cost curve, p. 388	Production function, p. 377
Average product of labor, p. 381	Explicit cost, p. 376	Marginal cost, p. 383	Short run, p. 375
Average total cost, p. 378	Fixed costs, p. 375	Marginal product of labor, p. 379	Technological change, p. 374
Average variable cost, p. 386	Implicit cost, p. 376	Minimum efficient scale, p. 389	Technology, p. 374
Constant returns to scale, p. 389	Law of diminishing returns, p. 379	Opportunity cost, p. 376	Total cost, p. 375
Diseconomies of scale, p. 389	Long run, p. 375		Variable costs, p. 375

11.1 Technology: An Economic Definition, pages 374–375

LEARNING OBJECTIVE: Define technology and give examples of technological change.

MyLab Economics   Visit **www.pearson.com/mylab/economics** to complete these exercises online and get instant feedback.

Summary

The basic activity of a firm is to use inputs, such as workers, machines, and natural resources, to produce goods and services. The firm's **technology** is the processes it uses to turn inputs into goods and services. **Technological change** refers to a change in the ability of a firm to produce a given level of output with a given quantity of inputs.

Review Questions

1.1 What is the difference between technology and technological change?

1.2 Is it possible for technological change to be negative? If so, give an example.

Problems and Applications

1.3 EOG, a Texas-based producer of oil and gas, is called the "Apple of oil" because of the company's history of developing innovative methods to extract energy from shale rock. Using one of EOG's innovations, called iSteer, the company can navigate through thousands of feet of rock with a drill bit that allows for greater recovery oil and gas than methods the company previously used. Briefly explain why economists would consider EOG's use of iSteer an example of technological change.

Source: Erin Ailworth, "Fracking 2.0: Shale Drillers Pioneer New Ways to Profit in Era of Cheap Oil," *Wall Street Journal*, March 30, 2017.

1.4 Which of the following are examples of a firm experiencing positive technological change?
   a. A fall in the wages JetBlue pays its mechanics leads it to lower its ticket prices.
   b. A training program makes a firm's workers more productive.
   c. An exercise program makes a firm's workers healthier and reduces the number of days the typical worker is absent.
   d. A firm cuts its workforce and is able to maintain its initial level of output.
   e. A firm rearranges the layout of its factory and finds that by using its initial set of inputs, it can produce exactly as much as before.

1.5 (Related to the Apply the Concept on page 374) Segment.com reorganized its office as part of its "anti-distraction campaign." According to an article in the *Wall Street Journal*, the company cut back on its internal text messaging service and moved "some of its communication back to email to reduce the number of notifications employees were receiving."
   a. Is it possible that this movement from a new technology—text messaging—to an older technology—e-mail—represented positive technological change at Segment? Briefly explain.
   b. Suppose that competition for software engineers results in Segment.com having to pay them higher salaries. Would the fact that the firm will now face an increased cost of providing its services be an example of negative technological change? Briefly explain.

Source: Rachel Feintzeig, "How One Firm Lowered Its Open-Office Noise," *Wall Street Journal*, November 15, 2016.

11.2 The Short Run and the Long Run in Economics, pages 375–378

LEARNING OBJECTIVE: Distinguish between the economic short run and the economic long run.

MyLab Economics   Visit **www.pearson.com/mylab/economics** to complete these exercises online and get instant feedback.

Summary

In the **short run**, a firm's technology and the size of its factory, store, or office are fixed. In the **long run**, a firm is able to adopt new technology and increase or decrease the size of its physical plant. **Total cost** is the cost of all the inputs a firm uses in production. **Variable costs** are costs that change as output changes. **Fixed costs** are costs that remain constant as output changes. **Opportunity cost** is the highest-valued alternative that must be given up to engage in an activity. An **explicit cost** is a cost that involves spending money. An **implicit cost** is a nonmonetary opportunity cost. The relationship between the inputs employed by a firm and the maximum output it can produce with those inputs is called the firm's **production function**. **Average total cost** is total cost divided by the quantity of output produced.

Review Questions

2.1 What is the difference between the short run and the long run? Is the amount of time that separates the short run from the long run the same for every firm?

2.2 Distinguish between a firm's fixed costs and variable costs and give an example of each.

2.3 What are implicit costs? How are they different from explicit costs?

2.4 What is the production function? What does the short-run production function hold constant?

Problems and Applications

2.5 Peter Reinhardt, CEO of Segment.com, made the following comment on his blog when discussing how the firm's noisy open office was lowering the productivity of its engineers: "We can't immediately ditch our open floor plan (although we're looking at various options for our next office.)" Why can't the firm immediately ditch its open floor plan? Is Reinhardt's remark about Segment.com's economic short run or its economic long run? Briefly explain.

Source: Peter Reinhardt, "Improving Our Focus by Measuring Sound Levels," segment.com, October 19, 2016

2.6 An article on fortune.com estimated that the cost of materials in Apple's iPhone 7 with 32 gigabytes of memory was $225. Apple was selling the iPhone 7 for $649. Can we conclude from this information that Apple is making a profit of about $424 per iPhone? Briefly explain.

Source: Don Reisinger, "Here's How Much the iPhone 7 Cost to Manufacture," fortune.com, September 20, 2016.

2.7 **(Related to the Apply the Concept on page 376)** Small business owner Jay Goltz described several decisions he made to reduce the fixed costs of his businesses, including replacing halogen lamps with LED lamps. Goltz noted, "I'm guessing that many business owners could save a lot more than pennies on their fixed costs, and those savings … fall right to the bottom line."

a. Why are the costs of electricity used to power the lights used in Mr. Goltz's businesses fixed costs?

b. Explain why Goltz wrote that reducing fixed costs results in savings that "fall right to the bottom line."

Source: Jay Goltz, "Not All Fixed Costs Are Truly Fixed," New York Times, May 25, 2011.

2.8 **(Related to the Apply the Concept on page 376)** For Jill Johnson's pizza restaurant, explain whether each of the following is a fixed cost or a variable cost.

a. The payment she makes on her fire insurance policy

b. The payment she makes to buy pizza dough

c. The wages she pays her workers

d. The lease payment she makes to the landlord who owns the building where her store is located

e. The $300-per-month payment she makes to her local newspaper for running her weekly advertisements

2.9 **(Related to the Apply the Concept on page 376)** An article in the *New York Times* on the airline industry described airlines as being "burdened by high fixed costs." What are likely to be the most important fixed costs for an airline? Are airlines likely to have particularly high fixed costs relative to their variable costs when compared with, say, an Old Navy clothing store or a Panera Bread restaurant? Briefly explain.

Source: Kevin Allison, "Warren Buffett, in a Switch, Warms to Airline Industry," *New York Times*, November 15, 2016.

2.10 Suppose that Bill owns an automobile collision repair shop. The following table shows how the quantity of cars Bill can repair per month depends on the number of workers he hires. Assume that he pays each worker $4,000 per month and his fixed cost is $6,000 per month. Using the information provided, fill in the missing values in the following table.

Quantity of Workers	Quantity of Cars per Month	Fixed Cost	Variable Cost	Total Cost	Average Total Cost
0	0	$6,000			—
1	20				
2	30				
3	40				
4	50				
5	55				

2.11 Suppose Jill Johnson operates her pizza restaurant in a building she owns in the center of the city. Similar buildings in the neighborhood rent for $4,000 per month. Jill is considering selling her building and renting space in the suburbs for $3,000 per month, but she decides not to make the move. She reasons: "I would like to have a restaurant in the suburbs, but I pay no rent for my restaurant now, and I don't want to see my costs rise by $3,000 per month." Evaluate Jill's reasoning.

2.12 When the DuPont chemical company first attempted to enter the paint business, it was not successful. According to a company report, in one year it "lost nearly $500,000 in actual cash in addition to an expected return on investment of nearly $500,000, which made a total loss of income to the company of nearly a million." Why did this report include as part of the company's loss the amount it had expected to earn—but didn't—on its investment in manufacturing paint?

Source: Alfred D. Chandler, Jr., Thomas K. McCraw, and Richard Tedlow, *Management Past and Present*, Cincinnati, OH: South-Western, 2000.

11.3 The Marginal Product of Labor and the Average Product of Labor, pages 379–383

LEARNING OBJECTIVE: Explain and illustrate the relationship between the marginal product of labor and the average product of labor.

Summary

The **marginal product of labor** is the additional output produced by a firm as a result of hiring one more worker. Specialization and division of labor cause the marginal product of labor to rise for the first few workers hired. Eventually, the **law of diminishing returns** causes the marginal product of labor to decline. The **average product of labor** is the total amount of output produced by a firm divided by the quantity of workers hired. When the marginal product of labor is greater than the average product of labor, the average product of labor increases. When the marginal product of labor is less than the average product of labor, the average product of labor decreases.

Review Questions

3.1 Draw a graph that shows the usual relationship between the marginal product of labor and the average product of labor. Why do the marginal product of labor and the average product of labor curves have the shapes you drew?

3.2 What is the law of diminishing returns? Does it apply in the long run?

Problems and Applications

3.3 Devra Gartenstein, a restaurant owner, made the following observation about preparing food: "Cooks become increasingly less productive as a kitchen becomes increasingly crowded."

　a. What do economists call the problem she is describing? What are its implications for the marginal product of labor for cooks?

　b. Do restaurant owners have a solution to this problem in the long run? Briefly explain.

　Source: Devra Gartenstein "Law of Diminishing Marginal Returns in Restaurant Operations," smallbusiness.chron.com.

3.4 Fill in the missing values in the following table.

Quantity of Workers	Total Output	Marginal Product of Labor	Average Product of Labor
0	0		
1	400		
2	900		
3	1,500		
4	1,900		
5	2,200		
6	2,400		
7	2,300		

3.5 Use the numbers from problem 3.4 to draw one graph that shows how total output increases with the quantity of workers hired and a second graph that shows the marginal product of labor and the average product of labor.

3.6 A student looks at the numbers in Table 11.3 on page 379 and draws this conclusion:

> The marginal product of labor is increasing for the first two workers hired, and then it declines for the next four workers. I guess each of the first two workers must have been hard workers. Then Jill must have had to settle for increasingly bad workers.

Do you agree with the student's analysis? Briefly explain.

3.7 **(Related to the Apply the Concept on page 381)** Briefly explain whether you agree with the following argument:

> Adam Smith's idea of the gains to firms from the division of labor makes a lot of sense when the good being manufactured is something complex like automobiles or computers, but it doesn't apply in the manufacturing of less complex goods or in other sectors of the economy, such as retail sales.

3.8 Sally looks at her college transcript and asks you, "How is this possible? My grade point average for this semester's courses is higher than my grade point average for last semester's courses, but my cumulative grade point average still went down from last semester to this semester." Explain to Sally how this outcome is possible.

3.9 The table below shows the quantity of workers and total output for a local pizza parlor. Answer the following questions based on the table.

Quantity of Workers	Total Output
0	0
1	5
2	—
3	19
4	24
5	28
6	26

　a. When the owner hires 4 workers, what is average product of labor?

　b. What is the marginal product of the fifth worker?

　c. If the marginal product of the second worker is 6, what is the total number of pizzas produced when 2 workers are hired?

　d. Assuming that the marginal product of the second worker is 6, with which worker hired does the law of diminishing returns set in?

11.4 The Relationship between Short-Run Production and Short-Run Cost, pages 383–386

LEARNING OBJECTIVE: Explain and illustrate the relationship between marginal cost and average total cost.

MyLab Economics   Visit **www.pearson.com/mylab/economics** to complete these exercises online and get instant feedback.

Summary

The **marginal cost** of production is the increase in total cost that results from producing another unit of output. The marginal cost curve has a U shape because when the marginal product of labor is rising, the marginal cost of output is falling, and when the marginal product of labor is falling, the marginal cost of output is rising. When marginal cost is less than average total cost, average total cost falls. When marginal cost is greater than average total cost, average total cost rises. Therefore, the average total cost curve also has a U shape.

Review Questions

4.1 What is the difference between the average cost of production and the marginal cost of production?

4.2 If the marginal product of labor is rising, is the marginal cost of production rising or falling? Briefly explain.

4.3 Explain why the marginal cost curve intersects the average total cost curve at the level of output where average total cost is at a minimum.

Problems and Applications

4.4 Older oil wells that produce fewer than 10 barrels of oil a day are called "stripper" wells. Suppose that you and a partner own a stripper well that can produce 8 barrels of oil per day, and you estimate that the marginal cost of producing another barrel of oil is $80. In making your calculation, you take into account the cost of labor, materials, and other inputs that increase when you produce more oil. Your partner looks over your calculation of marginal cost and says: "You forgot about that bank loan we received two years ago. If we take into account the amount we pay on that loan, it adds $10 per barrel to our marginal cost of production." Briefly explain whether you agree with your partner's analysis.

4.5 Is it possible for average total cost to be decreasing over a range of output where marginal cost is increasing? Briefly explain.

4.6 Suppose a firm has no fixed costs, so all its costs are variable, even in the short run.
   a. If the firm's marginal costs are continually increasing (that is, marginal cost is increasing from the first unit of output produced), will the firm's average total cost curve have a U shape? Briefly explain.
   b. If the firm's marginal costs are $5 at every level of output, what shape will the firm's average total cost have?

4.7 **(Related to Solved Problem 11.4 on page 385)** Santiago Delgado owns a copier store. He leases two copy machines for which he pays $20 each per day. He cannot increase the number of machines he leases without giving the office machine company six weeks' notice. He can hire as many workers as he wants, at a cost of $40 per day per worker. These are the only two inputs he uses to produce copies.
   a. Fill in the remaining columns in the following table.
   b. Draw the average total cost curve and marginal cost curve for Santiago's store. Do these curves have the expected shapes? Briefly explain.

Quantity of Workers	Quantity of Copies per Day	Fixed Cost	Variable Cost	Total Cost	Average Total Cost	Marginal Cost
0	0					
1	600					
2	1,100					
3	1,500					
4	1,800					
5	2,000					
6	2,100					

4.8 Is Jill Johnson correct when she states the following: "I am currently producing 10,000 pizzas per month at a total cost of $50,000. If I produce 10,001 pizzas, my total cost will rise to $50,011. Therefore, my marginal cost of producing pizzas must be increasing." Draw a graph to illustrate your answer.

4.9 Is Jill Johnson correct when she states the following: "I am currently producing 20,000 pizzas per month at a total cost of $75,000. If I produce 20,001 pizzas, my total cost will rise to $75,002. Therefore, my marginal cost of producing pizzas must be increasing." Draw a graph to illustrate your answer.

4.10 (This problem is somewhat advanced.) Using symbols, we can write that the marginal product of labor is equal to $\Delta Q/\Delta L$. Marginal cost is equal to $\Delta TC/\Delta Q$. Because fixed costs by definition don't change, marginal cost is also equal to $\Delta VC/\Delta Q$. If Jill Johnson's only variable cost (VC) is labor cost, then her variable cost equals the wage multiplied by the quantity of workers hired, or wL.
   a. If the wage Jill pays is constant, then what is ΔVC in terms of w and L?
   b. Use your answer to part (a) and the expressions given for the marginal product of labor and the marginal cost of output to find an expression for marginal cost, $\Delta TC/\Delta Q$, in terms of the wage, w, and the marginal product of labor, $\Delta Q/\Delta L$.
   c. Use your answer to part (b) to determine Jill's marginal cost of producing pizzas if the wage is $750 per week and the marginal product of labor is 150 pizzas. If the wage falls to $600 per week and the marginal product of labor is unchanged, what happens to Jill's marginal cost? If the wage is unchanged at $750 per week and the marginal product of labor rises to 250 pizzas, what happens to Jill's marginal cost?

11.5 Graphing Cost Curves, pages 386–387

LEARNING OBJECTIVE: Graph average total cost, average variable cost, average fixed cost, and marginal cost.

MyLab Economics Visit www.pearson.com/mylab/economics to complete these exercises online and get instant feedback.

Summary

Average fixed cost is equal to fixed cost divided by the level of output. **Average variable cost** is equal to variable cost divided by the level of output. Figure 11.5 on page 387 shows the relationship among marginal cost, average total cost, average variable cost, and average fixed cost. It is one of the most important graphs in microeconomics.

Review Questions

5.1 Where does the marginal cost curve intersect the average variable cost curve and the average total cost curve?

5.2 As the level of output increases, what happens to the difference between the value of average total cost and the value of average variable cost?

Problems and Applications

5.3 Suppose the total cost of producing 10,000 tennis balls is $30,000, and the fixed cost is $10,000.
   a. What is the variable cost?
   b. When output is 10,000, what are the average variable cost and the average fixed cost?
   c. Assume that the cost curves have the usual shape. Is the dollar difference between the average total cost and the average variable cost greater when the output is 10,000 tennis balls or when the output is 30,000 tennis balls? Explain.

5.4 One description of the costs of operating a railroad made the following observation: "The fixed … expenses which attach to the operation of railroads … are in the nature of a tax upon the business of the road; the smaller the [amount of] business, the larger the tax." Briefly explain why fixed costs are like a tax. In what sense is this tax smaller when the amount of business is larger?

Source: Alfred D. Chandler, Jr., Thomas K. McCraw, and Richard Tedlow, *Management Past and Present*, Cincinnati, OH: South-Western, 2000, pp. 2–27.

5.5 In the ancient world, a book could be produced either on a scroll or as a codex, which was made of folded sheets glued together, something like a modern book. One scholar has estimated the following variable costs (in Greek drachmas) of the two methods:

	Scroll	Codex
Cost of writing (wage of a scribe)	11.33 drachmas	11.33 drachmas
Cost of paper	16.50 drachmas	9.25 drachmas

Another scholar points out that a significant fixed cost was involved in producing a codex:

> In order to copy a codex … the amount of text and the layout of each page had to be carefully calculated in advance to determine the exact number of sheets … needed. No doubt, this is more time-consuming and calls for more experimentation than the production of a scroll would. But for the next copy, these calculations would be used again.

a. Suppose that the fixed cost of preparing a codex was 58 drachmas and that there was no similar fixed cost for a scroll. Would an ancient book publisher who intended to sell 5 copies of a book be likely to publish it as a scroll or as a codex? What if the publisher intended to sell 10 copies? Briefly explain.

b. Although most books were published as scrolls in the first century C.E., by the third century, most were published as codices. Considering only the factors mentioned in this problem, explain why this change may have taken place.

Sources: T. C. Skeat, "The Length of the Standard Papyrus Roll and the Cost-Advantage of the Codex," *Zeitschrift fur Papyrologie und Epigraphik*, Germany: Rudolf Habelt, 1982, p. 175; and David Trobisch, *The First Edition of the New Testament*, New York: Oxford University Press, 2000, p. 73.

5.6 **(Related to the Chapter Opener on page 372)** We saw in the chapter opener that some colleges and private companies have launched online courses that anyone with an Internet connection can take. The most successful of these massive open online courses (MOOCs) have attracted tens of thousands of students. Suppose that your college offers a MOOC and spends a total of $200,000 on one-time costs to have instructors prepare the course material and buy additional server capacity. The college administration estimates that the variable cost of offering the course will be $20 per student per course. This variable cost is the same, regardless of how many students enroll in the course.

a. Use this information to fill in the missing values in the following table:

Number of Students Taking the Course	Average Total Cost	Average Variable Cost	Average Fixed Cost	Marginal Cost
1,000				
10,000				
20,000				

b. Use your answer to part (a) to draw a cost curve graph to illustrate your college's costs of offering this course. Your graph should measure cost on the vertical axis and the quantity of students taking the course on the horizontal axis. Be sure your graph contains the following curves: average total cost, average variable cost, average fixed cost, and marginal cost.

5.7 Use the information in the graph to find the values for the following at an output level of 1,000.

a. Marginal cost
b. Total cost
c. Variable cost
d. Fixed cost

5.8 List the errors in the following graph. Carefully explain why the curves drawn this way are incorrect. In other words, why can't these curves be as they are shown in the graph?

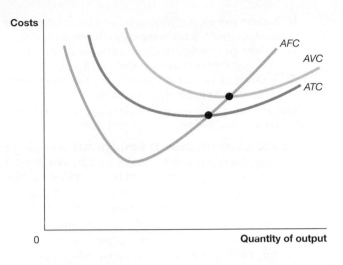

5.9 Explain how the events listed in (a) through (d) would affect the following costs at Southwest Airlines:
1. Marginal cost
2. Average variable cost
3. Average fixed cost
4. Average total cost
   a. Southwest signs a new contract with the Transport Workers Union that requires the airline to increase wages for its flight attendants.
   b. The federal government starts to levy a $20-per-passenger carbon emissions tax on all commercial air travel.
   c. Southwest decides on an across-the-board 10 percent cut in executive salaries.
   d. Southwest decides to double its television advertising budget.

11.6 Costs in the Long Run, pages 388–392

LEARNING OBJECTIVE: Explain how firms use the long-run average cost curve in their planning.

MyLab Economics   Visit **www.pearson.com/mylab/economics** to complete these exercises online and get instant feedback.

Summary

The **long-run average cost curve** shows the lowest cost at which a firm is able to produce a given level of output in the long run. For many firms, the long-run average cost curve falls as output expands because of **economies of scale**. **Minimum efficient scale** is the level of output at which all economies of scale have been exhausted. After economies of scale have been exhausted, firms experience **constant returns to scale**, where their long-run average cost curve is flat. At high levels of output, the long-run average cost curve turns up as the firm experiences **diseconomies of scale**.

Review Questions

6.1 What is the difference between total cost and variable cost in the long run?
6.2 What is minimum efficient scale? What is likely to happen in the long run to firms that do not reach minimum efficient scale?

6.3 What are economies of scale? What are four reasons that firms may experience economies of scale?
6.4 What are diseconomies of scale? What is the main reason that a firm eventually encounters diseconomies of scale as it keeps increasing the size of its store or factory?
6.5 Why can short-run average cost never be less than long-run average cost for a given level of output?

Problems and Applications

6.6 In describing the optimal size of an investment fund, a writer for the *Wall Street Journal* observed:

> … at first, bigger is better for both investors and managers…. Managing money is expensive. Small funds have many fixed costs…. If a fund is small, it can't generate enough fees to cover costs…. The result is that in terms of performance, funds should want to get big to cover costs and maximize returns, but not so big that diseconomies of scale erode returns.

Draw a graph of a long-run average cost curve for a typical firm in the investment fund industry. In your graph, draw and label the following.

a. A short-run average total cost curve for an investment fund that has not reached minimum efficient scale

b. A short-run average total cost curve for an investment fund that has reached minimum efficient scale

c. A short-run average total cost curve for an investment fund that experiences diseconomies of scale

d. A range of output within which investment funds experience constant returns to scale

Source: Wesley Gray, "Why Your Fund Manager May Not Have the Same Goal as You," *Wall Street Journal*, May 16, 2016.

6.7 (Related to **Solved Problem 11.6** on page 389) Mozambique has only recently become a major supplier of rubies. A *Wall Street Journal* article described how Gemfields, a mining company in Mozambique, increased its production of rubies in response to a growing demand for these gems:

> For centuries, the ruby trade… [was] centered in Southeast Asia, with stones plucked from the earth … by small, artisanal miners…. Because rubies have in the past been so rare, Thai cutters and polishers rarely focused on volumes or economies of scale. Gemfields looks to operate on a larger basis.

a. Draw a graph representing the long-run average cost curve for a representative firm that mines rubies. In your graph show the short-run average cost curve (ATC_1) for a firm that mines rubies by "plucking them from the earth" and the short-run average cost curve (ATC_2) for Gemfields that "looks to operate on a larger basis."

b. Will ATC_2 be lower than ATC_1 for all output levels? Briefly explain.

Source: Alexandra Wexler, "Sitting on a Trove of Rubies, Gemfields Looks to Create Fresh Demand," *Wall Street Journal*, April 17, 2017.

6.8 (Related to **Solved Problem 11.6** on page 389) Suppose that Jill Johnson has to choose between building a smaller restaurant and a larger restaurant. In the following graph, the relationship between costs and output for the smaller restaurant is represented by the curve ATC_1, and the relationship between costs and output for the larger restaurant is represented by the curve ATC_2.

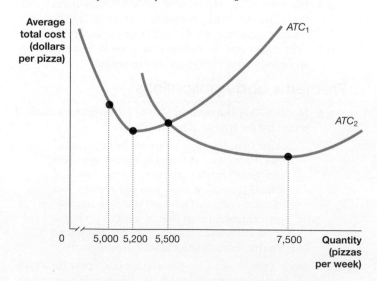

a. If Jill expects to produce 5,100 pizzas per week, should she build a smaller restaurant or a larger restaurant? Briefly explain.

b. If Jill expects to produce 6,000 pizzas per week, should she build a smaller restaurant or a larger restaurant? Briefly explain.

c. A student asks, "If the average cost of producing pizzas is lower in the larger restaurant when Jill produces 7,500 pizzas per week, why isn't it also lower when Jill produces 5,200 pizzas per week?" Give a brief answer to the student's question.

6.9 (Related to **Solved Problem 11.6** on page 389) At one point, Time Warner and the Walt Disney Company discussed merging their news operations. Time Warner owns Cable News Network (CNN), and Disney owns ABC News. After analyzing the situation, the companies decided that a combined news operation would have higher average costs than either CNN or ABC News had separately. Use a long-run average cost curve graph to illustrate why the companies did not merge their news operations.

Source: Martin Peers and Joe Flint, "AOL Calls Off CNN–ABC Deal, Seeing Operating Difficulties," *Wall Street Journal*, February 14, 2003.

6.10 (Related to the **Apply the Concept** on page 391) Suppose that Henry Ford had continued to experience economies of scale, no matter how large an automobile factory he built. Discuss what the implications of this would have been for the automobile industry.

6.11 In recent years, the United States has experienced large increases in oil production due in large part to a new technology, hydraulic fracturing ("fracking"). Fracking involves injecting a mixture of water, sand, and chemicals into rock formations at high pressure to release oil and natural gas. An article in the *Wall Street Journal* indicates that economies of scale in fracking may be considerably smaller than in conventional oil drilling. If this view is correct, what would the likely consequences be for the number of firms drilling for oil in the United States?

Source: Russell Gold and Theo Francis, "The New Winners and Losers in America's Shale Boom," *Wall Street Journal*, April 20, 2014.

6.12 (Related to the **Don't Let This Happen to You** on page 392) In his autobiography, T. Boone Pickens, a geologist, entrepreneur, and oil company executive, wrote:

> It's unusual to find a large corporation that's efficient…. When you get an inside look, it's easy to see how inefficient big business really is. Most corporate bureaucracies have more people than they have work.

Was Pickens describing diminishing returns or diseconomies of scale? Briefly explain.

Source: T. Boone Pickens, *The Luckiest Man in the World*, Washington, DC: Beard Books, 2000, p. 275.

6.13 (Related to the **Don't Let This Happen to You** on page 392) A writer for the *Wall Street Journal*, discussing the relatively poor performance of HSBC, a global bank with headquarters in the United Kingdom, noted, " [The poor performance] is further reason to ask whether the structure of such a large, global bank is working against it…. There remains a legitimate question whether the group is too big to manage." After reading this article, a student remarks: "It seems that the firm is suffering from diminishing returns." Briefly explain whether you agree with this remark.

Source: Paul J. Davies, "HSBC Shows the Diminished Value of Global Banks," *Wall Street Journal*, February 23, 2015.

Critical Thinking Exercises

CT11.1 Pick five firms from articles you find in sources such as your local newspaper, cnn.com, bloomberg.com, the *Wall Street Journal*, or the *New York Times* and describe the technology that each firm uses for its major product. Be sure to describe each firm's major inputs and outputs.

CT11.2 Chapter 1 described how economists use marginal analysis, and Chapter 10 used marginal analysis to understand consumer behavior. This chapter introduces another specific part of marginal analysis: marginal cost (MC). Suppose that a firm is thinking of expanding production by hiring more workers, who will help the firm produce more goods. The firm's managers calculate that the additional cost of hiring more workers is less than the additional revenue (also called marginal revenue) from selling more goods. Briefly explain whether you think the firm should expand production.

CT11.3 Often, many firms in an industry are located in the same geographic area. Examples include Hollywood (movies), Silicon Valley (information technology), Wall Street (finance), and Dalton, Georgia (carpets). Provide an additional example of firms in the same industry locating close together. Use the concepts from this chapter to explain why firms in an industry may decide to locate near each other.

CT11.4 Over the past 30 years in the United States, there has been a great expansion in the number of beer brewers. Can you think of two reasons this expansion might have occurred? Use concepts from this chapter and Chapter 10 in your answer.

LEARNING OBJECTIVE: Use isoquants and isocost lines to understand production and cost.

Using Isoquants and Isocost Lines to Understand Production and Cost

Isoquants

In this chapter, we studied the important relationship between a firm's level of production and its costs. In this appendix, we look more closely at how firms choose the combination of inputs to produce a given level of output. Firms usually have a choice about how they will produce their output. For example, Jill Johnson is able to produce 5,000 pizzas per week by using 10 workers and 2 ovens or by using 6 workers and 3 ovens. We will see that firms search for the *cost-minimizing* combination of inputs that will allow them to produce a given level of output. The cost-minimizing combination of inputs depends on two factors: technology—which determines how much output a firm receives from employing a given quantity of inputs—and input prices—which determine the total cost of each combination of inputs.

An Isoquant Graph

We begin by graphing the levels of output that Jill can produce using different combinations of two inputs: labor—the quantity of workers she hires per week—and capital—the quantity of ovens she uses per week. In reality, of course, Jill uses more than just these two inputs to produce pizzas, but nothing important would change if we expanded the discussion to include many inputs instead of just two. Figure 11A.1 measures the quantity of capital along the vertical axis and the quantity of labor along the horizontal axis. The curves in the graph are **isoquants**, which show all the combinations of two inputs—in this case capital and labor—that will produce the same level of output.

Isoquant A curve that shows all the combinations of two inputs, such as capital and labor, that will produce the same level of output.

MyLab Economics Animation

Figure 11A.1

Isoquants

Isoquants show all the combinations of two inputs—in this case capital and labor—that will produce the same level of output. For example, the isoquant labeled $Q = 5,000$ shows all the combinations of ovens and workers that enable Jill to produce that quantity of pizzas per week. At point A, she produces 5,000 pizzas using 3 ovens and 6 workers, and at point B, she produces the same output using 2 ovens and 10 workers. With more ovens and workers, she can move to a higher isoquant. For example, with 4 ovens and 12 workers, she can produce at point C on the isoquant $Q = 10,000$. With even more ovens and workers, she could move to the isoquant $Q = 13,000$.

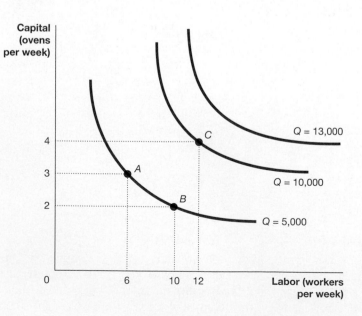

The isoquant labeled $Q = 5,000$ shows all the combinations of workers and ovens that enable Jill to produce that quantity of pizzas per week. For example, at point A, she produces 5,000 pizzas using 6 workers and 3 ovens, and at point B, she produces the same output using 10 workers and 2 ovens. With more workers and ovens, she can move to a higher isoquant. For example, with 12 workers and 4 ovens, she can produce at point C on the isoquant $Q = 10,000$. With even more workers and ovens, she could move to the isoquant $Q = 13,000$. The higher the isoquant—that is, the further to the upper right on the graph—the more output the firm produces. Although we have shown only three isoquants in this graph, there is, in fact, an isoquant for every level of output.   MyLab Economics Concept Check

The Slope of an Isoquant

Remember that the slope of a curve is the ratio of the change in the variable on the vertical axis to the change in the variable on the horizontal axis. Along an isoquant, the slope tells us the rate at which a firm is able to substitute one input for another while keeping the level of output constant. This rate is called the **marginal rate of technical substitution (MRTS)**.

We expect that the *MRTS* will change as we move down an isoquant. In Figure 11A.1, at a point like A on isoquant $Q = 5,000$, the isoquant is relatively steep. As we move down the curve, it becomes less steep at a point like B. This shape is the usual one for isoquants: They are bowed in, or convex. The reason isoquants have this shape is that as we move down the curve, we continue to substitute labor for capital. As the firm produces the same quantity of output using less capital, the additional labor it needs increases because of diminishing returns. Remember from the chapter that, as a consequence of diminishing returns, for a given decline in capital, increasing amounts of labor are necessary to produce the same level of output. Because the MRTS is equal to the change in capital divided by the change in labor, it will become smaller (in absolute value) as we move down an isoquant.   MyLab Economics Concept Check

Marginal rate of technical substitution (MRTS) The rate at which a firm is able to substitute one input for another while keeping the level of output constant.

Isocost Lines

A firm wants to produce a given quantity of output at the lowest possible cost. We can show the relationship between the quantity of inputs used and the firm's total cost by using an *isocost* line. An **isocost line** shows all the combinations of two inputs, such as capital and labor, that have the same total cost.

Isocost line All the combinations of two inputs, such as capital and labor, that have the same total cost.

Graphing the Isocost Line

Suppose that Jill has $6,000 per week to spend on capital and labor. Suppose, to simplify the analysis, that Jill can rent pizza ovens by the week. The table in Figure 11A.2 shows the combinations of capital and labor available to her if the rental price of ovens is $1,000 per week and the wage rate is $500 per week. The graph uses the data in the table to construct an isocost line. The isocost line intersects the vertical axis at the maximum number of ovens Jill can rent per week, which is shown by point A. The line intersects the horizontal axis at the maximum number of workers Jill can hire per week, which is point G. As Jill moves down the isocost line from point A, she gives up renting 1 oven for every 2 workers she hires. Any combination of inputs along the line or inside the line can be purchased with $6,000. Any combination that lies outside the line cannot be purchased because it would have a total cost to Jill of more than $6,000.   MyLab Economics Concept Check

The Slope and Position of the Isocost Line

The slope of the isocost line is constant and equals the change in the quantity of ovens divided by the change in the quantity of workers. In this case, in moving from any point on the isocost line to any other point, the change in the quantity of ovens equals −1, and the change in the quantity of workers equals 2, so the slope equals −1/2. Notice that with a rental price of ovens of $1,000 per week and a wage rate for labor of

Figure 11A.2

An Isocost Line

The isocost line shows the combinations of inputs with a total cost of $6,000. The rental price of ovens is $1,000 per week, so if Jill spends the whole $6,000 on ovens, she can rent 6 ovens (point A). The wage rate is $500 per week, so if Jill spends the whole $6,000 on workers, she can hire 12 workers (point G). As she moves down the isocost line, she gives up renting 1 oven for every 2 workers she hires. Any combination of inputs along the line or inside the line can be purchased with $6,000. Any combination that lies outside the line cannot be purchased with $6,000.

Combinations of Workers and Ovens with a Total Cost of $6,000			
Point	Ovens	Workers	Total Cost
A	6	0	(6 × $1,000) + (0 × $500) = $6,000
B	5	2	(5 × $1,000) + (2 × $500) = $6,000
C	4	4	(4 × $1,000) + (4 × $500) = $6,000
D	3	6	(3 × $1,000) + (6 × $500) = $6,000
E	2	8	(2 × $1,000) + (8 × $500) = $6,000
F	1	10	(1 × $1,000) + (10 × $500) = $6,000
G	0	12	(0 × $1,000) + (12 × $500) = $6,000

$500 per week, the slope of the isocost line is equal to the ratio of the wage rate divided by the rental price of capital, multiplied by −1, or −$500/$1,000 = −1/2. In fact, this result will always hold, whatever inputs are involved and whatever their prices may be: *The slope of the isocost line is equal to the ratio of the price of the input on the horizontal axis divided by the price of the input on the vertical axis multiplied by −1.*

The position of the isocost line depends on the level of total cost. Higher levels of total cost shift the isocost line outward, and lower levels of total cost shift the isocost line inward. This can be seen in Figure 11A.3, which shows isocost lines for total costs of $3,000, $6,000, and $9,000. We have shown only three isocost lines in the graph, but there is, in fact, a different isocost line for each level of total cost. **MyLab Economics** Concept Check

Figure 11A.3

The Position of the Isocost Line

The position of the isocost line depends on the level of total cost. As total cost increases from $3,000 to $6,000 to $9,000 per week, the isocost line shifts outward. For each isocost line shown, the rental price of ovens is $1,000 per week, and the wage rate is $500 per week.

Capital (ovens per week)

Combinations of workers and ovens that produce 5,000 pizzas but at higher total cost than at *A*

Cost-minimizing combination of workers and ovens

C

A

B

D *Q* = 5,000

Labor (workers per week)

Lower total cost than at *A* but output less than 5,000 pizzas

MyLab Economics Animation

Figure 11A.4

Choosing Capital and Labor to Minimize Total Cost

Jill wants to produce 5,000 pizzas per week at the lowest total cost. Point *B* is the lowest-cost combination of inputs shown in the graph, but this combination of 1 oven and 4 workers will produce fewer than the 5,000 pizzas needed. Points *C* and *D* are combinations of ovens and workers that will produce 5,000 pizzas, but their total cost is $9,000. The combination of 3 ovens and 6 workers at point *A* produces 5,000 pizzas at the lowest total cost of $6,000.

Choosing the Cost-Minimizing Combination of Capital and Labor

Suppose Jill wants to produce 5,000 pizzas per week. Figure 11A.1 on page 402 shows that there are many combinations of ovens and workers that will allow Jill to produce this level of output. There is only one combination of ovens and workers, however, that will allow her to produce 5,000 pizzas *at the lowest total cost*. Figure 11A.4 shows the isoquant $Q = 5,000$ along with three isocost lines. Point *B* is the lowest-cost combination of inputs shown in the graph, but this combination of 1 oven and 4 workers will produce fewer than the 5,000 pizzas needed. Points *C* and *D* are combinations of ovens and workers that will produce 5,000 pizzas, but their total cost is $9,000. The combination of 3 ovens and 6 workers at point *A* produces 5,000 pizzas at the lowest total cost of $6,000.

Figure 11A.4 shows that moving to an isocost line with a total cost of less than $6,000 would mean producing fewer than 5,000 pizzas. Being at any point along the isoquant $Q = 5,000$ other than point A would increase total cost above $6,000. In fact, the combination of inputs at point A is the only one on isoquant $Q = 5,000$ that has a total cost of $6,000. All other input combinations on this isoquant have higher total costs. Notice also that at point A, the isoquant and the isocost lines are tangent, so the slope of the isoquant is equal to the slope of the isocost line at that point.

Different Input Price Ratios Lead to Different Input Choices

Jill's cost-minimizing choice of 3 ovens and 6 workers is determined jointly by these two factors:

1. The technology available to her, as represented by her firm's isoquants
2. Input prices, as represented by her firm's isocost lines

If the technology of making pizzas changes, perhaps because new ovens are developed, her isoquants will be affected, and her choice of inputs may change. If her isoquants remain unchanged but input prices change, then her choice of inputs may also change. This fact can explain why firms in different countries that face different input prices may produce the same good using different combinations of capital and labor, even though they have the same technology available.

For example, suppose that in China, pizza ovens are higher priced and labor is lower priced than in the United States. In our example, Jill Johnson pays $1,000 per week to rent pizza ovens and $500 per week to hire workers. Suppose a businessperson

MyLab Economics Animation

Figure 11A.5

Changing Input Prices Affects the Cost-Minimizing Input Choice

As the graph shows, the input combination at point A, which was optimal for Jill, is not optimal for a businessperson in China. Using the input combination at point A would cost businesspeople in China more than $6,000. Instead, the Chinese isocost line is tangent to the isoquant at point B, where the input combination is 2 ovens and 10 workers. Because ovens cost more in China but workers cost less, a Chinese firm will use fewer ovens and more workers than a U.S. firm, even if it has the same technology as the U.S. firm.

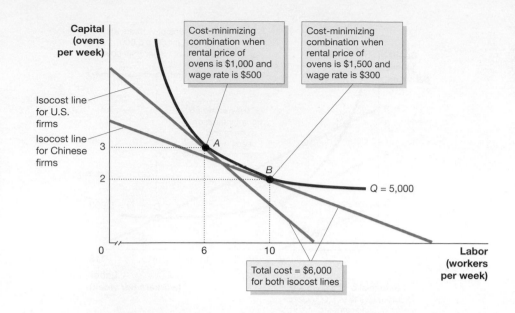

in China must pay a price of $1,500 per week to rent the identical pizza ovens but can hire Chinese workers who are as productive as U.S. workers at a wage of $300 per week. Figure 11A.5 shows how the cost-minimizing input combination for the businessperson in China differs from Jill's.

Remember that the slope of the isocost line equals the wage rate divided by the rental price of capital multiplied by −1. The slope of the isocost line that Jill and other U.S. firms face is −$500/$1,000, or −1/2. Firms in China, however, face an isocost line with a slope of −$300/$1,500, or −1/5. As Figure 11A.5 shows, the input combination at point A, which was optimal for Jill, is not optimal for a firm in China because it would cost that firm more than $6,000. Instead, the Chinese isocost line is tangent to the isoquant at point B, where the input combination is 2 ovens and 10 workers. This result makes sense: Because ovens cost more in China but workers cost less, a Chinese firm will use fewer ovens and more workers than a U.S. firm, even if it has the same technology as the U.S. firm.

MyLab Economics Concept Check

Solved Problem 11A.1

MyLab Economics Interactive Animation

Firms Responding to Differences in Input Price Ratios

David Autor, an economist at MIT, wrote, "When Nissan Motor Company builds cars in Japan, it makes extensive use of industrial robots to reduce labor costs. When it assembles cars in India, it uses robots far more sparingly." Explain why Nissan uses this strategy. Illustrate your answer with an isoquant–isocost line graph.

Source: David Autor, "The 'Task' Approach to Labor Markets: An Overview," *Journal of Labor Market Research*, Vol. 46, No. 3 (February 2013), pp. 185–199.

Solving the Problem

Step 1: **Review the chapter material.** This problem is about determining the optimal choice of inputs when input price ratios differ, so you may want to review the section "Different Input Price Ratios Lead to Different Input Choices," which begins on page 405.

Step 2: **Answer the question by explaining Nissan's strategy.** Nissan must be pursuing this strategy because labor costs are higher in Japan than in India. The higher cost of labor relative to capital (industrial robots) in Japan means that Nissan faces an isocost line that is steeper in Japan than in India. Assuming that Nissan's technology is the same in the two countries, the steeper isocost line in Japan will be tangent to the isoquant at a point that represents more capital and less labor than in India. This conclusion is illustrated by the graph in step 3.

Step 3: **Finish your answer by drawing a graph to illustrate your explanation in step 2.** Nissan will produce in Japan at point A, using L_J units of labor and K_J units of capital. It will produce in India at point B, using L_I units of labor and K_I units of capital.

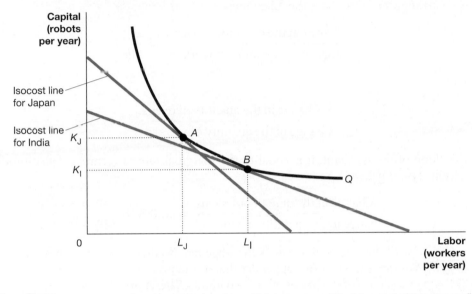

Your Turn: For more practice, do related problem 11A.6 on page 412 at the end of this appendix.

MyLab Economics Study Plan

Another Look at Cost Minimization

We know that consumers maximize utility when they consume each good up to the point where the marginal utility per dollar spent is the same for every good. We can derive a very similar cost-minimization rule for firms. Remember that at the point of cost minimization, the isoquant and the isocost line are tangent, so they have the same slope. Therefore, *at the point of cost minimization, the marginal rate of technical substitution (MRTS) is equal to the wage rate divided by the rental price of capital.*

The slope of the isoquant tells us the rate at which a firm is able to substitute labor for capital, *keeping the level of output constant.* The slope of the isocost line tells us the rate at which a firm is able to substitute labor for capital, *given current input prices.* Only at the point of cost minimization are these two rates the same.

When we move from one point on an isoquant to another, we end up using more of one input and less of the other input, but the level of output remains the same. For example, as Jill moves down an isoquant, she uses fewer ovens and more workers but produces the same quantity of pizzas. In this chapter, we defined the *marginal product of labor* (MP_L) as the additional output produced by a firm as a result of hiring one more worker. Similarly, we can define the *marginal product of capital* (MP_K) as the additional output produced by a firm as a result of using one more machine. So, when Jill uses fewer ovens by moving down an isoquant, she loses output equal to:

$$-\text{Change in the quantity of ovens} \times MP_K.$$

But she uses more workers, so she gains output equal to:

$$\text{Change in the quantity of workers} \times MP_L.$$

We know that the gain in output from the additional workers is equal to the loss from the smaller quantity of ovens because total output remains the same along an isoquant. Therefore, we can write:

$$-\text{Change in the quantity of ovens} \times MP_K = \text{Change in the quantity of workers} \times MP_L.$$

Loss in output from using fewer ovens

Gain in output from using more workers

If we rearrange terms, we have the following:

$$\frac{-\text{Change in the quantity of ovens}}{\text{Change in the quantity of workers}} = \frac{MP_L}{MP_K}.$$

Because:

$$\frac{-\text{Change in the quantity of ovens}}{\text{Change in the quantity of workers}}$$

is the slope of the isoquant, it is equal to the marginal rate of technical substitution (multiplied by negative 1). So, we can write:

$$\frac{-\text{Change in the quantity of ovens}}{\text{Change in the quantity of workers}} = MRTS = \frac{MP_L}{MP_K}.$$

The slope of the isocost line equals the wage rate (w) divided by the rental price of capital (r). We saw earlier in this appendix that at the point of cost minimization, the MRTS equals the ratio of the prices of the two inputs. Therefore:

$$\frac{MP_L}{MP_K} = \frac{w}{r}.$$

We can rewrite this to show that at the point of cost minimization:

$$\frac{MP_L}{w} = \frac{MP_K}{r}.$$

This last expression tells us that to minimize cost for a given level of output, a firm should hire inputs up to the point where the last dollar spent on each input results in the same increase in output. If this equality did not hold, a firm could lower its costs by using more of one input and less of the other. For example, if the left side of the equation were greater than the right side, a firm could rent fewer ovens, hire more workers, and produce the same output at lower cost. **MyLab Economics** Concept Check

Solved Problem 11A.2

MyLab Economics Interactive Animation

Determining the Optimal Combination of Inputs

Consider the information in the following table for Jill Johnson's restaurant:

Marginal product of capital	3,000 pizzas per oven
Marginal product of labor	1,200 pizzas per worker
Wage rate	$300 per week
Rental price of ovens	$600 per week

Briefly explain whether Jill is minimizing costs. If she is not minimizing costs, explain whether she should rent more ovens and hire fewer workers or rent fewer ovens and hire more workers.

Solving the Problem

Step 1: **Review the chapter material.** This problem is about determining the optimal choice of inputs by comparing the ratios of the marginal products of inputs to their prices, so you may want to review the section "Another Look at Cost Minimization," which begins on page 407.

Step 2: **Compute the ratios of marginal product to input price to determine whether Jill is minimizing costs.** If Jill is minimizing costs, the following relationship should hold:

$$\frac{MP_L}{w} = \frac{MP_K}{r}.$$

In this case, we have:

$$MP_L = 1,200$$

$$MP_K = 3,000$$

$$w = \$300$$

$$r = \$600.$$

So:

$$\frac{MP_L}{w} = \frac{1,200}{\$300} = 4 \text{ pizzas per dollar, and } \frac{MP_K}{r} = \frac{3,000}{\$600} = 5 \text{ pizzas per dollar.}$$

Because the two ratios are not equal, Jill is not minimizing cost.

Step 3: **Determine how Jill should change the mix of inputs she uses.** Jill produces more pizzas per dollar from the last oven than from the last worker. This indicates that she has too many workers and too few ovens. Therefore, to minimize cost, Jill should use more ovens and hire fewer workers.

Your Turn: For more practice, do related problems 11A.7 and 11A.8 on page 412 at the end of this appendix.

MyLab Economics Study Plan

Apply the Concept

MyLab Economics Video

Do National Football League Teams Behave Efficiently?

In the National Football League (NFL), the "salary cap" is the maximum amount each team can spend in a year on salaries for football players. Each year's salary cap results from negotiations between the league and the union representing the players. To achieve efficiency, an NFL team should distribute salaries among players so as to maximize the level of output—in this case, winning football games—given the constant level of cost represented by the salary cap. (Notice that maximizing the level of output for a given level of cost is equivalent to minimizing cost for a given level of output. To see why, think about the situation in which an isocost line is tangent to an isoquant. At the point of tangency, the firm has simultaneously minimized the cost of producing the level of output represented by the isoquant and maximized the output produced at the level of cost represented by the isocost line.)

In distributing the fixed amount of salary payments available, teams should equalize the ratios of the marginal productivity of players, as represented by their contribution to winning games, to the salaries players receive. Just as a firm may decide not to use a machine that has a very high marginal product if its rental price is very high, a football team may not want to hire a superstar player if the salary the team would need to pay is too high.

PA Images/Alamy Stock Photo

Did a rule change keep Cleveland from paying Myles Garrett of Texas A&M too much?

Economists Cade Massey, of the University of Pennsylvania, and Richard Thaler, of the University of Chicago, have analyzed whether NFL teams distribute their salaries efficiently. NFL teams obtain their players either by signing free agents—who are players whose contracts with other teams have expired—or by signing players chosen in the annual draft of eligible college players. The college draft consists of seven rounds, with the teams with the worst records the previous year choosing first. Massey and Thaler found that, in fact, NFL teams do not allocate salaries efficiently. In particular, the players chosen with the first few picks of the first round of the draft tend to be paid salaries that are much higher relative to their marginal products than are players taken later in the first round. A typical team with a high draft pick would increase its ability to win football games at the constant cost represented by the salary cap if it traded for lower draft picks, provided that it could find another team willing to make the trade. Why do NFL teams apparently make the error of not efficiently distributing salaries? Massey and Thaler argue that general managers of NFL teams tend to be overconfident in their ability to forecast how well a college player is likely to perform in the NFL.

General managers of NFL teams are not alone in suffering from overconfidence. Studies have shown that, in general, people tend to overestimate their ability to forecast an uncertain outcome. Because NFL teams tend to overestimate the future marginal productivity of high draft picks, they pay them salaries that are inefficiently high compared to salaries other draft picks receive. NFL teams were aware that they were probably overpaying high draft picks. In 2011, they negotiated a new contract with the NFL Players Union that limited the salaries drafted players can receive.

This example shows that the concepts developed in this chapter provide powerful tools for analyzing whether firms are operating efficiently.

Source: Cade Massey and Richard Thaler, "The Loser's Curse: Decision Making and Market Efficiency in the National Football League Draft," *Management Science*, Vol. 59, No. 7, (July 2013), pp. 1479–1495.

MyLab Economics Study Plan

Your Turn: Test your understanding by doing related problem 11A.14 on page 413 at the end of this appendix.

The Expansion Path

We can use isoquants and isocost lines to examine what happens as a firm expands its level of output. Figure 11A.6 shows three isoquants for a firm that produces bookcases. The isocost lines are drawn under the assumption that the machines used in producing bookcases can be rented for $100 per day and the wage rate is $25 per day. The point where each isoquant is tangent to an isocost line determines the cost-minimizing combination of capital and labor for producing that level of output. For example, 10 machines and 40 workers is the cost-minimizing combination of inputs for producing 50 bookcases per day. The cost-minimizing points *A*, *B*, and *C* lie along the firm's **expansion path**, which is a curve that shows the cost-minimizing combination of inputs for every level of output.

Expansion path A curve that shows a firm's cost-minimizing combination of inputs for every level of output.

An important point to note is that the expansion path represents the least-cost combination of inputs to produce a given level of output *in the long run*, when the firm is able to vary the levels of all of its inputs. We know, though, that in the short run, at least one input is fixed. We can use Figure 11A.6 to show that as the firm expands in the short run, its costs will be higher than in the long run. Suppose that the firm is currently at point *B*, using 15 machines and 60 workers to produce 75 bookcases per day. The firm wants to expand its output to 100 bookcases per day, but in the short run, it is unable to increase the quantity of machines it uses. Therefore, to expand output, it must hire more workers. The figure shows that in the short run, to produce 100 bookcases per day using 15 machines, the lowest costs it can attain are at point *D*, where it employs 110 workers. With a rental price of machines of $100 per day and a wage rate of $25 per day, in the short run, the firm will have total costs of $4,250 to produce 100 bookcases per day. In the long run, though, the firm can increase the

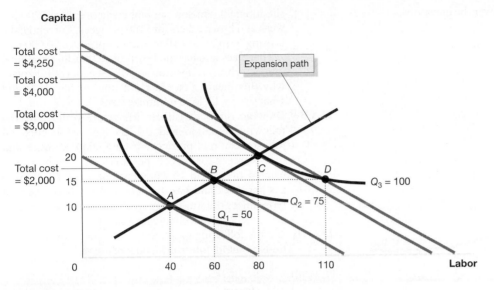

MyLab Economics Animation

Figure 11A.6

The Expansion Path

The tangency points *A*, *B*, and *C* lie along the firm's expansion path, which is a curve that shows the cost-minimizing combination of inputs for every level of output. In the short run, when the quantity of machines is fixed, the firm can expand output from 75 bookcases per day to 100 bookcases per day at the lowest cost only by moving from point *B* to point *D* and increasing the number of workers from 60 to 110. In the long run, when it can increase the quantity of machines it uses, the firm can move from point *D* to point *C*, thereby reducing its total costs of producing 100 bookcases per day from $4,250 to $4,000.

number of machines it uses from 15 to 20 and reduce the number of workers from 110 to 80. This change allows it to move from point *D* to point *C* on its expansion path and to lower its total costs of producing 100 bookcases per day from $4,250 to $4,000. The firm's minimum total costs of production are lower in the long run than in the short run.   MyLab Economics Concept Check   MyLab Economics Study Plan

Key Terms

Expansion path, p. 410

Isocost line, p. 403

Isoquant, p. 402

Marginal rate of technical substitution (MRTS), p. 403

11A Using Isoquants and Isocost Lines to Understand Production and Cost, pages 402–411

LEARNING OBJECTIVE: Use isoquants and isocost lines to understand production and cost.

MyLab Economics   Visit www.pearson.com/mylab/economics to complete these exercises online and get instant feedback.

Review Questions

11A.1   What is an isoquant? What is the slope of an isoquant?

11A.2   What is an isocost line? What is the slope of an isocost line?

11A.3   How do firms choose the optimal combination of inputs?

Problems and Applications

11A.4   Draw an isoquant–isocost line graph to illustrate the following situation: Jill Johnson can rent pizza ovens for $400 per week and hire workers for $200 per week. She is currently using 5 ovens and 10 workers to produce 20,000 pizzas per week and has total costs of $4,000. Make sure to label your graph to show the cost-minimizing input combination and the maximum quantity of labor and capital she can use with total costs of $4,000.

11A.5   Use the following graph to answer the questions.

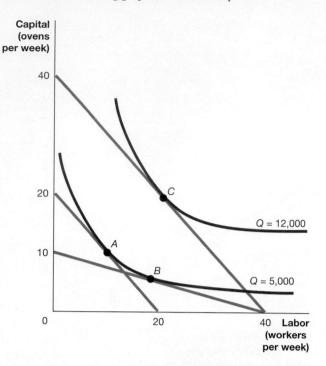

a. If the wage rate and the rental price of ovens are both $100 and total cost is $2,000, is the cost-minimizing point A, B, or C? Briefly explain.

b. If the wage rate is $25, the rental price of ovens is $100, and total cost is $1,000, is the cost-minimizing point A, B, or C? Briefly explain.

c. If the wage rate and the rental price of ovens are both $100 and total cost is $4,000, is the cost-minimizing point A, B, or C? Briefly explain.

11A.6   **(Related to Solved Problem 11A.1 on page 406)** During the eighteenth century, the American colonies had much more land per farmer than did Europe. As a result, the price of labor in the colonies was much higher relative to the price of land than it was in Europe. Assume that Europe and the colonies had access to the same technology for producing food. Use an isoquant–isocost line graph to illustrate why the combination of land and labor used in producing food in the colonies would have been different from the combination used to produce food in Europe.

11A.7   **(Related to Solved Problem 11A.2 on page 408)** Consider the information in the following table for Jill Johnson's restaurant:

Marginal product of capital	4,000
Marginal product of labor	100
Wage rate	$10
Rental price of pizza ovens	$500

Briefly explain whether Jill is minimizing costs. If she is not minimizing costs, explain whether she should rent more ovens and hire fewer workers or rent fewer ovens and hire more workers.

11A.8   **(Related to Solved Problem 11A.2 on page 408)** Draw an isoquant–isocost line graph to illustrate the following

situation: Jill Johnson can rent pizza ovens for $200 per week and hire workers for $100 per week. Currently, she is using 5 ovens and 10 workers to produce 20,000 pizzas per week and has total costs of $2,000. Jill's marginal rate of technical substitution (*MRTS*) equals –1. Explain why this means that she's not minimizing costs and what she could do to minimize costs.

11A.9   Draw an isoquant–isocost line graph to illustrate the following situation and the change that occurs: Jill Johnson can rent pizza ovens for $2,000 per week and hire workers for $1,000 per week. Currently, she is using 5 ovens and 10 workers to produce 20,000 pizzas per week and has total costs of $20,000. Then Jill reorganizes the way things are done in her business and achieves positive technological change.

11A.10   Use the following graph to answer the following questions about Jill Johnson's isoquant curve.

a. Which combination of inputs yields more output: combination A (3 ovens and 2 workers) or combination B (2 ovens and 3 workers)?

b. What will determine whether Jill selects A, B, or some other point along this isoquant curve?

c. Is the marginal rate of technical substitution (*MRTS*) greater at point A or point B?

11A.11   Draw an isoquant–isocost line graph to illustrate the following situation: Jill Johnson can rent pizza ovens for $2,000 per week and hire workers for $1,000 per week. She can minimize the cost of producing 20,000 pizzas per week by using 5 ovens and 10 workers, at a total cost of $20,000. She can minimize the cost of producing 45,000 pizzas per week by using 10 ovens and 20 workers, at a total cost of $40,000. She can minimize the cost of producing 60,000 pizzas per week by using 15 ovens and 30 workers, at a total cost of $60,000. Draw Jill's long-run average cost curve and discuss its economies of scale and diseconomies of scale.

11A.12   In Brazil, a grove of oranges is picked using 20 workers, ladders, and baskets. In Florida, a grove of oranges is picked using 1 worker and a machine that shakes the oranges off the trees and scoops up the fallen oranges. Using an isoquant–isocost line graph, illustrate why these two different methods are used to pick the same number of oranges per day in these two locations.

11A.13 Jill Johnson is minimizing the costs of producing pizzas. The rental price of one of her ovens is $2,000 per week, and the wage rate is $600 per week. The marginal product of capital in her business is 12,000 pizzas. What must be the marginal product of her workers?

11A.14 **(Related to the Apply the Concept on page 409)** If Cade Massey and Richard Thaler are correct, should the team that has the first pick in the draft keep the pick or trade it to another team for a lower pick? Briefly explain. Does the 2011 agreement that limits the salaries of drafted players affect your answer?

11A.15 Swift Ellis, Inc., manufactures running shoes. The following graph illustrates the combination of capital and labor (point A) that minimizes the firm's cost of producing 5,000 pairs of shoes. Suppose both the wage rate and the rental price of machinery doubles.

a. Draw a new isocost line to reflect this change in the wage rate and rental price of machinery.

b. Draw a new isoquant to show the combination of capital and labor that minimizes total cost, given the increase in input prices. Label this combination point B.

c. Comparing point A to point B, can we be sure that at point B the firm will be using more or less labor? More or less capital? Briefly explain.

Are Cage-Free Eggs the Road to Riches?

In recent years, the demand for healthier foods has increased. And many people are concerned that some animals being raised for food are not being treated humanely. More than 65,000 farms in the United States specialize in producing eggs. Until recently, most farmers raised chickens in cages that restrict their movement. Some farmers, though, have begun selling eggs produced using "cage-free" or "free-range" methods. Although the U.S. Department of Agriculture has not developed official definitions of these terms, chickens raised this way have significant room to move around, and some are raised outdoors.

Some consumers are willing to pay more for eggs produced by cage-free chickens, and by 2015, consumer demand for cage-free eggs had increased so much that farmers were able to sell these eggs for as much as double the price of eggs produced using conventional methods. The cost of raising cage-free chickens is higher because fewer chickens can be raised in an area of a given size, the chickens eat more because they are moving around, and some chickens die from being pecked by other chickens. But the higher price more than offset the higher cost, resulting in a larger profit. This larger profit attracted the notice of other egg farmers, one of whom noted: "Farming is about making a profit, and if someone is willing to pay us extra, we're going to do that."

By 2017, though, the profitability of selling cage-free eggs was declining. Increasing consumer demand had led more than 175 firms that sell eggs or use them in preparing food, including Panera Bread, Dunkin' Donuts, and McDonald's, to pledge to begin using only cage-free eggs. While you might expect that this increase in demand increased profits, it didn't because more farmers had begun using cage-free methods. According to U.S. Department of Agriculture data, in mid-2017, U.S. farms had more than 40 million cage-free chickens that were projected to lay

Alan Hopps/Moment Open/Getty Images

about 11 *billion* eggs during the year. While that was just 13 percent of total egg production in the United States, it was an increase from 10 percent in 2016 and from only 6 percent in 2015. The supply of cage-free eggs was growing more rapidly than the demand, causing the premium over the price of conventional eggs to shrink.

The process of new firms entering a profitable market and driving down prices and profits is found not only in agriculture. Throughout the economy, entrepreneurs are continually introducing new products or new ways of making products, which—when successful—enable them to earn an economic profit in the short run. But in the long run, competition among firms forces prices to the level where they just cover the costs of production. This process of competition is at the heart of the market system and is the focus of this chapter.

Sources: Stephanie Strom, "What to Make of Those Animal-Welfare Labels on Meat and Eggs," *New York Times*, January 31, 2017; Jayson Lusk, "Making Hens Cage-Free? You'll Shell Out for Eggs," *Wall Street Journal*, May 18, 2016; David Kesmodel, "Latest Flap on Egg Farms: Whether to Go 'Cage-Free,'" *Wall Street Journal*, March 11, 2015; "Walmart to Switch to All Cage-Free Eggs by 2025," Reuters, April 6, 2016; and U.S. Department of Agriculture data.

Chapter Outline & Learning Objectives

Economics in Your Life & Career

Are You an Entrepreneur?

Were you an entrepreneur during high school? If you babysat or mowed lawns for your neighbors, you were essentially an entrepreneur running a small business. How did you decide what price to charge for your services? You may have wanted to charge $25 per hour for babysitting or mowing lawns, but you probably charged much less. As you read the chapter, think about the competitive situation you faced as a teenage entrepreneur and try to determine why the prices received by most people who babysit and mow lawns are so low. You can check your answer against the one we provide on **page 441** at the end of this chapter.

An *industry* refers to all the firms selling a particular good or service—for instance, eggs, automobiles, or life insurance. Poultry farming is an example of a *perfectly competitive* industry. Firms in these industries are unable to control the prices of the products they sell and are unable to earn an economic profit in the long run for two main reasons:

1. Firms in these industries sell identical products.
2. It is easy for new firms to enter these industries.

Studying how perfectly competitive industries operate is the best way to understand how markets answer the fundamental economic questions discussed in Chapter 1:

- What goods and services will be produced?
- How will the goods and services be produced?
- Who will receive the goods and services produced?

Most industries, though, are not perfectly competitive. In most industries, firms do *not* produce identical products. And it may be difficult for new firms to enter some industries. There are thousands of industries in the United States. Although in some ways each industry is unique, industries share enough similarities that economists can group them into four market structures. In particular, any industry has three key characteristics:

1. The number of firms in the industry
2. The similarity of the good or service produced by the firms in the industry
3. The ease with which new firms can enter the industry

Economists use these characteristics to classify industries into the four market structures listed in Table 12.1.

Many industries, including restaurants, clothing stores, and other retailers, have a large number of firms selling products that are differentiated, rather than identical, and fall into the category of *monopolistic competition*. Some industries, such as computers and automobiles, have only a few firms and are *oligopolies*. Finally, a few industries, such as the delivery of first-class mail by the U.S. Postal Service, have only one firm and are *monopolies*. After discussing perfect competition in this chapter, we will devote a chapter to each of these other market structures.

Table 12.1

The Four Market Structures

	Market Structure			
Characteristic	Perfect Competition	Monopolistic Competition	Oligopoly	Monopoly
Number of firms	Many	Many	Few	One
Type of product	Identical	Differentiated	Identical or differentiated	Unique
Ease of entry	High	High	Low	Entry blocked
Examples of industries	• Growing wheat • Poultry farming	• Clothing stores • Restaurants	• Manufacturing computers • Manufacturing automobiles	• First-class mail delivery • Providing tap water

Perfectly Competitive Markets

12.1 LEARNING OBJECTIVE: Explain what a perfectly competitive market is and why a perfect competitor faces a horizontal demand curve.

Why are firms in a **perfectly competitive market** unable to control the prices of the goods they sell, and why are the owners of these firms unable to earn an economic profit in the long run? We can begin our analysis by listing the three conditions that make a market perfectly competitive:

1. There must be many buyers and many firms, all of which are small relative to the market.
2. All firms in the market must sell identical products.
3. There must be no barriers to new firms entering the market.

> **Perfectly competitive market** A market that meets the conditions of (1) many buyers and sellers, (2) all firms selling identical products, and (3) no barriers to new firms entering the market.

All three of these conditions hold in markets for agricultural products. For example, no single consumer or producer of apples buys or sells more than a tiny fraction of the total apple crop. The apples sold by each apple grower are identical, and there are no barriers to a new firm entering this market by purchasing land and planting apple trees. As we will see, it is the existence of many firms, all selling the same good, that keeps any single apple farmer from affecting the price of apples.

Although the market for apples meets the conditions for perfect competition, the markets for most goods and services do not. In particular, the second and third conditions are very restrictive. In most markets that have many buyers and sellers, firms do not sell identical products. For example, not all restaurant meals are the same, nor is all women's clothing the same. In later chapters, we will explore the common situation of monopolistic competition where many firms are selling similar but not identical products, and we will analyze industries that are oligopolies, where entry of new firms is difficult, and industries that are monopolies, where entry of new firms is impossible. In this chapter, we concentrate on perfectly competitive markets so we can use them as a benchmark to analyze how firms behave when they face the maximum possible competition.

A Perfectly Competitive Firm Cannot Affect the Market Price

Prices in perfectly competitive markets are determined by the interaction of demand and supply for the good or service. The actions of any single consumer or any single firm have no effect on the market price. Consumers and firms have to accept the market price if they want to buy and sell in a perfectly competitive market.

Because a firm in a perfectly competitive market is very small relative to the market and because it is selling exactly the same product as every other firm, it can sell as much as it wants without having to lower its price. If a perfectly competitive firm tries to raise its price, it won't sell anything at all because consumers will switch to buying the product from the firm's competitors. Therefore, the firm will be a **price taker** and will have to charge the same price as every other firm in the market. Although we don't usually think of firms as being too small to affect the market price, consumers are often in the position of being price takers. For instance, suppose your local supermarket is selling bread for $2.50 per loaf. You can load up your shopping cart with 20 loaves of bread, and the supermarket will gladly sell them all to you for $2.50 per loaf. But if you go to the cashier and offer to buy the bread for $2.49 per loaf, he or she will not sell it to you at that price. As a buyer, you are too small relative to the bread market to have any effect on the equilibrium price. Whether you leave the supermarket and buy no bread or you buy 20 loaves, you are unable to change the market price of bread by even 1 cent.

> **Price taker** A buyer or seller that is unable to affect the market price.

The situation you face as a bread buyer is the same one a wheat farmer faces as a wheat seller. There are about 150,000 farmers growing wheat in the United States. The market price of wheat is determined not by any individual wheat farmer but by the interaction of all the buyers and all the sellers in the wheat market. If any one wheat farmer has the best crop the farmer has ever had, or if any one wheat farmer stops growing wheat altogether,

Figure 12.1

A Perfectly Competitive Firm Faces a Horizontal Demand Curve

A firm in a perfectly competitive market is selling exactly the same product as all of the other firms in the market. Therefore, it can sell as much as it wants at the current market price, but it cannot sell anything at all if it raises the price by even 1 cent. As a result, the demand curve for a perfectly competitive firm's output is a horizontal line. In the figure, whether the wheat farmer sells 6,000 bushels or 15,000 bushels per year has no effect on the market price of $7.

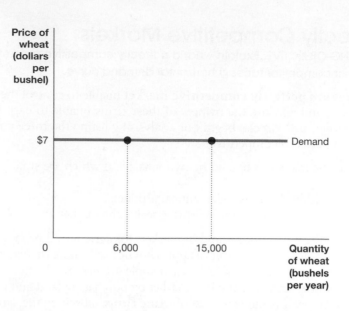

the market price of wheat will not be affected *because the market supply curve for wheat will not shift enough to change the equilibrium price by even 1 cent.* MyLab Economics Concept Check

The Demand Curve for the Output of a Perfectly Competitive Firm

Suppose Bill Parker grows wheat on a 250-acre farm in Washington State. Farmer Parker is selling wheat in a perfectly competitive market, so he is a price taker. Because he can sell as much wheat as he chooses at the market price—but can't sell any wheat at all at a higher price—the demand curve for his wheat has an unusual shape: It is horizontal, as shown in Figure 12.1. With a horizontal demand curve, Farmer Parker must accept the market price, which in this case is $7 per bushel. Whether Farmer Parker sells 6,000 bushels per year or 15,000 has no effect on the market price.

The demand curve for Farmer Parker's wheat is very different from the market demand curve for wheat. Panel (a) of Figure 12.2 shows the market for wheat. The demand curve in panel (a) is the *market demand curve for wheat* and has the normal downward slope we are familiar with from the market demand curves in Chapter 3.

Don't Let This Happen to You

Don't Confuse the Demand Curve for Farmer Parker's Wheat with the Market Demand Curve for Wheat

The demand curve for wheat has the normal downward-sloping shape. If the price of wheat goes up, the quantity of wheat demanded goes down, and if the price of wheat goes down, the quantity of wheat demanded goes up. But the demand curve for the output of a single wheat farmer is *not* downward sloping: It is a horizontal line. If an individual wheat farmer tries to increase the price he charges for his wheat, the quantity demanded falls to zero because buyers will purchase from one of the other 150,000 wheat farmers. But any one farmer can sell as much wheat as he or she can produce without needing to cut the price. Both of these

features of this market result from each wheat farmer being very small relative to the overall market for wheat.

When we draw graphs of the wheat market, we usually show the market equilibrium quantity in millions or billions of bushels. When we draw graphs of the demand for wheat produced by one farmer, we usually show the quantity produced in smaller amounts, such as thousands of bushels. It is important to remember this difference in scale when interpreting these graphs.

Finally, it is not just wheat farmers who have horizontal demand curves for their products; any firm in a perfectly competitive market faces a horizontal demand curve.

Your Turn: Test your understanding by doing related problem 1.7 on page 442 at the end of this chapter. MyLab Economics Study Plan

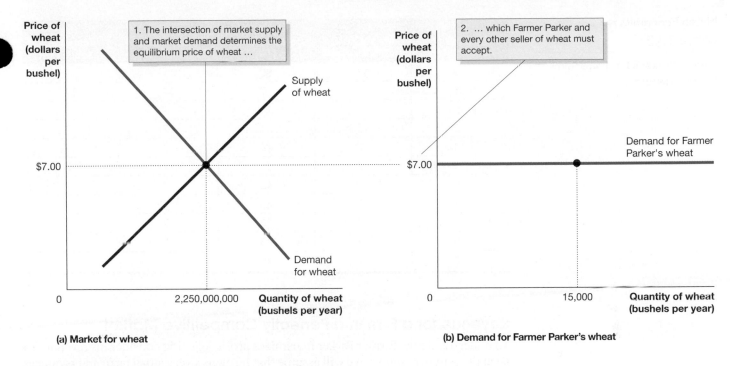

MyLab Economics Animation

Figure 12.2   **The Market Demand for Wheat versus the Demand for One Farmer's Wheat**

In a perfectly competitive market, price is determined by the intersection of market demand and market supply. In panel (a), the demand and supply curves for wheat intersect at a price of $7 per bushel. An individual wheat farmer like Farmer Parker cannot affect the market price for wheat. Therefore, as panel (b) shows, the demand curve for Farmer Parker's wheat is a horizontal line. To understand this figure, it is important to notice that the scales on the horizontal axes in the two panels are very different. In panel (a), the equilibrium quantity of wheat is 2.25 *billion* bushels, and in panel (b), Farmer Parker is producing only 15,000 bushels of wheat.

Panel (b) of Figure 12.2 shows the demand curve for Farmer Parker's wheat, which is a horizontal line. By viewing these graphs side by side, you can see that the price Farmer Parker receives for his wheat in panel (b) is determined by the interaction of all sellers and all buyers of wheat in the wheat market in panel (a). Notice, however, that the scales on the horizontal axes in the two panels are very different. In panel (a), the equilibrium quantity of wheat is 2.25 *billion* bushels. In panel (b), Farmer Parker is producing only 15,000 bushels, or less than 0.001 percent of market output. We need to use different scales in the two panels so we can display both of them on one page. Keep in mind this key point: Farmer Parker's output of wheat is very small relative to the total market output.   **MyLab Economics** Concept Check   **MyLab Economics** Study Plan

12.2 How a Firm Maximizes Profit in a Perfectly Competitive Market

LEARNING OBJECTIVE: Explain how a firm maximizes profit in a perfectly competitive market.

We have seen that Farmer Parker cannot control the price of his wheat. In this situation, how does he decide how much wheat to produce? We assume that Farmer Parker's objective is to maximize profit. This assumption is reasonable for most firms, most of the time. Remember that **profit** is the difference between total revenue (*TR*) and total cost (*TC*):

Profit Total revenue minus total cost.

$$\text{Profit} = TR - TC.$$

To maximize his profit, Farmer Parker should produce the quantity of wheat where the difference between the total revenue he receives and his total cost is as large as possible.

MyLab Economics Animation

Table 12.2

Farmer Parker's Revenue from Wheat Farming

(1) Number of Bushels (Q)	(2) Market Price (per bushel) (P)	(3) Total Revenue (TR)	(4) Average Revenue (AR)	(5) Marginal Revenue (MR)
0	$7	$0	—	—
1	7	7	$7	$7
2	7	14	7	7
3	7	21	7	7
4	7	28	7	7
5	7	35	7	7
6	7	42	7	7
7	7	49	7	7
8	7	56	7	7
9	7	63	7	7
10	7	70	7	7

Revenue for a Firm in a Perfectly Competitive Market

To understand how Farmer Parker maximizes profit, let's first consider his revenue. To keep the numbers simple, we will assume that he owns a very small farm and produces at most 10 bushels of wheat per year. Table 12.2 shows the revenue Farmer Parker will earn from selling various quantities of wheat if the market price for wheat is $7.

The third column in Table 12.2 shows that Farmer Parker's *total revenue* rises by $7 for every additional bushel he sells because he can sell as many bushels as he wants at the market price of $7 per bushel. The fourth and fifth columns in the table show Farmer Parker's *average revenue* and *marginal revenue* from selling wheat. His **average revenue (AR)** equals his total revenue divided by the quantity of bushels he sells. For example, if he sells 5 bushels for a total of $35, his average revenue is $35/5 = $7. Notice that his average revenue is also equal to the market price of $7. In fact, for any level of output, a firm's average revenue is always equal to the market price. To see why, first note that total revenue equals price times quantity ($TR = P \times Q$), and average revenue equals total revenue divided by quantity ($AR = TR/Q$). Therefore, $AR = TR/Q = (P \times Q)/Q = P$.

Average revenue (AR) Total revenue divided by the quantity of the product sold.

Farmer Parker's **marginal revenue (MR)** is the change in his total revenue from selling one more bushel:

Marginal revenue (MR) The change in total revenue from selling one more unit of a product.

$$\text{Marginal revenue} = \frac{\text{Change in total revenue}}{\text{Change in quantity}}, \text{ or } MR = \frac{\Delta TR}{\Delta Q}.$$

Each additional bushel Farmer Parker sells always adds $7 to his total revenue, so his marginal revenue is $7. Farmer Parker's marginal revenue is $7 per bushel because he is selling wheat in a perfectly competitive market and can sell as much as he wants at the market price. In fact, Farmer Parker's marginal revenue and average revenue are both equal to the market price. This point is important: *For a firm in a perfectly competitive market, price is equal to both average revenue and marginal revenue.* MyLab Economics Concept Check

Determining the Profit-Maximizing Level of Output

To determine how Farmer Parker can maximize profit, we have to consider his costs as well as his revenue. A wheat farmer has many costs, including the costs of seed and fertilizer, as well as the wages of farm workers. In Table 12.3, we bring together the revenue data from Table 12.2 with cost data for Farmer Parker's farm. Recall that a firm's *marginal cost* is the increase in total cost resulting from producing another unit of output.

We calculate profit in the fourth column by subtracting total cost in the third column from total revenue in the second column. The fourth column shows that as long as Farmer Parker produces between 3 and 9 bushels of wheat, he will earn a profit.

MyLab Economics Animation

Table 12.3

Farmer Parker's Profit from Wheat Farming

(1) Quantity (bushels) (Q)	(2) Total Revenue (TR)	(3) Total Cost (TC)	(4) Profit (TR – TC)	(5) Marginal Revenue (MR)	(6) Marginal Cost (MC)
0	$0.00	$10.00	–$10.00	—	—
1	7.00	14.00	–7.00	$7.00	$4.00
2	14.00	16.50	–2.50	7.00	2.50
3	21.00	18.50	2.50	7.00	2.00
4	28.00	21.00	7.00	7.00	2.50
5	35.00	24.50	10.50	7.00	3.50
6	42.00	29.00	13.00	7.00	4.50
7	49.00	35.50	13.50	7.00	6.50
8	56.00	44.50	11.50	7.00	9.00
9	63.00	56.50	6.50	7.00	12.00
10	70.00	72.00	–2.00	7.00	15.50

His maximum profit is $13.50, which he will earn by producing 7 bushels of wheat. Because Farmer Parker wants to maximize his profit, we would expect him to produce 7 bushels of wheat. Producing more than 7 bushels reduces his profit. For example, if he produces 8 bushels of wheat, his profit will decline from $13.50 to $11.50. The values for marginal cost given in the last column of the table help us understand why Farmer Parker's profit will decline if he produces more than 7 bushels of wheat: After the seventh bushel of wheat, rising marginal cost causes Farmer Parker's profit to decline.

In fact, comparing the marginal cost and marginal revenue at each level of output is an alternative method of calculating Farmer Parker's profit. We illustrate the two methods of calculating profit in Figure 12.3. We show the total revenue and total cost approach in panel (a) and the marginal revenue and marginal cost approach in panel (b).

(a) Total revenue, total cost, and profit

(b) Marginal revenue and marginal cost

MyLab Economics Animation

Figure 12.3   **The Profit-Maximizing Level of Output**

In panel (a), Farmer Parker maximizes his profit where the positive vertical distance between total revenue and total cost is the largest, which occurs at an output of 7 bushels. Panel (b) shows that Farmer Parker's marginal revenue (MR) is equal to a constant $7 per bushel. He maximizes profit by producing wheat up to the point where the marginal revenue of the last bushel produced is equal to its marginal cost, or MR = MC. In this case, at no level of output does marginal revenue exactly equal marginal cost. The closest Farmer Parker can come is to produce 7 bushels of wheat. He will not want to continue to produce once marginal cost is greater than marginal revenue because that would reduce his profit. Panels (a) and (b) show alternative ways of thinking about how Farmer Parker can determine the profit-maximizing quantity of wheat to produce.

Total revenue is a straight line on the graph in panel (a) because total revenue increases at a constant rate of $7 for each additional bushel sold. Farmer Parker's profit is maximized when the vertical distance between the line representing total revenue and the total cost curve is as large as possible. Just as we saw in Table 12.3, his maximum profit occurs at an output of 7 bushels.

The last two columns of Table 12.3 show the marginal revenue (MR) Farmer Parker receives from selling another bushel of wheat and his marginal cost (MC) of producing another bushel of wheat. Panel (b) of Figure 12.3 plots Farmer Parker's marginal revenue and marginal cost. Because marginal revenue is always equal to $7, it is a horizontal line at the market price. We have already seen that the demand curve for a perfectly competitive firm is also a horizontal line at the market price. *Therefore, the marginal revenue curve for a perfectly competitive firm is the same as its demand curve.* Farmer Parker's marginal cost of producing wheat first falls and then rises, following the usual pattern we discussed in Chapter 11, Section 11.4.

We know from panel (a) that profit is at a maximum at 7 bushels of wheat. In panel (b), profit is also at a maximum at 7 bushels of wheat. To understand why profit is maximized at the level of output where marginal revenue equals marginal cost, remember this key economic principle: *Optimal decisions are made at the margin.* Firms use this principle to decide the quantity of a good to produce. In deciding how much wheat to produce, Farmer Parker needs to compare the marginal revenue he earns from selling another bushel of wheat to the marginal cost of producing that bushel. The difference between the marginal revenue and the marginal cost is the additional profit (or loss) from producing one more bushel. As long as marginal revenue is greater than marginal cost, Farmer Parker's profit is increasing, and he will want to expand production. For example, he will not stop producing at 6 bushels of wheat because producing and selling the seventh bushel adds $7.00 to his revenue but only $6.50 to his cost, so his profit increases by $0.50. He wants to continue producing until the marginal revenue he receives from selling another bushel is equal to the marginal cost of producing it. At that level of output, he will make no *additional* profit by selling another bushel, so he will have maximized his profit.

By inspecting Table 12.3, we can see that there is no level of output at which marginal revenue exactly equals marginal cost. The closest Farmer Parker can come is to produce 7 bushels of wheat. He will not want to produce additional wheat once marginal cost is greater than marginal revenue because doing so would reduce his profit. For example, the eighth bushel of wheat adds $9.00 to his cost but only $7.00 to his revenue, so producing the eighth bushel *reduces* his profit by $2.00.

From the information in Table 12.3 and Figure 12.3, we can draw the following conclusions:

1. The profit-maximizing level of output is where the positive difference between total revenue and total cost is the greatest.
2. The profit-maximizing level of output is also where marginal revenue equals marginal cost, or $MR = MC$.

Both of these conclusions are true for any firm, whether or not it is in a perfectly competitive industry. We can draw one other conclusion about profit maximization that is true only of firms in perfectly competitive industries: For a firm in a perfectly competitive industry, price is equal to marginal revenue, or $P = MR$. So we can restate the $MR = MC$ condition as $P = MC$.

 ## 12.3 Illustrating Profit or Loss on the Cost Curve Graph

LEARNING OBJECTIVE: Use graphs to show a firm's profit or loss.

We have seen that profit is the difference between total revenue and total cost. We can also express profit in terms of *average total cost* (ATC). This approach allows us to show profit on the cost curve graph we developed in Chapter 11, Section 11.5.

We need to work through a few steps to determine the relationship between profit and average total cost. Because profit is equal to total revenue (*TR*) minus total cost (*TC*) and total revenue is price multiplied by quantity, we can write the following:

$$\text{Profit} = (P \times Q) - TC.$$

If we divide both sides of this equation by *Q*, we have:

$$\frac{\text{Profit}}{Q} = \frac{(P \times Q)}{Q} - \frac{TC}{Q},$$

or, because *TC/Q* equals *ATC*:

$$\frac{\text{Profit}}{Q} = P - ATC.$$

This equation tells us that profit per unit (or average profit) equals price minus average total cost. Finally, we obtain the equation for the relationship between total profit and average total cost by multiplying by *Q*:

$$\text{Profit} = (P - ATC) \times Q.$$

This equation tells us that a firm's total profit is equal to the difference between price and average total cost multiplied by the quantity produced.

Showing Profit on a Graph

Figure 12.4 shows the relationship between a firm's average total cost and its marginal cost that we discussed in Chapter 11, Section 11.4. In this figure, we also show the firm's marginal revenue curve (which is the same as its demand curve) and the area representing total profit. Using the relationship between profit and average total cost that we just determined, we can say that the area representing total profit has a height equal to (*P* − *ATC*) and a base equal to *Q*. This area is shown by the green-shaded rectangle.   **MyLab Economics** Concept Check

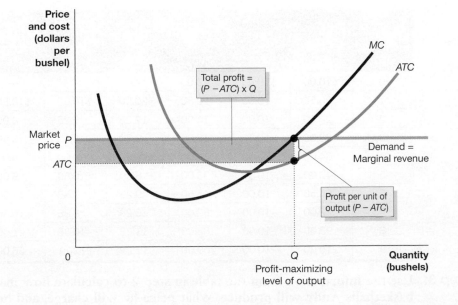

MyLab Economics Animation

Figure 12.4

The Area of Maximum Profit

A firm maximizes profit at the level of output at which marginal revenue equals marginal cost. The difference between price and average total cost equals profit per unit of output. Total profit equals profit per unit multiplied by the number of units produced. Total profit is represented by the area of the green-shaded rectangle, which has a height equal to (*P* − *ATC*) and a width equal to *Q*.

Solved Problem 12.3

Determining Profit-Maximizing Price and Quantity

Suppose that Andy sells basketballs in the perfectly competitive basketball market. His output per day and his costs are as follows:

Output per Day	Total Cost
0	$10.00
1	20.50
2	24.50
3	28.00
4	34.00
5	43.00
6	55.50
7	72.00
8	93.00
9	119.00

a. Suppose the current equilibrium price in the basketball market is $12.50. To maximize profit, how many basketballs will Andy produce, what price will he charge, and how much profit (or loss) will he earn? Draw a graph to illustrate your answer. Label your graph clearly and include Andy's demand, ATC, AVC, MC, and MR curves; the price he is charging; the quantity he is producing; and the area representing his profit (or loss).

b. Suppose the equilibrium price of basketballs falls to $6.00. Now how many basketballs will Andy produce, what price will he charge, and how much profit (or loss) will he make? Draw a graph to illustrate this situation, using the instructions in part (a).

Solving the Problem

Step 1: Review the chapter material. This problem is about using cost curve graphs to analyze perfectly competitive firms, so you may want to review the section "Illustrating Profit or Loss on the Cost Curve Graph," which begins on page 422.

Step 2: Calculate Andy's marginal cost, average total cost, and average variable cost. To maximize profit, Andy will produce the level of output where marginal revenue is equal to marginal cost. We can calculate marginal cost from the information given in the following table. We can also calculate average total cost and average variable cost in order to draw the required graph. Average total cost (ATC) equals total cost (TC) divided by the level of output (Q). Average variable cost (AVC) equals variable cost (VC) divided by output (Q). To calculate variable cost, recall that total cost equals variable cost plus fixed cost. When output equals zero, total cost equals fixed cost. In this case, fixed cost equals $10.00.

Output per Day (Q)	Total Cost (TC)	Fixed Cost (FC)	Variable Cost (VC)	Average Total Cost (ATC)	Average Variable Cost (AVC)	Marginal Cost (MC)
0	$10.00	$10.00	$0.00	—	—	—
1	20.50	10.00	10.50	$20.50	$10.50	$10.50
2	24.50	10.00	14.50	12.25	7.25	4.00
3	28.00	10.00	18.00	9.33	6.00	3.50
4	34.00	10.00	24.00	8.50	6.00	6.00
5	43.00	10.00	33.00	8.60	6.60	9.00
6	55.50	10.00	45.50	9.25	7.58	12.50
7	72.00	10.00	62.00	10.29	8.86	16.50
8	93.00	10.00	83.00	11.63	10.38	21.00
9	119.00	10.00	109.00	13.22	12.11	26.00

Step 3: Use the information from the table in step 2 to calculate how many basketballs Andy will produce, what price he will charge, and how

much profit he will earn if the market price of basketballs is $12.50. Andy's marginal revenue is equal to the market price of $12.50. Marginal revenue equals marginal cost when Andy produces 6 basketballs per day. So, Andy will produce 6 basketballs per day and charge a price of $12.50 per basketball. Andy's profit is equal to his total revenue minus his total costs. His total revenue equals the 6 basketballs he sells multiplied by the $12.50 price, or $75.00. So, his profit equals $75.00 − $55.50 = $19.50.

Step 4: **Use the information from the table in step 2 to illustrate your answer to part (a) with a graph.**

Step 5: **Calculate how many basketballs Andy will produce, what price he will charge, and how much profit he will earn when the market price of basketballs is $6.00.** Referring to the table in step 2, we can see that marginal revenue equals marginal cost when Andy produces 4 basketballs per day. He charges the market price of $6.00 per basketball. His total revenue is only $24.00, while his total costs are $34.00, so he will have a loss of $10.00. (Can we be sure that Andy will continue to produce even though he is operating at a loss? We answer this question in Section 12.4.)

Step 6: **Illustrate your answer to part (b) with a graph.**

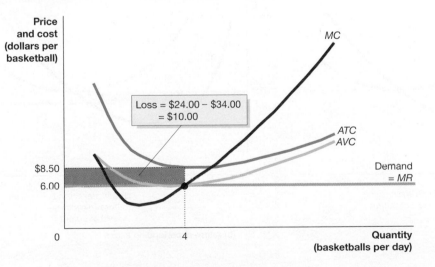

Your Turn: For more practice, do related problems 3.3 and 3.4 on pages 443–444 at the end of this chapter. MyLab Economics Study Plan

Don't Let This Happen to You

Remember That Firms Maximize Their Total Profit, *Not* Their Profit per Unit

A student examines the following graph and argues: "I think that a firm will want to produce at Q_1, not Q_2. At Q_1, the distance between price and average total cost is the greatest. So at Q_1, the firm will be maximizing its profit per unit." Briefly explain whether you agree with the student's argument.

The student's argument is incorrect because firms are interested in maximizing their *total* profit, not their profit per unit. We know that profit is not maximized at Q_1 because at that level of output, marginal revenue is greater than marginal cost. A firm can always increase its profit by producing any unit that adds more to its revenue than it does to its costs. Only when the firm has expanded production to Q_2 will it have produced every unit for which marginal revenue is greater than marginal cost. At that level of output, it will have maximized profit.

Your Turn: Test your understanding by doing related problem 3.5 on page 444 at the end of this chapter. MyLab Economics Study Plan

Illustrating When a Firm Is Breaking Even or Operating at a Loss

We have already seen that to maximize profit, a firm produces the level of output where marginal revenue equals marginal cost. But will the firm actually make a profit at that level of output? It depends on the relationship of price to average total cost. There are three possibilities:

1. $P > ATC$, which means the firm makes a profit
2. $P = ATC$, which means the firm *breaks even* (its total cost equals its total revenue)
3. $P < ATC$, which means the firm experiences a loss

Figure 12.4 on page 423 shows the first possibility, where the firm makes a profit. Panels (a) and (b) of Figure 12.5 show the situations where a firm breaks even

(a) A firm breaking even

(b) A firm experiencing a loss

MyLab Economics Animation

Figure 12.5   **A Firm Breaking Even and a Firm Experiencing a Loss**

In panel (a), price equals average total cost, and the firm breaks even because its total revenue will be equal to its total cost. In this situation, the firm makes zero economic profit. In panel (b), price is below average total cost, and the firm experiences a loss. The loss is represented by the area of the red-shaded rectangle, which has a height equal to $(ATC - P)$ and a width equal to Q.

or suffers a loss. In panel (a) of Figure 12.5, at the level of output at which $MR = MC$, price is equal to average total cost. Therefore, total revenue is equal to total cost, and the firm will break even, making zero economic profit. In panel (b), at the level of output at which $MR = MC$, price is less than average total cost. Therefore, total revenue is less than total cost, and the firm suffers a loss. In this case, maximizing profit amounts to *minimizing* loss.   MyLab Economics Concept Check   MyLab Economics Study Plan

Apply the Concept   MyLab Economics Video

Losing Money in the Restaurant Business

In a market system, a good or service becomes available to consumers only if an entrepreneur brings the product to market. Thousands of new businesses open every week in the United States. Each new business represents an entrepreneur risking his or her funds to earn a profit. Of course, there are no guarantees of success, and many new businesses experience losses rather than earn the profits their owners hoped for.

The restaurant business is intensely competitive, particularly in cities experiencing strong economic growth, where diners have many choices available and landlords can choose to rent their retail space to many alternative businesses. In 2017, restaurants in a number of cities had difficulty avoiding losses due primarily to rising costs. Fixed costs were rising because landlords were increasing rents, and marginal costs were rising because of increasing wages.

In big cities, restaurants compete with other small businesses for space. During periods of strong economic growth, landlords typically increase rents. The owner of one restaurant in New York City's Flatiron district announced that he was closing his restaurant after 15 years in business because "the lease is up and the rent is too damn high." Restaurants in some cities also were experiencing higher wage costs as a result of increases in the minimum wage and a federal requirement that businesses pay some managers higher wages once they had worked 40 hours in a week. With wages and salaries accounting for about 35 percent of the typical restaurant's costs, rising wages are a "punch to the gut," in the words of one restaurant manager.

There are many Asian restaurants in New York City. The following figure shows the effect of higher costs on a representative restaurant. At a price of $16 per bowl of ramen noodles (remember that this is New York!), the restaurant breaks even because at its profit-maximizing quantity of Q_1, its average total cost, shown by ATC_1 in the figure, also equals $16. An increase in the wages the restaurant pays its workers causes the marginal cost curve to shift up from MC_1 to MC_2 because the cost of preparing and serving an additional bowl of ramen has increased. The higher labor cost also increases the restaurant's average variable cost of making ramen and, therefore, its average total cost curve. An

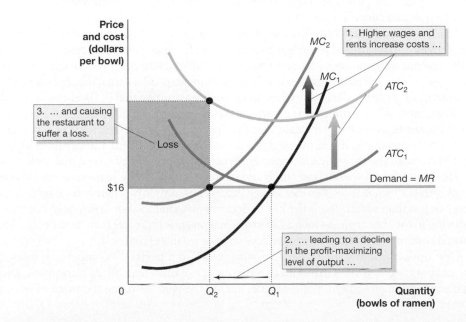

increase in rent increases the restaurant's average fixed cost. The combination of higher average variable cost and higher average fixed cost causes the restaurant's average total cost curve to shift up from ATC_1 to ATC_2. The restaurant's profit-maximizing quantity of bowls of ramen declines from Q_1 to Q_2, and, because average total cost is now greater than the price of \$16, the restaurant is suffering a loss, shown by the red-shaded rectangle in the figure.

Why wouldn't a restaurant in this situation raise its price at least to the level needed to break even? There are many Asian restaurants in New York City selling ramen noodles, and we have already seen that any firm that tries to raise the price of its product above the market price loses customers to competing firms. As the owner of the Ganso Japanese restaurants in Brooklyn put it after closing two of his locations: "You can't charge \$30 for a bowl of ramen." If losses of this type become widespread, it's unclear what will happen to restaurants in New York and other large cities, particularly to restaurants that are not part of national chains. William Wheaton, an economist at the Massachusetts Institute of Technology, gives one likely outcome: "As costs rise, the guys with deep pockets hang in there for a while, and the others close up." When an independent restaurant closes, the entrepreneur who started that business likely loses most of his or her investment.

Sources: Florence Fabricant, "Craftbar in Flatiron District Will Close This Spring," *New York Times*, February 3, 2017; Karen Stabiner, "Is New York Too Expensive for Restaurateurs? We Do the Math," *New York Times*, October 25, 2016; and Cara Eisenpress, "Restaurants Are Seeing Their Profits Devoured by Landlords and Labor Costs," crainsnewyork.com, January 23, 2017.

MyLab Economics Study Plan

Your Turn: Test your understanding by doing related problem 3.7 on page 444 at the end of this chapter.

12.4 Deciding Whether to Produce or to Shut Down in the Short Run

LEARNING OBJECTIVE: Explain why firms may shut down temporarily.

In panel (b) of Figure 12.5, we assumed that the firm would continue to produce even though it was operating at a loss. In the short run, a firm experiencing a loss has two choices:

1. Continue to produce
2. Stop production by shutting down temporarily

In many cases, a firm experiencing a loss will consider stopping production temporarily. Even during a temporary shutdown, however, a firm must still pay its fixed costs. For example, if the firm has signed a lease for its building, the landlord will expect to receive a monthly rent payment, even if the firm is not producing anything that month. Therefore, if a firm does not produce, it will suffer a loss equal to its fixed cost. This loss is the maximum the firm will accept as a result of producing. The firm will shut down if producing would cause it to lose an amount greater than its fixed cost.

A firm can reduce its loss below the amount of its total fixed cost by continuing to produce, provided that the total revenue it receives is greater than its variable cost. A firm can use the revenue over and above the amount of its variable cost to cover part of its fixed cost. In this case, a firm will have a smaller loss by continuing to produce than if it shuts down.

In analyzing a firm's decision to shut down, we are assuming that its fixed costs are *sunk costs*. Remember that a **sunk cost** is a cost that has already been paid and cannot be recovered. We assume, as is usually the case, that the firm cannot recover its fixed costs by shutting down. For example, if a farmer has taken out a loan to buy land, the farmer is legally required to make the monthly loan payment whether he grows any wheat that season or not. The farmer has to spend those funds and cannot get them back, *so the farmer should treat his sunk costs as irrelevant to his short-run decision making*. For any firm, whether total revenue is greater or less than *variable cost* is the key to deciding whether to shut down or to continue producing in the short run. As long as a firm's total revenue is greater than its variable cost, it should continue to produce no matter how large or small its fixed cost.

One option not available to a firm with losses in a perfectly competitive market is to raise its price. If the firm did raise its price, it would lose all its customers, and its sales would drop to zero. For example, during the past 20 years, the price of wheat

Sunk cost A cost that has already been paid and cannot be recovered.

has usually been high enough for a typical wheat farmer in the United States to at least break even. But in 2017, the price of wheat fell to about $4 per bushel from about $7 per bushel three years earlier. For some wheat farmers, $4 per bushel was below their break-even point. But any wheat farmer who tried to raise the price to $7 per bushel would have seen his or her sales quickly disappear because buyers could purchase all the wheat they wanted at $4 per bushel from the thousands of other wheat farmers.

The Supply Curve of a Firm in the Short Run

Remember that the supply curve for a firm tells us how many units of a product the firm is willing to sell at any given price. Notice that the marginal cost curve for a firm in a perfectly competitive market tells us the same thing. The firm will produce at the level of output where $MR = MC$. Because price equals marginal revenue for a firm in a perfectly competitive market, the firm will produce where $P = MC$. For any given price, we can determine from the marginal cost curve the quantity of output the firm will supply. *Therefore, a perfectly competitive firm's marginal cost curve is also its supply curve.* There is, however, an important qualification to this fact. We have seen that if a firm is experiencing a loss, it will shut down if its total revenue is less than its variable cost:

$$\text{Total revenue} < \text{Variable cost,}$$

or, in symbols:

$$(P \times Q) < VC.$$

If we divide both sides by Q, we have the result that the firm will shut down if:

$$P < AVC.$$

If the price drops below average variable cost, the firm will have a smaller loss if it shuts down and produces no output. So, *the firm's marginal cost curve is its supply curve only for prices at or above average variable cost.*

Recall that the marginal cost curve intersects the average variable cost where the average variable cost curve is at its minimum point. Therefore, as shown in Figure 12.6, the firm's supply curve is its marginal cost curve above the minimum point of the average variable cost curve. For prices below minimum average variable cost (P_{MIN}), the firm will shut down, and its output will drop to zero. The minimum point on the average variable cost curve is called the **shutdown point**, and it occurs at the output level Q_{SD}. The dark red line in Figure 12.6 shows the supply curve for the firm in the short run. **MyLab Economics** Concept Check

Shutdown point The minimum point on a firm's average variable cost curve; if the price falls below this point, the firm shuts down production in the short run.

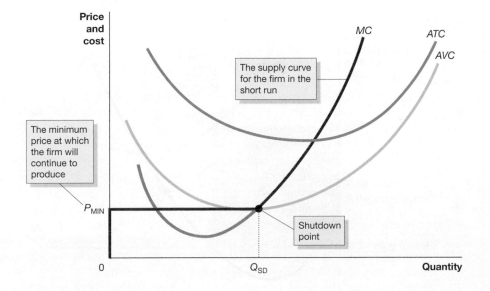

MyLab Economics Animation

Figure 12.6

The Firm's Short-Run Supply Curve

Because price equals marginal revenue for a firm in a perfectly competitive market, the firm will produce where $P = MC$. For any given price, we can determine the quantity of output the firm will supply from the marginal cost curve, so the marginal cost curve is the firm's supply curve. But the firm will shut down if the price falls below average variable cost. The marginal cost curve crosses the average variable cost at the firm's shutdown point at the output level Q_{SD}. For prices below P_{MIN}, the supply curve is a vertical line along the price axis, which shows that the firm will supply zero output at those prices. The red line is the firm's short-run supply curve.

Solved Problem 12.4

When to Shut Down a Farm

According to an article in the *Wall Street Journal*, a wheat farmer decided to take 170 acres out of production and plant grass on it rather than wheat because "that seemed like his only choice after spending about $6.50 a bushel on seed, fertilizer, fuel, and pesticides to grow wheat last year only to [sell the wheat for] . . . $2.90 a bushel."

a. Are the costs listed in the article variable costs or fixed costs? Briefly explain.

b. Can we calculate the farmer's loss per bushel of wheat from the information given? Briefly explain.

c. Provide an economic explanation for the farmer's decision to take these acres out of production. Illustrate your answer with a graph.

Solving the Problem

Step 1: **Review the chapter material.** This problem is about firms deciding whether to produce when price is below average total cost, so you may want to review the section "Deciding Whether to Produce or to Shut Down in the Short Run," which begins on page 428.

Step 2: **Answer part (a) by explaining whether the listed costs are variable costs or fixed costs.** The more wheat the farmer intends to grow, the more seed, fertilizer, fuel, and pesticides he needs to use. Because the costs of these inputs change as output changes, we can conclude that they are variable costs rather than fixed costs.

Step 3: **Answer part (b) by explaining whether we have enough information to calculate the farmer's loss per bushel of wheat.** His loss per bushel is equal to $P - ATC$. Recall that $ATC = AVC + AFC$. We are given information on the farmer's average variable cost, but not on his average fixed cost. Therefore, we don't have enough information to determine his loss per bushel.

Step 4: **Answer part (c) by providing an economic explanation for the farmer's decision to take the acres out of production.** We've seen that a firm will shut down if $P < AVC$. In that case, a firm will suffer a smaller loss by shutting down than by continuing to produce. We know that the farmer's average variable cost of growing wheat on these acres is $6.50, while the price of wheat is only $2.90. Therefore, the farmer will reduce his loss if he shuts down.

Step 5: **Finish answering the problem by drawing a graph to illustrate your answer from step 4.** Your graph should look like this one.

Note that at the profit-maximizing (in this case, loss-minimizing) level of output, Q_1, the market price of $2.90 per bushel is below the farmer's average variable cost of $6.50. The farmer would need the price of wheat to be P_1 in order to break even. If he were to produce at a price of $2.90, his loss would equal the area of the red-shaded rectangle. We know that this amount is greater than the loss he would suffer by shutting down because the market price is below his average variable cost.

Source: Jesse Newman and Patrick McGroarty, "The Next American Farm Bust Is upon Us," *Wall Street Journal*, February 8, 2017.

Your Turn: Test your understanding by doing related problems 4.8, 4.9, and 4.10 on page 446 at the end of this chapter.

MyLab Economics Study Plan

The Market Supply Curve in a Perfectly Competitive Industry

The market demand curve is determined by adding up the quantity demanded by each consumer in the market at each price (see Chapter 10, Section 10.2). Similarly, the market supply curve is determined by adding up the quantity supplied by each firm in the market at each price. Each firm's marginal cost curve tells us how much that firm will supply at each price. So, the market supply curve can be derived directly from the marginal cost curves of the firms in the market. Panel (a) of Figure 12.7 shows the marginal cost curve for one wheat farmer. At a price of $7, this wheat farmer supplies 15,000 bushels of wheat. If every wheat farmer supplies the same amount of wheat at this price

(a) Individual firm supply

(b) Market supply

MyLab Economics Animation

Figure 12.7 **Firm Supply and Market Supply**

We can derive the market supply curve by adding up the quantity that each firm in the market is willing to supply at each price. In panel (a), one wheat farmer is willing to supply 15,000 bushels of wheat at a price of $7 per bushel. If every wheat farmer supplies the same amount of wheat at this price and if there are 150,000 wheat farmers, the total amount of wheat supplied at a price of $7 will equal 15,000 bushels per farmer × 150,000 farmers = 2.25 billion bushels of wheat. This amount is one point on the market supply curve for wheat shown in panel (b). We can find the other points on the market supply curve by determining how much wheat each farmer is willing to supply at each price.

and if there are 150,000 wheat farmers, the total quantity of wheat supplied at a price of $7 will be:

15,000 bushels per farmer × 150,000 farms = 2.25 billion bushels of wheat.

Panel (b) shows a price of $7 and a quantity of 2.25 billion bushels as a point on the market supply curve for wheat. In reality, of course, not all wheat farms are alike. Some wheat farms supply more at the market price than the typical farm; other wheat farms supply less. The key point is that we can derive the market supply curve by adding up the quantity that each firm in the market is willing and able to supply at each price.

MyLab Economics Study Plan

MyLab Economics Concept Check

12.5 "If Everyone Can Do It, You Can't Make Money at It": The Entry and Exit of Firms in the Long Run

LEARNING OBJECTIVE: Explain how entry and exit ensure that perfectly competitive firms earn zero economic profit in the long run.

In the long run, unless a firm can cover all its costs, it will shut down and exit the industry. In a market system, firms continually enter and exit industries. In this section, we will see how profits and losses provide signals to firms that lead to entry and exit.

Economic Profit and the Entry or Exit Decision

Let's look more closely at how economists characterize the profit earned by the owners of a firm. Suppose Sacha Gillette decides to start her own business. After considering her skills and interests and preparing a business plan, she decides to start a cage-free egg farm rather than a restaurant or clothing boutique. After 10 years of effort, Sacha has saved $50,000, and she is able to borrow another $700,000 from a bank. With these funds, she buys the land, equipment, and chickens necessary to start her farm. She intends to sell the eggs in a local farmers' market. When someone invests her own funds in her firm, the opportunity cost to the firm is the return the funds would have earned in their best alternative use (see Chapter 11, Section 11.2). If Farmer Gillette could have earned a 10 percent return on her $50,000 in savings in their best alternative use—which might have been, for example, as a down payment on a small restaurant—then her egg business incurs a $5,000 opportunity cost. We can also think of this $5,000 as being the minimum amount that Farmer Gillette needs to earn on her $50,000 investment in her farm to remain in the industry in the long run.

Table 12.4 lists Farmer Gillette's costs. In addition to her explicit costs, we assume that she has two implicit costs: the $5,000 that represents the opportunity cost of the funds she invested in her farm and the $30,000 salary she could have earned managing someone else's farm instead of her own. Her total costs are $90,000. If the market

Table 12.4

Farmer Gillette's Costs per Year

Explicit Costs	
Water	$10,000
Wages	18,000
Fertilizer	12,000
Electricity	5,000
Payment on bank loan	10,000
Implicit Costs	
Forgone salary	30,000
Opportunity cost of the $50,000 she has invested in her farm	5,000
Total cost	**$90,000**

price of cage-free eggs is $3 per dozen and Farmer Gillette sells 50,000 dozen, her total revenue will be $150,000, and her economic profit will be $60,000 (total revenue of $150,000 minus total costs of $90,000). Recall that **economic profit** equals a firm's revenues minus all its costs, implicit and explicit.

Economic profit A firm's revenues minus all its costs, implicit and explicit.

Economic Profit Leads to Entry of New Firms
Unfortunately, Farmer Gillette is unlikely to earn an economic profit for very long. Suppose other farmers are just breaking even by selling regular eggs. In that case, they will have an incentive to switch to selling cage-free eggs so they can begin earning an economic profit. As we saw in the chapter opener, in recent years more farmers have been switching from producing eggs using conventional methods to using cage-free methods, in the hope of earning a higher profit. Remember that the more firms there are in an industry, the farther to the right the market supply curve is. Panel (a) of Figure 12.8 shows that as more farmers begin selling cage-free eggs, the market supply curve shifts to the right. Farmers will continue entering the market until the market supply curve has shifted from S_1 to S_2.

With the supply curve at S_2, the market price will fall to $2 per dozen. Panel (b) shows the effect on Farmer Gillette, whom we assume has the same costs as other egg farmers. As the market price falls from $3 to $2 per dozen, Farmer Gillette's demand curve shifts down, from D_1 to D_2. In the new equilibrium, Farmer Gillette is selling 40,000 dozen eggs, at a price of $2 per dozen. She and the other egg farmers are no longer earning any economic profit. They are just breaking even, and the return on their investment is just covering the opportunity cost of these funds. New farmers will stop entering the market because the rate of return from selling cage-free eggs is now no better than they can earn by selling regular eggs.

(a) Market for cage-free eggs sold in farmers' markets

(b) Farmer Gillette's farm

MyLab Economics Animation

Figure 12.8   **The Effect of Entry on Economic Profit**

Initially, Farmer Gillette and other farmers selling cage-free eggs are able to charge $3 per dozen and earn an economic profit. Farmer Gillette's economic profit is represented by the area of the green-shaded rectangle in panel (b). Panel (a) shows that as other farmers begin to sell cage-free eggs, the market supply curve shifts to the right, from S_1 to S_2, and the market price drops to $2 per dozen. Panel (b) shows that the falling price causes Farmer Gillette's demand curve to shift down from D_1 to D_2, and she reduces her output from 50,000 dozen eggs to 40,000. At the new market price of $2 per dozen, cage-free egg farmers are just breaking even: Their total revenue is equal to their total cost, and their economic profit is zero. Notice the difference in scale between the graphs in panels (a) and (b).

Will Farmer Gillette continue to sell cage-free eggs even though she is just breaking even? She will because she earns as high a return on her investment as she could earn elsewhere. It may seem strange that new firms will continue to enter a market until all economic profit is eliminated and that established firms remain in a market despite not earning any economic profit. But it seems strange only because we are used to thinking in terms of accounting profit rather than *economic* profit. Remember that accounting rules generally require that only explicit costs be included on a firm's financial statements. The opportunity cost of the funds Farmer Gillette invested in her farm—$5,000—and her forgone salary—$30,000—are economic costs, but neither is an accounting cost. So, although an accountant would see Farmer Gillette as earning a profit of $35,000, an economist would see her as just breaking even. Farmer Gillette must pay attention to her accounting profit when preparing her financial statements and when paying her income tax. But because economic profit takes into account all her costs, it gives a more accurate indication of the financial health of her farm.

Economic loss The situation in which a firm's total revenue is less than its total cost, including all implicit costs.

Economic Losses Lead to Exit of Firms Suppose some consumers decide that they no longer want to eat eggs, whether cage-free or not. Panel (a) of Figure 12.9 shows that the demand curve for cage-free eggs will shift to the left, from D_1 to D_2, and the market price will fall from $2 per dozen to $1.75. Panel (b) shows that as the price falls, a farmer like Sacha Gillette will move down her marginal cost curve to a lower level of output. At the lower level of output and lower price, she will be suffering an **economic loss** because she will not cover all her costs. As long as price is above average variable cost, she will continue to produce in the short run, even when suffering losses. But in the long run, firms will exit an industry if they are unable to cover all their costs. In this case, some farmers will switch from producing eggs to producing other agricultural products or will leave farming.

Panel (c) of Figure 12.9 shows that as firms exit from selling cage-free eggs, the market supply curve shifts to the left. Firms will continue to exit, and the supply curve will continue to shift to the left until the price has risen back to $2 and the market supply curve is at S_2. Panel (d) shows that when the price is back to $2, the remaining firms in the industry will be breaking even. **MyLab Economics** Concept Check

Long-Run Equilibrium in a Perfectly Competitive Market

We have seen that economic profits attract firms to enter an industry. The entry of firms forces down the market price until a typical firm is breaking even. Economic losses cause firms to exit an industry. The exit of firms forces up the equilibrium market price until the typical firm is breaking even. In **long-run competitive equilibrium**, entry and exit have resulted in the typical firm breaking even. In the long run, firms can also vary their scale by becoming larger or smaller (see Chapter 11, Section 11.6). The *long-run average cost curve* shows the lowest cost at which a firm is able to produce a given quantity of output in the long run. So, we would expect that in the long run, competition drives the market price to the minimum point on the typical firm's long-run average cost curve.

Long-run competitive equilibrium The situation in which the entry and exit of firms has resulted in the typical firm breaking even.

The long run in selling cage-free eggs appears to be several years, which is the amount of time it takes farmers to convert from using traditional methods of producing eggs to cage-free methods. As we discussed in the chapter opener, the number of farmers producing cage-free eggs has been rapidly increasing, but cage-free eggs are still more profitable than eggs produced using conventional methods. So we can predict that in the coming years more farmers will begin producing eggs using cage-free methods.

Firms in perfectly competitive markets are in a constant struggle to stay one step ahead of their competitors. They are always looking for new ways to provide a product, such as selling cage-free eggs. It is possible for firms to find ways to earn an economic profit for a while, but competition typically eliminates that profit in just a few years. This observation is not restricted to agriculture. In any perfectly competitive market, an opportunity to make an economic profit never lasts long. As Sharon Oster, an economist at Yale University, has put it, "If everyone can do it, you can't make money at it." **MyLab Economics** Concept Check

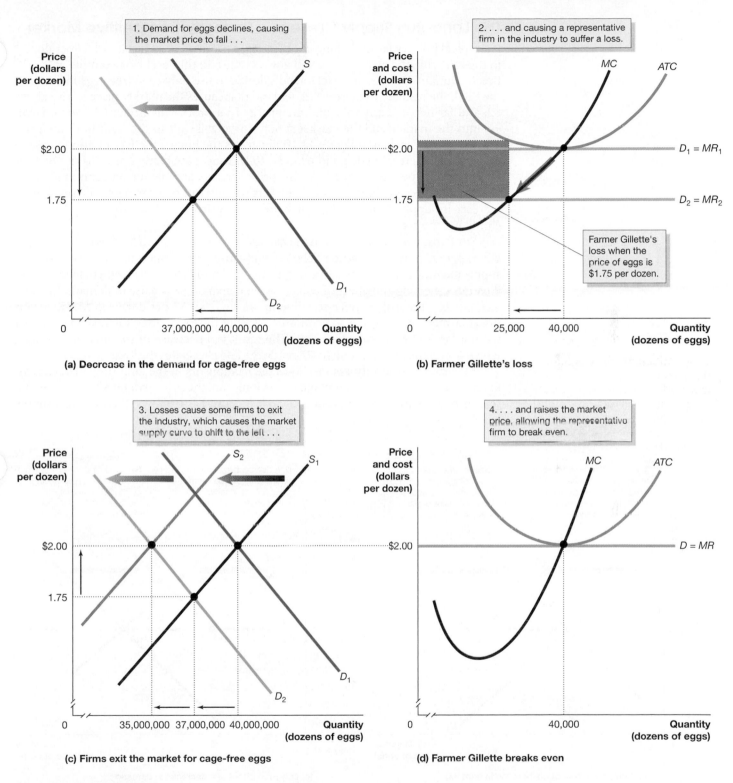

MyLab Economics Animation

Figure 12.9   **The Effect of Exit on Economic Losses**

When the price of cage-free eggs is $2 per dozen, Farmer Gillette and other farmers are breaking even. A total quantity of 40,000,000 dozen eggs is sold in the market. Farmer Gillette sells 40,000 dozen. Panel (a) shows a decline in the demand for cage-free eggs from D_1 to D_2 that reduces the market price to $1.75 per dozen. Panel (b) shows that the falling price causes Farmer Gillette's demand curve to shift down from D_1 to D_2 and her output to fall from 40,000 to 25,000 dozen. At a market price of $1.75 per dozen,

farmers have losses, represented by the area of the red-shaded rectangle. As a result, some farmers will exit the market, which shifts the market supply curve to the left. Panel (c) shows that exit continues until the supply curve has shifted from S_1 to S_2 and the market price has risen from $1.75 back to $2.00. Panel (d) shows that with the price back at $2.00, Farmer Gillette will break even. In the new market equilibrium in panel (c), total sales of cage-free eggs have fallen from 40,000,000 to 35,000,000 dozen.

The Long-Run Supply Curve in a Perfectly Competitive Market

If a typical poultry farmer selling cage-free eggs breaks even at a price of $2 per dozen, in the long run, the market price will always return to this level. For example, if Panera Bread, Dunkin' Donuts, and McDonald's decide to use only cage-free eggs in the food they sell, the result is an increase in demand that causes the market price to rise above $2, and farmers to earn an economic profit. That profit will attract additional farmers into the market, and the market supply curve will shift to the right until the price is back to $2. Panel (a) in Figure 12.10 illustrates the long-run effect of an increase in demand. An increase in demand from D_1 to D_2 causes the market price to rise temporarily from $2 per dozen to $3. At this price, farmers are making an economic profit selling cage-free eggs, but the profit attracts the entry of new farmers. The result is an increase in supply from S_1 to S_2, which forces the price back down to $2 per dozen and eliminates the economic profit.

Similarly, if a decrease in demand causes the market price to fall below $2, farmers will experience an economic loss. The loss will cause some farmers to exit the market, the supply curve will shift to the left, and the price will return to $2. Panel (b) in Figure 12.10 illustrates the long-run effect of a decrease in demand. A decrease in demand from D_1 to D_2 causes the market price to fall temporarily from $2 per dozen to $1.75. At this price, farmers are suffering an economic loss, but the loss causes some farmers to exit the market for selling cage-free eggs. The result is a decrease in supply from S_1 to S_2, which forces the price back up to $2 per dozen and eliminates the loss.

The **long-run supply curve** shows the relationship in the long run between market price and the quantity supplied. In the long run, the price will be $2 per dozen, no matter how many eggs are produced. So, as Figure 12.10 shows, the long-run supply

Long-run supply curve A curve that shows the relationship in the long run between market price and the quantity supplied.

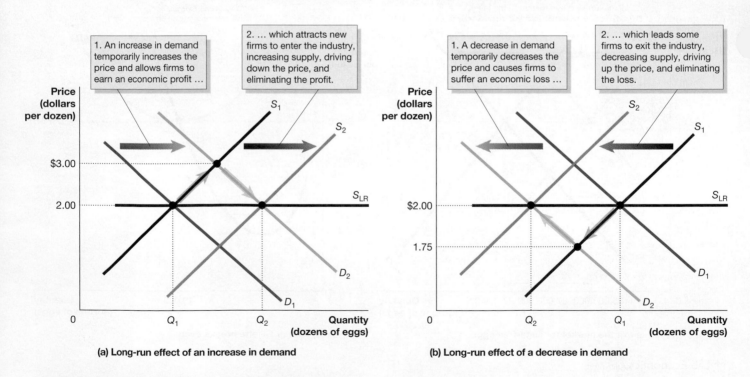

(a) Long-run effect of an increase in demand

(b) Long-run effect of a decrease in demand

MyLab Economics Animation

Figure 12.10 **The Long-Run Supply Curve in a Perfectly Competitive Industry**

Panel (a) shows that an increase in demand for cage-free eggs will lead to a temporary increase in price from $2.00 to $3.00 per dozen, as the market demand curve shifts to the right, from D_1 to D_2. The entry of new firms shifts the market supply curve to the right, from S_1 to S_2, which will cause the price to fall back to its long-run level of $2.00. Panel (b) shows that a decrease in demand will lead to a temporary decrease in price from $2.00

to $1.75 per dozen, as the market demand curve shifts to the left, from D_1 to D_2. The exit of firms shifts the market supply curve to the left, from S_1 to S_2, which causes the price to rise back to its long-run level of $2.00. The long-run supply curve (S_{LR}) shows the relationship between market price and the quantity supplied in the long run. In this case, the long-run supply curve is a horizontal line.

curve (S_{LR}) is a horizontal line at a price of $2. Remember that the price returns to $2 in the long run because at this price, a typical firm in the industry just breaks even. The typical firm breaks even because $2 is at the minimum point on the firm's average total cost curve. We can draw the important conclusion that *in the long run, a perfectly competitive market will supply whatever amount of a good consumers demand at a price determined by the minimum point on the typical firm's average total cost curve.*

Because the position of the long-run supply curve is determined by the minimum point on the typical firm's average total cost curve, anything that raises or lowers the costs of the typical firm in the long run will cause the long-run supply curve to shift. For example, if the cost of the feed for chickens permanently increases enough to add $0.25 per dozen to the average cost of producing cage-free eggs, the long-run supply curve will shift up by $0.25.   **MyLab Economics** Concept Check

Apply the Concept   **MyLab Economics** Video

In the Apple App Store, Easy Entry Makes the Long Run Pretty Short

One reason for the popularity of Apple's iPhones and iPads is the section of Apple's iTunes music and video store devoted to applications (or "apps"). By 2017, sales of apps on iTunes approached $30 billion. Major software companies, as well as individuals writing their first software programs, have posted games, calendars, dictionaries, and many other types of apps to the App Store, for which they receive 30 percent of the revenue their app generates.

But competition in the App Store is intense, particularly for games, with about 750 new games being added to the store *per day*. Hogrocket, a three-person company, developed the game "Tiny Invaders" and began selling it in the App Store in 2011. Initially, the company was successful in selling the app for $2.99. As we have seen, though, when firms earn an economic profit in a market, other firms have a strong economic incentive to enter that market. Competition from new games forced Hogrocket to lower the price of its game to $0.99. At that price, the company was unable to sell enough downloads to break even, and the firm had to shut down.

Economic profit can be rapidly competed away in the iTunes App Store.

With so many games to choose from, many people are unwilling to download one unless they can do so for free. Some app designers have tried the strategy of allowing apps to be downloaded for free while attempting to earn revenue by forcing users to see advertisements before the app opens or while it runs. Many people find these advertisements annoying, though, so developers have begun offering free apps that lack advertisements but where the developers earn revenue from users making in-app purchases. For instance, in the popular game "Candy Crush Saga," users are given free turns. After they have used them up, they can wait 30 minutes for another free turn or they can pay a small amount to immediately receive five more turns. Still, only about 3 percent of people who play these games make any in-app purchases. That leaves developers dependent on "whales," who make $50 to $100 per month in in-app game purchases. Only the best games can attract whale players and survive the intense competition of the App Store.

But even the most popular games eventually find their profitability undermined by competition. For instance, in Supercell's "Clash of Clans" game, players can slowly build up their villages' defenses and their armies for free or they can make an in-app purchase of "gems" to speed up the process. By 2017, Supercell's revenues from in-app purchases had begun to decline, which an article in the *Wall Street Journal* attributed to "fierce competition in the mobile gaming industry." Supercell also was suffering revenue declines from "Clash Royale," its follow-up game to "Clash of Clans." Other firms, including Rovio (maker of "Angry Birds") and Nintendo (maker of "Super Mario Run"), also experienced disappointing revenues from their mobile games.

In a competitive market, earning an economic profit in the long run is extremely difficult. And the ease of entering the market for smartphone and tablet apps has made the long run pretty short.

Leszek Kobusinski/Shutterstock

Sources: Dan Gallagher, "Why Super Mario's Run Was Short," *Wall Street Journal*, January 2, 2017; Matthias Verbergt, "'Clash of Clans' Maker Posts Revenue Fall amid Pokémon Competition," *Wall Street Journal*, February 15, 2017; Adam Satariano, "Angry Birds Maker Rovio May Cut Jobs in Revamp of Functions," bloomberg.com, February 15, 2017; and Sarah E. Needleman, "Mobile-Game Makers Try to Catch More 'Whales' Who Pay for Free Games," *Wall Street Journal*, May 10, 2015.

MyLab Economics Study Plan

Your Turn: Test your understanding by doing related problem 5.8 on page 447 at the end of this chapter.

Increasing-Cost and Decreasing-Cost Industries

Any industry in which the typical firm's average costs do not change as the industry expands production will have a horizontal long-run supply curve, like the one in Figure 12.10 on page 436. These industries, including the egg industry, are called *constant-cost industries*. It's possible, however, for the typical firm's average costs to change as an industry expands.

For example, if an input used in producing a good is available in only limited quantities, the cost of the input will rise as the industry expands. If only a limited amount of land is available on which to grow the grapes to make a certain variety of wine, an increase in demand for wine made from these grapes will result in competition for the land and will drive up its price. As a result, more of the wine will be produced in the long run only if the price rises to cover the typical firm's higher average cost. In this case, the long-run supply curve will slope upward. Industries with upward-sloping long-run supply curves are called *increasing-cost industries*.

Finally, in some cases, the typical firm's costs may fall as the industry expands. Suppose that someone invents a new smartphone that uses as an input a specialized memory chip that is currently produced only in small quantities. If demand for the smartphone increases, firms that produce smartphones will increase their orders for the memory chip. If there are *economies of scale* in producing a good, the average cost of producing it will decline as output increases (see Chapter 11, Section 11.6). If there are economies of scale in producing this memory chip, the average cost of producing it will fall, and competition will result in its price falling as well. This price decline, in turn, will lower the average cost of producing the new smartphone. In the long run, competition will force the price of the smartphone to fall to the level of the typical firm's new lower average cost. In this case, the long-run supply curve will slope downward. Industries with downward-sloping long-run supply curves are called *decreasing-cost industries*.

MyLab Economics Study Plan   **MyLab Economics** Concept Check

12.6 Perfect Competition and Economic Efficiency

LEARNING OBJECTIVE: Explain how perfect competition leads to economic efficiency.

Notice how powerful consumers are in a market system. If consumers want more cage-free eggs, the market will supply them. More cage-free eggs are supplied not because a government bureaucrat in Washington, DC, or an official in a farmers' association gives orders. The additional eggs are produced because an increase in demand results in higher prices and a larger profit from selling cage-free eggs. Farmers, trying to get the highest possible return on their investments, begin to switch from producing eggs the conventional way to producing eggs using cage-free methods. If consumers lose their taste for these eggs and demand falls, the process works in reverse.

Productive Efficiency

Productive efficiency The situation in which a good or service is produced at the lowest possible cost.

In a market system, consumers get as many cage-free eggs as they want, produced at the lowest average cost possible. The forces of competition will drive the market price to the typical firm's minimum average cost. **Productive efficiency** refers to the situation in which a good or service is produced at the lowest possible cost. As we have seen, perfect competition results in productive efficiency.

The managers of every firm strive to earn an economic profit by reducing costs. But in a perfectly competitive market, other firms quickly copy ways of reducing costs. Therefore, in the long run, only the consumer benefits from cost reductions.   MyLab Economics Concept Check

Solved Problem 12.6   MyLab Economics Interactive Animation

How Productive Efficiency Benefits Consumers

Financial writer Michael Lewis once remarked, "The sad truth, for investors, seems to be that most of the benefits of new technologies are passed right through to consumers free of charge."

a. What do you think Lewis means by the benefits of new technology being "passed right through to consumers free

of charge"? Use a graph like Figure 12.8 on page 433 to illustrate your answer.

b. Explain why this result is a "sad truth" for investors.

Solving the Problem

Step 1: **Review the chapter material.** This problem is about perfect competition and efficiency, so you may want to review the section "Perfect Competition and Economic Efficiency," which begins on page 438.

Step 2: **Use the concepts from this chapter to explain what Lewis means.** By "new technologies," Lewis means new products—such as smartphones, laptops with retina displays, or 4K television sets—or lower-cost ways of producing existing products. In either case, new technologies will allow firms to earn an economic profit for a while, but the profit will lead new firms to enter the market in the long run.

Step 3: **Use a graph like Figure 12.8 on page 433 to illustrate why the benefits of new technologies are "passed right through to consumers free of charge."** Figure 12.8 shows the situation in which a firm is making an economic profit in the short run but entry eliminates the profit in the long run. We can draw a similar graph to analyze what happens in the long run in the market for 4K televisions, which provide sharper, higher-resolution images than do conventional high-definition (HD) televisions.

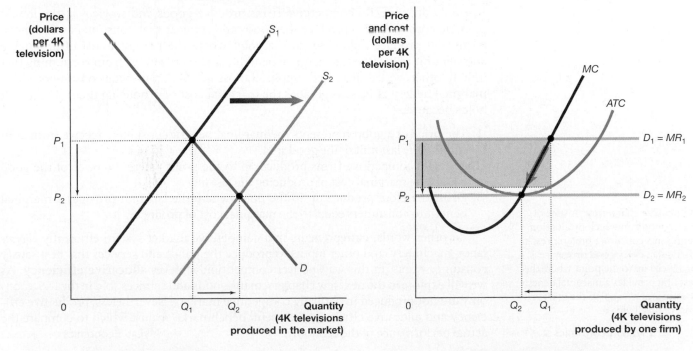

(a) Market for 4K televisions   (b) One firm selling 4K televisions

When 4K televisions were first introduced, prices were high, and only a few firms were in the market. Panel (a) shows that the initial equilibrium price in the market for 4K televisions is P_1. Panel (b) shows that at this price, the typical firm in the industry is earning an economic profit, which is shown by the green-shaded rectangle. The economic profit attracts new firms into the industry. This entry shifts the market supply curve from S_1 to S_2 in panel (a) and lowers the equilibrium price from P_1 to P_2. Panel (b) shows that at the new market price, P_2, the typical firm is breaking even. Therefore, 4K televisions are being produced at the lowest possible cost, and productive efficiency is achieved. Consumers receive the new technology "free of charge" in the sense that they only have to pay a price equal to the lowest possible cost of production.

Step 4: **Answer part (b) by explaining why the result in part (a) is a "sad truth" for investors.** We have seen in answering part (a) that in the long run, firms only break even on their investment in producing high-technology goods. This result implies that investors in these firms are also unlikely to earn an economic profit in the long run.

Extra Credit: Lewis is using a key result from this chapter: In the long run, the entry of new firms competes away economic profit. Notice that, strictly speaking, the high-technology industries Lewis is discussing are not perfectly competitive. Smartphones and 4K televisions, for instance, are not identical, and each firm in these industries produces a quantity large enough to affect the market price. However, as we will see in the next chapter, these deviations from perfect competition do not change the important conclusion that the entry of new firms benefits consumers by forcing prices down to the level of average cost. In fact, the price of 4K televisions dropped by more than 50 percent within three years of their first becoming widely available.

Source: Michael Lewis, "In Defense of the Boom," *New York Times*, October 27, 2002.

MyLab Economics Study Plan

Your Turn: For more practice, do related problems 6.6, 6.7, and 6.8 on pages 448–449 at the end of this chapter.

Allocative Efficiency

Not only do perfectly competitive firms produce goods and services at the lowest possible cost, they also produce the goods and services that consumers value most. Firms will produce a good up to the point where the marginal cost of producing another unit is equal to the marginal benefit consumers receive from consuming that unit. In other words, firms will supply all those goods that provide consumers with a marginal benefit at least as great as the marginal cost of producing them. This result holds because:

1. The price of a good represents the marginal benefit consumers receive from consuming the last unit of the good sold.
2. Perfectly competitive firms produce up to the point where the price of the good equals the marginal cost of producing the last unit.
3. Firms therefore produce up to the point where the last unit provides a marginal benefit to consumers equal to the marginal cost of producing it.

Allocative efficiency A state of the economy in which production represents consumer preferences; in particular, every good or service is produced up to the point where the last unit provides a marginal benefit to consumers equal to the marginal cost of producing it.

MyLab Economics Study Plan

In other words, entrepreneurs in a competitive market system efficiently *allocate* labor, machinery, and other inputs to produce the goods and services that best satisfy consumer wants. In this way, perfect competition achieves **allocative efficiency**. As we will explore in the next few chapters, many goods and services sold in the U.S. economy are not produced in perfectly competitive markets. Nevertheless, productive efficiency and allocative efficiency are useful benchmarks against which to compare the actual performance of the economy.

MyLab Economics Concept Check

Continued from page 415

Economics in Your Life & Career

Are You an Entrepreneur?

At the beginning of the chapter, we asked you to think about why you can charge only a relatively low price for babysitting or mowing lawns. In the chapter, we saw that firms selling products in competitive markets can't charge prices higher than competing firms charge. The market for babysitting and mowing lawns is very competitive because in most neighborhoods, there are many teenagers willing to supply these services. The price you can charge for babysitting may not be worth your time when you are 20 but is enough to cover the opportunity cost of a 14-year-old who is eager to enter the market. And the barriers to entering the babysitting and lawn-mowing markets are very low. So, in your career as a teenage entrepreneur, you may have become familiar with one of the lessons of this chapter: A firm in a competitive market has no control over price.

Conclusion

The competitive forces of the market impose relentless pressure on firms to produce new and better goods and services at the lowest possible cost. Firms that fail to adequately anticipate changes in consumer tastes or that fail to adopt the latest and most efficient technology do not survive in the long run. In the nineteenth century, the biologist Charles Darwin developed a theory of evolution based on the idea of the "survival of the fittest." Only the plants and animals that are best able to adapt to the demands of their environment are able to survive. Darwin first realized the important role that the struggle for existence plays in the natural world after reading early nineteenth-century economists' descriptions of the role it plays in the economic world. Just as "survival of the fittest" is the rule in nature, so it is in the economy.

At the start of this chapter, we saw that there are four market structures: perfect competition, monopolistic competition, oligopoly, and monopoly. Now that we have studied perfect competition, in the following chapters we move on to the other three market structures.

Visit **MyLab Economics** for a news article and analysis related to the concepts in this chapter.

CHAPTER SUMMARY
AND PROBLEMS

Key Terms

Allocative efficiency, p. 440

Average revenue (AR), p. 420

Economic loss, p. 434

Economic profit, p. 433

Long-run competitive equilibrium, p. 434

Long-run supply curve, p. 436

Marginal revenue (MR), p. 420

Perfectly competitive market, p. 417

Price taker, p. 417

Productive efficiency, p. 438

Profit, p. 419

Shutdown point, p. 429

Sunk cost, p. 428

 12.1 ## Perfectly Competitive Markets, pages 417–419

LEARNING OBJECTIVE: Explain what a perfectly competitive market is and why a perfect competitor faces a horizontal demand curve.

MyLab Economics   Visit **www.pearson.com/mylab/economics** to complete these exercises online and get instant feedback.

Summary

A **perfectly competitive market** must have many buyers and sellers, firms must be producing identical products, and there must be no barriers to new firms entering the market. The demand curve for a good or service produced in a perfectly competitive market is downward sloping, but the demand curve for the output of one firm in a perfectly competitive market is a horizontal line at the market price. Firms in perfectly competitive markets are **price takers**, and their sales drop to zero if they attempt to charge more than the market price.

Review Questions

1.1 What are the three conditions for a market to be perfectly competitive?

1.2 What is a price taker? When are firms likely to be price takers?

1.3 Draw a graph showing the market demand and supply curves for corn and the demand curve for the corn produced by one corn farmer. Be sure to indicate the market price and the price the corn farmer receives.

Problems and Applications

1.4 Indicate whether each of the following is a perfectly competitive market. For each market that is not perfectly competitive, explain why it is not.
  a. Corn farming
  b. Coffee shops
  c. Automobile manufacturing
  d. New home construction

1.5 **(Related to the Chapter Opener on page 414)** By 2017, McDonald's had stopped selling Chicken McNuggets and other products made from chickens that had been fed antibiotics. The change increased McDonald's costs, but an article in the *Wall Street Journal* noted that "McDonald's ability to raise its prices is limited because of stiff competition." Does this "stiff competition" mean that the demand

curve for McDonald's Chicken McNuggets is horizontal? Briefly explain.

Source: David Kesmodel, Jacob Bunge, and Annie Gasparro, "McDonald's to Curb Antibiotics in Chicken," *Wall Street Journal*, March 4, 2015.

1.6 The late Nobel Prize–winning economist George Stigler once wrote, "the most common and most important criticism of perfect competition … [is] that it is unrealistic." If few firms sell identical products in markets where there are no barriers to entry, why do economists believe that the model of perfect competition is important?

Source: George Stigler, "Perfect Competition, Historically Contemplated," *Journal of Political Economy*, Vol. 65, No. 1, February 1957, pp. 1–17.

1.7 **(Related to the Don't Let This Happen to You on page 418)** Explain whether you agree with the following remark:

> According to the model of perfectly competitive markets, the demand curve for wheat should be a horizontal line. But this can't be true: When the price of wheat rises, the quantity of wheat demanded falls, and when the price of wheat falls, the quantity of wheat demanded rises. Therefore, the demand curve for wheat is not a horizontal line.

1.8 The financial writer Andrew Tobias described an incident that occurred when he was a student at the Harvard Business School: Each student in the class was given large amounts of information about a particular firm and asked to determine a pricing strategy for the firm. Most of the students spent hours preparing their answers and came to class carrying many sheets of paper with their calculations. Tobias came up with the correct answer after just a few minutes and without having made any calculations. When his professor called on him in class for an answer, Tobias stated: "The case said the XYZ Company was in a very competitive industry … and the case said that the company had all the business it could handle." Given this information, what price do you think Tobias argued the company should charge? Briefly explain. (Tobias says the class greeted his answer with "thunderous applause.")

Source: Andrew Tobias, *The Only Investment Guide You'll Ever Need*, Boston: Houghton Mifflin Harcourt, 2016, pp. 7–8.

1.9 In 2017, two beer drinkers in California filed a lawsuit against Kona Brewing Company, which sells Kona beer. The beer drinkers claimed that Kona was marketed as if it were brewed in Hawaii, but the beer is actually brewed in Oregon, Washington, Tennessee, and New Hampshire. If the market for beer were perfectly competitive, would the location of breweries matter to consumers? Briefly explain.

Source: Cameron Miculka, "Suit Alleges Misrepresentation by Kona Brewing Co. Owner," westhawaiitoday.com, March 3, 2017.

12.2 How a Firm Maximizes Profit in a Perfectly Competitive Market, pages 419–422

LEARNING OBJECTIVE: Explain how a firm maximizes profit in a perfectly competitive market.

MyLab Economics Visit **www.pearson.com/mylab/economics** to complete these exercises online and get instant feedback.

Summary

Profit is the difference between total revenue (*TR*) and total cost (*TC*). **Average revenue (AR)** is total revenue divided by the quantity of the product sold. A firm maximizes profit by producing the level of output where the difference between revenue and cost is the greatest. This is the same level of output where marginal revenue is equal to marginal cost. **Marginal revenue (MR)** is the change in total revenue from selling one more unit.

Review Questions

2.1 Explain why it is true that for a firm in a perfectly competitive market, $P = MR = AR$.

2.2 Explain why at the level of output where the difference between *TR* and *TC* is at its maximum positive value, *MR* must equal *MC*.

2.3 Explain why it is true that for a firm in a perfectly competitive market, the profit-maximizing condition $MR = MC$ is equivalent to the condition $P = MC$.

Problems and Applications

2.4 A student argues: "To maximize profit, a firm should produce the quantity where the difference between marginal revenue and marginal cost is the greatest. If a firm produces more than this quantity, then the profit made on each additional unit will be falling." Briefly explain whether you agree with this reasoning.

2.5 Why don't firms maximize revenue rather than profit? Briefly explain whether a firm that maximized revenue would be likely to produce a smaller or larger quantity than if it were maximizing profit.

2.6 Refer to Table 12.3 on page 421. Suppose the price of wheat falls to $5.50 per bushel. How many bushels of wheat will Farmer Parker produce, and how much profit will he make? Briefly explain.

2.7 Refer to Table 12.3 on page 421. Suppose that the marginal cost of wheat is $0.50 higher for every bushel of wheat produced. For example, the marginal cost of producing the eighth bushel of wheat is now $9.50. Assume that the price of wheat remains $7 per bushel. Will this increase in marginal cost change the profit-maximizing level of production for Farmer Parker? Briefly explain. How much profit will Farmer Parker make now?

2.8 In Table 12.3 on page 421, what is Farmer Parker's fixed cost? Suppose that his fixed cost increases by $10. Will this increase change the profit-maximizing level of production for Farmer Parker? Briefly explain. How much profit will Farmer Parker make now?

12.3 Illustrating Profit or Loss on the Cost Curve Graph, pages 422–428

LEARNING OBJECTIVE: Use graphs to show a firm's profit or loss.

MyLab Economics Visit **www.pearson.com/mylab/economics** to complete these exercises online and get instant feedback.

Summary

From the definitions of profit and average total cost, we can develop the following expression for the relationship between total profit and average total cost: Profit = $(P - ATC) \times Q$. Using this expression, we can determine the area showing profit or loss on a cost curve graph: The area of profit or loss is a rectangle with a height equal to price minus average total cost (for profit) or average total cost minus price (for loss) and a base equal to the quantity of output.

Review Questions

3.1 Draw a graph showing a firm that is making a profit in a perfectly competitive market. Be sure your graph includes the firm's demand curve, marginal revenue curve, marginal cost curve, average total cost curve, and average variable cost curve, and make sure to indicate the area representing the firm's profit.

3.2 Draw a graph showing a firm that is operating at a loss in a perfectly competitive market. Be sure your graph includes the firm's demand curve, marginal revenue curve, marginal cost curve, average total cost curve, and average variable cost curve, and make sure to indicate the area representing the firm's loss.

Problems and Applications

3.3 **(Related to Solved Problem 12.3 on page 424)** Frances sells pencils in the perfectly competitive pencil market. Her output per day and her total cost are shown in the following table:

Output per Day	Total Cost
0	$1.00
1	2.50
2	3.50
3	4.20
4	4.50
5	5.20
6	6.80
7	8.70
8	10.70
9	13.00

a. If the current equilibrium price in the pencil market is $1.80, how many pencils will Frances produce, what price will she charge, and how much profit (or loss) will she make? Draw a graph to illustrate your answer. Your graph should be clearly labeled and should include Frances's demand, ATC, AVC, MC, and MR curves; the price she is charging; the quantity she is producing; and the area representing her profit (or loss).

b. Suppose the equilibrium price of pencils falls to $1.00. Now how many pencils will Frances produce, what price will she charge, and how much profit (or loss) will she make? Show your work. Draw a graph to illustrate this situation, using the instructions in part (a).

c. Suppose the equilibrium price of pencils falls to $0.25. Now how many pencils will Frances produce, what price will she charge, and how much profit (or loss) will she make?

3.4 (Related to Solved Problem 12.3 on page 424) Review Solved Problem 12.3 and then answer the following: Suppose the equilibrium price of basketballs falls to $2.50. Now how many basketballs will Andy produce? What price will he charge? How much profit (or loss) will he make?

3.5 (Related to the Don't Let This Happen to You on page 426) A student examines the following graph and argues: "I believe that a firm will want to produce at Q_1, not at Q_2. At Q_1, the distance between price and marginal cost is the greatest. Therefore, at Q_1, the firm will be maximizing its profit." Briefly explain whether you agree with the student's argument.

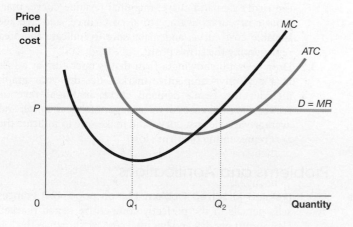

3.6 An article in the *Wall Street Journal* discussing the financial results for General Electric Co. (GE) for the first quarter of 2017 reported that, compared with the same quarter in the previous year, the firm's revenue had fallen from $27.94 billion to $27.66 billion, while its profit had increased from $228 million to $653 million. How is it possible for GE's revenue to decrease but its profit to increase? Doesn't GE have to maximize its revenue to maximize its profit? Briefly explain.

Source: Thomas Gryta and Joshua Jamerson, "General Electric, Still Weighed by Energy, Boosts Profit amid Cost Cutting Plan," *Wall Street Journal*, April 21, 2017.

3.7 (Related to the Apply the Concept on page 427) Suppose that most wheat farms are suffering losses. Now suppose that a new scientific study shows that eating four slices of whole wheat bread per day is an effective means of weight control, lowers blood pressure, and reduces the likelihood of heart disease. Assume that this study leads to the typical wheat farm earning an economic profit. Use two graphs to illustrate the effect of the release of the study: one graph showing the effect on the market for wheat and another graph showing the effect on a representative wheat farm. Be sure your graph for the wheat market shows any shifts in the market demand and supply curve and any changes in the equilibrium market price. Be sure that your graph for the representative farm includes its marginal revenue curve, marginal cost curve, average total cost curve, any change in its demand curve, and the area showing its loss before the release of the study and its profit after the release.

3.8 The following graph represents the situation of Marguerite's Caps, a firm selling caps in the perfectly competitive cap industry:

a. How much output should Marguerite produce to maximize her profit?

b. How much profit will she earn?

c. Suppose Marguerite decides to quit the cap industry and shut down. What would her loss be?

12.4 Deciding Whether to Produce or to Shut Down in the Short Run, pages 428–432

LEARNING OBJECTIVE: Explain why firms may shut down temporarily.

MyLab Economics   Visit **www.pearson.com/mylab/economics** to complete these exercises online and get instant feedback.

Summary

In deciding whether to shut down or produce in the short run, a firm should ignore its *sunk costs*. A **sunk cost** is a cost that has already been paid and that cannot be recovered. In the short run, a firm continues to produce as long as its price is at least equal to its average variable cost. A perfectly competitive firm's **shutdown point** is the minimum point on the firm's average variable cost curve. If price falls below average variable cost, the firm shuts down in the short run. For prices above the shutdown point, a perfectly competitive firm's marginal cost curve is also its supply curve.

Review Questions

4.1 What is the difference between a firm's shutdown point in the short run and in the long run? Why are firms willing to accept losses in the short run but not in the long run?

4.2 What is the relationship between a perfectly competitive firm's marginal cost curve and its supply curve?

4.3 How is the market supply curve derived from the supply curves of individual firms?

Problems and Applications

4.4 Consider a firm in each of the following three situations. For each situation, carefully explain whether the firm will produce in the short run or shut down in the short run.

	Situation 1	Situation 2	Situation 3
Price	$10	$10	$10
Quantity	1,000	1,000	1,000
Variable cost	$5,000	$5,000	$11,000
Fixed cost	$5,000	$6,000	$5,000
Marginal cost of 1,000th unit	$10	$10	$10

4.5 Ed Scahill produces desk lamps in the perfectly competitive desk lamp market.
  a. Fill in the missing values in the table in the next column.
  b. Suppose the equilibrium price in the desk lamp market is $50. How many desk lamps should Ed produce, and how much profit will he make?
  c. If next week the equilibrium price of desk lamps drops to $30, should Ed shut down? Explain.

Output per Week	Total Cost	AFC	AVC	ATC	MC
0	$100				
1	150				
2	175				
3	190				
4	210				
5	240				
6	280				
7	330				
8	390				
9	460				
10	540				

4.6 Matt Rafferty produces hiking boots in the perfectly competitive hiking boots market.
  a. Fill in the missing values in the following table.

Output per Week	Total Cost	AFC	AVC	ATC	MC
0	$100.00				
1	155.70				
2	205.60				
3	253.90				
4	304.80				
5	362.50				
6	431.20				
7	515.10				
8	618.40				
9	745.30				
10	900.00				

  b. Suppose the equilibrium price in the hiking boots market is $100. How many pairs of boots should Matt produce, what price should he charge, and how much profit will he make?
  c. If next week the equilibrium price of boots drops to $65, how many pairs of boots should Matt produce, what price should he charge, and how much profit (or loss) will he make?
  d. If the equilibrium price of boots falls to $50, how many pairs of boots should Matt produce, what price should he charge, and how much profit (or loss) will he make?

4.7 The following graph represents the situation of a perfectly competitive firm. Indicate on the graph the areas that represent the following:

a. Total cost
b. Total revenue
c. Variable cost
d. Profit or loss

Briefly explain whether the firm will continue to produce in the short run.

4.8 **(Related to Solved Problem 12.4 on page 430)** A columnist for the *Wall Street Journal* discussed the fact that some firms were buying existing drilling operations in Canadian oil sands regions. These operations would not have been profitable to build from scratch but were profitable to operate given that they were already built because, as the columnist said, "The key is the distinction between fixed and variable costs. While the fixed investment in new oil sands projects is prohibitive, variable costs can be in the low $20 range per barrel." The columnist estimated that the fixed cost of a new oil sands drilling operation could be $95 per barrel. At the time the column was written, the price of oil was about $50 per barrel.

a. Assuming that variable cost of an existing oil sands operation is $20 per barrel and the price of oil is $50 per barrel, how much were the companies selling these drilling operations losing per barrel?
b. At a price of $50 per barrel, were the companies buying the existing drilling operations earning a profit of $30 per barrel? If not, explain what information we would need to calculate their profit.

Source: Spencer Jakab, "Plenty of Cash Lies Buried on Canada's Oil Sands," *Wall Street Journal*, March 20, 2017.

4.9 **(Related to Solved Problem 12.4 on page 430)** Suppose you decide to open a copy store. You rent store space (signing a 1-year lease to do so), and you take out a loan at a local bank and use the money to purchase 10 copiers. Six months later, a large chain opens a copy store two blocks away from yours. As a result, the revenue you receive from your copy store, while sufficient to cover the wages of your employees and the costs of paper and utilities, doesn't cover all your rent and the interest and repayment costs on the loan you took out to purchase the copiers. Briefly explain whether you should continue operating your business.

4.10 **(Related to Solved Problem 12.4 on page 430)** According to an article in the *Wall Street Journal*, in 2007 the insurance company AXA Equitable signed a long-term lease on 2 million square feet of office space in a skyscraper on Sixth Avenue in Manhattan in New York City. In 2013, AXA decided that it needed only 1.7 million square feet of office space, so it subleased 300,000 square feet of space to several other firms. Although AXA is paying a rent of $88 per square foot on all 2 million square feet it is leasing, it is only receiving $40 per square foot from the firms to which it is subleasing the 300,000 square feet. Briefly explain why AXA's actions might make economic sense in the short run. Would these actions make sense in the long run? Briefly explain.

Source: Molly Hensley-Clancy, "A Slump on Sixth Avenue," *Wall Street Journal*, June 16, 2013.

 12.5 **"If Everyone Can Do It, You Can't Make Money at It": The Entry and Exit of Firms in the Long Run, pages 432–438**

LEARNING OBJECTIVE: Explain how entry and exit ensure that perfectly competitive firms earn zero economic profit in the long run.

MyLab Economics   Visit **www.pearson.com/mylab/economics** to complete these exercises online and get instant feedback.

Summary

Economic profit is a firm's revenue minus all its costs, implicit and explicit. **Economic loss** is the situation in which a firm's total revenue is less than its total cost, including all implicit costs. If firms make an economic profit in the short run, new firms enter the industry until the market price has fallen enough to wipe out the profit. If firms suffer an economic loss, firms exit the industry until the market price has risen enough to wipe out the loss. **Long-run competitive equilibrium** is the situation in which the entry and exit of firms has resulted in the typical

firm breaking even. The **long-run supply curve** shows the relationship between market price and the quantity supplied.

Review Questions

5.1 When are firms likely to enter an industry? When are they likely to exit an industry?

5.2 Briefly explain whether a firm earning zero economic profit will continue to produce in the long run.

5.3 Describe the shape of the long-run supply curve in a perfectly competitive market. Suppose that a perfectly competitive market is initially at long-run equilibrium and then there is a permanent decrease in the demand for the product. Draw a graph showing how the market adjusts in the long run.

Problems and Applications

5.4 Suppose an assistant professor of economics is earning a salary of $75,000 per year. One day she quits her job, sells $100,000 worth of bonds that had been earning 3 percent per year, and uses the funds to open a bookstore. At the end of the year, she shows an accounting profit of $80,000 on her income tax return. What is her economic profit?

5.5 **(Related to the Chapter Opener on page 414)** The following questions are about long-run equilibrium in the market for cage-free eggs.

a. As described in the chapter opener, in 2017 was the market for cage-free eggs in long-run equilibrium? Briefly explain.

b. What would we expect to happen to the price of cage-free eggs and the quantity of cage-free eggs produced in the long run? Briefly explain.

c. As of 2017, the U.S. Department of Agriculture (USDA) did not have detailed guidelines for egg farmers to follow before they could claim that the eggs they sell were laid by cage-free chickens. Some animal rights activists were pushing for the USDA to enact stricter guidelines than many egg farmers were following voluntarily. Such guidelines would be likely to significantly raise the cost of producing cage-free eggs. Suppose that the USDA begins to require these stricter guidelines. What effect will this increase in cost have on the long-run price of cage-free eggs? In the long run, will the quantity of cage-free eggs be larger, smaller, or the same as it would have been without the USDA adopting the guidelines? Briefly explain.

Source: Stephanie Strom, "What to Make of Those Animal-Welfare Labels on Meat and Eggs," *New York Times*, January 31, 2017.

5.6 In panel (b) of Figure 12.9 on page 435, Sacha Gillette reduces her output from 40,000 to 25,000 dozen eggs when the price falls to $1.75. At this price and this output level, she is operating at a loss. Why doesn't she just continue charging the original $2.00 and continue producing 40,000 dozen eggs?

5.7 An article in the *Wall Street Journal* noted that demand for organic foods was growing rapidly in the United States. According to the article, "meat and egg companies like Pilgrim's Pride Corp., Perdue Farms Inc. and Cal-Maine Foods Inc. are … expanding organic production, boosting demand for organic animal feed." But this development hadn't benefited U.S. farmers as much as they had hoped: "U.S. organic-farming groups say that an influx of foreign grain has been a chief factor in slashing prices for organic corn by about 30% in 2016." Illustrate the effects of these developments using two graphs: One graph should illustrate what happened in the market for organic corn and should include shifts in demand and supply indicated by the developments described. The other graph should show what happened to the situation of a representative U.S. farmer growing organic corn. Be sure to correctly label all the curves in your graphs

Source: Jacob Bunge, "Organic Food Sales Are Booming; Why Are American Farmers Crying Foul?" *Wall Street Journal*, February 21, 2017.

5.8 **(Related to the Apply the Concept on page 437)** In 2017, Apple reported that since its iTunes App Store had opened in 2008, third-party app developers had earned more than $60 billion and currently employed 1.4 million people. Yet, as we've seen, because of intense competition, many game developers can only break even on the games they develop. Given this outcome, would we expect individuals and companies to continue developing games in the long run? Briefly explain.

Source: Tripp Mickle, "Apple's App Store Sales Top $28 Billion," *Wall Street Journal*, January 5, 2017.

5.9 Suppose that currently the market for gluten-free spaghetti is in long-run equilibrium at a price of $3.50 per box and a quantity of 4 million boxes sold per year. If the demand for gluten-free spaghetti permanently increases, which of the following combinations of equilibrium price and equilibrium quantity would you expect to see in the long run? Carefully explain why you chose the answer you did.

a. A price of $3.50 per box and a quantity of 4 million boxes

b. A price of $3.50 per box and a quantity of more than 4 million boxes

c. A price of more than $3.50 per box and a quantity of more than 4 million boxes

d. A price of less than $3.50 per box and a quantity of less than 4 million boxes

5.10 Suppose that each of the following is true: (1) The laptop computer industry is perfectly competitive, and the firms that assemble laptops do not also make the displays or screens; (2) the laptop display industry is also perfectly competitive; and (3) because the demand for laptop displays is currently relatively small, firms in the laptop display industry have not been able to take advantage of all the economies of scale in laptop display production. Use a graph of the laptop computer market to illustrate the long-run effects on equilibrium price and quantity in the laptop computer market of a substantial and sustained increase in the demand for laptop computers. Use another graph to show the effect on the cost curves of a typical firm in the laptop computer industry. Briefly explain your graphs. Do your graphs indicate that the laptop computer industry is a constant-cost industry, an increasing-cost industry, or a decreasing-cost industry?

5.11 In 2015, cocoa prices rose 13 percent from the previous year, the fourth straight year in which prices increased. However, by the end of 2016 cocoa prices fell. Edward George, the head of research at Ecobank, commented, "Everyone's like, wow. There's a lot of cocoa out there." Much of the world's supply of cocoa beans is grown in West Africa.

a. Assume that the market for cocoa beans is perfectly competitive and was in long-run equilibrium in 2012. Draw two graphs: one showing the world market for cocoa beans and one showing the market for the cocoa beans grown by a representative farmer.

b. Assume that there was an increase in the worldwide demand for chocolate in 2013. In the graphs you drew in part (a), show the short-run effect of the demand increase.

c. Explain why the supply of cocoa beans increased and the price decreased in 2016. Show the effect of this increase in supply on the graphs you drew in part (b).

Source: Katherine Dunn, "Too Much Chocolate: In Sharp Turn Around, Cocoa Prices Drop," *Wall Street Journal*, December 8, 2016.

5.12 Suppose that at the beginning of a year, the price of corn is $3.80 per bushel, and 14 billion bushels are harvested. There are approximately 400,000 corn farmers, so the average output per farmer is about 350,000 bushels. The following graphs assume that the market for corn is initially in long-run equilibrium. Favorable weather during the year increases the total corn harvest to 16 billion bushels. Assume that no other factors affect the market for corn.

a. What percentage of the total corn output did the average corn farmer produce at the beginning of the year?

b. Show on the graph for the total market for corn and the graph for the typical farm any changes that occur in the short run as a result of the increase in the corn harvest. Be sure to note whether any curves shift and whether there are any changes in the equilibrium price or the equilibrium quantities.

c. Show on the graph for the total market for corn and the graph for the typical farm any changes that occur in the long run as a result of the increase in the corn harvest. Be sure to note whether any curves shift and whether there are any changes in the equilibrium price or the equilibrium quantities.

12.6 | **Perfect Competition and Economic Efficiency, pages 438–441**

LEARNING OBJECTIVE: Explain how perfect competition leads to economic efficiency.

MyLab Economics Visit **www.pearson.com/mylab/economics** to complete these exercises online and get instant feedback.

Summary

Perfect competition results in **productive efficiency**, which means that goods and services are produced at the lowest possible cost. Perfect competition also results in **allocative efficiency**, which means the goods and services are produced up to the point where the last unit provides a marginal benefit to consumers equal to the marginal cost of producing it.

a. How much profit is Karl earning?

b. Does the current situation of Karl's firm illustrate productive efficiency or allocative efficiency? If so, briefly explain how.

Review Questions

6.1 Why are consumers so powerful in a market system?

6.2 What is meant by *allocative efficiency*? What is meant by *productive efficiency*? Briefly discuss the difference between these two concepts.

6.3 How does perfect competition lead to allocative efficiency and productive efficiency?

Problems and Applications

6.4 The chapter states, "Firms will supply all those goods that provide consumers with a marginal benefit at least as great as the marginal cost of producing them." A student objects to this statement, arguing, "I doubt that firms will really do this. After all, firms are in business to make a profit; they don't care about what is best for consumers." Evaluate the student's argument.

6.5 The following graph represents the situation of Karl's Kumquats, a kumquat grower.

6.6 (Related to Solved Problem 12.6 on page 439) Discuss the following statement: "In a perfectly competitive market, in the long run consumers benefit from reductions in costs, but firms don't." Don't firms also benefit from cost reductions because they are able to earn larger profits?

6.7 (Related to Solved Problem 12.6 on page 439) Suppose you read the following item in a newspaper article, under the headline "Price Gouging Alleged in Pencil Market":

Consumer advocacy groups charged at a press conference yesterday that there is widespread price gouging in the sale of pencils. They released a study showing that whereas the average retail price of pencils was $1.00, the average cost of producing pencils was only $0.50. "Pencils can be produced without complicated machinery or highly skilled workers, so there is no justification for companies charging a price that is twice what it costs them to produce the product. Pencils are too important in the life of every American for us to tolerate this sort of price gouging any longer," said George Grommet, chief spokesperson for the consumer groups. The consumer groups advocate passing a law that would allow companies selling pencils to charge a price no more than 20 percent greater than their average cost of production.

Do you believe such a law would be advisable in a situation like this? Explain.

6.8 **(Related to Solved Problem 12.6 on page 439)** Sony suffered losses selling televisions from 2004 to 2013, before finally earning a small profit on this business from 2014 to 2016. Given the strong consumer demand for plasma, LCD, and LED television sets, shouldn't Sony have been able to raise prices to earn a profit during that decade of losses? Briefly explain.

Source: "Sony Consolidated Financial Results for the Third Quarter Ended December 31, 2016," December 31, 2016.

6.9 An article in the *Wall Street Journal* discusses the visual effects industry, which is made up of firms that provide visual effects for films and television programs. The article noted, "Blockbusters ... often have thousands of visual effects shots. Even dramas and comedies today can include hundreds of them." But the article also noted that the firms producing the effects have not been very profitable. Some firms have declared bankruptcy, and the former general manager of one firm was quoted as saying, "A good year for us was a 5% return." If demand for visual effects is so strong, why is it difficult for the firms that supply them to make an economic profit?

Source: Ben Fritz, "Visual Effects Industry Does a Disappearing Act," *Wall Street Journal*, February 22, 2013.

6.10 Hedrick Smith was a foreign correspondent for the *New York Times* who lived in the Soviet Union in the 1970s, a period when the country had a planned economy rather than a market system. In a book he wrote about everyday life in the Soviet Union, Smith made the following observations about shopping in Moscow:

At first it seemed ... that the stores were pretty well stocked. Only as we began to shop in earnest ... did the Russian consumer's predicament really come through to me. First, we needed textbooks for our children ... and found that the sixth-grade textbooks had run out.... We tried to find ballet shoes for our 11-year-old daughter... only to discover that in this land of ballerinas, ballet shoes size 8 were unavailable in Moscow.... I tried to find shoes for myself. They were out of anything in my size but sandals or flimsy, lightweight shoes that the clerk, with one look at me, recommended against buying. "They won't last," he admitted.

a. Judging by Smith's observations, briefly explain whether the Soviet Union achieved allocative efficiency in the production of sixth-grade textbooks, ballet shoes, and men's shoes.

b. Can we tell from these observations whether the Soviet Union achieved productive efficiency in the production of sixth-grade textbooks, ballet shoes, and men's shoes? Briefly explain.

Source: Hedrick Smith, *The Russians*, New York: Ballantine Books, 1977, p. 77.

Critical Thinking Exercises

CT12.1 In a perfectly competitive market in the long run, can you say anything definite about the elasticity of the market supply curve? Can you say anything definite about the elasticity of the market demand curve? Briefly explain.

CT12.2 Suppose a perfectly competitive firm finds a way to reduce its fixed cost. Briefly explain whether each of the following will change for the firm. Use a graph to illustrate your answer.
  a. Average total cost
  b. Profit
  c. Average variable cost
  d. Marginal cost
  e. Average fixed cost
  f. The firm's supply curve

CT12.3 Some professions, like hair cutting or hair braiding, are fairly close to perfectly competitive. These professions sometimes succeed in getting the government to establish licensing requirements that deter some competitors from entering the profession. Why might these professions want to impose such licensing requirements? Use the concepts from this chapter to explain your answer. Why might the government choose to impose such requirements?

Monopolistic Competition: The Competitive Model in a More Realistic Setting

Will Panera's "Clean Food" Advantage Last?

Few industries are as competitive as the restaurant industry. In most downtowns, it's not unusual to see several restaurants open and then quickly close, sometimes after just a few months. To succeed, restaurants need to distinguish, or *differentiate*, their food from other restaurants' food. Louis Kane and Ron Shaich founded the firm that became Panera Bread in 1981. Although they originally concentrated on selling baked goods and breakfast foods, by the late 1990s, the firm had expanded to serve a variety of sandwiches, soups, and salads throughout the day.

Panera, like Chipotle Mexican Grill and Shake Shack, operates "fast-casual restaurants," which prepare fresh food quickly but do not offer table service. These restaurants serve food that many consumers consider healthier because it is made with higher-quality ingredients than the food at traditional fast-food restaurants, such as Taco Bell and McDonald's. In 2017, Ron Shaich, now serving as chair of Panera's board of directors, announced that its 2,000 restaurants had completed a two-year process of converting to serving only "clean food"—food containing no artificial preservatives, sweeteners, or other additives. He pointed out that other fast-casual restaurants and fast-food restaurants were unable to make this claim.

When we discussed the situation of firms in perfectly competitive markets in Chapter 12, we saw that these markets share three key characteristics:

1. There are many firms.
2. All firms sell identical products.
3. There are no barriers to new firms entering the industry.

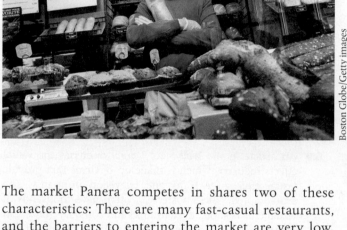

Boston Globe/Getty images

The market Panera competes in shares two of these characteristics: There are many fast-casual restaurants, and the barriers to entering the market are very low. But the products that Panera and its competitors sell are differentiated rather than identical. So, the market is monopolistically competitive rather than perfectly competitive.

Can Panera continue to succeed? The process of converting to "clean food" required a substantial investment, but do consumers actually care enough about food ingredients for the investment to pay off? And if they do, will Panera's competitors begin serving "clean food" as well, reducing the advantages Shaich hoped to gain? As we will see, most monopolistically competitive firms are unable to earn an economic profit in the long run.

Sources: Julie Jargon, "What Panera Had to Change to Make Its Menu 'Clean,'" *Wall Street Journal*, February 20, 2017; Craig Giammona, "Panera Becomes First Chain to Label Added Sugar in Beverages," bloomberg.com, March 31, 2017; and "The No-No List," panerabread.com, March 14, 2017.

Chapter Outline & Learning Objectives

 13.1 Demand and Marginal Revenue for a Firm in a Monopolistically Competitive Market, page 452
Explain why a monopolistically competitive firm has downward-sloping demand and marginal revenue curves.

 13.2 How a Monopolistically Competitive Firm Maximizes Profit in the Short Run, page 454
Explain how a monopolistically competitive firm maximizes profit in the short run.

 13.3 What Happens to Profits in the Long Run? page 457
Analyze the situation of a monopolistically competitive firm in the long run.

 13.4 Comparing Monopolistic Competition and Perfect Competition, page 462
Compare the efficiency of monopolistic competition and perfect competition.

 13.5 How Marketing Differentiates Products, page 465
Define marketing and explain how firms use it to differentiate their products.

 13.6 What Makes a Firm Successful? page 466
Identify the key factors that determine a firm's success.

Economics in Your Life & Career

Can You Operate a Successful Restaurant?

After you graduate, you plan to realize your dream of opening an Italian restaurant. You have many decisions to make in operating your restaurant. Will it be "family style," with sturdy but inexpensive furniture, or will it be more elegant, with nice furniture, tablecloths, and candles? Will you offer a full menu or concentrate on pasta dishes made with your grandmother's secret sauce? The decisions you make will distinguish your restaurant from competitors. What's likely to happen in the restaurant market in your hometown after you open your restaurant? How successful are you likely to be? Try to answer these questions as you read this chapter. You can check your answers against those we provide on **page 468** at the end of this chapter.

Many markets in the U.S. economy are similar to the restaurant market: They have many buyers and sellers, and the barriers to entry are low, but the goods and services offered for sale are differentiated rather than identical. Examples of these markets include coffee houses, movie theaters, supermarkets, and furniture stores. In fact, the majority of the firms you buy from are competing in **monopolistically competitive** markets.

We have seen how perfect competition benefits consumers and results in economic efficiency. Will these same desirable outcomes also hold for monopolistically competitive markets? This question is important because monopolistically competitive markets are common.

13.1 Demand and Marginal Revenue for a Firm in a Monopolistically Competitive Market

LEARNING OBJECTIVE: Explain why a monopolistically competitive firm has downward-sloping demand and marginal revenue curves.

If the Panera restaurant located a mile from where you live raises the price of a turkey sandwich from $7.00 to $7.50, it will lose some, but not all, of its customers. Some customers will switch to buying their sandwiches at another restaurant, but other customers will be willing to pay the higher price for a variety of reasons: This restaurant may be closer to them, or they may prefer Panera's turkey sandwiches to similar sandwiches at competing restaurants. So, a Panera restaurant will face a downward-sloping demand curve, unlike a wheat farmer, who will sell no wheat if he raises his price and who, therefore, faces a horizontal demand curve.

The Demand Curve for a Monopolistically Competitive Firm

Figure 13.1 shows how a change in price affects the quantity of turkey sandwiches Panera sells. The increase in the price from $7.00 to $7.50 decreases the quantity of sandwiches sold from 3,000 per week to 2,400 per week.   **MyLab Economics** Concept Check

Marginal Revenue for a Firm with a Downward-Sloping Demand Curve

For a firm in a perfectly competitive market, the demand curve and the marginal revenue curve are the same (see Chapter 12, Section 12.2). A perfectly competitive firm faces a horizontal demand curve and does not have to cut the price to sell a larger quantity. A monopolistically competitive firm, however, must cut the price to sell more, so its marginal revenue curve will slope downward and will be below its demand curve.

The data in Table 13.1 illustrate this point. To keep the numbers simple, let's assume that your local Panera restaurant is very small and sells at most 11 turkey

Figure 13.1

The Downward-Sloping Demand Curve for Turkey Sandwiches at Panera

If a Panera restaurant increases the price of its turkey sandwiches, it will lose some, but not all, of its customers. In this case, raising the price from $7.00 to $7.50 reduces the quantity of sandwiches sold from 3,000 per week to 2,400. Therefore, unlike a perfect competitor, a Panera restaurant faces a downward-sloping demand curve.

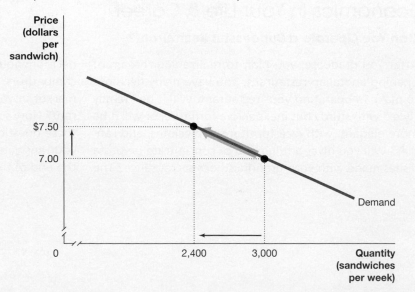

Sandwiches Sold per Week (Q)	Price (P)	Total Revenue (TR = P × Q)	Average Revenue $\left(AR = \dfrac{TR}{Q}\right)$	Marginal Revenue $\left(MR = \dfrac{\Delta TR}{\Delta Q}\right)$
0	$10.00	$0.00	—	—
1	9.50	9.50	$9.50	$9.50
2	9.00	18.00	9.00	8.50
3	8.50	25.50	8.50	7.50
4	8.00	32.00	8.00	6.50
5	7.50	37.50	7.50	5.50
6	7.00	42.00	7.00	4.50
7	6.50	45.50	6.50	3.50
8	6.00	48.00	6.00	2.50
9	5.50	49.50	5.50	1.50
10	5.00	50.00	5.00	0.50
11	4.50	49.50	4.50	−0.50

MyLab Economics Animation

Table 13.1

Demand and Marginal Revenue at a Panera Restaurant

sandwiches per week. If this Panera charges a price of $10.00 or more, all of its potential customers will buy their turkey sandwiches somewhere else. If it charges $9.50, it will sell 1 turkey sandwich per week. For each additional $0.50 this Panera reduces the price, it increases the number of sandwiches it sells by 1. The third column in the table shows how the firm's *total revenue* changes as it sells more turkey sandwiches. The fourth column shows the firm's revenue per unit, or its *average revenue*. Average revenue is equal to total revenue divided by quantity. Because total revenue equals price multiplied by quantity, dividing by quantity leaves just price. Therefore, *average revenue is always equal to price*. This result will be true for firms selling in any of the four market structures (see Chapter 12).

The last column in Table 13.1 shows the firm's marginal revenue, or the change in total revenue as the firm sells 1 more sandwich. For a perfectly competitive firm, the additional revenue received from selling 1 more unit is just equal to the price. That will *not* be true for this Panera restaurant because to sell another sandwich, it has to reduce the price. When the firm cuts the price by $0.50, one good thing happens, and one bad thing happens:

- **The good thing.** It sells 1 more sandwich; we can call this the *output effect*.
- **The bad thing.** It receives $0.50 less for each sandwich that it could have sold at the higher price; we can call this the *price effect*.

Figure 13.2 illustrates what happens when the firm cuts the price from $7.50 to $7.00. Selling the sixth sandwich adds the $7.00 price to the firm's revenue; this is the

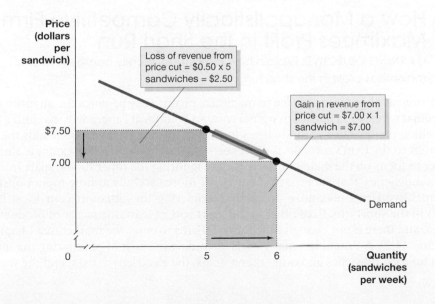

MyLab Economics Animation

Figure 13.2

How a Price Cut Affects a Firm's Revenue

If a local Panera restaurant reduces the price of a sandwich from $7.50 to $7.00, the number of sandwiches it sells per week will increase from 5 to 6. Its marginal revenue from selling the sixth sandwich will be $4.50, which is equal to the $7.00 additional revenue from selling 1 more sandwich (the area of the green rectangle) minus the $2.50 loss in revenue from selling the first 5 sandwiches for $0.50 less each (the area of the red rectangle).

MyLab Economics Animation

Figure 13.3

The Demand and Marginal Revenue Curves for a Monopolistically Competitive Firm

Any firm that has the ability to affect the price of the product it sells will have a marginal revenue curve that is below its demand curve. We plot the data from Table 13.1 to create the demand and marginal revenue curves. After the tenth sandwich, marginal revenue becomes negative because the additional revenue received from selling 1 more sandwich is smaller than the revenue lost from receiving a lower price on the sandwich that could have been sold at the original price.

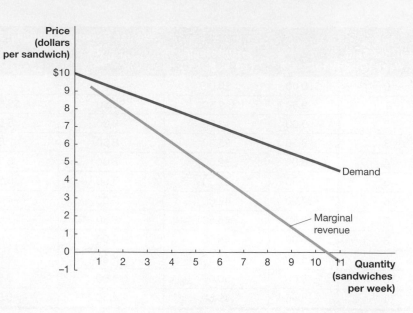

MyLab Economics Study Plan

output effect. But this Panera now receives a price of $7.00, rather than $7.50, on the first 5 sandwiches sold; this is the price effect. As a result of the price effect, the firm's revenue on these 5 sandwiches is $2.50 less than it would have been if the price had remained at $7.50. So, the firm has gained $7.00 in revenue on the sixth sandwich and lost $2.50 in revenue on the first 5 sandwiches, for a net change in revenue of $4.50. Marginal revenue is the change in total revenue from selling 1 more unit. Therefore, the marginal revenue of the sixth sandwich is $4.50. Notice that the marginal revenue of the sixth sandwich is far below its price of $7.00. In fact, for each additional sandwich this Panera sells, marginal revenue will be less than price. There is an important general point: *Every firm that has the ability to affect the price of the good or service it sells will have a marginal revenue curve that is below its demand curve.* Only firms in perfectly competitive markets, which can sell as many units as they want at the market price, have marginal revenue curves that are the same as their demand curves.

Figure 13.3 plots the data from Table 13.1 and shows the relationship between the demand curve and the marginal revenue curve for your local Panera. Notice that after the tenth sandwich, marginal revenue becomes negative because the additional revenue received from selling 1 more sandwich is smaller than the revenue lost from receiving a lower price on the sandwiches that could have been sold at the original price.

MyLab Economics Concept Check

 13.2 ## How a Monopolistically Competitive Firm Maximizes Profit in the Short Run

LEARNING OBJECTIVE: Explain how a monopolistically competitive firm maximizes profit in the short run.

All firms use the same approach to maximize profit: They produce the quantity where marginal revenue is equal to marginal cost. So your local Panera will maximize profit by selling the quantity of sandwiches for which the last sandwich sold adds the same amount to the firm's revenue as to its costs. (We want to keep this example simple in order to focus on the main points, so we are ignoring the other foods, apart from turkey sandwiches, that Panera sells.) Let's look more carefully at how monopolistically competitive firms maximize profit by considering the situation your local Panera faces in the short run. Recall that in the short run, at least one factor of production is fixed, and there is not enough time for new firms to enter the market (see Chapter 11, Section 11.2). A Panera has many costs, including the cost of purchasing the ingredients for its sandwiches and other menu items, the electricity it uses, and the wages of its employees. Recall that a firm's *marginal cost* is the increase in total cost resulting from producing another unit of output. We have seen that for many firms, the marginal cost curve has a U shape. We will assume that the marginal cost curve for this Panera has the usual shape.

We combine the revenue data for this Panera from Table 13.1 with cost data to create the table in Figure 13.4. The graphs in Figure 13.4 plot the data from the table. In panel (a), we see how this Panera can determine its profit-maximizing quantity and price. As long as the marginal cost of selling 1 more sandwich is less than the marginal

Sandwiches Sold per Week (Q)	Price (P)	Total Revenue (TR)	Marginal Revenue (MR)	Total Cost (TC)	Marginal Cost (MC)	Average Total Cost (ATC)	Profit
0	$10.00	$0.00	—	$6.00	—	—	–$6.00
1	9.50	9.50	$9.50	11.00	$5.00	$11.00	–1.50
2	9.00	18.00	8.50	15.50	4.50	7.75	2.50
3	8.50	25.50	7.50	19.50	4.00	6.50	6.00
4	8.00	32.00	6.50	24.50	5.00	6.13	7.50
5	7.50	37.50	5.50	30.00	5.50	6.00	7.50
6	7.00	42.00	4.50	36.00	6.00	6.00	6.00
7	6.50	45.50	3.50	42.50	6.50	6.07	3.00
8	6.00	48.00	2.50	49.50	7.00	6.19	–1.50
9	5.50	49.50	1.50	57.00	7.50	6.33	–7.50
10	5.00	50.00	0.50	65.00	8.00	6.50	–15.00
11	4.50	49.50	–0.50	73.50	8.50	6.68	–24.00

(a) Profit-maximizing quantity and price for a monopolistic competitor

(b) Short-run profit for a monopolistic competitor

MyLab Economics Animation

Figure 13.4 **Maximizing Profit in a Monopolistically Competitive Market**

To maximize profit, a Panera restaurant needs to sell sandwiches up to the point where the marginal revenue from selling the last sandwich is just equal to the marginal cost. As the table shows, selling the fifth sandwich—point A in panel (a)—adds $5.50 to the firm's costs and $5.50 to its revenues. The firm then uses the demand curve to find the price that will lead consumers to buy this quantity of sandwiches (point B). In panel (b), the green rectangle represents the firm's profit. The rectangle has a height equal to $1.50, which is the $7.50 price minus the average total cost of $6.00, and it has a base equal to the quantity of 5 sandwiches. So, for this Panera, profit equals $1.50 × 5 = $7.50.

revenue, the firm should make and sell additional sandwiches. For example, increasing the quantity of sandwiches sold from 3 per week to 4 per week increases cost by $5.00 but increases revenue by $6.50. So, the firm's profit is increased by $1.50 as a result of selling the fourth sandwich.

As this Panera sells more sandwiches, rising marginal cost eventually equals marginal revenue, and the firm sells the profit-maximizing quantity of sandwiches. Marginal cost equals marginal revenue with the fifth sandwich, which adds $5.50 to the firm's costs and $5.50 to its revenues—point A in panel (a) of Figure 13.4. The demand curve tells us the price at which the firm is able to sell 5 sandwiches per week. In Figure 13.4, if we draw a vertical line from 5 sandwiches up to the demand curve, we can see that the price at which the firm can sell 5 sandwiches per week is $7.50 (point B). We can conclude that for this Panera, the profit-maximizing quantity is 5 sandwiches, and the profit-maximizing price is $7.50. If the firm sells more than 5 sandwiches per week, its profit will fall. For example, selling a sixth sandwich adds $6.00 to its costs and only $4.50 to its revenues. So, its profit will fall from $7.50 to $6.00.

Panel (b) adds the average total cost curve for this Panera. The panel shows that the average total cost of selling 5 sandwiches is $6.00. Recall from Chapter 12, Section 12.3 that:

$$\text{Profit} = (P - ATC) \times Q.$$

In this case, profit = ($7.50 − $6.00) × 5 = $7.50. The green rectangle in panel (b) of Figure 13.4 shows the amount of profit. The rectangle has a base equal to Q and a height equal to $(P - ATC)$, so its area equals profit.

Notice that, unlike a perfectly competitive firm, which produces where $P = MC$, a monopolistically competitive firm produces where $P > MC$. This Panera charges a price of $7.50, although marginal cost is $5.50. For a perfectly competitive firm, price equals marginal revenue, $P = MR$. Therefore, to fulfill the $MR = MC$ condition for profit maximization, a perfectly competitive firm will produce where $P = MC$. $P > MR$ for a monopolistically competitive firm because the firm's marginal revenue curve is below its demand curve. Therefore, a monopolistically competitive firm will maximize profit by producing where $P > MC$.

MyLab Economics Study Plan

MyLab Economics Concept Check

Solved Problem 13.2

MyLab Economics Interactive Animation

Does Minimizing Cost Maximize Profit at Apple?

Suppose Apple finds that the relationship between the average total cost of producing iPhones and the quantity of iPhones produced is as shown in the following graph. Will Apple maximize profit if it produces 800,000 iPhones per month? Briefly explain.

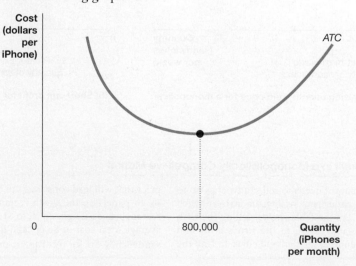

Solving the Problem

Step 1: **Review the chapter material.** This problem is about how monopolistically competitive firms maximize profit, so you may want to review the section "How a Monopolistically Competitive Firm Maximizes Profit in the Short Run," which begins on page 454.

Step 2: **Discuss the relationship between minimizing cost and maximizing profit.** Firms often talk about the steps they take to reduce costs. The graph shows that by producing 800,000 iPhones per month, Apple will minimize its average cost of production. But remember that minimizing cost is not the firm's ultimate goal; the firm's ultimate goal is to maximize profit. Depending on demand, a firm may maximize profit by producing a quantity that is either larger or smaller than the quantity that would minimize average total cost.

Step 3: **Draw a graph that shows Apple maximizing profit at a quantity where average cost is not minimized.** Note that in the graph, average total cost reaches a minimum at a quantity of 800,000, but profit is maximized at a quantity of 600,000.

Your Turn: For more practice, do related problem 2.5 on page 471 at the end of this chapter.

MyLab Economics Study Plan

What Happens to Profits in the Long Run?

13.3 LEARNING OBJECTIVE: Analyze the situation of a monopolistically competitive firm in the long run.

Remember that a firm makes an economic profit when its total revenue is greater than all of its costs, including the opportunity cost of the funds invested in the firm by its owners. Because cost curves include the owners' opportunity costs, the Panera restaurant represented in Figure 13.4 on page 455 is making an economic profit. This economic profit gives entrepreneurs an incentive to enter this market and establish new firms. If a Panera is earning an economic profit selling turkey sandwiches, new restaurants serving similar food are likely to open in the same area.

How Does the Entry of New Firms Affect the Profits of Existing Firms?

As new restaurants open near your local Panera, the firm's demand curve will shift to the left. The demand curve will shift because the Panera will sell fewer sandwiches at each price when there are additional restaurants in the area. The demand curve will also become more elastic because consumers have additional restaurants from which to buy turkey sandwiches, so the Panera will lose more sales if it raises its prices. Figure 13.5 shows how the demand curve for your local Panera shifts as new firms enter its market.

(a) A monopolistic competitor may earn a short-run profit

(b) A monopolistic competitor's profit is eliminated in the long run

MyLab Economics Animation

Figure 13.5 How Entry of New Firms Eliminates Profit

Panel (a) shows that in the short run, your local Panera faces the demand and marginal revenue curves labeled "Short run." With this demand curve, the restaurant can charge a price above average total cost (point A) and make a profit, shown by the green rectangle. But this profit attracts new firms to enter the market, which shifts the demand and marginal revenue curves to the curves labeled "Long run" in panel (b). Because price is now equal to average total cost (point B), the restaurant breaks even and no longer earns an economic profit.

In panel (a) of Figure 13.5, the short-run demand curve shows the relationship between the price of turkey sandwiches and the quantity of sandwiches this Panera sells per week before the entry of new firms. With this demand curve, this Panera can charge a price above average total cost—shown as point A in panel (a)—and make a profit. But this profit attracts additional restaurants to the area and shifts the demand curve for this Panera's turkey sandwiches to the left. As long as this Panera is making an economic profit, there is an incentive for additional restaurants to open in the area and sell turkey sandwiches, and the demand curve will continue shifting to the left. As panel (b) shows, eventually the demand curve will have shifted to the point where it is just touching—or tangent to—the average total cost curve.

In the long run, at the point where the demand curve is tangent to the average total cost curve, price is equal to average total cost (point B), the firm is breaking even, and it no longer earns an economic profit. In the long run, the demand curve is also more elastic because the more restaurants there are in the area, the more sales this Panera will lose to other restaurants if it raises its price.

Don't Let This Happen to You

Don't Confuse Zero Economic Profit with Zero Accounting Profit

Remember that economists count the opportunity cost of the owner's investment in a firm as a cost. Suppose you invest $200,000 opening a pizza parlor, and the return you could earn on those funds each year in a similar investment—such as opening a sandwich shop—is 10 percent. Therefore, the annual opportunity cost of investing the funds in your own business is 10 percent of $200,000, or $20,000. This $20,000 is part of your profit in the accounting sense, and you would have to pay taxes on it. But in an economic sense, the $20,000 is a cost. In long-run equilibrium, we would expect that entry of new firms would keep you from earning more than 10 percent on your investment. So, you would end up breaking even and earning zero economic profit, even though you were earning an accounting profit of $20,000.   MyLab Economics Study Plan

Your Turn: Test your understanding by doing related problem 3.7 on page 473 at the end of this chapter.

Of course, it is possible that a monopolistically competitive firm will suffer an economic loss in the short run. As a consequence, the owners of the firm will not be covering the opportunity cost of their investment. We expect that, in the long run, firms will exit an industry if they are suffering an economic loss. If firms exit, the demand curve for the output of a remaining firm will shift to the right. This process will continue until the representative firm in the industry is able to charge a price equal to its average total cost and break even. Therefore, in the long run, monopolistically competitive firms will experience neither an economic profit nor an economic loss. Table 13.2 summarizes the short run and the long run for a monopolistically competitive firm.

MyLab Economics Concept Check

Table 13.2

The Short Run and the Long Run for a Monopolistically Competitive Firm

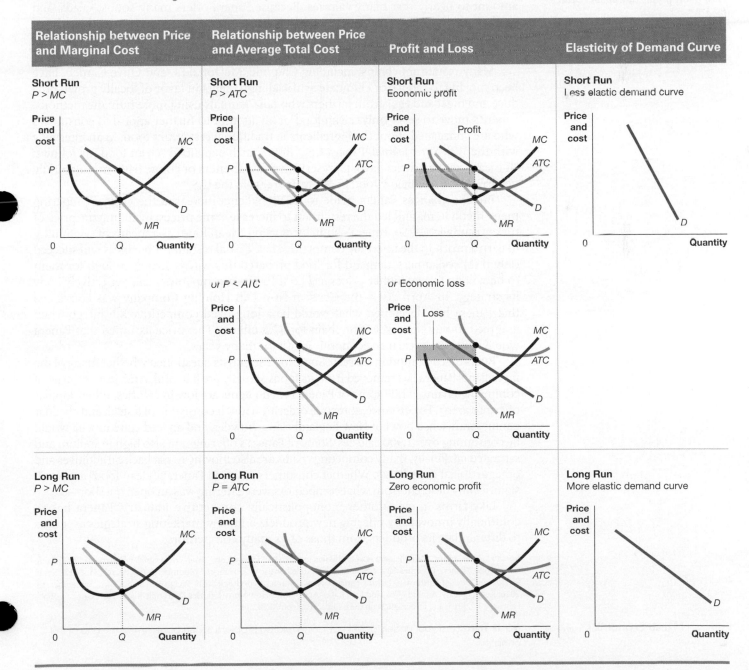

Relationship between Price and Marginal Cost	Relationship between Price and Average Total Cost	Profit and Loss	Elasticity of Demand Curve
Short Run $P > MC$	**Short Run** $P > ATC$	**Short Run** Economic profit	**Short Run** Less elastic demand curve
	or $P < ATC$	or Economic loss	
Long Run $P > MC$	**Long Run** $P = ATC$	**Long Run** Zero economic profit	**Long Run** More elastic demand curve

Apply the Concept

MyLab Economics Video

Is "Clean Food" a Sustainable Market Niche for Panera?

Ann Hermes/MACSM/AP Images

How many people care about "clean food"?

A burger, French fries, and a soft drink. Or a pepperoni pizza with extra cheese. For generations, these were typical meals for many teenagers and young adults. Today, however, some people view these traditional fast-food meals as unhealthy. "Fast-casual" restaurants such as Panera have benefitted from that view. The pioneer in the fast-casual restaurant niche was Chipotle Mexican Grill, whose founder, Steve Ells, recognized that there was a market for restaurants that serve healthier food than fast-food restaurants and provide speedier service than traditional table-service restaurants.

But Chipotle and some other fast-casual restaurants have had problems attracting consumers hoping to eat healthier foods because many of their menu items are high in calories. A 20-year old woman who is moderately active can consume about 2,200 calories per day without gaining weight. According to an article in the *New York Times*, a single Chipotle meal of a carnitas burrito, chips and guacamole, and a Coke would amount to nearly that many calories. Because Panera offers many soups, salads, and sandwiches, its offerings tend to be lower in calories. Panera promoted this advantage by becoming the first fast-casual chain to prominently show calorie counts on its menus and on display boards in the area where cashiers take orders.

Many restaurant chains, including Chipotle, McDonald's, and Olive Garden, have been moving to reduce or eliminate artificial ingredients in favor of locally grown produce and meat and eggs from farmers who raise animals using more humane methods. Panera's move to serve only "clean food" is an attempt to further appeal to consumers who are concerned about the ingredients in traditional restaurant food. In an interview with the *Wall Street Journal*, Panera CEO Ron Shaich explained "clean food" as follows: "It means zero artificial flavors, preservatives, sweeteners or colors from non-naturally occurring sources in any food in our restaurants in the U.S."

But the changes Panera made to its ingredients increased the cost of preparing many menu items and led the restaurant to increase some prices, including the price of turkey sandwiches. So, Panera's strategy of using "clean food" as a means of continuing to earn a profit in the intensely competitive fast-casual restaurant business will succeed only if (1) consumers' demand for food prepared this way is strong enough for them to be willing to pay higher prices *and* (2) if Panera's competitors can't effectively copy its strategy. In April 2017, the German firm JAB Holding Company was convinced that Panera had developed what would be a long-lived competitive advantage when it agreed to buy the restaurant chain for $7.5 billion. This price assumed that Panera would continue to earn an economic profit for many years.

But is that assumption correct? Some food scientists questioned whether many of the ingredients Panera has removed from its foods actually are harmful. And, just as is true of competing chains, while some of Panera's menu items are low in calories, other popular offerings aren't. For instance, someone ordering a lunch consisting of a steak and cheddar panini sandwich, a bowl of New England clam chowder, and an iced caffè mocha would be consuming over 1,900 calories. Some of Panera's offerings are also high in sodium and saturated fat. Finally, many competing chains are also moving to cut back on additives and other artificial ingredients. Whether consumers will find Panera's "clean food" approach significantly different from what competitors were offering was an open question.

Like firms in every other monopolistically competitive industry, Panera has to continually innovate by offering new products and new marketing strategies as it tries to differentiate its products from those of its many competitors.

Sources: Julie Jargon, "What Panera Had to Change to Make Its Menu 'Clean,'" *Wall Street Journal*, February 20, 2017; Craig Giammona, "Panera Becomes First Chain to Label Added Sugar in Beverages," bloomberg.com, March 31, 2017; Kavin Senapathy, "Should Customers Fall for Panera's New Gimmick? Food Scientists Weigh In," forbes.com, September 13, 2016; Kevin Quealy, Amanda Cox, and Josh Katz, "At Chipotle, How Many Calories Do People Really Eat?" *New York Times*, February 17, 2015; and information on the panerabread.com Web site.

MyLab Economics Study Plan

Your Turn: Test your understanding by doing related problem 3.9 on page 474 at the end of this chapter.

Is Zero Economic Profit Inevitable in the Long Run?

The economic analysis of the long run shows the effects of market forces over time. Owners of monopolistically competitive firms, of course, do not have to passively accept this long-run result. The key to earning an economic profit is either to sell a differentiated product or to find a way of producing an existing product at a lower cost. If a monopolistically competitive firm selling a differentiated product is earning a profit, the profit will attract the entry of additional firms, and the entry of those firms will eventually eliminate the firm's profit. If a firm introduces new technology that allows it to sell a good or service at a lower cost, competing firms will eventually duplicate that technology and eliminate the firm's profit. *But this result holds only if the firm stands still and fails to find new ways of differentiating its product or fails to find new ways of lowering the cost of producing its product.*

The owner of a competitive firm is in a position like that of Ebenezer Scrooge in Charles Dickens's *A Christmas Carol*. When the Ghost of Christmas Yet to Come shows Scrooge visions of his own death, he asks the ghost, "Are these the shadows of the things that Will be, or are they shadows of things that May be, only?" The shadow of the end of their profits haunts owners of every firm. Firms try to continue earning a profit by reducing costs, by improving their products, by providing exceptional customer service, or by convincing consumers that their products are indeed different from what competitors offer. To stay one step ahead of its competitors, a firm has to offer consumers goods or services that they perceive to have greater *value* than those that competing firms offer. Value can take the form of product differentiation that makes the good or service more suited to consumers' preferences, or it can take the form of a lower price.

MyLab Economics Concept Check   **MyLab Economics** Study Plan

Solved Problem 13.3

MyLab Economics Interactive Animation

Red Robin Abandons an Experiment in Fast-Casual Restaurants

In 2011, Red Robin Burgers, a chain of more than 400 full-service restaurants, announced that it would open 12 fast-casual restaurants. In 2016, the company announced that it would close nine of those restaurants and abandon the fast-casual approach in the remaining three. As an article in the *Wall Street Journal* put it, the company had learned that "there is nothing fast—or easy—about breaking into the highly competitive market in fast-casual dining." A spokesman for the company said that Red Robin's fast-casual restaurants were "not performing as well as company officials had hoped" and were "not differentiated enough from the full-service, larger Red Robin restaurants."

a. Draw a graph similar to Figure 13.4, panel (b) for a representative Red Robin fast-casual restaurant.

Your graph should show two demand curves: one showing the situation where the restaurant is making a profit (which is what the firm's managers hoped for), and one where the restaurant is suffering a loss (which is what actually occurred). Be sure that your graph shows the restaurant's average total cost curve and marginal cost curve, as well as the marginal revenue curve for each of the two demand curves.

b. In explaining the failure of Red Robin's fast-casual restaurants, why did the spokesman specify that they were not sufficiently differentiated from the company's full-service restaurants?

Solving the Problem

Step 1: **Review the chapter material.** This problem is about how a monopolistically competitive firm maximizes profit, so you may want to review the section "How a Monopolistically Competitive Firm Maximizes Profit in the Short Run," which begins on page 454.

Step 2: **Answer part (a) by drawing a graph that shows demand at a Red Robin fast-casual restaurant as the company's managers expected it to be and as it actually was.** For simplicity, the graph assumes that hamburgers are the only item the restaurant sells. Demand curve D_1 shows the situation where the restaurant is earning a profit, as the company's managers hoped it would. The profit-maximizing quantity of hamburgers is Q_1, and the profit-maximizing price is P_1. We know the restaurant is earning a profit because we can see on the vertical axis that P_1 is greater than ATC_1. Demand curve D_2 shows the actual situation where the restaurant is suffering a loss. The profit-maximizing quantity of hamburgers is now Q_2, and the profit-maximizing price is P_2. The restaurant is suffering a loss because P_2 is less than ATC_2.

Step 3: **Answer part (b) by explaining why it was important for Red Robin to differentiate its fast-casual restaurants from its regular restaurants.** Red Robin restaurants have been around for decades, and most customers expect a sit-down meal with a server coming to their table to take their order—which will most likely be a hamburger. Fast-casual restaurants provide faster service, typically with more limited menus that feature healthier options (although the Shake Shack chain has had success providing fast-casual service selling hamburgers). People who liked full-service Red Robin restaurants were already eating there. To draw business away from fast-casual restaurants, Red Robin had to attract new customers by offering an experience that was different than in full-service Red Robin restaurants. In the end, the company failed to convince enough consumers that its fast-casual restaurants were sufficiently different from its full-service restaurants, and the firm had to abandon the effort.

Sources: Austen Huffard, "Red Robin Retreats from Fast-Casual Dining Experiment," *Wall Street Journal*, October 5, 2016; and Lisa Jennings, "Red Robin Closes, Rebrands 12 Fast-Casual Burger Works Units," nrn.com, October 3, 2016.

MyLab Economics Study Plan   **Your Turn:** For more practice, do related problems 3.10 and 3.11 on page 474 at the end of this chapter.

13.4 Comparing Monopolistic Competition and Perfect Competition

LEARNING OBJECTIVE: Compare the efficiency of monopolistic competition and perfect competition.

We have seen that monopolistic competition and perfect competition share the characteristic that in long-run equilibrium, firms earn zero economic profit. As Figure 13.6 shows, however, there are two important differences between long-run equilibrium in the two markets:

Figure 13.6 Comparing Long-Run Equilibrium under Perfect Competition and Monopolistic Competition

In panel (a), a perfectly competitive firm in long-run equilibrium produces at Q_{PC}, where price equals marginal cost, and average total cost is at a minimum. The perfectly competitive firm is both allocatively efficient and productively efficient. In panel (b), a monopolistically competitive firm produces at Q_{MC}, where price is greater than marginal cost, and average total cost is not at a minimum. As a result, the monopolistically competitive firm is neither allocatively efficient nor productively efficient. The monopolistically competitive firm has excess capacity equal to the difference between its profit-maximizing level of output and the productively efficient level of output.

- Monopolistically competitive firms charge a price greater than marginal cost.
- Monopolistically competitive firms do not produce at minimum average total cost.

Excess Capacity under Monopolistic Competition

Recall that a firm in a perfectly competitive market faces a perfectly elastic demand curve that is also its marginal revenue curve. Therefore, the firm maximizes profit by producing the quantity where price equals marginal cost. As panel (a) of Figure 13.6 shows, in long-run equilibrium, a perfectly competitive firm produces at the minimum point of its average total cost curve.

Panel (b) of Figure 13.6 shows that the profit-maximizing level of output for a monopolistically competitive firm comes at a level of output where price is greater than marginal cost, and the firm is not at the minimum point of its average total cost curve. A monopolistically competitive firm has *excess capacity*: If it increased its output, it could produce at a lower average total cost.   MyLab Economics Concept Check

Is Monopolistic Competition Inefficient?

We previously discussed the difference between productive efficiency and allocative efficiency (see Chapter 12, Section 12.6):

- *Productive efficiency* refers to the situation in which a good is produced at the lowest possible cost. For productive efficiency to hold, firms must produce at the minimum point of the average total cost curve.
- *Allocative efficiency* refers to the situation in which every good or service is produced up to the point where the last unit provides a marginal benefit to consumers equal to the marginal cost of producing it. For allocative efficiency to hold, firms must charge a price equal to marginal cost.

In a perfectly competitive market, both productive efficiency and allocative efficiency are achieved, but in a monopolistically competitive market, neither is achieved. Does it matter? Economists have debated whether monopolistically competitive markets being neither productively nor allocatively efficient results in a significant loss of well-being to society in these markets compared with perfectly competitive markets.   MyLab Economics Concept Check

How Consumers Benefit from Monopolistic Competition

Looking again at Figure 13.6, you can see that the key difference between the monopolistically competitive firm and the perfectly competitive firm is that the demand curve for the monopolistically competitive firm slopes downward, while the demand curve for the perfectly competitive firm is a horizontal line. The demand curve for the monopolistically competitive firm slopes downward because the good or service the firm is selling is differentiated from those being sold by competing firms. The perfectly competitive firm is selling a good or service identical to those being sold by its competitors. Remember that *firms differentiate their products to appeal to consumers.* For example, when Panera restaurants begin offering chicken avocado melt sandwiches, when Apple begins selling smartphones with larger screens, when General Mills introduces Apple-Cinnamon Cheerios, or when PepsiCo introduces Diet Wild Cherry Pepsi, they are all attempting to attract and retain consumers through product differentiation. The success of these product differentiation strategies indicates that some consumers find these products preferable to the alternatives. Consumers, therefore, are better off than they would have been had these companies not differentiated their products.

We can conclude that consumers face a trade-off when buying the product of a monopolistically competitive firm: They are paying a price that is greater than marginal cost, and the product is not being produced at minimum average cost, but they benefit from being able to purchase a product that is differentiated and more closely

MyLab Economics Study Plan   suited to their tastes.   MyLab Economics Concept Check

---

🔴 Apply the Concept   MyLab Economics Video

One Way to Differentiate Your Restaurant? Become a Ghost!

Bloomberg/Getty images

Are "ghost" restaurants the future of big city dining?

To differentiate themselves from the competition, firms try to anticipate changes in consumer tastes and to adapt their products or develop new products that fit those changed tastes. Doing so can be difficult for restaurants, though, because consumers often associate a restaurant with a particular type of food or style of service. As we saw in Solved Problem 13.3, Red Robin failed when it tried to open fast-casual restaurants because consumers identified it too strongly with burgers served in traditional table-service restaurants. Similarly, in 2017, McDonald's CEO Steve Easterbrook announced that the company would abandon attempts to compete with fast-casual restaurants by offering healthier meal options and return to its fast-food roots. McDonald's had added more salads, snack wraps, and items similar to those found at Panera and other fast-casual restaurants, but it was unable to successfully compete for consumers who liked those foods. Instead, McDonald's decided to concentrate on improving the taste and quality of its hamburgers and other traditional menu items. As one McDonald's executive put it, "We don't need to be a different McDonald's, but a better McDonald's."

In 2013, Todd Millman and Peter Schatzberg came up with a solution to the problem of restaurants being too closely identified with one type of food: When consumer tastes change, just start a new restaurant with a new menu. Building new brick-and-mortar restaurants every few months would be extremely costly, but all of Millman and Schatzberg's restaurants exist only online. In 2017, their Green Summit Group operated nine "restaurants" in New York City and nine in Chicago, but all of the food was prepared from a single location in each city. Customers ordered food for delivery through the Grubhub app. The 18 different "restaurants" that Millman and Schatzberg operate exist only as logos on Web sites and on the containers the food is delivered in. Most people using the app don't realize that they aren't ordering from a brick-and-mortar restaurant.

Schatzberg argues that for restaurants appealing to younger consumers, "variety is key…. If you can have vegan, vegetarian, chicken and shrimp, you can cater to a broader audience. It's a variety of categories, and variety within the categories." Being online only allows Green Summit to quickly add new menu items: "Quinoa bowls—I had that epiphany in the morning, and we launched in the afternoon." The company can also drop menu items quickly, as it did when consumers in Midtown Manhattan failed to order as many Middle Eastern dishes as had been expected.

Are Green Summit and other "ghost restaurants" the wave of the future in the restaurant business? For the next few years, these firms are likely to account for an increasing share of food sales as more people purchase food online and as ghost restaurants are able to quickly respond to changes in consumer tastes. But these restaurants also face some obstacles to expanding. Their menus usually don't include foods with multiple sauces or other ingredients that might spill during delivery. In addition, delivery time is generally longer than for pizza and similar foods that have long dominated the home-delivery segment of the market. The time it takes for delivery also makes it harder for ghost restaurants to compete with Panera, Chipotle, and other fast-casual restaurants. According to online reviews, the food delivered from ghost restaurants sometimes arrives cold. It remains to be seen if ghost restaurants can overcome these problems and seize a large share of the market in the long run.

Sources: Robert Channick, "9 Restaurants, 1 Kitchen, No Dining Room—Virtual Restaurants Open for Online Delivery," chicagotribune.com, March 27, 2017; Cara Eisenpress, "Behold 'Ghost Restaurants': Order Online, but Don't Try to Show Up for Dinner," crainsnewyork.com, February 22, 2016; and Neal Ungerleider, "Hold the Storefront: How Delivery-Only 'Ghost' Restaurants Are Changing Takeout," fastcompany.com, January 20, 2017.

Your Turn: Test your understanding by doing related problem 4.7 on page 475 at the end of this chapter.

MyLab Economics Study Plan

13.5 How Marketing Differentiates Products

LEARNING OBJECTIVE: Define marketing and explain how firms use it to differentiate their products.

Firms can differentiate their products through **marketing**, which refers to all the activities necessary for a firm to sell a product to a consumer. Marketing includes activities such as determining which product to sell, designing the product, advertising the product, deciding how to distribute the product—for example, in retail stores or through a Web site—and monitoring how changes in consumer tastes are affecting the market for the product. Peter F. Drucker, a leading business strategist, described marketing as follows: "It is the whole business seen from the point of view of its final result, that is, from the consumer's point of view…. True marketing … does not ask, 'What do we want to sell?' It asks, 'What does the consumer want to buy?'"

For monopolistically competitive firms to earn an economic profit and defend the profit from competitors, they must differentiate their products. Firms use two marketing tools to differentiate their products: brand management and advertising.

Marketing All the activities necessary for a firm to sell a product to a consumer.

Brand Management

Brand management The actions of a firm intended to maintain the differentiation of a product over time.

Once a firm has succeeded in differentiating its product, it must try to maintain that differentiation over time through **brand management**. As we have seen, whenever a firm successfully introduces a new product or a significantly different version of an old product, it earns an economic profit in the short run. But the success of the firm inspires competitors to copy the new or improved product, and, in the long run, the firm's economic profit will be competed away. Firms use brand management to postpone the time when they will no longer be able to earn an economic profit.   MyLab Economics Concept Check

Advertising

An innovative advertising campaign can make even long-established and familiar products, such as Coke or McDonald's Big Mac hamburgers, seem more desirable than competing products. When a firm advertises a product, it is trying to shift the demand curve for the product to the right and to make it more inelastic. If the firm is successful, it will sell more of the product at every price, and it will be able to increase the price it charges without losing as many customers. Of course, advertising also increases a firm's costs. If the increase in revenue that results from the advertising is greater than the increase in costs, the firm's profit will increase.   MyLab Economics Concept Check

Defending a Brand Name

To defend a brand name, a firm can apply for a *trademark*, which grants legal protection against other firms using its product's name.

One threat to a trademarked name is the possibility that it will become so widely used for a type of product that it will no longer be associated with the product of a specific company. Courts in the United States have ruled that when this happens, a firm is no longer entitled to legal protection of the brand name. For example, "aspirin," "escalator," and "thermos" were originally all brand names of the products of particular firms, but each became so widely used to refer to a type of product that none remains a legally protected brand name. Firms spend substantial amounts of money trying to prevent this from happening. Coca-Cola, for example, employs people to travel to restaurants around the country and order a "Coke" with their meal. If the restaurant serves Pepsi or some other cola, rather than Coke, Coca-Cola's legal department sends the restaurant a letter reminding the owner that "Coke" is a trademarked name and not a generic name for any cola. Similarly, Xerox Corporation spends money on advertising to remind the public that "Xerox" is not a generic term for making photocopies.

Legally enforcing trademarks can be difficult. Estimates are that each year, U.S. firms lose hundreds of billions of dollars in sales worldwide as a result of unauthorized use of their trademarked brand names. U.S. firms often find it difficult to enforce their trademarks in the courts of some foreign countries, although recent international agreements have increased the legal protections for trademarks.

Firms that sell their products through franchises rather than through company-owned stores encounter the problem that if a franchisee does not run his or her business well, the firm's brand may be damaged. Firms can take steps to keep such damage from happening. For example, automobile firms send "roadmen" to visit their dealers to make sure the dealerships are clean and well maintained and that the service departments employ competent mechanics and are well equipped with spare parts. Similarly, McDonald's sends employees from corporate headquarters to visit McDonald's franchises to make sure the bathrooms are clean and the French fries are hot.   MyLab Economics Concept Check

MyLab Economics Study Plan

13.6 What Makes a Firm Successful?

LEARNING OBJECTIVE: Identify the key factors that determine a firm's success.

A firm's owners and managers control some of the factors that make a firm successful and allow it to earn an economic profit. The most important of these is the firm's ability to differentiate its product or to produce it at a lower average cost than competing

MyLab Economics Animation

Figure 13.7

What Makes a Firm Successful?

The factors under a firm's control—the ability to differentiate its product and the ability to produce it at lower cost—combine with factors beyond its control to determine the firm's profitability.

Source: Adapted from Figure 9.2 in David Besanko, David Dranove, Mark Shanley, and Scott Schaefer, *The Economics of Strategy*, 6th ed., New York: John Wiley & Sons, Inc., 2012, p. 295.

firms. A firm that successfully does one or both of these things creates *value* for its customers. Consumers will buy a product if they believe it meets a need not met by competing products or if its price is below that of competitors.

Some factors that affect a firm's profitability are not directly under the firm's control. Certain factors will affect all the firms in a market. For example, rising prices for jet fuel will reduce the profitability of all airlines. When many consumers decided that rather than buy DVDs, they preferred to download or stream movies from Netflix, iTunes, or Amazon, the profitability of all stores selling DVDs was reduced.

Sheer chance also plays a role in business, as it does in all other aspects of life. A struggling McDonald's franchise may see its profit increase dramatically after the county unexpectedly decides to build a new road nearby. Many businesses in Florida, including restaurants, hotels, and resorts, experienced a marked drop in customers and profits as a result of the effects of Hurricane Irma in September 2017. Figure 13.7 illustrates the important point that factors within the firm's control and factors outside the firm's control interact to determine the firm's profitability. **MyLab Economics** Concept Check

MyLab Economics Study Plan

Apply the Concept

MyLab Economics Video

Is Being the First Firm in the Market a Key to Success?

Some business analysts argue that the first firm to enter a market can have important *first-mover advantages*. By being the first to sell a particular good, a firm may find its name closely associated with the good in the public's mind, as, for instance, Amazon is closely associated with online shopping or eBay is associated with online auctions. This close association may make it more difficult for new firms to enter the market and compete against the first mover.

Surprisingly, though, recent research has shown that the first firm to enter a market often does *not* have a long-lived advantage over later entrants. Consider, for instance, the market for pens. Until the 1940s, the only pens available were fountain pens that had to be refilled frequently from an ink bottle and used ink that dried slowly and smeared easily. In October 1945, entrepreneur Milton Reynolds introduced the first ballpoint pen, which did not need to be refilled. When it went on sale at Gimbels department store in New York City, it was an instant success. Although the pen had a price of $12—the equivalent of about $160 at today's prices—hundreds of thousands were sold, and Milton Reynolds became a millionaire. Unfortunately, it didn't last. Although Reynolds had guaranteed that his pens would write for two years—later raised to five years—in fact, the pens often leaked and frequently stopped writing after only limited use. Sales began to collapse, the flood of pens returned under the company's guarantee wiped out its profit, and within a few years, Reynolds International Pen Company stopped selling pens

Studiomode/Alamy Stock Photo

Although not first to market, Bic ultimately was more successful than the firm that pioneered ballpoint pens.

in the United States. By the late 1960s, firms such as Bic, selling inexpensive—but reliable—ballpoint pens, dominated the market.

What happened to the Reynolds International Pen Company turns out to be more the rule than the exception. For example, Apple's iPod was not the first digital music player to appear on the U.S. market. Both SaeHan's MPMan and Diamond's Rio PMP 300 were released in the United States in 1998, three years before the iPod. The Japanese firm NTT DoCoMo introduced the first widely adopted smartphone in 1999, and BlackBerry introduced a smartphone in the United States shortly thereafter. By 2016, neither firm was still producing smartphones. Similarly, although Hewlett-Packard currently leads the market for laser printers, with a market share of more than 35 percent, it did not invent the laser printer. Xerox invented the laser printer, and IBM sold the first commercial laser printers, although neither firm is important in the market today. As another example, Procter & Gamble was not the first firm to sell disposable diapers when it introduced Pampers in 1961. Microsoft's Internet Explorer was not the first Web browser; before Internet Explorer, there was Netscape; before Netscape, there was Mosaic; and before Mosaic, there were several other Web browsers that for a time looked as if they might dominate the market. In 2004 Microsoft introduced the SPOT smartwatch, but the company discontinued it in 2008, when it failed to find many buyers. In all these cases, the firms that were first to introduce a product ultimately lost out to other companies that arrived on the scene later but did a better job of providing consumers with products that were more reliable, less expensive, more convenient, or that otherwise provided greater value.

Sources: David George-Cosh and Jacquie McNish, "BlackBerry Outsourcing Handset Business," *Wall Street Journal,* September 28, 2016; Steven P. Schnaars, *Managing Imitation Strategies: How Later Entrants Seize Markets from Pioneers,* New York: The Free Press, 1994; and Gerard J. Tellis and Peter N. Golder, *Will and Vision: How Latecomers Grow to Dominate Markets,* Los Angeles: Figueroa Press, 2006.

MyLab Economics Study Plan

Your Turn: Test your understanding by doing related problem 6.5 on page 477 at the end of this chapter.

Continued from page 451

Economics in Your Life & Career

Can You Operate a Successful Restaurant?

At the beginning of the chapter, we asked you to think about how successful you are likely to be in opening an Italian restaurant in your hometown. As you saw in this chapter, if your restaurant is successful, other people are likely to open competing restaurants, and all your economic profit will eventually disappear. Your new competitors will sell Italian food, but it won't be exactly like yours. Each restaurant will have its own ideas on how best to appeal to people who like Italian food. Unless your food is very different from your competitors' food—or your service is much better—in the long run, you will be unable to charge prices high enough to allow you to earn an economic profit.

In a monopolistically competitive market, free entry will reduce prices and lead to zero economic profit in the long run. In addition to lowering prices, competition benefits consumers by leading firms to offer somewhat different versions of the same product; for example, two Italian restaurants will rarely be exactly alike.

Conclusion

In this chapter, we applied to the more common market structure of monopolistic competition many of the ideas about competition we developed in discussing perfect competition. At the end of Chapter 12, we concluded: "The competitive forces of the market impose relentless pressure on firms to produce new and better goods and services at the lowest possible cost. Firms that fail to adequately anticipate changes in consumer tastes or that fail to adopt the latest and most efficient production technology do not survive in the long run." These conclusions are as true for fast-casual restaurants and firms in other monopolistically competitive markets as they are for wheat farmers and cage-free egg farmers in perfectly competitive markets.

In the next two chapters, we discuss the remaining market structures: oligopoly and monopoly.

Visit **MyLab Economics** for a news article and analysis related to the concepts in this chapter.

CHAPTER SUMMARY AND PROBLEMS

Key Terms

Brand management, p. 466

Marketing, p. 465

Monopolistic competition, p. 452

13.1 Demand and Marginal Revenue for a Firm in a Monopolistically Competitive Market, pages 452–454

LEARNING OBJECTIVE: Explain why a monopolistically competitive firm has downward-sloping demand and marginal revenue curves.

MyLab Economics   Visit www.pearson.com/mylab/economics to complete these exercises online and get instant feedback.

Summary

A firm competing in a **monopolistically competitive** market sells a differentiated product. Therefore, unlike a firm in a perfectly competitive market, it faces a downward-sloping demand curve. When a monopolistically competitive firm cuts the price of its product, it sells more units but must accept a lower price on the units it could have sold at the higher price. As a result, its marginal revenue curve is downward sloping. Every firm that has the ability to affect the price of the good or service it sells will have a marginal revenue curve that is below its demand curve.

Review Questions

1.1 What are the most important differences between perfectly competitive markets and monopolistically competitive markets? Give two examples of products sold in perfectly competitive markets and two examples of products sold in monopolistically competitive markets.

1.2 Why does a local McDonald's face a downward-sloping demand curve for its Quarter Pounders? If a McDonald's raises the price of Quarter Pounders above the prices other local fast-food restaurants charge for hamburgers, won't it lose all its customers?

1.3 With a downward-sloping demand curve, why is average revenue equal to price? Why is marginal revenue less than price?

Problems and Applications

1.4 There are about 400 wineries in California's Napa Valley. Describe the reaction of consumers if the owner of one of the wineries—Chip Case's Wine Emporium—raises the price of his wine by $5.00 per bottle, assuming the following:
  a. The industry is perfectly competitive.
  b. The industry is monopolistically competitive.

1.5 Purell announced that the new chemical formula for its hand sanitizer was so effective that "just 1 squirt of Purell Advanced Hand Sanitizer kills as many germs as two squirts of any other national brand." If Purell succeeds in convincing consumers that its claim is correct, would its demand curve become more elastic or less elastic? Briefly explain.

1.6 Fill in the missing values in the following table, which shows the demand for snow skiing lessons per day at a resort in Vermont:

Snow Skiing Lessons per Day (Q)	Price (P)	Total Revenue (TR = P × Q)	Average Revenue ($AR = \dfrac{TR}{Q}$)	Marginal Revenue ($MR = \dfrac{\Delta TR}{\Delta Q}$)
0	$80.00			
1	75.00			
2	70.00			
3	65.00			
4	60.00			
5	55.00			
6	50.00			
7	45.00			
8	40.00			

1.7 There are many wheat farms in the United States, and there are also more than 2,000 Panera Bread restaurants. Why, then, does a Panera restaurant face a downward-sloping demand curve, while a wheat farmer faces a horizontal demand curve?

1.8 Is it possible for marginal revenue to be negative for a firm selling in a perfectly competitive market? Is it possible for marginal revenue to be negative for a firm selling in a monopolistically competitive market? Briefly explain.

1.9 In the following graph, consider the marginal revenue of the eleventh unit sold. When the firm cuts the price from $5.00 to $4.75 to sell the eleventh unit, what area in the graph shows the output effect, and what is the dollar value of the output effect? What area in the graph shows the price effect, and what is the dollar value of the price effect? What is the marginal revenue of the eleventh unit?

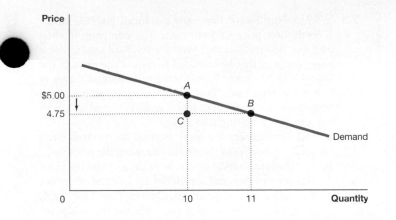

1.10 Sally runs a vegetable stand. The following table shows two points on the demand curve for the heirloom tomatoes she sells:

Price	Quantity Demanded per Week
$5.00	100,000
$3.25	200,000

a. What would Sally's marginal revenue be from lowering the price of tomatoes from $5.00 to $3.25?
b. Calculate the output effect and the price effect from lowering the price to $3.25.

13.2 How a Monopolistically Competitive Firm Maximizes Profit in the Short Run, pages 454–457

LEARNING OBJECTIVE: Explain how a monopolistically competitive firm maximizes profit in the short run.

MyLab Economics   Visit www.pearson.com/mylab/economics to complete these exercises online and get instant feedback.

Summary

A monopolistically competitive firm maximizes profit at the level of output where marginal revenue equals marginal cost. Price equals marginal revenue for a perfectly competitive firm, but price is greater than marginal revenue for a monopolistically competitive firm. Therefore, unlike a perfectly competitive firm, which produces where $P = MC$, a monopolistically competitive firm produces where $P > MC$.

Review Questions

2.1 Why doesn't a monopolistically competitive firm produce where $P = MC$, as a perfectly competitive firm does?

2.2 Isabella runs a pet salon. She is currently grooming 125 dogs per week. If instead of grooming 125 dogs, she grooms 126 dogs, she will add $68.50 to her costs and $60.00 to her revenues. What will be the effect on her profit of grooming 126 dogs instead of 125 dogs?

2.3 If Daniel sells 350 hamburgers at a price of $3.25 each, and his average cost of producing 350 hamburgers is $3.00 each, what is his profit?

Problems and Applications

2.4 Maria manages a bakery that specializes in ciabatta bread, and she has the following information on the bakery's demand and costs:

Ciabatta Bread Sold per Hour (Q)	Price (P)	Total Cost (TC)
0	$6.00	$3.00
1	5.50	7.00
2	5.00	10.00
3	4.50	12.50
4	4.00	14.50
5	3.50	16.00
6	3.00	17.00
7	2.50	18.50
8	2.00	21.00

a. To maximize profit, how many loaves of ciabatta bread should Maria sell per hour, what price should she charge, and how much profit will she make?
b. What is the marginal revenue Maria receives from selling the profit-maximizing quantity of ciabatta bread? What is the marginal cost of producing the profit-maximizing quantity of ciabatta bread?

2.5 (Related to Solved Problem 13.2 on page 456) Suppose a firm producing table lamps has the following costs:

Quantity (Q)	Average Total Cost (ATC)
1,000	$15.00
2,000	9.75
3,000	8.25
4,000	7.50
5,000	7.75
6,000	8.50
7,000	9.75
8,000	10.50
9,000	12.00

Ben and Jerry are managers at the company, and they have this discussion:

Ben: We should produce 4,000 lamps per month because that will minimize our average cost.

Jerry: But shouldn't we maximize profit rather than minimize cost? To maximize profit, don't we need to take demand into account?

Ben: Don't worry. By minimizing average cost, we will be maximizing profit. Demand will determine how high the price we can charge will be, but it won't affect our profit-maximizing quantity.

Evaluate the discussion between the two managers.

2.6 (Related to the Chapter Opener on page 450) According to an article in the *Wall Street Journal*, in 2015 and 2016, Panera suffered from lower profits in part because of the costs of implementing its "clean food" strategy. Draw a graph showing the effect of this cost increase on the price of Panera's turkey sandwiches, on the quantity of turkey sandwiches Panera sells, and on its profit. Be sure that your graph includes Panera's demand, marginal revenue, marginal cost, and average total cost curves. Your graph should show changes in any of the curves. For simplicity, assume that Panera's clean food strategy doesn't affect the demand for its turkey sandwiches.

Source: Maria Armental, "Panera's Quarterly Results Beat Projections," *Wall Street Journal*, February 7, 2017.

2.7 William Germano served as the vice president and publishing director at the Routledge publishing company. He once gave the following description of how a publisher might deal with an unexpected increase in the cost of publishing a book:

> It's often asked why the publisher can't simply raise the price [if costs increase].... It's likely that the editor [is already] ... charging as much as the market will bear.... In other words, you might be willing to pay $50.00 for a ... book on the Brooklyn Bridge, but if ... production costs [increase] by 25 percent, you might think $62.50 is too much to pay, though that would be what the publisher needs to charge. And indeed the publisher may determine that $50.00 is this book's ceiling—the most you would pay before deciding to rent a movie instead.

a. According to what you have learned in this chapter, how do firms adjust the price of a good when there is an increase in cost? Use a graph to illustrate your answer.

b. Does the model of monopolistic competition seem to fit Germano's description? If a publisher does not raise the price of a book following an increase in its production cost, what will be the result?

c. How would the elasticity of demand for published books affect the ability of the publishing company to raise book prices when costs increase?

Source: William Germano, *Getting It Published: A Guide to Scholars and Anyone Else Serious about Serious Books*, 3rd ed., Chicago: University of Chicago Press, 2016, p. 130.

2.8 In 1916, Ford Motor Company produced 500,000 Model T Fords, at a price of $440 each. The company made a profit of $60 million that year. Henry Ford told a newspaper reporter that he intended to reduce the price of the Model T to $360, and he expected to sell 800,000 cars at that price. Ford said, "Less profit on each car, but more cars, more employment of labor, and in the end we get all the total profit we ought to make."

a. Did Ford expect the total revenue he received from selling Model Ts to rise or fall following the price cut?

b. Use the information given above to calculate the price elasticity of demand for Model Ts. Use the midpoint formula to make your calculation. (See Chapter 6, page 186, if you need a refresher on the midpoint formula.)

c. What would the average total cost of producing 800,000 Model Ts have to be for Ford to make as much profit selling 800,000 Model Ts as it made selling 500,000 Model Ts? Is this smaller or larger than the average total cost of producing 500,000 Model Ts?

d. Assume that Ford would make the same total profit when selling 800,000 cars as when selling 500,000 cars. Was Henry Ford correct in saying he would make less profit per car when selling 800,000 cars than when selling 500,000 cars?

2.9 Use the following graph for Elijah's Burgers to answer the questions.

a. If Elijah produces at the profit-maximizing level of output, how much is his total revenue? How much is his total cost? Briefly explain your calculations.

b. How much economic profit is Elijah earning? Briefly explain your calculation.

13.3 What Happens to Profits in the Long Run? pages 457–462

LEARNING OBJECTIVE: Analyze the situation of a monopolistically competitive firm in the long run.

MyLab Economics Visit www.pearson.com/mylab/economics to complete these exercises online and get instant feedback.

Summary

If a monopolistically competitive firm earns an economic profit in the short run, entry of new firms will eliminate the profit in the long run. If a monopolistically competitive firm is suffering an economic loss in the short run, exit of existing firms will eliminate the loss in the long run. Monopolistically competitive firms continually struggle to find new ways of differentiating their products as they try to stay one step ahead of other firms that are attempting to copy their success.

Review Questions

3.1 What effect does the entry of new firms have on the demand curve of an existing firm in a monopolistically competitive market?

3.2 What is the difference between zero accounting profit and zero economic profit?

3.3 Under what circumstances might a monopolistically competitive firm continue to earn an economic profit as new firms enter its market?

3.4 In the following graph, reproduced from the answer to Solved Problem 13.3, indicate the area representing the Red Robin restaurant's profit when the demand curve is D_1 and the area representing its loss when the demand curve is D_2.

Problems and Applications

3.5 (Related to the Chapter Opener on page 450) Panera Bread restaurants have been a very popular "fast-casual" dining option—with better food choices than fast-food restaurants like McDonald's and faster service and lower prices than traditional restaurants. Panera's profit per restaurant is much greater than McDonald's. Ten years from now, would you expect Panera's economic profit per restaurant to be higher, lower, or about the same as it is today? Briefly explain.

3.6 Suppose Angelica opens a small store near campus, selling beef brisket sandwiches. Use the graph below, which shows the demand and cost for Angelica's beef brisket sandwiches, to answer the following questions.

a. If Angelica wants to maximize profit, how many beef brisket sandwiches should she sell per day, and what price should she charge? Briefly explain your answer.

b. How much economic profit (or loss) is Angelica earning? Briefly explain.

c. Is Angelica likely to continue selling this number of beef brisket sandwiches in the long run? Briefly explain.

3.7 (Related to the Don't Let This Happen to You on page 458) A student remarks:

> If firms in a monopolistically competitive industry are earning an economic profit, new firms will enter the industry. Eventually, a representative firm will find that its demand curve has shifted to the left until it is just tangent to its average total cost curve and the firm is earning zero profit. Because firms are earning zero profit at that point, some firms will leave the industry, and the representative firm will find that its demand curve will shift to the right. In long-run equilibrium, price will be above average total cost by just enough so that each firm is just breaking even.

Briefly explain whether you agree with this analysis.

3.8 The market for athletic shoes is intensely competitive. In 2016, Sports Authority, one of the firms in the market, declared bankruptcy and closed its 460 stores. An Associated Press article discussed the effect of the closings of the Sports Authority stores on Foot Locker's store in the New York City borough of Manhattan and quoted Foot Locker's CEO as stating: "We realized a long time ago that we couldn't be everything to everybody [in one store]. We have definitive brands and experiences."

a. Draw a graph showing the effect on Foot Locker's Manhattan store of the exit of competing Sports Authority stores. Be sure that your graph includes the Foot Locker store's demand, marginal revenue, marginal cost, and average total cost curves. Your graph should show changes in any of the curves. It should also show any changes in the area representing the store's economic profit (or loss). Be sure to explain any assumptions you are making.

b. Why would Foot Locker's CEO emphasize that the store will have "definitive brands and experiences?" Wouldn't trying to be "everything to everybody" be a better strategy because the store might attract a larger number of customers? Briefly explain.

Source: Associated Press, "Foot Locker to Play Up the Store Experience," crainsnewyork.com, August 29, 2016.

3.9 **(Related to the Apply the Concept on page 460)** In March 2017, an article in the *Wall Street Journal* discussed an announcement by Chipotle Mexican Grill that it had succeeded in changing its recipes with the goal of stripping "its burritos down to ingredients customers could find in their own pantries." The article noted, "Chipotle has always sought to stand out with fresher offerings than its competitors, but many fast food chains in recent years have tried to make their menus simpler and healthier." We've seen that Panera Bread spent two years changing its recipes as part of its "clean food" strategy. Are the strategies used by Panera, Chipotle, and other chains likely to give them the ability to earn an economic profit in the long run? If not, why do they bother pursuing these strategies?

Source: Annie Gasparro, "Chipotle Removes Preservatives from Its List of Ingredients," *Wall Street Journal*, March 28, 2017.

3.10 **(Related to Solved Problem 13.3 on page 461)** At the end of 2016, as the company suffered losses, Red Robin CEO Denny Marie Post announced that the company was increasing the number of lower-priced items on its menus. In particular, the restaurant would increase the number of meals priced at $6.99 from one to four. An article on marketwatch.com quoted the CEO as saying, "We see our recent upturn in traffic … as validation of our decision to refocus on everyday value … and improved speed-to-table."

a. In increasing the number of lower-priced menu items, is Red Robin more likely to be reacting to competition from McDonald's or from Panera Bread? In emphasizing improved service time ("speed-to-table"), is Red Robin more likely to be reacting to competition from McDonald's or Panera Bread? Briefly explain.

b. Would these two strategies be an example of a firm in a monopolistically competitive industry attempting to differentiate its product? If not, briefly explain why the CEO may have decided to pursue these strategies.

Source: Tonya Garcia, "Red Robin Earnings Miss, but Shares Pop on Turnaround Potential," marketwatch.com, November 4, 2016.

3.11 **(Related to Solved Problem 13.3 on page 461)** In recent years, McDonald's has faced increased competition from other fast-food restaurants. In an attempt to differentiate itself from fast-food competitors, McDonald's has responded by remodeling some restaurants to include kiosks that customers can use to pay for their orders and to request table service. Remodeling a restaurant can cost as much as $60,000. McDonald's expects that customers will spend more on food when they order with kiosks. Suppose McDonald's begins to earn an economic profit in the restaurants offering table service and kiosks.

a. How are other fast-food restaurants likely to respond?

b. Is this new strategy likely to enable McDonald's to earn an economic profit in the long run? Briefly explain.

Source: Julie Jargon, "McDonald's Table Service: Fast Food Redefined," *Wall Street Journal*, November 18, 2016.

3.12 An article in the *Wall Street Journal* discussed the sidewalk vegetable stands in New York City's Chinatown. About 80 of these small vegetable stands operate along a handful of streets in that neighborhood. Most supermarkets buy vegetables from large wholesalers. In contrast, the entrepreneurs who run the stands in Chinatown buy from smaller wholesalers located in the neighborhood. These wholesalers, in turn, buy primarily from smaller family farms, some located overseas. Because these wholesalers make several deliveries per day, the owners of the stands do not have to invest in substantial storage space and the refrigerators that supermarkets use to keep vegetables fresh. The reporter compared prices for vegetables sold by these stands with vegetables sold by her supermarket: "In almost every case, Chinatown's prices were less than half what I would pay at the supermarket. Among the bargains: broccoli for 85 cents a pound, $1 each for pomegranates, oranges for a quarter."

a. Is it likely that the owners of these vegetable stands are earning an economic profit? Briefly explain.

b. Why doesn't competition among supermarkets drive the prices of vegetables they sell down to the prices of the vegetables sold in the Chinatown stands?

Source: Anne Kadet, "Why Fruits and Veggies Are So Crazy Cheap in Chinatown," *Wall Street Journal*, June 24, 2016.

13.4 **Comparing Monopolistic Competition and Perfect Competition, pages 462–465**

LEARNING OBJECTIVE: Compare the efficiency of monopolistic competition and perfect competition.

MyLab Economics Visit **www.pearson.com/mylab/economics** to complete these exercises online and get instant feedback.

Summary

Perfectly competitive firms produce at a quantity where price equals marginal cost and at minimum average total cost. Perfectly competitive firms achieve both allocative and productive efficiency. Monopolistically competitive firms produce at a quantity where price is greater than marginal cost and above minimum average total cost. Monopolistically competitive firms do not achieve either allocative or productive efficiency. Consumers face a trade-off when buying the product of a monopolistically competitive firm: They are paying a price that is greater than marginal cost, and the product is not being produced at minimum average total cost, but they benefit from being able to purchase a product that is differentiated and more closely suited to their tastes.

Review Questions

4.1 What are the differences between the long-run equilibrium of a perfectly competitive firm and the long-run equilibrium of a monopolistically competitive firm?

4.2 Why is a monopolistically competitive firm not productively efficient? In what sense does a monopolistically competitive firm have excess capacity?

4.3 Why is a monopolistically competitive firm not allocatively efficient?

4.4 Does the fact that monopolistically competitive markets are not allocatively or productively efficient mean that there is a significant loss in economic well-being to society in these markets? In your answer, be sure to define what you mean by "economic well-being."

Problems and Applications

4.5 A student makes the following comment:

> I can understand why a perfectly competitive firm won't earn a profit in the long run because it charges a price equal to marginal cost. But a monopolistically competitive firm can charge a price greater than marginal cost, so why can't it continue to earn a profit in the long run?

How would you answer this question?

4.6 Consider the following graph.

a. Is it possible to say whether this firm is a perfectly competitive firm or a monopolistically competitive firm? If so, explain how you are able to make this determination.

b. Does the graph show a short-run equilibrium or a long-run equilibrium? Briefly explain.

c. What quantity on the graph represents long-run equilibrium if the firm is perfectly competitive?

4.7 **(Related to the Apply the Concept on page 464)** In Chicago, Green Summit appears to be running nine different restaurants, with names such as Butcher Block, Milk Money, and Leafage. In reality, all the food for these restaurants is cooked in one central kitchen, and none of the restaurants have physical locations. The brands exist only as Web sites and on the delivery containers. An article on chicagotribune.com quoted the firm's CEO as saying, "I don't really think anybody cares. They just want really high-quality food."

a. If nobody cares whether a restaurant exists as a physical place, why does Green Summit have a Web site for each restaurant and packaging printed with each restaurant's name and logo? Aren't Green Summit's costs higher than if it just had a single name and one Web site?

b. Does Green Summit's strategy increase or decrease productive efficiency in the restaurant business? Does the strategy increase or decrease allocative efficiency? Does it increase or decrease the well-being of its customers? Briefly explain.

Source: Robert Channick, "9 Restaurants, 1 Kitchen, No Dining Room—Virtual Restaurants Open for Online Delivery," chicagotribune.com, March 27, 2017.

4.8 Consider the following graph.

a. At the profit-maximizing level of output, how much economic profit is this firm earning? Briefly explain.

b. Is this firm allocatively efficient? Is it productively efficient? Briefly explain.

4.9 An article in the *Wall Street Journal* described the marketing philosophy of Whole Foods Market, a supermarket chain that sells many food products that have no preservatives or artificial sweeteners (Amazon.com acquired Whole Foods after this article was published):

> Whole Foods has long divided its 462 stores into 11 regions, each with distinct product offerings like local maple syrup and gourmet pickles. A quarter of Whole Foods shoppers that visited the chain in the past month did so for items they couldn't find elsewhere.... For those who shopped at Wal-Mart Stores

Inc., only 3% said exclusive brands were the top draw.

a. Explain why Whole Foods does not achieve productive efficiency by offering its customers "distinct product offerings" and "exclusive brands."

b. Briefly explain how Whole Foods' product differentiation may benefit its customers more than if the supermarkets achieved allocative and productive efficiency.

Source: Annie Gasparro and Heather Haddon, "Whole Foods Aims to Cut Prices but Keep Its Cachet," *Wall Street Journal*, April 16, 2017.

 ## How Marketing Differentiates Products, pages 465–466

LEARNING OBJECTIVE: Define marketing and explain how firms use it to differentiate their products.

MyLab Economics Visit www.pearson.com/mylab/economics to complete these exercises online and get instant feedback.

Summary

Marketing refers to all the activities necessary for a firm to sell a product to a consumer. Firms use two marketing tools to differentiate their products: brand management and advertising. **Brand management** refers to the actions of a firm intended to maintain the differentiation of a product over time. When a firm has established a successful brand name, it has a strong incentive to defend it. A firm can apply for a *trademark*, which grants legal protection against other firms using its product's name.

Review Questions

5.1 Define *marketing*. Is marketing just another name for advertising?

5.2 Why are many companies so concerned about brand management?

Problems and Applications

5.3 Draw a graph that shows the effect on a firm's profit when it increases spending on advertising but the increased advertising has *no* effect on the demand for the firm's product.

5.4 A skeptic says, "Marketing research and brand management are unnecessary. If a company wants to find out what customers want, it should simply look at what they're already buying." Do you agree with this comment? Explain.

5.5 In 2016, Howard Shultz announced that he would step down as CEO of Starbucks to establish luxury coffee shops that would charge as much as $12 for a cup of coffee. Although some analysts questioned whether many consumers would be willing to pay such high prices for coffee, Erich Joachimsthaler, an executive at a brand-strategy

consulting firm, believes the projects could be successful. Joachimsthaler compared the market for coffee to the market for beer, which has experienced competition from small craft breweries. "They [established companies such as Coors and Anheuser-Busch InBev] never protected themselves from the high end…. I think Starbucks sees that the middle is slowing down."

a. Briefly explain what Joachimsthaler means by the "high end" and "the middle is slowing down." What relevance do his observations have for the success of Schultz's project?

b. Briefly explain whether Schultz establishing luxury coffee shops illustrates:
  • Product differentiation
  • Marketing
  • Brand management

Source: Julie Jargon, "Middle-Market Woes Inspire Starbucks's Bet on Luxury Coffee," *Wall Street Journal*, December 5, 2016.

5.6 Some companies have done a poor job protecting the images of their products. For example, Hormel's Spam brand name is widely ridiculed and is associated with annoying commercial messages received via e-mail. Think of other cases of companies failing to protect their brand names. What can companies do about the situation? Should the companies rebrand their products?

5.7 JustFab is an online fashion retailer that analyzes information about customers obtained from its Web site to gauge the clothing they like most and the frequency of their purchases. This information has enabled the company to respond quickly to changes in fashion trends and to better control its inventory. The type of customer data JustFab gathers is not available to retailers that sell only in brick-and-mortar stores. Briefly explain the contribution that JustFab's use of customer data can make to its marketing efforts.

Source: Loretta Chao, "JustFab Finds Managing Fashion Inventories Is Both Science and Art," *Wall Street Journal*, July 1, 2015.

What Makes a Firm Successful? pages 466–468

LEARNING OBJECTIVE: Identify the key factors that determine a firm's success.

MyLab Economics Visit www.pearson.com/mylab/economics to complete these exercises online and get instant feedback.

Summary

A firm's owners and managers control some of the factors that determine the profitability of the firm. Other factors affect all the firms in the market or result from chance, so they are not under

the control of the firm's owners. The interactions between factors the firm controls and factors it does not control determine its profitability.

Review Questions

6.1 What are the key factors that determine the profitability of a firm in a monopolistically competitive market?

6.2 How might a monopolistically competitive firm continually earn an economic profit?

Problems and Applications

6.3 In 2008, Gogo became the first company to offer Wi-Fi service on commercial aircraft. It provides the service primarily through ground-based cellular towers. Many air travelers find the $30 price Gogo charges on a cross-country flight to be very high because the speeds offered are too slow to stream movies or other content. Gogo faces competition from newer services that use satellites rather than ground-based towers, which enables them to offer much higher speeds at half the price Gogo charges. According to an article in the *Wall Street Journal*, in late 2016, Gogo was "rolling out an advanced satellite-based network" that would allow it to offer higher speeds at a lower price. A number of airlines, though, were considering switching to competing services.
   a. Will copying its competitors by offering a faster, lower-priced service likely allow Gogo to recapture its market share?
   b. Unlike its competitors, Gogo had to spend substantial amounts to build a network of ground-based cellular towers. It has to abandon those towers as it switches to a satellite-based network. Is the cost of those towers a disadvantage to Gogo as it competes with the new firms entering the industry? Briefly explain.
   Source: Thomas Gryta and Andy Pasztor, "Gogo Plans to Speed Up In-Flight Internet Service … in 2018," *Wall Street Journal*, September 28, 2016.

6.4 7-Eleven, Inc., operates more than 20,000 convenience stores worldwide. Edward Moneypenny, 7-Eleven's chief financial officer, was asked to name the biggest risk the company faced. He replied, "I would say that the biggest risk that 7-Eleven faces, like all retailers, is competition … because that is something that you've got to be aware of in this business." In what sense is competition a "risk" to a business? Why would a company in the retail business need to be particularly aware of competition?
   Source: Company Report, "CEO Interview: Edward Moneypenny—7-Eleven, Inc.," The Wall Street Transcript Corporation, February 24, 2003.

6.5 **(Related to the Apply the Concept on page 467)** A firm that is first to market with a new product frequently discovers that there are design flaws or problems with the product that were not anticipated. For example, the ballpoint pens made by the Reynolds International Pen Company often leaked. What effect do such problems cause for the innovating firm, and how do these unexpected problems create possibilities for other firms to enter the market?

6.6 Wealthy investors often invest in hedge funds. Hedge fund managers use investors' money to buy stocks, bonds, and other investments with the intention of earning high returns. But a column in the *Wall Street Journal* noted that managers who earned a high return for a few years were "smart or lucky," and it can be difficult for investors to determine which they were. Is it ever easy to determine whether a firm making an economic profit is doing so because of the skills of the firm's managers or because of luck? Briefly explain.
   Source: James Mackintosh, "Every Stock Picking Opportunity Is a Way to Lose Money Too," *Wall Street Journal*, January 16, 2017.

Critical Thinking Exercises

CT13.1 Suppose that a perfectly competitive firm finds a way to differentiate its product and become a monopolistically competitive firm.
   a. Explain how the graph showing the firm's demand, marginal revenue, and cost curves would change as a result. Be sure to mention whether anything happens to each curve.
   b. Explain whether you think this firm would be earning a profit in its new position as a monopolistically competitive firm.

CT13.2 For this exercise, your instructor may assign you to a group. Perhaps you've thought about being an entrepreneur and have a product or service in mind. If you haven't, think of a product or service now. Each member of the group should briefly describe his or her product or service. The group should pick one of the products or services mentioned and develop a brief plan for selling it. How well do your group's plans conform to the ideas in Section 13.5?

CT13.3 Section 13.5 describes how firms differentiate their products. You've likely flown on an airliner and know that all airline seats are basically the same, particularly in coach. Think about what service an airline is selling when you buy a ticket for a particular seat. Conduct online research to find out how airlines differentiate their services. Write two paragraphs summarizing your findings.

Apple, Spotify, and the Music Streaming Revolution

Few industries have experienced the disruptive force of technology the way the music industry has. For decades prior to the 1990s, large recording companies such as Universal Music Group, EMI, Warner Music, and Columbia dominated the music industry.

By the mid-1990s, though, the music industry faced a serious threat from the development by engineers in Germany of a new way of storing music. MP3 files compressed the amount of information—computer bits—on a physical CD to be small enough to make downloading songs from the Internet feasible. Many people bought CDs, converted the songs on them to MP3 files, and posted the songs to the Internet, where they were available for anyone to download for free, in violation of the copyright laws.

In 2001, Apple introduced the iPod, the first successful portable MP3 player. As CD sales declined sharply, most record companies became willing to sell music in Apple's iTunes store, which opened in 2003 and allowed people to legally download millions of songs for $0.99 each. Although Apple gave the record companies a 70 percent share of the revenue from downloads, that didn't come close to replacing what the record companies and musicians were losing from the collapse of CD sales.

Apple's iTunes was tremendously successful, but it did not put an end to digital piracy. By 2015, many consumers were switching from buying individual songs to streaming songs from YouTube or other sites without purchasing them. Several companies offered plans that allowed people to stream for free, although with advertisements similar to those on commercial radio stations. Spotify, a music streaming service based in Sweden, and Alphabet's Google Play Music offered subscription plans that allowed unlimited streaming for $9.99 per month without advertisements. In 2015, Apple began offering Apple Music to

A. Aleksandravicius/Shutterstock

compete with Spotify and Google Play Music. In 2016, Amazon launched Amazon Unlimited Music at a price of $7.99 per month for customers of its Amazon Prime expedited shipping service or $3.99 per month for owners of an Echo voice-activated device.

An industry like music streaming that includes only a few firms is an *oligopoly*. In an oligopoly, a firm's profitability depends on its interactions with other firms. In these industries, firms must develop *business strategies*, which involve not just deciding what price to charge and what quantity to produce but also how much to advertise, which new technologies to adopt, how to manage relationships with suppliers, and which new markets to enter.

Because there are relatively few firms competing in an oligopolistic industry, each firm must continually react to other firms' actions or risk a substantial decline in sales. In this chapter, we focus on strategic interactions among firms.

Sources: Dan Seifert, "Amazon's Full On-Demand Streaming Music Service Launches Today," theverge.com, October 12, 2016; Brian X. Chen, "Taylor Swift Scuffle Aside, Apple's New Music Service Is Expected to Thrive," *New York Times*, June 28, 2015; and Hannah Karp, "Apple iTunes Sees Big Drop in Music Sales," *Wall Street Journal*, October 24, 2014.

Chapter Outline & Learning Objectives

Economics in Your Life & Career

If You Were Managing a Walmart, Would You Cut the Price of a PlayStation 4?

You are a manager at Walmart and are responsible for setting the prices of consumer electronics. Currently, you are charging $399 for a PlayStation 4 game system, which is the same price being charged by Amazon, Best Buy, and Target. Your assistant manager makes the following proposal: "Let's cut the price to $349. By selling for $50 less than our competitors, we will gain a lot of their customers and increase our profit." Do you accept this proposal? As you read this chapter, try to answer this question. You can check your answer against the one we provide on **page 499** at the end of this chapter.

In studying perfectly competitive and monopolistically competitive industries, our analysis focused on how to determine a firm's profit-maximizing price and quantity. We concluded that firms maximize profit by producing where marginal revenue equals marginal cost. To determine marginal revenue and marginal cost, we used graphs that included the firm's demand, marginal revenue, and marginal cost curves. In this chapter, we will study oligopoly, a market structure in which a small number of interdependent firms compete. In analyzing oligopoly, we cannot rely on the same types of graphs we use in analyzing perfect competition and monopolistic competition—for two reasons:

1. We need to use economic models that allow us to analyze the more complex business strategies of large oligopoly firms. These strategies involve more than choosing the profit-maximizing price and quantity.

2. Even in determining the profit-maximizing price and quantity for an oligopoly firm, demand curves and cost curves are not as useful as in the cases of perfect competition and monopolistic competition. We are able to draw the demand curves for competitive firms by assuming that the prices these firms charge have no effect on the prices other firms in their industries charge. This assumption is realistic when each firm is small relative to the market. It is not a realistic assumption, however, for firms that are as large relative to their markets as Apple, General Motors, or Walmart.

When large firms cut their prices, their rivals in the industry often—but not always—respond by also cutting their prices. Because we don't know for sure how other firms will respond to a price change, we don't know the quantity an oligopolist will sell at a particular price. In other words, it is difficult to know what an oligopolist's demand curve will look like. As we have seen, a firm's marginal revenue curve depends on its demand curve. If we don't know what an oligopolist's demand curve looks like, we also don't know what its marginal revenue curve looks like. Because we don't know marginal revenue, we can't calculate the profit-maximizing quantity and the profit-maximizing price the way we do for competitive firms.

The approach we use in this chapter to analyze competition among oligopolists is called *game theory*. Game theory can be used to analyze any situation in which groups or individuals interact. In the context of economic analysis, game theory is the study of the decisions of firms in industries where the profit of each firm depends on its interactions with other firms. It has also been applied to strategies used in other contexts, such as international trade negotiations, political campaigns, and medical students choosing residency programs.

14.1 Oligopoly and Barriers to Entry
LEARNING OBJECTIVE: Show how barriers to entry explain the existence of oligopolies.

Oligopoly A market structure in which a small number of interdependent firms compete.

An **oligopoly** is an industry with only a few firms. This market structure lies between competitive industries, which have many firms, and monopolies, which have only a single firm. One measure of the extent of competition in an industry is the *concentration ratio*. Every five years, the U.S. Bureau of the Census publishes four-firm concentration ratios that measure the fraction of each industry's sales accounted for by its four largest firms. Most economists believe that a four-firm concentration ratio greater than 40 percent indicates that an industry is an oligopoly.

However, concentration ratios have the following flaws as measures of the extent of competition in an industry:

1. They do not include the goods and services that foreign firms export to the United States.

2. They are calculated for the national market, even though the competition in some industries, such as restaurants or college bookstores, is mainly local.

3. They do not account for competition that sometimes exists between firms in different industries. For example, Walmart is included in the discount department store industry but also competes with firms in the supermarket industry and the retail toy store industry.

Some economists prefer another measure of competition, known as the *Herfindahl-Hirschman Index* (see Chapter 15, Section 15.5). Despite their shortcomings, concentration ratios can provide a general idea of the extent of competition in an industry.

Table 14.1 lists examples of oligopolies in manufacturing and retail trade (along with representative firms from each industry). The Bureau of the Census does not track the streaming music industry separately, but in 2017, just a few firms—including Apple, Spotify, Google, and Tidal—accounted for more than 90 percent of paid music streaming subscriptions, making the industry an oligopoly.

Barriers to Entry

Why do oligopolies exist? Why aren't there many more firms in the computer, discount department store, beer, aircraft, or music streaming industries? Recall that new firms will enter industries when existing firms are earning an economic profit. But new firms often have difficulty entering an oligopoly. Anything that keeps new firms from entering an industry in which firms are earning an economic profit is called a **barrier to entry**. Three important barriers to entry are economies of scale, ownership of a key input, and government-imposed barriers.

Barrier to entry Anything that keeps new firms from entering an industry in which firms are earning economic profits.

Economies of Scale The most important barrier to entry is **economies of scale**, which exist when a firm's long-run average costs fall as the firm increases output (see Chapter 11, Section 11.6). The greater the economies of scale, the smaller the number of firms that will be in the industry. Figure 14.1 illustrates this point.

Economies of scale The situation in which a firm's long-run average costs fall as the firm increases output.

Table 14.1

Examples of Oligopolies in Retail Trade and Manufacturing

Retail Trade		Manufacturing	
Industry	Four-Firm Concentration Ratio	Industry	Four-Firm Concentration Ratio
Discount department stores (Walmart and Target)	97%	Cigarettes (Phillip Morris and R.J. Reynolds)	88%
Warehouse clubs and supercenters (Sam's Club and BJ's Wholesale Club)	94%	Beer (Anheuser-Busch and MillerCoors)	88%
College bookstores (Barnes & Noble and Follett)	75%	Aircraft (Boeing and Lockheed Martin)	80%
Hobby, toy, and game stores (Toys"R"Us and Michael's)	72%	Breakfast cereal (Kellogg's and General Mills)	79%
Radio, television, and other electronic stores (Best Buy and Apple)	70%	Dog and cat food (Hills and Nestlé Purina)	68%
Athletic footwear stores (Footlocker and Champs)	68%	Automobiles (General Motors and Ford)	60%
Pharmacies and drugstores (Walgreens and CVS Caremark)	63%	Chocolate and chocolate candy (Mars and Hershey)	48%

Source: U.S. Census Bureau, *Concentration Ratios*. (The values for manufacturing are for 2012; the values for retail trade are for 2007.)

Figure 14.1

Economies of Scale Help Determine the Extent of Competition in an Industry

An industry will be competitive if the minimum point on the typical firm's long-run average cost curve ($LRAC_1$) occurs at a level of output that is a small fraction of total industry sales, such as Q_1. An industry will be an oligopoly if the minimum point comes at a level of output that is a large fraction of industry sales, such as Q_2.

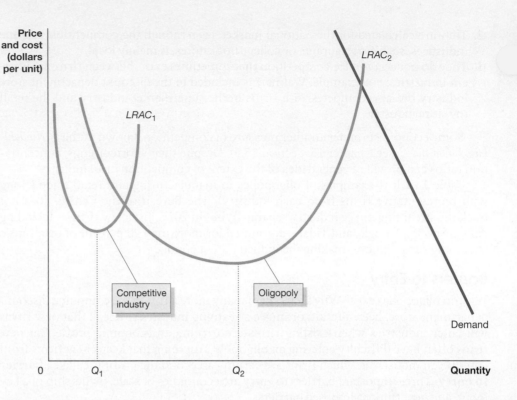

If economies of scale are relatively unimportant in the industry, the typical firm's long-run average cost curve (*LRAC*) will reach a minimum at a level of output (Q_1 in Figure 14.1) that is a small fraction of total industry sales. The industry will have room for a large number of firms and will be competitive. If economies of scale are significant, the typical firm will not reach the minimum point on its long-run average cost curve (Q_2 in Figure 14.1) until it has produced a large fraction of industry sales. In that case, the industry will have room for only a few firms and will be an oligopoly.

Economies of scale can explain why there is much more competition in the restaurant industry than in the music streaming industry. Because very large restaurants do not have significantly lower average costs than smaller restaurants, the restaurant industry has room for many firms. In contrast, a large music streaming firm such as Spotify has much lower average costs than would a small music streaming firm, partly because a large firm can spread the high fixed costs of streaming music—including very large server capacity, large research and development costs for its app, and the costs of the complex accounting necessary to keep track of the payments to the musicians and other copyright holders whose songs are being streamed—over a much larger quantity of subscriptions sold.

Ownership of a Key Input If production of a good requires a particular input, then control of that input can be a barrier to entry. For many years, the Aluminum Company of America (Alcoa) controlled most of the world's supply of high-quality bauxite, the mineral needed to produce aluminum. The only way other companies could enter the industry to compete with Alcoa was to recycle aluminum. The De Beers Company of South Africa was able to block competition in the diamond market by controlling the output of most of the world's diamond mines. Until the 1990s, Ocean Spray had very little competition in the market for fresh and frozen cranberries because it controlled almost the entire supply of cranberries. Even today, Ocean Spray controls about 65 percent of the cranberry crop through agreements with 650 cranberry growers.

Government-Imposed Barriers Firms sometimes try to convince the government to impose barriers to entry. Many large firms employ *lobbyists* to persuade state legislators and members of Congress to pass laws that are favorable to the economic interests of the firms. There are tens of thousands of lobbyists in Washington, DC, alone. Top lobbyists command annual salaries of $300,000 or more, which indicates the value firms place on their activities. Three important government-imposed barriers to entry are patents, licensing requirements, and restrictions on international trade.

A **patent** gives a firm the exclusive right to a new product for a period of 20 years from the date the patent application is filed with the government. Governments use patents to encourage firms to carry out research and development of new and better products and better ways of producing existing products. Output and living standards increase faster when firms devote resources to research and development, but a firm that spends money to develop a new product may not earn much profit if other firms can copy the product. For example, the pharmaceutical company Merck spends more than $5 billion per year on developing new prescription drugs. If rival companies could freely produce these new drugs as soon as Merck developed them, most of the firm's investment would be wasted. Because Merck can patent a new drug, the firm can charge higher prices during the years the patent is in force and make an economic profit on its successful innovation.

Governments also restrict competition through *occupational licensing*. For example, doctors and dentists in every state need licenses to practice. Licensing has expanded in recent years, though, to include occupations such as teeth whitening, irrigation contracting, and art therapy. Almost one-quarter of workers in the United States now have jobs that require a license. Acquiring a license can be a long and expensive process, frequently requiring completing a training or certification program approved by a licensing board. The justification for licensing laws is to protect the public from incompetent practitioners, but by restricting the number of people who can enter the licensed occupations, the laws also raise prices. Studies have shown that states that make it harder to earn a dentist's license have prices for dental services that are about 15 percent higher than in other states. Similarly, states that require a license for out-of-state firms to sell contact lenses have higher prices for contact lenses. When state licenses are required for occupations such as hair braiding or yoga instruction, restricting competition is the main result.

Governments also impose barriers to entering some industries by imposing tariffs and quotas on foreign competition. A *tariff* is a tax on imports, and a *quota* limits the quantity of a good that can be imported into a country (see Chapter 9, Section 9.4). A quota on foreign sugar imports severely limits competition in the U.S. sugar market. As a result, U.S. sugar companies can charge prices that are much higher than the prices companies outside the United States charge.

> **Patent** The exclusive right to a product for a period of 20 years from the date the patent application is filed with the government.

Apply the Concept

MyLab Economics Video

Got a Great Recipe for Cookies? Don't Try Selling Them in Wisconsin or New Jersey

If you enjoy baking, you may have developed your own tasty recipes. Or you may have become very good at baking cookies and cakes from your grandmother's recipes. You may even decide to make some extra money selling your baked goods. But if you lived in Wisconsin or New Jersey in 2017, selling baked goods out of your home or apartment was illegal.

In New Jersey, no one can legally sell baked goods unless the food is prepared in a commercial kitchen that has been inspected by the state government's Department of Health and Senior Services. Meeting this requirement would typically cost you $15,000 or more. Wisconsin requires anyone selling baked goods to obtain a license from the state and to prepare the food in a commercial kitchen that is subject to state inspection. In both states, legislators have argued that the laws are necessary to ensure that cakes and cookies are prepared under sanitary conditions. Critics of the laws point out, though, that large quantities of cakes and cookies are given away each

Fuse/Corbis/Getty Image

Does this home baker threaten small commercial bakeries in her area?

year in New Jersey and Wisconsin at church, school, and charity events. Few people report becoming ill from eating this food. Small home bakeries in the 48 states that allow them have also not resulted in an increase in food-borne illnesses.

In recent years, California, Minnesota, and Texas have repealed their laws banning the sale of home-baked goods. According to a report by the Institute for Justice, a group that opposes such laws, repeal led to more than 1,000 new home bakery businesses being established in each state. Typically, these businesses are operated part time and have revenues of just a few thousand dollars per year. But most of those revenues have come at the expense of commercial bakeries and other existing businesses that are selling fewer baked goods because of the new competition from home bakers. Opposition from businesses in Wisconsin and New Jersey that fear similar losses may be the key reason that attempts to repeal the ban on selling home-baked goods have failed in those states. The speaker of the Wisconsin Assembly explained his opposition to repeal: "While it's important that Wisconsin attracts new entrepreneurs, it should not be at the expense of our small businesses that are currently meeting the standards and regulations." Similarly, a news report noted opposition to a similar bill in the New Jersey state legislature from bakery owners who argued that "it gives home bakers an unfair advantage over ... traditional bakeries." But a lawyer representing three home bakers suing the state of Wisconsin on the grounds that the ban violates the state constitution asserted, "Protecting other businesses from competition is not a legitimate government interest."

As we saw in the *Apply the Concept* on page 256 of Chapter 8, many economists and policymakers are concerned that the rate at which new businesses are formed in the United States has slowed significantly in recent years. During the 2016 presidential campaign, Hillary Clinton and Donald Trump agreed that the federal government should take steps to reduce barriers to people wanting to open new businesses. But state legislatures, rather than Congress, typically enact occupational licenses and other barriers to opening small businesses, such as the ban on selling home-baked goods in Wisconsin and New Jersey.

Sources: Spencer Kent, "N.J. May Become Last State with Ban on Sales of Homemade Baked Goods," nj.com, April 27, 2017; Erica Jedynak and Heather Russinko, "Don't Even Think about Selling Grandma's Homemade Cookies," *Wall Street Journal*, December 2, 2016; Joe Moszczynski, "Home Bakers Pushing for Law to Allow Them to Sell Goodies to Public," nj. com, August 25, 2013; Nick Sibilla, "Over 3,000 Bakers Are Now in Business, after Minnesota Eased Restrictions on Selling Homemade Food," ij.org, February 16, 2017; and Anna Thomas Bates, "'Cookie Bill' Would Allow Home Bakers to Sell Their Goods," jsonline.com, April 26, 2017.

MyLab Economics Study Plan

Your Turn: Test your understanding by doing related problem 1.10 on page 501 at the end of this chapter.

In summary, to earn an economic profit, all firms would like to charge a price well above average total cost, but earning an economic profit attracts new firms to enter the industry. Eventually, the increased competition forces the price down to average total cost, and firms just break even. In an oligopoly, barriers to entry prevent—or at least slow down—entry, which allows firms to earn an economic profit over a longer period.   **MyLab Economics** Concept Check

MyLab Economics Study Plan

Game theory The study of how people make decisions in situations in which attaining their goals depends on their interactions with others; in economics, the study of the decisions of firms in industries where the profits of a firm depend on its interactions with other firms.

 14.2 Game Theory and Oligopoly

LEARNING OBJECTIVE: Use game theory to analyze the strategies of oligopolistic firms.

As we noted at the beginning of the chapter, economists analyze oligopolies by using *game theory*, which was developed during the 1940s by the mathematician John von Neumann and the economist Oskar Morgenstern. **Game theory** is the study of how people make decisions in situations in which attaining their goals depends on their interactions with others. In oligopolies, the interactions among firms are crucial in determining profitability because the firms are large relative to the market.

In all games—whether poker, chess, or Monopoly—the interactions among the players are crucial in determining the outcome. In addition, games share three key characteristics:

1. *Rules* that determine what actions are allowable
2. *Strategies* that players employ to attain their objectives in the game
3. *Payoffs* that are the results of the interactions among the players' strategies

In business situations, the rules of the "game" include not just laws that a firm must obey but also other factors beyond a firm's control—at least in the short run—such as its production function. A **business strategy** is a set of actions that a firm takes to achieve a goal, such as maximizing profit. The *payoff* is the profit a firm earns as a result of how its strategies interact with the strategies of other firms. The best way to understand the game theory approach is to look at an example.

> **Business strategy** Actions that a firm takes to achieve a goal, such as maximizing profits.

A Duopoly Game: Price Competition between Two Firms

In this simple example, we use game theory to analyze price competition in a *duopoly*—an oligopoly with two firms. We assume that Apple and Spotify are the only two firms selling subscriptions for music streaming. In 2017, in exchange for a $9.99 per month subscription charge, the firms allowed individuals to stream millions of songs. (Both firms offered a discounted charge of $4.99 to college students.) Some industry analysts thought that the firms needed to charge $14.99 per month to become consistently profitable. Let's focus on the pricing decisions Apple and Spotify face. We assume that the managers of the two firms have to decide whether to charge $9.99 or $14.99 for subscriptions. Which price will be more profitable depends on the price the other firm charges. Choosing a price is an example of a business strategy. In Figure 14.2, we organize the possible outcomes that result from the actions of the two firms into a **payoff matrix**, which is a table that shows the payoffs that each firm earns from every combination of strategies by the firms.

> **Payoff matrix** A table that shows the payoffs that each firm earns from every combination of strategies by the firms.

Apple's profit is shown in gold, and Spotify's profit is shown in blue. Each of the four quadrants of the payoff matrix shows the results of different combinations of strategies the two firms use. For example, if Apple and Spotify both charge $14.99 per month for unlimited music streaming, we are in the upper-left quadrant, which shows that each firm will make a profit of $10 million per month. If Apple charges the lower price of $9.99, while Spotify charges $14.99, Apple will gain many of Spotify's customers. Apple's profit will be $15 million, and Spotify's profit will be only $5 million. Similarly, if Spotify charges $9.99, while Apple charges $14.99, Apple's profit will be only $5 million, while Spotify's profit will be $15 million. If both firms charge $9.99, each will earn a profit of $7.5 million per month.

Clearly, the firms will be better off if they both charge $14.99 per month. But will they both charge this price? One possibility is that Apple's managers and Spotify's managers will get together and *collude* by agreeing to charge the higher price. **Collusion**

> **Collusion** An agreement among firms to charge the same price or otherwise not to compete.

MyLab Economics Animation

Figure 14.2

A Duopoly Game

Spotify's profit is shown in blue, and Apple's profit is shown in gold. Spotify and Apple will each make a profit of $10 million per month on sales of streaming music subscriptions if they both charge $14.99. However, each firm has an incentive to undercut the other by charging a lower price. If both firms charge $9.99, they will each make a profit of only $7.5 million per month.

	Apple	
	$14.99	**$9.99**
Spotify **$14.99**	Apple earns $10 million / Spotify earns $10 million profit	Apple earns $15 million / Spotify earns $5 million profit
Spotify **$9.99**	Apple earns $5 million / Spotify earns $15 million profit	Apple earns $7.5 million / Spotify earns $7.5 million profit

is an agreement among firms to charge the same price or otherwise not to compete. Unfortunately for Apple and Spotify—but fortunately for their customers—collusion is against the law in the United States and Europe. The government can fine companies that collude and send the managers involved to prison.

Apple's managers can't legally discuss their pricing decision with Spotify's managers, so they have to predict what the other managers will do. Suppose Apple's managers are convinced that Spotify's managers will charge $14.99. In this case, Apple's managers will definitely charge $9.99 because doing so will increase Apple's profit from $10 million to $15 million. But suppose that, instead, Apple's managers are convinced that Spotify's managers will charge $9.99. Then Apple's managers also will definitely charge $9.99 because that will increase their profit from $5 million to $7.5 million. In fact, regardless of which price Spotify's managers decide to charge, Apple's managers are better off charging $9.99. So, we know that Apple's managers will choose a price of $9.99 per month.

Now consider the situation from the point of view of Spotify's managers. They are in the same position as Apple's managers, so we can expect them to make the same decision to charge $9.99 per month. In this situation, both firms have a *dominant strategy*. A **dominant strategy** is the best strategy for a firm, no matter what strategies other firms use. The result is an equilibrium where both firms charge $9.99 per month. This situation is an equilibrium because each firm is maximizing profit, *given the price chosen by the other firm*. In other words, neither firm can increase its profit by changing its price, given the price chosen by the other firm. An equilibrium in which each firm chooses the best strategy, given the strategies chosen by other firms, is called a **Nash equilibrium**, named after the late Nobel Laureate John Nash of Princeton University, a pioneer in the development of game theory. MyLab Economics Concept Check

Dominant strategy A strategy that is the best for a firm, no matter what strategies other firms use.

Nash equilibrium A situation in which each firm chooses the best strategy, given the strategies chosen by other firms.

Firm Behavior and the Prisoner's Dilemma

Notice that the equilibrium in Figure 14.2 is not very satisfactory for either firm. The firms earn $7.5 million in profit each month by charging $9.99, but they could instead earn $10 million in profit if they both charge $14.99. By "cooperating" and charging the higher price, they would have achieved a *cooperative equilibrium*. In a **cooperative equilibrium**, players cooperate to increase their mutual payoff. We have seen, though, that the outcome of this game is likely to be a **noncooperative equilibrium**, in which each firm pursues its own self-interest.

A situation like the one in Figure 14.2, in which pursuing dominant strategies results in noncooperation that leaves everyone worse off, is called a **prisoner's dilemma**. The game gets its name from the problem two suspects face when arrested for a crime. If the police lack other evidence, they may separate the suspects and offer each a reduced prison sentence in exchange for confessing to the crime and testifying against the other suspect. Because each suspect has a dominant strategy to confess to the crime, they will both confess and serve a jail term, even though they would have gone free if they had both remained silent. MyLab Economics Concept Check

Cooperative equilibrium An equilibrium in a game in which players cooperate to increase their mutual payoff.

Noncooperative equilibrium An equilibrium in a game in which players do not cooperate but pursue their own self-interest.

Prisoner's dilemma A game in which pursuing dominant strategies results in noncooperation that leaves everyone worse off.

Don't Let This Happen to You

Don't Misunderstand Why Each Firm Ends Up Charging a Price of $9.99

It is tempting to think that Apple and Spotify would each charge $9.99 rather than $14.99 for a month of unlimited music streaming because each is afraid that the other firm will charge $9.99. In fact, fear of being undercut by the other firm charging a lower price is not the key to understanding each firm's pricing strategy. Notice that charging $9.99 is the most profitable strategy for each

firm, regardless of which price the other firm decides to charge. For example, even if Apple's managers somehow knew for sure that Spotify's managers intended to charge $14.99, Apple would still charge $9.99 because its profits would be $15 million instead of $10 million. Spotify's managers are in the same situation. That is why charging $9.99 is a dominant strategy for both firms.

Your Turn: Test your understanding by doing related problem 2.8 on page 502 at the end of the chapter. MyLab Economics Study Plan

Solved Problem 14.2

Is Offering a College Student Discount a Prisoner's Dilemma for Apple and Spotify?

Spotify and Apple Music both charge $9.99 per month for unlimited music streaming. Spotify introduced a reduced price of $4.99 for college students, which after a delay Apple decided to match. In an attempt to attract more college students away from Spotify, Apple decided to allow students to receive the discount for four years, rather than for just one year, as Spotify does. But some industry analysts questioned whether either firm could earn a profit if they continued their current pricing. Spotify has grown rapidly, but it had yet to earn a profit by the end of 2016, which caused one analyst to hope: "Maybe profitability will start to become a priority too."

Construct a payoff matrix for Apple Music and Spotify, using the following hypothetical information:

- If neither firm offers a college student discount, each firm earns a profit of $7 million per month.
- If both firms offer a college student discount, each firm earns a profit of $5 million per month.

- If Apple Music offers a college student discount and Spotify doesn't, Apple Music earns a profit of $9 million, and Spotify earns a profit of $4 million.
- If Spotify offers a college student discount and Apple Music doesn't, Spotify earns a profit of $9 million, and Apple Music earns a profit of $4 million.

a. If Apple Music wants to maximize profit, will it offer a college student discount? Briefly explain.

b. If Spotify wants to maximize profit, will it offer a college student discount? Briefly explain.

c. Is there a Nash equilibrium to this game? If so, what is it?

d. Does your analysis allow you to predict whether Spotify is likely to expand the term of its college student discount from one year to four to match the term of Apple Music's discount?

Solving the Problem

Step 1: **Review the chapter material.** This problem uses payoff matrixes to analyze a business situation, so you may want to review the section "A Duopoly Game: Price Competition between Two Firms," which begins on page 485.

Step 2: **Construct the payoff matrix.** Note that your payoff matrix should look similar to Figure 14.2.

		Apple	
		Don't Offer	**Offer**
Spotify	**Don't Offer**	Spotify earns $7 million profit / Apple earns $7 million profit	Spotify earns $4 million profit / Apple earns $9 million profit
	Offer	Spotify earns $9 million profit / Apple earns $4 million profit	Spotify earns $5 million profit / Apple earns $5 million profit

Step 3: **Answer part (a) by showing that Apple Music has a dominant strategy of offering a college student discount.** If Spotify doesn't offer the discount, Apple Music will make $9 million if it offers the discount but only $7 million if it doesn't. If Spotify offers the discount, Apple Music will make $5 million if it offers the discount but only $4 million if it doesn't. Therefore, offering the discount is a dominant strategy for Apple Music.

Step 4: **Answer part (b) by showing that Spotify has a dominant strategy of offering a college student discount.** Spotify is in the same situation as Apple Music, so it also has a dominant strategy of offering the discount.

Step 5: **Answer part (c) by showing that there is a Nash equilibrium for this game.** Both firms offering a college student discount is a Nash equilibrium. Given that Apple Music is offering the discount, Spotify's best strategy is to offer the service. Given that Spotify is offering the discount, Apple Music's best strategy is to offer it. Therefore, offering a college student discount is the optimal decision for both firms, *given the decision by the other firm.*

Step 6: **Answer part (d) by predicting whether Spotify is likely to match Apple's terms for the student discount.** The logic of the prisoner's dilemma analysis would lead us to predict that Spotify will extend the time limit to use the college student discount from one year to four years. Failing to match Apple's terms would likely cause Spotify to lose some sales to Apple, just as Apple's initial failure to offer a college student discount caused it to lose some sales to Spotify.

Extra Credit: This game is another example of the prisoner's dilemma. Apple Music and Spotify would be more profitable if neither offered a college student discount. Each firm's dominant strategy is to offer the discount, however, so they end up in an equilibrium where both offer the discount, and both earn a reduced profit. As we will see in the next section, though, it's possible that there may be a way out of the prisoner's dilemma for firms in this type of situation. In fact, in 2017, some industry analysts expected that Spotify and Apple Music would eventually both increase prices in order to become profitable.

Sources: Nathan Olivarez-Giles, "Apple Music Is Now Half Price for Students," *Wall Street Journal*, May 6, 2016; and Mia Shanley, "Spotify Could Become Profitable in 2017," businessinsider.com, December 1, 2016.

MyLab Economics Study Plan

Your Turn: For more practice, do related problems 2.9 and 2.10 on page 502 at the end of this chapter.

Can Firms Escape the Prisoner's Dilemma?

Although the prisoner's dilemma game seems to show that cooperative behavior always breaks down, we know that people often cooperate to achieve their goals, and firms find ways to cooperate by not competing on price. The reason the basic prisoner's dilemma story is not always applicable in the real world is that it assumes the game will be played *only once*. Most business situations, however, are repeated over and over. For example, consider the following situation: Suppose that in a small town, the only places to buy a pizza are Domino's and Pizza Hut. Assume that the managers will charge either $12 or $10 for a large pepperoni pizza. Panel (a) of Figure 14.3 gives the payoff matrix. Notice that each manager has an incentive to charge the lower price. Once again, the firms appear to be caught in a prisoner's dilemma. But the managers will not play this game only once; each day they will decide again what price to charge for a pizza. In the language of game theory, the managers are playing a *repeated game*, where the losses from not cooperating are greater than in a game played only once, and players can employ *retaliation strategies* against other players who don't cooperate. As a result, firms have a greater incentive to cooperate.

Panel (a) of Figure 14.3 shows that Domino's and Pizza Hut are earning $150 less per day by both charging $10 instead of $12 for the pizza. Every day that passes with both stores charging $10 increases the total amount lost: A year of charging $10 will cause each store to lose more than $50,000 in profit. This lost profit increases the incentive for the store managers to cooperate by *implicitly* colluding. Remember that *explicit* collusion—such as the managers meeting and agreeing to charge $12—is illegal. But if the managers can find a way to signal each other that they will charge $12, they may be within the law.

Suppose that Domino's and Pizza Hut both advertise that they will match the lowest price offered by any competitor—and in our simple example, they are each other's only competitor. These advertisements are signals to each other that they intend to charge $12 for a pizza. The signal is clear because each restaurant knows that if it charges $10, the other restaurant will automatically retaliate by also lowering its price to $10. The offer to match prices is a good *enforcement mechanism* because it guarantees that if either restaurant fails to cooperate and charges the lower price, the competing restaurant will automatically punish that restaurant by also charging the lower price. As Figure 14.3 shows, the restaurants have changed the payoff matrix they face.

With the original payoff matrix in panel (a), there are no advertisements about matching prices, and each restaurant makes more profit if it charges $10 when the other charges $12. The advertisements about matching prices change the payoff matrix

Pizza Hut

(a) The payoff matrix with no offer to match prices

If Domino's and Pizza Hut each advertise that they will match their competitor's price, the payoff matrix changes from the matrix in panel (a) to the matrix in panel (b).

Equilibrium changes from this outcome in panel (a) to this outcome in panel (b).

(b) The payoff matrix with an offer to match prices

MyLab Economics Animation

Figure 14.3

Changing the Payoff Matrix in a Repeated Game

Domino's and Pizza Hut can change the payoff matrix for selling pepperoni pizzas by advertising that each will match its competitor's price. This retaliation strategy provides a signal that one restaurant charging a lower price will be met automatically by the other restaurant charging a lower price. In the payoff matrix in panel (a), there is no advertisement about matching prices, and each restaurant benefits if it charges $10 when the other charges $12. In the payoff matrix in panel (b), after advertising that they will match prices, the managers have only two choices: They can charge $12 and receive a profit of $500 per day, or they can charge $10 and receive a profit of $350 per day. The equilibrium shifts from the prisoner's dilemma result of both restaurants charging the low price and receiving low profits to both restaurants charging the high price and receiving high profits.

to the one shown in panel (b). Now the managers can charge $12 and receive a profit of $500 per day, or they can charge $10 and receive a profit of $350 per day. The equilibrium shifts from the prisoner's dilemma result of both managers charging the low price and receiving low profits to a result where both charge the high price and receive the high profits. An advertisement offering to match competitors' prices might seem to benefit consumers, but game theory shows that it actually may hurt consumers by allowing implicit collusion that keeps prices high.

Another form of implicit collusion is **price leadership**, in which one firm takes the lead in announcing a price change that other firms in the industry then match. For example, through the 1970s, General Motors (GM) would announce a price change in the fall at the beginning of a model year, and Ford and Chrysler would match GM's price change. In some cities, one construction firm will set prices for construction jobs, and other firms will charge the same prices in an attempt to avoid competition that will lower prices, particularly when bidding on government projects. In a number of cases in recent years, this type of implicit collusion has evolved into illegal explicit collusion when construction firms have arranged to take turns winning government contracts at an agreed on price.   MyLab Economics Concept Check

Price leadership A form of implicit collusion in which one firm in an oligopoly announces a price change and the other firms in the industry match the change.

Apply the Concept   MyLab Economics Video

Are the Big Four Airlines Colluding?

Coordinating prices is easier in some industries than in others. Fixed costs in the airline industry are very large, and marginal costs are very small. The marginal cost of flying one more passenger from Chicago to New York is no more than a few dollars: the cost of another snack served and a little additional jet fuel. As a result, airlines often engage in last-minute price cutting to fill the remaining empty seats on a flight. Even a low-price ticket will increase marginal revenue more than marginal cost. As with other oligopolies, if all airlines cut prices, industry profits will decline. Airlines therefore

Casey Martin/Alamy Stock Photo

Are U.S. airlines engaging in implicit collusion?

continually adjust their prices while at the same time monitoring their rivals' prices and retaliating against them for either cutting prices or failing to go along with price increases.

In recent years, mergers in the airline industry have increased the possibility of implicit collusion. In 2017, just four airlines—American, Delta Airlines, United, and Southwest—flew 80 percent of all passengers, a sharp increase from their 40 percent share in 2007. Smaller airlines, such as JetBlue, Spirit Airlines, and Allegiant Air, provided competition on some routes, but the four big airlines were the only ones offering service between many pairs of cities. In 2013, when American was merging with US Airways, the U.S. Department of Justice (DoJ) threatened to go to court to block the merger unless the airlines agreed to give up landing slots at some airports to smaller competitors. When the airlines agreed to this condition, the DoJ approved the merger. Two years later, though, the DoJ began investigating whether the big four airlines were illegally colluding.

In particular, the DoJ was concerned when top managers of all four major airlines publicly stated that they intended to undertake only modest increases in capacity by buying additional planes or flying additional routes. Adding more capacity would mean having more tickets to sell, which would increase the likelihood of price cutting to fill the seats. Were these announcements an example of implicit price collusion, or were they just routine discussions by top managers of their firms' future plans? As one airline industry analyst put it, "If you're listening as a Justice Department attorney, you'd say, 'Wait a minute, these guys are all saying the same thing, and that can't just happen naturally, can it?'" But a lawyer who defends firms accused of collusion was skeptical that the DoJ could prove its case without evidence of an explicit agreement, which he doubted had occurred: "I'd be shocked if they got together in a smoke-filled room and agreed to cut capacity." This analysis appears to have been correct because in early 2017, the DoJ decided that it had been unable to find sufficient evidence to bring charges against the airlines for collusion.

Some economists and policymakers remain concerned about the level of competition in the U.S. airline industry. Although JetBlue and other smaller airlines provide vigorous competition at some airports, other airports are dominated by one or two carriers that often avoid price competition. For instance, the merger of American and US Airways gave the combined company a greater than 75 percent share of flights originating in Philadelphia. American's ticket prices rose sharply after the merger. The federal government does not allow airlines with more than 25 percent foreign ownership to operate flights between U.S. cities, reducing potential competition. Europe has looser restrictions of foreign airlines, which may help explain why airline fares are lower per mile in Europe than in the United States.

Some airline passengers wonder whether policies of charging for checked luggage or heavy use of overbooking—selling more tickets for a flight than there are seats on the plane—that the big four airlines have adopted indicate collusion. The practice of overbooking was in the spotlight in April 2017, when a ticketed passenger on a United flight was injured while being forcibly removed from a plane after he declined to give up his seat to a United employee.

As we will see in Chapter 15, Section 15.5, the federal government can have difficulty deciding whether firms in an oligopoly are colluding. When collusion occurs, consumers pay higher prices and receive inferior service.

Sources: "A Lack of Competition Explains the Flaws in American Aviation," *Economist*, April 22, 2017; Brent Kendall and Susan Carey, "Obama Antitrust Enforcers Won't Bring Action in Airline Probe," *Wall Street Journal*, January 11, 2017; Christopher Drew, "Airlines under Justice Dept. Investigation over Possible Collusion," *New York Times*, July 1, 2015; Jack Nicas, Brent Kendall, and Susan Carey, "Justice Department Probes Airlines for Collusion," *Wall Street Journal*, July 1, 2015; and Susan Carey and Jack Nicas, "Airlines' New Normal: More Seats, Fewer Flights," *Wall Street Journal*, July 2, 2015.

MyLab Economics Study Plan   **Your Turn:** Test your understanding by doing related problems 2.14, 2.15, and 2.16 on page 503 at the end of this chapter.

Cartels: The Case of OPEC

In the United States, firms cannot legally meet to agree on what prices to charge and how much to produce. But suppose they could. Would this be enough to guarantee that their collusion would be successful? The example of the Organization of the Petroleum Exporting Countries (OPEC) indicates that the answer to this question is "no." OPEC has 12 members, including Saudi Arabia, Kuwait, and other Arab countries, as well as Iran, Venezuela, and Nigeria. Together, these countries own more than 75 percent of the world's proven crude oil reserves, although they supply only about 35 percent of the total oil sold each year. OPEC operates as a **cartel**, which is a group of firms that collude by agreeing to restrict output to increase prices and profits. The members of OPEC meet periodically and agree on quotas, which are quantities of oil that each country agrees to produce. The quotas are intended to reduce oil production well below the competitive level to force up the price of oil and increase the profits of member countries.

> **Cartel** A group of firms that collude by agreeing to restrict output to increase prices and profits.

Figure 14.4 shows oil prices from 1972 to mid-2017. The blue line shows the price of a barrel of oil in each year. Prices in general have risen since 1972, which has reduced the amount of goods and services that consumers can purchase with a dollar. The red line corrects for general price increases by measuring oil prices in terms of the dollar's purchasing power in 2017. The figure shows that OPEC succeeded in raising the price of oil during the mid-1970s and early 1980s, although political unrest in the Middle East and other factors also affected the price of oil during these years. Oil prices had been below $3 per barrel in 1972 but rose to more than $39 per barrel in 1980, which was more than $120 measured in dollars of 2017 purchasing power. The figure also shows that OPEC has had difficulty sustaining the high prices of 1980 in later years, although oil prices rose sharply between 2004 and mid-2008, in part due to increasing demand from China and India. In the past few years, OPEC has also had difficulty maintaining oil prices because of a surge in U.S. production as oil companies have used "fracking" techniques to recover oil from shale deposits.

Game theory helps us understand why oil prices have fluctuated. If every member of OPEC cooperates and produces the low output level dictated by its quota, prices will be high, and the cartel will earn large profits. (Even though OPEC cannot raise prices as high as it did before U.S. production increased, it can still increase world oil prices if all of its

MyLab Economics Animation

Figure 14.4 **Oil Prices, 1972 to mid-2017**

The blue line shows the price of a barrel of oil in each year. The red line measures the price of a barrel of oil in terms of the purchasing power of the dollar in 2017. By reducing oil production, OPEC was able to raise the world price of oil in the mid-1970s and early 1980s. Sustaining high prices has been difficult over the long run, however, because OPEC members often exceed their output quotas.

Source: Federal Reserve Bank of St. Louis.

Figure 14.5

The OPEC Cartel with Unequal Members

Because Saudi Arabia can produce much more oil than Nigeria, its output decisions have a larger effect on the price of oil. In the figure, Low Output corresponds to cooperating with the OPEC-assigned output quota, and High Output corresponds to producing at maximum capacity. Saudi Arabia has a dominant strategy to cooperate and produce a low output. Nigeria, however, has a dominant strategy not to cooperate and instead produce a high output. Therefore, the equilibrium of this game will occur with Saudi Arabia producing a low output and Nigeria producing a high output.

	Nigeria	
	Low Output	**High Output**
Low Output (Saudi Arabia)	Saudi Arabia earns $100 million profit / Nigeria earns $10 million profit	Saudi Arabia earns $75 million profit / Nigeria earns $15 million profit
High Output (Saudi Arabia)	Saudi Arabia earns $80 million profit / Nigeria earns $7 million profit	Saudi Arabia earns $60 million profit / Nigeria earns $10 million profit

members agree to restrict production.) Once the price has been driven up, however, each member has an incentive to stop cooperating and to earn even higher profits by increasing output beyond its quota. But if no country sticks to its quota, total oil output will increase, and profits will decline. In other words, OPEC is caught in a prisoner's dilemma.

If the members of OPEC always exceeded their production quotas, the cartel would have no effect on world oil prices. In fact, the members of OPEC periodically meet and assign new quotas that, at least for a while, enable them to restrict output enough to raise prices. Two factors explain OPEC's occasional success at behaving as a cartel. First, the members of OPEC are participating in a repeated game. As we have seen, being in a repeated game increases the likelihood of a cooperative outcome. Second, Saudi Arabia has far larger oil reserves than any other member of OPEC. Therefore, it has the most to gain from high oil prices and a greater incentive to cooperate. To see this, consider the payoff matrix shown in Figure 14.5. To keep things simple, let's assume that OPEC has only two members: Saudi Arabia and Nigeria. In Figure 14.5, "Low Output" corresponds to cooperating with the OPEC-assigned output quota, and "High Output" corresponds to producing at maximum capacity. The payoff matrix shows the profits received per day by each country.

We can see that Saudi Arabia has a strong incentive to cooperate and maintain its low output quota. By keeping output low, Saudi Arabia can by itself significantly raise the world price of oil, increasing its own profits as well as those of other members of OPEC. Therefore, Saudi Arabia has a dominant strategy of cooperating with the quota and producing a low output. Nigeria, however, cannot by itself have much effect on the price of oil. Therefore, Nigeria has a dominant strategy of not cooperating and instead producing a high output. The equilibrium of this game will occur with Saudi Arabia producing a low output and Nigeria producing a high output. In fact, OPEC often operates in just this way. Saudi Arabia will cooperate with the quota, while the other 11 members produce at capacity. Because this is a repeated game, however, Saudi Arabia will occasionally produce more oil than its quota to intentionally drive down the price and retaliate against the other members for not cooperating.

14.3 Sequential Games and Business Strategy

LEARNING OBJECTIVE: Use sequential games to analyze business strategies.

We have been analyzing games in which both players move simultaneously. In many business situations, however, one firm will act first, and then other firms will respond. These situations can be analyzed using *sequential games*. We will use sequential games to analyze two business strategies: deterring entry and bargaining between firms. To keep things simple, we consider situations that involve only two firms.

Deterring Entry

In Section 14.1, we saw that barriers to entry are a key to firms continuing to earn an economic profit. Can firms create barriers to deter new firms from entering an industry? Some research in game theory has focused on this question. Suppose that Apple and Dell are the only makers of very thin, light laptop computers. One factor firms consider in pricing a new product is the effect different prices have on the likelihood that competitors will enter the market. A high price might lead to a large profit if other firms do not enter the market, but if a high price attracts entry from other firms, it might actually result in a smaller profit. A low price, by deterring entry, might lead to a larger profit. Assume that managers at Apple have developed a very thin, light laptop before Dell has and are considering what price to charge. To break even by covering the opportunity cost of the funds used, laptops must provide a minimum rate of return of 15 percent on Apple's investment. If Apple has the market for this type of laptop to itself and charges a price of $800, it will earn an economic profit by receiving a return of 20 percent. If Apple charges a price of $1,000 and has the market to itself, it will receive a higher return of 30 percent.

It seems clear that Apple should charge $1,000 for its laptops, but the managers are worried that Dell might also begin selling this type of laptop. If Apple charges $800 and Dell enters the market, Apple and Dell will divide up the market, and both will earn only 5 percent on their investments, which is below the 15 percent return each firm needs to break even. If Apple charges $1,000 and Dell enters, although the market will still be divided, the higher price means that each firm will earn 16 percent on its investment.

Apple and Dell are playing a sequential game because Apple makes the first move—deciding what price to charge—and Dell responds. We can analyze a sequential game by using a *decision tree*, like the one shown in Figure 14.6. The boxes in the figure represent *decision nodes*, which are points where the firms must make the decisions contained in the boxes. At the left, Apple makes the initial decision of what price to charge, and then Dell responds by either entering the market or not. The decisions made are shown beside the arrows. The *terminal nodes*, in green at the right side of the figure, show the resulting rates of return.

Let's start with Apple's initial decision. If Apple charges $1,000, then the arrow directs us to the upper gold decision node for Dell. If Dell decides to enter, it will earn a 16 percent rate of return on its investment, which represents an economic profit because it is above the opportunity cost of the funds involved. If Dell doesn't enter, Apple will earn 30 percent, and Dell will not earn anything in this market (indicated by the dash). Apple's managers can conclude that if they charge $1,000 for their laptops, Dell will enter the very thin, light laptop market, and both firms will earn 16 percent on their investments.

If Apple decides to charge $800, then the arrow directs us to the lower gold decision node for Dell. If Dell decides to enter, it will earn only a 5 percent rate of return. If it doesn't enter, Apple will earn 20 percent, and Dell will not earn anything in this

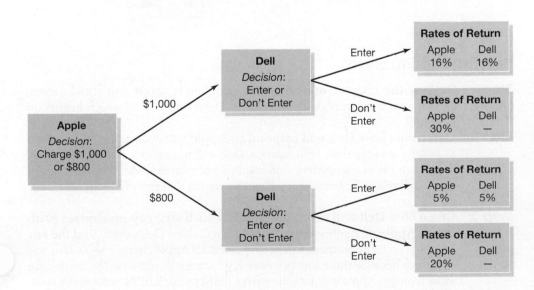

MyLab Economics Animation

Figure 14.6

The Decision Tree for an Entry Game

Apple earns its highest return if it charges $1,000 for its very thin, light laptop and Dell does not enter the market. But at that price, Dell will enter the market, and Apple will earn only 16 percent. If Apple charges $800, Dell will not enter because Dell will suffer an economic loss by receiving only a 5 percent return on its investment. Therefore, Apple's best decision is to deter Dell's entry by charging $800. Apple will earn an economic profit by receiving a 20 percent return on its investment. Note that the dashes (—) indicate the situation where Dell does not enter the market and so makes no investment and receives no return.

market. Apple's managers can conclude that if they charge $800, Dell will not enter, and Apple will earn 20 percent on its investment.

This analysis should lead Apple's managers to conclude that they can charge $1,000 and earn 16 percent—because Dell will enter—or they can charge $800 and earn 20 percent by deterring Dell's entry. Using a decision tree helps Apple's managers make the correct choice and charge $800 to deter Dell's entry into this market. Note that our discussion is simplified because we are ignoring other characteristics, apart from price, on which the firms also compete. In practice, Apple charged a relatively high price for its lightweight laptop, the MacBook Air, which caused Dell to enter the market with the lower-priced XPS 15z Ultrabook. Apple's managers believed that the MacBook Air's features would remain attractive to consumers, despite the XPS 15z Ultrabook having a lower price.   **MyLab Economics** Concept Check

Solved Problem 14.3   MyLab Economics Interactive Animation

Is Deterring Entry Always a Good Idea?

Like any other business strategy, deterring entry is a good idea only if it has a higher payoff than alternative strategies. Use the following decision tree to decide whether Apple should deter Dell from entering the market for very thin, light laptops. Assume that each firm must earn a 15 percent return on its investment to break even.

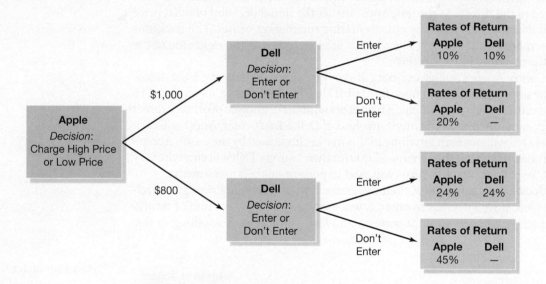

Solving the Problem

Step 1: **Review the chapter material.** This problem is about sequential games, so you may want to review the section "Deterring Entry," which begins on page 492.

Step 2: **Determine how Dell will respond to Apple's decision.** If Apple charges $1,000 for its very thin, light laptops, Dell will not enter the market because the return on its investment represents an economic loss. If Apple charges $800, Dell will enter because it will earn a return that represents an economic profit.

Step 3: **Given how Dell will react, determine which strategy maximizes profits for Apple.** If Apple charges $1,000, it will deter Dell's entry, and the rate of return on its investment will be 20 percent. If Apple charges $800, Dell will enter, but because these low prices will substantially increase the market for these laptops, Apple will actually earn a higher return of 24 percent. By splitting the market with Dell at a lower price, Apple earns a higher return than it would have if it had the whole market to itself at a high price.

Step 4: **State your conclusion.** Like any other business strategy, deterrence is worth pursuing only if the payoff is higher than for other strategies. In this case, expanding the market for very thin, light laptops by charging a lower price has a higher payoff for Apple, even given that Dell will enter the market.

Your Turn: For more practice, do related problem 3.3 on page 504 at the end of this chapter.

MyLab Economics Study Plan

Bargaining

The success of many firms depends on how well they bargain with other firms. For example, firms often must bargain with their suppliers over the prices they pay for inputs. Suppose that TruImage is a small firm that has developed software that improves how pictures from digital cameras or smartphones are displayed on computer screens. TruImage currently sells its software only on its Web site and earns a profit of $2 million per year. Dell informs TruImage that it is considering installing the software on every new computer Dell sells. Dell expects to sell more computers at a higher price if it can install TruImage's software on its computers. The two firms begin bargaining over what price Dell will pay TruImage for its software.

The decision tree in Figure 14.7 illustrates this bargaining game. At the left, Dell makes the initial decision about what price to offer TruImage for its software, and then TruImage responds by either accepting or rejecting the contract offer. Suppose that Dell offers TruImage a contract price of $30 per copy for its software. If TruImage accepts this contract, its profit will be $5 million per year, and Dell will earn $10 million in additional profit. If TruImage rejects the contract, its profit will be the $2 million per year it earns selling its software on its Web site, and Dell will earn zero additional profit.

Now, suppose Dell offers TruImage a contract price of $20 per copy. If TruImage accepts this contract, its profit will be $3 million per year, and Dell will earn $15 million in additional profit. If TruImage rejects this contract, its profit will be the $2 million it earns selling its software on its Web site, and Dell will earn zero additional profit. Clearly, for Dell, a contract price of $20 per copy is more profitable, while for TruImage, a contract price of $30 per copy is more profitable.

Suppose TruImage attempts to obtain a favorable outcome from the bargaining by telling Dell that it will reject a $20-per-copy contract price. If Dell believes this threat, then it will offer TruImage a $30-per-copy contract price because Dell is better off with the $10 million additional profit that will result from TruImage accepting the contract than with the zero additional profit Dell will earn if TruImage rejects the $20-per-copy contract price. This result is a Nash equilibrium because neither firm can increase its profit by changing its choice—*provided that Dell believes TruImage's threat.* But

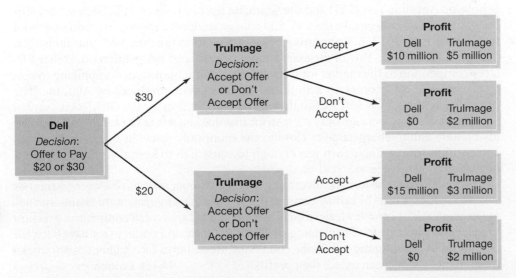

MyLab Economics Animation

Figure 14.7

The Decision Tree for a Bargaining Game

Dell earns the highest profit if it offers a contract price of $20 per copy and TruImage accepts the contract. TruImage earns the highest profit if Dell offers it a contract of $30 per copy and it accepts the contract. TruImage may attempt to bargain by threatening to reject a $20-per-copy contract. But Dell knows this threat is not credible because once Dell has offered a $20-per-copy contract, TruImage's profits are higher if it accepts the contract than if it rejects it.

is TruImage's threat credible? Once Dell has offered TruImage the $20 contract price, TruImage's choices are to accept the contract and earn $3 million or reject the contract and earn only $2 million. Because rejecting the contract reduces TruImage's profit, TruImage's threat to reject the contract is not credible, and Dell should ignore it.

As a result, we would expect Dell to use the strategy of offering TruImage a $20-per-copy contract price and TruImage to use the strategy of accepting the contract. Dell will earn an additional profit of $15 million per year, and TruImage will earn a profit of $3 million per year. This outcome is called a *subgame-perfect equilibrium*. A subgame-perfect equilibrium is a Nash equilibrium in which no player can make himself or herself better off by changing his or her decision at any decision node. In our simple bargaining game, each player has only one decision to make. As we have seen, Dell's profits are highest if it offers the $20-per-copy contract price, and TruImage's profits are highest if it accepts the contract. Typically, in sequential games of this type, there is only one subgame-perfect equilibrium.

Managers use decision trees like those in Figures 14.6 and 14.7 in business planning because they provide a systematic way of thinking through the implications of a strategy and of predicting the reactions of rivals. We can see the benefits of decision trees in the simple examples considered here. In the first example, Apple's managers can conclude that charging a low price is more profitable than charging a high price. In the second example, Dell's managers can conclude that TruImage's threat to reject a $20-per-copy contract is not credible.

MyLab Economics Study Plan   **MyLab Economics** Concept Check

14.4 The Five Competitive Forces Model

LEARNING OBJECTIVE: Use the five competitive forces model to analyze competition in an industry.

We have seen that the number of competitors in an industry affects a firm's ability to charge a price above average total cost and earn an economic profit. The number of firms is not the only determinant of the level of competition in an industry, however. Michael Porter of the Harvard Business School has developed a model that shows how five competitive forces determine the overall level of competition in an industry.

In this section, we briefly discuss each of the five competitive forces: (1) competition from existing firms, (2) the threat from potential entrants, (3) competition from substitute goods or services, (4) the bargaining power of buyers, and (5) the bargaining power of suppliers.

Competition from Existing Firms

We have already seen that competition among firms in an industry can lower prices and profits. Consider another example: Educational Testing Service (ETS) produces the Scholastic Aptitude Test (SAT) and the Graduate Record Exam (GRE). High school students applying to college take the SAT, and college students applying to graduate school take the GRE. In 2017, ETS charged a price of $54.50 to take the SAT, and it charged $205 to take the GRE. Part of the explanation for this large price difference is that ETS faces competition in the market for tests given to high school students applying to college, where the SAT competes with the ACT Assessment, produced by ACT, Inc. The price to take the ACT is $56.50. But there is no competition for the GRE. As we saw in Section 14.2, when there are only a few firms in a market, it is easier for them to implicitly collude and to charge a price close to the monopoly price. In this case, however, competition from a single firm was enough to cause ETS to keep the price of the SAT near the competitive level.

Competition in the form of advertising, better customer service, or longer warranties can also reduce profits by raising costs. In recent years, several restaurant chains, including Panera Bread, Chipotle Mexican Grill, and McDonald's, have felt competitive pressure to reduce or eliminate food containing additives and meat and poultry that have been fed antibiotics or raised under inhumane conditions. Restaurants face higher costs to make these changes, which can reduce their profits.   **MyLab Economics** Concept Check

The Threat from Potential Entrants

Firms face competition from companies that currently are not in the market but might enter. We have already seen how actions taken to deter entry can reduce profits. In our hypothetical example in the previous section, Apple charged a lower price and earned less profit to deter Dell's entry. Business managers often take actions aimed at deterring entry. Some of these actions include advertising to create product loyalty, introducing new products—such as slightly different cereals or toothpastes—to fill market niches, and setting lower prices to keep profits at a level that makes entry less attractive. As we saw in the chapter opener, Apple entered the market for streaming music in 2015. Spotify had hoped to deter Apple's entry by keeping its monthly subscription charge at $9.99—a price at which it struggled to earn a profit. Apple, however, was willing to match that price and appeared confident that it would eventually be able to earn a profit on its service.   MyLab Economics Concept Check

Competition from Substitute Goods or Services

Firms are always vulnerable to competitors introducing a new product that fills a consumer need better than their current product does. Consider the encyclopedia business. For decades, many parents bought expensive and bulky encyclopedias for their children attending high school or college. By the 1990s, computer software companies such as Microsoft were offering electronic encyclopedias that sold for a small fraction of the price of printed encyclopedias. Encyclopedia Britannica and the other encyclopedia publishers responded by cutting prices and launching advertising campaigns aimed at showing the superiority of printed encyclopedias. Still, profits continued to decline, and by the end of the 1990s, most printed encyclopedias had disappeared. Eventually, the free Web site Wikipedia made it difficult for firms to sell even low-priced electronic encyclopedias, and Microsoft and most other firms discontinued producing them.   MyLab Economics Concept Check

The Bargaining Power of Buyers

If buyers have enough bargaining power, they can insist on lower prices, higher-quality products, or additional services. Automobile companies, for example, have significant bargaining power in the tire market, which tends to lower tire prices and limit the profitability of tire manufacturers. Some retailers have significant buying power over their suppliers. For instance, Walmart has required many of its suppliers to alter their distribution systems because it wants to reduce the inventories it holds in its warehouses. In the face of online competition from Amazon, Walmart has pushed for price cuts from even its largest suppliers, such as Procter & Gamble, which makes household products including Tide laundry detergent and Crest toothpaste.   MyLab Economics Concept Check

The Bargaining Power of Suppliers

If many firms can supply an input and the input is not specialized, the suppliers are unlikely to have the bargaining power to limit a firm's profit. For instance, suppliers of paper napkins to McDonald's restaurants have very little bargaining power. With only a single or a few suppliers of an input, however, the purchasing firm may face a high price. During the 1930s and 1940s, for example, the Technicolor Company was the only producer of the cameras and film that studios needed to produce color movies. Technicolor charged the studios high prices to use its cameras, and it had the power to insist that only its technicians could operate the cameras. The only alternative for the studios was to make black-and-white movies.

As with other competitive forces, the bargaining power of suppliers can change over time. For instance, when IBM chose Microsoft to supply the operating system for its personal computers, Microsoft was a small company with very limited bargaining power. As Microsoft's Windows operating system became standard in more than 90 percent of personal computers, this large market share increased Microsoft's bargaining power with computer manufacturers.   MyLab Economics Concept Check   MyLab Economics Study Plan

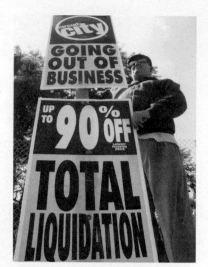

Damian Dovarganes/AP Images

Although Circuit City's business strategy had once been widely admired, the company declared bankruptcy in 2009.

Apply the Concept

MyLab Economics Video

Can We Predict Which Firms Will Continue to Be Successful?

For years, economists and business strategists believed that market structure was the most important factor in explaining the ability of some firms to continue earning economic profits. For example, most economists argued that during the first few decades after World War II, steel companies in the United States earned an economic profit because barriers to entry were high, there were few firms in the industry, and competition among firms was low. In contrast, restaurants were seen as less profitable because barriers to entry were low, and the industry was intensely competitive. One problem with this approach to analyzing the profitability of firms is that it does not explain how firms in the same industry can have very different levels of profit.

Today, economists and business strategists put greater emphasis on the characteristics of individual firms and the strategies their managers use to continue to earn economic profits. This approach helps explain why Nucor continues to be a profitable steel company, while Bethlehem Steel, at one time the second-largest steel producer in the United States, was forced into bankruptcy. It also explains why Amazon, which began in the 1990s as a small company Jeff Bezos started in Seattle, Washington, with a handful of employees, became the leading online retailer, while many other online retailers that were started at the same time have long since disappeared.

Is it possible to draw general conclusions about which business strategies are likely to be successful in the future? A number of business analysts have tried to identify strategies that have made firms successful and have recommended those strategies to other firms. Although books with these recommendations are often bestsellers, they have a mixed record in identifying winning strategies. For instance, in 1982, Thomas J. Peters and Robert H. Waterman, Jr., published *In Search of Excellence: Lessons from America's Best-Run Companies*. The book was favorably reviewed by business magazines and sold more than 3 million copies. Peters and Waterman identified 43 companies that were the best at using eight key strategies to "stay on top of the heap." But just two years after the book was published, an article in *BusinessWeek* pointed out that 14 of the 43 companies were experiencing significant financial difficulties. The article noted: "It comes as a shock that so many companies have fallen from grace so quickly—and it also raises some questions. Were these companies so excellent in the first place?"

In 2002, Jim Collins published *Good to Great: Why Some Companies Make the Leap ... and Others Don't*, with the goal of determining how companies can "achieve enduring greatness." Although this book also sold 3 million copies, not all of the 11 "great companies" it identified were able to remain successful. For instance, Circuit City was forced to file for bankruptcy in 2009, and the Federal National Mortgage Association ("Fannie Mae") avoided bankruptcy only after the federal government took it over in 2008.

These two books, and many others like them, provide useful analyses of the business strategies of successful firms. That many of the firms highlighted in these books are unable to sustain their success should not be surprising. Many successful strategies can be copied—and often improved on—by competitors. Even in oligopolies, competition can quickly erode profits and even turn a successful firm into an unsuccessful one. It remains difficult to predict which currently successful firms will maintain their success.

Sources: Thomas J. Peters and Robert H. Waterman, Jr., *In Search of Excellence: Lessons from America's Best-Run Companies*, New York: HarperCollins Publishers, 1982; Jim Collins, *Good to Great: Why Some Companies Make the Leap ... and Others Don't*, New York: HarperCollins Publishers, 2001; "Oops. Who's Excellent Now?" *BusinessWeek*, November 5, 1984; and Steven D. Levitt, "From Good to Great ... to Below Average," *New York Times*, July 28, 2008.

MyLab Economics Study Plan

Your Turn: Test your understanding by doing related problem 4.6 on page 505 at the end of this chapter.

Continued from page 479

Economics in Your Life & Career

If You Were Managing a Walmart, Would You Cut the Price of a PlayStation 4?

At the beginning of this chapter, we asked you to suppose you were a manager at Walmart and were considering a proposal to cut the price you were charging for a PlayStation 4 game system from $399 to $349. The purpose of the price cut would be to increase profit by attracting some consumers who would otherwise buy the game system from Best Buy, Target, or Amazon. In this chapter, we have seen that managers of large firms may be tempted to charge low prices in an attempt to attract customers from other firms, but such a strategy invites retaliation from those firms. If all firms cut their prices—in this case, from $399 to $349—they will likely all end up reducing their profits. In game theory, this result is called a prisoner's dilemma. Because pricing PlayStations is actually a repeated game with the retailers involved selling the game system in competition over a long period of time, a better strategy for you is to reject the advice and maintain the $399 price. The result will be a cooperative equilibrium, in which the firms all charge a high price—a result that is good news for the profits of Walmart and its competitors but bad news for consumers!

Conclusion

Firms are locked in a never-ending struggle to earn an economic profit. As we have noted several times, competition erodes economic profits. Even in the oligopolies discussed in this chapter, firms have difficulty earning an economic profit in the long run. We have seen that firms attempt to avoid the effects of competition in various ways, including occupying a secure niche in the market, engaging in implicit collusion with competing firms, or persuading the government to impose barriers to entry.

Visit MyLab Economics for a news article and analysis related to the concepts in this chapter.

Key Terms

Barrier to entry, p. 481

Business strategy, p. 485

Cartel, p. 491

Collusion, p. 485

Cooperative equilibrium, p. 486

Dominant strategy, p. 486

Economies of scale, p. 481

Game theory, p. 484

Nash equilibrium, p. 486

Noncooperative
equilibrium, p. 486

Oligopoly, p. 480

Patent, p. 483

Payoff matrix, p. 485

Price leadership, p. 489

Prisoner's dilemma, p. 486

14.1 Oligopoly and Barriers to Entry, pages 480–484

LEARNING OBJECTIVE: Show how barriers to entry explain the existence of oligopolies.

MyLab Economics Visit www.pearson.com/mylab/economics to complete these exercises online and get instant feedback.

Summary

An **oligopoly** is a market structure in which a small number of interdependent firms compete. **Barriers to entry** keep new firms from entering an industry. The three most important barriers to entry are economies of scale, ownership of a key input, and government barriers. Economies of scale are the most important barrier to entry. **Economies of scale** exist when a firm's long-run average costs fall as it increases output. Government barriers include patents, licensing, and barriers to international trade. A **patent** is the exclusive right to a product for a period of 20 years from the date the patent application is filed with the government.

Review Questions

1.1 What is an oligopoly? Give three examples of oligopolistic industries in the United States.

1.2 What do barriers to entry have to do with the extent of competition in an industry? What is the most important reason that some industries, such as music streaming, are dominated by just a few firms?

1.3 Give an example of a government-imposed barrier to entry. Why would a government be willing to erect barriers to firms entering an industry?

Problems and Applications

1.4 Michael Porter has argued that "the intensity of competition in an industry is neither a matter of coincidence nor bad luck. Rather, competition in an industry is rooted in its underlying economic structure." What does Porter mean by "economic structure"? What factors besides economic structure might be expected to determine the intensity of competition in an industry?
Source: Michael Porter, *Competitive Strategy: Techniques for Analyzing Industries and Competitors*, New York: The Free Press, 1980, p. 3.

1.5 An article in *Forbes* described these characteristics of the airline industry: "Airlines aren't like normal consumer businesses.... Infrastructure including aircraft, gates and runways takes years to put in place. Capacity rebalancing

in response to demand shifts isn't easy and idle infrastructure of this magnitude is very expensive." Do the characteristics referred to in the article help explain why the airline industry is an oligopoly? Briefly explain.
Source: Kevin O'Marah, "The Lesson of the Delta Disaster: Flying Is Too Cheap," *Forbes*, August 11, 2016.

1.6 A column on forbes.com discussed Google, Apple, Facebook, and Amazon, all of which operate in oligopolistic markets. The column argued that the concerns of some policymakers and economists about the market power of these firms may be overstated because "history teaches us that in a fast-moving industry, driven by fast-changing technologies, barriers to entry may be far less significant than one might believe."
   a. What does the columnist mean by "barriers to entry"? Name one barrier to entry a new firm would face in competing with:
      i. Google in online advertising
      ii. Apple in smartphones
      iii. Facebook in social media apps
      iv. Amazon in online retailing
   b. How might "fast-changing technology" reduce the importance of each barrier to entry that you identified in part a.?
Source: Jeremy Ghez, "Why U.S. Tech Giants Might Not Dominate the World after All," forbes.com, November 16, 2016.

1.7 While a professor at the Harvard Business School, the late Thomas McCraw wrote, "Throughout American history, entrepreneurs have tried, sometimes desperately, to create big businesses out of naturally small-scale operations. It has not worked." What advantage would entrepreneurs expect to gain from creating "big businesses"? Why would entrepreneurs fail to create big businesses with "naturally small-scale operations"? Illustrate your answer with a graph showing long-run average costs.
Source: Thomas K. McCraw, ed., *Creating Modern Capitalism*, Cambridge, MA: Harvard University Press, 1997, p. 323.

1.8 The following graph illustrates the average total cost curves for two automobile manufacturing firms: Little Auto and Big Auto. Under which of the following conditions would you expect to see the market composed of firms like Little Auto, and under which conditions would you expect to see the market dominated by firms like Big Auto?

a. When the market demand curve intersects the quantity axis at fewer than 1,000 units

b. When the market demand curve intersects the quantity axis at more than 1,000 units but fewer than 10,000 units

c. When the market demand curve intersects the quantity axis at more than 10,000 units

1.9 Alfred Chandler, who was a professor at the Harvard Business School, once observed, "Imagine the diseconomies of scale—the great increase in unit costs—that would result from placing close to one-fourth of the world's production of shoes, or textiles, or lumber into three factories or mills!" The shoe, textile, and lumber industries are very competitive, with many firms producing each of these products. Briefly explain how Chandler's observation helps explain why these industries are competitive.

Source: Alfred D. Chandler, Jr., "The Emergence of Managerial Capitalism," in Alfred D. Chandler, Jr., and Richard S. Tedlow, *The Coming of Managerial Capitalism*, New York: Irwin, 1985, p. 406.

1.10 **(Related to the Apply the Concept on page 483)** The North Carolina State Board of Dental Examiners had been requiring that only licensed dentists be allowed to sell teeth-whitening services. The board brought legal action against hair salons and spas that also offered these services, arguing that only licensed dentists have the training to ensure that consumers aren't injured in the teeth-whitening process. In 2015, the U.S. Supreme Court ruled that a federal government agency had the authority to stop the board from preventing non-dentists from offering teeth-whitening services. According to a news report, the federal agency argued that "the dental board was motivated by financial self-interest, not health concerns."

a. Predict the effect of the Supreme Court ruling on the price and quantity of teeth-whitening services offered in North Carolina.

b. Can we be sure that the result of the decision will be to increase the well-being of consumers of teeth-whitening services in the state? Briefly explain.

Source: Brent Kendall, "Supreme Court Affirms FTC Antitrust Authority over Licensing Boards," *Wall Street Journal*, February 25, 2015.

14.2 | Game Theory and Oligopoly, pages 484–492

LEARNING OBJECTIVE: Use game theory to analyze the strategies of oligopolistic firms.

MyLab Economics Visit **www.pearson.com/mylab/economics** to complete these exercises online and get instant feedback.

Summary

Because an oligopoly has only a few firms, interactions among those firms are particularly important. **Game theory** is the study of how people make decisions in situations in which attaining their goals depends on their interactions with others; in economics, it is the study of the decisions of firms in industries where the profits of each firm depend on its interactions with other firms. A **business strategy** refers to actions taken by a firm to achieve a goal, such as maximizing profit. Oligopoly games can be illustrated with a **payoff matrix**, which is a table that shows the payoffs that each firm earns from every combination of strategies by the firms. One possible outcome in oligopoly is **collusion**, which is an agreement among firms to charge the same price or otherwise not to compete. A **cartel** is a group of firms that collude by agreeing to restrict output to increase prices and profits. In a **cooperative equilibrium**, firms cooperate to increase their mutual payoff. In a **noncooperative equilibrium**, firms do not cooperate but pursue their own self-interest. A **dominant strategy** is a strategy that is the best for a firm, no matter what strategies other firms choose. A **Nash equilibrium** is a situation in which each firm chooses the best strategy, given the strategies chosen by other firms. A situation in which pursuing dominant strategies results in noncooperation that leaves everyone worse off is called a **prisoner's dilemma**. Because many business situations are repeated games, firms may end up implicitly colluding to keep prices high. With **price leadership**, one firm takes the lead in announcing a price change, which is then matched by the other firms in the industry.

Review Questions

2.1 Give brief definitions of the following concepts.
  a. Game theory
  b. Cooperative equilibrium
  c. Noncooperative equilibrium
  d. Dominant strategy
  e. Nash equilibrium
  f. Price leadership

2.2 Why do economists refer to the methodology for analyzing oligopolies as game theory?

2.3 What is the difference between explicit collusion and implicit collusion? Give an example of each. What is a cartel?

2.4 What is a prisoner's dilemma game? Is the outcome of the game likely to be different in a repeated game? Briefly explain.

Problems and Applications

2.5 Bob and Tom are two criminals who have been arrested for burglary. The police put Bob and Tom in separate cells. They offer to let Bob go free if he confesses to the crime and testifies against Tom. Bob also is told that he will serve a 15-year prison sentence if he remains silent while Tom confesses. If Bob confesses and Tom also confesses, they will each serve a 10-year sentence. Separately, the police make the same offer to Tom. Assume that Bob and Tom know that if they both remain silent, the police have only enough evidence to convict them of a lesser crime, and they will both serve 3-year sentences.

    a. Use the information provided to write a payoff matrix for Bob and Tom.

    b. Does Bob have a dominant strategy? If so, what is it?

    c. Does Tom have a dominant strategy? If so, what is it?

    d. What prison sentences do Bob and Tom serve? How might they have avoided this outcome?

2.6 Under "early decision" college admission plans, students apply to a college in the fall and, if they are accepted, they must enroll in that college. Some critics of early decision plans, including some college presidents, argue that the plans put too much pressure on students to decide early in their senior year in high school which college to attend. Some college administrators have proposed abolishing early decision plans, but as a columnist in the *New York Times* noted, "It's more prevalent than ever, with some selective schools using it to fill upward of 40 percent of their incoming freshman class." If many college administrators believe that early decision plans should be abolished, why do their schools continue to use them? Can game theory help analyze this situation?

    Source: Frank Bruni, "The Plague of 'Early Decision,'" *New York Times*, December 21, 2016.

2.7 For several years, a professor at Johns Hopkins University used the following grading scheme for his final exam: He would give an A to the student with the highest score. The grades of the remaining students were then based on what percentage their scores were of the top student's score. But at the end of one semester, the students in his class decided to boycott the final exam. They stood in the hallway outside the classroom but did not enter the room to take the exam. After waiting for a time, the professor cancelled the exam and, applying his grading scale, gave everyone in the class an A on the exam. An article in the *New York Times* about this incident observes: "This is an amazing game theory outcome, and not one that economists would likely predict." Do you agree with this observation that game theory indicates the students' strategy was unlikely to work? Briefly explain.

    Source: Catherine Rampell, "Gaming the System," *New York Times*, February 14, 2013.

2.8 **(Related to the Don't Let This Happen to You on page 486)** A student argues, "The prisoner's dilemma game is unrealistic. Each player's strategy is based on the assumption that the other player won't cooperate. But if each player assumes that the other player *will* cooperate, the 'dilemma' disappears." Briefly explain whether you agree with this argument.

2.9 **(Related to Solved Problem 14.2 on page 487)** Coca-Cola and Pepsi both spend large amounts on advertising, but would they be better off if they didn't? Their television commercials and online ads are usually not designed to convey new information about their products. Instead, they are designed to capture each other's customers. Construct a payoff matrix using the following hypothetical information:

- If neither firm advertises, Coca-Cola and Pepsi each earn a profit of $750 million per year.
- If both firms advertise, Coca-Cola and Pepsi each earn a profit of $500 million per year.
- If Coca-Cola advertises and Pepsi doesn't, Coca-Cola earns a profit of $900 million, and Pepsi earns a profit of $400 million.
- If Pepsi advertises and Coca-Cola doesn't, Pepsi earns a profit of $900 million, and Coca-Cola earns a profit of $400 million.

    a. If Coca-Cola wants to maximize profit, will it advertise? Briefly explain.

    b. If Pepsi wants to maximize profit, will it advertise? Briefly explain.

    c. Is there a Nash equilibrium to this advertising game? If so, what is it?

2.10 **(Related to Solved Problem 14.2 on page 487)** UPS and FedEx both struggle to deliver the surge of packages they receive during the December holiday season. According to an article in the *Wall Street Journal*, in 2014, both firms considered charging Amazon and other firms rates that would be 10 percent higher for packages delivered during the week before Christmas. Such higher rates would likely have increased the profits of both firms. Neither UPS nor FedEx actually raised rates during the 2014 holiday season, but both firms did raise them during the 2016 holiday season. Use game theory to explain why in 2014 neither firm raised rates during the holiday season, but two years later both firms did.

    Sources: Laura Stevens, "UPS, FedEx Got Back on Time This Holiday," *Wall Street Journal*, December 29, 2014; and Paul Ziobro, "UPS Earnings: What to Watch," *Wall Street Journal*, January 30, 2017.

2.11 An economist argues that with respect to advertising in some industries, "gains to advertising firms are matched by losses to competitors" in the industry. Briefly explain the economist's reasoning. If his reasoning is correct, why do firms in these industries advertise?

    Source: Craig L. Garthwaite, "Demand Spillovers, Combative Advertising, and Celebrity Endorsements," *American Economic Journal: Applied Economics*, Vol. 6, No. 2, April 2014, p. 76.

2.12 World War I began in August 1914 and on the Western Front quickly bogged down into trench warfare. In Belgium and northern France, British and French troops were dug into trenches facing German troops a few hundred yards away. The troops continued firing back and forth until a remarkable event occurred, which historians have labeled "The Christmas Truce." On Christmas Eve, along several sectors of the front, British and German troops stopped firing and eventually came out into the area between the trenches to sing Christmas carols and exchange small gifts. The truce lasted until

Christmas night in most areas of the front, although it continued until New Year's Day in a few areas. Most of the troops' commanding officers were unhappy with the truce—they would have preferred the troops to keep fighting through Christmas—and in the future they often used a policy of rotating troops around the front so that the same British and German troops did not face each other for more than relatively brief periods. Can game theory explain why the Christmas Truce occurred? Can game theory help explain why the commanding officers' strategy was successful in reducing future unauthorized truces?

Source: Robert M. Sapolsky, "The Spirit of the 1914 Christmas Truce," *Wall Street Journal*, December 19, 2014.

2.13 In 2017, Best Buy had the following price matching policy posted to its Web site:

> At the time of sale, we price match all local retail competitors (including their online prices) and we price match products shipped from and sold by these major online retailers: Amazon.com, Bhphotovideo.com, Crutchfield.com, Dell.com, HP.com, Newegg.com, and TigerDirect.com.

Is Best Buy's policy likely to result in lower prices or higher prices on televisions and other products it sells in competition with Amazon and local brick-and-mortar stores? Briefly explain.

Source: "Best Buy Price Match Guarantee," bestbuy.com, April 30, 2017.

2.14 (Related to the Apply the Concept on page 489) The U.S. Department of Justice investigated whether the four major U.S. airlines were colluding. Some analysts believed the airlines were restraining increases in capacity by failing to buy more planes or fly additional routes in order to reduce pressure to cut ticket prices. An airline industry analyst commented on the investigation, "I don't sense that the executives talk to each other. They actually hate each other, truth be told. But with so few of them left, there's almost a natural oligopoly."

a. What does the analyst mean by "a natural oligopoly"?

b. Would it be necessary for the airline executives to talk to each other to collude? Briefly explain.

Source: Christopher Drew, "Airlines under Justice Dept. Investigation over Possible Collusion," *New York Times*, July 1, 2015.

2.15 (Related to the Apply the Concept on page 489) Airlines sometimes find themselves in price wars. Consider the following game: Delta and United are the only two airlines flying the route from Houston, Texas to Omaha, Nebraska. Each firm has two strategies: Charge a high price or charge a low price.

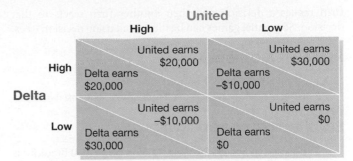

a. What (if any) is the dominant strategy for each firm?

b. Is this game a prisoner's dilemma?

c. How could repeated playing of the game change the strategy each firm uses?

2.16 (Related to the Apply the Concept on page 489) For many years, airlines would post proposed changes in ticket prices on computer reservation systems several days before the new ticket prices went into effect. Eventually, the federal government took action to end this practice. Now airlines can post prices on their reservation systems only for tickets that are immediately available for sale. Why would the federal government object to the old system of posting prices before they went into effect?

Source: Scott McCartney, "Airfare Wars Show Why Deals Arrive and Depart," *Wall Street Journal*, March 19, 2002.

2.17 Finding dominant strategies is often a very effective way of analyzing a game. Consider the following game: Microsoft and Apple are the two firms in the market for operating systems. Each firm has two strategies: Charge a high price or charge a low price.

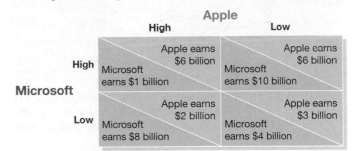

a. What (if any) is the dominant strategy for each firm?

b. Is there a Nash equilibrium? Briefly explain.

2.18 Suppose there are four large manufacturers of toilet tissue. The largest of these manufacturers announces that it will raise its prices by 15 percent due to higher paper costs. Within three days, the other three large toilet tissue manufacturers announce similar price hikes. Would this decision to raise prices be evidence of explicit collusion among the four companies? Briefly explain.

14.3 ## Sequential Games and Business Strategy, pages 492–496

LEARNING OBJECTIVE: Use sequential games to analyze business strategies.

MyLab Economics Visit **www.pearson.com/mylab/economics** to complete these exercises online and get instant feedback.

Summary

Recent work in game theory has focused on actions firms can take to deter the entry of new firms into an industry. Deterring entry can be analyzed using a sequential game, where first one firm makes a decision and then another firm reacts to that decision. Sequential games can be illustrated using decision trees.

Review Questions

3.1 What is a sequential game?

3.2 How are decision trees used to analyze sequential games?

Problems and Applications

3.3 **(Related to Solved Problem 14.3 on page 494)** Bradford is a small town that currently has no fast-food restaurants. McDonald's and Burger King both are considering entering this market. Burger King will wait until McDonald's has made its decision before deciding whether to enter. McDonald's will choose between building a large store and building a small store. Once McDonald's has made its decision about the size of the store it will build, Burger King will decide whether to enter this market. Use the following decision tree to decide the optimal strategy for each company. Does your answer depend on the rate of return that owners of fast-food restaurants must earn on their investments to break even? Briefly explain.

3.4 When Microsoft announced a new version of its Xbox One video game console, it said the console would have a price of $499. Later, Sony announced that its new

PlayStation 4 video game console would have a price of $399. An article on the event where Microsoft introduced the new console noted that the firm's spokesperson "started by showing off features like live-television technology and the ability to video-chat through its Skype service." According to the article, not until nearly halfway through the presentation did the Microsoft spokesperson mention the new games the console could play.

a. Why in announcing a new video game console would Microsoft focus its presentation on features of the console other than its ability to play games?

b. Was it an advantage to Sony that Microsoft announced the price of the Xbox One before Sony announced the price of the PlayStation 4? Briefly explain.

Source: Ian Sherr and Daisuke Wakabayashi, "Xbox One to Launch at $499, PlayStation 4 at $399," *Wall Street Journal*, June 10, 2013.

3.5 Suppose that in the situation shown in Figure 14.7 on page 495, TruImage's profit is $1.5 million if the firm accepts Dell's contract offer of $20 per copy. Now will Dell offer TruImage a contract for $20 per copy or a contract for $30 per copy? Briefly explain.

3.6 Refer to Figure 14.5 on page 492. Consider the entries in the row of the payoff matrix that correspond to Saudi Arabia choosing "Low Output." Suppose the numbers change so that Nigeria's profit is $15 million when Nigeria chooses "Low Output" and $10 million when it chooses "High Output."

a. Create the payoff matrix for this new situation, assuming that Saudi Arabia and Nigeria choose their output levels simultaneously. Is there a Nash equilibrium to this game? If so, what is it?

b. Draw the decision tree for this situation using the values from the payoff matrix you created in part (a), assuming that Saudi Arabia and Nigeria make their decisions sequentially: First, Saudi Arabia chooses its output level, and then Nigeria responds by choosing its output level. Is there a Nash equilibrium in this game? If so, what is it?

c. Compare your answers to parts (a) and (b). Briefly explain the reason for any differences in the outcomes of these two games.

14.4 The Five Competitive Forces Model, pages 496–498

LEARNING OBJECTIVE: Use the five competitive forces model to analyze competition in an industry.

MyLab Economics Visit **www.pearson.com/mylab/economics** to complete these exercises online and get instant feedback.

Summary

Michael Porter of the Harvard Business School argues that the state of competition in an industry is determined by five competitive forces: competition from existing firms, the threat from new entrants, competition from substitute goods or services, the bargaining power of buyers, and the bargaining power of suppliers.

Review Questions

4.1 Describe the five competitive forces model.

4.2 Does the strength of each of the five competitive forces remain constant over time? Briefly explain.

Problems and Applications

4.3 Briefly explain which of the five competitive forces is involved in each of these business developments.

a. The effect on Apple as Microsoft introduces the Surface Laptop computer

b. The effect on McDonald's as White Castle and Taco Bell start selling breakfast food

c. The effect on Target retail stores when Harry's razors cuts into Gillette's share of the razor market

d. The effect on the publishing firm Hachette when Amazon bargains to lower the prices of the books Hachette sells on Amazon's site

e. The effect on the AMC movie theater chain of IMAX increasing the fees it charges to theaters to use its technology

4.4 Michael Porter argued that in many industries, "strategies converge and competition becomes a series of races down identical paths that no one can win." Briefly explain whether firms in these industries will likely earn economic profits.

Source: Michael E. Porter, "What Is Strategy?" *Harvard Business Review*, November–December 1996, p. 64.

4.5 (Related to the Chapter Opener on page 478) When Apple first launched Apple Music, singer Taylor Swift refused to allow her album *1989*, which had been the best-selling album of the year, to be made available for the service because Apple did not intend to pay royalties on songs it streamed during an initial three-month period when the service would be free to subscribers. In response, Apple changed its policy and agreed to pay royalties during those three months, even though doing so reduced its profit. Do singers typically have substantial bargaining power with Apple, Spotify, and the other streaming services? Briefly explain.

Source: Mike Ayers and Ethan Smith, "Taylor Swift Is Now Making '1989' Available on Apple Music," *Wall Street Journal*, June 25, 2015.

4.6 (Related to the Apply the Concept on page 498) In the preface to the 2004 reprint of *In Search of Excellence*, Thomas Peters and Robert Waterman wrote: "Our main detractors point to the decline of some of the companies we featured. They miss the point.... We weren't writing *Forever Excellent*, just as it would be absurd to expect any great athlete not to age." Is the analogy the authors make between great firms and great athletes accurate? Should we expect firms to become less successful as they age, just as athletes do?

Source: Thomas Peters and Robert H. Waterman, Jr., "Authors' Note: Excellence 2003," in *In Search of Excellence: Lessons from America's Best-Run Companies*, New York: HarperCollins, 2004 (original edition 1982).

4.7 Under Armour, Inc., was founded in 1996 by Kevin Plank, a 23-year-old former University of Maryland football player. The company specializes in manufacturing and selling athletic and casual apparel made from synthetic material that repels moisture. The company does not have patents on the fabric it uses or on its manufacturing process. Use Michael Porter's five competitive forces model to analyze the competition Under Armour faces in the athletic and casual apparel industry.

Source: Katherine Arline, "Porter's Five Forces: Analyzing the Competition," *Business News Daily*, February 18, 2015.

4.8 Movie studios split ticket revenues with the owners of the movie theaters that show their films. When a movie is no longer being shown in theaters, theater owners earn nothing further from the film, but studios continue to earn revenue when the movie is available for home viewing on DVD, Blu-ray, streaming, and cable. Theater owners would prefer that the time between when a movie appears in theaters and when it becomes available for home viewing be as long as possible. Typically, movies are not available for home viewing for at least 90 days after they are first shown in theaters. An article in the *Wall Street Journal* in 2017 noted a possible change to this system: "Hollywood studios are preparing to upend decades of tradition by releasing movies at home less than 45 days after they debut on the big screen." The article went on to note, "Studio executives say they would prefer to reach a deal with theaters, one reason they have been reluctant to unilaterally announce a new policy." Typically, would you expect that the profits of movie studios are more at risk from the bargaining power of theaters, or would you expect that the profits of theaters are more at risk from the bargaining power of movie studios? Have streaming and other online ways of watching movies changed the relative bargaining power of movie studios and theater owners? Briefly explain.

Source: Ben Fritz, "From Multiplex to Living Room, in 45 Days or Less," *Wall Street Journal*, March 26, 2017.

Critical Thinking Exercises

CT14.1 For this exercise, your instructor may assign you to a group. Each group member should do all of the following.
  a. Search sources such as a local newspaper, cnn.com, bloomberg.com, the *Wall Street Journal*, or the *New York Times* for one firm that he or she believes is in a monopolistically competitive industry and another firm that is in an oligopoly.
  b. For each firm selected, write down the source of your information and briefly explain why you think the firm is in an industry that is monopolistically competitive or in an industry that is an oligopoly.
  c. Meet as a group and select the best example of a monopolistically competitive firm and the best example of an oligopoly firm. Describe the reason the group decided on its specific examples by identifying several characteristics and behaviors of each firm.

CT14.2 If 3-D printing technology vastly reduced economies of scale for the production of cars, how would car companies' pricing strategies change? What kind of market structure might come about after the change?

CT14.3 In Chapters 11 through 14, you read about firms in several types of market structures. Which feature varied most in these chapters: the firms' costs or the demand for the firms' products?

15

Monopoly and Antitrust Policy

A Monopoly on Lobster Dinners in Maine?

A *New York Times* article written from Stonington, Maine, explained, "Lobsters are flooding the market here." The reporter observed that the huge lobster harvest was not good news for fishermen because "the law of supply and demand has forced the price down to a 40-year low" of $1.35 per pound. Yet shortly after this article appeared, a columnist for *Slate,* an online magazine, had dinner with his father at the only lobster restaurant in Stonington, The Fisherman's Friend. He was surprised that the restaurant charged $20.99 for each dinner.

How could The Fisherman's Friend charge so much for a lobster dinner when the price of lobsters was so low? The answer is that The Fisherman's Friend is the *only* seafood restaurant in Stonington. The *Slate* reporter and his father couldn't eat at "the competitor next door" because there wasn't one. To eat lobster while staying in Stonington, they had to either eat at that restaurant or buy lobsters in a supermarket and cook them. In other words, The Fisherman's Friend has a *monopoly* on selling seafood dinners in that town.

Few firms in the United States are monopolies because in a market system whenever a firm earns an economic profit, typically other firms will enter that market. Therefore, it is very difficult for a firm to remain the only provider of a good or service. Only if the gap between the price of lobsters and the price of lobster dinners in Stonington fails to attract a competitor would The Fisherman's Friend be able to maintain its monopoly. (The restaurant was recently renamed the Harbor View Store & Stonecutters Kitchen.)

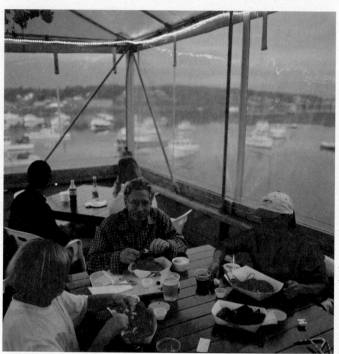

Katja Heinemann/Robert Harding World Imagery

Although not common, monopolies are worth studying because they provide a benchmark for how firms behave when they face little or no competition. In this chapter, we will build a model to analyze monopolies. We will also discuss government policies toward monopoly. These *antitrust policies* have been a subject of debate among economists and policymakers for more than 100 years.

Sources: Katharine Q. Seelye, "In Maine, More Lobsters Than They Know What to Do With," *New York Times*, July 28, 2012; and Matthew Yglesias, "The Mystery of the Market Price," www.slate.com, August 21, 2012.

Chapter Outline & Learning Objectives

Economics in Your Life & Career

Can a Business Run from Your Dorm Be a Monopoly?

You and your roommate Fatma hear students complaining about the lack of food services on campus on Saturday and Sunday evenings, so you come up with an idea for a business: You will buy rolls, lunch meat, lettuce, and tomatoes and become the sole seller of submarine sandwiches in your school's dormitories on those evenings. You believe that there will be many hungry customers when students return to campus from the library and off-campus events. What price will you charge for the subs?

Fatma argues that because your business is a monopoly, you can charge prices much higher than what local shops charge for subs during the day; hungry students will have to buy your subs or stay hungry until the following day. You want to make a profit from your business but are not sure whether Fatma is right. Is your business a monopoly? Should you charge high prices for your subs? As you read this chapter, try to answer these questions. You can check your answers against those we provide on **page 530** at the end of this chapter.

A lthough few firms are monopolies, the economic model of monopoly can be quite useful. As we have seen, even though perfectly competitive markets are rare, the competitive market model provides a benchmark for how a firm acts when it is in an industry, such as farming, with many firms that all supply the same product. Monopoly provides a benchmark for the other extreme, where a firm is the only one in its industry and, therefore, faces no competition from other firms. The monopoly model is also useful in analyzing situations in which firms agree to *collude*, or not compete, and act together as if they were a monopoly. As we will discuss in this chapter, collusion is illegal in the United States, but it occasionally happens.

Monopolies pose a dilemma for the government. Should the government allow monopolies to exist? Are there circumstances in which the government should actually promote the existence of monopolies? Should the government regulate the prices monopolies charge? In this chapter, we will explore these public policy issues.

15.1 Is Any Firm Ever Really a Monopoly?

LEARNING OBJECTIVE: Define monopoly.

Monopoly A firm that is the only seller of a good or service that does not have a close substitute.

A **monopoly** is a firm that is the only seller of a good or service that does not have a close substitute. Because substitutes of some kind exist for just about every product, are there actually any monopolies? The answer is "yes," provided that the substitutes are not "close" substitutes. But how do we decide whether a substitute is a close substitute? A narrow definition of monopoly that some economists use is that a firm has a monopoly if it can ignore the actions of all other firms. In other words, if a firm can ignore the prices other firms charge, it has a monopoly because other firms must not be producing close substitutes. For example, candles are a substitute for electric lights, but your local electric company can ignore candle prices because however low the price of candles becomes, almost no customers will give up using electric lights and switch to candles. Therefore, your local electric company is clearly a monopoly.

Many economists, however, use a broader definition of *monopoly*. For example, consider again The Fisherman's Friend restaurant in Stonington, Maine, that we discussed in the chapter opener. Does this restaurant have a monopoly? Substitutes for lobsters dinners certainly exist. If the price of lobster dinners is too high, people will switch to eating at a restaurant that serves steak or some other food. So, The Fisherman's Friend does not meet the narrow definition of a monopoly. Many economists, however, would still label the restaurant a monopoly.

We have seen that when firms earn an economic profit, we can expect new firms to enter the industry, and in the long run, the economic profit is competed away (see Chapter 12, Section 12.5). The Fisherman's Friend's profit will not be competed away as long as it is the *only* seller of lobster dinners. A reporter noted, "Stonington is a great place to visit. But it's also a very small town." So, it's possible that no other seafood restaurants will choose to open in the town. If so, The Fisherman's Friend has a monopoly because there are no other firms selling a substitute close enough that its economic profit will be competed away.

MyLab Economics Study Plan

MyLab Economics Concept Check

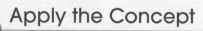

Apply the Concept

MyLab Economics Video

Is the NCAA a Monopoly?

In 1905, President Theodore Roosevelt was disturbed by the 18 deaths and many injuries college football players had suffered during the previous season. A meeting took place at the White House between Roosevelt and several college presidents to discuss rule changes that would make the game safer. This meeting eventually led to the establishment of the National Collegiate Athletic Association (NCAA) in 1910. NCAA rules now govern men's and women's athletics at more than 1,200 institutions. On its Web site, the NCAA states, "The National Collegiate Athletic Association is a membership-driven organization dedicated to safeguarding the well-being of student-athletes and equipping them with the skills to succeed on the playing field, in the classroom and throughout life." Some economists wonder whether the NCAA's rules might also have other goals.

Harvard University economist Robert Barro claims that the NCAA is effectively a monopoly. Nearly all colleges want their teams to participate in NCAA tournaments and other events. Those colleges therefore have to agree to the NCAA's rules. Included in those rules are limits on the number of scholarships that a college can award student athletes and a prohibition on paying salaries to athletes. These restrictions reduce the cost to colleges of running their athletic programs. Noting that very few college athletes go on to careers in professional sports, Barro argued that "many college basketball players come from poor families…. Absent the NCAA, such a student would be able to amass significant cash during a college career. With the NCAA in charge, this student remains poor." The NCAA defends its restrictions on scholarships and its prohibition on paying salaries to athletes as a way of preserving the amateur status of collegiate sports.

Rodger Mallison/Fort Worth Star-Telegram/ TNS/Alamy Stock Photo

Do NCAA rules preserve the ideal of amateurism in college sports, or are they violations of federal antitrust laws?

Because the NCAA does not directly control the operations of the athletic departments of the member colleges, some economists argue that it is more accurate to think of the organization as a cartel than as a monopoly. As we saw in Chapter 14, Section 14.2, when discussing the Organization of the Petroleum Exporting Countries (OPEC), a cartel is a group of firms that collude by agreeing to restrict output to increase prices and profits. The NCAA restricts the number of games the member schools' teams can play, effectively restricting output. For decades, the NCAA also restricted the number of college football and basketball games that could be televised. Some larger schools did not support these restrictions, however, and in 1982, the University of Georgia and the University of Oklahoma sued the NCAA under the federal antitrust laws. As we will see in Section 15.5, the antitrust laws are aimed at eliminating collusion and promoting competition among firms. In 1984, the Supreme Court decided the case against the NCAA, noting that "good motives alone will not validate an otherwise anticompetitive practice." In the years since the decision, college football and basketball broadcasts have greatly increased.

The federal courts have ruled against some of the NCAA's rules, such as the one restricting television broadcasts, but as of 2017, the courts had not provided a final judgment on many of the group's other rules. Nevertheless, the NCAA has agreed to loosen one of its key rules by allowing colleges the freedom to reimburse athletes for the *full* cost of attending college, as determined by federal government guidelines. This cost is typically several thousand dollars per year more than an athlete pays for tuition, books, and room and board because it includes food, clothing, and the cost of travel between the campus and the student's home. The NCAA's defenders argue that its rules and restrictions are necessary to preserve the ideal of amateurism in college sports and to make it possible for colleges to offer students the opportunity to participate in sports that do not generate much revenue from ticket sales and broadcasting rights, while preserving the ability of smaller schools to compete with larger schools. The organization's critics believe that many of the NCAA's regulations and restrictions are inconsistent with antitrust laws and argue that they should be removed.

Sources: Steve Berkowitz and A. J. Perez, "Supreme Court Will Not Consider the Ed O'Bannon Antitrust Case against NCAA," usatoday.com, October 3, 2016; Sharon Terlep, "Colleges Don't Need to Pay Athletes Beyond Attendance Costs," *Wall Street Journal,* September 30, 2015; Gary Becker, "The NCAA as a Powerful Cartel," becker-posnerblog.com, April 3, 2011; Robert L. Barro, "The Best Little Monopoly in America," bloomberg.com, December 9, 2002; "Who We Are," ncaa.org; and Michael A. Leeds and Peter von Allmen, *The Economics of Sports,* 5th ed., Boston: Pearson, 2014.

Your Turn: Test your understanding by doing related problem 1.6 on page 531 at the end of this chapter.

MyLab Economics Study Plan

15.2 Where Do Monopolies Come From?

LEARNING OBJECTIVE: Explain the four main reasons monopolies arise.

Because monopolies do not face competition, every firm would like to have a monopoly. But to have a monopoly, barriers to entering the market must be so high that no other firms can enter. *Barriers to entry* may be high enough to keep out competing firms for four main reasons:

1. Government action blocks the entry of more than one firm into a market.
2. One firm has control of a key resource necessary to produce a good.
3. There are important *network externalities* in supplying the good or service.
4. Economies of scale are so large that one firm has a *natural monopoly*.

Government Action Blocks Entry

As we will discuss in Section 15.5, governments ordinarily try to promote competition in markets, but sometimes governments take action to block entry into a market. In the United States, governments block entry in two main ways:

1. By granting a *patent*, *copyright*, or *trademark* to an individual or a firm, giving it the exclusive right to produce a product
2. By granting a firm a *public franchise*, making it the exclusive legal provider of a good or service

Patent The exclusive right to a product for a period of 20 years from the date the patent application is filed with the government.

Patents, Copyrights, and Trademarks The U.S. government grants patents to firms that develop new products or new ways of making existing products. A **patent** gives a firm the exclusive right to a new product for a period of 20 years from the date the patent application is filed with the government. Because Apple has a patent on the iOS operating system for smartphones, other firms can't sell their versions of iOS. The government grants patents to encourage firms to spend money on the research and development necessary to create new products. If other firms could freely copy iOS, Apple would probably not have spent the time and money necessary to develop it. Sometimes a firm is able to maintain a monopoly in the production of a good without patent protection, provided that it can keep secret how the product is made.

Patent protection is critical to pharmaceutical firms because they start research and development work on a new prescription drug an average of 12 years before the drug is available for sale. A firm applies for a patent about 10 years before it begins to sell the product. The average 10-year delay between the government granting a patent and the firm actually selling the drug is due to the federal Food and Drug Administration's requirements that the firm demonstrate that the drug is both safe and effective. Therefore, during the period before the drug can be sold, the firm will have significant costs to develop and test it. If the drug does not successfully make it to market, the firm will have a substantial loss.

Once a drug is available for sale, the profits the firm earns from the drug will increase throughout the period of patent protection—which is usually about 10 years—as the drug becomes more widely known to doctors and patients. After the patent has expired, other firms are free to legally produce chemically identical drugs called *generic drugs*. Gradually, competition from generic drugs will eliminate the profit the original firm had been earning. For example, when patent protection expired for Glucophage, a diabetes drug manufactured by Bristol-Myers Squibb, revenue from the drug declined by more than $1.5 billion in the first year due to competition from 12 generic versions of the drug produced by other firms. When the patent expired on Prozac, an antidepressant drug manufactured by Eli Lilly, revenue dropped by more than 80 percent. Most economic profit from selling a prescription drug is eliminated 20 years after the drug is first offered for sale.

A *trademark* grants a firm legal protection against other firms using its product's name. Trademarks are also called *brand names*. The U.S. Patent and Trademark Office defines a trademark as "any word, name, symbol, device, or any combination, used or intended to be used to identify and distinguish the goods/services of one seller or provider from those of others, and to indicate the source of the goods/services." Firms often vigorously defend their trademarks, including by filing lawsuits against other firms for selling goods that infringe on their trademarks. For example, Christian Louboutin filed a lawsuit against Yves Saint Laurent, claiming that Yves Saint Laurent had infringed on Christian Louboutin's trademark on women's shoes with red soles. A court ruled that Yves Saint Laurent could use red on soles only when that color contrasted with the color of the upper part of the shoe.

Apply the Concept

MyLab Economics Video

Does Hasbro Have a Monopoly on Monopoly?

To receive a copyright, patent, or trademark, a work has to be substantially new. Once a work no longer has legal protection, it is in the *public domain* and available to be freely used. It wouldn't be possible, for example, to make small changes to Mark Twain's novel *Huckleberry Finn* and then claim copyright on the book because it has been in the public domain for decades. (If you drew new illustrations for the book, however, it would be possible to copyright those illustrations independently of the text of the book.)

CaseyMartin/Shutterstock

Hasbro's trademark on its Monopoly game prevents other companies from creating and selling similar games using the same name.

Hasbro is the multinational U.S. company that owns Monopoly, one of the world's most popular board games. The company estimates that more than 275 million copies of the game have been sold, and it is available in 43 languages. According to Hasbro, Charles Darrow invented the game in the 1930s. After selling many homemade copies, Darrow sold the game to Parker Brothers. In 1935, the U.S. Patent and Trademark Office issued Parker Brothers a trademark on the use of the name Monopoly for a board game. Hasbro bought Parker Brothers in 1991. Trademarks, unlike patents and copyrights, never expire, so Hasbro continues to have a trademark on the name Monopoly.

Economics professor Ralph Anspach of California State University, San Francisco, received an unexpected lesson in the law of trademarks when he decided in the 1970s to sell a game about competition that he titled Anti-Monopoly. The game was a hit, selling 200,000 copies the first year. Parker Brothers sued Anspach on the grounds that his game infringed on its Monopoly trademark. In the course of defending the lawsuit, Anspach believed he had uncovered evidence that in 1904, a woman named Elizabeth Magic had developed The Landlord's Game, which was very similar to Monopoly. The game was never trademarked and was played for years on the East Coast. According to Anspach, Darrow became aware of The Landlord's Game in the mid-1930s, made a few changes to it, and sold it to Parker Brothers in 1935. A federal appeals court largely agreed with Anspach that given the history of the game, the name Monopoly was in the public domain and so couldn't be trademarked. Congress later amended the law, though, in a way that reinstated the Parker Brothers trademark. Eventually, Anspach and Hasbro worked out a settlement under which Anspach was allowed to sell his Anti-Monopoly game under a license from Hasbro.

Losing the trademark on its Monopoly game would have cost Hasbro millions of dollars per year because other companies could have begun to market similar games using the same name. The long legal fight the company had with Professor Anspach illustrates that companies consider it critical to retain exclusive control of their products.

Sources: Mary Pilon, "How a Fight over a Board Game Monopolized an Economist's Life," *Wall Street Journal*, October 20, 2009; Ralph Anspach, *The Billion Dollar Monopoly® Swindle*, 2nd ed., Bloomington, IN: Xlibris, 2007; and Rachel Doepker, "Monopoly Patented," Business Reference Services, Library of Congress, www.loc.gov/rr/business/businesshistory/December/monopoly.html.

Your Turn: Test your understanding by doing related problem 2.9 on page 532 at the end of this chapter.

MyLab Economics Study Plan

Just as the federal government grants a new product patent or trademark protection, it grants creators of books, films, and pieces of music **copyright** protection, which is the exclusive right to use the creation during the creator's lifetime.

Copyright A government-granted exclusive right to produce and sell a creation.

The creator's heirs retain this exclusive right for 70 years after the creator's death. In effect, copyrights create monopolies for the copyrighted items. Without copyrights, individuals and firms would be less likely to invest in creating new books, films, and software.

Public franchise A government designation that a firm is the only legal provider of a good or service.

Public Franchises In some cases, the government grants a firm a **public franchise** that allows it to be the only legal provider of a good or service. For example, state and local governments often designate one company as the sole provider of electricity, natural gas, or water.

Occasionally, a government may decide to provide certain services directly to consumers through a *public enterprise*. Public enterprises are more common in Europe than in the United States. For example, the governments in most European countries own the railroad systems. In the United States, many city governments provide water and sewage service rather than rely on private firms. Congress has given the U.S. Postal Service the exclusive right to deliver first-class mail. No other company can legally deliver a letter to your mailbox. **MyLab Economics** Concept Check

Control of a Key Resource

Another way for a firm to become a monopoly is by controlling a key resource. Firms rarely gain this control because most resources, including raw materials such as oil or iron ore, are widely available from a variety of suppliers. There are, however, a few prominent examples of monopolies based on control of a key resource, such as the Aluminum Company of America (Alcoa) and the International Nickel Company of Canada.

For many years, until the 1940s, Alcoa either owned or had long-term contracts to buy nearly all of the available bauxite, the mineral needed to produce aluminum. Without access to bauxite, competing firms had to use recycled aluminum, which limited the amount of aluminum they could produce. Similarly, the International Nickel Company of Canada controlled more than 90 percent of available nickel supplies. Competition in the nickel market increased when the Petsamo nickel fields in northern Russia were developed after World War II.

In the United States, a key resource for a professional sports team is a large stadium. The teams that make up the major professional sports leagues—Major League Baseball, the National Football League, the National Hockey League, and the National Basketball Association—usually either own or have long-term leases with the stadiums in major cities. Control of these stadiums is a major barrier to new professional baseball, football, hockey, or basketball leagues forming. **MyLab Economics** Concept Check

Apply the Concept
MyLab Economics Video

Are Diamond Profits Forever? The De Beers Diamond Monopoly

The most famous monopoly based on control of a raw material is the De Beers diamond mining and marketing company of South Africa. Before the 1860s, diamonds were extremely rare. Only a few pounds of diamonds were produced each year, primarily from Brazil and India. Then in 1870, enormous deposits of diamonds were discovered along the Orange River in South Africa. It became possible to produce thousands of pounds of diamonds per year, and the owners of the new mines feared that the price of diamonds would plummet. To avoid financial disaster, the mine owners decided in 1888 to merge and form De Beers Consolidated Mines, Ltd.

De Beers became one of the most profitable and longest-lived monopolies in history. The company carefully controlled the supply of diamonds to keep prices high. As new diamond deposits were discovered in Russia and Zaire, De Beers was able to maintain prices by buying most of the new supplies.

Because diamonds are rarely destroyed, De Beers has always worried about competition from the resale of stones. Heavily promoting diamond engagement and wedding rings with the slogan "A Diamond Is Forever" was a way around this problem. Because engagement and wedding rings have great sentimental value, they are seldom resold, even by the heirs of the original recipients. De Beers advertising has been successful even in some countries, such as Japan, that had no custom of giving diamond engagement rings. As the populations in De Beers's key markets age, its advertising in recent years has focused on middle-aged men presenting diamond rings to their wives as symbols of financial success and continuing love and on women buying "right-hand rings" for themselves.

Over the years, competition has gradually increased in the diamond business. By 2000, De Beers directly controlled only about 40 percent of world diamond production. The company became concerned about how much it was spending to buy diamonds from other sources to keep them off the market. It decided to abandon its strategy of attempting to control the worldwide supply of diamonds and to concentrate instead on differentiating its diamonds by relying on its name recognition. Each De Beers diamond is now marked with a microscopic brand—a "Forevermark"—to reassure consumers of its high quality. Other firms, such as BHP Billiton, which owns mines in northern Canada, have followed suit by branding their diamonds. De Beers has also become concerned about the increased supply of synthetic diamonds. It has developed technology to detect whether a diamond is synthetic rather than natural (mined) and hopes to convince consumers to continue buying natural diamonds. Whether consumers will pay attention to brands on diamonds and whether they will care about the difference between synthetic and natural diamonds remains to be seen, although in 2017, De Beers, which had become part of the Anglo American mining company, maintained about a 35 percent share of the diamond market.

Ed Rooney/Alamy Stock Photo

De Beers promotes the sentimental value of diamonds as a way to maintain its position in the diamond market.

Sources: Scott Patterson and Alex MacDonald, "De Beers Tries to Counter a Growing Threat: Man-Made Diamonds," *Wall Street Journal*, November 6, 2016; Alex MacDonald, "De Beers Brings Oppenheimer Era to End," *Wall Street Journal*, October 3, 2012; Edward Jay Epstein, "Have You Ever Tried to Sell a Diamond?" *Atlantic Monthly*, February 1982; and Donna J. Bergenstock, Mary F. Deily, and Larry W. Taylor, "A Cartel's Response to Cheating: An Empirical Investigation of the De Beers Diamond Empire," *Southern Economic Journal*, Vol. 73, No. 1, July 2006, pp. 173–189.

Your Turn: Test your understanding by doing related problem 2.10 on page 532 at the end of this chapter.

MyLab Economics Study Plan

Network Externalities

There are **network externalities** in the consumption of a product if its usefulness increases with the number of people who use it. If you owned the only HD television in the world, for example, it would not be very valuable because firms would not have an incentive to develop HD programming. The more HD televisions there are in use, the more valuable they become to consumers.

Some economists argue that network externalities can serve as barriers to entry. For example, in the early 1980s, Microsoft gained an advantage over other software companies by developing MS-DOS, the operating system for the first IBM personal computers. Because IBM sold more computers than any other company, software developers wrote many application programs for MS-DOS. The more people who used MS-DOS–based programs, the greater the value to a consumer of using an MS-DOS–based program. By the 1990s, Microsoft had replaced MS-DOS with Windows. Today, Windows has an 85 percent share in the market for personal computer operating systems, with Apple's operating system having a 10 percent share, and other operating systems, including the open-source Linux system, having shares of about 1 percent or less. If another firm introduced a new operating system, some economists argue that relatively few people would use it initially, and few applications would run on it, which would limit the operating system's value to other consumers.

eBay was the first Internet site to attract a significant number of people to its online auctions. Once many people began to use eBay to buy and sell collectibles, antiques, and many other products, it became a more valuable place to buy and sell. Yahoo.com, Amazon.com, and other Internet sites eventually started online auctions,

Network externalities A characteristic of a product in which its usefulness increases with the number of consumers who use it.

but they had difficulty attracting buyers and sellers. On eBay, a buyer expects to find more sellers, and a seller expects to find more potential buyers than on other auction sites.

As these examples show, from a firm's point of view, network externalities can set off a *virtuous cycle*: If a firm can attract enough customers initially, it can attract additional customers because the value of its product has been increased by more people using it, which attracts even more customers, and so on. With products such as computer operating systems and online auctions, it might be difficult for new firms to enter the market and compete away the profit being earned by the first firm in the market.

Economists debate, however, the extent to which network externalities are important barriers to entry in the business world. Some economists argue that Microsoft and eBay have dominant positions primarily because they are efficient in offering products that satisfy consumer preferences rather than because of the effects of network externalities. In this view, the advantages firms gain from network externalities would not be enough to protect them from competing firms offering better products. For example, many people have switched from computers to tablets and smartphones that run on Apple's iOS or Google's Android operating system, making Microsoft's domination of computer operating systems less important. **MyLab Economics** Concept Check

Natural Monopoly

Natural monopoly A situation in which economies of scale are so large that one firm can supply the entire market at a lower average total cost than can two or more firms.

Economies of scale exist when a firm's long-run average cost falls as it increases the quantity of output it produces (see Chapter 11, Section 11.6). A **natural monopoly** occurs when economies of scale are so large that one firm can supply the entire market at a lower average total cost than can two or more firms. In that case, there is "room" in the market for only one firm.

Figure 15.1 shows the average total cost curve for a firm producing electricity and the total demand for electricity in the firm's market. Notice that the average total cost curve is still falling when it crosses the demand curve at point A. If the firm is a monopoly and produces 30 billion kilowatt-hours of electricity per year, its average total cost of production will be $0.04 per kilowatt-hour. Suppose instead that two firms are in the market, each producing half the market output, or 15 billion kilowatt-hours per year. Assume that each firm has the same average total cost curve. The figure shows that producing 15 billion kilowatt-hours would move each firm back up its average cost curve so that the average cost of producing electricity would rise to

Figure 15.1

Average Total Cost Curve for a Natural Monopoly

With a natural monopoly, the average total cost curve is still falling when it crosses the demand curve (point A). If only one firm is producing electric power in the market, and it produces where the average cost curve intersects the demand curve, average total cost will equal $0.04 per kilowatt-hour of electricity produced. If the market is divided between two firms, each producing 15 billion kilowatt-hours, the average cost of producing electricity rises to $0.06 per kilowatt-hour (point B). In this case, if one firm expands production, it can move down the average total cost curve, lower its price, and drive the other firm out of business.

$0.06 per kilowatt-hour (point B). In this case, if one of the firms expands production, it will move down the average total cost curve. With lower average costs, it will be able to offer electricity at a lower price than the other firm can offer. Eventually, the other firm will be driven out of business, and the remaining firm will have a monopoly. Because a monopoly would develop automatically—or *naturally*—in this market, it is a natural monopoly.

Natural monopolies are most likely to occur in markets where fixed costs are very large relative to variable costs. For example, a firm that produces electricity must make a substantial investment in machinery and equipment necessary to generate the electricity and in the wires and cables necessary to distribute it. Once the firm makes the initial investment, however, the marginal cost of producing another kilowatt-hour of electricity is relatively small.　　　**MyLab Economics** Concept Check

MyLab Economics Study Plan

15.3 How Does a Monopoly Choose Price and Output?

LEARNING OBJECTIVE: Explain how a monopoly chooses price and output.

Like every other firm, a monopoly maximizes profit by producing where marginal revenue equals marginal cost. A monopoly differs from other firms in that *a monopoly's demand curve is the same as the market demand curve for the product*. With perfect competition, the market demand curve for wheat is very different from the demand curve for the wheat produced by any one farmer (see Chapter 12, Section 12.1). If, however, one farmer had a monopoly on wheat production, the two demand curves would be exactly the same.

Marginal Revenue Once Again

Recall that firms in perfectly competitive markets—such as a farmer in the wheat market—face horizontal demand curves. These firms are *price takers*. All other firms, including monopolies, are *price makers*. If price makers raise their prices, they will lose some, but not all, of their customers. Therefore, they face both a downward-sloping demand curve and a downward-sloping marginal revenue curve. Let's review why a firm's marginal revenue curve slopes downward if its demand curve slopes downward.

Remember that when a firm cuts the price of a product, one good thing happens, and one bad thing happens:

- **The good thing.** The firm sells more units of the product.
- **The bad thing.** The firm receives less revenue from each unit than it would have received at the higher price.

For example, consider the table in Figure 15.2, which shows information on the market for Comcast's basic cable package. To operate a cable system in a city, firms typically need a license from the city government. Comcast is the only cable television available in some cities, effectively giving it a monopoly on cable service. For simplicity, we assume that a particular market has only 10 potential subscribers. If Comcast charges a price of $60 per month for this basic package, it won't have any subscribers. If it charges a price of $57, it sells 1 subscription. At $54, it sells 2 subscriptions, and so on. Comcast's total revenue is equal to the number of subscriptions sold per month multiplied by the price. The firm's average revenue—or revenue per subscription sold—is equal to its total revenue divided by the quantity of subscriptions sold. Comcast is particularly interested in marginal revenue because marginal revenue tells the firm how much its revenue will increase if it cuts the price to sell 1 more subscription.

Notice that Comcast's marginal revenue is less than the price for every subscription sold after the first subscription. To see why, think about what happens if Comcast cuts the price of its basic cable package from $42 to $39, which increases its subscriptions sold from 6 to 7. Comcast increases its revenue by the $39 it receives for the seventh subscription. But it also loses revenue of $3 per subscription on the first 6 subscriptions

Subscribers per Month (Q)	Price (P)	Total Revenue (TR = P × Q)	Average Revenue (AR = TR/Q)	Marginal Revenue (MR = ΔTR/ΔQ)
0	$60	$0	–	–
1	57	57	$57	$57
2	54	108	54	51
3	51	153	51	45
4	48	192	48	39
5	45	225	45	33
6	42	252	42	27
7	39	273	39	21
8	36	288	36	15
9	33	297	33	9
10	30	300	30	3

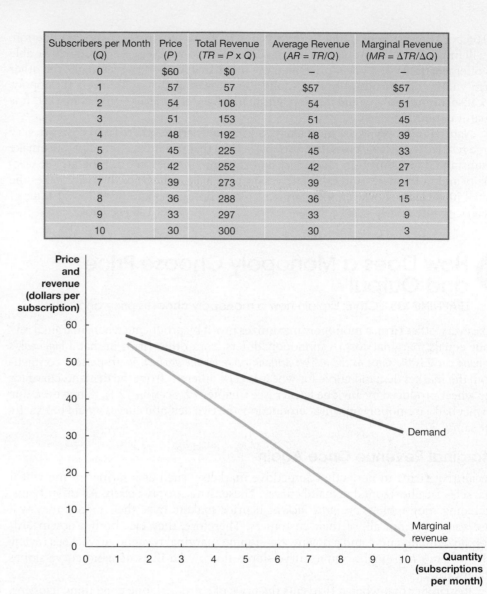

MyLab Economics Animation

Figure 15.2

Calculating a Monopoly's Revenue

Comcast faces a downward-sloping demand curve for subscriptions to basic cable. To sell more subscriptions, it must cut the price. By cutting the price, Comcast gains revenue from selling more subscriptions but loses revenue from selling at a lower price the subscriptions that it could have sold at a higher price. The firm's marginal revenue is the change in revenue from selling another subscription. We can calculate marginal revenue by subtracting the revenue lost as a result of a price cut from the revenue gained. The table shows that Comcast's marginal revenue is less than the price for every subscription sold after the first subscription. Therefore, Comcast's marginal revenue curve will be below its demand curve.

because it could have sold them at the old price of $42. So, its marginal revenue on the seventh subscription is $39 − $18 = $21, which is the value shown in the table. The graph in Figure 15.2 plots Comcast's demand and marginal revenue curves, based on the information in the table. **MyLab Economics** Concept Check

Profit Maximization for a Monopolist

Figure 15.3 shows how Comcast combines the information on demand and marginal revenue with information on average and marginal costs to decide how many subscriptions to sell and what price to charge. We assume that the firm's marginal

(a) Profit-maximizing quantity and price for a monopolist

(b) Profit for a monopolist

MyLab Economics Animation

Figure 15.3 **Profit-Maximizing Price and Output for a Monopoly**

Panel (a) shows that to maximize profit, Comcast should sell subscriptions up to the point where the marginal revenue from selling the last subscription equals its marginal cost (point A). In this case, both the marginal revenue from selling the sixth subscription and the marginal cost are $27. Comcast maximizes profit by selling 6 subscriptions per month and charging a price of $42 (point B). In panel (b), the green rectangle represents Comcast's profit. The rectangle has a height equal to $12, which is the price of $42 minus the average total cost of $30, and a base equal to the quantity of 6 cable subscriptions. Comcast's profit therefore equals $12 × 6 = $72.

cost and average total cost curves have the typical U shapes we encountered in previous chapters. In panel (a), we see how Comcast can calculate its profit-maximizing quantity and price. As long as the marginal cost of selling one more subscription is less than the marginal revenue, the firm should sell additional subscriptions because it is adding to its profit. As Comcast sells more cable subscriptions, rising marginal cost will eventually equal marginal revenue, and the firm will be selling the profit-maximizing quantity of subscriptions. Comcast maximizes profit with the sixth subscription, which adds $27 to the firm's costs and $27 to its revenues—point A in panel (a) of Figure 15.3. The demand curve indicates that Comcast can sell 6 subscriptions for a price of $42 per month. We can conclude that Comcast's profit-maximizing quantity of subscriptions is 6, and its profit-maximizing price is $42.

Panel (b) shows that the average total cost of 6 subscriptions is $30 and that Comcast can sell 6 subscriptions at a price of $42 per month (point B on the demand curve). Comcast is making a profit of $12 per subscription: the price of $42 minus the average cost of $30. Its total profit is $72 (= 6 subscriptions × $12 profit per subscription), which is shown by the area of the green-shaded rectangle in the figure. We could also have calculated Comcast's total profit as the difference between its total revenue and its total cost. Its total revenue from selling 6 subscriptions is $252. Its total cost equals its average total cost multiplied by the number of subscriptions sold, or $30 × 6 = $180. So, its profit is $252 − $180 = $72.

Note that even though Comcast is earning an economic profit, new firms will *not* enter the market unless they can obtain licenses from the city. If it holds the only license, Comcast has a monopoly and will not face competition from other cable operators. Therefore, if other factors—such as demand and its costs—remain unchanged, Comcast will be able to continue to earn an economic profit, even in the long run.

MyLab Economics Concept Check   MyLab Economics Study Plan

Solved Problem 15.3

MyLab Economics Interactive Animation

Finding the Profit-Maximizing Price and Output for a Cable Monopoly

Suppose that Comcast has a cable monopoly in Philadelphia. The following table gives Comcast's demand and cost per month for subscriptions to basic cable. (For simplicity, we once again keep the number of subscribers artificially small.)

Price	Quantity	Total Revenue	Marginal Revenue $\left(MR = \dfrac{\Delta TR}{\Delta Q} \right)$	Total Cost	Marginal Cost $\left(MC = \dfrac{\Delta TC}{\Delta Q} \right)$
$27	3			$56	
26	4			73	
25	5			91	
24	6			110	
23	7			130	
22	8			151	

a. Fill in the missing values in the table.

b. If Comcast wants to maximize profit, what price should it charge, and how many cable subscriptions per month should it sell? How much profit will Comcast make? Briefly explain.

c. Suppose the city government imposes a $25-per-month tax on Comcast. Now what price should Comcast charge, how many subscriptions should it sell, and what will its profit be?

Solving the Problem

Step 1: **Review the chapter material.** This problem is about finding the profit-maximizing quantity and price for a monopolist, so you may want to review the section "Profit Maximization for a Monopolist," which begins on page 516.

Step 2: **Answer part (a) by filling in the missing values in the table.** Remember that to calculate marginal revenue and marginal cost, you divide the change in total revenue or total cost by the change in quantity.

We don't have enough information from the table to fill in the values for marginal revenue and marginal cost in the first row.

Price	Quantity	Total Revenue	Marginal Revenue $\left(MR = \dfrac{\Delta TR}{\Delta Q} \right)$	Total Cost	Marginal Cost $\left(MC = \dfrac{\Delta TC}{\Delta Q} \right)$
$27	3	$81	—	$56	—
26	4	104	$23	73	$17
25	5	125	21	91	18
24	6	144	19	110	19
23	7	161	17	130	20
22	8	176	15	151	21

Step 3: **Answer part (b) by determining the profit-maximizing quantity and price.** We know that Comcast will maximize profit by selling subscriptions up to the point where marginal cost equals marginal revenue. In this case, that means selling 6 subscriptions per month. From the information in the first two columns, we know Comcast can sell 6 subscriptions at a price of $24 each.

Comcast's profit is equal to the difference between its total revenue and its total cost: Profit = \$144 − \$110 = \$34 per month.

Step 4: **Answer part (c) by analyzing the effect of the tax.** The tax is a fixed cost to Comcast because it is a flat \$25 no matter how many subscriptions it sells. Because the tax doesn't affect Comcast's marginal revenue or marginal cost, the profit-maximizing level of output has not changed. So, Comcast will still sell 6 subscriptions per month at a price of \$24, but its profit will fall by the amount of the tax, from \$34 per month to \$9 per month.

Your Turn: For more practice, do related problems 3.4 and 3.5 on page 533 at the end of this chapter.   MyLab Economics Study Plan

---

Don't Let This Happen to You

Don't Assume That Charging a Higher Price Is Always More Profitable for a Monopolist

In answering part (c) of Solved Problem 15.3, it's tempting to argue that Comcast should increase its price to make up for the tax. After all, Comcast is a monopolist, so why can't it just pass along the tax to its customers? The reason it can't is that Comcast, like any other monopolist, must pay attention to demand. Comcast is not interested in charging high prices for the sake of charging high prices; it is interested in maximizing profit. Charging a price of \$1,000 per month for a basic cable subscription sounds good, but if no one will buy at that price, Comcast would hardly be maximizing profit.

To look at it another way, before the tax is imposed, Comcast has already determined that \$24 per month is the price that will maximize its profit. After the tax is imposed, it must determine whether \$24 is still the profit-maximizing price. Because the tax has not affected Comcast's marginal revenue or marginal cost (or had any effect on consumer demand), \$24 is still the profit-maximizing price, and Comcast should continue to charge it. The tax reduces Comcast's profit but doesn't cause it to increase the price of cable subscriptions.

MyLab Economics Study Plan

Your Turn: Test your understanding by doing related problem 3.8 on page 533 at the end of this chapter.

15.4 Does Monopoly Reduce Economic Efficiency?

LEARNING OBJECTIVE: Use a graph to illustrate how a monopoly affects economic efficiency.

We have seen that a perfectly competitive market is economically efficient (see Chapter 12, Section 12.6). How would economic efficiency be affected if instead of being perfectly competitive, a market were a monopoly? *Economic surplus* provides a way of characterizing the economic efficiency in a market. *Equilibrium in a perfectly competitive market results in the greatest amount of economic surplus, or total benefit to society, from the production of a good or service* (see Chapter 4, Section 4.2). What happens to economic surplus under a monopoly? We can begin the analysis by considering the hypothetical case of what would happen if the market for smartphones begins as perfectly competitive and then becomes a monopoly.

Comparing Monopoly and Perfect Competition

Panel (a) in Figure 15.4 illustrates the situation if the market for smartphones is perfectly competitive. Price and quantity are determined by the intersection of the demand and supply curves. Remember that none of the individual firms in a perfectly competitive industry has any control over price. Each firm must accept the price determined by the market. Panel (b) shows what happens if the smartphone market becomes a monopoly. We know that the monopoly will maximize profit by producing where marginal revenue equals marginal cost. To do this, the monopoly reduces the quantity

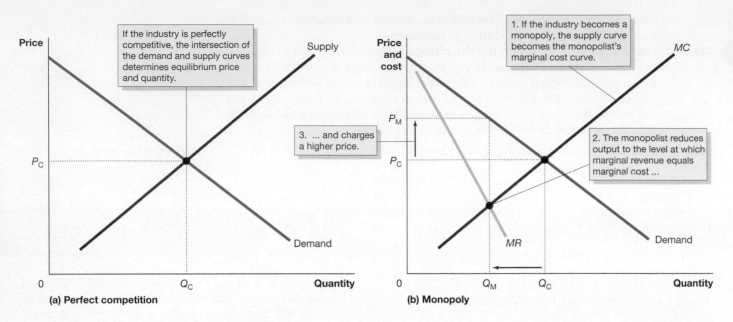

MyLab Economics Animation

Figure 15.4 **What Happens if a Perfectly Competitive Industry Becomes a Monopoly?**

In panel (a), the market for smartphones is perfectly competitive, and price and quantity are determined by the intersection of the demand and supply curves. In panel (b), the perfectly competitive smartphone market becomes a monopoly. As a result, we have the following:

1. The industry supply curve becomes the monopolist's marginal cost curve.
2. The monopolist reduces output to where marginal revenue equals marginal cost, Q_M.
3. The monopolist raises the price from P_C to P_M.

of smartphones that would have been produced if the industry were perfectly competitive and increases the price. Panel (b) illustrates an important conclusion: *A monopoly will produce a smaller quantity and charge a higher price than would a perfectly competitive industry producing the same good.*   MyLab Economics Concept Check

Measuring the Efficiency Losses from Monopoly

Figure 15.5 uses panel (b) from Figure 15.4 to illustrate how monopoly affects consumers, producers, and the efficiency of the economy. Recall that *consumer surplus* measures the net benefit received by consumers from purchasing a good or service (see Chapter 4,

MyLab Economics Animation

Figure 15.5

The Inefficiency of Monopoly

A monopoly charges a higher price, P_M, and produces a smaller quantity, Q_M, than a perfectly competitive industry, which charges price P_C and produces Q_C. The higher price reduces consumer surplus by the area equal to the rectangle A and the triangle B. Some of the reduction in consumer surplus is captured by the monopoly as producer surplus, and some becomes deadweight loss, which is the area equal to triangles B and C.

Section 4.1). We measure consumer surplus as the area below the demand curve and above the market price. The higher the price, the smaller the consumer surplus. Because a monopoly raises the market price, it reduces consumer surplus. In Figure 15.5, the loss of consumer surplus is equal to rectangle *A* plus triangle *B*. Remember that *producer surplus* measures the net benefit to producers from selling a good or service. We measure producer surplus as the area above the supply curve and below the market price. The increase in price due to monopoly increases producer surplus by an amount equal to rectangle *A* and reduces it by an amount equal to triangle *C*. Because rectangle *A* is larger than triangle *C*, we know that a monopoly increases producer surplus compared with perfect competition.

Economic surplus is equal to the sum of consumer surplus and producer surplus. By increasing price and reducing the quantity produced, the monopolist has reduced economic surplus by an amount equal to the areas of triangles *B* and *C*. This reduction in economic surplus is called *deadweight loss* and represents the loss of economic efficiency due to monopoly.

The best way to understand how a monopoly causes a loss of economic efficiency is to recall that price is equal to marginal cost in a perfectly competitive market. As a result, a consumer in a perfectly competitive market is always able to buy a good if she is willing to pay a price equal to the marginal cost of producing it. As Figure 15.5 shows, the monopolist stops producing smartphones at a point where the price is well above marginal cost. Consumers are unable to buy some smartphones for which they would be willing to pay a price greater than the marginal cost of producing them. Why doesn't the monopolist produce these additional smartphones? Because the monopolist's profit is greater if it restricts output and forces up the price. A monopoly produces the profit-maximizing level of output but fails to produce the efficient level of output from the point of view of society.

We can summarize the effects of monopoly as follows:

1. Monopoly causes a *decrease* in consumer surplus.
2. Monopoly causes an *increase* in producer surplus.
3. Monopoly causes a deadweight loss, which represents a reduction in economic efficiency.   MyLab Economics Concept Check

How Large Are the Efficiency Losses Due to Monopoly?

We know that there are relatively few monopolies, so the loss of economic efficiency due to monopoly must be small. Many firms, though, have **market power**, which is the ability of a firm to charge a price greater than marginal cost. The analysis we just completed shows that some loss of economic efficiency will occur whenever a firm has market power and can charge a price greater than marginal cost, even if the firm is not a monopoly. The only firms that do *not* have market power are firms in perfectly competitive markets, which must charge a price equal to marginal cost. Because few markets are perfectly competitive, *some loss of economic efficiency occurs in the market for nearly every good or service*.

Is the total loss of economic efficiency due to market power large or small? It is possible to put a dollar value on the loss of economic efficiency by estimating for every industry the size of the deadweight loss triangle, as in Figure 15.5. The first economist to do this was Arnold Harberger of the University of California, Los Angeles. His estimates—largely confirmed by later researchers—indicated that the total loss of economic efficiency in the U.S. economy due to market power is relatively small. According to his estimates, if every industry in the economy were perfectly competitive, so that price were equal to marginal cost in every market, the gain in economic efficiency would equal less than 1 percent of the value of total production in the United States, or less than $600 per person.

The loss of economic efficiency is small primarily because true monopolies are very rare. In most industries, competition keeps price much closer to marginal cost than would be the case in a monopoly. The closer price is to marginal cost, the smaller the size of the deadweight loss.   MyLab Economics Concept Check

Market power The ability of a firm to charge a price greater than marginal cost.

Market Power and Technological Change

Some economists argue that the economy may actually benefit from firms having market power. This argument is most closely identified with Joseph Schumpeter, an Austrian economist who spent many years as a professor of economics at Harvard. Schumpeter argued that economic progress depends on technological change in the form of new products. For example, the replacement of horse-drawn carriages by automobiles, the replacement of ice boxes by refrigerators, and the replacement of mechanical calculators by electronic computers all represent technological change that significantly raised living standards. In Schumpeter's view, new products unleash a "gale of creative destruction" that drives older products—and, often, the firms that produce them—out of the market. Schumpeter was not concerned that firms with market power would charge higher prices than perfectly competitive firms:

> It is not that kind of [price] competition which counts but the competition from the new commodity, the new technology, the new source of supply, the new type of organization ... competition which commands a decisive cost or quality advantage and which strikes not at the margins of the profits and outputs of the existing firms but at their foundations and their very lives.

Economists who support Schumpeter's view argue that the introduction of new products requires firms to spend funds on research and development. It is possible for firms to raise this money by borrowing from investors or banks. But investors and banks are usually skeptical of ideas for new products that have not yet passed the test of consumer acceptance in the market. As a result, firms are often forced to rely on their profits to finance the research and development needed for new products. Because firms with market power are more likely to earn an economic profit than are perfectly competitive firms, they are also more likely to carry out research and development and launch new products. In this view, the benefits that consumers receive from these new products outweigh the higher prices firms with market power charge.

Some economists disagree with Schumpeter's views. These economists point to the number of new products developed by smaller firms, including, for example, Steve Jobs and Steve Wozniak inventing the first Apple computer in Jobs's garage, and Larry Page and Sergey Brin inventing the Google search engine as graduate students at Stanford. As we will see in the next section, government policymakers continue to struggle with the issue of whether, on balance, large firms with market power are good or bad for the economy.

MyLab Economics Study Plan

MyLab Economics Concept Check

15.5 Government Policy toward Monopoly

LEARNING OBJECTIVE: Explain how the government regulates monopoly.

Because monopolies reduce consumer surplus and economic efficiency, most governments have policies that regulate their behavior. **Collusion** refers to an agreement among firms to charge the same price or otherwise not to compete (see Chapter 14, Section 14.2). In the United States, *antitrust laws* are designed to prevent monopolies and collusion. Governments also regulate firms that are natural monopolies, often by controlling the prices they charge.

Collusion An agreement among firms to charge the same price or otherwise not to compete.

Antitrust Laws and Antitrust Enforcement

The first important law regulating monopolies in the United States was the Sherman Act, which Congress passed in 1890 to promote competition and prevent the formation of monopolies. Section 1 of the Sherman Act outlaws "every contract, combination in the form of trust or otherwise, or conspiracy in restraint of trade." Section 2 states that "every person who shall monopolize, or attempt to monopolize, or combine or conspire with any other person or persons, to monopolize any part of the trade or commerce ... shall be deemed guilty of a felony."

Law	Date Enacted by Congress	Purpose
Sherman Act	1890	Prohibited "restraint of trade," including price fixing and collusion. Also outlawed monopolization.
Clayton Act	1914	Prohibited firms from buying stock in competitors and from having directors serve on the boards of competing firms.
Federal Trade Commission Act	1914	Established the Federal Trade Commission (FTC) to help administer antitrust laws.
Robinson–Patman Act	1936	Prohibited firms from charging buyers different prices if the result would reduce competition.
Cellar–Kefauver Act	1950	Toughened restrictions on mergers by prohibiting any mergers that would reduce competition.

Table 15.1

Important U.S. Antitrust Laws

The Sherman Act targeted firms in several industries that had combined during the 1870s and 1880s to form "trusts." In a trust, the firms were operated independently but gave voting control to a board of trustees. The board enforced collusive agreements for the firms to charge the same price and not to compete for each other's customers. The most notorious of the trusts was the Standard Oil Trust, organized by John D. Rockefeller. In the years following passage of the Sherman Act, business trusts disappeared, but the term **antitrust laws** has lived on to refer to the laws aimed at eliminating collusion and promoting competition among firms.

The Sherman Act prohibited trusts and collusive agreements, but it left several loopholes. For example, it was not clear whether it would be legal for two or more firms to merge to form a new, larger firm that would have substantial market power. A series of Supreme Court decisions interpreted the Sherman Act narrowly, and the result was a wave of mergers at the turn of the twentieth century. Included in these mergers was U.S. Steel Corporation, which was formed from dozens of smaller companies. U.S. Steel, organized by J. P. Morgan, was the first billion-dollar corporation, and it controlled two-thirds of steel production in the United States. The Sherman Act also left unclear whether any business practices short of outright collusion were illegal.

To address the loopholes in the Sherman Act, in 1914, Congress passed the Clayton Act and the Federal Trade Commission Act. Under the Clayton Act, a merger was illegal if its effect was "substantially to lessen competition, or to tend to create a monopoly." The Federal Trade Commission Act set up the Federal Trade Commission (FTC), which was given the power to police unfair business practices. The FTC has brought lawsuits against firms employing a variety of business practices, including deceptive advertising. In setting up the FTC, Congress divided the authority to police mergers. Currently, both the Antitrust Division of the U.S. Department of Justice (DOJ) and the FTC are responsible for merger policy. Table 15.1 lists the most important U.S. antitrust laws and the purpose of each.   **MyLab Economics** Concept Check

Antitrust laws Laws aimed at eliminating collusion and promoting competition among firms.

Apply the Concept

MyLab Economics Video

Have Generic Drug Firms Been Colluding to Raise Prices?

As we saw in Section 15.2, patents provide pharmaceutical firms with an economic incentive to undertake the costly research necessary to develop new drugs. After 20 years, a patent on a drug expires, and other firms can legally produce the same drug. Drugs without patent protection are called *generic drugs*. About 88 percent of

Rob Byron/Shutterstock

The federal government has investigated the prices that Mylan and other firms charge for generic drugs.

all prescriptions doctors write in the United States are for generic drugs. It's common for the price of a drug to drop by 50 percent or more when it loses patent protection and several firms begin selling generic versions. Because competition can be intense in the market for generic drugs, firms have a strong incentive to break the antitrust laws and collude to raise prices.

In early 2017, two executives at Heritage Pharmaceuticals Inc., a small pharmaceutical firm, pleaded guilty to colluding with other firms to fix the prices of two drugs: doxycycline hyclate (an antibiotic) and glyburide (a drug used to treat diabetes). The names of the other firms involved were not made public at that time, but the DOJ conducted a wide-ranging probe into the pricing of more than 20 generic drugs. Mylan Pharmaceuticals has been subjected to substantial criticism for the price it charges for its EpiPen, which is used to counteract the effects of severe allergies. Mylan holds a patent on the EpiPen, which helps shield it from competition from other firms. But Mylan also sells a number of generic drugs, including doxycycline hyclate, for which it has the largest market share. While Mylan denied colluding with other firms to fix the prices of generic drugs, in 2017, the DOJ subpoenaed its records, along with the records of a dozen other firms. Federal investigators also searched the offices of another pharmaceutical firm, Perrigo.

In 2016, a report to Congress by the U.S. General Accountability Office (GAO) indicated that between 2010 and 2015, more than 300 of the 1,441 generic drugs studied had "had at least one extraordinary price increase of 100 percent or more." The report also noted that "the extraordinary price increases generally persisted for at least 1 year and most had no downward movement after the extraordinary price increase." Were these price increases the result of collusion? The GAO report drew no conclusions but noted, "Manufacturers reported that competition, determined by the price and availability of the same drug from other manufacturers, is the primary driver of generic drug prices, as less competition could drive prices higher."

The DOJ appeared skeptical of the manufacturers' explanation for high prices, particularly in light of the Heritage executives having pleaded guilty to price fixing. A DOJ press release included the following statement from an FBI agent participating in the investigation: "Conspiring to fix prices on widely-used generic medications skews the market, flouts common decency—and very clearly breaks the law…. The FBI stands ready to investigate and hold accountable those who willfully violate federal antitrust law."

Whether the DOJ's investigation would indeed discover that many firms had been colluding to fix the prices of generic drugs was not yet known as of late 2017. Such cases can be hard for the government to prove in court because, as an article in the *Wall Street Journal* noted, "Courts have set a high bar for price-collusion cases, requiring a written document or other evidence of an agreement among companies to follow each other on prices." However it turns out, the investigation is an example of attempts by the government to keep firms from artificially restricting competition to raise prices. As we have seen, higher prices reduce consumer surplus and economic efficiency.

Sources: Jeremy Roebuck, "Ex-N.J. Pharma Execs Admit to Fixing Generic Drug Prices," philly.com, January 10, 2017; Tom Schoenberg, David McLaughlin, and Sophia Pearson, "U.S. Generic Drug Probe Seen Expanding After Guilty Pleas," bloomberg.com, December 14, 2016; Jonathan D. Rockoff, "Perrigo Says Investigators Searched Its Offices in Generic-Drug Probe," *Wall Street Journal*, May 4, 2017; U.S. General Accountability Office, "Generic Drugs Under Medicare," August 2016; and U.S. Department of Justice, "Former Top Generic Pharmaceutical Executives Charged with Price-Fixing, Bid-Rigging, and Customer Allocation Conspiracies," justice.gov, December 14, 2016.

MyLab Economics Study Plan

Your Turn: Test your understanding by doing related problem 5.6 on page 535 at the end of this chapter.

Mergers: The Trade-off between Market Power and Efficiency

Horizontal merger A merger between firms in the same industry.

The federal government regulates business mergers because if firms gain market power by merging, they may use that market power to raise prices and reduce output. As a result, the government is most concerned with **horizontal mergers**, or mergers between firms in the same industry. Two airlines or two candy manufacturers merging are examples of a horizontal merger. Horizontal mergers are more likely to increase market power than **vertical mergers**, which are mergers between firms at different stages in the production of a good. An example of a vertical merger would be a merger between a company making soft drinks and a company making plastic bottles.

Vertical merger A merger between firms at different stages in the production of a good.

Federal regulators deal with two factors that can complicate evaluating horizontal mergers:

1. **The extent of the market.** The "market" that firms are in is not always clear. For example, if Hershey Foods wants to merge with Mars, Inc., maker of M&Ms, Snickers, and other candies, what is the relevant market?

   - If the government looks just at the candy market, the newly merged company would have more than 70 percent of the market, a level at which the government would likely oppose the merger.
   - If the government looks at the broader market for snacks, Hershey and Mars compete with makers of potato chips, pretzels, and peanuts—and perhaps even producers of fresh fruit. With this broader definition of the market, the market shares of Hershey and Mars would likely be too low for federal regulators to oppose their merger.
   - If the government looked at the very broad market for food, then both Hershey and Mars have very small market shares, and there would be no reason for federal regulators to oppose their merger.

   In practice, the government defines the relevant market on the basis of whether there are close substitutes for the products being made by the merging firms. In this case, potato chips and the other snack foods mentioned are not close substitutes for candy. So, the government would consider the candy market to be the relevant market and would oppose the merger, on the grounds that the new firm would have too much market power.

2. **Possible increases in economic efficiency.** The second factor that complicates merger policy is the possibility that the newly merged firm might be more efficient than the merging firms were individually. For example, one firm might have an excellent product but a poor distribution system for getting the product into the hands of consumers. A competing firm might have built a great distribution system but have an inferior product. Allowing these firms to merge might be good for both the firms and consumers. Or, two competing firms might each have an extensive system of warehouses that are only half full, but if the firms merged, they could consolidate their warehouses and significantly reduce their average costs.

Most of the mergers that come under the scrutiny of the Department of Justice and the FTC are between large firms. For simplicity, though, let's consider a case in which all the firms in a perfectly competitive industry want to merge to form a monopoly. As we saw in Figure 15.5 on page 520, as a result of this merger, prices will rise and output will fall, leading to a decline in consumer surplus and economic efficiency. But what if the larger, newly merged firm actually is more efficient than the smaller firms were? Figure 15.6 shows a possible result.

If the merger doesn't affect costs, we have the same result as in Figure 15.5: Price rises from P_C to P_M, quantity falls from Q_C to Q_M, consumer surplus declines, and there is a loss of economic efficiency. If the monopoly has lower costs than the competitive firms, it is possible for price to decline and quantity to increase. In Figure 15.6, note that after the merger MR crosses MC at the new profit-maximizing quantity, Q_{Merge}. The demand curve shows that the monopolist can sell this quantity of the good at a price of P_{Merge}. Therefore, the price declines after the merger from P_C to P_{Merge}, and the quantity increases from Q_C to Q_{Merge}. We have the following seemingly paradoxical result: *The newly merged firm has a great deal of market power, but consumers are better off and economic efficiency is increased because the firm is more efficient.* Of course, sometimes a

MyLab Economics Animation

Figure 15.6   **A Merger That Makes Consumers Better Off**

This figure shows the result of all the firms in a perfectly competitive industry merging to form a monopoly. If the merger does not affect costs, the result is the same as in Figure 15.5 on page 520: Price rises from P_C to P_M, quantity falls from Q_C to Q_M, consumer surplus declines, and a loss of economic efficiency results. If, however, the monopoly has lower costs than the perfectly competitive firms, as shown by the marginal cost curve shifting to MC after the merger, it is possible that the price of the good will actually decline from P_C to P_{Merge} and that output will increase from Q_C to Q_{Merge} following the merger.

merged firm will be more efficient and have lower costs, and other times it won't. Even if a merged firm is more efficient and has lower costs, the lower costs may not offset the increased market power of the firm enough to increase consumer surplus and economic efficiency.

As you might expect, whenever large firms propose a merger, they claim that the newly merged firm will be more efficient and have lower costs. They realize that without these claims, the Department of Justice and the FTC, along with the court system, are unlikely to approve the merger.   **MyLab Economics** Concept Check

The Department of Justice and FTC Merger Guidelines

For many years after the passage of the Sherman Act in 1890, lawyers from the Department of Justice enforced the antitrust laws. The lawyers rarely considered economic arguments, such as the possibility that consumers might be made better off by a merger if economic efficiency were significantly improved. This situation began to change in 1965, when Donald Turner became the first PhD economist to head the Antitrust Division of the Department of Justice. Under Turner and his successors, economic analysis shaped antitrust policy. In 1973, the Economics Section of the Antitrust Division was established and staffed with economists who evaluate the economic consequences of proposed mergers.

Economists played a major role in the development of merger guidelines by the Department of Justice and the FTC in 1982. The guidelines made it easier for firms considering a merger to understand whether the government was likely to allow the merger or to oppose it. The guidelines, which were modified in 2010, have three main parts:

1. Market definition
2. Measure of concentration
3. Merger standards

Market Definition A market consists of all firms making products that consumers view as close substitutes. Economists can identify close substitutes by looking at the effect of a price increase. If the definition of a market is too narrow, a price increase will cause firms to experience a significant decline in sales—and profits—as consumers switch to buying close substitutes.

Identifying the relevant market involved in a proposed merger begins with a narrow definition of the industry. For a hypothetical merger of Hershey Foods and Mars, Inc., economists might start with the candy industry. If all firms in the candy industry increased price by 5 percent, would their profits increase or decrease? If profits would increase, the market is defined as being just these firms. If profits would decrease, economists would try a broader definition—say, by adding in potato chips and other snacks. Would a price increase of 5 percent by all firms in the broader market raise profits? If profits increase, the relevant market has been identified. If profits decrease, economists consider a broader definition. Economists continue the process until a market has been identified.

Measure of Concentration A market is *concentrated* if a relatively small number of firms have a large share of total sales in the market. A merger between firms in a market that is already highly concentrated is very likely to increase market power. A merger between firms in an industry that has a very low concentration is unlikely to increase market power and can be ignored. The guidelines use the *Herfindahl-Hirschman Index (HHI)* of concentration, which squares the market shares of each firm in the industry and adds up the values of the squares. The following are some examples of calculating HHI:

- 1 firm, with 100 percent market share (a monopoly):

$$\text{HHI} = 100^2 = 10,000.$$

- 2 firms, each with a 50 percent market share:

$$\text{HHI} = 50^2 + 50^2 = 5,000.$$

- 4 firms, with market shares of 30 percent, 30 percent, 20 percent, and 20 percent:

$$\text{HHI} = 30^2 + 30^2 + 20^2 + 20^2 = 2,600.$$

- 10 firms, each with a 10 percent market share:

$$\text{HHI} = 10 \times (10)^2 = 1,000.$$

Merger Standards Table 15.2 shows how the Department of Justice and the FTC use the HHI calculation for a market to evaluate proposed horizontal mergers according to these standards.

The merger guidelines state that increases in economic efficiency will be taken into account and can lead to approval of a merger that otherwise would be opposed, but the burden of showing that the efficiencies exist lies with the merging firms:

> The merging firms must substantiate efficiency claims so that the [Department of Justice and the FTC] can verify by reasonable means the likelihood and magnitude of each asserted efficiency…. Efficiency claims will not be considered if they are vague or speculative or otherwise cannot be verified by reasonable means. **MyLab Economics** Concept Check

Table 15.2

Federal Government Standards for Horizontal Mergers

Value of the Herfindahl-Hirschman Index (HHI) of a Market after a Merger	Amount by Which the Merger Increases the HHI	Antitrust Action by Federal Regulators
Less than 1,500	Increase doesn't matter	Merger will be allowed.
Between 1,500 and 2,500	Fewer than 100 points	Merger is unlikely to be challenged.
Between 1,500 and 2,500	More than 100 points	Merger may be challenged.
Greater than 2,500	Fewer than 100 points	Merger is unlikely to be challenged.
Greater than 2,500	Between 100 and 200 points	Merger may be challenged.
Greater than 2,500	More than 200 points	Merger is likely to be challenged.

Regulating Natural Monopolies

If a firm is a natural monopoly, competition from other firms will not play its usual role of forcing price down to the level where the company earns zero economic profit. As a result, local or state *regulatory commissions* usually set the prices for natural monopolies, such as firms selling natural gas or electricity. What price should these commissions set? Economic efficiency requires the last unit of a good or service produced to provide an additional benefit to consumers equal to the additional cost of producing it (see Chapter 12, Section 12.6). We can measure the additional benefit consumers receive from the last unit by the price of the product, and we can measure the additional cost to the monopoly of producing the last unit by marginal cost. Therefore, to achieve economic efficiency, regulators should require that the monopoly charge a price equal to its marginal cost. There is, however, an important drawback to doing so, as illustrated in Figure 15.7, which shows the situation of a typical regulated natural monopoly.

Remember that with a natural monopoly, the average total cost curve is still falling when it crosses the demand curve. If unregulated, the monopoly will charge a price equal to P_M and produce Q_M. To achieve economic efficiency, regulators should require the monopoly to charge a price equal to P_E. The monopoly will then produce Q_E. But here is

MyLab Economics Animation

Figure 15.7 **Regulating a Natural Monopoly**

A natural monopoly that is not subject to government regulation will charge a price equal to P_M and produce Q_M. If government regulators want to achieve economic efficiency, they will set the regulated price equal to P_E, and the monopoly will produce Q_E. But P_E is below average total cost, and the monopoly will suffer a loss, shown by the red rectangle. Because the monopoly will not continue to produce in the long run if it suffers a loss, government regulators set a price equal to average total cost, which is P_R in the figure. The resulting production, Q_R, will be below the efficient level.

the drawback: P_E is less than average total cost, so the monopoly will be suffering a loss, shown by the area of the red-shaded rectangle. In the long run, the owners of the monopoly will not continue in business if they are experiencing a loss. Realizing this, most regulators will set the regulated price, P_R, equal to the level of average total cost at which the demand curve intersects the *ATC* curve. At that price, the owners of the monopoly are able to break even on their investment by producing the quantity Q_R, although this quantity is below the efficient quantity, Q_E.   MyLab Economics Concept Check   MyLab Economics Study Plan

Solved Problem 15.5   MyLab Economics Interactive Animation

What Should Your College Charge for a MOOC?

In Chapter 11, we observed that some colleges offer massive open online courses (MOOCs). We saw that the fixed cost of offering an online course is relatively high because instructors must develop new syllabi, exams, and teaching notes, as well as determine when and how to interact with their students. But after the course is placed online, the marginal cost of providing instruction to an additional student is low and will be constant rather than U shaped. Suppose that your college decides to offer a calculus course as a MOOC that students anywhere in the world can take, whether they are enrolled in your college or not. The figure shows the demand and cost situation for the MOOC.

a. The faculty member who designed the course argues: "I think the course should be priced so that the maximum number of students enroll." Which price should this faculty member favor? Briefly explain.

b. An economics professor argues: "I think the course should be priced so as to achieve economic efficiency." Which price should this faculty member favor? Briefly explain.

c. The dean of the college argues: "I think the course should be priced to maximize the profit the college earns, so these funds can be used to pay some other expenses." Which price should the dean favor? Briefly explain.

d. You are a member of a student committee that is asked to recommend a price for the course, and you argue: "I think the college should charge a price so that it just breaks even on the course." What price should you recommend? Briefly explain.

e. How much profit (or loss) will the college make on the course if it charges each of the prices you found in your answers to parts (a), (b), (c), and (d)?

Solving the Problem

Step 1: **Review the chapter material.** This problem is related to the discussion of pricing in a situation of natural monopoly, so you may want to review the section "Regulating Natural Monopolies," which begins on page 528.

Step 2: **Begin your answer by noting that the situation in the figure is similar to the situation of a natural monopoly, as shown in Figure 15.7.** Because the graph shows the average total cost curve for the MOOC as still falling when it crosses the demand curve, effectively this MOOC is a natural monopoly, and we can employ the analysis of prices shown in Figure 15.7 to answer the questions.

Step 3: **Answer part (a) by explaining which price will maximize the number of students enrolling in the course.** The graph shows that the maximum number of students to take the course will occur when the price equals 0 and the demand curve intersects the quantity axis.

Step 4: **Answer part (b) by explaining which price will result in economic efficiency.** Economic efficiency occurs where price equals marginal cost. In the graph, the price should be set at $20 to achieve economic efficiency.

Step 5: **Answer part (c) by explaining which price will maximize the profit the college will earn from the course.** To maximize profit, the college should charge a price that results in a quantity demanded at which marginal revenue equals marginal cost. In the graph, the price that maximizes profit equals $75.

Step 6: **Answer part (d) by explaining which price will result in the college just breaking even on the course.** To break even, the college should charge a price equal to average total cost. In the graph, at a price of $44, price is equal to average total cost, and the college just breaks even on the course.

Step 7: **Answer part (e) by calculating the profit (or loss) the college will make if it charges each of the prices you found in the earlier parts of the problem.** The following table shows the calculation of profit (or loss) for each price.

If the college charges this price ...	it will earn revenue of ...	and have a total cost equal to ...	So, the college will ...
0	0	the average total cost of $36 per student multiplied by the 24,000 students who enroll, or $36 × 24,000 = $864,000.	suffer a loss of $864,000 (0 − $864,000 = −$864,000).
$20	$20 × 20,000 = $400,000	$38 × 20,000 = $760,000.	suffer a loss of $360,000 ($400,000 − $760,000 = −$360,000).
$75	$75 × 10,000 = $750,000	$60 × 10,000 = $600,000.	earn a profit of $150,000 ($750,000 − $600,000 = $150,000).
$44	$44 × 16,000 = $704,000	$44 × 16,000 = $704,000.	break even.

MyLab Economics Study Plan

Your Turn: For more practice, do related problems 5.12 and 5.13 on page 536 at the end of this chapter.

Continued from page 507

Economics in Your Life & Career

Can a Business Run from Your Dorm Be a Monopoly?

At the beginning of the chapter, we asked whether the submarine sandwich business you and your roommate, Fatma, start in your dorm is a monopoly and whether you should charge high prices for the subs to increase your profit.

In this chapter, we have seen that a monopoly is a firm that is the only seller of a good or service that does not have a close substitute. Even though you and Fatma would be the only sellers of submarine sandwiches on campus during the evening hours on Saturdays and Sundays, there could be other options for hungry students. For example, students could buy food from nearby off-campus restaurants, have food delivered from those restaurants, or buy from on-campus vendors that are open earlier in the day. Most goods have substitutes, and you and Fatma should realize that for many students, pizza and hamburgers from local restaurants are good substitutes for subs. High prices are likely to lead many of your customers to search for those substitutes.

Conclusion

The more intense the level of competition among firms, the better a market works. If a market is a monopoly, then, compared with the situation in which the market is perfectly competitive, the price of the good or service is higher, output is lower, and consumer surplus and economic efficiency are reduced. Fortunately, true monopolies are rare. Even though most firms resemble monopolies in being able to charge a price above marginal cost, most markets have enough competition to keep the efficiency losses from market power low.

Visit **MyLab Economics** for a news article and analysis related to the concepts in this chapter.

Key Terms

Antitrust laws, p. 523

Collusion, p. 522

Copyright, p. 511

Horizontal merger, p. 524

Market power, p. 521

Monopoly, p. 508

Natural monopoly, p. 514

Network externalities, p. 513

Patent, p. 510

Public franchise, p. 512

Vertical merger, p. 525

15.1 Is Any Firm Ever Really a Monopoly? pages 508–509

LEARNING OBJECTIVE: Define monopoly.

MyLab Economics Visit www.pearson.com/mylab/economics to complete these exercises online and get instant feedback.

Summary

A **monopoly** exists only in the rare situation in which a firm is producing a good or service for which there are no close substitutes. A narrow definition of monopoly that some economists use is that a firm has a monopoly if it can ignore the actions of all other firms. Many economists favor this broader definition of monopoly: A firm has a monopoly if no other firms are selling a substitute close enough that the firm's economic profit is competed away in the long run.

Review Questions

1.1 What is a monopoly? Can a firm be a monopoly if close substitutes for its product exist?

1.2 If you own the only hardware store in a small town, do you have a monopoly?

Problems and Applications

1.3 The great baseball player Ty Cobb had a reputation for being very thrifty. Near the end of his life, he was interviewed by a reporter who was surprised to find that Cobb used candles, rather than electricity, to light his home. From Ty Cobb's point of view, was the local electric company a monopoly?

1.4 An article in the *New Yorker* noted, "The Bronx [borough of New York City] is home to 1.5 million people, two hundred thousand public-school students, eleven colleges and universities, and a single general-interest bookstore—

a Barnes & Noble, located in the Bay Plaza shopping center." The article also noted that this bookstore closed at the end of 2016. Would the only bookstore in the Bronx, or any other city, be considered a monopoly? If so, why would it have closed?

Source: Andrew Boryga, "The Bronx Loses Its Only Bookstore," *New Yorker*, October 28, 2016.

1.5 Harvard Business School started using case studies—descriptions of strategic problems encountered at real companies—in courses in 1912. Today, Harvard Business Publishing (HBP) sells its case studies to about 4,000 colleges worldwide. HBP is the sole publisher of Harvard Business School's case studies. What criteria would you use to determine whether HBP has a monopoly on the sale of business case studies to be used in college courses?

1.6 (Related to the Apply the Concept on page 508) In discussing the NCAA, the late Nobel Laureate Gary Becker, an economist, wrote, "It is impossible for an outsider to look at these [NCAA] rules without concluding that their main aim is to make the NCAA an effective cartel that severely constrains competition among schools for players."

a. What is a cartel? In what ways does the NCAA act like a cartel?

b. Who gains and who loses as a result of the NCAA acting like a cartel? If you are a student who does not play intercollegiate sports but who is enrolled at a school with prominent sports teams, such as the University of Alabama or Ohio State University, does the NCAA acting as a cartel make you better off or worse off? Briefly explain.

Source: Gary Becker, "The NCAA as a Powerful Cartel," becker-posnerlog.com, April 4, 2011.

15.2 Where Do Monopolies Come From? pages 510–515

LEARNING OBJECTIVE: Explain the four main reasons monopolies arise.

MyLab Economics Visit www.pearson.com/mylab/economics to complete these exercises online and get instant feedback.

Summary

To have a monopoly, barriers to entering the market must be so high that no other firms can enter. Barriers to entry may be high enough to keep out competing firms for four main reasons: (1) A government blocks the entry of more than one firm into a market by issuing a **patent**, which is the exclusive right to make a product for 20 years, a **copyright**, which is the exclusive right to produce and sell a creation, or a *trademark*, which grants a firm legal protection against other firms using its product's name, or by giving a firm a **public franchise**, which is the right to be the only legal provider of a good or service; (2) one firm has control of a key raw material necessary to produce a good; (3) there are important *network externalities* in supplying the good or service; or (4) economies of scale are so large that one firm has a *natural monopoly*. **Network externalities** refer to a characteristic of a product where its usefulness increases with the number of consumers who use it. A **natural monopoly** is a situation in which economies of scale are so large that one firm can supply the entire market at a lower average cost than can two or more firms.

Review Questions

2.1 What are the four most important ways a firm becomes a monopoly?

2.2 If patents, copyrights, and trademarks reduce competition, why does the federal government grant them?

2.3 What is a public franchise? Are all public franchises natural monopolies?

2.4 What is "natural" about a natural monopoly?

Problems and Applications

2.5 The U.S. Postal Service (USPS) is a monopoly because the federal government has blocked entry into the market for delivering first-class mail. Is the USPS also a natural monopoly? How can we tell? What would happen if the law preventing competition in this market were removed?

2.6 An article in the *Wall Street Journal*, discussing large high-tech firms such as Amazon, Microsoft, and Google, stated, "Today's high-tech giants may not be monopolies in the most classic sense…. [Demand] for technology products and services keeps increasing…. That leaves a lot of potential upside for a small group of big players that already have demonstrated that scale matters."
   a. Why would high-technology firms not be considered monopolies in the "classic sense"?
   b. Why would the article state that for the most profitable high-technology firms, "scale matters"?
   Source: Dan Gallagher, "Tech's Titans Go from Big to Bigger," *Wall Street Journal*, April 27, 2017.

2.7 For most of the 1800s, the United States did not recognize the copyrights of books written by foreign authors. As a result, many U.S. publishers printed "pirated"—unauthorized—editions of Charles Dickens and other British authors without paying them royalties. A history of book publishing noted, "[U.S.] publishers claimed that pirating [foreign] works allowed their prices to remain low, which in turn made the works more accessible to the public at large." There were (eventually successful) attempts in Congress to recognize foreign copyrights in exchange for other countries recognizing U.S. copyrights. At the time, one U.S. publisher described these efforts as the "clamor of two hundred authors against the interests of fifty-five million people." Do copyright laws benefit authors at the expense of readers? If so, why does the U.S. Constitution give Congress the right to enact copyright laws?
   Source: J. P. Romney and Rebecca Romney, *Printer's Error: Irreverent Stories from Book History*, New York: Harper, 2017, pp. 218, 227.

2.8 The German company Koenig & Bauer has 90 percent of the world market for presses that print currency. Discuss the factors that would make it difficult for new companies to enter this market.

2.9 (Related to the Apply the Concept on page 511) Why should it matter legally whether Professor Anspach is correct that Hasbro's Monopoly game closely resembles a game that had been played for decades before Charles Darrow claimed to have invented it? Does it matter economically? Briefly explain.

2.10 (Related to the Apply the Concept on page 512) Why was De Beers worried that people might resell their old diamonds? How did De Beers attempt to convince consumers that previously owned diamonds were not good substitutes for new diamonds? How did De Beers's strategy affect the demand curve for new diamonds? How did De Beers's strategy affect its profit?

2.11 In a magazine article, a writer explained that the provision of electric power in the United States consists of two processes: the generation of electricity and the distribution of electricity. The writer argued that "power distribution is a natural monopoly…. But … there's … no reason why the people who generate the electricity … should be the same people who own the power lines."
   a. Why would the distribution of electric power be a natural monopoly?
   b. Why would the generation of electric power *not* be a natural monopoly?
   Source: Tim Worstall, "Which Should We Have: Public Utilities or Regulated Private Monopolies?" *Forbes*, March 24, 2013.

2.12 In China, the government owns many more firms than do governments in the United States. A former Chinese government official argued that a number of government-run industries such as oil refining were natural monopolies. Is it likely that oil refining is a natural monopoly? How would you be able to tell?
   Source: Shen Hong, "Former State Assets Regulator: SOE Monopolies 'Natural,'" *Wall Street Journal*, January 4, 2012.

2.13 Suppose that the quantity demanded per day for a product is 90 when the price is $35. The following table shows costs for a firm with a monopoly in this market:

Quantity (per day)	Total Cost
30	$1,200
40	1,400
50	2,250
60	3,000

Briefly explain whether this firm has a natural monopoly.

15.3 How Does a Monopoly Choose Price and Output? pages 515–519

LEARNING OBJECTIVE: Explain how a monopoly chooses price and output.

MyLab Economics Visit **www.pearson.com/mylab/economics** to complete these exercises online and get instant feedback.

Summary

Monopolists face downward-sloping demand and marginal revenue curves and, like all other firms, maximize profit by producing where marginal revenue equals marginal cost. Unlike a perfect competitor, a monopolist that earns an economic profit does not face the entry of new firms into the market. Therefore, a monopolist can earn an economic profit even in the long run.

Review Questions

3.1 What is the relationship between a monopolist's demand curve and the market demand curve? What is the relationship between a monopolist's demand curve and its marginal revenue curve?

3.2 In what sense is a monopolist a *price maker*? Will charging the highest possible price always maximize a monopolist's profit? Briefly explain.

3.3 Draw a graph that shows a monopolist earning a profit. Be sure your graph includes the monopolist's demand, marginal revenue, average total cost, and marginal cost curves. Be sure to indicate the profit-maximizing level of output and price.

Problems and Applications

3.4 **(Related to Solved Problem 15.3 on page 518)** Ed Scahill has acquired a monopoly on the production of baseballs (don't ask how) and faces the demand and cost situation shown in the following table.

Price	Quantity (per week)	Total Revenue	Marginal Revenue	Total Cost	Marginal Cost
$20	15,000			$330,000	
19	20,000			365,000	
18	25,000			405,000	
17	30,000			450,000	
16	35,000			500,000	
15	40,000			555,000	

a. Fill in the remaining values in the table.

b. If Ed wants to maximize profit, what price should he charge, and how many baseballs should he sell? How much profit (or loss) will he make? Draw a graph to illustrate your answer. Your graph should be clearly labeled and should include Ed's demand, ATC, AVC, AFC, MC, and MR curves; the price he is charging; the quantity he is producing; and the area representing his profit (or loss).

c. Suppose the government imposes a tax of $50,000 per week on baseball production. Now what price should Ed charge, how many baseballs should he sell, and what will his profit (or loss) be?

d. Suppose that the government raises the tax in part (c) to $70,000. Now what price should Ed charge, how many baseballs should he sell, and what will his profit (or loss) be? Will his decision on what price to charge and how much to produce be different in the short run than in the long run? Briefly explain.

3.5 **(Related to Solved Problem 15.3 on page 518)** Use the information in Solved Problem 15.3 to answer the following questions.

a. What will Comcast do if the tax is $36 per month instead of $25? (*Hint:* Will its decision be different in the long run than in the short run?)

b. Suppose that the flat per-month tax is replaced with a tax on the firm of $25 per cable subscriber. Now how many subscriptions should Comcast sell if it wants to maximize profit? What price should it charge? What is its profit? (Assume that Comcast will sell only the quantities listed in the table.)

3.6 Before inexpensive pocket calculators were developed, many science and engineering students used slide rules to make numerical calculations. Slide rules are no longer produced, which means nothing prevents you from establishing a monopoly in the slide rule market. Draw a graph showing the situation your slide rule firm would be in. Be sure to include on your graph your demand, marginal revenue, average total cost, and marginal cost curves. Indicate the price you would charge and the quantity you would produce. Are you likely to make a profit or a loss? Show this area on your graph.

3.7 Does a monopolist have a supply curve? Briefly explain. (*Hint:* Look again at the definition of a supply curve in Chapter 3 on page 83 and consider whether this definition applies to a monopolist.)

3.8 **(Related to the Don't Let This Happen to You on page 519)** A student argues: "If a monopolist finds a way of producing a good at lower cost, he will not lower his price. Because he is a monopolist, he will keep the price and the quantity the same and just increase his profit." Do you agree? Use a graph to illustrate your answer.

3.9 When homebuilders construct a new housing development, they usually sell to a single cable television company the rights to lay cable. As a result, anyone buying a home in that development is not able to choose between competing cable companies. Some cities have begun to ban such exclusive agreements. Williams Township, Pennsylvania, decided to allow any cable company to lay cable in the utility trenches of new housing developments. The head of the township board of supervisors argued: "What I would like to see and do is give the consumers a choice. If there's no choice, then the price [of cable] is at the whim of the provider." In a situation in which the consumers in a housing development have only one cable company available, is the price really at the whim of the company? Would a company in this situation be likely to charge, say, $500 per month for basic cable services? Briefly explain.

Source: Sam Kennedy, "Williams Township May Ban Exclusive Cable Provider Pacts," (Allentown, PA) *Morning Call*, November 5, 2004.

3.10 Will a monopoly that maximizes profit also be maximizing revenue? Will it be maximizing output? Briefly explain.

15.4 Does Monopoly Reduce Economic Efficiency? pages 519–522

LEARNING OBJECTIVE: Use a graph to illustrate how a monopoly affects economic efficiency.

MyLab Economics   Visit www.pearson.com/mylab/economics to complete these exercises online and get instant feedback.

Summary

Compared with a perfectly competitive industry, a monopoly charges a higher price and produces a smaller quantity, which reduces consumer surplus and economic efficiency. Some loss of economic efficiency will occur whenever firms have **market power** and can charge a price greater than marginal cost. The total loss of economic efficiency in the U.S. economy due to market power is small, however, because true monopolies are very rare. In most industries, competition will keep price much closer to marginal cost than would be the case in a monopoly.

Review Questions

4.1 The late Nobel Laureate economist George Stigler wrote that the "purely 'economic' case against monopoly is that it reduces aggregate economic welfare…. When the monopolist raises prices above the competitive level in order to reap his monopoly profits, customers buy less of the product, less is produced, and society as a whole is worse off."

    a. Draw a graph similar to Figure 15.5 on page 520. In your graph indicate the price that is at what Stigler refers to as "the competitive level." Compare this price to the price at which the firm earns "monopoly profits."

    b. Use your graph to explain why society is worse off when a monopolist charges a price that earns monopoly profits rather than when price is set at the "competitive level."

    Source: George J. Stigler, "Monopoly," *The Concise Encyclopedia of Economics*, www.econlib.org/library/Enc/Monopoly.html.

4.2 Explain why market power leads to a deadweight loss. Is the total deadweight loss from market power for the economy large or small?

Problems and Applications

4.3 **(Related to the Chapter Opener on page 506)** Suppose that a second seafood restaurant opens in Stonington, Maine. Will consumer surplus and economic efficiency necessarily increase? Briefly explain.

4.4 The late economist Harvey Leibenstein argued that the loss of economic efficiency in industries that are not perfectly competitive is often understated. He argued that when competition is weak, firms are under less pressure to adopt the best techniques or to hold down their costs. He referred to this effect as "x-inefficiency." If

x-inefficiency causes a firm's marginal costs to rise, use a graph to show that the deadweight loss in Figure 15.5 on page 520 understates the true deadweight loss caused by a monopoly.

4.5 Most cities own the water system that provides water to homes and businesses. Some cities charge a flat monthly fee, while other cities charge by the gallon. Which method of pricing is more likely to result in economic efficiency in the water market? Be sure to refer to the definition of *economic efficiency* in your answer. Why do you think the same method of pricing isn't used by all cities?

4.6 Review the concept of externalities from Chapter 5, page 148. If a market is a monopoly, will a negative externality in production always lead to a quantity being produced that is greater than the economically efficient quantity? Use a graph to illustrate your answer.

4.7 Suppose that the city has given Fernando a monopoly selling baseball caps at the local minor league stadium. Use the following graph to answer the questions.

    a. What quantity will Fernando produce, and what price will he charge?

    b. How much profit will Fernando earn?

    c. Review the definition of allocative efficiency. If Fernando produced at the allocatively efficient level of output, what quantity would he produce?

    d. How much deadweight loss does Fernando create by acting like a monopolist rather than a perfect competitor? (Assume that the marginal cost curve is linear—a straight line—between the two relevant points.)

15.5 Government Policy toward Monopoly, pages 522–530
LEARNING OBJECTIVE: Explain how the government regulates monopoly.

MyLab Economics   Visit **www.pearson.com/mylab/economics** to complete these exercises online and get instant feedback.

Summary

Because monopolies reduce consumer surplus and economic efficiency, governments often regulate them. Firms that are not monopolies have an incentive to avoid competition by **colluding**, or agreeing to charge the same price or otherwise not to compete. In the United States, **antitrust laws** are aimed at deterring monopoly, eliminating collusion, and promoting competition among firms. The Antitrust Division of the U.S. Department of Justice and the Federal Trade Commission share responsibility for enforcing the antitrust laws, including regulating mergers between firms. A **horizontal merger** is a merger between firms in the same industry. A **vertical merger** is a merger between firms at different stages of production of a good. Local governments often regulate the prices charged by natural monopolies.

Review Questions

5.1 What is the purpose of the antitrust laws? Who is in charge of enforcing these laws?

5.2 What is the difference between a horizontal merger and a vertical merger? Which type of merger is more likely to increase the market power of a newly merged firm?

5.3 Why would it be economically efficient to require a natural monopoly to charge a price equal to marginal cost? Why do most regulatory agencies require natural monopolies to charge a price equal to average cost instead?

Problems and Applications

5.4 Food service firms buy meat, vegetables, and other foods and resell them to restaurants, schools, and hospitals. US Foods and Sysco are by far the largest firms in the industry. In 2015, these firms were attempting to merge to form a single firm. A news story quoted one restaurant owner as saying, "There was definite panic in the restaurant industry … when the merger was announced. They know they're going to get squeezed."
  a. Analyze the effect on the food service market of US Foods and Sysco combining. Draw a graph to illustrate your answer. For simplicity, assume that the market was perfectly competitive before the firms combined and would be a monopoly afterward. Be sure your graph shows changes in the equilibrium price, the equilibrium quantity, consumer surplus, producer surplus, and deadweight loss.
  b. Why would restaurant owners believe they would be "squeezed" by this development?
  c. Ultimately, the merger did not occur because the Federal Trade Commission was successful in suing to stop it. The judge who decided the case wrote, "The proposed merger of the country's first and second largest broadline foodservice distributors is likely to cause the type of industry concentration that Congress sought

to curb at the outset before it harmed competition." Briefly explain what the judge meant by "industry concentration" and what the results will be of a merger that harms competition.
  Sources: Brent Kendall, "Judge Explains Reasons for Blocking Sysco-US Foods Merger," *Wall Street Journal*, June 28, 2015; Tess Stynes, "Sysco Extends Merger Pact with U.S. Foods to May," *Wall Street Journal*, March 9, 2015; and Annie Gasparro and Jesse Newman, "Restaurants Fear Clout of a New Food Giant," *Wall Street Journal*, January 6, 2014.

5.5 In 2016, telecommunications company AT&T reached an agreement to buy TimeWarner, which owns cable networks, magazines, and a film studio. In an interview with the *Wall Street Journal*, the CEOs of the two firms "played down concerns that the deal wouldn't get regulatory approval, again asserting that the deal is vertical in nature, rather than eliminating a competitor."
  a. What did the CEOs mean by saying that the merger was "vertical in nature"?
  b. Why would federal antitrust regulators be less likely to oppose a merger that was "vertical in nature" than one that eliminated a competitor?
  c. If the deal doesn't eliminate a competitor, what do the firms hope to gain from it?
  Source: Deepa Seetharaman and Thomas Gryta, "AT&T CEO Says Time Warner Deal Not about Raising Prices," *Wall Street Journal*, October 25, 2016.

5.6 **(Related to the Apply the Concept on page 523)** An article in the *Wall Street Journal* on the DOJ's investigation into possible price fixing by pharmaceutical firms selling generic drugs noted, "Agreements among companies to set prices or to divide up markets have long been illegal under federal antitrust law."
  a. When did price fixing first become illegal under federal law? Why does the federal government care if firms collude to fix the prices of the products they sell?
  b. The article also noted that to secure a court conviction in a price-fixing case, "there must be evidence of an agreement among companies to follow each other on prices, such as a written document or telephone conversation or a meeting." Why do the courts require such a high standard of proof in a price-fixing case? Shouldn't evidence that all companies are charging the same price for a generic drug be sufficient evidence that collusion has happened? Briefly explain.
  Source: Peter Loftus, Brent Kendall, and Christopher M. Matthews, "Generic-Drug Firms Face Possible Collusion Charges," *Wall Street Journal*, November 3, 2016.

5.7 An article in the *Wall Street Journal* quoted a DOJ antitrust official as saying, "Mergers between substantial competitors, especially in already concentrated industries, can give companies far too much power over the markets in which they operate."
  a. What does the official mean by a "concentrated industry"?
  b. What does he mean by "power over the markets in which they operate"?

c. The article also quoted the official as saying that mergers might benefit the public "when they bring together complementary assets, people and ideas that help lower production costs or spur greater innovation." Will these positive aspects of a merger always be enough to offset the negative aspects you discussed in answering part (b) of this problem? Briefly explain.

Source: Brent Kendall, "Justice Official Voices Concern over Mergers Between Major Competitors," *Wall Street Journal*, June 16, 2016.

5.8 Draw a graph like Figure 15.6 on page 526 that shows a merger lowering costs. On your graph, show consumer surplus and producer surplus before a merger and consumer surplus and producer surplus after a merger.

5.9 Look again at the section "The Department of Justice and FTC Merger Guidelines," which begins on page 526. Evaluate the following situations.

a. A market initially has 20 firms, each with a 5 percent market share. Of the firms, 4 propose to merge, leaving a total of 17 firms in the industry. Are the Department of Justice and the Federal Trade Commission likely to oppose the merger? Briefly explain.

b. A market initially has 5 firms, each with a 20 percent market share. Of the firms, 2 propose to merge, leaving a total of 4 firms in the industry. Are the Department of Justice and the Federal Trade Commission likely to oppose the merger? Briefly explain.

5.10 The following table shows the market shares during the first three months of 2017 for companies in the U.S. personal computer (PC) market, which includes desktop PCs and laptops, but not tablet computers, such as iPads.

Company	Market Share
Lenovo	20%
Hewlett-Packard	20
Dell	15
ASUS	7
Apple	7
Acer	6
Others	25

Use the information in the section "The Department of Justice and FTC Merger Guidelines," which begins on page 526, to predict whether the Department of Justice and the Federal Trade Commission would be likely to oppose a merger between Apple and Dell. Assume that "Others" in the table consists of five firms, each of which has a 5 percent share of the market.

Source: Juli Clover, "Worldwide Mac Sales up Slightly as PC Market Continues to Decline in Q1 2017," www.macrumors.com, April 11, 2017.

5.11 Consider the natural monopoly shown in Figure 15.7 on page 528. Assume that the government regulatory agency sets the regulated price, P_R, at the level of average total cost at which the demand curve intersects the ATC curve. If the firm knows that it will always be able to charge a price equal to its average total cost, does it have an incentive to reduce its average cost? Briefly explain.

5.12 **(Related to Solved Problem 15.5 on page 529)** Use the following graph of a monopoly to answer the questions.

a. What quantity will the monopoly produce, and what price will the monopoly charge?

b. Suppose the monopoly is regulated. If the regulatory agency wants to achieve economic efficiency, what price should it require the monopoly to charge? How much output will the monopoly produce at this price? Will the monopoly make a profit if it charges this price? Briefly explain.

5.13 **(Related to Solved Problem 15.5 on page 529)** Use the following graph of a monopoly to answer the questions.

a. What quantity will the monopoly produce, and what price will the monopoly charge?

b. Suppose the government decides to regulate this monopoly and imposes a price ceiling of $18 (in other words, the monopoly can charge less than $18 but can't charge more). Now what quantity will the monopoly produce, and what price will the monopoly charge? Will every consumer who is willing to pay this price be able to buy the product? Briefly explain.

Critical Thinking Exercises

CT15.1 Monopolists are generally very large firms. Does this observation mean that monopolists will always earn a profit? Carefully explain your answer.

CT15.2 In recent chapters, we explored different types of industries that firms may be in, including: perfect competition (Chapter 12), monopolistic competition (Chapter 13), and monopoly (Chapter 15). While they are very different, there is a common method firms use to determine how much of a good or service to produce. What is that method? As part of your answer, include a graph for each type of firm.

CT15.2 The graphs for monopoly and monopolistic competition are quite similar, but the details of each of the graphs are different. Write a paragraph explaining the differences.

16

Pricing Strategy

Walt Disney Discovers the Magic of Big Data

If you manage a business, what price should you charge for your product? As we have seen in earlier chapters, the answer seems straightforward: Charge a price that results in your selling the quantity where marginal revenue equals marginal cost. For many businesses, though, the answer is not so straightforward. For example, many businesses charge customers different prices, based on differences in their willingness to pay for the product. The Walt Disney Company charges different prices for entry into its Magic Kingdom park in Florida, depending on a customer's age, home address, and occupation. Children, Florida residents, and members of the military pay lower prices than do people who do not fall into those categories. How does Disney determine which price to charge which group?

Disney offers a variety of products that it needs to price correctly as it tries to maximize profit. How should it price a "vacation package" that includes a stay in a Disney resort hotel, tickets to enter the park, and meals? How should it price souvenirs in the parks? Will opening the parks very early or keeping them open very late result in people paying more for tickets? The answers to these types of questions depend on consumers' preferences. Firms have found it easier to determine consumers' preferences by using *big data*, which refers to the collection and analysis of massive amounts of data, with the goal of measuring aspects of people's behavior. For example, do people who stay in the most expensive Disney World hotels visit the parks for more hours than people who stay in less expensive hotels? How much do sales of souvenirs decline when Disney increases their prices? With enough data, Disney can answer these types of questions.

In recent years, Disney has greatly increased its ability to collect data by having visitors to its parks wear MagicBands around their wrists. Visitors use the bands to enter the park, buy souvenirs, pay for meals, and enter rides. The bands have chips that automatically record data and enter them into Disney's information technology system. The bands

Charles Ridgway/Alamy Stock Photo

are an example of the "Internet of Things"—networks of devices that directly communicate data to computers, without the need for humans to enter the data. The MagicBands program and associated technology have cost Disney about $1 billion to implement, which indicates the importance to the company of gathering and analyzing data on its customers' preferences.

Disney and other firms use such methods to implement *pricing strategies* to increase their profits. In this chapter, we will study some of these pricing strategies.

Sources: Shelly Palmer, "Data Mining Disney—A Magical Experience," huffingtonpost.com, May 11, 2015; Elizabeth Miller Coyne, "The Disney Take on Big Data's Value," thenewip.net, January 13, 2015; and Brooks Barnes, "At Disney Parks, a Bracelet Meant to Build Loyalty (and Sales)," *New York Times*, January 7, 2013.

16.1 Pricing Strategy, the Law of One Price, and Arbitrage, page 540

Define the law of one price and explain the role of arbitrage.

16.2 Price Discrimination: Charging Different Prices for the Same Product, page 542

Explain how a firm can increase its profits through price discrimination.

16.3 Other Pricing Strategies, page 551

Explain how some firms increase their profits by using odd pricing, cost-plus pricing, and two-part tariffs.

Economics in Your Life & Career

Should You Charge More Than One Price to See the Movies in Your Theater?

AMC Entertainment is the largest movie theater chain in the United States. Suppose AMC hires you to manage one of its theaters, and you have some discretion on setting ticket prices. Should you charge one flat price for tickets, whether the movie is shown in the afternoon or at night and whether the ticket buyer is a student, a senior citizen, or of another age? Should you always charge the same price for popcorn? As you read this chapter, try to answer these questions. You can check your answers against the ones we provide on **page 556** at the end of this chapter.

I n previous chapters, we saw that entrepreneurs continually seek out economic profit. Using pricing strategies is one way firms can attempt to increase their economic profit. One of these strategies, called *price discrimination*, involves firms charging different prices for the same good or service, as Disney does when setting admission prices at Walt Disney World. In this chapter, we will see how a firm can increase its profit by charging a higher price to consumers who value the good more and a lower price to consumers who value the good less.

We will also analyze the widely used strategies of *odd pricing* and *cost-plus pricing*. Finally, we will analyze situations in which firms are able to charge consumers one price for the right to buy a good and a second price for each unit of the good purchased, a strategy economists call a *two-part tariff*.

16.1 Pricing Strategy, the Law of One Price, and Arbitrage

LEARNING OBJECTIVE: Define the law of one price and explain the role of arbitrage.

We saw in the chapter opener that sometimes firms can charge different prices for the same good. In fact, many firms rely on economic analysis to practice *price discrimination* by charging higher prices to some customers and lower prices to others. Some firms, such as Disney, practice a sophisticated form of price discrimination by using *big data* methods to gather and analyze information on consumers' preferences and their responsiveness to changes in prices. Managers can use this analysis to rapidly adjust the prices of their goods and services. This practice of rapidly adjusting prices, called *yield management*, has been particularly important to airlines and hotels. There are limits, though, to the ability of firms to charge different prices for the same product. The key limit is the possibility that in some circumstances consumers who can buy a good at a low price will resell it to consumers who would otherwise have to buy at a high price.

Arbitrage

According to the *law of one price*, identical products should sell for the same price everywhere. Let's explore why the law of one price usually holds true. Suppose that, on average, used cars sell for $2,000 more in Atlanta than in San Francisco. Anyone who lives in San Francisco could buy used cars and ship them to Atlanta. They could sell them in Atlanta through online advertising on Craigslist or other sites. Buying a product in one market at a low price and reselling it in another market at a high price is called *arbitrage*. The profits received from engaging in arbitrage are called *arbitrage profits*.

As people take advantage of the price difference to earn arbitrage profits, the supply of used cars in Atlanta will increase, and the price of used cars in Atlanta will fall. At the same time, the supply of used cars in San Francisco will decrease, and the price of used cars in San Francisco will rise. Eventually, the arbitrage process will eliminate most, but not all, of the price difference. Some price difference will remain because sellers must pay to ship cars to Atlanta and to list them for sale online. The costs of carrying out a transaction—by, for example, shipping used cars across the country—are called **transactions costs**. The law of one price holds exactly *only if transactions costs are zero*. As we will soon see, in cases in which it is impossible to resell a product, the law of one price will not hold, and firms will be able to practice price discrimination. Apart from this important qualification, we expect that arbitrage will result in a product selling for the same price everywhere.

MyLab Economics Concept Check

Transactions costs The costs in time and other resources that parties incur in the process of agreeing to and carrying out an exchange of goods or services.

Solved Problem 16.1

MyLab Economics Interactive Animation

Is Arbitrage Just a Rip-off?

People are often suspicious of arbitrage. Buying something at a low price and reselling it at a high price exploits the person buying at the high price—or does it? Is this view correct? If so, do the auctions of collectibles on eBay serve any useful economic purpose?

Solving the Problem

Step 1: **Review the chapter material.** This problem is about arbitrage, so you may want to review the section "Arbitrage," on page 540. If necessary, also review the discussion of the benefits from trade in earlier chapters (see Chapters 2 and 9).

Step 2: **Use the discussion of arbitrage and the discussion in earlier chapters of the benefits from trade to answer the questions.** Many of the goods on eBay have been bought at low prices and are being resold at higher prices. In fact, some people supplement their incomes by buying collectibles and other goods at garage sales and reselling them on eBay. Does eBay serve a useful economic purpose? Economists would say that it does. Consider the case of Chip, who buys collectible movie posters and resells them on eBay. Suppose Chip buys a *Wonder Woman* poster at a garage sale for $30 and resells it on eBay for $60. Both the person who sold to Chip at the garage sale and the person who bought from him on eBay must have been made better off by the deals, *or they would not have made them*. Chip has performed the useful service of locating the poster and making it available for sale on eBay. In carrying out this service, Chip has incurred costs, including the opportunity cost of his time spent searching garage sales, the opportunity cost of the funds he has tied up in posters he has purchased but not yet sold, and the cost of the fees eBay charges him.

It is easy to sell goods on eBay, so over time, competition among Chip and other movie poster dealers should cause the difference between the prices of posters sold at garage sales and the prices on eBay to shrink until they are equal to the dealers' costs of reselling the posters, including the opportunity cost of their time.

Your Turn: For more practice, do related problems 1.5 and 1.6 on page 557 at the end of this chapter.

MyLab Economics Study Plan

Why Don't All Firms Charge the Same Price?

The law of one price may appear to be violated even where transactions costs are zero and a product can be resold. For example, different Web sites may sell what seem to be identical products for different prices. We can resolve this apparent contradiction if we look more closely at what "product" an Internet Web site—or another business—actually offers for sale.

Suppose you want to buy a Blu-ray disc of *Star Wars: The Last Jedi*. You research prices online and get the results shown in Table 16.1. Would you automatically buy from one of the last two sites listed because of their low prices? Before you answer, consider what each of these sites offers.

As we have discussed, firms differentiate the products they sell in many ways (see Chapter 13, Section 13.1). One way is by providing faster and more reliable delivery than competitors, as Amazon.com and walmart.com have done. New Internet sellers who lack that reputation will have to differentiate their products on the basis of price, as the two fictitious firms listed in the table have done. So, the difference in the prices of products offered on Web sites does *not* violate the law of one price. A Blu-ray disc Amazon.com offers for sale is not the same product as a Blu-ray disc JustStartedin-BusinessLastWednesday.com offers for sale.

MyLab Economics Concept Check   MyLab Economics Study Plan

Table 16.1

Which Internet Retailer Would
You Buy From?

Product: *Star Wars: The Last Jedi* Blu-ray Disc		
Company	Price	What does this site offer you?
Amazon.com	$22.96	• Fast delivery to your home. • Secure packaging. • Easy payment to your credit card using a secure method that keeps your credit card number safe from computer hackers.
walmart.com	22.96	• Fast delivery to your home. • Secure packaging. • Easy payment to your credit card using a secure method that keeps your credit card number safe from computer hackers.
WaitForeverForYourOrder.com	21.50	Low price
JustStartedinBusinessLastWednesday.com	20.25	Low price

 ## 16.2 Price Discrimination: Charging Different Prices for the Same Product

LEARNING OBJECTIVE: Explain how a firm can increase its profits through price discrimination.

We saw at the beginning of this chapter that the Walt Disney Company charges different prices for the same product: admission to Disney World. Charging different prices to different customers for the same good or service when the price differences are not due to differences in cost is called **price discrimination**. But doesn't price discrimination contradict the law of one price? Why doesn't the possibility of arbitrage profits lead people to buy at the low price and resell at the high price?

The Requirements for Successful Price Discrimination

In order to successfully practice price discrimination, a firm must:

1. Possess market power.
2. Have some customers with a greater willingness to pay for the product than other customers and be able to identify which customers have the greater willingness to pay.
3. Be able to divide up—or *segment*—the market for the product so that consumers who buy the product at a low price are not able to resell it at a high price. In other words, price discrimination will not work if arbitrage is possible.

A firm selling in a perfectly competitive market cannot practice price discrimination because it can only charge the market price. For example, a farmer will be unable to sell any eggs at a price higher than the market price because consumers have many other farmers they can buy eggs from. Because most firms do not sell in perfectly competitive markets, they have market power and can set the price of the goods they sell.

Many firms may also be able to determine that some consumers have a greater willingness to pay for a product than others. However, the third requirement—that markets be segmented so that consumers buying at a low price will not be able to resell the product—can be difficult to fulfill. For example, some people really love Big Macs and would be willing to pay $10 rather than do without one. Other people would not be willing to pay a penny more than $1 for a Big Mac. Even if McDonald's could identify differences in the willingness of consumers to pay for Big Macs, it would not be able to charge them different prices. Suppose McDonald's knows that Joe is willing to pay $10,

Price discrimination Charging different prices to different customers for the same product when the price differences are not due to differences in cost.

Don't Let This Happen to You

Don't Confuse Price Discrimination with Other Types of Discrimination

Price discrimination is not the same as discrimination based on race or gender. Discriminating on the basis of arbitrary characteristics, such as race or gender, is illegal under the federal government's civil rights laws. Price discrimination is legal because it involves charging people different prices on the basis of their willingness to pay rather than on the basis of arbitrary characteristics. There is a gray area, however, when companies charge different prices on the basis of gender. For example, insurance companies usually charge women lower prices than men for automobile insurance. The courts have ruled that this is not illegal discrimination under the civil rights laws because women, on average, have better driving records than men. Because the costs of insuring men are higher than the costs of insuring women, insurance companies are allowed to charge men higher prices. Notice, though, that this is not actually price discrimination as we have defined it here. Price discrimination involves charging different prices for the same product *where the price differences are not due to differences in cost.*

MyLab Economics Study Plan

Your Turn: Test your understanding by doing related problem 2.10 on page 559 at the end of this chapter.

---

whereas Jill will pay only $1. If McDonald's tries to charge Joe $10, he will just have Jill buy a Big Mac for him.   **MyLab Economics** Concept Check

An Example of Price Discrimination

Only firms that can keep consumers from reselling a product are able to practice price discrimination. When buyers cannot resell the product, the law of one price does not hold. For example, movie theaters know that many people are willing to pay more to see a movie in the evening than during the afternoon. As a result, theaters usually charge higher prices for tickets to evening showings than for tickets to afternoon showings. They keep these markets separate by making the tickets to afternoon showings a different color or by having the time printed on them and by having a ticket taker examine the tickets. That practice makes it difficult for someone to buy a lower-priced ticket in the afternoon and use the ticket to gain admission to an evening showing.

Figure 16.1 illustrates how the owners of movie theaters use price discrimination to increase their profits. The marginal cost to the movie theater owner from another person attending a showing is very small: a little more wear on a theater seat and a little more spilled popcorn to be swept from the floor. In previous chapters, we assumed that the marginal cost curve has a U shape. In Figure 16.1, we assume for simplicity that marginal cost is a constant $0.50, shown as a horizontal line. Panel (a) shows the demand for afternoon showings. In this segment of its market, the theater should maximize profit by selling the quantity of tickets for which marginal revenue equals marginal cost, or 450 tickets. We know from the demand curve that the theater can sell 450 tickets at a price of $8.50 per ticket. Panel (b) shows the demand for evening showings. Notice that charging $8.50 per ticket would *not* be profit maximizing in this market. At a price of $8.50, the theater sells 650 tickets, which is 125 more tickets than the profit-maximizing quantity of 525. By charging $8.50 for tickets to afternoon showings and $11.00 for tickets to evening showings, the theater has maximized profit.

Figure 16.1 also illustrates another important point about price discrimination: When firms can practice price discrimination, they will charge customers who are less sensitive to price—those whose demand for the product is *less elastic*—a higher price and charge customers who are more sensitive to price—those whose demand is *more elastic*—a lower price. In this case, the demand for tickets to evening showings is less elastic, so the price charged is higher, and the demand for tickets to afternoon showings is more elastic, so the price charged is lower.   **MyLab Economics** Concept Check

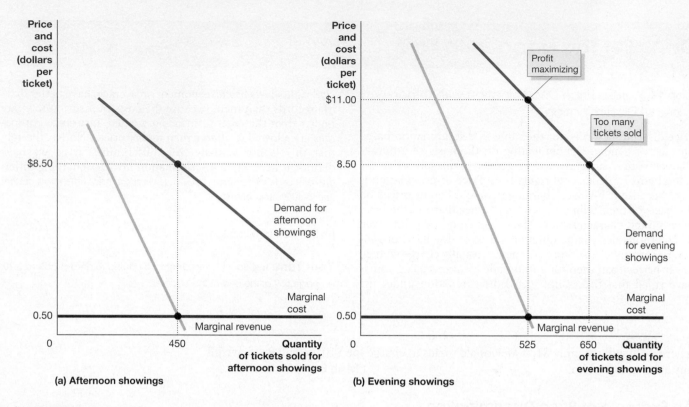

Figure 16.1   **Price Discrimination by a Movie Theater**

Fewer people want to go to the movies in the afternoon than in the evening. In panel (a), the profit-maximizing price for a ticket to an afternoon showing is $8.50. Charging this same price for evening showings would not be profit maximizing, as panel (b) shows. At a price of $8.50, the theater would sell 650 tickets to evening showings, which is more than the profit-maximizing number of 525 tickets. To maximize profit, the theater should charge $11.00 for tickets to evening showings.

Solved Problem 16.2

How Apple Uses Price Discrimination to Increase Profits

During the summer of 2017, Apple was selling MacBook Pro laptop computers with 13-inch retina displays on its Web site and in its retail stores for $1,299. But college students and faculty members could buy the same laptop from Apple for $1,199. Why would Apple charge different prices for the same laptop, depending on whether the buyer is an education customer? Draw two graphs to illustrate your answers: one for the general public and one for education customers.

Solving the Problem

Step 1:   Review the chapter material. This problem is about using price discrimination to increase profits, so you may want to review the section "Price Discrimination: Charging Different Prices for the Same Product," which begins on page 542.

Step 2:   Explain why charging different prices to education customers and other customers will increase Apple's profit. It makes sense for Apple to charge different prices if education customers have a different price elasticity of demand than do other customers. In that case, Apple will charge the market segment with the less elastic demand a higher price and the market segment with the more elastic demand a lower price. Because Apple is charging education customers the lower price, they must have a more elastic demand than do other customers.

Step 3:   Draw a graph to illustrate your answer. Your graphs should look like the following ones, where we have chosen hypothetical quantities to illustrate the ideas. As in the case of movie theaters, you can assume for simplicity that marginal cost is constant; in the graph we assume that marginal cost is $400.

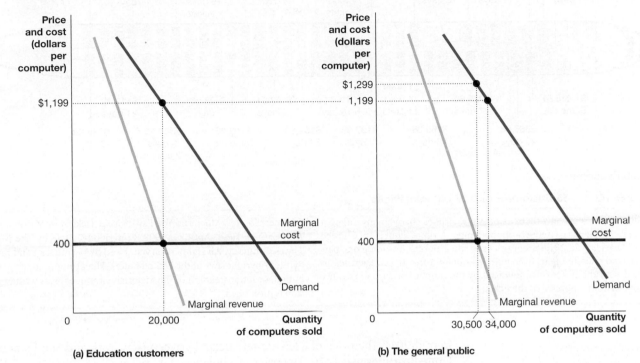

(a) Education customers

(b) The general public

Panel (a) shows that in the education customers segment of the market, marginal revenue equals marginal cost at 20,000 laptops sold. Therefore, Apple should charge a price of $1,199 to maximize profits. But if Apple also charges $1,199 in the general public segment of the market, shown in panel (b), it will sell 34,000 laptops, which is more than the profit-maximizing quantity. By charging $1,299 to the general public, Apple will sell 30,500 laptops, the profit-maximizing quantity. We have shown that Apple maximizes its profits by charging education customers a lower price than it charges the general public.

Your Turn: For more practice, do related problem 2.11 on page 559 at the end of this chapter.

MyLab Economics Study Plan

Airlines: The Kings of Price Discrimination

Airline seats are a perishable product. Once a plane has taken off from Chicago for Los Angeles, any seat that has not been sold on that particular flight will never be sold. In addition, the marginal cost of flying one additional passenger is low. As a result, airlines have a strong incentive to manage prices to fill as many seats as possible on each flight.

Airlines divide their customers into two main categories: business travelers and leisure travelers. Business travelers often have inflexible schedules, can't commit until the last minute to travel on a particular day, and, most importantly, are not very sensitive to changes in price. The opposite is true for leisure travelers: They are flexible about when they travel, willing to buy their tickets well in advance, and sensitive to changes in price. Based on what we discussed earlier in this chapter, you can see that airlines will maximize profits by charging business travelers higher ticket prices than leisure travelers, but they need to determine who is a business traveler and who is a leisure traveler. Traditionally, airlines made this determination by requiring people who want to buy a ticket at the leisure price to buy 14 days in advance and to stay at their destination over a Saturday night. Anyone unable to meet these requirements must pay a much higher price. Business travelers end up paying the higher ticket price because they often cannot make their plans 14 days in advance of their flight and don't want to stay over a weekend. The gap between leisure fares and business fares is often substantial. For example,

MyLab Economics Animation

Figure 16.2 **33 Customers and 27 Different Prices**

To fill as many seats on a flight as possible, airlines charge many different ticket prices. The 33 passengers on this United Airlines flight from Chicago to Los Angeles paid 27 different prices for their tickets, including one passenger who used frequent flyer miles to obtain a free ticket. Each seat is labelled with the ticket price followed by the number of days in advance that the customer purchased the ticket.

in mid-2017, the price of a leisure-fare ticket between New York and San Francisco on United Airlines was $410. The price of a business-fare ticket was $708.

The airlines go well beyond a single leisure fare and a single business fare in their pricing strategies. Although they ordinarily charge high prices for tickets sold only a few days in advance, airlines are willing to reduce prices for seats that they doubt they will be able to sell at current prices. Since the late 1980s, airlines have employed economists and mathematicians to construct computer models of the market for airline tickets. To calculate a suggested price each day for each seat, these models take into account factors that affect the demand for tickets, such as the season of the year, the length of the route, the day of the week, and whether the flight typically attracts primarily business or leisure travelers. This practice of continually adjusting prices to take into account fluctuations in demand is called *yield management*.

Since the late 1990s, Internet sites such as Priceline.com have helped the airlines to implement yield management. On Priceline.com, buyers commit to paying a price of their choosing for a ticket on a particular day and agree that they will fly at any time on that day. This approach gives airlines the opportunity to fill seats that otherwise would have gone empty, particularly on late-night or early-morning flights, even though the price may be well below the normal leisure fare. In 2001, several airlines came together to form the Internet site Orbitz, which became another means of filling seats at discount prices. In fact, the chance that you paid the same price for your airline ticket as the person sitting next to you has become quite small. Figure 16.2 shows an actual United Airlines flight from Chicago to Los Angeles. The 33 passengers on the flight paid 27 different prices for their tickets, including one passenger who used frequent flyer miles to obtain a free ticket.

MyLab Economics Concept Check

Apply the Concept

MyLab Economics Video

Big Data and the Rise of Dynamic Pricing

As we saw in the chapter opener, to improve their price setting, Disney and other firms are using big data to gather information on their customers. When firms use these data to determine how responsive different groups of customers are to changes in price, the firms are engaging in what economists call price discrimination.

The word *discrimination* has unfavorable connotations, so many firms call their pricing strategies *yield management, price optimization,* or *dynamic pricing.* The last term has become popular because it reflects the idea that prices are continually adjusted as new data become available.

Airlines' initial efforts at price discrimination didn't require much data. They could distinguish business travelers from leisure travelers by this simple requirement: To receive a lower price, customers had to purchase a ticket well in advance and stay over a weekend at their destinations. Today, airlines charge many different prices on most flights, and the prices are determined by sophisticated software that processes huge amounts of data on many factors that might affect the responsiveness of passengers to changes in ticket prices on a particular flight, such as whether the flight attracts primarily leisure travelers or primarily business travelers; the weather forecast in the originating and destination cities; how many flights competing airlines are offering; the number of seats currently unsold on this and competing flights; and whether conventions, large professional conferences, major concerts, or sporting events are occurring in the destination city. For example, analysis of big data indicated that leisure travelers are more likely to book fares during a weekend, while business travelers are more likely to book fares on Friday for the following week. As a result, one study found that airlines charge prices that are 13 percent higher on tickets sold on Fridays than on tickets sold on Sundays.

Tasfoto/Alamy Stock Photo

Airlines use sophisticated software to determine the many different prices they charged these passengers.

Similar pricing strategies have become widespread. For instance, according to an article in the *Wall Street Journal*, until recently the Indianapolis Zoo charged a flat admission fee of $16.95. After the zoo implemented a dynamic pricing strategy, the fee ranged between $8 and $30, "based on advance sales and expected demand. [The zoo] discounts cold weekdays in February and boosts prices after school groups book dozens of tickets. Since introducing such dynamic pricing . . . the zoo's admission revenue has grown 12%." Some ski resorts and professional sports teams have adopted comparable strategies.

Online retailers such as Amazon have become skilled at analyzing big data. When you log on to a Web site, its servers can gather important information about you, including your location—which can be determined from your Internet Protocol (IP) address—and your browsing history. If the site already has your e-mail address, it may be able to use an Internet data firm to discover your age, race, gender, and income and adjust prices on the basis of this information. One conclusion retailers have drawn is that because more consumers are online during the workday, it makes sense to raise prices in the morning and reduce them in the evening. Some retailers have gone beyond such simple changes and implemented sophisticated data-based pricing strategies, although they are often reluctant to discuss them publicly.

Reporters for the *Wall Street Journal* conducted an experiment to see if they could discover an online price strategy used by the Web site of Staples, the office supply store. They logged on to the site from computers in many different places and found that the Web site displayed different prices for several items based on the zip code from which the person logged on. For example, some people saw a price of $15.79 for a Swingline stapler, while other people saw a price of $14.29 for the same stapler. Similarly, some people saw a price of $28.49 for a 12-pack of Bic rollerball pens, while other people saw a price of $25.99. Staples's managers declined to explain their pricing strategy, so the reporters carried out a statistical analysis of the characteristics of the zip codes. The most important characteristic turned out to be whether a zip code was within 20 miles of an OfficeMax or Office Depot store, which are Staples's main competitors. Because people living in zip codes close to a rival store would be more responsive to changes in Staples's prices, they were likely to see the low price, and people in zip codes far away from a rival store were likely to see the high price.

Automobile insurance companies typically call their pricing strategies price optimization. Because the rates insurance companies charge usually have to be approved by state government agencies, some of the companies' price optimization policies have been the subject of public debate. Typically, automobile insurance companies have set policy premiums on the basis of the likelihood of a policyholder having an accident. For example, data show that young unmarried males are more likely to have accidents than are people in other demographic groups. Similarly, drivers who have previously had an accident are more likely to have future accidents than are drivers who have not had accidents. So, those groups are charged higher premiums. In recent years, though, some insurance companies have used analysis of big data to charge higher premiums not just for high-risk drivers but also for drivers who are likely to have a lower responsiveness to premium increases. For example, people who have only a high school degree or who have continued to purchase a policy from the same company over many years tend to be less responsive to premium increases than are people with college degrees or who change companies frequently. Some state regulatory agencies are critical of these pricing strategies and have been pressuring insurance companies to return to setting premiums primarily on the basis of how likely a driver is to have an accident.

When firms adopt pricing strategies like the ones we've described, typically some consumers gain by paying lower prices, while other consumers lose by paying higher prices. As a group, though, consumers lose because, if successful, dynamic pricing strategies increase firms' revenues. The more consumers pay for the same quantity of goods, the worse off they are.

Sources: Jerry Useem, "How Online Shopping Makes Suckers of Us All," theatlantic.com, May 2017; Scott McCartney, "The Worst Day to Buy a Plane Ticket," *Wall Street Journal*, December 9, 2015; Jack Nicas, "Now Prices Can Change from Minute to Minute," *Wall Street Journal*, December 14, 2015; Tracy Samilton, "Being a Loyal Auto Insurance Customer Can Cost You," npr.org, May 8, 2015; and Jennifer Valentino-Devries, Jeremy Singer-Vine, and Ashkan Soltani, "Websites Vary Prices, Deals Based on Users' Information," *Wall Street Journal*, December 24, 2012.

MyLab Economics Study Plan   **Your Turn:** Test your understanding by doing related problems 2.12, 2.13, and 2.14 on page 559 at the end of this chapter.

───●

Perfect Price Discrimination

If a firm knew every consumer's willingness to pay and could keep consumers who bought a product at a low price from reselling it, the firm could charge every consumer a different price. In this case of *perfect price discrimination*—also known as *first-degree price discrimination*—each consumer would have to pay a price equal to the consumer's willingness to pay and, therefore, would receive no consumer surplus. To see why, remember that consumer surplus is the difference between the highest price a consumer is willing to pay for a product and the price the consumer actually pays (see Chapter 4, Section 4.1). But if the price the consumer pays is the maximum he or she would be willing to pay, there is no consumer surplus.

Figure 16.3 shows the effects of perfect price discrimination. To simplify the discussion, we assume that the firm is a monopoly and that it has constant marginal and average total costs. Panel (a) shows the case of a monopolist that cannot practice price discrimination and, therefore, can charge only a single price for its product. The monopolist maximizes profit by producing the level of output where marginal revenue equals marginal cost (see Chapter 15, Section 15.3). Recall that the economically efficient level of output occurs where price is equal to marginal cost, which is the level of output in a perfectly competitive market. Because the monopolist produces where price is greater than marginal cost, the monopolist causes a loss of economic efficiency equal to the area of the deadweight loss triangle in the figure.

Panel (b) shows the situation of a monopolist practicing perfect price discrimination. Because the firm can charge each consumer the maximum each consumer is willing to pay, its marginal revenue from selling one more unit is equal to the price of that unit. Therefore, the monopolist's marginal revenue curve becomes equal to its demand curve, and the firm will continue to produce up to the point where price is equal to marginal cost. It may seem like a paradox, but the ability to practice perfect price discrimination causes the monopolist to produce the efficient level of output.

(a) A monopolist that cannot practice price discrimination

(b) A monopolist practicing perfect price discrimination

MyLab Economics Animation

Figure 16.3   **Perfect Price Discrimination**

Panel (a) shows the case of a monopolist that cannot practice price discrimination and, therefore, can charge only a single price for its product. The graph shows that to maximize profit, the monopolist will produce the level of output where marginal revenue equals marginal cost. The area of the green-shaded rectangle shows the resulting profit. Given the monopoly price, the area of the blue-shaded triangle shows the amount of consumer surplus in this market. The economically efficient level of output occurs where price equals marginal cost. Because the monopolist stops production at a level of output where price is above marginal cost, there is a deadweight loss equal to the area of the yellow-shaded triangle. In panel (b), the monopolist is able to practice perfect price discrimination by charging a different price to each consumer. The result is to convert both the consumer surplus and the deadweight loss from panel (a) into profit.

By doing so, the monopolist converts the consumer surplus *and* the deadweight loss in panel (a) into profit. In both panel (a) and panel (b), the profit shown is also producer surplus.

Even though the result in panel (b) is more economically efficient than the result in panel (a), consumers clearly are worse off because the amount of consumer surplus has been reduced to zero. We probably will never see a case of perfect price discrimination in the real world because firms typically do not know how much each consumer is willing to pay and, therefore, cannot charge each consumer a different price. Still, this extreme case helps us to see the two key results of price discrimination:

1. Profit increases.
2. Consumer surplus decreases.

Perfect price discrimination improves economic efficiency. Can we also say that this will be the case if price discrimination is less than perfect? Often, less-than-perfect price discrimination will improve economic efficiency. But under certain circumstances, it may actually reduce economic efficiency, so we can't draw a general conclusion.   **MyLab Economics** Concept Check

Price Discrimination across Time

Firms are sometimes able to engage in price discrimination over time. With this strategy, firms charge a higher price for a product when it is first introduced and a lower price later. Some consumers are *early adopters* who will pay a high price to be among the first to own certain new products. This pattern helps explain why Blu-ray players, digital cameras, and 4K televisions all sold for very high prices when they were first introduced. After the demand of the early adopters was satisfied, the companies reduced prices to attract more price-sensitive customers. For example, the price of Blu-ray players dropped by 95 percent within five years of their introduction.

Some of the price reductions over time for these products were also due to falling costs, as companies took advantage of economies of scale, but some represented price discrimination across time.

Book publishers routinely use price discrimination across time to increase profits. Hardcover editions of novels have much higher prices and are published months before paperback editions. For example, the hardcover edition of John Grisham's novel *Camino Island* was published in June 2017 at a price of $28.95. The paperback edition was published in April 2018 for $9.99. Although this difference in price might seem to reflect the higher costs of producing hardcover books, in fact, it does not. The marginal cost of printing another copy of the hardcover edition is about $1.50. The marginal cost of printing another copy of the paperback edition is only slightly less, about $1.25. So, the difference in price between the hardcover and paperback editions is explained primarily by differences in demand. John Grisham's most devoted fans want to read his next book at the earliest possible moment and are not very sensitive to price. Many casual readers are also interested in his books but will read something else if the price of his latest book is too high.

As Figure 16.4 shows, a publisher will maximize profit by segmenting the market—in this case, across time—and by charging a higher price to the less elastic market segment and a lower price to the more elastic segment. (This example is similar to our earlier analysis of movie tickets in Figure 16.1 on page 544.) If the publisher had skipped the hardcover and issued only the paperback version at a price of $9.99 when the book was first published in June, its revenue would

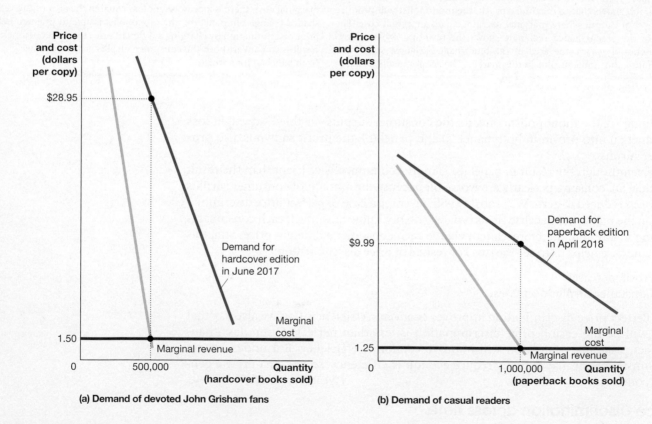

(a) Demand of devoted John Grisham fans

(b) Demand of casual readers

MyLab Economics Animation

Figure 16.4 **Price Discrimination across Time**

Publishers issue most novels in hardcover editions at high prices to satisfy the demand of the novelists' most devoted fans. Later, publishers issue paperback editions at much lower prices to capture sales from casual readers. In panel (a), with a marginal cost of $1.50 per copy for a hardcover edition, the profit-maximizing level of output is 500,000 copies, which can be sold at a price of $28.95. In panel (b), the more elastic demand of casual readers and the slightly lower marginal cost result in a profit-maximizing output of 1,000,000 for the paperback edition, which can be sold at a price of $9.99.

have dropped by the number of readers who bought the hardcover edition multiplied by the difference in price between the hardcover and paperback editions, or 500,000 × ($28.95 − $9.99) = $9,480,000.   **MyLab Economics** Concept Check

Can Price Discrimination Be Illegal?

When discussing monopoly, we saw that Congress has passed *antitrust laws* to promote competition (see Chapter 15, Section 15.5). Price discrimination may be illegal if its effect is to reduce competition in an industry. In 1936, Congress passed the Robinson–Patman Act, which outlawed price discrimination that reduced competition. The act also contained language that could be interpreted as making illegal *all* price discrimination not based on differences in cost. In the 1960s, the Federal Trade Commission sued Borden, Inc., under this act because Borden was selling the same evaporated milk for two different prices. Cans with the Borden label were sold for a high price, and cans the company sold to supermarkets to be repackaged as the supermarkets' private brands were sold for a much lower price. The courts ultimately ruled that Borden had not violated the law because the price differences increased, rather than reduced, competition in the market for evaporated milk. In recent years, the courts have interpreted the Robinson–Patman Act narrowly, allowing firms to use the types of price discrimination described in this chapter.   **MyLab Economics** Concept Check   **MyLab Economics** Study Plan

16.3 Other Pricing Strategies

LEARNING OBJECTIVE: Explain how some firms increase their profits by using odd pricing, cost-plus pricing, and two-part tariffs.

In addition to price discrimination, firms use many other pricing strategies, depending on the nature of their products, the level of competition in their markets, and the characteristics of their customers. In this section, we consider three important strategies: odd pricing, cost-plus pricing, and two-part tariffs.

Odd Pricing: Why Is the Price $2.99 Instead of $3.00?

Many firms use *odd pricing*—for example, charging $4.95 instead of $5.00, or $199 instead of $200. Surveys show that 80 to 90 percent of the products sold in supermarkets have prices ending in "9" or "5" rather than "0." Odd pricing has a long history. In the early nineteenth century, most goods in the United States were sold in general stores and did not have fixed prices. Instead, prices were often determined by haggling, much as prices of new cars are often determined today by haggling on dealers' lots. Later in the nineteenth century, when most products began to sell for a fixed price, odd pricing became popular.

There are two common explanations for the origin of odd pricing. One explanation is that in the nineteenth century, goods imported from Great Britain had a reputation for high quality. When the prices of British goods in British currency were translated into U.S. dollars, the result was an odd price. Because customers connected odd prices with high-quality goods, even sellers of domestic goods charged odd prices. The other explanation is that odd pricing began as an attempt to guard against employee theft. An odd price forced an employee to give the customer change, reducing the likelihood that the employee would simply pocket the customer's money without recording the sale.

Whatever the origins of odd pricing, why do firms still use it today? The most obvious answer is that an odd price, say $9.99, somehow seems significantly cheaper than $10.00. Some people in retailing refer to the *left-digit effect*, meaning that consumers focus on the leftmost digit in a price. But do consumers really have this illusion? To find out, three market researchers conducted a study. Economists can estimate demand curves statistically. If consumers have the illusion that $9.99 is significantly cheaper than $10.00, they will demand a greater quantity of goods at $9.99 than the estimated demand curve predicts. The researchers surveyed consumers about their willingness to purchase six different products at a series of prices. Ten of the prices were either odd cent prices—99 cents or 95 cents—or odd dollar prices—$95 or $99. Nine of these 10 odd prices resulted in an odd-price effect, with the quantity demanded being greater than predicted using the estimated demand curve. The study provides some evidence that using odd prices makes economic sense.

Another study involved catalogs for women's clothing. With the cooperation of the clothing firm, some women were mailed catalogs with even dollar prices and other women received catalogs with prices ending in 99 cents. The women receiving the catalogs with prices ending in 99 cents bought 8 percent more clothes than the women receiving catalogs with even dollar prices.

Many firms have begun to use sales strategies that rely on insights from *behavioral economics*, which is the study of situations in which people make choices that do not appear to be economically rational (see Chapter 10, Section 10.4). Odd pricing is an old strategy that is consistent with the modern analysis of behavioral economics.

MyLab Economics Concept Check

Why Do McDonald's and Other Firms Use Cost-Plus Pricing?

Many firms use *cost-plus pricing*, which involves adding a percentage *markup* to average total cost. With this pricing strategy, the firm first calculates average total cost at a particular level of production, usually equal to the firm's expected sales. The firm then applies a percentage markup, say 30 percent, to the estimated average total cost to arrive at the price. For example, if average total cost is $100 and the percentage markup is 30 percent, the price will be $130. For a firm selling multiple products, the markup is intended to cover all costs, including those that the firm cannot assign to any particular product. For example, the work performed by the employees in the accounting and finance departments at McDonald's applies to all of McDonald's products and can't be assigned directly to Big Macs or Happy Meals.

Apply the Concept

MyLab Economics Video

Cost-Plus Pricing in the Publishing Industry

Book publishing companies incur substantial costs for editing, designing, marketing, and warehousing books. These costs are difficult to assign directly to any particular book. Most publishers arrive at a price for a book by applying a markup to their production costs, which are usually divided into plant costs and manufacturing costs. Plant costs include typesetting the manuscript and preparing graphics or artwork for printing. Manufacturing costs include the costs of printing, paper, and binding the book.

Consider the following example for a hypothetical new book by Adam Smith, *How to Succeed at Economics without Really Trying*. We will assume that the book is 250 pages long, the publisher expects to sell 5,000 copies, and plant and manufacturing costs are as given in the following table.

Plant Costs		
	Typesetting	$3,500
	Other plant costs	2,000
Manufacturing Costs		
	Printing	$5,750
	Paper	6,250
	Binding	5,000
Total Production Cost		
		$22,500

With total production cost of $22,500 and production of 5,000 books, the per-unit production cost is $22,500/5,000 = $4.50. Many publishers multiply the unit production cost number by 7 or 8 to arrive at the retail price they will charge customers in bookstores. In this case, multiplying by 7 results in a price of $31.50 for the book. The markup seems quite high, but publishers typically sell books to bookstores at a 40 percent discount. Although a customer in a bookstore will pay $31.50 for the book—or less, of course, if it is purchased from a bookseller that discounts the retail price—the publisher receives only $18.90. The difference between the $18.90 received from the bookstore and the $4.50 production cost equals the cost of editing, marketing, warehousing, paying a royalty to the author of the book, and all other costs, including the opportunity cost of the investment in the firm by its owners, plus any economic profit the owners receive.

Source: Beth Luey, *Handbook for Academic Authors*, 5th ed., New York: Cambridge University Press, 2010.

Your Turn: Test your understanding by doing related problem 3.8 on page 561 at the end of this chapter.

MyLab Economics Study Plan

We have seen that firms maximize profit by producing the quantity at which marginal revenue equals marginal cost and charging a price that will lead consumers to buy that quantity. The cost-plus approach doesn't appear to maximize profit unless the cost-plus price turns out to be the same as the price that will cause the marginal revenue earned on the last unit to equal the unit's marginal cost. Economists have two views of cost-plus pricing. One is that it is simply a mistake that firms should avoid. The other view is that cost-plus pricing helps a firm come close to the profit-maximizing price when either marginal revenue or marginal cost is difficult to calculate.

Small firms often like cost-plus pricing because it is easy to use. Unfortunately, these firms can fall into the trap of mechanically applying a cost-plus pricing rule, which may result in charging prices that do not maximize profit. The most obvious problems with cost-plus pricing are that (1) it ignores demand, and (2) it focuses on average total cost rather than marginal cost. If a firm's marginal cost is significantly different from its average total cost at its current level of production, cost-plus pricing is unlikely to maximize profit.

Despite these problems, cost-plus pricing is used by some large firms that have the knowledge and resources to devise a better method of pricing if cost-plus pricing fails to maximize profit. Economists conclude that using cost-plus pricing may be the best way to determine the optimal price in two situations:

1. When marginal cost and average total cost are roughly equal
2. When a firm has difficulty estimating its demand curve

In fact, most large firms, such as automobile manufacturers, that use cost-plus pricing do not just mechanically apply a markup to their estimate of average total cost. Instead, they adjust the markup to reflect their best estimate of current demand. A large firm is likely to have a pricing policy committee that adjusts prices based on the current state of competition in the industry and the current state of the economy. If competition is strong in a weak economy, the pricing committee may decide to set price significantly below the cost-plus price.

In general, firms that take demand into account will charge lower markups on products that are more price elastic and higher markups on products that are less elastic. Supermarkets, where cost-plus pricing is widely used, have markups in the 5 to 10 percent range for products with more elastic demand, such as soft drinks and breakfast cereals, and markups in the 50 percent range for products with less elastic demand, such as fresh fruits and vegetables. MyLab Economics Concept Check

How Can Using Two-Part Tariffs Increase a Firm's Profit?

Some firms require consumers to pay an initial fee for the right to buy their product and an additional fee for each unit of the product purchased. For example, many golf and tennis clubs require members to buy an annual membership in addition to paying a fee each time they use the golf course or a tennis court. Sam's Club and Costco

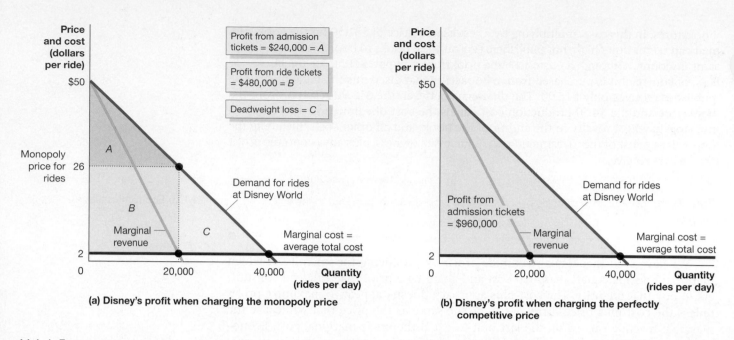

MyLab Economics Animation

Figure 16.5 A Two-Part Tariff at Disney World

In panel (a), Disney charges the monopoly price of $26 per ride ticket and sells 20,000 ride tickets. Its profit from *ride tickets* is shown by the area of rectangle *B*, or $480,000. If Disney is in the position of knowing every consumer's willingness to pay, it can also charge a price for *admission tickets* that would result in the total amount paid for admission tickets being equal to total consumer surplus from the rides. Total consumer surplus from the rides equals

the area of the triangle, *A*, or $240,000. So, when charging the monopoly price, Disney's total profit equals $480,000 + $240,000 or $720,000. In panel (b), Disney charges the perfectly competitive price of $2, which results in a quantity of 40,000 ride tickets sold. At the lower ride ticket price, Disney can charge a higher price for admission tickets, which will increase its total profits from operating the park to the area of the green triangle, or $960,000.

Two-part tariff A situation in which consumers pay one price (or tariff) for the right to buy as much of a related good as they want at a second price.

require consumers to pay a membership fee before shopping at their stores. Wireless companies, such as AT&T and Sprint, sometimes charge a monthly fee and then have a per-minute charge after a certain number of minutes have been used. Economists call this pricing strategy a **two-part tariff**.

The Walt Disney Company is in a position to use a two-part tariff by charging consumers for admission to Walt Disney World or Disneyland and also charging them to use the rides in the parks. When Disneyland in California first opened, the admission price was low, but people had to purchase tickets to go on the rides. Today, you pay a high price for admission to Disneyland or Disney World, but the rides are free once you're in the park. Figure 16.5 helps us understand which of these pricing strategies is more profitable for Disney. The numbers in the figure are simplified to make the calculations easier.

Once visitors are inside the park, Disney is in the position of a monopolist: No other firm is operating rides in Disney World. So, we can draw panel (a) in Figure 16.5 to represent the market for rides at Disney World. This graph looks like the standard monopoly graph (see Chapter 15, Section 15.3). (Note that the marginal cost of another rider is quite low. We assume that it is a constant $2 and equal to the average total cost.) It seems obvious—but it will turn out to be wrong!—that Disney should determine the profit-maximizing quantity of ride tickets by setting marginal revenue equal to marginal cost. In this case, the result would be 20,000 ride tickets sold per day at a price of $26 per ride. Disney's profit from selling *ride tickets* is shown by the area of rectangle *B*. The area equals the difference between the $26 price and the average total cost of $2, multiplied by the 20,000 tickets sold, or ($26 − $2) × 20,000 = $480,000. Disney also has a second source of profit from selling *admission tickets* to the park. Given the $26 price for ride tickets, what price would Disney be able to charge for admission tickets?

For simplicity, let's make the following three assumptions: (1) The only reason people want admission to Disney World is to go on the rides, (2) all consumers have the same individual demand curve for rides, and (3) Disney knows what this demand curve is. This last assumption allows Disney to practice perfect price discrimination. More realistic assumptions would make the outcome of the analysis somewhat different but would not affect the main point of how Disney uses a two-part tariff to increase its profit. With these assumptions, we can use the concept of consumer surplus to calculate the maximum total amount consumers would be willing to pay for admission. Remember that consumer surplus is equal to the area below the demand curve and above the price line, shown by the area of triangle A in panel (a). Consumers would not be willing to pay more for admission to the park than the consumer surplus they receive from the rides. In panel (a) of Figure 16.5, the total consumer surplus when Disney charges a price of $26 per ride is $240,000. (This number is easy to calculate if you remember that the formula for the area of a triangle is $\frac{1}{2} \times$ base $\times$ height, or $\frac{1}{2} \times 20,000 \times \$24$.) Disney can set the price of admission tickets so that the *total* amount spent by buyers would be $240,000, which is the entire consumer surplus from the rides. So, Disney's total profit from Disney World would be the $240,000 it receives from admission tickets plus the $480,000 in profit from the rides, or $720,000 per day.

Is this the most profit Disney can earn from selling admission tickets and ride tickets? The answer is "no." The key to understanding why is to notice that *the lower the price Disney charges for ride tickets, the higher the price it can charge for admission tickets.* Lower-priced ride tickets increase consumer surplus from the rides and, therefore, increase the willingness of buyers to pay a higher price for admission tickets. In panel (b) of Figure 16.5, we assume that Disney acts as it would in a perfectly competitive market and charges a price for ride tickets that is equal to marginal cost, or $2. Charging this price increases consumer surplus—*and* the maximum total amount that Disney can charge for admission tickets—from $240,000 to $960,000. (Once again, we use the formula for the area of a triangle to calculate the area of the green-shaded triangle in panel (b): $\frac{1}{2} \times 40,000 \times 48 = \$960,000$.) Disney's profit from the rides will decline to zero because it is now charging a price equal to average total cost, *but its total profit from Disney World will rise from $720,000 to $960,000 per day.* Table 16.2 summarizes this result.

What is the source of Disney's increased profit from charging a price equal to marginal cost? Disney has converted what was deadweight loss when it charged the monopoly price—the area of triangle C in panel (a)—into consumer surplus. Disney then turns this consumer surplus into profit by increasing the price of admission tickets.

Note the following about the outcome of a firm using an optimal two-part tariff:

1. Because price equals marginal cost at the level of output supplied, the outcome is economically efficient.
2. All consumer surplus is transformed into profit.

Observe that, in effect, Disney is practicing perfect price discrimination. As we noted in our discussion of perfect price discrimination on page 548, Disney's use of a two-part tariff has increased the amount of the product—in this case, rides at Disney World—consumers are able to purchase but has eliminated consumer surplus. Although it may seem paradoxical, consumer surplus was actually higher when consumers were being charged the monopoly price for the rides.

	Monopoly Price for Rides	Competitive Price for Rides
Profit from admission tickets	$240,000	$960,000
Profit from ride tickets	480,000	0
Total profit	**720,000**	**960,000**

Table 16.2

Disney's Profit per Day from Different Pricing Strategies

The solution to the paradox is that although consumers pay a lower price for the rides when Disney employs a two-part tariff, the overall amount they pay to be at Disney World increases.

Disney actually does follow the profit-maximizing strategy of charging a high price for admission to the park and a very low price—zero—for the rides. It seems that Disney could increase its profits by raising the price for the rides from zero to the marginal cost of the rides. But the marginal cost is so low that it would not be worth slowing the rate that guests are able to enter rides by making them swipe their MagicBands at ride entrances. Finally, note that in practice Disney can't convert all consumer surplus into profit because (1) the demand curves of customers are not all the same, and (2) even with the help of the big data it has been collecting in the past few years, Disney does not know precisely what these demand curves are.

MyLab Economics Study Plan

MyLab Economics Concept Check

Continued from page 539

Economics in Your Life & Career

Should You Charge More Than One Price to See the Movies in Your Theater?

At the beginning of the chapter, we asked you to suppose that AMC Entertainment hires you to manage a movie theater. Should you charge one flat price for tickets whether the movie is being shown in the afternoon or at night and whether the ticket buyer is a student, a senior citizen, or of another age? Should you always charge the same price for popcorn?

As we've seen in this chapter, firms try to use pricing strategies to increase their profit. A movie theater will try to charge different prices to different consumers, based on their willingness to pay. If you have two people of about the same age, one a student and one not, you might assume that the student has a lower income and therefore a lower willingness to pay than the nonstudent, and the movie theater would like to charge the student a lower price. To practice this form of price discrimination, you can instruct an employee to ask to see a student ID to ensure that the theater is giving the discount only to students.

Would it also make sense for you to practice price discrimination at the concession stand? It is likely that a student will also have a lower willingness to pay for popcorn, and you can check for a student ID at the time of purchase, but unlike with the entry ticket, you will have a difficult time preventing the student from giving the popcorn to a nonstudent once the student has made the purchase.

Because it is easier to limit resale in movie admissions, we often see theaters charge different prices for different groups. Because it is difficult to limit resale of popcorn and other movie concessions, theaters typically charge everyone the same price.

Conclusion

Firms in perfectly competitive industries must sell their products at the market price. For firms in other industries—which means, of course, the vast majority of firms—pricing is an important part of the strategy used to maximize profit. We have seen in this chapter, for example, that if firms can successfully segment their customers into different groups on the basis of the customers' willingness to pay, the firms can increase their profits by charging different segments different prices.

Visit **MyLab Economics** for a news article and analysis related to the concepts in this chapter.

Key Terms

Price discrimination, p. 542   Transactions costs, p. 540   Two-part tariff, p. 554

16.1 ## Pricing Strategy, the Law of One Price, and Arbitrage, pages 540–542

LEARNING OBJECTIVE: Define the law of one price and explain the role of arbitrage.

MyLab Economics   Visit www.pearson.com/mylab/economics to complete these exercises online and get instant feedback.

Summary

According to the *law of one price*, identical products should sell for the same price everywhere. If a product sells for different prices, it will be possible to make a profit through *arbitrage*: buying a product at a low price and reselling it at a high price. The law of one price will hold as long as arbitrage is possible. Arbitrage is sometimes blocked by high **transactions costs**, which are the costs in time and other resources incurred to carry out an exchange or because the product cannot be resold. Another apparent exception to the law of one price occurs when companies offset the higher price they charge for a product by providing superior or more reliable service to customers.

Review Questions

1.1 What is the law of one price? What is arbitrage?

1.2 Does a product always have to sell for the same price everywhere? Briefly explain.

Problems and Applications

1.3 Economist Richard Thaler of the University of Chicago noted that most economists consider arbitrage to be one way "that markets can do their magic." Briefly explain the role arbitrage can play in helping markets work.

Source: Richard H. Thaler, "Unless You Are Spock, Irrelevant Things Matter in Economic Behavior," *New York Times*, May 8, 2015.

1.4 Prices for many goods are higher in the city of Shenzhen on the mainland of China than in the city of Hong Kong. An article in the *Economist* noted that "individuals can arbitrage these differences through what effectively amounts to smuggling."

a. Explain what the article means when it notes that individuals can "arbitrage these price differences."

b. Ultimately, what would you expect the result to be of individuals engaging in this arbitrage? Is your answer affected by the fact that the government of China requires a visa for Shenzhen residents to visit Hong Kong and regulates the number of trips that can be made between the two cities in a given year? Briefly explain.

Source: "Restrictions on Travel to Hong Kong by Shenzhen Residents," *Economist*, April 13, 2015.

1.5 **(Related to Solved Problem 16.1 on page 541)** In 2016, Walmart closed 150 stores in the United States and deeply discounted the merchandise in them. Some people bought the merchandise at these low prices and resold it on Amazon, eBay, and other sites. An article in the *Wall Street Journal* described one reseller who "sent three employees in a 26-foot truck to the nearest closing Walmart, about 160 miles south. . . . They hauled off $35,000 in merchandise, like Legos and Star Wars pajamas, which he said he expects to sell for as much as $100,000 on Amazon."

a. Is the reseller making a $65,000 profit on these goods? Briefly explain.

b. Is the reseller exploiting the people who buy these goods from him on Amazon? Briefly explain.

Source: Greg Bensinger, "Wal-Mart Closures Bring out the Amazon Sellers," *Wall Street Journal*, January 29, 2016.

1.6 **(Related to Solved Problem 16.1 on page 541)** Suspicions about arbitrage have a long history. For example, Valerian of Cimiez, a Catholic bishop who lived during the fifth century, wrote, "When something is bought cheaply only so it can be retailed dearly, doing business always means cheating." What might Valerian think of eBay? Do you agree with his conclusion? Briefly explain.

Source: Michael McCormick, *The Origins of the European Economy: Communications and Commerce, A.D. 300–900*, New York: Cambridge University Press, 2001, p. 85.

16.2 ## Price Discrimination: Charging Different Prices for the Same Product, pages 542–551

LEARNING OBJECTIVE: Explain how a firm can increase its profits through price discrimination.

MyLab Economics   Visit www.pearson.com/mylab/economics to complete these exercises online and get instant feedback.

Summary

Price discrimination occurs if a firm charges different prices for the same product when the price differences are not due to differences in cost. Three requirements must be met for a firm to successfully practice price discrimination: (1) A firm must possess market power; (2) some consumers must have a greater willingness to pay for the product than other consumers, and firms must be able to know what consumers are willing to pay; and (3) firms must be able to divide up—or segment—the market for the product so that consumers who buy the product at a low price cannot resell it at a high price. In the case of *perfect price discrimination*, each consumer pays a price equal to his or her willingness to pay.

Review Questions

2.1 What is price discrimination? Under what circumstances can a firm successfully practice price discrimination?

2.2 In 2017, the Rock and Roll Hall of Fame and Museum charged the following admission prices:

Demographic	Admission Price
Adults	$23.50
College students	$18.00
Seniors (65 and older)	$21.25
Children between 6 and 12	$13.75
Military personnel	$19.00

Use the admission prices to rank these groups based on their elasticities of demand from highest to lowest.

Source: www.rockhall.com.

2.3 What is perfect price discrimination? Is it likely to ever occur? Is perfect price discrimination economically efficient? Briefly explain.

Problems and Applications

2.4 Some people—usually business travelers—have a very strong desire to fly to a particular city on a particular day, and airlines charge these travelers higher ticket prices than they charge other people, such as families who are planning vacations months in advance. Some people really like Big Macs, and other people only rarely eat Big Macs, preferring to eat other food for lunch on most days. Consider the following possible explanations of why airlines can charge different people different prices while McDonald's can't and briefly explain which explanation is correct.

1. In most cities, there are laws against charging different people different prices for food products.
2. Most people don't pay attention to prices when buying plane tickets, so the airlines can charge different prices without it being noticed.
3. People don't like hamburgers as much as they used to, so McDonald's has to keep cutting the prices it charges everyone.
4. People can't resell airline tickets, so people buying them at low prices can't resell them at high prices. People can resell hamburgers more easily.

2.5 Lexmark charges lower prices for its printer cartridges in some foreign countries than it charges in the United States. An article in the *Wall Street Journal* explained how a company in West Virginia bought Lexmark printer cartridges from retailers in foreign countries and resold the cartridges for higher prices in the United States.
   a. What must Lexmark be assuming about the price elasticity of demand for printer cartridges in the United States relative to the price elasticity of demand for printer cartridges in these foreign countries?

   b. Is Lexmark likely to be able to continue to price discriminating in this way? Briefly explain.

   Source: Daniel Hemel and Lisa Larrimore Ouellette, "How 'Price Discrimination' Helps Less-Affluent Countries," *Wall Street Journal*, March 20, 2017.

2.6 While in Shanghai, China, to teach an MBA course, Craig Richardson, an economics professor from Winston-Salem State University, asked his American students to haggle with sellers in a market where prices for the same items can vary widely. Professor Richardson explained that the same item with the same sticker price at different market stalls can have a final price that varies "by 1,500% or more, depending on the negotiating skills of the buyer."
   a. Do Shanghai merchants practice price discrimination? Briefly explain.
   b. Which consumers are likely to pay the highest prices for similar items in the Shanghai market?

   Source: Craig J. Richardson, "An Econ Lesson in a Shanghai Market," *Wall Street Journal*, July 6, 2015.

2.7 **(Related to the Chapter Opener on page 538)** When asked what was most valuable about the big data Disney was collecting from its MagicBands program, the executive in charge of the program stated, "The biggest value comes from being able to segment customers into better, smarter segments so you know what is going on and can act on those segments." Briefly explain his reasoning.

   Source: Elizabeth Miller Coyne, "The Disney Take on Big Data's Value," thenewip.net, January 13, 2015.

2.8 **(Related to the Chapter Opener on page 538)** In 2017, Disney offered a complex variety of ticket options for admission to Walt Disney World.
   a. Disney charged different prices for one-day tickets to its Disney World parks, depending on the time of the year. Summer and the winter holiday season had the highest ticket prices, while most weeks in the winter and spring had the lowest. But people buying tickets that could be used for more than one day paid the same price whatever time of the year they attended. Briefly explain what assumptions Disney must be making for this pricing strategy to increase its profit.
   b. A Disney World guide book notes that families have many different ticket options to choose from and that, "adding to the complexity, Disney's reservation agents are trained to avoid answering…which ticket option is 'best.' Many families, we suspect, become overwhelmed…and simply purchase a more expensive ticket with more features than they'll use." Can the complexity of Disney's ticket options be a form of price discrimination? If so, which people are likely to pay the higher ticket prices and which people the lower ticket prices?

   Source: Bob Sehlinger and Len Testa, *The Unofficial Guide to Walt Disney World, 2017*, Birmingham, AL: AdventureKEEN, 2017, p. 61.

2.9 In early 2017, a headline in the *Wall Street Journal* read: "Pricey Virtual-Reality Headsets Slow to Catch On." Is it possible that Sony, Facebook, and the other firms producing virtual-reality headsets were better off keeping prices high when initially offering them for sale, even if the result was a smaller quantity sold? Briefly explain.

   Source: Sarah E. Needleman, "Pricey Virtual-Reality Headsets Slow to Catch On," *Wall Street Journal*, February 14, 2017.

2.10 **(Related to the Don't Let This Happen to You on page 543)** A columnist on forbes.com offered the following advice to retailers practicing price discrimination: "Consumers don't much like the idea of other people getting better deals than are offered to them, and retailers need to be careful not to turn *differentiated* pricing into *discriminatory* pricing. There has to be a legal and ethical rationale for offering different prices to different customers." What would be a legally acceptable reason for offering different prices to different customers? What would be a legally unacceptable reason? Are there situations in which price discrimination might be legally acceptable but ethically unacceptable? Briefly explain.

Source: Nikki Baird, "Dynamic Pricing: When Should Retailers Bother?" forbes.com, April 18, 2017.

(a) Market 1

(b) Market 2

2.11 **(Related to Solved Problem 16.2 on page 544)** Use the graphs above to answer the questions.
   a. If this firm wants to maximize profit, what price will it charge in Market 1, and what quantity will it sell?
   b. If this firm wants to maximize profit, what price will it charge in Market 2, and what quantity will it sell?

2.12 **(Related to the Apply the Concept on page 546)** Jason Furman and Tim Simcoe, who were at the time chair of and a senior economist for President Barack Obama's Council of Economic Advisors, wrote, "Economists have studied [price discrimination] for many years, and while big data seems poised to revolutionize pricing practice, it has not altered the underlying principles. . . . Those principles suggest that [price discrimination] is often good for both firms and their customers." Furman and Simcoe described "need-based financial aid for college students" as an example of price discrimination that is good for consumers.
   a. What do Furman and Simcoe mean by "underlying principles"?
   b. In what sense is need-based financial aid an example of price discrimination? Is financial aid good for both colleges and students? Briefly explain.

Source: Jason Furman and Tim Simcoe, "The Economics of Big Data and Differential Pricing," www.whitehouse.gov/blog/2015/02/06/economics-big-data-and-differential-pricing, February 6, 2015.

2.13 **(Related to the Apply the Concept on page 546)** The Danish firm a2i Systems A/S sells software that helps service stations implement dynamic pricing strategies for gasoline sales. Service stations that use the software typically offer lower prices in the morning than in the afternoon and even raise prices when competing stations with very low prices have long lines. In an article in the *Wall Street Journal*, the firm's CEO noted, "This is not a matter of stealing more money from your customer. It's about making margin on people who don't care, and giving away margin to people who do care."
   a. What does the CEO mean by "margin"?
   b. Briefly explain how these pricing strategies "make margin" on customers who don't care and "give away margin" on customers who do care.

Source: Sam Schechner, "Why Do Gas Station Prices Constantly Change? Blame the Algorithm," *Wall Street Journal*, May 8, 2017.

2.14 **(Related to the Apply the Concept on page 546)** Many supermarkets provide regular shoppers with "loyalty cards." By swiping the card when checking out, a shopper receives reduced prices on a few goods, and the supermarket compiles information on all the shoppers' purchases. Some supermarkets have switched from giving the same price reductions to all shoppers to giving shoppers differing price reductions depending on their shopping history. A manager at one supermarket that uses this approach said, "It comes down to understanding elasticity at a household level."
   a. Is the use of loyalty cards that provide the same price discounts for every shopper who uses them a form of price discrimination? Briefly explain.
   b. Why would making price discounts depend on a shopper's buying history involve "understanding elasticity at a household level"? What information from a shopper's buying history would be relevant in predicting the shopper's response to a price discount?

Source: Stephanie Clifford, "Shopper Alert: Price May Drop for You Alone," *New York Times*, August 9, 2012.

2.15 Fernando has a monopoly on sales of pizzas in the small town of North Key Largo, Florida. Use the following information on the demand for Fernando's pizzas to answer the questions.

Price	Quantity Demanded
$30	0
25	1
20	2
15	3
10	4
5	5
0	6

a. If Fernando can produce pizzas at a constant cost of $5 per pizza, how many pizzas does he produce, what price does he charge, and how much profit does he make?

b. If Fernando is able to engage in perfect price discrimination, what is his total revenue for 3 pizzas? What is his marginal revenue from the third pizza?

c. If Fernando is able to engage in perfect price discrimination, how many pizzas does he produce, and how much profit does he make?

d. Draw a graph showing producer surplus, consumer surplus, and deadweight loss if Fernando does not price discriminate. Draw a second graph showing producer surplus, consumer surplus, and deadweight loss if Fernando practices perfect price discrimination.

16.3 Other Pricing Strategies, pages 551–556

LEARNING OBJECTIVE: Explain how some firms increase their profits by using odd pricing, cost-plus pricing, and two-part tariffs.

MyLab Economics   Visit **www.pearson.com/mylab/economics** to complete these exercises online and get instant feedback.

Summary

In addition to price discrimination, firms use odd pricing, cost-plus pricing, and two-part tariffs as pricing strategies. Firms use *odd pricing*—for example, charging $1.99 rather than $2.00—because consumers tend to buy more at odd prices than would be predicted from estimated demand curves. With *cost-plus pricing*, firms set the price for a product by adding a percentage markup to average total cost. Using cost-plus pricing may be a good way to come close to the profit-maximizing price when marginal revenue or marginal cost is difficult to measure. Some firms can require consumers to pay an initial fee for the right to buy their product and an additional fee for each unit of the product purchased. Economists refer to this situation as a **two-part tariff**. Sam's Club, cellphone companies, and many golf and tennis clubs use two-part tariffs in pricing their products.

Review Questions

3.1 What is odd pricing?

3.2 What is cost-plus pricing? Is using cost-plus pricing consistent with a firm maximizing profit? How does the elasticity of demand affect the percentage price markup that firms use?

3.3 Give an example of a firm using a two-part tariff as part of its pricing strategy.

Problems and Applications

3.4 One leading explanation for odd pricing is that it allows firms to trick buyers into thinking they are paying less than they really are. If this explanation is correct, in what types of markets and among what groups of consumers would you be most likely to find odd pricing? Should the government ban this practice and force companies to round up their prices to the nearest dollar? Briefly explain.

3.5 Instacart is a Web-based firm that offers home delivery of groceries. It buys the groceries in regular brick-and-mortar supermarkets, marks up the prices it pays, and then charges consumers the higher prices in exchange for making home deliveries. According to an article in the *Wall Street Journal*, Instacart marks up the price of potato chips by 26 percent, but it marks up the price of eggs by only 2.5 percent. Is it likely that Instacart believes that the demand for potato chips is more elastic or less elastic than the demand for eggs? Briefly explain.

Source: Greg Bensinger and Willa Plank, "A $5.39 Bag of Chips? Doing the Math on an Instacart Order," *Wall Street Journal*, January 15, 2015.

3.6 A review of Kappo Masa, a popular restaurant in New York City, noted, "The markup that New York restaurants customarily add to retail wine and sake prices is about 150 percent. The average markup at Kappo Masa is 200 percent to 300 percent." Even 150 percent is a much larger markup than the markups restaurants use to price the meals they serve. Why do restaurants use a higher markup for wine than for food, and why might a popular restaurant mark up the price of wine more than an average restaurant does?

Source: Pete Wells, "Restaurant Review: Kappo Masa on the Upper East Side," *New York Times*, January 6, 2015.

3.7 An article in the *Wall Street Journal* gave the following explanation of how products were traditionally priced at Parker Hannifin Corporation:

> For as long as anyone at the 89-year-old company could recall, Parker used the same simple formula to determine prices of its 800,000 parts—from heat-resistant seals for jet engines to steel valves that hoist buckets on cherry pickers. Company managers would calculate how much it cost to make and deliver each product and add a flat percentage on top, usually aiming for about 35%. Many managers liked the method because it was straightforward.

Is it likely that this system of pricing maximized the firm's profit? Briefly explain.

Source: Timothy Aeppel, "Seeking Perfect Prices, CEO Tears up the Rules," *Wall Street Journal*, March 27, 2007.

3.8 (Related to the Apply the Concept on page 552) Would you expect a publishing company to use a strict cost-plus pricing system for all its books? How might you find some indication about whether a publishing company actually is using cost-plus pricing for all its books?

3.9 Many colleges and universities have popular teams in one sport (usually football or basketball) for which there is a shortage of tickets for the teams' home games. In response to the shortage, some of the schools require people to make "charitable" contributions to the college or buy seat licenses that allow them to purchase season tickets. Referring to this practice, economist Phil Miller explained that this "is the two-part tariff that is so common in business these days . . . a person pays a flat fee to essentially get the right to buy a product and then has to pay again to buy the product. It's a way to obtain higher profits."

    a. Why would schools use a two-part tariff rather raising prices to eliminate shortages of tickets for their popular sports teams? (*Hint:* Refer to Chapter 10, Section 10.3.)

    b. Would the use of online brokers (for example, StubHub) that allow buyers of season tickets to resell tickets result in greater economic efficiency in this market? Explain briefly.

    Source: Phil Miller, "The Use of the Two-Part Tariff in College Ticket Pricing," *The Sports Economist*, June 17, 2010.

3.10 During the nineteenth century, the U.S. Congress encouraged railroad companies to build transcontinental railways across the Great Plains by giving them land grants. At that time, the federal government owned most of the land on the Great Plains. The land grants consisted of the land on which the railway was built and alternating sections of 1 square mile each on either side of the railway to a distance of 6 to 40 miles, depending on the location. The railroad companies were free to sell this land to farmers or anyone else who wanted to buy it. The process of selling the land took decades. Some economic historians have argued that the railroad companies charged lower prices to ship freight because they owned so much land along the tracks. Briefly explain the reasoning of these economic historians.

3.11 (Related to the Chapter Opener on page 538) If you visited Disneyland between 1955 and 1982, most rides would have required a ticket—in addition to the ticket necessary to enter the park. Explain why this pricing strategy earned Disney a lower profit than the current strategy of requiring visitors to purchase a ticket to enter the park but not requiring an additional ticket to be purchased for each ride.

3.12 Thomas Kinnaman, an economist at Bucknell University, analyzed the pricing of garbage collection:

> Setting the appropriate fee for garbage collection can be tricky when there are both fixed and marginal costs of garbage collection. . . . A curbside price set equal to the average total cost of collection would have high garbage generators partially subsidizing the fixed costs of low garbage generators. For example, if the time that a truck idles outside a one-can household and a two-can household is the same, and the fees are set to cover the total cost of garbage collection, then the two-can household paying twice that of the one-can household has subsidized a portion of the collection costs of the one-can household.

Briefly explain how a city might solve this pricing problem by using a two-part tariff in setting the garbage collection fees it charges households.

    Source: Thomas C. Kinnaman, "Examining the Justification for Residential Recycling," *Journal of Economic Perspectives*, Vol. 20, No. 4, Fall 2006, pp. 219–232.

Critical Thinking Exercises

CT16.1 For this exercise, your instructor may assign you to work with another student.

    a. With your partner, survey 10 people (perhaps fellow students in other classes or family members and friends) and ask them about their views on price discrimination. Use specific examples of price discrimination but do not actually use the term *price discrimination* in talking with the people you interview.

    b. Write a summary of your findings.

    c. Compare the answers from the people you interviewed with how economists view price discrimination.

    d. *Bonus:* Do you think that you would get different answers from students if your survey question mentioned student discounts? Briefly explain.

CT16.2 In 2017, major U.S. airlines started to offer tickets with a lower level of service for a lower price. Someone buying one of these tickets cannot store her carry-on bag in overhead storage, is in the last group to board, and has a seat assigned at the gate. Many airlines call this service "Basic Economy." News reports about this new class of airline ticket were often critical of the airlines, but how do you think an economist might view the airlines' new strategy?

CT16.3 Read "Amazon Introduces Discounted Monthly Prime Offer for Customers Receiving Government Assistance," from http://phx.corporate-ir.net/phoenix.zhtml?c=176060&p=irol-newsArticle&ID=2279027. Briefly explain whether Amazon is practicing price discrimination with this new offering.

17

The Markets for Labor and Other Factors of Production

Rio Tinto Mines with Robots

When most people think of coal and iron mines, they picture workers wearing lamp helmets and carrying shovels and picks. The London-based mining company Rio Tinto is changing that perception. At Rio Tinto's large iron mines in the Pilbara region of the Australian Outback, robotic machines now carry out many traditional mining jobs. The company uses large robotic drills to dig for iron ore deposits. Employees at computer consoles 800 miles away, in the city of Perth, control the operation of the drills. In the mines, the company uses machines to collect and load ore on 76 driverless trucks that bring the ore to trains for transport to the coast and then shipment abroad. The trucks, which are built in the United States by the Japanese company Komatsu, rely on sensors to safely drive in and around the mines. The company is currently using conventional trains to transport the ore to the coast for shipment, but it plans to introduce robotic trains that can be operated remotely.

Rio Tinto was able to introduce robotic machines into its mining operations thanks to developments in computer technology, the Global Positioning System (GPS), and robotics. The company's mining operations are another example of the "Internet of Things," in which devices directly communicate data to computers, without requiring people to enter the data. Rio Tinto had to pay high wages, often $100,000 or more per year, to attract miners and truck drivers to work in such a remote location as Pilbara. These high wages increased the company's incentive to adopt new robotic technology. In 2017, Rio Tinto's CEO Jean-Sébastien Jacques estimated that the driverless trucks reduced costs by 15 percent compared with trucks that use drivers.

Many companies have begun using new robotic technology to substitute capital for labor. Although robots are most widespread in manufacturing, particularly in assembling

Amy Coopes/AFP/Getty Images

automobiles, Amazon is planning to open grocery stores that use cameras and sensors to automatically charge customers and eliminate checkout lines and cashiers. Some people see the spread of robotic technology as a boon to the economy that will lead to higher living standards, but other people fear that robots will reduce the demand for labor enough to leave some workers permanently unemployed.

Throughout this book, we have used the model of demand and supply to analyze the markets for goods and services. As we will see, this model can also help us analyze important issues concerning the market for labor, including the effect of robotics.

Sources: John Dagge, "Rio Tinto Paves Road to Its Future with Rise of the Robots," heraldsun.com.au, April 12, 2017; Laura Stevens, "Amazon Delays Opening of Cashierless Store to Work out Kinks," *Wall Street Journal*, March 27, 2017; Matthew Hall, "Forget Self-Driving Google Cars, Australia Has Self-Driving Trucks," smh.com.au, October 20, 2014; and Timothy Aeppel, "Be Calm, Robots Aren't About to Take Your Job, MIT Economist Says," *Wall Street Journal*, February 25, 2015.

Chapter Outline & Learning Objectives

 17.1 The Demand for Labor, page 564
Explain how firms choose the profit-maximizing quantity of labor to employ.

 17.2 The Supply of Labor, page 568
Explain how people choose the quantity of labor to supply.

17.3 Equilibrium in the Labor Market, page 570
Explain how equilibrium wages are determined in labor markets.

17.4 Explaining Differences in Wages, page 577
Use demand and supply analysis to explain how compensating differentials, discrimination, and labor unions cause wages to differ.

17.5 Personnel Economics, page 585
Discuss the role personnel economics can play in helping firms deal with human resources issues.

 17.6 The Markets for Capital and Natural Resources, page 588
Show how equilibrium prices are determined in the markets for capital and natural resources.

Economics in Your Life & Career

When Should You Give an Employee a Raise?

Suppose you own a local sandwich shop and Sophia is one of your employees. She has worked in the shop for a year and asks you for a raise. She tells you that she is a good employee, with a good attitude and work ethic. She explains that she has learned to make sandwiches more quickly, track inventory more accurately, and work the cash register more effectively than when you hired her. Will you give her a raise? As you read this chapter, try to answer this question. You can check your answer against the one we provide on **page 591** at the end of this chapter.

Factors of production Labor, capital, natural resources, and other inputs used to produce goods and services.

Firms use **factors of production**—such as labor, capital, and natural resources—to produce goods and services. For example, the Rio Tinto mining company uses labor (the operators who remotely control its robotic equipment), capital (driverless trucks and other robotic equipment), and natural resources (iron ore) to produce the iron the company exports from Australia to other countries around the world. In this chapter, we will explore how firms choose the profit-maximizing quantity of labor and other factors of production. The interaction between firms' demand for labor and households' supply of labor determines the equilibrium wage rate.

Because there are many different types of labor, there are many different labor markets. The equilibrium wage in the market for professional athletes in major sports leagues is much higher than the equilibrium wage in the market for college professors. We will analyze why. We will also analyze how factors such as discrimination, unions, and compensation for dangerous or unpleasant jobs help explain differences in wages. We will then look at *personnel economics*, which is concerned with how firms can use economic analysis to design their employee compensation plans. Finally, we will analyze the markets for other factors of production.

17.1 The Demand for Labor

LEARNING OBJECTIVE: Explain how firms choose the profit-maximizing quantity of labor to employ.

Until this point in the book, we have concentrated on consumer demand for final goods and services. The demand for labor is different from the demand for final goods and services because it is a *derived demand*. A **derived demand** for a factor of production depends on the demand for the good the factor produces. You demand an Apple iPhone because of the utility you receive from making phone calls, texting, using Snapchat, playing games, and listening to music. Apple's demand for the labor to make iPhones is derived from the underlying consumer demand for iPhones. As a result, we can say that Apple's demand for labor depends primarily on two factors:

Derived demand The demand for a factor of production; it depends on the demand for the good the factor produces.

1. The additional iPhones Apple can produce if it hires one more worker
2. The additional revenue Apple receives from selling the additional iPhones

(In fact, Apple's suppliers, rather than Apple itself, manufacture the iPhone. For simplicity, we are assuming here that Apple does the manufacturing.)

The Marginal Revenue Product of Labor

Let's consider an example. To keep the main point clear, we'll assume that in the short run, Apple can increase production of iPhones only by increasing the quantity of labor it employs. The table in Figure 17.1 shows the relationship between the quantity of workers Apple hires, the quantity of iPhones it produces, the additional revenue from selling the additional iPhones, and the additional profit from hiring each additional worker.

For simplicity, we are keeping the scale of Apple's factory very small. We will also assume that Apple is a perfect competitor both in the market for selling smartphones and in the market for hiring labor. As a result, Apple is a *price taker* in both markets. Although this assumption is not realistic, the basic analysis would not change if we assumed that Apple can affect the price of smartphones and the wage paid to workers. Suppose that Apple can sell as many iPhones as it wants at a price of $200 and can hire as many workers as it wants at a wage of $600 per week. Remember that the additional output a firm produces as a result of hiring one more worker is called the **marginal product of labor** (see Chapter 11, Section 11.3). In the table in Figure 17.1, we calculate the marginal product of labor as the change in total output as each additional worker is hired. Because of the *law of diminishing returns*, the marginal product of labor declines as a firm hires more workers.

Marginal product of labor The additional output a firm produces as a result of hiring one more worker.

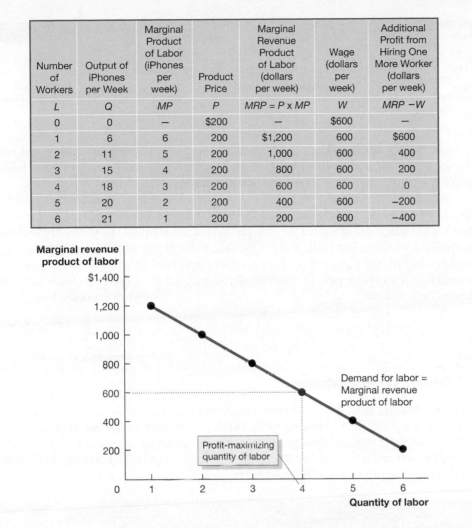

Number of Workers	Output of iPhones per Week	Marginal Product of Labor (iPhones per week)	Product Price	Marginal Revenue Product of Labor (dollars per week)	Wage (dollars per week)	Additional Profit from Hiring One More Worker (dollars per week)
L	Q	MP	P	MRP = P × MP	W	MRP − W
0	0	—	$200	—	$600	—
1	6	6	200	$1,200	600	$600
2	11	5	200	1,000	600	400
3	15	4	200	800	600	200
4	18	3	200	600	600	0
5	20	2	200	400	600	−200
6	21	1	200	200	600	−400

MyLab Economics Animation

Figure 17.1

The Marginal Revenue Product of Labor and the Demand for Labor

The marginal revenue product of labor equals the marginal product of labor multiplied by the price of the good. The marginal revenue product curve slopes downward because diminishing returns cause the marginal product of labor to decline as the firm hires more workers. A firm maximizes profit by hiring workers up to the point where the wage equals the marginal revenue product of labor. The marginal revenue product of labor curve is the firm's demand curve for labor because it tells the firm the profit-maximizing quantity of workers to hire at each wage. For example, using the demand curve shown in this figure, if the wage is $600, the firm will hire 4 workers.

When deciding how many workers to hire, a firm is not interested in how much *output* will increase as it hires another worker but in how much *revenue* will increase as it hires another worker. In other words, what matters is how much the firm's revenue will rise when it sells the additional output it can produce by hiring one more worker. We can calculate this amount, which is called the **marginal revenue product of labor (MRP)**, by multiplying the additional output produced by the product price. For example, consider what happens if Apple increases the number of workers hired from 2 to 3. The table in Figure 17.1 shows that hiring the third worker allows Apple to increase its weekly output of iPhones from 11 to 15, so the marginal product of labor is 4 iPhones. The price of the iPhones is $200, so the marginal revenue product of the third worker is 4 × $200, or $800. In other words, Apple adds $800 to its revenue as a result of hiring the third worker. In the graph, we plot the values of the marginal revenue product of labor at each quantity of labor.

To decide how many workers to hire, Apple compares the additional revenue it earns from hiring another worker to the increase in its costs from paying that worker. The difference between the additional revenue and the additional cost is the additional profit (or loss) from hiring one more worker. This additional profit is shown in the last column of the table in Figure 17.1 and is calculated by subtracting the wage from the marginal revenue product of labor. As long as the marginal revenue product of labor is greater than the wage, Apple's profit is increasing, and it should continue to hire more workers. When the marginal revenue product of labor is less than the wage, Apple's profit is falling, and it should hire fewer workers. When the marginal revenue product of labor is equal to the wage, Apple has maximized its profit by hiring the optimal number of workers. The values in the table show that Apple should hire 4 workers.

Marginal revenue product of labor (MRP) The change in a firm's revenue as a result of hiring one more worker.

Table 17.1

The Relationship between the Marginal Revenue Product of Labor and the Wage

When . . .	the firm . . .
$MRP > W$,	should hire more workers to increase profit.
$MRP < W$,	should hire fewer workers to increase profit.
$MRP = W$,	is hiring the optimal number of workers and is maximizing profit.

If Apple hires a fifth worker, the marginal revenue product of $400 will be less than the wage of $600, and its profit will fall by $200. Table 17.1 summarizes the relationship between the marginal revenue product of labor and the wage.

We can see from Figure 17.1 that if Apple has to pay a wage of $600 per week, it should hire 4 workers. If the wage rises to $1,000, then applying the rule that profit is maximized where the marginal revenue product of labor equals the wage, Apple should hire only 2 workers. Similarly, if the wage falls to $400 per week, Apple should hire 5 workers. In fact, the marginal revenue product curve tells a firm how many workers it should hire at any wage rate. In other words, *the marginal revenue product of labor curve is the demand curve for labor.* **MyLab Economics** Concept Check

Solved Problem 17.1

MyLab Economics Interactive Animation

Hiring Decisions by a Firm That Is a Price Maker

We have assumed that Apple can sell as many iPhones as it wants without having to cut the price. A firm in a perfectly competitive market is in this situation. These firms are *price takers.* Suppose instead that a firm has market power and is a *price maker,* so that to increase sales, it must reduce the price.

Assume that Apple faces the situation shown in the following table. Fill in the missing values and then determine the profit-maximizing quantity of workers for Apple to hire. Briefly explain why hiring this quantity of workers is profit maximizing.

(1) Quantity of Labor	(2) Output of iPhones per Week	(3) Marginal Product of Labor	(4) Product Price	(5) Total Revenue	(6) Marginal Revenue Product of Labor	(7) Wage	(8) Additional Profit from Hiring One Additional Worker
0	0	—	$200		—	$500	—
1	6	6	180			500	
2	11	5	160			500	
3	15	4	140			500	
4	18	3	120			500	
5	20	2	100			500	
6	21	1	80			500	

Solving the Problem

Step 1: **Review the chapter material.** This problem is about determining the profit-maximizing quantity of labor for a firm to hire, so you may want to review the section "The Demand for Labor," which begins on page 564.

Step 2: **Fill in the missing values in the table.** As Apple hires more workers, it sells more iPhones and earns more revenue. You can calculate how revenue increases by multiplying the quantity of iPhones produced—shown in column (2)—by the price—shown in column (4). Then you can calculate the marginal revenue product of labor as the change in revenue as each additional worker is hired. (Notice that in this case, marginal revenue product is *not* calculated by multiplying the marginal product by the product price. Because Apple is a price maker, its marginal revenue from selling additional iPhones is less than the price of iPhones.) Finally, you can calculate the additional profit from hiring one more worker by subtracting the wage—shown in column (7)—from each worker's marginal revenue product.

(1) Quantity of Labor	(2) Output of iPhones per Week	(3) Marginal Product of Labor	(4) Product Price	(5) Total Revenue	(6) Marginal Revenue Product of Labor	(7) Wage	(8) Additional Profit from Hiring One Additional Worker
0	0	—	$200	$0	—	$500	—
1	6	6	180	1,080	$1,080	500	$580
2	11	5	160	1,760	680	500	180
3	15	4	140	2,100	340	500	−160
4	18	3	120	2,160	60	500	−440
5	20	2	100	2,000	−160	500	−660
6	21	1	80	1,680	−320	500	−820

Step 3: **Use the information in the table to determine the profit-maximizing quantity of workers to hire.** To determine the profit-maximizing quantity of workers to hire, you need to compare the marginal revenue product of labor with the wage. Column (8) makes this comparison by subtracting the wage from the marginal revenue product. As long as the values in column (8) are positive, the firm should continue to hire workers. The marginal revenue product of the second worker is $680, and the wage is $500, so column (8) shows that hiring the second worker will add $180 to Apple's profit. The marginal revenue product of the third worker is $340, and the wage is $500, so hiring the third worker would reduce Apple's profit by $160. Therefore, Apple will maximize profit by hiring 2 workers.

Your Turn: For more practice, do related problem 1.6 on page 592 at the end of this chapter.

MyLab Economics Study Plan

The Market Demand Curve for Labor

We can determine the market demand curve for labor in the same way we determine the market demand curve for a good—by adding up the quantity of the good demanded by each consumer at each price (see Chapter 10, Section 10.2). To find the market demand curve for labor, we add up the quantity of labor demanded by each firm at each wage, holding constant all other variables that might affect the willingness of firms to hire workers.

MyLab Economics Concept Check

Factors That Shift the Market Demand Curve for Labor

In constructing the demand curve for labor, we held constant all variables—except for the wage—that would affect the willingness of firms to demand labor. An increase or a decrease in the wage causes *an increase or a decrease in the quantity of labor demanded*, which we show by a movement along the demand curve. If any variable other than the wage changes, the result is *an increase or a decrease in the demand for labor*, which we show by a shift of the demand curve. The following are the five most important variables that cause the labor demand curve to shift:

1. **Increases in human capital. Human capital** represents the accumulated knowledge and skills that workers acquire from formal training and education or from life experiences. For example, a worker with a college education generally has more skills and is more productive than a worker who has only a high school diploma. If workers become more educated and are therefore able to produce more output per day, the demand for their services will increase, shifting the labor demand curve to the right.

Human capital The accumulated knowledge and skills that workers acquire from formal training and education or from life experiences.

2. **Changes in technology.** As new and better machinery and equipment are developed, workers who use them become more productive. This effect causes the labor demand curve to shift to the right over time.

3. **Changes in the price of the product.** The marginal revenue product of labor depends on the price a firm receives for its output. A higher price increases the marginal revenue product and shifts the labor demand curve to the right. A lower price shifts the labor demand curve to the left.

4. **Changes in the quantity of other inputs.** Workers are able to produce more if they have more machinery and other inputs available to them. The marginal product of labor in the United States is higher than the marginal product of labor in most other countries in large part because U.S. firms provide workers with more machinery and equipment. Over time, workers in the United States have had increasing amounts of other inputs available to them, which has increased their productivity and caused the labor demand curve to shift to the right.

5. **Changes in the number of firms in the market.** If new firms enter the market, the labor demand curve will shift to the right. If firms exit the market, the demand for labor will shift to the left. The result is similar to the effect that increasing or decreasing the number of consumers in a market has on the demand for a good.

MyLab Economics Study Plan

MyLab Economics Concept Check

 17.2 The Supply of Labor

LEARNING OBJECTIVE: Explain how people choose the quantity of labor to supply.

Now that we have discussed the demand for labor, we can consider the supply of labor. Of the many trade-offs each of us faces in life, one of the most important is how to divide up the 24 hours in a day between labor and leisure. Every hour spent posting to Snapchat, walking in a park, or in other forms of leisure is one hour less spent working. Because in devoting an hour to leisure we give up an hour's earnings from working, the *opportunity cost* of leisure is the wage. The higher the wage we could earn working, the higher the opportunity cost of leisure. Therefore, as the wage increases, we tend to take less leisure and work more. As Figure 17.2 shows, the result is that the labor supply curve for most people is upward sloping.

Although we normally expect the labor supply curve for an individual to be upward sloping, it is possible that at very high wage levels, the labor supply curve of an individual might be *backward bending*, so that higher wages actually result in a *smaller* quantity of labor supplied, as shown in Figure 17.3. To understand why, recall the definitions of the *substitution effect* and the *income effect* (see Chapter 3, Section 3.1 and Chapter 10, Section 10.1). The substitution effect of a price change refers to the fact that an increase in price makes a good more expensive *relative* to other goods. In the case of a wage change, the substitution

MyLab Economics Animation

Figure 17.2

The Labor Supply Curve

As the wage increases, the opportunity cost of leisure increases, causing individuals to supply a greater quantity of labor. Therefore, the labor supply curve is upward sloping.

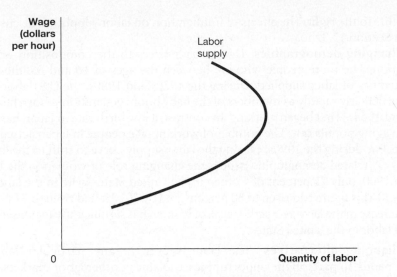

MyLab Economics Animation

Figure 17.3

A Backward-Bending Labor Supply Curve

As the wage rises, a greater quantity of labor is usually supplied. As the wage rises above a certain level, the individual is able to afford more leisure even though the opportunity cost of leisure is higher. The result may be that an increase in the wage leads to a smaller quantity of labor supplied.

effect refers to the fact that an increase in the wage raises the opportunity cost of leisure and causes a worker to devote *more* time to working and less time to leisure.

The income effect of a price change refers to the change in the quantity demanded of a good that results from changes in consumer purchasing power as the price changes. An increase in the wage will clearly increase a consumer's purchasing power for any given number of hours worked. For a normal good, the income effect leads to a larger quantity demanded. Because leisure is a normal good, the income effect of a wage increase will cause a worker to devote *less* time to working and more time to leisure. So, the substitution effect of a wage increase causes a worker to supply a larger quantity of labor, but the income effect causes a worker to supply a smaller quantity of labor. Whether a worker supplies more or less labor following a wage increase depends on whether the substitution effect is larger than the income effect.

Figure 17.3 shows the common case of the substitution effect being larger than the income effect at low levels of wages—so the worker supplies a larger quantity of labor as the wage rises—and the income effect being larger than the substitution effect at high levels of wages—so the worker supplies a smaller quantity of labor as the wage rises. For example, suppose an attorney has become quite successful and can charge clients very high fees. Or suppose a rock band has become very popular and receives a large payment for every concert. In these cases, there is a high opportunity cost for the lawyer to turn down another client to take a longer vacation or for the band to turn down another concert. But because their incomes are already very high, they may decide to give up additional income for more leisure. In this case, for the lawyer or the rock band, the income effect is larger than the substitution effect, and a higher wage causes them to supply *less* labor.

The Market Supply Curve of Labor

We can determine the market supply curve of labor in the same way we determine a market supply curve of a good. We find the market supply curve of a good by adding up the quantity of the good supplied by each firm at each price (see Chapter 12, Section 12.4). Similarly, we find the market supply curve of labor by adding up the quantity of labor supplied by each worker at each wage, holding constant all other variables that might affect the willingness of workers to supply labor. MyLab Economics Concept Check

Factors That Shift the Market Supply Curve of Labor

In constructing the market supply curve of labor, we hold constant all other variables that would affect the willingness of workers to supply labor, except the wage. If any of these other variables change, the market supply curve will shift. The following are the three most important variables that cause the market supply curve of labor to shift:

1. **Increasing population.** As the population grows due to the number of births exceeding the number of deaths and due to immigration, the supply curve of labor

shifts to the right. The effects of immigration on labor supply are discussed further in Section 17.3.

2. **Changing demographics.** *Demographics* refers to the composition of the population. The more people who are between the ages of 16 and 65, the greater the quantity of labor supplied. During the 1970s and 1980s, the U.S. labor force grew particularly rapidly as members of the baby boom generation—born between 1946 and 1964—first began working. In contrast, a low birth rate in Japan has resulted in an aging population. The number of working-age people in Japan actually began to decline during the 1990s, causing the labor supply curve to shift to the left.

A related demographic issue is the changing role of women in the labor force. In 1900, only 21 percent of women in the United States were in the labor force. By 1950, this figure had risen to 30 percent, and by 2017 it had risen to 57 percent. This increase in the *labor force participation* of women has significantly increased the supply of labor in the United States.

3. **Changing alternatives.** The labor supply in any particular labor market depends, in part, on the opportunities available in other labor markets. For example, declining sales at department stores such as Macy's and JCPenney have led to layoffs at those firms. Many workers have left the market for labor at brick-and-mortar retail stores—causing the labor supply curve to shift to the left—and entered other markets, causing the labor supply curves to shift to the right in those markets. People who have lost jobs or who have low incomes are eligible for unemployment insurance and other payments from the government. The more generous these payments are, the less pressure unemployed workers have to quickly find another job. In many European countries, it is much easier than in the United States for unemployed workers to replace a larger fraction of their wage income with government payments. Many economists believe generous unemployment benefits help explain the higher unemployment rates experienced in some European countries.

MyLab Economics Study Plan

MyLab Economics Concept Check

 ## Equilibrium in the Labor Market

LEARNING OBJECTIVE: Explain how equilibrium wages are determined in labor markets.

In Figure 17.4, we bring together labor demand and labor supply to determine equilibrium in the labor market. We can use demand and supply to analyze changes in the equilibrium wage and the level of employment for the entire labor market, and we can also use it to analyze markets for different types of labor, such as baseball players or college professors.

MyLab Economics Animation

Figure 17.4

Equilibrium in the Labor Market

As in other markets, equilibrium in the labor market occurs where the demand curve for labor and the supply curve of labor intersect.

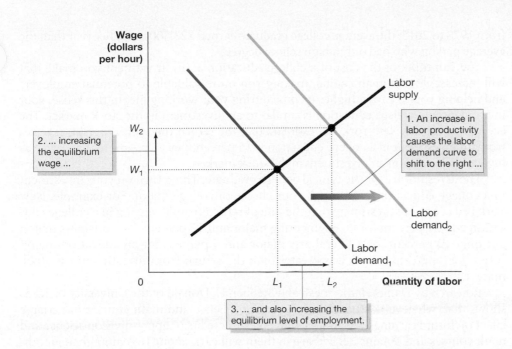

MyLab Economics Animation

Figure 17.5

The Effect of an Increase in Labor Demand

Increases in labor demand will cause the equilibrium wage and the equilibrium level of employment to rise:

1. If the productivity of workers rises, the marginal revenue product increases, causing the labor demand curve to shift to the right.
2. The equilibrium wage rises from W_1 to W_2.
3. The equilibrium level of employment rises from L_1 to L_2.

The Effect on Equilibrium Wages of a Shift in Labor Demand

In many labor markets, increases over time in labor productivity will cause the demand for labor to increase. As Figure 17.5 shows, if labor supply is unchanged, an increase in labor demand will increase both the equilibrium wage and the number of workers employed.   **MyLab Economics** Concept Check

Apply the Concept   MyLab Economics Video

Is Investing in a College Education a Good Idea?

You pay a cost to attend college: both the monetary cost of paying for tuition, books, and other expenses and the nonmonetary opportunity cost of delaying your entry into the workforce. Is the cost worth it?

Most people realize the value of a college education. As the following graph shows, in 2017, full-time workers aged 25 and over with a college degree earned more per week than other workers; for example, they earned 2.5 times as much as high school dropouts. The earnings premium from a college education has persisted over time. A study by economists at the Federal Reserve Bank of New York estimated that over the period

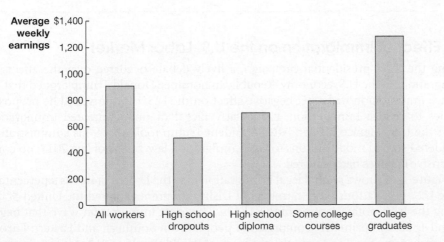

Source: U.S. Bureau of Labor Statistics, "Usual Weekly Earnings of Wage and Salary Workers, First Quarter 2017," April 18, 2017.

from 1970 to 2013, the average college graduate earned $23,500 more per year than the average person who had only a high school degree.

You can think of the cost of a college education as an investment you make that will increase your human capital, making you more valuable to potential employers and helping you to earn a higher income during your working life. In this sense, your investment in a college education is similar to an investment in the stock market. The economists at the New York Fed estimate that the return the typical person receives from an investment in a college education is 15 percent per year—more than twice as high as the return on an investment in the stock market.

These results are for the typical college graduate. The return on your investment in a college education varies with your choice of college major. For example, New York Fed economists estimate that the rate of return from investing in a college education was 21 percent for an engineering major and 17 percent for a business major, but only 12 percent for a liberal arts major and 9 percent for an education major. (Even the 9 percent return was greater than the return from investing in the stock market.)

Research by Daniel Hamermesh and Stephen G. Donald of the University of Texas shows that, whatever a student's major, taking science and math courses has a large effect on future earnings: "A student who takes 15 credits of upper-division science and math courses and obtains a B average in them will earn about 10% more than an otherwise identical student in the same major . . . who takes no upper-division classes in these areas." This result held even after adjusting for a student's SAT score.

In economic recessions when unemployment in the economy rises, college graduates are less likely to lose their jobs and are likely to experience smaller declines in wages than are high school graduates. Research by Joseph Altonji, Lisa Kahn, and Jamin Speer of Yale University indicates that people with certain college majors fare better during recessions than people with other college majors. For example, during years when the economy is not in recession, economics majors earn about 25 percent more than the average of all college graduates. During recessions, economics majors earn about 35 percent more than the typical college graduate, as their earnings decline by less. If graduating from college is a good idea, majoring in economics is a particularly good idea—and taking some science and math courses isn't a bad idea, either!

Sources: Joseph G. Altonji, Lisa B. Kahn, and Jamin D. Speer, "Cashier or Consultant? Entry Labor Market Conditions, Field of Study, and Career Success," *Journal of Labor Economics*, Vol. 34, No. S1, Pt. 2, January 2016, pp. S361–S401; Claire Cain Miller, "A College Major Matters Even More in a Recession," *New York Times*, June 20, 2014; Jaison R. Abel and Richard Deitz, "Do the Benefits of College Still Outweigh the Costs?" Federal Reserve Bank of New York, *Current Issues in Economics and Finance*, Vol. 20, No. 3, 2014; and Daniel S. Hamermesh and Stephen G. Donald, "The Effect of College Curriculum on Earnings: An Affinity Identifier for Non-Ignorable Non-Response Bias," *Journal of Econometrics*, Vol. 144, No. 2, June 2008, pp. 479–491.

MyLab Economics Study Plan   **Your Turn:** Test your understanding by doing related problem 3.3 on page 594 at the end of this chapter.

The Effect of Immigration on the U.S. Labor Market

During the 2016 presidential campaign, a lively debate occurred over the effects of immigration on the U.S. economy. Republican nominee Donald Trump argued that on balance immigration had a net negative effect on the U.S. economy, and he proposed policies to reduce immigration, particularly illegal or undocumented immigration across the U.S.–Mexico border. After President Trump took office, his administration considered several modifications to U.S. immigration law, but as of late 2017, no comprehensive changes had occurred.

Figure 17.6 shows annual legal immigration into the United States as a percentage of the U.S. population. Large numbers of Irish immigrants entered the United States during the Irish potato famine of the 1840s. The great immigration wave that began around 1880 was primarily comprised of people from Southern and Eastern Europe and largely came to an end with the outbreak of World War I in 1914. After an increase in immigration following the war, Congress passed the Immigration Act of 1924,

MyLab Economics Animation

Figure 17.6   **Legal Immigration into the United States**

Prior to the early 1920s, there were few restrictions on immigration into the United States. Congressional legislation limited immigration from the 1920s through the mid-1960s, until Congress eased restrictions with passage of the Immigration Act of 1965. A surge in immigration followed passage of the Immigration Act of 1990. Currently, foreign-born residents make up about 13.5 percent of the U.S. population.

Sources: U.S. Department of Homeland Security, *Yearbook of Immigration Statistics 2015*, Table 1; and Susan B. Carter et al., eds., *Historical Statistics of the United States, Millennial Edition Online*, Series Aa7.

which resulted in lower rates of immigration until Congress passed less restrictive legislation in 1965. The Immigration Act of 1990 raised ceilings on legal immigration and resulted in a temporary surge in immigration. In recent years, the bulk of immigrants have come from Latin America, particularly Mexico, and Asia, particularly China and India. In 2015, the foreign-born population was about 43 million (including about 11 million undocumented immigrants), which was about 13.5 percent of the total U.S. population of about 320 million.

Policymakers and economists have debated the overall effects of immigration on the U.S. economy. The most direct effect of immigration is to increase the labor supply. As Figure 17.7 shows, if labor demand is unchanged, an increase in labor supply due to immigration will decrease the equilibrium wage while increasing the number of workers employed.

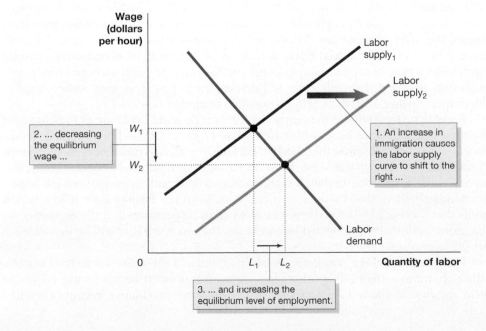

MyLab Economics Animation

Figure 17.7

The Effect of an Increase in Labor Supply Due to Immigration

Increases in labor supply will cause the equilibrium wage to fall but the equilibrium level of employment to rise:
1. Immigration causes the labor supply curve to shift to the right.
2. The equilibrium wage falls from W_1 to W_2.
3. The equilibrium level of employment increases from L_1 to L_2.

The analysis in Figure 17.7 is simplified because it assumes that there is only a single national labor market, while in reality there are many regional labor markets as well as different markets for different types of labor. It also assumes that immigration does not affect the demand for labor, which it may if, for example, immigrants are responsible for innovations that raise productivity and, therefore, the demand for labor. The great immigration wave from 1880 to 1914 appears to have had a surprisingly small effect on average wages. Some economists believe that the increase in the labor supply due to immigration helped spur the rise of high-productivity mass-production methods in the automobile and other industries. The resulting increase in the marginal product of labor increased labor demand sufficiently to offset the increase in labor supply, leaving the average wage rate largely unchanged. Economists' estimates of the effect on wages of recent immigration vary, but there is some consensus that immigration is likely to have reduced the wages of low-skilled native-born workers. Such a result is consistent with the outcome shown in Figure 17.7, under the assumption that increased immigration has not affected the demand for labor in the market for unskilled workers.

Currently, legal immigrants to the United States are on average older and somewhat more likely to be college graduates than the native-born population, while undocumented immigrants are younger and significantly less likely to be college graduates. Both legal and undocumented male immigrants are more likely to be employed than are native-born males, while women immigrants are less likely to be employed than are native-born women.

The economic and non-economic effects of immigration are too wide-ranging to be analyzed in this text but include such issues as (1) the increasing fraction of STEM (science, technology, engineering, and mathematics) workers who are immigrants and the contributions these workers make to technological progress in the United States; (2) the effect of immigrants on local governments' social services and school budgets; (3) the rate at which new immigrants assimilate to U.S. society; (4) the role of immigration in maintaining population growth during a period of declining U.S. birth rates; and (5) the concentration of immigrant workers in certain industries, including farming, construction, hotels, and restaurants.

MyLab Economics Study Plan   **MyLab Economics** Concept Check

Apply the Concept   MyLab Economics Video

Will You Compete with a Robot for a Job—Or Work with One?

Will you have trouble finding a job because robots will eventually become sophisticated enough to replace people in a wide range of occupations? Economists who have studied the effects of robots are divided in their answers to this question. First, although there is no universally agreed upon definition of robots, most economists consider them to be a type of capital that performs sophisticated physical activities that previously only people performed. So the self-driving trucks Rio Tinto uses, as described in the chapter opener, are robots, while a personal computer is not.

Fears that firms will permanently reduce their demand for labor as they increase their use of capital date back at least to the late 1700s in England, when textile workers known as *Luddites*—after their leader Ned Ludd—smashed machinery in an attempt to save their jobs. Since that time, the term Luddite has described people who oppose increases in capital because they fear the increases will result in permanent job losses. Economists believe that these fears often stem from the *lump-of-labor fallacy*, which holds that there is only a fixed amount of work to be performed in the economy. So the more work that is performed by machines, the less work that will be available for people to perform.

However, capital is a *complement* to labor, as well as a substitute for it. For instance, although some automobile workers lost their jobs as firms began to use robots to weld car chassis, the remaining workers became more productive because they had additional capital to work with, and their productivity resulted in higher wages. In fact, most economists agree that the main reason that the wages of workers today are much higher than they were 100 years ago is that workers today are much more productive because they have more capital to work with. Higher productivity can also reduce firms' costs, leading to lower prices. Lower prices increase the quantity of goods demanded and, therefore, the demand for labor.

Will this long-run trend toward ever higher productivity and wages continue as more of the increases in capital involve robots and other new technologies associated with the Internet of Things? Most economists are optimistic that these new technologies will lead to higher productivity and wages, although some economists take a more pessimistic view. For example, Carl Benedikt Frey and Michael A. Osborne of the University of Oxford estimate that as many as 47 percent of U.S. workers could lose their current jobs to robots and other new technology. Seth Benzell of Boston University and colleagues argue that it is possible that although the higher productivity due to robots will result in lower prices of goods and services, this benefit will be offset by the lower wages workers earn after losing their current jobs.

Economists have also looked at the effects of robots and other new technologies on particular occupations. David Autor, of the Massachusetts Institute of Technology, has divided workers into three broad categories: highly skilled workers, middle-skilled workers, and low-skilled workers. We can use labor demand and supply analysis to explain the trends in employment and wages in these three categories of workers:

1. **Highly skilled workers, such as doctors, lawyers, managers, and software engineers.** Both employment and wages in these occupations have generally increased in recent years. In this category of workers, robots and other new technologies are often complementary to workers. As a result, the productivity of these workers has increased, raising the demand for them. For instance, Rio Tinto has substantially increased its demand for network technicians with mechanical engineering and electrical engineering skills to maintain and remotely operate its robotic drills and trucks. The figure below shows the demand curve for these workers shifting to the right, from Labor demand$_1$ to Labor demand$_2$, resulting in an increase in the equilibrium wage and in the equilibrium quantity of workers employed. The labor supply curve in these occupations is likely to be relatively inelastic because these workers have skills and specialized training—some have advanced degrees—which means it takes substantial time before rising wages significantly increase the quantity of labor supplied.

2. **Middle-skilled workers, such as salespeople, office workers, carpenters, plumbers, and factory workers.** Both employment and wages in these occupations have generally declined in recent years. In this category, robots and new

technology are often substitutes for workers; for instance, the robotic truck and drill technology at Rio Tinto's mines are a substitute for the drivers and drill operators the company previously employed. The largest user of robots in the United States is the automobile industry. Although automobile sales in the United States reached a record high in 2016, automobile manufacturers produced this level of output using 30 percent fewer workers than they employed as recently as 2000. The figure below shows the demand curve for these workers shifting to left, from Labor demand$_1$ to Labor demand$_2$, resulting in a decrease in the equilibrium wage and in the equilibrium quantity of workers employed. (Note, though, that in the case of automobile workers, rising productivity resulted in higher wages.)

3. **Lower-skilled workers, such as food workers, health care aides, janitors, and flight attendants.** Employment has generally increased in these occupations in recent years, but wages have declined. Robots and new technology have relatively little effect on the workers in this category. For the most part, robots have not replaced servers in restaurants, home health care aides, and similar workers. Nor are the new technologies complements to the tasks—cooking, cleaning, helping the elderly—these workers perform. New technologies have therefore not had a significant effect on the demand for these workers. (Although the aging of the population and rising incomes have increased demand for the services some of these workers provide, for simplicity, we will ignore this fact.) The figure below shows the labor demand curve as unchanged. However, some workers from the second category—factory workers and office workers, for example—who have lost their jobs have shifted into the occupations in this third category, causing the labor supply curve to shift to the right, from Labor supply$_1$ to Labor supply$_2$, resulting in an increase in the equilibrium quantity of workers employed but a decrease in the equilibrium wage.

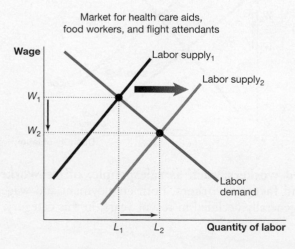

The process of workers and firms adapting to robots and other new technologies is ongoing, and economists continue to debate what the long-run consequences of these technologies will be.

Sources: Carl Benedikt Frey and Michael A. Osborne, "The Future of Employment: How Susceptible Are Jobs to Computerisation?" www.oxfordmartin.ox.ac.uk, September 17, 2013; Mira Rojanasakul and Peter Coy, "More Robots, Fewer Jobs," bloomberg.com, May 8, 2017; Timothy Aeppel, "What Clever Robots Mean for Jobs," *Wall Street Journal*, February 24, 2015; Seth G. Benzell et al., "Robots Are Us: Some Economics of Human Replacement," National Bureau of Economic Research, Working Paper No. 20941, February 2015; and David H. Autor, "Polanyi's Paradox and the Shape of Employment Growth," in Federal Reserve Bank of Kansas City, *Re-Evaluating Labor Market Dynamics*, 2014, pp. 129–177.

Your Turn: Test your understanding by doing related problem 3.8 on page 595 at the end of this chapter.

MyLab Economics Study Plan

17.4 Explaining Differences in Wages

LEARNING OBJECTIVE: Use demand and supply analysis to explain how compensating differentials, discrimination, and labor unions cause wages to differ.

A key conclusion of our discussion of the labor market is that the equilibrium wage equals the marginal revenue product of labor. The more productive workers are and the higher the price for which workers' output can be sold, the higher the wages workers will receive. We can expand on this conclusion by using the demand and supply model to analyze why wages differ. For instance, many people wonder why professional athletes are paid so much more than most other workers. Figure 17.8 shows the demand and supply curves for Major League Baseball players and the demand and supply curves for college professors.

Consider the marginal revenue product of baseball players, which is the additional revenue a team owner will receive from hiring one more player. Baseball players are hired to produce baseball games that are then sold to fans, who pay admission to baseball stadiums, and to radio and television stations, cable systems, and apps that broadcast or stream the games. Because a Major League Baseball team can sell each baseball game for a large amount, the marginal revenue product of baseball players is high. The supply of people with the ability to play Major League Baseball is also very limited. As a result, the average annual salary of the 750 Major League Baseball players was $4,470,000 in 2017.

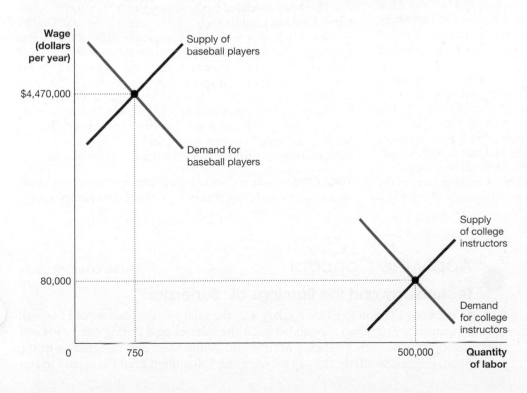

MyLab Economics Animation

Figure 17.8

Baseball Players Are Paid More Than College Instructors

The marginal revenue product of baseball players is very high, and the supply of people with the ability to play Major League Baseball is low. The result is that the 750 Major League Baseball players receive an average wage of $4,470,000. The marginal revenue product of college professors is much lower, and the supply of people with the ability to be college professors is much higher. The result is that the 500,000 full-time college instructors in the United States receive an average wage of $80,000, far below the average wage of baseball players.

The marginal revenue product of full-time college instructors is much lower than for baseball players. College instructors are hired to produce college educations that are sold to students and their parents. Although one year's college tuition is quite high at many colleges, hiring one more full-time instructor allows a college to admit at most a few more students. So, the marginal revenue product of a college instructor is much lower than the marginal revenue product of a baseball player. There are also many more people who possess the skills to be a college instructor than who possess the skills to be a Major League Baseball player. As a result, the average annual salary of the country's 500,000 full-time college instructors was about $80,000 in 2017.

We can use this analysis to answer the additional question of why the best professional athletes tend to end up in the largest cities. For example, in 2017, the highest-paid baseball player was Los Angeles Dodgers pitcher Clayton Kershaw, whose salary was $33 million. Why are the Dodgers willing to pay Kershaw more than other teams such as the Pittsburgh Pirates or Kansas City Royals would? Kershaw's marginal product—which we can think of as the extra games a team will win by employing him—should be about the same in Los Angeles as in Pittsburgh or Kansas City. But his *marginal revenue product* will be higher in Los Angeles. Because the Dodgers play in the second-largest metropolitan area in the United States, the number of Dodgers fans is much larger than the number of Pittsburgh or Kansas City fans, so winning additional games will result in a greater increase in attendance at Dodgers games than it would at Pirates or Royals games. It will also result in a greater increase in people watching Dodgers games on television or as streaming video. Therefore, the Dodgers are able to sell the extra wins that Kershaw produces for much more than the Pirates or Royals could. This difference explains why the Dodgers are willing to pay Kershaw much more than the Pirates or Royals would.

Don't Let This Happen to You

Remember That Prices and Wages Are Determined at the Margin

You have probably heard some variation of the following remark: "We could live without baseball, but we can't live without the trash being hauled away. In a more rational world, trash collectors would be paid more than baseball players." This remark seems logical: The total value to society of having the trash hauled away certainly is greater than the total value of baseball games. But wages—like prices—do not depend on total value but on *marginal* value. The *additional* baseball games the Los Angeles Dodgers have won by employing Clayton Kershaw, rather than a less skilled pitcher, has resulted in millions of dollars in increased revenue. The supply of people with the ability to play Major League Baseball is very limited. The supply of people with the ability to be trash collectors is much greater. If a trash-hauling firm hires another worker, the *additional* trash-hauling services it can now offer will bring in a

relatively small amount of revenue. The *total* value of baseball games and the *total* value of trash hauling are not relevant in determining the relative salaries of baseball players and trash collectors.

This point is related to the *diamond and water paradox* Adam Smith noted in 1776 in his book *The Wealth of Nations*. On the one hand, water is very valuable—we literally couldn't live without it—but its price is very low. On the other hand, apart from a few industrial purposes, diamonds are used only for jewelry, yet their price is quite high. We resolve the paradox by noting that the price of water is low because the supply is very large, and the additional benefit consumers receive from the last gallon purchased is low. The price of diamonds is high because the supply is very small, and the additional benefit consumers receive from the last diamond purchased is high.

Your Turn: Test your understanding by doing related problem 4.5 on page 595 at the end of this chapter.   **MyLab Economics** Study Plan

Apply the Concept   MyLab Economics Video

Technology and the Earnings of "Superstars"

The gap between Clayton Kershaw's salary and the salary of the lowest-paid baseball players is much greater than the gap between the salaries paid during the 1950s and 1960s to top players such as Mickey Mantle and Willie Mays and the salaries of the lowest-paid players. Similarly, the gap between the $30 million Brad Pitt is paid to star in a movie and the salary paid to an actor in a minor role is much greater than the gap between the salaries paid during the 1930s and 1940s to stars such as Clark Gable and Cary Grant and the salaries paid to bit players. In fact, in most areas of sports and entertainment, the highest-paid performers—the "superstars"—now have much higher incomes relative to other members of their professions than was true a few decades ago.

The increase in the relative incomes of superstars is mainly due to technological advances. The spread of cable television and online streaming has increased the number of potential viewers of Dodgers games, but many of those viewers will watch only if the Dodgers are winning. This growth in viewers increases the value to the Dodgers of winning games and, therefore, increases Kershaw's marginal revenue product and the salary he can earn.

With Blu-ray discs, DVDs, streaming video, Netflix, and pay-per-view cable, the value to movie studios of producing a hit movie has greatly risen. Not surprisingly, movie studios have also increased their willingness to pay large salaries to stars such as Brad Pitt and Leonardo DiCaprio because they think these superstars will significantly increase the chances that a film will be successful.

This process has been going on for a long time. For instance, before the invention of the motion picture, anyone who wanted to see a play had to attend the theater and see a live performance. Limits on the number of people who could see the best actors and actresses perform created an opportunity for many more people to succeed in the acting profession, and the gap between the salaries earned by the best actors and the salaries earned by average actors was relatively small. Today, when a hit movie starring Brad Pitt is available on DVD or streaming, millions of people will buy or rent it, and they will not be forced to spend money to see a less popular actor, as their great-great-grandparents might have been.

Why does Clayton Kershaw earn more today relative to the typical baseball player than baseball stars did in the 1950s and 1960s?

MyLab Economics Study Plan

Your Turn: Test your understanding by doing related problems 4.7 and 4.8 on pages 595–596 at the end of this chapter.

Differences in marginal revenue products are the most important factor in explaining differences in wages, but they are not the whole story. To provide a more complete explanation for differences in wages, we must take into account three important aspects of labor markets: compensating differentials, discrimination, and labor unions.

Compensating Differentials

Suppose Paul runs a pizza parlor and acquires a reputation for being a bad boss who yells at his workers and is generally unpleasant. Two blocks away, Brendan also runs a pizza parlor, but he is always very polite to his workers. We would expect in these circumstances that Paul will have to pay a higher wage than Brendan to attract and retain workers. A difference in wages that compensates workers for unpleasant aspects of a job is called a **compensating differential**.

If working in a dynamite factory requires the same degree of training and education as working in a semiconductor factory but is much more dangerous, a larger number of workers will want to work making semiconductors rather than dynamite. As a consequence, the wages of dynamite workers will be higher than the wages of semiconductor workers. We can think of the difference in wages as being the price of risk. As each worker decides on his or her willingness to assume risk and decides how much higher the wage must be to compensate for assuming more risk, wages will adjust so that dynamite factories will pay wages that are just high enough to compensate workers who choose to work there for the extra risk they assume. Only when workers in dynamite factories have been fully compensated with higher wages for the additional risk they assume will dynamite companies be able to attract enough workers.

Compensating differential A difference in wages that compensates workers for unpleasant aspects of a job.

K.C. Alfred/U-T San Diego/ZUMA Press Inc/Alamy Stock Photo

One surprising implication of compensating differentials is that *laws protecting the health and safety of workers may not make workers better off*. To see this point, suppose that dynamite factories pay wages of $35 per hour and semiconductor factories pay wages of $30 per hour, with the $5 difference in wages being a compensating differential for the greater risk of working in a dynamite factory. Suppose that the government passes a law regulating the manufacture of dynamite in order to improve safety in dynamite factories. As a result of this law, dynamite factories are no longer any more dangerous than semiconductor factories. Once this change occurs, the wages in dynamite factories will decline to $30 per hour, the same as in semiconductor factories. Are workers in dynamite factories any better or worse off? Before the law was passed, their wages were $35 per hour, but $5 per hour was a compensating differential for the extra risk they were exposed to. Now the extra risk has been eliminated, but their wages are only $30 per hour. The conclusion seems to be that dynamite workers are no better off as a result of the safety legislation.

This conclusion is true, though, only if the compensating differential actually does compensate workers fully for the additional risk. Nobel Laureate George Akerlof of Georgetown University and William Dickens of the Brookings Institution have argued that the psychological principle known as *cognitive dissonance* might cause workers to underestimate the true risk of their jobs. According to this principle, people prefer to think of themselves as intelligent and rational and tend to reject evidence that seems to contradict this image. Because working in a very hazardous job may seem irrational, workers in such jobs may refuse to believe that the jobs really are hazardous. Akerlof and Dickens present evidence that workers in chemical plants producing benzene and workers in nuclear power plants underestimate the hazards of their jobs. If Akerlof and Dickens are correct, the wages of these workers will not be high enough to compensate them fully for the risk they have assumed. So, in this situation, safety legislation may make workers better off. **MyLab Economics** Concept Check

Discrimination

Economic discrimination The practice of paying a person a lower wage or excluding a person from an occupation on the basis of an irrelevant characteristic such as race or gender.

Table 17.2 shows that in the United States, white males on average earn more than the other groups listed. One possible explanation for this fact is **economic discrimination**, in which an employer pays a person a lower wage or excludes a person from an occupation on the basis of an irrelevant characteristic such as race or gender.

If employers discriminated by hiring only white males for high-paying jobs or by paying white males higher wages than other groups working the same jobs, white males would have higher earnings, as Table 17.2 shows. However, excluding groups from certain jobs or paying one group more than another has been illegal in the United States since the passage of the Equal Pay Act of 1963 and the Civil Rights Act of 1964. Nevertheless, it is possible that employers are ignoring the law and practicing economic discrimination.

Most economists believe that only part of the gap between the wages of white males and the wages of other groups is due to discrimination. Instead, some of the gap is explained by three main factors:

1. Differences in education
2. Differences in experience
3. Differing preferences for jobs

Table 17.2

Why Do White Males Earn More Than Other Groups?

Group	Weekly Earnings
White males	$1,025
White females	827
Black males	756
Hispanic males	725
Black females	672
Hispanic females	623

Note: The values are median weekly earnings for full-time wage and salary workers aged 25 and older. Persons of Hispanic origin can be of any race.

Source: U.S. Bureau of Labor Statistics, "Usual Weekly Earnings of Wage and Salary Workers, First Quarter 2017," April 18, 2017.

Differences in Education Some of the difference between the incomes of white workers and the incomes of black workers can be explained by differences in education. Historically, African Americans and Hispanics have had less schooling than have whites. The gap has narrowed significantly over the years, but it has not completely closed. A higher percentage of white students graduate on time from public high schools than do African-American or Hispanic students. Similarly, a higher percentage of the white population aged 25 and older graduates from college than is true of the African-American or Hispanic populations. Studies have shown that differing levels of education can account for a significant part of the gap between the earnings of different ethnic groups. Some of the difference in educational levels may reflect past and current discrimination by governments in failing to provide equal educational opportunities.

Differences in Experience Women are much more likely than men to leave their jobs for a period of time after having a child. Women with several children will sometimes have multiple interruptions in their careers. Some women leave the workforce for several years until their children are of school age. As a result, on average, women with children have less workforce experience than do men of the same age. Because workers with greater experience are, on average, more productive, the difference in levels of experience helps explain some of the difference in earnings between men and women. Providing some support for this explanation is the fact that while married women earn about 25 percent less than married men, women who have never been married—and whose careers are less likely to have been interrupted—earn about 9 percent less than men who have never been married.

Differing Preferences for Jobs Significant differences exist between the types of jobs held by women and men:

- Women represent 90 percent or more of the people employed in some relatively low-paying jobs, such as preschool teachers, dental assistants, and childcare workers.
- Men represent more than 90 percent of the people employed in some relatively high-paying jobs, such as airline pilots, engineering managers, and electricians.

Although the overrepresentation of women in low-paying jobs and men in high-paying jobs may be due, in part, to discrimination, it is also likely to reflect differences in job preferences between men and women. For example, because many women interrupt their careers—at least briefly—when their children are born, they are more likely to take jobs where work experience is less important. More women may also be likely to take jobs, such as teaching, that allow them to be home in the afternoons when their children return from school.

The Difficulty of Measuring Discrimination When two people are paid different wages, discrimination may be the explanation. But differences in productivity or preferences may also be an explanation. Labor economists have attempted to measure how much of the differences in wages between black workers and white workers and between men and women is due to discrimination and how much is due to other factors. Unfortunately, it is difficult to precisely measure differences in productivity or in worker preferences. As a result, we can't know exactly the extent of economic discrimination in the United States today.

Solved Problem 17.4

MyLab Economics Interactive Animation

Is Passing "Comparable Worth" Legislation a Good Way to Close the Gap between Men's and Women's Pay?

As we have seen, because of either discrimination or differing preferences, certain jobs are filled primarily by men, and other jobs are filled primarily by women. On average, the "men's jobs" have higher wages than the "women's jobs." Some commentators have argued that many "men's jobs" are more highly paid than "women's jobs," despite the jobs being comparable in terms of the education and skills required and the working conditions involved. These commentators have argued that the earnings gap between men and women could be closed at least partially if the government required employers to pay the same wages for jobs that have *comparable worth*. Many economists are skeptical of these proposals because they believe allowing markets to determine wages results in a more efficient outcome.

Suppose that electricians are currently being paid a market equilibrium wage of $800 per week, and dental assistants are being paid a market equilibrium wage of

$500 per week. Comparable-worth legislation is passed, and a study finds that an electrician and a dental assistant have comparable jobs, so employers will now be required to pay workers in both jobs $650 per week. Analyze the effects of this requirement on the market for electricians and on the market for dental assistants. Be sure to use demand and supply graphs.

Solving the Problem

Step 1: **Review the chapter material.** This problem is about economic discrimination, so you may want to review the section "Discrimination," which begins on page 580.

Step 2: **Draw the graphs.** When the government sets the price in a market, the result is a surplus or a shortage, depending on whether the government-mandated price is above or below the competitive market equilibrium (see Chapter 4, Section 4.3). A wage of $650 per week is below the market wage for electricians and above the market wage for dental assistants. Therefore, we expect the requirement to result in a shortage of electricians and a surplus of dental assistants.

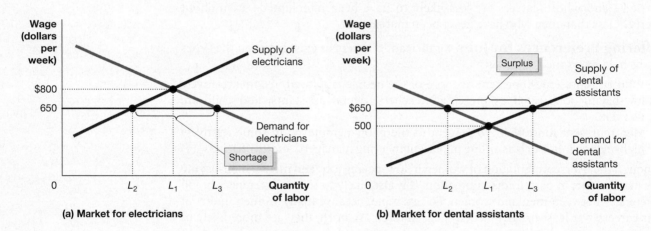

(a) Market for electricians   **(b) Market for dental assistants**

In panel (a), without comparable-worth legislation, the equilibrium wage for electricians is $800, and the equilibrium quantity of electricians hired is L_1. Setting the wage for electricians below equilibrium at $650 reduces the quantity of labor supplied in this occupation from L_1 to L_2 but increases the quantity of labor demanded by employers from L_1 to L_3. The result is a shortage of electricians equal to $L_3 - L_2$, as shown by the bracket in the graph.

In panel (b), without comparable-worth legislation, the equilibrium wage for dental assistants is $500, and the equilibrium quantity of dental assistants hired is L_1. Setting the wage for dental assistants above equilibrium at $650 increases the quantity of labor supplied in this occupation from L_1 to L_3 but reduces the quantity of labor demanded by employers from L_1 to L_2. The result is a surplus of dental assistants equal to $L_3 - L_2$, as shown by the bracket in the graph.

Extra Credit: Most economists are skeptical of government attempts to set wages and prices as comparable-worth legislation would require. Supporters of comparable-worth legislation, by contrast, see differences between men's and women's wages as being mainly due to discrimination and see government legislation as a solution.

MyLab Economics Study Plan   **Your Turn:** For more practice, do related problems 4.15 and 4.16 on page 597 at the end of this chapter.

Apply the Concept

MyLab Economics Video

Does Greg Have an Easier Time Finding a Job Than Jamal?

One difficulty in accurately measuring economic discrimination is that two workers may not only differ in race and gender but also in characteristics that employers expect will affect the workers' productivity. If Worker A is hired instead of Worker B, is it because A is a white male, while B is a black female, or is it because of A's and B's other characteristics?

Marianne Bertrand of the University of Chicago and Sendhil Mullainathan of Harvard University found an ingenious way of gaining insight into the extent of economic discrimination. They responded to help wanted ads in newspapers by sending identical résumés, with the exception that half of the résumés were assigned an African-American–sounding name and half were assigned a white-sounding name (The names were selected by examining birth certificates for names that were nearly always given to either white babies or to African-American babies). In other words, the characteristics of these fictitious people were the same, except for their names. Bertrand and Mullainathan based their artificial résumés on actual résumés, so the artificial résumés included the characteristics that actual job applicants think are relevant to employers in assessing the applicants' productivity. In the absence of discrimination, résumés with African-American–sounding names, such as Jamal Jones, should have been as likely to get job interviews as the identical résumés with white-sounding names, such as Greg Baker. Bertrand and Mullainathan sent out more than 5,000 résumés to many different employers who were advertising for jobs in sales, administrative support, clerical services, and customer services. They found that employers were 50 percent more likely to interview workers with white-sounding names than workers with African-American–sounding names.

As a further test for the presence of discrimination, the authors divided résumés into high and low quality categories. High quality résumés might include extra computer skills, volunteer work, or military experience. Although whites submitting higher quality résumés were significantly more likely to be interviewed, African Americans were not. Bertrand and Mullainathan conclude that the results of their experiment show that "differential treatment by race . . . appears to still be prominent in the U.S. labor market."

Ronnie Kaufman/Larry Hirshowitz/Blend Images/Alamy Stock Photo

Does having an African-American–sounding name make it more difficult to find a job?

Sources: Marianne Bertrand and Sendhil Mullainathan, "Are Emily and Greg More Employable Than Lakisha and Jamal? A Field Experiment on Labor Market Discrimination," *American Economic Review*, Vol. 94, No. 4, September 2004, pp. 991–1013; and David Neumark, "Detecting Discrimination in Audit and Correspondence Studies," *Journal of Human Resources*, Vol. 47, No. 4, Fall 2012, pp. 1128–1157.

Your Turn: Test your understanding by doing related problems 4.17 and 4.18 on page 597 at the end of this chapter.

MyLab Economics Study Plan

Does It Pay to Discriminate? Many economists believe that in the long run, markets can undermine economic discrimination. One reason is that *employers who discriminate pay an economic penalty*. To see why, let's consider a simplified example. Suppose that men and women are equally qualified to be airline pilots and that, initially, airlines do not discriminate. In Figure 17.9, we divide the airlines into two groups: "A" airlines and "B" airlines. If neither group of airlines discriminates, we would expect them to pay an equal wage of $1,100 per week to both men and women pilots. Now suppose that "A" airlines decide to break the law and discriminate by firing all their women pilots. This action will reduce the supply of pilots to these airlines and, as shown in panel (a), will force up the wage from $1,100 to $1,300 per week. At the same time, as women fired from the jobs with "A" airlines apply for jobs with "B" airlines, the supply of pilots to "B" airlines will increase, and the equilibrium wage will fall from $1,100 to $900 per week. All the women pilots will end up being employed at the nondiscriminating airlines and will be paid a lower wage than the men who are employed by the discriminating airlines.

But this situation cannot persist for two reasons. First, male pilots employed by "B" airlines will also receive the lower wage. This lower wage gives them an incentive

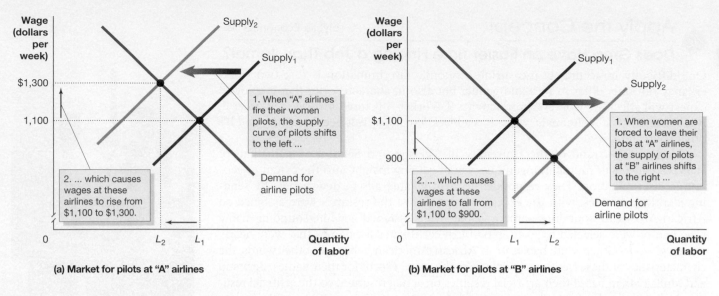

MyLab Economics Animation

Figure 17.9   **Discrimination and Wages**

In this hypothetical example, we assume that initially neither "A" airlines nor "B" airlines discriminate. As a result, men and women pilots receive the same wage of $1,100 per week at both groups of airlines. We then assume that "A" airlines discriminate by firing all their women pilots. Panel (a) shows that discrimination reduces the supply of pilots to "A" airlines and raises the wage paid by these airlines from $1,100 to $1,300. Panel (b) shows that discrimination increases the supply of pilots to "B" airlines and lowers the wage paid by these airlines from $1,100 to $900. All the women pilots will end up being employed at the nondiscriminating airlines and will be paid a lower wage than the men who are employed by the discriminating airlines.

to quit their jobs at "B" airlines and apply at "A" airlines, which will shift the labor supply curve for "B" airlines to the left and the labor supply curve for "A" airlines to the right. Second, "A" airlines are paying $1,300 per week to hire pilots who are no more productive than the pilots being paid $900 per week by "B" airlines. As a result, "B" airlines will have lower costs and will be able to charge lower prices. Eventually, high-price "A" airlines will lose their customers to low-price "B" airlines and will be driven out of business. The market will have imposed an economic penalty on the discriminating airlines. So, discrimination will not persist, and the wages of men and women pilots will become equal.

Can we conclude from this analysis that competition in markets will eliminate all economic discrimination? Unfortunately, this optimistic conclusion is not completely accurate. We know that until the Civil Rights Act of 1964 was passed, some firms in the United States refused to hire black workers. Even though this practice had persisted for decades, nondiscriminating competitors did not drive these firms out of business. Why not? There were three important factors:

1. **Worker discrimination.** In some cases, white workers refused to work alongside black workers. As a result, some industries—such as the important cotton textile industry in the South—were all white. Because of discrimination by white workers, an entrepreneur who wanted to use low-cost black labor might need to hire an all-black workforce. Some entrepreneurs tried this approach, but because black workers had been excluded from these industries, they often lacked the skills and experience to form an effective workforce.
2. **Customer discrimination.** Some white consumers were unwilling to buy from companies in certain industries if they employed black workers. This discrimination was not a significant barrier in manufacturing industries, where consumers would not know the race of the workers producing the good. It was, however, a problem for firms in industries in which workers came into direct contact with the public.
3. **Negative feedback loops.** Our analysis in Figure 17.9 assumed that men and women pilots were equally qualified. However, if discrimination makes it difficult

for a member of a group to find employment in a particular occupation, his or her incentive to be trained to enter that occupation is reduced. Consider the legal profession as an example. In 1952, future Supreme Court Justice Sandra Day O'Connor graduated third in her class at Stanford University Law School and was an editor of the *Stanford Law Review*, but for some time she was unable to get a job as a lawyer because in those years, many law firms would not hire women. Given such bleak job prospects, it's not surprising that relatively few women entered law school. As a result, a law firm that did not discriminate would have been unable to hire women lawyers at a lower salary and use this cost advantage to drive discriminating law firms out of business. Notice the difference between this situation and the airline example discussed earlier. In this situation, an unfortunate feedback loop was in place: Few women prepared to become lawyers because many law firms discriminated against women, and nondiscriminating law firms were unable to drive discriminating law firms out of business because there were too few women lawyers available.

Most economists agree that the market imposes an economic penalty on firms that discriminate, but because of the factors just discussed, it may take the market a very long time to eliminate discrimination entirely. The passage of the Civil Rights Act of 1964, which outlawed hiring discrimination on the basis of race and sex, greatly sped up the process of reducing economic discrimination in the United States.   **MyLab Economics** Concept Check

Labor Unions

Workers' wages can differ depending on whether the workers are members of **labor unions**, which are organizations of employees that have the legal right to bargain with employers about wages and working conditions. If a union is unable to reach an agreement with a company, it has the legal right to call a *strike*, which means its members refuse to work until a satisfactory agreement has been reached. *Industrial unions*, such as the United Automobile Workers, attempt to organize all or most workers in an industry into a union. Craft unions, such as the International Brotherhood of Electrical Workers, organize workers with a particular skill or training, who may work in a variety of industries. In 2017, about 6 percent of private-sector and 34 percent of public-sector workers were members of a union. A smaller fraction of the labor force is unionized in the United States than in most other high-income countries.

In 2016, U.S. workers who were in unions earned an average of $1,004 per week, while nonunion workers earned an average of $802. Do union members earn more than nonunion members because they are in unions? The answer might seem to be "yes," but many union workers are in industries, such as automobile manufacturing, in which their marginal revenue products are high, so their wages would be high even if they were not unionized. Economists who have attempted to estimate statistically the effect of unionization on wages have concluded that being in a union increases a worker's wages about 10 percent, holding constant other factors, such as the industry the worker is in.   **MyLab Economics** Concept Check

> **Labor union** An organization of employees that has a legal right to bargain with employers about wages and working conditions.

MyLab Economics Study Plan

Personnel Economics

17.5

LEARNING OBJECTIVE: Discuss the role personnel economics can play in helping firms deal with human resources issues.

Traditionally, labor economists have focused on issues such as the effects of labor unions on wages or the determinants of changes in average wages over time. They have spent less time analyzing *human resources issues*, which address how firms hire, train, and promote workers and set their wages and benefits. In recent years, some labor economists, including Edward Lazear of Stanford University and William Neilson of the University of Tennessee, have begun exploring the application of economic analysis to human resources issues. This new focus has become known as **personnel economics**.

> **Personnel economics** The application of economic analysis to human resources issues.

Figure 17.10

Paying Car Salespeople by Salary or by Commission

This figure compares the compensation a car salesperson receives if she is on a straight salary of $800 per week and if she receives a commission of $200 for each car she sells. With a straight salary, she receives $800 per week, no matter how many cars she sells. This outcome is shown by the horizontal line in the figure. If she receives a commission of $200 per car, her compensation will increase with every car she sells, as shown by the upward-sloping line. If she sells fewer than 4 cars per week, she would be better off with the $800 salary. If she sells more than 4 cars per week, she would be better off with the $200-per-car commission.

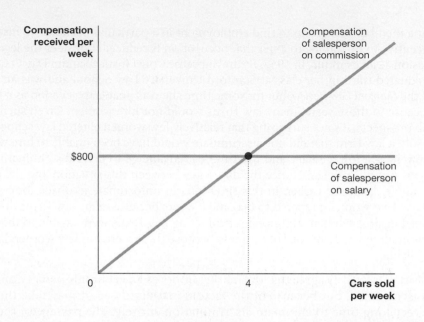

Personnel economics analyzes the link between differences among jobs and differences in the way workers are paid. Jobs have different skill requirements, require more or less interaction with other workers, have to be performed in more or less unpleasant environments, and so on. Firms need to design compensation policies that take into account these differences among jobs. Personnel economics also analyzes other human resources policies, such as promotions, training, and pensions. In this brief overview, we look only at compensation policies.

Should Workers' Pay Depend on How Much They Work or on How Much They Produce?

One issue personnel economics addresses is when workers should receive *straight-time pay*—a certain wage per hour or salary per week or month—and when they should receive *commission* or *piece-rate pay*—a wage based on how much output they produce.

Suppose that Anne owns a car dealership and is trying to decide whether to pay her salespeople a salary of $800 per week or a commission of $200 on each car they sell. Figure 17.10 compares the compensation a salesperson would receive under the two systems, according to the number of cars the salesperson sells.

With a straight salary, the salesperson receives $800 per week, no matter how many cars she sells, which is shown by the horizontal line in Figure 17.10. If she receives a commission of $200 per car, her compensation will increase with every car she sells, as shown by the upward-sloping line. A salesperson who sells fewer than 4 cars per week would earn more by receiving a straight salary of $800 per week. A salesperson who sells more than 4 cars per week would be better off receiving the $200-per-car commission. We can identify two advantages Anne would receive from paying her salespeople commissions rather than salaries: She would attract and retain the most productive employees, and she would provide an incentive to her employees to sell more cars.

Suppose that other car dealerships are all paying salaries of $800 per week. If Anne pays her employees on commission, any of her employees who are unable to sell at least 4 cars per week can improve their pay by going to work for one of her competitors. And any salespeople at Anne's competitors who can sell more than 4 cars per week can raise their pay by quitting and coming to work for Anne. Over time, Anne will find her least productive employees leaving, and she will be able to hire new employees who are more productive.

Paying a commission also increases the incentive Anne's salespeople have to sell more cars. If Anne paid a salary, her employees would receive the same amount no matter how few cars they sold. An employee on salary might decide on a particularly hot or cold day that it was less trouble to stay inside the building than to go out on the car lot to greet potential customers. An employee on commission would know that the additional effort expended on selling more cars would be rewarded with additional compensation. **MyLab Economics** Concept Check

Apply the Concept
MyLab Economics Video

A Better Way to Sell Contact Lenses

Many firms rely on salespeople to sell their goods. By one estimate, firms spend about three times as much on paying their salespeople as they do on advertising. Evidence on how salespeople respond to different ways of being compensated can be difficult to obtain. This difficulty arises partly because firms are often reluctant to discuss the details of their compensation plans with people outside the firm and partly because the connection between a firm's compensation plan and its sales can be difficult to determine, given other factors that may affect a firm's sales.

Sanjog Misra of Rochester University and Harikesh Nair of Stanford University were able to overcome some of these difficulties when a large contact lens manufacturer agreed to provide them with details of the firm's compensation plan and with detailed data on compensation received and sales made by individual salespeople. The firm used its salespeople to market its contact lenses to ophthalmologists and opticians. It had no way of closely monitoring its salespeople's effort, so it needed to rely on its compensation plan to motivate them. The salespeople received a salary and could also earn a commission on sales over an assigned quarterly quota of the number of lenses sold. The commission was capped, though, so salespeople did not receive a commission on lenses sold above a ceiling amount. Firms often use ceilings to avoid paying "windfall" commissions that might result when a new product is introduced that proves very popular and sales rise sharply even without much effort from the firms' salespeople. A firm might also increase a salesperson's quota if he or she consistently exceeds it. Raising output quotas is sometimes called "ratcheting."

Misra and Nair discovered that the firm's compensation plan was inefficient. Salespeople appeared to work harder just before the end of a calendar quarter in order to satisfy their sales quotas. They also appeared to reduce their effort once they had met their quotas. The researchers found that salespeople were often reluctant to exceed their quotas for fear the firm would increase—ratchet up—their quota in future quarters.

To reduce these inefficiencies, Misra and Nair recommended that the firm eliminate the sales quotas and compensation ceilings and move to a compensation plan that consisted of a straight commission on sales. The firm accepted the recommendation, and after implementing the new plan, sales increased by more than 20 percent, or nearly $80,000 per salesperson per quarter. The higher compensation under the new plan succeeded in increasing the sales force's effort. The increase in the firm's revenue more than offset the increase in its compensation cost, resulting in a 6 percent increase in the firm's profit.

Sociologists sometimes question whether worker productivity can be increased through the use of monetary incentives. The experience of this contact lens firm provides a clear example of workers reacting favorably to the opportunity to increase work effort in exchange for higher compensation.

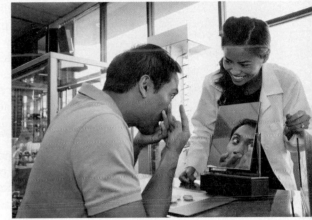

Peathegee Inc/Blend Images/Getty Images

A contact lens manufacturer increased its profit by taking the advice of economists to compensate its salespeople with a straight commission on sales.

Source: Sanjog Misra and Harikesh S. Nair, "A Structural Model of Sales-Force Compensation Dynamics: Estimation and Field Implementation," *Quantitative Marketing and Economics,* Vol. 9, No. 3, September 2009, pp. 211–257.

Your Turn: Test your understanding by doing related problems 5.5, 5.6, and 5.7 on page 598 at the end of this chapter.

MyLab Economics Study Plan

Other Considerations in Setting Compensation Systems

The discussion so far has indicated that companies will find it more profitable to use a commission or piece-rate system of compensation rather than a salary system. In fact, many firms continue to pay their workers salaries, which means they are paying their workers on the basis of how long they work rather than on the basis of how much they produce. Firms may choose a salary system for several good reasons:

- **Difficulty measuring output.** Often firms have difficulty attributing output to any particular worker. For example, an engineering firm may carry out a project using teams of workers whose individual contributions are difficult to distinguish. On assembly lines, such as those used in the automobile industry, the amount produced by each worker is determined by the speed of the line, which is set by managers rather than by workers. Managers at many firms perform such a wide variety of tasks that measuring their output would be costly, if it could be done at all.

- **Concerns about quality.** If workers are paid on the basis of the number of units produced, they may become less concerned about quality. An office assistant who is paid on the basis of the quantity of documents prepared may become careless about how many errors the documents contain. In some cases, there are ways around this problem; for example, the assistant may be required to correct the mistakes on his or her own time, without pay.

- **Worker dislike of risk.** Piece-rate or commission systems of compensation increase the risk to workers because sometimes output declines for reasons not connected to the worker's effort. For example, if there is a very snowy winter, few customers may show up at Anne's auto dealership. Through no fault of their own, her salespeople may have great difficulty selling any cars. If they are paid a salary, their income will not be affected, but if they are on commission, their incomes may drop to low levels. The flip side of this is that by paying salaries, Anne assumes a greater risk. During a snowy winter, her payroll expenses will remain high even though her sales are low. With a commission system of compensation, her payroll expenses will decline along with her sales. But owners of firms are typically better able to bear risk than are workers. As a result, some firms may find that workers who would earn more under a commission system will prefer to receive a salary to reduce their risk. In these situations, paying a lower salary may reduce the firm's payroll expenses compared with what they would have been under a commission or piece-rate system.

Personnel economics is a relatively new field, but it holds great potential for helping firms deal more efficiently with human resources issues.   MyLab Economics Concept Check

MyLab Economics Study Plan

 17.6

The Markets for Capital and Natural Resources

LEARNING OBJECTIVE: Show how equilibrium prices are determined in the markets for capital and natural resources.

The approach we have used to analyze the market for labor can also be used to analyze the markets for other factors of production. We have seen that the demand for labor is determined by the marginal revenue product of labor because the value to a firm of hiring another worker equals the increase in the firm's revenue from selling the additional output it can produce by hiring the worker. The demand for capital and the demand for natural resources are determined in a similar way.

The Market for Capital

Physical capital includes machines, equipment, and buildings. Firms sometimes buy capital, but we will focus on situations in which firms rent capital. A chocolate manufacturer renting a warehouse and an airline leasing a plane are examples of firms renting capital. Like the demand for labor, the demand for capital is a derived demand.

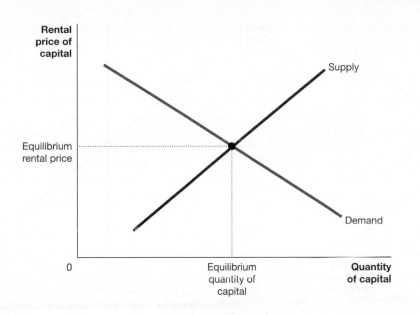

MyLab Economics Animation

Figure 17.11

Equilibrium in the Market for Capital

The rental price of capital is determined by demand and supply in the market for capital. In equilibrium, the rental price of capital is equal to the marginal revenue product of capital.

When a firm is considering increasing its capital by, for example, employing another machine, the value it receives equals the increase in the firm's revenue from selling the additional output it can produce by employing the machine. The *marginal revenue product of capital* is the change in the firm's revenue as a result of employing one more unit of capital. We have seen that the marginal revenue product of labor curve is the demand curve for labor. Similarly, the marginal revenue product of capital curve is the demand curve for capital.

Firms producing capital goods face increasing marginal costs, so the supply curve of capital goods is upward sloping. Figure 17.11 shows equilibrium in the market for capital. In equilibrium, suppliers of capital receive a rental price equal to the marginal revenue product of capital, just as suppliers of labor receive a wage equal to the marginal revenue product of labor.   **MyLab Economics** Concept Check

The Market for Natural Resources

The market for natural resources can be analyzed in the same way as the markets for labor and capital. When a firm is considering employing more natural resources, the value it receives equals the increase in the firm's revenue from selling the additional output it can produce by buying the natural resources. So, the demand for natural resources is also a derived demand. The *marginal revenue product of natural resources* is the change in a firm's revenue as a result of employing one more unit of natural resources, such as a barrel of oil. The marginal revenue product of natural resources curve is also the demand curve for natural resources.

Although the total quantity of most natural resources is ultimately fixed—as the humorist Will Rogers once remarked: "Buy land. They ain't making any more of it"—in many cases, the quantity supplied still responds to the price. For example, although the total quantity of oil deposits in the world is fixed, an increase in the price of oil will result in an increase in the quantity of oil supplied during a particular period. The result, as shown in panel (a) of Figure 17.12, is an upward-sloping supply curve. In some cases, however, the quantity of a natural resource that will be supplied is fixed and will not change as the price changes. The land available at a busy intersection is fixed, for example. In panel (b) of Figure 17.12, we illustrate this situation with a supply curve that is a vertical line, or perfectly inelastic. The owner of a factor of production that is in fixed supply receives an **economic rent** (or **pure rent**). In this case, the price of the factor is determined only by demand. For example, if a new highway diverts much of the traffic from a previously busy intersection, the demand for the land will decline, and the price of the land will fall, but the quantity of the land will not change.   **MyLab Economics** Concept Check

Economic rent (or pure rent) The price of a factor of production that is in fixed supply.

Figure 17.12   **Equilibrium in the Market for Natural Resources**

In panel (a), the supply curve of a natural resource is upward sloping. The price of the natural resource is determined by the interaction of demand and supply. In panel (b), the supply curve of the natural resource is a vertical line, indicating that the quantity supplied does not respond to changes in price. In this case, the price of the natural resource is determined only by demand. The price of a factor of production with a vertical supply curve is called an *economic rent*, or *pure rent*.

Monopsony

Monopsony The situation in which a firm is sole buyer of a factor of production.

We have analyzed the case of *monopoly*, where a firm is the sole *seller* of a good or service (see Chapter 15). What happens if a firm is the sole *buyer* of a factor of production? This case, which is called **monopsony**, is comparatively rare. An example is a firm in an isolated town—perhaps a lumber mill in a small town in Washington or Oregon—that is the sole employer of labor in that location. In the nineteenth and early twentieth centuries, some coal mining firms were the sole employers in certain small towns in West Virginia, and some pineapple plantations were the sole employers on certain small islands in Hawaii. In these cases, not only would the firm own the mill, mine, or plantation, but it would also own the stores and other businesses in the town. Workers would have the choice of working for the sole employer in the town or moving to another town.

We know that a firm with a monopoly in an output market takes advantage of its market power to reduce the quantity supplied to force up the market price and increase its profits. A firm that has a monopsony in a factor market would employ a similar strategy: It would restrict the quantity of the factor demanded to force down the price of the factor and increase profit. A firm with a monopsony in a labor market will hire fewer workers and pay lower wages than would be the case in a competitive market. Because fewer workers are hired than would be hired in a competitive market, monopsony results in a deadweight loss. Monopoly and monopsony have similar effects on the economy: In both cases, a firm's market power results in a lower equilibrium quantity, a deadweight loss, and a reduction in economic efficiency compared with a competitive market.

In some cases, monopsony in labor markets is offset by worker membership in a labor union. A notable example of this is professional sports. For instance, Major League Baseball effectively has a monopsony on employing professional baseball players. (Although independent baseball leagues exist, none of the best players play for these teams, and the teams pay salaries that are a small fraction of those paid by Major League Baseball teams.) The monopsony power of the owners of Major League Baseball teams is offset by the power of the Major League Baseball Players Association, the union that represents baseball players. Bargaining between the representatives of Major League Baseball and the players' union has resulted in baseball players being paid something close to what they would be receiving in a competitive market.   MyLab Economics Concept Check

The Marginal Productivity Theory of Income Distribution

We have seen that in equilibrium, each factor of production receives a price equal to its marginal revenue product. We can use this fact to explain the distribution of income. Marginal revenue product represents the value of a factor's marginal contribution to producing goods and services. Therefore, individuals will receive income equal to the marginal contributions to production from the factors of production they own, including their labor. The more factors of production an individual owns and the more productive those factors are, the higher the individual's income will be. This approach to explaining the distribution of income is called the **marginal productivity theory of income distribution**. The theory was developed by John Bates Clark, who taught at Columbia University in the late nineteenth and early twentieth centuries.   MyLab Economics Concept Check

Marginal productivity theory of income distribution The theory that the distribution of income is determined by the marginal productivity of the factors of production that individuals own.

MyLab Economics Study Plan

Continued from page 563

Economics in Your Life & Career

When Should You Give an Employee a Raise?

At the beginning of this chapter, we asked you to suppose that you own a local sandwich shop and that one of your employees asks you for a raise.

One way for you to measure the value of an employee is by estimating how many dollars her work generates for the sandwich shop: her marginal revenue product. If the employee has become better at her job and has gained new skills, she may have become a more productive employee. A key to your decision about whether to grant the employee a raise is whether this increased productivity has resulted in increased revenue for your sandwich shop. If it has, then you are likely to have to raise her wage or see her quit to take a job at a competing business.

Conclusion

In this chapter, we used the demand and supply model to explain why wages differ among workers. The demand for workers depends on their productivity and on the prices firms receive for the output the workers produce. The supply of workers to an occupation depends on the wages and working conditions employers offer and the skills they require. The demand and supply for labor can also help us analyze issues such as economic discrimination and the effect of labor unions.

Visit MyLab Economics for a news article and analysis related to the concepts in this chapter.

Key Terms

Compensating differentials, p. 579

Derived demand, p. 564

Economic discrimination, p. 580

Economic rent (or pure rent), p. 589

Factors of production, p. 564

Human capital, p. 567

Labor union, p. 585

Marginal product of labor, p. 564

Marginal productivity theory of income distribution, p. 591

Marginal revenue product of labor (MRP), p. 565

Monopsony, p. 590

Personnel economics, p. 585

17.1 The Demand for Labor, pages 564–568

LEARNING OBJECTIVE: Explain how firms choose the profit-maximizing quantity of labor to employ.

MyLab Economics Visit www.pearson.com/mylab/economics to complete these exercises online and get instant feedback.

Summary

Factors of production are labor, capital, natural resources, and other inputs used to produce goods and services. The demand for labor is a **derived demand** because it depends on consumers' demand for goods and services. The additional output produced by a firm as a result of hiring another worker is called the **marginal product of labor**. The amount by which a firm's revenue will increase as a result of hiring one more worker is called the **marginal revenue product of labor (MRP)**. A firm's MRP curve is its demand curve for labor. Firms maximize profit by hiring workers up to the point where the wage is equal to the MRP. We find the market demand curve for labor by adding up the quantity of labor demanded by each firm at each wage, holding constant all other variables that might affect the willingness of firms to hire workers. The most important variables that shift the labor demand curve are changes in human capital, technology, the price of the product, the quantity of other inputs, and the number of firms in the market. **Human capital** is the accumulated training and skills that workers possess.

Review Questions

1.1 In what sense is the demand for labor a derived demand?

1.2 What is the difference between the marginal product of labor and the marginal revenue product of labor?

1.3 Why is the demand curve for labor downward sloping?

1.4 What are the five most important variables that cause the market demand curve for labor to shift?

Problems and Applications

1.5 Frank Gunter owns an apple orchard. He employs 87 apple pickers and pays them each $8 per hour to pick apples, which he sells for $1.60 per box. If Frank is maximizing profit, what is the marginal revenue product of the last worker he hired? What is that worker's marginal product?

1.6 (Related to **Solved Problem 17.1** on page 566) Fill in the missing values in the following table for Terrell's Televisions.

Number of Workers (L)	Output of Televisions per Week (Q)	Marginal Product of Labor (television sets per week) (MP)	Product Price (P)	Marginal Revenue Product of Labor (dollars per week)	Wage (dollars per week) (W)	Additional Profit from Hiring One More Worker (dollars per week)
0	0		$300		$1,800	
1	8		300		1,800	
2	15		300		1,800	
3	21		300		1,800	
4	26		300		1,800	
5	30		300		1,800	
6	33		300		1,800	

a. From the information in the table, can you determine whether this firm is a price taker or a price maker? Briefly explain.

b. Use the information in the table to draw a graph like Figure 17.1 on page 565 that shows the demand for labor by this firm. Be sure to indicate the profit-maximizing quantity of labor on your graph.

1.7 State whether each of the following events will result in a movement along the market demand curve for labor in electronics factories in China or whether it will cause the market demand curve for labor to shift. If the demand curve shifts, indicate whether it will shift to the left or to the right and draw a graph to illustrate the shift.

a. The wage rate declines.

b. The price of smartphones declines.

c. Several firms exit the smartphone market in China.

d. Chinese high schools introduce new vocational courses in assembling electronic products.

1.8 Baseball writer Rany Jazayerli assessed then Kansas City Royals outfielder Jose Guillen as follows: "Guillen has negative value the way his contract stands." How could a baseball player's contract cause him to have negative value to a baseball team?

Source: Rany Jazayerli, "Radical Situations Call for Radical Solutions," www.ranyontheroyals.com, June 6, 2009.

1.9 Two employers made the following comments about a proposed increase in the federal minimum wage:

> Dillon Edwards, founder of Parlor Coffee: "[The increase] should definitely be [to] more than [$8.75 an hour]. . . . It needs to be at least in double digits."

> Beth Fahey, owner of Creative Cakes: "If you raise the minimum wage . . . I can't raise everybody. If I do, the price of a doughnut is going to be $3 and nobody's going to buy it."

Briefly explain for which employer the marginal revenue product of labor is likely to be greater.

Source: Leslie Josephs and Adam Janofsky, "As Minimum Wages Rise, Smaller Firms Get Squeezed," *Wall Street Journal*, June 11, 2015.

17.2 The Supply of Labor, pages 568–570

LEARNING OBJECTIVE: Explain how people choose the quantity of labor to supply.

MyLab Economics   Visit **www.pearson.com/mylab/economics** to complete these exercises online and get instant feedback.

Summary

As the wage increases, the opportunity cost of leisure increases, causing individuals to supply a greater quantity of labor. Normally, the labor supply curve is upward sloping, but it is possible that at very high wage levels, the supply curve might become backward bending. This outcome occurs when someone with a high income is willing to accept a somewhat lower income in exchange for more leisure. We find the market labor supply curve by adding up the quantity of labor supplied by each worker at each wage, holding constant all other variables that might affect the willingness of workers to supply labor. The most important variables that shift the labor supply curve are increases in population, changing demographics, and changing alternatives.

Review Questions

2.1 How can we measure the opportunity cost of leisure? What are the substitution effect and the income effect resulting from a wage change? Why is the supply curve of labor usually upward sloping?

2.2 What are the three most important variables that cause the market supply curve of labor to shift?

Problems and Applications

2.3 Daniel was earning $65 per hour and working 45 hours per week. Then Daniel's wage rose to $75 per hour, and as a result, he now works 40 hours per week. What can we conclude from this information about the income effect and the substitution effect of a wage change for Daniel?

2.4 Uber, the ride-hailing service, increases the price of a ride when demand increases, as happens, for instance, on New Year's Eve or during a snowstorm. An article in the *New York Times* discussed how new Uber drivers respond

to fluctuations in the wages they earn: "Many of these drivers appeared to have an income goal in mind and stopped when they were near it, causing them to knock off sooner when their hourly wage was high and to work longer when their wage was low." On the basis of this information, what does the labor supply curve for new Uber drivers look like? Draw a graph to illustrate your answer.

Source: Noam Scheiber, "How Uber Drivers Decide How Long to Work," *New York Times*, September 4, 2016.

2.5 Most labor economists believe that many adult males are on a vertical section of their labor supply curves. Use the concepts of income and substitution effects to explain under what circumstances an individual's labor supply curve would be vertical.

Source: Robert Whaples, "Is There Consensus among American Labor Economists? Survey Results on Forty Propositions," *Journal of Labor Research*, Vol. 17, No. 4, Fall 1996.

2.6 Suppose that a large oil field is discovered in Michigan. By imposing a tax on the oil, the state government is able to eliminate the state income tax on wages. What is likely to be the effect on the labor supply curve in Michigan?

2.7 A columnist in the *New York Times* noted that the U.S. labor supply "in the next decade is expected to expand at less than half the pace of the 1960s, 1970s and 1980s." What explains these changing growth rates in the U.S. labor supply?

Source: Eduardo Porter, "The Payoff in Delaying Retirement," *New York Times*, March 5, 2013.

2.8 State whether each of the following events will result in a movement along the market supply curve of agricultural labor in the United States or whether it will cause the market supply curve of agricultural labor to shift. If the supply curve shifts, indicate whether it will shift to the left or to the right and draw a graph to illustrate the shift.
  a. The agricultural wage rate declines.
  b. Wages outside agriculture increase.
  c. The law is changed to allow for unlimited immigration into the United States.

17.3 **Equilibrium in the Labor Market, pages 570–577**
LEARNING OBJECTIVE: Explain how equilibrium wages are determined in labor markets.

MyLab Economics   Visit www.pearson.com/mylab/economics to complete these exercises online and get instant feedback.

Summary

The intersection between labor supply and labor demand determines the equilibrium wage and the equilibrium level of employment. If labor supply is unchanged, an increase in labor demand will increase both the equilibrium wage and the number of workers employed. If labor demand is unchanged, an increase in labor supply will lower the equilibrium wage and increase the number of workers employed.

Review Questions

3.1 If the labor demand curve shifts to the left and the labor supply curve remains unchanged, what will happen to the equilibrium wage and the equilibrium level of employment? Illustrate your answer with a graph.

3.2 If the labor supply curve shifts to the left and the labor demand curve remains unchanged, what will happen to the equilibrium wage and the equilibrium level of employment? Illustrate your answer with a graph.

Problems and Applications

3.3 (Related to the Apply the Concept on page 571) Over time, the gap between the wages of workers with college degrees and the wages of workers without college degrees has been increasing. Shouldn't this gap have raised the incentive for workers to earn college degrees, thereby increasing the supply of college-educated workers and reducing the size of the gap?

3.4 An article in the *Wall Street Journal* discussed why the hotel workers' union in New York City was against a proposal for more hotels to be built in Midtown Manhattan: "The union is concerned that rapid hotel development shrinks room prices and profit margins, driving down the wages of its members." Is the union's reasoning consistent with the economic analysis in this chapter? Briefly explain.
Source: Laura Kusisto, "City, Union Seek Hotel Limit in Grand Central Area," *Wall Street Journal*, June 17, 2014.

3.5 Sean Astin, who played the hobbit Sam in *The Lord of the Rings* movies, wrote the following about an earlier film he had appeared in: "Now I was in a movie I didn't respect, making obscene amounts of money (five times what a teacher makes, and teachers do infinitely more important work)." Are salaries determined by the importance of the work being done? If not, what are salaries determined by?
Source: Sean Astin with Joe Layden, *There and Back Again: An Actor's Tale*, New York: St. Martin's Press, 2004, p. 35.

3.6 In the Immigration Act of 1990, Congress established the H-1B visa program, intended to allow U.S. firms to hire foreign workers in areas such as the physical sciences,

computer programing, and engineering. John Bound and Nicolas Morales of the University of Michigan and Gaurav Khanna of the University of California, San Diego, studied the effects of the H-1B program on the market for computer science (CS) workers in the United States in the years from 1994 to 2001, during which the Internet first became important for the operations of U.S. firms. They found that the visa program may have had effects on labor demand in two ways: (1) if immigrant CS workers were responsible for innovations, such as improving the functioning of Web sites, that required more CS workers to be hired, and (2) if U.S. firms hiring immigrant CS workers reduced the likelihood that the firms would have hired foreign technology firms to carry out CS work. They noted, "If computer scientists are a sufficient spur to innovation, or if domestic employers can readily offshore CS work, any negative effects that an increase in the number of foreign CS workers might have on the domestic high-skill workforce would be offset by increases in the domestic demand for computer scientists."

a. Draw a demand and supply graph of the market for CS workers in the United States to illustrate the authors' argument. Be sure to indicate on your graph any effects of the H-1B visa program on the demand and supply curves.

b. The authors estimate that the H-1B visa program resulted in a reduction of about 4 percent in the wages U.S. CS workers would otherwise have received. Does this conclusion allow you to determine whether the program had a greater effect on labor demand or on labor supply? Briefly explain.

Source: John Bound, Nicolas Morales, and Gaurav Khanna, "Understanding the Economic Impact of the H-1B Program on the U.S.," National Bureau of Economic Research, Working Paper No. 23153, February 2017.

3.7 Following the 2016 Major League Baseball season, the market for home run hitters who were free agents and available to sign with any team was unexpectedly quiet. Players such as Edwin Encarnacion and Chris Carter signed for lower salaries and for fewer years than either they or their agents had expected. Here are two explanations for the relatively low salary offers:

1. Mark Shapiro, president and CEO of the Toronto Blue Jays, explained, "There has been a shift . . . in how people value . . . defense and some of the other aspects of players' games."

2. Brian Cashman, general manager of the New York Yankees, blamed the weak market on a greater-than-normal number of power hitters who were free agents: "The chessboard was set up with more participants than there were chairs."

Draw two graphs depicting the demand and supply for home run hitters. In the first graph, illustrate a change in the market that is consistent with Mark Shapiro's explanation for the decline in salaries. In the second graph, illustrate a change in the market that is consistent with Brian

Cashman's explanation for the decline in salaries. Briefly explain your graphs.

Source: Jared Diamond, "Home Runs Are No Longer Paying the Bills," *Wall Street Journal*, March 1, 2017.

3.8 (Related to the Apply the Concept on page 574) During the same period that robots and other new technologies have been affecting the labor market, there has been an increase in imports to the United States of manufactured goods—including shoes, clothing, and automobiles— from countries in which workers receive lower wages. In addition, some U.S. firms have engaged in "offshoring," in which they move some operations—such as telephone help lines—to other countries where wages are lower.

a. Are the workers most likely to lose their jobs to robots also likely to be affected by these developments? Briefly explain.

b. By looking at changes in equilibrium wages in the affected industries, can we distinguish the effects of increased use of robots, increased foreign imports, and increased offshoring? Briefly explain.

17.4 Explaining Differences in Wages, pages 577–585

LEARNING OBJECTIVE: Use demand and supply analysis to explain how compensating differentials, discrimination, and labor unions cause wages to differ.

MyLab Economics Visit www.pearson.com/mylab/economics to complete these exercises online and get instant feedback.

Summary

The equilibrium wage is determined by the intersection of the labor demand curve and the labor supply curve. Some differences in wages are explained by **compensating differentials**, which are higher wages that compensate workers for unpleasant aspects of a job. Wages can also differ because of **economic discrimination**, which involves paying a person a lower wage or excluding a person from an occupation on the basis of irrelevant characteristics, such as race or gender. **Labor unions** are organizations of employees that have the legal right to bargain with employers about wages and working conditions. Being in a union increases a worker's wages about 10 percent, holding constant other factors, such as the industry the workers are in.

Review Questions

4.1 What is a compensating differential? Give an example.

4.2 Define *economic discrimination*. Is the fact that one group in the population has higher earnings than other groups evidence of economic discrimination? Briefly explain.

4.3 In what sense do employers who discriminate pay an economic penalty? Is this penalty enough to eliminate discrimination? Briefly explain.

Problems and Applications

4.4 (Related to the Chapter Opener on page 562) An article in the *Wall Street Journal* on the use of driverless trucks at Rio Tinto's Australian mines observed, "The new equipment cut many driving jobs. . . . But the reductions will be partly offset by new types of work. The company now needs more network technicians . . . a hybrid of electrical and mechanical engineering that hardly existed five years ago." Is it likely that total employment at Rio Tinto's mines will have increased or decreased as a result of its use of robots? Are the *average* wages Rio Tinto pays

likely to be higher or lower? Are the wages of the truck drivers who were replaced by robots likely to end up higher or lower in the drivers' new jobs? Briefly explain your answers.

Source: Timothy Aeppel, "What Clever Robots Mean for Jobs," *Wall Street Journal*, February 24, 2015.

4.5 (Related to the Don't Let This Happen to You on page 578) Joe Morgan is a sportscaster and former baseball player. After he stated that he thought the salaries of Major League Baseball players were justified, a baseball fan wrote the following to Rob Neyer, a sports columnist:

> Mr. Neyer,
>
> What are your feelings about Joe Morgan's comment that players are justified in being paid what they're being paid? How is it ok for A-Rod [Alex Rodriguez, at the time a player on the New York Yankees] to earn $115,000 per GAME while my boss works 80 hour weeks and earns $30,000 per year?

How would you answer this fan's questions?

Source: ESPN.com, August 30, 2002.

4.6 Through the 2016 season, Nick Saban's record as the head football coach at the University of Alabama was 119 wins and 19 losses. The $11.125 million salary the university paid him in 2017 was the highest received by any college football coach. Yet ESPN commentator Scott Van Pelt argued, "Alabama is still getting a bargain in Nick Saban, and I guarantee you that they know that." How could the University of Alabama be getting a bargain despite paying Saban such a high salary?

Source: Ben George, "ESPN's Scott Van Pelt Explains Why Nick Saban Is Underpaid," espn929.com, May 4, 2017.

4.7 (Related to the Apply the Concept on page 578) A business columnist for the *New York Times* estimated that the wealth of J.K. Rowling, author of the Harry Potter novels, at $1.2 *billion*. The columnist observed, "Along with other famous authors, entertainers and sports stars, Ms. Rowling has also benefited from globalization and technology advances." What technology advances is he likely referring to? Why would those advances increase Rowling's wealth compared with the wealth of a similarly popular author of, say, the 1960s?

Source: James B. Stewart, "In the Chamber of Secrets: J.K. Rowling's Net Worth," *New York Times*, November 24, 2016.

4.8 **(Related to the Apply the Concept on page 578)** Why are there superstar basketball players but no superstar plumbers?

4.9 The following table is based on a summary of a survey conducted by the Bureau of Labor Statistics. There are wide differences in the median wages of the occupations listed—for example, between air traffic controllers and actors. (Half the workers in an occupation earn more than the median wage and half earn less.) But there are also significant variations in wages within occupations. The highest-paid workers in any of the occupations earned more than the lowest-paid workers in any of the other occupations. For each of the following occupations, provide one reason large variations exist between the tenth and ninetieth percentile wages:

  a. Athletes
  b. Real estate brokers
  c. Lawyers
  d. Postsecondary (or college) teachers

Occupation	Employment	Median Wage	10th Percentile Wage	90th Percentile Wage
Actors	59,210	$41,203	$18,720	>$187,200
Athletes	11,520	43,350	20,190	>187,200
Veterinarians	62,470	87,590	52,530	157,390
Chiropractors	29,830	66,720	31,440	143,760
Real estate brokers	38,720	57,360	23,880	178,770
Physicists	16,790	109,600	54,930	184,650
Economists	18,680	95,710	50,440	170,780
Lawyers	603,310	114,970	55,400	>187,200
Postsecondary teachers	1,522,210	63,010	28,950	138,720
Air traffic controllers	22,860	122,340	67,070	172,000

Source: Elka Torpey, "Same Occupation, Different Pay: How Wages Vary," U.S. Department of Labor Statistics, May 2015.

4.10 Sam Goldwyn, a movie producer during Hollywood's Golden Age in the 1930s and 1940s, once remarked about one of his stars: "We're overpaying him, but he's worth it."

  a. In what sense did Goldwyn mean that he was overpaying this star?
  b. If he was overpaying the star, why would the star have still been worth it?

4.11 Prior to the early twentieth century, a worker who was injured on the job could collect damages only by suing his employer. To sue successfully, the worker—or his family, if the worker had been killed—had to show that the injury was due to the employer's negligence, that the worker did not know the job was hazardous, and that the worker's own negligence had not contributed to the accident. These lawsuits were difficult for workers to win, and even workers who had been seriously injured on the job often were unable to collect any damages from their employers. Beginning in 1910, most states passed workers' compensation laws that required employers to purchase insurance that would compensate workers for injuries suffered on the job. A study by Price Fishback of the University of Arizona and Shawn Kantor of the University of California, Merced, shows that after the passage of workers' compensation laws, wages received by workers in the coal and lumber industries fell. Briefly explain why passage of workers' compensation laws would lead to a decrease in wages in some industries.

Source: Price V. Fishback and Shawn Everett Kantor, "Did Workers Pay for the Passage of Workers' Compensation Laws?" *Quarterly Journal of Economics*, Vol. 110, No. 3, August 1995, pp. 713–742.

4.12 The following table is similar to Table 17.2 on page 580, except that it includes the earnings of Asian males and females. Does the fact that Asian males are the highest-earning group in the table affect the likelihood that economic discrimination is the best explanation for why earnings differ among the groups listed in the table? Briefly explain your argument.

Group	Weekly Earnings
Asian males	$1,271
White males	1,025
Asian females	921
White females	827
Black males	756
Hispanic males	725
Black females	672
Hispanic females	623

Source: U.S. Bureau of Labor Statistics, "Usual Weekly Earnings of Wage and Salary Workers, First Quarter 2017," April 18, 2017.

4.13 During the 1970s, many women changed their minds about whether they would leave the labor force after marrying and having children or whether they would be in the labor force most of their adult lives. In 1968, the National Longitudinal Survey asked a representative sample of women aged 14 to 24 whether they expected to be in the labor force at age 35. Twenty-nine percent of white women and 59 percent of black women responded that they expected to be in the labor force at that age. In fact, when these women were 35 years old, 60 percent of those who were married and 80 percent of those who were unmarried were in the labor force. In other words, many more women ended up being in the labor force than expected to be when they were of high school and college age. What effect did this fact have on the earnings of these women? Briefly explain.

Source: Claudia Goldin, *Understanding the Gender Gap: An Economic History of American Women*, New York: Oxford University Press, 1990, p. 155.

4.14 Lawrence Katz, an economist at Harvard, was quoted in a newspaper article as arguing that differences between the incomes of male physicians and female physicians "are largely explained by individual choices." He also noted that discrimination could account for part of the gap, "though it isn't clear how much."

a. What did Katz mean by "individual choices"? How can individual choices result in differences between how much men and women are paid?

b. Why is it difficult to estimate how much of the gap between what men and women are paid is due to discrimination?

Source: Josh Mitchell, "Women Notch Progress," *Wall Street Journal*, December 4, 2012.

4.15 (Related to **Solved Problem 17.4** on page 581) Use the following graphs to answer the questions.

Market for trash collectors

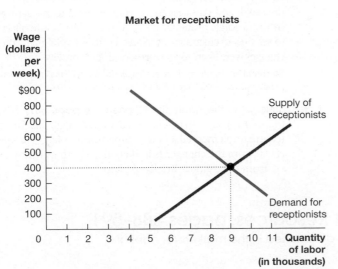

Market for receptionists

a. What is the equilibrium quantity of trash collectors hired, and what is the equilibrium wage?

b. What is the equilibrium quantity of receptionists hired, and what is the equilibrium wage?

c. Briefly discuss why trash collectors might earn a higher weekly wage than receptionists.

d. Suppose that comparable-worth legislation is passed, and the government requires that trash collectors and receptionists be paid the same wage, $500 per week. Now how many trash collectors will be hired, and how many receptionists will be hired?

4.16 (Related to **Solved Problem 17.4** on page 581) In most universities, economics professors receive higher salaries than English professors. Suppose that the government requires that from now on, all universities must pay economics professors the same salaries as English professors. Use demand and supply graphs to analyze the effect of this requirement.

4.17 (Related to the **Apply the Concept** on page 583) Why might employers be more likely to interview a job applicant with a white-sounding name than an applicant with an African-American–sounding name? Leaving aside legal penalties, will employers who follow this practice incur an economic penalty? Briefly explain.

4.18 (Related to the **Apply the Concept** on page 583) Many firms include on their employment applications a box that job seekers are asked to check if they have ever been convicted of a crime. Some firms automatically reject applicants who check the box. As a result, some people with criminal convictions have difficulty finding a job, which may increase the likelihood that they will commit another crime. Some states and cities have enacted "ban the box" legislation that forbids firms from asking about criminal histories on job applications, although typically the firms are allowed to ask such questions in job interviews. A study by Jennifer L. Doleac of the University of Virginia and Benjamin Hansen of the University of Oregon found that ban the box legislation significantly reduces the probability of employment among young male African-American job applicants. The economists noted that ban the box legislation "does not address employers' concerns about hiring those with criminal records, and so could increase discrimination against groups that are more likely to include recently-incarcerated ex-offenders." Briefly explain why this result might have occurred. Relate your answer to the reasons firms might be more likely to interview an applicant with a white-sounding name even if the applicant's résumé was identical to that of an applicant with a black-sounding name.

Source: Jennifer L. Doleac and Benjamin Hansen, "Does 'Ban the Box' Help or Hurt Low-Skilled Workers? Statistical Discrimination and Employment Outcomes When Criminal Histories Are Hidden," National Bureau of Economic Research, Working Paper No. 22469, July 2016.

4.19 Daniel Hamermesh, an economist at the University of Texas, has done a great deal of research on labor markets. According to an article in *Forbes*, Hamermesh wrote that "below-average-looking men earn 17% less than those considered good-looking, while below-average-looking females earn 12% less than their attractive counterparts." Is this difference in earnings due to economic discrimination? Briefly explain.

Source: Susan Adams, "Does Beauty Really Pay?" *Forbes*, August 30, 2011.

17.5 Personnel Economics, pages 585–588

LEARNING OBJECTIVE: Discuss the role personnel economics can play in helping firms deal with human resources issues.

MyLab Economics Visit www.pearson.com/mylab/economics to complete these exercises online and get instant feedback.

Summary

Personnel economics is the application of economic analysis to human resources issues. One insight of personnel economics is that the productivity of workers can often be increased if firms move from straight-time pay to commission or piece-rate pay.

Review Questions

5.1 What is personnel economics?

5.2 What are the two ways that the productivity of a firm's employees may increase when a firm moves from straight-time pay to commission or piece-rate pay? If piece-rate or commission systems of compensating workers have important advantages for firms, why don't more firms use them?

Problems and Applications

5.3 A study found that the number of jobs in which firms used bonuses, commissions, or piece rates to tie workers' pay to their performance increased from an estimated 30 percent of all jobs in the 1970s to 40 percent in the 1990s. Why would systems that tie workers' pay to how much they produce have become increasingly popular with firms? The same study found that these pay systems were more common in higher-paid jobs than in lower-paid jobs. Briefly explain this result.

Source: Thomas Lemieux, W. Bentley MacLeod, and Daniel Parent, "Performance Pay and Wage Inequality," *Quarterly Journal of Economics*, Vol. 124, No. 1, February 2009, pp. 1–49.

5.4 Research by economists Susan Helper, Morris Kleiner, and Yingchun Wang found that the use of pay-for-performance, or piece-rate pay, has declined in manufacturing industries in recent decades. In a summary of this research, Lester Picker explained, "This change has come about with the adoption of modern manufacturing

systems in which firms produce a greater variety of products to a more demanding quality and delivery standard."

a. What characteristics determine whether a salary system or a piece-rate system is likely to be more profitable for a manufacturing firm?

b. Why would modern systems "in which firms produce a greater variety of products to a more demanding quality and delivery standard" than manufacturers used previously result in firms choosing to pay their workers salaries rather than use piece rates?

Source: Lester Picker, "The Decline of 'Piece Rate' Compensation in Manufacturing," *The Digest*, National Bureau of Economic Research.

5.5 (Related to the Apply the Concept on page 587) In most jobs, the harder you work, the more you earn. Some workers would rather work harder and earn more; others would rather work less hard, even though as a result they earn less. Suppose, though, that all workers at a company fall into the "work harder and earn more" group. Suppose also that the workers all have the same abilities. In these circumstances, would output per worker be the same under an hourly wage compensation system as under a piece-rate system? Briefly explain.

5.6 (Related to the Apply the Concept on page 587) For years, the Goodyear Tire & Rubber Company compensated its sales force by paying a salesperson a salary plus a bonus, based on the number of tires he or she sold. Eventually, Goodyear made two changes to this policy: (1) The basis for the bonus was changed from the *quantity* of tires sold to the *revenue* from the tires sold; and (2) salespeople were required to get approval from corporate headquarters in Akron, Ohio, before offering to sell tires to customers at reduced prices. Explain why these changes were likely to increase Goodyear's profits.

Source: Timothy Aeppel, "Amid Weak Inflation, Firms Turn Creative to Boost Prices," *Wall Street Journal*, September 18, 2002.

5.7 (Related to the Apply the Concept on page 587) When the contact lens firm discussed in the *Apply the Concept* feature implemented a new compensation plan, who benefited from the change? Is it likely that there were any losers from the change? Briefly explain.

17.6 The Markets for Capital and Natural Resources, pages 588–591

LEARNING OBJECTIVE: Show how equilibrium prices are determined in the markets for capital and natural resources.

MyLab Economics Visit www.pearson.com/mylab/economics to complete these exercises online and get instant feedback.

Summary

The approach used to analyze the market for labor can also be used to analyze the markets for other factors of production. In equilibrium, the price of capital is equal to the marginal

revenue product of capital, and the price of natural resources is equal to the marginal revenue product of natural resources. The price received by a factor that is in fixed supply is called an **economic rent** (or **pure rent**). A **monopsony** is a situation in which a firm is the sole buyer of a factor of production. According to the **marginal productivity theory of income distribution**, the distribution of income is determined by the marginal productivity of the factors of production individuals own.

Review Questions

6.1 In equilibrium, what determines the price of capital? What determines the price of natural resources? What is an economic rent?

6.2 What is a monopsony?

6.3 What is the marginal productivity theory of income distribution?

Problems and Applications

6.4 Adam operates a pin factory. Suppose that Adam faces the situation shown in the following table and that the cost of renting a machine is $550 per week.

   a. Fill in the missing values in the table and determine the profit-maximizing number of machines for Adam to rent. Briefly explain why renting this number of machines is profit maximizing.

   b. Draw Adam's demand curve for capital.

Number of Machines	Output of Pins (boxes per week)	Marginal Product of Capital	Product Price (dollars per box)	Total Revenue	Marginal Revenue Product of Capital	Rental Cost per Machine	Additional Profit from Renting One Additional Machine
0	0	—	$100		—	$550	
1	12		100			550	
2	21		100			550	
3	28		100			550	
4	34		100			550	
5	39		100			550	
6	43		100			550	

6.5 Many people have predicted, using a model like the one in panel (b) of Figure 17.12 on page 590, that the price of natural resources should rise consistently over time in comparison with the prices of other goods because the demand curve for natural resources is continually shifting to the right, while the supply curve must be shifting to the left as natural resources are used up. However, the relative prices of most natural resources have not been increasing. Draw a graph showing the demand and supply for natural resources that can explain why prices haven't risen even though demand has.

6.6 In 1879, economist Henry George published *Progress and Poverty*, which became one of the best-selling books of the nineteenth century. In this book, George argued that all existing taxes should be replaced with a single tax on land. Tax incidence refers to the actual division of the burden of a tax between buyers and sellers in a market (see Chapter 4, Section 4.4). If land is taxed, how will the burden of the tax be divided between the sellers of land and the buyers of land? Illustrate your answer with a graph of the market for land.

6.7 The total amount of oil in the earth is not increasing. Does this mean that in the market for oil, the supply curve is perfectly inelastic? Briefly explain.

6.8 In a competitive labor market, imposing a minimum wage should reduce the equilibrium level of employment. Will this result still hold if the labor market is a monopsony? Briefly explain.

Critical Thinking Exercises

CT17.1 A columnist for the *New York Times* discussed the book *Academically Adrift*, written by sociologists Richard Arum and Josipa Roksa. Locate and read the column and note what factor affecting the demand for labor the columnist describes. Discuss how this factor affects the demand for labor. The column was written in 2014. Has anything changed in the years since then that would affect your answer? Briefly explain.

   Source: Kevin Carey, "The Economic Price of Colleges' Failures," *New York Times*, September 2, 2014.

CT17.2 Section 17.4 of this chapter explains that the pay of professional athletes depends on their marginal revenue product (*MRP*). You likely know that college football and basketball are very popular sports, so presumably some college athletes have high *MRP*s. Yet beyond tuition and board, college athletes are not paid. What might be an economic reason for the difference in pay between college athletes and professional athletes?

CT17.3 If you follow professional sports, you likely know that many leagues, such as the National Football League, have salary caps for teams. That is, the amount a team can pay its players is limited. Why might leagues adopt salary caps? *Hint:* Consider how the pay of professional athletes is explained in this chapter.

Public Choice, Taxes, and the Distribution of Income

Should Your Small Business Be Taxed Like Apple?

How should the federal government tax businesses? The corporate income tax applies to corporations, but as we saw in Chapter 8, most businesses in the United States are sole proprietorships, not corporations. If you open a bakery, run a bicycle repair shop, or sell movie posters on eBay, you are likely a sole proprietor and will pay the federal personal income tax—not the corporate income tax—on your profit.

For many years, the U.S. corporate income tax rate was among the highest in the world. In 2017, Congress and President Donald Trump enacted legislation cutting the top corporate tax rate from 35 percent to 21 percent. The tax rate was also lowered for some "income pass-through businesses." Sole proprietorships and most partnerships are pass-through businesses, so the tax rate owners of some of these businesses pay was cut substantially from the top personal income tax rate of 39.6 percent. President Trump stated that the purpose of cutting tax rates was to increase economic growth. Some policymakers and economists noted, though, that a significant share of the benefits of the tax cuts went to high-income individuals, particularly those who own corporate stock or who own pass-through businesses that are eligible to be taxed at the new lower rate. As a result, these critics argued, the tax cuts will make the distribution of income more unequal.

The debate over President Trump's tax reform proposal wasn't unusual. When Presidents John F. Kennedy and Ronald Reagan proposed significant cuts in income taxes that they argued would increase economic efficiency, critics claimed that the tax cuts rewarded high-income taxpayers and increased income inequality. Although the basic purpose of taxes is to pay for the government's spending, over the years, Congress and the president have used taxes to

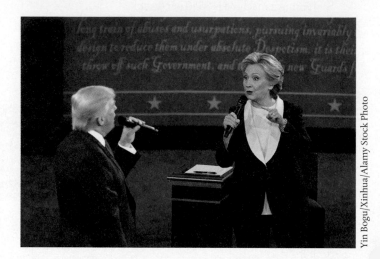

Yin Bogu/Xinhua/Alamy Stock Photo

try to achieve other policy objectives including promoting home ownership, employer-provided medical insurance, solar power, and the use of ethanol in gasoline. Some of these objectives have been controversial. During the 2016 presidential election, Democratic nominee Hillary Clinton proposed increasing taxes on some high-income individuals and using the funds to finance government programs aimed at raising living standards for people with lower incomes.

Understanding the tax system and the criteria economists use to evaluate it is important in analyzing the role of the government in the economy. Among the questions we consider in this chapter are: Has the tax code increased or reduced economic efficiency? Has government policy had much effect on the distribution of income? If not, what explains trends in income inequality?

Sources: Michael C. Bender and Richard Rubin, "Trump Plans to Seek Tax Rate of 15% on Owner-Operated Companies," *Wall Street Journal*, April 25, 2017; Josh Zumbrun, "Economists Say President Donald Trump's Agenda Would Boost Growth—A Little," *Wall Street Journal*, May 11, 2017; and Julie Hirschfeld Davis and Alan Rappeport, "White House Proposes Slashing Tax Rates, Significantly Aiding Wealthy," *New York Times*, April 26, 2017.

Public Choice, page 602

Describe the public choice model and use it to analyze government decision making.

 The Tax System, page 606

Explain the tax system in the United States, including the principles that governments use to create tax policy.

 Tax Incidence Revisited: The Effect of Price Elasticity, page 614

Explain the effect of price elasticity on tax incidence.

18.4 **Income Distribution and Poverty,** page 617

Discuss income distribution and income mobility and the role of policy in addressing these issues.

Economics in Your Life & Career

Which Is Better: A $500 Raise or $500 toward Health Insurance?

Suppose you own a bike shop with 15 employees. You have trouble retaining employees because competing bike shops are paying higher wages. You think increasing your employees' compensation by $500 per year would make working at your bike shop more attractive. One employee requests that instead of increasing her wage by $500 you reduce by that amount the premium she pays for the health insurance plan you offer employees. Why would she make that request? Wouldn't anyone prefer to have $500 in cash rather than $500 contributed to a health insurance plan? As you read this chapter, try to answer this question. You can check your answer against the one we provide on **page 629** at the end of this chapter.

Public choice model A model that applies economic analysis to government decision making.

We have seen that the government plays a significant role in helping the market system work efficiently by providing secure rights to private property and an independent court system to enforce contracts (see Chapter 2, Section 2.3). We have also seen that the government itself must sometimes supply goods—known as *public goods*—that private firms will not supply (see Chapter 5, Section 5.4). But how do governments decide which policies to adopt? The late Nobel Laureate James Buchanan and the late Gordon Tullock, of George Mason University, along with other economists, developed the **public choice model**, which applies economic analysis to government decision making. In the next section, we will explore how public choice can help us understand how policymakers make decisions.

In the following sections, we will discuss the principles that governments use to create tax policy. In particular, we will see how economists identify which taxes are most economically efficient. At the end of this chapter, we will discuss the extent to which government policy—including tax policy—affects the distribution of income.

18.1 Public Choice

LEARNING OBJECTIVE: Describe the public choice model and use it to analyze government decision making.

In earlier chapters, we explained the decisions of households and firms by assuming that they act to make themselves as well off as possible. In particular, we have assumed that households choose the goods they buy to maximize their utility and that firms choose the quantities and prices of the goods they sell to maximize profit. Because government policy plays an important role in the economy, we need to consider how government policymakers—such as senators, governors, presidents, and state legislators—arrive at their decisions. One of the key insights from the public choice model is that policymakers are no different from consumers or managers of firms: A policymakers is likely to pursue his or her own self-interest, even if it conflicts with the public interest. In particular, we expect that public officials will take actions that are likely to result in their being reelected.

How Do We Know the Public Interest? Models of Voting

It is possible to argue that elected officials simply represent the preferences of the voters who elect them. After all, it would seem logical that voters will not reelect a politician who fails to act in the public interest. A closer look at voting, however, makes it less clear that politicians are simply representing the views of the voters.

The Voting Paradox Many policy decisions involve multiple alternatives. Consider, for instance, the trade-offs members of Congress face because the size of the federal budget is limited. To take a simple example, suppose that there is $1 billion available in the budget, and Congress must choose whether to spend it on *only one* of three alternatives: (1) research on breast cancer, (2) subsidies for mass transit, or (3) increased border security. Assume that the votes of members of Congress will represent the preferences of their constituents. We might expect that Congress will vote for the alternative favored by a majority of voters. In fact, though, there are circumstances in which majority voting will fail to result in a consistent decision. For example, suppose for simplicity that there are only three voters, and they have the preferences shown at the top of Table 18.1.

In the table, we show the three policy alternatives in the first column. The remaining columns show the voters' rankings of the alternatives. For example, Lena would prefer to see the money spent on cancer research. Her second choice is mass transit, and her third choice is border security. What happens if a series of votes are taken in which each pair of alternatives is considered in turn? The bottom of Table 18.1 shows the results of these votes. If the vote is between spending the money on cancer research and spending the money on mass transit, cancer research wins because Lena and

Policy	Lena	David	Kathleen
Cancer research	1st	2nd	3rd
Mass transit	2nd	3rd	1st
Border security	3rd	1st	2nd

Votes	Outcome
Cancer research versus mass transit	Cancer research wins
Mass transit versus border security	Mass transit wins
Border security versus cancer research	Border security wins

Table 18.1

The Voting Paradox

David both prefer spending the money on cancer research rather than on mass transit. So, if the votes of members of Congress represent the preferences of voters, we have a clear verdict, and the money is spent on breast cancer research. Suppose, though, that the vote is between spending the money on mass transit and spending the money on border security. Then, because Lena and Kathleen prefer spending on mass transit to spending on border security, mass transit wins. Now, finally, suppose the vote is between spending on cancer research and spending on border security. Surprisingly, border security wins because that is what David and Kathleen prefer. The outcome of this vote is surprising because if voters prefer cancer research to mass transit and mass transit to border security, we would expect that consistency in decision making would ensure that they prefer cancer research to border security. But in this example, the collective preferences of the voters turn out not to be consistent. The failure of majority voting to always result in consistent choices is called the **voting paradox**.

This example is artificial because we assumed that there were only three alternatives, there were only three voters, and a simple majority vote determined the outcomes. In fact, though, the late Nobel Laureate Kenneth Arrow of Stanford University demonstrated mathematically that the failure of majority votes to always represent voters' preferences is a very general result. The **Arrow impossibility theorem** states that no system of voting can be devised that will consistently represent the underlying preferences of voters. This theorem suggests that there is no way through democratic voting to ensure that the preferences of voters are translated into policy choices. In fact, the Arrow impossibility theorem indicates that voting might lead to shifts in policy that may not be efficient. For instance, which of the three alternatives for spending the $1 billion Congress will actually choose would depend on the order in which the alternatives happen to be voted on, which might change from one year to the next. So, for economic issues, such as the funding of public goods, we cannot count on the political process to necessarily result in an efficient outcome. In other words, the "voting market"—as represented by elections—may often do a less efficient job of representing consumer preferences than do markets for goods and services.

The Median Voter Theorem In practice, many political issues are decided by a majority vote. In those cases, what can we say about which voters' preferences the outcome is likely to represent? An important result, known as the **median voter theorem**, states that the outcome of a majority vote is likely to represent the preferences of the voter who is in the political middle. To take another simplified example, suppose there are five voters, and their preferences for spending on breast cancer research are shown in Figure 18.1. Their preferences range from Kathleen, who prefers to spend nothing on breast cancer research—preferring the funds to be spent on other programs or for federal spending to be reduced and taxes lowered—to Lena, who prefers to spend $6 billion.

In this case, David is the median voter because he is in the political middle; two voters would prefer to spend less than he does, and two voters would prefer to spend more than he does. To see why the median voter's preferences are likely to prevail, consider first a vote between David's preferred outcome of spending $2 billion and a proposal to spend $6 billion. Because only Lena favors $6 billion and the other voters all prefer

Voting paradox The failure of majority voting to always result in consistent choices.

Arrow impossibility theorem A mathematical theorem that holds that no system of voting can be devised that will consistently represent the underlying preferences of voters.

Median voter theorem The proposition that the outcome of a majority vote is likely to represent the preferences of the voter who is in the political middle.

Figure 18.1

The Median Voter Theorem

The median voter theorem states that the outcome of a majority vote is likely to represent the preferences of the voter who is in the political middle. In this case, David is in the political middle because two voters want to spend more on breast cancer research than he does, and two voters want to spend less. In any vote between a proposal to spend $2 billion and a proposal to spend a different amount, a proposal to spend $2 billion will win.

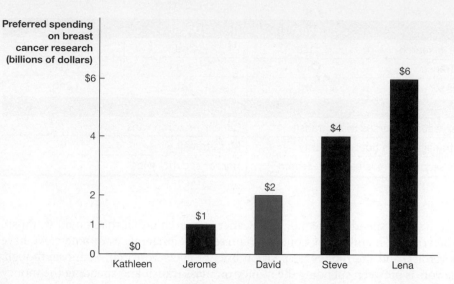

spending less, the proposal to spend $2 billion would win four votes to one. Similarly, consider a vote between spending $2 billion and spending $1 billion. Three voters prefer spending more than $1 billion, and only two prefer spending $1 billion or less, so the proposal to spend $2 billion will win three votes to two. Only the proposal to spend $2 billion will have the support of a majority when paired with proposals to spend a different amount. Notice also that the amount spent as a result of the voting is less than the amount that would result from taking the simple average of the voter's preferences, which would be $2.6 billion.

One implication of the median voter theorem is that the political process tends to serve individuals whose preferences are in the middle but not those individuals whose preferences are far away from the median. There is an important contrast between the political process, which results in collective actions in which everyone is obliged to participate, and the market process, in which individuals are free to participate or not. For instance, even though Kathleen would prefer not to spend government funds on breast cancer research, once a majority has voted to spend $2 billion, Kathleen is obliged to go along with the spending—and the taxes required to fund the spending. This outcome is in contrast with the market for goods and services, where if, for instance, Kathleen disagrees with the majority of consumers who like iPhones, she is under no obligation to buy one. Similarly, even though Lena and Steve might prefer to pay significantly higher taxes to fund additional spending on breast cancer research, they are obliged to go along with the lower level of spending that the majority approved. If Lena would like to have her iPhone gold plated, she can choose to do so, even if the vast majority of consumers would consider such spending a waste of money. **MyLab Economics** Concept Check

Government Failure?

The voting models we have just considered indicate that individuals are less likely to see their preferences represented in the outcomes of government policies than in the outcomes of markets. The public choice model goes beyond this observation to question whether the self-interest of policymakers is likely to cause them to take actions that are inconsistent with the preferences of voters, even where those preferences are clear. In the next sections, we examine five key concepts that help explain this outcome.

Rent Seeking Economists usually focus on the actions of individuals and firms as they attempt to make themselves better off by interacting in markets. The public choice model shifts the focus to attempts by individuals and firms to engage in **rent seeking**, which is the use of government action to make themselves better off at the expense of others. One of the benefits of the market system is that it channels self-interested behavior in a way that benefits society as a whole. Although Apple developed the iPhone to make a profit, its actions increased the well-being of millions of consumers.

Rent seeking Attempts by individuals and firms to use government action to make themselves better off at the expense of others.

When Samsung introduced the Galaxy to compete with the iPhone, it was also motivated by the desire for profit, but it further increased consumer well-being by expanding the choice of smartphones available to consumers. Rent seeking, in contrast, can benefit a few individuals or firms at the expense of all other individuals and firms. For example, U.S. sugar firms have successfully convinced Congress to impose a quota on imports of sugar (see Chapter 9, Section 9.4). The quota has benefited the owners of U.S. sugar firms and the people who work for them but has reduced consumer surplus, hurt U.S. candy companies and their workers, and reduced economic efficiency.

Because firms can benefit from government intervention in the economy, as the sugar companies have benefited from the sugar quota, they are willing to spend money to influence government policymakers. Members of Congress, state legislators, governors, and presidents need funds to finance their election campaigns. So, these policymakers may accept campaign contributions from rent-seeking firms and may be willing to introduce *special-interest legislation* on their behalf.

Logrolling and Rational Ignorance Two other factors help explain why rent-seeking behavior can sometimes succeed. It may seem puzzling that the sugar quota has been enacted when it helps very few workers and firms. Why would members of Congress vote for the sugar quota if they do not have sugar companies in their districts? One possibility is *logrolling*, which refers to the situation in which a member of Congress votes to approve a bill in exchange for favorable votes from other members on other bills. For example, a member of Congress from Texas might vote for the sugar quota, even though none of the member's constituents will benefit from it. In exchange, members of Congress from districts where sugar producers are located will vote for legislation the member of Congress from Texas would like to see passed. As Pennsylvania Senator Pat Toomey put it after his attempt to eliminate the sugar quota was voted down: "They circle the wagons, work together, protect each others' interests." This *vote trading* may result in a majority of Congress supporting legislation that benefits the economic interests of a few while harming the economic interests of a much larger group.

But if the majority of voters are harmed by rent-seeking legislation, how does it get passed, even given the effects of logrolling? Consider another possible explanation for the survival of the sugar quota. Although total consumer surplus declines by $2.59 billion per year because of the sugar quota, when it is spread across a population of 325 million, the loss per person is only about $8. Because the loss is so small, most people do not take it into account when deciding who to vote for, and many people are not even aware that the sugar quota exists. Other voters may be convinced to support restrictions on trade because the jobs saved by tariffs and quotas are visible and often highly publicized, while the jobs lost because of these restrictions and the reductions in consumer surplus receive less notice. Because becoming informed on an issue may require time and effort and the economic payoff is often low, some economists argue that many voters are *rationally ignorant* of the effect of rent-seeking legislation. In this view, because voters frequently lack an economic incentive to become informed about legislation, the preferences of voters do not act as a constraint on legislators voting for rent-seeking legislation.

Regulatory Capture One way in which the government intervenes in the economy is by establishing a regulatory agency or commission that is given authority over a particular industry or type of product. For example, no firm is allowed to sell prescription drugs in the United States without first receiving authorization from the Food and Drug Administration (FDA). Ideally, regulatory agencies will make decisions in the public interest. The FDA should weigh the benefits to patients from quickly approving a new drug against the costs if a drug with potentially dangerous side effects is approved without thorough testing. However, because the firms being regulated have a financial stake in the regulatory agency's actions, the firms have an incentive to try to influence those actions. In extreme cases, this influence may lead the agency to make decisions that are in the best interests of the firms being regulated, even if these actions are not in the public interest. In that case, the agency has been subject to *regulatory capture* by the industry being regulated. Some economists point to the Interstate Commerce Commission (ICC) as an example of regulatory capture. Although Congress has since abolished the ICC, for decades it determined the prices that railroads and long-distance trucking firms could charge to haul freight. Congress originally established the ICC to safeguard the interests of consumers, but some economists have argued that for many years the ICC operated to suppress competition, which was in the interests of the railroads and trucking firms rather than in the interests of consumers. Economists debate the extent to which regulatory capture explains the decisions of some government agencies.

The presence of externalities can lead to market failure, which is the situation in which the market does not supply the economically efficient quantity of a good or service (see Chapter 5, Section 5.1). Public choice analysis indicates that *government failure* can also occur. For the reasons we have discussed in this section, it is possible that government intervention in the economy may reduce economic efficiency rather than increase it. Economists disagree about the extent to which government failure results in serious economic inefficiency in the U.S. economy. Most economists, though, accept the basic argument of the public choice model that policymakers may have incentives to intervene in the economy in ways that do not promote efficiency and that proposals for such intervention should be evaluated with care.   **MyLab Economics** Concept Check

Is Government Regulation Necessary?

The public choice model raises important questions about the effect of government regulation on economic efficiency. Can we conclude that Congress should abolish agencies such as the Food and Drug Administration (FDA), the Environmental Protection Agency (EPA), and the Federal Trade Commission (FTC)? In fact, most economists agree that these agencies can serve useful purposes. For instance, the EPA can help correct the effect of externalities, such as the pollution that some companies emit as they produce goods. Regulatory agencies can also improve economic efficiency in markets where consumers have difficulty obtaining the information they need to make informed purchases. For example, consumers have no easy way of detecting bacteria and other contaminants in food or determining whether prescription drugs are safe and effective. The FDA was established in 1906 to monitor the nation's food supply following newspaper accounts of unsanitary practices in many meatpacking plants.

Although government regulation can clearly provide important benefits to consumers, we need to take into account the costs of regulations. Recent estimates indicate that the costs of federal regulations may be several thousand dollars per taxpayer. Economics can help policymakers devise regulations that provide benefits to consumers

MyLab Economics Study Plan   that exceed their costs.   **MyLab Economics** Concept Check

 The Tax System

18.2

LEARNING OBJECTIVE: Explain the tax system in the United States, including the principles that governments use to create tax policy.

Regardless of how the size of government and the types of activities it engages in are determined, government spending has to be financed. The government primarily relies on taxes to raise the revenue it needs. Some taxes, such as those on cigarettes or alcohol, are intended to discourage what society views as undesirable behavior in addition to raising revenue. These are the most widely used taxes:

- **Individual income taxes.** The federal government, most state governments, and some local governments tax the wages, salaries, and other income of households and the profits of small businesses, which, as we saw in the chapter opener, are typically taxed at the same rate as wages and salaries. The individual income tax is the largest source of revenue for the federal government. Because low-income people do not pay federal individual income taxes, in recent years nearly half of all households have paid no federal income tax.

- **Social insurance taxes.** The federal government taxes wages and salaries to raise revenue for the Social Security and Medicare programs. *Social Security* makes payments to retired workers and to disabled individuals. *Medicare* helps pay the medical expenses of people over age 65. The Social Security and Medicare taxes are often called *payroll taxes*. As the U.S. population has aged, payroll taxes have increased. By 2017, more than three-quarters of taxpayers paid a greater amount in payroll taxes than in federal individual income taxes. The federal government and state governments also tax wages and salaries to raise revenue for the unemployment insurance system, which makes payments to workers who have lost their jobs.
- **Sales taxes.** Most state and local governments tax retail sales of most products. More than half the states exempt groceries from the sales tax, and a few states also exempt clothing.
- **Property taxes.** Most local governments tax homes, offices, factories, and the land they are built on. In the United States, the property tax is the largest source of funds for public schools.
- **Excise taxes.** The federal government and some state governments levy excise taxes on specific goods, such as gasoline, cigarettes, and beer.

An Overview of the U.S. Tax System

Panels (a) and (b) of Figure 18.2 show the revenue sources of the federal, state, and local governments. Panel (a) shows that the federal government raises more than 75 percent of its revenue from the social insurance taxes and individual income taxes. Corporate

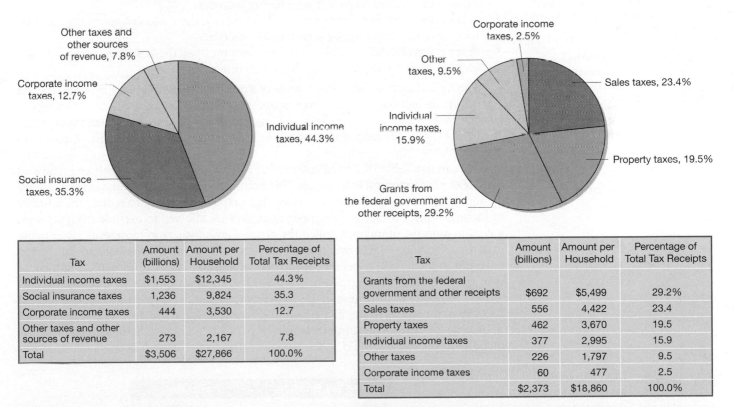

Tax	Amount (billions)	Amount per Household	Percentage of Total Tax Receipts
Individual income taxes	$1,553	$12,345	44.3%
Social insurance taxes	1,236	9,824	35.3
Corporate income taxes	444	3,530	12.7
Other taxes and other sources of revenue	273	2,167	7.8
Total	$3,506	$27,866	100.0%

Tax	Amount (billions)	Amount per Household	Percentage of Total Tax Receipts
Grants from the federal government and other receipts	$692	$5,499	29.2%
Sales taxes	556	4,422	23.4
Property taxes	462	3,670	19.5
Individual income taxes	377	2,995	15.9
Other taxes	226	1,797	9.5
Corporate income taxes	60	477	2.5
Total	$2,373	$18,860	100.0%

(a) Sources of federal government revenue, 2016

(b) Sources of state and local government revenue, 2016

MyLab Economics Animation

Figure 18.2   **Federal, State, and Local Sources of Revenue, 2016**

Panel (a) shows that individual income taxes are the most important source of revenue for the federal government, and social insurance taxes are the second most important source. Panel (b) shows that state and local governments receive large grants from the federal government, in part to help pay for federally mandated programs like Medicaid. Many local governments depend on property taxes to raise most of their tax revenue.

Source: U.S. Bureau of Economic Analysis.

income taxes and excise taxes account for much smaller fractions of federal revenues. In 2016, federal revenues of all types amounted to more than $3.5 trillion, or $27,866 per household. Over the past 40 years, federal revenues as a share of gross domestic product (GDP—the value of all the final goods and services produced in the U.S. economy) have typically remained in a fairly narrow range between 17 percent and 19 percent, with a low of 16 percent in 2009 and a high of 21 percent in 2000.

Panel (b) shows that state and local governments rely on a different mix of revenue sources than does the federal government. In the past, the largest source of revenue for state and local governments was sales taxes. State and local governments also receive large grants from the federal government, which in 2016 were their largest source of revenue. These grants are intended in part to pay for programs that the federal government requires state and local governments to carry out. These programs, often called *federal mandates*, include the *Medicaid* program, which finances health care for many low-income people, and the Temporary Assistance for Needy Families (TANF) program, which provides financial assistance to poor families. Local governments also raise substantial revenue from property taxes. Many local school districts, in particular, rely almost entirely on revenues from property taxes. **MyLab Economics** Concept Check

Progressive and Regressive Taxes

Economists often categorize taxes on the basis of the percentage of their income that people at different income levels pay in taxes:

Regressive tax A tax for which people with lower incomes pay a higher percentage of their income in tax than do people with higher incomes.

Progressive tax A tax for which people with lower incomes pay a lower percentage of their income in tax than do people with higher incomes.

- A tax is **regressive** if people with lower incomes pay a higher percentage of their income in tax than do people with higher incomes.
- A tax is **progressive** if people with lower incomes pay a lower percentage of their income in tax than do people with higher incomes.
- A tax is *proportional* if people with lower incomes pay the same percentage of their income in tax as do people with higher incomes.

The federal income tax is an example of a progressive tax. To see why, note first the important distinction between a tax rate and a tax bracket. A *tax rate* is the percentage of income paid in taxes. A *tax bracket* is the income range within which a tax rate applies. Table 18.2 shows the federal income tax brackets and tax rates for single taxpayers in 2017.

We can use Table 18.2 to calculate what Matt, a single taxpayer with an income of $100,000, pays in federal income tax. This example is somewhat simplified because we are ignoring the *exemptions* and *deductions* that taxpayers can use to reduce the amount of income subject to tax. For example, taxpayers are allowed to exclude from taxation a certain amount of income, called the *personal exemption*, that represents basic living expenses. Ignoring Matt's exemptions and deductions, he will have to make the tax payment to the federal government shown in Table 18.3. Matt's first $9,325 of income is in the 10 percent bracket, so he pays $932.50 in taxes on that part of his income. His next $28,625 of income is in the 15 percent bracket, so he pays $4,293.75. His next $53,950 of income is in the 25 percent bracket, so he pays $13,487.50. His last $8,100 of income is in the 28 percent bracket, so he pays $2,268, which brings his total federal income tax bill to $20,981.75. **MyLab Economics** Concept Check

Table 18.2

Federal Income Tax Brackets and Tax Rates for Single Taxpayers, 2017

Income Tax Brackets	Tax Rate
$0–$9,325	10%
$9,326–$37,950	15
$37,951–$91,900	25
$91,901–$191,650	28
$191,651–$416,700	33
$416,701–$418,400	35
Over $418,400	39.6

Source: Internal Revenue Service.

On Matt's ...	Matt pays tax of ...
first $9,325 of income	$932.50
next $28,625 of income	4,293.75
next $53,950 of income	13,487.50
last $8,100 of income	2,268.00
His total federal income tax payment is	$20,981.75

Table 18.3

Federal Income Tax Paid on
Taxable Income of $100,000

Apply the Concept

MyLab Economics Video

Which Groups Pay the Most in Federal Taxes?

In the chapter opener, we mentioned the ongoing debate over whether to increase taxes on people with high incomes. To evaluate this debate, it's useful to know how much each income group pays of the total taxes collected by the federal government. The following table shows projections for 2017 by the Tax Policy Center, with taxpayers divided into quintiles from the 20 percent with the lowest income to the 20 percent with the highest income. The last row shows taxpayers whose incomes put them in the top 1 percent. Column (1) shows the percentage of total income earned by each income group. Column (2) shows the percentage of all federal taxes—including Social Security and Medicare payroll taxes—paid by each income group. Column (3) shows the average federal tax rate for each group, calculated by dividing total taxes paid by total income.

Income Category	(1) Share of Total Income Earned	(2) Share of Total Federal Taxes Paid	(3) All Federal Taxes Paid as a Fraction of Income (average federal tax rate)
Lowest 20%	4.4%	1.0%	4.2%
Second 20%	8.7	3.9	8.8
Third 20%	14.2	10.0	14.0
Fourth 20%	20.8	18.4	17.6
Highest 20%	52.1	66.6	25.7
Total	100.0%	100.0%	20.0%
Highest 1%	15.3	25.1	32.9

Note: Columns may not sum to precisely 100% due to rounding.
Source: Urban-Brookings Tax Policy Center, Tables T17-0042 and T17-0054, March 17, 2017.

The data in column (2) show that the 20 percent of taxpayers with the highest incomes pay about 67 percent of federal taxes, which is greater than their 52 percent share of total income earned, as shown in column (1). Only taxpayers in the highest quintile pay a larger share of taxes than their share of income. Taxpayers whose incomes put them in the top 1 percent pay more than 25 percent of federal taxes. Many individuals in the lowest quintile of income, particularly those with children, receive tax credits from the federal government so that they in effect pay negative taxes. Column (3) indicates that average tax rates rise as income rises.

If we look at just the federal individual income tax considered separately from the payroll tax and other federal taxes, the results are similar. In 2017:

- Taxpayers in the top 1 percent of the income distribution were projected to earn 15 percent of all income while paying 38 percent of all federal individual income taxes.
- The top 20 percent of the income distribution earned 52 percent of all income while paying 84 percent of individual taxes.
- The bottom 40 percent of the income distribution earned 13 percent of all income but actually paid *negative* 3 percent of federal individual income taxes when taking into account tax credits, such as the child tax credit.

We can conclude that the federal tax system is highly progressive. Whether the system should be made more or less progressive remains a topic of political debate.

MyLab Economics Study Plan

Your Turn: Test your understanding by doing related problem 2.10 on page 632 at the end of this chapter.

Marginal and Average Income Tax Rates

Marginal tax rate The fraction of each additional dollar of income that must be paid in taxes.

Average tax rate Total tax paid divided by total income.

The fraction of each additional dollar of income that must be paid in taxes is called the **marginal tax rate**. The **average tax rate** is the total tax paid divided by total income. When a tax is progressive, as is the federal income tax, the marginal and average tax rates differ. For example, in Table 18.3, Matt had a marginal tax rate of 28 percent because that is the rate he paid on the last dollar of his income. But his average tax rate was:

$$\left(\frac{\$20,981.75}{\$100,000.00} \right) \times 100 = 21.0\%.$$

His average tax rate was lower than his marginal tax rate because the first $91,900 of his income was taxed at rates below his marginal rate of 28 percent.

The marginal tax rate is a better indicator than the average tax rate of how a change in a tax will affect people's willingness to work, save, and invest. For example, if Matt is considering working longer hours to raise his income, he will use his marginal tax rate to determine how much extra income he will earn after taxes. He will ignore his average tax rate because it does not represent the taxes he must pay on the *additional* income he earns. The higher the marginal tax rate, the lower the return he receives from working additional hours and the less likely he is to work those additional hours. MyLab Economics Concept Check

The Corporate Income Tax

The federal government taxes the profits earned by corporations under the *corporate income tax*. Like the individual income tax, the corporate income tax is progressive, with the lowest tax rate being 15 percent and the highest being 35 percent. Unlike the individual income tax, however, where relatively few taxpayers are taxed at the highest rate, many corporations are in the 35 percent tax bracket.

Economists debate the costs and benefits of a separate tax on corporate profits. The corporate income tax ultimately must be paid by a corporation's owners—who are its shareholders—or by its employees, in the form of lower wages, or by its customers, in the form of higher prices. Some economists argue that if the purpose of the corporate income tax is to tax the owners of corporations, it would be better to do so directly by taxing the owners' incomes rather than by taxing the owners indirectly through the corporate income tax. Individual taxpayers already pay income taxes on the dividends and capital gains they receive from owning stock in corporations. In effect, the corporate income tax "double taxes" earnings on individual shareholders' investments in corporations. An alternative policy that avoids this double taxation would be for corporations to calculate their total profits each year and send a notice to each shareholder, indicating the shareholder's portion of the profits. Shareholders would then be required to include this amount as taxable income on their personal income tax. Under another alternative policy, the federal government could continue to tax corporate income through the corporate income tax but allow individual taxpayers to receive corporate dividends and capital gains tax free. MyLab Economics Concept Check

International Comparison of Corporate Income Taxes

In recent years, a number of countries have cut corporate income taxes to increase investment spending and growth. Table 18.4 compares corporate income tax rates in several high-income countries. The tax rates given in the table include taxes at all levels of government. In the United States, for example, they include taxes imposed on

Country	Tax Rate in 2000	Tax Rate in 2017
Canada	42%	27%
France	37	33
Germany	52	30
Ireland	24	13
Italy	41	24
Japan	42	31
Spain	35	25
Sweden	28	22
United Kingdom	30	20
United States	40	40

Table 18.4

Corporate Income Tax Rates around the World

Note: The rates given include taxes at all levels of government. In the United States, the rate includes state as well as federal taxes.

Source: KPMG, *KPMG's Corporate and Indirect Tax Survey, 2017.*

corporate profits by state governments as well as by the federal government. The table shows that of the countries listed, only the United States did not reduce its corporate income tax rate between 2000 and 2017. Ireland has been particularly successful in using lower corporate income tax rates to attract foreign corporations to locate facilities there. Lower tax rates have led Microsoft, Intel, and Dell, among other U.S. firms, to base some of their operations in Ireland. The table also shows that corporate income tax rates are higher in the United States than in other high-income countries.

The relatively high U.S. corporate tax rate has led many large U.S. firms with significant sales in foreign countries to avoid returning profits earned in those countries back to the United States. By keeping their profits overseas, these U.S. firms do not have to pay U.S. taxes on them, although the funds are also not available to be spent in the United States. As a result, many large U.S. firms pay a marginal tax rate well below the 40 percent rate indicated in Table 18.4. As part of President Trump's tax reform proposal mentioned in the chapter opener, the top corporate tax rate would be cut to 20 percent. The United States is unusual in that it imposes taxes on corporate earnings wherever they are earned, but it allows corporations to postpone paying the taxes until the profits are brought back to the United States. As a result, many U.S. corporations keep the bulk of their overseas profits outside the United States. They can't use these funds in the United States to build new facilities or engage in research and development, and they can't return them to shareholders. President Trump proposed sharply reducing the tax that U.S. corporations pay on their foreign profits. As of late 2017, it was unclear which, if any, of President Trump's proposals Congress might enact.   **MyLab Economics** Concept Check

Evaluating Taxes

We have seen that to raise revenue, governments have available a variety of taxes. In selecting which taxes to use, governments take into account the following goals and principles:

- The goal of economic efficiency
- The ability-to-pay principle
- The horizontal-equity principle
- The benefits-received principle
- The goal of attaining social objectives

The Goal of Economic Efficiency We can briefly review the effect of taxes on economic efficiency (see Chapter 4, Section 4.4). A government tax on an activity raises the cost of engaging in that activity, so less of the activity will occur. Figure 18.3 uses a demand and supply graph to illustrate this point for a sales tax. A sales tax increases the cost of supplying a good, which causes the supply curve to shift up by

Figure 18.3

The Efficiency Loss from a Sales Tax

This figure reviews the discussion of the efficiency loss from a tax (see Chapter 4, Section 4.4). A sales tax increases the cost of supplying a good, which causes the supply curve to shift up, from S_1 to S_2. Without the tax, the equilibrium price of the good is P_1, and the equilibrium quantity is Q_1. After the tax is imposed, the equilibrium price rises to P_2, and the equilibrium quantity falls to Q_2. After paying the tax, producers receive P_3. The government receives tax revenue equal to the green-shaded rectangle. Some consumer surplus and some producer surplus become tax revenue for the government, and some become deadweight loss, shown by the yellow-shaded triangle. The deadweight loss is the *excess burden* of the tax.

Excess burden A measure of the efficiency loss to the economy that results from a tax having reduced the quantity of a good produced; also known as the deadweight loss.

the amount of the tax. In the figure, the equilibrium price rises from P_1 to P_2, and the equilibrium quantity falls from Q_1 to Q_2. When a good is taxed, less of it is produced.

The government collects tax revenue equal to the tax per unit multiplied by the number of units sold. The green-shaded rectangle in Figure 18.3 represents the government's tax revenue. Although sellers appear to receive a higher price for the good—P_2—the price they receive after paying the tax falls to P_3. Because the price consumers pay has risen, consumer surplus has fallen. Because the price producers receive has also fallen, producer surplus has fallen. Some of the reduction in consumer surplus and producer surplus becomes tax revenue for the government. The rest of the reduction in consumer surplus and producer surplus is equal to the deadweight loss from the tax and is shown in the figure by the yellow-shaded triangle. The deadweight loss is called the *excess burden* of the tax. The **excess burden** is a measure of the efficiency loss to the economy that results from the tax having reduced the quantity of the good produced. *A tax is efficient if it imposes a small excess burden relative to the tax revenue it raises.*

Economists believe that to improve the economic efficiency of a tax system, the government should reduce its reliance on taxes that have a high deadweight loss relative to the revenue raised. The tax on interest earned from savings is an example of a tax with a high deadweight loss because savings often come from income that has already been taxed once. Therefore, taxing interest earned on savings from income that has already been taxed is essentially double taxation.

There are other examples of significant deadweight losses of taxation. High taxes on work can reduce the number of hours a person works, as well as how hard the person works or whether the person starts a business. In each case, the reduction in the taxed activity—here, work—generates less government revenue, and people are worse off because the tax encourages them to change their behavior.

Taxation can have substantial effects on economic efficiency by altering incentives to work, save, or invest. A good illustration of this effect can be seen in the large differences between annual hours worked in Europe and in the United States. Europeans typically work fewer hours than do Americans. According to an analysis by Nobel Laureate Edward Prescott of Arizona State University, this difference was not always present. In the early 1970s, when European and U.S. tax rates on income were comparable, European and U.S. hours worked per employee were also comparable. Prescott finds that virtually all of the difference between labor supply in the United States and labor supply in France and Germany since that time is due to differences in their tax systems.

The administrative burden of a tax represents another example of the deadweight loss of taxation. Individuals spend many hours during the year keeping records for income tax purposes, and they spend many more hours prior to April 15 preparing their tax returns. The opportunity cost of this time is billions of dollars each year and represents an administrative burden of the federal income tax. For corporations, complexity in tax planning results in substantial expenditures on accountants and software with the goal of minimizing the corporations' tax liabilities. The federal government also has to devote resources to enforcing the tax laws. The administrative burden that the complexity of the corporate income and individual income tax codes places on households, firms, and the government represents a loss of economic efficiency.

Wouldn't tax simplification reduce the administrative burden and the deadweight loss of taxation? The answer is "yes." So why is the tax code complicated? In part, complexity arises because the political process has resulted in different types of income being taxed at different rates, requiring rules to limit taxpayers' ability to avoid taxes by shifting income from one category to another. In addition, interest groups seek to pay lower taxes, while the majority of taxpayers, who do not benefit from these "tax loopholes," find it difficult to organize a drive for a simpler tax system.

The Ability-to-Pay Principle The *ability-to-pay principle* holds that when the government raises revenue through taxes, it is fair to expect a greater share of the tax burden to be borne by people who have a greater ability to pay. To follow this principle, the government should attempt to achieve *vertical equity* by raising more taxes from people with high incomes than from people with low incomes. The federal income tax is consistent with the ability-to-pay principle. The sales tax, in contrast, is not consistent with the ability-to-pay principle because, on average, low-income people spend a larger fraction of their income than do high-income people. As a result, low-income people will pay a greater fraction of their income in sales taxes than will high-income people.

The Horizontal-Equity Principle The *horizontal-equity principle* states that people in the same economic situation should be treated equally. Although this principle seems desirable, it is not easy to follow in practice because it is sometimes difficult to determine whether two people are in the same economic situation. For example, two people with the same income are not necessarily in the same economic situation. Suppose one person does not work but receives an income of $50,000 per year entirely from interest received on bonds, and another person receives an income of $50,000 per year from working at two jobs 16 hours a day. In this case, we could argue that the two people are in different economic situations and should not pay the same tax. Although policymakers and economists usually consider horizontal equity when evaluating proposals to change the tax system, it is not a principle they can easily follow.

The Benefits-Received Principle According to the *benefits-received principle*, people who receive the benefits from a government program should pay the taxes that support the program. For example, if a city operates a marina that private boat owners use, the government can raise the revenue to operate the marina by levying a tax on the boat owners. Raising the revenue through a general income tax that both boat owners and non–boat owners pay would be inconsistent with the benefits-received principle. Because the government has many programs, however, it would be impractical to identify and tax the beneficiaries of every program.

The Goal of Attaining Social Objectives The tax code is sometimes used to attain social objectives. Here are two examples: (1) Congress has promoted home ownership by making the interest borrowers pay on home mortgages—loans households take out to buy homes—deductible from the individual income taxes they owe; (2) Congress also has exempted from the individual income tax compensation employees receive in the form of health insurance and certain other *fringe benefits*. If you receive a $1,000 raise, you must pay federal income taxes on that amount. If, instead, your employer spends an additional $1,000 to provide you with health insurance, the amount is not taxed.

Some economists and policymakers have questioned whether provisions like these in the tax code violate the principle of horizontal equity. A homeowner receives a significant financial advantage not available to a renter in comparable economic circumstances. Similarly, someone whose employer provides generous health insurance benefits receives a significant advantage not available to someone whose employer doesn't offer health insurance or who offers an inexpensive policy with only limited coverage. In designing the federal tax code, Congress has to balance its pursuit of social objectives against the goals and principles of tax policy that we listed earlier.

MyLab Economics Study Plan

MyLab Economics Concept Check

18.3 Tax Incidence Revisited: The Effect of Price Elasticity

LEARNING OBJECTIVE: Explain the effect of price elasticity on tax incidence.

Tax incidence The actual division of the burden of a tax between buyers and sellers in a market.

There is an important difference between who is legally required to send a tax payment to the government and who actually bears the burden of a tax (see Chapter 4, Section 4.4). Recall that the actual division of the burden of a tax between buyers and sellers in a market is known as **tax incidence**. We can go beyond the basic analysis of tax incidence and consider how the price elasticity of demand and price elasticity of supply affect how the burden of a tax is shared between consumers and firms.

If the government imposes a 10-cent-per-gallon federal excise tax on gasoline, consumers will pay the majority of the tax because the elasticity of demand for gasoline is smaller than the elasticity of supply. In fact, we can draw a general conclusion: *When the demand for a product is less elastic than the supply, consumers pay the majority of the tax on the product. When demand for a product is more elastic than the supply, firms pay the majority of the tax on the product.*

Figure 18.4 shows why this conclusion is correct: D_1 is inelastic between points A and B, and D_2 is elastic between points A and C. With demand curve D_1, the 10-cent-per-gallon tax raises the market price of gasoline from $3.00 (point A) to $3.08 (point B) per gallon, so consumers pay 8 cents of the tax, and firms pay 2 cents. With D_2, the market price rises only to $3.02 (point C) per gallon, and consumers pay only 2 cents of the tax. With demand curve D_2, sellers of gasoline receive only $2.92 per gallon after paying the tax. So, the amount they receive per gallon after taxes falls from $3.00 to $2.92 per gallon, and they pay 8 cents of the tax.

MyLab Economics Study Plan

MyLab Economics Concept Check

MyLab Economics Animation

Figure 18.4

The Effect of Elasticity on Tax Incidence

When demand is more elastic than supply, consumers bear less of the burden of a tax. When supply is more elastic than demand, firms bear less of the burden of a tax. D_1 is inelastic between points A and B, and D_2 is elastic between points A and C. With demand curve D_1, a 10-cent-per-gallon tax raises the equilibrium price from $3.00 (point A) to $3.08 (point B), so consumers pay 8 cents of the tax, and firms pay 2 cents. With D_2, a 10-cent-per-gallon tax on gasoline raises the equilibrium price only from $3.00 (point A) to $3.02 (point C), so consumers pay 2 cents of the tax. Because in this case producers receive $2.92 per gallon after paying the tax, their share of the tax is 8 cents per gallon.

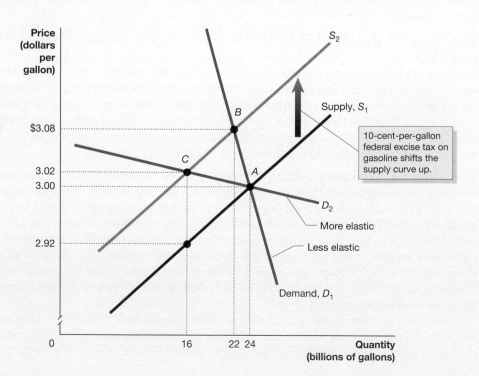

Don't Let This Happen to You

Don't Confuse Who Pays a Tax with Who Bears the Burden of the Tax

Consider the following statement: "Of course, I bear the burden of the sales tax on everything I buy. I can show you my sales receipts with the 6 percent sales tax clearly labeled. The seller doesn't bear that tax. I do."

The statement is incorrect. To understand why it is incorrect, think about what would happen to the price of a product if the sales tax on it were eliminated. Figure 18.4 shows that the price of the product would fall because the supply curve would shift down by the amount of the tax. The equilibrium price, however, would fall by less than the amount of the tax.

(If you doubt that this statement is correct, draw the graph to convince yourself.) So, the gain from eliminating the tax would be received partly by consumers in the form of a lower price but also partly by sellers in the form of a new price that is higher than the amount they received from the old price minus the tax. Therefore, the burden from imposing a sales tax is borne partly by consumers and partly by sellers.

In determining the burden of a tax, what counts is not what is printed on the receipt for a product but how the price of a product changes as a result of the tax.

Your Turn: Test your understanding by doing related problem 3.4 on page 633 at the end of this chapter. **MyLab Economics** Study Plan

Apply the Concept

MyLab Economics Video

Do Corporations Really Bear the Burden of the Federal Corporate Income Tax?

At a campaign appearance, 2012 Republican presidential candidate Mitt Romney encountered hecklers who suggested that taxes on corporations be raised. Romney responded by saying: "Corporations are people, my friend." The hecklers responded: "No, they're not!" To which Romney responded: "Of course they are. Everything corporations earn ultimately goes to people. Where do you think it goes?" Romney was correct that corporations are legal persons in the eyes of the law. But there is a larger question: Who actually pays the corporate income tax? The incidence of the corporate income tax is one of the most controversial questions in the economics of tax policy. It is straightforward to determine the incidence of the gasoline tax using demand and supply analysis. Determining the incidence of the corporate income tax is more complicated because economists disagree about how corporations respond to the tax.

A study by the Congressional Budget Office stated:

Sorbis/Shutterstock

Will these consumers be paying part of Apple's corporate income tax when they buy an Apple product?

> A corporation may write its check to the Internal Revenue Service for payment of the corporate income tax, but the money must come from somewhere: from reduced returns to investors in the company, lower wages to its workers, or higher prices that consumers pay for the products the company produces.

Most economists agree that some of the burden of the corporate income tax is passed on to consumers in the form of higher prices. There is also some agreement that, because the corporate income tax reduces the rates of return received by investors, it results in less investment in corporations. This reduced investment means workers have less capital available to them. When workers have less capital, their productivity and their wages both fall (see Chapter 17, Section 17.1). In this way, some of the burden of the corporate income tax is shifted from corporations to workers in the form of lower wages. The Congressional Budget Office (CBO) has estimated that about 25 percent of the burden of the corporate income tax is in the form of lower wages. Other studies have estimated that lower wages may account for as much as 90 percent of the burden. The deadweight loss or excess burden from the corporate income tax is substantial. A CBO study estimated that this excess burden could equal more than half of the revenues raised by the tax. This estimate would make the corporate income tax one of the most inefficient taxes imposed by the federal government.

As we saw in the chapter opener, in 2017, the Trump administration proposed a wide-ranging overhaul of the tax system that would include substantial cuts in the corporate income tax rate. One part of the proposal would also reduce the tax rate on "pass-through" businesses, which are businesses, like sole proprietorships and partnerships, whose owners pay taxes on their business income at the individual rate rather than the corporate rate. To reduce their tax liability, owners of some firms have structured the firms so that the income they earn is taxed at the most favorable rate. As two economists at the Brookings Institution observed, "The effort, cost, and complexity of structuring businesses and business activities to minimize taxes is inefficient and wasteful." Narrowing or eliminating the gap between the tax rate on corporate income and the tax rate on business pass-through income could help reduce some of this inefficiency.

Sources: Aaron Krupkin and Adam Looney, "9 Facts about Pass-Through Businesses," brookings.edu, May 17, 2017; Michael Cooper et al., "Business in the United States: Who Owns It and How Much Tax Do They Pay?" U.S. Department of the Treasury, Office Tax Analysis, Working Paper No. 104, October 2015; Congressional Budget Office, *The Distribution of Household Income and Federal Taxes, 2008 and 2009*, July 2012; Jennifer C. Gravelle, "Corporate Tax Incidence: A Review of Empirical Estimates and Analysis," Congressional Budget Office, Working Paper No. 2011-01, June 2011; Ashley Parker, "'Corporations Are People,' Romney Tells Iowa Hecklers Angry over His Tax Policy," *New York Times*, August 11, 2011; and Congressional Budget Office, "The Incidence of the Corporate Income Tax," March 1996.

MyLab Economics Study Plan

Your Turn: Test your understanding by doing related problem 3.5 on page 633 at the end of this chapter.

Solved Problem 18.3

MyLab Economics Interactive Animation

The Effect of Price Elasticity on the Excess Burden of a Tax

Explain whether you agree with the following statement: "For a given supply curve, the excess burden of a tax will be greater when demand is less elastic than when it is more elastic." Illustrate your answer with a demand and supply graph.

Solving the Problem

Step 1: **Review the chapter material.** This problem is about both excess burden and tax incidence, so you may want to review the section "Evaluating Taxes," which begins on page 611, and the section "Tax Incidence Revisited: The Effect of Price Elasticity," which begins on page 614.

Step 2: **Draw a graph to illustrate the relationship between tax incidence and excess burden.** Figure 18.4 on page 614 is a good example of the type of graph to draw. Be sure to indicate the areas representing excess burden.

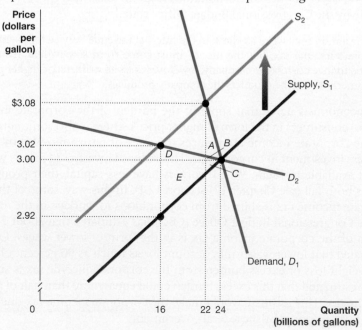

Step 3: **Use the graph to evaluate the statement.** For a given supply curve, when demand is more elastic, as with demand curve D_2, the fall in equilibrium quantity is greater than when demand is less elastic, as with demand curve D_1. The deadweight loss when demand is less elastic is shown by the area of the triangle made up of areas *A*, *B*, and *C*. The deadweight loss when demand is more elastic is shown by the area of the triangle made up of areas *B*, *C*, *D*, and *E*. The area of the deadweight loss is clearly larger when demand is more elastic than when it is less elastic. Recall that the excess burden of a tax is measured by the deadweight loss. Therefore, when demand is less elastic, the excess burden of a tax is *smaller* than when demand is more elastic. We can conclude that the statement is incorrect. The key to this result is that the equilibrium quantity after the tax is smaller than with a less elastic demand curve than with a more elastic demand curve. This larger decline in quantity results in a larger decline in economic surplus (which is the sum of consumer surplus and producer surplus) and a greater excess burden.

Your Turn: For more practice, do related problems 3.9 and 3.10 on page 633 at the end of this chapter.

MyLab Economics Study Plan

18.4 Income Distribution and Poverty

LEARNING OBJECTIVE: Discuss income distribution and income mobility and the role of policy in addressing these issues.

No country has complete income equality. Inevitably, some individuals will have very high incomes, and some individuals will have very low incomes. But how unequal is the distribution of income in the United States today? How does it compare with the distribution of income in the United States in the past or with the distribution of income in other countries today? What determines the distribution of income? And, to return to an issue raised at the beginning of this chapter, how does the tax system affect the distribution of income? We will explore these questions in this section.

Measuring the Income Distribution and Measuring Poverty

Tables 18.5 and 18.6 show that the distribution of income clearly is unequal. Table 18.5 shows that in 2016, while 21 percent of U.S. households had annual incomes less than $25,000, the top 28 percent of households had incomes greater than $100,000.

Table 18.6 divides households in the United States into five groups, from the 20 percent with the lowest incomes to the 20 percent with the highest incomes. The fraction of total income received by each of the five groups is shown for selected years. Table 18.6 reinforces the fact that income is unequally distributed in the United States. The first row shows that in 2016, the 20 percent of U.S. households with the lowest incomes received only 3.1 percent of all income, while the 20 percent with the highest incomes received 51.5 percent of all income.

Annual Income	Percentage of All Households
$0–$24,999	21%
$25,000–$49,999	22
$50,000–$74,999	17
$75,000–$99,999	12
$100,000–$199,999	21
$200,000 and above	7

Source: Jessica L. Semega, Kayla R. Fontenot, and Melissa A. Kollarr, U.S. Census Bureau, Current Population Reports, P60–259, *Income and Poverty in the United States: 2016*, Washington, DC: U.S. Government Printing Office, September 2017.

Table 18.5

The Distribution of Household Income in the United States, 2016

Table 18.6

How Has the Distribution of Income in the United States Changed over Time?

Year	Lowest 20%	Second 20%	Middle 20%	Fourth 20%	Highest 20%
2016	3.1%	8.3%	14.2%	22.9%	51.5%
2000	3.6	8.9	14.8	23.0	49.8
1990	3.9	9.6	15.9	24.0	46.6
1980	4.3	10.3	16.9	24.9	43.7
1970	4.1	10.8	17.4	24.5	43.3
1960	3.2	10.6	17.6	24.7	44.0
1950	3.1	10.5	17.3	24.1	45.0
1936	4.1	9.2	14.1	20.9	51.7

Sources: Jessica L. Semega, Kayla R. Fontenot, and Melissa A. Kollarr, U.S. Census Bureau, Current Population Reports, P60–259, *Income and Poverty in the United States: 2016*, Washington, DC: U.S. Government Printing Office, September 2017. U.S. Census Bureau, *Income in the United States, 2002*, P60–221, September 2003; and U.S. Census Bureau, *Historical Statistics of the United States, Colonial Times to 1970*, Washington, DC: U.S. Government Printing Office, 1975.

Table 18.6 also shows that over time, there have been some changes in the distribution of income. There was a moderate decline in inequality between 1936 and 1980, followed by an increase in inequality during the years after 1980. We will discuss some reasons for the recent increase in income inequality later in this chapter.

The Poverty Rate in the United States Some of the discussion of the distribution of income focuses on poverty. The federal government has a formal definition of poverty that was first developed in the early 1960s. According to this definition, a family is below the **poverty line** if its annual income is less than three times the amount necessary to purchase the minimum quantity of food required for adequate nutrition. In 2017, the poverty line was $24,600 for a family of four. Figure 18.5 shows the **poverty rate**, or the percentage of the U.S. population that was poor during each year between 1960 and 2016. Between 1960 and 1973, the poverty rate declined by half, falling from 22 percent to 11 percent of the population. In the past 40 years, however, the poverty rate has declined very little. In 2016, it was actually higher than it was in 1969.

Different groups in the population have substantially different poverty rates. Table 18.7 shows that while the overall poverty rate in 2016 was 12.7 percent, the rates among women who head a family with no husband present, among black people, and among Hispanic people were much higher. The poverty rates for white and Asian people, as well as for families headed by married couples, were below average.

MyLab Economics Concept Check

Poverty line A level of annual income equal to three times the amount of money necessary to purchase the minimum quantity of food required for adequate nutrition.

Poverty rate The percentage of the population that is poor according to the federal government's definition.

MyLab Economics Animation

Figure 18.5

Poverty in the United States, 1960–2016

The poverty rate in the United States declined from 22 percent of the population in 1960 to 11 percent in 1973. Over the past 40 years, the poverty rate has fluctuated between 11 and 15 percent of the population.

Source: Jessica L. Semega, Kayla R. Fontenot, and Melissa A. Kollarr, U.S. Census Bureau, Current Population Reports, P60–259, *Income and Poverty in the United States: 2016*, Washington, DC: U.S. Government Printing Office, September 2017.

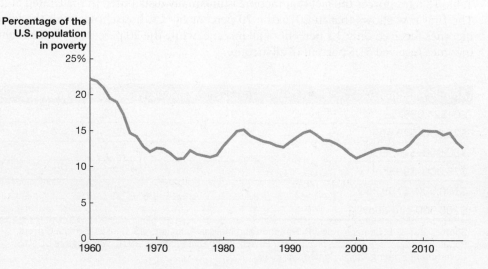

Group	Poverty Rate
Total population	12.7%
Female head of family, no husband present (all races)	28.8
Blacks	22.0
Hispanics	19.4
Asians	10.1
White, not Hispanic	8.8
Married couple families (all races)	5.1

Note: Hispanics can be of any race.

Source: Jessica L. Semega, Kayla R. Fontenot, and Melissa A. Kollarr, U.S. Census Bureau, Current Population Reports, P60–259, *Income and Poverty in the United States: 2016*, Washington, DC: U.S. Government Printing Office, September 2017.

Table 18.7

Poverty Rates Vary across Groups, 2016

Showing the Income Distribution with a Lorenz Curve

Figure 18.6 presents the distribution of income using a **Lorenz curve**, which shows the distribution of income by arraying incomes from lowest to highest on the horizontal axis and indicating the cumulative fraction of income earned by each fraction of households on the vertical axis. If the distribution of income were perfectly equal, a Lorenz curve would be a straight line because the first 20 percent of households would earn 20 percent of total income, the first 40 percent of households would earn 40 percent of total income, and so on. Panel (a) of Figure 18.6 shows a Lorenz curve for the actual distribution of income in the United States in 1980 and another curve for the distribution of income in 2016, using the data from Table 18.6. We know that income was distributed more unequally in 2016 than in 1980 because the Lorenz curve for 2016 is farther away from the line of equal distribution than is the Lorenz curve for 1980.

Lorenz curve A curve that shows the distribution of income by arraying incomes from lowest to highest on the horizontal axis and indicating the cumulative fraction of income earned by each fraction of households on the vertical axis.

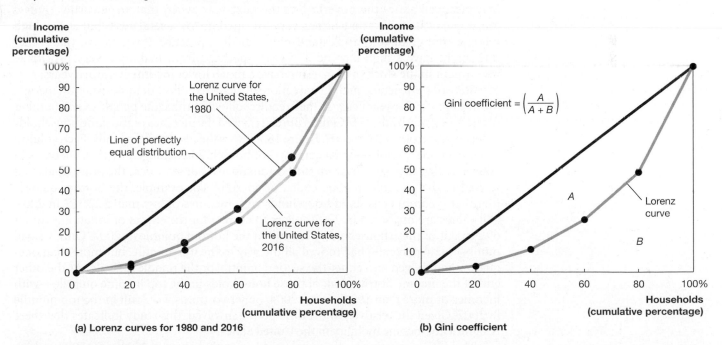

(a) Lorenz curves for 1980 and 2016

(b) Gini coefficient

MyLab Economics Animation

Figure 18.6 **The Lorenz Curve and Gini Coefficient**

In panel (a), the Lorenz curves show the distribution of income by arraying incomes from the lowest to the highest on the horizontal axis and indicating the cumulative fraction of income by each fraction of households on the vertical axis. The straight line represents perfect income equality. Because the Lorenz curve for 1980 is closer to the line of perfect equality than the Lorenz curve for 2016, we know that income was more equally distributed in 1980 than in 2016. In panel (b), we show the Gini coefficient, which is equal to the area between the line of perfect income equality and the Lorenz curve—area A—divided by the whole area below the line of perfect equality—area A plus area B. The closer the Gini coefficient is to 1, the more unequal the income distribution.

Panel (b) illustrates how to calculate the *Gini coefficient*, which is one way of summarizing the information provided by a Lorenz curve. The Gini coefficient is equal to the area between the line of perfect income equality and the Lorenz curve—area *A* in panel (b)—divided by the whole area below the line of perfect equality—area *A* plus area *B* in panel (b). Or:

$$\text{Gini coefficient} = \left(\frac{A}{A + B} \right).$$

If the income distribution were completely *equal*, the Lorenz curve would be the same as the line of perfect income equality, area *A* would be zero, and the Gini coefficient would be zero. If the income distribution were completely *unequal*, area *B* would be zero, and the Gini coefficient would equal 1. Therefore, the greater the degree of income inequality, the greater the value of the Gini coefficient. In 1980, the Gini coefficient for the United States was 0.403. In 2016, it was 0.481, which tells us again that income inequality increased between 1980 and 2016. **MyLab Economics** Concept Check

Problems in Measuring Poverty and the Distribution of Income

The measures of poverty and the distribution of income that we have discussed to this point may be misleading for two reasons. First, these measures are snapshots in time that do not take into account *income mobility*, which refers to changes in an individual's or a family's income over time. Second, they ignore the effects of government programs meant to reduce poverty.

Income Mobility in the United States We expect that most people will not remain in the same place on the income distribution their whole lives. When you graduate from college, your income will rise as you assume a new job. A family may be below the poverty line one year because the main wage earner is unemployed but may rise well above the poverty line the next year, when that wage earner finds a job. A medical student may have a very low income for several years but a very high income after graduating and establishing a medical practice. It is also true that someone might have a high income one year—perhaps from making a very profitable investment in the stock market—and have a much lower income in future years.

Statistics on income mobility are more difficult to collect than statistics on income during a particular year because they require following the same people over a number of years. A study by the U.S. Census Bureau tracked the incomes of the same households for each year from 2004 to 2007. Figure 18.7 shows the results of the study. Each column represents one quintile—or 20 percent—of households, arranged by their incomes in 2004. Reading the columns from the bottom up, we can see where the households that started in that quintile in 2004 ended up in 2007. For example, the bottom quintile (the first column) consists of households with incomes of less than $22,367 in 2004. (All values are measured in 2007 dollars to correct for the effects of inflation.) About 69 percent of these households were still in the bottom quintile in 2007. Only a small number—1.6 percent—had moved all the way to the top quintile, but more than one-quarter had moved into either the second quintile or the middle quintile. At the other end of the income distribution, of those households in the top income quintile—with incomes of more than $92,886—in 2004, only two-thirds were still in the top quintile in 2007. Given the relatively short time period involved, this study indicates that there is significant income mobility in the United States.

The U.S. economy experienced rapid growth between 2004 and 2007, which may have increased the degree of income mobility. However, an earlier study by Peter Gottschalk of Boston College and Sheldon Danziger of the University of Michigan also provides evidence of significant income mobility. In that study, only 47 percent of people who were in the lowest 20 percent of incomes in 1968 were still in the lowest bracket in 1991. More than 25 percent had incomes in 1991 that put them in the middle- or higher-income brackets. Of those people who were in the highest-income bracket in 1968, only 42 percent were still in the highest bracket in 1991. Almost 8 percent of this group had fallen to the lowest-income bracket.

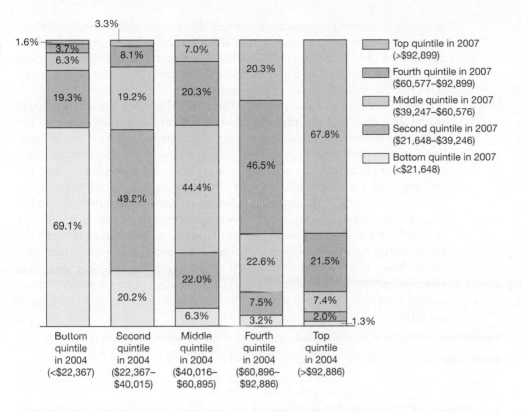

MyLab Economics Animation

Figure 18.7

Income Mobility in the United States, 2004–2007

Each column represents one quintile—or 20 percent—of households, arranged by their incomes in 2004. Reading the columns from the bottom up, we can see where the households that started in that quintile in 2004 ended up in 2007. Only 69 percent of the households that were in the bottom quintile of income in 2004 were still in the bottom quintile in 2007. Only 68 percent of the households that were in the top quintile of income in 2004 were still in the top quintile in 2007.

Note: Incomes are in 2007 dollars to correct for the effects of inflation.

Source: U.S. Census Bureau, "Dynamics of Economic Well-Being: Movements in the U.S. Income Distribution, 2004–2007," *Current Population Reports*, P70–124, March 2011.

Some economists and policymakers are concerned, though, that the extent of economic mobility in the United States may have declined over time and that mobility may now be lower in the United States than in Canada and Western Europe. For example, a study by Markus Jäntti, of Stockholm University in Sweden, and colleagues found that 42 percent of U.S. males who began life in the bottom quintile of the income distribution remained there as adults. In contrast, only 25 percent of Danish males and 30 percent of British males born into the bottom quintile remained there as adults.

Finally, another study by the U.S. Census Bureau found that of people who were poor at some time during the years 2004–2006, about half were in poverty for four months or less. Of the people who were poor in January 2004, only about 23 percent remained in poverty every month through December 2006. Only 2.8 percent of the U.S. population was poor every month during those three years.

Solved Problem 18.4

MyLab Economics Interactive Animation

What's the Difference between Income Mobility and Income Inequality?

An article in the *Wall Street Journal* observed, "The distinction between economic mobility and income inequality… is important at a time when politicians are using the words almost interchangeably."

a. What is the difference between income inequality and economic mobility?

b. Do you agree that it is important for members of Congress and other policymakers to understand the difference? Briefly explain.

Solving the Problem

Step 1: **Review the chapter material.** This problem is about income mobility, so you may want to review the section "Income Mobility in the United States," which begins on page 620.

Step 2: **Answer part (a) by defining income inequality and economic mobility.** The income distribution shows how total income is distributed across the population. A common way of illustrating the income distribution is to show what percentage of total income is earned by different percentages of the population, as in Table 18.6 on page 618. The distribution of income typically refers to the situation *in a particular year*. Income mobility looks at how a person's or a family's income changes *over time*.

Step 3: **Answer part (b) by discussing whether the difference between income inequality and income mobility is important for policymakers.** The distinction between the two concepts is important for policymakers because rapid income mobility might offset income inequality if a low-income person has a high probability of rising to a higher income level over time. On the one hand, a person might be born into a low-income family but may rise to the middle of the income distribution or higher by the time she is in her 40s. On the other hand, high levels of income inequality combined with low levels of income mobility would be a greater cause for concern because the result would be that the typical low-income person at any particular time would have only a low probability of rising to a higher income level over time. For instance, someone who takes a low-paying, entry-level job immediately after leaving school would still be in a similar position when he is in his 40s.

Sources: Damian Paletta, "New Data Muddle Debate on Economic Mobility," *Wall Street Journal*, January 23, 2014.

MyLab Economics Study Plan   **Your Turn:** For more practice, do related problem 4.12 on page 635 at the end of this chapter.

The Effect of Taxes and Transfers A second reason the conventional statistics on poverty and income distribution may be misleading is that they omit the effects of government programs. Because of government programs, there is a difference between the income people earn and the income they actually have available to spend. The data in Table 18.6 on page 618 show the distribution of income before taxes are paid. We have seen that at the federal level, taxes are progressive, meaning that people with high incomes pay a larger share of their incomes in taxes than do people with low incomes. Therefore, income remaining after taxes is more equally distributed than is income before taxes. The table also does not include income from *transfer payments* individuals receive from the government, such as Social Security payments to retired and disabled people. The Social Security system has been very effective in reducing the poverty rate among people older than 65. In 1960, 35 percent of people over age 65 in the United States had incomes below the poverty line. By 2016, only 9 percent of people over age 65 had incomes below the poverty line.

Individuals with low incomes also receive noncash benefits, such as health insurance through the Medicare program, food stamps, free school lunches, and rent subsidies. The government's Supplemental Nutrition Assistance Program, more commonly called the *food stamp program*, has been a particularly important noncash benefit. Under this program, individuals with low incomes can buy, at a discount, coupons to purchase food in supermarkets. In 2017, about 43 million people participated in this program, at a cost to the federal government of $70 billion. Because individuals with low incomes are more likely to receive transfer payments and other benefits from the government than are individuals with high incomes, the distribution of income is more equal if we take these benefits into account.

A study by the Congressional Budget Office (CBO) analyzed the effects of federal taxes and transfer programs on the distribution of income in 2013, the most recent year for which data are available. The first column of Table 18.8 shows the ratio of the highest income quintile of households to each of the lower quintiles, with income measured before taxes are paid and transfers are received. The second column shows the same ratios after household income is adjusted to take into account taxes and transfers. The table shows that taking into account taxes and transfers makes a significant difference to the income distribution, particularly with respect to the gap between the highest and lowest quintiles. Before the effects of taxes and transfers, the top quintile has about 16 times

Quintile	Ratio of Highest Income Quintile to Other Income Quintiles *before* Taxes and Transfers	Ratio of Highest Income Quintile to Other Income Quintiles *after* Taxes and Transfers
Lowest 20%	16.0	8.0
Second 20%	8.1	4.5
Middle 20%	4.8	3.2
Fourth 20%	2.9	2.3
Highest 20%	1.0	1.0

Table 18.8

The Effect of Taxes and Transfers on the Distribution of Household Income in the United States, 2013

Source: Congressional Budget Office, *The Distribution of Household Income and Federal Taxes, 2013,* June 8, 2016.

the income of the lowest quintile. Taking into account the effects of taxes and transfers, the top quintile has about 8 times the income of the lowest quintile. The CBO study looked at only the effects of federal tax and transfer policies. Taking into account the effects of state and local tax and transfer policies would likely further reduce the inequality of the income distribution. **MyLab Economics** Concept Check

Explaining Income Inequality

The novelists Ernest Hemingway and F. Scott Fitzgerald supposedly once had a conversation about the rich. Fitzgerald said to Hemingway: "You know, the rich are different from you and me." To which Hemingway replied: "Yes. They have more money." Although witty, Hemingway's joke doesn't help answer the question of why the rich have more money. We can consider several factors that help explain income inequality.

Differences in Returns to the Factors of Production One answer to the question of why incomes differ is given by the *marginal productivity theory of income distribution* (see Chapter 17, Section 17.6). In equilibrium, each factor of production receives a payment equal to its marginal revenue product. The more factors of production a person owns, the more productive those factors are, and the higher the price the output that can be produced with those factors can be sold for, the higher the person's income will be.

The most important factor of production that most people own is their labor. Therefore, the income they earn depends on how productive they are and on the prices of the goods and services their labor helps produce. Baseball player Clayton Kershaw earned a salary of $33 million in 2017 because he is a very productive player, and his employer, the Los Angeles Dodgers, can sell tickets and television, radio, and streaming rights to the baseball games Kershaw plays in for a high price. Individuals who help to produce goods and services that can be sold for only a low price earn lower incomes.

A person's productivity depends in part on his or her **human capital**, which refers to the accumulated knowledge and skills that workers acquire from formal training and education or from life experiences. Human capital is not equally distributed across workers. For example, some people have degrees in software engineering that prepare them for high-paying jobs, while other people drop out of high school and are prepared primarily for lower-paying jobs.

Many people own other factors of production beyond their labor. For example, many people own capital by owning stock in corporations or by owning shares in mutual funds or exchange-traded funds that buy the stock of corporations. Ownership of capital is not equally distributed, and income earned from capital is more unequally distributed than income earned from labor. Some people supply entrepreneurial skills by starting and managing businesses. Their income is increased by the profits from these businesses.

Human capital The accumulated knowledge and skills that workers acquire from formal training and education or from life experiences.

The Effects of Technological Change and International Trade We saw
in Table 18.6 that income inequality has increased during the past 30 years. Two factors that appear to have contributed to this increase are technological change and expanding

international trade. As we saw in Chapter 17, Section 17.3, rapid technological change, particularly the development of information technology, has led to the substitution of robots and other technology for unskilled and semi-skilled workers, including some salespeople, office workers, and factory workers. The new technologies have been complements to other workers, including professionals, managers, and software engineers, increasing their productivity. As a result, there has been a decline in the wages of many unskilled and semi-skilled workers relative to the wages of more highly skilled workers.

Economists Lawrence Katz and Claudia Goldin of Harvard University argue that over the long run, income inequality in the United States has been driven by a race between technological change, which destroys unskilled jobs and increases the returns to skilled jobs, and education, which prepares workers for skilled jobs. Rising educational attainment between 1910 and the 1970s narrowed the income distribution by reducing the relative wages of skilled workers. Educational attainment in the United States since the 1970s has increased more slowly, leading to rising relative wages of skilled workers.

Expanding international trade has put some U.S. workers, such as those in many manufacturing industries, in competition with foreign workers to a greater extent than in the past. This competition has caused the wages of some unskilled workers to decline relative to the wages of workers who do not face this competition. Some economists have also argued that the incomes of low-income workers have been depressed by competition with workers who have immigrated to the United States.

The Effects of Assortative Mating Some economists have noted an increase in assortative mating that may have increased income inequality. *Assortative mating* refers to marriages between people with similar educations. Research by Jeremy Greenwood of the University of Pennsylvania and colleagues shows that the tendency for men and women of similar educational backgrounds to marry has increased substantially since 1960. Assortative mating increases income inequality across households because, as we saw in Chapter 17, Section 17.3, people with more years of education tend to earn higher incomes.

To take a simple example of assortative mating, consider two women, one with a master's degree in engineering who has an income of $125,000 per year and one who dropped out of high school and has an income of $25,000 per year; and two men, one with a master's degree and an income of $125,000 and one a high-school dropout with an income of $25,000. If the man and woman with master's degrees marry each other and the two high-school dropouts marry each other, one household will have an income of $250,000 per year, and the other will have an income of $50,000 per year. But if the two people with master's degrees each marry one of the high-school dropouts, the two households will each have incomes of $150,000. Greenwood and colleagues estimate that in 2005, if people married each other without regard to educational background, then the Gini coefficient measure of income inequality would have been reduced from 0.45 to 0.34, a reduction of almost 25 percent.

Luck Finally, as with everything else in life, earning an income is subject to good and bad luck. A poor person who becomes a millionaire by winning the state lottery is an obvious example, as is a person whose earning power drastically declines as a result of a debilitating illness or accident. So, we can say that as a group, the people with high incomes are likely to have greater-than-average productivity and own greater-than-average amounts of capital. They are also likely to have experienced good luck. As a group, people with low incomes are likely to have lower-than-average productivity and own lower-than-average amounts of capital. They are also likely to have been unlucky. **MyLab Economics** Concept Check

Policies to Reduce Income Inequality

The factors that determine the income distribution are complex and not easily affected by government policies. Some economists and policymakers have concluded that attempts by the federal government to reduce income inequality are likely to be ineffective and may even be counterproductive if the policies slow the rate of economic growth, thereby limiting gains for lower-income workers. Nevertheless, policymakers and economists have made a number of proposals aimed at reducing income inequality.

Reducing Inequality through Taxes and Transfers As Table 18.8 on page 623 shows, federal tax and transfer programs already have a significant effect on the distribution of income. Some policymakers and economists argue that the after-tax distribution of income could be made more equal if the top marginal tax rate were to rise from the current 39.6 percent closer to the 70 percent rate that prevailed prior to 1980. (Because this rate applied to very high incomes and because the tax code contained additional deductions that have since been eliminated, many fewer people used to pay this top marginal rate than pay the top rate today.) Higher-income people are more likely than lower-income people to own assets, such as stocks and bonds, and the returns people receive on their financial assets often receive favorable tax treatment. For example, people who own stock in corporations receive dividend payments and earn *capital gains* if they sell the stock for a profit. Both dividends and capital gains are taxed at rates that are lower than the top marginal individual income tax rates. Raising taxes on dividends and capital gains could potentially reduce the after-tax inequality of incomes.

Other economists and policymakers are skeptical of the idea that raising taxes is an efficient way to reduce income inequality. These economists argue that higher marginal tax rates will discourage work, saving, and investment, thereby slowing economic growth and increases in incomes for all groups. Similarly, they argue that higher taxes on dividends and capital gains will reduce incentives to save and invest. They also argue that past periods of high marginal tax rates have seen higher-income people devote time and money to *tax avoidance*, which involves searching for provisions of the tax code that will allow individuals to reduce their tax payments. Resources spent on tax avoidance add to the excess burden of the tax code.

As we've seen, in 2017, the Trump administration proposed reducing the tax rate that many small business owners, as sole proprietors, pay on their business earnings. Reducing this rate may provide incentives for people to open new businesses and help provide the funds to expand existing businesses. In addition, tax simplification, which involves reducing the complexity of the tax code, would reduce the record keeping and other administrative costs, which are a particularly significant burden on small businesses. As we saw in Chapter 8, Section 8.1, the United States has experienced a dramatic slowdown in the number of small businesses opening each year. Because unskilled workers are more likely to be hired by small businesses, policies that strengthen small businesses may help reduce income inequality. In addition, licensing requirements imposed by state and local governments have made it difficult for some workers to enter occupations that would increase their earnings.

Because of exemptions and deductions, the lower 40 percent of the income distribution does not pay the federal individual income tax. But all workers must pay the payroll taxes that fund the Social Security and Medicare programs from the first dollar they earn. Some policymakers and economists have advocated reducing the federal payroll tax to boost the after-tax incomes of lower-income workers. Others have proposed an increase in the Earned Income Tax Credit, which provides payments to low-income workers.

Reducing Inequality through Improvements in Human Capital Many economists believe that workers who acquire skills that are complementary to the new technologies being developed will be able to find jobs that pay higher wages. For example, as we saw in Chapter 17, as mining company Rio Tinto introduced robots into its iron ore mines, it increased its demand for workers with the skills to service and program the robots. Policymakers in both political parties have proposed expanding enrollments in community colleges and in apprenticeship programs in order to increase the number of workers with technical training. Apprenticeship programs are typically sponsored by firms that seek workers with particular skills. These programs have long played an important part in worker training in some countries, including Germany and the United Kingdom. They have been less popular among workers and firms in the United States, and the number of workers enrolled in them has declined over the past 10 years. The recent policy proposals are an attempt to reverse that decline.

Other policymakers have focused on ensuring that workers obtain basic skills through improvements in K–12 education, particularly in low-income urban areas. Some proposals have focused on expanding preschool programs to provide low-income children with skills that can help them succeed in kindergarten and later grades. Research showing that children from single-parent households are less likely to finish high school or acquire basic skills has led some policymakers to propose programs aimed at providing support to these households.

Economists have not arrived at a consensus about what has caused the increase in income inequality or about the likely effects of the proposals that have been made to reverse the increase. Policymakers will undoubtedly continue to have a spirited debate over these policies. **MyLab Economics** Concept Check

Apply the Concept
MyLab Economics Video

Who Are the 1 Percent, and How Do They Earn Their Incomes?

In recent years, concerns about increasing inequality have often focused on the top 1 percent of the income distribution. During 2012, the "Occupy Wall Street" movement, which held demonstrations against income inequality in New York and other cities, used the slogan "We are the 99%" to indicate what they saw as the unfair advantages the 1 percent received at the expense of the rest of the population. The French economist Thomas Piketty's book *Capital in the Twenty-First Century* received considerable publicity due to the author's controversial analysis of income inequality and, in particular, the rise in the share of income earned by people at the top of the income distribution.

In 2016, an annual income from all sources of more than $675,000 was necessary to be in the top 1 percent of all households in the United States. The share of total income earned by households in this group rose from about 9 percent in 1979 to about 19 percent in 2016. The group's share of federal individual income taxes paid increased from 18 percent to 31 percent. The debate over the reasons for the increased share of income earned by the top 1 percent mirrors the debate over the broader increase in income inequality, with some of the same potential causes being cited.

As with any other income group, the same people are not in the top 1 percent of income earners every year. Each year some people rise into the group, and some people fall out of it. Nevertheless, the typical occupations of people in the top 1 percent have been part of the debate over income inequality and have influenced the discussion about possible policy measures that Congress and the president might take to reduce it. Some policymakers and economists have argued that investment bankers and other people working for financial firms dominate the top 1 percent of income earners in the United States. However, the following figure, which reflects research by Jon Bakija of Williams College, Adam Cole of the Treasury Department, and Bradley T. Heim of Indiana University, shows that financial professionals make up fewer than 14 percent of the top 1 percent. Executives and managers of nonfinancial firms are the largest group in the top 1 percent (31 percent), with doctors and other medical professionals being the second-largest group (16 percent).

Some policymakers have proposed reducing income inequality by increasing taxes on capital gains, which represent increases in prices of assets, such as stocks or bonds. Currently, capital gains are taxed at lower rates than is wage and salary income. A Congressional Budget Office analysis of tax data showed, however, that earnings from capital gains are not the primary source of income for the top 1 percent:

- Less than 20 percent of the income of the top 1 percent is typically in the form of capital gains.

- Nearly 60 percent of their income is in the form of wages and salaries or income from operating a business.
- The amount of income the top 1 percent earned from operating a business increased from 14 percent in 1979 to 23 percent in 2013, which may indicate that entrepreneurial activity (rather than earnings from capital gains) has become a more important way of generating a high income, rather than a less important way, as some policymakers have argued.

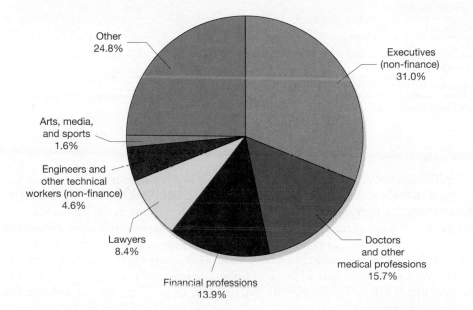

Some high-income households, such as members of the Walton family (heirs to Sam Walton, founder of Walmart), earn most of their income from the return on inherited wealth. However, research by Steven Kaplan of the University of Chicago and Joshua Rauh of Stanford has shown that the currently wealthy are much *more* likely to be the first in their family to run a firm and much *less* likely to have been born into a wealthy family than was true in the 1980s.

The debate over the top 1 percent will undoubtedly continue to be a particularly contentious part of the larger debate on income inequality in the United States.

Sources: Congressional Budget Office, *The Distribution of Household Income and Federal Taxes, 2013*, June 2016; Jon Bakija, Adam Cole, and Bradley T. Heim, "Jobs and Income Growth of Top Earners and the Causes of Changing Income Inequality: Evidence from U.S. Tax Return Data," April 2012; James Ppierson, "The Truth about the 'One Percent,'" *Wall Street Journal*, February 18, 2014; Thomas Piketty, *Capital in the Twenty-First Century*, Cambridge, MA: Harvard University Press, 2014; and Steven N. Kaplan and Joshua Rauh, "It's the Market: The Broad-Based Rise in the Return to Top Talent," *Journal of Economic Perspectives*, Vol. 27, No. 3, Summer 2013, pp. 35–56.

Your Turn: Test your understanding by doing related problem 4.13 on page 635 at the end of this chapter.

MyLab Economics Study Plan

Income Distribution and Poverty around the World

How does income inequality in the United States compare with income inequality in other countries? Table 18.9 compares for several countries the ratio of total income received by the 20 percent of the population with the highest incomes and the 20 percent with the lowest incomes. The United States has the most unequal distribution of income of any high-income country in the world, although there are some developing countries in which the distribution of income is more unequal. Of course, we have to make such comparisons with care because transfer payments are not counted in these income measures. For example, the Social Security and Medicare systems in the United States are much more generous than the corresponding systems in Japan but less generous than those in France and Germany.

Table 18.9

Income Inequality around
the World

Country	Ratio of Income Received by Highest 20% to Income Received by Lowest 20%
United States	16.6
Canada	13.3
China	10.0
Italy	5.7
United Kingdom	4.6
Germany	4.6
France	4.5
Sweden	3.7
Japan	3.0

Sources: The World Bank; Eurostat; and Statistics Canada.

MyLab Economics Study Plan

Although poverty remains a problem in high-income countries, it is a much larger problem in low-income countries. The level of poverty in much of sub-Saharan Africa, in particular, is a human catastrophe. In 2017, the poverty line in the United States for a family of four was an annual income of $24,600, but economists often use a much lower threshold income of $1.25 per day when calculating the rate of poverty in poor countries. Table 18.10 shows estimates from Maxim Pinkovskiy of the Federal Reserve Bank of New York and Xavier Sala-i-Martin of Columbia University using this measure of the poverty line. Their estimates indicate that in 1970, about 27 percent of the population of the developing world was poor. (The developing world excludes high-income countries such as the United States, Japan, Canada, and the countries of Western Europe.) By 1992, the poverty rate had declined to less than 12 percent, and by 2010, it was less than 5 percent. The greatest reduction in poverty has taken place in Asia, including China, where the majority of people were poor in 1970, while very few are poor today. Poverty rates remain high in sub-Saharan Africa, although even in those countries poverty has been much reduced. Why has poverty fallen more dramatically in Asia than in sub-Saharan Africa? The key explanation is that the countries of Asia have had higher rates of economic growth than have the countries of sub-Saharan Africa. Recent economic research demonstrates a positive relationship between economic growth and the incomes of lower-income people.

MyLab Economics Concept Check

Table 18.10

Poverty Has Declined
Dramatically around the World
Since 1970

Region	Percentage of the Population in Poverty		
	1970	1992	2010
Developing world	26.8%	11.8%	4.5%
East Asia	58.8	11.5	0.4
South Asia	20.1	10.5	1.6
Middle East and North Africa	8.4	0.5	0.5
Latin America	11.6	3.3	2.0
Sub-Saharan Africa	39.9	37.4	24.4

Note: The methods used to estimate poverty rates in 1970 are different from the methods used to estimate poverty rates for 1992 and 2010, so the results are not completely comparable.

Sources: Xavier Sala-i-Martin and Maxim Pinkovskiy, "Parametric Estimations of the World Distribution of Income," National Bureau of Economic Research, Working Paper No. 15433, October 2009. Copyright © 2009 by Xavier Sala-i-Martin and Maxim Pinkovskiy. Reprinted by permission; and Xavier Sala-i-Martin and Maxim Pinkovskiy, "Lights, Camera, ... Income! Estimating Poverty Using National Accounts, Survey Means, and Lights," Federal Reserve Bank of New York Staff Reports, Staff Report No. 669, January 2015, Table X.

Continued from page 601

Economics in Your Life & Career

Which Is Better: A $500 Raise or $500 toward Health Insurance?

At the beginning of this chapter, we asked you to suppose that you owned a bike shop and that you were thinking of increasing your employees' compensation by $500 per year to make it more competitive with what other local bike shops were paying. We asked you to explain why one of your employees requested the $500 in the form of a reduction in what she has to pay for the health insurance you provide rather than as salary.

We saw in the chapter that in order to encourage firms to offer health insurance, the federal government does not tax employees on the amount that employers spend providing them with health insurance. So, the employee realizes that if she receives the $500 as salary, she will have to pay tax on that amount, but if you spend the $500 to reduce her health insurance premiums, the government won't tax the increase in her compensation. This example is one of many ways in which Congress uses the tax code to achieve social objectives, thereby increasing its complexity.

Conclusion

A saying attributed to Benjamin Franklin is that "nothing in this world is certain but death and taxes." But which taxes? The tax system represents a balance among the principles of economic efficiency, ability to pay, payment for benefits received, and achievement of social objectives. As we saw in Chapter 1, policymakers often face a trade-off between economic efficiency and equity. Ultimately, whether the tax code should be used to pursue policies such as reducing income inequality is a normative question. Economics alone cannot decide the issue.

Visit **MyLab Economics** for a news article and analysis related to the concepts in this chapter.

Key Terms

Arrow impossibility theorem, p. 603	Human capital, p. 623	Poverty line, p. 618	Regressive tax, p. 608
Average tax rate, p. 610	Lorenz curve, p. 619	Poverty rate, p. 618	Rent seeking, p. 604
Excess burden, p. 612	Marginal tax rate, p. 610	Progressive tax, p. 608	Tax incidence, p. 614
	Median voter theorem, p. 603	Public choice model, p. 602	Voting paradox, p. 603

 18.1 ## Public Choice, pages 602–606
LEARNING OBJECTIVE: Describe the public choice model and use it to analyze government decision making.

MyLab Economics Visit **www.pearson.com/mylab/economics** to complete these exercises online and get instant feedback.

Summary

The **public choice model** applies economic analysis to government decision making. The observation that majority voting may not always result in consistent choices is called the **voting paradox**. The **Arrow impossibility theorem** states that no system of voting can be devised that will consistently represent the underlying preferences of voters. The **median voter theorem** states that the outcome of a majority vote is likely to represent the preferences of the voter who is in the political middle. Individuals and firms sometimes engage in **rent seeking**, which is the use of government action to make themselves better off at the expense of others. Although government intervention can sometimes improve economic efficiency, public choice analysis indicates that *government failure* can also occur, reducing economic efficiency.

Review Questions

1.1 What is the public choice model?

1.2 What is the difference between the voting paradox and the Arrow impossibility theorem?

1.3 What is rent seeking, and how is it related to regulatory capture?

1.4 What is the relationship between market failure and government failure?

Problems and Applications

1.5 Will the preferences shown in the following table lead to a voting paradox? Briefly explain.

Policy	Lena	David	Kathleen
Cancer research	1st	2nd	3rd
Mass transit	2nd	1st	1st
Border security	3rd	3rd	2nd

1.6 Many political observers have noted that Republican presidential candidates tend to emphasize their conservative positions on policy issues while running for their party's nomination, and Democratic presidential candidates tend to emphasize their liberal positions on policy issues while running for their party's nomination. In the general election, though, Republican candidates tend to downplay their conservative positions, and Democratic candidates tend to downplay their liberal positions. Can the median voter theorem help explain this pattern? Briefly explain.

1.7 Briefly explain whether you agree with the following argument:

> The median voter theorem will be an accurate predictor of the outcomes of elections when a majority of voters have preferences very similar to those of the median voter. When the majority of voters have preferences very different from those of the median voter, the median voter theorem will not lead to accurate predictions of the outcomes of elections.

1.8 An article in the *Economist* on the work of the late Nobel Laureate James Buchanan made the following observation: "It was important…to understand the ways that government could fail systematically."

a. What does *government failure* mean in this context? How does public choice theory help us understand how "government could fail systematically"?

b. The same article noted that "rent-seeking is a very useful concept to have around when thinking about policy." What is rent seeking? Why is the concept useful when thinking about policy?

Source: "Don't Hate the Player, Hate the Game," *Economist*, January 17, 2013.

1.9 Jason Furman served as the chairman of the White House Council of Economic Advisers under President Obama. In an opinion column in the *Wall Street Journal* discussing President Trump's tax reform proposal, Furman noted the need "for seriously revamping America's inefficient business-tax system to unlock stronger economic growth." But he also observed that tax reform is even more difficult than reforming the health care system "since it touches a larger fraction of the economy and threatens more powerful vested interests."

a. Briefly explain what Furman means by "powerful vested interests."

b. If tax reform leads to stronger economic growth, shouldn't a majority of Congress support it even if vested interests oppose the reform? Why then has tax reform legislation been difficult for Congress to pass?

Source: Jason Furman, "How to Make Tax Reform Bipartisan," *Wall Street Journal*, April 2, 2017.

1.10 In Chapter 4, Section 4.3, we discussed the federal government's agricultural program, which is often called the "farm bill." Because the U.S. Department of Agriculture administers the Supplemental Nutrition Assistance Program (SNAP), more generally known as the food stamp program, its funding is included in the farm bill. Some members of Congress believe that spending on SNAP should be reduced. In an article in the *Washington Post*, Marion Nestle of New York University was quoted as arguing: "[The program is] at great risk, and what has saved it from being chopped up into little pieces is that it's in the Farm Bill and therefore logrolled with agricultural supports." Briefly explain what Nestle means by "logrolling" and evaluate her argument.

Source: Chris Mooney and John Wagner, "Trump Picks Sonny Perdue for Agriculture Secretary," washingtonpost.com, January 19, 2017.

1.11 An article describing the work of James Buchanan observed, "Buchanan and other public choice theorists altered the debate by proposing that government may not really correct problems in the marketplace because of the wealth trading, or rent seeking, that occurs during the legislative process." The same article included the following statement by Buchanan: "I was greatly influenced by Knut Wicksell's admonition that economists cease acting as if government were a benevolent despot."
  a. Explain why James Buchanan and other public choice economists believed that government policymakers do not act as "benevolent despots."
  b. Why would "rent seeking" be an impediment to government attempts to correct "problems in the marketplace"?

Source: Robert L. Formaini, "James M. Buchanan," *Economic Insights*, Federal Reserve Bank of Dallas, Vol. 2, No. 2, 2003.

 18.2

The Tax System, pages 606–614

LEARNING OBJECTIVE: Explain the tax system in the United States, including the principles that governments use to create tax policy.

MyLab Economics Visit **www.pearson.com/mylab/economics** to complete these exercises online and get instant feedback.

Summary

Governments raise the funds they need through taxes. The most widely used taxes are income taxes, social insurance taxes, sales taxes, property taxes, and excise taxes. Governments take into account several important objectives when deciding which taxes to use: efficiency, ability to pay, horizontal equity, benefits received, and attaining social objectives. A **regressive tax** is a tax for which people with lower incomes pay a higher percentage of their incomes in tax than do people with higher incomes. A **progressive tax** is a tax for which people with lower incomes pay a lower percentage of their incomes in tax than do people with higher incomes. The **marginal tax rate** is the fraction of each additional dollar of income that must be paid in taxes. The **average tax rate** is the total tax paid divided by total income. When analyzing the effect of taxes on how much people are willing to work, save, or invest, economists focus on the marginal tax rate rather than the average tax rate. The **excess burden** of a tax is the efficiency loss to the economy that results from a tax having reduced the quantity of a good produced.

Review Questions

2.1 Which type of tax raises the most revenue for the federal government? What is the largest source of revenue for state and local governments?

2.2 What is the difference between a *progressive tax* and a *regressive tax*? Give an example of each.

2.3 What is the difference between a marginal tax rate and an average tax rate? Which is more important in determining the effect of a change in taxes on economic behavior?

2.4 Briefly discuss each of the five goals and principles governments consider when deciding which taxes to use.

Problems and Applications

2.5 An article in a Federal Reserve publication noted that "nearly all taxes create some market inefficiency in the form of deadweight loss." The article further noted that when something is taxed, the result is "an outcome in which both [buyers and sellers] would gain from more production."
  a. Briefly explain why taxes result in deadweight loss.
  b. If buyers and sellers would gain from more production of a good or service that is taxed, why doesn't more of the good or service get produced?

Source: Tim Sablik, "Taxing the Behemoths," Federal Reserve Bank of Richmond, *Econ Focus*, Third Quarter 2013.

2.6 In 2017, voters in Santa Fe, New Mexico, rejected a proposed tax on sugary drinks that would have raised soft drink prices by 2 cents per ounce. A Santa Fe newspaper reported that in a lower-income district, 73 percent voted against the tax. In two higher-income districts, the vote was evenly split between supporters and opponents of the tax. Do the results of the vote suggest that the tax would have been regressive or progressive? Briefly explain.

Source: "The Soda Tax Class Revolt," *Wall Street Journal*, May 3, 2017.

2.7 The federal government imposes a tax on sales of cigarettes. The federal Centers for Disease Control and Prevention compiled the data shown in the following table.

Percentage of Adults Who Are Current Cigarette Smokers, 2015	
At or above the poverty level	15.5%
Below the poverty level	29.5%

Based on these data, is the federal cigarette tax progressive or regressive? Be sure to define *progressive tax* and *regressive tax* in your answer.

Source: Ahmad Jamal et al., "Current Cigarette Smoking among Adults—United States, 2005–2015," *Morbidity and Mortality Weekly Report*, Vol. 65, No. 44, November 11, 2016.

2.8 Use the information in Table 18.2 on page 608 to calculate the total federal income tax paid, the marginal tax rate, and the average tax rate for people with the following incomes. (For simplicity, assume that these people have no exemptions or deductions from their incomes.)
   a. $25,000
   b. $125,000
   c. $300,000

2.9 Use the following table to answer the questions.

Annual Income	Tax Liability
$15,000	$0
30,000	4,500
45,000	11,250
60,000	21,000
75,000	30,000

   a. What is the average tax rate at each income level?
   b. Based on these data, is the tax progressive or regressive? Briefly explain.
   c. Is it possible to determine, based on these data, the marginal tax rate of someone earning $65,000 per year? Briefly explain.

2.10 **(Related to the Apply the Concept on page 609)** President Barack Obama proposed legislation that Congress failed to enact that would have included the so-called "Buffett Rule," named after billionaire Warren Buffett, who noted that he was paying a lower tax rate than his secretary. The Buffett Rule would set a new tax rate for those earning incomes of more than $1 million per year.
   a. Looking at the table on page 609 for the percentage of federal taxes paid by the different income categories, is Mr. Buffett's situation of paying a lower tax rate than his secretary typical of the highest 1 percent of U.S. income earners?
   b. According to an article in the *New York Times*, "[Buffett's] income comes mostly from his investments, which are taxed at the capital gains rate of 15 percent. His secretary is most likely paid a salary and bonus, which would be taxed as ordinary income, at a rate that goes as high as 35 percent." What are capital gains? Which goals and principles of evaluating taxes are relevant to considering whether the federal government should continue to tax capital gains at a lower rate than ordinary income? Briefly explain.

Source: Paul Sullivan, "'Buffett Rule' Is More Complicated Than Politics Suggest," *New York Times*, September 23, 2011.

2.11 Currently, the Social Security and Medicare programs are funded by payroll taxes rather than by the federal personal income tax. In 2017, the payroll tax for Social Security was 12.4 percent on wage, salary, and self-employment income up to $127,200. (Half of the tax is collected from employers and half from employees.) Above that income level, the tax dropped to zero. The Medicare tax was 2.9 percent on all wage, salary, and self-employment income. Some economists and policymakers have proposed eliminating the payroll tax and shifting to funding Social Security and Medicare out of the federal personal income tax. Would this proposal make the federal income tax system as a whole more progressive or less progressive? Briefly explain.

2.12 Almost all states levy sales taxes on retail products, but about half of them exempt purchases of food. In addition, virtually all services are exempt from state sales taxes. Evaluate these tax rate differences, using the goals and principles of taxation discussed on pages 611–614.

2.13 Suppose the government eliminates the federal income tax and replaces it with a consumption tax. With a consumption tax, individuals pay a tax on only the part of their income they spend rather than save. Think about the effect of this change on the market for automobiles. Can you necessarily tell what will happen to the price and quantity of automobiles? Briefly explain.

18.3 Tax Incidence Revisited: The Effect of Price Elasticity, pages 614–617
LEARNING OBJECTIVE: Explain the effect of price elasticity on tax incidence.

MyLab Economics   Visit **www.pearson.com/mylab/economics** to complete these exercises online and get instant feedback.

Summary

Tax incidence is the actual division of the burden of a tax. In most cases, buyers and sellers share the burden of a tax levied on a good or service. When the elasticity of demand for a product is smaller in absolute value than the elasticity of supply, consumers pay the majority of the tax on the product. When the elasticity of demand for a product is larger in absolute value than the elasticity of supply, sellers pay the majority of the tax on the product.

Review Questions

3.1 What does *tax incidence* mean?
3.2 Briefly discuss the effect of price elasticity of supply and demand on tax incidence.

Problems and Applications

3.3 Cecil Bohanon, an economist at Ball State University, and Brian Pizzola, an economist with the accounting firm Ernst & Young, used a proposed tax on income earned by credit card lenders in Minnesota to explain how tax incidence is determined. The tax, which state lawmakers did not pass, would have been imposed on lenders who charged credit card customers more than 15 percent interest on their balances. Bohanon and Pizzola explained that many of those who paid high interest rates were consumers with fewer other sources of credit, and there was nothing to prevent lenders from further raising interest rates after the tax was imposed. John Spry, an economist at St. Thomas University, stated that the proposed tax was "highly regressive…twenty percent of the new tax would be paid by Minnesota families with the lowest 10 percent of income. Thirty-seven percent of the tax would be paid by families with the lowest 20 percent of income."

a. Explain why John Spry believed that the proposed tax would have been "highly regressive."

b. Do Bohanon and Pizzola believe the elasticity of demand of those who would have been most affected by the tax was more or less elastic than the elasticity of supply of credit card lenders? Briefly explain.

Source: Cecil Bohanon and Brandon Pizzola, "Who Pays the Tax? Theoretical and Empirical Considerations of Tax Incidence," Mercatus Center, September 24, 2012.

3.4 (Related to the Don't Let This Happen to You on page 615) According to an article in the *New York Times*, some New Yorkers were deciding to buy existing condominiums (condos) rather than newly constructed condos. One reason given was that some buyers "seek to avoid the 1.825 percent transfer tax that buyers must pay on a brand-new condo. (In resales, the seller pays the tax.)" Analyze this reason for buying a resale rather than a new condo.

Source: Teri Karush Rogers, "Mint Condition, Low Miles," *New York Times*, May 29, 2009.

3.5 (Related to the Apply the Concept on page 615) Business historian John Steele Gordon noted in a *Wall Street Journal* column that the first federal corporate income tax was enacted in 1909, before passage of the Sixteenth Amendment made a federal income tax constitutional. According to Gordon, Congress enacted the corporate income tax because of "the political pressure to tax the rich." Is the corporate income tax an efficient means of taxing the rich? Briefly explain.

Source: John Steele Gordon, "Top 10 Reasons to Abolish the Corporate Income Tax," *Wall Street Journal*, December 29, 2014.

3.6 (Related to the Chapter Opener on page 600) In 2017, the Trump administration proposed changes to the federal tax code, including reducing the top corporate income tax rate from 35 percent to 15 percent. An article in the *Wall Street Journal* noted, "A tax overhaul could give companies more incentive to invest."

a. What type of investments is the article referring to? Why would cutting the corporate income tax rate lead companies to engage in more investment?

b. Some policymakers and economists are critical of cuts in the corporate income tax rate because they argue that such cuts increase income inequality. Does the incidence of the corporate income tax matter in evaluating this argument? Briefly explain.

Source: Nick Timiraos and Andrew Tangel, "Can Trump Deliver 3% Growth? Stubborn Realities Stand in the Way," *Wall Street Journal*, May 15, 2017.

3.7 According to an article in the *New York Times*, when the French government imposed a new tax on sales of beer, it estimated that the retail price of beer would rise by the equivalent of 6 cents per half pint. A spokesman for the beer industry argued that the actual increase in price would be 25 cents per half pint. Discuss the differences between the French government's and the beer industry's estimates of the price elasticity of demand for beer.

Source: Aurelien Breeden, "Beer Lovers Fear an Unequal Tax Bite in Wine Country," *New York Times*, November 26, 2012.

3.8 Governments often have multiple objectives in imposing a tax. In each part of this question, use a demand and supply graph to illustrate your answer.

a. If the government wants to minimize the excess burden from excise taxes, should these taxes be imposed on goods that have price-elastic demand or on goods that have price-inelastic demand?

b. Suppose that rather than minimizing excess burden, the government is most interested in maximizing the revenue it receives from the tax. In this situation, should the government impose excise taxes on goods that have price-elastic demand or on goods that have price-inelastic demand?

c. Suppose that the government wants to discourage smoking and drinking alcohol. Will a tax be more effective in achieving this objective if the demand for these goods is price elastic or if the demand is price inelastic?

3.9 (Related to Solved Problem 18.3 on page 616) Use the following graph of the market for cigarettes to answer the questions.

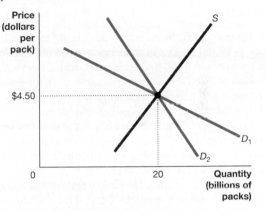

a. If the government imposes a 10-cent-per-pack tax on cigarettes, will the price consumers pay rise more if the demand curve is D_1 or if the demand curve is D_2? Briefly explain.

b. If the government imposes a 10-cent-per-pack tax on cigarettes, will the revenue the government collects be greater if the demand curve is D_1 or if the demand curve is D_2? Briefly explain.

c. If the government imposes a 10-cent-per-pack tax on cigarettes, will the excess burden from the tax be greater if the demand curve is D_1 or if the demand curve is D_2? Briefly explain.

3.10 (Related to Solved Problem 18.3 on page 616) Explain whether you agree with the following statement: "For a given demand curve, the excess burden of a tax will be greater when supply is less price elastic than when it is more price elastic." Illustrate your answer with a demand and supply graph.

3.11 Suppose the government decides to tax sales of pizzas. Use the following graph to answer the questions.

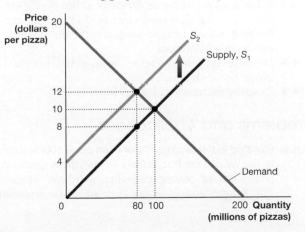

a. How much of a per unit tax does the government impose on pizzas?

b. Before the tax, what price do consumers pay for pizza? How does the price consumers pay change after the tax?

c. Before the tax, what price do sellers receive? How does the price sellers receive change after the tax?

d. Are consumers or producers bearing a greater burden of this tax? Briefly explain.

18.4 Income Distribution and Poverty, pages 617–628

LEARNING OBJECTIVE: Discuss income distribution and income mobility and the role of policy in addressing these issues.

MyLab Economics Visit www.pearson.com/mylab/economics to complete these exercises online and get instant feedback.

Summary

In the United States, there was a decline in income inequality between 1936 and 1980, and there has been an increase in income inequality between 1980 and today. A **Lorenz curve** shows the distribution of income by arraying incomes from lowest to highest on the horizontal axis and indicating the cumulative fraction of income earned by each fraction of households on the vertical axis. About 13 percent of Americans are below the **poverty line**, which is defined as the annual income equal to three times the amount necessary to purchase the minimum quantity of food required for adequate nutrition. Over time, there has been significant income mobility in the United States. The United States has a more unequal distribution of income than do other high-income countries. The *marginal productivity theory of income distribution* states that in equilibrium, each factor of production receives a payment equal to its marginal revenue product. The more factors of production an individual owns and the more productive those factors are, the higher the individual's income will be. **Human capital** is the accumulated knowledge and skills that workers acquire from formal training and education or from life experiences. Economists and policymakers have been debating policies to reduce income inequality. The **poverty rate**—the percentage of the population that is poor—has been declining in most regions around the world, with the important exception of sub-Saharan Africa.

Review Questions

4.1 Discuss the extent of income inequality in the United States. Has inequality in the distribution of income in the United States increased or decreased over time? Briefly explain.

4.2 Define *poverty line* and *poverty rate*. How has the poverty rate changed in the United States since 1960?

4.3 What is a Lorenz curve? What is a Gini coefficient? If a country had a Gini coefficient of 0.48 in 1960 and 0.44 in 2018, would income inequality in the country have increased or decreased?

4.4 Describe the main factors economists believe cause inequality of income.

4.5 Describe the trend in global poverty rates.

Problems and Applications

4.6 (Related to the Chapter Opener on page 600) In a column in the *Washington Post*, Robert J. Samuelson wrote, "As for what's caused greater inequality, we're also in the dark. The Reagan and Bush tax cuts are weak explanations,

because gains have occurred in pretax incomes.... Up to a point, inequality is inevitable and desirable."

a. What are pretax incomes?

b. Do you agree with Samuelson's argument that income inequality may be inevitable and desirable? Briefly explain.

Source: Robert J. Samuelson, "The Rich and the Rest," *Washington Post*, April 18, 2007.

4.7 A column in the *New York Times* observed that the "growing trend of 'assortative mating' is a major cause of income inequality."

a. What is assortative mating?

b. How can assortative mating contribute to income inequality?

c. If assortative mating is a major cause of income inequality, what are the likely consequences for government policies intended to reduce income inequality?

Source: John Tierney, "For Couples, Time Can Upend the Laws of Attraction," *New York Times*, June 29, 2015.

4.8 Use the following Lorenz curve graph to answer the questions.

a. Did the distribution of income become more equal in 2018 than it was in 2017, or did it become less equal? Briefly explain.

b. If area A = 2,150, area B = 250, and area C = 2,600, calculate the Gini coefficient for 2017 and the Gini coefficient for 2018.

4.9 Draw a Lorenz curve showing the distribution of income for the five people in the following table.

Name	Annual Earnings
Lena	$70,000
David	60,000
Steve	50,000
Jerome	40,000
Lori	30,000

4.10 **(Related to the Chapter Opener on page 600)** An article in the *New York Times* noted that a proposal by 2016 Democratic presidential candidate Hillary Clinton would "increase taxes on the wealthiest Americans to combat a widening gap between rich and poor."
   a. Currently, does the effect of federal taxes make the distribution of income more or less equal? Briefly explain.
   b. What are the benefits and drawbacks of using the federal income tax code to reduce income inequality?
   Source: Amy Chozick, "Hillary Clinton Offers Her Vision of a 'Fairness Economy' to Close the Income Gap," *New York Times*, July 13, 2015.

4.11 Robert Hall of Stanford University and Nicholas Petrosky-Nadeau of the Federal Reserve Bank of San Francisco used the U.S. Census Bureau's Survey of Income and Program Participation (SIPP) to divide households into four income levels, or quartiles. They found that in 2013, households in the lowest quartile earned 62 percent of their income from working, while households in the highest quartile earned 96 percent of their income from working. What might explain the difference in the percentage of income earned by working between these two groups? Is your answer relevant to determining the effects of government policy on reducing income inequality? Briefly explain.
   Source: Robert Hall and Nicolas Petrosky-Nadeau, "Changes in Labor Participation and Household Income," *FRBSF Economic Letter*, February 1, 2016.

4.12 **(Related to Solved Problem 18.4 on page 621)** Evaluate the following statement: "Policies to redistribute income are desperately needed in the United States. Without such policies, the roughly 13 percent of the population that is currently poor has no hope of ever climbing above the poverty line."

4.13 **(Related to the Apply the Concept on page 626)** In an article in the *Wall Street Journal*, Edward Lazear of Stanford University was quoted as saying, "There is some good news.... Most of the inequality reflects an increase in returns to 'investing in skills.'" Why would it be good news if it were true that most of the income inequality in the United States reflected an increase in returns to investing in skills?
   Source: Greg Ip and John D. McKinnon, "Bush Reorients Rhetoric, Acknowledges Income Gap," *Wall Street Journal*, March 26, 2007.

4.14 Why do economists often use a lower poverty threshold for low-income countries than for high-income countries such as the United States? Is there a difference between *relative* poverty and *absolute* poverty? Briefly explain.

4.15 Suppose that a country has 20 million households. Ten million are poor households that each have labor market earnings of $20,000 per year, and 10 million are rich households that each have labor market earnings of $80,000 per year. If the government enacted a marginal tax of 10 percent on all labor market earnings above $20,000 and transferred this money to households earning $20,000, would the incomes of the poor rise by $6,000 per year? Briefly explain.

Critical Thinking Exercises

CT18.1 Go to the website for the Pew Research Center (www.pewresearch.org), find the article "Political Polarization in the American Public," and read the introduction. Does the chart at the beginning of the article imply that the median voter theorem no longer applies to the United States? Explain your answer in a paragraph.

CT18.2 For this exercise, your instructor may assign you to a group.
   a. Each person in the group should reread Section 18.2.
   b. Each person should identify some point(s) in these pages that he or she finds surprising.
   c. The group members should discuss with each other what they found surprising and compare their answers.
   d. The group should prepare a brief report on what the group members found surprising.

CT18.3 Watch "Hans Rosling's 200 Countries, 200 Years, 4 Minutes - The Joy of Stats - BBC Four," at www.youtube.com/watch?v=jbkSRLYSojo. Does this video support one of the main points of "Income Distribution and Poverty around the World" at the end of Section 18.4? Did you find this video surprising? If so, briefly explain why.

GLOSSARY

A

Absolute advantage The ability of an individual, a firm, or a country to produce more of a good or service than competitors, using the same amount of resources.

Accounting profit A firm's net income, measured as revenue minus operating expenses and taxes paid.

Adverse selection The situation in which one party to a transaction takes advantage of knowing more than the other party to the transaction.

Allocative efficiency A state of the economy in which production is in accordance with consumer preferences; in particular, every good or service is produced up to the point where the last unit provides a marginal benefit to society equal to the marginal cost of producing it.

Antitrust laws Laws aimed at eliminating collusion and promoting competition among firms.

Arrow impossibility theorem A mathematical theorem that holds that no system of voting can be devised that will consistently represent the underlying preferences of voters.

Asset Anything of value owned by a person or a firm.

Asymmetric information A situation in which one party to an economic transaction has less information than the other party.

Autarky A situation in which a country does not trade with other countries.

Automatic stabilizers Government spending and taxes that automatically increase or decrease along with the business cycle.

Average fixed cost Fixed cost divided by the quantity of output produced.

Average product of labor The total output produced by a firm divided by the quantity of workers.

Average revenue (AR) Total revenue divided by the quantity of the product sold.

Average tax rate Total tax paid divided by total income.

Average total cost Total cost divided by the quantity of output produced.

Average variable cost Variable cost divided by the quantity of output produced.

B

Balance sheet A financial statement that sums up a firm's financial position on a particular day, usually the end of a quarter or year.

Barrier to entry Anything that keeps new firms from entering an industry in which firms are earning economic profits.

Behavioral economics The study of situations in which people make choices that do not appear to be economically rational.

Black market A market in which buying and selling take place at prices that violate government price regulations.

Bond A financial security that represents a promise to repay a fixed amount of funds.

Brand management The actions of a firm intended to maintain the differentiation of a product over time.

Budget constraint The limited amount of income available to consumers to spend on goods and services.

Business strategy Actions that a firm takes to achieve a goal, such as maximizing profits.

C

Cartel A group of firms that collude by agreeing to restrict output to increase prices and profits.

Centrally planned economy An economy in which the government decides how economic resources will be allocated.

***Ceteris paribus* ("all else equal") condition** The requirement that when analyzing the relationship between two variables—such as price and quantity demanded—other variables must be held constant.

Circular-flow diagram A model that illustrates how participants in markets are linked.

Coase theorem The argument of economist Ronald Coase that if transactions costs are low, private bargaining will result in an efficient solution to the problem of externalities.

Collusion An agreement among firms to charge the same price or otherwise not to compete.

Command-and-control approach A policy that involves the government imposing quantitative limits on the amount of pollution firms are allowed to emit or requiring firms to install specific pollution control devices.

Common resource A good that is rival but not excludable.

Comparative advantage The ability of an individual, a firm, or a country to produce a good or service at a lower opportunity cost than competitors.

Compensating differential A difference in wages that compensates workers for unpleasant aspects of a job.

Competitive market equilibrium A market equilibrium with many buyers and sellers.

Complements Goods and services that are used together.

Constant returns to scale The situation in which a firm's long-run average costs remain unchanged as it increases output.

Consumer surplus The difference between the highest price a consumer is willing to pay for a good or service and the actual price the consumer pays.

Cooperative equilibrium An equilibrium in a game in which players cooperate to increase their mutual payoff.

Copyright A government-granted exclusive right to produce and sell a creation.

Corporate governance The way in which a corporation is structured and the effect that structure has on the corporation's behavior.

Corporation A legal form of business that provides owners with protection from losing more than their investment should the business fail.

Coupon payment An interest payment on a bond.

Cross-price elasticity of demand The percentage change in the quantity demanded of one good divided by the percentage change in the price of another good.

D

Deadweight loss The reduction in economic surplus resulting from a market not being in competitive equilibrium.

Demand curve A curve that shows the relationship between the price of a product and the quantity of the product demanded.

Demand schedule A table that shows the relationship between the price of a product and the quantity of the product demanded.

Demographics The characteristics of a population with respect to age, race, and gender.

Derived demand The demand for a factor of production; it depends on the demand for the good the factor produces.

Direct finance A flow of funds from savers to firms through financial markets, such as the New York Stock Exchange.

Diseconomies of scale The situation in which a firm's long-run average cost rises as the firm increases output.

Dividends Payments by a corporation to its shareholders.

Dominant strategy A strategy that is the best for a firm, no matter what strategies other firms use.

Dumping Selling a product for a price below its cost of production.

E

Economic discrimination The practice of paying a person a lower wage or excluding a person from an occupation on the basis of an irrelevant characteristic such as race or gender.

Economic efficiency A market outcome in which the marginal benefit to consumers of the last unit produced is equal to its marginal cost of production and in which the sum of consumer surplus and producer surplus is at a maximum.

Economic growth The ability of the economy to increase the production of goods and services.

Economic loss The situation in which a firm's total revenue is less than its total cost, including all implicit costs.

Economic model A simplified version of reality used to analyze real-world economic situations.

Economic profit A firm's revenues minus all of its implicit and explicit costs.

Economic rent (or **pure rent**) The price of a factor of production that is in fixed supply.

Economic surplus The sum of consumer surplus and producer surplus.

Economic variable Something measurable that can have different values, such as the number of people employed in manufacturing.

Economics The study of the choices people make to attain their goals, given their scarce resources.

Economies of scale The situation in which a firm's long-run average cost falls as it increases the quantity of output it produces.

Elastic demand The case where the percentage change in quantity demanded is *greater* than the percentage change in price, so the price elasticity is *greater* than 1 in absolute value.

Elasticity A measure of how much one economic variable responds to changes in another economic variable.

Endowment effect The tendency of people to be unwilling to sell a good they already own even if they are offered a price that is greater than the price they would be willing to pay to buy the good if they didn't already own it.

Entrepreneur Someone who operates a business, bringing together the factors of production—labor, capital, and natural resources—to produce goods and services.

Equity The fair distribution of economic benefits.

Excess burden A measure of the efficiency loss to the economy that results from a tax having reduced the quantity of a good produced; also known as the deadweight loss.

Excludability The situation in which anyone who does not pay for a good cannot consume it.

Expansion path A curve that shows a firm's cost-minimizing combination of inputs for every level of output.

Explicit cost A cost that involves spending money.

Exports Goods and services produced domestically and sold in other countries.

External economies Reductions in a firm's costs that result from an increase in the size of an industry.

Externality A benefit or cost that affects someone who is not directly involved in the production or consumption of a good or service.

F

Factor market A market for the factors of production, such as labor, capital, natural resources, and entrepreneurial ability.

Factors of production Labor, capital, natural resources, and other inputs used to make goods and services.

Fee-for-service A system under which doctors and hospitals receive a payment for each service they provide.

Fixed costs Costs that remain constant as output changes.

Free market A market with few government restrictions on how a good or service can be produced or sold or on how a factor of production can be employed.

Free riding Benefiting from a good without paying for it.

Free trade Trade between countries that is without government restrictions.

G

Game theory The study of how people make decisions in situations in which attaining their goals depends on their interactions with others; in economics, the study of the decisions of firms in industries where the profits of a firm depend on its interactions with other firms.

Globalization The process of countries becoming more open to foreign trade and investment.

H

Health care Goods and services, such as prescription drugs, consultations with a doctor, and surgeries, that are intended to maintain or improve a person's health.

Health insurance A contract under which a buyer agrees to make payments, or *premiums*, in exchange for the provider's agreeing to pay some or all of the buyer's medical bills.

Human capital The accumulated knowledge and skills that workers acquire from formal training and education or from life experiences.

I

Implicit cost A nonmonetary opportunity cost.

Imports Goods and services purchased domestically that are produced in other countries.

Income effect The change in the quantity demanded of a good that results from the effect of a change in price on consumer purchasing power, holding all other factors constant.

Income elasticity of demand A measure of the responsiveness of the quantity demanded to changes in income, measured by the percentage change in the quantity demanded divided by the percentage change in income.

Income statement A financial statement that shows a firm's revenues, costs, and profit over a period of time.

Indifference curve A curve that shows the combinations of consumption bundles that give the consumer the same utility.

Indirect finance A flow of funds from savers to borrowers through financial intermediaries such as banks. Intermediaries raise funds from savers to lend to firms (and other borrowers).

Inelastic demand The case where the percentage change in quantity demanded is *less* than the percentage change in price, so the price elasticity is *less* than 1 in absolute value.

Inferior good A good for which the demand increases as income falls and decreases as income rises.

Interest rate The cost of borrowing funds, usually expressed as a percentage of the amount borrowed.

Isocost line All the combinations of two inputs, such as capital and labor, that have the same total cost.

Isoquant A curve that shows all the combinations of two inputs, such as capital and labor, that will produce the same level of output.

L

Labor union An organization of employees that has a legal right to bargain with employers about wages and working conditions.

Law of demand A rule that states that, holding everything else constant, when the price of a product falls, the quantity demanded of the product will increase, and when the price of a product rises, the quantity demanded of the product will decrease.

Law of diminishing marginal utility The principle that consumers experience diminishing additional satisfaction as they consume more of a good or service during a given period of time.

Law of diminishing returns The principle that, at some point, adding more of a variable input, such as labor, to the same amount of a fixed input, such as capital, will cause the marginal product of the variable input to decline.

Law of supply A rule that states that, holding everything else constant, increases in price cause increases in the quantity supplied, and decreases in price cause decreases in the quantity supplied.

Liability Anything owed by a person or a firm.

Limited liability A legal provision that shields owners of a corporation from losing more than they have invested in the firm.

Long run The period of time in which a firm can vary all its inputs, adopt new technology, and increase or decrease the size of its physical plant.

Long-run average cost curve A curve that shows the lowest cost at which a firm is able to produce a given quantity of output in the long run, when no inputs are fixed.

Long-run competitive equilibrium The situation in which the entry and exit of firms has resulted in the typical firm breaking even.

Long-run supply curve A curve that shows the relationship in the long run between market price and the quantity supplied.

Lorenz curve A curve that shows the distribution of income by arraying incomes from lowest to highest on the horizontal axis and indicating the cumulative fraction of income earned by each fraction of households on the vertical axis.

M

Macroeconomics The study of the economy as a whole, including topics such as inflation, unemployment, and economic growth.

Marginal analysis Analysis that involves comparing marginal benefits and marginal costs.

Marginal benefit The additional benefit to a consumer from consuming one more unit of a good or service.

Marginal cost The change in a firm's total cost from producing one more unit of a good or service.

Marginal product of labor The additional output a firm produces as a result of hiring one more worker.

Marginal productivity theory of income distribution The theory that the distribution of income is determined by the marginal productivity of the factors of production that individuals own.

Marginal rate of substitution (MRS) The rate at which a consumer would be willing to trade off one good for another.

Marginal rate of technical substitution (MRTS) The rate at which a firm is able to substitute one input for another while keeping the level of output constant.

Marginal revenue (MR) The change in total revenue from selling one more unit of a product.

Marginal revenue product of labor (MRP) The change in a firm's revenue as a result of hiring one more worker.

Marginal tax rate The fraction of each additional dollar of income that must be paid in taxes.

Marginal utility (MU) The change in total utility a person receives from consuming one additional unit of a good or service.

Market A group of buyers and sellers of a good or service and the institution or arrangement by which they come together to trade.

Market demand The demand by all the consumers of a given good or service.

Market economy An economy in which the decisions of households and firms interacting in markets allocate economic resources.

Market equilibrium A situation in which quantity demanded equals quantity supplied.

Market failure A situation in which the market fails to produce the efficient level of output.

Market power The ability of a firm to charge a price greater than marginal cost.

Market-based reforms Changes in the market for health care that would make it more like the markets for other goods and services.

Marketing All the activities necessary for a firm to sell a product to a consumer.

Median voter theorem The proposition that the outcome of a majority vote is likely to represent the preferences of the voter who is in the political middle.

Microeconomics The study of how households and firms make choices, how they interact in markets, and how the government attempts to influence their choices.

Minimum efficient scale The level of output at which all economies of scale are exhausted.

Mixed economy An economy in which most economic decisions result from the interaction of buyers and sellers in markets but in which the government plays a significant role in the allocation of resources.

Monopolistic competition A market structure in which barriers to entry are low and many firms compete by selling similar, but not identical, products.

Monopoly A firm that is the only seller of a good or service that does not have a close substitute.

Monopsony The situation in which a firm is sole buyer of a factor of production.

Moral hazard Actions people take after they have entered into a transaction that make the other party to the transaction worse off.

N

Nash equilibrium A situation in which each firm chooses the best strategy, given the strategies chosen by other firms.

Natural monopoly A situation in which economies of scale are so large that one firm can supply the entire market at a lower average total cost than can two or more firms.

Network externality A situation in which the usefulness of a product increases with the number of consumers who use it.

Noncooperative equilibrium An equilibrium in a game in which players do not cooperate but pursue their own self-interest.

Normal good A good for which the demand increases as income rises and decreases as income falls.

Normative analysis Analysis concerned with what ought to be.

O

Oligopoly A market structure in which a small number of interdependent firms compete.

Opportunity cost The highest-valued alternative that must be given up to engage in an activity.

P

Partnership A firm owned jointly by two or more persons and not organized as a corporation.

Patent The exclusive right to a product for a period of 20 years from the date the patent application is filed with the government.

Patient Protection and Affordable Care Act (ACA) Health care reform legislation passed by Congress and signed by President Barack Obama in 2010.

Payoff matrix A table that shows the payoffs that each firm earns from every combination of strategies by the firms.

Perfectly competitive market A market that meets the conditions of (1) many buyers and sellers, (2) all firms selling identical products, and (3) no barriers to new firms entering the market.

Perfectly elastic demand The case where the quantity demanded is infinitely responsive to price and the price elasticity of demand equals infinity.

Perfectly inelastic demand The case where the quantity demanded is completely unresponsive to price and the price elasticity of demand equals zero.

Personnel economics The application of economic analysis to human resources issues.

Pigovian taxes and subsidies Government taxes and subsidies intended to bring about an efficient level of output in the presence of externalities.

Positive analysis Analysis concerned with what is.

Poverty line A level of annual income equal to three times the amount of money necessary to purchase the minimum quantity of food required for adequate nutrition.

Poverty rate The percentage of the population that is poor according to the federal government's definition.

Present value The value in today's dollars of funds to be paid or received in the future.

Price ceiling A legally determined maximum price that sellers may charge.

Price discrimination Charging different prices to different customers for the same product when the price differences are not due to differences in cost.

Price elasticity of demand The responsiveness of the quantity demanded to a change in price, measured by dividing the percentage change in the quantity demanded of a product by the percentage change in the product's price.

Price elasticity of supply The responsiveness of the quantity supplied to a change in price, measured by dividing the percentage change in the quantity supplied of a product by the percentage change in the product's price.

Price floor A legally determined minimum price that sellers may receive.

Price leadership A form of implicit collusion in which one firm in an oligopoly announces a price change and the other firms in the industry match the change.

Price taker A buyer or seller that is unable to affect the market price.

Principal–agent problem A problem caused by agents pursuing their own interests rather than the interests of the principals who hired them.

Prisoner's dilemma A game in which pursuing dominant strategies results in noncooperation that leaves everyone worse off.

Private benefit The benefit received by the consumer of a good or service.

Private cost The cost borne by the producer of a good or service.

Private good A good that is both rival and excludable.

Producer surplus The difference between the lowest price a firm would be willing to accept for a good or service and the price it actually receives.

Product market A market for goods—such as computers— or services—such as medical treatment.

Production function The relationship between the inputs employed by a firm and the maximum output it can produce with those inputs.

Production possibilities frontier (PPF) A curve showing the maximum attainable combinations of two goods that can be produced with available resources and current technology.

Productive efficiency A situation in which a good or service is produced at the lowest possible cost.

Profit Total revenue minus total cost.

Progressive tax A tax for which people with lower incomes pay a lower percentage of their income in tax than do people with higher incomes.

Property rights The rights individuals or businesses have to the exclusive use of their property, including the right to buy or sell it.

Protectionism The use of trade barriers to shield domestic firms from foreign competition.

Public choice model A model that applies economic analysis to government decision making.

Public franchise A government designation that a firm is the only legal provider of a good or service.

Public good A good that is both nonrival and nonexcludable.

Q

Quantity demanded The amount of a good or service that a consumer is willing and able to purchase at a given price.

Quantity supplied The amount of a good or service that a firm is willing and able to supply at a given price.

Quota A numerical limit a government imposes on the quantity of a good that can be imported into the country.

R

Regressive tax A tax for which people with lower incomes pay a higher percentage of their income in tax than do people with higher incomes.

Rent seeking Attempts by individuals and firms to use government action to make themselves better off at the expense of others.

Rivalry The situation that occurs when one person's consumption of a unit of a good means no one else can consume it.

S

Scarcity A situation in which unlimited wants exceed the limited resources available to fulfill those wants.

Separation of ownership from control A situation in a corporation in which the top management, rather than the shareholders, controls day-to-day operations.

Short run The period of time during which at least one of a firm's inputs is fixed.

Shortage A situation in which the quantity demanded is greater than the quantity supplied.

Shutdown point The minimum point on a firm's average variable cost curve; if the price falls below this point, the firm shuts down production in the short run.

Single-payer health care system A system, such as the one in Canada, in which the government provides health insurance to all of the country's residents.

Social benefit The total benefit from consuming a good or service, including both the private benefit and any external benefit.

Social cost The total cost of producing a good or service, including both the private cost and any external cost.

Socialized medicine A health care system under which the government owns most of the hospitals and employs most of the doctors.

Sole proprietorship A firm owned by a single individual and not organized as a corporation.

Stock A financial security that represents partial ownership of a firm.

Stockholders' equity The difference between the value of a corporation's assets and the value of its liabilities; also known as *net worth*.

Substitutes Goods and services that can be used for the same purpose.

Substitution effect The change in the quantity demanded of a good that results from a change in price making the good more or less expensive relative to other goods, holding constant the effect of the price change on consumer purchasing power.

Sunk cost A cost that has already been paid and cannot be recovered.

Supply curve A curve that shows the relationship between the price of a product and the quantity of the product supplied.

Supply schedule A table that shows the relationship between the price of a product and the quantity of the product supplied.

Surplus A situation in which the quantity supplied is greater than the quantity demanded.

T

Tariff A tax imposed by a government on imports.

Tax incidence The actual division of the burden of a tax between buyers and sellers in a market.

Technological change A positive or negative change in the ability of a firm to produce a given level of output with a given quantity of inputs.

Technology The processes a firm uses to turn inputs into outputs of goods and services.

Terms of trade The ratio at which a country can trade its exports for imports from other countries.

Total cost The cost of all the inputs a firm uses in production.

Total revenue The total amount of funds a seller receives from selling a good or service,

calculated by multiplying price per unit by the number of units sold.

Trade The act of buying and selling.

Trade-off The idea that, because of scarcity, producing more of one good or service means producing less of another good or service.

Tragedy of the commons The tendency for a common resource to be overused.

Transactions costs The costs in time and other resources that parties incur in the process of agreeing to and carrying out an exchange of goods or services.

Two-part tariff A situation in which consumers pay one price (or tariff) for the right to buy as much of a related good as they want at a second price.

U

Unit-elastic demand The case where the percentage change in quantity demanded is *equal to* the percentage change in price, so the price elasticity is equal to 1 in absolute value.

Utility The enjoyment or satisfaction people receive from consuming goods and services.

V

Variable costs Costs that change as output changes.

Vertical merger A merger between firms at different stages in the production of a good.

Voluntary exchange A situation that occurs in markets when both the buyer and the seller of a product are made better off by the transaction.

Voluntary export restraint (VER) An agreement negotiated between two countries that places a numerical limit on the quantity of a good that can be imported by one country from the other country.

Voting paradox The failure of majority voting to always result in consistent choices.

W

Wall Street Reform and Consumer Protection Act (Dodd-Frank Act) Legislation passed during 2010 that was intended to reform regulation of the financial system.

World Trade Organization (WTO) An international organization that oversees international trade agreements.

COMPANY INDEX

SUBJECT **INDEX**

Key terms and the page on which they are defined appear in **boldface.**

CREDITS

Chapter 1: *page 5:* John Hechinger, "FBI Presses Banks to Boost Security as Robberies Rise," *Wall Street Journal,* October 8, 2002.

Chapter 4: *page 121:* Daniel K. Fetter, "The Home Front: Rent Control and the Rapid Wartime Increase in Home Ownership," *Journal of Economic History,* Vol. 76, No. 4, December 2016, pp. 1001–1043.

Chapter 5: *page 151:* Ronald H. Coase, "The Problem of Social Cost," *Journal of Law and Economics,* Vol. 3, October, 1960, pp. 1–44.

Chapter 6: *page 192, Table 6.2: "Estimated Real-World Price Elasticities of Demand,"* Kelly D. Brownell and Thomas R. Frieden, "Ounces of Prevention—The Public Policy Case for Taxes on Sugared Beverages," *New England Journal of Medicine,* April 30, 2009; Sheila M. Olmstead and Robert N. Stavins, "Comparing Price and Non-Price Approaches to Urban Water Conservation," Resources for the Future, Discussion paper 08–22, June 2008; Jonathan E. Hughes, Christopher R. Knittel, and Daniel Sperling, "Evidence of a Shift in the Short-Run Price Elasticity of Gasoline Demand," *Energy Journal,* Vol. 29, No. 1, January 2008; Robert P. Trost, Frederick Joutz, David Shin, and Bruce McDonwell, "Using Shrinkage Estimators to Obtain Regional Short-Run and Long-Run Price Elasticities of Residential Natural Gas Demand in the U.S.," George Washington University Working Paper, March 13, 2009; Lesley Chiou, "Empirical Analysis of Competition between Wal-Mart and Other Retail

Channels," *Journal of Economics and Management Strategy,* Vol. 18, No. 2, Summer 2009; Judith Chevalier and Austan Goolsbee, "Price Competition Online: Amazon versus Barnes and Noble," *Quantitative Marketing and Economics,* Vol. 1, No. 2, June 2003; Henry Saffer and Frank Chaloupka, "The Demand for Illicit Drugs," *Economic Inquiry,* Vol. 37, No. 3, July 1999; "Response to Increases in Cigarette Prices by Race/Ethnicity, Income, and Age Groups—United States, 1976–1993," *Morbidity and Mortality Weekly Report,* July 31, 1998; James Wetzel and George Hoffer, "Consumer Demand for Automobiles: A Disaggregated Market Approach," *Journal of Consumer Research,* Vol. 9, No. 2, September 1982; Jerry A. Hausman, "The Price Elasticity of Demand for Breakfast Cereal," in Timothy F. Bresnahan and Robert J. Gordon, eds., *The Economics of New Goods,* Chicago: University of Chicago Press, 1997; K. J. Duffey, et al., "Food price and diet and health outcomes: 20 years of the CARDIA Study," *Archives of Internal Medicine,* Vol. 170, No. 5, March 8, 2010, pp. 420–6; Christopher J. Ruhm, et al., "What U.S. Data Should Be Used to Measure the Price Elasticity of Demand for Alcohol," *Journal of Health Economics,* Vol. 31, No. 16, December 2012; Susan Dynarski, Jonathan Gruber, and Danielle Li, "Cheaper By the Dozen: Using Sibling Discounts at Catholic Schools to Estimate the Price Elasticity of Private School Attendance," NBER Working Paper 15461, October 2009; and U.S. Department of Agriculture, Economic Research Service; Peter Cohen, et al., "Using Big Data to

Estimate Consumer Surplus: The Case of Uber," National Bureau of Economic Research, Working Paper No. 22627, September 2016.

Chapter 7: *page 245:* John Cogan, Glenn Hubbard, and Daniel Kessler, *Healthy, Wealthy, and Wise: 5 Steps to a Better Health Care System,* Second edition, Stanford, California: The Hoover Institution Press, 2011.

Chapter 8: *page 269–270:* Michael Lewis, "The End," *Portfolio,* December 2008.

page 271 (in boxed feature): Virginia Postrel, "How to Save Twitter Two Pennies at a Time," bloomberg.com, March 29, 2017.

Chapter 10: *page 337:* Gary Becker and Kevin M. Murphy, *Social Economics,* Cambridge, MA: Harvard University Press, 2000, p. 9.

page 340: Steffen Andersen, et al., "Stakes Matter in Ultimatum Game," *American Economic Review,* Vol. 101, No. 7, December 2011, pp. 3427–3439.

page 347–348: Richard H. Thaler and Cass R. Sunstein, *Nudge: Improving Decisions about Health, Wealth, and Happiness,* revised and expanded edition, New York: Penguin Books, 2009; Dhruv Khullar, "How Behavioral Economics Can Produce Better Health Care," New York Times, April 13, 2017; Daniella Meeker, Jeffrey A. Linder, Craig R. Fox, et al., "Effect of Behavioral Interventions on Inappropriate Antibiotic Prescribing among Primary Care Practices," *Journal of the American Medical Association,*

Vol. 315, No. 6, February 9, 2016, pp. 562–570; and Adam M. Grant and David A. Hoffman, "It's Not All about Me: Motivating Hand Hygiene among Health Care Professionals by Focusing on Patients," *Psychological Science,* Vol. 22, No. 12, November 10, 2011.

Chapter 11: *page 389* Norihiko Shirouzu and Sebastian Moffett, "As Toyota Closes in on GM, Quality Concerns Also Grow," *Wall Street Journal,* August 4, 2004.

Chapter 12: *page 434;* Sharon M. Oster, *Modern Competitive Analysis,* Third Edition, New York: Oxford University Press, 1999.

Chapter 13: *page 465:* Peter F. Drucker, *Management: Tasks, Responsibilities, Practices,* New York: Harper & Row, 1974, pages 63–64.

Chapter 15: *page 522:* Joseph Schumpeter, *Capitalism, Socialism, and Democracy,* New York: Harper and Row, 1942, p. 84.

page 527: U.S. Department of Justice, *Horizontal Merger Guidelines Issued by the U.S. Department of Justice and the Federal Trade Commission, April 8, 1997,* updated June 25, 2015.

Chapter 18: *page 624:* Claudia Goldin and Lawrence Katz, *The Race Between Education and Technology,* Cambridge, MA: Harvard University Press, 2008.

Jeremy Greenwood, Nezih Guner, Georgi Kocharkov, and Cezar Santos, "Marry Your Like: Assortative Mating and Income Inequality," *American Economic Review,* Vol. 104, No. 5, May 2014, pp. 348–53.